shakespearean criticism

"Thou art a Monument without a tomb,
And art alive still while thy Book doth
     live
And we have wits to read and praise to
give."

*Ben Jonson, from the preface
to the First Folio, 1623.*

MR. WILLIAM

SHAKESPEARES

COMEDIES,
HISTORIES, &
TRAGEDIES.

Publifhed according to the True Originall Copies.

Martin Droeshout fculpfit London.

LONDON
Printed by Isaac Iaggard, and Ed. Blount. 1623.

Frontispiece to the First Folio (1623). By permission of the Folger Shakespeare Library.

ISSN 0883-9123

Volume 70

shakespearean criticism

Criticism of
William Shakespeare's Plays and Poetry,
from the First Published Appraisals
to Current Evaluations

Lynn M. Zott
Project Editor

GALE®

THOMSON

GALE

Detroit • New York • San Diego • San Francisco • Cleveland • New Haven, Conn. • Waterville, Maine • London • Munich

THOMSON
GALE

Shakespearean Criticism, Vol. 70

Project Editor
Lynn M. Zott

Editorial
Jenny Cromie, Kathy D. Darrow, Elisabeth Gellert, Edna M. Hedblad, Julie Keppen, Jelena O. Krstović, Michelle Lee, Jessica Menzo, Thomas J. Schoenberg, Lawrence J. Trudeau, Russel Whitaker

Research
Nicodemus Ford, Sarah Genik, Tamara C. Nott, Tracie A. Richardson

Permissions
Margaret Chamberlain

Imaging and Multimedia
Robert Duncan, Lezlie Light, Kelly A. Quin

Product Design
Michael Logusz

Composition and Electronic Capture
Carolyn Roney

Manufacturing
Stacy L. Melson

LIBRARY OF CONGRESS CATALOG CARD NUMBER 86-645085

ISBN 0-7876-5999-1
ISSN 0883-9123

Contents

Preface vii

Acknowledgments ix

SC Contents, by Volume xi

Literary Criticism Series Advisory Board xv

Preface

*S*hakespearean Criticism (*SC*) provides students, educators, theatergoers, and other interested readers with valuable insight into Shakespeare's drama and poetry. A multiplicity of viewpoints documenting the critical reaction of scholars and commentators from the seventeenth century to the present day derives from hundreds of periodicals and books excerpted for the series. Students and teachers at all levels of study will benefit from *SC*, whether they seek information for class discussions and written assignments, new perspectives on traditional issues, or the most noteworthy of analyses of Shakespeare's artistry.

Scope of the Series

Volumes 1 through 10 of the series present a unique historical overview of the critical response to each Shakespearean work, representing a broad range of interpretations.

Volumes 11 through 26 recount the performance history of Shakespeare's plays on the stage and screen through eyewitness reviews and retrospective evaluations of individual productions, comparisons of major interpretations, and discussions of staging issues.

Volumes 27 through 56 in the series focus on criticism published after 1960, with a view to providing the reader with the most significant modern critical approaches. Each volume is ordered around a theme that is central to the study of Shakespeare, such as politics, religion, or sexuality. The topic entry that introduces each volume is comprised of general essays that discuss this theme with reference to all of Shakespeare's works. Following the topic entry are several entries devoted to individual works.

Beginning with volume 57 in the series, *SC* provides a works-based approach; each of the four entries contained in a regular volume focuses on a specific Shakespearean play or poem. The entries will include the most recent criticism available on the works, as well as earlier criticism not previously included in *SC*. Select volumes contain topic entries comprised of essays that analyze various topics, or themes, found in Shakespeare's works. Past topic entries have covered such subjects as Honor, Jealousy, War and Warfare, and Elizabethan Politics.

Until volume 48, published in October 1999, *SC* compiled an annual volume of the most noteworthy essays published on Shakespeare during the previous year. The essays, reprinted in their entirety, were recommended to Gale by an international panel of distinguished scholars.

Organization of the Book

An *SC* entry consists of the following elements:

- The **Introduction** contains background information that introduces the reader to the work or topic that is the subject of the entry and outlines modern interpretations of individual Shakespearean topic, plays, and poems.

- Reprinted **Criticism** for each entry consists of essays arranged chronologically under a variety of subheadings to facilitate the study of different aspects of the play, poem, or topic. This provides an overview of the major areas of concern in the analysis of Shakespeare's works, as well as a useful perspective on changes in critical evaluation over recent decades. The critic's name and the date of composition or publication of the critical work are given at the beginning of each piece of criticism. Unsigned criticism is preceded by the title of the source in which it appeared. Footnotes are reprinted at the end of each essay or excerpt. In the case of excerpted criticism, only those footnotes that pertain to the excerpted texts are included.

- A complete **Bibliographical Citation** of the original essay or book precedes each piece of criticism.

- Critical essays are prefaced by **Explanatory Notes** as an aid to students using *SC*. The explanatory notes summarize the criticism that follows.

- Each volume includes such **Illustrations** as reproductions of images from the Shakespearean period, paintings and sketches of eighteenth- and nineteenth-century performers, photographs of modern productions, and stills from film adaptations.

- An annotated bibliography of **Further Reading** appears at the end of each entry and suggests resources for additional study. In some cases, significant essays for which the editors could not obtain reprint rights are included here.

Indexes

A **Cumulative Character Index** identifies the principal characters of discussion in the criticism of each play and non-dramatic poem.

A **Cumulative Topic Index** identifies the principal topics in the criticism and stage history of each work. The topics are arranged alphabetically, by topic.

A **Cumulative Topic Index, by Play** identifies the principal topics in the criticism and stage history of each work. The topics are arranged alphabetically, by play.

Citing *Shakespearean Criticism*

When writing papers, students who quote directly from any volume in the Literary Criticism Series may use the following general format to footnote reprinted criticism. The first example pertains to material drawn from periodicals, the second to material reprinted from books.

Tetsuya Motohashi. "Body Politic and Political Body in *Coriolanus*," in *Forum for Modern Language Studies* XXX, no. 2 (April 1994): 97-112; reprinted in *Shakespearean Criticism*, vol. 50, ed. Kathy D. Darrow (Farmington Hills, Mich.: The Gale Group, 2000), 119-128.

Mary Hamer. "Authority and Violence," in *William Shakespeare: Julius Caesar* (Northcote House, 1998), 12-20; reprinted in *Shakespearean Criticism*, vol. 50, ed. Kathy D. Darrow (Farmington Hills, Mich.: The Gale Group, 2000), 230-34.

Suggestions are Welcome

Readers who wish to suggest new features or topics to appear in future volumes, or who have other suggestions or comments are cordially invited to call, write, or fax the Project Editor:

Project Editor, Literary Criticism Series
The Gale Group
27500 Drake Road
Farmington Hills, MI 48331-3535
1-800-347-4253 (GALE)
Fax: 248-699-8054

Acknowledgments

The editors wish to thank the copyright holders of the excerpted criticism included in this volume and the permissions managers of many book and magazine publishing companies for assisting us in securing reproduction rights. We are also grateful to the staffs of the Detroit Public Library, the Library of Congress, the University of Detroit Mercy Library, Wayne State University Purdy/Kresge Library Complex, and the University of Michigan Libraries for making their resources available to us. Following is a list of the copyright holders who have granted us permission to reproduce material in this volume of *SC*. Every effort has been made to trace copyright, but if omissions have been made, please let us know.

PHOTOGRAPHS APPEARING IN *SC*, VOLUME 70, WERE RECEIVED FROM THE FOLLOWING SOURCES:

SC Contents, by Volume

Literary Criticism Series Advisory Board

The members of the Gale Group Literary Criticism Series Advisory Board—reference librarians and subject specialists from public, academic, and school library systems—represent a cross-section of our customer base and offer a variety of informed perspectives on both the presentation and content of our literature criticism products. Advisory board members assess and define such quality issues as the relevance, currency, and usefulness of the author coverage, critical content, and literary topics included in our series; evaluate the layout, presentation, and general quality of our printed volumes; provide feedback on the criteria used for selecting authors and topics covered in our series; provide suggestions for potential enhancements to our series; identify any gaps in our coverage of authors or literary topics, recommending authors or topics for inclusion; analyze the appropriateness of our content and presentation for various user audiences, such as high school students, undergraduates, graduate students, librarians, and educators; and offer feedback on any proposed changes/enhancements to our series. We wish to thank the following advisors for their advice throughout the year.

Antony and Cleopatra

For further information on the critical and stage history of *Antony and Cleopatra,* see *SC,* Volumes 6, 17, 27, 47, and 58.

INTRODUCTION

Regarded as one of Shakespeare's most compelling love stories, *Antony and Cleopatra* is often seen as an anomaly among critics because, despite its apparently tragic ending, the play ends on a triumphant note. Although Antony and Cleopatra both die at the play's end, they deny Octavius Caesar victory and achieve immortality as lovers. The tragedy of the play is also undercut by the comic elements that appear throughout the course of the drama. The play's genre, which encompasses the comic, heroic, tragic, and romantic, comprises one area of intense critical analysis. Critics are also concerned with the language used in *Antony and Cleopatra,* and examine the rhetorical styles of the characters as well as Shakespeare's use of metaphor and imagery. Investigations of the characters in the play are concerned to some degree with the Elizabethan understanding of the characters as fictional entities and as historical personages. In modern stage productions of *Antony and Cleopatra,* the dynamic relationship between the two lovers is typically of most interest to spectators as well as reviewers.

Antony, Cleopatra, and Caesar are the most heavily scrutinized characters in *Antony and Cleopatra.* Some critics focus their character analyses on the way in which these characters might have been received by Elizabethan audiences. Robert P. Kalmey (1978) argues that the Elizabethan conception of Octavius Caesar was two-pronged. According to Kalmey, Elizabethans praised Caesar as an ideal prince only after he was crowned emperor. Prior to this event, Kalmey maintains, Caesar was condemned by Elizabethans who saw him as a tyrant who fueled the fires of civil war to further his own ambitions. Like Kalmey, Theodora A. Jankowski (1989) is interested in the Elizabethan take on Shakespeare's characters, specifically Cleopatra and her resemblance to Queen Elizabeth. Jankowski notes that although both women used their bodies for political purposes, Cleopatra should not be taken as an allegorical representation of Elizabeth. Jankowski states that the similarities between the women suggest Shakespeare's awareness of the fact that a successful female sovereign was an anomaly in a patriarchal society, and of the particular problems Elizabeth faced in ruling England. Taking a similar approach to the issue of Cleopatra's characterization, Imtiaz Habib (2000) also finds a connection between Cleopatra and Elizabeth.

Habib, however, suggests that Cleopatra's blackness and seductive nature, in conjunction with the indolence of Egypt as a nation, is contrasted with the nobility of England, and the white and virginal Queen Elizabeth. Habib also comments on the black woman of Shakespeare's *Sonnets* and her relationship to Cleopatra. Additionally, Habib maintains that the critical connection between Cleopatra's political impotency and her sexual power is her race, which Habib demonstrates was understood to be black and ethnic in the eyes of historians and of Shakespeare. Coppélia Kahn (see Further Reading) centers her study on the rivalry between Octavius Caesar and Antony. Kahn contends that Caesar campaigns against Antony not only to demonize Cleopatra and paint her as Rome's archenemy, but to completely discredit Antony as a rival. Kahn goes on to examine the relationship between Caesar and Antony from Antony's point of view, commenting on what Antony hoped to accomplish through his suicide, and also discussing how his death would have been interpreted according to Renaissance ideas regarding suicide.

The sense of triumph at the play's end is an important element of modern stage productions of *Antony and Cleopatra.* In her review of the 1999 production of the play staged at the Southmark Globe Theatre in London and directed by Giles Block, Lois Potter (1999) comments that the director's vision of the play emphasized the victory of "a gloriously human couple." Potter additionally singles out members of this all-male cast for praise; she finds that Mark Rylance's Cleopatra offered new insights into the character and the play as a whole, and that John McEnery's performance as Enobarbus was exceptional as well. Patrick Carnegy (1999) and Russell Jackson (2000) review another recent production of *Antony and Cleopatra,* staged by the Royal Shakespeare Company at Stratford-upon-Avon and directed by Steven Pimlott. Although Carnegy criticizes Alan Bates, as Antony, for stumbling over many of his lines, he gives high praise to Frances de la Tour's performance as Cleopatra, and to the production as a whole. Likewise, Jackson is equally taken with de la Tour's Cleopatra and finds Bates's Antony to be likeable and energetic, but decidedly unheroic.

Many aspects of the language, style, and generic structure of *Antony and Cleopatra* fascinate modern critics. Robert D. Hume (1973) offers a detailed examination of the ways in which language, rhythm, and rhetorical habit are used for the purposes of character differentiation and development. For example, Hume observes that Antony's language reflects his vacillation between the worlds of Rome and Egypt, and that Cleopatra's imaginative language and varied rhythms are contrasted with Caesar's straightforward and regular verse. In another comparison between the language of Caesar and Cleopatra, Hume comments that the melodiousness arising from Cleopatra's use of assonance is set against the cacophony generated by Caesar's alliteration. Like Hume, Rosalie L. Colie (1974) explores the styles of speech used in *Antony and Cleopatra.* Colie focuses on the contrast between the Attic and Asiatic styles of speech and how these styles were understood in the Renaissance as encompassing not just rhetorical patterns, but moral and cultural differences as well. Colie explains that Atticism, the style preferred by Caesar, is characterized by plain, direct speech, while Asianism, which is more sensuous, self-indulgent, and imaginative, is the style used by both Cleopatra and Antony. Furthermore, Colie examines the language Antony and Cleopatra use with each other, commenting that their love transcends conventional hyperbole; in their creation of new forms of overstatement, the lovers employ a language reflective of the instability of their love. Donald C. Freeman (1999) uses the theory of cognitive metaphor to evaluate the figurative language found in *Antony and Cleopatra.* Freeman identifies the major image schemes used in the play and demonstrates the way these inform our understanding of the play's treatment of Antony, Cleopatra, and Rome. In terms of genre, *Antony and Cleopatra* encompasses elements of the comic, heroic, tragic, and romantic. J. L. Simmons (1969) demonstrates the ways in which the structure of the play follows the pattern of other Shakespearean comedies. Simmons finds that the contrast between Rome and Egypt is mirrored by the contrasts between court and tavern in the *Henry IV* plays, between Venice and Belmont in *The Merchant of Venice,* and between court and forest in *A Midsummer Night's Dream* and *As You Like It.* Taking another approach to the debate over the play's genre, R. J. Dorius (see Further Reading) discusses the interaction between the tragic, heroic, and romantic elements of the play, arguing that Shakespeare's treatment of love and of Cleopatra is at the center of the controversy regarding the relationship between tragedy and romance in *Antony and Cleopatra.*

OVERVIEWS AND GENERAL STUDIES

John Turner (essay date 1995)

SOURCE: Turner, John. Introduction to *The Tragedie of Anthonie, and Cleopatra,* by William Shakespeare, edited by John Turner, pp. 13-29. New York: Prentice Hall/ Harvester Wheatsheaf, 1995.

[*In the following essay, Turner examines Shakespeare's treatment of Rome in* Antony and Cleopatra, *suggesting that his view of the empire was fueled by an imaginative return to the "honour culture" of late medieval aristocrats. Turner also comments on the major relationships within the play, and on the love poetry of* Antony and Cleopatra.]

The stage upon which *The Tragedie of Anthonie, and Cleopatra* is enacted is a site upon which competitors meet. . . .

I am using the word 'competitor' in that precise but ambiguous sense which it enjoys throughout the play, and which, according to the *OED,* it enjoyed for the century between 1579 and 1681: a sense fluctuating between 'rival' and 'associate', and implying both the competition and collaboration that today—though we still speak of 'fellow-competitors' in a race—are usually thought to be mutually incompatible.

It is no accident that the period of the word's ambiguity coincides so closely with the period of the greatest efflorescence of court society in Britain, as succeeding monarchs sought to 'gentle' their aristocracy and disarm their code of honour by drawing them to court, where their behaviour might be overseen and their energies directed towards an honours system managed by the crown.[1] Here was a society alive and anxious with 'the ebb and flow of friendships and rivalries, alliances and ruptures, loyalties and betrayals' as courtiers vied incessantly for prestige, now competing with and now competing against one another.[2] The slipperiness of the word, that is, precisely mirrored the slipperiness of court society: what Wyatt at the start of our period called 'the slipper top / Of court's estate', and what Marvell at its end called 'giddy favour's slippery hill'.[3]

Yet although the structural ambiguity of the term 'competition' belongs to the contemporary world of court society, aristocratic life had previously been characterised by an even greater sense of political instability. *The Tragedie of Anthonie, and Cleopatra,* in its attempt to imagine the Rome of the triumvirate, returns to the honour culture of the late mediaeval aristocracy, before it had yielded to the power and ideology of a centralised monarchy with a providentialist view of history. It returns to an honour culture haunted by the belief 'that Fate, irrational, incomprehensible and uncontrollable, rules over human history'.[4] To the man of honour, all the critical moments of his life had seemed 'hag-ridden by Fate'; and it is no accident that the chief focus of Shakespeare's play, in describing the competitiveness of the life of honour, should fall upon the instability of its alliances, the unpredictability of its military encounters and, more generally, upon the mutability of all earthly fortunes. It is not that Shakespeare 'was using the Roman Empire as a symbol for the sublunar world' unsustained by divine order and love.[5] His point, I think, was political rather than theological: he was depicting the endemic instability of a dying culture and the determined efforts of Caesar to bring about a new order, centralised and stabilised under his own imperial power.

There is something of the play's sense of mutability in North's *Plutarch,* where we find that Anthony had 'often-times proved both the one and the other fortune' and that he was 'throughly acquainted with the divers chaunges and fortunes of battells'.[6] But as the poems of Wyatt and

Marvell intensify Seneca's sense of the slipperiness of court society, so too does Shakespeare's play intensify Plutarch's picture of the fickleness of Fortune. Its swirling sequences of short scenes, with their peripateias, their multiple perspectives, their giddy rangings across the globe and their collapsing of a decade's history into a three-hour entertainment, all enhance this effect—especially in the Folio text before us, where the absence of division into acts and scenes casts us adrift from our familiar bearings.[7] Throughout the play we witness the human attempts to make meaning, and to win an honourable place in history, under the threat of constant erasure from the fluxes and refluxes of fortune. The power that makes is the power that mars: in Anthony's own words, 'That which is now a Horse, even with a thoght / the Racke dislimes, and makes it indistinct / As water is in water'. It is this power of fortune that Caesar sets out to master.

When the claims of Rome and Egypt compete for Anthony's attention and loyalty at the start of the play, he replies as follows, in a passage justly famous for its poetic beauty:

> Let Rome in Tyber melt, and the wide Arch
> Of the raing'd Empire fall: Heere is my space,
> Kingdomes are clay:

'Heere is my space': it is indeed a question of space. If these words are taken naturalistically, they refer to the space allotted by the drama to Egypt, and in particular to Cleopatra's court; and in their passionate rejection of Rome, they suggest that the most important competition in the play will prove to be that between Anthony and Caesar. If we consider the words metadramatically, however, as Raymond Williams has pointed out,[8] we shall see that the space towards which Anthony gestures is also the theatrical space around him: the actor, in competition with the rest of the cast, is indicating the arena which he hopes to fill with his own particular speaking voice and, beyond that, the city with whose attractions the play is competing in its search for an audience. I want to explore each of these two points in turn, before returning to my opening claim that the First Folio text too is a space which we must understand as a site of competition. In each case, we shall find that what is at stake is the peculiar nature of the poetry that Shakespeare wrote for this play, and his growing awareness as a dramatist of the equivocal status of human beings as poets, story-tellers, spinners of narrative, in a world where—the conflictual and multivocal nature of the dramatic form itself drives home the point[9]—the competition for power, and thus for hegemonic control over the narratives of others, was felt to alienate and denature the individual self.

* * *

Anthony's claim that his space is here—in Egypt, in Cleopatra's court, even perhaps in Cleopatra's arms—is a characteristically indirect admission of his harassed sense of Caesar's inescapable presence, even in his absence. It is

not paradoxical, I think, but true to say that the competition between Anthony and Caesar is the most important human relationship in the play; and the evidence of this is to be found in the scene with the Soothsayer.

> His Cocks do winne the Battaile, still of mine,
> When it is all to naught: and his Quailes ever
> Beate mine (inhoopt) at odd's. I will to Egypte:
> And though I make this marriage for my peace,
> I'th'East my pleasure lies.

It is Caesar's cocks and quails that drive Anthony back to Egypt; his love for Cleopatra, his pleasure in the East, seem here no more than rationalisations of his primary superstitious dread of Caesar. It is a question, it seems, of 'Naturall lucke'; and however much we seek to translate these words into a discourse more familiar to us today—discussing the sexual competition between the rising young man and the declining man in his mid-life crisis, for example, or contrasting the focused self-possession of the new man with the reckless magnanimity of the old—Anthony himself is bound by the language of the fortune-teller. 'Whose Fortunes shall rise higher / *Cæsars* or mine?': the man of honour, dependent upon his own resolve to win prestige, is haunted by the sense of his own impotence, fearful that the world lies fatefully beyond his control and that his will is doomed to be overthrown by the fellow-contrary power of Fortune.

The centrality of Caesar to the play means that the love between Anthony and Cleopatra—powerful and real though it is—must be understood in relation to the Rome that has produced it. 'Let Rome in Tyber melt': their love is a dissolution, a melting, an overflowing of all the measures of time and place upon which Rome depends, and its very existence depends upon having those measures to transgress. There is, in other words, no self-authenticating language of pleasure in the play. From the licentiousness of Charmian's talk at the start to the malapropisms of the Clown at the end, the discourses of pleasure subvert the moral and linguistic grammar whose purpose is to order them; but they cannot create a coherent world of their own. The opening tableau of the play makes the point perfectly for us. With eternity upon their lips but with Roman soldiers and messengers by their sides, the two lovers dream of a 'new Heaven, new Earth'; and yet these new worlds of which they dream are no more than the resorts of fantasy to dissolve the intolerable tensions of the old. Love can only realise itself in opposition to duty, Egypt in opposition to Rome. But it is not enough to talk of antithesis here: whether we speak of Rome and Egypt, of duty and love, of Caesar and Cleopatra or of Apollo and Dionysus,[10] we must remember Jonathan Dollimore's insistence, quoting Derrida, that 'binary oppositions are "a violent hierarchy" where one of the two terms forcefully governs the other'.[11] The hierarchy here serves Rome and is held in place by a culture of demonisation that sees Cleopatra as a 'great Faiery' or a 'Witch', dependent upon whether she is in or out of favour with Anthony; it is a world in which love is linguistically structured as a spell, a charm, a magical fascination.

Hence, of course, the danger in describing the play as a 'love-tragedy'; for the label, through its very familiarity, may blind us to precisely those connections that we are being invited to make—the connections between love and history, both personal and political. Anthony and Cleopatra themselves, at certain moments of their lives—though, importantly, not at others—speak of their love as absolute, magical, transcendental; they identify one another with mythical figures, especially with Venus and Mars; and they strive to make their love the stuff of legend, so that they might become what Caesar finally calls them: 'a payre so famous' that no grave can hold their like. Moved we may be; but we should not be taken in. For there is no such thing as love; there are endless varieties of experience that are called love, and we need to understand them in their variety. The interesting questions are always the particular ones: what is understood by 'love' in each case? why do people fall in love with certain people and not with others? why, in so doing, do they sometimes speak of Love rather than of love? The purpose of these questions is to return the seemingly overwhelming experience of love back to the totality of its material history in order to understand it fully; and here the play can help us.

For it helps to deconstruct those aristocratic—and, later, bourgeois—reifications which have seen Love as a kind of Fate, a transcendental power which was impossible to resist. The Venus and the Cupid of the aristocratic culture of the late sixteenth century—like the Eros of the bourgeois culture of the late nineteenth century—ensnared their victims in a passionate game whose fascination obscured the political realities of the society in which it was played out. The young aristocrat who went to court to enjoy the pleasures of love unwittingly submitted to the royal power of surveillance as he did so; excelling in the field of love, he lay down his arms in the field of war, and thus confirmed the power of his sovereign. Here in *The Tragedie of Anthonie, and Cleopatra,* it is this same connection between love and politics that is laid bare. It is the *distraction* of love that we see, in both senses of the word: a passionate excitement that, in engulfing the reason, seduces the military man from the noble pursuit of honour amongst his fellow-competitors.

It is perhaps a question of punctuation in the narratives we tell, of whether 'love' should be the last word in the sentences we spin; and here too the Folio can help us. For how should we punctuate the title of the play? It is an important question, to which the Folio has two answers. In the heading of the play—the version that I have preferred here, for its capacity to surprise—there is a comma after Anthonie; but on the running title at the head of each page, the comma is gone. There is no single answer; the play has two titles, each with different implications—and each might be said to epitomise something really present within the text. If we omit the comma, we are encouraged to think of Anthony and Cleopatra as constituting in some sense a single unit of thought—as though their tragedy is the consequence of their love, enabling the two of them together to constitute a reality greater than they do apart.

But if the comma is inserted, it divides their destinies, opens up their different experiences of love for separate scrutiny in their different political contexts, and draws our attention to those distinctions which their poetry labours to dissolve.

For the love-poetry of Anthony and Cleopatra is a poetry of dissolution. There are, of course, many other kinds of poetry in the play; but it is the love-poetry that has attracted most attention—and understandably so, because of its great beauty. Yet beauty, like love, is always of a particular kind, and must be not only admired but characterised. 'Kingdomes are clay': the plangency of such verse derives from its curious blend of transgressive defiance and regressive yearning, and exists from the start in a curiously paradoxical relationship with time and place. For its aristocratic recklessness, its fine prodigality of word and emotion, is also a wilful neglect of the real world where aristocratic honour must be won. This is Aristotelian liberality run to excess. Kingdoms are *not* clay; but the energy of the poetry springs from the insatiable need to say that they are. The lovers are driven to dematerialise the material; to transform the untransformable; to build out of words a home that can never be built out of bricks. The beauty of their verse, in other words, for all its defiant aspiration, is also a function of its commitment to illusion; it is plangent because it overlooks (in both senses of the word) the facts of daily life which usually provide imagination with its materials to work upon. But the imagination here is driven into counter-creation; it must evolve a counter-narrative to efface the history that Caesar is engaged in writing.

The crowning achievement of such counter-narrative, of course, occurs at the end of the play, when Cleopatra in defeat draws herself up in the full pomp of her regalia and rhetoric.

> Give me my Robe, put on my Crowne, I have
> Immortall longings in me. Now no more
> The juyce of Egypts Grape shall moyst this lip.
> Yare, yare, good *Iras*; quicke: Me thinkes I heare
> *Anthony* call: I see him rowse himselfe
> To praise my Noble Act. I heare him mock
> The lucke of *Cæsar,* which the Gods give men
> To excuse their after wrath. Husband, I come . . .

The verse is beautiful, spell-binding; but its theological beliefs are illusion. Cleopatra's declaration of the supremacy of love in the next life only serves to disclose the supremacy of Caesar's power in this. The queen who will shortly see the asp that is killing her as a baby sucking her to sleep is compelled to transform the world in verse because she has failed to transform it in fact. This dissociation between imagination and reality is Caesar's real victory. Cleopatra dismisses his triumph as 'lucke', as she later dismisses Caesar himself as 'Asse, unpolicied'. But she is wrong; it is not a question of luck but of successful policy. He could not stall with Anthony, he says, in the whole world, and so he prepared himself for the moment when their uneasy collaboration would break down into a deadly rivalry. Here is a man determined to owe nothing to luck and fortune. An old world at the last gives way to a new; and an older kind of competition gives way to a kind that we should recognise today.

* * *

'Heere is my space': the actor saying these words may also gesture towards the theatrical arena around him, and in so doing spark off a series of reflections about the relationship between theatre and 'real life' that might naturally culminate in contemplating the theatricality of Cleopatra's death.

In one sense, of course, in Jacobean London as today, theatre was very much a part of that 'real life'. It was a flourishing commercial enterprise in competition with other businesses to attract audiences; and the actor who declared the theatre to be his space was also declaring the source of his income, in a world where everyone was busy making a living. But in another sense, theatre was—and still is—a place apart. In Jacobean London, the marginality of the theatre was inscribed in its geographical exclusion outside the city walls. It was a place dangerous to the physical and the moral health of its audience, a place where crowds could gather, where actors could impersonate their betters, and where the pretensions of power and the self-interest of ideology could be exposed simply by the productions and reproductions of the new dramatic form. Right from the start, that is, capitalism generated space for its own critique.

Yet neither money nor satire could wholly satisfy the new dramatists, who also needed to feel the social and political centrality of their own practice; and here, I think, they were often disappointed. There is an excess in their satirical railing that suggests a consciousness of their own marginality; and the sense of theatre as illusion, which is so pervasive in the later works of Shakespeare, suggests a similar awareness. No doubt this sense was also in part a reaction to the conditions of working in the theatre, with its devotion to make-believe and its rapid turnover of material. In the theatre it is art that is short-lived, life that is long; and the form that Sidney thought capable of embodying eternal verities appeared hauntingly ephemeral to Shakespeare. Cleopatra's death, in its theatricality, embodies perfectly his sense of the paradoxical status of dramatic art; for the beauty of her verse, even as she speaks it, discloses its most powerful effects as illusion. Art, it seems, is denatured by the same market-place that prompts it.

Yeats once speculated that 'there is some one myth for every man, which, if we but knew it, would make us understand all he did and thought'. Shakespeare's myth, he went on, referring to *Hamlet* and the second tetralogy of History Plays as his examples, 'describes a wise man who was blind from very wisdom, and an empty man who thrust him from his place, and saw all that could be seen from very emptiness'.[12] If there is perhaps one single myth informing Shakespeare's work, I should say that it depicts the displacement of the corrupt poetry of a vestigial aristocratic code of honour by the mean-spirited prose of an emergent machiavellianism; and that this myth—which with various modifications informs plays like *Hamlet,* the second tetralogy, the Tragedies and, of course, the play before us now, *The Tragedie of Anthonie, and Cleopatra*—has its roots in Shakespeare's sense of the history of his own lifetime, as the flawed glamour of Essex and his friends, including Shakespeare's own patrons, had been thrust from places of influence at court by the pragmatism of Cecil and his supporters.[13]

The competition between Caesar and Anthony, in other words, is not simply the history of two incompatible personalities; it is also the history of the cultural clash between two incompatible ways of seeing the world, each of which is grounded in a different material reality. It was a history found in Plutarch but shaped in sixteenth-century London, with the events of the two historical periods assimilated into a single myth that offers to interpret them both. Caesar's triumph at the end of the play creates for its audience a picture of the prehistory of its own present; Augustan Rome becomes the cradle of the modern world—a world from which the poetry of honour and love has disappeared, along with their material base in aristocratic power and the early court societies of the Renaissance. All that remains is Caesar, whom Jonathan Dollimore has likened to Machiavelli's Prince: 'inscrutable and possessed of an identity which becomes less fixed, less identifiable as his power increases'.[14] Ben Jonson had already in *The Poetaster* (1601) introduced Augustus Caesar to the English stage,[15] portraying him as an idealised ruler whose sense of the importance of moral temperance, social hierarchy and literary patronage was perhaps intended as coercive flattery of Elizabeth herself. But Shakespeare's Octavius—still to proclaim himself the Emperor Augustus—is no such ideal figure; he is a model of prudence and watchfulness, a puritan whose denatured realpolitik seems to epitomise Shakespeare's own sense of the political life that succeeded the disarming of the aristocracy.

What is missing from this picture of Caesar, however, is the poetry that honour, beauty and love evoke from him at two critical moments in the play: on his first appearance he celebrates the heroism of Anthony's soldiership in the Alps, and on his last he celebrates Cleopatra's 'strong toyle of Grace' and the fame that she and 'her *Anthony*' will enjoy as lovers. It is true that in each case his tribute is expedient; and yet it also seems true that each is profoundly felt. His poetry is moving. In other words, the dissociation between imagination and realpolitik that Caesar is irresistibly imposing upon the world is replicated within his own subjectivity. He is, of course, too canny to succumb to its tragic potential; it is Enobarbus' role in the play to do this, and the fact that Shakespeare has made the character who played so small a role in Plutarch so central to his own play is proof of his interest in the dissociation that Caesar has brought about.

For the true heir of Caesar is the dramatist himself, together with his play and the playhouse in which it is enacted. Here in the marginal place of the playhouse, in the marginal time of the play, the dramatist too recalls the flawed poetry of honour, beauty and love that have gone from the world. He recalls them critically, without nostalgia, in a critique of the meanness of the world that survives; and yet his play is implicated in that world by its existence as a commodity in the market-place. This paradoxical relationship of conformity and unconformity between the new work of dramatic art and the new world emerging around it constitutes the subtext to the closing words of the play:

> their Story is
> No lesse in pitty, then his Glory which
> Brought them to be lamented. Our Army shall
> In solemne shew, attend this Funerall,
> And then to Rome. Come *Dolabella,* see
> High Order, in this great Solemnity.

One story is brought to its ritual conclusion, but another goes on; once Anthony and Cleopatra are buried in Egypt, Caesar will return to Rome. Yet despite Caesar's wish to have the last word, to be master of the narrative he tells and the funeral he stages, the competition between himself and Anthony still continues. It continues, as we have seen, within his individual sensibility; and it continues too within the sensibility of the dramatist and his audience, as the 'solemne shew' of his tragedy is produced and reproduced again and again in performance. The competition between Caesar and Anthony is thus constantly regenerated as part of the paradox of an art which both collaborates with the economic activities of its society and criticises them in the name of a greater richness and vitality—a richness and vitality which, though flawed in all their manifestations hitherto, nevertheless persist in making their lack felt through an imaginative hunger which Caesar, for all his wealth, cannot feed.

* * *

The text of *The Tragedie of Anthonie, and Cleopatra* too, as it is produced and reproduced in print and in performance, has become a site of competition, though in a different way, befitting the new ambiguities structured into bourgeois scholarship; it has become a site where generations of editors, from the First Folio on, have collaborated and vied with one another in the attempt to establish and to annotate a text which is both authentic and comprehensible.

What is striking about this long history of editorial work is that, until the last ten years or so, it has tended to produce texts that are more suitable for the armchair than the theatre: texts that have the completeness, self-consistency and grammatical correctness of a novel, together with long and learned notes to satisfy the scholar, the lexicographer and the cultural historian. What is missing—interesting and valuable though such editions are—is twofold: a recognition of the theatrical potential of Shakespeare's

texts, and a recognition of their original (and continuing) status as what Jonathan Bate calls 'vital, mutable theatrical scripts',[16] to be shaped differently according to the requirements of different theatrical performances. For there is, in other words, no authentic script of any Shakespearean play; nor could the sudden discovery of an original manuscript provide one. It is true that the First Folio texts which we are reproducing in this series have misprints, errors, mispunctuations and enigmas in them, and that it remains the duty of an editor to try to find sense in nonsense. Yet their incompletenesses, inconsistencies and incorrectnesses are useful in reminding us of the status in the Elizabethan and Jacobean theatre of the playscripts that we are dealing with; and, of course, they also enable us to inspect the processes of emendation that they no doubt began and that have been going on ever since.

It is once again a question of narrative and of how we punctuate that narrative. Each added stage-direction, each emendation and each gloss involves us in the construction of a narrative; and each narrative involves competition with our fellow-editors, as our narrative converges upon—or diverges from—theirs. *The Tragedie of Anthonie, and Cleopatra* does not raise the same kind of fundamental editorial problems that bedevil plays like *Hamlet* and *King Lear,* where there are different texts in existence with rival claims to be authoritative; the First Folio of *The Tragedie of Anthonie, and Cleopatra* is the only text that we have. The questions it raises are thus always local and particular; and yet they are interesting, as the following three examples may show.

First, at the end of the play, when Cleopatra has secured herself in her monument and is negotiating with Proculeius, the Folio suddenly assigns him two speeches together, the second one of which begins: 'You see how easily she may be surpriz'd'. The intended stage-business is clear: troops have been smuggled into the monument, and Cleopatra finds herself under arrest. Precisely how the operation is carried out is not stated in the Folio; but some editions, including the Arden, on the authority of Plutarch, assign the operation—and the second of Proculeius' two speeches—to Gallus, whom Caesar was preparing to use in some unspecified task in the previous scene. The Arden editor, in developing this narrative, is able to praise Proculeius' honesty and corroborate Anthony's dying judgment of him: 'None about *Cæsar* trust, but *Proculeius*'. He is also able to clear Shakespeare from the charge of 'bad craftsmanship'[17]—that is, of introducing an expectation and not fulfilling it—by suggesting a compositorial error that transferred the name of Proculeius from the text to the speech-heading that should have read '*Gallus*'. Charlton Hinman too suspects that compositorial error made it necessary, for reasons of space, to drop material from the original manuscript here.[18] Yet why should we assume that Shakespeare's manuscript was complete in this way? Such an idea of a finished work of Art is not necessarily appropriate to a play-script which, as Hinman himself goes on to say, can be 'finished only in performance',[19] when the details of entrances, exits and other stage-business can finally be thrashed out. There is enough in the Folio text from which to fashion a production; and it may be a strength and not a weakness that the whole of this final scene should be so open. It leaves a great deal to the technical and imaginative resources of the playhouse; and in so doing, it underlines the inscrutability of Caesar's character and behaviour, and emphasises finally the disastrous unreliability of Anthony as a judge of character. It all depends what narrative we want to tell; but I can see no good reason to add new stage-directions to the printed text.

Second, a few lines later in the play, there is a famous moment when Cleopatra, in conversation with Dolabella, praises Anthony's unrivalled generosity of spirit:

> For his bounty,
> There was no winter in't: an autumn 'twas
> That grew the more by reaping:

Or so she usually says. But in the Folio she says: 'An *Anthony* it was, / That grew the more by reaping'. Although acknowledging its orthographical unlikelihood, the Arden editor calls the emendation from 'autumn' to 'Anthony' brilliant, and adds that it gives 'admirable sense, and that the turn of imagination is thoroughly Shakespearean, whereas *Antony* gives no sense at all'.[20] What is at issue here is an ideal of poetic decorum quite at odds with the spirit of hyperbole driving Cleopatra. Her metaphor overflows the measure because she can find no words other than the name of the man himself to express the qualities she thinks he had. As once she had said that 'my Oblivion is a very *Anthony*', so now her speechlessness is vindicated in the ineffableness of Anthony's virtue. Words and metaphors are at breaking-point, and to tidy them up is to go against the grain of the whole passage. Once again, of course, it depends upon what narrative we want to tell. But the key test of the lines should surely be whether or not they make sense in the theatre, not whether they reach the standard of some idealised Shakespeare with whose imaginative workings we feel ourselves to be intimate. This example may stand for a number of emendations in modern editions that aim to tidy up the syntax or the imagery of people who are in a state of excitement; and in these cases I think we should be especially reluctant to emend the Folio text.

Third, when Caesar is saying farewell to Octavia before she leaves with Anthony, he urges her:

> Sister, prove such a wife
> As my thoughts make thee, and as my farthest Band
> Shall passe on thy approofe:

The last clause here is condensed and its meaning difficult to tease out. The New Cambridge edition quotes approvingly the gloss of Dr Johnson: 'as I will venture the greatest pledge of security on the trial of thy conduct'.[21] According to this explanation, Caesar will only let his honour stand surety for his sister's virtue if her conduct merits it; he may refuse if he so pleases, and she of course may misbehave if she so pleases. Now it is true that Octavia may misbehave, and that he may refuse to stand surety for her; but the drive of the honour code is to occlude both the woman's freedom to act as she wishes and the man's freedom to dissociate himself from his family and friends. Caesar feels—or he talks as though he does—that his honour is already, of necessity, pledged on behalf of his sister's conduct, and that he will only be able to circulate freely amongst men of honour as long as his word passes for currency amongst them. 'What is a man but his promise?':[22] therefore, in the chiastic structuring of his sentence, he works hard to bind Octavia's freedom so that she will prove herself only in such a way as to be approved within the circles of honourable men. Hence my own interpretation of his final clause: 'so as even my uttermost pledge as to your merits shall be vindicated and found acceptable when other people come to inspect and approve them'. It is this emphasis upon the policing of the honour code that is lacking from Dr Johnson's explanation. Perhaps he thought more naturally in terms of the individual protestant ethic rather than in terms of the essentially social nature of the honour code. But for whatever reason, the difference at issue shows how even the smallest gloss involves editors in the construction of rival narratives in a competition to see which shall command the most assent.

These are indeed only small examples of the processes involved in every emendation and gloss; the endnotes are full of countless others, and every editor of course could tell a similar story. It is perhaps no coincidence, however, that each example discussed here should date back to the eighteenth century—to Theobald twice and once to Dr Johnson—when modern methods of editing Shakespeare were laid dowm, when drama was often excluded from the categories of respectable literature, and when art was something to be consumed in the pleasurable solitude of the drawing-room rather than created in the vulgar public arena of the theatre. It is against that tradition that this edition of the First Folio is launched. 'Heere is my space': it is perhaps a new space for most performers and readers alike, and one which may help them to remember the true status of Shakespearean texts as play-scripts; to keep alive a sense of their theatrical openness which is also a kind of danger; and to do so particularly here, in the case of a play written to commemorate the flawed but overflowing vitality of a disorderly world which had all but vanished before the new order of the heirs of Caesar—'the little o'th'earth', Cleopatra calls them (though only in the Folio text), whose only glory comes from the light cast by Anthony. For this is the abiding power of *The Tragedie of Anthonie, and Cleopatra*: that it continues to articulate a dissociation characteristic of our culture. No matter whether we consider it in its history or in our own present, it still reproduces its fundamental antithesis, which still remains a 'violent hierarchy' and a potential source of tragedy: the tragedy of the dissociation between romantic images of beauty, vitality and freedom and our disillusioned experiences of competition in the everyday worlds of home, work and political power.

Notes

1. See Rosalie Colie, 'Reason and Need: *King Lear* and the "Crisis of the Aristocracy"', in Rosalie L. Colie and F. T. Flahiff (eds), *Some Facets of 'King Lear': Essays in Prismatic Criticism* (Toronto: University of Toronto Press, 1974), for an interesting account of the way that the Tudor state had set out 'to gentle the armigerous aristocracy' (p. 186).

2. Graham Holderness, Nick Potter and John Turner, *Shakespeare: Out of Court* (London: Macmillan, 1990) p. 19. The allusion is to a study of competition in *Love's Labour's Lost.*

3. Sir Thomas Wyatt's poem 'Stand, whoso list, upon the slipper top' is a translation of the same passage from Seneca as Andrew Marvell's 'The Second Chorus from Seneca's Tragedy "Thyesetes"'.

4. Mervyn James, 'English Politics and the Concept of Honour 1485-1642', *Past and Present,* Supplement 3 (The Past and Present Society, 1978), p. 7. The whole of this long essay has much to offer to a student of *The Tragedie of Anthonie, and Cleopatra.*

5. Charles A. Hallett, 'Change, Fortune, and Time: Aspects of the Sublunar World in *Antony and Cleopatra*', in *Journal of English and Germanic Philology,* vol. LXXV (1976) p. 87.

6. Quoted in Geoffrey Bullough, *Narrative and Dramatic Sources of Shakespeare* vol. V (London: Routledge & Kegan Paul, 1964), p. 302.

7. It is worth remembering Charlton Hinman's caution about the conventional act-scene divisions found in editions of Shakespeare: 'they tend to foster mistaken notions both of the principles by which Shakespeare constructed his plays and of the manner in which they were meant to be staged'; in *The Norton Facsimile: The First Folio of Shakespeare* (New York: W.W. Norton, 1968), p. xxiv.

8. Raymond Williams, *Drama in Performance* (Harmondsworth: Penguin, 1972), p. 69. Chapter 4 of this book is a pioneering analysis of the First Folio as a text for performance.

9. See Raymond Williams, in the Afterword to Jonathan Dollimore and Alan Sinfield (eds), *Political Shakespeare: New Essays in Cultural Materialism* (Manchester: Manchester University Press, 1985), p. 238, for a discussion of the political implications of the 'multivocal' and 'interactive' form of the new drama.

10. There is a good discussion of the play in Nietzschean terms during the last chapter of Michael Long's *The Unnatural Scene: A Study in Shakespearean Tragedy* (London: Methuen, 1976), pp. 220-59.

11. Jonathan Dollimore, 'The Dominant and the Deviant: A Violent Dialectic', in *Critical Quarterly* vol. 28, nos. 1 and 2 (1986), p. 190.

12. W. B. Yeats, 'At Stratford-on-Avon', in *Essays and Introductions* (London: Macmillan, 1969) p. 107.

13. A connection between Essex and Mark Antony had already been drawn by friends of Fulke Greville, urging him to destroy his own tragedy about the story of Antony and Cleopatra. See Bullough, *Narrative and Dramatic Sources of Shakespeare,* pp. 216-17.

14. Jonathan Dollimore, *Radical Tragedy: Religion, Ideology and Power in the Drama of Shakespeare and his Contemporaries* (Brighton: Harvester Press, 1984), p. 208.

15. A comparison of Jonson's and Shakespeare's pictures of Augustus Caesar may be found in the last five pages of Howard Erskine-Hill's essay, 'Antony and Octavius: The Theme of Temperance in Shakespeare's "Antony and Cleopatra"', in *Renaissance and Modern Studies.* vol. XIV (1970), pp. 26-47.

16. Jonathan Bate, 'Shakespeare's Tragedies as Working Scripts', in *Critical Survey,* vol. 3, no. ii (1991), p. 126.

17. See the Arden edition of *Antony and Cleopatra* (London: Methuen, 1954), p. 254.

18. See Hinman, *The Norton Facsimile,* p. xvii.

19. *Ibid.,* p. xiii.

20. Arden edition, p. 214.

21. New Cambridge edition of *Antony and Cleopatra* (Cambridge: Cambridge University Press, 1990), p. 155.

22. These words, epitomising the honour code of the aristocracy, were spoken by Lord Darcy in 1536 to justify military confederacy against the crown. They are quoted in Mervyn James, 'English Politics and the Concept of Honour, 1485-1642', p. 29.

CHARACTER STUDIES

Robert P. Kalmey (essay date 1978)

SOURCE: Kalmey, Robert P. "Shakespeare's Octavius and Elizabethan Roman History." *Studies in English Literature 1500-1900* 18, no. 2 (spring 1978): 275-87.

[*In the following essay, Kalmey examines the Elizabethan conception of Octavius Caesar, and finds that Elizabethans praised Caesar as an ideal prince only after he was crowned emperor. Prior to this event, Kalmey maintains, Caesar was condemned by Elizabethans who saw him as a tyrant who fueled the fires of civil war to further his own ambitions.*]

Few readers of *Antony and Cleopatra* have overlooked the contempt with which Cleopatra condemns as mere hollow words the paltry machinations of Octavius Caesar to take her captive. "He words me, girls, he words me, that I should not / Be noble to myself" (V.ii.190-191: *Arden Shakespeare,* ed. M. R. Ridley). Nor have readers neglected the irony Cleopatra articulates that Octavius, who has conquered Brutus, Sextus Pompey, Lepidus, Lucius Antonius, and Marc Antony, should so easily and deftly be humiliated by the personal will of a defeated queen. Speaking to the asp at her breast, Cleopatra defines her final contemptuous image of Octavius: "O, couldst thou speak, that I might hear thee call great Caesar ass, / Unpolicied!" (V.ii.305-307).

In spite of Cleopatra's final scathing assessment of the character of Octavius, it is a persistent commonplace in modern criticism to place Octavius in the role of an ideal prince who stands as the moral superior of the dissolute Antony, and who therefore deserves to accede to the governance of Rome because of his political rectitude and moral superiority. J. E. Phillips was the first of the modern critics to emphasize an honorific character for Octavius in his study of the state and the governor in the Roman plays.[1] More recently, Maurice Charney and J. Leeds Barroll, apparently accepting and following Phillips' assertions, perpetuate the critical assessment of Octavius as the ideal prince. Charney claims "that in Elizabethan histories and comparable works, the reputation of Octavius was very high; he was seen as the ideal Roman emperor. . . ."[2] The commonplace of the character of Octavius as ideal prince persists into contemporary criticism as Julian Markels in his study of the theme of order in *Antony and Cleopatra, The Pillar of the World,* observes that "Octavius is no villain but, like King Henry V, whom he so resembles in character, the agent of political order renewing itself."[3] It is easier for critics to think of Octavius, who plots bloody civil war in *Julius Caesar* and betrayal in *Antony and Cleopatra,* as "no villain" in politics if they may find resonance for this value judgment from other critics who value Octavius' moral rectitude highly. Roy Battenhouse, for instance, finds Octavius morally temperate and prudent—a man of Roman virtue whose "achievement" Shakespeare respects, however limited to pragmatic values Octavius may be.[4] According to this view, Octavius governs himself with rectitude and asceticism in order to achieve his goal of Emperorship. Battenhouse then contrasts the temperate Octavius to the intemperate Antony and Cleopatra. According to Battenhouse, in a critical view highly popular with many readers of otherwise diverse critical persuasions, conscientious Octavius wins the world from dissolute Antony and distracted Cleopatra, who win a merely "ironic" bliss of eroticism.[5] Although A. P. Riemer finds that Octavius "does not have the play's full endorsement" and that Octavius is "ambivalent," he does affirm Octavius as "magnanimous . . . noble, well-intentioned, and generally just."[6] Riemer, like Battenhouse, finds any sense of transcendence of the world for Antony and Cleopatra ambiguous and contradicted by their sheer worldly lust.[7] Even Honor Matthews, who does not share

Phillips', Battenhouse's, and Riemer's reservations about the absolute transcendent value of Antony and Cleopatra's love, asserts that Octavius' "place in history was . . . a peculiarly honourable one, to the Elizabethan imagination."[8]

But if we accept the above assessments of Octavius' character in the play, we find ourselves holding up as an avowed Elizabethan ideal prince and moral man one whose final and definitive character is fixed in the play as "ass, / Unpolicied!" Furthermore, with whom do our sympathies reside in *Antony and Cleopatra?* Surely not with the cold and passive virtue of Octavia or with the equally cold, though active, calculations and betrayals of her aggressive brother, Octavius. For this reason, an alternative critical nexus has won more adherents than the co-existing one described above. Many modern critics have identified Octavius not as a temperate and moral apogee in *Antony and Cleopatra,* but as its moral perigee. He is seen in this view as the evil and impelling force of the material and base world against the increasingly transcendent love of Antony and Cleopatra. The clearest assessment of Octavius' character as it functions in opposition to the drama of transcendence in the play may be found in the criticism of Maynard Mack, Thomas McFarland, Sigurd Burckhardt, and Matthew Proser, where we find, amid some inevitable variation not important here, a valuational dialectic between, on the one hand, the world of plotting Octavius in which fortunes rise and fall in mutability and death, and on the other hand, the world of "immortal longings" (V.ii.280) from which Antony calls and to which Cleopatra, responding, aspires.[9] The valuational dialectic leads to an ontological distinction that these critics recognize: the world of Octavius is the repository for Cleopatra's "baser" elements, water and earth (V.ii.288-289); her refined elements of "fire, and air" transcend Octavius' world, and have their being in immortality and eternity.[10]

My purpose now is not to explore in detail these two main strands of criticism on *Antony and Cleopatra*; rather, I hope to suggest that each of the two recurrent but different kinds of assessment of *Antony and Cleopatra* builds support upon mutually exclusive judgments of the character and function of Octavius. I seek instead to offer evidence of a pervasive Elizabethan concept of Octavius that has two distinct parts to it: the distinction made in the Elizabethan histories of Rome, to be analyzed below, holds that Octavius is to be honored as positive example of the ideal prince *only after* he is crowned Emperor in Rome after the defeat of Antony; *before* this precise occasion, the same Elizabethan histories of Rome characterize Octavius as a vicious tyrant who foments bloody civil war and a reign of terror solely for his personal gain. In their condemnation of rebellious, unbridled ambition which breeds civil war, the Elizabethan historians of Rome follow the main stream of Tudor historiography so thoroughly documented by E. M. W. Tillyard, Lily Campbell, and Irving Ribner.[11]

The distinction made by Elizabethan historians of Rome between the early ambitious tyrant Octavius and the later

Emperor Augustus is entirely consistent with Shakespeare's dramatization of Octavius in *Antony and Cleopatra,* and in *Julius Caesar* as well, strictly and wholly within the time *prior* to his becoming Emperor of Rome. This precise limitation within the two plays, and within *Antony and Cleopatra* in particular, suggests a clear circumference of definition about the character of Octavius contained within the historical pattern when he functions as immoral tyrant—not in any sense an honorific character in contrast with which pejorative judgments may be delivered against the love of Antony and Cleopatra. If we can become aware of the common distinction between early tyrant and later Emperor in Octavius' life repeatedly made for literate Elizabethans by their contemporary historians of ancient Rome, we may find that the precise historical place Octavius held in "the Elizabethan imagination" serves to support those critics who assess *Antony and Cleopatra* as a drama of transcendent love and being over a world subjugated to the bloody lust of ambition and power.

As a triumvir, then, Octavius is revealed in Elizabethan histories of Rome as a pernicious demagogue; as a crowned emperor, he is presented as an ideal prince—like the reigning Tudor monarch. In both cases the Elizabethan historians emphasize moral lessons to be observed by their readers: early in his rise to power, Octavius exemplifies the horrors attendant on the demagogic subversion of the commonweal; later, as emperor, Octavius exemplifies the great Tudor image of the ideal prince, an analogue of Queen Elizabeth. In both *Antony and Cleopatra* and *Julius Caesar,* Octavius appears *only* as a triumvir in the process of accumulating power; he has not yet become emperor even at the end of *Antony and Cleopatra.* It is an unnecessary hypothesis to posit that Shakespeare deliberately followed the distinction between the demagogue Octavius and the emperor Octavius Caesar Augustus. It is enough to observe that his plays dramatize only the demagogue Octavius, and to be familiar ourselves as critics with the distinction in the Elizabethan histories of Rome merely as a precedent, nothing more, for the distinction between immoral triumvir and ideal prince in the Elizabethan understanding of the character of Octavius.

When the Elizabethan historians of Rome judged an historical character, they examined him within a framework of moral instruction advocated for an individual who would conduct himself properly, as the historians so often exhort, within the commonweal. Octavius Caesar Augustus was one of the more significant figures upon whom the Elizabethan historians of Rome directed moral judgment.

Specifically, in his analysis of *Julius Caesar* and *Antony and Cleopatra,* J. E. Phillips places great importance on a concept of Elizabethan political theorists and propagandists that establishes Octavius as "a great ruler."[12] Phillips places Shakespeare within the tradition of those influenced by the "great ruler" concept of Octavius. Phillips cites three prime authorities for his concept of Octavius as "great ruler": George More, Chelidonius, and Thomas Elyot. He quotes from the latter, who cites Suetonius in support of the "great ruler" concept of Octavius. Although much in Suetonius' life of Octavius Caesar Augustus illustrates the rule of a great monarch whose dominions included most of the civilized world, much also in Suetonius characterizes Octavius as a vicious tyrant determined to satisfy his own lust for power regardless of the cost for others. Phillips neglects to mention that the tyrant Octavius appears not only in Suetonius, but in literally hundreds of pages of Elizabethan Roman history as well. We turn now to the Elizabethan histories of Rome to document the widespread characterization of Octavius Caesar as an ambitious and overreaching tyrant.

When we consider the great praise traditionally accorded to Octavius, as Augustus Caesar, for his fruitful rule as emperor, at first it appears strange that some final judgments of him should be so reserved. In *Augustus,* H. Seile completes his essay with an enigmatic opinion: "It had beene an ineffable benefit to the Commonwealth of Rome, if eyther he had never dyed, or never beene borne."[13] The empire of Augustus was established at great cost to the Roman commonweal. Writing of the murder of Julius Caesar, William Fulbecke judges that Rome could have returned to the most peaceful and fruitful years of the Republic except for the personal ambition of Caesar's heir, Octavius: "the common-weale did seeme to have rolled herselfe into the state of her pristinate libertie, and it had returned unto the same, if either Pompey had not left sonnes, or Caesar had not made an heire."[14] Seile also develops a similar conclusion: "the Commonwealth might have recovered Liberty, if . . . Caesar had left no heire."[15] Fulbecke questions the right of Octavius to "succeed" to the imperial position of Julius Caesar, because the privilege and honours were given to Caesar alone, not to his lineage. The hasty crime of Brutus and Cassius permitted Octavius to fashion a just cause for aspiring to Caesar's position of power: "But if Caesar's death had bene attended, till naturall dissolution, or just proceeding had caused it, his nephews entrie into the monarchie might well have bene barred and intercepted: because these honors were annexed and appropriated to Caesars person. And if patience might have managed their wisdomes, though there had bene a Caesar, yet should there never have bene an Augustus."[16]

What were the sources of the reluctance and regret which permeate the adverse opinions of Octavius? It was popular among the Elizabethan historians of Rome (probably following Suetonius) to credit Octavius with creating most of the discords with Antony. Octavius sought only to satisfy his personal ambition. Rome had been the victim of several civil wars, and never could benefit from more. Sir Thomas North recounts Octavius' plottings: after Antony had repulsed his attempts to become consul, he began to work the Senate against Antony and to subvert the commonweal to his own gain.[17] He delivered speeches against Antony;[18] he spread throughout the city rumor and dissension.[19] His most treacherous and irresponsible plot is revealed by Suetonius: "by the advice and persuasion of some he set certaine persons privily in hand to murder Antonius."[20] Although the murder plot was discovered before effected, Octavius was successful in his campaign to blacken the image of Antony. Cicero assisted Octavius by helping to turn the Senate against Antony,[21] and, according to North, civil war followed as a direct result.[22]

Even after a peace had been devised between Antony and Octavius, the young Caesar used his rival's absence from Rome as an opportunity for sowing more civil dissension.[23] In this situation, Octavius willfully destroyed a peace established specifically to avoid the upheavals caused by his earlier dissensions.[24] Octavius' unscrupulous scheming aroused the disapproval of the Senate on one notable occasion. Suetonius writes that in assembly with the Senate Octavius read Antony's will, "the better to proove and make good that he had degenerated."[25] Appian, too, describes the incident and the Senate reaction: "So he [Octavius] went, and tooke it [the will] away, and first by himselfe redde it, and noted what might be sayde agaynst it. Then he called the Senate, and redde it openly, whereat many were grieved, thinking it not reasonable that a mans minde for his death, shoulde bee scanned whylest he was alive."[26]

Octavius' willingness to sacrifice the well-being of others in order to achieve his personal goals extended to his own sister, Octavia. In Mexia, Octavius advises her to join Antony so that she might have "occasion to fall out with him (as Plutarch recounteth in the life of Antony) if she were not well entertained."[27] In Seile's *Augustus,* Octavius is seen to be still more devious, for he outwardly affects concern for Octavia's welfare as he hopes her noble demeanor in the face of Antony's scorn will move the Romans to despise Antony.[28] Appian, too, clearly indicates Octavius' sacrifice of his sister's welfare to his own political ambitions.[29] Octavius thus used his sister as bait to lead Rome into civil war with Antony. After Octavia's rejection at the hands of Antony, Octavius takes advantage of the disrespect which his rival incurs: "Octavian began openly to complaine of Marcus Antonius, and to shew himselfe his enemie."[30] In these ways, Octavius deliberately drew Rome closer to civil war.

Fulbecke defines with characteristic Tudor dread the macrocosmic upheavals involved in the tempest of a state at civil war: "And, as in the yearely conversion of the heavens, it commeth to passe, that the starres jogged together do murmure and threaten tempest, so with the alteration of the Romane state, before Octavius founded his Monarchie, the whole globe of the earth with civill and forraine warre, with fight on sea and land was terribly shaken."[31] The young Caesar exploits the world in order to establish his power firmly and exclusively. Suetonius lists five major civil wars Octavius engaged in: Mutina, Philippi, Perusium, Sicily, and Actium.[32] Appian's whole history is concerned with the Roman civil wars previous to Octavius' monarchy—*An Auncient Historie and Exquisite Chronicle of the Romanes Warres* (1578). The wars of Octavius occupy over two hundred pages alone.[33] He and

Antony march on Rome to demand favors by the force of arms, creating a panic in the city.[34] Octavius extorts the consulship from Rome, and proceeds to incite another civil war. Mexia, too, records the originator of the struggle with Pompey: "Octavian remaining in Rome, grew mightie, and in great estimation; so likewise he became covetous: and as the companie and neighborhood of Sextus Pompeius in Sicilia was displeasing unto him, so would he have been glad to have any occasion to warre against him: and so hee determined, and prepared a great fleete for the purpose."[35] The battles between Octavius and Pompey were many, but the final one "without doubt was one of the most cruell in the world."[36]

In order to explain why Octavius brought such catastrophe to Rome, the Elizabethan historians of Rome often explored his motives for the several plots and civil wars. Fulbecke exposes the speciousness of Octavius' role as avenger for the murder of Julius Caesar: "no commonweale can be without men of aspiring humours, and when such a murder is wrought they find present occasion to tumultuate, knowing that Anarchie breedeth confusion, & that it is best fishing in a troubled streame: making a glorius pretece to revenge the death of a Prince, though in heart & in truth, they beare greater affection to the monarchie remaining, then to the Monarcke who is taken away."[37] Octavius seeks to stir Rome into a great civil tumult out of which he may emerge supreme in power.

The early dispute with Antony offers a significant example of Octavius' ability to create discord, and to use the subsequent upheaval to further his ambition to become sole ruler of Rome. Octavius maneuvers the Senate into opposition with Antony and his army. The Senate has no army to oppose him, but Octavius does. The Senate therefore must grant Octavius great military and civil powers in order to protect itself from Antony's army. Thus Octavius gains power by stabilizing the discord he created.[38] In Seile's *Augustus,* Octavius schemes to have the army that will challenge Antony led by Hirtius and Pansa, the ruling consuls, so that he will stand to gain most with least risk to himself.[39] Octavius, then, ensures his own succession to power by killing personally the two consuls.[40]

Later, when Octavius and Antony make war as allies, North testifies to their rapacity: "when they had driven all the natural Italians out of Italy, they gave their soldiers their lands and towns, to which they had no right: and moreover the only mark they shot at in all this war they made, was but to overcome and reign."[41] They did nothing to avoid the misery brought to all Italy by their wars.[42] In a similar manner, Mexia accounts for their neglect of the commonweal: "But the truth is, they both desired to bee Lords of the whole, and in my opinion, vainglorie, ambition, covetousnes, and envie, moved them thereto, each of them putting his determination in effect, calling and levying forces and aides; so as the whole world in a manner, either of the one side or other, was moved and troubled therewith."[43] Mexia cites "principally Octavian," whose greed and ambition overwhelms all other motives in the quest for world domination.[44]

The offences of Octavius against the commonweal were many, but none so corrupt, none so destructive, nor none so cruel as the proscription by the Triumvirate. Upon the announcement of proscription, Appian recounts, the city suffered violent and unnatural omens that reflect the cruelty of Octavius.[45] The Triumvirate, supposedly conceived to preserve the peace, became an instrument by which to fulfill personal ambition. Octavius, Antony, and Lepidus, according to North, "could hardly agree whom they would put to death: for every one of them would kill their enemies, and save their kinsmen and friends. Yet at length, giving place to their greedy desire to be revenged of their enemies, they spurned all reverence of blood and holiness of friendship at their feet."[46] Mexia, also, stresses the perverted standards of friendship displayed by the Triumvirs: "In this proscription and league which they made . . . they concluded also each of them to kill his enemies, and the one delivering them into the others hands, having more respect and care to be revenged of an enemie, then to the saving of a friend: and so was made the most cruell and most inhumane proscription and butcherie that ever was seene or heard of, giving and exchaunging friends and kinsmen, for enemies and adversaries."[47] Appian, too, notes that not only the commonweal was sacrificed in order to achieve personal power, but friends readily were murdered.[48] Among the dead were 300 Senators and 2000 noble Romans, "so great power had ambition and hatred in the hearts of these three men."[49] The irony of the Triumvirate's action compared with the purpose of its existence is clear in Appian: "It seemed wonderful to them to consider, that other Cities being undone by sedition, have bin preserved againe by agreement. This Cittie, the devision of the rulers hadde consumed, and their agreement, broughte it to desolation."[50] Octavius' rule is compared to the sacking of a city, and his care of the commonweal likened to sedition. Octavius is clearly condemned as a tyrant in Seile's *Augustus*: "The poor Romans had not changed the Tyranny [of Julius Caesar], but the Tyrants. Yea they had three for one into the bargaine."[51]

The time of the proscriptons was, Seile assures us, "a lamentable and ruthful time, good and bad, rich and poore, being alike subject to the slaughter."[52] Mexia dramatizes the discord and sorrow which seized Rome and Italy under the rule of the Triumvirs: "And presently those which by them were condemned and proscript, were by their commandement put to death, being sought out in al parts & places, ransacking their houses, and confisking their goods: In the execution whereof there was so great confusion, sorrow and heaviness in the citie of Rome, and almost in al Italie, as the like was never seene nor heard of therein by man."[53] So neglected was morality, Appian observes, that murder was rewarded by the Triumvirs: "there was greate suddayne slaughter, and diverse kyndes of murders, and cuttings off of heads to be shewed for rewardes sake. . . . The condemned persons heads were brought before the seats in the common place, that they that had brought them, might receive their goods."[54] Values were inverted by the proscriptions so that the trust people had

for one another was destroyed. Because this trust formed the basis for social order, the loss of it meant social chaos. So extensive was the destruction of society that families were torn apart by murders and betrayals.[55]

Even Eutropius, who sees Octavius as the great monarch, admits that his paragon of princes did willfully "detayne the weale publique, by force of armes."[56] North allows that Octavius at first opposed the idea of proscription, but he admits that "when the sword was once drawn, he was no less cruel than the other two."[57] Suetonius attributes to him the same initial reluctance followed by an excess of vigorous cruelty,[58] and affirms that his motive in carrying out the proscription was to gain personal power: Octavius "professed openly, That hee had determined no other end of the saide proscription, but that hee might have liberty still to proceede in all things as he would."[59] Octavius, according to Mexia's figurative emphasis, "plotting the Triumvirat . . . shed so much bloud and such execution, that there was not any streete in Rome, but was stained with civill bloud."[60]

North's final word on the proscriptions presents a fit conclusion to the abundant catalogue of historical opinion damning Octavius: "In my opinion there was never a more horrible, unnatural, and crueller change than this was. For thus changing murther for murther, they did as well kill those whom they did forsake and leave unto others, as those also which others left unto them to kill: but so much more was their wickedness and cruelty great unto their friends, for that they put them to death being innocents, and having no cause to hate them."[61]

In other events under his direction, Octavius appears barbarous and savage. Suetonius, for example, mentions his cruelty to the prisoners at Philippi,[62] his mass execution at Perusia,[63] and his plucking out of Gallius' eyes.[64]

The significance of the common indictment against Octavius' tyranny by the several historians is that nearly all the acts condemned were committed *before* Octavius became emperor. Most of the historians damn Octavius' neglect of the commonweal while he strove to attain absolute power; most praise him for his care *after* he had obtained it. He is both the ambitious and ruthless tyrant, and the benevolent monarch. Mexia comprehends the complexity of Octavius: "he happened wisely and uprightly to governe that, which by force and cunning he had gotten."[65] As the ambitious and cruel triumvir, Octavius violates constituted civil order (always an evil act in Tudor histories) in his desire to accumulate all power to himself.

Awareness of the sharp distinction maintained by so many Elizabethan historians between Octavius the ambitious tyrant and Octavius the great ruler may lead us, in turn by analogy, to be more sharply aware that Shakespeare has presented only a calculating and cruel tyrant Octavius in *Julius Caesar* and *Antony and Cleapatra*. He has not yet become emperor at the end of *Antony and Cleapatra*, and Cleopatra, like the Elizabethan historians of Rome, holds his bloody civil war victories in abhorrent contempt.

Notes

1. J. E. Phillips, *The State in Shakespeare's Greek and Roman Plays* (New York, 1940), pp. 198-200.

2. Maurice Charney, *Shakespeare's Roman Plays: The Function of Imagery in the Drama* (Cambridge, Mass., 1961), p. 91; J. Leeds Barroll, "Shakespeare and Roman History," *MLR,* 53 (1958), 327-343; also cited by Charney, p. 229, n. 9. In a later article, Professor Barroll makes a broad claim about how in Elizabethan times Octavius Caesar "was considered an eminently impressive historical figure" ("The Characterization of Octavius," *Shakespeare Studies,* 6 [1972], p. 252 and nn. 26, 44). Others share Professor Barroll's view: see Brents Stirling, *Unity in Shakespearean Tragedy* (New York, 1956), pp. 165, 179, where Octavius Caesar appears in "a choric function" against a diminished Antony and Cleopatra; and Daniel Stempel, "The Transmigration of the Crocodile," *SQ,* 7 (1956), 63-66.

3. Julian Markels, *The Pillar of the World* (Columbus, Ohio, 1968), p. 126.

4. Roy W. Battenhouse, *Shakespearean Tragedy* (Bloomington, Indiana, 1969), pp. 172-173.

5. Battenhouse, pp. 174-183.

6. A. P. Riemer, *A Reading of Shakespeare's "Antony and Cleopatra"* (Sydney, 1968), pp. 12, 38-39.

7. Riemer, pp. 76, 81. Riemer offers a helpful survey of *Antony and Cleopatra* in his first and third chapters, and points out how Virgil K. Whitaker, *The Mirror up to Nature* (San Marino, 1965) and Brents Stirling, *Unity in Shakespearean Tragedy* (New York, 1956), especially, support his own assessment of the play's irresolute conclusion in the alleged contradictions, paradoxes, and ironies generated by the lovers' self-interest and lust.

8. Honor Matthews, *Character and Symbol in Shakespeare's Plays* (New York, 1969; copyright 1962), p. 66. See pp. 206-207 for affirmation of Antony and Cleopatra's transcendent love.

9. Maynard Mack, "Introduction" to his Pelican edition of *The Tragedy of Antony and Cleopatra* (Baltimore, 1960), pp. 21-23; and in *"Antony and Cleopatra*: The Stillness and the Dance" in *Shakespeare's Art: Seven Essays,* ed. Milton Crane (Chicago, 1973), p. 91, Professor Mack observes that "Nothing seems to be granted finality in *Antony and Cleopatra,* perhaps not even death"; Thomas McFarland, *Tragic Meanings in Shakespeare* (New York, 1966), pp. 98-100, 120-26; Sigurd Burckhardt, "The King's Language: Shakespeare's Drama as Social Discovery," *Antioch Review,* 21 (1961), 386, quoted in Matthew Proser, *The Heroic Image in Five Shakespearean Tragedies* (Princeton, 1965), p. 174; Proser's distinction between the world of Octavius and the world of Antony and Cleopatra comes to most succinct focus on

p. 176. Drawing on Professor Mack's criticism, Janet Adelman affirms the transcendence of Antony and Cleopatra in *The Common Liar: An Essay on "Antony and Cleopatra"* (New Haven, 1973), pp. 156-157, 196 n. 20. Northrop Frye identifies "a superhuman vitality" that Cleopatra draws out of Antony leading them together into the discovery of a transcendence in "the appearance of another world that endures no master" (*Fools of Time: Studies in Shakespearean Tragedy* [Toronto, 1967], pp. 73-74). Harold Fisch finds transcendence in the mythological archetypes of Mars and Venus, Osiris and Isis, Cupid and Psyche in "'Antony and Cleopatra:' The Limits of Mythology," *Shakespeare Survey,* 23 (1970), 59-67. Professor Fisch cites work by Raymond B. Waddington, *"Antony and Cleopatra*: What Venus Did with Mars," *Shakespeare Studies,* 2 (1966), 210-227, and sees Cleopatra's death as "ritual apotheosis," "deserved punishment" by providence for sins, and transcending marriage ceremony leading to "her strong toil of grace" as a "heavenly and transcendent virtue" (pp. 66-67). For a sampling of other critics who define transcendence in *Antony and Cleopatra,* see Joseph A. Bryant, *Hippolyta's View* (Lexington, Ky., 1961), pp. 179-180, 183-188, and pp. 177-179, 188, for a pejorative view of Octavius; S. L. Bethell, *Shakespeare and the Popular Dramatic Tradition* (London, 1944), pp. 166, 168; David Kaula, "The Time Sense of *Antony and Cleopatra*," *SQ,* 15 (1964), 223; J. L. Simmons, *Shakespeare's Pagan World: The Roman Tragedies* (Charlottesville, 1973), pp. 15, 163; Robert Ornstein, "The Ethic of the Imagination: Love and Art in *Antony and Cleopatra*" in *The Later Shakespeare, Stratford-upon-Avon Studies 8,* ed. John Russell Brown and Bernard Harris (London, 1966), pp. 31-46, for transcendence by means of art; and Theodore Spencer, *Shakespeare and the Nature of Man,* 2nd ed. (New York, 1966), p. 174.

10. Proser, p. 229. The drama of transcendence is not missed by all those critics who find high values in the character of Octavius: see Markels, p. 150, for "transformation" and "apotheosis" in death; and Matthews, pp. 206-207, for transcendence of the material world (cf. n. 8, above).

11. E. M. W. Tillyard, *Shakespeare's History Plays* (New York, 1946), passim, esp. pp. 64-70; Lily B. Campbell, *Shakespeare's "Histories": Mirrors of Elizabethan Policy* (San Marino, 1958; copyright 1947); see also her *Tudor Conceptions of History and Tragedy in "A Mirror for Magistrates"* (Berkeley, 1936), and "The Use of Historical Patterns in the Reign of Elizabeth," *HLQ* 1 (1938); Irving Ribner, *The English History Play in the Age of Shakespeare* (Princeton, 1957). See also Leonard F. Dean, "Tudor Theories of History Writing," *University of Michigan Contributions in Modern Philology,* No. 1 (1941), 1-24; Herbert Weisinger, "Ideas of History during the Renaissance," *JHI,* 6 (1945), 415-435; and W. R. Trimble,

"Early Tudor Historiography, 1485-1548," *JHI,* 11 (1950), 30-41.

12. Phillips, p. 199.

13. H. Seile, *Augustus: or, an essay* (London, 1632), p. 227.

14. William Fulbecke, *An Historicall Collection of the Continuall Factions of the Romans and Italians* (London, 1601), p. 17.

15. *Augustus,* p. 27.

16. Fulbecke, p. 171.

17. *Shakespeare's Plutarch: Being a Selection From The Lives in North's Plutarch,* ed. W. W. Skeat (London, 1904), p. 166. (Hereafter cited as North.)

18. *Augustus,* pp. 31-32.

19. Appian, *An Auncient Historie and Exquisite Chronicle of the Romanes Warres,* trans. W. B. (London, 1578), p. 181.

20. Suetonius, *The History of the Twelve Caesars,* trans. P. Holland (1606) in *The Tudor Translations,* XXI (London, 1899), p. 187.

21. Pedro Mexia, *The Historie of all the Romane Emperors,* Englished by W. T. (London, 1604), p. 29.

22. North, p. 167.

23. *Augustus,* p. 52. See also Mexia, p. 42.

24. North, p. 202.

25. Suetonius, pp. 92-93.

26. Appian, p. 383.

27. Mexia, p. 41. See also North, p. 199.

28. *Augustus,* pp. 55-56.

29. Appian, pp. 380-381.

30. Mexia, p. 41.

31. Fulbecke, p. 18.

32. Suetonius, pp. 86-87.

33. See Books 3 and 4.

34. Appian, p. 189. See also Mexia, p. 30.

35. Mexia, p. 36.

36. Mexia, p. 39.

37. Fulbecke, p. 172.

38. Appian, pp. 181-197.

39. *Augustus,* pp. 33-35.

40. Suetonius, p. 88.

41. North, pp. 145-146.

42. Appian, pp. 311-312.

43. Mexia, p. 42.

44. Mexia, p. 41.

45. Appian, p. 230.

46. North, p. 169.

47. Mexia, p. 31. See also *Augustus,* pp. 41-42.

48. See Appian, pp. 230-231.

49. Mexia, p. 31.

50. Appian, pp. 236-237. See also p. 231.

51. *Augustus,* pp. 43-43.

52. *Augustus,* p. 42.

53. Mexia, p. 31.

54. Appian, pp. 235-237.

55. Appian, p. 236.

56. Eutropius, *A Briefe Chronicle, where in are described shortlye the Originall, and the successive estate of the Romaine weale publique,* trans. N. Howard (London, 1564), fol. 69v. Richard Reynoldes, *A Chronicle of all the noble Emperours of the Romaines* (London, 1571), also praises the *emperor* Augustus, not the *aspiring* Octavius.

57. North, p. 236.

58. Suetonius, p. 101-102.

59. Suetonius, p. 102.

60. Mexia, p. 27.

61. North, p. 169.

62. Suetonius, p. 89.

63. Suetonius, p. 90.

64. Suetonius, pp. 102-103.

65. Mexia, p. 51.

Theodora A. Jankowski (essay date 1989)

SOURCE: Jankowski, Theodora A. "'As I Am Egypt's Queen': Cleopatra, Elizabeth I, and the Female Body Politic." In *Assays: Critical Approaches to Medieval and Renaissance Texts,* Vol. V, edited by Peggy A. Knapp, pp. 91-110. Pittsburgh: University of Pittsburgh Press, 1989.

[*In the following essay, Jankowski identifies the similarities and differences between Queen Elizabeth and Shakespeare's Cleopatra, and notes that although both women used their bodies for political purposes, Cleopatra should not be viewed as a direct allegorization of Elizabeth. Jankowski also claims that the parity between the two women* reveals Shakespeare's interest in the difficulties Elizabeth faced as a woman attempting to be an effective ruler in patriarchal England.]

In his 1558 pamphlet, *The First Blast of the Trumpet Against the Monstrous Regiment of Women,* John Knox argued that no woman could be a sovereign ruler because

> the immutable decree of God . . . hath subiected her to one membre of the congregation, that is to her husband. . . . So that woman by the lawe of God . . . is vtterly forbidden to occupie the place of God in the offices aforesaid, which he hath assigned to man, whome he hath appointed and ordeined his lieutenant in earth.[1]

That dour Protestant directed these words primarily against the two reigning Catholic monarchs, Mary Tudor of England and Mary Stuart of Scotland. The pamphlet, however, appeared after the Protestant Elizabeth Tudor replaced her sister Mary on the throne of England. Yet despite the irony of Knox's "blasting" the monarch who would come to be known as a champion of the Protestant cause, his negative reactions to a female sovereign notably echoed those of many of his fellow subjects.

The extreme patriarchalism of Renaissance society made it virtually impossible for a woman to attain power in any sphere, especially politics.[2] Renaissance works of political theory nearly always focused on how a male ruler could secure, enjoy, or extend his power within a society that was most definitely patriarchal and, therefore, *used* to being ruled by a man.[3] Even if heredity decreed that a woman should rule, society provided her with no patterns of behavior to follow. Male monarchs, in contrast, were products of a society whose major components—civil, ecclesiastical, familial—consisted of a ruling father figure who groomed chosen "sons" to take over his role. Even the formula for proclaiming a new ruler—"the king is dead, long live the king"—reinforces, as Jean Wilson reminds us, the Renaissance assumption that all rulers were male.[4]

Elizabeth I was aware of her anomalousness from the beginning of her reign but, unlike her sister, Mary, used it to insure her position on the throne. One particular strategy she used was to play on the notion of the monarch's two bodies, a notion which for her had to have a somewhat different meaning than for male monarchs. This notion was devised to deal with the paradox that kings died but the crown endured. Marie Axton very clearly defines the concept in terms of Elizabeth:

> For the purposes of law it was found necessary by 1561 to endow the Queen with two bodies: a *body natural* and a *body politic*. . . . The body politic was supposed to be *contained within the natural body of the Queen*. When lawyers spoke of this body politic they referred to a specific quality: the essence of *corporate perpetuity*. The Queen's natural body was subject to infancy, infirmity, error and old age; her body politic, created out of a combination of faith, ingenuity and practical expediency, was held to be immortal.[5]

Given this concept of dualities, Elizabeth's anomalousness could be glossed over. Her body natural may have been female, but her subjects could easily accept, as she did herself in her Tilbury speech (1588), her body politic as male.

But the mere existence of the queen's two bodies did not resolve the sometimes rival claims of these bodies. Elizabeth had to make some very definite choices regarding these two bodies to insure the success of her reign. What she did was to make her body natural serve her body politic. She opted to remain a virgin and to forgo the roles of wife and mother. She made this decision part of her political theory by claiming either that she was married to England or her subjects, or that the English people were her children. This decision had two very specific positive results: first, her position as virgin queen harked back to the Mariolatry of medieval England and implied that Elizabeth as virgin was essentially a deity; second, her decision to remain a virgin eliminated the possibility (and fear) that a consort could usurp her power over the throne of England.

Recently, critics have been exploring some of the various strategies the queen used for dealing with the complexity of her gender position within a patriarchal society. Leah Marcus has argued that Elizabeth developed a political rhetoric which successfully supported the legal fiction of herself as "king." While she often used "queen," Elizabeth habitually referred to herself as "prince," a term which in the sixteenth century clearly referred to a male ruler. Gradually she adopted more sexually ambiguous formulas: "the Queen's majesty," "the Queen's most excellent majesty in her princely nature considering," or "Monarch and prince sovereign." As Marcus rightly observes, "subtly, perhaps not always consciously, [the queen] constructed a vocabulary of rule which was predominantly male."[6]

These legal and rhetorical ploys became the underpinnings of the political fictions Elizabeth used to contain her threatening anomaly. It is important to remember, as Louis Adrian Montrose cogently argues, that the reign of a woman sovereign was threatening to the strictly patriarchal society she ruled, for: "as the female ruler of what was, at least in theory, a patriarchal society, Elizabeth incarnated a contradiction at the very center of the Elizabethan sex gender system. . . . [She] was a cultural anomaly: and this anomalousness—at once divine and monstrous—made her powerful and dangerous."[7] Elizabeth's royal fictions, then, were of necessity paradoxical. They had to present her as a powerful sovereign who was capable of successfully ruling England, yet, at the same time, they had to assure her populace that her reign posed them no threat. She managed to accomplish this dual purpose, as Jonathan Goldberg indicates, by offering her subjects a "show of love." So successful was she that her "loving behaviour preconceived in the People's heades upon these considerations was then thoroughly confirmed, and indeede emplanted a wonderfull hope in them touchyinge her woorthy Governement in the reste of her Reyne."[8] In offering these shows of love, the queen was essentially wooing her people to her. She was aware that a woman was not thought of as a ruler and so could not assume the loyalty of her subjects. She had to win it.

In contrast, the entrance of Elizabeth's successor, James I, into London reinforced the innate power any male monarch could draw upon in a patriarchal society. Goldberg maintains that "sexual *domination* is implied in James's ravishing entrance" (p. 30) to the city, for the king arrived "like a bridegroom entering the bride" (p. 31). Since James could rely upon the existing metaphors and formulas of a patriarchal society, his fictions were not essential for establishing his power. Elizabeth had no such social tropes to draw upon. She was forced to become a consummate fiction-maker creating an elaborate political icon partially out of whole cloth, partially out of a symbolic list of strong women who were not necessarily rulers.[9]

Louis Montrose's recent work examines the ways in which Elizabeth secures her position on the throne through the uses of consciously iconographic fictions.[10] He quotes Elizabeth as telling Leicester: "I will have here but one Mistress and no Master" ("Shaping," 78). Montrose's statement—"to be her own mistress, her own master, the Queen had to be everyone's mistress and no one's" (78)—ties in very closely with both the concept of the queen's two bodies and the most powerful of Elizabeth's fictions, the virgin queen. The queen who adopted a virgin existence for political reasons could be—and often was—the "mistress" of everyone. She was the "mistress" of all her people as well as those courtiers and foreign princes she favored. Yet, given the social attitudes of the time, the queen could only support her political status as "multimistress" by being, in effect, actually a virgin. Thus, Elizabeth, to be successful in the fictions she created, had to make her body natural subordinate to her body politic by agreeing to give up a life of female sexuality in her body natural. Only two sexual options were open to her as a Renaissance woman: *actual* mistress to all men, or whore; "mistress" to only one, or wife. The former option would have violated accepted patriarchal religious and social custom, thus causing the queen to lose credibility as a monarch. The latter, while allowing her to retain credibility, would have effectively reduced her power by making her a wife, by definition in the Renaissance, a creature subservient to a husband/consort.

Once Elizabeth had made the decision to fuse her political and natural bodies into the image of the perpetual virgin, a strategy for successful rule presented itself. By becoming an official virgin, Elizabeth effectively removed herself from being seen as a "normal" woman—a powerless creature in the Renaissance political scheme. By redefining herself as a virgin—a woman who is "different" in very fundamental ways from other women, namely in her non-dependence on men to define her existence—Elizabeth defined herself as a powerful creature in Renaissance terms and assumed the power usually reserved exclusively for Renaissance men.

As the virginal "mistress of all," Elizabeth was able to use the Petrarchan conventions of courtship to suit her own purposes. Traditionally, the male lover courted the often distant beloved. Elizabeth turned the convention around so that she became the Petrarchan lover who courted not a mistress, but a consort. Her skill in such courtship is obvious in her negotiations for a French husband. Elizabeth initially entered into marriage negotiations with the French in 1570 for two reasons. First, an heir of her body would insure and solidify her dynasty—thus blunting Mary Stuart's claims to the throne of England—as well as rendering assassination of the English sovereign an ineffectual political ploy. Second, the end of the third civil war in France meant that country would be free once again to annoy England. Thus, a marriage between Elizabeth and a French prince could eliminate both the fear of Elizabeth dying childless and the fear of French intervention in English affairs. Various difficulties intervened to prevent the marriage, but in April of 1572 the queen signed the Treaty of Blois with France against Spain. As Elizabeth's biographer, J. E. Neale, indicates, the queen's alliance with France "against the ruler of the Netherlands . . . ended her dangerous isolation and paralysed French interference in her dealings with Mary and Scotland" without requiring her to marry.[11] In fact, she managed to gain all of the political advantages a marriage with a French prince would have provided without having to sacrifice any of her sovereignty at home.

By 1578, a changed political situation made it again necessary to consider strengthening the English alliance with France. But popular opposition to a French Catholic husband caused Elizabeth to slow down negotiations until 1580 when a Spanish-papal alliance made it even more necessary for Elizabeth to ally with France. When the Duc d'Alençon finally arrived in England in October of 1581, he signed not a marriage contract, but an agreement for Elizabeth to finance his campaign in the Netherlands. But this agreement also bound Alençon to support the anti-Guise faction in France, a move which effectually prevented his brother, Henry III, from siding with Elizabeth's Guise enemies. With this agreement, Elizabeth achieved a mighty diplomatic victory: "She had outwitted Henry III and Catherine de'Medici, got the substance of an alliance with France—and was still unmarried."[12] Elizabeth continued to make promises to marry Alençon—promises that strengthened his credit on the money markets—but by February of 1582 he was out of England. The courtship, according to Neale, "had served her purpose, for she had succeeded in keeping out of the Netherlands, and had frightened Philip with the prospect of an Anglo-French alliance" (p. 259). These incidents show to what extent Elizabeth used courtship—and the consequent promise of marriage—as a political strategy. Her courtships were not designed to be physically consummated in marriage, for that would have violated her position as virgin queen, but to be politically consummated in treaty or formal agreement. By thus retaining control of her sexuality, Elizabeth retained her power on the throne and redefined the concept of the female body politic. It

Judi Dench as Cleopatra and Anthony Hopkins as Mark Antony in a 1987 production of Antony and Cleopatra *at Olivier Theatre in the National Theatre.*

became—through her uniting of her natural and political bodies—a powerful political tool.

In his queen of Egypt, Shakespeare created a female character who also used her body as a political tool. However, in direct contrast to Queen Elizabeth, Cleopatra is represented as uniting her body natural and her body politic by literally "using" her blatant sexuality to insure her power on the throne.[13] Shakespeare is definitely aware of the anomalousness of the female sovereign's position and his creation of Cleopatra can be seen as a reflection upon the problems Elizabeth faced in trying to rule successfully in patriarchal Renaissance England.[14] By displacing the situation of Antony and Cleopatra to Egypt, Shakespeare was able to explore these questions of the nature of female rule free from the possibility of court censure. For, although Shakespeare clearly does not use Cleopatra as an allegory for Queen Elizabeth, he does endow her with Elizabeth's talent for using fictions in order to reinforce her power on the throne. As we have seen, Elizabeth's major fiction of virgin queen united her body natural and body politic to serve her political ends, which were to insure her place on the throne and prevent her marriage to a consort who could potentially wrest power from her. Like Elizabeth, Shakespeare's Cleopatra is shown to have

developed a successful strategy for rule that is based on uniting her body natural and her body politic. Unlike Elizabeth, she does this by making her political adversaries—the representatives of Rome—her lovers and binding them to her by bearing them children. In the Egypt Shakespeare has devised—an Egypt where "the holy priests / Bless [Cleopatra], when she is riggish"[15]—the granting of sexual favors becomes his character's main tool for obtaining and securing power. Shakespeare has demonstrated that Cleopatra has been using this technique long before she encountered Mark Antony. Pompey, in Act II, scene vi, calls to mind the story of Cleopatra's earlier connection with Julius Caesar. Caesar supported Cleopatra's claims to the throne of Egypt after she had appeared to him as a hoyden rolled up in a mattress (II, vi, 70). As Caesar's lover and the mother of his child, Cleopatra was able to secure her power on the throne. That she may have used the same technique to secure her power over Gnaeus Pompey may be deduced from Antony's calling attention to this previous liason (III, xiii, 117).

Cleopatra is similarly shown to use her sexuality to serve her political ends when she appears to Antony as Venus on the Cydnus (II, ii). In this scene, described by Enobarbus, we are presented with her most well-known fiction for securing power. This elaborate fiction of herself as a love/ fertility goddess seems designed solely to seduce Antony to her table and her bed. But the seduction is not simply sexual. Before Cleopatra's arrival, Antony had been "Enthron'd i' the market-place" (II, ii, 215). But once she does arrive, he suddenly finds himself "alone, / Whistling to the air" (215-16) for all the inhabitants of the city find themselves drawn to Cleopatra. Would it not cause a defect in nature, we are told, the air itself would have left Antony to gaze upon the queen of Egypt. The authority of Antony's rulership—symbolized by his enthronement—seems quite dubious given Cleopatra's power to call the people to her even while Antony is holding court. Given this context, we can see Antony's submission to Cleopatra as political as well as sexual. This dual submission is reinforced by Agrippa's recalling her similar effect on Julius Caesar: "Royal wench! / She made great Caesar lay his sword to bed; / He plough'd her, and she cropp'd" (226-28). The reference to both Antony and Caesar in such a few lines reinforces the similarity of the representation of Cleopatra's conquest of them. Her appealing to them both on a purely sexual level and bearing them children results in their "laying their swords to bed." This image is, of course, sexual, but it is also symbolic of both men giving up their masculine power of rulership—symbolized by the sword—wholly to Cleopatra.[16] That Mark Antony follows a pattern Caesar has established is further reinforced in act II, scene v, line 23, where Cleopatra reminds her waiting women that she has worn Antony's sword. Thus we can clearly see that Cleopatra is represented as using her sexual power to first conquer the sexual and then the political power of both Caesar and Antony. The swords can, of course, be seen as phallic images of male sexual and gender power, but they are also symbols of military and political power. Only defeated kings and generals take off or give up their swords to their conquerors.

Although Cleopatra has been ruling Egypt successfully, she is shown as finding herself in the odd position of having to validate—or to seem to have Rome validate—her position on the throne. As with all her major "policy statements," Cleopatra is represented as making this one with a regal presentation of herself, her consort, and her heirs:

> I' the market-place, on a tribunal silver'd,
> Cleopatra and himself in chairs of gold
> Were publicly enthron'd: at the feet sat
> Caesarion, whom they call my father's son,
> And all the unlawful issue that their lust
> Since then hath made between them. Unto her
> He gave the stablishment of Egypt, made her
> Of lower Syria, Cyprus, Lydia,
> Absolute queen.

(III, vi, 3-11)

Clearly this scene is problematical. It is described by Octavius "as 'tis reported" (19) and we have no evidence as to the trustworthiness or the point of view of the reporter.[17] As a result, the character Octavius perceives Antony, his antagonist, to be the creator of it. He cannot conceive that a mere female ruler could mount such a celebration of

power. Antony is the representative of the only real power Octavius acknowledges—Roman power—so he *must* be the instigator of the scene, the bestower of power.[18] Yet Shakespeare has shown us that while Antony has no talent for regal spectacles, Cleopatra stages and uses them constantly—on the Cydnus (II, ii), for example, and in her Pyramid (V, ii). The queen of Egypt also appears here "In the habiliments of the goddess Isis" (17) with no indication that Antony appears in similar regal or divine garb. He is merely seated in a golden chair. Also, as I have indicated in my discussion of act II, scene ii, the fact that Antony may set himself up in a marketplace does not necessarily mean that the Egyptian people—or Cleopatra— accept him as a ruler. It is clear to me, therefore, that this enthronement is simply the visual representation of Cleopatra's conquering Antony and her setting him up as her consort. The fact that both Caesar's and Antony's children are part of this presentation indicates that the scene is, indeed, Cleopatra's. Further, Cleopatra's only reference to Antony as "Emperor" occurs in act V, scene ii, line 76 when he is dead and no longer a threat to her political sovereignty.

Unconsciously or not, Shakespeare has created a female figure within whose seemingly gratuitous voluptuousness lies a clever strategy for successful rule. Uniting her body natural and her body politic has allowed Cleopatra to use her body natural's sexuality as a means by which she can gain power in her body politic. She is represented as having ruled successfully in Egypt for many years by coopting the power of those sent to conquer her by "conquering" them sexually and making them her lovers. She has also secured the continuance of her dynasty through the production of various heirs who are destined to succeed *her,* and not their Roman fathers.

One way to understand the significance of Cleopatra's strategy of rule is to see that she makes of her body a different "text" than Renaissance patriarchal constructions of woman allowed.[19] Typically, the male body was represented as an integrated, complete, male body in which the reason of the "head" controls the emotion/will of the "body" itself. Reason—that quality that separates man from the beasts—should control emotion to such a degree, in fact, that man should attain the Aristotelian "mean." The hierarchical arrangement of head over body is reinforced by the hierarchical positioning of man as the rational "head" over woman as the emotion-bound "body." This idea of the socially accepted complete and integrated male body in opposition to the socially unacceptable female body is present in *Antony and Cleopatra*. Octavius Caesar, the representative of Rome and, therefore, the character who determines Roman values in the play, is just such a complete and integrated male figure. In terms of the play, Octavius can only be defined by his position as Roman ruler. His complete devotion to the mean—as well as to an integrated, unitary selfhood—causes him to be seen as somewhat two-dimensional when compared to Antony. In fact, Octavius's refusal to take part in the celebrations on Pompey's galley reinforces his desire to retain a singular and immutable selfhood:

ANTONY.

> Be a child o' the time.

OCTAVIUS.

> Possess it, I'll make answer:
> But I had rather fast from all, four days,
> Than drink so much in one.

(II, vii, 98-101)

This belief that the body should be one (male) thing representing that patriarchal society it belongs to is one of the major reasons why the character Octavius cannot accept the changes Antony has undergone in Egypt. For most readers of the play, Antony can be seen as general and soldier, lover and politician, triumvir and emperor. His fullness is both his nature and his strength. For Octavius, however, Antony's fullness is his weakness. For Octavius, Antony should be only the man whose retreat from Modena "Was borne so like a soldier, that [his] cheek / So much as lank'd not" (I, iv, 70-71). The soldier's body is a strong and important image in the Roman empire.[20] As the man who gallantly survived the disastrous retreat from Modena with no ill effects, Antony becomes the image of an accepted male role in Roman society. Antony's soldier's reason managed to keep his body so under control that he maintained his "mean" and did not seem to suffer the excess that one would expect of someone on a starvation march. Thus, what Octavius, and Rome in the person of Enobarbus, admire about Antony is his ability to have a body which can be seen as a "text" for one specific ideal of Roman behavior. So strongly is Antony identified with his "soldier's body" that he is denigrated by Romans of all classes—from Octavius to Scarus—when he seems to act in any way that appears contrary to this sense of himself. Enobarbus, in fact, so completely accepts this singular view of Antony that he deserts him when he feels that his general has ceased to be a soldier.

Octavius is shown to turn against Antony once the soldier's body has changed, has become something else, has become something perhaps created by Cleopatra or tainted by her sexuality. Like Enobarbus and Scarus, Octavius can identify with the soldier who retreated from Modena. He fears the man who returns from Egypt to negotiate with him because that man has ceased to be the symbol of inflexible, immutable, male selfhood with whom Octavius can identify. No longer simply a Roman soldier, Antony has learned some of the values of the fluid and mutable Egyptian life. Later, once he finally returns to Egypt, he scorns the "boy Caesar" (III, xiii, 17), and is not completely unwilling to call attention to the "grizzled head" (17) he bears as both Cleopatra's lover and her general. Even though his Roman suicide shows how Antony is represented as retaining much of his Roman attitude toward his body, his speech to the clouds (IV, xiv, 2-14) shows how far he has moved from that rigid Roman selfhood to a willingness to accept the variability of life that Cleopatra and her realm promise him.

Octavius's fear of Cleopatra is based on the fact that he is the representative of a society that has very clearly defined gender roles which are based on how the body is perceived. This society, like that of Renaissance England, has created as its norm an image of an integrated male body ruled by the "head." In contrast, it has created an image of a female body that is the opposite of the male body and is controlled by emotion rather than reason. In order to deal with the essential cultural fear of woman and woman's sexual power over man, this society has attempted to control female power by strategies that involve dismemberment and/or silence.

Francis Barker indicates that the effect of patriarchal power "in one of its more spectacular forms" can be seen in "the delight to be had in dismembering a woman's body" (p. 86). The ultimate aim of this symbolic dismemberment is to grant power to a man through destruction of an adversary/woman. Barker analyzes this theory in terms of Andrew Marvell's poem, "To His Coy Mistress," in which the poet never speaks to or of his mistress as a "complete" woman, but rather as a collection of discrete pieces: "Thine Eyes," "thy Forehead," "each Breast," "every part," "the rest." The ultimate effect of this dismemberment of the female body—"uttered within a syntax more reminiscent of taxonomy than of the expectations of love poetry" (p. 89)—is its silence. As her body is torn apart, the mistress's ability to speak is also dismembered and in place of lover and mistress are two very different people: "the inexorable male voice which utters the poem" and "an empty place" (p. 91).

Nancy J. Vickers also speaks of the strategy of dismemberment as a way of silencing women. She examines the male fear of women in the context of the Diana-Actaeon myth as it appears in certain of Petrarch's poems. Petrarch's Actaeon-like speaker attempts to prevent his Diana from dismembering him by focusing only upon individual aspects of her body—her hair, hand, foot, and eyes—rather than upon the whole woman. Vickers thus shows a clear connection between the male fear of female power and the Renaissance insistence upon female silence. Speech becomes power; to deny a woman speech is to effectively deny her power.[21]

The effects of this "dismembered" view of women can be seen in *Antony and Cleopatra* in the characters of Octavia and Fulvia, two women who use more traditional means to try to gain power or exist within the patriarchal power structure of Rome. Octavia is shown as accepting the traditional woman's position as subservient to her brother Octavius for she is, as Caesar says, "a great part of myself" (III, ii, 24). She is virtually his object to use as he will and allows herself to become a political wife to Antony as a result of "The power of Caesar, and / His power unto Octavia" (II, ii, 143-44).[22] Octavia has the potential to be an ideal wife since she "is of a holy, cold, and still conversation" (II, vi, 119-20). She is shown to deny herself so readily, in fact, that she effectively loses the power of public speech, communicating almost exclusively in whispers to Octavius (III, ii). In this she becomes as voiceless as Marvell's mistress or Petrarch's Diana, as described by Barker and Vickers. In direct contrast to the "statue" Octavia (III, iii, 21), Cleopatra never loses her power of speech. With her speech she controls Octavia, like Caesar, by devising an entirely new "creature" to suit her own view of what she feels Octavia should be (II, iii). As Catherine Belsey indicates, speech is symbolic of power in patriarchal society: "To speak is to possess meaning, to have access to the language which defines, delimits and locates power. To speak is to become a subject. But for women to speak is to threaten the system of differences which gives meaning to patriarchy."[23] This is so for Cleopatra. Like the women of the romances, she remains "in command," as Inga-Stina Ewbank points out, because she maintains control of her rhetoric, of the resources of language.[24] Abandoned by Antony, Octavia's only place is as a silent shadow behind her brother in Rome. "Chaste, silent, and obedient"—to use Suzanne Hull's phrase—Octavia represents the ideal Renaissance woman.[25]

If Octavia can be seen as accepting the ideal silent, dismembered female body of the patriarchy, Fulvia can be seen as refusing this identification. By contrast, she is shown as trying to assume the role—and by extension the "body"—of a man and gain power by leading her armies against Rome.[26] This is a dangerous stance. Fulvia does not realize that her Amazonian role—essentially a direct usurpation of male military means to power—allows her to be viewed as a direct threat to male authority. Her death underlines her unsuccessful attempts to use specifically male means to power. Cleopatra is represented as adopting neither the "morally correct" behavior of Octavia, nor the military power of Fulvia.

In direct contrast to these women characters, Cleopatra is never shown as silenced or dismembered and is thus like a male body, though committed to mutability in a way very different from the marble-constant Romans. Cleopatra is shown neither as a part of anyone, like Octavia, nor as a part of herself—eyes, mouth, genitals, etc. She is always presented as a *complete* body, but not one that is rigid and immutable. Her body is highly eroticized and desirable, yet at the same time it is the body of a goddess (II, ii; III, vi; V, ii) or a mother (V, ii). It becomes "wrinkled deep in time" (I, v, 24) as she passes from her "salad days" (I, v, 73) to her current age and it can be burnt by the sun (I, v, 28) or blown to abhorring by water flies (V, ii, 59-60). In its ability to be complete and mutable, therefore, it is quite different both from the accepted female body that is silent, dismembered, or a male plaything, and from the accepted male body that is fixed and immutable. Thus, Shakespeare has represented Cleopatra's body as being something vitally different from existing Renaissance stereotypes of male and female bodies.

Given the change Shakespeare makes in the nature of Cleopatra's body, he still has to have her deal—as Queen Elizabeth dealt—with the male fear of female power as well as the seemingly paradoxical patriarchal belief that "female power" is a contradiction in terms. One strategy Elizabeth used to deal with the male fear of female power

was to present herself as androgynous. She often used male rhetoric—as Leah Marcus has indicated—to refer to herself in official documents or pronouncements, such as her speech at Tilbury where she affirmed that the heart and stomach that resided in her weak and feeble female body was, indeed, kingly, that is, male. Elizabeth consciously tried to deal with the Renaissance perception of the inadequacy of female power by implying that her androgynous power was greater than the sum of its male and female parts. Although willing to appear in armor as defender of her realm, the queen deliberately shunned comparison with Amazons who were perceived as threats to male social systems.[27] Elizabeth's androgyny allowed her to avoid the destructive extremes of both male and female power and locate a middle ground where she could positively unite the qualities of each sort of power.

Cleopatra's androgyny is implied in act II, scene v, lines 22-23, where she puts her "tires and mantles" upon Antony and wears "his sword Philippan." However, unlike Elizabeth at Tilbury, this vision of the verbally adept Cleopatra complete with Antony's surrogate penis comes dangerously close to the type of destructive female as outlined by Vickers[28] and dangerously close to the Renaissance image of the Amazon as female destructive power set up in opposition to patriarchal society. But by claiming power through a symbolic dismemberment and its accompanying marginalization, Cleopatra uses the very techniques Barker and Vickers describe male poets as using to marginalize women. The men Cleopatra is shown to marginalize are her political opponents. Though she does not dismember Octavius, she marginalizes him by referring to him as a child—"scarce-bearded Caesar" (I, i, 21). Antony is reduced to a surrogate penis. While he is alive, Cleopatra takes his sword to wear leaving him the symbolic trappings of a marginalized femininity, as Octavius indicates: [Antony] is not more manlike / Than Cleopatra; nor the queen of Ptolemy / More womanly than he" (I, iv, 5-7), Antony's death is lamented in the phallic line "The soldier's pole is fall'n" (IV, xv, 65). But, unlike Petrarch's Laura, Cleopatra is never punished for a behavior that is consciously threatening to male beliefs. While I agree that her wearing Antony's sword is an attempt to show her taking control of a power that can only be called male, Shakespeare rewards her for her audacity by allowing her to become a powerful and successful ruler. Shakespeare manages to accomplish this by showing that Cleopatra's power is different from that of the Amazon who simply mimics the destructive power of patriarchy. Shakespeare shows us that Cleopatra uses power in a more creative and generative way, as indicated by Peter Erickson:

> The play invites us to reconsider the traditional definition of masculinity as an identity founded on military success. . . . Antony and Cleopatra engage in a gender-role exchange that enlarges but does not erase the original and primary sexual identity of each. . . . Instead, what is involved is a crossing back and forth over a boundary no longer seen as a rigid barrier dividing the two sexes into two absolutely separate groups.[29]

Erickson sees act II, scene v as an attempt by Antony and Cleopatra to *share*—rather than simply to *exchange*—power in a sort of "heterosexual androgyny" (p. 133). Yet Cleopatra is not depicted as making androgyny as important a part of her political strategy as Elizabeth did, and so uses it rarely. Nevertheless, Cleopatra can be seen as revolutionary not only because she is a woman who holds regal power, but because she creates a new and much broader kind of female power out of existing, if limiting, strategies of male power.

Although Shakespeare has shown Cleopatra throughout the play to be as successful a ruler in Egypt as Elizabeth is in England, at the end she seems to abandon her own theory of rule. While she bargains as well as she can with Proculeius (V, ii), there is a sense that her dealings with him are merely superficial. What is even more curious is that she does not attempt to use her sexuality to control Octavius. In her one brief encounter with him Cleopatra does not act the temptress, or indeed any of her other favored roles. Instead, she treats Octavius as her conqueror:

> Sir, the gods
> Will have it thus, my master and my lord
> I must obey. . . .
>
> . . . .
>   Sole sir o'the world,
> . . . .
>   I have
> Been laden with like frailties, which before
> Have often sham'd our sex.
>
> . . . .
> My Master, and my lord!
>
> (V, ii, 114-16; 119; 121-23; 189)

Although Cleopatra is fully aware of Caesar's plot against her—"He words me, girls, he words me, that I should not / Be noble to myself" (V, ii, 190-91)—she never tries to bring him under her sway. That she creates an elaborate final image of herself as dead queen of Egypt and eternal Isis to counter Octavius's plan to parade her in triumph through Rome does not eliminate the fact that this is not her traditional way of dealing with a political adversary. Octavius has not been turned into a lover, as Julius Caesar and Antony had been; Cleopatra has merely allowed him to witness her last role.

I see Cleopatra as being forced to abandon her previously successful strategies for rule because of her relationship to Antony. Cleopatra's political tactics are based on sexual use of her body natural to serve her political purposes. Her love for Antony and her devotion to him—"Husband, I come" (V, ii, 286)—cause her to refrain from using her body natural in a political manner. Since she has given her heart to Antony, she has, essentially, given away her body natural and removed it from service to her body politic. Thus, she is at a disadvantage when meeting Octavius, for she is without the major component of her political bargaining strategy. She has to rely on her wits alone, without her sexuality, to subdue Octavius. This partial power is not sufficient. Cleopatra is forced to destroy both

her bodies in a final fiction that manages to satisfy them both. Her magnificent death scene convinces Octavius that Cleopatra died as a queen: "Bravest at the last, / She levell'd at our purposes, and being royal / Took her own way" (V, ii, 333-35), yet also as a lover: "but she looks like sleep, / As she would catch another Antony / In her strong toil of grace" (V, ii, 344-46). Cleopatra may be defeated, but a paradoxical sense of triumph surrounds her at her end so that we wonder whether she has really won or lost.

Ultimately, it is difficult not to see Cleopatra's triumph as that of a woman ruler who manages to rule successfully despite overwhelming social pressures. Like Elizabeth I—whom Shakespeare seems to have had in mind when he created her—Cleopatra is shown to work against existing patriarchal stereotypes to create a strategy for rule that works within the conditions of her society. She is represented as actively using her body natural's sexuality to support her body politic's place on the throne. Also like Elizabeth, Cleopatra manages to counter the threats caused by the fear of female power by creating a more positive, more androgynous kind of power. Shakespeare even manages to go beyond this examination of women in positions of power to consider the dilemma of those women in patriarchal society—as represented by Octavia and Fulvia—who are not able to create successful strategies for dealing with the restrictive social conditions and social fears that control their existence.

By reading Cleopatra through the text of Queen Elizabeth I's strategies for rule, a figure somewhat different from the "traditional" one appears. This reading is a direct result of my persistent exasperation with what can be called the "traditional" reading of Cleopatra's character, namely that which sees her as the whore who ruined a great triumvir but, at the end, was conquered by love and took her life in remorse.[30] What annoys me most about this reading is its proponents' willingness to be blinded by Dryden's "all for love" romanticism and their unwillingness to examine the political space in which Cleopatra's character is figured. My own reading of *Antony and Cleopatra* is informed by the new work in historicist criticism and the feminist readings it has produced.[31] Historicist criticism, as Louis Montrose sees it, is a critical practice which strives

> to resituate canonical literary texts among the multiple forms of writing, and in relation to the non-discursive practices and institutions, of the social formation in which those texts have been produced—while, at the same time, recognizing that this project of historical resituation is necessarily the textual construction of critics who are themselves historical subjects.
>
> (p. 6)

Thus, in an attempt to examine just how Shakespeare explores questions of female rule in his creation of Cleopatra, I have examined the strategies Queen Elizabeth I used to both create and employ a specific kind of female power in a world which was hostile to the thought of female power in any form. My historicist method of analysis—a method that uses literary and nonliterary materials to examine how the question of female political power is represented and managed in the Renaissance—is somewhat at odds with feminist criticism which has not traditionally concerned itself with an examination of female political power. However, my reading is clearly feminist in intent. Therefore, I term my particular reading of Cleopatra "historicist-feminist."

As a female ruler who took power and controlled the various aspects of her rule, Elizabeth challenged and subverted in an essential way the established Renaissance ideology of patriarchal rule. Yet to subvert this major ideology in such an essential way was highly dangerous. There was no telling how long Elizabeth could survive as queen—given her society's views of ruling women as expressed by John Knox—if she consistently subverted the major ideology to such a degree. So she contained her subversion within the accepted female paradigm of a contained female sexuality—virginity. Her genius lay in maintaining the tension between the power of her subversion and the fiction of her submission within her containment, thus enabling her to retain her power on the throne while reducing the threat of her female sexuality.

In *Antony and Cleopatra,* one can examine just this question of the subversion of ideology through the character Cleopatra. The difference between Cleopatra and Elizabeth is that Shakespeare has allowed Cleopatra to subvert the ruling Roman (English) ideology to an even greater degree than Elizabeth by living as a sexually fulfilled woman. Elizabeth sacrificed her sexuality to contain her subversion; Shakespeare allows Cleopatra literally to use her sexuality to gain her power and to create the subversive ideology of her reign. In this way, her power is enormous and shown to be a major threat to the established patriarchal ideology of Rome. Cleopatra is not shown to take steps, as Elizabeth had done, to contain her power. Shakespeare takes these steps. His depiction of Cleopatra's refusal to use her sexuality to dominate Octavius and his representation of her acceptance of death become the means by which her subversion is contained.

Instead of the simple tale of the great general ruined, *Antony and Cleopatra* becomes an important examination of the nature of power, the differences between various types of powers, and the means by which dominant ideologies are displayed and subverted. Further, Shakespeare's representation of Cleopatra becomes an examination of the means by which a female monarch can secure regal power even within a society whose basic tenets have denied her, as a woman, virtually all power. *Antony and Cleopatra,* then, becomes a text of female political theory which owes its creation, I maintain, to the earlier text written by Queen Elizabeth I herself.

Notes

1. John Knox, *The First Blast of the Trumpet Against the Monstrous Regiment of Women* (1558; rpt. New York: Da Capo, 1972), pp. 16-17. Spelling modernized as regards tildas and long *s*.

2. Lawrence Stone, *The Family, Sex and Marriage in England 1500-1800* (New York: Harper & Row, 1977), pp. 591, 623.

3. Specifically, such works as: Niccolò Machiavelli, *Il Principe* (1513), Thomas More, *Utopia* (1515-16), Desiderius Erasmus, *Institutio princips christiani* (1516), Baldesar Castiglione, *Il Cortegiano* (1528), and Thomas Elyot, *The Boke Named the Gouernour Devised by Sir Thomas Elyot, Knight* (1531).

4. Jean Wilson, *Entertainments for Elizabeth I* (Woodbridge: D. S. Brewer and Totowa, N.J.: Rowan and Littlefield, 1980), p. 3.

5. Marie Axton, *The Queen's Two Bodies: Drama and the Elizabethan Succession* (London: Royal Historical Society, 1977), p. 12. Axton's work, as the title indicates, focuses on drama of the Elizabethan period that was concerned with urging the queen to marry and produce an heir, thus insuring the succession. Axton bases her generalizations on Edmund Plowden's reference to the monarch's two bodies in 1561, as reported by F. W. Maitland in "The Crown as Corporation," in *Collected Papers,* ed. H. A. L. Fisher (Cambridge: Cambridge University Press, 1911), and on Ernst Kantorowicz's *The King's Two Bodies* (Princeton, N.J.: Princeton University Press, 1957). Axton feels that Kantorowicz "did not explore the Elizabethan setting in any depth" (p. 15). Louis Adrian Montrose, "'Shaping Fantasies': Figurations of Gender and Power in Elizabethan Culture," *Representations* 1 (1983), 61-94, esp. 77, also mentions the concept of the queen's two bodies.

6. Leah S. Marcus, "Shakespeare's Comic Heroines, Elizabeth I, and the Political Uses of Androgyny," in *Women in the Middle Ages and the Renaissance,* ed. Mary Beth Rose (Syracuse, N.Y.: Syracuse University Press, 1986), pp. 135-53.

7. Montrose, "'Shaping Fantasies,'" 77, 78.

8. Jonathan Goldberg, *James I and the Politics of Literature* (Baltimore: Johns Hopkins University Press, 1983), p. 30. Goldberg is quoting a contemporary reaction to Elizabeth's first procession through London in 1558/9.

9. Frances A. Yates, *Astraea: The Imperial Theme in the Sixteenth Century* (London: Routledge & Kegan Paul, 1975), pp. 153-82.

10. Louis Montrose, "'Eliza, Queene of Shepheardes,' and the Pastoral of Power," *ELH* 10 (1980), 153-82.

11. J. E. Neale, *Queen Elizabeth I* (1934; rpt. Harmondsworth, U.K.: Penguin, 1960), p. 226.

12. Ibid., p. 257.

13. Robert S. Miola, *Shakespeare's Rome* (Cambridge: Cambridge University Press, 1983). Miola observes that, "threatened on all sides by hostile forces, both Dido and Cleopatra ensnare important Roman soldiers in nets of luxury and concupiscence" (p. 123).

14. Helen Morris, "Queen Elizabeth I 'Shadowed' in Cleopatra," *Huntington Library Quarterly* 32 (1969), 271-78, and Keith Rinehart, "Shakespeare's Cleopatra and England's Elizabeth," *Shakespeare Quarterly* 23 (1972), 81-86. Morris maintains that the Cleopatra in North's Plutarch "must" have reminded Shakespeare of Queen Elizabeth and "this resemblance was at the back of his mind while he was writing the play." Rinehart indicates that parallels exist between Elizabeth and Cleopatra because "both were queens regnant, both used courtship as a mainstay of their statecraft, and both attained apotheosis of a sort as female deities." Janet Adelman, *The Common Liar: An Essay on "Antony and Cleopatra"* (New Haven, Conn.: Yale University Press, 1973), points out that Antony's reference to Cleopatra as "this great fairy" (IV, viii, 12) can be read as a reference to Elizabeth I as Gloriana, the Faerie Queene (p. 65).

15. William Shakespeare, *Antony and Cleopatra,* ed. M. R. Ridley, The Arden Shakespeare (London: Methuen, 1982), II, ii, 239-40. All further references to the play will be to this edition.

16. "Agrippa associates Cleopatra's sexuality with the fecundity of nature [in II, ii, 227-28]. . . . The wordplay makes the point very tidily: the sword is unmistakably both a sexual and a military weapon; and the military must be put aside (or laid to bed) before the sexual can be literally laid to bed, or put to use. In the image, the sword has been beaten into a plowshare: there are suggestions of that great generative sympathy in nature which occurs only when Mars succumbs to Venus and lays his sword to bed" (Adelman, *The Common Liar,* p. 95). Barbara J. Bono, *Literary Transvaluation* (Berkeley and Los Angeles: University of California Press, 1984), argues that Cleopatra uses Antony "to advance her political schemes for the resurgence of Alexander's empire" (p. 159).

17. Janet Adelman, in *The Common Liar,* points out many times that "in *Antony and Cleopatra,* information of all kinds is unreliable" and "we frequently find that we can make no judgment at all" regarding the reliability of any evidence that is reported, Roman or Egyptian (pp. 34, 29).

18. Richard S. Ide, *Possessed with Greatness: The Heroic Tragedies of Chapman and Shakespeare* (Chapel Hill, N.C.: University of North Carolina Press, 1980) believes that, in this scene, "Cleopatra . . . herself has been bewitched by the new political stature Antony has given her" (p. 112). Barbara J. Bono, *Literary Transvaluation,* indicates that "Cleopatra is politically astute and wins from Antony a promise to 'piece / Her opulent throne with kingdoms' (I, v, 45-46). This local Egyptian naturalistic interpretation culminates in their ritual coronation at Alexandria, where Cleopatra 'In the habiliments of the goddess Isis' watches Antony proclaim her and their children rulers of the East (III, vi, 17). But this coronation of the earthly Isis and her Bacchic consort provokes full-scale Roman opposition" (p. 207). Bono forgets that Julius Caesar's child figures in this enthronement as well as Antony's children and that Shakespeare did not tell us that Antony appeared in the guise of Bacchus.

19. Francis Barker, "Into the Vault," in *The Tremulous Private Body: Essays on Subjection,* ed. Francis Barker (London: Methuen, 1984); Nancy J. Vickers, "Diana Described: Scattered Woman and Scattered Rhyme," *Critical Inquiry* 8 (1981), 265-79; and Michael D. Bristol, *Carnival and Theater: Plebeian Culture and the Structure of Authority in Renaissance England* (New York: Methuen, 1985).

20. Miola, *Shakespeare's Rome,* points out that Caesar and Antony share "a common heritage: the Roman tradition of military honor" (p. 129).

21. Vickers, "Diana Described," 273, 278-79.

22. Eve Kosofsky Sedgwick, *Between Men: English Literature and Male Homosocial Desire* (New York: Columbia University Press, 1985), observes that men in patriarchal society often "consolidate partnership with authoritative males in and through the bodies of females" (p. 38).

23. Catherine Belsey, *The Subject of Tragedy* (London: Methuen, 1985), p. 191.

24. Inga-Stina Ewbank, "Shakespeare's Portrayal of Women: A 1970's View," in *Shakespeare: Pattern of Excelling Nature,* ed. David Bevington and Jay L. Halio (Newark, Del.: University of Delaware Press, 1978), pp. 222-29, esp. p. 224.

25. Suzanne W. Hull, *Chaste, Silent and Obedient: English Books For Women 1475-1640* (San Marino, Calif.: Huntington Library, 1982). Carol Thomas Neely, *Broken Nuptials in Shakespeare's Plays* (New Haven, Conn.: Yale University Press, 1985) sees Octavia as "victimized" by Antony and Octavius (p. 144).

26. Phyllis Rackin, "Anti-Historians: Women's Roles in Shakespeare's Histories," *Theater Journal* 37 (1985), 329-44, indicates that Margaret of Anjou is, in some ways, like Fulvia. Margaret is "a virago who defies her husband [and] leads armies into battle . . . [and] has a 'tiger's heart wrapped in a woman's hide'" (p. 336).

27. Celeste Turner Wright, "The Amazons in Elizabethan Literature," *SP* 73 (1940), 433-56, esp. pp. 433, 449, 456, and Simon Shepherd, *Amazons and Warrior Women: Varieties of Feminism in Seventeenth Century Drama* (New York: St. Martin's Press, 1981), p. 14.

28. Indeed, Adelman, *The Common Liar,* observes that a clothing exchange "inevitably suggests a disastrous

exchange of sexual authority and consequently a violation of the proper hierarchical relation between man and woman. This disturbance in sexual hierarchy can be seen morally as a violation of the proper hierarchical relation between reason and will" (p. 91).

29. Peter Erickson, *Patriarchal Structures in Shakespeare's Drama* (Berkeley and Los Angeles: University of California Press, 1985), pp. 131, 133. Miola speaks of the "vision of sexual passion as emasculating and antithetical to the male business of war" (p. 139). He also suggests that Egypt is "a reign of transshifting shapes and forms where men behave like women, women behave like men, and both act like gods" (p. 129).

30. Michael Steppat, *The Critical Reception of Shakespeare's "Antony and Cleopatra" From 1607 to 1905* (Amsterdam: Grüner, 1980), analyzes historical attitudes toward Cleopatra. Robert E. Fitch, "No Greater Crack?" *Shakespeare Quarterly* 19 (1968), 3-17, provides a limited, but helpful, survey. A more detailed compendium of critical attitudes toward the queen of Egypt can be found in L. T. Fitz, "Egyptian Queens and Male Reviewers: Sexist Attitudes in *Antony and Cleopatra* Criticism," *Shakespeare Quarterly* 28 (1977), 297-316. Janet Adelman, *The Common Liar,* also examines much of the critical history of attitudes toward Cleopatra in her various notes.

31. I refer specifically to the works by Barker, Belsey, Bristol, Erickson, Marcus, Montrose, Rackin, Sedgwick, and Vickers mentioned above, but additionally to those by Stephen Greenblatt, *Renaissance Self-Fashioning* (Chicago: University of Chicago Press, 1980) and *The Power of Forms in the English Renaissance,* ed. Greenblatt (Norman, Okla.: Pilgrim Books, 1982); Louis Montrose, "Renaissance Literary Studies and the Subject of History," *English Literary Renaissance* 16 (1986), 5-12; Jean E. Howard, "The New Historicism in Renaissance Studies," *English Literary Renaissance* 16 (1986), 13-43; and Marilyn L. Williamson, *The Patriarchy of Shakespeare's Comedies* (Detroit: Wayne State University Press, 1986), which deal with theoretical and practical aspects of historicist criticism.

Imtiaz Habib (essay date 2000)

SOURCE: Habib, Imtiaz. "Cleopatra and the Sexualization of Race." In *Shakespeare and Race: Postcolonial Praxis in the Early Modern Period,* pp. 157-205. Lanham, Md.: University Press of America, 2000.

[*In the following essay, Habib suggests that in* Antony and Cleopatra, *Shakespeare contrasted noble England and the white, virginal Queen Elizabeth with the torpor of Egypt and its black and wanton ruler, Cleopatra.*]

Think on me
That am with Phoebus's amorous pinches black
And wrinkled deep in time?

Antony and Cleopatra 1.5.27-29

I

If *Titus Andronicus* was a failure to construct empire, *Antony and Cleopatra* may be a renewed attempt using this time as the object of subjugation a black female monarch of an alternative empire. It is a renewed effort also to reify through the idea of a fabulously re-imagined Rome the idea of empire, to vindicate it by writing it on whatever lies beyond it—in this case the East and Egypt. What is revisited is the archetypal European colony in Africa on the eve of its colonization, Egypt at the moment of its becoming a Roman province. Concomitantly, it is also an attempt to vindicate noble Rome-England and the memory of a white virgin Elizabeth against an indolent Egypt and a black seductive Cleopatra. This is a national instinct whose strength is reflected for example in a work like Anne Bradstreet's poem, "In Honor of that High and Mighty Princess Queen Elizabeth of Happy Memory," in which Elizabeth is as glorious as Cleopatra is ignoble and shameful (*Works* 11:86-89; cited in Nyquist 86).[1] As Kim Hall puts it, "Rome is England's imagined forefather in Empire, and *Antony and Cleopatra* provides an object lesson in imperial history" (*Things of Darkness* 160).

Also, if *Othello* is a revision of the black male subject of *Titus Andronicus* as has been argued earlier,[2] *Antony and Cleopatra* is a revision of the black female subject of the *Sonnets* (Ericson, *Patriarchal Structures* 125-27; Estrin 178-79, Ronald Macdonald 87). If *Othello* was an emancipatory myth of the black man in power, *Antony and Cleopatra* is an emancipatory myth of the black woman in power, both being singular cases in early modern English drama and in Shakespeare respectively. At the same time, Cleopatra's apprehension of being written by Rome "I' th' posture of a whore" (5.2.221) recalls and parallels the dark prostitute of the *Sonnets* that the black female subaltern has already become.

The tropic proximity, for analytical purposes, between the resistant black woman of the *Sonnets* and the defiant non-European queen in *Antony and Cleopatra* has to be the starting point for a postcolonial inquiry into the discursive politics implicit in the representation of Cleopatra. This proximity is a part of what John Gillies has said is the compelling sense in which in Shakespeare "exoticism in general controls ethnicity in particular." But this produces "a . . . relation" *as well as* instead of "*rather than* a kind of character" as Gillies has evasively put it (99 emphasis added), for it is the former that guides the textual design of the latter. As the relations that bind the *Sonnets* to *Antony and Cleopatra* are a product of early English colonialism's continual re-thematization of itself so the character that is revisited is the female ethnic alien. That such a dramatic personification is now conceived not as an invasive or intrusive presence in colonialism's own "geographic or moral center" as was the black woman in the *Sonnets* but as something encountered in "an outward . . . adventure beyond [those] geographical and moral" confines (Gillies 112), is indicative of the early colonial English imagination's developing struggle with its knowledge of its ethnic and sexual other. The female ethnic subject is by a symbolic act of distancing and expulsion now re-imagined in a legendary historical landscape in which the act of subjugation can be rehearsed afresh. The powerful female ethnic subject may have left its traces in other conflicted Shakespearean mimetic explorations of power-ful "dangerous . . . fully sexual and threatening" women such as Gertrude, Goneril and Regan, Lady Macbeth and Volumina that are approximately coterminous with Cleo-patra as some have argued (Ericson, *Patriarchal Structures* 124; Adelman, *Suffocating Mothers* 177), but to posit particularly its reappearance in *Antony and Cleopatra* is to recover the cogency of its inevitable intertextual effect in later Shakespeare.[3]

The revival of the black female subject in the play, which has been the object of some critical notice only in the last decade, is, however, a contestatory phenomena played out between the colonial poet, the male protagonist and Cleo-patra herself.[4] The similarities between Cleopatra and the *Sonnets*' black woman, and between the former's play and the latter's poems noted by Peter Ericson (*Patriarchal Structures* 125-28) are persuasive. But to suggest that Cleopatra is Shakespeare's reclamation of the "dark woman" of the *Sonnets* (125) is to assume a simplistic relationship between discourse, author and work. As Barbara Estrin has instead argued, in the language of sexual loss and the struggle for recompense that is com-mon to both the play and poem (129) it is the "female character, who aware of the possibility of loss, embraces it as a means of expressing her nature" (178). But if the limitations of a certain kind of white feminist critical practice[5] confine that "nature" in Estrin's analysis to be by silent assumption white and to deny all cognizance of Cleopatra's color, it does point to the recusant politics of desire and memory that are re-played through the colonial-patriarchal imagination. Janet Adelman's discussion of fantasies of maternal origin in Shakespeare (*Suffocating Mothers* 174-88) is useful for making it possible for Cleo-patra to be seen as the resistant reconfigured focus of Shakespeare's recovery of the lost masculinity of the *Son-nets*. This struggle between a revisionist collective and personal memory working through the playwright and the unpredictable re-play of the discursive subject of the black woman that is Cleopatra constitutes the field of interven-tion for a postcolonial critical poetics in the play.

II

Shakespeare is forced to return to the repressed black female subject in *Antony and Cleopatra* in his thoughts of empire, since as Robert Young has said the subliminal heart of the colonial/imperial instinct may be the dream of sexual dominion over a resistant black woman (earlier cited Chapter 1). As Lucy Hughes-Hallett aptly puts it,

The image of an Eastern country as a woman and of a Western male—whether military aggressor, mystic, scholar or tourist—as her heterosexual lover is one so commonplace as to pervade all Western thinking about the East . . . In it an erotic code is used to represent a political reality: the pornographic image of a woman bound and helpless becomes the metaphor for a conquered country.

Whether for Asia or for Africa, the Western "rhetoric of imperialism and heterosexuality are inextricably inter-twined" (207).[6] This is an unconscious Anglo-European collective urge that is startlingly caught for instance in the graphic portrait of the rape of a black woman by three white men that was painted by the Dutch painter Christian van Couwenbergh in 1632 (Scobie, "African Women in Early Europe" 149-52).[7] It is also implicit in exotic, sup-posedly eye witness Elizabethan descriptions of Egypt, such as the anonymous one recorded in Hakluyt, that Lucy Hughes-Hallett has cited:

There are innumerable barks rowing to and fro laden with gallant girls and beautiful dames, which with sing-ing, eating, drinking and feasting take their solace. The women of this country are most beautiful and go in rich attire bedecked with gold, precious stones, and jewels of great value, but chiefly perfumed with odours, and are very libidinous, and the men likewise.

(209)

The same popular thinking fuels the more symptomatic scenarios of Robert Burton shortly afterwards describing the mentality of the Orient as "the savouring of animal existence; the pleasant languor, the dreamy tranquillity . . . which in Asia stand in lieu of the vigorous, intensive, passionate life of the West" (Hughes-Hallett 216). As Ania Loomba has pointed out, these are the stereotypical quali-ties that commonly attach to both Cleopatra and her people in the sixteenth century popular English imagination (*Gender, Race, Renaissance Drama* 79).

To cite Hughes-Hallett again, on the political thematics of such urges,

The other is not only the adversary. She/he/it is also the promised consummation of all unconsummatable desire.

The other might be a geographical space; it might equally well be a woman, for women like foreigners, were strange to Western men and the realms of the East, like women, invited penetration and possession (206)

. . . . .

And place and woman are not only metaphors for each other (sexual intercourse equals annexation, conquest equals rape), they are also symbolic of something else—of the "ill-defined rapture" of that which is otherwise denied

(223).[8]

To this can be added the reminder of Loomba, who says "In colonialist discourse, the conquered land is often explicitly endowed with feminine characteristics in contrast to the masculine attributes of the colonizer" (*Gender, Race, Renaissance Drama* 78).

What triggers Shakespeare's return to the black woman is the relatively more formalized imperialism of James's court compared to Elizabeth's. The difference between Elizabeth's court and James's, as Kim Hall has demonstrated, is a difference between a cautious insularity and an eager internationalism (with unfortunately accelerated colonial consequences), and that is neatly caught in the thematic distance between Elizabeth's personal motto *semper eadem* (always one) and James's *rex pacificus* (royal peacemaker). If the colonial instinct in the Elizabethan reign was a surreptitious discovery, in the subsequent one it is a formal declaration, the chastity of the earlier monarch serving, as Kim Hall aptly puts it, as a figure for the "closing off of England from foreign powers," as compared to the marriage of the latter one which could be seen as nationally embodying "the creation of bonds with outsiders" (126-27). The colonialist projects that are busily institutionalized from the beginning of the seventeenth century, in the formal incorporation of trading companies such as the Virginia, the Guinea, and the East India companies, are paralleled by James's well-known adoption of Great Britain as England's official title, and which is an extension of the solitary and unofficial invocation of England as "an empire" in the reign of his predecessor.[9] The renewed metropolitanism of Jacobean cultural agenda is spelled out by James's encouragement of lavish civic spectacles, particularly the opulent pageants such as those for which Inigo Jones was commissioned to construct decorative public architecture, as well as the elaborate masques that were a staple of early seventeenth century London's courtly entertainment. These declare an internationalist ambition with its attendant nascent multiculturalism that is the quintessential underpinning of the imperial-colonial dream. Not inappropriately, James is routinely regarded by contemporary critical commentators of *Antony and Cleopatra* and its seventeenth century English political background as a re-born Augustus (Hunt 120, Nyquist 96, Whitney 85).

Domesticated black aliens, both live ones as in James's own marriage as well as impersonated representations as in Jonson's *Masque of Blackness,* embody a growing English need to display/demonstrate (particularly to already visibly internationalist-colonialist countries such as Spain and Portugal) a self image of political-cultural self mastery through dominion over others.[10] One of the most palpable manifestations of this urge, and which has startling resonances with *Antony and Cleopatra* is a famous Jacobean incident that is not, however, usually associated with this play. The marriage in 1614 of one of the members of the first English colonial settlers in Virginia, John Rolfe, to the Indian princess Pocahontas, the daughter of Powhattan, is usually connected to *The Tempest* because of the supposed ethnological proximity of Pocahontas to Caliban and because of the way the incident's direct English colonial history suggests the background of that

later play. But if the difference between the Western Indian and the African and the Asiatic is for the moment ignored as it in fact always was in the early colonial English racial imagination, the incident has compelling affiliations with the imperial colonial discourse that writes *Antony and Cleopatra* seven years earlier and that in fact predicts it. As Paul Brown, one of the most effective discussants of the incident in the light of *The Tempest,* has himself put it, Rolfe's letter to the Governor seeking permission for the match "confirms Rolfe in the position of colonizer and Pocahontas in the position of the savage other," and Rolfe's encounter with Pocahontas "serves to confirm the civil subject in that self-knowledge which ensures self-mastery." Literally echoing the situation of the *Antony and Cleopatra,* Rolfe is the European colonizer who like Antony in the process of subduing the margins joins it (in marriage) and threatens the integrity of the center which he is supposed to uphold. James's initial anger at Rolfe's "treachery" duplicates Caesar's ire at Antony's affiliation with Egypt. The eventual approval of Pocahontas, as "Lady Rebecca," and her admission to English civil society is however the completion of her colonization, implicit in her death in England soon afterwards (Paul Brown 49-50). The greater and more useful political-cultural metonymies of this incident with *Antony and Cleopatra* as opposed to *The Tempest* lie in the gender parallelism of Pocahontas and Cleopatra and in the power struggle of which both are formally a focus. To cite Paul Brown's words again,

> The discourse of sexuality in fact offers the critical nexus for the various domains of colonialist discourse . . .
>
> (51)

> What lurks in Rolfe's "secrete bosome" is a desire for a savage female (49), [and] Rolfe's letter reorients potentially truant sexual desire within the confines of a duly ordered and supervised civil relationship.
>
> (51)

Played out in popular drama, such an instinct appears in the spate of seventeenth century plays that describe the successful physical subjugation of or moral victory over African or African-based kingdoms and potentates by European/Roman ruling orders such as in Thomas Dekker's *Lust's Dominion* (1600), John Marston's *Sophonisba* (1606), Philip Massinger's *The Bondmen* (1623) and Thomas Heywood's *2 The Fair Maid of the West* (1630). Specifically, such an instinct is also evident in the numerous court representations of Cleopatra and other conquered foreign queens in the Stuart court, such as in *The Masque of Queens* in 1609 in which James's wife herself took part (Russ McDonald 305). If such dramatizations also include black females, that phenomenon can be contextualized by a possible Stuart courtly memory of the captive African women in the Scottish courts of James's ancestors cited earlier, and generally by the expedience of using the subjugation of dangerously empowered black women to write the text for a compliant white womanhood that is the collective cultural instinct of the early modern English nationalist project. The subduing of the powerful black woman that is Cleopatra in *Antony and Cleopatra* in 1606 derives considerable charge from the energy of these overlapping cultural discourses.

The blackness/ethnic origin of the historical, and in consequence, of the fictional Shakespearean, Cleopatra, can be established along the lines of four kinds of inquiries/interrogations of conventional opinion. *First,* the common assertion that the Ptolemies were notoriously eugenic, being very careful of preserving their blood in marriage even to the extent of familial inter-breeding (Holland 56, Hughes-Hallett 14, 15), needs to be mediated by Alexander's and Caesar's documented prescriptive practices of inter-racial unions (the former pointed out by Gillies 113, and the latter by Hughes-Hallett herself 37). Although the strong possibility of Cleopatra's mixed blood and of her consequently being colored is still contested by most scholars who believe that even for their mistresses the Ptolemies, following the Pharaonic practice of preserving blood line by marrying their own kin, chose "upper-class Greeks" (Holland 57), it should be remembered that the Pharaohs themselves were not immune to conducting exogamic unions, as did Amenhotep III when he married the Nubian commoner Tiye in 1428 B.C. (Simon 57). If the Ptolemies could be said to follow the other Pharaonic practice, they could arguably be said to also draw precedence from this.

Second, Cleopatra's location in most modern scholarly sources exclusively within the Ptolemaic dynasty as Ptolemy XII's daughter ignores the double possibility of one of her grandparents as well as of her mother being Egyptian. As is the consensus of established scholarship, Cleopatra's father was the illegitimate offspring of Ptolemy IX (Soter II) ("Ptolemy XII Auletes," *Britannica*; "The Ptolemies" *Cambridge Ancient History* 9:788 [genealogical map]).[11] The illegitimacy of Ptolemy XII, which was the reason for his difficulty in getting Rome's support for his rulership ("Ptolemy XII Auletes," *Britannica*), effectively precludes any Ptolemaic immaculateness in his daughter's blood. Royal illegitimacy for the Ptolemies, and apparently for the Romans too in their understanding of Ptolemaic succession practices, meant a birth that was not the product of Ptolemaic inbreeding. It did not mean more generally the product of an unlegalized sexual union as it means today, and even if it could be stretched to fit the modern meaning the chances are that such unions remained unauthorized because they did not fit the Ptolemaic eugenic prescription for royal marriages because one of the partners was not of Ptolemaic blood. Among the few modern scholars who point to the inevitable gradual mixing of Macedonian-Ptolemaic and native Egyptian blood from the time of Ptolemy IV Philopator is the British classicist Sir Paul Harvey, who believes that because of Philopator's recruitment of native troops in his victorious battle against Antiochus III in 217 B.C. Egyptian influence in and penetration of Ptolemaic political and civic life increased to the point that "A mixed Graeco-Egyptian race was gradually formed" (353).[12]

Who Cleopatra's mother was is also unknown, and hence the possibility of her ethnic matrilineal descent cannot be simply dismissed. That, like her father, Cleopatra's own maternal origins are obscured (whether or not she was the daughter of the woman that Ptolemy XII married, Cleopatra V Tryphaena, is unclear, being unspecified in most sources), suggests an interesting reason for her name, "Thea Philopater" which meant "Goddess Loving Her Father" ("Cleopatra VII Thea Philopator," *Britannica*). Some scholars believe that Cleopatra's mother was "a Nubian woman," an assertion supportable in terms of the evidence of Pharaonic unions with Nubians cited earlier.[13] Although no portraits of her exist, the depiction of her in both of the two coins that were minted by her orders in her youth and later arguably exhibit mixed African-Egyptian and European features. . . . Her recognition of her mixed lineage may have been what prompted Cleopatra, an otherwise accomplished linguist by all accounts, to be the first of the Ptolemies to bother to learn Egyptian ("Cleopatra VII Thea Philopator," *Britannica*). As one of her most respected modern biographers Hans Volkmann pointed out, like her father she had little popularity with the "upper stratum of the Alexandrian population" (62). Although most scholarly opinions steadfastly refuse to consider Cleopatra as anything but Macedonian Greek they consistently admit that she was, to a degree unprecedented in her ancestors, close to and deeply involved in native Pharaonic Egyptian cultural life, that her "thoughts and feelings . . . were certainly far closer to the Egyptian world than we have so far assumed" (Volkmann 207), and that she was "primarily an Egyptian Queen" (*Cambridge Ancient History* 9:321).[14] If in all historical narratives—Greek and Roman—Cleopatra consciously identifies with, and fights (against Rome) for her Egyptian kingdom, and foregrounds her national/political and social/cultural difference in doing so, it is hard to understand how she can be considered exclusively European. A mixed color and lineage for Cleopatra is thus highly likely, exactly what would be signified by the word "tawny" that Cleopatra uses to refer to herself in Shakespeare's play.

Third, it is not what she was ethnically (whether or not that is knowable), but what she was in early modern English popular imagination that has more to say about her ethnicity in Shakespeare. In Elizabethan thinking she is both European, such as in Daniel (Nyquist), and non-European, in more than the three instances that Janet Adelman pointed out (*Common Liar* 185-86). These include Robert Greene in his *Ciceronis amor* 1589 who said that Cleopatra was "a black Egyptian" and that to Antony her "blackest ebon was brighter than whitest ivory" (quoted by Hughes-Hallett 201), George Gascoigne in his "In Praise of a gentlewoman who though she were not very faire, yet was she as hard fauoured as might be" who marginally notes that Cleopatra was "Egyptian," (186) and Samuel Brandon in his *The Virtuous Octavia* who wondered how Cleopatra's "sun-burnt beauty" could please "[Antony's] sight" (186; also quoted by Hughes-Hallett 202). In addition to these, Kim Hall further cites Aemilia Lanyer as referring to Cleopatra in her *Salve Deus Rex Judaeorun* as "a blacke Egyptian" and Elizabeth Cary in her *Tragedy of Mariam* describing Cleopatra as "a brown Egyptian" (*Things of Darkness* 183-5). Even as late as the eighteenth century Colley Cibber has Cleopatra describe herself as an "Egyptian . . . born too near the glowing sun" (Hughes-Hallett 202).

Shakespeare twice explicitly paints her as colored—once in the "tawny front" reference in Act 1, and later in the "Phoebus" reference as black. Adelman's warnings about not taking literally every Elizabethan/Shakespearean use of the word black to mean skin color (*Common Liar* 184-85), which are fueled more by a contemporary postmodern nervousness in talking about race than any great danger of misunderstanding Shakespeare, need to be mediated by the reverse reminder very usefully articulated by Kim Hall that all uses of the word in Shakespeare should not automatically be construed to be metaphorical either (*Things of Darkness* 70).[15] The character's contextual history (see note 11 above), which Adelman herself points out in the pages immediately following her warning, make the phenotypical denotations of the references unavoidable. As Linda Charnes has insisted, it is particularly crucial not to ignore Cleopatra's identity as a black woman in view of the fact that she is the only one in the play who describes herself and that self description is black (127). Conversely, there are no specific signals of her "whiteness" in the play. That is, as Kim Hall has put it, "Shakespeare is at pains to make us see a black Cleopatra" (*Things of Darkness* 154). It is difficult to fathom the ideological assumptions that would make it compelling to ignore these deliberate indications, as the play's conventional exegesis has done.[16]

Furthermore, the play, as Linda Charnes has acutely explained it, is not about transcendent love but about the politics of empire (137-41) that underwrites that thematic. This can be seen in the way that the eugenic forsaking of the colored woman as the necessity of Western empire construction functions as the European cultural paratext for the Antony Cleopatra story. As Hughes-Hallett citing classical Roman sources has brilliantly reminded us, conceived within a few years of Cleopatra's death Virgil's original Augustus-inspired plan for the ultimate epic that would demonstrate the triumph of Roman-European nobility and imperial fortitude over the temptations of the world was not Aeneas's affair with the Carthaginian African queen Dido but Antony's with Cleopatra (60-61).[17] What necessitated the change from this plan to what became the substance of the *Aeneid* was a didactic improvement over history: the mythic demonstration of the ability of a European ruler (Aeneas) tempted by a seductive African female potentate (Dido) to uphold and return dutifully to his own world and lineage, over and against the historical record of precisely such an inability in a Roman conqueror (Antony) who charmed by his non-European/colored Egyptian queen (Cleopatra) actually could not and did not. To slightly paraphrase Maynard Mack, Antony's desertion of Rome for an African queen was to be reversed by Aeneas's disavowal of an African queen for Roman greatness

(cited by Ronald Macdonald 97n9). With the political damage controlled, the event could begin its historical journey as the legend of a passionate though regrettable extramarital affair, but not an extra-ethnic one. In the subsequent transmission of the Antony and Cleopatra story a century later the elements of a narrative of passion already coexist within the history of a political struggle, as for instance in Plutarch who in connecting Cleopatra to his own Greek background sees Antony's relationship with her more as adulterous than miscegenic (Gillies 115).[18] If in Chaucer the pair are characters of love, in the works of Dante, Boccaccio and Spenser they are sensual profligates.

The containment and diffusion of the subversive political potential of the non-European queen who defied Rome is effected, in other words, through the simultaneous transformation of her as an avatar of love and the denigration of her in terms of her sensual excess and in terms of the erotic passion that she both comes to stands for and ignites in Antony. It is not therefore surprising that while for Shakespeare's contemporaries the narrative's political interest/content is sometimes more foregrounded and sometimes less, it is never absent. Thus, in Marlowe's *Dido,* Fulke Greville's self suppressed play (Bullough 5:216; Hughes-Hallett 139),[19] Elizabeth Cary's *The Tragedy of Mariam,* Aemilia Lanyer's *Salve Deux Judaeorum* (Kim Hall, *Things of Darkness* 183-85) as well as in Robert Anton's (Wilders 11) and Richard Reynolde's (Charnes 137) allusive comments about Cleopatra's "horrible crimes" and "murthers" respectively, the moral-aesthetic marking down of Cleopatra is the vehicle of a visible English national-political self pointing. In contrast, in the Countess of Pembroke's adaptation of Robert Garnier's *Marc Antoine,* Daniel's Senecan drama and Gascoigne's and Greene's poems cited earlier, the elementalism of the lovers' passions is more a human tragedy than a national-imperial danger to be guarded against. This variable but ubiquitous political interest/content is what shapes the supposed love thematics of the Antony Cleopatra legend in popular representations such as Shakespeare's play. As Charnes describes it, the "production of legendary love, can be one of the most effective ways to deflect, defuse and contain perceptions of irreconcilable political differences" (138).[20]

The play's politics can be seen also in the way that an implicitly Orientalist-racist cultural agenda masquerades as the thematics of love in its critical and theatrical history starting from Charles Sedley and John Dryden, albeit less overtly in the former than in the latter.[21] In both not only are Antony and Cleopatra "kind, heroic and faithful lovers" (Ridley xxxviii), but as Charnes observes, Cleopatra is painted as "explicitly white" (203n48), which is a telling demonstration of the hidden political instincts of the love theme. In eighteenth century productions such as those of David Garrick in Drury Lane in 1759 "the emphasis of the play was significantly altered" and "[i]t became essentially a tragedy of love played out within a sketchy political context" (Wilders 15). If nineteenth century romantic critics such as Schlegel, Coleridge, Swinburne, and Victor Hugo collectively propagated "the intensity and imaginative force of love" in the play (Spevack, Variorum *Antony and Cleopatra* 641-47), Victorian productions so radically re-shaped the play that "mostly the political and military" scenes were cut out (Wilders 18).[22] This tradition fed the mid twentieth century's more influential critical judgments of the play, as for instance those of Wilson Knight, Dover Wilson and Reuben Brower that saw the play as articulating the poetics of an impossible transcendent love (Spevack 642). As the calm pronouncement of the editor of one of the most recent scholarly editions of the play has it, "The play is a dramatization of a tragic and celebrated love affair" (Wilders 1). Wilders's opinion echoes that of his predecessor's, M. R. Ridley's magisterial declaration in his 9th Arden Shakespeare edition of the play in 1954 that "In the first place it is a love tragedy" ("Introduction" xliii).

In Ridley's view of the play, which is as implicitly racist as his now-infamous view of Othello's blackness (7th Arden Shakespeare *Othello* "Introduction"), we are offered "a thrill, a quickening of the pulses, a brief experience in a region where there is an unimagined vividness of life" (xlvii). What Ridley does not admit is the extent to which this view is predicated on the exotic black female subject, the way in which the "thrill," "the quickening pulses," are all fueled by white European colonial patriarchy's secret fascination of that which it has forbidden for itself because it is threateningly different but that which it also cannot forget and about which it can fantasize only in some imaginary place removed from the norm. This is the mythic East that is Ridley's unspecified but nonetheless revealing "region" of "unimagined vividness." The comment exemplifies Hughes-Hallett's description of the European colonialist sexual fantasy of the black/colored woman as the Other as a subliminal drive for sexual fulfillment of that which is desired but unattainable and which because of that is all the more desired, and of how non-Europe (Asia or Africa) functions as the only symbolic space in which such fantasies can be materialized (206; 222-24). These interestedly orientalist scholarly re-castings of the play between the seventeenth and the twentieth centuries, in fabulist scenarios of erotic passion, thus implicitly trace an archetypally colonial European fantasy of sex and power in a symbolic political landscape. Such a fantasy is the discursive agenda of the play's thematics of love, and it is one which its critical and theatrical histories both reflect and transmit. From a postcolonial standpoint the "love" thematization of *Antony and Cleopatra* is also the subjugation, through the whitening, of the politically powerful black woman.

III

The spatial and ideological binaries that in traditional criticism hold Shakespeare's Rome and Egypt apart also enact a textual program of reclaiming the imperial (Roman) state through the exclusion of both gender and race. The construction of the white masculinity of the European state, signalled through the play's early dismissal of the

ineffective and docile Fulvia and the relegation to the narrative background of a dutiful Octavia rendered irrelevant in the play of Caesarist global politics (both of whom while being positive comparative makers against Cleopatra are unsatisfactory surrogates of woman compared to her), is aimed not just at the female abundance that is Cleopatra that Janet Adelman has pointed to but also at the imagined place of the racial other that is Egypt. The alien-ness of the female-sexual wild which is also the foreign-ness of the racial-cultural wild is the expelled ground of difference on which the imperial national imaginary is to be nourished.

The colonial author-function's mimetic encasement of the black female subject, in simultaneously incorporating an indictment of race and a containment of gender, sexualizes race and racializes sexuality, because the colonial-patriarchal notion of imperial nationhood is predicated on a selective appropriation of bodies for the continuance of a male ethnically exclusionist political order.[23] The double mimetic track of the mutually interactive racial-sexual marking of Cleopatra achieves the obliteration of the black female subject by blurring her reality and making her visibility fictional. Her fictionalized reality, together with the illusion of her power, serves only to validate the actuality of a white western world order, just as the myth of Othello's generalship had done earlier. She is the site of subjugation, in Kim Hall's terms "the imperial text" (*Things of Darkness* 159), on which the political life of colonial patriarchy is to be semiotically exercised. These suppressive instincts that rule the play's colonial-patriarchal representative agenda thus both confirm and extend the metropolitan construction that has been the Shakespearean colonial author function's ongoing discursive enterprise.

The mimetic incarceration of the reinvoked black female subject through the sexualization of race and the racialization of sexuality in Cleopatra is implicit in the play's selected moment of narrative entry. Not only are the play's famous opening lines an announcement of deliberate specular painting and pointing, the creation of a political frieze with a specific political lesson, the vehicular logic of its teaching turns on a discreet ascription of moral failure to an inferiority that is both racial and sexual. As Philo's multiple, expostulatory verbal emphases, "Those," "Look where they come! / Take but good note, and you shall see . . ." "Behold and see," sharply locate "the goodly eyes . . . [and] . . . the captain's heart" of the formerly global triumvirate "pillar of the world" that was Antony as the "strumpet's fool", their urgently reductive rhetoric combines "tawny front" with "gipsy" to naturalize the "lust" that is Cleopatra (1.1.1-13). The moral defectiveness, and hence unnatural-ness, of Antony is based on the unspokenly axiomatic naturalness of the affinity of tawny-gipsy with lustful, in which lustful-female-strumpet means tawny-gipsy and vice-versa, a natural semantic association that Antony either has not remembered or is ignoring.[24] The particular pressure of Philo's construction is to encourage a questioning of Antony's behavior but not of the debilitating sexuality of the black woman the synonymous negativity of whose skin color and sexuality is thus silently preserved. This prescriptive cultural campaign, which is all the more effective because of its demotic location in the sidelines of the high ground of Antony and Cleopatra's playing space, scripts Cleopatra's degeneracy as neither *and* both woman and black throughout the play.

The same esthetic stereophonically played from different speaking positions in the play constitutes Cleopatra as the site of a difference that is to be marked in a public space concertedly between her ethnicity and gender. "[C]ommodifiable material" for the social performance of male others, her simultaneous denigration and exoticization (Charnes 119) is a function of the variable, interdependent, use her race and her sex have for Roman self construction. Simultaneously "Royal wench" (to Agrippa 2.2.227) and "Egypt's widow" (to Pompey 2.1.37), her sexuality is non-specific, being both sweet and stale, and extends to a universal archetype of sexuality that is her "salt[y]" lustfulness (Pompey 2.1.21), even as what lends particular salaciousness to that sexuality is that it is Egyptian (as also in Agrippa's "Rare Egyptian" 2.2.218). This is the exotic item of public consumption that is Enobarbus's diagnostic identification of her as "Egyptian dish" (2.6.126), a left-over Caesarist "morsel" that can on occasion be cold even for Antony's eating (3.13.116). The generally voyeuristic political-civic space of these constructions, occasioned by the political consultancy of Roman triumvirs re-mapping their imperial domain or by the speculative gossip of subordinates interpreting the high events of their superiors or even by the displeasure of her Roman lover, objectify Cleopatra as the common property of popular Roman patriarchal social opinion feasting on the foreign in both the female and the alien. The relative ethnic spareness of these constructions do not constitute the play's marginal interest in race as Nyquist (96), as well as the editor of the most recent Oxford Shakespeare text of the play believe (Neill, *Tempest* 87), but a sign of racial marking's imbrication in the denigration of gender in the colonial agenda of the play's text.

The mutually supportive deployment of racial insculpture and sexual blackening in the negative construction of the black female subject in Cleopatra is also visible in the myth of her politically empowered status in the play. As has been noted (Loomba, *Gender, Race, Renaissance Drama* 75-76, 127-29, Nyquist 94-95), Cleopatra's queenship/rulership is a trivial textual decoration devoid of any real political power. Instead of the subtle multi-lingual diplomat and nationalist politician that is the historical figure,[25] the Shakespearean Cleopatra is an indolent despot with no visible political life whose sole activities are partying, amusing herself and waiting for Antony, as for instance in 1.5. when drunk with lethargy she wants to sleep time itself away, and in 2.5 when she wants to drown herself in music. Her queenliness is written as a nugatory womanliness merely, her rulership is visibly located more in the pursuit of personal desire rather than in the exercise of public responsibility and concern for community and kingdom. As Adelman has put it, "Her queenship is . . .

implicit, her subjects invisible" (*Suffocating Mothers* 191). She is presented always in the object position never in the subject, so that in the play's beginning moment as well as later when Antony has come to her she is merely reactive, waiting for *him* to decide to stay or to go. When Octavius attacks Egypt with his forces she follows Antony's plans of battle despite being Queen of Egypt with considerable forces of her own. Her political actions to defend Egypt are presented not like those of a capable political leader in a mutually beneficial alliance with a foreign power but like those of a vulnerable wife who unable to cope with the world by herself can only help her husband. That she even manages to be present in a war that has officially been declared against *her* and not Antony ("Is't not denounced against us?" 3.7.5), is only due to the miraculous success of her insistence against all contrary opinion ("Why should we not be there in person?" 3.7.5-6, and "A charge we bear in'th war / And as the president of my kingdom, will / Appear there for a man. Speak not against it" 3.7.16-18). Her political power allows only the operation of her private desires, enabling her to "unpeople Egypt" in fury if she ever loses Antony (1.5.78). That power is the source only of the plenitude of her leisure, spent endlessly with her waiting women in personal fantasies of pleasure.

Accordingly, when Enobarbus has to explain to Maecenas and Agrippa her political impact he has to describe her sexually as both the personification and the cause of carnal appetite: "Other women cloy the appetites they feed, / She makes hungry where most she satisfies." In this archetypal European patriarchal dream of women as the object of endless sexual feeding, as a passive timeless sex organ waiting to ceaselessly satisfy man, the "infinite variety" that "age cannot wither" (2.2.233-37), the wondrousness of the portrait depends discreetly on an essential coquettishness in Cleopatra that is its object to establish.[26] A composite of many imaginable surfaces but not of any revealing depths, her textual space in short is that of the one dimensional immemoriality of stereotype, interdependently typifying despotic potentate and lascivious woman. The clear logic of this portraiture, as both Loomba, (*Gender, Race, Renaissance Drama* 127) and Nyquist (95) have pointed out, is the separation of womankind from any significant political power by trivializing the former's use of the latter. At the same time, Cleopatra has the potential to be a serious sexual-political danger for the estate of man. What makes her political position dangerous is her gender, which could make her personify the female's subjugation of colonial-patriarchal man. Conversely, what makes her sexuality dangerous is that it is given added potency by her political position as queen.

What needs to be stressed here, however, is that the connecting link in the inverse relationship between Cleopatra's political impotence and her sexual potency is her racialization. In the play's imperial-colonial European gaze, what codes the mimetic values of her inept politics and her powerful sexuality is her racial identity, which is thus the middle term as it were in the triadic paradigm of empire-race-sexuality. For the imperial-racial European male the tautological antithesis of Cleopatra's political status and her sexual identity acquires a particular necessity in terms of the unsuitability of an ethnic woman in power, since if white womankind in power is dangerous the empowered colored woman must be doubly so. Thus, while the danger of womankind in power is reflected in Tudor tracts such as John Knoxe's *First Blast of the Trumpet Against the Monstrous Regiment of Women* in 1558, such discourses out of local as well ideological necessity make their point through the examples of foreign women, which can be Scottish women such as Mary Queen of Scots or European women such as Margaret of Parma of Mary of Lorraine (Shepherd 22), or the non-European woman as the mythic Amazon figure of Tudor-Stuart travel literature that by its difference is subliminally such a primordial threat to Anglo-European civic life (Shepherd 13-17; Laura Brown 130-32).[27] An example of the latter is the poem by Anne Bradstreet cited at the beginning of this chapter, in which as Nyquist explains, even if "Eliza" is a white "Amazon" (referring to the "manly" Queen at Tilbury) her "amazonomachy" demonstrates patently the superiority of her rulership over that of Asiatic Amazon figures such as Tomris, Semiramis and Cleopatra (85-86).[28] So, obscured by these overlapping interactions between the denigration of the alien female ruler's gender and the trivialization of her political ability, Cleopatra's racial marking remains for the most part blocked from direct analytical sight, alternately being stood in by femininity's lassitude and by the corruption of its rule, with, in the process, her blackness passing unspokenly for white in the play's critical afterlife.

A function of Cleopatra's textual colonization is to position her in an indeterminate space outside of kinship ties, in which her race and her gender help to cloak each other. Not only is she disconnected from a particular social imaginary, she is shorn of a visible family history, having neither parents nor children. If the former occurs in the guise of historical irrelevance, the latter happens as the result of a deliberate mimetic agenda that constructs her outside of the human continuity of generative time. The sterilization/isolation of the black female subject is necessarily the exposition of her uniqueness, the projection of the singleness of her being in distinction from the carefully nursed multiplicitousness of white European colonial patriarchy's family life. As the seductive other woman who steals Antony from the patient wifedom first of Fulvia and then of Octavia, Cleopatra is also the denatured entity whose sexuality overrides her maternal potential and whose blocked maternal urges impede the play of her sexual life. The former is implicit in the suppression of her children in the text's entire depiction of her liaison with Antony, and in the surfacing of her maternal concern only after she and Antony have been defeated by Caesar and she sues to have her children assigned "The circle of the Ptolemies for her heirs" (3.12.18).[29] The confused maternal instinct is also resurgent in Cleopatra when, after Antony's death, in applying the asp to herself to commit suicide she refers to it as "my baby at my breast / That sucks the nurse asleep" (5.2.309-10). Correspondingly, her blocked

maternality's impediment of her sexual life is implicit in Charmian's comment to the soothsayer, in response to his prophecy of a future ill-fortune for her, about the possible bastardy of any children she might have, "Then belike my children shall have no names" (1.2.35-36). Since the scene as a whole is a key example of the festive home life of Cleopatra's female court as Charles Whitney has seminally shown ("Charmian's Laughter"), Charmian's words are a reference to Cleopatra's children as well. Overall, what the scene delineates is a vibrant sexuality that is interrupted by longings for a maternal domesticity that is also unavailable.[30]

What ultimately mandates the denial of either wifehood or motherhood to Cleopatra is the whoredom of her race, in the representative colonial gaze of her authoring the eugenic finality of her unsuitability to breed. She is situated in other words in a primal locale discovered by European man, a creature bereft of the dense network of genetic obligation/familial associations that comprise the history of personal life. Unsurprisingly, denied any soliloquies she has no interiority, no privateness, and is shown always in company even if in exclusive ones, in the idle inner circle of her waiting women.[31] This is to say that as Cleopatra's maternality and sexuality are mutually blocked, the impact of her gender is diffused. As her gender is rendered intangible (which is its mythologization) so is her ethnicity (which is its erasure), ethnicity and gender being the twin foundational markers of identity in the colonial economy of cultural difference. The more Cleopatra's sexuality is played up the more mythic it becomes, and since in the colonial view her sexuality is a token of her race (the foreign/colored woman as always lascivious), the more mythic is her sexuality correspondingly the more fictional is her race.

Thus, if at one level both her political inefficiency and her puissant sexuality, as well as her racial sexuality and her sexual race, each have an inverse relationship within themselves in European construction, at another level her gender and her ethnicity have a direct relationship. What this means is that her race and her sexuality are played against each other as well as with each other. This is a symptom of what a contemporary postcolonial/black British feminist, has described as "the division *between* (as well as) within structures of identification," and of the fact that "the nature of identification" is both "antagonistic" as well as "divisive" (Sara Ahmed 158). The inverse linkage between Cleopatra's ethnicity and her gender is a function of her being a negative marker simultaneously to Fulvia and Octavia and to a Romanized Stuart rulership in the play's first half, whereas the direct relationship is a necessity of the undermining of her individual emotional-psychic being in the play's second half. If the racial-sexual inversion is an instinct of early colonial English national self construction, the racial-sexual synchronicity is the reflex of an exclusionist social imaginary defining itself through prescriptive notions of compliant white womanhood. Together, the play's twin mimetic processes of invertedly and directly connecting Cleopatra's ethnicity and gender serve to complete the circuit of her discursive incarceration.

Enabling/Empowering the complex bind of these dual representative processes in the play is the colonial author-function's memory of the subject of the black woman in the *Sonnets*. If the specificity of that personal authorial narrative is what underwrites the intertextual thematics obtaining generally between the *Sonnets* and *Antony and Cleopatra* as noted by Ericson (*Patriarchal Structures*) and Estrin and others, it is also what tropically connects Africa to Egypt, with the former re-fashioning the latter in the colonial text's geographic-cultural imagination. If the black female subject of the *Sonnets* was the domesticated subaltern in the metropolis, she reappears in *Antony and Cleopatra,* by a symbolic act of expulsion and regression as it were, as the again-as-yet unsubjugated black female at the margins of European empire, in which Cleopatra's royal stature is a metaphoric reconstruction of the unconquered self agency of the black woman in the wild. The two paradigms, of the colonized black women in the metropolis and the yet-to be-vanquished African-Egyptian queen, connect to form a closed system of intertextual relations within which the sexualization of race and the racialization of sexuality can endlessly repeat and renew themselves.

As the text's external/surface mythos is a collective early colonial English revisionist history of a male political order resisted by a colored female ruling order, so its internal/subliminal thematics is the Shakespearean author function's corrective re-enactment of the memory of the renitent discursive subject of the black woman of the *Sonnets,* the former being the cultural cue for the resurgence of the latter's poetic existence. In both cases the enterprise of recovery is in the service of a lost white idealized masculinity (Adelman 177-78), an unfulfilled eugenic homosocial imaginary, that struggles to establish itself over an unsubdued black desire. A mnemonic battleground, between the colonial poet's reparative memory of desire and the suppressed black female subject's awakened desire of memory, the play is thus the site of contestation between on the one hand an imperialist-colonialist national-social as well as a personal memory that strives to re-make experience and on the other hand an elided black female subject that re-writes itself into that memory making. If this critical framework is the point of departure for a postcolonial inquiry into the racial politics of Shakespeare's black/African queen, the specific target of its intervention is the unpredictable re-play of the poetic subject of the black woman that is Cleopatra in the resistance of its colonial inscription, the reflux of its seizure of the drama's narrative discourse.

IV

Located within overlapping mimetic regimes that deploy racial marking and sexual denigration concurrently against each other at multiple levels, the textual reflex of the incarcerated discursive subject of the black woman that is Cleopatra is the performative unpredictability of the racialized female in the compliance of its colonized cultural destiny. As both the substance and the play of her self life, unpredictability recusantly re-performs the elided memory of the black woman in her scripting as Cleopatra. In other words, unpredictability is the modality of the discursive subject of the colonized black woman's de-scribing/re-writing of her construction as a consumable commodity of the colonial-patriarchal social imagination, passed around in the *Sonnets* between the poet, his fair friend and the salaciousness of a boyish public opinion, and in *Antony and Cleopatra* between Antony, Octavius, Caesar and the ignominy of snickering male Roman report. In the face of a homosocial memory of desire, thus, unpredictability is the colonized black female's assertion of a racial-gendered desire of remembrance, her own invocation of the same two mimetic agendas that have historically incarcerated her being not a defeatist contradiction but the necessary ambivalence of the colonized gendered "subject's migratory and hybrid passage into being" (Sara Ahmed 165). The discursive effect of the black woman's tactical trope of unpredictability on the level of textual design, as will be evident later, is the generic confusion for which *Antony and Cleopatra* has been conventionally noted.

If in colonial time-space, culture, and history, memory is a structuration of experience, an imposition of form on formlessness, a shaping of meaning out of the pre-meaning of anterior forms of consciousness (Sara Ahmed 162), unpredictability is the alterity of this phenomenon. So, unpredictability is an anti-memory memory, a phenomenology that is the obverse of expectation and of the script of causality. Furthermore, unpredictability is the indeterminacy of language, the breakage of cultural writing through the disruption of anomalous local speech, an excess that makes talking a frenzy of self affirmation (what Michel de Certeau calls an "ecstasy") and a contestation of the historical/political assumptions that write the psychology of both the individual and the social body. Concurrently, unpredictability is the recalcitrance of sight, the deliberate self-effacement with which the colonized black female subject invokes the claim of her visibility by denying the conditions of her historical presentation. Cumulatively therefore, if memory, language, sight aim at knowing, unpredictability aims at the unknowingness of knowing, at exposing the hegemonic agenda of the legibility that is knowledge.

Most central to an interventionist postcolonial critical practice, however, is the predictive foundation of the notion of unpredictability in Gayatri Spivak's formulation in her essay "The Rani of Sirmur," in "the absence of a text that can 'answer back'", in the "dubious place of the free will of the sexed subject as female" (268). This is the formulation that Benita Parry has subsequently identified as Spivak's key locale of recuperating resistance in the colonial encounter (Parry 41).[32] In the essay, in the process of her archival examination of the nineteenth century colonial British appropriation of the lands and administration of the terminally ill (and hence deposed) Raja of Sirmur in the Simla Hills of Northeastern India through their attempt to manipulate the Rani to rule by proxy in the name of her under-age son and the Rani's counter resolve to instead immolate herself on her husband's funeral pyre in the Indian tradition of *Sati,* Spivak finds the Rani "caught . . . between imperialism and patriarchy" (268). On the one hand, if in traditional Brahminical patriarchy the practice of widow self-immolation was a "manipulation of female *subject*-formation" to accept suicide as the "good woman's desire," for the widow within that patriarchal tradition to embrace *Sati* was to seize the "signifier of woman as exception." On the other hand, to be dissuaded by the British "after a decision, was . . . a mark of real free choice, a choice of freedom." It is between these "two contending versions of freedom,"—that of "[Indian/colonized] patriarchal subject-formation and imperialist [British/colonial] object-constitution"—that Spivak finds "the dubious place of the free will of the sexed subject as female," even though in this instance Spivak suggests that it was "successfully effaced" and "thoroughly undermined" (268-69), since the British archival records, typically needing the figure of the Rani only for "the territorial/commercial interests of the East India Company" (263), are silent about the rest of the Rani's story. The Rani's ultimate decision, even if it was archivally recoverable, cannot be read simply as an acceptance of the one or the other of the two choices she faces but as a contravention of both.

Spivak's analysis of this material, which is more prognostic than enunciative, is useful nevertheless for the theoretical possibilities they open up for recomposing the will of the "gendered subaltern" in comparable historical situations and cultural texts. The parallels between the Rani's historical situation and Cleopatra's are striking. Both are inscribed by the exchange between local power and colonial disenfranchisement, and between female agency and patriarchal control. The unreadable track of the Rani's will that Spivak is pointing to, as it negotiates precariously between and against the two discourses that bear down on her and that together describe the double colonization of the female subaltern subject, cyphers the semantic codes of the history that will write that subject. This is the thematic indeterminacy that supplements the archival unavailability, both of the end of the Rani's story as well as of the alternative Egyptian substance of Cleopatra's life in Roman imperial record and in the early colonial popular English text. The "dubiety" of the free will of the female sexed subject is precisely its unpredictable potency, and in that comprises a pertinent interpretative analog to the unpredictability that is the modality of the black gendered colonized subject's reclamation of her self life as Cleopatra. To appropriate Spivak's paradigmatic formulation about a nineteenth century colonized Indian historical woman and apply it *backwards* to an analysis of a seventeenth century popular English dramatic representation of a historical figure from antiquity is not the stretched anachronism that it might seem but rather a *radical reverse tracing* of the critical process that the intellectual historian

Dominick La Capra described as the "repetition-displacement of the past into the present as it necessarily bears on the future" (Spivak 250).[33] Such reverse application of the "repetition-displacement" procedure is, in other words, symptomatically for postcolonial studies, the use of the pressures of the present to restore the elisions of the past. Specifically, to do so in Cleopatra's case is to reconstruct the elided subjectivity of the colonized black female within her objectification in the popular early modern English imagination.

The unpredictable self play of the textual subject of the black woman that is Shakespeare's Cleopatra is the dismembering of the demotic mythic memoriality that is her discursive constitution in the play, and which in turn is her subversion of the colonial author-function's personal memory of her. As the subject of representation the black woman's memorialization has happened twice already, in the Anglo-European mythic paratext that has staged her as Cleopatra in the seventeenth century English cultural consciousness, and in the poet's private narrative of the black woman in the *Sonnets*. It is against the play of this compound, already-completed memorial construction that the unpredictability of the black woman's textual self presence writes itself in the play, destroying/confronting that which has already been culturally remembered with the disruptions of an exigent present that has not been memorially inscribed. Thus, in the play's opening act as Antony prepares officiously to leave her for Roman duty, rupturing the enactment of his departure is her reminder to him of how when he had first arrived in Egypt he had "sued staying:"

> Then was the time for words; no going then,
> Eternity was in our lips and eyes,
> Bliss in our brows' bent; none our parts so poor
> But was a race of heaven. They are so still,
> Or thou, the greatest soldier of the world,
> Art turn'd the greatest liar.

> (1.3.33-39)

The obtrusive reminder reclaims the sovereignty of action from an Antony who leaves and a Cleopatra who sues to hold him back, to a Cleopatra who had agreed to an Antony's original plea to stay, thereby reestablishing however momentarily a Cleopatra who can just as equivocally let him now be gone: "Nay, pray you seek no color for your going, / But bid farewell and go" (1.3.33-34). The slipped alternative memory evident here is also corroborated later by Enobarbus's account of their first meeting in which within the glamour of the description of Cleopatra's arrival at Cydnus the discreet detail of the Egyptian queen's will prevailing over the Roman conqueror's survives: "Upon her landing, Antony sent to her; / Invited her to supper. She replied / It should be better he became her guest" (2.2.219-21).

Thus also in the play's opening movement, fissuring the script of her constructed remembrance, "Sir, you and I must part, but that's not it; / Sir, you and I have loved, but that's not it; / That you know well," is a "Something it is I would—," that is the nominal catachresis that exceeds the articulation of memory. This is the naming of "my oblivion" that is the antithesis of remembering itself, the anti-memory over which memory presides: "And I am all forgotten" (1.3.87-91). Antony's departure, otherwise the imperial Roman's brusque leaving of his Eastern conquest, is achieved through the "kill[ing]" of Cleopatra's "becomings" and her "unpitied folly," a clumsy leave-taking that his brave show of rapport, "Come / Our separation so abides and flies / That thou, residing here, goes yet with me" (1.3.102-4), cannot hide. This is to say that unpredictability interrupts the normalizing mandate of official memory—the Roman Antony must come, love the Egyptian Cleopatra, and leave for Rome—with the compulsions of an unremembered self that is beyond the reach of such a mandate and that while unable to reverse the teleology of such a narrative robs it of its ideological charge.

To put it in another way, unpredictability as anti-memory is the uncontained subjectivity of the individual colonized consciousness as opposed to the regulated objectivity of colonial public thought, and its object is the undermining of the efficacy of the latter's functioning. Quintessentially, unpredictability's anti-memory is also the gendered subaltern's counter-memory of race, as it were the thought without a name within the smooth nominal hierarchy of imperial account. So, after Antony has left for Rome and Cleopatra self-teasingly wonders why Antony should think of her, "Think on me / That am with Phoebus' amorous pinches black, / And wrinkled deep in time?" (1.5.27-29), the interrogative enunciation masks the desire for its precise opposite: to be thought of. The contrariety of the sudden reflection of her skin color, the signal importance of which is indicated by its being otherwise the sole instance in the play, lies in its daring phenotypical self-problematization, in its positing of the seeming difficulty of a white Antony in a popular etiolatory imperial Roman consciousness remembering a black Cleopatra as the precise reason for the desirability of his doing so. The challenge of the reflection is also thus the reclamation of her self value beneath her performance of the very myth that obliterates it. As this is the unthinking that challenges the colonial thought that mythically constructs her, it is "the delicious poison" with which she "feeds" herself (1.5.26-29). As Joyce Green MacDonald has put it, "Her dark skin, in terms of the well-known proverb from the period, is a literal emblem of the impossibility—or at least extreme difficulty—of the task that the Romans have set themselves in conquering Egypt" ("Sex, Race, and Empire" 69). In sum, Cleopatra's textually unprepared and unique color conscious self recollection is what contemporary black British feminist theoretical analysis would describe as the refutation of "the racialist logic that demands the purification of colour" by the renegade "reminder of an-Other that refuses to inhabit these terms and returns . . . only as a threat" (Sara Ahmed 159).

Her anti-memory has the power to make and unmake the reality of her fiction, so that the memory of her love for

Antony as well as the love she had for Caesar before him are both authenticated expediently by *her,* as Charmian reminds her in the same scene, "I sing [of Caesar] but after you" (1.5.73), and as she herself demonstrates when on hearing of Antony's marriage to Octavia she begins to think again of Caesar: "In praising Antony I have disprais'd Caesar" (2.5.108). The expedience of her momentarily resurgent alternative memory is the unavoidable imbrication of the colonized black woman's "love" of her colonial European lover in the politics of her historical survival. The unpredictability of her anti-memory is in other words the protection of the sovereignty of her self, her intervention in the retrospective colonial organization of experience in which she is included. Thus, within the colonially designed script of her dalliance with Antony, in her swearing loyalty to him as a way of seeking his forgiveness for having betrayed him in the first sea fight against Caesar, her unforewarned remembrance of her maternality is her anti-memory's furtive seizure of that part of her life which that script has disallowed even as she cooperates with that disallowance:

Ant.

> Cold-hearted toward me?

Cleo.

> Ah, dear, if I be so, . . .
>   The next Caesarion smite
> Till by degrees the memory of my womb,
> Together with my brave Egyptians all . . .
> Lie graveless. . . .

> (3.13.158-66)

Similarly, after Antony's death, the unsubdued residue of her female consciousness is what feeds Cleopatra's momentary contra-memory of herself as "No more but e'en a woman, and commanded / By such poor passion as the maid that milks and does the meanest chares" (4.15.73-75). The unexpected bucolic self-cameo, with its invocation of youthfulness and sexual innocence in deliberate contradiction of the earlier self pointing to age and sexual experience, is the gendered subaltern subject's discursive repossession of the freedom of her imaginary life beyond the ends of her colonial narrative, otherwise one clear example of the Spivakian "dubious place of the free will of the female sexed subject."

If by play's end it is Cleopatra more than Caesar who writes the memory of Antony, she does so in a manner that contains its absurd alterity, coding the mythos of imperial recollection with the incongruity of its antitype:

> I dreamt there was an emperor Antony . . .
> His legs bestrid the ocean; his reared arm
> Crested the world . . .
> His delights
> Were dolphin-like; they showed his back above
> The element they lived in . . .

> (5.2.76-90)

Frank Zotter as Eros, Leon Pownall as Antony, Lewis Gordon as Enobarbus, Edward Atienza as Lepidus, and Stephen Ouimette as Octavius Caesar in Act II, scene ii of the 1993 Stratford Festival production of Antony and Cleopatra.

As Linda Charnes has shown, the illogicality of an Antony straddling the ocean and at the same time swimming in it like a dolphin, represents "a panegyric at once contradictory and true" (143), pointing to the perforation of a public mnemonic ritual by the anti-mnemonism of the very subjective consciousness that is made to validate it and that by that very act instead steals attention for itself. Furthermore, to the extent that Antony is the play's "primary absent object of desire," the "idealized masculinity" which Adelman says is part of the play's project of recovery (*Suffocating Mothers* 177, 180-81), that is, the focus of the text's recuperative homosocial imaginary, the rhetorical uncertainty of Cleopatra's chosen remembrance of him destabilizes the possibility of that recuperation by inscribing in effect the inherent instability of the male posturing that is the patriarchal enterprise. Conversely, this implicit anti-memory of the male positions *her* on the ideological high ground of the play's politics of gender, re-establishing her in what was going to be the drama of her negation.[34] Encompassing, then, the triple coordinates of race, sex and empire, that is to say the worlds of the social, the psychic and the imperial, unpredictability's anti-memory is the colonized black female subject's re-tabulation of the public memoir of herself, the mechanism of her spectral counter-life against the record of her colonial history.

Unpredictability as the discursive subject of the black woman's oppositional self performance within the mimetic codes of her colonial text is also the indeterminacy of her language, the verbal inexplicability through which Cleopatra preserves the mastery of her fictional life. With Antony, her unpredictability as linguistic indeterminacy takes the form of a talking performance that blocks the visibility of her speaking position, shields her rhetorical intention and hence guards the legibility of her sovereign self. In the play's opening scene, in the triple solipsistic contestation of Antony's gratuitous desires that she performs, Cleopatra's own verbal intentions are left unexposed, and with them is left intact the independence of her own options of action. Her challenge of his professions of love, "If it be love indeed, tell me how much," not only debars his deferral of the semantic trap she leads him into, "There's beggary in love that can be reckoned," but also effectively imposes her authority over their emotional transaction:

"I'll set a bourne how far to be belov'd." Turning to the matter of his supposed disinterest in his wife's feelings or his claimed indifference to Caesarist and Roman political directive the news of either or both of which may be in the messenger's brief that Antony does not want to hear, she dares him to prove himself:

> Nay hear them . . .
> Thou blushest Antony, and that blood of thine
> Is Caesar's homager; else so thy cheek pays shame
> When shrill-tongu'd Fulvia scolds.

But Antony's compliance, by affirmatively kissing her on the spot, "the nobleness of life / Is to do thus [embracing]," is merely grounds for her to return to her original inquiry about the sincerity of his feelings for her: "Excellent falsehood! Why did he marry Fulvia and not love her?" (1.1.14-41). The shifting track of this inquisition of Antony's ethical and political mettle, which is repeated in part in 1.3., not only puts Antony in the object position but also secures the unintelligibility of Cleopatra's choices for anyone but herself. Within her historical moment as the conquered Egyptian queen as well as in her discursive/ fictional location as the colonized black woman, the inscrutability of Cleopatra's verbal practice transforms the colonial lover's attempted emotional-psychological bonding of the gendered subaltern into her reverse hold over him.

If language is a "tacit" agreement of social order and a guarantee of the continuance of its structural performance as Ronald Macdonald observed in his discussion of the play (87), between the two principal domains of its operation, writing and speech, is manifested two versions of its power: language as control which is the documentativeness, enforced uniformity and conformity of writing, and language as speech which is the immediacy, the contextual specificity and the radical independence of talking.[35] If the former with its ability to seize and carry away meaning from phenomena and incarcerate it in the elsewhere of written script is the tool and space of colonial control, the latter with its grounding in its particular location and hence its ability to resist intellectual transportation (Certeau, *Writing of History* 215-16) is the medium and arena of anti-colonial resistance. Linguistic indeterminacy in speech is therefore also Cleopatra's unpredictable disruption of the colonial social order that surrounds her, another function of the colonized black female's tactical unpredictability as the means of her self survival. If Cleopatra's alienness in her early colonial English mimesis is her linguistic excess as Ania Loomba suggests, that excess is not merely because she talks more than any other woman in Shakespeare ("Shakespeare and Cultural Difference" 175), but because her use of language violates the political order that sanctions it, unmaking the social reality that it is entrusted to build. Expectedly more evident in her interaction with the innumerable messengers that are the ventriloquist voice of the Roman center's imperial authority, the tactical transgression that is her linguistic indeterminacy in speech underlies in particular the episode of her treatment of the messenger who brings her news of Antony's marriage to Octavia in 2.5.

The cruelty of Cleopatra's treatment of the messenger is the violence of the discursive subject of the colonized black woman's rejection of the colonial conventions of expressive signification and of her defense of her right in her colonized domain to the social politics of meaning construction in words. The suddenness of her response, which is the mark of the unpredictable self play of the gendered subaltern's protective self suzerainty, turns on the truth-effects of the messenger's news and on the resultant situation they try to impose on her: "He's bound unto Octavia . . . For the best turn i'th bed . . . Madam, he's married to Octavia" (2.5. 58-60). The "truth" of the messenger's news is the "lie" of Cleopatra's value and Egypt's in the esteem of Antony and Rome: Antony's marriage to the proper Octavia is the trivialization of Cleopatra's civic worth (as unfit for the social contract of marriage) and in consequence the dismissal of Egypt's social and sexual civility by the high culture of Europe, particularly since she herself as monarch is the symbol and determinant of the civilization of her kingdom. The seeming calmness of the messenger, "I that do bring that news made not the match" (68) and his insistence on the exclusive validity of his verbal representation, "I have made no fault" (74), is what fuels the particular ferocity of her retaliation, "The most infectious pestilence upon thee! *Strikes him down* . . . Hence, horrible villain, or I'll spurn thine eyes / Like balls before me; I'll unhair thy head. *She hales him up and down* . . . Rogue, thou hast lived too long. *Draws a knife*'" (61-64). If as Queen of her country, colonized or not, she cannot be only the hearer of news but also the maker of it (Ronald Macdonald 87), she cannot also be merely the recipient of "truth" but also the creator of it. This is to say that as language is the register of her political and social reality, it is that she will re-make to defend the historical existence of herself. This is her psychological *parole* to the imperial *langue* of Rome, her reclamation of the legality of her narrative currency as opposed to the authority of Roman meaning.

She tries therefore to roll back the linguistic reality of this development by forcing the messenger to unsay what he says, and belie the truth of his words, and in that expose the lie of the social order that he represents in validation of the truth of hers. Her specific instruction to him, "Say tis not so," as well as her repeated questions "He is married? . . . He is married?" counteracts the messenger's iterative emphasis of the substance of his message, "He's married, madam" (92) "He's married to Octavia," (101), which he thus performs four times in the scene, and it is thematically contextualized by her explanation that

> Though it be honest it is never good
> To bring bad news. Give to a gracious message
> An host of tongues, but let ill tidings tell
> Themselves when they be felt.

> (84-88)

This is the thematic of her linguistic indeterminacy, of the sovereignty of her local speech over the language of global-colonial history, that is, of the right of the receiving situation in the periphery to determine the semantics of linguistic representation over the interested hermeneutics of the sending center. To "let ill tidings / Tell themselves when they be felt" is to oppose the predetermination of imperial account with the phenomenological exigencies of its local application, as it were to make history that has already happened re-perform itself if it can but on a more level terrain. It is these retrograde interpretative instincts that undergird her pointed reply to the messenger's exasperated question, "Should I lie, madam?": "Oh, I would thou didst" (94-95).

As it so happens, the "lie" of the messenger's Roman "truth," which is conversely the "truth" of Cleopatra's "lie" that the messenger is here balking from, is grounded in the fact of Octavia's marriage being meaningless and in name only, and has already been vindicated by Antony himself, when in confirmation of the soothsayer's prognosis that his prosperity does not lie in Rome he says: "And though I make this marriage for my peace / I'th East my pleasure lies" (2.3.38-39). That it is the mandate of her contestatory "truthful" lies that prevails over Rome's "lying" truths is implicit in the messenger's carefully negative description of Ocatavia later in deference to the "truth" of Cleopatra's beauty: "[S]he [Octavia] is low-voiced . . . She creeps . . . She shows a body rather than a life" (3.3.13-19). If in these scenes the operation of the linguistic indeterminacy of Cleopatra's speech through the mandate of her "truthful" lying, is humorous, that humor is the deliberate subversion of the solemnity of her imperial history and her mechanism for undermining the "lies" of her colonial record. This is the excess of her talking that makes it simultaneously a frenzied self location and a critique of the colonial historical/cultural imaginary that imprints the body and the *socius*. As she demonstrates that Roman "truths" do not apply in Egypt, so she establishes that the social conventions of "truth" and "meaning" that are used to bind that community cannot be used to bind this.

The linguistic indeterminacy of Cleopatra's speech as the play of expediently chosen meaning as her tactical prerogative in her colonized situation is also evident in the scenes of her negotiation with Thidias in 3.13 and subsequently with Caesar in 5.2. Her determination not to mean what she says is her franchise to protect the sancity of her social order and of her ethical standing as its guarantor against the incursions of the colonial one that seeks to replace it. The hidden semantics of her special speech is in fact her matching of Rome's articulation of its particular agenda in the guise of a seeming objectivity, of using, in other words, its duplicitous language to out-talk it. If Thidias's official Roman re-presentation of her story with Antony as one in which she "He [Caesar] knows that you embrac[ed] not Antony / As you did love, but as you feared him," aims at displacing the grammar of her free will in her relationship with Antony with the bonded accents of a fearful and conquered potentate who will now be safe-housed in supposedly beneficial Caesarist custody, her agreement with

him, "He [Caesar] . . . knows / What is most right. Mine honour was not yielded / But conquer'd merely" (3.13.56-62), is merely her paying back the coin of Rome's meaningless verbal currency in kind, of blocking dictional duplicity with itself. If Thidias and Caesar's language offer her false knowledge while "knowing" her, she replies in kind, offering them false knowledge of herself while instead "knowing" them. If knowledge given (Caesar means to be her benefactor) is an imposition (Cleopatra should accept his patronage), she resists that imposition by giving back to them a false knowledge of herself (she accepts his patronage), thereby checking that incursion and subverting that power exchange.

Her interview with Caesar in the fifth act is a compound rendition of the same linguistic politics, in which what she lies about is the truth that will redeem her from total Roman effacement. In it what she makes Seleucus do is to not just reveal the "lie" of her honest account of her assets but through it to do something else: make Caesar believe through the apparently accidental third-party exposure of the secret hoarding of her valuables that she intends to live. The complete obscurity of her use of words here, doubly insulated by the vehemence of her attacks on Seleucus, is precisely what guarantees the success of the suicide with which she will ultimately defeat the Roman seizure of herself and of her kingdom. This will be her out-wording of Caesar's "word[ing]" of her to prevent her from "be[ing] noble to [herself]" (5.2.190-91). So, she will live, but not in the manner the Romans understand it: she lives in the moral triumph of having killed herself rather than fall into their hands. In both instances, the function of her words is to invite their own deconstruction in their audience, within which the integrity of her codes of meaning and the freedom of her own intentionality remain undisturbed. All together, Cleopatra's linguistic indeterminacy, in its verbal inscrutability, its deliberate excess, and its seizure of the conventions of meaning construction to rupture the colonizer's political power and disrupt his social order, is the vocal register of her unpredictability, the tongue through which the resistant subalternity of the colonized black woman speaks herself.

Unpredictability is also the recusancy of sight, the contrary self-seeing that is also the secret self-knowing and which together are the beginnings of historical identity. Lost in the overlap between two counteractive avenues of self identification Cleopatra is made visible by neither. Connected to an European-Greek Ptolemaic line which because of its transplantational history is not fully available to her, and to an Egyptian-African one the full purity of which she will always lack, she has only the uncertain luminescence of a Bakhtinian *exotopia* by which to know and show herself, the liminal identarian consciousness of a simultaneous insider/outsider-ship through which to build an understanding and a projection of herself in time and history.[36] Her self sight is therefore her rejection of the conditions of her historical visibility, which neither reveal nor conceal her psychic being. Her struggle for satisfactory ocular presence is consequently manifest not so much in any gestures of pronounced self painting as in her effacement of the elements of her mis-presentation. The moments in which she does try to visualize herself, as for instance in the "phoebus," "womb," or "maid" references cited earlier, have the panoptic clarity of hindsight and memory and are significant for the self pictures they etch. The continuum of an ontological self awareness that is necessarily indefinable and works through visual postponement is however another equally significant aspect of her struggle to be seen. Its contradictory insistence on see-able presence through its cancellation of that seeeability constitutes the tactical reluctance of sight that is one more dimension of the unpredictability of the discursive subject of the black woman in Cleopatra.

At the beginning, if a happy Antony wants to see a happy Cleopatra she shows him a sad one, if a healthy Antony wants to see a healthy Cleopatra she shows him a sick one and vice-versa: "If you find him sad / Say I am dancing; if in mirth, report / That I am sudden sick" (1.3.3-5). This can work in literal or parodic excess with the same effect. In the fourth act if an angry Antony wants to see a repentant Cleopatra heartstruck with anguish for having betrayed him, she shows him a Cleopatra so tormented as to have killed herself: "to th' monument . . . go tell him I have slain myself. / Say the last I spoke was 'Antony'" (4.13.7-10). At the play's end if a triumphant Caesar wishes to see a subdued Cleopatra she shows him an excessively subdued one that is a cover for the defiance underneath. Her posture of submission here, "My master and my lord / I must obey" (5.2.116-17), is as she explains later, "the way / To fool their preparation, and to conquer / Their most absurd intents" (5.2.225-26). In all of these instances, she retains control over her visual presence by negating the effect people want to see. When she dies, she shows herself not in the languishment Rome might expect (in Plutarch having at least once seen her thus) but in the robes of an unvanquished majesty: "Show me . . . like a queen" (5.2.227). It is this constantly removed sight of herself that is responsible for the curious, perpetual deferral of herself that Catherine Belsey has described as the secret of Cleopatra's textual-thematic seduction ("Cleopatra's Seduction" 42-46).

If the colonial portrait of Cleopatra as the possessed black female potentate is that of a spectacle, of the sort that Enobarbus says would have diminished Antony's reputation as a "traveller" had he not seen her (1.2.153-55), the visual strategy of the gendered-colored subaltern is, as Linda Charnes has observed, to return that spectacle to the spectator without showing anything of herself in it (128-29). She manipulates the staging of the appearance of herself to subvert the spectacular values of that staging. If the colonial imagination expects her to arrange her demise in the European accents of a royal death, she designs hers deliberately in the style of an Asiatic Egyptian one, in the death by snake bite that not only declines the preferred European self killing by sword or dagger that is Antony's method but that also clearly identifies her with the Egyptian mythology of the Isis goddess with whom she

wishes to be seen in history. The contrary visual self representation is also the discursive response of the subject of the colonized black woman to the antitheatricality and antifeminism of popular early modern English drama that Jyotsna Singh, among others, has noted ("Renaissance Antitheatricality, Antifeminism"). Her negative visualism corresponds as well to the necessary theatricality of discursive subjectivity that Linda Charnes has insisted on (127, 158-59), but deployed here particularly in the instance of a gendered raciality that shows itself in a performance of seeing that destroys the false sight of itself. The discursive subject of the black woman's unpredictable anti-visualism is, in sum, the modality of race's self-viewing through the opposition of colonialism's viewership of it, that is through the invisibility that emerges through its dismissal of the visibility that colonialism gives it. This is the lacuna within which race can construct the expedient sameness of its difference in a postcolonial domain.

In the processive combination of its anti-memory, linguistic indeterminacy and anti-visualism, the unpredictability of the discursive subject of the black woman in Cleopatra aims inevitably at the unknowability that is at once its colonial destiny and its anti-colonial desire. This involves the same reversible play of power implicit in the politics of knowledge that was operative in Othello's subaltern life. To reinvoke that argument here, knowledge is not only the primary condition of the operation of power and the optimal requirement of its occurrence, but also within the colonial moment the tactical high ground in the struggle for control between colonizer and colonized. So, if in Edward Said's terms to know is to possess (*Orientalism* 32, 36-37), then that which is unknown is also that which is unpossessed. Thus, if what constitutes the alien-ness of the alien is its unknowability, then that which marks the alien's path of self enfranchisement is its refusal to be known. Within a political esthetic it is not that to be unknown is to be free but that to be known as unknowable is to enjoy a certain measure of existential self agency. This is the subjective reclusion of the colonized self that is resistant to the penetration and inscriptions of the colonizer's global imperatives. In this sense a persistent unknowability is the strategic disposition of the colonized subject, and with respect to the life of its race and gender the basic means of its destruction of the epistemology that has enabled its disenfranchisement. On the level of language, sight, and the collective memory that is resurrected as social convention, it becomes a counter to the naturalization of the colonizing process. Cleopatra's unknowability as the constant endpoint of the black gendered subaltern's multifarious unpredictability, otherwise the "infinite variety" that is her colonial cultural blazon, is her signal interactive objective throughout her mimetic performance in her colonial text.

The effect of Cleopatra's indefinability that Antony reflects in act one is in the very complaint with which he prefaces his words:

> Fie, wrangling queen,
> Whom everything becomes—to chide, to laugh,

To weep; whose every passion fully strives
To make itself (in thee) fair and admir'd!

(1.1.48-51)

What unspokenly prompts this indulgent protest of Cleopatra's many-sided contrariness is her denial through it of the privilege of familiarity, which is the privilege that knowing brings and which will be the facilitator of Antony's way with her on the psychic as well as the political planes. That "way" is patriarchy's manipulative power in the heterosexual exchange and colonialism's surreptitious assumption of rulership in the locales of its emergence. As Antony's repeated exclamations of incomprehension later in the same act reveal, "What's the matter?" (1.3.18), "How now, lady?" (1.3.39), the subjugated black woman's refusal to yield to her colonial lover-conqueror a uniform legibility confuses his self mastery and thereby retains as merely contingent the political reality that has allowed him to approach her. Even in that initial approach, in Enobarbus's famous account of their first meeting, whereas Antony waits to meet her on land, she arrives by water, and as noted earlier as he invites her to supper she invites him instead to join her. The purpose of this constant "cross-[ing]" of him as Charmian at one point fearfully puts it (1.3.9), is to keep elusive the idea of her political disenfranchisement and to create the illusion instead of her power over him. As Enobarbus describes it, she draws the crowds, not him, and he is left alone with neither public attendance nor political recognition, in a posture of near-vacuous imbecility: "And Antony / Enthron'd i'th' market place, did sit alone, / Whistling to th' air" (2.2.214-16). If her unknowability therefore suggests a possibility of role reversal in their colonial relationship, a substitution of her disempowerment and passivity by his empowered active self sovereignty and vice-versa, and that will be a deface-ment of the achievements of colonial-patriarchal power, that is reflected in the cross dressing with which she blurs the limits of her historical confinement: "Ere the ninth hour, I drunk him to his bed / Then put my tires and mantles on him, whilst / I wore the sword Philippan" (2.5.21-23). This playful exchange of her "tires and mantles" for his "sword Philippan," that is, of her Egyptian womanliness for his male Roman conquerorship, is nevertheless a semiotic of her dissolution of the fixity of her political and sexual location, and hence a destruction of the ability of either to essentially read her.

Two of the strongest instances of the unknowability that is the ultimate practice of the unpredictability of the discursive subject of the black woman are however Cleopatra's bizarre naval conduct and the difficult mimesis of her suicide. The inexplicability of her flight at both of the two sea battles that finally seal Antony's defeat by Octavius, which is unexplained as well in all of the ancient historical accounts of her, connects to the semiotic of changeability that she advertises in her deliberate association with water (as in her decision to appear initially before Antony on the river, and in her support of him later to fight Octavius by sea), in life and in her discursive after-life in the popular early colonial English cultural master

text. As the nineteenth century Egyptian nationalist dramatist Ahmed Shawqui surmised, the political rationale of her sudden abandonment of the fight is the ensuring of her own survival by making the two competing colonial figures destroy themselves (Hughes-Hallett 297). This is not to entirely negate her relationship with Antony but to ground that relationship in the fundamental political choices within which she is bound, that is, to unavoidably balance the instincts of her psychic life with the particular pressures of her historical moment. If her ships at Actium carry her wealth (a detail that the colonial text leaves out [Volkmann 185], but the impress of which surfaces nonetheless in that text to underwrite her unexpected action in it), they are what will finance her fortunes, with Antony or without him. The advantage of the tactical flex-ibility that her unknowable action here affords is implicit as a matter of fact in Antony's ability later in Taenarum, to which he flees following Cleopatra, to use that same wealth to both equip his remaining commanders for their own flights to safety (3.11.9-24) and to facilitate his and Cleopatra's return to Egypt to reorganize themselves. If the unknowability of her behavior in this episode appears to invite its misinterpretation as her treachery, that is of little consequence as the brevity of Antony's accusations of her and his quick reconciliation with her within a mere twenty-four lines shows (3.11.51-75). More importantly, that misinterpretation allows her the opportunity to choose the time, the venue and the terms of her moral self vindica-tion without in the meanwhile conceding the material posi-tion that will enable that recovery. Overall, what the deliberate obscurity of her naval action at Actium does is to preserve a separation of her own political fortunes from those of her embattled colonial lover, not necessarily in support of his vengeful imperial rival and political superior but in favor of herself. This is the black gendered subaltern's inevitable and instinctive choice of expedience as the political ethic of her self survival, the impalpable esthetics of contingency with which she must combat the oppressions of her colonial experience and the means by which she can temporize the material finality of her histori-cal fate. This is also linked to the tactic of shifting-ness, to her ability to change the locale of her self performance at will, that Charnes has discussed (110-111, 135).

In the second and final sea-fight at Alexandria (4.12.), the unknowability of her behavior lies not in any of her own actions *per se*, but in her culpability in the actions of oth-ers that might be attributable to her: the defection of her entire fleet to Octavius in the very opening moments of the final engagement. In the physical separation of herself and her fleet (she is obviously not on her ships when they defect), is the equivocal distance between her motivation and its physical manifestation. Buried in the uncertainty of whether or not she authorizes that defection, is the rupture of the identity of action that can externally write her, and thereby the incidence of the ethical-psychological illeg-ibility that protects the play of her self agency. The real ambiguity of her intention, caught in the convincing surprise with which she meets Antony's anger after the episode, "Why is my lord enraged against his love?" (31), consists in the episode's concurrent projection of her power and her powerlessness, of her ability to command her forces and her inability to control them. Paradoxically, she can be in the defection as well as in her resistant location with Antony, that is, on two psychological planes at once. This is nothing other than the simultaneity of the victimization and recusant self-will with which the colonized subject performs its colonial narrative. The complex unknowability of her intentional location in this episode makes possible the critical postulate that the black gendered subaltern's historical self being is more than the sum of her visible actions and that she cannot be known through any unitary hermeneutics of her mimetic behavior. If the fight for signs is the fight for life, and if one's actions are the exposed signatures of one's being, then the discursive subject of the colonized black woman in Cleopatra fights for her right not to be written/known only through the signs of her observable representative existence.[37]

As an elusive unknowability is the particular sign under which the discursive subject of the black woman in Cleopatra textually lives, so the ultimate demonstration of that unknowability is its rendering of Cleopatra's death in mimetic terms that radically contradict what they project. Her extinction may be her historical destiny but her staging of it refuses that extinction by making her suicide the vehicle of her triumphing over the inscriptive control of the colonial forces that vanquish her. The text of that future scripting, both in the early colonial English text's received cultural history of her as well as in its eager imagination of the actual physical conditions of its own re-play of that script, is stated four times in the last two acts: in Antony's angry rebuke of her in 4.12.33-34, in Cleopatra's own fearful evocation of it in 5.2.53-56, in Dolabella's confirmation of it in 5.2.199-201, and finally in Cleopatra's own famous iteration of it before she prepares to die: "I shall see / Some squeaking Cleopatra boy my greatness / I'th posture of a whore" (5.2.219-21). The particular valencies of this quadruple repetition, of this textual drumbeat as it were, is the advertisement of her material fate that is the colonizer's prerogative. This is the colonizer's ideological justification of his military-economic conquest, the reflexive benefit of his self glorification through his denigration of the colonized.[38] In preferring to die rather than be the object of this Roman scurrility, Cleopatra, like Othello, terminates the cultural game of imperial patriarchy's writing of its other by writing out herself. The manner of that dying, however, both performs the exoticization of her that is the imperative of her colonial discourse and contests it, which is to say she Egyptianizes her Roman death. In doing so she prevents her death from essentializing her memory even while establishing it.

That suicide is the Roman way of dealing with dishonor and defeat Cleopatra knows from the examples of Brutus and Cassius in the Caesarist civil war. She also knows it from the precedent of her colonial-lover's death. But her particular execution of that ritual of dying is something that Rome cannot know, and because of that her suicide performs instead her own inimitability rather than any transparent Roman values. As Antony's was a male version of that ritual self killing, hers is going to be a female one, manifested as earlier noted in her pronounced association with the exotic Egyptian female mother-goddess Isis and with her symbol of the asp or *uraeus,* which in pharaonic "hieroglyphic writing was the determinative sign for the word 'goddess'" (Volkmann 207). The obfuscatory semiotic of this association is also perfectly congruent with the "multiplicit[ousness]" and "portmanteau nature" of the Isis myth (Hughes-Hallett 80) itself. Furthermore, that Isis was to Romans the goddess of foreigners (Hughes-Hallett 80) translates the Roman familiarity of the ritual of her suicide into the unfamiliarity of an alien practice, thereby inserting the ethnic-gendered foreign-ness of her self into the transparency of the colonial-patriarchal knowing of her. Concurrently, as Antony's self killing was marked by a blundering ineptitude, this is going to be distinguished by an elegant efficiency that will reify the social standing of the subjugated black female over the imperial-colonial male even in death. In these backcrossed racial-sexual features her suicide thus uses the very racialization-sexualization of herself that is her colonial burden to confuse any homogenous clarity in the notion of herself that might be the gateway to her cultural incarceration in the future history of the colonizer's community.

Still further, if in substance the act of suicide is a gesture of self cancellation as in Brutus's, Cassius's and Antony's case, Cleopatra's deliberate staging of it is a statement of self assertion in the face of extinction. This is signalled in the elaborateness of her final dressing routine, which begins with the imperious order of "Go, fetch my best attires" in 5.2.227 and continues over fifty two lines to the conscious flourish of "Give me my robes. Put on my crown / I have immortal longings in me" in 5.2.279. The same opacity is achieved in the choice of her method of death by a snake's bite, which displays her dying but not immediately the cause of it, so that in Octavius's wondering, "The manner of their deaths? / I do not see them bleed" (5.2.337-38) her demise refuses to offer the thematic closure that it otherwise could have been colonially expected to yield. Her death therefore presents the memorial claim of her life not by its self explanatoriness but by its traces of lingering mystery. It is precisely her death's stylistic thwarting of a thematic finality that prompts her colonial conqueror's quick compensatory propagandist authorization of her story as one of love, "She shall be buried by her Antony / No grave upon the earth shall clip in it / A pair so famous" (5.2.358-60), that critical commentary has noted in her colonial text (Charnes 138), and that historical and investigative journalistic analyses has traditionally identified in the cultural paratext that produced that text (Hughes-Hallett 38-42).[39] In doing all these things simultaneously Cleopatra's suicide retains the integrity of her being by projecting its indecipherability, and which is a quintessential manifestation of the necessary dubiety of the Spivak-ian "free will of the female sexed subject" in its colonial location.

In general, unpredictability's location in the "dubious place of the free will of the female-sexed subject" is helped considerably by, and profitably shades into, the potent notion of Irigaray-an *jouissance* and the vital post-feminist heuristic of Haraway-ian *cyborgism,* both in turn being derivatives of Lacanian revisionist post-Freudian psychoanalysis. If for Luce Irigaray "No singular form(s) . . . can complete the becomings of the desire of a woman," so that "what comes to pass in the *jouissance* of woman is in excess of it[womanhood]" (*Irigaray Reader* 55), and "female *jouissance* is a dimension that is never complete and never reversible" (*Irigaray Reader* 190), for Donna Haraway "The cyborg is a condensed image of both imagination and reality," an idea that "takes *pleasure* in the confusion of boundaries and . . . *responsibility* in their construction . . . an ultimate self united at last from all dependency" (598). To these can be added the relatedness of unpredictability to the "subversive repetition" that Judith Butler has said interrupts the processing of colonial identity and the spatial design of the social text (*Gender Trouble* 140-43; Ang-Lygate 182). This is not dissimilar to Gayatri Spivak's own notion of "interruption," as "a place of the reinscription of the dialectic into deconstruction," and as a necessity "which allows something to function" (*Postcolonial Critic* 110). These multiple paradigms all contribute pertinent interpretative methodologies for tracking the operation of anti-memory, linguistic indeterminacy, recusant self-sight, and unknowability in the play of Cleopatra's strategically unpredictable textual behavior. Within the "dubious place of the free will of the female sexed subject," the additional critical imperatives of *jouissance, cyborgism,* and subversive repetition or necessary interruption, help to make Cleopatra's unpredictability a psychic natural condition of historical response that dissolves the binary prophylactics of racial and sexual othering upon which colonialism historically depends.

The discernible effect of the unpredictability of the discursive subject of the black woman in Cleopatra can be seen if the analytical Jamesonian symbolic design of her textual landscape is clearly understood. In that symbolic design, Antony is the Shakespearean colonial author function, Caesar and his Rome the homosocial imaginary that is writing him, and Cleopatra the discursive subject of the black woman the surviving authorial memory of whose desire is the occasion for the colonial text of *Antony and Cleopatra.* In this representative discursive scenario the success of Cleopatra's unpredictability in subverting Caesarist-Roman patriarchal social and psychic self constructions such as its national-imperial dutifulness and the resolute nobility of its manhood, is also the discursive subject of the black woman's obstruction of the recovery of the lost homosocial order of the *Sonnets* that is the Shakespearean author-function's subliminal cue for its memory of her in the play. The retained integrity of Cleopatra's fecund Egyptian-feminine principle against the sterile white masculinity of the Roman order is then the

vindication of the black woman's ethnic and gendered being over the white patriarchal world of her early modern English authoring. Additionally, if the history of the Roman naming of August, to commemorate the final subjugation of the East by the West in Octavius's ultimate sacking of Egyptian power on the month of Cleopatra's death in August 10, 30 B.C., also contains within it the memory of the Eastern colored monarch's defiance of European hegemony and sustains through that her foundational impact on world history (Volkmann 213), that has an analogous resonance with the date of *Antony and Cleopatra*'s actual first performance. Since the scholarly consensus for that date, "late 1606" (Bevington A18, *Riverside* 1343, Wilders 1), locates the play in the second half of that year, the proximity of that calendric location to August temptingly marks the play's performance as a double survival, of the memory of the black woman in the *Sonnets* through the memory of the historical black figure of Cleopatra in the received Stuart history of the naming of the month of the latter's theatrical reappearance.

The specific achievements of the unpredictability of the subject of the black woman in Cleopatra, which is basically the failure of the popular colonial text's attempt to negatively manipulate the discourses of race and gender against each other, can also be seen ultimately in the resultant hybridity of its textual architecture. This is the conflation of the instincts of tragedy, history, comedy, and romance in the play text that has traditionally comprised the problem of its generic confusion in postmodern critical commentary (Spevack 621-34). If in Aristotelian patriarchal formalism tragedy is male, appropriating thematic markers such as morality, responsibility, duty, culture, and state, and comedy and romance are female, deploying tropes of love, marriage, festivity, nature, and social relations, the play's teleology is synchronously tragic and comic and not diachronously so. Because of Cleopatra's textual contrariety, the play succeeds in celebrating neither state nor marriage, neither Rome or Antony nor Cleopatra or Egypt. The generic hybridization that her unpredictability effects is also thereby her seizure of the discursive control of her colonial narration. The fact that most of the instances of the unpredictability of the black woman in Cleopatra discussed in this section appear in Shakespeare from her cultural history (in Plutarch for instance), is merely proof of the intrinsic recursivity of the subject of the black woman in all her discursive re-performances, and that is a part of the larger recalcitrance of the racial subaltern in all the renditions of its cultural history that has been the basic insistence of this book.

V

The abstract speculativeness of the tracing that this chapter has attempted of the black woman's resistant struggle, from her subliminal presence in the *Sonnets* to her surfacing in the black classical Egyptian queen's foundational discursive contestation of the re-play of her story in *Antony and Cleopatra,* merely describes the critical difficulties attendant upon such a project. The convolutions of such an interventionist exercise threaten the very clarity of its results. For instance, the foregoing explanation of Cleopatra's unpredictability must perforce itself be false, not only because of the expedient expository selectiveness of its apparata and evidentiality, nor only because of the inevitable gender appropriation that is the critical space of its male authoring (see note 33), but because unpredictability must logically be inexplicable. The failure of unpredictability's discursive transparency can therefore be the ultimate proof of its success in its colonial text, and in its imbrication in the black woman's recalcitrant shadow life in Cleopatra, but the guarantee of her discursive survival conversely lies only in the obscurity of such an interpretative space.

These difficulties define the deep structures of the black woman's incarceration in her colonial author's ongoing cultural imagination and warn against any simplistic notions of her recoverability. They suggest at best the ethical necessity of reading her colonial narrative against its cultural grain, of dismantling the semantic codes of its imperial syntax, in the hope not of resurrecting her but of making evident the programs of her elision. That *Antony and Cleopatra* marks the *terminus quo* of the black woman's contrary discursive after-life in Shakespeare, being replaced for the last time by early English colonialism's self educative master myth of the black man in the wild in *The Tempest,* means that the black woman can live only in the agendas of critical practices that continue to question her absence in Shakespeare's canonic formations.

Notes

1. The strength of this urge can be seen in the fact that Bradstreet was an immigrant to the American colony in 1630, and the poem was written there.

2. On this, also see Gillies who, notwithstanding his overall interest in seeing *Othello*'s connections with *The Merchant of Venice* rather than with *Titus,* says nevertheless that "All Shakespearean moors inherit Aaron's paradox" (112).

3. In Ericson's view Cleopatra also combines "aspects of the youthful, sacrificial, beneficent, redemptive type" of Shakespearean female characters such as Ophelia, Desdemona, Cordelia as well as Marina, Perdita and Miranda (*Patriarchal Structures* 124), but he does not explain, and it is difficult to see, the logic of this grouping.

4. The relative paucity of re-assessments of *Antony and Cleopatra* along the lines of race discourse compared to the volume of such work on Shakespearean texts such as *Othello* or *The Tempest* that has emerged in the last decade, has been described by some as "a conspiracy of silence" (Nyquist 87). Following Adelman's work, the few race based revaluations of the play within the last decade include the studies of Adelman, Loomba (*Gender, Race, Renaissance Drama*), Kim Hall (*Things of Darkness*), Charnes, Ericson (*Patriarchal Structures*), Nyquist and Joyce MacDonald ("Sex, Race, and Empire in *Antony and Cleopatra.*").

5. The problematic phenomenon of woman being tacitly *white,* noted by Barbara Nyquist for instance with regard to Cleopatra (87), has been seen by both Anne McClintock (183-84) and Judith Butler (*Bodies that Matter* 181) as the result of postmodern European feminism's prioritization of sexual difference over racial difference (cited by Sara Ahmed 157-58).

6. Despite its journalistic pedigree, Hughes-Hallett's deservedly much-cited book is so thoroughly researched as to be a minefield of information, and though not self consciously theoretical is rich in theoretical and critical insights. My reliance on this work here is for this reason.

7. The comments of the Swiss historian Hans Werner DeBrunner on this painting that Scobie cites are telling:

> . . . in a dramatic way, the painter accuses Europeans of brutal abuse of Africans . . . The African woman belongs to the dream world of primal psychological conceptions . . . All these representations and descriptions of African women show a common tendency: to imagine in the African woman a being sometimes dangerous, sometimes amusing, always different and possibly even doomed to perdition.

(152)

The painting may recall at least one real life incident, the rape of a black woman and her abandonment on a remote island by the crew of Francis Drake's crew on his third trip round the world (Kim Hall, *Things of Darkness* 152).

8. Jack D'Amico's remark about *Antony and Cleopatra* itself is similar:

> . . . through Enobarbus, Shakespeare reveals the deeper appeal of a world that attracts the Western foreigner not only because it allows him a vacation from the rules of his homeland but also because it takes him into the more seductive realm of transformation where none of the old rules applies.

(154).

9. Richard Helgerson, in his essay, "Language Lessons," citing two recent studies, credits the Tudor Cambridge mathematician and astrologer, John Dee, for being the first early modern English source of this associative phrase (292).

10. Even though James's marriage took place in Scotland when he was the Scottish James IV the details of the entertainment that he arranged for the ceremony—having four naked Africans run in the snow before the marriage party's carriage—are a part of what I am describing as the more deliberately imperialist ambitions of his government and politics. As is now well known that infamous episode involved the death of one of the Africans from exposure to the extreme cold (Kim Hall, *Things of Darkness* 128).

11. This is not the only instance. As the same map shows, and as *The Cambridge Ancient History* points out, Ptolemy Apion was also the product of the union of Ptolemy VII Euergetes II with a concubine (316). Clearly, Ptolemaic blood was less "pure" than a certain kind of interested historical scholarship would fondly like to believe.

12. Earlier in his otherwise helpful article, Harvey confuses Ptolemy IX with Ptolemy XI and Ptolemy XII himself with his son Ptolemy XIII (352). It is possibly this same error that is replicated by both Clarke and Rogers, cited below.

13. John Henrik Clarke, citing Pierre Loupous (126). However, Clarke, as well as J. A. Rogers whom he cites, both confuse Ptolemy IX with Ptolemy XI (the former was Soter II, the latter was Alexander II).

14. The gradual Egyptianization of the Ptolemies from the time of Philopator up to Cleopatra, would seem to corroborate Martin Bernal's otherwise contested thesis (in *Black Athena*) about the reverse cultural colonialism of the Greeks by the ancient Egyptians.

15. It is revealing that after herself laying the grounds for a racial analysis of the play in her first book (*Common Liar*) Adelman proceeds to ignore the implications of Cleopatra's color in her second, otherwise acutely argued book, *Suffocating Mothers*. Another example of the recalcitrance to talk about race in current criticism is Charles Whitney's essay, "Charmian's Laughter," which despite its very helpful analysis of the connections between Shakespeare's Egyptian Cleopatra and her court and early modern English gypsies, confines itself to a capable class analysis (that focuses attention on Charmian rather than Cleopatra) while remaining disinterested in any exploration of the racial construction of the play. He bypasses any racial question with merely a cursory acknowledgment of the subject with the word "oriental" at two points in his essay. This, presumably, is the phenomenon that Nyquist has aggressively described as "a conspiracy of silence" (earlier cited in note 3).

16. Although Adelman's belief in the blackness of Shakespeare's Cleopatra is cautiously expressed, she herself cites no less than five cogent reasons for the probability of Shakespeare's audience to regard Cleopatra as an "African queen", among which two of the more compelling ones are that Cleopatra, in the "to blanch an Ethiop" reference in lines 223-25, "uses current [Elizabethan] theory to explain her color suggests that Shakespeare imagined her as the proverbial Elizabethan Ethiopean," and that given the Tudor assumptions about the sexual profligacy of Africans if Cleopatra was meant to be lascivious she had to be thought of as African (*Common Liar* 187-88). For the direct connection in Virgil between Cleopatra and Dido also see John Wilders's "Introduction" in his recent Arden Shakespeare edition of the play (66).

17. See also Wilders 66, and Pelling 17, whom Wilders cites.

18. This is probably the origin of the notion of both the historical and the fictional Cleopatra's "whiteness" in popular and scholarly thinking from medieval through modern times. Plutarch's Europeanizing of Cleopatra completes the classical rewriting of the political effects of the pair's relationship. If the strategy of the Virgilian move was not only to roll back the subversive power of the black queen by making the lover abandon her but also to remove her altogether from direct visibility by making Dido stand in for her, Plutarch's treatment extends this process of Cleopatra's effacement by making her unequivocally white.

19. Hughes-Hallett, who citing Geoffrey Bullough points this out, infers the play's content was political on the grounds that Fulke Greville suppressed it for fear of offending the Queen at a time when she was sensitive to criticism:

> Sir Fulke Greville, Shakespeare's contemporary, wrote a tragedy of Antony and Cleopatra, but burnt the manuscript in fear that its chief characters, 'having some childish wantonness,' might be identified with Elizabeth I and her rejected favorite, the Earl of Essex. Essex was in disgrace, and the Queen was sensitive to any criticism; it was no time, Greville judged, to publish a play censuring a ruler for 'forsaking empire to follow sensuality.'
>
> (139)

20. This is to say that love and politics are not separate but inextricably connected, that desire and passion have origins and consequences in the political life of the world. It is this caveat that, in my discussions of the play later in this chapter, silently conflates Antony's and Caesar's positions. His situation apparently between the Western imperial-colonial patriarchy of Rome on the one hand and the counter-politics of Cleopatra's Eastern Egypt and of his lover-ship of Cleopatra on the other, that has been noted in most commentary (by Charnes, for instance, 112-15), does not in the long view of Cleopatra's racial-colonized politics of survival afford him a significantly different discursive location than Caesar's. He is for her merely the focus of a different kind of strategy than Caesar, and without suggesting that her involvement with him is simply duplicitous my assumption is that involvement is predicated on the tactical advantage he represents for her historically. For a similar explanation of the complexity of Cleopatra's "love" see Charnes's explanation of love "as poetic construct" and as "realpolitik" (*Notorious Identity* 144).

21. Nyquist feels that the political agenda of Sedley's play is a kind of revivalist republicanism whereas Dryden's is a direct challenge to that (100).

22. It is therefore not surprising that, as Martin Bernal has argued, the "whitening" of ancient Egypt oc-

curred in the nineteenth century, until which time and going back to antiquity Eqypt was always regarded as African and black (iv, 2, 243). In early modern England, Bernal points out, "the fact that the name Gypsy (or Egyptian) was given to people from North-West India shows that in the 15th century the Egyptians were seen as archetypally dark people" (242).

23. My focusing on the negative racial-sexual discursive intermixture in Shakespeare's Cleopatra is paralleled by Jenny Sharpe's formulation of "the sexed subject of Victorian England [as] also a racial identity", and my critical intention behind this focusing, as will be evident shortly, is also echoed by her emphasis on the "need [for] a critical model that can accommodate, on the one hand, female power and desire, and, on the other hand, gender restrictions and sexual subordination" (11).

24. As that formidable eighteenth century Shakespearean editor, Samuel Johnson, glibly put it, "*Gypsy* is used here, both in the original meaning for an *Egyptian,* and in its *accidental* sense, for a *bad* woman" (Spevack 7). Likewise, a recent editor of the play in glossing the "tawny front" and "gipsy" reference has explained, "Gipsies began to appear in England in the early sixteenth century and were thought to have come from Egypt. 'Gipsy' was a contemptuous term for a promiscuous woman. Hence Cleopatra is here described as a gipsy, an Egyptian and a whore" (Wilders 91). For an extended eye-opening discussion of what the "gypsy" reference could have meant to Jacobean audiences aware of English gypsies and of their illegitimate status, see Charles Whitney's essay, "Charmian's Laughter."

25. For Cleopatra's visibly active role in Antony's war preparation against Caesar, see Volkmann 154-55.

26. Enobarbus may be responding to the awe-struck Agrippa's essentialist question about what Cleopatra is like, but the cue of the conversation is squarely political: the speakers are part of the administrative staff of competing Roman political and military personalities who have met to negotiate a difficult but necessary alliance between themselves. The specific context of Enobarbus's portrait of Cleopatra is also political: he is describing how Cleopatra first met Antony and overcame him with her dazzling physical presence. Noticeably, in Enobarbus's description, that conquest has no political qualities.

27. What Knoxe said was that,

> To promote a woman to beare rule, superioritie, dominion or empire above any realm, nation. or citie, is repugnant to nature, contumelie to God, a thing most contrarious to his reveled will and approved ordinance, and finallie it is the subversion of good order, of all equitie and justice.
>
> (Shepherd 23)

Coinciding with Elizabeth's accession to the throne, and with the fact of her necessary and generally admirable reign, however, Knoxe's statement was quickly qualified by John Calvin ("that there were occasionally women so endowed . . . that they were raised up by divine authority . . . to condemn the inactivity of men" Knoxe 17, Shepherd 24) and Edmund Spenser ("Unless the heavens them lift to lawful soveraintie," *Faerie Queene* 5.5.25), not only to clearly position Elizabeth as the exception to this view, but also to make such exceptional women a vehicle of God's admonishment to a community of inactive or incapable men. The misogyny of such attacks, as Shepherd points out, is partly contextualized by the instances of Catholic female rulers (Shepherd 24), but their larger serviceability remains bound within the performance of a racialized gender discourse. For a discussion of the early modern Anglo-European provenance of "Amazonomachy" see, in addition to Shepherd and Brown, Stephen Orgel's essay "Jonson and the Amazons."

28. For effective recent studies of the connections between Cleopatra and Elizabeth in Elizabethan cultural practice see the essays by Rhinehart and Jankowski.

29. The deliberateness of the suppression of Cleopatra's children in Shakespeare is evident in the fact that other Elizabethan texts do mention them. For instance, Charles Whitney has pointed out that in the Countess of Pembroke's translation of Garnier's *Antonie,* Charmian elaborately mentions Cleopatra's children as a strong reason for the latter not to commit suicide (72), a reference that in Shakespeare appears only obliquely in the soothsayer scene cited above.

30. The other supposed maternal markings of Cleopatra that Adelman has discussed, such as the "womb" reference in 3.5.163 (*Suffocating Mothers* 186), do not so much show her located in and attached to maternality as detached and separated from it. Insofar as the "womb" reference is a "memory" it is a part not of her mimetic presentation but of her response to it, a function of her anti-memory as will be evident later in this chapter.

31. The only visible moment of uninterrupted reflection she has is her quiet speech in 5.2.1-8 when after Antony's death she begins to think of suicide. But even then her maids are with her.

32. This important essay written in her mid-to-late career is symptomatic of Spivak's increasing focus later on what she has subsequently termed as her central critical interest:

> the one most consistently exiled from episteme . . . the disenfranchised woman, the figure I have called 'the gendered subaltern' . . . [h]er continuing heterogeneity, her continuing subalternization and loneliness, have defined the subaltern subject for me.
>
> (*Postcolonical Critic* 102-3)

I find now that my work is coalescing around strange single figures like the Rani of Sirmur.

(*Postcolonial Critic* 116)

33. Spivak goes on in the essay to correct La Capra's "psychoanalytical metaphor for transformative disciplinary practice" as an inevitable "catachresis," in which the reconstruction of the past is also "a genealogy of the historian" (251), in direct candid proof of which she says "My Indian example could thus be seen as a nostalgic investigation of the lost roots of my own identity" (252). My own acquiescence to this confessional prerequisite is simply the admission of my interest in the racial and sexual minority histories not only over and through which popular canonical European cultural mastertexts such as Shakespeare's are constructed but against which they are transmitted in contemporary discourse. While not thereby indulging in the kind of "congratulatory self marginalization" that Spivak has warned against (quoted in Bahri 4), as a Bangladeshi male scholar teaching a canonical Anglo-European author and period in the U.S. my connection to "minority discourses" is, I would assume, obvious. The fact of my gender, and of my particular national origins on the periphery of the power hub of the Indian subcontinent, give me a compoundedly self counteractive critical identity (as a Bangladeshi I am as disempowered in the U.S. as I am in the Indian subcontinent, while as a male I am privileged in both locations) that is both my advantage and my difficulty.

34. While Adelman also sees clearly the value of Cleopatra's speech about Antony in terms of its appropriative memorial reconstruction, she finds the speech restorative of Cleopatra's position (and of the bountiful maternality of the female against the sterility of the Octavian-Roman male regime) only through her recovery of an ideal memory of the male in Antony (*Suffocating Mothers* 183-84).

35. The distinction I am suggesting here is obviously indebted to the Swiss linguist Ferdinand de Saussure's notion of the difference between *langue* and *parole* in which "Language is a social phenomenon, whereas speech is an individual one," and particularly to the socio- and ethno- logic validation of that distinction in post-Saussurian linguistics (Ducrot and Todorov 118), and my appropriation of Certeau's ideas about the power of speech has resonances with Mikhail Bakhtin's concept of *heteroglossia* (earlier cited Chapter 3 note 19).

36. For an explanation of Mikhail Bakhtin's coinage of the term see Chapter 3.

37. This is only to claim in a postcolonial pedagogy a particular significance for what might otherwise also be a generally valid idea.

38. This is reflected neatly in the historical Octavius's insistence to the Roman senate at the outset of his campaign that his wars with Antony not be represented as a civil war but as a war against Egypt and its Queen as "a righteous and holy war, a '*bellum iustum pium*'" (Volkmann 170), despite the lack of any direct or exclusive interaction between Egyptian and Roman forces.

39. In proclaiming her "sad love story" Octavius is actually establishing his own "nobility" in the eyes of his own imperial constituency, thereby transforming his deliberate Roman colonial conquest of her and of Egypt into a "human tragedy."

Works Cited

Adelman, Janet. *The Common Liar: An Essay on Antony and Cleopatra.* New Haven: Yale University Press, 1973.

————. *Suffocating Mothers: Fantasies of Maternal Origin in Shakespeare's Plays, Hamlet to The Tempest.* New York: Routledge, 1992.

Ahmed, Sara. "Its a Sun-tan, isn't it? Autobiography as an Identificatory Practice." *Black British Feminism.* Ed. Heidi Safia Mirza. London: Routledge, 1997. 153-67.

Bahri, Deepika. "Disembodying the Corpus: Postcolonial Pathology in Tsitsi Dangarembga's *Nervous Conditions.*" *Postmodern Culture* 5.1 (1994): 1-15. An electronic journal at http://muse.jhu.edu/journals/postmodern_culture.

Bakhtin, Mikhail M. *The Dialogic Imagination: Four Essays by Mikhail Bakhtin.* Ed. M. Holquist. Austin: University of Texas Press, 1981.

Bernal, Martin. *Black Athena: The Afroasiatic Roots of Classical Civilization.* 2 vols. New Brunswick, N.J.: Rutgers University Press, 1987.

Bradstreet, Anne. *The Works of Anne Bradstreet.* Ed. Jeannine Hensley. Cambridge, Mass.: Belknap Press of Harvard University Press, 1981.

Brown, Laura. "Amazons and Africans: Gender, Race and Empire in Daniel Defoe." Margo Hendricks and Patricia Parker Ed. *Women, "Race," and Writing in the Early Modern Period.* New York: Routledge, 1994.

Bullough, Geoffrey, Ed. *Narrative and Dramatic Sources of Shakespeare.* 8 vols. London: Columbia University Press, 1964.

Butler, Judith. *Bodies That Matter: On the Discursive Limits of "Sex."* New York: Routledge, 1993.

Charnes, Linda. *Notorious Identity: Materializing the Subject in Shakespeare.* Cambridge, Mass.: Harvard University Press, 1993.

Clarke, John Henrik. "African Warrior Queens." *Black Women in Antiquity.* Ed. Ivan Van Sertima. London: Transaction Books, 1985. 123-34.

D'Amico, Jack. *The Moor in English Renaissance Drama.* Tampa: University of South Florida Press, 1991.

Ducrot, Oswald, and Tzvetan Todorov. Ed. *Encyclopedic Dictionary of the Sciences of Language.* 1979; rpt. Baltimore: Johns Hopkins Press, 1994.

Ericson, P. *Patriarchal Structures in Shakespeare's Drama.* Berkeley: University of California Press, 1985.

Gillies, John. *Shakespeare and the Geography of Difference.* New York: Cambridge University Press, 1994.

Hall, Kim. *Things of Darkness: Economies of Race and Gender in Early Modern England.* Ithaca: Cornell University Press, 1995.

Harvey, Sir Paul. *The Oxford Companion to Classical Literature.* 1937; rpt. Oxford: Clarendon Press, 1969.

Helgerson, Richard. "Language Lessons: Linguistic Colonialism, Linguistic Postcolonialism, and the Early Modern English Nation." *The Yale Journal of Criticism* 11.1 (1998): 289-99.

Hughes-Hallett, Lucy. *Cleopatra: Histories, Dreams and Distortions.* New York: Harper and Row, 1990.

La Capra, Dominick. *Rethinking Intellectual History: Texts, Contexts, Language.* Ithaca: Cornell University Press, 1983.

Loomba, Ania. *Gender, Race, Renaissance Drama.* Manchester (U.K.): Manchester University Press, 1989.

MacDonald, Joyce Green. "Sex, Race, and Empire in Shakespeare's *Antony and Cleopatra.*" *Literature and History* 5.1 (1996): 60-77.

McClintock, Anne. *Imperial Leather: Race, Gender, and Sexuality in the Colonial Conquest.* London: Routledge, 1995.

Nyquist, Mary. "'Profuse, proud Cleopatra:' 'Barbarism,' and Female Rule in Early Modern English Republicanism." *Women's Studies* 24.1-2 (1994): 85-131.

Orgel, Stephen. "Jonson and the Amazons." Elizabeth D. Harvey and Katherine Eisaman Maus ed. *Soliciting Interpretations: Literary Theory and Seventeenth Century English Poetry.* Chicago: University of Chicago Press, 1990. 119-39.

Pelling, C. B. R. Ed. *Life of Antony.* Cambridge (U.K.): Cambridge University Press, 1988.

Sharpe, Jenny. *Allegories of Empire.* Minneapolis: University of Minnesota, 1993.

Shepherd, Simon. *Amazons and Warrior Women: Varieties of Feminism in Seventeenth Century Drama.* New York: St. Martin's Press, 1981.

Spevack, Marvin. ed. *Antony and Cleopatra.* A New Variorum edition of Shakespeare. New York: Modern Language Association of America, 1990.

Spivak, Gayatri. *The Postcolonial Critic: Interviews, Strategies, Dialogues.* New York: Routledge, 1990.

Volkmann, Hans. *Cleopatra: A Study in Politics and Propaganda.* London: Elek Books, 1958.

Whitney, Charles. "Charmian's Laughter: Women, Gypsies and Festive Ambivalence in *Antony and Cleopatra.*" *The Upstart Crow* 14 (1994): 67-88.

Wilders, John. Ed. *Antony and Cleopatra.* The Arden Shakespeare. Third Series. London: Methuen, 1995.

PRODUCTION REVIEWS

Patrick Carnegy (review date 1999)

SOURCE: Carnegy, Patrick. "Wanton Self-Destruction." *The Spectator* 283, no. 8917 (3 July 1999): 41-2.

[*In the following review, Carnegy offers a mostly favorable assessment of the Royal Shakespeare Company's production of* Antony and Cleopatra *at Stratford-upon-Avon for the Summer-Winter 1999-2000 season, directed by Steven Pimlott. Although Carnegy criticizes Alan Bates, as Antony, for stumbling over many of his lines, he gives high praise to Frances de la Tour's performance as Cleopatra.*]

'Men's judgements,' as Enobarbus, Antony's sometime friend and shrewdest observer, remarks, 'are a parcel of their fortunes.' For Enobarbus, and for Steven Pimlott's new production, Antony's tragedy is his loss of judgement. His ill-fortune is shown as lying more in his stars than in Cleopatra's arms. We see an Antony whose behaviour is driven by *ennui,* even by what Sartre called nausea. Behold the man of power, the 'triple pillar of the world', now grown bored with omnipotence.

Cleopatra is one reason for him to go on living, drink is another. The one sure thing about Alan Bates's Antony is that it's already all up with him, a man who knows he's marked for death and will revel while he may. This is a Dionysus matched against the Pentheus of Guy Henry's coldly calculating Caesar. It's not his dalliance with Cleopatra that antagonises friends but his wanton self-destruction.

What, then, of Antony's relationship with the serpent of old Nile? Shakespeare doesn't show its growth, catching it only at its maturity and tracing its downward curve and the pathos of its valedictory upsurge. Cleopatra has no need of alcohol. Her intoxication is Antony. From first to last in Frances de la Tour's magnificent performance, she doesn't really know him. At the end, she recognises that her vision of a hero whose 'legs bestrid the ocean; his reared arm crested the world . . . He was as rattling thunder' may have been no more than a dream. If Alan Bates is substantial enough in his exuberant dissolution, de la Tour's infatuation is instability itself. The drama is of her transformation from 'the whore of Egypt', playing infantile games to hold her man, into regal queen who longs to call him 'husband'.

It's only with the approach of death that, too late, they sober up into a semblance of what they must have been. When Antony rounds on Cleopatra for her navy's desertion, the embers rekindle. But his reproaches are really self-reproaches. Love flames again in his manic jealousy on discovering Cleopatra bent over the hand of Caesar's luckless emissary. As Caesar closes in on the triumvir who's so carelessy redistributing choice morsels of the Empire, Antony's death parodies that of the romantic hero. It's a botched, cowardly suicide, triggered by a blubbering eunuch's false news of Cleopatra's death. All judgment gone, he fails to see that *this* was the messenger he should have whipped, a jackanapes who gets off with no more than a bystander's boot to his ample *gluteus maximus*.

Antony, famously, strips off the disgraced 'sevenfold shield of Ajax' to meet his end: 'Unarm, Eros. The long day's task is done . . .' Alan Bates manages the ignominious death as best he may, but as elsewhere fumbles too many of his lines into inaudibility. De la Tour's Cleopatra paints her face and robes herself as Egypt's golden queen, rising to greatness through her pain and pride as she prepares to die. She does so a ritual victim, strewing the ground with sand and absolving her attendants by sponging their necks with water. In all this de la Tour gives the performance of a lifetime, with heartrending delivery of the poetry of her 'immortal longings'.

The visual setting that Steven Pimlott and his designer Yolanda Sonnabend provide is of a rich but finely disciplined theatricality, drawing on Pimlott's experience in opera and Sonnabend's in ballet.

The bare boards of the theatre's new wooden oval, used so successfully in *A Midsummer Night's Dream* and *Othello,* are now closely carpeted in charcoal grey. Three towering glass surfaces, framed like dressing-mirrors, reflect the action back on itself. Behind them, the outlines of an emblematic pyramid and sinuous hieroglyphs eventually lift to herald the chill dawn of Caesar's victorious entry. The transitions between Rome and Egypt are swiftly accomplished by Hugh Vanstone's lighting which knows how to make this exposed stage seem a private prison or a public palace. Sonnabend's penchant for luxuriant invention is focused into costumes which hit off to perfection the contrast between the suave austerity of Caesar's milieu and the oriental pleasures of Cleopatra's court—Antony cockily celebrates his return from Rome by affecting a sumptuous kaffiyeh.

Pimlott's theatrical language borrows from oriental mime. Malcolm Storry's sonorous Enobarbus wills the life out of him by pounding his naked chest. Cleopatra and her maids haul on invisible ropes to bring up the dying Antony who's clearly visible slumped in a chair behind them. Corpses quit the stage on their feet. The one moment that didn't read was when Antony's friend and appointed executioner,

the ironically named Eros, seemed not to have turned the sword on himself but to have thrust it into Antony and calmly walked off. Not the right message at that crucial juncture. It will doubtless be corrected. All in all, this is a compelling view of the work and not to be missed.

Lois Potter (review date 1999)

SOURCE: Potter, Lois. "Shakespeare Performed: Roman Actors and Egyptian Transvestites." *Shakespeare Quarterly* 50, no. 4 (winter 1999): 508-17.

[*In the following excerpted review of the Southmark Globe Theatre's all-male production of* Antony and Cleopatra, *directed by Giles Block, Potter praises many of the performances of the major characters, finding in particular that Mark Rylance's Cleopatra uncovered new meaning in the play. Potter comments that the director's vision of the play emphasized the victory of "a gloriously human couple."*]

In its 1999 season the Southwark Globe took up several challenges from its critics: to prove that it could do Shakespearean tragedy as well as comedy, to adopt more Elizabethan conventions (in this case, all-male casts for *Julius Caesar* and *Antony and Cleopatra*), and to perform a new play. To make room for the last of these, which opened after I left, there were no plays by Shakespeare's contemporaries this year; I suspect that they will mostly be relegated to the small indoor theater when it finally materializes, and that the same will be true of new plays. The Globe theater has also taken notice of last season's complaints about problems seeing and hearing the actors. The pillars have new, slimmer bases; though actors can no longer stand on them, a little more of the forestage can now be seen from the side. This year each production has had a "Master of Play" and "Master of Verse," and the work of these coyly named individuals, especially the latter, has made a difference. While some of the actors occasionally sounded as if they were forcing their voices, most could make themselves heard even above the sound of a helicopter. The stage movement was also much more inventive, with most actors apparently comfortable about playing to the whole of their audience instead of just the quadrant directly in front of the stage. . . .

. . . [I]t was Giles Block's production of *Antony and Cleopatra* that everyone was waiting for. Mark Rylance may or may not have been the age of the now-unknown Jacobean actor who originally played one of the greatest female roles of all time. It didn't matter; his performance as Cleopatra was a genuine revelation of aspects of the play and the role that I have never seen exploited before. It gained, for instance, from the audience's double awareness of character and actor, particularly when he was physically threatening other characters or doing one of Cleopatra's quick transitions between sinking into a faint and deciding not to bother after all. This Cleopatra, as several reviewers said, really did look as if she might decide at any time to hop forty paces through the public street. Barefoot much of the time and dressed like a gypsy, she played the second scene with the messenger wearing chopines and a feathered headdress, thus carefully giving herself every advantage when she asked whether Octavia was "as tall as me." Following Plutarch's account, Rylance also gave us a Cleopatra who had shaved her head and lacerated her face in mourning for Antony, thus making the final transformation with robe and crown even more stunning than usual.

In most productions it is Antony who is shown to be suffering from divided longings and Cleopatra who acts on blind impulse. Here, however, Paul Shelley's Antony became the object of love—both Cleopatra's and Enobarbus's—rather than an autonomous subject. He was a creature of instinct, never needing to brood over what he was going to do next. His generosity on hearing that Enobarbus had left him was so rapid and spontaneous that it went largely unnoticed, as did his instant forgiveness when he learned that Cleopatra was still alive after all; the death of Eros (who slit his own throat) shocked the audience more than it did him. In all three cases I would have liked him to take a few seconds longer to register, or let the audience register, the enormity of what he was not saying. Cleopatra was allowed far greater interiority; she actually heard Enobarbus's sarcastic comments on Antony's deteriorating judgment (usually treated as an aside) and her gradual realization that her lover was no longer a superman gave her a shared understanding, delicately indicated, of Enobarbus's state of mind. This sympathy between the two people who love Antony most is not in the text, but then this play, unlike Julius Caesar, has a subtext—at least, that's how I would describe such lines as Cleopatra's "Then Antony—but now—Well, on."

There were other fine performances. John McEnery's Enobarbus was admirably clear, understatedly funny, and able to span the barge speech, the sarcastic one-liners, and the difficult death scene. Mark Lewis Jones, good in all his roles, stood out as the amiably second-rate Pompey. Danny Sapani as Charmian revealed a comic range that he had conscientiously repressed as Brutus, while James Gillan was a remarkably convincing Iras. As the messenger who gets mauled by Cleopatra, Roger Gartland had a wonderful moment in their second scene, when she offered him gold for the second time and he registered a horrified suspicion that the cycle of reward and attack was about to start again. On the other hand, I found most of the Romans, especially Octavius (Ben Walden), somewhat colorless, and I suspect that the director was simply not very interested in this half of the conflict. In some productions this would have been a disaster. For this one it didn't seem to matter. I have rarely seen an interpretation so little concerned with the difference between the Roman and Egyptian worldviews.

Was the final effect tragic? Is it ever? Block seems to me to see the play as the triumph of a gloriously human couple. The speed at which events moved, matched by that of the characters themselves as they danced and dashed across their world stage, made it easier to enjoy the comedy than to respond to the sense of "greatness going off" or the suggestiveness of the moment (surprisingly ineffective, at least in the previews) when music from under the earth hints at the end of an era. This may be why the most moving part of the play was the minitragedy of Enobarbus, who ironically dies in public yet so lost in his own grief as to be unaware that he has an audience. Perhaps we are overinclined to associate tragedy with interiority and silence and do not know how to respond to a play that takes place entirely in public. Yet the company tried to play as many lines as possible out front. They duly glared at us whenever they complained about the unreliability of the common people; the anonymous servant's lament that Lepidus should "be called into a huge sphere and not . . . be seen to move in't" was played as a joke about acting minor parts at the Globe; after his one military victory, Antony assured us (rather unconvincingly) that he owed it all to us. The fact that such moments could be achieved only by forcing the lines marks the difference between Antony and Cleopatra and the season's other plays. Both its historical setting and its Jacobean context imply an audience whose role is (as Philo says at the start) to "behold and see" rather than to affect events. . . .

Russell Jackson (review date 2000)

SOURCE: Jackson, Russell. "Shakespeare at Stratford-upon-Avon: Summer and Winter, 1999-2000." *Shakespeare Quarterly* 51, no. 2 (summer 2000): 217-29.

[*In the following excerpted review, Jackson comments on the Royal Shakespeare Company's production of* Antony and Cleopatra *at Stratford-upon-Avon, directed by Steven Pimlott. In particular, Jackson finds Frances de la Tour's performance of Cleopatra outstanding, and notes that Alan Bates's Antony, while amiable, is somewhat unheroic.*]

In my previous report on Shakespeare at Stratford-upon-Avon I wondered more in sorrow than in anger what kind of artistic policy the RSC might lay claim to.[1] Whether or not in the course of the "Summer Festival Season" the company found a policy, they certainly acquired a stage, which may amount to the same thing. The 1500-seat proscenium-arch main house, with whose architecture directors and designers have struggled since it opened in 1932, was remodeled under the direction of the company's resident designer, Anthony Rowe. For the summer season the company installed a deep, elliptical platform stage, on which the principal action of each play was performed. The space upstage of the proscenium arch was relegated to providing background images or (for long stretches of some of the season's plays) simply closed off from view. In order to make the actors visible to spectators at the back of the topmost level, the new platform was higher than in previous attempts to bring the stage forward (such as that of the 1976 season). Consequently, the front two rows of stalls on either side of it became "restricted-view" seats, and the performers' horizontal sight line was slightly above the heads of the audience in the middle and rear stall seats.

But two other elements of the past twelve months' work in Stratford were definitely signs of policy: an increased attention to clarity of speech (reinforced by company voice classes) and the designation of the main season, from March to September, as a "summer festival." The voice work—together with the remodeled stage—addressed directly some criticisms made in recent years by giving speech and action priority over scenic display. . . .

For *Antony and Cleopatra,* directed by Steven Pimlott with designs by Yolanda Sonnabend, the forestage was backed by three tall mirrors that could be instantly rendered transparent to reveal a background of gold geometric shapes against a dark backdrop. By means of these mirrors a character in Alexandria could be "present" at a scene in Rome and *vice-versa.* On the right and left, stacked against the proscenium arch, were Egyptian and Roman accoutrements of the kind normally associated with the play: standards and weapons inscribed with the empire's "S.P.Q.R.", feather fans, the odd *ankh.* In defiance of this reminder of performance traditions, there was no standard-wielding, *Aïda*-style marching or fanning in this production. The milieu at first suggested an Alexandrian nightclub in the middle of the twentieth century, with cocktail glasses and cigarettes. Philo delivered his opening speech directly to the audience from the front of the stage (Demetrius did not appear), while upstage to the audience's right a group of courtiers huddled round what seemed to be a *chaise longue.* On "Behold and see" the group parted to reveal Antony and Cleopatra. At some early performances they were unequivocally in the last stages of cunnilingus, and later in the run they were discovered in a more decorous postcoital position, he with his head in her lap. Either way, the director was announcing a no-holds-barred version of court life in Alexandria, which suited the fearlessness of Frances de la Tour's Cleopatra. De la Tour is not conventionally good-looking but has a commanding stature, a strong, melodious contralto voice, and a winning quality of emotional openness. Conventions of Egyptian glamour were not going to be served in this rawly passionate performance, which ignored no chance for comedy and made no bones about the queen's desire for physical and emotional satisfaction. In her treatment of both the departing Antony and of the hapless messenger who reports on Antony's marriage she was formidable and quick-witted, turning on a sixpence from nostalgia to anger or from humor to indignation. With Thidias (in 3.13) her condescension could not conceal her sense of the need to survive. Her raising of Antony to the monument (in fact he was pulled across the stage and placed in a chair) was allowed an element of the ridiculous, but the lament after his death was heartrending.

In the final scene, for which the geometric lumber-room upstage was cleared out to reveal the brick wall at the rear, Cleopatra was costumed in a simple shift. The betrayal of her by her steward was by now an irrelevance, rather than any kind of victory for the smoothly magnanimous Caesar. After Caesar's departure she prepared for death. In a long, silent ritual she made up her face before donning the robe that presented her in formal grandeur for the first time. According to a convention established earlier in the

production, after her "death" she discarded a garment and walked off. De la Tour did this simply and without fussing over the arrangement of her shift so that often her breasts were exposed, and in some later performances she left the stage completely naked.

The principal male role in this play raises interesting questions about the relationship between theatrical and other kinds of heroism. An Antony needs to command whatever stage he has been put on. Alan Bates was amiable, energetic, but unheroic. It was difficult to perceive in this shaggy, kindly figure the warrior who has gone to seed but easy to understand that he was good company. Bates is a fine exponent of characters whose self-destructive or wayward behavior has obliged them to take refuge in a winning but desperate degree of charm. Here his strongest scene was the parley with his fellow triumvirs in Rome, in which Antony's ease of manner contrasted with the stiffness and vocal deliberation of Guy Henry's Octavius Caesar. Antony was master of the table as of the situation, handing out bread rolls and dispensing wine. That he should ever have bestrid the world like a colossus did seem fanciful. The genuine subtleties and strengths of the performance were best appreciated from the middle of the stalls: projection on the scale required by the Stratford main house seemed not to be at the actor's command. In purely physical terms Enobarbus (Malcolm Storry) was more convincing as a fighting man. His was also a performance of wit and feeling, in which the delicious absurdity of the barge speech was savored and the conflict between reason and affection was fully explored. In his death scene Enobarbus beat at his chest with one fist ("I am alone the villain of the earth") in a gesture reminiscent of harrowing scenes of grief familiar from Balkan news reports and also suggestive of a literal breaking of the heart. According to the production's established custom, he then walked off, leaving his jacket behind him. . . .

Note

1. See my "Shakespeare at Stratford-upon-Avon, 1996-98: or the Search for a Policy," *Shakespeare Quarterly* 50 (1999): 185-205.

THEMES

William Blissett (lecture date 1962)

SOURCE: Blissett, William. "Dramatic Irony in *Antony and Cleopatra.*" *Shakespeare Quarterly* 18, no. 2 (spring 1967): 151-66.

[*In the following essay, originally delivered as a lecture in 1962, Blissett explores* Antony and Cleopatra*'s use of dramatic irony, focusing in particular on the dramatic irony generated from the nature of the theater and from the audiences' interpretations of the play's characters and events.*]

ANT.

    Ho now, Enobarbus!

ENO.

    What's your pleasure, sir?

ANT.

    I must with haste from hence.

ENO.

    Why, then we kill all our women. We see how mortal
    an unkindness is to them; if they suffer our departure,
    death's the word.[1]

Antony, one may imagine, looks a little distraught; and a slight operatic tremolo carries over from the well-turned *bel canto* tribute to his late wife Fulvia. Enobarbus knows his man even if he does not know the news: his remarks are dry and pointed—ironic, in a sense recognized in Shakespeare's time, that is, in the rhetorical mode described as the "dry mock".[2] The relationship of the two characters might also have been called *eironeia* by the Greeks: the element of boastfulness and pretence in Antony at this moment, and often in the play, brings him close to the comic type of the *alazon*; and the tendency of Enobarbus to belittle and deflate makes him an *eiron*. *Eiron* is to *alazon* as pin to balloon.[3]

But the situation itself is an instance of dramatic irony in the modern sense: that is, one of the persons on the stage knows more than the other, and the spectator knows more than either, indeed than both. Antony knows of Fulvia's death and of the strong exigencies that recall him to Rome, and so the foolery of Enobarbus rebounds upon himself—to be deftly caught by the quick-witten *eiron* and thrown again with better aim when he says, "The tears live in an onion that would water this sorrow." But Enobarbus too has superior insight and sees, as the momentarily resolved Antony cannot, how painful the parting with Cleopatra will be—funny and painful, a combination beloved of the ironic character and the ironic writer.[4] And the audience can see and appraise both the committed and the detached man—Antony, a "plain man without subtlety" though given to a somewhat Asiatic style of speech and life,[5] and Enobarbus, a man of sharper perception and more pointed, less rotund, rhetoric. Thus the spectators experience here the proper pleasure of the theater, that sense of comprehending the motives of the actors and the inner form and flow of the action that we call dramatic irony.[6]

It may be useful to go over the same passage again. On hearing of Fulvia's death, Antony resolves to leave "the present pleasure" for what he believes to be duty or honor in Rome; he calls Enobarbus, and Enobarbus asks, "What is your pleasure, sir?" A perfectly normal question, yet ironic in the context. Antony replies, "I must with haste from hence." The spectator may or may not recall that Julius Caesar's virtue and boast was *celeritas*: he will be noticing, from this point on, that resolute and prompt ac-

tion is ever the mark of the Roman—of Antony when stirred by Roman thoughts, of Octavius Caesar; and to be taken by surprise always the mark of the loser in the power-struggle, first Pompey, then Antony, for

> Celerity is never more admir'd
> Than by the negligent.

"Why, then we kill all our women", Enobarbus answers: "We see how mortal an unkindness is to them; if they suffer our departure, death's the word." What exactly is the dramatic irony here? There is first the irony from outside the play. "Death's the word", we might have told Enobarbus from the vantage point of our superior knowledge of history, death for Cleopatra and her women, for Antony and himself. But there is also an irony within the play that makes us note this speech and say, "Be careful, witty man, lest you prove a prophet." A prophet he does prove: immediately, when we behold Cleopatra's winds and waters; ultimately, when Cleopatra lets it be thought that Antony's unkindness has indeed been mortal and so precipitates his death and hers.[7] From the beginning, the audience appraises Enobarbus as ironically as he appraises the other characters.

What I have tried to gain by looking so intently at this rather unemphatic passage are the senses of irony and the terms of reference for the ensuing study. Irony the trope; the *eiron* as a comic mask confronting and deflating the *alazon*; the dramatic irony that springs from the very nature of the theater; that which comes from information outside the play; that which arises from the audience's cumulative act of interpretation whereby in its state of recollection and attention it performs prodigies of memory and anticipation, responding to the play phase by phase and as a totality. Such an approach will not, of course, arrive at a full reading of *Antony and Cleopatra,* though it will be possible to raise the time-honored questions of the structural strength or weakness of the play and whether or not the world is well lost when the phoenix and the turtle (or, alternatively, the sensualist and the woman in whose arms such men perish) are fled in a mutual flame from hence.[8]

The universally known story of Antony and Cleopatra creates in the mind of the spectator a sort of pre-existing play. He knows that the Roman Republic has departed forever and that the Roman Empire is about to be established—and that the Empire will go the way of the Republic. He knows that maverick Antony will be defeated by imperial Caesar—a great ruler, a great dissembler, a cold comedian, "one of the most odious of the world's successful men".[9] He knows—as who has ever forgotten?—Cleopatra, fatal, regal, meretricious, tragic. He knows further that this action, so apparently decisive in its time, the battle of East against West, of Oriental *levitas* against Roman *gravitas,* has proved not to be the central event of all time, even of its time: its opulence shadowed and its rhetoric quite hushed by the dayspring of the Christian era, to which Shakespeare as it were over the heads of all the characters of his play makes repeated allusion, no doubt thereby pleasing the wiser sort among his auditory.

Given this initial readiness to respond and interpret, dramatic irony is present from the beginning, even in expository passages and first lines. The opening speech—Nay, the opening word—does the Roman thing and sets going the opposition of pleasure and duty, the East and the West; it also, as if in spite of Philo's grave intention, expresses Antony's very defects in heroic, hyperbolical terms—his "dotage" being compared to a river bursting its banks, his very bondage being heroic, like a Mars not knowing he is netted. Thinking (and such a thought is ironic) that this cannot be all, we look and see visible in Antony all the Roman pillar-like stature, all the limiting folly or hamartia that Philo's words led us to expect, but those words pale beside the protagonist's opening lines. For a man in Egyptian bondage, Antony speaks like an emperor with a glimpse of the apocalypse. But involved in the glory of this apocalypse is the destruction of Rome and of that part of himself that may be likened to a Roman structure:

> Let Rome in Tiber melt, and the wide arch
> Of the rang'd empire fall!

The speech thus magnificently begun discandies into turgidity, and the whole is a verbal accompaniment to an embrace of the mutual pair which this early in the play will excite embarrassed laughter, and to a dismissal of the messenger from Rome, an action of which an audience, always eager for news, cannot approve. Any spectator will take an instant liking to Antony, glowingly alive and virile among the women and the eunuchs; nevertheless, we begin to form a desire for him to hearken to the voice of duty, and sure enough, before the scene changes from Egypt, he is exclaiming, "These strong Egyptian fetters I must break, Or lost myself in dotage"—dotage, Philo's word. He breaks them, but only after a scene that we expect him to dominate but which Cleopatra steals easily, heckling to tatters his studied and correct speech of leave-taking and then giving him leave to go. If the play were to pause a moment here, all would agree that return he must: if Antony like Hercules must simply choose between Pleasure and Virtue, he must simply choose Virtue.[10]

The play cannot pause but goes on to unfold itself in a second phase. Instead of speculating further, one must see and appraise this other set of values, this other style of life, that Antony has chosen with our concurrence. Young Caesar enters and addresses old Lepidus like a schoolmaster dictating notes. Already the future Augustus has adopted his uncle's trick of referring to himself as if he were a historical personage. Impersonal he shows himself at once to be, and cold and impassive. Alexandria, that we have seen and he has not, is recognizable but only barely recognizable in the bleak light of his account; he reinforces the Hercules parallel by his allusion to the story of the hero made effeminate by Omphale;[11] and he sums up his

lesson for Lepidus with a comment on Antony's weakness, the pitiless truth of which prepares the audience for Caesar's final victory, Antony's final defeat.

Lepidus replies in images whose helpless inconsistency effectively cancels him out thus early in the play and renders ironic all arrangements based on his being counted as a figure of weight.[12]

> I must not think there are
> Evils enow to darken all his goodness:
> His faults, in him, seem as the spots of heaven,
> More fiery by night's blackness. . . .

Thus far the tentative thematic opposition of Pleasure and Duty holds, for Antony is not returning to enjoy the company of Caesar and Lepidus. But as this second phase of the play develops, we look in vain for some cause at stake in the struggle that Antony has joined. Antony before leaving Egypt, Caesar here, are both given speeches expressing contempt for the common people—they draw together on this unamiable ground; but neither yet is moved by anything but considerations of personal power, which Pompey threatens.[13]

Pompey duly appears. Will he perhaps embody some identifiable force for good or evil in the commonwealth? His first speech is as damaging to him as the first speech of Lepidus had been:

> If the great gods be just, they shall assist
> The deeds of justest men.

This piece of specious pagan pietism is spoken to his two lieutenants, pirates by trade, and Pompey's moral capital falls through a hole in his toga. And when news of Antony's return is brought, Pompey at first refuses to believe it, then comforts himself that it is he who

> Can from the lap of Egypt's widow pluck
> The ne'er-lust-wearied Antony.

We recognize him now for a certain loser. Before the alliance is even made, the audience knows as all the world does that only two of the triumvirate count; but we and only we know that the threat to them from outside has no strength of purpose. Thus there is not the slightest military or political suspense. The audience can therefore give its full attention to the figure Antony cuts in his new surroundings. As duty dissolves into power, and the claims of power lose their urgency, the other term, pleasure, must inevitably be reappraised, and the second phase of the play will melt into the third.

The reappraisal is accomplished in the long and complex scene that brings the triumvirs together. It opens with the feeble Lepidus begging Enobarbus to entreat his captain to soft and gentle speech, in reply to which Enobarbus momentarily steps out of his role of dry commentator to do some of Antony's boasting for him. The two great men at this point make their entrance, from opposite directions.

Can a spectator without a smile watch the elaborate pretense of each to be deeply preoccupied with affairs of state and unaware of the other's approach? Can he without laughter watch their hackles rise as each tries to induce the other to sit down at his bidding? Neither has yielded yet. Antony, who is at a moral disadvantage, attacks; Caesar parries, counterattacks, scores. Antony retreats, admitting first that he could not rule his wife, then that he did not receive Caesar's messenger because

> Three kings I had newly feasted, and did want
> Of what I was i'th'morning.

With each such admission he shrinks nearer to Caesar's size. Only when they are evenly matched—itself a victory for Caesar—do Caesar's men recall the present danger and the need for reconciliation. Here Enobarbus protests against the imposture and falsity of the accord at the summit that seems imminent, and is silenced. He then stands, a "considerate stone", while the shrivelled Antony struts in the speech that draws an incredulous snort of contempt and marks the nadir of our esteem for him—"I am not married, Caesar".[14] A marriage is promptly arranged to link the two greatest men in the world; they leave the stage; the scene is over? Not quite. Just at the point when the mean spirit of Caesar seems dominant, Cleopatra nods us to her and from Alexandria steals the greatest Roman scene of the play.

"She's a most triumphant lady, if report be square unto her." No need to specify that Cleopatra and not Octavia is meant. Observe how regally she can appropriate to herself the Roman word "triumphant"—worthy of triumphing; worthy too, we shall come to realize, of being led in triumph. The great description that follows prepares for Antony's return to Egypt and for the failure of the alliance with Caesar. Ultimately, it prepares for Cleopatra's similar emergence, after the death of Antony, to dominate the last scenes of the play, which would else have been Caesar's; and here and now it decides the audience is irrevocably in favor of Egypt and makes ironic every speech and action before Antony's return. It is in the glow of this great passage that we appraise the false bonhomie on Pompey's galley and the footling point of honor that costs the wretched Pompey his world, that we see the encounter of the newly married couple and smile at the irony of Antony's first words to his bride—

> The world, and my great office, will sometimes
> Divide me from your bosom—

that we hear the warning, an echo of our own judgment, of the Soothsayer to Antony to separate himself from Caesar's withering genius. In this same glow we see Cleopatra herself in the scenes with the Messenger. Her outburst of anger is ironic in coming just at the time that we are sure that she is safe. We are impressed at how quickly she comes to share our insight. In contrast to the other major persons of the play (even the *eiron*, Enobarbus), Cleopatra is never long regarded ironically by the audience.

As Rome comes to represent something less than duty, Egypt becomes something more than pleasure, and now that Antony has finally chosen the East, his earlier promise to piece Cleopatra's opulent throne with kingdoms is vividly brought to mind by Caesar's report that he has done so, and in the process assumed an oriental divine kingship.[15] Far more than any other Renaissance treatment of the story,[16] Shakespeare's play gives an astonishingly accurate and concise impression of two incompatible worlds and ways of life—the cult of pleasure and fertility and the great goddess in the East, and in the West the Roman combination of stoic apathy and assent to the political juggernaut, as expressed with lapidary force in Caesar's words of cold comfort to his sister:

> Let determin'd things to destiny
> Hold unbewail'd their way.[17]

Shakespeare does, however, omit from Plutarch one comment made on the meeting of Antony and Cleopatra at Cydnus which might seem most apposite for these purposes: that "there went a rumour in the people's mouths, that the goddess Venus was come to play with the god Bacchus, for the general good of all Asia."[18] It is appropriate, I think, to pause for a moment and ask why, for the answer will bear directly on the play and especially on the phase we are now entering. First, the general good of Asia matters to Shakespeare and to us not at all: such political interest as there is in the action must be concentrated in Rome. Secondly, Shakespeare can make no use of Dionysus. Dionysus in the modern world (we need to be reminded) is largely the discovery of Friedrich Nietzsche and other demonic professors; for Shakespeare he bore the name and nature of Bacchus—the "plumpy Bacchus with pink eyen" of the song on Pompey's galley, a figure quite without dignity. The historic Antony began his political career by identifying his public image with his supposed ancestor, Hercules, and only later in his Greek and Egyptian phases graduated, so to speak, to the more sophisticated and Eastern, more universal and less cultishly military and masculine figure, Dionysus.[19] But it appears from the text that Shakespeare could do so much with Hercules that a second mythical identification would merely have caused confusion. A mythical identification need not be complete, consistent, or always present: it is like a constellation—a few points are sufficient for the picture. But it should be a clear and single picture. Let us see how the playwright makes use of the Hercules theme to afford to the auditor who recognizes it an additional insight into the action and the characters and hence that superior knowledge of which dramatic irony is the product.

Though a favorite patron of soldiers, Hercules was not himself a soldierly figure, and so Antony's military stature is built up first by reference to Mars. Philo's "plated Mars", Enobarbus' "let him speak as loud as Mars", Cleopatra's "though he be painted one way like a Gorgon, The other way's a Mars", all establish Antony's soldiership on a superhuman scale. But almost concurrent with the first of these and continuing longer and of much greater mythical moment, since they allude to actions charged with meaning and not just to a conventional metonymic figure, are the Hercules references, some overt, some covert.

Hercules is of sanguine temperament—warm, impulsive, unreflective, great in physique, terrible in wrath, outstanding in powers of endurance and enjoyment, and Marc Antony has the physique and temperament to profit by his claim to descent from the legendary hero.[20] "This Herculean Roman" has performed prodigies of endurance in the Alpine campaign and enjoyed prodigious pleasure in Alexandria. In reference to his ancestor's holding the earth on his shoulder, Cleopatra speaks of Antony as the "demi-Atlas of the world". But three parallels in the story of Hercules and Antony are played upon, at the beginning, the middle, and the end. One has already been observed: it is the hero's choice of Virtue over Pleasure, Hercules at the crossroads at the beginning of his career. The second identifies Cleopatra with the virago Omphale. Antony, Caesar complains,

> Is not more manlike
> Than Cleopatra, nor the queen of Ptolemy
> More womanly than he. . . .

The indulgence of sensual passion (for so the Renaissance misread and moralized the legend) makes a man effeminate—a statement that everyone from Caesar's time to Shakespeare's would regard as a truism. The picture comes to focus here when Cleopatra recalls how

> I laughed him out of patience; and that night
> I laugh'd him into patience, and next morn,
> Ere the ninth hour, I drunk him to his bed;
> Then put my tires and mantles on him, whilst
> I wore his sword Philippan.

It recalls the story of the infatuated Hercules, "with his great beard and furious countenance, in womans attire, spinning at *Omphales* commaundement", and prompts the comment that "the representing of so strange a power in love procureth delight: and the scornefulness of the action stirreth laughter". For so Sir Philip Sidney speaks of this scene of what we should call irony.[21]

"By Hercules I think I am i'th'right", says the common soldier who tries to plead the cause of military common-sense to Antony, and it is the historically and dramatically appropriate way to swear. In the strange quiet scene between the first battle and the second the reedy music under ground is taken as proof that "the god Hercules, whom Antony lov'd, now leaves him."[22] Placed as it is, not before the final defeat but before Antony's only victory, this effect is well timed. Somewhere Antony must win or we will doubt his soldiership, which cannot depend entirely upon report; he must win so that we will glory with him, and so the victory is placed just at the moment that we know that his doom is sealed. Because we must never consider the possibility of his final victory, this melancholy shadow (darkened by the desertion of Enobarbus) must frame his golden hour, and later, when he greets his victorious followers, he must, to point the

irony further, hail them as "all Hectors", thereby recalling the greatest, warmest, most sympathetic of doomed warriors.

Within a few minutes' playing time, Antony, betrayed as he believes by Cleopatra, makes for himself the identification with Hercules in his death agony that has long been anticipated:

> The shirt of Nessus is upon me, teach me,
> Alcides, thou mine ancestor, thy rage.
> Let me lodge Lichas on the horns o'the moon,
> And with those hands that grasped the heaviest club,
> Subdue my worthiest self. The witch shall die.

Omphale earlier, here the witch. Parallel to the Hercules theme is the theme of a Circe-like enchantress binding the hero with erotic magic.[23] The gipsy queen, like her servant the soothsayer, can read a little in "nature's infinite book of secrecy", and knows the properties of things as well as the qualities of people: mandragora, for example. In Gerarde's *Herball* (1597) Shakespeare could have learned of the mandrake that "the wine wherein the roote hath been boiled or infused, provoketh sleep, and asswageth paine." Most of its other associations and legends he would find scornfully dismissed by Gerarde, but perhaps useful for poetic purposes—the identification of the plant with Reuben's love-apples in the book of Genesis, the magical aphrodisiac that made Rachel fruitful; its human shape; the folk belief that it grows from the secretions of a hanged man. In keeping with the image of liquification in the play, when Antony is away Cleopatra drinks a soporific love-potion distilled of a homunculus. Further, the playwright may have known that the mandrake was sometimes called *Circeium*.[24] Circe, and Venus, and Eve, with the love-apple and the serpent, the potion of sleep and love made from the man-like plant—all these associations have combined by the second half of the play and generate their full charge when Antony is called "the noble ruin of her magic", when he hails her in victory as "this great Fairy", in defeat as "thou spell", and "the witch", and exclaims

> O this false soul of Egypt! this grave charm,
> Whose eye beck'd forth my wars, and call'd them home;
> Whose bosom was by crownet, my chief end,
> Like a right gipsy, hath at fast and loose
> Beguil'd me, to the very heart of loss.

The moving weight of the Hercules and of the Circe patterns (both of which come into clearer view in the latter part of the play) no less than the outward action and its traditional interpretation, would seem inevitably to lead to the spectacle of the destruction of the hero by a harlot sorceress. And yet most readers and spectators will say that such is not the dominant but only a recessive impression of the play.

Part of the counter-effect that Shakespeare achieves in this penultimate phase of the action is established by the permanent destruction of our esteem for the Roman way of life, as embodied in Caesar, whom we reject as a human being, and in Octavia, whom we try to warm to and fail. Again, the identification of Cleopatra with Isis does more than add variety: it also serves to neutralize her identification with Circe, for in the moral allegory current in the Renaissance, Circe-figures are evil, Venus-figures are double, and Isis-figures are loving, maternal, and beneficent.[25] And further, when Cleopatra robs her Hercules of his sword, she stands to him as a sinister Omphale; but when the shirt of Nessus is upon him, though he calls her witch, her role is that of Deianeira, the loving wife of Hercules and innocent cause of his death. But the chief countervailing agent to prevent the obvious interpretation of the play is Enobarbus.

Enobarbus wanted Antony to return to Egypt, as we did, and yet as Antony falls into dotage and dishonor he speaks our comment aloud, and this part of the play is given over to a most unusual and unexpected encounter of *eiron* and *alazon* in which it is the *eiron* who comes to be regarded the more ironically by the audience, as being ultimately the more ignorant of his true condition.

Herculean Antony is recognizable to any Elizabethan as a sanguine man. In the first scene Cleopatra taunts him—

> Thou blushest, Antony, and that blood of thine
> Is Caesar's homager. . . .

Caesar, just as clearly, is, as the Romans would say, *aridus* in distinction to Antony's *genialis*.[26] The buoyancy of the sanguine man, his ruddy complection and warm moist handshake, are in Antony's case combined with frequent reminders of his time of life, a golden autumn. In returning to golden Alexandria, the granary of the ancient world, he is returning to his natural habitat.

In his earlier scenes Enobarbus is presented as a somewhat prudent, somewhat cynical follower of Antony, temperamentally similar to his master. He has shown good judgment in mocking Antony's excesses, in gauging political realities in Rome, and in rising to a description of that wonderful piece of work, Cleopatra. Now he can move more fully into his role of choric commentator and *eiron*—an *eiron* who is a subtle and perceptive person feigning not stupidity but plainness and common-sense.

He it is who warns Antony not to fight by sea, who (with Scarus) describes the shameful defeat, who, when many are deserting, yet resolves to follow the wounded chance of Antony. When next we see him, Cleopatra is asking, "What shall we do, Enobarbus?" and he answers, "Think, and die." This is exactly what he does, in his own person, and as the representative of that part of us that looks upon Antony from the outside in cold appraisal. Antony in defeat sends a resounding, ranting challenge to the victorious Caesar, and Enobarbus left alone hardens and sharpens to a needle-like wit. Irony the rhetorical figure we observe in his speech; the ironist at work on the boaster; but also, I suggest, dramatic irony.[27] Does Enobarbus see everything

that the spectator does in his world and his own role when he speaks thus?

> Yes, like enough! High-battled Caesar will
> Unstate his happiness, and be stag'd to the show
> Against a sworder! I see men's judgements are
> A parcel of their fortunes, and things outward
> Do draw the inward quality after them,
> To suffer all alike, that he should dream,
> Knowing all measures, the full Caesar will
> Answer his emptiness; Caesar, thou hast subdued
> His judgement too.

The full Caesar, empty Antony? Whose judgement now is a parcel of his fortunes? The audience by this time sees and understands more than the most perceptive person on the stage.

Enobarbus continues, with the irony of detachment,[28] looking upon his own moral conflict with the same dispassion as he has shown toward Antony, but not realizing that such abstraction ensures the victory of the baser motive. That his judgment is corrupted, that our observer cannot see what is before him, is proved immediately in the encounter of Caesar's man Thidias with Cleopatra, in which Enobarbus imputes to her on insufficient evidence the disloyalty he has allowed himself to contemplate. When Thidias suggests that the Queen has embraced Antony only out of fear, her reply is more noncommittal even than silence—a simple "O!" He goes on to speak of Caesar:

> The scars upon your honour, therefore, he
> Does pity, as constrained blemishes,
> Not as deserv'd.

And she answers with a most politic, astute, and ironic ambiguity:

> He is a god, and knows
> What is most right. Mine honour was not yielded,
> But conquer'd merely.

The second statement depends entirely upon assent to the first, that Caesar is a god—a belief that neither she nor Thidias holds, or believes the other to hold. And yet Enobarbus so misses the point that he goes to get Antony and says, aside:

> Sir, sir, thou art so leaky
> That we must leave thee to thy sinking, for
> Thy dearest quit thee.

Enobarbus is shortly to witness the rage of Antony at the sight of Thidias kissing Cleopatra's hand (a rage gloriously refreshing to us who do not wish a hero to be always patient) and the reconciliation of the lovers. Once again it is *alazon* and *eiron* when Antony calls for one more gaudy night, and Enobarbus comments that "a diminution in our captain's brain Restores his heart."

Enobarbus' desertion is accomplished at the time the god Hercules also departs, to the sound of music under the earth.[29] The element of earth is to be his from now on. Antony at the end wishes to fight Caesar in the fire and in the air, and Cleopatra still later is to exclaim, "I am air and fire, my other elements I give to baser life." Their lower elements have already departed in Enobarbus. Regretting his perfidy almost immediately, the renegade is struck down by an acute melancholia, the humour of earth as Antony's sanguine is the humour of air. "I will joy no more", he says, and when the soldier appears, bearing gold and exclaiming, "Your Emperor continues still a Jove", Enobarbus realizes the full magnitude of his loss. Calling himself "the villain of the earth", he resolves to seek

> Some ditch wherein to die: the foul'st best fits
> My latter part of life.

It is in a ditch, mixture of the two baser elements, that he addresses to the moon his last words:

> O sovereign mistress of true melancholy,
> The poisonous damp of night dispunge upon me,
> That life, a very rebel to my will,
> May hang no longer on me. Throw my heart
> Against the flint and hardness of my fault,
> Which being dried with grief, will break to powder,
> And finish all foul thoughts. . . .

Bradley says, "Enobarbus simply dies",[30] but this is wide of the mark. Enobarbus the *eiron* and the Enobarbus in the spectator perish for the defect of their *eironeia* and sink out of consideration. The play is purged of melancholy, self-regard, and self-pity. Shakespeare is thus able to omit Antony's retirement in defeat to a hermitage of misanthropy, his Timonaeum[31] (perhaps saving the conception for another play). Black vesper's pageants, of which Antony sings in a beautiful aria, are pageants of air in a fading realm of light and have nothing in them of poisonous damp.

Treatments of *Antony and Cleopatra* usually make some attempt at an Aristotelian statement of the tragedy of Antony—his outstandingness and limitation of character issuing into a risky course of action that can have no other outcome but destruction, the final catastrophic reversal of situation however affording to hero and audience a recognition of reality not otherwise to be gained.[32] And yet this is one play with one ending, not two plays with two. How does Shakespeare solve his structural problem and prevent half the interest of the play from dying with Antony?

The first thing he does is ruthlessly to disappoint normal tragic expectation. The death-speeches of a man who has been superbly eloquent in two plays, with their short phrases and sinking rhythms, do not rise to a full grandeur or memorability or finality, and Cleopatra steals the scene—as she had stolen their early scene of parting, as she had stolen the great scene of the triumvirs.

Then news of Antony's death is brought to Caesar, and the "universal landlord" is touched:

> When such a spacious mirror's set before him
> He needs must see himself.

The mirror for magistrates—fortune's vicissitudes as a warning to the victor: that is what Maecenas means, but why do we smile inwardly? Only the sight of Caesar can touch Caesar? That, certainly, and we may recall Caesar's words to Antony newly wedded to Octavia—"You take with you a great part of myself; use me well in't." But we think also that if Caesar sees only himself—what might happen to his sort of man in his sort of life—in the death of Antony, how little he sees, how blind he is. Thus dramatic irony survives into act five, for the wise young Caesar of the first act is no wiser in the last.

The great passage descriptive of Cleopatra had blazed in the cold light of Rome; the comparable passage that completes the characterization of Antony is delayed until after his death. To the captured, distraught, dishevelled Queen, a young staff-officer, unknown to her and to us, one of Caesar's men with great things awaiting him on the new frontier, enters to take charge:

> Most noble Empress, you have heard of me?

Cleopatra, without interest, without looking: "I cannot tell."

> Assuredly you know me.

Again, a most discouraging lack of interest:

> No matter, sir, what I have heard or known.
> You laugh when boys or women tell their dreams
> Is't not your trick?

It is just his trick, and so he can but stammer, "I understand not, madam."

> I dreamt there was an Emperor Antony.
> O such another sleep, that I might see
> But such another man.

Dolabella attempts to interrupt: "If it might please ye. . . ."

> His face was as the heav'ns, and therein stuck
> A sun and moon, which kept their course and lighted
> The little O, the earth.

Securely, Antony is of fire and air, enskied in Hercules' bosom.[33] Dolabella begins to forget himself and attend to Cleopatra: "Most sovereign creature . . .". But Cleopatra goes on with a colossal, more than Herculean image, combining it with the golden bounty of autumn and the image of the kingly dolphin that loves mankind and playfully leaps out of its own element into a higher one. Then she asks,

> Think you there was, or might be such a man
> As this I dreamt of?

Dolabella's reply is the last whisper of the dead and discredited *eiron*, Enobarbus: "Gentle madam, no." Cleopatra obliterates him, using the same image of nature overgoing art that had been applied to herself in the comparable great passage, and from this point Dolabella is a changed man. These few moments have for him rapidly recapitulated the movement of the play; his words confirm the spectator in his judgment of its meaning:

> Hear me, good madam,
> Your loss is as yourself, great; and you bear it
> As answering to the weight: would I might never
> O'ertake pursued success, but I do feel,
> By the rebound of yours, a grief that strikes
> My very heart at root.

This briefest of encounters makes it religion for him to obey Cleopatra, and he discloses Caesar's plan to lead her in triumph. The stature of Antony, the fascination of Cleopatra, are still being freshly revealed in act five.

Dramatic expectation, even after the death of Antony, is likewise reaching new heights. The stage is now set for a *scène à faire,* the long-awaited confrontation of Caesar and Cleopatra. They meet on equal terms—he victorious through all the world, she in total defeat; he planning to trick her, she knowing the plan and resolved to thwart it. The victor enters, attended by his train, he looks around, and, blind fool, asks the ridiculous question, "Which is the Queen of Egypt?" The arid man cannot by taking thought become genial, and all his speeches of carefully prepared cordiality cannot conceal what he has revealed in that question.[34] Not even when his ascendency in the world has added to it a moral ascendancy, when Cleopatra is laughably exposed by her treasurer, does he become any more than Fortune's knave, a minister of her will; and Cleopatra's words to the eunuch hit the frosty boy:

> Prithee go hence,
> Or I shall show the cinders of my spirits
> Through th'ashes of my chance: wert thou a man,
> Thou wouldst have mercy on me.

The lass unparalleled has quite put down the ass unpolicied.

Comment on the remainder of the play I pretermit, though in the encounter of Cleopatra with the old rustic there is irony in the words, an ironic mixture of the funny and the painful in the situation, and dramatic irony of the thematic sort in our Biblical recollections of a woman, a serpent, and death. As for the death scene itself: the whole play has been groping toward this moment, this *kairos,*[35] in which Cleopatra finds her nick of time and Caesar for all his celerity sends too slow a messenger.

I have used the word *kairos* as being common to natural philosophy and theology. I must say something before concluding about the contribution to the experience of dramatic irony made by the scriptural references, the meaning of which, of course, is open to the audience and closed to every actor in the play. These have frequently been noticed, but not to my knowledge collected for comment.

Some serve to remind us that, great as the world of the play and its historical action are, they are not all. We are told that Antony feasted three kings, as if to prompt us to ask what three kings. Herod of Jewry is likewise mentioned several times, usually as part of the political action as derived from Plutarch;[36] but when Cleopatra in comic fury vows "That Herod's head I'll have", we laugh at the scrambled reminder of Herod and Salome and John the Baptist.[37] And very early in the play Charmian asks the Soothsayer for an excellent fortune: "Let me be married to three kings in a forenoon, and widow them all: let me have a child at fifty, to whom Herod of Jewry may do homage." Again the three kings, again Herod, now the Christ child, who will be born when Charmian would have been about fifty—or perhaps John the Baptist, whose mother was past childbearing.[38] These passages are ironic in that we smile at the ignorance of the Egyptians.

So do we at the Romans'. Antony in his exuberance at agreeing to marry Octavia, says to Caesar: "Let me have thy hand: further this act of grace"; but Caesar returns Antony's "thou" with the formal "you", and the graciousness, in any sense, of this act of grace is questioned. Caesar is later proclaimed by a messenger to be "full of grace", and he himself states:

> The time of universal peace is near:
> Prove this a prosp'rous day, the three-nook'd world
> Shall bear the olive freely.

But it is only a messenger, not an angel, and we know that it is not Caesar who is full of grace, not he the Prince of Peace.

A last cluster of scriptural references deserves separate treatment. Antony's grand reply to Cleopatra's demand to know how far she is beloved—"Then must thou needs find out new heaven, new earth"—sounded the hyperbolical note, the note of *hubris* and *alazoneia,* early in the play and was remote indeed from the Apocalypse to which it alludes.[39] But when in the latter part of the play there are ten more recollections of the Book of Revelation, a point of view is surely established for ironical interpretation. Cleopatra seems identified with the harlot, with whom have committed fornication the kings of the earth, who has glorified herself and lived wantonly, who has said in her heart, I sit being a queen, and am no widow, and shall see no mourning. Such an identification fits in with the Circean figure of the gypsy queen. But the image of poisoned hail, the horror of being left unburied, the phrase "abysm of hell", are drawn from the same source but are not similarly linked with an existing pattern of symbols: rather, they belong to a cluster of their own, whose moment of greatest concentration occurs when Antony's men find him still alive after falling on his sword. "The star is fallen", says one: a star falls from heaven in Rev. viii:10; "And time is at his period", says another, recalling the promise that time should be no more—Rev. x:6; "Alas and woe", one cries, echoing Rev. viii:13; and Antony says, "Let him that loves me strike me dead." "Not I", say several, recalling that men shall desire to die, and death shall fly from them—Rev. ix:6. When Antony dies, it is to Cleopatra as if the sun were smitten and darkened; and again, her words to Dolabella recall the description of the angel—Rev. x:1-6. But in her death scene she is prepared as a bride trimmed for her husband. What infinite variety—so to transmigrate from the harlot of the Apocalypse to the New Jerusalem!

At this point an orderly retreat must be sounded or we shall be identifying, or contrasting, Antony with the suffering Servant on the basis of an allusion to a messianic psalm in "the hill of Basan",[40] an allusion too lonely and remote to have much force in the theater, however potent it may be in a "spatial" account of the play's imagery. I have argued that perceptions and judgments of great subtlety can be expected of an audience, but only as part of the unfolding dramatic experience, which in this perhaps more than any other play is shifting and fluid. At the beginning we share the simple nature, the singly divided nature, of an Antony, but by the end have arrived at a vision of Cleopatra's variety and the varying shore of the world. "These strong Egyptian fetters I must break", Antony declares at the beginning; but when he returns victorious from the second battle, Cleopatra reverses, increases, complicates the force of the image when she greets him thus:

> Lord of lords,
> O infinite virtue, com'st thou smiling from
> The world's great snare uncaught?

And at the very end, Caesar himself returns for the last time to the image of the net, softened and (ironically) sanctified:

> she looks like sleep
> As she would catch another Antony
> In her strong toil of grace.

Notes

This paper was presented at the North-Central Regional Conference of the Renaissance Society of America in Cleveland, April, 1962.

1. All quotations are taken from the New Arden text, edited by M. R. Ridley (London, 1954).

2. For the senses of "irony" in English, see Norman Knox, *The Word Irony and its Context, 1500-1755* (Durham, N.C., 1961).

3. F. M. Cornford, *The Origins of Attic Comedy* (London, 1914), pp. 136-137; G. G. Sedgewick, *Of Irony Especially in Drama,* second edition (Toronto, 1948), chapter one, and p. 50, where Antony is called a self-deceiver and Enobarbus an ironist.

4. A. R. Thompson, *The Dry Mock* (Berkeley, Calif., 1948), pp. 11 and 247: here a mixture of the painful and the funny is held to be of the essence of dramatic irony. G. Wilson Knight in *The Imperial Theme* (London, 1958), p. 254, observes of *Antony and Cleopatra* that a "certain sportive spirit stirs the play's surface into ripples of shimmering laughter." Certainly it differs in this regard from all previous treatments of the story, which are grave and moralistic.

5. R. H. Carr, ed., *Plutarch's Lives . . . in North's Translation* (Oxford, 1938), p. 184, Antony's plainness; p. 164, his Asiatic style.

6. I take my conception of dramatic irony largely from Sedgewick, *Of Irony,* pp. 48-49 and *passim;* see also my article on Macbeth, "The Secret'st Man of Blood", *SQ,* X (1959), 397-408.

7. In *Poets on Fortune's Hill* (London, 1952), p. 138, J. F. Danby observes: "Even if we read Enobarbus's words as irony, the double-irony that works by virtue of the constant ambivalence in the play still turns them back to something resembling the truth."

8. For an account of Cleopatra's conquests among the critics after Johnson, see Daniel Stempel, "The Transmigration of the Crocodile", *SQ,* VII (1956), 59-61. Cf. Bernard Shaw's preface to *Three Plays for Puritans.*

9. E. M. Forster, *Alexandria* (New York, 1961), p. 29; but see the reference by F. M. Dickey, *Not Wisely But Too Well* (San Marino, Calif., 1957), to "the Augustus whom the Elizabethans regarded as the ideal prince", p. 183, and his note to J. E. Phillips, *The State in Shakespeare's Greek and Roman Plays* (New York, 1940), pp. 198-200.

10. Erwin Panofsky, *Hercules am Scheidewege* (Studien der Bibliothek Warburg, XVIII, Leipzig & Berlin, 1930); Hallett Smith, *Elizabethan Poetry* (Cambridge, Mass., 1952), pp. 293-296.

11. An explicit likening of Cleopatra to Omphale is to be found in the "Comparison of Demetrius with Antonius", appended to Plutarch's *Life of Antony*: see E. A. J. Honigmann, "Shakespeare's Plutarch", *SQ,* X (1959), 27. The identification was used from the first by Octavius for propaganda purposes: see Hans Volkmann, *Cleopatra,* T. J. Cadoux, tr. (London, 1953), p. 139.

12. The absurdity of the passage was drawn to my attention by the poet George Johnston. B. T. Spencer makes the best case for it in "*Antony and Cleopatra* and the Paradoxical Metaphor", *SQ,* IX (1958), 375. J. A. Bryant, quoting this speech in *Hippolyta's View* (Lexington, Ky., 1961), p. 177, finds Lepidus "equal to Antony only in charity", which is charitable. J. F. Danby, in *Poets on Fortune's Hill,* p. 147, finds Lepidus "judicious", which is injudicious.

13. The absence of political issues in the play has often been maintained—by M. W. MacCallum, *Shake-*

speare's Roman Plays (London, 1910), pp. 306, 345; by Willard Farnham, *Shakespeare's Tragic Frontier* (Berkeley, Calif., 1950), p. 204; by William Rosen, *Shakespeare and the Craft of Tragedy* (Cambridge, Mass., 1960), p. 123. Against these stand J. E. Phillips, *The State in Shakespeare's Greek and Roman Plays,* who thinks that the problem of order is the theme of the play, and Dickey and Stempel, who follow him in this regard.

14. I disagree with the usual interpretation here—with Brents Stirling, *Unity in Shakespearian Tragedy* (New York, 1956), p. 166, who says that Antony "gains his stature through contrast with Octavius"; with Willard Farnham, who sees him as taking "exactly the right course" with Octavius, p. 176; with Maurice Charney, *Shakespeare's Roman Plays* (Cambridge, Mass., 1961), who praises his "admirable diplomacy" and "political ability", pp. 83-84; and with J. A. Bryant, p. 177, who praises each specific act of Antony in Rome and says that his behavior "measurably increases our respect for him".

15. For the Roman fear of Eastern political and religious domination and the abandonment of Rome as center and capital, see *Aeneid,* VIII, 685-688, 705-706; Horace, *Epode IX,* 2; Ovid, *Met.* XV, 826; also Volkmann, *Cleopatra,* esp. p. 136.

16. Dickey, *Not Wisely But Too Well,* chapters 10 and 11.

17. Plutarch, p. 216: "It was predestined that the government of all the world should fall into Octavius Caesar's hands".

18. Plutarch, p. 186.

19. H. Jeanmaire, *Dionysos: Histoire du Culte de Bacchus* (Paris, 1951), pp. 274, 428, 453, 465 ff. Plutarch, pp. 183, 220.

20. Plutarch, pp. 166, 196. MacCallum, p. 336, and others have pointed out that Shakespeare's Antony is a more grandiose and opulent—*i.e.,* Herculean—figure than Plutarch's, though it should be noted that Antony does not share the character of Hercules the builder and civilizer. For the saga and interpretation of Hercules in antiquity see Gilbert Murray, "Hercules, 'The Best of Men'", *Greek Studies* (Oxford, 1946), pp. 106-126; and Andrew Runni Anderson, "Hercules and his Successors", *Harvard Studies in Classical Philology,* XXXIX (1928), 7-58.

21. *Sidney's Apologie for Poetrie,* ed. J. C. Collins (Oxford, 1945), p. 55. See also Ariosto, *Orlando Furioso,* Sir John Harington, tr., Canto 7, stanzas 19 and 49; Tasso, *Jerusalem Liberated,* Edward Fairfax, tr., 16: 5-6; 20: 118; and Spenser, *The Faerie Queene,* the episode of Artegall's subjection to Radegund, Book V, canto 5.

22. Plutarch, p. 235, recounts the desertion of Bacchus, not Hercules. It is perhaps significant that Antony's Parthian campaign, which bore something of the character of a Bacchic rout, is the only important episode in Antony's later career omitted by Shakespeare.

23. The Homeric Circe reached the Renaissance interpreted and moralized, and emerges in its literature in such figures of Ariosto's Alcina, Tasso's Armida, and Spenser's Acrasia. See Merritt Y. Hughes, "Spenser's Acrasia and the Circe of the Renaissance", *JHI,* IV (1943), 381-399.

24. C. J. S. Thompson, *The Mystic Mandrake* (London, 1934), pp. 21, 188 ff.; J. G. Frazer, "Jacob and the Mandrakes", *PBA,* VIII (1917-18), 59-79; G. Elliot Smith, *The Evolution of the Dragon* (Manchester, 1919), pp. 192-206; John Gerarde, *The Herball* (London, 1597), pp. 280-282.

25. The main literary sources are the eleventh book of Apuleius, translated by Adlington (1566), and the essay on Isis and Osiris in Plutarch's *Moralia,* translated by Holland (1603). Sidney praises the Plutarchan essay in the *Apologie,* pp. 45-46. See also Michael Lloyd, "Cleopatra as Isis", *Shakespeare Survey 12* (1959), pp. 88-94.

26. R. B. Onians, *The Origins of European Thought* (Cambridge, 1951), p. 225.

27. Sedgewick, p. 50, speaks of Enobarbus (and the Duke in *Measure for Measure* and Prospero) as ironists, "shapes that are half-character, half-spectator, moving in the stage illusion with something of the sympathy and the detachment of the spectator himself."

28. Sedgewick, p. 13, defines this as "the attitude of mind held by a philosophic observer when he abstracts himself from the contradictions of life and views them all impartially, himself perhaps included in the ironic vision."

29. Maurice Charney, in "Shakespeare's Antony: A Study of Image Themes", *SP,* LIV (1957), 158, discusses this scene as an example of the "theme of dispersal" that pervades the play.

30. A. C. Bradley, *Oxford Lectures on Poetry* (Oxford, 1955), p. 284. Cf. Plutarch, p. 223, where Domitius does simply die.

31. Plutarch, p. 229.

32. Sylvan Barnet, "Recognition and Reversal in *Antony and Cleopatra*", *SQ,* VIII (1957), 331-334.

33. Charney, *Shakespeare's Roman Plays,* pp. 80-81, on the devaluation of the world theme.

34. See Volkmann, p. 203, where he cites Dio's narrative of the meeting, in which Octavius is unmoved by the siren. Stempel, p. 63, praises him for resisting the temptress.

35. Onians, p. 347; also Volkmann, pp. 218-219.

36. Plutarch, pp. 221, 231, 232.

37. Onians, p. 157, reminds us that the head was regarded in antiquity—and later—as the source of fertility and procreation. *Caput Iohannis in disco* replaced the pagan fertility god at midsummer. Shakespeare, who so often echoes archaic patterns of thought, may partake of this complex of associations when he has Antony say, "To the boy Caesar send this grizzled head."

38. See MacCallum, p. 347, note 1, quoting Zielinski.

39. This paragraph follows closely an article by Ethel Seaton, "*Antony and Cleopatra* and the *Book of Revelation*", RES, XXII (1946), 219-224.

40. J. A. Bryant, p. 180, contrasts the Christlike submissiveness of the Psalmist with Antony's anger. This is well-argued, but I still think the allusion to be the only serious poetic fault of the play.

J. L. Simmons (essay date 1969)

SOURCE: Simmons, J. L. "The Comic Pattern and Vision in *Antony and Cleopatra*." *ELH* 36, no. 3 (September 1969): 493-510.

[*In the following essay, Simmons explores the ways in which the structure and thematic interests of* Antony and Cleopatra *are reflective of elements of Shakespearean comedy.*]

Antony and Cleopatra is in the anomalous position of being Shakespeare's delightful tragedy. Death for Cleopatra has lost its terror if not its sting. The fear of something after or simply the horror of cessation is not a part of the effect, an effect all tragedy works with to some degree. Instead, the grave offers a victory:

> No grave upon the earth shall clip in it
> A pair so famous.
>
> (V.ii.362-363)[1]

Throughout the play the love-death imagery has pointed to this embracing grave, to some "mettle in death" that only a saint, certainly no tragic personage, can descry. By being absolute for death, Cleopatra and her Antony become absolute in death and achieve the eternal embrace and the acme of worldly fame, their two motivating ideals. The sense of triumph in the final scene, with the corollary of Caesar's "defeat," is thus very strong, and some of the most enthusiastic pages of Shakespearean criticism have been written on its unique effect and its reflexiveness upon the entire play. But in this final scene, that conflict in the play between poetry and action continues, the conflict between love's idealistic aspiration for "new heaven, new earth" and the imperfect realities imposed by the "dungy earth." L. C. Knights cautions us: "[Cleopatra] may speak of the baby at her breast that sucks the nurse asleep; but it

is not, after all, a baby—new life; it is simply death."[2] The effect, however, is not simplistic. An ambivalence of response is caused by a merging of the tragic with what is essentially the comic vision:[3] a clown appropriately brings on the means of death.

The full extent and function of comedy within the tragic movement of the play have not been explored. A. C. Bradley remarked on the comic tone, especially in the first half, as working against the tragic effect of the Great Four and as a symptom of Shakespeare's trying "something different";[4] but Bradley's Hegelian view of tragedy did not critically accommodate this difference. Single aspects of comedy in the play have been treated, particularly that of critical comedy. Harold Goddard emphasizes the comic exposure of worldly power, admitting that "satire" is not quite the word.[5] Brents Stirling finds the entire play satirical in nature, and he treats it in a manner akin to O. J. Campbell's investigation of Shakespeare's "satirical tragedy."[6] But, since the play cannot substantiate for Stirling a moral norm, it easily becomes anyone's guess what is satirical and what is not. The world of the satirist, as Alvin Kernan defines it, is "a battlefield between a definite, clearly understood good . . . and an equally clear-cut evil."[7] Since the world of *Antony and Cleopatra* is marked by the absence of a "clearly understood good," the simple norm for judgment must be extrapolated. Matthew N. Proser is much more persuasive in treating the critical comedy "as a qualifying point of view," but this facet of comedy needs to be placed within a larger comic pattern and as a part of a comic vision, beyond laughter, which Proser felicitously captures when he dubs Cleopatra the "queen of comedy."[8]

The structure of the play follows a familiar pattern of Shakespearean comedy. The worlds of Egypt and Rome are analogous to the tavern and court of *Henry IV*, Venice and Belmont in *The Merchant of Venice*, and the forest and court of *A Midsummer-Night's Dream* and *As You Like It*—to what Northrop Frye calls the "green world of comedy" and the "red and white world of history."[9] In Egypt, as in Falstaff's tavern, the sanctions and restrictions of society have been overturned into one endless holiday spirit:

> There's not a minute of our lives should stretch
> Without some pleasure now.
>
> (I.i.46-47)

The "now" is the only reality, a constant present in which the considerations and responsibilities of past and future do not exist. Cleopatra is as little concerned with time as Falstaff, unless hours were to be measured by her means of pleasure. When her companion in the revels has departed, she might as well "sleep out this great gap of time." She is more the queen of non-rule than of misrule:

> But that your royalty
> Holds idleness your subject, I should take you
> For idleness itself.
>
> (I.iii.91-93)

As in the Saturnalia, this idleness is an open defiance of the workaday world with its business of unquestioned aims, its rigid conventions and values. By making no serious pretense of being other than it is, Egypt remains invulnerable to the normal world's moralistic attack, as after Antony's Roman rebuke, just cited, Cleopatra can parry the thrust with a profession of true feeling:

> 'Tis sweating labour
> To bear such idleness so near the heart
> As Cleopatra this.

The public world of Rome, on the other hand, with its gap between moral appearance and moral reality, is wide open to comic exposure, especially since Rome makes no allowance for the private, natural man. Personal feelings and relations, along with all loyalties, are subsumed under public affairs and ambitions. Octavia is immaculate, but she is first and last a pawn of Roman policy. This world's comic flaw is in pretending to be perfect and in justifying its demand for complete commitment to it by professing the ideal of honor as a reality. But honor, as we see in Octavius, cannot survive untarnished by the realities of policy and imperfect man.

Egypt offers personal freedom for the life of the emotions, a life which is either denied by the rigidity of Rome or compartmented into degraded subordination. (For Octavius, a "tumble" with Cleopatra is "not amiss.") In the true holiday spirit of Egypt, humanity in all its infinite variety becomes of interest in and for itself, not just as a social body to be controlled:

> . . . and all alone
> To-night we'll wander through the streets and note
> The qualities of people.

(I.i.52-54)

The very activity, as Katherine Mansfield ecstatically observed, is "so *true* a pleasure of lovers."[10] And it is love, of course, that the green world fosters, "the triumph of life over the waste land,"[11] itself a holiday which releases the absurd along with the best of the individual spirit. Love generates its own idealism, its own claim to perfection and demand for absolute commitment, which comedy questions without discarding in the dual spirit of Rosalind-Ganymede. In the usual progression of Shakespearean comedy, love leads to marriage, always "the plot of comedy," according to Geoffrey Bush; and "it is the women of comedy who by their own natural philosophy arrange the happy ending."[12] Thus a reconciliation between the two worlds is effected by this public act which returns the lovers to the world, now a freer world which, after the comic purgation, acknowledges and grants a place for the individual spirit.

The pattern and thematic concerns of *Antony and Cleopatra* therefore support the many facets of Shakespearean comedy. The pure holiday spirit of Egypt encourages the radically comic, sometimes bordering on farce. The conflict of Egypt and Rome engenders critical comedy. In the Roman scenes Shakespeare even comes close to a comedy of manners, perhaps because for the only time in his career he is treating a historical subject in which the welfare of the state has little relevance. Above all, the comedy of love is the basis of the protagonists' tragedy.

Nowhere more than in the aspiration of love does the comic spirit emerge. The desire for perfect realization of the emotional life creates the attraction of the green world. This desire grows out of the human need to celebrate and even re-establish the Golden Age. It perforce must be an indictment of that real world which drives the comic lovers from its precincts. Frye summarizes the basis of the two worlds and their inevitable conflict:

> We spend our lives partly in a waking world we call normal and partly in a dream world which we create out of our own desires. Shakespeare endows both worlds with equal imaginative power, brings them opposite one another, and makes each world seem unreal when seen by the light of the other. . . . His distinctive comic resolution . . . is a detachment of the spirit born of this reciprocal reflection of two illusory realities.[13]

This conflict is complicated further, as Hegel recognized, by the limitation not of the dream or of the real world but of the aspirer himself as the instrument for fulfilling the dream. "In such a case what substance there is only exists in the individual's imagination. . . ."[14] Hegel, strangely enough, is more explicit about the nature of the comic resolution and comes close to defining Frye's "detachment of the spirit":

> But inasmuch as the comic element wholly and from the first depends upon contradictory contrasts, not only of ends themselves on their own account, but also of their content as opposed to the contingency of the personal life and external condition, the action of comedy requires a *resolution* with even more stringency than the tragic drama. In other words, in the action of comedy the contradiction between that which is essentially true and its specific realization is more fundamentally asserted.

> That which, however, is abrogated in this resolution is not by any means either the *substantive* being or the *personal* life as such.

The aspiration, though incapable of fulfillment, is not denied its value. The aspirer is reconciled to the limitations of himself and the world but "remains at bottom unbroken and in good heart to the end," by rising superior to contradictions involved in his aspiration even though suffering "the dissolution of its aims and realization."

The comparison of *Antony and Cleopatra* and *Henry IV* has lain on the surface of criticism for many years. W. J. Courthope described Antony as "a Henry V without his power of self-control."[15] Others have compared Cleopatra and Falstaff.[16] Ernest Schanzer was the first to see the earlier work as the closest analogue to the later "in its effect on the play's structure and on the whole organization of its material";[17] but he does not suggest what is the essence of their similarity, that the two worlds of comedy have been transplanted into genuine history. The workaday world becomes the history of England and of Rome instead of, say, Theseus' court; it now determines that the *genre* is history and tragedy, respectively, not comedy. But there is one essential difference between the comic patterns in the two plays. In *Henry IV,* there is no reconciliation on the comic level. As C. L. Barber points out regarding the famous rejection, "Hal's lines, redefining his holiday with Falstaff as a dream, and then despising the dream, seek to invalidate that holiday pole of life, instead of including it. . . ."[18] The green world has served its function in reflecting two very limited moral environments and in allowing Hal to establish a third possibility. But that third possibility is not a reconciliation, because it has room for the advice of Bolingbroke and none for that of Falstaff. Whatever limitations this may mean for Hal (and *Henry V* strongly urges that there are many), the fault is primarily Falstaff's; for it is he who refuses reconciliation and insists on having both worlds on his own terms. Moreover, the fact that this historical world is English gives it an absolute sanction; therefore individual considerations, even for this world's ideal king, are finally beside the point. If our comic sense, then, is rather jarred by the rejection of Falstaff, it is because the two strains in the play and the expectations they arouse are at the last moment yoked by violence together, a violent yoking which enables Shakespeare to create powerful drama out of an event foreshadowed and ordained from the very first.

In *Antony and Cleopatra* our comic expectations are fulfilled in the tragedy, but not by Antony. He, like Hal, stands between two worlds. In Egypt, before the return to Rome, Antony could say with the Prince, "If all the year were playing holidays, / To sport would be as tedious as to work." The holiday wears thin; the search for "some pleasure" masks and finally generates boredom. But because there is no place at all in Rome for a reconciliation with this spirit (the ludicrous scene on Pompey's ship might be considered a vain attempt), Antony's tragedy is assured. He insists upon a comic reconciliation which is shown to be impossible. No total rejection of Cleopatra is called for: the morality of Rome simply does not justify such a sacrifice, neither does its destiny nor the welfare of its people. If the perfect freedom of the holiday is rejected, so is the opposite pole of denying all outlet for the expressive heart.

The comic dilemma becomes the tragic dilemma, as is underlined by the fate of Enobarbus.[19] He is a character from the comic world who would have found a place very near the center of a comic reconciliation. He is firmly grounded in reality and good sense but with ironic detachment. Therefore he can be a part of the Roman world but rise above its absurdity through his comic awareness. The pretentions of Octavius and Antony's reconciliation offer a good opportunity for his characteristic voice:

ENO.

> Or, if you borrow one another's love for the instant, you may, when you hear no more words of Pompey,

return it again. You shall have time to wrangle in when you have nothing else to do.

ANT.

> Thou art a soldier only. Speak no more.

ENO.

> That truth should be silent I had almost forgot.

(II.ii.103 ff.)

With this awareness and detachment Enobarbus can also acknowledge the naturalness and the attractiveness of Egypt. While he sees the flaws of both worlds, he remains firmly committed to the life of martial Rome and pays tribute to Cleopatra's greatness.

Enobarbus holds a superior moral position in *Antony and Cleopatra* because he sees a proper place for Cleopatra and Egypt in the soldier's life. He becomes, in fact, the greatest support for Antony's desire to maintain both worlds. However, there is never for him any question of what choice should be made if a choice becomes necessary. As he tells Antony, when hearing of his determination to leave Egypt:

> Under a compelling occasion let women die. It were pity to cast them away for nothing, though, between them and a great cause, they should be esteemed nothing.

(I.ii.141 ff.)

Several readers have heard the sexual overtones, as sounded in *Hamlet,* in the last "nothing,"[20] and it certainly clarifies Enobarbus' position. When a soldier's activity is required, women are reduced, if not quite literally to nothing, to their most naturalistic and unsentimental function. Since life is not made up of endless compelling occasions (unless, like Octavius, one is creating those occasions), Cleopatra has her place as more than "nothing." And Enobarbus appreciates that place more than anyone except Antony:

> Age cannot wither her nor custom stale
> Her infinite variety. Other women cloy
> The appetites they feed, but she makes hungry
> Where most she satisfies; for vilest things
> Become themselves in her, that the holy priests
> Bless her when she is riggish.

(II.ii.240-245)

The tribute is dazzling because, confining himself entirely to the level of lust, Enobarbus projects Antony's transcendentalism while reveling in the sensual. Even as only a courtesan she defies the reality of lust ("Past reason hunted, and no sooner had / Past reason hated"); as a whore she achieves a sainthood of sorts. Such a woman is not to be thrown over lightly. Enobarbus never evinces concern over his certain knowledge that Antony will return to Egypt. Knowing the simple political reality, that the "pair of chaps" are going to "grind the one the other" regardless of

Antony, Eros, Cleopatra, and Attendants in Act III, scene xi of Antony and Cleopatra.

Cleopatra, Enobarbus can point out no moral significance in Antony's return. There is no reason why a soldier should not have his battle and his woman.

In the fatal and climactic decision before the disaster at Actium, however, Antony attempts to combine his absolute commitment both to honor and to love. Enobarbus comically exposes the tragic folly:

> If we should serve with horse and mares together,
> The horse were merely lost; the mares would bear
> A soldier and his horse.
>
> . . . . .
>
> . . . 'tis said in Rome
> That Photinus an eunuch and your maids
> Manage this war.
>
> (III.vii.8 ff.)

Antony and Cleopatra's view is different. With Antony once more the Egyptian, Cleopatra can sound like a Roman. Her own honor has been touched:

> Is't not denounc'd against us? Why should not we
> Be there in person?
>
> (III.vii.5-6)

All of her poison, it seems, has been purged. Whereas Antony condemned her "idleness" in the opening scene, she comically reverses the situation, rebuking him:

> Celerity is never more admir'd
> Than by the negligent.
>
> ANT.
>
> A good rebuke,
> Which might have well becom'd the best of men
> To taunt at slackness.
>
> (III.vii.25-28)

Shakespeare has drastically altered Plutarch's account of her motivations: in the source she followed Antony in order to assure his not returning to Octavia, insisting on a sea-battle purely for her own safety. Instead, Shakespeare allows a glimpse of Antony's ideal reconciliation, with the qualification of its comic absurdity: we have a king and a queen, two public figures, who are assuring their absolute position in the world for their private love. To this change of the source, Shakespeare joins the determining factor of Antony's honor: if they are to be absolute, he must fight Octavius at sea "For that he dares us to't." Again it is Enobarbus who very simply underscores the imperfect reality which Antony's idealism must ignore:

> So hath my lord dar'd him to single fight.

Antony's ideals of love and honor join in precipitating the fall. Honor is blind to the reason of strategy; but, in spite of that, Antony's side is slightly ahead (III.x.11-13) at the crucial moment in the battle. But Cleopatra is of course unable to sustain her role, one which would demand the exclusion of all sensual, feminine nature, of all that both generates poison and prevents her from being a Fulvia. She cannot be a man, and her flight prompts Antony's choice, in spite of both lovers, between lust and honor, between a suddenly jaded world and the world of history.

In a reconciliation and purging of Antony's two imperfect worlds, Enobarbus' voice would have been the happiest. When this reconciliation fails to take place and, instead, the mutual intrusion leads to disaster, he deserts. He is forced by reason into a choice which in the comic world would have been unreasonable: he is made to deny the spiritual reality of the heart's affections. With perfect poetic justice, his heart breaks. Shakespeare has subtly prepared us for Enobarbus' mistake: in his undercutting of Roman honor, in his inability to see more than the sensual possibilities of Egypt, he has shown his reason to be attuned primarily to the harshest reality. He has exposed the folly and absurdity, but he is clearly not prepared to give his life for the substance of aspiration behind that folly and absurdity. The comic "plain man" cannot survive in this tragic world. Instead of earning "a place i' th' story," and conquering "him that did his master conquer," he must be ranked "A master-leaver and a fugitive." Shakespeare, by allowing Enobarbus a tragic recognition of his mistake, has given glory to a name which has little "place" in Plutarch's "story"; but the true greatness belongs to those who refuse to make this impossible choice.

Antony refuses, finally, to choose, even though he makes many choices:

> What our contempts do often hurl from us,
> We wish it ours again. The present pleasure,
> By revolution low'ring, does become
> The opposite of itself.

(I.ii.127-130)

To get to the moral cause of his revolving attractions and revulsions is to recognize the particular moral environment of the play as well as the comic-tragic dilemma. Antony, in his quest for absolute value, is denied a focus for absolute commitment since all the means are partial. Ideally the perfection of the circle encompasses Rome and Egypt, but the realities of sensual love and of political power are mutually exclusive. To succeed, Antony must bestride the ocean, his reared arm cresting the world. On the imaginative and poetic level, the true circle exists; in the realm of action, the circle becomes Antony's wheel of fire.

Although he is defeated and even cheated by two worlds, in his death Antony embraces both what he was, the noblest Roman, and what he has, the Egyptian. The two cannot, however, be reconciled for him. But Schanzer is wrong in claiming that the play suggests "no third moral order," as does *Henry IV*.[21] A reconciliation exists in what Geoffrey Bush calls "the perfect image" of comedy:

> The vision of both the comedies and the histories belongs to the effort of the mind toward certainty and conclusion. The great plans of Bacon and Spenser, in this widest sense, belong to the same argument of hope; their vision is the vision of comedy. The endeavor toward certainty is an attempt to reach a settlement with the world that is contained in a single and absolute commitment; it is an endeavor toward the perfect shape of truth, and toward the recovery of an original wholeness in which fact is gathered into an arrangement that transfigures it.[22]

In *Antony and Cleopatra* it is the heroine who does this manipulating of fact, thus finding the wholeness which has eluded Antony. She steps forward like the "queen of comedy," arranging the happy ending of marriage and thereby winning the admiration and approval of the Roman world's highest moral sense. The comic purging and reconciliation take place to our delight while we are moved by the tragedy of its requiring the lovers' death. The only room allowed them in the world is a grave. But the world also grants to them (and here is the tragic reconciliation) the height of fame.

Cleopatra's delay in effecting the conclusion has prompted almost as much wrong-headed criticism as Hamlet's. Certain observations need to be made. When Samuel Daniel began his *Tragedie of Cleopatra* (1594) with a heroine determined to die, he was faced with the dramatic

problem of justifying her delay.[23] He solved the problem by stressing her lack of means, the necessity of putting Caesar off his guard, and her attempt to arrange for her children's safety. Drama was never Daniel's *forte* and his Senecan models offered no assistance; but he does have a card up his sleeve for the account of her death, reported by the Nuntius who brought Cleopatra the basket of figs. As she is about to apply the asp, suddenly she experiences a conflict "twixt Life and Honor"; "she must shew that life desir'd delay." This conflict then occupies over thirty lines of allegorical description.

Shakespeare faced the same problem of delay, though only for the length of a crowded scene. It begins with Cleopatra's proud resolution; then Proculeius, Dolabella, and Caesar enter successively for an interview. When all are gone she immediately sends for the countryman, her means of death since Proculeius has seized and disarmed her. Stated this way, the events tell of no delay: she obviously cannot apply an asp to her breast until all Romans are off-stage. Fortunately, there is a question of delay, of what Richard Harrier has called her "double-mindedness."[24] For whatever reason, Cleopatra desires the confrontation with Caesar, holds back most of her fortune, seeks confirmation of what is to be her fate at Caesar's hands, and, finally, admits the "woman" in her which would fight "resolution." To just what extent the "woman" has been struggling we have no way of knowing.[25] But Shakespeare leaves that struggle and wavering as the dominant impression of her delay by making Daniel's other reasons either ambiguous (the tricking of Caesar in the Seleucus episode) or unemphatic (the fate of her children, her lack of means).

We ask many questions in this final scene, but one which should never have been asked is "Does she kill herself to be with Antony or to escape Caesar?"[26] No one asks the question of Antony when he pictures to Eros the alternative of Caesar's triumph even after the decision to join Cleopatra in death. The question insists on a false separation of love and personal honor which Antony's experience should not allow us to make. If the play has demonstrated anything, it is that there can be no integrity in love without honor, no heroical love at all. Putting the question another way—"Would Cleopatra have lived if she could have made her own terms with Caesar?"—we are involved in the real dramatic suspense of the final act, the suspense on which hangs the tragic and comic reconciliation.

Cleopatra's inexhaustible desire for life, even at her moment of leaving it, distinguishes her tragedy from all other Shakespearean tragic deaths, certainly including Antony's. She may be weary of the world, but not of life. Shakespeare accepted this inescapable fact of her nature which Daniel could only treat allegorically in the Nuntius' description of her last fight between Life and Honor. But Shakespeare's triumph was in refusing to change her nature merely to let history have its way. His Cleopatra unites her "double-mindedness"—Life and Honor—by envisioning death as the absolute fulfillment of life, as a triumphant reconciliation of the contradictions which had denied its realization in the world. This affords the comic victory which ironically emerges while we fear that her desire for life will ruin everything. Instead, it glorifies everything.

It is not usually noted that Cleopatra's determination to rejoin Antony occurs only when the countryman is approaching with the basket of figs. Before this point, the possibility is not even suggested. At the end of Act Four, when she resolves to follow "the high Roman fashion," Antony is "wither'd," "fall'n," "cold." The world, which had equaled heaven while he lived, is now "No better than a sty." She speaks of her "resolution," but death is only death, "the secret house." In spite of her profession, this end is not for Cleopatra; undermining her words, her messenger in the following scene reveals her desire to know Caesar's "intents." Her ploy is too ambiguous for us totally to reject her determination. Her position will not change so much as add new dimensions. At this point, however, the vision of her tragedy is no higher than Antony's: it merely accepts the defeat, accepts the conflict which has caused it, and ushers the protagonists out with a modicum of face-saving honor and without a glimmer of understanding.

When next we see her, at the beginning of the final scene, her vision of death has enlarged:

> My desolation does begin to make
> A better life. 'Tis paltry to be Caesar.
> Not being Fortune, he's but Fortune's knave,
> A minister of her will. And it is great
> To do that thing that ends all other deeds,
> Which shackles accidents and bolts up change,
> Which sleeps, and never palates more the dung,
> The beggar's nurse and Caesar's.

Here she is the Senecan philosopher, but Cleopatra is not going to triumph through philosophy. However, she now speaks of "A better life," already a thrust beyond "the secret house of death"; and the conditions of that life are those which from the first scene of the play Antony has shown to be the necessary conditions for their ideal love: deeds, accidents, change, and especially the dung have indeed caused their downfall. But her vision of death as sleep cannot appeal long to Cleopatra. She will never shed all of the dung in her nature; her love for Antony has its beginning in the flesh. Likewise, her attempt to echo Antony's "Kingdoms are clay" is no more genuine for her than it was for her momentarily blinded lover. Caesar himself may be paltry, but to be in his position is not. The glory of earthly power growing out of those kingdoms will be a part of her final vision as will the love growing out of the dung: Cleopatra will still be Queen, her lover "an Emperor Antony." Her grandiose philosophy in this passage finally avoids all that is important in the play by rejecting both the good and the evil of life, by eliminating the significance of all human action in the name of Fortune. Both world and love are well lost. The final dimension will emerge when Cleopatra fills this sleep of death with the imaginative substance of a dream.

Cleopatra's great powers of imagination were established for us after Antony's departure for Rome. David Kaula sees her idleness as promoting "an incessant imaginative activity which carries her freely beyond the here and now. . . ."[27] Cleopatra, however, in a comic exchange with the eunuch Mardian, places the generation of it firmly in the genitalia: "'Tis well for thee / That, being unseminar'd, thy freer thoughts / May not fly forth of Egypt" (I.v.10-12). Her physical longing then creates a preview of the masterpiece in the final act: Antony is "The demi-Atlas of this earth, the arm / And burgonet of men."

In addition to physical longing, her capture by Proculeius has added a new urgency to her imaginative activity. In the desperation of the moment, she can evoke death in the most brutal of images, not "the secret house" or last sleep, but that death which takes babes, beggars, and dogs. With the receptive Dolabella, however, her freer thoughts begin to range once more, this time beyond the world of nature where there is nothing left remarkable. Physical longing extends into spiritual longing, as her vision is of an Antony standing like Colossus on the earth but rising into the spheres. Bestriding the ocean, Antony unites Egypt and Rome into one world. Soldier and lover are fused, as Proser points out;[28] Antony is absolute Emperor. Moreover, as a purely natural force, he is perfected: like Spenser's Adonis in Venus' garden, Antony will be endangered no more by winter; in him the generation of spring and autumn merge.[29] This is not the Antony of the play, as Knights astringently observes; nor is this the world of the play. But it is the Antony and the world of the lovers' aspiration.

If the drama invites us to evaluate her vision, the charge of "something self-deceiving and unreal" misses the mark.[30] Cleopatra is not deluded; the vision, as she prefaces it, is from a dream of what Antony was:

> I dreamt there was an Emperor Antony—
> O, such another sleep, that I might see
> But such another man!

Only after the poetic creation does she bring in the relevance and the criterion of actuality. She asks the conditionally realistic Dolabella:

> Think you there was or might be such a man
> As this I dreamt of?

Dol.

> Gentle madam, no.

Cleo.

> You lie, up to the hearing of the gods!
> But, if there be or ever were one such,
> It's past the size of dreaming. Nature wants stuff
> To vie strange forms with fancy; yet, t' imagine
> An Antony were nature's piece 'gainst fancy,
> Condemning shadows quite.

Cleopatra is consciously fighting all the grim realism in the world. She must protect her vision from the two charges of the realists that would make life unbearable: the ideal is impossible; dreams are meaningless. Through paradox and even contradiction, she defends her vision with a defense of poetry, for poetry, finally, is what this brave new world would destroy. If she rejects Dolabella's simple negative, she insists on no simple positive ("But, *if* there be or ever were . . ."). She leaves open the possibility of realization and goes on to the more important matter of the substance of her vision; for Dolabella, the realist, would "laugh when boys or women tell their dreams." In three lines, she gives the essence of Sidney's defense of poetry's truth and Aristotle's justification (by way of Sidney) for poetry's place in the world of men. Imperfect nature may not be able to compete in "strangeness" with the fanciful jumblings of dreams—those "strange forms" of the fancy's mere sensual construction. But the poet, because he knows what perfection is, can glimpse through fallen nature the marvelous forms of Ideal Nature. He is not bound like Dolabella or the historian to what has been but imagines what might have been and what should be.

Cleopatra reaches the universal (*an* Antony) through the aid, but not the limitation, of the specific (*the* Antony), as the highest art works with nature, not against it. She therefore is also drawing the important distinction between two Renaissance conceptions of art—one praised, one feared—which Spenser shows us respectively in the Garden of Adonis and the Garden of Acrasia. She is bringing about the return of nature to its original perfection, not concealing truth but revealing it. Her art here, as Goddard has suggested,[31] is in marked contrast to that which Enobarbus describes in his famous passage; there fancy had striven with nature to deceive, to appeal only to the senses:

> O'erpicturing that Venus where we see
> The fancy outwork nature.

> (II.ii.205-206)

Now Cleopatra insists that her art is Nature's masterpiece, as Polixenes assures Perdita in *The Winter's Tale*:

> Yet Nature is made better by no mean
> But Nature makes that mean; so, over that art
> Which you say adds to Nature, is an art
> That Nature makes.

> (IV.iv.89-92)

Cleopatra convinces Dolabella. He swears by his and his world's highest value, "pursu'd success," that he is in perfect sympathy. He also observes what we now feel for the first time, that Cleopatra has risen to the moral stature of Antony and is capable of responding to his love and aspiration in kind:

> Your loss is as yourself, great; and you bear it
> As answering to the weight.

Her vision has condemned shadows quite, the shadows of fancy and the shadows of nature which obscure true form. It also entirely eliminates the shadows of death.

Since her dream is real, the sleep of death, where she might see "such another man," is now filled with life. Because she is defeating Caesar in death as well as reconciling the tragically comic contradictions, there is neither jarring nor "relief" when a clown helps her bring about the happy ending.[32] His comic confusions of sexuality with death, death with life, and life with immortality laugh the complexities of the play into affirmation. Will the worm eat her? Cleopatra wants to know:

> You must not think I am so simple but I know the devil himself will not eat a woman. I know that a woman is a dish for the gods, if the devil dress her not. But truly, these same whoreson devils do the gods great harm in their women; for in every ten that they make, the devils mar five.

David Stempel, who sees Cleopatra as the villain in a political play, hears "the misogynic bias" of the traditional satires on women,[33] but that is only half of the clown's attitude, as it is only half of the play. Exactly half, the clown says. A woman may become so evil that even the devil fears her. But woman is created by the gods and is worthy of the gods if the devil has not corrupted her. The odds are fifty-fifty. If half of the picture is the medieval condemnation of women, the other half is the medieval glorification. Shakespeare's point of view is not unlike that of Robert Burton, who could likewise stress the very worst dangers in man's love for a woman and who also triumphed over the caveat that the topic "is too light for a divine, too comical a subject":

> So Siracides himself speaks as much as may be for and against women, so doth almost every philosopher plead pro and con, every poet thus argues the case (though what cares *vulgus hominum* what they say?); so can I conceive peradventure, and so canst thou: when all is said, yet since some be good, some bad, let's put it to the venture.[34]

Cleopatra's snare is finally a "toil of grace." Her desire to call Antony "husband" is a reconciliation of flesh with spirit and, though belatedly, of the lovers with the world. In the moral environment of the play, however, their tragedy is inevitable because they demand the perfection of new heaven and new earth without revelation of what must burn away. The peace of Augustus, however ironic and limited, will offer the time for that birth which will clarify the significance of man's ability to love and his desire for honor. But for these pre-Christians, in a world where the lovers can have no other means to rise but the flesh and earthly glory, these means, with their possibilities of substance and worth, are not rejected, just as the Renaissance did not reject them. Man's ability to transcend the clay, however limited on his own, is still the distinction between man and beast. The grandest irony of *Antony and Cleopatra* is that even the member of the audience who approaches it with moral or Christian expectations is forced, finally, to approve the lovers. Even without grace, the humanistic possibilities of man and his poetic imagination can at least point him upward and suggest that time, space, and death are not the final realities.

Notes

1. George Lyman Kittredge, ed., *Antony and Cleopatra* (Boston, 1941). All references are to this edition.

2. *Some Shakespearean Themes* (London, 1959), p. 149.

3. This suggestion was made, without elaboration, by Geoffrey Bush, *Shakespeare and the Natural Condition* (Cambridge, Mass., 1956), p. 130.

4. "Shakespeare's *Antony and Cleopatra*," in *Oxford Lectures on Poetry* (London, 1909), pp. 284-285.

5. *The Meaning of Shakespeare* (Chicago, 1951), pp. 573 ff.

6. *Unity in Shakespearian Tragedy* (New York, 1956), pp. 157-192.

7. *The Cankered Muse* (New Haven, Conn., 1959), pp. 21-22.

8. *The Heroic Image in Five Shakespearean Tragedies* (Princeton, 1965), pp. 189 ff.

9. "The Argument of Comedy," *English Institute Essays 1948,* ed. D. A. Robertson, Jr. (New York, 1949), p. 70. In the following paragraphs, I am also generally indebted to C. L. Barber, *Shakespeare's Festive Comedy* (Princeton, 1959); and Geoffrey Bush, *op. cit.*

10. J. Middleton Murry, ed., *Journal of Katherine Mansfield* (New York, 1927), p. 207.

11. Frye, p. 67.

12. Bush, pp. 24, 27.

13. Frye, pp. 72-73.

14. *The Philosophy of Fine Art,* trans. F. P. B. Osmaston (London, 1920), IV, 303-305.

15. In *Antony and Cleopatra,* ed. H. H. Furness, Jr., New Variorum Shakespeare (Philadelphia, 1907), p. 489.

16. See, for example, Bradley, "Shakespeare's *Antony and Cleopatra*," pp. 299-300; and Harold S. Wilson, *On the Design of Shakespearian Tragedy* (Toronto, 1957), pp. 172-173.

17. *The Problem Plays of Shakespeare* (London, 1963), pp. 162-167.

18. Barber, p. 219.

19. For Enobarbus' comic role in the play, see Elkin C. Wilson, "Shakespeare's Enobarbus," in *Joseph Quincy Adams Memorial Studies,* ed. James G. McManaway et al. (Washington, D. C., 1948), pp. 391-408.

20. See, for example, Leo Kirschbaum, "Shakespeare's Cleopatra," *Shakespeare Assoc. Bulletin,* XIX (1944), 170 n. 13.

21. Schanzer, pp. 166-167.

22. Bush, p. 36.

23. I take the Senecan play only for a comparative instance. Nevertheless, there is much evidence that Shakespeare was influenced by Daniel's treatment. For a good summary of the evidence, see Arthur M. Z. Norman, "Daniel's *The Tragedie of Cleopatra* and *Antony and Cleopatra*," *SQ,* IX (1958), 11-18.

24. "Cleopatra's End," *SQ,* XIII (1962), 64.

25. For some good words of caution regarding interpretation of "Shakespeare's Dramatic Vagueness," see the article of that title by Fredson Bowers, *Virginia Quarterly Review,* XXXIX (1963), 475-484.

26. L. J. Mills, "Cleopatra's Tragedy," *SQ,* XI (1960), 159. The importance of this question for Willard Farnham (*Shakespeare's Tragic Frontier* [Berkeley-Los Angeles, 1950], pp. 194-203) vitiates his fine chapter on the play. See Eugene M. Waith, *The Herculean Hero* (London, 1962), p. 214 n. 6: "Although devotion to Antony is not the sole reason for her suicide, fear of disgrace in Rome is not so much an alternative reason as a supporting one."

27. "The Time Sense of *Antony and Cleopatra*," *SQ,* XV (1964), 221.

28. Proser, p. 183.

29. "For his bounty, / There was no winter in't; an autumn 'twas / That grew the more by reaping." The image describes the natural world in the Golden Age or in the prelapsarian garden. See Spenser's *FQ,* II-I.vi.42: "There is continuall Spring, and harvest there / Continuall, both meeting at one tyme"; Milton's *PL,* V.394-5: "*Spring* and *Autumn* here / Danc'd hand in hand"; Shakespeare's *Tempest,* IV.i.114-5: "Spring come to you at the farthest / In the very end of harvest!"

30. Knights, p. 149. For Knights, therefore, Shakespeare makes it clear that the love is finally "discarded or condemned." Derek Traversi (in *Shakespeare: The Roman Plays* [London, 1963] pp. 186 ff.) also emphasizes the "self-deception" of Cleopatra's dream and "the origin in unreality" (p. 195).

31. Goddard, pp. 589-590.

32. For Bradley (*Shakespearean Tragedy* [London, 1904], p. 62) Shakespeare's bringing on the countryman at this point was "the acme of audacity."

33. "The Transmigration of the Crocodile," *SQ,* VII (1956), 70.

34. *The Anatomy of Melancholy* III.2.v.5 (in Everyman's Library edition, III.253).

Robert D. Hume (essay date 1973)

SOURCE: Hume, Robert D. "Individuation and Development of Character through Language in *Antony and Cleopatra*." *Shakespeare Quarterly* 24, no. 3 (summer 1973): 280-300.

[*In the following essay, Hume analyzes the way in which language functions in the play and demonstrates how*

Shakespeare used language in order to distinguish and develop the characters in Antony and Cleopatra.]

In some of Shakespeare's plays—*Love's Labour's Lost,* for example—a linguistic character-typology is quite plain. In others it is less evident. Few of us would say with Tolstoy that all of Shakespeare's characters sound alike, but neither would many say with Pope that we could properly assign all the speeches if the speakers were unidentified. Studies of Shakespeare's language have tended to be either technical and descriptive or devoted to the general poetic effect of the language, particularly the imagery.[1] Here I wish to study not the general effect but the specific function of the language as it contributes to the dramatization of individual characters.[2] I have selected *Antony and Cleopatra* as my example for a number of reasons. First, it exhibits Shakespeare's style in full maturity. Second, none of its characters (save the Clown) is sharply differentiated for satiric purposes or on social grounds. Third, the contribution of the characters' language to the impression they create seems to me striking, and it has been seriously underrated. S. L. Bethell has gone so far as to argue that "there is, in fact, no attempt to differentiate characters by the verse they speak, except to some extent with Octavius Caesar, whose verse is normally dull and flat and impersonal, or else staccato as he issues orders."[3] I wish to show, on the contrary, that the characters are sharply differentiated by their language.

Explanation of my method is clearly in order. Two general points should be made clear. First, I am interested only in what seems to contribute significantly to the aesthetic impact of the play; that is, I am not using the work as a linguistic sample or document. Second, I am unwilling to depend on "orthographic" data.[4] So the evidence I wish to consider can be described in the following three categories: sound, rhetoric, and personal habit.[5]

I. Sound:
　　1. Words: different characters may use words which emphasize different consonant or vowel sounds.
　　2. Rhythm: regularity, irregularity, and length of sentence-span contribute to our reaction to a character.

II. Rhetoric:
　　1. The patterns of a character's thought may be an index to his ways of thinking.
　　2. The terms (including imagery) used by and about a person—his habitual language—help characterize him.

III. Deviations:
　　Certain personal habits or deviations from more normal usage—e.g., repetition, wordplay, ellipsis—contribute strikingly to the impression a character makes.

Having described such categories I wish to ignore them, as categories, as far as possible. To present evidence of this sort analytically by character or type of evidence is to oversimplify. Here I prefer to start by describing the basic structural contrasts in characteristic language, and then to proceed to show in further detail how they function within the pattern and context of the play. I offer this analysis not

in the hope of finding evidence for a radical reinterpretation of *Antony and Cleopatra,* but simply to show in some detail how the distinctively personal speech of each individual contributes to our apprehension of his character.

I

In this section I wish to discuss the structural (as opposed to the atmospheric) significance of the language. Certainly recurrent images do help characterize a play, though as Wolfgang Clemen says, "we are generally quite unaware of the fact that they create atmosphere," since "such expressions appear to us entirely natural in their place."[6] (Much the same thing, I believe, can be said of their contribution to character.) Various sorts of imagery have been noted in *Antony and Cleopatra*. Caroline Spurgeon calls attention to images of grandeur; Clemen offers an excellent discussion of the significance of sea, astronomical, light-dark, and fortune imagery, while pointing out the duality of the descriptions of Cleopatra; two recent studies show how Shakespeare used death imagery to create anticipation of his conclusion.[7]

But here I am concerned with the relation of language to character, or, more specifically, with demonstrating the contribution of language to contrasts between characters. There are six characters in *Antony and Cleopatra* who by virtue of prominence or function are of particular significance. To lend substance to what can seem like insubstantial assertions of differences, I have worked from lists (appended in the footnotes) of what seems to me "striking" language. This procedure is necessarily somewhat subjective: I have simply listed for each character words and phrases which are repeated or somehow distinctive. Some phrases are too standard to attract such attention[8]; others (Clemen's sea-images, for instance) are evidently meant to characterize the play, but do not divide among individual characters. But though in their very nature these lists cannot be definitive, they can serve as a rough index to characteristic language.

Consider the basic conflicts of the play. Antony, Caesar, and Lepidus, the "triple pillars of the world," are being challenged by Pompey. Antony and Caesar (as their language indicates) are by far the most powerful of the four. When they come into conflict Antony is torn between the appeals of Rome and Egypt. Structurally, Caesar is set against Cleopatra with Antony vacillating between the positions they represent. The Roman world is coldly rational and proper; the Egyptian is emotional, at once exalted and degraded. In Enobarbus we are shown in microcosm the dilemma of Antony's followers, torn between personal loyalty and Roman rationality. These basic conflicts and contrasts are reinforced by parallel divisions in the characters' language; what I wish to demonstrate initially is just how sharply Shakespeare individuated his characters.

To start with the most obvious example, consider Lepidus, who is allegedly coequal with Antony and Caesar.[9] He says almost nothing, usually contenting himself with such interjections as "here's more news" (I.iv.33).[10] What is remarkable is the concentration in so few lines of so many phrases like "beseech," "entreat," "let me," and "pray you"; he is always begging in a bleating voice to which the sound of "beseech" and "entreat" seems very appropriate. He is obsequious even to Enobarbus:

> Good Enobarbus, 'tis a worthy deed,
> And shall become you well, to entreat your captain
> To soft and gentle speech.

(II. ii. 1-3)

The address "*good* Enobarbus" is characteristic of Lepidus almost to the point of caricature, though "noble" is his more usual form.[11] The use of "your captain" makes it sound as though he thinks of Caesar as his own—which is substantially true. *Quiet* is another of his motifs (none of Antony's "thunder" for him); he dislikes "loud" dispute (l. 21) and is continually begging for "soft" and "gentle" speech, for he fears "passion" and wishes to "stir no embers up" (ll. 12-13). When, in a polite afterthought, Antony says "Let us, Lepidus, / Not lack your company" (II. ii. 169-70), Lepidus replies: "*Noble* Antony, / Not *sickness* should detain me" (ll. 170-71; my italics). Lepidus thinks in small, everyday terms; for him, sickness is as grand a thing as might oppose his going. Antony might have said: "the gods themselves shall not prevent me." Only twice does Lepidus' speech rise above the timid and pedestrian, and both times it is concerning Antony (I. iv. 10-15; III. ii. 65-66).[12] Clearly Lepidus is not the man to stand his ground against Antony and Caesar.

In a similar way Pompey's relative ineffectuality is underscored.[13] *Honor* and *justice* are his key concepts. For example, II. vi. 8-23 is on the theme of honor and justice to his father as a reason for his actions; ll. 26-29 are about Antony taking his father's house; in ll. 39-46 he objects to Antony's ingratitude; in ll. 53-56 he says that his heart will never be subject to fortune; that is, honor will direct him, not selfish motives. And indeed, on this ground, Pompey refuses Menas' offer to make him "the earthly Jove" by killing the others (II. vii. 72-79). Pompey claims equality with the "triple pillars," but linguistically he does not place himself on their level. Caesar and Antony are called (in play) "Jupiter" and "the god of Jupiter" (III. ii. 9-10), and Antony is regularly described in terms of the gods, but Pompey appeals to the gods as superior powers (II. i. 1-5; 50-52).[14] And when a compromise is reached Pompey sounds like Lepidus when he says, "I crave our composition may be written" (II. vi. 58).

In the principal conflict of the play Antony and Caesar are opposed, with the views and demands of Rome and Egypt as a background. The characteristic Egyptian language of Cleopatra is utterly different from the speech of Caesar; there is no significant overlap whatever. It has long been recognized that Antony and Cleopatra exhibit a striking duality in their imagery.[15] The grand is set against the degraded. There is a soaring, often astronomical terminol-

ogy which they use again and again: heaven, moon, sun, earth, stars, space, kingdom, wide arch of ranged empire, world, ocean, fire, air, tree imagery, great sphere, eternity, orb, thunder. Set against this imagery of transcendental grandeur are terms of degradation, poison, treachery, and decay: snakes, slime, poison, serpents, cistern, discandying, gnats, flies, sty, dung, mud, breeding serpent's poison, ooze, creeps, dungy earth. This combination of the high and low accurately mirrors the ambiguous nature of the protagonists, and it can be seen again in the terms used to describe them.[16]

Caesar's language is nothing like this.[17] What is startling about it is its almost total lack of vivid terms or striking characteristics. When Caesar wishes to be vivid he speaks in terms of "hoop," "fortress," and "cement," for he is an immensely practical man, but as a rule he is very sparing of images and descriptive terms. Even in his relatively higher flights Caesar remains pedestrian: he thinks of "an army for an usher," or a "mate in empire." And almost every instance of vivid speech or grand description from Caesar is occasioned by Antony. Caesar normally states matters of fact, occasionally marked by the intrusion of a moral stance: he disapproves of sex and revelry (e.g., I. iv. 16-33; 55-71; II. vii. 98-99; III. vi. 1-11). There is never any grandeur in Caesar's speech, and never anything degraded. He speaks with contempt and loathing of the common people, but usually in such rather abstract terms as a "common body . . . lackeying the varying tide"; his strongest description of them is as "knaves that smell of sweat," which is far less vivid than Cleopatra's

> mechanic slaves
> With greasy aprons, rules, and hammers shall
> Uplift us to the view. In their thick breaths,
> Rank of gross diet, shall we be enclouded,
> And forced to drink their vapor.

(V. ii. 209-13)

Cleopatra feels intensely all that she describes. Caesar does not. His abstract and dispassionate speech gives the impression that he is a man of little feeling or imagination. Only Octavia seems to rouse any personal feeling in him (III. ii.; vi.).

Antony's vacillation between the Roman and Egyptian worlds is clearly reflected in his language. The bulk of his characteristic terms he shares with Cleopatra: astronomy, mud, melting, death. But when his dormant ambition is stirred he can take the Roman view, as in "These strong Egyptian fetters I must break / Or lose myself in dotage" (I. ii. 112-13; cf. Philo, I. i. 1-10). When Antony decides to return to Rome (I. ii.) and after he has suffered defeat (III. xii., xiii.; IV. xii.), he uses such terms as "Egyptian fetters," "dotage," "enchanting queen" (picking up the Roman view that Cleopatra was ensnaring him by witchcraft), "morsel cold . . . trencher," "foul Egyptian," "charm," "gypsy," "spell," "witch." As the scene by scene list shows, when in Rome Antony hardly ever uses "Egyptian" terms. In fact, he uses very little striking imagery at all; competing with Caesar, Antony adopts his language. Thus in II. ii. he uses horse-world imagery (cf. Caesar, V. i. 39-40), and in II. iii. building terms (1. 6; cf. Caesar, III. ii. 29-31).

Cleopatra's imagery is mostly of the dual Egyptian variety already mentioned. She also uses some of the widely prevalent sea-imagery (e.g., "anchor his aspect," I. v. 33). Her wiles and cunning charm appear in such expressions as "trade in love" (II. v. 2) or "amorous pinches" (I. v. 28), and particularly in her fishing imagery, the ambivalence in which is expressed by Caesar as he surveys her dead body: she looks "as she would catch another Antony / In her strong toil of grace" (V. ii. 345-46). This peculiar ambivalence is found again and again. For instance, like Antony, Cleopatra uses "melting" to describe both death and the supremacy of love (a pointed coupling): compare "Let Rome in Tiber melt" (I. i. 33) with "the crown o' th' earth doth melt" (IV. xv. 63).[18] And when Cleopatra threatens a messenger she proposes to melt gold and pour it down his throat (II. v. 34-35). But while there is a certain grandeur to these uses of "melt," both protagonists can also use "melt" and "discandy" in an unpleasant way when they refer to dissolution into formless stickiness (e.g., III. xiii. 165; IV. xii. 22).

In the range of the imagery we can see latent the development of the whole play. Caesar's language does not possess the grandeur which makes the protagonists tragic, but neither does it reflect the degradation which is their undoing. The play balances precariously between extremes. We do not have here a glorification of "all for love"; rather, as in Marlowe's *Doctor Faustus,* we are shown a tragic fall, though with a persuasive and sensitive presentation of the temptation. Caesar's condemnation of the lovers is far from being the whole story, but close study of characteristic language can serve to remind us not to overromanticize them. Antony and Cleopatra are grand, but they clearly suffer from folly and degradation, and this is unerringly reflected in the language used by and about them.

Perhaps our best perspective on Antony and Cleopatra is through Enobarbus.[19] He alone of the other characters straddles the Roman and Egyptian worlds. He is equally at home among Roman soldiers (II. vi.) and in the seamy luxury of Cleopatra's court (I. ii.). He can call Cleopatra Antony's "Egyptian dish" (II. vi. 123), but understands very well her appeal. It is no accident that the "barge speech" is his, for though the hyperbolic language "belongs" to Cleopatra, the sensitivity and perceptiveness of the description are Enobarbus' own. Even when he is being sarcastic to Antony at her expense, his response to her charm is plain (e.g., I. ii. 143-48). Like Antony, Enobarbus would be quite incapable of walking into the presence of Cleopatra and her ladies, and enquiring, as Caesar does, "which is the Queen of Egypt?" (V. ii. 112).

Enobarbus' character is underscored by his language, which is plain, blunt, and down-to-earth. His imagery is concrete and earthy; he thinks naturally in everyday terms:

food, drink, weather, and sex. For him gods are tailors, women clothes, fortune a sword cut, and onions the source of tears. Caesar too is a practical man, but his speech has nothing like the concreteness characteristic of Enobarbus, who draws easily on such common occupations as hunting and sailing for his metaphors (e.g., "the wounded chance of Antony," and "my reason sits in the wind against me," III. x. 36-37). In Enobarbus we can follow the reactions of a sturdy, sensible Roman who is bound by personal loyalty and some imaginative sympathy to Antony. Not surprisingly, since Enobarbus' ultimate commitment is to Antony, his characteristic imagery of food, drink, and water is given ambiguous connotations. What can seem merely blunt and convivial can become unpleasant, as in

> Then, world, thou hast a pair of chaps, no more;
> And throw between them all the food thou hast,
> They'll grind the one the other.
>
> (III. v. 12-14)

and "Egyptian dish," or "valor preys on reason."[20]

What should be evident now—even from so cursory an inspection of "characteristic" language—is that there are strikingly personal linguistic characterizations and contrasts in *Antony and Cleopatra.* Two techniques are in evidence. When Shakespeare merely sketched in a character he strongly emphasized a few traits. Pompey's preoccupation with honor and justice (incongruous in these surroundings), and Lepidus' bleating "beseech" theme and soft-quiet-gentle motif are clear indications that they will not survive. Such a technique applied at greater length would quickly lead to gross caricature, but used in brief it is an economical way of indicating character. In the fuller presentation of the other four there is no need for such shorthand. Instead, each one is allowed to speak in appropriate, thoroughly individual terms.

"Horizontally," the radical split in imagery between Rome and Egypt emphasizes the incommensurability of their standards. Antony wavers between them but must choose decisively, for they are mutually exclusive. Consequently Caesar, totally committed to Rome, can have no understanding of what motivates him. "Vertically," the extreme duality of the Egyptian imagery contains the essential paradox of the tragedy. The Egyptian way is base; it leads to ruin and death. Not surprisingly, both lovers are selfish and treacherous. Yet somehow there is something in their lives exalted beyond the comprehension of Caesar. That we feel their grandeur is largely a function of their imagery, for there is little in their self-indulgent folly to rouse esteem in us. It is the highest part of their feeling as it comes through the language which affects us and commands our admiration.

II

My object in this section is to analyze the linguistic contrasts as Shakespeare sets them up at the outset of the play; in the next I will follow their development. I do not wish to seem to overstress the first appearances of the characters. I am concentrating on them because it seems to me that Shakespeare went to some trouble to indicate immediately through language the nature of each person. Characteristic language may later be subordinated to the exigencies of plot, but at the outset it is emphasized in order to establish it firmly. We might say that Shakespeare started by offering a set of contrasts, some of whose components he later altered as the progression of the play demanded.

Antony's relation to Cleopatra is shown immediately in the first scene. He speaks of love in terms of heaven and earth (ll. 15, 17); the grandiosity of his declaration of love exceeds by far in its sweep and force anything Caesar will say in the course of the play:

> Let Rome in Tiber melt and the wide arch
> Of the ranged empire fall! Here is my space,
> Kingdoms are clay: our dungy earth alike
> Feeds beast as man. The nobleness of life
> Is to do thus; when such a mutual pair
> And such a twain can do't, in which I bind,
> On pain of punishment, the world to weet
> We stand up peerless.
>
> (I. i. 33-40)

Here at once we have the "Egyptian" combination of grand and base, empire versus dungy earth and feeding. Though the phrases are short, they lend themselves to forceful declamation (note the alliterations of the final lines). Antony's response to the arrival of messengers with news is "Grates me! The sum" (l. 18)—irresponsible, but very much the reply of a man utterly used to command.

For all this, it is Cleopatra who holds the initiative. Her fanciful speculation about the news (ll. 19-24) leaves Antony gasping, "How, my love?" (l. 24). In I. iii. she again demonstrates her ability to keep him off balance, as his responses show: "Now, my dearest queen" (l. 17); "What's the matter?" (l. 18); "The gods best know" (l. 24); "Cleopatra" (l. 26); "Most sweet queen" (l. 31); "How now, lady?" (l. 39). Here it is only with the utmost trouble that Antony manages to assert his Roman ambition. Cleopatra is supposed to be a fascinating woman of infinite variety. Shakespeare could not describe her physical charms, and the first scene is as close as he dared come to a love scene with these slightly tawdry middle-aged lovers; so he had to find some other way of indicating Cleopatra's appeal. In large part he managed this by giving her varied rhythms and an unpredictable imagination which, as we have seen, leaves Antony's slower mind floundering far behind.

CLEO.

> Nay, hear them, Antony.
> Fulvia perchance is angry; or who knows
> If the scarce-bearded Caesar have not sent
> His pow'rful mandate to you, 'Do this, or this;
> Take in that kingdom, and enfranchise that.
> Perform't, or else we damn thee.'

ANTONY

> How, my love?

CLEO.

> Perchance? Nay, and most like:
> You must not stay here longer, your dismission
> Is come from Caesar; therefore hear it, Antony.
> Where's Fulvia's process? Caesar's I would say?
>   both?
> Call in the messengers. As I am Egypt's Queen,
> Thou blushest, Antony, and that blood of thine
> Is Caesar's homager: else so thy cheek pays shame
> When shrill-tongued Fulvia scolds. The messengers!
>
> (ll. 19-32)

Here Cleopatra stops and goes; she can pause quickly three times in succession and then pour out an unbroken line. The freedom of her verse helps convey, as no mere description could do, her infinite variety. Particularly early in the play, when she is rather skittish, the rhythm of her speech is highly variable.

No variety at all is Caesar's characteristic. His verse is clear and regular; it must be delivered at an even rate, for the regular pauses and the sameness of words adapted to crisp pronunciation make much variation impractical. All this contributes to the "flat" quality noted by Bethell. Cleopatra's verse, in a dramatic contrast of "Egyptian" versus "Roman," particularly lends itself to variation in speed and emphasis. The irregular pattern of her pauses practically demands a reading of irregular ebb and flow, so the reader can accelerate and slow down again without an awkward scramble. The result is a personal speaking voice quite distinct from Caesar's impersonal formality.

We meet Antony's fellow triumvirs as they are discussing his dereliction of duty. Caesar's first words are a self-justification, a particular habit of his (I. iv. 1-10). Lepidus' response is revealing:

> I must not think there are
> Evils enow to darken all his goodness:
> His faults, in him, seem as the spots of heaven,
> More fiery by night's blackness; hereditary
> Rather than purchased, what he cannot change
> Than what he chooses.
>
> (ll. 10-15)

This reads quickly and lightly. It is the speech of a man habitually deferential; neither Antony nor Caesar would start a speech "I must not think. . . ." The grand images of this speech "belong" to Antony. Compare Caesar's reply:

> You are too indulgent. Let's grant it is not
> Amiss to tumble on the bed of Ptolemy,
> To give a kingdom for a mirth, to sit
> And keep the turn of tippling with a slave,
> To reel the streets at noon, and stand the buffet
> With knaves that smell of sweat. . . .
>
> (ll. 16-21)

Here alliteration and plosive consonants create the dominant sound. "T," "d," "k," and "g" are prominent. Caesar's crisp consonants give a sense of hardness which Lepidus' milder speech does not convey—it is impossible to say "to tumble on the bed of Ptolemy" very mildly. Lepidus "must not think"; he is unwilling to render judgment. Caesar does so in four words: "You are too indulgent." In the discussion which ensues Caesar has about fifty lines, a nameless messenger fifteen, and Lepidus two interjections: "Here's more news" (33) and "'Tis pity of him" (71). At the end of the scene Lepidus' final comment underlines his subservient place:

> Farewell, *my lord*. What you shall know meantime
> Of stirs abroad, I shall *beseech* you, sir,
> To *let me* be partaker.
>
> (ll. 81-83; my italics)

No doubt should remain about the probability of Lepidus' deposition.

Our introduction to Pompey (II.i.) undercuts him less drastically than this, but nonetheless its import is clear-cut. His first words establish his "justice" motif: "If the great gods be just, they shall assist / The deeds of justest men" (ll. 1-2). In his first extended speech Pompey muses on his position:

> I shall do well:
> The people love me, and the sea is mine;
> My powers are crescent, and my auguring hope
> Says it will come to th' full. Mark Antony
> In Egypt sits at dinner, and will make
> No wars without doors. Caesar gets money where
> He loses hearts. Lepidus flatters both,
> Of both is flattered; but he neither loves,
> Nor either cares for him.
>
> (II.i.8-16)

He starts here with a firm declarative statement and adduces evidence in support of it. His self-applied, possibly astronomical image marks him as a leader of magnitude, which he is. The language is firm enough, though a little "soft" by Caesar's consonantal standards. What is lacking are logical connectives: there is no proposition in this catalog of data and Pompey appears to be reassuring himself. This impression is strengthened by his reaction to the news that Caesar and Lepidus are in the field. First he denies it: "Where have you this? 'Tis false" (l. 18). Next he pooh-poohs the idea: "He dreams: *I know* they are in Rome together, / Looking for Antony" (ll. 19-20; my italics). Finally, he goes into an elaborate invocation, asking that Antony may not be roused:

> But all the charms of love,
> *Salt* Cleopatra, *soften* thy waned lip!
> Let *witchcraft* join with beauty, *lust* with both!
> Tie up the libertine in a field of *feasts*,
> Keep his brain *fuming*. Epicurean cooks
> Sharpen with *cloyless sauce* his *appetite*,
> That *sleep* and *feeding* may prorogue his honor
> Even till a Lethe'd dulness—
>
> (ll. 20-27; my italics)

The rhythm here is as dreamy as Pompey's hope that Cleopatra will lull Antony into inaction. Notice that the speech is a denigration of the senses. Pompey's overriding concerns are honor and justice, and in the design of the play these are set against the sensual life which Cleopatra represents. Though the contrast is less developed, Pompey is as far on one side of Caesar as Cleopatra is on the other. If Antony is torn between the sensual world of Cleopatra and the power politics of Caesar, so he has, as Caesar does not, some sense of the "honor" of which Pompey speaks (l. 26). Morally, Pompey takes much the view of Antony's revels that Caesar does: compare his attitude toward the "amorous surfeiter" (l. 33) with Caesar's condemnation of "lascivious wassails" (I.iv.56).

Faced with certain news of Antony's arrival, Pompey reacts revealingly:

> I could have given less matter
> A better ear. Menas, I did not think
> This amorous surfeiter would have donned his helm
> For such a petty war. His soldiership
> Is twice the other twain. But let us rear
> The higher opinion that our stirring
> Can from the lap of Egypt's widow pluck
> The ne'er lust-wearied Antony.
>
> (ll. 31-38)

The use of "petty war," as has been noted, belies the grand imagery of his first speech. And as his first sentence indicates, Pompey rather flinches from the bad news. Compare Antony's firm "Well, what worst?" (I.ii.90). His first reaction is discouragement, but then he manages to interpret the news as testimony to his own importance. Again we may feel that Pompey is trying to reassure himself. He *is* honest enough to recognize that the triumvirs will probably settle their own differences long enough to face him (ll. 42-49), but after this chain of clear reasoning he throws it all up: "Be't as our gods will have't. It only stands / Our lives upon to use our strongest hands" (ll. 50-51). This is irrelevant to what has gone before. Pompey accepts the challenge and will fight as best he can, but with a feeling of fatalism which bodes his chances no good.

Pompey is noble, but less than logical (ellipsis is a characteristic of his—see ll. 16, 36, 49) as becomes strikingly apparent in his confrontation with the triumvirs (II. vi.). He opens with a disconcertingly disconnected sentence: "Your hostages I have, so have you mine; / And we shall talk before we fight" (ll. 1-2). The hostages are not, of course, the prime reason for the parley, as this implies. Caesar's characteristic reply is precise, logical, and utterly to the point:

> Most meet
> That *first* we come to words, and *therefore* have we
> Our written purposes before us sent;
> Which *if* thou hast considered, let us know
> *If* 'twill tie up thy discontented sword. . . .
>
> (ll. 2-6; my italics)

Pompey's reply (ll. 8-23) is an elliptical harangue which does not answer Caesar's question. He grandly pictures his fleet as angering the ocean (ll. 20-21), but for all his blustering the tense of "meant" (l. 21) indicates clearly that he has already been stopped. Here again (as in II.i.19-27) Pompey speaks with vigor and conviction about something which is wishful thinking; he is deriving satisfaction from thinking about his plans even after he knows he will not carry them through. Caesar's response to this diatribe is merely "Take your time" (l. 23), after which Pompey gets off onto the subject of his father's house (ll. 26-29).

Lepidus asks "from the present" (l. 30) how he takes their offer, and Caesar adds acidly "There's the point" (l. 31). But after repeating the terms (ll. 34-39) Pompey again digresses: "Know then / I came before you here a man prepared to take this offer; but Mark Antony / Put me to some impatience . . ." (l. 39ff.). Pompey never does state his acceptance (we may infer it from the handshake of l. 48) until he implies it by asking that the agreement be written (ll. 58-59). It comes as no surprise when we learn (III. v.) that Pompey has fared badly in this world of *Realpolitik*.

III

By III. vii. the final development of the play has begun. Briefly, we may consider what has changed. Pompey and Lepidus have been squeezed out and Antony has opted for Cleopatra and Egypt rather than Octavia and Rome. In Enobarbus' image the world has become a "pair of chaps" (Antony and Caesar) which can only "grind" each other. Here, all diversions past, we have the basic conflict of the play.

Caesar and Cleopatra remain essentially constant throughout; it is Antony who wobbles between the positions they represent. As we have seen, his "striking" imagery almost disappears while he is in Rome. We can follow the process of this change. In I. i. we have the Antony of "Let Rome in Tiber melt and the wide arch / Of the ranged empire fall!" (ll. 33-34). In I. ii. Cleopatra notes that "A Roman thought hath struck him" (l. 79); conscience striken, Antony adopts the Roman terminology as he exclaims "These strong Egyptian fetters I must break / Or lose myself in dotage" (ll. 112-13). By I. iii. his voice is firm and commanding (ll. 41-56); the images of breeding and creeping make Antony's speech here more vivid than Caesar's, but it is rhythmically steady and controlled in a way that his initial speeches are not (cf. I.i.48-55).

When we next see Antony (II. ii.) it is hard to distinguish his speech from Caesar's. Roused and Roman, Antony is definitely a man to reckon with. His verse becomes, like Caesar's, flat, his thought logical, precise, and reservedly argumentative.

> You do mistake your business: my brother never
> Did urge me in his act. I did inquire it
> And have my learning from some true reports

That drew their swords with you. Did he not rather
Discredit my authority with yours,
And make the wars alike against my stomach,
Having alike your cause?

　　　　　　　　　　　　　　　　　　(ll. 45-51)

There is very little striking imagery in this scene, though note that Antony and Caesar do employ a similar image of control. "The third o' th' world is yours, which with a snaffle / You may pace easy, but not such a wife" (Ant. ll. 63-64); "Yet if I knew / What hoop should hold us staunch, from edge to edge / O' th' world I would pursue it" (Caes. ll. 114-16).

The Banquet Scene (II. vii.), seemingly so inorganic, is actually an excellent index to character. It permits us to observe all of the major male characters under "Egyptian" circumstances. The odd discussion of Nile, slime, ooze, serpents, and crocodiles both reminds us of Cleopatra, Antony's "serpent of old Nile," and contributes to the atmosphere of Egyptian sensuality. Caesar does nothing but complain in terms of chilly disapproval, responding to a toast:

> I could well forbear't.
> It's monstrous labor when I wash my brain
> And it grows fouler.

　　　　　　　　　　　　　　　　　　(ll. 97-99)

> Possess it, I'll make answer;
> But I had rather fast from all four days
> Than drink so much in one.

　　　　　　　　　　　　　　　　　　(ll. 100-102)

Antony's reply is "Be a child o' th' time" (l. 99). Antony, Enobarbus, and even Pompey are all able to relax and enjoy themselves (Lepidus has been carried out); Caesar cannot, for "graver business" (l. 119) is always on his mind. It is Caesar's impatient and disgusted speech starting "What would you *more?*" (l. 118; my italics) that breaks up the party.

The Banquet Scene marks the end of the initial development of the play; it is plain by then that Pompey and Lepidus will vanish, leaving Antony to contend with Caesar. The party is also the last of a series of scenes designed to keep in our minds a steady contrast of Rome and Egypt. (Cleopatra appears directly in I. v., II. v., and III. iii.; Enobarbus describes her at length in II. ii.)[21] At this point Antony is like—in the image he applies to Octavia—"the swan's down feather / That stands upon the swell at full of tide, / And neither way inclines" (III. ii. 48-50). Unfortunately, we are not shown the actual process of Antony's decision to return to Egypt; it would be interesting to study his language. Of course we are never in much doubt about what he is going to do (see II. iii. 38-40, and Enobarbus, II. vi. 123). Presumably we are meant to realize that Cleopatra is steadily on his mind, just as she is kept in ours, and her hold on him is such that even Roman ambition cannot break it.

Definition of Cleopatra's hold is beyond the scope of this essay, but we can profitably enquire into the linguistic manifestations of her infinite variety and fascination, particularly as she is contrasted with Caesar. In general the euphony of Cleopatra's assonance is set against the cacophony of Caesar's alliteration. Compare the sound of Cleopatra's first speech (I. i. 19-24; quoted above) with Caesar's "to tumble on the bed of Ptolemy." In the one there is a variety (subtly varied) of "a" sounds; in the other it is clicking consonants which set the tone. Cleopatra repeats two names over and over: "Antony," and "Charmian," which have in common her typical elongated "a" sound. The names which Caesar uses and re-uses all lend themselves well to his crisp pronunciation: Agrippa, Thidias, Octavia, Dolabella. Indeed, though Caesar uses more polysyllabic words than the others, he generally takes those which are easy to speak quickly: e.g., "lascivious," "contestation," "contemning," "publicly," "stablishment," "ostentation," "habiliments." Caesar's characteristic speech is a combination of these crisp polysyllabic words and short ones, ordered to permit brisk, steady delivery.

> You may see, Lepidus, and henceforth know
> It is not Caesar's natural vice to hate
> Our great competitor. From Alexandria
> This is the news: he fishes, drinks, and wastes
> The lamps of night in revel; is not more manlike
> Than Cleopatra, nor the queen of Ptolemy
> More womanly than he; hardly gave audience, or
> Vouchsafed to think he had partners. You shall find
>   there
> A man who is the abstract of all faults
> That all men follow.
>
>   (I. iv. 1-10)

Caesar uses words which can be got out quickly: he would not use a phrase like Cleopatra's "Tawny-finned fishes" (II. v. 12), for it would slow his delivery.

To discuss characteristic differences in the sound of the words is risky, for our impressions are unavoidably subjective, but it seems worth hazarding some cautious generalizations. In a sensitive, though very personal essay on *Antony and Cleopatra*, G. Wilson Knight remarks on the "preeminence of thin or feminine vowel sounds, 'e' and 'i',"[22] and he quotes some twenty-five prominent examples, including "by the fire that quickens Nilus' slime," "her infinite variety," "intrinsicate," "dislimns," "that great medicine hath with his tinct gilded thee" (I. v. 36-37), "discandying," "terrene." What Knight failed to note is that about three-quarters of these phrases are used by Antony and Cleopatra and include some of their most characteristic terms, while most of the rest are used about them. Knight goes on to suggest that the thin vowels and a light "ing" ending are set against the "rich, yet elongated" vowel sound of "sun," "moon," "burn," "world," and the like.[23] Quite right, I think. From this I would conclude—or suggest at least—that Antony and Cleopatra share a characteristic vowel sound (thin "i" and "e" balanced against richer "o" and "a") in noticeable contrast to Caesar, whose characteristic sound is consonantal.

Consider also the difference between Caesar and Cleopatra in their patterns of thought. Caesar is relentlessly logical. His speeches move smoothly from premises or evidence to conclusion (e.g., V. ii. 179-88) without repetition, digression, or ellipsis. In a striking dramatic contrast, one of Cleopatra's prime characteristics is verbal repetition and parallelism.

> O well-divided disposition! *Note him,*
> *Note him,* good Charmian, 'tis the man; but *note him.*
> *He was not sad,* for he would shine on those
> That make their looks by his; *he was not merry. . . .*
>
>   (I. v. 53-56; my italics)

Such repetition occurs again and again throughout the play.[24] Notice too Enobarbus' uncharacteristic repetitions as he argues with her: "But why, why, why?" (III. vii. 2); "is it, is it?" (l. 4). In the same scene we see Antony again firmly under Cleopatra's spell, and it is with a repetition that he reaffirms his disastrous decision: "By sea, by sea" (l. 40).[25] It may be that the repetition is merely for emphasis, but is it just accident that the verbal habit is Cleopatra's and that the decision is essentially hers (l. 28)? And in IV. xv. Antony seems to reaffirm his commitment to Cleopatra as he repeats, "I am dying, Egypt, dying" (ll. 18, 41).

Thus Cleopatra's repetition and parallelism are set against the logical progression of Caesar's speech. Where Caesar works out an idea, Cleopatra usually just sets one up. Very seldom does she work steadily toward a conclusion as he does; she either jumps to it immediately or has no interest in one. Her refutation of coldheartedness, for instance (III. xiii. 158-67), is vivid but static. She builds on a single idea, but without extending it in a logical framework. She says merely: if I am so, then. . . . In Caesar's characteristic pattern this would go: I would rather . . . than be considered that, *therefore* I cannot be so. Cleopatra's speeches are displays of feeling or intuition which, unlike Caesar, she never troubles to justify. Thus she can reach a conclusion without preamble (V. ii. 191) or take four positions in as many speeches, jumping to the next as Antony opens his mouth to object to the last (I. iii. 19-39). Perhaps it is not merely fanciful to say that the static quality and emotional basis of her thought can be associated with the sloth and self-indulgence which the Romans find characteristic of "Egypt." But no mere description does justice to Cleopatra's feminine flip-flops of logic, scrambles of idiom, and mincing, mousing tones, and it is these characteristics, not her queenliness, that make her so fascinating a woman.

In the third and fourth acts Antony shifts back and forth between Roman and Egyptian language, just as he wavers between caring about the war and caring about Cleopatra. Immediately after his first defeat (III. xi.) Antony is so disgusted with himself that he is little inclined to reproach Cleopatra, though he has good cause to do so. His state of mind may be reflected and signalled by the spectacular incidence of verbal repetition in his speech.[26] After his final defeat (IV. xii.) Antony rails against Cleopatra in Roman terms, calling her "foul Egyptian," "triple turned whore," "charm," "gypsy," "spell," and "witch." At other times he alternates between manic exhilaration (IV. iv., viii.) and gloomy forebodings (IV. ii.). Only occasionally, as in his response to Enobarbus' defection (IV. v.), does his language seem to reflect genuine self-insight rather than a sophistic attempt to bolster his own morale.

III. xiii. displays the gamut of Antony's feelings. He can be both firm and noble ("Let her know't," l. 16), and foolishly assertive (ll. 20-28). As he feels his authority "melt" from him (l. 90), he tries to reaffirm his identity: "I am Antony yet" (ll. 92-93). Shakespeare played with this notion. Who is Antony? The Roman who snaps at Cleopatra with a contempt worthy of Caesar: "I found you as a morsel cold upon / Dead Caesar's trencher" (ll. 116-17)? Or is Antony "himself again" (as Cleopatra believes, ll. 186-87) when he says "come, / Let's have one other gaudy night" (ll. 182-83)? But for all his wobbling Antony is a ruined man and he has already declared for "Egypt." When he is told that Cleopatra is dead (IV. xiv.) Antony considers his own life at an end: "Unarm, Eros. The long day's task is done, / And we must sleep" (ll. 35-36). With his death certain Antony's speech stabilizes as he regains his clear sense of purpose. Compare the hysterical imbalance of "Hence, saucy eunuch, peace! / She hath betrayed me and shall die the death" (ll. 25-26) with the firm assurance of:

> Thrice-nobler than myself!
> Thou teachest me, O valiant Eros, what
> I should, and thou couldst not. My queen and Eros
> Have by their brave instruction got upon me
> A nobleness in record. But I will be
> A bridegroom in my death, and run into't
> As to a lover's bed.
>
> (IV. xiv. 95-101)

We can trace a similar progression in Enobarbus' speech, and it is worth doubling back to examine his development. Enobarbus is, as we have seen, a blunt and down-to-earth character; Kent-like, he enjoys a "plainness" which "nothing ill becomes" him (II. vi. 78-79). He serves as an observer in the play. His perspective is basically Roman but he has become involved in Egyptian corruption and seems perfectly at home amidst the lubricious voluptuousness of Cleopatra's Court (I. ii. 1-73).[27] Enobarbus' speech varies from humorous and colloquial-sounding prose (e.g., I. ii. 130-41) to the extravagantly elaborate "barge speech." His "Roman" speech is of two sorts. Talking in prose with Menas he coldly and accurately assesses the state of affairs, taking the "Roman" view of Cleopatra and all she represents: "He will to his Egyptian dish again" (II. vi. 123). In verse Enobarbus is less rough-sounding; nonetheless his speech remains vigorous and concrete. At his most formal Enobarbus can speak with the sturdy logic and steady rhythm of Caesar:

> Most worthy sir, you therein throw away
> The absolute soldiership you have by land,

> Distract your army, which doth most consist
> Of war-marked footmen, leave unexecuted
> Your own renowned knowledge, quite forgo
> The way which promises assurance, and
> Give up yourself merely to chance and hazard
> From firm security.
>
> (III. vii. 41-48)

It is this Roman logic which makes Enobarbus question the wisdom of staying with Antony (III. x. 35-37). In III. xiii. he coldly analyzes Antony's downfall (ll. 3-12, 29-37) and his logical condemnation of Antony's making "his will / Lord of his reason" (ll. 3-4) leads him to an internal debate:

> Mine honesty and I begin to square.
> The loyalty well held to fools does make
> Our faith mere folly: yet he that can endure
> To follow with allegiance a fall'n lord
> Does conquer him that did his master conquer
> And earns a place i' th' story.
>
> (III. xiii. 41-46)

Always before Enobarbus has, like Caesar, moved sturdily from evidence to conclusion. Here, when he is perplexed, there is a rhetorical change: his thought breaks and he sets up a balanced contrast. Feeling and reason conflict and Enobarbus' puzzlement is reflected in his sentence structure. Throughout this key scene Enobarbus' debate serves as counterpoint to Antony's vacillations (note how skilfully Enobarbus' speeches are inserted along the way) and at the end of the scene Enobarbus' decision is a cutting commentary on Antony's apparent revival:

> Now he'll outstare the lightning. To be furious
> Is to be frightened out of fear, and in that mood
> The dove will peck the estridge; and I see still
> A diminution in our captain's brain
> Restores his heart. When valor preys on reason,
> It eats the sword it fights with: I will seek
> Some way to leave him.
>
> (ll. 195-201)

As he chooses the rational, "Roman" solution Enobarbus' speech reverts to its usual firm, logical progression, and it is in the same characteristic language that he recognizes his mistake (IV. vi.). In view of his final choice of feeling over reason it is worth noting that Enobarbus, like Cleopatra, thinks of death in terms of a ditch in which to die (IV. vi. 38; cf. V. ii. 57), refers to the "blessed moon," and calls death upon himself in the "Egyptian" image of "poisonous damp" (IV. ix. 7, 13). In Enobarbus' fate we can see that Antony and Cleopatra cannot be judged merely by the standards of common sense and Roman logic.

As the end of the play approaches, the language of the protagonists firms and broadens. Antony's speech, heretofore in alternating balance between the Roman and Egyptian, becomes rich and poetic, intensely imaginative:

> Off, pluck off:
> The sevenfold shield of Ajax cannot keep
> The battery from my heart. O, cleave, my sides!

Heart, once be stronger than thy continent,
Crack thy frail case! Apace, Eros, apace. . . .
I will o'ertake thee, Cleopatra, and
Weep for my pardon. So it must be, for now
All length is torture: since the torch is out,
Lie down, and stray no farther. Now all labor
Mars what it does; yea, very force entangles
Itself with strength: seal then, and all is done.
Eros!—I come, my queen.—Eros!—Stay for me.
Where souls do couch on flowers, we'll hand in hand,
And with our sprightly port make the ghosts gaze:
Dido and her Aeneas shall want troops,
And all the haunts be ours.—Come Eros, Eros!

(IV. xiv. 37-54)

Note here the repetitions—particularly of Eros; thus as Antony approaches his love-death he is continually calling on *love*—the grand imagery of Ajax and continent, and the image of light extinguished (cf. Cleopatra, IV. xv. 85). The language reflects Antony's new firmness and clarity of purpose; no longer is he torn and uncertain. During the period of the battles Antony seems belittled or mocked by grand or astronomical references (e.g., III. xiii. 91-93), but now with his new resolution "sun," "world," "star," and "Jove" again seem natural comparisons for him. Cleopatra too begins to show a new firmness and purpose in her language. As she is increasingly committed to her relationship with Antony her rhythm smooths out and her verse lengthens. She gives full rein to a surging vitality which sweeps away the rhythmic stops and starts of her early speeches; her skittishness vanishes as her sense of commitment grows.

Give me my robe, put on my crown, I have
Immortal longings in me. Now no more
The juice of Egypt's grape shall moist this lip.
Yare, yare, good Iras; quick. Methinks I hear
Antony call: I see him rouse himself
To praise my noble act. . . .
                              Husband, I come:
Now to that name my courage prove my title!
I am fire and air; my other elements
I give to baser life.

(V. ii. 279-89)

How different this is from the early Cleopatra:

Give me mine angle, we'll to th' river: there,
My music playing far off, I will betray
Tawny-finned fishes. My bended hook shall pierce
Their slimy jaws; and as I draw them up,
I'll think them every one an Antony,
And say, 'Ah ha! y' are caught!'

(II. v. 10-15)

As their deaths approach, the language of the protagonists rises to the sublime. If it did not do so, the end of the tragedy would be flat indeed, for Shakespeare seems to have gone out of his way to surround the conclusion with unglamorous circumstances. Antony bungles even his own suicide (IV. xiv. 103), and we must not forget that despite her grand resolution (IV. xv. 86-88—in Roman terms)

Cleopatra does explore the possibility of coming to terms with Caesar. Her deceit is ludicrously exposed by Seleucus (V. ii. 148), and her quibbling with the Clown (l. 249) makes us wonder whether she is really still much the same person who earlier trifled with Mardian (I. v.). Nonetheless, tragic grandeur remains. It is almost wholly a function of the language, for these aged and dissipated lovers are ambiguous figures at best.

The grandiosity of the death scenes is a result of intense concentration of the "high" Egyptian imagery and the exalted frame of mind which it reflects.

O sun,
Burn the great sphere thou mov'st in, darkling stand
The varying shore o' th' world!

(IV.xv.9-11)

O, see, my women,
The crown o' th' earth doth melt. My lord!
O, withered is the garland of the war,
The soldier's pole is fall'n: young boys and girls
Are level now with men. The odds is gone,
And there is nothing left remarkable
Beneath the visiting moon.

(ll. 62-68)

Granville-Barker correctly calls this "little better than ecstatic nonsense,"[28] but somehow it successfully conveys the higher part of the lovers' feelings. For all that their love has a tawdry side, in its highest part it is sublime and it carries them to heights undreamt of by Caesar, who is quite incapable of such feeling—or speeches. The sublimity of the love-deaths is emphasized by the dull flatness of the speech with which Caesar concludes the play.

Most probable
That so she died: for her physician tells me
She hath pursued conclusions infinite
Of easy ways to die. Take up her bed,
And bear her women from the monument.
She shall be buried by her Antony.
No grave upon the earth shall clip in it
A pair so famous. High events as these
Strike those that make them; and their story is
No less in pity than his glory which
Brought them to be lamented. Our army shall
In solemn show attend this funeral,
And then to Rome. Come, Dolabella, see
High order in this great solemnity.

(V.ii.351-64)

Caesar enters thirty-three lines from the end; it is his place to assert his authority and provide some sort of epitaph. It takes him twenty-three lines to satisfy his interest in "the manner" of Cleopatra's death. One can scarcely help feeling that his perfunctory compliment to the famous pair reveals his utter incomprehension of their complexity and sublimity.[29]

I do not want to draw conclusions from all this, since only in a general way is this essay designed to prove anything beyond its specific observations. It is, indeed, doubly hard to substantiate generalizations convincingly in material of this sort because they must rest on cumulative impressions. So there is nothing definitive here. I have merely tried to point out what seem to me striking contrasts in characteristic language, rhythm, and rhetorical habit, hoping to contribute to an understanding of how character is embedded in language. I do believe that in these terms we can better understand how Shakespeare obtains his effects—and what these effects are meant to be. For language is an index to character and it offers a valuable way of checking our general impressions and letting us anchor them in the text of the play.

It should be plain that in *Antony and Cleopatra* language is not merely the vehicle of the action; rather, it parallels and reinforces the conflicts of the play, indicates what is going to happen and helps tell us why. We can, laboriously, define analytically the various sorts of contrasts which are present—in rhetoric, the logic of Caesar versus the ellipticity of Pompey; in sound, the vowels of Cleopatra against the consonants of Caesar; in imagery, the rich imaginativeness of Antony and Cleopatra versus the barrenness of Caesar—but the significance of such linguistic typology lies in its cumulative impact, an impact so subtly contrived in this play that the spectator is seldom conscious of the artistry which moves him.

Notes

1. For example, Helge Kökeritz, *Shakespeare's Pronunciation* (New Haven, 1953); Hilda Hulme, *Explorations in Shakespeare's Language* (New York, 1962); Sister Miriam Joseph, *Shakespeare's Use of the Arts of Language* (New York, 1947). More general studies are F. E. Halliday, *The Poetry of Shakespeare's Plays* (London, 1954); and Wolfgang Clemen, *The Development of Shakespeare's Imagery* (New York, n.d.; orig. ed. 1936).

2. Caroline Spurgeon long ago suggested that imagery could be used to trace the changes in Falstaff's character (*Shakespeare's Imagery* [Cambridge, Eng., 1965; orig. 1935], Appendix VII, pp. 377-80), and M. M. Morozov has demonstrated the consistency with which Shakespeare associated images with characters and the way in which shifts in "characteristic" imagery can reflect the development of a play ("The Individualization of Shakespeare's Characters Through Imagery," *Shakespeare Survey* 2 [1949], pp. 83-106).

When characters are satirized they are often set apart by their speech. For discussion of this technique see Arthur H. King, *The Language of Satirized Characters in Poëtaster* (Lund Studies in English X; Lund, 1941), and, more specifically, Leonard Prager, "The Language of Shakespeare's Low Characters: An Introductory Study," Unpubl. Diss. (Yale, 1957). Here, however, I am concerned with a less obvious kind of linguistic individualization. I am well aware that we tend to read speeches in accordance with our

conception of the characters to whom they belong (see the *caveat* of James Sutherland, "How the Characters Talk," in *Shakespeare's World*, Sutherland and Hurstfield edd., [New York, 1964], p. 119); such a warning may serve to make us more critical of our impressions, but it should not rule out all attempts at this kind of investigation.

3. *"Antony and Cleopatra,"* repr. in *Shakespeare: The Tragedies,* ed. Alfred Harbage (Englewood Cliffs, N.J., 1964), p. 153.

4. On the questionable reliability of such evidence see A. C. Partridge, *Orthography in Shakespeare and Elizabethan Drama* (London, 1964).

5. In connection with "sound" it should be recollected that Shakespeare probably wrote each part with a specific actor's voice in mind for it.

6. Clemen, p. 160.

7. Spurgeon, pp. 349-54; Clemen, chap. 16; Katherine Vance Macmullan, "Death Imagery in *Antony and Cleopatra,*" SQ, XIV (1963), 399-410; Sheila M. Smith, "'This Great Solemnity': A Study of the Presentation of Death in *Antony and Cleopatra,*" ES, XLV (1964), 163-76.

8. E.g., "fortunes proud" (II. v. 69); "vulgar fame" (III. xiii. 119); death's "pestilent scythe" (III. xiii. 194); "like a man of steel" (IV. iv. 33); "hacked targets . . . brazen din" (IV. viii. 31, 36); "tearing groan" (IV. xiv. 31).

9. References are to the Pelican edition, ed. Maynard Mack (Baltimore, 1960).

10. *Lepidus.* For characteristic and striking words and phrases of Lepidus, see the following passages: I. iv. 12-13, 82, 83. II. ii. 1, 2, 3, 13, 14, 17, 20, 21, 22, 23, 83, 98, 102, 170. II. iv. 1. II. vi. 29. II. vii. 24, 26, 27, 40, 47. III. ii. 65-66.

11. Hence the ironic point of Agrippa's "noble Lepidus" (III. ii. 6).

12. The latter case (III. ii. 65-66) is debatable, for the whole passage is fraught with problems; but the remark is plainly addressed to Antony, Octavia, or both, and the astronomical reference does fit the pattern associated with Antony.

13. *Pompey* (characteristic words and phrases): II. i. 1, 2, 21, 22, 23, 24, 25, 26, 27, 33. II. vi. 10, 58. II. vii. 75, 76.

14. Pompey apparently once speaks of himself in the terms of astronomical self-reference we associate with Antony's grandeur ("My powers are crescent," II. i. 10), though he promptly undermines the effect by calling the threat he poses "petty" (l. 34), but on the evidence of the *OED* the astronomical connotation for "crescent" seems dubious at this date.

15. *Antony* (characteristic words and phrases): I. i. 17, 33, 33-34, 35, 36. I. ii. 105, 112, 113, 124, 126, 181,

188, 190. I. iii. 48, 50, 68-69. II. ii. 63-64, 97. II. iii. 1, 6. II. vii. 17, 20, 22, 58-59, 99, 106, 107. III. ii. 48-50. III. iv. 8, 22, 24. III. vii. 20, 57. III. xi. 1-2, 13, 54, 57, 60. III. xiii. 20, 90, 95, 109, 113, 116, 117, 145, 147, 153, 154, 193. IV. ii. 6, 37, 44. IV. viii. 3, 12, 18, 38. IV. x. 3. IV. xii. 10, 13, 16, 18, 21, 22, 23, 25, 30, 38, 45, 47. IV. xiv. 10, 11, 14, 36, 40-41, 46, 51, 56, 57-59, 100. IV. xv. 18, 41.

Cleopatra (characteristic words and phrases): I. ii. 79. I. iii. 35, 37, 63, I. v. 23, 25, 27, 28, 30-31, 33, 37, 59, 73, 78. II. v. 2, 12, 13, 25, 34-35, 64, 78, 79, 80, 94, 95. III. iii. 20, 21, 45. III. vii. 15. III. xi. 55. III. xiii. 39, 55, 61, 159, 160, 162, 163, 165, 166. IV. viii. 17-18. IV. xv. 9, 10, 11, 25-26, 36, 62, 63, 68, 76, 77, 78, 85, 87, 89. V. ii. 7, 17, 51, 57, 58, 59, 79, 80, 81, 82, 83, 84, 85, 86, 88-89, 91, 209-212, 220-21, 240, 241, 243, 279, 280, 288-89, 294, 302, 303, 304, 308.

16. Thus Antony is called "plated Mars" (I. i. 4), "Herculean Roman" (I. iii. 84), "demi-Atlas" (I. v. 23), "a Mars" (II. v. 117), "a Jove" (IV. vi. 29), a "star" (IV. xiv. 106), and "crown o' th' earth" (IV. xv. 63), but he can also be called "a strumpet's fool" (I. i. 13), "a doting mallard" (III. x. 20), and "old ruffian" (IV. i. 4). Similarly Cleopatra, a "royal wench" (II. ii. 227) and "lass unparalleled" (V. ii. 315), is called "gypsy" (I. i. 10; IV. xii. 28), "Egyptian dish" (II. vi. 123), "ribaudred nag of Egypt," "cow in June" (III. x. 10, 14), and "triple-turned whore" (IV. xii. 13). She herself understands the Roman point of view (I. ii. 79), and can refer to herself in the Roman food imagery as "a morsel for a monarch" (I. v. 31).

17. *Caesar* (characteristic words and phrases): I. iv. 17, 21, 43, 46. II. ii. 115-16. II. vii. 98-99. III. ii. 29-31. III. vi. 44. IV. i. 4. V. i. 15, 16, 19, 39-40, 43. V. ii. 183, 346.

18. Compare also the various uses of "dislimns," "cannot hold . . . shape," "dissolve," and "melt."

19. *Enobarbus* (characteristic words and phrases): I. ii.11-12, 44, 145, 146, 147, 158-60, 161, 163, 165, 166. II. ii. 5-8, 110, 179, 183, 191-206, 207-219, 221, 225, 227, 238. II. vi. 73, 84, 86, 92, 104, 117-119, 123, 124. II. vii. 93, 104, 112-17. III. ii. 5, 20, 51, 59. III. v. 12-14, 13. III. vii. 7. III. x. 36, 36-37. III. xiii. 35, 63, 64, 199, 200. IV. ii. 24, 34, 35. IV. vi. 38. IV. ix. 7, 13, 17.

20. Compare the similar way in which breeding imagery (often used by Antony and Cleopatra) is made ambiguous throughout the play. Idleness hatches ills (I. ii. 125-26); "breeding" may yield "a serpent's poison" (ll. 188-90); "mud" breeds the "crocodile" (II. vii. 24-27); Enobarbus objects to serving "with horse and mares together" (III. vii. 7); Cleopatra is called "a cow in June" (III. x. 14); yet Antony and Cleopatra swear, rather grandly (irresponsibly?) by "the fire that quickens Nilus' slime" (e.g., I. iii. 68-

69). In this play the usual connotations of birth and fertility are sharply modified: ought this to influence our reaction to Cleopatra's final "baby at my breast" (V. ii. 308), usually taken as a symbol of fertile married love? In view of the irony already inherent in the statement, I think so.

21. That III. iii. follows II. v. without a break in time seems proof that Shakespeare was deliberately trying to keep Cleopatra in the forefront of the mind of his audience.

22. G. Wilson Knight, *The Imperial Theme* (London, 1963; orig. 1931), p. 201.

23. Knight, pp. 202-203. I do not agree with Knight's general conclusion that this lack of "sonority" contributes to a "tragedy . . . taken lightly, almost playfully," though I feel that he is quite right when he notes that Othello, Lear, and Timon all have a deeper, richer note in their speech.

24. "Music, music" (II. v. 1); "But yet . . . but yet . . . but yet" (ll. 50-52); "thou say'st . . . thou say'st" (56); "majesty . . . majesty" (III. iii. 20-21); "my lord . . . my lord" (III. xi. 54); "pardon . . . pardon, pardon" (61, 68); "Antony, Antony, Antony"; "help . . . help . . . help, help" (IV. xv. 11-13); "I dare not, dear; dear . . . I dare not" (21-22); "come, come" (29); "come, come, come" (37); "welcome, welcome" (38); "what, what" (83); "women, women" (84; again 90); "he words me . . . he words me" (V. ii. 191); "yare, yare good Iras; quick" (282); "peace, peace" (307).

25. Antony's repetition as he justifies himself to Caesar ("not so, not so," II. ii. 56) I take as essentially just deprecatory.

26. "Be gone . . . be gone . . . be gone" (III. xi. 8, 10, 15); "pray you" (four times: 17, 22, 24); the numerous "I have" constructions; "no, no, no, no, no" (29); "fie, fie, fie" (31); "yes . . . yes" (35).

27. M. M. Mahood suggests in her *Shakespeare's Wordplay* (London, 1957), pp. 166-67, that it is the role of involved observer which accounts for Enobarbus' frequent puns, which are certainly a noticeable characteristic of his speech (see particularly IV. ii. 8).

28. Harley Granville-Barker, *Prefaces to Shakespeare* (2 vols; London, 1961; orig. 1930), I, 422.

29. Caesar shows more feeling at the news of Antony's death (V.i.), perhaps because, as Maecenas says, "when such a spacious mirror's set before him, / He needs must see himself" (ll. 34-35). Caesar does see Antony's demise in earth-shaking terms (ll. 14-19), but his image of their conflict is of a pair of horses who "could not stall together / In the whole world" (ll. 39-40), and he interrupts his disquisition upon Antony to speak to a messenger (ll. 49-51).

Rosalie L. Colie (essay date 1974)

SOURCE: Colie, Rosalie L. "*Antony and Cleopatra*: The Significance of Style." In *Shakespeare's Living Art*, pp. 168-207. Princeton, N.J.: Princeton University Press, 1974.

[*In the following essay, Colie examines the play's use of Attic and Asiatic styles of speech, explaining that Atticism, the style preferred by Caesar, is characterized by plain, direct speech, while Asianism, which is more sensuous, self-indulgent, and imaginative, is the style used by both Cleopatra and Antony. Colie contends that in the Renaissance, these styles were studied not just as rhetorical effects, but as indicators of morality and cultural differences.*]

I

Like earlier chapters, this one is concerned with a particular manifestation of Shakespeare's control over style and styles. By definition, Shakespeare was a very stylish writer indeed, conscious of the range of stylistic alternatives available to him, concerned to honor the particular decorums of style and to extend (even to subverting those official decorums) the possibilities of expressive style. We have looked at his analytic prodigality in *Love's Labour's Lost,* as well as his counterpointing of epigrammatic and sonnet styles in his *Sonnets*: we have seen both how closely style is tied up with topic, subject, and moral tone, and how far away from these it can pull. In *Othello,* the charged passages in sonnet-language owe their impact to Shakespeare's significant control over the resources of that "language," his ability to make *topos,* epithet, and cliché resound with the generic meanings of a whole tradition of sonneteering. *Antony and Cleopatra* relies on that language too—a whole piece could be written on its unmetaphoring of standard love-conventions—but it is with another stylistic paradigm that I am concerned here. As in the sonnets, where Shakespeare exploited the *ping* and *pong*[1] of two different short-form genres, in *Antony and Cleopatra* he transposed the *ping* and *pong* of another literary paradigm rejuvenated in the Renaissance; and once again, his penetrating literary eye, fixed on the implications of a stylistic cliché, reopened the whole question of appropriate style in tragedy.

This time, the paradigm so examined was an ancient antithesis brought into contemporary prominence in the argument over expository prose styles, that is, the polemic over the "Attic" and "Asiatic" styles which, as an offshoot of the polemic over strict Ciceronianism, preoccupied such men as Lipsius, Muret, Montaigne, Bacon, Browne, and even Robert Burton. In *Antony and Cleopatra,* I think, Shakespeare subjected to scrutiny the personal, psychological, and cultural meanings implicit in that polemic, dealing with the very stereotypes of moral life that had, long before when Greeks confronted Persians, given rise to the terms in the first place—and, typically, examined those styles in the lives of his hero and his heroine.[2]

Obviously, Shakespeare was skilled in constructing dramatic characters who speak in what seems "personal"

styles—one thinks at once of such confrontations as that of Hal with Falstaff, or of Hotspur with Glendower; of Hamlet with Polonius, Hamlet with the Gravedigger; of Iago with Othello—or even of Iago with Cassio; of Kent with Cornwall, of Cordelia with her sisters, of Lear with his Fool. The list of such episodes, in which with the greatest economy so much is revealed about character, class, and motivation, is very long.

In *Love's Labour's Lost,* as we have seen, the playwright translated something else, the degrees of social hierarchy and occupation, into linguistic styles, managing therewith to mock the pretensions both of hierarchy and of occupations.

Underneath the nonsense with words in *Love's Labour's Lost,* a point of considerable importance is being made: that words' artifice does not reflect the real behavior of men and women. Well within the comic mode, the gaps are opened between *res* and *verbum,* between pathos and its expression, even between personality and life-style, and shown to be traps where individual preferences, drives, and even personalities can be lost. Language is played with, criticized, and praised, but all in terms of comedy—although the comedy in which these questions are raised rejects the standard comic solution. The play moves within, at, and beyond the limits of conventional language, nonetheless always celebrating the resources of the language it sometimes chastises. We are shown the predestination in language, and its flexibility as well, but no one is by these means predestined to suffer forever, as at the play's end languages are readjusted lightheartedly to fit the characters' new understanding of society and of themselves.

In other plays quite unlike *Love's Labour's Lost,* we hear language used in contexts where *language* itself is crucial:[3] even in what used to be called "interpolations," such as the Porter's speech in *Macbeth,* or the Gravedigger's exchange with Hamlet, we now hear thematic supports for central events and tendencies in the plays. Kent's linguistic disguises, manifestly "garments" the man chose to put on, nonetheless display an honesty which Cornwall, Oswald, and the wicked sisters, all speaking in their own persons, cannot call up. Lear's great speeches demonstrate, as Edgar said, "reason in madness";[4] Coriolanus' inarticulate utterances portray with great purity the struggle of polity with pride. In *Julius Caesar* (as to some extent in *Coriolanus* as well) critics have seen in the spare language the playwright's effort to match his style to his austere subject, to achieve a peculiarly "Roman" style.[5] And in both plays, *la questione della lingua,* or at least *dello stile,* is written deeply into the plot: action turns on *how* men speak as well as what they say, appropriately enough, in plays about Roman political life.

The high point of *Julius Caesar* and its greatest set-piece is a rhetorical contest, in which two considerable orators compete for public favor in the matter of Caesar's death. Brutus was a stoic—except for Monteverdi's Seneca, the most attractive stoic ever staged—whose mode of speech is properly "plain." He tries, as the stoic rhetoric urged, to represent "himself" in his words and his syntax.[6] In the case at hand, such self-representation is of prime importance, since on the authority of Brutus' integrity the conspirators' justification can be said to rest. Although in the source Shakespeare used, Plutarch tells us a great deal about Mark Antony's speech at Caesar's funeral, he attempts no version of that speech itself—its invention was Shakespeare's own, who did not flinch from the task; and Brutus' speech is entirely Shakespeare's interpolation into the story. Brutus' reputation as an Atticist—thus, as a plain speaker and proponent of a rhetorical style designed to match the directness of the person using it—was well-known; so was Antony's predilection for Asianism, recorded so fully by Plutarch.[7] By picking up hints from Plutarch and the rhetoric-books, Shakespeare could treat Brutus and Antony as the living exemplars of what might otherwise have been mere *topoi*: he could make them live the styles in which they chose to speak.

At the same time, he glanced at aspects of the current controversy over prose-style which reanimated an ancient polarity. Greeks had, naturally enough, characterized Persians and others to the east of Athens as "Asiatic," meaning sensuous, sybaritic, self-indulgent, rich, materialist, decorated, soft. According to the paradigm, Asiatics lived a life of ease, delicacy, even of sloth, surrounded by ornate works of art and elaborate amusements for body and spirit. Gradually, the moral disapproval leveled at their eastern neighbors came to be applied to a style of oratory conceived as "like" Persian life, a style formally complex, ornate, decorated, and elaborate. Naturally, a simple, direct, relatively plain style was "Attic."[8] Needless to say, what was Attic and what was Asiatic varied considerably according to context, period, and generation: a given style can always be seen as plainer or more ornate than some other, and what was Attic to one generation sometimes seemed Asiatic to the next. In Rome, the debate recurred, centered on Cicero's style or styles, which to one generation (Cicero's own) appeared clear, intelligible, and direct, matching style to matter—and thus Attic; but to the next generation, which sought to reform it, elaborate, overly-wrought, untruthfully formal—thus artificial and Asiatic.[9] In late humanism, the terms of the debate were revived, this time appropriately over "Ciceronianism," the formally correct style established by precedents in Cicero's works, that instrument by which humanists sought to purify their Latin of scholastic barbarisms. Morris Croll and others[10] have presented valuable analyses and hypotheses of this prose-*agon* of the late Renaissance, and upon their writings I lean with gratitude. Not all Croll's normative statements are acceptable now without qualification. Even his hypothesis has borne considerable rethinking; but his paradigm of Attic and Asiatic is of immense use, and illuminates much not only about prose-styles but also about the range of poetic styles in that highly rhetorical period, when writers, trained from boyhood on rhetorical exercises, practised with immense control their vernacular skills. What the notions of "Attic" and "Asiatic" do for us, then,

is to provide us with a *ping* and *pong,* a range of comparison, for Renaissance styles.[11] By comparing one passage with another, one style with another, we can get some sense of what seemed "plain" and what "ornate" to contemporary readers interested in such matters.

The decisive oratorical contest in *Julius Caesar* is a case in point: we know that Shakespeare recognized in the two orators representatives of the two styles. In the competition between Brutus and Mark Antony for the people's approbation, the playwright used styles as marks of characterization for both personality and motive. The obvious difference between Brutus' style and Antony's points directly to the differences in their characters. In the play, Brutus speaks first, in prose, a device designed to show his relative directness and sincerity. If we examine that plain prose of his, though, we see it not simply as an expression of his naked personality (such as Attic theorists advocated for their style), for from his style we can read how sophisticated Brutus was, how studied in the rhetoric of the schools:

> Romans, countrymen, and lovers, hear me for my cause, and be silent, that you may hear. Believe me for mine honour, and have respect to mine honour, that you may believe. Censure me in your wisdom, and awake your senses, that you may the better judge.

It sounds straight: it is too often circular.

> As Caesar loved me, I weep for him; as he was fortunate, I rejoice at it; as he was valiant, I honour him; but, as he was ambitious, I slew him. There is tears, for his love; joy, for his fortune; honour, for his valour; and death, for his ambition. Who is here so base, that would be a bondman? If any, speak; for him have I offended. Who is here so rude, that would not be a Roman? Who is here so vile, that will not love his country? If any, speak; for him have I offended.

> (III.ii.13-17, 25-34)

Syntactical regularity of this sort is not accidental; Brutus was an orator, who knew his craft: his particular job this time was to demonstrate in his speech, and thus in his person, that his motives in a complicated situation were above reproach. The speech certainly exploits directness—"I slew him" is an admirably uncompromising statement of responsibility assumed. All the same, that frankness is elaborated in beautiful polysyndeta, zeugma, and parison, all going to show that even the plain-speaking Brutus knew in his bones how to make speeches and had, long before Julius Caesar's death, submitted his natural, unretouched personality to the finish of the rhetorical schools.

Brutus was an honorable man: when Mark Antony enters the Forum with Caesar's body, Brutus leaves the platform to him, enjoining the crowd to listen to whatever Antony has to say. What that was, is too well-known to warrant quotation: Mark Antony wins over the people in a long oration several times broken by applause and by the speaker's own display of emotion. In Antony's words, "I am no orator, as Brutus is, / But (as you know me all) a plain blunt man" (III.ii.219-20), an Attic appeal apparently entirely untutored, we can read truth and trickery. Antony was, as he said, no orator—officially; but he had studied the rhetorical arts in Athens, where he had been drawn to Asianism, as Plutarch tells us. What he displays is a style more intimate, more moving—and far more demagogic than Brutus'. Of course, by his false modesty, Antony means to imply that he has no skill in rhetoric and that his speech, therefore, cannot be expected to move the crowd, which had no need to be on guard against his wiles. In that implication, of course, Antony lies.

Shakespeare's confronting of these two styles is highly complex: he does not rely on a simplistic or moralistic paradigm, that "simple" is honest ("kersey noes") and "fancy" deceitful—but manages rather to show the limitations in the characters of both men, at once displayed and concealed by the styles they use. In the simplest ways, the two speeches are set in opposition: Brutus speaks prose, Antony verse. Since verse is by definition more decorated than prose, to that extent Antony's is the more decorated speech. Brutus' speech, though, is *syntactically* more formal by far—in other words, more structured, more Ciceronian—and has a firm structural consistency which Antony's by design lacks. Antony's flexible oration shifts from the formality of its beginning—"I come to bury Caesar, not to praise him"; "If it were so, it was a grievous fault, / And grievously hath Caesar answer'd it"—to an astonishing frankness and intimacy at its end:

> Good friends, sweet friends, let me not stir you up
> To such a sudden flood of mutiny.
> They that have done this deed are honourable.
> What private griefs they have, alas, I know not,
> That made them do it. . . .
> For I have neither wit, nor words, nor worth,
> Action, nor utterance, nor the power of speech
> To stir men's blood; I only speak right on.

(III.ii.211-16; 223-25)

In this artful and insidious speech, the grammatical members are plain but varied, more "naturally" disposed than those in the oration of the stoical Brutus. In one sense, signalized by shifting syntax and broken tone, Antony's language is "plainer," answers more honestly to his mood, and is thus more "Attic" than Brutus'. Brutus' syntax is elaborate, carefully-constructed, balanced, but his *tone* is consistent and direct and his whole oration markedly economical. Antony's tone fluctuates and shifts as the refrain "And Brutus is an honourable man" measures its altering direction. Again and again that refrain returns us to the tonic, showing Antony's remarkable way with words—and with his words, his way with his hearers' emotions. In sum, in their oratory we can hear the differences between the two men: Brutus' innocence shines out compared with Antony's guile; Brutus' self-deception is plain beside Antony's manifest scheming.

Mark Antony had indeed "studied eloquence": his rhetoric is active, emotional, moving, and ultimately victorious

over the relatively more neutral, more correct rhetoric of his opponent. The tricks of irony and sensationalism in Antony's repertory win over the fickle, casual populace, with important political results. But we must realize how *political* both men are, how they both use forensic oratory as a political weapon. Brutus seeking to damp down, Antony to stoke, the potential fires of popular wrath, both men address themselves in entirely different styles to their different tasks. Underneath Brutus' sincerity, we are aware of how consciously he plays upon that sincerity; in Antony's speech, we come to realize equally the man's love for Caesar and the artfulness of his own political intent.

Mark Antony's style, too, fits his character as given in the play. He makes no high pretensions to virtue; we see him temporizing with the conspirators after the murder, and we are early told that for all his talents Mark Antony is a dissolute young man. From his speech we sense his political acumen and, perhaps, his ambition—and the fluidity of his temperament as well: no one attending to his rhetoric alone would judge his personal rectitude to be higher than Brutus'. In *Julius Caesar,* Shakespeare dealt in the problems of politics, as of character and motive; nothing is simple here—not even the rhetoric officially designated as "plain." Caesar was and was not a tyrant; Brutus was a good man seduced with lamentable ease; Antony a clever and expedient man, at the same time more loyal than would conventionally be supposed from his casual behavior and his slippery rhetoric. In the play's stylistic *paragone,* all this is implicit: Brutus' honesty and self-deception, Antony's loyalty and his political skills, the cloudy ethics of the whole matter, the deep chasm separating the self-centered patricians from the unstable populace on whose favor their authority so peculiarly rested. Among so much that he has done, Shakespeare has here examined not only the motives of political men engaged by enormous power, but the problematics of public utterance as well, by means of which such motives were traditionally displayed—and concealed.

II

In *Antony and Cleopatra,* the problem of style, although equally telling, is set entirely differently. Oratory and public speaking are not at issue in this play, are not the plot-elements they are in both *Julius Caesar* and *Coriolanus.* Nor is style displayed at the outer surface of the play, as in *Love's Labour's Lost* styles are animated into personality. Nonetheless, its peculiar language is a major force in the play, as critics from Dr. Johnson to Maurice Charney have pointed out; in comparison to the plainer speech of the other Roman plays, the verbal richness of *Antony and Cleopatra* demands attention not only for its spectacular imagery but also as a function of the play's subject. As in *Julius Caesar,* where the economical style seems properly mated to its severe subject, so in *Antony and Cleopatra* the abundance of the language seems to match the richness of its subject, the fertility of the Egyptian setting, the emotional largesse of hero and heroine. The play's language bursts with energy and vigor; figures abound; of figures, as Charney so cleverly shows,[12] hyperbole is particularly common, that overreacher of the figures of speech. Indeed, the figures are so numerous and so rich that at times they seem almost to crowd out other meanings, to stop the action and the plot, to force attention to their resonances alone. Enobarbus' speech on Cleopatra is one example, the most famous of the play's set-pieces; Cleopatra's memories of the absent Antony, her paean to Dolabella, Antony's evaluations of his own emotional and worldly situations raise speech above the movement of plot.

Magniloquence fascinates both hearers and speakers. Antony's "normal" decisions to undertake his Roman responsibilities as triumvir and husband vanish in the hue and cry raised by his emotions and expressed immediately in the language he uses. More markedly, Enobarbus' famous detachment gives way before his recognition of Cleopatra's sources of power. In his great comment on her qualities his magniloquence rolls out to contrast with the plainness and irony of his previous speeches about her. In that speech, Enobarbus abandons himself to Cleopatra, and thereby gives himself away: from his response to her, apparently so out of character, we feel the force of her enchantment. Indeed, Enobarbus' giving way to grandiloquence seems an almost sexual abandon before her; the cynical and experienced Roman soldier, suspicious of Egypt and its ways, cannot and will not contain his climactic praise of the Queen.

Though the language seems at times to crowd out action and judgment, it does not crowd out meaning, for much of the meaning of this play, as one critic has argued, resides in the characters' attitudes to the language they use.[13] The stated, plotted action of the play is in itself grand enough to require no rival in language: the range of the play is epic, over the whole Mediterranean world which was, in the Roman context, the whole world altogether. Action and scene oscillate[14] between the poles of Rome and Egypt. From the beginning, in Philo's first speech, Rome and Egypt are set off against one another, in the shapes of Caesar and Octavia on the one side, Cleopatra on the other. The two locales, with their properly representative *dramatis personae,* seem to struggle for domination over Mark Antony's spirit and will. Like his great ancestor, the god Hercules, Antony stood at the crossroads of duty and sensuality, of self-denial and self-indulgence. Rome is duty, obligation, austerity, politics, warfare, and honor: Rome is public life. Egypt is comfort, pleasure, softness, seduction, sensuousness (if not sensuality also), variety, and sport: Egypt promises her children rich, languorous pleasures and satisfactions. Rome is business, Egypt is foison; Rome is warfare, Egypt is love. Egypt is "the East," where the beds are soft—and what "beds" can mean is never scanted in this play. To keep us aware of Cleopatra's power, the Romans, in their own eyes contemptuous of her life, show themselves as fascinated by Cleopatra's reputation as a bedfellow as Antony is by the actuality. Egypt is florid, decorated, deceitful, artful, opulent, sensual, idle; is "inflatus," "solutus," "tumens," "superfluens," "redundans," "enervis," "inanus."[15] I took this list of Latin adjec-

tives from various critiques, not of the fleshpots of Egypt, but of the Asiatic style; these epithets can, within the frame of this play, be transferred to the loose, ungirt life in Alexandria, the life to which, according to the source, Antony was inclined by temperament and which, in the end, he chooses as his own.

The question at issue is another dimension of style from those already discussed: not style as garment, or as chosen rhetoric or self-presentation, not style as manipulative instrument, but style as fundamental morality, style as life. Style of speech necessarily reveals personality, values, and ethics: one recognizes both the rectitude and the chilliness of Octavia, the silliness of Lepidus, the policy of Dolabella, from the way they speak as well as from what they say. In the speeches of Antony, Cleopatra, Octavius, Enobarbus, we recognize not just the varying moods of the speakers but their complex inner natures as well. How otherwise, indeed, could we ever assume anything about dramatic characters? Language must act to indicate quality and character, but here it does more: by reaching to the heart of the moral problems faced by Antony and Cleopatra, the language of their play makes us realize anew the ingrained connection between speech and style of life. The "square" of Roman speech and Roman life has its values, which we recognize the more easily as we see those values betrayed by Romans;[16] the "foison" of Egypt, both its fertility and its corruption, find expression in the *agon.* If one felt that the play were only an essay in style as life-style, then one might draw back from it as superficial and trivial; but *Antony and Cleopatra* seems to be more than a presentation-play of theatrical and unpersoned types, more also than the *psychomachia* to which it is occasionally reduced.[17] One thing that makes the play so compelling is that it *is* all these things—show, morality, exercise of power; it *is* a study in cheapness as well as in extravagance and costliness. Its chief characters are undisguisedly selfish and often trivial; in what lies its force? The language is one indicator, again, for the very style, with its grandioseness and hyperbolical explosions, finally points to the real problem: the efforts of two powerful, wilful, commanding personalities to bring their styles of living, their ingrained alien habits, into line with one another, for no reason other than love.

In a sense quite different from that of the morality-play, *Antony and Cleopatra* is about morality, about *mores* and ways of life—not by any means just about sexual morality, although problems of sexuality are not ignored—but about lives lived in moral terms. "Style" is—especially in the Attic-Asiatic polarity—a moral indicator, but here displayed as deeply thrust into the psychological and cultural roots of those ways of life. In this play, a given style is never merely an alternative way of expressing something: rather, styles arise from cultural sources beyond a character's choice or control.[18]

At the beginning of the play, this does not seem to be the case: Antony doffs and dons Egyptian and Roman styles, of speech and of life, apparently at will and at need. By the play's end, he has settled for a manner of speech and behavior proved by his decisive final actions to be the signature of his inmost nature. That is to say, his style can be seen not only to express his deepest sense of self, but also to relate to the consequences of his life-choices.[19] It is possible—indeed, it was the classical view, which Plutarch tried hard to present—to see Mark Antony's life as ruined by Cleopatra, to see the play, then, as a struggle between *virtus* and *voluptas*[20] in which Antony fails to live up to his ancestor Hercules' example *in bivio*. But as Plutarch takes pains to tell us, and as Shakespeare in *Julius Caesar* lets us know clearly enough, there was much in Antony's temperament, bred though it was in Rome, to explain why the pull of Egypt was so strong upon him, and from Enobarbus we know how strong that pull was on anyone. Though there is a structural and thematic contrast in the play between Rome and Egypt, the scenes alternating to give us that strong sense of oscillation between these poles, the play is not so simple as a straight contest between their different values.

Seen from one perspective, Rome dominates the play: Rome's wide arch covers the epic scene, Roman policy decides the order of events and the order therefore of these important private lives. The play begins and ends with expressions of the Roman point of view; by Roman standards, Antony perishes for his failure as a Roman. But seen from another angle, Egypt commands the play, where the action begins and ends and where all the major episodes take place. In this respect, the oscillation between the two localities makes it difficult to identify a single and certain source of power. Further, the two areas are not really kept polar: Rome and Egypt interpenetrate each other, just as past history continually penetrates the play's present. Rome's impact on Egypt has helped make Cleopatra what she is; and Antony's Roman-ness flaws his pleasure in Egypt, even as his Egyptian experience dulls his Roman arrangements. Together and apart, Antony and Cleopatra recall their own and each other's past; Octavius speaks of Antony's and his shared past; Pompey takes the action he does because of events long over before the play begins. We see Antony unwillingly come to accept the fact that his present has been shaped by his past behavior, or that his "Rome" can never be an unqualified value again. Cleopatra dies as a Roman, or so she thinks—but does so in a *décor* undeniably Egyptian, and by a means particularly local. Her attributes, the iconographical details she chooses for her last tableau, are entirely Egyptian, but her suicide is itself the final Roman gesture consciously chosen.

Nor is the mixture of Rome and Egypt in her accidental: deep in her experience lay the same Julius Caesar who had such a marked effect on both Mark Antony and Octavius Caesar. Before the play's beginning, Cleopatra and her Egypt had been Romanized; by its end, she is once more Romanized, and her Egypt has finally fallen to Roman rule. Indeed, throughout the play, Egypt is constantly open to Rome: Cleopatra's relation to Julius Caesar, to Pompey, to Antony, even her efforts to charm Octavius, are symbolic

of her country's dependency upon Rome's dominion. The presence at her court (a court "hers" only by the conqueror's grace) of so many Romans, full of what she calls with distaste "Roman thoughts," assures that the force of Rome upon Egypt is never unfelt, even at the height of Egyptian wassail.

However he may think of himself, Antony is a Roman soldier; Roman soldiers are always with him, even at the moment of his death. When he is away from Egypt, Roman messengers bring Cleopatra news of him and of affairs in Rome. He himself was sent to Egypt as a political administrator; he is succeeded at the play's end by Caesar himself, the last of a series of Romans proclaiming the dominion of the empire, Thidias, Dolabella, Proculeius. People die *à la romaine*: Enobarbus, Eros, Antony, Cleopatra, Charmian, Iras. Antony is borne to die his long-drawn-out death after the high Roman fashion; Cleopatra promises a like death, in which she shall be "marble constant" at the end of a life lived, publicly and privately, in significantly "infinite variety." There is no altering Roman historical destiny, however captivating Egypt and the Egyptian way of life may be.

As the play begins, we are instructed to take Roman virtues for granted as the measure from which Antony has fallen off, but as it develops, we are shown more and more to criticize in Rome.[21] No one could be sillier than Lepidus, one of the triple pillars of the world, grosser and more clownish than any Egyptian; nor more opportunistic than Menas, whose master regrets only that Menas forced him to veto his schemes. Octavius calculates ever; Pompey seeks his own ambitious ends; Octavius' relation to Roman polity is hardly self-subordinating. Further and most important, when he is "Roman," Antony is at his least attractive—in his relations to his Roman wives, Fulvia and Octavia, both dismissed in his mind's economy as terms of political function. As the play advances, the notion of Rome becomes more and more tarnished, particularly in the great orgy-scene in which even Octavius' tongue "splits what it speaks," and Lepidus is carried drunk to bed (a scene unmatched in the play by the "sensual" Egyptians so constantly criticized by these same Roman tongues). In that scene, the grossness of Rome is unequivocally displayed in the unbending ambitions of Caesar, the jealousy of the triumvirs, the thinness of Pompey's honor, Menas' crude hankering after power, the heroes' dancing to their roundsong. Into such hands the world has been delivered. Of course "Egypt" offers no moral improvement over this—Cleopatra lies from first to last, to others and to herself. We are never in doubt of her duplicity, but its naturalness comes to seem worthy in comparison to the slyness of Octavius and of the "trustworthy" Proculeius. Cleopatra's is a consistent and therefore honest duplicity: her policy is innocence itself compared to the masterful and automatic deceptions of the politic Octavius. More: life in its natural spontaneity is set against machination, as Cleopatra faces Octavius symbolically and in fact. Against such an opposition, all the more obviously can Cleopatra be seen to satisfy a universal human need: though she makes hungry where most she satisfies, both hunger and satisfaction are natural enough. The Roman hunger for power can never be filled; in it there is always something barren, inhuman, and perverse—but Cleopatra can allay, even as she rekindles, one Roman's hunger for the satisfactions of love.

III

The question at issue is not so much the value of Rome set against the value of Egypt, clear as these are, as it is the private relation between Antony and Cleopatra, a relation always colored by their different backgrounds and local loyalties. Normally speaking, it is not considered admirable, nor even sensible, for a man of public position to jeopardize his career for a woman. When the man is Antony, well-married in Rome and well-supplied elsewhere, and the woman Cleopatra, full of experience and of years, it is easy enough to see the matter with Roman eyes as a dissolute business between middle-aged sensualists having a last fling while they can, sinking into sloth and indolence and letting the affairs of empire go hang. Further, there is opportunism even in this love affair—that Cleopatra's political position was immensely strengthened by Antony's presence in Egypt, Caesar's sharp observations make plain. The suspicion certainly exists that she loves Antony for what he can do for her as well as for what he is to her.

The play begins with a Roman inductor, who takes the worst for granted. Philo (what a name for him!) evaluates the major characters according to accepted Roman standards; his critical speech breaks off as Antony and Cleopatra enter to act out what he has just, so degradingly, described as their typical behavior:

> Nay, but this dotage of our general's
> O'erflows the measure: those his goodly eyes,
> That o'er the files and musters of the war
> Have glow'd like plated Mars, now bend, now turn
> The office and devotion of their view
> Upon a tawny front: his captain's heart,
> Which in the scuffles of great fights hath burst
> The buckles on his breast, reneges all temper
> And is become the bellows and the fan
> To cool a gipsy's lust.
>   Look, where they come:
> Take but good note, and you shall see in him
> The triple pillar of the world transform'd
> Into a strumpet's fool: behold and see.

(I.i.1-13)

The hero and heroine then enter, to act out their tableau of mutual absorption. They behave with freedom towards each other—perhaps with abandon, indeed—but *not* as strumpet and fool. Their language, that of lovers bent on ideal expression, is thus quite counter to Philo's assessment of them:

CLEO.:

If it be love indeed, tell me how much.

ANT.:

There's beggary in love that can be reckon'd.

CLEO.:

I'll set a bourn how far to be belov'd.

ANT.:

Then must thou needs find out new heaven, new earth.

(I.i.14-17)

The inflation of their language may strike us, but hardly as exceptional in any pair of lovers mutually absorbed. Rather, theirs is the common rhetoric of love, unspecified and generalized, seeking to express inexpressible heights and depths of feeling. Cosmic analogies are habitually called up by lovers less involved than these in the "real" world; the fact that Antony and Cleopatra are so deeply involved in the factual political world lends poignancy, irony, and a kind of accuracy to their occupational hyperbole. The "new heaven, new earth" of their love, created by them for themselves alone, must substitute for the real geography around them, the Mediterranean world over which their influence and the play's action range. Symbolic geography is invoked, with its real referents: Rome, Alexandria, Athens, Sicily, Sardinia, Parthia, Judea, Media, Mesopotamia, Syria, Armenia, Cyprus, Lydia, Cilicia, Phoenicia, Libya, Cappadocia, Paphlagonia, Thrace, Arabia, Pontus all testify to the reach of Rome, whose "universal peace," proclaimed by Caesar, was endangered by Antony's withdrawal from the world-scene in wilful, careless, selfish pursuit of private satisfactions.

All this real world, then, was insufficient for these two—but more important than that, it was also too much for them. To keep their love safe, they must shut out the actual world in hopes of finding a new space for themselves small enough[22] to exclude occupations other than love, large enough to contain their exalted imaginations. In this play, the common literary metaphor of lovers' giving up the world for love is taken as the literal *donnée*: meaning pours back to give substance to the cliché, as the play teaches something of the human cost involved in neglecting the serious public world, the glories and woes of war and administration, for love of one woman.

Antony and Cleopatra speak "excessively" from the beginning, in an idiom familiar enough in love-poetry.[23] But it is worth noting that they are not alone in this habit of overstatement: Philo's initial speech is wholly cast in terms of excess. He degrades the amorous exploits of his commander with Egypt's queen, certainly: his account of that commander's military accomplishments is as excessive as his contumelious commentary on Antony's amatory achievements. Antony's eyes in war "glow'd like plated Mars"; "his captain's heart . . . burst the buckles on his breast." Caesar's speech too follows the pattern of overstatement: he makes the same kind of contrast of Antony's "lascivious wassails" and "tumblings on the bed of

Ptolemy" to his astonishing endurance at Modena and on the Alps (I.iv.55-71). Whatever Antony does, it seems, "o'erflows the measure"—but the Romans can *recognize* excess only in Antony's un-Roman acts: the heroic rest is, to them, natural in a Roman. Excess, then, is culturally conditioned: men recognize as excessive only what they regard as "too much," so that Romans who valued military extravagance as much as Cleopatra valued extravagant pleasures could find in her Antony much to praise. When Octavius denounces Antony's self-indulgence, he calls him "A man who is the abstract of all faults / That all men follow." Who could be more than this, an epitome of ill? Taking exception to Octavius' statement, Lepidus casts his comments in terms equally hyperbolical:

> I must not think there are
> Evils enow to darken all his goodness:
> His faults in him, seem as the spots of heaven,
> More fiery by night's blackness.
>
> (I.iv.10-13)

What are we to make of Antony, then? What are we to make of his present love-experience, judged by Philo as tawdry and low, judged by the lovers as quite past the reach of expression? In fact, what do Antony and Cleopatra *do*? We are told (by Romans) how they pass their time, in behavior characterized as "Asiatic" in the extreme. Egypt is, certainly, "the East," regularly so designated in the play. As queen, Cleopatra is often addressed by her country's name; when she dies, she is called "the eastern star," that is, the planet Venus. What Antony and Cleopatra do, evidently, is live by the attributes of the Asiatic style; they act out, they and the Romans tell us, a life-style gaudy, loose, ungirt, decorated, artful, contrived, and deceitful. The Egyptian court is an idle, opulent, sensual, Asiatic place, where men are effeminate and women bold. Mardian the eunuch exists to remind us of what can happen to a man in such an environment, and we see Antony unmanned in various symbolic ways. Normal decorum is constantly breached by this general, this queen. Drunk, Antony will not hear his messages from Rome; playing with Cleopatra, he relinquishes his armor to her and dresses in her "tires and mantles." She takes his sword away, and though she returns it before their battle, she disarms him entirely in the midst of a real battle, by more critical means. Publicly she ignores him, however preoccupied with him privately. Nor is she manly, for all the dressing in armor and proclaiming herself a man's equal before the last battle. At Actium she flees out of fear, and retires in the last pitch as well: when Antony is dying before her eyes, she will not emerge from her monument, nor even open its doors that he may easily be brought in to her—because, she says, she is afraid.

In Egypt men feast and sleep. "The beds in the East are soft" in many ways. Both defeat and victory are celebrated in Egypt by one other gaudy night, and Caesar seems to acknowledge this Egyptian need for self-indulgence when, to reassure the captive Cleopatra, he urges her to "Feed and sleep." Though the meanings of "sleep" deepen radically by the end of the play, at the beginning and for the most part, "sleep" is a sign of Egyptian indolence and womanishness. Festivities are unmanly too; Caesar says of his great competitor:

> From Alexandria
> This is the news: he fishes, drinks, and wastes
> The lamps of night in revel; is not more manlike
> Than Cleopatra; nor the queen of Ptolemy
> More womanly than he.
>
> (I.iv.3-7)

His last comment may indicate Caesar's limitations as a judge of human character, but it also sums up the Roman attitude to Egypt, a place merely of "lascivious wassails." The way most Romans think of Cleopatra, it is no wonder that she shrinks, at the end, from being carried through Rome to see "some squeaking Cleopatra boy my greatness / I' the posture of a whore." She knows how she is named in Rome, because in his rage Antony tells her:

> I found you as a morsel, cold upon
> Dead Caesar's trencher; nay, you were a fragment
> Of Gnaeus Pompey's, besides what hotter hours,
> Unregister'd in vulgar fame, you have
> Luxuriously pick'd out.
>
> (III.xiii.116-20)

Again and again, "appetite" is a word used to cover all satisfactions. Feasting and love (or, better, sex) are equated, as in the passage just quoted. Cleopatra is often reduced to food—by Enobarbus, speaking of Antony, "He will to his Egyptian dish again"; by herself, in her youth "a morsel for a monarch," although those were, as she says, her "salad days," when she was both greener and colder than she later became.[24] Pompey speaks man-to-man to Antony of "your fine Egyptian cookery" (II.vii.63-65) and, later, of the "cloyless sauce" that Egypt proves for Antony.

Unquestionably the preoccupation with sex and with the shared sexuality of Antony and Cleopatra runs as an undercurrent through the play. The difference between Egyptian and Roman talk of sex is instructive: Charmian and the Soothsayer, Cleopatra and the Eunuch, speak playfully and naturally; Enobarbus speaks cynically to and about Antony, on "death," on horses and mares; and the other Romans show their prurience and crudity when they speak, as they compulsively do, about the subject. The imagery too carries its sexual meanings: Cleopatra's "sweating labour" joins with the imagery of bearing and of weight to remind us of the woman's part in the act of love. This language in turn conjoins with the marvelous and varied horse-imagery[25] which reaches its peak as she imagines the absent Antony on horseback: "O happy horse, to bear the weight of Antony!" Such language assumes sexuality to be a normal part of life; the Nile-imagery, with its "quickenings" and "foison" references, suggests procreation and creation as part of a natural cycle. Nature provides reproductive images for sexuality, and war another sort. The constant reference to swords, in fact as in image, keeps manliness ever at the forefront of our

Michael Mawson as Agrippa, Lewis Gordon as Enobarbus, Stephen Ouimette as Octavius Caesar, Frank Zotter as Eros, Ronn Sarosiak as Maecenas, Leon Pownall as Antony, Edward Atienza as Lepidus, Derek J. Sangster as a Roman Soldier, Jeffrey Kuhn as Scarus, Matthew Penn as Demetrius, Paul Miller as Dolabella, Geoffrey Tyler as a Pirate, Françoise Balthazar as a Dancing Girl, Gerry Mackay as Varrius, and Michael Simpson as Menas in Act II, scene vii of the 1993 Stratford Festival production of Antony and Cleopatra.

awareness, as it is at the forefront of the dramatic characters' awareness, too.[26]

There is more than the suggestion, then, that love is no more than appetite or a drive; if that were all there was to love, the Roman view of this affair would be correct, Cleopatra simply a whore and Antony besotted, "ne'er lust-wearied." But can a man remain "ne'er lust-wearied" by the same woman, however infinite her variety, if she is merely a whore, however aristocratic her birth?[27] Enobarbus, in so many ways faithful to Antony and Cleopatra in spite of his disapproval of their behavior, sees something more in her and tries to say what that "more" is. Once again, significantly, he speaks in terms of food—"Other women cloy / The appetites they feed, but she makes hungry, / Where most she satisfies." Mere sexuality, strong sexual love, idealized love: however it is described, the emotions shared by Antony and Cleopatra challenge the heroic world of Roman military organization.

This miracle of love (or whatever it is) we do not see acted out onstage. Indeed, we never see Antony and Cleopatra alone, as we do Romeo and Juliet, Desdemona and Othello. What we see is something quite different: a man and a woman playing, quarreling, making up; a woman sulking, pretending to anger, flying into real rages, running away from danger, flirting even in deep disgrace and danger. Except on Roman tongues, there is little that can be called shameless or lascivious in Cleopatra's or Antony's utterances about love: her language on this preoccupying subject is remarkably clean—which is not the case with Roman commentators on these spectacular lovers.

To make so commonplace, so vulgar a mixture into a woman worth losing the world for is a considerable task for any playwright. Our playwright accomplishes it by fairly simple, even domestic, means. His Cleopatra has, among other things, a girlish, hoydenish companionability. She is obviously amusing company; she will try anything once. She has a lovely imagination and considerable command of language. She tries to rise to occasions, and sometimes she does. We hear much of Cleopatra's whoredom, and we see Antony blundering after her, twice fatally; we hear him speak of the less pleasant side of his love, of the "Egyptian fetters" which tie him in Alexandria, of his "dotage," and later, when he misses her in Rome, of his "pleasure" with Cleopatra. There is every reason to think very little of Cleopatra—although, to balance her crudities (as when she had a salt-fish attached to Antony's line), we are made to see that even in her breaches of decorum, her riggishness, her foolish middle age, she is delightful. She is earthy, and down-to-earth;[28] her sudden accessions of realism puncture both the romanticizing of the lovers and Antony's simplistic view of love and Cleopatra as satisfaction to his appetite. This woman is something more:

> Sir, you and I must part . . .
> Sir, you and I have lov'd. . . .

>   (I.iii.87-88)

> In praising Antony, I have disprais'd Caesar . . .
> I am paid for't now.

>   (II.v.107-109)

> Think you there was, or might be such a man
> As this I dreamt of?

>   (V.ii.93-94)

>   Antony
> Shall be brought drunken forth, and I shall see
> Some squeaking Cleopatra boy my greatness
> I' the posture of a whore.

>   (V.ii.218-20)

When her ironical common sense pierces her own theatricals, her charm is irresistible: though she rarely acts on that knowledge, we see that at moments she knows herself and the precarious, politicking world she lives in. It is this side of her, the practical, real woman, that is picked up in Charmian's farewell epithet: to "a *lass* unparallel'd." Age, apparently, could not wither her, nor a rakish life, nor child-bearing.

But in her first parting from Antony, as in her exchange with Dolabella after Antony's death and just before her own, Cleopatra's common sense rises to something greater:

> Sir, you and I must part, but that's not it:
> Sir, you and I have lov'd, but there's not it. . . .

The facts are clear enough—but they do not provide Cleopatra with an explanation for the pressure of her feelings, that this love for Antony is unduly significant, that parting from him must radically diminish her. Her sentence loses its direction as she seeks to express the "more" of her feeling for him:

> That you know well, something it is I would,—
> O, my oblivion is a very Antony,
> And I am all forgotten!

>   (I.iii.89-91)

As she later says, she wants to sleep out "the great gap of time" that Antony is away from her; in his absence, even by herself, she is, imaginatively, "forgotten" and therefore does not exist. Both Antony and Cleopatra speak feelingly and movingly about their sense of identity lost. Part of their tragedy lies in Antony's feeling himself dissolve when he is with her, and Cleopatra's feeling her "nothingness" when he is not with her.

Cleopatra makes clear that her love for Antony is fully sexual; but, as has been noted,[29] this emphasis comes in reverie, not in lascivious action or exchange. What is significant, surely, is that in a life given to sexual conquest and enjoyment, her relation to Antony means more to her than anything else. It is not that Cleopatra does not want to be reminded of her old connection with Caesar; it is that she knows its qualitative difference from the connection with Antony. Certainly Cleopatra does not shirk the facts of her sexual past; however giddy and irresponsible her behavior with Antony, though, she knows that for him, she has quit being a rake. For her, sexuality is never just the "pleasure" that Antony implies early in the play it is for him. It has (at last, one has the impression) risen above itself to become love of a sort that defies definition in psychological ways, not just in "literary" ways.[30] Indeed, in literary ways, the lovers' extreme preoccupation with one another is almost *too* resonant to the conventional language of love: as in *Othello,* but in an entirely different context, the petrarchan mixture of love and war has here been actualized in the necessary conditions, unmetaphored into actuality, of everday life for this general and this queen. But the love-poet's transcendent aim is the same as theirs: how to express the indefinable love they share, a love that to unsympathetic onlookers seems ordinary enough, vulgar enough, but to the lover experiencing it inexpressibly glorious and valuable. Their language is pitched at the familiar literary goal, to make the "new heaven, new earth" of lovers' cliché into a universe for their exclusive dwelling. Their *folie à deux* is in part a matter of language, manipulated to record heightened experience and to displace both conventional and particular renditions of their experience by others.

Cleopatra's imagination particularly works at this task: if sex is the reality and imagination the fantasy of love, then the two fuse in Cleopatra's speech in Antony's absence from her, when she imagines him as he at that very moment actually *is*:

> Stands he, or sits he?
> Or does he walk? or is he on his horse?

>   (I.v.19-20)

Her sexual memories crowd into the single line, "O happy horse, to bear the weight of Antony!" Her images of weight, realistic enough in any woman's experience of love, come to their culmination in the terrible scene of Antony's death, as she draws him into her monument:

> How heavy weighs my lord!
> Our strength is all gone into heaviness,
> That makes the weight.
>
> (IV.xv.32-34)

The reality is there, although not displayed to us, of the children she has borne him; "the lap of Egypt's widow," as Pompey so rudely said, has actually held Antony and known what it was to do so. Finally, to her "demi-Atlas" she attributes more weight than any man can carry; she turns her love into an even more colossal personage than the world will recognize or can, in the person of Dolabella, accept.

IV

In this habit of stretching expression, of trying to say more than words or figures habitually allow, lies some clue to the effect on each other of these lovers. They make each other feel that age is no bar to living fully; they make each other feel, not still alive, but more than usually alive, a feeling, however illusory, which can exercise curious power over a man and a woman more than commonly experienced. The connection between them, obviously, is quite different from other experiences they have had; Cleopatra knows this from the beginning of the play, and we witness Antony coming to know it too.[31] It is precisely his marriage to Octavia, with all its chilly merits, that teaches him what Cleopatra is to him. In their view of each other, Antony and Cleopatra are more than lifesize. So Cleopatra speaks truth in her great speech of hyperbole about Antony:

> I dreamt there was an Emperor Antony.
> O such another sleep, that I might see
> But such another man! . . .
> His face was as the heavens, and therein stuck
> A sun and moon, which kept their course, and lighted
> The little O, the earth. . . .
> His legs bestrid the ocean, his rear'd arm
> Crested the world: his voice was propertied
> As all the tuned spheres, and that to friends:
> But when he meant to quail, and shake the orb,
> He was as rattling thunder. For his bounty,
> There was no winter in 't: an autumn 'twas
> That grew the more by reaping: his delights
> Were dolphin-like, they show'd his back above
> The element they liv'd in: in his livery
> Walk'd crowns and crownets: realms and islands were
> As plates dropp'd from his pocket.
>
> (V.ii.76-92)

Antony has then finally turned into that "new heaven, new earth" he had told Cleopatra in the first scene she must find as the appropriate bound of their love. Microcosm and macrocosm change places: the earth is smaller than this man, as the common cosmic metaphor expands into all space and more-than-time in the images of ever-ripe autumn and a creature, the dolphin, transcending his natural element.[32] Correspondence imagery involving worlds in different scales—the cosmos, however thought of; macrocosm and microcosm; stars and eyes—is so common in sixteenth- and seventeenth-century poetry as to be mere cliché, and certainly at one level, all Cleopatra is doing in this magnificent speech is making more extravagant a notion already hyperbolical at its base. But in this particular case of lovers, the standard hyperbole has its peculiar reality to "match" this particular psychological and political situation. In the imagery, the larger world has been contracted into the limits of Antony's body (normally a microcosm), and Antony's body in turn enlarged encompasses and surpasses the macrocosm to which originally it had been likened. In fact, this is what happened to these lovers: "the world," in this case half or a third of the civilized world which was under their control, was rejected in favor of the "little world," quite literally, of man. "Bodies" are very important in the play, and although Antony and Cleopatra speak with remarkable delicacy about each other's bodies and their own bodily sensations in love, this speech gives the literary justification for that physical love. Hyperbolic metaphor that it is, this speech at the same time unmetaphors its literary content by making plain the crucial importance to these lovers of their finite, particular, well-worn bodies.

Cleopatra does not linger on the fantasy, but asks Dolabella, with the realism characteristic of her:

> Think you there was, or might be such a man
> As this I dreamt of?
>
> (V.ii.93-94)

To that, Roman Dolabella can only respond, "Gentle madam, no"—which serves to arouse Cleopatra to still more immense reaches of imagery, to language rejecting anything nature can offer as fit comparison to the wonder that Antony was. This time momentary realism touched off, as it habitually does not, the reassertion of hyperbole's value. Hyperbole becomes "true"—and yet even that hyperbolical language is not "enough" for the intense feelings between these two overreachers of life. In the references within the play, they are always more than merely human, more than triumvir and queen: Cleopatra was, we hear, more beautiful than the most beautiful picture of Venus. Art cannot render her, nor can nature's works render Antony. In her eulogy of him, Cleopatra never denies his manhood—"My man of men," she says, and she should know—but the manhood she attributes to him no ordinary mortal can aspire to. His bounty was endless—and his treatment of Enobarbus suggests that this is so—his delights transcendent. His empire was to be prodigal of imperial power—"as plates dropp'd from his pocket." Compare that magnificence with Caesar's careful accounting of Mark Antony's distribution of empire in III.vi: for Caesar, these political entities which Mark Antony gave away were no mere "plates" but the extended possessions of Rome, to be protected, at cost, for Rome's sake.

Cleopatra's imagination is as bountiful as Antony's generosity. Her language is rich as her habitat, and she is, as both detractors and admirers point out, histrionic to a degree. She stages herself at Cydnus; she stages herself as dead for Antony; she stages herself for her death. She speaks and is spoken of in theatrical terms of scene, act, and stage; she is a creature of impulse and whim, which she tries out on her audiences, acting to Dolabella, to Caesar, to Antony, acting even with her familiar maids. That habit of acting stands her in good stead in her determination to outwit Caesar at the end. Reversing Marx's famous quip, this play first acts out in farce what becomes tragedy a second time through. Cleopatra pretends to be dead—trivially, but with horrible results for Antony—before she dies in earnest. The theme of death echoes throughout the play—the lovers know, long before the crisis, the cost of their choice. Enobarbus plays on the slang term, "death," for sexual intercourse, when Antony first tells him he must be gone; his cynicism can seem justified to an audience which sees Cleopatra feign illness and death. Her coquetry, charming within the domestic protections of her court, is fatal on the battlefield. It is worth noting that for the deceit which cost him his life, Mark Antony never reproaches her; instead, he promises to be "A bridegroom in my death, and run into 't / As to a lover's bed." She too equates love and death: "The stroke of death is as a lover's pinch, / Which hurts, and is desir'd." She dies to join Mark Antony—"Husband, I come"—as his wife, taking for granted the meaning of a simple social act which could never take place in the Roman world during their lives. Put in the simplest terms, the word "death" is gradually ennobled by what happens in the play—but not before its seamier implications have all been laid before us.

So the play begins to live up to itself. As Philo's crudity is submerged under the lovers' flood of words, again and again the nasty turns out to have its noble aspect too, the Gorgon indeed becomes Mars. Because the playwright never shirks the unpleasantness, the triviality, even the occasional brutality of the lovers, because he always allows them to recognize and to reveal the compulsiveness of their love, its literal extremity, that love's peculiar force begins to take its confirmation from the radical action and the extreme language. As we watch the hyperbole coming true, we recognize a maturing of emotions more than life-size to begin with, commanding a space of their own making, relying on their mutual respect for their own worth. The simplicity, singleheartedness, and intensity of this faulty human love, magnificent in spite of the lovers' politics and duplicity, in spite of the inevitable deceits of their world, come to seem a far greater achievement, against greater odds, than the successful Roman quest for power.

And for this, as we shall see, there is theoretical precedent in Longinus' defense of the style Antony and his acquaintances used, a style designed to express generosity, magnitude, magnanimity; a style, as he put it, "with the true ring of a noble mind."[33] Though Shakespeare does not slight the cultural structure and construction of any style—Roman, Egyptian here, Navarrese elsewhere—he is

concerned in this play with the significance of a personal style within the cultural matrix, with what Longinus called "μεγαλοφροσύνη." Though we know, from Philo's initial speech, of Antony's capacity for greatness and perceive, in his dealings with Enobarbus and Cleopatra, his magnanimity in the face of terrible losses, he still has to live up to the nobility of his soul and to the elevation of his speech. Still more Cleopatra, unused to Roman gestures of magnanimity: from riggish, rakish queen who plays tricks with a man's honor and his life, she must grow into the moral capacities her hyperbole seems to make light of.

The risks are great—how does a man, how can a woman, leave off grandiose and bombastic play-acting, even to the roles of god and goddess, to die as heroes? The lovers set their sights high from the start: chose as their models superhuman figures from Roman mythology—Antony in the play's first speech is likened to Mars, Cleopatra unmistakably to Venus.[34] They act out that archetypal coupling throughout their lives, even to receiving mockery like the gods of Venus and Mars. Cleopatra is a goddess of love in her disguises, both the Roman Venus and the Egyptian Isis: she celebrated her greatest political triumph, over Antony and by his means over Rome, dressed "in the habiliments of the goddess Isis," as Caesar in outrage reports. Isis was also a moon-goddess, whose variability, reflected in the feminine psychology, is made much of in the play; her "habiliments," as Plutarch tells us in another place, are varicolored, to show her involvement with all nature—with light as well as dark, fire as well as water, life as well as death, beginning as well as ending. These robes are singularly appropriate to Cleopatra: they symbolize all matter and "afford many disclosures of themselves, and opportunities to view them as they are changed about in various ways."[35] Cleopatra is too much a woman, variable and faulty, to "be" either Venus or Isis, but she takes the part of both of them; posing as these goddesses, she occasionally takes on some of their meanings, as Antony on occasion takes on some of the meanings attributed to Mars and Hercules.[36] In addition, this pair is too intermingled in one another for such an interpretation: whatever their natural attributes making them godlike, Antony and Cleopatra are a man and a woman to each other and to the world.[37]

Although it is as a man that she most values him, Cleopatra symbolically and actually unmans Antony. We hear of her dressing him in her clothes, as Omphale did Hercules.[38] His decline from perfect manhood to something less than that is part of Antony's tragedy. In this play, however, the facts of the Roman idea of manhood are examined again and again and found wanting, particularly in respect to the very quality Antony so lavishly displays, magnanimity. He was a generous, a prodigal man, but always a man large of spirit. Largesse is his attribute, in all senses. He gave away his goods to his soldiers in defeat; his graciousness drove the defected Enobarbus to his shamefast death. To Antony's naturally great character Octavius stands in cheerless contrast; and no one in Rome, ever, is shown as rising to Antony's heights of grace. Again and again we are brought up against the hard realization that if to be a Roman is to be so narrow and calculating as Octavius, so vulgar as Pompey, so divided as Enobarbus, then Antony has surely chosen the better part. Octavius speaks beautifully of Antony's death:

> The breaking of so great a thing should make
> A greater crack. The round world
> Should have shook lions into civil streets,
> And citizens to their dens. The death of Antony
> Is not a single doom; in the name lay
> A moiety of the world.
>
> (V.i.14-19)

Beautiful words indeed to eulogize a dead colleague and opponent—but Caesar cannot help calculating the man's worth: "A moiety of the world."[39] That coveted demi-monde is at last his; the reckoning is over, the world brought under Caesar's universal landlordism. The "boy" has become, as Cleopatra names him, "Sole sir of the world." After the briefest respite in honor of his dead "mate in empire," Caesar turns back to the business of the world and lays his plans for the future. To such a man, it is difficult not to prefer the prodigal old ruffian, who can assert, and mean it, "There's beggary in love that can be reckon'd," who can risk and lose his moiety (or his third) of the world for something which, however flawed, he valued above himself.

For Antony is no standard Roman, as the Romans testify. Men *speak* of his greatness of character and action, his stature in virtue and in vice. Men *act* to honor those qualities: his soldiers love him; his servant kills himself rather than stab his master; Enobarbus dies of having betrayed him. Philo can speak of him only in hyperbolical terms; so, in spite of themselves, can Caesar and Lepidus. In everyone's mind, this man was aggrandized and enlarged above the commonalty of men. Like his ancestor Hercules, Antony does things no other man can do, on a scale on which no other man can do them. It is not Cleopatra alone who feels this, but everyone who knows him. When we compare this Antony with the man duped twice by Cleopatra, or with the man causing Caesar's messenger to be beaten, or the man feasting, joking, and making love with Cleopatra, we see the range of the problem Shakespeare set himself—and we must suspect that some of this hyperbole is merely bombast. But when his imagination is fired by Cleopatra, Antony *can* do great deeds at arms. He conquered the entire East and redistributed its countries (without consulting Rome) among Cleopatra and her children. When she arms him, he defeats the Romans at odds, and returns to tell her his "gests" that day. At his death, when an ordinary man might well have nagged, he looks to an Elysium in which he and she shall outdo Aeneas and Dido; he warns her to look after her safety and, like the great lover he is, dies on a kiss. No trace remains of his rage at her, no trace of reproach for her false message: with his own life he was prodigal; with hers, he was generous.

These are the gestures to match an hyperbolical style, the behavior so admired by Longinus: the gestures of the over-reaching man whose imagination is larger than the stage it must act upon. For Antony, the two "stand up peerless"; Cleopatra remembers that

> Eternity was in our lips, and eyes,
> Bliss in our brow's bent; none our parts so poor,
> But was a race of heaven.
>
> (I.iii.35-37)

For her he was, finally, truly Herculean, a "demi-Atlas," a colossus whose "legs bestrid the ocean"; he was greater than the arch of empire itself: he was her world. For him, she could make herself into Venus and Isis, could "be" ageless and infinitely desirable, immortal, more than human. They read their stature from their mutual view of one another. Their ideas of themselves and of each other may have been unrealistic, vain, self-flattering, and self-deceitful, but they reflected what can never be readily explained, the peculiar sense of well-being and power a man and woman in love can give each other. So their clumsy games, their open lovemaking and open quarreling, their flirtations, their drinking, their mockery, turn somehow from nonsense and bombast into legitimate hyperbole, into a language forever on the stretch to express what had not been expressed before. Far from ideal lovers, Antony and Cleopatra demand a language for their love which rejects conventional hyperbole and invents and creates new overstatements, new forms of overstatement. In the language itself, we can read the insatiability of their love, as the language seems to make hungry, too, where most it satisfies. Nothing is enough for these two, not even the most extravagant figures of speech.

The language Antony and Cleopatra use, the language others use about them, is stretched at its upper and lower limits, to express their high and low gestures as bigger than lifesize. It is interesting that Antony and Cleopatra do not bewitch others' imaginations only by their charismatic presence; their great qualities are praised, described, referred to, and criticized mostly in their absence. These two are watched by a world fascinated even when disapproving; they are staged in a play of their own making, with the world as their willing audience. But they do not really play for that audience: their imaginative acting is all for each other, and in their mutual absorption they do not care who happens to look on at the spectacle. Of course the Romans cannot keep their eyes off them; beneath the language of official disapproval, one can see Roman fascination with this un-Roman style of life, with this abundant, prodigal, excessive manner of doing things. Their bounty knows no winter but is, in Antony's word, always "foison."

V

Ripeness, overripeness: certainly the images of fertility, in particular the Nile-imagery, stresses life-giving, fecundity, creation; and, with these good qualities, also corruption and rotting. Action can corrupt; so can inaction. In Caesar's image for the variable Roman people, the famous "vagabond flag" passage, we read of one kind of rotting; in Antony's inaction we see another. The flag is dissolved in the stream's current; "solutus," dissolved, was one word of disapprobation applied to the Asiatic style, and (as Charney points out) images of dissolution and deliquescence abound in the play.[40] We see things dissolve and resolve—the liaison with Cleopatra, the marriage with Octavia. Antony vacillates between his Roman alliances and his Egyptian delights, choosing now the one, now the other. The tide is against him, literally at Actium, figuratively on land as well. And yet one is not surprised at this particular literalization of water-images of dissolution, for the metaphor has gained power through the play until, in Antony's great speech about himself, we see that he thinks of himself as formless, his shape lost. The metaphor of dissolution is overtly made use of through the play—"Let Rome in Tiber melt," Antony cries at the beginning; "Authority melts from me," he says near the end of his life. Cleopatra too speaks in this image: "Melt Egypt into Nile." If she should ever play him false, then "dissolve my life." Both use the neologism "discandy," Cleopatra in a hyperbolical assertion of love, Antony in connection with his melting authority:

> The hearts
> That spaniel'd me at heels, to whom I gave
> Their wishes, do discandy, melt their sweets
> On blossoming Caesar.
>
> (IV.xii.20-23)

The most important of the dissolution-passages is Antony's speech about himself as a cloud in which shapes continually shift, dissolve, and reform until "The rack dislimns, and makes it indistinct, / As water is in water." When he finds his Roman form again and dies "a Roman, by a Roman / Valiantly vanquish'd," Cleopatra says of him, "The crown o' the earth doth melt," into a nothingness she feels as palpable. To mark Cleopatra's death, Charmian calls for cosmic dissolution, "Dissolve, thick cloud, and rain, that I may say / The gods themselves do weep" (V.ii.298-99).

Peculiarly enough, other words characteristically applied in denigration to the Asiatic style are picked up and openly developed in the powerful imagery of this play. "Enervis" is such a word—Antony and Cleopatra taunt each other with idleness (I.ii.113-14, 127; III.xiii.90-92), and Antony accuses himself of "slackness" (III.vii.27). The notion of effeminacy is related to the notion of idleness and, in Enobarbus' last speech to Antony, is explicitly connected with melting. Enobarbus weeps ("I, an ass, am onion-eyed"), and asks Antony to stop talking—"for shame / Transform us not to women" (IV.ii.35-36). "Inanis," empty, is another word played in the imagery: "vacancy" occurs, in connection with voluptuousness (I.iv.26), and in Enobarbus' attempt to praise Cleopatra (II.vi.216). By all odds the most significant use in the play of such a term is the imagery and the practice of enlargement, of blowing up. The Asiatic style was "inflatus": we have seen how Cleopatra continually enlarged her idea of Antony, until in her

paean to Dolabella of Antony's greatness she outdid her hyperbolical habits of rhetoric. There is, too, much about inflation in the play's language. In the first speech of Philo, in which so much of the play's implications, sexual and other, lie coiled, Antony is said to have "become the bellows and the fan / To cool a gipsy's lust." Primarily, the bellows blows up, the fan cools: but *both* can actually blow up and both can cool. On her barge, Cleopatra has magical fans, apparently, also both blowing and cooling: the "winds did seem / To glow the delicate cheeks which they did cool, / And what they undid did." (II.ii.203-205). Breathless, Cleopatra breathes forth her power; in her, Enobarbus assures his hearers, defect becomes perfection. Antony and Cleopatra, then, "inflate" each other—or, to put the same thing more gracefully, they inspirit each other. For those Atticists who polemicized against the Asiatic style, such "inflation" was bad because it was untrue to nature and gave false impressions of fact. Now, Antony and Cleopatra may have had, and have fostered, false impressions about themselves and each other; but they were trying to do something else, something highly respectable and highly poetic: to give utterance to their own convictions and sensations of being larger than life, which in turn demanded a style of expression more spacious than that used by the ruck of mankind. By means of the style, ever on the reach for an undefined "more," the infinite longings of these figures can be understood: but, furthermore, by means of this twice-heightened speech, the play examines not only the values of an enriched style, but the values of the life it seeks to match. The play is a study in richness and ripeness, necessarily also a study in overripeness as well, a study even of corruption. But never may we conclude, in morality vein, that these last qualities are valueless, that the people who speak so are simply megalomaniac and self-deluded. Indeed, what emerges from the play is something quite different, the affirmation of the values, qualified by an awareness of its dangers, of such a way of life.

As one works through the play, several things become clearer: at the beginning, Antony speaks hyperbolically, bombastically: his honest heartfelt emotions, mingled with an ironic self-criticism, are reserved for his realization of Fulvia's death. It is Cleopatra who checks his overstatement, questions the sincerity of his hyperbole ("Excellent falsehood"; "Hear the ambassadors"). Mocking him, she is still besotted with him; no less than Antony is she manipulable by her love. Both Antony and Cleopatra suffer from self-surpassing rages, she at the messenger, he at her apparent and real betrayals of him; hyperbole operates there in both language and gesture. By the third act, something has begun to happen which demonstrates the identity of the lovers: the hyperbolical style with which Antony began the play now issues from Cleopatra's mouth:

> Ah, dear, if I be so,
> From my cold heart let heaven engender hail,
> And poison it in the source, and the first stone
> Drop in my neck: as it determines, so
> Dissolve my life; the next Caesarion smite
> Till by degrees the memory of my womb,

Together with my brave Egyptians all,
By the discandying of this pelleted storm,
Lie graveless, till the flies and gnats of Nile
Have buried them for prey!

(III.xiii.158-67)

It is Antony now who says, "I am satisfied," evidently needing that assurance to go on with the "chronicle" of which he feels himself to be a part. Early in the play, Antony and Cleopatra are separately hyperbolical; as their unity grows, they adapt to each other's modes of speech. These lovers are in many ways temperamentally alike, and they become more so as their meaning for each other becomes more conscious and more motivating in their lives. In the third act, as they pitch their lives together once more, their most hyperbolical speeches of love are signs of their deepening unity with one another, the more poignant for their violent and frequent misunderstandings.

To speak as they do, so grandly, so magnificently, so frankly in hyperbole, is in Antony's and Cleopatra's nature. They are true to one aspect of the Attic (or "Senecan") prescription, after all, in that they express "themselves" truly in their language—this is to say, then, that their style *must* in honesty be bombastic, which according to Attic prescription should mean that their style matches the variability and shoddiness of their characters, discovers beneath their bluster and shouting mere fustian cheapness, secondhand emotions, and sleazy intentions. Longinus was fully aware of how close the elevated style was to bombast: it is almost as if Shakespeare set himself to examine Longinus' problem fully in this play, to test out against human actions and human speech the human aspiration for sublimity.

Antony's habits of speech reach toward and respond to the fundamental grandeur of his nature, as his actions increasingly confirm the propriety and integrity of his grand style. That Enobarbus adopts the hyperbolical mode—that Plutarch adopts it, indeed—to render Cleopatra's magnificence, tells us much about the "real" application of an inflated and hyperbolical style. In Enobarbus' mouth we are invited to recognize things as they are: Enobarbus knows *ping* from *pong,* Rome from Egypt. For better and for worse, Enobarbus is a Roman, speaks as a Roman, acts as a Roman. Yet to this man is given the great speech about Cleopatra, its figures stretching farther and farther as the speech goes on and as he realizes the difficulties involved in making anyone who has not experienced her charm understand what this woman is. Like his master, vacillating between Rome and Egypt in his own life, Enobarbus seems to opt for Rome against Egypt. At his end he chooses neither place, but rather chooses a man, a human being involved with both symbolic places and, for him, transcending both. From his relation to Mark Antony, Enobarbus took his final definition, to die with his betrayed master's name on his lips. By the pull of hyperbole, of overstatement, of inflation, and of magnanimity on such a man, we can measure the power of Antony for Cleopatra—and, just because of his greatness, can measure her power

for him. The two lovers confirm each other and themselves—so much we might expect. Enobarbus, with his excursions beyond his habitual style and behavior, not wanting to do so, nonetheless confirms them from outside themselves.

In his set-speech on Cleopatra, Enobarbus had called upon a natural miracle to attest to her power:

Antony
Enthron'd i' the market-place, did sit alone,
Whistling to the air; which, but for vacancy,
Had gone to gaze on Cleopatra too,
And made a gap in nature.

(II.ii.214-18)

Even in figure, though, this miracle cannot take place: there is no gap in nature, nor in this play, however crowded things are by the space Antony and Cleopatra take up, by the bruit of their presence, the bustle of their companionship. To stretch the metaphor, the play's dominant style is not one of vanity, although there are vanities enough blatantly set forth in the protagonists' characters. They are self-centered and self-indulgent—but they are not self-satisfied. They look to each other forever for more; they criticize each other and themselves. In their lives, however lived out in the Asiatic style, in dissoluteness, inflation, swelling, enervation, slackness, effeminacy, and idleness, these two do *not* decay. Their satisfactions breed hunger; their desire neither stales nor cloys, not even at the moments in which they die. Finally, their desire can be seen to be a particular kind of love, a kind of love rarely made romantic, firmly based in shared sexual experience. Out of such love, each can think only of the other at the time of death.

Even when they are idle, Antony and Cleopatra make a stir in the world. This is perhaps part of the tragedy (though not in Renaissance terms): that public figures cannot afford private joys.[41] In the modern jargon, there is no solution to their problems either of aspiring temperament or of historical situation. They could not do without each other and, their world being what it was, they could not live comfortably with each other. But imagine alternative solutions: suppose Antony *had* gone back to live in Rome with Octavia and their daughters (present in Plutarch but excised from the play); the political struggle with Caesar could hardly have failed to come to a head, for Caesar, if not Antony, had to find opportunity for quarrel. Suppose Cleopatra had gone back to her philanderings with eastern potentates and Roman ambassadors: could she have restrained herself from political troublemaking, out of boredom if nothing else? Or, turning the matter about still more, how could Antony have lived among Romans whose view of Cleopatra was as extreme as his own, though at quite the other end of the scale? Could he have endured the silliness of Lepidus, the calculations of Octavius, the prurience of Menas and the rest, their eagerness to vulgarize personal experiences beyond their capacities to imagine? Character has something to do with "fate"—the struggle with Caesar would have come in the end, without the satisfaction for Antony of having chosen for Cleopatra, without the heroics at his death which, self-deceiving or not, eased him into Elysium with the conviction that his life had been worth its trouble and pain, and that his final disgrace was canceled by his grandiose final gestures of love.

This is a curious play, resting on an ambivalent concept of love impossible to sum up, to categorize, or to define. We learn throughout that desire can remain insatiable, that vacillation breeds corruption, that rewards in one sphere exact penalties in another. Cleopatra's fans heated where they cooled, what they undid, did. So Cleopatra: she undid Antony, but also she made of him not so much what she wanted him to be—indeed, in that she failed—as what *he* wanted to be. Certainly one cannot draw as a general conclusion from this play that an intense connection between a man and a woman justifies all else, justifies all the neglect, the idleness, the betrayals, the prodigality of lives and honor. Shakespeare shows us, unmistakably, that it does not, by the play's eternal balancing of one thing against another, its long vacillation between the bombastic and the sublime, its constant qualification of virtue by fault, of vice by virtue. But on balance, it is obvious that those experiences, from whatever source, which can elevate human beings are judged more favorably than those which do not; that those human beings who can be elevated are nobler than those whose nature is too small to permit such enlargement. With all its qualifications and all its defects admitted, proclaimed, displayed, the love of Antony and Cleopatra is nonetheless affirmed, the strumpet and the strumpet's fool grow into the imaginative warrior and the theatrical queen. There is no denying their excesses, which are examined, studied, and reassessed both by the speakers within the play and by the audience watching the excesses demonstrated onstage. We learn that in such excess, life itself can reside. Though it threatens to rot, and seems at times to have corrupted the lovers, their style of living affirms their life—and that despite the deaths of the proceedings.

Indeed, in the deaths we see the value of the lives. Antony says that he dies as a Roman, but he bungled his death all the same, both by letting Eros die before him, and by not killing himself outright. However significant the "elevation" of Antony into Cleopatra's tomb, it is an awkward business;[42] the queen's failure to open the tomb lays stress, just at the worst moment, on the weakest side of her nature. Antony's dying skirts bombast the while, and we may assume that his failure to die efficiently in the Roman style is one mark Egypt laid upon him.

His beauty of character, though, emerges clearly through this uncomfortable death-scene: in spite of the cluminess, what we remember is Antony's magnanimity and Cleopatra's high poetry. Antony affirms in his manner of dying both the Roman and the eastern sides of his nature; Cleopatra too comes to accept Roman ways, even to embrace them in her own death. Her contemptuous fear of "Roman thoughts" in the first act gives way before her desire to emulate Antony and to die, like him, "in the high Roman fashion." Her suicide, though, cannot be said to be pure Roman: she had done research into painless ways to die; she chose the Nile worm as a suitable weapon; she arranged the spectacle of her death with a care and love inappropriate to Roman suicide. In both suicides, a Roman pattern has been expanded and enriched by Egyptian opulence and Egyptian decoration, not least in the ornate style in which both Antony and Cleopatra take leave of their world. The actual world has shrunk away from them; in expectation of Elysium in each other's company, they affirm the larger world of their fantastic and extravagant imagination, which their love had brought into being. The play's language affirms that determination to enlarge life: even at the end, Cleopatra speaks as woman, lover, and mother. After all, it is only by Roman tongues that the hero and heroine are spoken of as mere voluptuaries, softened and weakened by self-indulgence and excess. Antony's and Cleopatra's speech is consistently vigorous, various, copious, vivid, liveliest in those remarkable passages where excessive behavior, excessive sensation, excessive emotions are given their due.

Even though it threatens to do so, this hyperbolical play does not get out of hand: its images are as closely controlled as those of the other late tragedies. Further, the richness and decoration of the language, in passages of passionate disgust as in passages of grandiloquent elevation, match the richness of temperament which confers upon their characters the privilege of an equal elevation. What at first sounds like bombast in Antony's speech is naturalized in the course of the play, until his way of speaking becomes a standard against which other men are judged. Of effeminacy, slackness, or idleness, Antony's behavior may sometimes be accused—but never his language, nor Cleopatra's. From first to last what emerges is its affirmation of activity, of creativity, of unending and unendingly interesting emotional process. Till their very last breaths, these persons change and develop, to involve the audience in that development toward greatness. During the course of the play, then, Antony and Cleopatra grow into their rhetorical measure. At the play's start, Philo had called a spade a spade, or even a shovel; in contrast, Antony and Cleopatra spoke in love's arrogant, idealized overstatements. By the end of the play, Philo's linguistic practice is blocked out by Antony's hyperbole coming true, until we too believe that "the nobleness of life" is for such lovers to embrace. Until the very end, we are never quite sure of Cleopatra, such is the oscillation of the play and the woman between extremes, from rejection to reunion, from reviling to reaffirmation, from lie to truth, from denigration to encomium.

By their manner of dying, these figures are known: the Roman world, with all its real space, could not house the love of Antony for Cleopatra. That Antony lost his place in the real world, lost that world altogether, is made to seem unimportant beside the imaginative satisfactions of his emotional life. What Antony and Cleopatra do and say represents them: for all their own vacillation and oscillation, they turn out to be true in their ultimate commitment to each other. Antony dies with energy and (oddly enough) enthusiasm; Cleopatra looks to her last moment and beyond it, both on earth and in Elysium—she remains alive, feeling, imagining, to her last breath. Both catch and express their visions of the new heaven, new earth, seen always in terms of each other and of being with each other. They die as they had lived, beyond definition, in expectation of more. It is the strength, the vividness, the vigor of excess which this play presents, examines, criticizes, and ultimately, with full understanding, confirms, in a language of hyperbole built to match the size and scope of the subject. In the *ping* and *pong* of plain and grandiloquent styles, now one seeming to lead and now the other, Shakespeare manages to show us the problem and the problematics, in moral as in literary terms, at the heart of style. By sinking the notions associated with the Asiatic style back into life itself, in the play's dramatic action he can examine and assess both the style and the style of life in terms of each other, and to see them as one. He can demonstrate, then, by the peculiarly literary device of a stylistic *agon,* the moral problematics of dimension, can manage to make acceptable—more, to make admirable and comprehensible—the values of an honestly ostentatious style.

Notes

1. See E. H. Gombrich, *Art and Illusion* [New York, 1960], pp. 370, 381.

2. My chapter owes much to earlier studies of the play, especially to Maurice Charney's *Shakespeare's Roman Plays* [Cambridge, 1961], chapters 1 and 4. My hypothesis states, more overtly and probably more pedantically than Charney's, that Shakespeare deliberately animated a stylistic paradigm in this play, a paradigm polemically discussed in his lifetime and of which he was aware, in order to re-examine interchangeable relations of verbal style to style in living and (far more important) to cultural style. See also Benjamin T. Spencer, "*Antony and Cleopatra* and the Paradoxical Metaphor," [*Shakespeare Quarterly*], IX (1958), 373-78; [Matthew N.] Proser, *The Heroic Image in Five Shakespearean Plays* [Princeton, 1965]; Madeleine Doran, *The Endeavors of Art* (Madison, 1954), pp. 245-50; and [Sigurd] Burckhardt, *Shakespearean Meanings* [Princeton, 1968].

3. See chapter 1. . . .

4. Sheldon P. Zitner, "*King Lear* and its Language" [in *Some Facets of King Lear: Essays in Prismatic Criticism,* edited by Rosalie Colie and F. T. Flahiff. Toronto: University of Toronto Press, 1974.]; "Shakespeare's Secret Language" (unpublished paper).

5. See, in particular, Charney, chapter 5; and James L. Calderwood, "*Coriolanus*: Wordless Meanings and Meaningless Words," [*Studies in English Literature, 1500-1900,*] VI (1966), 211-24.

6. For the theory behind this concept of "matching," see Gombrich, *Art and Illusion,* pp. 29, 73, 116-18, 188-89.

7. Plutarch, *The Lives of the Noble Grecians and Romanes,* tr. Thomas North (London, 1595), p. 969.

8. M. von Wilamowitz-Möllendorf, "Asianismus und Atticismus," *Hermes,* XXXV (1900), 1-52; Eduard Norden, *Die antike Kunstprosa* (Leipzig, 1915-1918); G. L. Hendrickson, "The Original Meaning of the Ancient Characters of Style," *American Journal of Philology,* XXVI (1905), 248-90; C. N. Smiley, "Seneca and the Stoic Theory of Literary Style," *Wisconsin Studies in Language and Literature,* III (1919), 50-61; A. D. Leeman, *Orationis Ratio: the Stylistic Theories and Practice of the Orators, Historians, and Philosophers* (Amsterdam, 1963); F. Quadlbauer, *Die antike Theorie der genera dicendi* (Vienna, 1958).

9. Cicero himself exemplifies this process: see *Tusc. Disp.,* II, i; *Brutus,* xiii, 51; lxxxii, 284-lxxiv, 291; *Orator,* viii, 27-31; xxiii, 76-xxvi, 90.

10. Morris W. Croll, in essays now conveniently collected in *Style, Rhetoric, and Rhythm* (Princeton, 1966); see also George Williamson, *The Senecan Amble* (Chicago, 1951); Brian Vickers, *Francis Bacon and Renaissance Prose* (Cambridge, 1968); and E. R. Curtius, *European Literature and the Latin Middle Ages* [New York, 1953] pp. 67-68.

11. Gombrich's ping-pong paradigm perforce alters the moral intention of Winters' division of poetic styles into plain and ornate.

12. Charney, pp. 79ff.

13. Charney, *Roman Plays,* pp. 93ff; and see John Danby, "The Shakespearean Dialectic: An aspect of *Antony and Cleopatra,*" in *Poets on Fortune's Hill* (London, 1952); William Rosen, *Shakespeare and the Craft of Tragedy* (Cambridge, Mass., 1960); Robert Ornstein, "The Ethic [*sic*] of Imagination: Love and Art in *Antony and Cleopatra,*" *The Later Shakespeare, Stratford-upon-Avon Studies,* VIII (1966); Maynard Mack, Introduction to *Antony and Cleopatra* (Pelican Shakespeare, Baltimore, 1960), p. 19.

14. "Oscillate" is Danby's word; see also Northrop Frye, *Fools of Time* (Toronto, 1967), pp. 70-71; Mack, Introduction, pp. 19-20; Ernest Schanzer, *The Problem Plays of Shakespeare* (New York, 1965), pp. 138-39; Charney, pp. 93ff.; Dipak Nandy, "The Realism of *Antony and Cleopatra,*" in *Shakespeare in a Changing World,* ed. Arnold Kettle (London, 1964), pp. 172-94.

15. Leeman, pp. 140-41.

16. The point is made by many critics; see Julia Markels, *The Pillar of the World* (Columbus, 1968), pp. 35, 41-43.

17. See, e.g., J. Leeds Barroll, "Enobarbus' Description of Cleopatra," *Texas Studies in Language and Literature* (1958), pp. 61-68.

18. I do not here speak of Antony's self-deception, of which Proser and Markels write so well, so much as of the *cultural* force of his language, with its sources in Roman ideas of magnanimity and greatness as well as in Roman ideas of duty and service. There is, also, a major literary source for Antony's speech and self-presentation, in the *Aeneid*—though Antony, as his references to Aeneas and Dido indicate, did not choose (like Aeneas) to subdue his passions to his mission: Antony is, in this sense, a reviser of the story. For this, as for much else, I am indebted to discussions with Roger Hornsby.

19. See Arnold Stein, "The Image of Antony: Lyric and Tragic Imagination," reprinted in *Essays in Shakespearean Criticism,* ed. James L. Calderwood and Harold E. Toliver (Englewood Cliffs, 1970), pp. 560-75.

20. Barroll, *passim*; Schanzer, p. 155. This notion is qualified in the work of Barbara Bono (still unpublished) and of Raymond Waddington: see below, footnote 34.

21. Again, most critics comment on this: see Markels, pp. 35, 41-43; Ornstein, p. 393, for especially interesting comments.

22. On world-imagery, see Charney, pp. 82-93, an extremely perceptive analysis.

23. See Stein, *passim*; though their language relies on expression conventionally assigned to lovers, Antony's and Cleopatra's speech, with its curiously generalized, unspecified imagery, suggests an enlarged range of love. Theirs is, in language as in life, an *extreme* love, fully human but at the edge of human capacity.

24. Charney, pp. 102-104.

25. G. Wilson Knight, *The Imperial Theme* (repr. London, 1965), pp. 212, 213, collects the imagery of horses in this play, and comments on the different associations it calls up.

26. Charney, pp. 127-29.

27. For this, see Markels, especially p. 150.

28. This in spite of the fact that she is "all air and fire": the elements, earth, water, air, and fire, are all used in connection with Cleopatra, a world in herself.

29. Ornstein, p. 391.

30. One way in which Caesar is made to seem young, inexperienced, and closed to human experience is that he is completely unaware of this aspect of either Antony or Cleopatra.

31. Again, Mr. Markels seems to me the critic who preeminently expresses both the universally human and the particular, specific experience of love depicted in this play.

32. Another "philosophical" suggestion of Antony's being more than a man lies in the implications of this simile, in which a creature "transcends" its element: so he, a man, becomes (at least in Cleopatra's imagination) a god. See also Ruth Nevo, "The Masque of Greatness," [*Shakespeare Studies*], III (1967), 111-28, for the "gigantism" of the play, and the "cosmic contrived into a pageant."

33. Longinus, *On the Sublime* (LCL), pp. 144-45.

34. I have been greatly helped in the matter of the mythographic element of this play by the published work of Raymond B. Waddington, "Antony and Cleopatra: 'What Venus Did with Mars,'" [*Shakespeare Studies*], II (1966); and of Harold Fisch, "*Antony and Cleopatra*: the Limits of Mythology," [*Shakespeare Survey*], XXIII (1970), 59-68 (whose argument seems to me too fine-spun, particularly in his reliance on Christian myth); and by the unpublished work of Barbara Bono, which reaches very subtle and illuminating conclusions about the play. See also Adrien Bonjour, "From Shakespeare's Venus to Cleopatra's Cupids," [*Shakespeare Studies*], XVI (1963), 73-80.

35. Plutarch, *Isis and Osiris, Moralia,* V; see Michael Lloyd, "Cleopatra as Isis," [*Shakespeare Studies*], XII (1959).

36. Eugene M. Waith, Jr., *The Herculean Hero in Marlowe, Chapman, Shakespeare, and Dryden* (New York, 1962), discusses this aspect of Antony's character and behavior; see also Plutarch, *Lives,* p. 913, for Antony's self-comparison to Hercules, and p. 921 for Cleopatra as Venus. It is important to note that Shakespeare excises from his play Plutarch's many references to Antony as Bacchus; mention of Bacchus, in the Roman orgy, is made in specifically Roman associations. See J. Leeds Barroll, "Shakespeare and the Art of Character," [*Shakespeare Studies*], III (1967), 159-235.

37. Cf. Markels, and Barbara Bono's unpublished work.

38. Waith, p. 113; Schanzer, p. 158.

39. On this point, see Terence Eagleton, *Shakespeare and Society* (New York, 1967), p. 127.

40. Charney, pp. 18-19; 137-40; Danby, p. 131.

41. See Markels, chapter 2.

42. Charney, pp. 134-36, is valuable on Antony's "elevation."

Donald C. Freeman (essay date 1999)

SOURCE: Freeman, Donald C. "'The rack dislimns': Schema and Metaphorical Pattern in *Antony and Cleopatra.*" *Poetics Today* 20, no. 3 (fall 1999): 443-60.

[*In the following essay, Freeman uses the theory of cognitive metaphor to evaluate the figurative language found in* Antony and Cleopatra.]

Any approach to metaphor hoping to enhance centuries of scholarship on Shakespeare's dramatic language faces an onerous burden of proof, the more so when the play under discussion is *Antony and Cleopatra*. The play's lushness of figurative language has attracted hosts of both New Critics and traditional philologists. Many have commented on the play's vast compass—one made possible in large part by the cosmic imagery that Shakespeare so frequently employs.

The great German Shakespearean Wolfgang Clemen (1962 [1951]: 160), for example, remarked more than sixty years ago that *Antony and Cleopatra* summons "to our minds again and again the image of the wide ocean and of the immeasurably vast world." At about the same time, Caroline Spurgeon (1935: 352) pointed out how the play "fills the imagination with the conception of beings so great that physical size is annihilated and the whole habitable globe shrinks in comparison with them."

This commentary anticipated much of what has followed. Many of Clemen's and Spurgeon's successors have remarked on the relationship of *Antony and Cleopatra*'s imagery to its grand physical, political, and spiritual landscapes, but only in the most general terms. Seeking to refocus our attention from the play's "verbal figure" to what he called "dramatic metaphor," Maurice Charney (1961: 7) fails to specify what aspect of the play's figuration is thus constitutive of its form. T. A. McAlindon (1973: 187) describes the play's language as a "grandiose blend of mythology and hyperbole," without explaining the components or consequences of that blend. G. Wilson Knight (1951: 289) notices *Antony and Cleopatra*'s "massively spatialized technique" without the kind of detailed analysis that would show how the play's nonspatial entities come to be perceived in spatial terms.

Although readings of this sort can be incomplete or imprecise, I find them in many respects intuitively satisfying. In what follows, I start from these intuitions, seeking to articulate and ground them in a theory of metaphor that depends on a theory of mind. I shall argue that the cognitive approach to metaphor[1] provides analyses of figurative language that are sufficiently detailed and coherent so that the interpretations they yield can be assessed against competing interpretations. Further, I claim, motivated cognitive analyses of one skein of a literary artwork's figurative language generalize perspicuously to analyses of other figurative patterns in the same artwork or in other works by the same poet. Finally, following the argument sketched out in D. Freeman 1995, I will seek to demonstrate that the notion of metaphorical projection as a property of mind logically prior to properties of language enables the critic of poetic language to characterize within the cognitive framework not only figurative patterns in literary language, but analogous figurative patterns in other elements of the artwork as well.

This interrelatedness of metaphorical patterning in *Antony and Cleopatra* emerges when we examine the processes of metaphorical projection that constitute the play's figurative language. We begin with an account of the cognitive templates, the image and conceptual schemas constituting the source domains from which we metaphorically project elements and structure into abstract target domains, the entities that are metaphorized.

For *Antony and Cleopatra,* the key image schemas are, I shall argue, those of CONTAINER, LINKS, and PATH, which fuse variously with one another (for discussion of these schemas, see Johnson 1987: 113-27). Thus Antony's courage and passion, and later his grief, as we shall see, are figured in terms of liquids swelling within the CONTAINER of his body; the LINK schema appears as marriage bonds and ties of loyalty; the PATH schema emerges as Antony describes how at the Battle of Actium he turned his ship to follow the fleeing Cleopatra instead of pressing the attack. And in what I regard as the play's climactic speech, as Antony reads in the changing clouds his utter dissolution, the CONTAINER schema fuses with the key metaphorical projection KNOWING IS SEEING (for a detailed discussion, see Sweetser 1990: 37-40) to inscribe that dissolution in a metaphorical density and richness adumbrated at the play's very start and sustained until its final lines. We understand Antony as a grand failure because the container of his Romanness "dislimns": it can no longer outline and define him even to himself. Conversely, we understand Cleopatra at her death as the transcendent queen of "immortal longings" because the container of her mortality can no longer restrain her: unlike Antony, she never melts, but sublimates from her very earthly flesh to ethereal fire and air.

The audience first hears of Antony through an all-too-accurate report from his lieutenant Philo, in a speech dominated by metaphors projected from the CONTAINER schema:[2]

> Nay, but this dotage of our general's
> O'erflows the measure . . .
>   His captain's heart,
> Which in the scuffles of great fights hath burst
> The buckles on his breast, reneges all temper
> And is become the bellows and the fan
> To cool a gypsy's lust.
>
>   (1.1.1-2, 6-10)

The scant tolerance that the hard-edged Roman military code allots to a general's dalliance is metaphorized as a container, a measuring cup that cannot hold the liquid of Antony's grand passion;[3] but before Cleopatra distracted him, as Philo recalls, Antony's heart had been a container with such enormous capacity for the liquid of courage that it burst the containing fetters of his armor.

Later we are to see Antony's heart-container swell again, but it does so because it "o'erflows the measure" of grief at Cleopatra's reported death. Antony would have his heart "crack" not the armor that contains his martial courage, but the very body that contains that heart:

O, cleave, my sides!
Heart, once be stronger than thy continent;
Crack thy frail case!

(4.14.40-42)

At Antony's death, Cleopatra understands his body in identical terms: "This case of that huge spirit now is cold" (4.15.9).

This proliferation of metaphors projected from the CON-TAINER schema, and their function as containers of the liquids of passionate love, martial courage, and grief, are significant. For, as we will see, what critics have characterized as the play's shifting perspective on Antony and Cleopatra is accomplished by a similar three-stage progression in its central metaphors: from those in which the robust and solid outline of Rome, political authority, and all that they contain melt into the liquid of those passions; to those in which the liquid of those passions evaporates into ever changing cloud shapes; and finally to the death vision of Cleopatra's "marble-constant" body-container sublimating directly into her nobler elements of "fire and air."

But even Cleopatra's ethereal final state fails to reduce the ambiguity of "their story," as Octavius Caesar terms it in tidying up the play's last scene. *Antony and Cleopatra* is, from its first to its forty-second and final scene, a play that paradoxically is also dominated by the physical action of seeing and its subtextual metaphor KNOWING IS SEEING— and about the unreliability of both. These concerns are most closely brought together in Antony's speech to the bemused Eros near the end of act 4 about the evanescence of shapes we see in clouds, and hence of our perception and knowledge generally. Ironically, at the same time that Antony mediates upon the contingent nature of vision, he is under the impression that Cleopatra has betrayed him with Caesar, and shortly will fatally wound himself because of his "knowledge" that Cleopatra has committed suicide.

The CONTAINER schema dominates the metaphors of *Antony and Cleopatra* from the very start. Cleopatra announces teasingly to Antony that she will "set a bourn how far to be beloved" (1.1.16); Antony, for his part, immediately seeks to transcend that boundary within which Cleopatra has contained their love, in explicitly biblical language (as Wilders [1995: 92n] observes): "Then must thou needs find out new heaven, new earth." Given the many cases in which love is metaphorized as a liquid, it follows naturally that a play so concerned with passion should be dominated by containers. For Antony, the container of the Rome-world is confining, limiting, a "measure," while the container of the Egypt-world is liberating, a capacious domain in which he can explore "new heaven, new earth." The contrast between the two is epitomized in one of the play's most famous speeches:

Let Rome in Tiber melt, and the wide arch
Of the ranged empire fall! Here is my space!
Kingdoms are clay!

(1.1.34-36)

The traditional view of this passage as dominated by an image of "melting"[4] is only a beginning. In the play and to Antony, Rome represents the sharply defined "measure" that conspicuously fails to contain the liquid of what to Philo is Antony's "dotage," and to Antony is his grand passion. For Rome to "melt" is for it to lose its defining shape, the boundary that contains the civic and military codes that it stands for, perhaps reified for Shakespeare's audience in the symmetrically arched aqueducts and ruler-straight roads that the Roman Empire extended even to the distant province of Britain. Once it melts into a liquid, Rome cannot be "marble-constant"; once it has become part of the Tiber, Rome and what it represents are consubstantial with the heated and fructifying liquid that produces "my serpent of old Nile," as "indistinct [from Egypt] / As water is in water" (4.14.10-11).

Antony relies on the same projection from the CONTAINER schema into his Roman and military characteristics when Cleopatra's servants are slow to respond to his summons:

Authority melts from me. Of late, when I cried "Ho,"
Like boys unto a muss, kings would start forth
And cry "Your will?" Have you no ears? I am
Antony yet.

(3.13.95-98)

Along with the sharply outlined periphery of his Roman authority has melted, for Antony, the crystal-clear hierarchy, social order, and values of Roman "measure." These do not play well in "my space" of Alexandria, where he has just seen (or thinks he has seen) Cleopatra being courted by Thidias, the messenger of his enemy.

After his defeat at Actium, Antony realizes in the same projection his own military, political, and moral collapse. What has "melted from" him has melted upon Octavius:

The hearts
That spanieled me at heels, to whom I gave
Their wishes, do discandy, melt their sweets
On blossoming Caesar, and this pine is barked
That overtopped them all.

(4.12.20-24)

The solid form of Antony's soldiers and their Roman courage and Roman loyalty are represented metonymically as "hearts," as was Antony's courage at the beginning of the play. These hearts and the Roman qualities they represent now "discandy," lose their outward shape and internal crystalline structure, the periphery that makes the many soldiers into one body, and the regular and articulated internal relations that give them structure as a disciplined military unit.[5] The liquid thus created cascades upon and thickens the protecting military shell of the solid Roman Caesar. The immediately following metaphor invokes the generic schema GOOD IS UP, as Antony describes himself as "this pine . . . that overtopped them all." But instead of metaphorizing Antony's loss of that status in the traditional terms of the pine's being cut down or lopped off at the top, Shakespeare describes it as the loss of the tree's bark, its containing and protecting boundary.[6]

Antony's habit of understanding a containing shape as his status, his standing in the world, extends as well to his own life when, having been (falsely) informed by her eunuch Mardian that Cleopatra is dead, he intones to his loyal retainer:

> Unarm, Eros. The long day's task is done
> And we must sleep . . .
>   Off! pluck off!
> The sevenfold shield of Ajax cannot keep
> The battery from my heart . . .
>   . . . since the torch is out,
> Lie down, and stray no farther. Now all labour
> Mars what it does—yea, very force entangles
> Itself with strength.

(4.14.35-36, 38-40, 47-50)

In "unarming," Antony removes his last containing shape, a once-defining suit of armor that becomes only a pile of "bruised pieces" (4.14.43), as have his Romanness, his identity as a military leader ("You [bruised pieces] have been nobly borne"), and now his very being as Cleopatra's lover. Immediately following this projection is, again, a crucial conceptual metaphor, LIFE IS A DAY, in which the events of his military loss at Actium and his amatory loss of Cleopatra are reified as the action of suicide, ending the day of his life;[7] later in the speech, the reading of "unarming" as suicide is further reinforced by the generic metaphor LIFE IS LIGHT, as Antony's torch is out, and he is contained, "entangled," fettered by the very martial force that is his way of life and that the "bruised pieces" of his now-discarded armor have represented.

Cleopatra uses metaphors of melting and discontainment altogether differently. Until the very end of the play, they are for her solely instruments of hyperbole (on this point see Doran 1976: 154-81)—indeed, one might argue that they ironically reduce Antony's cosmic metaphoric flights. Cleopatra flies into a rage when a messenger tells her of Antony's politically motivated marriage to Octavia: "Melt Egypt into Nile, and kindly creatures / Turn all to serpents!" (2.5.77-78). But, although she echoes Antony's use of the same metaphor, Cleopatra is not calling herself to another world. Nor, having given the messenger gold for what she thinks is good news about Antony, does Cleopatra propose to destroy the measure of value that gold represents when, after reinterpreting the message, she screeches, "The gold I give thee will I melt and pour / Down thy ill-uttering throat" (2.5.34-35). The Roman gossip about Antony's "levity" and her frivolous efforts (by Roman standards) at making war not love infuriate her ("Sink, Rome, and their tongues rot / That speak against us!" [3.7.15-16]), but she is merely expressing frustration and resentment, not calling for the dissolution of an entire culture.

Her response to Antony's death, however, is quite different:

> The crown o'th' earth doth melt. My lord!
> O, withered is the garland of the war,
> The soldier's pole is fallen . . .

(4.15.65-67)

Cleopatra understands her lover's death not just as the dissolution of a way of life, as Antony understands Rome, but as the entire world losing its containing periphery, represented in the crown that loses its defining shape. With that periphery is lost all human social organization, metonymized in the garland that becomes, in turn, a metonym for the military triumphs of Antony's "melt[ed]" career. Antony's toppled war standard, detumescent for all time,[8] can no longer stand as a rallying point for Antony's troops.

In the play's many metaphors of melting, the foregrounded feature of the CONTAINER schema is its role as a giver of shape, a definer of periphery, rather than the traditional distinction (see Lakoff and Johnson 1999: 380-82) between inside and outside that this schema's projections so frequently emphasize. This confining, structuring aspect also is foregrounded in the many instances of metaphors projected from the LINKS schema in *Antony and Cleopatra,* where the links are, chiefly, not those of service or love, as they are, for example, in *King Lear* (see D. Freeman 1993). Instead, the dominant feature of the LINKS projections in *Antony and Cleopatra* is that of imprisonment, constraint of movement—for example, where the linked elements are, as one might expect, Antony and Cleopatra, and the linking medium is enchantment: "These strong Egyptian fetters I must break, / or lose myself in dotage" (1.2.121-22; notice that Antony describes himself as did Philo in the play's opening line); "I must from this enchanting queen break off" (1.2.135).

Marriages also are understood in *Antony and Cleopatra* as imprisoning, limiting bonds, not the enriching links of kinship, service, or reciprocal love. Cleopatra characterizes Antony's marriage to Fulvia as

> Riotous madness,
> To be entangled with those mouth-made vows
> Which break themselves in swearing!

(1.3.30-32)

The linking medium between Antony and Fulvia consists, in Cleopatra's view, of vows made only with the mouth, not the spirit, which entangle rather than fruitfully join their makers, and are fragile in the extreme—as opposed to the "fetters" that join her to Antony—and more like the self-defeating force that "entangles / Itself with strength."

Antony's marriage to Octavia is described several times as a bond or a knot, but, except for a remark by Cleopatra's messenger ("He's bound unto Octavia," 2.5.58), the linked entities in this marriage bond are not Antony and Octavia as husband and wife, as the conventional projection would have us understand them, but Antony and Caesar as shaky political allies. Agrippa suggests this *mariage de convenance*:

To hold you in perpetual amity,
To make you brothers, and to knit your hearts
With an unslipping knot, take Antony
Octavia to his wife . . .

(2.2.132-35)

And as Caesar sees off Octavia for her marriage to Antony, he likewise understands the marriage not as a link
between the couple, but between himself and Antony, with
his sister as the bonding medium that sustains their
relationship for now, but that in time can become the
means of destroying it. The bonding medium, Octavia, can
become an instrument that invades the container of the
very relationship it is supposed to strengthen:

Most noble Antony,
Let not the piece of virtue [Octavia] which is set
Betwixt us, as the cement of our love
To keep it builded, be the ram to batter
The fortress of it.

(3.2.27-31)

For Cleopatra, the foregrounded aspect of the LINKS schema
is less that of imprisonment than that of entrapment. She
sees Antony as a fish that she will bond to herself with the
trap of a hook and line:

My bended hook shall pierce
Their slimy jaws, and, as I draw them up,
I'll think them every one an Antony,
And say, "Ah, ha! You're caught!"

(2.5.12-15)

The linked entities are Cleopatra as angler and Antony as
fish; the linking medium is the fishing line with its barbed
hook; Cleopatra is thus the enactor of a strategy, with Antony as the dumb object. She employs the same metaphor
(if a different mechanism) in describing the relationship
among Antony, Egypt, and the world (importantly, the
outside world), when she greets him upon his temporarily
successful return from the land phase of the battle of Actium:

Lord of lords!
O infinite virtue! Com'st thou smiling from
The world's great snare uncaught?

(4.8.16-18)

Here the entrapment metaphor merges the LINKS and CON-
TAINER schemata. Antony and the world are the linked elements, and the putative linking element is the "world's
great snare." That link, which would have drawn Antony
into the container of the world's trap, fails, however,
because the link between him and Cleopatra is stronger,
and its bonding medium is metaphorized in the path he
must follow to return from the outside world to Egypt.
Antony here is not a mindless fish, but a wily animal who
escapes the world's trap; the ironic subtext is that he
escapes that trap only because he is linked by the medium
of his return journey to an ultimately much more confining
one.

Cleopatra understands even life itself in terms of the LINK
schema rather than the conventional LIFE IS A DAY or LIFE
IS LIGHT metaphors that Antony employs:

Come, thou mortal wretch,
With thy sharp teeth this knot intrinsicate
Of life at once untie.

(5.2.302-4)

The "knot intrinsicate" is in the linking medium—one
might almost say that it creates that medium. The knot ties
together two ropes or bands, creating a single bond linking
the entities of Cleopatra and life. We might also see the
knot as Cleopatra's body-container binding her life, or
spirit, within itself ("As sweet as balm, as soft as air"
[5.2.311]). That container's periphery will be penetrated
from without by the asp's bite: "Dost thou not see my
baby at my breast / That sucks the nurse asleep?" (5.2.307-
8). The power of this image derives from the fact that
Shakespeare reverses every element of the folk conception
of infant nursing.[9] In that conception the nurse or mother
inserts part of her body, the nipple of her breast, into the
mouth of the baby. Here the asp puts part of its body, the
fangs located in its mouth, into Cleopatra's breast.
Mother's milk proceeds from mother to child, giving life;
the asp's venom proceeds from it to Cleopatra, giving
death. The impelling force of mother's milk is the baby's
suction from within the mother to within itself; the impelling force of the asp's venom is its own injection from
within itself to within its victim.

The association of Cleopatra with containing traps
continues until the very end of the play, where Caesar,
gazing upon her corpse, sees her "As she would catch
another Antony / In her strong toil of grace" (5.2.346-47),
the containing trap of her allure that already has proven
superior to the "world's great snare" and at the same time
is one of the linking elements constituting the "strong
Egyptian fetters" with which she binds herself to Antony.

A third aspect of confinement or compulsion in a cognitive-
metaphoric analysis of *Antony and Cleopatra* appears in
the play's many metaphors of towing. This source domain
involves chiefly the LINKS schema, but also has elements of
the PATH and CONTAINER schemata, particularly with the
strong overtones of binding and controlling that dominate
its appearance in this play. To be towed or led is to proceed
along the path of the towing force while being linked to
the exerter of that force. That path is both determined and
contained by that towing force's direction and speed.

These towing metaphors are densest after Antony's defeat
at Actium, but they are well prepared for. As Lepidus,
Caesar, and Antony celebrate their short-lived agreement
aboard Pompey's galley, Pompey curiously picks up and
metaphorically extends Menas's offer ("Let me cut the
cable, / And when we are put off, fall to their throats"
[2.7.72-73]) to sever the galley's link to the land so that
the triumvirs can be murdered in a containing environment
that Pompey controls. But he demurs:

> Thou must know
> 'Tis not my profit that does lead mine honour;
> Mine honour, it.

> (2.7.76-78)

Pompey would have Menas believe that his honor is a towing force, not a towed object, implying that to cut the galley's mooring cable would be to call in question that status of his honor (a concern for Pompey only because Menas wants him involved in and politically liable for the proposal before it is consummated). Menas immediately situates Pompey's honor in the world of realpolitik, using a metaphor likewise projected from the LINKS schema, but with stronger overtones of the PATH schema:

> For this,
> I'll never follow thy palled fortunes more.
> Who seeks, and will not take, when once 'tis offered,
> Shall never find it more.

> (2.7.82-85)

Menas reverses the force dynamic[10] that structures Pompey's view of his own honor. Menas "follow[s]," is attracted along the path of, Pompey's fortunes. But these fortunes are for Menas only his own profit. When Pompey asserts that what is led by his honor is his own profit, Menas disengages himself from the path and force dynamic of Pompey (= "fortunes"), itself subject to a towing force that Menas cannot understand and over which he has no control.

Caesar, for his part, portrays himself to his followers as predominantly a man of peace reluctantly dragged by the force of simple justice into a war contrary to his nature:

> Go with me to my tent, where you shall see
> How hardly I was drawn into this war,
> How calm and gentle I proceeded still
> In all my writings.

> (5.1.73-76)

With Antony's death, Cleopatra's main fear is that she will be imprisoned, constrained, and towed along as a prisoner in the force dynamic of Caesar's triumphal spectacle ("Know, sir [Proculeius], that I will not wait pinioned at your master's court . . . Shall they hoist me up / And show me to the shouting varletry / Of censuring Rome?" [5.2.51-52, 54-56]; "He'll [Caesar] lead me, then, in triumph" [5.2.108]). Antony clearly has the same metaphor in mind, if less explicitly, as he pleads with Eros to kill him:

> Wouldst thou be windowed in great Rome, and see
> Thy master thus with pleached arms, bending down
> His corrigible neck, his face subdued
> To penetrative shame, whilst the wheeled seat
> Of fortunate Caesar, drawn before him, branded
> His baseness that ensued?

> (4.14.73-78)

Antony would, with his arms pinioned (an ironically appropriate consequence of those "strong Egyptian fetters"),

be one of a long queue of prisoners attached to a linking rope, forced to march at the pace of Caesar's chariot in the procession of his triumph just as his passion for Cleopatra tied him by his heartstrings to her rudder at Actium.

In that climactic battle we see the densest occurrence of these metaphors. But Antony's troops see that he is being towed long before the battle itself, as Canidius remarks of his general's decision to give battle at sea, rather than on land where he has the advantage: "so our leader's led / And we are women's men" (3.7.69-70). Men, leaders, and Roman generals prototypically set direction along the path of events; they do not follow paths blazed by others, as Antony cries out in anguish to Cleopatra when they rejoin in Alexandria:

> O, whither hast thou led me, Egypt? See
> How I convey my shame out of thine eyes
> By looking back what I have left behind
> 'Stroyed in dishonour . . .
> 　　Egypt, thou knewst too well
> My heart was to thy rudder tied by th' strings,
> And thou shouldst tow me after.

> (3.11.51-54, 56-58)

As Canidius has predicted, Cleopatra is now the leader; Antony is the led. This metaphor of towing projected from the LINKS schema continues as Antony in effect interprets, conveys, or convoys,[11] his military shame from Cleopatra's very gaze itself. What he figuratively sees reflected in her eyes is himself, and to his rear, the procession of the fleet that he led, even as he in turn permitted himself to be led by Cleopatra's abrupt departure from the sea battle. Cleopatra as the tower leads Antony's heart (that in military combat was wont in better days to "burst / The buckles on his breast") by the linking medium of its strings; her rudder sets the course for him and for his troops. Antony and Cleopatra are linked, but the force dynamics governing that link are precisely the reverse of what they should be in time of war. "These strong Egyptian fetters" have wreaked their final and most potent damage.

The last consequence of that damage is, of course, the death of both the title characters, in which we find the paradoxically most containing and most liberating of the entire PATH-LINKS-CONTAINER metaphorical nexus. Both principals perceive their deaths as headlong rushes along a path into a container; in this respect, the overarching metaphorical pattern of *Macbeth* (see D. Freeman 1995: 706-7) is epitomized in the last major segment of *Antony and Cleopatra*.

For Antony, that container is the wedding bed, and the force impelling him along the path into that bed is the bridegroom's prototypically intense sexuality; yet, ironically, Shakespeare plays out the *Liebestod* theme so that Antony, the great military and sexual swordsman, winds up being penetrated by his own weapon:

> But I will be
> A bridegroom in my death, and run into't
> As to a lover's bed.

> (4.14.100-102)

Like Antony, Cleopatra metaphorizes her death as a containing structure into which she hastens, impelled by the intense force of her passionate grief. Later, she depicts her death as a containing force that likewise maintains her ascendancy over the forces of time and circumstance by fettering them:

> Then is it sin
> To rush into the secret house of death
> Ere death dare come to us?
>
> (4.15.84-86)

> And it is great
> To do that thing that ends all other deeds;
> Which shackles accidents and bolts up change . . .
>
> (5.2.4-6)

Even, or perhaps especially, in death, Cleopatra maintains her own autonomy: she is not led in Caesar's triumph, but, as Caesar himself points out, opposes his goals (and hence the PATH in terms of which we understand progress toward goals) and chooses her own path for the journey of her death:

> Bravest at the last,
> She levelled at our purposes and, being royal,
> Took her own way.
>
> (5.2.334-36)

And in what is perhaps the most startling of the metaphors in which we are asked to understand her death, Cleopatra obliterates the solid, containing periphery of her body not by melting, as Antony had sought for Rome and Roman-ness, but by sublimation, transmuting the "marble-constant" solidity of her physicality from a solid directly into a gas: "I am fire, and air; my other elements / I give to baser life" (5.2.288-89). Having towed Antony by his heartstrings from the battle of Actium to final defeat and immurement in her tower at Alexandria, Cleopatra now follows his imaginary example in conceiving of her death.

For Cleopatra has been preceded in thus perceiving her end by Antony's anguished parable to the uncomprehending Eros about the death of his standing and reputation. Fresh from his defeat before Alexandria and the "discandying" of his troops' hearts, Antony ironically defines for Eros, in a brief lesson about Gestalt perception, the final consequence of letting Rome in Tiber melt. The speech depends upon the metaphorical projection KNOWING IS SEEING and is in the form of an exemplum about the contingent nature of human knowledge:

> Eros, thou yet behold'st me? . . .
> Sometime we see a cloud that's dragonish,
> A vapour sometime like a bear or lion,
> A towered citadel, a pendant rock,
> A forked mountain, or blue promontory
> With trees upon't that nod unto the world
> And mock our eyes with air. Thou hast seen these
>   signs?

> They are black vesper's pageants. . . .
> That which is now a horse, even with a thought
> The rack dislimns and makes it indistinct
> As water is in water. . . .
> My good knave Eros, now thy captain is
> Even such a body. Here I am Antony,
> Yet cannot hold this visible shape, my knave.
>
> (4.14.1-14)

Near the end of a play in which, as the foregoing analysis suggests, the unambiguous, clearly outlined containing peripheries of Rome, empire, and military loyalty have, for an Antony rightly termed dissolute, melted into the liquids of passion and mercurial favor, he fully plays out his association of a containing and defining shape with his status, his standing in the world, and his very existence.

Antony implicates the hapless Eros in the act of seeing and cognizing, and invites him to imagine acts of seeing (and hence of knowing) shapes of cloud vapor to which our imagination imputes a defining periphery and structure. These acts become increasingly discrete and detailed, from a cloud that is only somewhat like a dragon, to a vapor that is somewhat like one or another animal (bears and lions are vaguely big four-legged animals), a fortress with towers, a rock hanging from a mountainside, a headland with trees blowing in the wind. These visions "mock our eyes with air"; when we see these vapors, our imagination causes us to inscribe perimeters around them and give them shape—for a moment, to indulge the illusion that these imaginary perimeters contain and delimit real objects.

But they do not, for the Gestalt perception created by the outline that our imagination momentarily imposes on these vaporous entities can be "dislimned,"[12] have its defining boundary and inner coherence destroyed, by a moment's change in the general background, or "rack"[13] of clouds that have provided the "data" for this evanescent "perception." Our vision, and with it, our knowledge, even our confidence in what and how we know, can be obliterated, and obliterated far more thoroughly than the Tiber can melt Antony's Rome or the Nile Cleopatra's Egypt. What we once knew with confidence can become—with a change in the background of that cloud formation that is no more tangible or discernible than a thought—mere vapor once again, as impossible to distinguish from what surrounds it as one kind of water is from another—say, water of Tiber from water of Nile.

And now, for the uncomprehending Eros, as he watches his idol come unglued before his eyes, comes the moral. Antony the man, and all he once represented (significantly, "thy captain")—Rome, the military ethos, leadership, stability, his own existence, perhaps existence itself—become as contingent against a background of the new dispensation's shifting values and alliances as are the shapes that our imagination limns against a background of vaporous shapes that appear and disappear at a moment's notice. He is "even such a body" as those clouds; like them, he "cannot hold this visible shape": the outline that we and Eros (and everyone) see and therefore know to contain him (for KNOWING IS SEEING)—citizenship, military rank, family, reputation, standing, armor—can "un-appear" at the slightest shift in the political winds.

Those winds obliterate the "visible shape" that once contained Antony's heart (the same organ that Philo had seen "burst its buckles" in the military sphere): the heart that in turn contained a million more hearts in the bodies of the troops contained by the military ethos and the force of Antony's leadership; those same hearts that now "do discandy, melt their sweets / On blossoming Caesar."[14]

If we sought for the sake of argument to interpret *Antony and Cleopatra* with Cleopatra as its dominating hero-figure, the major argument would rest, I suggest, on the fact that Antony's vision and knowledge of himself is defined, and in the end undefined, by his Romanness. Cleopatra, by contrast, sees him even in death as "past the size of dreaming . . . nature's piece 'gainst fancy, / Condemning shadows quite" (5.2.96, 98-99).

On this analysis, Cleopatra is the truly subversive force against Rome, for she threatens not merely Roman hegemony but Roman epistemology. The Rome personified in Octavius Caesar constructs itself as a sharply outlined, demarcated entity, and its might as concrete, structured, tangible, measurable, and, above all, visible; Cleopatra, for her part, exempts herself not only from conventional morality but the force of time and even the laws of physics. Small wonder, then, that when the grimly politic Octavius Caesar (maker of a marriage whose linking bonds, as we have seen, were not between his own sister and Antony but between himself and Antony) issues his first post-Cleopatran orders, they are detailed instructions in how to see, how to know, how to interpret: "Come, Dolabella, see / High order in this great solemnity" (5.2.364-65).

Dolabella is ordered to create a funeral ceremony that its viewers will see and know as the Octavian New World Order. The lovers' funeral must "keep the square": fancy must not outwork nature; Antony's deliquescent Rome, Cleopatra's sublimated fire and air, must be—and be seen to be—buried by the book, linked forever—but also contained forever—in the basest of the four classical elements. Rome must never melt again.

Notes

1. I assume general familiarity with this body of work, in which the most recent studies, in addition to those in this volume, include Gibbs 1994; Steen 1994; Morse 1994; D. Freeman 1993, 1995; Turner 1991, 1996; and M. Freeman 1997.

2. Citations are from Wilders 1995.

3. For the standard account of LOVE IS A FLUID IN A CONTAINER, see Kövesces 1988: 43-44.

4. See, among many others, Knight 1951: 232-39.

5. Wilders 1995: 223 gives a good historical account of "discandy"; the *OED* citation is "To melt or dissolve out of a candied or solid condition."

6. In *Measure for Measure,* Shakespeare uses this same metaphor in a way that more clearly reveals its operation, as Isabella describes how Claudio will lose his honor if he does not sacrifice himself for her: "In such a [nature], as you consenting to't, / Would bark your honour from that trunk you bear, / And leave you naked" (3.1.71-73 [the text is Lever 1965]). An important interpretive point about Antony's use of this figure is enhanced by a cognitive analysis. We might be tempted to read Antony-as-tallest-tree phallically. But that reading does violence to the figure's immediate context, in which, I would argue, there is no phallic imagery but a great deal of container-as-periphery imagery. The bark as periphery that protects the tree's vital substance maps into the candied shell as periphery that protects the vital substance of Antony's military ethos. The container reading explains more of the figure's element than does the phallic reading. Although *Antony and Cleopatra* has great many phallic images, this is not one of them. For discussion of how cognitive analysis yields a metatheory of literary interpretation, see D. Freeman 1998.

7. Unsurprisingly, Antony's and Cleopatra's deaths are metaphorized in identical terms: "[*Antony.*] The long day's task is done, / And we must sleep . . ." (4.14.35-36). "[*Iras.*] . . . the bright day is done, / And we are for the dark" (5.2.192-93).

8. Perhaps this is what is meant by Cleopatra's "The odds is gone" (4.15.68).

9. For a cognitive account of parental nurturance that sets out these elements in more detail, see Lakoff 1996: 108-29. This passage lends itself particularly well to a blended-space analysis of the sort articulated in other essays in this volume and elsewhere in current scholarship on metaphor. But the blending analysis does not, to my mind, account for the broad range of figurative language and other metaphorized elements (stage business, plot, character) characteristic of dramatic poetry. The theory of blended mental spaces provides rich new insights into the figurative language of short, self-contained poems (see, e.g., M. Freeman 1997) and of longer, narrative works like novels (see Vimala Herman's essay in this volume), where novelist, various narrators, and reader are situated differently. But this aproach seems rather confining, in its present form, for the rich heterogeneity of dramatic art.

10. The following discussion draws much of its conceptual framework from Leonard Talmy's pioneering research in force dynamics. A good introduction to this work is to be found in Talmy 1983.

11. The etymological relationship of *convey* in the sense of conveying meaning, significance (*OED, v.,* 9.b.)

was closer to *convoy* in Shakespeare's time. Like *convoy*, *convey* carried naval overtones.

12. *OED, v.* "dislimn": (1) "To obliterate the outlines of (anything limned); to efface, blot out."

13. *OED, sb.* "rack": (3b) "driving mist or fog." But in light of the other Shakespearean illustration offered for this sense (*The Tempest*, 4.1.156), "The great Globe it selfe . . . shall dissolue, And . . . Leaue not a racke behinde," it would seem that the more nearly correct sense for "rack" here is (3a), "Clouds, or a mass of cloud, driven before the wind in the upper air." Wilders 1995: 254n apparently shares this view.

14. Rosalie Colie (1974: 199-200) has written about Antony's climactic speech in terms very similar to the foregoing—as Antony's "dissolution." What her analysis fails to account for, in my view, is how this dissolution of Antony's selfhood works not only with other metaphors of melting in the play, but with Shakespeare's metaphorical account of what in Antony is dissolved: the sharply etched outline of his civic and military status.

References

Charney, Maurice: 1961 *Shakespeare's Roman Plays: The Function of Imagery in the Drama* (Cambridge: Harvard University Press).

Clemen, Wolfgang: 1962 [1951] *The Development of Shakespeare's Imagery* (New York: Hill and Wang).

Colie, Rosalie: 1974 *Shakespeare's Living Art* (Princeton, NJ: Princeton University Press).

Doran, Madeleine: 1976 *Shakespeare's Dramatic Language* (Madison: University of Wisconsin Press).

Freeman, Donald C.: 1993 "'According to my bond': *King Lear* and Re-Cognition," *Language and Literature* 2: 1-18; 1995 "'Catch[ing] the nearest way': *Macbeth* and Cognitive Metaphor," *Journal of Pragmatics* 23: 689-708; 1998 "Making Literary Arguments," paper delivered at the Universidad de Granada.

Freeman, Margaret H.: 1997 "Grounded Spaces: Deictic *-self* Anaphors in the Poetry of Emily Dickinson," *Language and Literature* 7: 7-28.

Gibbs, Raymond W., Jr.: 1994 *The Poetics of Mind: Figurative Thought, Language, and Understanding* (Cambridge: Cambridge University Press).

Johnson, Mark: 1987 *The Body in the Mind: The Bodily Basis of Meaning, Imagination, and Reason* (Chicago: University of Chicago Press).

Knight, G. Wilson: 1951 *The Imperial Theme* (London: Methuen).

Kövesces, Zoltán: 1988 *The Language of Love: The Semantics of Passion in Conversational English* (London: Associated University Presses).

Lakoff, George: 1996 *Moral Politics: What Conservatives Know That Liberals Don't* (Chicago: University of Chicago Press).

Lakoff, George, and Mark Johnson: 1999 *Philosophy in the Flesh: The Embodied Mind and Its Challenge to Western Thought* (New York: Basic Books).

McAlindon, T. A.: 1973 *Shakespeare and Decorum* (London: Macmillan).

Morse, David Wayne: 1994 "Metaphor as a Framework for Formulaic Poetry," Ph.D. diss., University of Southern California.

Shakespeare, William: 1965 *The Arden Shakespeare: Measure for Measure*, edited by J. W. Lever (London: Routledge); 1995 *The Arden Shakespeare: Antony and Cleopatra*, edited by John Wilders (London: Routledge).

Spurgeon, Caroline F. E.: 1935 *Shakespeare's Imagery and What It Tells Us* (Cambridge: Cambridge University Press).

Steen, Gerard: 1994 *Understanding Metaphor in Literature: An Empirical Approach* (London: Longman).

Sweetser, Eve: 1990 *From Etymology to Pragmatics: Metaphorical and Cultural Aspects of Semantic Structure* (Cambridge: Cambridge University Press).

Talmy, Leonard: 1983 "How Language Structures Space," in *Spatial Orientation: Theory, Research, and Application*, edited by Herbert Pick and Linda Acreodolo, 225-82 (New York: Plenum).

Turner, Mark: 1991 *Reading Minds: The Study of English in the Age of Cognitive Science* (Princeton, NJ: Princeton University Press); 1996 *The Literary Mind* (New York: Oxford University Press).

FURTHER READING

Criticism

Charney, Maurice. "The Imagery of *Antony and Cleopatra*." In *Shakespeare's Roman Plays: The Function of Imagery in the Drama*, pp. 79-141. Cambridge: Harvard University Press, 1961.

> Studies *Antony and Cleopatra*'s use of the imagery related to dimension and scope, demonstrating the way such imagery expresses the hyperbole characterizing the style of the play.

Dorius, R. J. "Love, Death, and the Heroic" and "The Triumph of Imagination: Act V." In *How to Read Shakespearean Tragedy*, edited by Edward Quinn, pp. 295-310; 339-49. New York: Harper's College Press, 1978.

> Discusses the interaction between tragic, heroic, and romantic elements in the play, and contends that much

of the divergence of opinion regarding the play's genre is rooted in the way Shakespeare's treatment of love and of Cleopatra are interpreted.

Hamilton, Donna B. "*Antony and Cleopatra* and the Tradition of Noble Lovers." *Shakespeare Quarterly* 24, no. 3 (summer 1973): 245-52.

Examines the literary tradition that views Antony and Cleopatra as truthful and faithful lovers, and suggests that Shakespeare drew on these accounts for inspiration.

Herbert, T. Walter "A Study of Meaning in *Antony and Cleopatra*." In . . . *All These to Teach: Essays in Honor of C. A. Robertson,* edited by Robert A. Bryan, Alton C. Morris, A. A. Murphree, and Aubrey L. Williams, pp. 47-66. Gainesville: University of Florida Press, 1965.

Offers an overview of the play's setting, action, poetry, and characters informed by an understanding of Elizabethan culture and beliefs.

Kahn, Coppélia. "Antony's Wound." In *Roman Shakespeare: Warriors, Wounds, and Women,* pp. 110-43. London: Routledge, 1997.

Focuses on the rivalry between Octavius Caesar and Antony, and claims that Caesar campaigns against Antony not only in order to portray Cleopatra as an enemy of Rome, but also to eliminate Antony as a serious rival.

MacMullan, Katherine Vance. "Death Imagery in *Antony and Cleopatra*." *Shakespeare Quarterly* 14, no. 4 (autumn 1963): 399-410.

Investigates the death imagery that Shakespeare employed in *Antony and Cleopatra,* focusing on the interconnectedness of the themes of love and death.

Miola, Robert S. "*Antony and Cleopatra*: Rome and the World." In *Shakespeare's Rome,* pp. 116-63. Cambridge: Cambridge University Press, 1983.

Explores Shakespeare's treatment of Rome and its relationship to Egypt in *Antony and Cleopatra,* as well as on the relationship of Shakespeare's portrayal of Rome in *Antony and Cleopatra* to his depiction of the empire in *Julius Caesar.*

Nandy, Dipak. "The Realism of *Antony and Cleopatra*." In *Shakespeare in a Changing World,* edited by Arnold Kettle, pp. 172-94. New York: International Publishers, 1964.

Interprets Antony's experience in the play as a discovery of his true relationship to Rome, personified by Octavius Caesar, and Egypt, represented by Cleopatra.

Rinehart, Keith. "Shakespeare's Cleopatra and England's Elizabeth." *Shakespeare Quarterly* 23, no. 1 (winter 1972): 81-6.

Demonstrates the likelihood that Shakespeare used Queen Elizabeth as a model for his portrayal of Cleopatra.

Thomas, Vivian. "Realities and Imaginings in *Antony and Cleopatra*." In *Shakespeare's Roman Worlds,* pp. 93-153. London: Routledge, 1989.

Examines the ways in which Shakespeare adapted his source material in order to portray Antony and Cleopatra in a manner attractive enough to encourage the sympathy of audiences.

Williamson, Marilyn. "The Political Context in *Antony and Cleopatra*." *Shakespeare Quarterly* 21, no. 3 (summer 1970): 241-51.

Stresses the importance of the aspects of *Antony and Cleopatra* that relate directly to Plutarch's historical narrative, maintaining that Shakespeare's use of his source was intended to demonstrate relevant political lessons, lessons which are taught through studying Antony and Cleopatra not just as lovers, but as rulers.

A Midsummer Night's Dream

For further information on the critical and stage history of *A Midsummer Night's Dream,* see *SC,* Volumes 3, 12, 29, 45, and 58.

INTRODUCTION

One of Shakespeare's most popular plays, *A Midsummer Night's Dream* is often considered a lighthearted comedy. It traces the romantic escapades of four young Athenian lovers lost on a midsummer night in a forest ruled by fairies. The dreamlike events that occur in the enchanted wood are framed by court scenes dominated by Theseus, ruler of Athens. Another group of characters, designated as rustics, artisans, or mechanicals, and led by Bottom the weaver, inhabit the play and enhance its comedic effects. Despite the play's obvious comic design, a number of critics have also identified within *A Midsummer Night's Dream* darker undertones. Theseus refers to a war with the Amazons in which he conquered his wife Hippolyta, and Titania's interlude with Bottom, who has been transformed into a man with a donkey's head, is suggestive of bestiality. The play performed by the mechanicals, although staged in a hilarious and bumbling manner, is itself a tragedy. The resulting effect of the weaving of comic and tragic elements, the structure and characters supporting this effect, and the myths influencing the play's content have all become areas of modern critical scrutiny.

Bottom figures prominently in analyses of *A Midsummer Night's Dream.* Jan Kott (1987) focuses on Bottom's metamorphosis, contending that the perverse carnival atmosphere in the Bottom-Titania interludes contradicts theatrical conventions typically associated with masques and court entertainments. Kott concludes that while Shakespeare's depiction of Bottom's transformation allows for both light and serious readings of the play, either interpretation is fraught with contradiction. Philip C. McGuire (1989) examines the significance of Egeus, Hermia's father, to *A Midsummer Night's Dream.* McGuire focuses on Egeus's silence in Act IV, scene i, when Theseus states that he will overturn the Athenian law requiring that Hermia marry Demetrius, whom her father has chosen. McGuire notes that Egeus is silent at this point in both the Quarto and the Folio; however, at the wedding ceremony in Act V, the Folio specifies that Egeus is present whereas the Quarto does not. Given this textual discrepancy, McGuire speculates on how Egeus's silence should be interpreted, maintaining that it may indicate consent, perhaps even reconciliation with Hermia, or it may be interpreted as his withdrawal from Athenian society. In contrast to critics who have focused on the contentious elements in *A Midsummer Night's Dream,* Tom Clayton (1999) assesses the comedy's lighter aspects. Clayton downplays the bestial implications of the Bottom-Titania interlude and highlights the civil nature of the relationship between Theseus and Hippolyta.

Many critics have argued that an examination of the relationship between the tragic and comic elements in *A Midsummer Night's Dream* is an important step to understanding the design of the play. While some scholars have attempted to demonstrate that the tragic and comic elements complement each other, Clifford Earl Ramsey (1977) underscores the distinct differences in their form and structure. Ramsey examines the scenic structure of the play, maintaining that it expresses diversity and opposition, and yet it also emphasizes harmony and integration. According to the critic, the scenic structure ultimately underscores the play's dual themes of the power of love and the power of imagination. Taking another approach, Richard H. Cox (1982) explores the way in which Shakespeare shaped his poetic imagination within the confines of comedy. Cox examines Shakespeare's comic treatment of the traditionally serious Theseus as well as the serious social subtext of the mechanicals' comic actions. Through these characters, Cox contends, Shakespeare didactically addressed weighty issues related to civic life within the framework of comedy. Similarly, Virgil Hutton (1985) explores the ways in which Shakespeare used comedy to camouflage the tragic content of *A Midsummer Night's Dream.* Hutton argues that Shakespeare raised religious and philosophical issues in the play, primarily in his treatment of the mechanicals, and outlines the ways in which the mechanicals' production of *Pyramus and Thisby* contrasts with the experiences of the lovers in the wood. Hutton demonstrates that the tragic world of Pyramus and Thisby resembles real life more than that of the dreamlike world of the four lovers. A. D. Nuttall (2000) traces the somber elements of *A Midsummer Night's Dream* to its mythic sources. Recounting the cruel depiction of Theseus in Greek myth, Nuttall demonstrates the careful, yet incomplete manner in which Shakespeare attempted to disguise Theseus's past. Furthermore, Nuttall reveals the dark background of the fairies and discusses the disturbing images evoked through Bottom's transformation and his interlude with Titania. Yet in his comic handling of Theseus, the fairies, and Bottom, Nuttall argues, Shakespeare offered a negotiation between comedy and tragedy, resulting in an exorcism of the fear evoked by the play's more sinister aspects.

The subtle balance of tragic and comic elements in the play presents significant challenges to modern directors of *A Midsummer Night's Dream.* Russell Jackson reviews a stage production of the play directed by Michael Boyd for the 1999-2000 season at Stratford-upon-Avon. Jackson analyzes the production's emphasis on the forest as the locus of sexuality, and comments on how the director deftly combined the sinister and comic elements of the play. The critic also praises Boyd's use of dance and movement in the production, noting that the dances evoked images of ancient fertility rites. Mark Thornton Burnett (2000) discusses two versions of the comedy directed by Adrian Noble, one a 1994-95 stage version, and the other Noble's 1996 film adaptation. While the staging achieved widespread critical acclaim, the film version received predominantly negative criticism. Burnett provides a reexamination of the film, concentrating on its style and "postmodern aspirations" and noting the way in which it successfully exploited and evoked childhood experience and children's stories. Many critics have assessed Michael Hoffman's 1999 film adaptation of *A Midsummer Night's Dream*. John Bemrose (1999) praises the performances of Kevin Kline as Bottom and Michelle Pfeiffer as Titania, but faults the film for interpreting the play in a modern and "tedious" Hollywood manner. Jim Welsh (1999) maintains that while Hoffman's film has its charm, it comes up lacking in both style and substance compared to the 1935 film by Max Reinhardt and William Dieterle. In another mixed review, Richard Alleva (1999) censures Hoffman for reducing Shakespeare's conception of "multi-layered emotionality" in *A Midsummer Night's Dream*. Alleva finds Pfeiffer's Titania to be "gracelessly spoken" and states that Kline's interpretation of Bottom transforms the weaver into an emotionally fragile clown of a man, although, Alleva adds, such a portrayal does work within the scope of Hoffman's film.

OVERVIEWS AND GENERAL STUDIES

Tom Clayton (essay date 1999)

SOURCE: Clayton, Tom. "'So quick bright things come to confusion': or, What Else was *A Midsummer Night's Dream* About?"[1] In *Shakespeare: Text and Theater,* edited by Lois Potter and Arthur F. Kinney, pp. 62-91. Newark: University of Delaware Press, 1999.

[*In the following essay, Clayton highlights the brighter, more lighthearted aspects of* A Midsummer Night's Dream, *emphasizing the civilized and complementary features of the relationship between Theseus and Hippolyta and downplaying the bestial connotation in the relationship between the transformed Bottom and Titania.*]

In the now ancient history of Shakespeare's birth-quatercentenary year of 1964, it would not have been easy to find in the year's publications a pair of perspectives less alike than those of R. W. Dent,

Rather than being a foe to good living, poetic imagination can be its comfort and its guide, far "more yielding" than most dreams. Whether *A Midsummer Night's Dream* has an unplumbed "bottom" as well as its inescapable Bottom, I hesitate to say. But it provides us "a most rare vision," one that offers us a disarmingly unpretentious defense of poetry by the greatest of England's poets;

and Jan Kott: "The *Dream* is the most erotic of Shakespeare's plays. In no other tragedy or comedy of his, except *Troilus and Cressida,* is the eroticism expressed so brutally."[2]

Each essay was original in its own way. Dent's is historical in emphasis, modest in assertion, and consistently illuminating, a classic. Kott's was groundbreaking, rough—"brutal"?—and provocative, and has been widely influential, especially as partial source of what is probably the most famous production of the century, Peter Brook's, in 1970 (see Halio 48-69). Brook's preface to Kott's book suggests why: it "is Poland that in our time has come closest to the tumult, the danger, the intensity, the imaginativeness and the daily involvement with the social process that made life so horrible, subtle and ecstatic to an Elizabethan" (x-xi).[3] True or not, the perception had its sway. Kott revealed and dwelt on the darker side of Shakespeare—or he projected it, or both. In any case, it was a side especially congenial to the time and has become durably postmodern. Accordingly, something of the character of Shakespeare's *Dream* has been thrust into the shade in succeeding decades, and critical editions as well as productions have undergone their own notable, not always unquestionable, alterations in the past decade or so.[4] My aim here is to try to restore light and a measure of balance of perspective in a few of *Dream*'s quarters that have suffered neglect or occasionally worse.

Theatrical production cannot stand still, of course, and by no means every *Dream* should ring changes on moonlight, roses, and transcendental imagination. But some recent professional productions have seemed to perform everything but the script, often adhering to the letter but relentlessly violating the spirit, something few living playwrights would readily permit. "Adaptation . . . of one sort or another seems to be the rule, . . . but how far can one carry this process and still call it Shakespeare?" (Halio 7). A view current among post-literary academics at present is that nothing has perennial value because all is culturally determined, including "Shakespeare" and his (currency) value. But this view is routinely falsified by individual and collective experience in the reading and often in the theater.

Performance and understanding begin with the script and text. For plays with more than one substantive text, the ultimate witness is the one inferred to be closer to holograph, usually but not always the longer—with *Hamlet* the longest—version.[5] "Holograph" may be foul papers (most often), fair copy, or revised manuscript; with inferred scribal transcript (Shakespeare's, anonymous, or by Ralph

Crane) intervening between print and holograph (of whatever kind). Revisionists argue that "revised" versions showing signs of "promptbook" influence and accordingly closer to theatrical practice are more authoritative, at least as far as their additions, cuts, and other alterations are concerned. But the assumption that the "more theatrical" text is the "better" is circular and rests on a somewhat limited view of genre, intention, and effect.

The modern textual situation of *Dream* was "stable" until 1986, when the *Oxford Shakespeare* innovated in incorporating F's—the Folio's—assignment to Egeus and Lysander of speeches in 5.1 that are Philostrate's and Theseus', respectively, in Q1 (1600), the sole wholly substantive text and the most authoritative as the source of Q2, in turn the source of most of F. The received explanation is that Q1 came from autograph foul papers, and F from Q2 altered here and there from a playhouse promptbook. It is easy enough to see expediency as a hypothetical reason for such changes in performance, but not as a good reason to adopt them, much less as revisions supposed to be by Shakespeare. In fact, they serve well enough to open up anew the question of *extent* in so-called Shakespearean revision.

"'TIS STRANGE, MY THESEUS" (5.1.1)

The critical and performing fate of these dramatic and mythical lovers has been mixed, especially in the past quarter century: not infrequently, Hippolyta has been aggrandized, Theseus demonized.[6] The script seems to give them about equal measure, a suggestion Shakespeare didn't need but Plutarch supplied in explaining the end of the war brought to Athens "within the precinct of the very cittie it selfe" by the Amazons:

> at the ende of foure moneths, peace was taken betwene them by meanes of one of the women called Hyppolita. . . . Nevertheles, some saye that she was slayne (fighting on Theseus side). . . . In memorie whereof, the piller which is joyning to the temple of the Olympian ground, was set up in her honour. *We are not to marvell, if the historie of things so auncient, be founde so diversely written.*
>
> (Bullough 386, 387)

Amen. So much context explains the mythic site and character of Theseus' recently most infamous lines, the first two of

> Hippolyta, I woo'd thee with my sword,
> And won thy love doing thee injuries;
> But I will wed thee in another key,
> With pomp, with triumph, and with revelling.
>
> (1.1.16-19)

His subject is the familiar progress of wooing, winning, wedding, with the paradox that the wars of myth were paradoxically the scene of contest turned to courtship; but the wedding will be triumphant "in another" and its own traditional "key."

The plotline of the impending nuptials of Theseus and Hippolyta constitutes *Dream*'s opening; it is joined in 2.1 by the alienation-reconciliation and amatory-management plotline of Oberon, Titania, and Puck/Robin that constitutes the closing. The parallels are obvious enough, and significant; and much has been written that is sensitive and wise about the propriety of doubling Theseus/Oberon and Hippolyta/Titania, which was certainly done as early as 1661 (Holland 96-97). But two points need making about doubling. First, doubling (to economize, for example) does not entail special affinities between the characters doubled. Second, and just as important, affinities between two characters may be seen without their doubling.

Theseus was clearly intended to be overshadowed at the end by Oberon and company, the inescapable effect of the order of events, with the diurnal world of waking reason giving way to the nocturnal world of dreamtime and imagination. But Theseus is no less important for that: if the day needs the night for rest and dreaming, night needs the day for enlightenment and exercise; and Theseus' reason transcends its own limitations, through his imagination (sic) and sentiment, which it is partly the business of his two act-5 setpieces—"More strange than true" and "The kinder we"—to demonstrate. One might say that if there were not a Theseus to deliver these speeches, a speaker might have had to be created from scratch. Not, of course, that the speeches came first, but they have a primacy and significance that *Dream* would be different and the worse for being without.

Theseus and Hippolyta are never separated, appearing together in 1.1, 4.1, and 5.1; and their dialogue is very much reciprocal from the opening exchange to their last banter on "Pyramus and Thisbe" (5.1.300-05).[7] Her mere four-and-a-half lines in the opening subscene have served every interpretative purpose, but they are sufficient in content and context to convey mutuality more readily than they can, without strain, express discontent and aloofness:

> Four days will quickly steep themselves in night;
> Four nights will quickly dream away the time;
> And then the moon, like to a silver bow
> [New] bent in heaven, shall behold the night
> Of our solemnities.
>
> (1.1.7-11)

In *Dream,* Theseus has a good deal of the country squire about him, and Hippolyta herself is on the horsy side, the two of them dog-fanciers together in their telling exchange in 4.1, just before they come upon the sleeping lovers. The pair's mutuality, similarity of expression, and shared "lifestyle"—as Anglo-Athenian-mythical country gentry—are far more in evidence than is a raw or even cooked competitiveness here, where their speeches even run to nearly equal length: Theseus has three lines opening (4.1.109-11), then she seven (112-18) and he eight-and-a-half, his last line completed by the transitional "But soft, what nymphs are these?" (119-27). This pattern of easy reciprocity obtains throughout, even when they disagree.

Theirs is, on the showing, a civil(ized) relationship of "mutual love and good liking";[8] and *that* is expressed most succinctly by "*my* Theseus" (5.1.1): one doesn't address a stranger to one's affections thus, and this is the opening note of act 5.

The social motion of their duologue here is marked by the echoing of Hippolyta's "'Tis *strange*" in (1) Theseus' extended reply beginning "More *strange* than true," and (2) Hippolyta's closing, "But howsoever, *strange* and *admirable*"—'to be wondered at,' with a trace of 'deserving admiration' (l. 27). The speeches of both express the complementarity of the speakers, as well as their differences, which are also complementary. Theseus' skeptical voice of reason confidently pronouncing in error transcends the limitations of what he "may believe" when it comes to the poet, whose flights of imagination are exquisitely and accurately described; in spite of himself, he speaks for the play and of the play, and of himself at one remove, if not for Shakespeare. But how not?

Some now hastily if not facilely dismiss Theseus and this setpiece by inflating the truisms that (1) his view should not be taken for Shakespeare's; (2) he is wrong about the imagination and much else, and Hippolyta is right; and (3) Theseus himself is an "antique" figment of imagination and therefore a butt of his own joke. But "*antic* fables"—bizarre narratives—is almost certainly correct, despite the fact that most current editions have "*antique* fables," as in Q1.[9] This is a problem of appropriate modern spelling, but it is not clear why editors who often follow F prefer Q1 here. Since "antique" makes inferior sense otherwise, one supposes the preference due to its ready association with Theseus, who is routinely faulted, accordingly, for disbelieving in his own mythical identity. No one can resist this joke who hasn't been pressed to explain how the "fables" *just told* are "antique" meaning ancient.

Theseus is not wrong about the value of "cool reason," even if it has limitations as applied here. But if he is "wrong" about the imagination, he nevertheless brings his own powerful imagination into play to deprecate the poet, who could scarcely be better appreciated by downright eulogy. Did Shakespeare give Theseus these splendid lines to make him risibly pompous and transcendently wrong? The former not really, the latter most certainly, in a special way.

There is general acceptance of Dover Wilson's argument that Shakespeare added the poet to a shorter speech on the imagination of the lover and the madman, which affords a ready explanation for mislining and overcrowded lines in Q1 at that point.[10] Whether the poet arrived at once or on second thought, he dominates the speech as we have it:

> The poet's eye, in a fine frenzy rolling,
> Doth glance from heaven to earth, from earth to heaven;
> And as imagination bodies forth
> The forms of things unknown, the poet's pen

> Turns them to shapes, and gives to aery nothing
> A local habitation and a name.

> (12-17)

Even delivered with skepticism and irony, this is breathtaking, a towering tribute to the poet as vates *and* as maker. It is a masterstroke to make Theseus its author, the rational skeptic pronouncing judgment on the irrationality of the imagination by using its highest resources to do so, condemning and commending simultaneously—to its and the poet's credit. Theseus may be talking through his philosopher's hat, but he has been given the poet's own eloquence to do it with. Transported by imagination unawares, he returns to practicalities with his last four lines—*and* those of the original version of the speech (if the poet *was* added). Hippolyta's rejoinder, sound, sympathetic, reasonable, and appreciative, complements Theseus' sweeping survey by bringing "something of great constancy" into the space of the poet's shapes and airy nothing. She is made utterly gracious in joining him at an esthetic distance from the object of their contemplation: "howsoever, strange and admirable." One of the most notable things about the exchange is that Theseus' imagination exceeds his reason here, and Hippolyta's reason her imagination—ultimately to the harmony and credit of them both.

In both exchanges of genial one-upmanship or simple disagreement Hippolyta fares as well as Theseus or better. It is (as always already) easy to read the gender wars into them. But the two characters read and perform most cohesively and intelligibly, and with least strain, as social and personal—and military—equals of partly shared background: mythic nobility from different countries of the classical and post-classical mind joined in late-Renaissance (or Early Modern) English-poetical matrimony.

The only non-fairy in the play who mentions fairies at all—twice—is Theseus. The lovers nowhere show the slightest awareness of their existence, even though Theseus' "fairy toys" implies that fairies figured in the lovers' accounts. For us to supply fairies to their hypothetical account would be to forget about the "discrepant awareness" of dramatic characters and ourselves, who know so much more than they.[11] Bottom alone has "reason" to swear there are fairies, but he does no such thing. The only bare *hint* of fairies by others is Demetrius' "I wot not by what power / (But by some power it is)" (4.1.164-65): fairy power, but *he* knows not that. Whatever the lovers' fables, as Hippolyta logically infers—she does not intuit—their experience was real and shared, and the fairies are no less real to us or, invisible, to them.

Theseus has *two* setpieces, or "arias,"[12] in act 5, so it might seem curious that the first gets far more attention than the second, "the kinder we" (89-105), which has often been ignored and is now read by some as hypocritical. But the speech seems in earnest for both Shakespeare and Theseus, and there are no textual grounds, as opposed to categorical aprioristic judgments, for taking it otherwise. It is in earnest for good reason, its theme *noblesse oblige,* which might not be necessary in a genuinely classless society of the sort the world has yet to see. Where there are inequalities, their effects are substantially ameliorated when the more fortunate—or powerful—show care for the less. And where there is personal contact between power and vulnerability, kindness finds a way to level differences in some degree. "The kinder we" episode speaks well for Theseus, and it appears to speak also for the play, not pompously preaching but eloquently pleading, with metaphor, anecdote, and subsequent example, advocating compassion of attitude and *noblesse oblige* in behavior, a socioethical message of some importance in Shakespeare's day and once again—rather urgently—in our own. The affluent and socially sophisticated find this banal and bourgeois. Directors who find it so, who wish to concentrate on other matters, or who do not like Theseus, either make the delivery effete and ineffectual or cut the speech.[13]

Both Theseus' speech itself and the dialogue that precedes it make a case for obligatory as well as obliging kindness that is in no way offset by the comic mockery of the courtiers during the performance of "Pyramus and Thisbe," although there is obvious *theoretical* inconsistency. But this entire part of the play is a rich amalgam of the serious and the comic that in a sympathetic production has no trouble with either the serious or the—superficially—inconsistent comedy. Told colorfully and wittily by Philostrate how bad the homespuns' play is (61-70), Theseus asks, "What are they that do play it?" "Hard-handed men that work in Athens here, / Which never labor'd in their minds till now," etc. His response is, "And we will hear it." This is ad hominem with benevolence. Warned a second time by Philostrate that "it is nothing, nothing in the world; / Unless you can find *sport in their intents*" (78-79), Theseus insists that "I will hear that play; / For never any thing can be amiss / When simpleness and duty tender it" (80-82). "Find sport" prepares for the courtiers' comments, and "their intents" stresses the primacy of intentions and the applicability of the golden rule in such cases. The homespuns are honored in having their play preferred, and audiences diverted by shortcomings of which the players are unaware and that they have no need to know.[14]

Hippolyta's "He says they can do nothing in this *kind*" elicits Theseus' cheerful asteism, "The *kind*er we" (85-89), the beginning of Shakespeare's setpiece and Theseus' poetic and substantial reflections on sympathetic imagination illuminated with the colors of rhetoric everywhere present in Shakespeare's earlier plays. "What *poor duty* cannot do, noble respect / Takes it in might, not merit" (91-92) at once defines noblesse oblige ("magnanimous or generous consideration," Foakes 120); gives an allegorical instance with personification; and concludes with an elliptical and emphatic short line strikingly expressive in its use of "might," a signal instance of pointed antanaclasis. "Might" is used to mean both "power" ("might" is more powerful than "merit") and potentiality (what they "might"

do).[15] An exemplum follows as a general anecdote based on Theseus' past experience:

> Where I have come, great clerks have purposed
> To greet me with premeditated welcomes;
> Where I have seen them shiver and look pale,
> Make periods in the midst of sentences,
> Throttle their practic'd accent in their fears,
> And in conclusion dumbly have broke off,
> Not paying me a welcome.

Their failure became success, however, because,

> Trust me, sweet,
> Out of this silence yet I pick'd a welcome;
> And in the modesty of *fearful* duty,

complementing the earlier "*poor* duty"

> I read as much as from the rattling tongue
> Of saucy and audacious eloquence.
> Love, therefore, and tongue-tied simplicity
> In least speak most, to my capacity.
>
> (5.1.93-105)

Hippolyta's "It must be your imagination then, and not theirs" (5.1.214), though ironic, spells out what is implied throughout this speech, in which Theseus advocates and exercises the very faculty of imagination he decried in theory at the beginning of the scene, a benign inconsistency to his moral credit.

The Amazonian Hippolyta, entirely at home in the Athenian court, joins the men in commenting wittily (and in prose) on the play and performance: "Indeed he [Quince] hath played on this prologue like a child on a recorder—a sound, but not in government" (122-23). When Wall walks off, her "This is the silliest stuff that ever I heard" (210) elicits Theseus'—thematic and didactic—reply, "The best in this kind are but shadows; and the worst are no worse, if imagination amend them. . . . If we imagine no worse of them than they of themselves, they may pass for excellent men" (211-18). Her next comment, "I am a-weary of this moon. Would he would change!" (251), together with Theseus' response, epitomizes the complex of dramatic effects centering on "Pyramus and Thisbe," a theatrical and literary three-ring circus of burlesque (meta)drama, witty commentary, and extemporaneous and illicit dialogue by the players with their immediate audience—with the seriously humane undercurrent rising to the surface here, again, with Theseus' answer concerning Moon: "It appears by his small light of discretion that he is in the wane; but *yet in courtesy, in all reason,* we must stay the time" (254-55). For *this* function of reason Theseus deserves credit that he is now seldom accorded by critics.

The last of Theseus and the courtiers is Theseus' speech concluding,

> This palpable-gross play hath well beguil'd
> The heavy gait of night. Sweet friends, to bed.

A fortnight hold we this solemnity,
In nightly revels and new jollity. [*Exeunt.*]

(367-70)

The jokes made by the courtiers about the palpable-gross play can be played as callous and as overheard and taken so by the players, in which case the audience will be disconcerted accordingly; it is just as obvious in the dialogue and often in performance that they are neither.[16] In fact, the entire social event centering on "Pyramus and Thisbe" is at once hugely comic and tacitly serious in its performing and the reasons for its being preferred. The punctuation of the drama by courtiers' comments is made more bond than brake, and this is still more so with the interaction between courtiers and players, notably Pyramus (184-87), Moon (257-59), and Pyramus again, rising from the dead to reassure Demetrius about Wall and offer the options of a terminal epilogue or a Bergomask (351-54). The latter is shortly forthcoming, bringing to an end "Pyramus and Thisbe" and, soon after, the play of the courtiers of Athens. Then with the fairies the *Dream* resumes.

"Do You Amend It Then; It Lies in You"
(2.1.118)

Oberon and Titania are not Theseus and Hippolyta. They are a married king and queen different from their mythical, aristocratic human counterparts in being folkloric supernaturals. Their behavior is that of (im)mortals with higher powers, like Greek-mythical gods except that the fairies are better behaved and motivated. Their estrangement and reconciliation is the central plot-line, even the main plot determining the progress of all other plots; at the center of it, in turn, is the fairy-queen-and-commoner romance of Titania and Bottom, its catalyst the refusal of Titania to give Oberon the changeling boy. Notwithstanding that he is the subject of a custody fight (as well as one with dire meteorological consequences, Titania claims), it is not very common for critics to discuss the *boy*'s interests; and he does not routinely appear, since he is not among the dramatis personae. According to the social norms implicit in the relations between the principals, it must be about the time that the boy would be fairy bar mitzvahed and join the men—or elder fairies—if he is ready to be a "henchman." So, in the patriarchal fairy culture, *his* interests are best served by his joining Oberon. Moreover, while Oberon "beg"s Titania to give him the boy, she withholds him, not for *his* sake but for the sake of his deceased mother, her late votary. The loyalty part of the sentiment is creditable but the rest and the effects are not: withholding the boy is made a willful refusal to yield responsibly and sympathetically to Oberon's begging: it has no evident benefits for the boy, the boy's deceased mother, herself, or Oberon, now or hereafter.

It is easy and now common to take the situation out of the play or away from the dialogue, anachronize it, and paraphrase it into male bullying and female righteous resistance; but the particular wording of the dialogue stresses the play's principled view of the relative right and wrong of the case, with Oberon given the dialogue to have the better of it, despite Titania's speaking at much greater length and with considerable rhetorical force—and extraordinary poetical eloquence.[17] One could scarcely claim that all of Oberon's responses should be mild in delivery, as most are in phrasing, because some are clearly meant not to be (e.g., 2.1.63);[18] but they are mostly laconic (excepting 74-80) and matter-of-fact; it is Titania's speeches that are lengthy and heated. Oberon is hardly guiltless in his mischievous reaction, but his pitying her and regretting his harshness show him twice "human." To her famous setpiece on the disordered state of the land (2.1.81-117), he replies mildly,

Do you amend it then; it lies in you.
Why should Titania cross her Oberon?
I do but *beg* a little changeling boy,
To be my henchman.

(2.1.118-21)

He repeats his appeal plaintively and companionably: "Give me that boy, and I will go with thee" (143). He is refused, Titania leaves, and the plot thickens and in degree darkens—more in some productions than in others: "Well, go thy way. Thou shalt not from this grove / Till I torment thee for this injury" (2.1.146-47). If it is his "torment," it is Titania's "injury"; or vice versa.

It is apparently Titania's jealousy that prompts her to accuse him of infidelity in courting the pastoral figment "Phillida" and of coming here from India because

. . . the bouncing Amazon,
Your buskin'd mistress, and your warrior love,[19]
To Theseus must be wedded, and you come
To give their bed joy and prosperity.

(70-73)

A supernatural kindness, *and* they come to share in conferring it. The reciprocal "*forgeries* of jealousy" are important not because they seem true but because they evaporate as soon as the quarrel ceases—with Oberon having the boy as henchman and Titania being released from the effects of love-in-idleness.[20]

Oberon's "I wonder if Titania be awak'd; / Then what it was that next came in her eye, / Which she must dote on in extremity" (3.2.1-3) can be taken to express some solicitude as well as eagerness to hear the worst, but the comic worst is what it heralds: it is an audience incitement with characterological detail. The denouement is 4.1.46-103, in the middle of which is an imperative that cries out for a youth musical, "rock the ground whereon these sleepers be" (86); and I am familiar with at least one rock-musical version, *The Dream*, directed by Chris Bond at the Half Moon Theatre in Mile End Road, London, in the spring of 1984.[21] The reunited couple indeed "will tomorrow midnight solemnly / Dance in Duke Theseus' house triumphantly, / And bless it to all fair prosperity" (4.1.88-90)—and so they do and so ends the play. The reconciliation of Oberon and Titania thus completes the harmonizing of the play's lovers eight and expresses it in the way and spirit of the time of Sir John Davies's nearly contemporary *Orchestra* (1594) in a dance.[22]

FLOWER POWER: THE DOTING AND THE ANTI-DOTE

Three are anointed into redirected affections: Titania and Lysander in 2.2 (27-34, 78-82), and Demetrius in 3.2 (102-09). Oberon initiates the dotings—and later supplies the antidote—with the best intentions, except for his practical joke played on Titania by means of flower power such that "The juice of it on sleeping eyelids laid / Will make or man or woman madly dote / Upon the next live *creature* that it sees" (2.1.170-72). Invisible, he sympathetically apostrophizes Helena, just departed in pursuit of Demetrius: "Fare thee well, nymph. Ere he do leave this grove, / Thou shalt fly him, and he shall seek thy love" (2.1.245-46). And he directs Puck, in disastrously general terms but according to his best lights (he hasn't seen Hermia and Lysander), to anoint the eyes of the "disdainful youth" in "Athenian garments" (2.2.260-66). So much for Hermia's Lysander, for the nonce.

Much concern is expressed by Demetriologists: is he restored to his original love, or is he *compelled* by Oberon's psychopharmacology to love Helena for evermore? He *is* anointed with the doting flower: "Flower of this purple dye, / Hit with Cupid's archery, / Sink in apple of his eye" (3.2.102-4). Both the "flower" and Demetrius' Lysander-like infatuated exclamations of adoration upon awakening and seeing Helena seem to say so. So also says the fact that Lysander is cured of doting by a different, antidotal herb that Puck is supposed to "crush . . . into Lysander's eye," which with its "liquor hath this virtuous property, / To take from thence all error with his might, / And make his eyeballs roll with wonted sight" (3.2.366-69). But though Demetrius is anointed with the flower that makes Titania and Lysander dote, his seems a case of homeopathic medicine, in effect a cure of the infection of doting upon Hermia's eyes (1.1.230) that, unlike the others, he had contracted without floral influence.

And the incantation over Demetrius is different from that over the others. Shakespeare attuned the heptasyllabic incantations accompanying each of the anointings to the individual case and left little room for doubt about any.[23] Sympathetic as before with the young lovers' plight, Oberon sends Puck to fetch Helena, saying he "will charm" Demetrius' "eyes against she do appear" (3.2.99). His incantation is carefully distinctive:

> When *his love* he doth espy,
> Let her shine as gloriously
> As the Venus of the sky.
> When thou wak'st, if she be by,
> Beg of her for remedy.
>
> (3.2.102-09)

"His love" is unequivocally specific, by contrast with the incantation over Lysander, meant for Demetrius but made

general in expression by Puck as in Oberon's instructions: "When thou wak'st, let love forbid / Sleep his seat on thy eyelid" (2.2.79-80). "His love" contrasts all the more with the horridly specific incantation over Titania—"What thou seest when thou dost wake, / Do it for thy true-love take; . . . / Wake when *some vile thing* is near" (2.2.27-28, 34). The "apple of his eye" (pupil, but object, too) is equally specific, and "Beg of her for remedy" says that Demetrius needs no other *and* no antidote, which he has had already.

Finally, Demetrius is made to be at pains to explain his case to Theseus (and to us) thus:

> . . . my good lord, I wot not by what power
> (But by some power it is), my love to Hermia
> (Melted as the snow) seems to me now
> As the remembrance of an idle gaud,
> Which in my childhood *I did dote upon*;
> And all the faith, the virtue of my heart,
> The object and the pleasure of mine eye,
> Is only Helena. To her, my lord,
> Was I betrothed ere I [saw] Hermia;
> But like a sickness did I loathe this food;
> *But, as in health, come to my natural taste,*
> Now I do wish it, love it, long for it,
> And will for evermore be true to it.
>
> (4.1.164-76)[24]

These measured but enthusiastic lines have the ring of sincerity and truth, and are some distance from the sheer infatuation and excess of the lovers in a trance.

The others' "doting" is cured by applying the "anti[-]dote"—with an implicit etymological joke; Shakespeare uses "antidote" once only, without jest, in *Macbeth,* who yearns for "some sweet oblivious antidote" to "Cleanse the stuff'd bosom" (5.3.43-44). The spells of curative reanointing are equally differentiated: wittily ironical and generic in Lysander's case (3.2.448-63), personal and affectionate in Titania's.

> Be as thou wast wont to be;
> See as thou wast wont to see.
> Dian's bud [o'er] Cupid's flower
> Hath such force and blessed power.
> Now, my Titania, wake you, my sweet queen.
>
> (4.1.71-75)

But suppose Demetrius *were* in a permanent trance. True love is partly that, and for lasting and reciprocated love it is a small—and unconscious—price to pay. Oberon prophesies (or proclaims), "back to Athens shall the lovers wend / With league whose date till death shall never end" (3.2.372-73).

Bottom's deliverance is Puck's removing of the ass-head with a single line of unceremonious blank verse: "Now, when thou wak'st, with thine own fool's eyes peep" (4.1.84).

BOTTOM, BESTIALITY, AND NOBLESSE OBLIGE

The rise of the phallus in *Dream* production probably dates from Peter Brook's priapic scenario for his post-

1960s *Dream* (1970). What still had some shock value then—even after *Hair* (1968) and *Oh, Calcutta!* (1969), but this was Shakespeare—has come to be *de rigueur* in many quarters of the book trade as well as on stage, as witness the covers or dust jackets of (1) Selbourne's *Making of "A Midsummer Night's Dream"* (1982), with its photograph of Bottom borne sitting on the backs of his fellows, one of whom has a fisted, upraised forearm thrust up between Bottom's legs; (2) the Oxford/World's Classics edition (1994), with 1628 woodcut of Robin Goodfellow with notable erection (1628); and (3) *Shakespeare in Performance*: *"A Midsummer Night's Dream"* (1994), without phallics but with Titania topless (for all practical purposes, near-transparent body stocking notwithstanding). Few major productions since Brook's have failed to show the pressure of Kott and Brook.

But Bottom's conduct as Titania's pampered and enthralling gentle-mortal guest is unexceptionably punctilious and as courtly as it can be, which in its way is very: Titania's "ear is much enamour'd" of "his note" (3.1.138), and he is "a very paramour for a sweet voice," as Quince malapropises later (4.2.11-12). I doubt whether the conceit of Bottom's copulating with Titania much precedes Brook's 1970 production, but it has certainly been rampant since. I agree entirely with part of Holland's comment, "What is so remarkable about Titania's night with Bottom is not a subdued, suppressed sexual bestiality that has only been properly uncovered in the twentieth century but rather the innocence which transforms something that might so easily have been full of animal sexuality into something touchingly naïve" (73); but the "sexual bestiality" seems to me not so much "properly uncovered" as untimely ripped. Such explicit eroticism is distinct from bawdy, a wholly different and typically comic and Shakespearean way of mediating sexuality in art. Titania says presumably with reference to the dewfall that "The moon, methinks, looks with a watery eye, / And when she weeps, weeps every little flower, / Lamenting some enforced chastity" (3.1.198-200). This is not a proclamation of celibacy but neither is it of sex at any price: it explicitly deplores sex by force. In a recent RSC production at the Royal Shakespeare Theatre, by something of a compromise Bottom and Titania, in decorous, half-dressed semi-private, copulated modestly and traditionally in the "missionary position," in a huge, inverted umbrella.[25]

It seems worth noting a quite different form of conceit in a glancing sally of ecclesiastical satire, or witticism without the satire, in Quince's exclamation, "Bless thee, Bottom, bless thee! Thou art translated" (3.1.118-19), from one sort of ass to another, as it were. This must have been accompanied by Quince's making the sign of the cross, and it quite possibly carried an allusion to a bishop's mitre and episcopal "translation" from see to shining see. Robin also uses the word in "I . . . left sweet Pyramus translated there" (3.2.31-32).

Bottom rises to the requirements of his courtly translation and himself practices noblesse oblige, the particular form

of socially benevolent behavior that Helena speaks for more generally as "manners," a value well above the "honor" of the infatuated young men and their brash devotion to their mistress Helena, and correspondingly harsh rejection of their sometime favorite, Hermia. Perhaps partly because the idea of "manners" has contracted from a stronger moral purport to something close to mere etiquette, it tends to be not much noticed in *Dream,* but, as already noted in connection with Theseus, it is certainly there and important, to Shakespeare as to his characters and some of his contemporaries. Bottom is at his gracious best as an ideal courtier translated favorite of the fairy queen (3.1, 4.1), and she is not wholly fool to find him "as wise as thou art beautiful" (3.1.148)—in manners, if not to the unbiased eye.[26] Titania tells her fairy courtiers to "Be kind and courteous to this gentleman" and "do him courtesies" (164, 174), and Bottom responds in kind with genial humor as he learns the fairies' names (179-96). And so he continues in 4.1 until he has "an exposition of sleep come upon me" (39), when the court fairies leave and Titania ends their dialogue with "Sleep thou, and I will wind thee in my arms. / . . . O how I love thee! How I dote on thee!" (40-45). The lack of stage directions at this point might be taken as performance latitude if not license for licentiousness. But both Q1 and F have Oberon present "behind" (i.e., "unseen," eds.) for the entire action, which could hardly pass uninterrupted if it were played as in some recent productions and Oberon were truly "jealous Oberon." After Titania's last line, both she and Bottom inferentially now sleeping, Oberon bids "Welcome, good Robin. Seest thou this sweet sight? / Her dotage now I do begin to pity" (46-47).

DREAM AS MORE THAN DREAM

The manifold ramifications of literary and figurative dream in *Dream* have understandably occupied the attention and sometimes obsessed the imagination of theatrical and academic exponents alike, often with a regrettable suppressing of the play's socioethical implications. That these were important to Shakespeare is evident in the emphasis they receive in *Dream,* comic at one end of the aesthetic scale in Bottom's delightful attempt, like Christopher Sly's, to rise to the greatness thrust upon him; serious at the other end to the point of—near—deadly earnest in the discord between the lovers. Helena as sentient victim is one of Shakespeare's most persuasive spokespersons for the theme:

HELENA.

> *If you were civil and knew courtesy,*
> You would not do me thus much injury. . . .
> If you were men, as men you are in show,
> You would not use a gentle lady so.

> (3.2.147-48, 151-52)

The sentiment is significant enough—as well as dramatically pertinent and compelling—to be repeated, still more plaintively and with a keen sense of the modes of mockery, when Helena includes her dearest, oldest friend Hermia:

If you have any pity, grace, or manners,
You would not make me such an argument.

(3.2.241-42)

What is said here is—again—socially important, unequivocal, and psychologically and philosophically true, not less now than in Shakespeare's day. To bury such humane and ethical sentiments in stage business, gender psychology, and mesmerism is to maim the play and abuse the audience and its civil culture simultaneously.

Demetrius remarks that "It seems to me / That yet we sleep, we dream" (4.1.193-94); and the lovers' experience, including Titania's and Bottom's, is very dreamlike, whereas much of the play's internal experience is less so, even as it centers *on* the fairies. And yet. Bottom's dream "hath no bottom" because he hath it, for good and always.

BLESS THEE, AEGEUS, BLESS THEE, THOU ART TRANSLATED; or WHENCE AND WHITHER A PATERNAL SENEX IRATUS AND A PANTALOON?

Disappearing without a trace in act 4, Egeus by his incorrigible irritability and intolerance would seem to have written himself out of the script before the matrimonial action of act 5 (in Q1), pronouncing his own epitaph, in effect, with his terminal Shylock-like, epizeuxis-laden lines calling for "the law, the law upon his [Lysander's] head," etc. (4.1.154-59). Among important recent editions, only the Oxford and Norton *Complete Works,* and the Oxford/World's Classics single-play text, replace Q1's act-5 Philostrate with F's Egeus and give some of Theseus' Q1 lines to Lysander (F).[27] The reasons were critical judgment and a belief that Folio changes represent Shakespearean revision, especially if they seem to have a theatrical orientation.[28] The scholarly consensus (both Oxfords included) is that Q1 (1600) derives from autograph foul papers, whereas F derives from Q2 (the 1619 reprint disguised as "1600") to some extent collated with and reflecting the promptbook, "the source for many of F's substantive variants from Q" (279). William B. Long, Randall McLeod, and others have argued that the playbook of Shakespeare's day was nothing like so orderly and consistent as Greg's and textual posterity's theoretical "prompt-book," an entity of importance in modern theatrical practice (see, e.g., Maguire 23 f. and Long 125-43). "If a rule is needed for judging what happened to a playwright's manuscript in the theater, it should be, 'as little as possible'" (Long 127); and only as much as was essential to clarify performance.

There is no very specific evidence for dating act 5 changes involving Egeus and Lysander. F's act divisions postdate 1609;[29] the F stage direction, "'Tawyer with a Trumpet before them'" (5.1.125.1/TLN 1924), probably "originated in a relatively late revival," since there is no known record of Tawyer "(presumably William)" before 1624.[30] Yet Taylor argues for other Folio variants:

> Some of these clearly originate in the prompt-book; others are clearly necessary; others involve the alteration of Q readings which seem acceptable to a casual or even an alert reader, and which therefore can hardly have originated in the whims of an unassisted printing-house 'editor'. Without strong evidence to the contrary, one must therefore assume that the prompt-book is the authority for all added or substantially altered Folio directions and speech-prefixes. Some of these variants might derive from late revivals, over which Shakespeare had no control; but none certainly do, and only the act divisions and Tawyer's name can be confidently associated with performances later than those in the mid 1590s. Although each direction has been considered on its merits, we have found no reason to doubt that the bulk of the Folio directions represent the play as originally and authoritatively staged. Those directions which clearly envisage a different staging from that implied by Q seem to us to be dramatic improvements for which Shakespeare was probably responsible.

(279-80)

This is a good example of what appears to be the Folio bias in action and effect. If there were no such bias, one might expect the practice described above to be reversed, thus: "Although each [F variant] has been considered on its merits, we have found no reason to doubt that the bulk of the [Q1] directions represent the play as originally and authoritatively staged"—or at least authoritatively conceived and composed, since authority qualifies conception and composition better than it can qualify staging as such. Such quartos as Q1 are (and historically were) certainly—as well as by definition—closer to their authorial origins than was "the prompt-book," a playbook of usually mixed authority lying somewhere between holograph and F. From his study of manuscript playbooks of the period, in this case especially *John a Kent and John a Cumber,* William B. Long concludes,

> On the basis of this earliest surviving example, the difference between the literary document—the fair copy of the play manuscript sold to the company by a fledgling playwright nevertheless aware of an ongoing theatrical tradition—and the theatrical document—the play as adapted to playing needs by the company—was merely seven short annotations indicating how few markings a given company felt it necessary to employ in its playbook.

(139-40)

Critical judgment of variants is not easily separated from assumptions or inferences about their origin, and these work in a circle—hermeneutic, not necessarily vicious: if the F variants are thought superior, they must have come from an authoritative source. Since it has been demonstrated that F was set from Q2 (1619), the ultimate source of "Shakespearean" alterations had to be "the prompt-book," from which details were copied into the copy of Q2. It seems likely that such details were copied from the promptbook, but it seems quite as likely—even more likely, to my way of thinking—that some changes made in Q2 between 1619 and 1623 reflected evolving theatrical practice unconnected with Shakespeare. If so, which changes were Shakespeare's?

Deborah Cass as Titania, Tony Van Bridge as Bottom, and the Fairies in Act IV, scene i of the 1960 Stratford Festival production of
A Midsummer Night's Dream.

Since there is no apparent theatrical reason for Egeus to replace Philostrate—the same actor could have played both parts without altering the script[31]—the purpose must have been to bring back and reconcile Egeus, who otherwise disappears in act 4, very like Shylock in *The Merchant of Venice*—dismissed to unhappiness, as it were. Holland notes that "audiences are unlikely to object if Egeus proves to be the person at court who fulfills that role [of Master of Revels], as in Bill Alexander's 1986 production" (267-68). Alexander went only half way, however; he rejected F's Lysander and "retained the quarto's assignment to Theseus of V.i.44-60" (Halio 82). And "audiences are unlikely to object" is not compelling: is it a reason for making a change? Of course, Egeus' newly and miraculously congenial and solicitous presence can be defended thematically, socially, structurally, symbolically, and otherwise as necessary and transcendently fulfilling, supremely imaginative, and therefore profoundly Shakespearean: nothing comes easier than symmetry, sentiment, and sophistry. Less grandly, it ties up loose ends and satisfies supposed audience expectations or

desires—good enough theatrical and commercial reasons for making changes, but slight and arbitrary in this instance.

In F these perfunctory changes of speech assignment could have been made by virtually anyone—especially incompletely (one of the six speeches is still Philostrate's in F at 5.1.76). Shakespeare's complicity cannot in reason be forced much further than Brooks's description of a "change Shakespeare cannot have wished for, though he might acquiesce in it as an expedient" (xxxii). Even if Shakespeare made the change—how shall we know?—he must have done so mechanically and in haste, altering nothing for sense or consonance, merely reassigning speeches. This is hardly what one would expect of the author of the inferred addition of the poet to the company of the lover and madman in Theseus' great setpiece, or of any other addition or revision with content enough to evaluate. In short, there seems no reason to dignify such "revision" by finding Shakespeare guilty of it. It should be axiomatic that a "revision" anyone could execute—above all a cut but any purely mechanical change as well—not only need not but should not be assigned to Shakespeare—or to any other playwright—without strong positive reasons.

The respective stage directions are

Enter Theseus, Hyppolita, and Philostrate. Q1, TLN 1736

Enter Theseus, Hippolita, Egeus and his Lords. F, TLN 1792

The sole business assuredly Shakespeare's is Q1's, which opens with a subscene's intimate conversation between Theseus and Hippolyta that Philostrate need not overhear even if "present" for 1-27.

Replying to Theseus' enquiry, Philostrate (or Egeus) says, "There is a brief how many sports are ripe. / Make choice of which your Highness will see first" (42-43). This has no stage direction in Q1 and needs none; it has none in F, which could well use something to explain how not Theseus, to whom the brief is offered (Q1), but Lysander (*Lis.* F), comes to read the titles of the entertainments, with Theseus responding only with a comment on each. In Q1 Theseus both reads the title and makes the comment, which has obvious stageworthiness and makes sense of Philostrate's presentation lines. Theseus is the ruler, after all. Here Brooks follows Q1 but the Oxford et al. follow F. Holland explains,

> While some commentators have worried why Lysander should be given the task, whether Philostrate has had his place usurped or has turned away in a huff, and whether the hierarchies and niceties of court behaviour have been disrupted, the dialogue certainly works more effectively when split between Lysander and Theseus, involving one more character in the action.
>
> (265)

Whether F's version works more effectively depends very much upon what confidence and ingenuity are invested in performance, but it seems quite as gratuitous as the reassignment of Philostrate's lines to Egeus. There is no cogent explanation available for either and not much to be said for them in effect, whatever may be said of them in theory, so there is little reason to think they are Shakespeare's. Instances of virtually certain Shakespearean revision there are, Theseus' setpiece poet probably prominent among them.[32] But it requires no strain to conclude that there was less Shakespearean revision than has recently been asserted.

THE EPILOGUE OF PUCK AND ROBIN

These are one and the same fairy with the significant but long-neglected difference that "Puck" is *a* Puck, a species of fairy.[33] In *Dream* he is identified for us first by a nameless fairy as "that shrewd and knavish sprite / Call'd Robin Goodfellow" (2.2.33-34), very likely a propitiatory name.[34] The fairy adds, "Those that Hobgoblin call you, and sweet Puck, / You do their work, and they shall have good luck. / Are not you he?" General awareness of the distinction considerably postdated Katharine Briggs's *Anatomy of*

Puck (1959). Both "Puck" and "Robin" occur together as speech headings (with and without abbreviation) in the earliest editions (Qq, F), but "Puck" has been the received normalization. Only recently has "Robin" become the normalized—unambiguous—speech heading, in the Oxford (and Norton) editions. "Puck" may well survive, however, since it is traditional and everyone knows who is intended: though there are many fairies in *Dream,* there is only one Puck.[35]

Shakespeare sometimes seems to mark by name the changing faces and functions of this character obedient to the letter of command but mischief-loving most of the time, who is thoroughly benign in the terminal couplet of the Epilogue, but with darker edges and affinities manifested here and there before. In 3.2, for example, Oberon bids "Robin, overcast the night," and "The starry welkin cover thou anon / With drooping fog as black as Acheron" (355-57). "Puck" (his speech heading in Qq, F) replies,

> My fairy lord, this must be done with haste,
> For Night's swift dragons cut the clouds full fast,
> And yonder shines Aurora's harbinger,
> At whose approach, ghosts, wand'ring here and there,
> Troop home to churchyards. Damned spirits all,
> That in crossways and floods have burial,
> Already to their wormy beds are gone.
> For fear lest day should look their shames upon,
> They willfully themselves exile from light,
> And must for aye consort with black-brow'd Night.
>
> (3.2.378-87)

From this poetical digression into the world of *Hamlet* or *Macbeth* he is quickly recalled by Oberon's reminder that "we are spirits of another sort." "Puck" assumes the darker character again and flirts with a pre-Gothic genre when he enters, alone, after the lovers have gone to bed, beginning, "Now the hungry lion roars," and going on to other gloomy and chilling "Now" events in

> Now it is the time of night
> That the graves, all gaping wide,
> Every one lets forth his sprite,
> In the church-way paths to glide,

a deliberate, spine-tingling, ghost-story warmup (371-82) before he modulates to "we fairies . . . / Now are frolic" and his present office: "I am sent with broom before / To sweep the dust behind the door" (390).

Is anything to be made of the separate names and designations? Is the Puck a sinister species given to recalcitrance at best, and Robin an exceptional member with a better nature made evident as such by the use of his name? Or to put that differently, is anything to be made of the uses of "his" multiple names in the play—in the text, the stage directions, and the speech headings? Brooks notes that the "most striking variations [in speech-prefixes] are between 'Puck' and some version of 'Robin Goodfellow'. These can readily be understood as corresponding each to the aspect of the character then uppermost in Shakespeare's mind" (xxiv). This plausible and intelligent interpretation may well be right. His detailed "explanation of how they came to alternate in the Q1 text" (xxiv-v) distinguishes between "Puck" as Oberon's messenger and "Robin" as the mischief-maker "acting on his own initiative."

I am inclined to see (the) "Puck" as having the darker nature, "Robin" as the more sociable. But the distribution of names in *Dream* does not seem to support the distinction (or Brooks's). The names occur in dialogue only nine times. In stage directions and speech headings they distribute pretty much—not by formes but—by the printer's sheet in Q1, with "Robin" in sheets B, D, and F; and "Puck" in C and E.[36] Uses in the dialogue are not much more evidently deliberate *except* in the Epilogue.

There has been no grave harm done in normalizing to "Puck" (or "Robin") throughout, but doing so—like normalizing to the personal name "Othello" or "Shylock"—obscures a distinction and a conjunction that the inconsistent speech-headings of the early editions emphasize, presumably inadvertently: the identity of the individual and the anomaly of the group ("Moor," "Jew," "Puck"). Shakespeare himself seems to use both in close proximity and interchangeably but for the meter: "Welcome, good Robin. Seest thou this sweet sight?" (4.1.45/ TLN 1513), where "Puck" would be unmetrical; "And, gentle Puck, take this transformed scalp" (63/1531), where either name could be used, depending upon "transforme/ 'd."[37] In that context both names have a positive valence, even if "good" is mainly phatic and "gentle" reflects status more than behavior (oxymoronically), itself as much phatic as flattering.

In any case, editorial normalizing and a sense of the interchangeability of names seem to have prevented readers from noting the Epilogue's—differential—use of both names. The stage direction says "Enter Pucke," and "Pucke"—5.1.370.1-71/TLN 2080-81, H3v—speaks the "prologue" to the fairies' song and dance; but "Robin"—l. 423/2133, H4—speaks the Epilogue.[38] Whether these differential speech headings represent deliberate division of character is doubtful, but in the Epilogue the use of both names appears to make a significant distinction between a threatening generic Puck and the obliging individual Robin. As "an honest Puck"—the Real Thing—the first appeals for "unearned luck / Now to scape the serpent's tongue" (432-33), promising "amends ere long" (434) if favored (cf. 2.1.32-43); but at the same time slyly threatens with "Else *the Puck* a liar call" (435), a very imprudent thing to do. After the Puck-in-effect concludes *his* part with "So, goodnight unto you all," by contrast, Robin-in-effect adds a genial terminal couplet, "Give me your hands, if we be friends, / And *Robin* shall restore amends" (437-38)—a clear advance from "amends ere long" (434).

It is no accident that the Epilogue, characteristically (for fairies) in heptasyllabics, opens with a falling rhythm in a trochaic-tetrameter couplet, and closes with a rising rhythm in an iambic-tetrameter couplet. The only other variation is an iambic-tetrameter line (431) beginning what is in effect the second octave. The first octave is impersonal and collective (beginning "we shadows"), and asks the "Gentles" to "think but this," that they have been asleep and dreaming; and "not [to] reprehend" a "theme / . . . yielding but a dream" (427-28).[39] It concludes equally generally, "If you pardon, we will mend" (430). Then the second octave turns personal with "I . . . an honest Puck" and "me" (Puck and/or Robin), and the semi-formal "Gentles" gives way to "if we be friends" (437), audience and Robin together. One takes "me" to be "Robin" exclusively, because he is named in the next, last line; but the point seems to be that the audience's giving their hands brings out the reciprocating Robin in the Puck. Anyhow, all are one in this conclusion.

Perhaps a pause cueing applause was intended or practiced between "So goodnight unto you all"—which has a terminal ring—and the closing couplet, "Give me your hands," which is affably forthcoming—and does mean "applaud," of course, the practical purport of all epilogues. But here the phrase must surely have been intended also to initiate hand-shaking. It is used in that way by Shakespeare many times with "hand" and four to six other times with "hands." Nearest in sense is *Julius Caesar* with Brutus' "Give me your hands all over, one by one" (2.1.112); and *The Tempest,* where Alonso says to Ferdinand and Miranda, "Give me your hands. / Let grief and sorrow still embrace his heart / That doth not wish you joy!" (5.1.213-15).[40] The gesture of taking hands is exactly right for Robin here, and it must have been the business of public performance in Shakespeare's day, when "the crowd of 'understanders'" would be "jostling alongside the amphitheatre platforms" (Gurr 179). With an elevated platform like the new Bankside Globe's, the natural action accompanying the lines would be the speaker's bending or kneeling to take the hands of spectators closest to the platform, whether right to right hand or, more likely, one by each hand, two by two.

"At the end" of Brook's *Dream,* "Puck and all his colleagues deliberately broke the magic—the magic created by theatre—by advancing into the audience on his final lines . . . and shaking hands with everyone they could reach. But of course such a tactic subtly continues the magic as well, making it linger in a way analogous to Puck's last speech, which both breaks and extends the illusion" (Dawson 24-25). The notion that *all* Puck does is invite applause is so deeply ingrained that no one seems to have remarked that Brook in effect rediscovered and elaborated on what must have been the original design, though Trewin comes close: "Puck, in his last two lines, . . . is inviting applause. Peter Brook interpreted the first words literally: his Puck (John Kane) jumped from the stage and came through the house, shaking hands left and right, the rest of the company at his heels. That was, and is, a fitting end to *A Midsummer Night's Dream*: all, on stage or off, must be at peace beneath the visiting moon" (105).

Such an "interactive" gesture, rather Michelangelic, makes an energetic kindred connection between the persons in and of the theater, and symbolically between the dramatic "shadows" brought together by the play for communal performance: of roles on the stage by players, and understanding and appreciation—their roles—off the stage by audience and spectators—for we too are shadows as such stuff as dreams—including this one—are made on, whose own little lives are rounded with a sleep. The script itself, itself shared, is the shadow of dialogue passing from actor to auditor and spectator, and through author, scribe, and printer (and editor) to reader: withal from poet-playwright to admirers of his making.

Notes

1. Or perhaps "Like." G. K. Hunter: "The question that is central to my discussion is . . . less 'what is this play about?' than 'what is this play like?'" (5). Unless otherwise specified, quotations are taken from the *Riverside Shakespeare,* 2nd ed.; and italics used for emphasis within quotations are mine unless otherwise specified. For familiarity's sake, I refer to Robin Goodfellow as "Puck" throughout.

2. Dent, "Imagination in *A Midsummer Night's Dream,*" 129; Kott, "Titania and the Ass's Head," in *Shakespeare Our Contemporary,* published in Poland in 1961 as *Szkice o Szekspirze,* in the U.S. in English in 1964, 175.

3. The two influenced each other, Brook through his 1955 production of *Titus Andronicus,* Kott by his book and through personal association. See Brook's Preface.

4. This is not meant to imply that there were not many—sometimes egregious—departures in preceding centuries, especially in production, on which see Halio, chs. 1-2.

5. The most substantial survey of contemporary thinking is to be found in Wells and Taylor's indispensable *Textual Companion*; see the condensed "Summary of Control-Texts," 145-47; and cf. the introduction to "Shakespeare's Text" in *Riverside* 55-69.

6. Belittling Theseus goes some way back; cf. even Young 138, 139; he quotes Hippolyta's 5.1.23-27 all or in part 4 times: [vii] epigraph with only 5 lines of Theseus' speech immediately preceding, 8, 140, and 180 as the last 2 lines of his book; since the title is *Something of Great Constancy,* this is not surprising.

7. Hippolyta has only 1.56% of *Dream*'s words by comparison with Theseus' 10%. Bottom has the highest percentage of all at 12.6 (10.3 as himself and 2.3 as Pyramus); Helena has 11.3 and Oberon 10. These figures should in general surprise no one, since the speakers variously speak best as well as most, except for Hippolyta, whose paucity of dialogue is quite sufficient in quality and content to articulate the

queen she is. The use of *word* counts eliminates the arbitrary disparity between verse and prose arising from "line counts" in editions of different size and design (e.g., quarto vs. folio). Spevack's *Concordance* provides the data for word counts based on *Riverside* (1st ed.).

8. See the section of this title and the whole of Cressy's chap. 10 on "Courtship and the Making of Marriage" (233-66).

9. For example, the New Arden and the Oxfords + Norton read *antique*. Pelican (1959, rev. 1971) and *Riverside* (1974, 1997) read "antic fables" (anticke F). As *OED2* notes, the spelling "antique" was used sometimes (as presumably in Q1) for the different word, "antic" (see both *antic* and *antique*).

10. "Wilson showed that if the irregular lines were removed, the text would still make excellent sense. . . . As W. W. Greg has said, 'There is no escaping the conclusion that in this we have the original writing, which was supplemented by fresh lines crowded into the margin so that their metrical structure was obscured.' . . . The obvious way of accounting for confusions in lineation in the quarto is to suppose that they result from alterations and reworkings made by the author in the course of composition" (Foakes 137).

11. The useful term is Bertrand Evans's.

12. "Several major speeches in this play are important not because they further the action or elaborate a character, but because they represent an explicit verbal development of ideas hinted at in other parts of the play. They are as it were arias in which snatches of melody heard elsewhere are fully developed" (Wells, ed. *Dream* 24).

13. In two post-1970s productions about a decade apart at the Tyrone Guthrie Theater, Minneapolis, director Liviu Ciulei did the former (1985) and Joe Dowling the latter (1997).

14. "Rude mechanicals" rather than "hempen homespuns" (both borrowed from Puck) is the form of reference preferred by most contemporary commentators.

15. *Might* as the third-person subjunctive of *may* (*OED2* v1). The New Variorum *Dream* records the difficulties of earlier editors with this passage; e.g., Johnson's note begins, "The sense of this passage as it now stands, if it has any sense, is this." Steevens alone seems to have recognized the wordplay, which has persistently gone unnoticed: "'In *might*' is, perhaps, an elliptical expression for *what might have been*" (210). It is apt and usual to gloss by the proverb, "To take the will for the deed" and "Everything is as it is taken" (Tilley, Dent, W393).

16. Demetrius' "No wonder, my lord; one lion may [speak], when many asses do" (153-54) *works* as a

joke fitting the ineptitude rather than as a snide judgment on the men playing their parts. It has been suggested that Moon is distraught by the courtiers' comments (232-45) and shows it when to Lysander's "Proceed, Moon" he replies, obligingly, "All that I have to say is to tell you that the lanthorn is the moon, I the man i' th' moon, this thorn-bush my thorn-bush, and this dog my dog" (257-59). He certainly could be played distraught, but at the expense of the manifest comic design, where the jokes and sociability, not the personal feelings of the player, are consistently foregrounded.

17. Notable exchanges and speeches by or about Oberon in this connection are 2.1.18-80, 118-47, 175-85; 3.2.374-77; 4.1.45-63, 70-82, 84-90 (87: "Now thou and I are new in amity").

18. In slanted productions Oberon tends to wax stentorian at every opportunity given or taken, partly on the hint, no doubt, of Puck's telling a fairy that "The King doth keep his revels here to-night; / Take heed the Queen come not within his sight; / For Oberon is passing fell and wrath," etc. (2.1.18-31). Puck's hyperbolical description expresses his swaggering for effect.

19. Neither "mistress" nor "love" implies coition; the case on this evidence is one of courtly courtship.

20. Greenblatt's reading differs: "Oberon and Titania have, we learn, long histories of amorous adventures; they are aware of each other's wayward passions; and, endowed with an extraordinary eroticizing rhetoric, they move endlessly through the spiced, moonlit night" (Norton 810-11). The character with a long history of amorous adventures is Theseus, four of whose liaisons are mentioned by Oberon (Perigenia, Aegles, Ariadne, and Antiopa; 2.1.77-80) in reproaching Hippolyta for her love of Theseus. Hippolyta and Antiopa are plainly differentiated here, but they were alternative names of the same Amazon, Antiopa/e the more common.

21. I saw it on 22 May. As an exuberant adaptation, it was arguably closer to the spirit—and therefore to the original letter—of *Dream* than many a recent "production." Bottom also played electric bass in the rock group providing the music, the "Hempen Homespuns."

22. The *orchestra* in ancient Greek and Greece was a dancing place. Shakespeare's *Rape of Lucrece,* in rhyme royal like *Orchestra,* also was printed in 1594.

23. Heptasyllabics are a distinctive verse-form of the fairies in *Dream* (though Puck usually speaks in pentameters) and of the Shakespearean Weïrd Sisters (but not Hecate) in *Macbeth,* among other uses. It has been written that "the brief waves of verse in other meters" than blank verse "serve mainly to change the rhythm or to provide a verse mode more appropriate for certain kinds of characters. The fair-

ies . . . signal their peculiar status (at least part of the time) through tetrameter couplets" (Wright 114). But (acatalectic, octosyllabic) tetrameters are the exceptions to heptasyllabic lines rather than the rule; and trochaics are still less frequent than occasional iambic tetrameters—e.g., the first two and last two lines of the Epilogue.

Heptasyllabics have a unique and variously exploitable lilt, and they are perhaps the most sense-enforcing kind of verse: the lines are almost invariably regular and the stresses especially serviceable in forcing the sense(s) and emphases intended. But most of Shakespeare's verse, including his blank verse, expresses its intended sense partly through meter, so it is a mistake to decide upon the sense and rhetoric of the words before entertaining the meter's dictates. This is one reason why it is useful for actors to understand versification—not technically, but functionally and semantically.

24. Demetrius' waking declaration of love for Helena (3.2.137-44) is similar to Lysander's (2.2.102-05, 111-22) and is taken so by Helena, but this is part of the (not uneasy) comedy of mistaken identity at midplay: "There's no art / to find the mind's construction in the face" (*Macbeth* 1.4.11-12)—or in the amatory utterance.

25. Dir. Adrian Noble, 1994-95; I saw it at the RST on 25 August 1994. In the 1970s *a tergo* became fashionable in productions of Jacobean tragedy, especially *The Changeling.*

26. Greenblatt finds him "the most flatulently absurd of the mechanicals" (Norton 807).

27. The F-based New Variorum *Dream* reads likewise.

28. So far as I know, no one has made a strong case for the changes. Oxford cites Barbara Hodgdon's "Gaining a Father" as making a critical case for following F with Egeus, but her case is mainly rhetorical. She dismisses Brooks's thoughtful argument in favor of Q1's Philostrate as "mask[ing] only slightly the subjectivity of equating Shakespeare's wishes with his own; I would counter his argument by noting that rejections of the Folio variants as theatrical expediency are themselves speculative" (535). She handles the awkwardness of Egeus as "our usual manager of mirth" by saying that, "since Theseus asks four questions in rapid succession, all of which have to do with the evening's entertainment, *it is most unlikely that an audience will pick up on* only one and thus question Philostrate's absence. Even if they do, the inconsistency is of a kind Shakespeare is all too famous for elsewhere" (538).

29. "The King's men appear not to have made use of such intervals before about 1609 (see Taylor, 'The Structure of Performance')" (*Textual Companion* 279b).

30. *Textual Companion* 279b; if "Tawyer" came so late, why not Egeus and Lysander? "William Tawyer, as

we know from the record of his burial ['June 1625, at St. Saviour's, Southwark'], was 'Mr. Heminges man'" (Brooks xxx). Extrapolating backward by way of Heminges, who was associated with Shakespeare's company from 1594 on, Berger infers that "Tawyer and his trumpet . . . could have been added at any time after the composition of the foul papers in the mid-1590s" (xi), whenever he was old enough, but we do not know when he was born.

31. And "Assertions that" the change "was made for reasons of doubling are unfounded and implausible" (*Textual Companion* 285a, 5.1.0.1/1700.1n).

32. Recent writings on revision are by now legion, among the seminal works being those by Warren (1978), Urkowitz (1980), the collection edited by Taylor and Warren (1983), and Ioppolo (1991).

33. In "All we like sheep . . ." elsewhere in this collection Susan Snyder includes consideration of Puck/Robin as an editorial problem in deciding how to designate characters in speech headings and stage directions.

34. Used in full otherwise only—and curiously, given its unnecessary length, which seems not likely to be authorial—in Q1 SDs (2.1.0.1/TLN 367, 3.2.0.1/988, and 4.1.45.1/1512).

35. "Robin Goodfellow, hobgoblins and pucks all belonged to the same group [genus?] of fairies. . . . Scot [*Discovery of Witchcraft*, 1584] lists all three as distinct and separate types of 'bug[bear]s'" (Holland 35).

36. Spellings vary: "Pu," "Puck," and "Pucke"; and "Ro," "Rob," "Robi," and "Robin." All could be Shakespearean. Some are instances of "decremental repetition," which occurs also in the Shakespearean pages of the MS of *Sir Thomas More* (see Clayton, "Today" 67, 73).

37. The word occurs with both 'd and ed pronunciations in Shakespeare.

38. Cf. Brooks: at 5.1.371 "on his mission as Oberon's and the fairies' harbinger, he enters and speaks as 'Puck'; but he addresses the audience in the Epilogue in the folk-lore character familiar to them: the epilogue prefix is Robin, and the last line promises: 'Robin shall restore amends.' Yet in the course of his address he has called himself 'the Puck' and 'an honest Puck' (l. [431]). By this time, no doubt, both appellations, 'Robin' and 'Puck', were always present in Shakespeare's mind" (xxv).

39. No one seems to gloss "theme," but perhaps it is not superfluous to give *OED2* 1b: "A subject treated by action (instead of by discourse, etc.); hence, that which is the cause of or for specified action, circumstance, or feeling; matter, subject. Obs."—and note that the first examples are from Shakespeare: *Titus Andronicus* 5.2.80 ("See heere he comes, and I

must play my theame"); and *Hamlet*. "Hamlet. Why I will fight with him vppon this Theme" (5.1.289) and "*Queen*. "Oh my sonne, what Theame? *Hamlet*. I lou'd Ophelia [etc.]."

40. The other plurals of the kind are *Richard II* 3.3.202 and *The Taming of the Shrew* 2.1.318. Two misleading "concordance cousins" are *Henry VI, Part 3*, 4.6.38 and *The Two Noble Kinsmen* 5.3.109; in these the speaker asks for the hands of two in order to join them together (Henry VI to Warwick and Clarence, Theseus to Emily and Arcite).

Works Cited

Briggs, Katharine. *The Anatomy of Puck*. London: Routledge and Kegan Paul, 1959.

Bullough, Geoffrey. *Narrative and Dramatic Sources of Shakespeare*. Vol. 7 (Major Tragedies). New York: Columbia University Press, 1973.

Clayton, Thomas. "Today We Have Parting of Names: A Preliminary Inquiry into Some Editorial Speech-(Be)headings in *Coriolanus*." In *Shakespeare's Speech-Headings*. Edited by George Walton Williams. Newark: University of Delaware Press, 1997. 61-99.

Cressy, David. *Birth, Marriage, and Death: Ritual, Religion, and the Life-Cycle in Tudor and Stuart England*. New York: Oxford University Press, 1997.

Dawson, Anthony B. *Watching Shakespeare: A Playgoers' Guide*. London: Macmillan Press, 1988.

Dent, R. W. "Imagination in *A Midsummer Night's Dream*." *Shakespeare Quarterly* 15 (1964): 115-29.

———. *Shakespeare's Proverbial Language: An Index*. Berkeley: University of California Press, 1981.

Evans, Bertrand. *Shakespeare's Comedies*. Oxford: Clarendon Press, 1960.

Gurr, Andrew. *The Shakespearean Stage 1574-1642*. 3rd ed. Cambridge: Cambridge University Press, 1992.

Halio, Jay L. *Shakespeare in Performance: "A Midsummer Night's Dream."* Manchester and New York: Manchester University Press, 1994.

Hodgdon, Barbara. "Gaining a Father: The Role of Egeus in the Quarto and the Folio." *Review of English Studies* NS 37 (1986): 534-42.

Hunter, G. K. *English Drama 1586-1642: The Age of Shakespeare*. Oxford History of English Literature 6. Oxford: Clarendon Press, 1997.

Ioppolo, Grace. *Revising Shakespeare*. Cambridge, MA: Harvard University Press, 1991.

Kott, Jan. "Titania and the Ass's Head." Translated by Boleslaw Taborski. In *Shakespeare Our Contemporary*. Rev edn. 1965, 171-90. London: Methuen & Co Ltd., 1967.

Long, William B. "*John a Kent and John a Cumber*: An Elizabethan Playbook and Its Implications." *Shakespeare and Dramatic Tradition: Essays in Honor of S. F. Johnson.* Edited by W. R. Elton and William B. Long. Newark: University of Delaware Press, 1989, 125-43.

Maguire, Laurie E. *Shakepearean Suspect Texts: The "Bad" Quartos and their Contexts.* Cambridge: Cambridge University Press, 1996.

Selbourne, David. *The Making of* [Brook's] "*A Midsummer Night's Dream.*" London: Methuen, 1982.

Shakespeare, William. *A Midsummer Night's Dream.* Edited by Harold F. Brooks. New Arden Shakespeare. London: Methuen & Co Ltd, 1979.

———. Edited by R. A. Foakes. New Cambridge Shakespeare. Cambridge: Cambridge University Press, 1984.

———. Edited by Horace Howard Furness. 1895. New Variorum Shakespeare. New York: Dover Publications, Inc., 1963.

———. Edited by Trevor R. Griffiths. Shakespeare in Production. Cambridge: Cambridge University Press, 1996.

———. Edited by Peter Holland. World's Classics. Oxford: Oxford University Press, 1994.

———. Edited by Gary Taylor (John Jowett, "Scrutinizer"). In *William Shakespeare: The Collected Works.* Oxford: Clarendon Press, 1986.

———. Edited by Stanley Wells. New Penguin Shakespeare. Harmondsworth: Penguin Books Ltd., 1967.

———. *A Midsummer Night's Dream 1600* [Q1]. Prepared by Thomas L. Berger. Malone Society Reprints. Oxford: Oxford University Press, 1995.

———. *The Norton Facsimile: The First Folio of Shakespeare.* Prepared by Charlton Hinman. New York: W. W. Norton & Company Inc., 1968.

———. *The Norton Shakespeare.* Edited by Stephen Greenblatt (general editor), Walter Cohen, Jean E. Howard, and Katharine Eisaman Maus. New York: W. W. Norton, 1997.

———. *The Riverside Shakespeare.* 2d ed. Edited by G. Blakemore Evans. Boston: Houghton Mifflin Company, 1997.

———. *William Shakespeare: The Complete Works.* Edited by Stanley Wells and Gary Taylor. Oxford: Clarendon Press, 1986.

Spevack, Marvin, comp. *A Complete and Systematic Concordance to the Works of [the Riverside, 1st ed.] Shakespeare.* Hildesheim: Georg Olms, 1968-80.

Taylor, Gary, and Michael Warren, eds. *The Division of the Kingdoms: Shakespeare's Two Versions of "King Lear."* Oxford Shakespeare Studies. Oxford: Clarendon Press, 1983.

Tilley, Morris Palmer. *A Dictionary of the Proverbs in England in the Sixteenth and Seventeenth Centuries.* Ann Arbor: University of Michigan Press, 1950.

Trewin, J. C. *Going to Shakespeare.* London: George Allen & Unwin, 1978.

Urkowitz, Steven. *Shakespeare's Revision of "King Lear."* Princeton: Princeton University Press, 1980.

Warren, Michael J. "Quarto and Folio *King Lear* and the Interpretation of Albany and Edgar." In *Shakespeare, Pattern of Excelling Nature.* Edited by David Bevington and Jay L. Halio. Newark: University of Delaware Press, 1978.

Wells, Stanley, and Gary Taylor. *William Shakespeare: A Textual Companion.* Oxford: Clarendon Press, 1987.

Wright, George T. *Shakespeare's Metrical Art.* Berkeley: University of California Press, 1988.

Young, David P. *Something of Great Constancy: The Art of "A Midsummer Night's Dream."* New Haven: Yale University Press, 1966.

Gail Kern Paster and Skiles Howard (essay date 1999)

SOURCE: Paster, Gail Kern and Skiles Howard, eds. Introduction to A Midsummer Night's Dream: *Texts and Contexts,* edited by Gail Kern Paster and Skiles Howard, pp. 1-9. Boston: Bedford/St. Martin's, 1999.

[*In the following essay, Paster and Howard survey the themes and central action of* A Midsummer Night's Dream *and provide a general review of critical trends.*]

A Midsummer Night's Dream is enchanting, lyrical, and very funny. So say generations of readers and audiences captivated by the play's eclectic mingling of lovers, fairies, and artisan actors in an action filled with mythological allusions and moved by the combined power of love, magic, and self-conscious theatricality. Thematically, the play stands forth as a comedy about romantic desire and the trials of imagination. Its two central actions—the love chase of Hermia, Helena, Lysander, and Demetrius and the encounter between a metamorphosed Bottom and the fairy queen Titania—symbolize the arbitrary power of lovers' imaginations to transform the beloved from just another human being into an incomparable individual. In its framing and subsidiary actions—the nuptial festivities of Theseus and Hippolyta and the artisans' hilarious rehearsal and performance of their version of "Pyramus and Thisbe"—the play extends its social reach to bring figures from classical legend together with humble (but aspiring) workingmen. In the melding of these comic materials, Shakespeare suggests that courtship, marriage, and putting on a play have much in common. All three are unpredictable, creative enterprises requiring daring, hope, and a willingness to look foolish in the eyes of others.

In the Athens of Theseus, the protocols of love are full of comic potential. Bottom opines wisely to Titania that "reason and love keep little company together nowadays" (3.1.119-20). In this summary judgment and commonplace wisdom, only the qualifying adverb "nowadays" is suspect. Nothing in the play's texture of allusion and mythology suggests that love was *ever* rational or comprehensible to the spectator from the outside or the desiring subject from within. In action, the onset of love produces events that are painful and/or hilarious to witness. From the opening of the play, Shakespeare hints at what troubles lovers in the passage from courtship to marriage. Theseus has had to conquer a woman's desire for autonomy—symbolized here by the Amazon Hippolyta. The four young lovers have to conquer various obstacles, both internal and external, ranging from the volatility of male desire to the opposition of Hermia's father and the mutual suspicions harbored by all four of them. These young lovers, while seeming overwhelmed by passion, have reason to be suspicious of love. When the men change from loving Hermia to loving Helena, their change of heart is violently expressed as hatred for the disavowed one: "Hang off, thou cat, thou burr," Lysander shouts to the bewildered Hermia, "Or I will shake thee from me like a serpent!" (3.2.260-61). Lysander and Demetrius seem to know no intermediate form of address to the women, oscillating between extremes of adoration and degradation. Oberon has transformed their vision, has altered the object of their desire, but he is not responsible for everything that Lysander and Demetrius say. And, given Oberon's (mis)management of his powers to create and destroy desire through magical love juice, the three couples at the end of the play will need fairy blessings and more to stay faithful to one another, to bear and raise happy children, and to keep their houses from harm.

For their part, the fairy spouses quarrel so bitterly over custody of Titania's foster child that Oberon is moved to punish and humiliate his queen by causing her to dote absurdly on Bottom. When Puck reports how it came to pass that "Titania waked and straightway loved an ass," Oberon replies with delight: "This falls out better than I could devise" (3.2.34-35). But its depiction of love as irrational, sudden, and even self-destructive does not prevent *A Midsummer Night's Dream* from finally endorsing romantic love as the basis of marriage, even if such endorsement requires myth, magic, and amnesia for its consummation. "These things seem small and undistinguishable," Demetrius says with puzzlement when the four lovers awake after their strife-filled night in the woods, "Like far-off mountains turnèd into clouds" (4.1.182-83). The job of comedy—so the play's joyous conclusion implies—is to imagine the attainment of long life, true love, and good children not as an arbitrary accident of fortune but as a reward for suffering, albeit the limited and predictable kind of suffering that goes here under the fanciful rubric of romantic misadventure in the woods. Perhaps it is this complex combination of recognition and endorsement that has recommended the play to generation after generation of playgoers.

Its enduring popularity and its undeniable charm are proof of *A Midsummer Night's Dream*'s greatness as comedy.

But questions other than the play's greatness have also preoccupied scholars for a long time; we intend to address them, at least in part, through the documents included in this volume. In the last two decades, much literary scholarship has been engaged in showing that Shakespeare's plays, including the romantic comedies, are deeply entwined in the sociocultural circumstances of early modern England. In the case of *A Midsummer Night's Dream,* understanding of the play has been complicated and deepened by critical attention to the political tensions and social conflicts embedded in its contextual history. Scholars have investigated, for example, the play's reproduction of the social structures of rank and gender. They have noted that the play treats Peter Quince and his fellow laboring men as less than fully adult. The mechanicals even seem to acquiesce in such infantilizing treatment, referring repeatedly to themselves as "every mother's son." Some scholars have wondered whether this affectionate but somewhat condescending portrayal is linked, defensively, to Elizabethan social tensions in the wake of widespread unrest and local uprisings in the mid-1590s (Leinwand, "'I believe'"); others have seen the mechanicals as a complexly ironic self-representation by Shakespeare the professional man of the theater, as a playful strategy for distancing his company of the Lord Chamberlain's Men from amateur players (Montrose, *Purpose* 205).

As with the mechanicals, so with other elements of the play: tracing out the play's complex interconnections with its culture has led scholarship in many directions. Thus some scholars have wished to follow the leads offered by the text's geographical allusions to "the farthest step of India" (2.1.69), where Titania's beloved foster child was born and whence Oberon has come to witness the wedding of Hippolyta to Theseus. In these geographical references, post-colonialist critics argue, we may glimpse the early traces of England's imperial future and its emerging preoccupation with the structures of racial and geographical difference (Hendricks). For feminist historians in particular, the play's opening allusion to the conquered Amazons and Theseus's strange pronouncement to Hippolyta that he has "won thy love doing thee injuries" (1.1.17) have prompted historical and theoretical critique. Feminists have noted the gender tensions, the note of complaint directed at all women, implied in the impatient bridegroom Theseus's comparison of the moon to "a stepdame or a dowager / Long withering out a young man's revenue" (1.1.5-6). Rather than dismissing the opening dispute between Hermia and her father as merely the generic furniture of comedy, the romantic conflict required to move the action, scholars have paid serious historical attention to the generational, gender, and religious tensions suggested by so prominent a disagreement over whose desire counts most in the matter of marital choice. To them, Theseus's dictum to Hermia that "to you your father should be as a god" (1.1.47) sounds less like a patriarch's serene orthodoxy and more like his embattled hope. And, of course, cultural historians of all stripes have sought to understand the full force and political implications of the play's several allusions to Queen Elizabeth. It is she, and not Titania, whom literate Elizabethans would have identified as "the fairy queen," whether or not they had read Edmund Spenser's great romantic poem. More specifically, in *A Midsummer Night's Dream,* it is Elizabeth to whom Oberon refers as "a fair vestal thronèd by the west," the "imperial vot'ress" (2.1.158, 163). In the play's mythmaking, she alone is said to be immune to the lovebolts of Cupid, in her "maiden meditation, fancy-free" (164).

Flattering acknowledgment of offstage royal beings is characteristic—indeed virtually required—of court entertainments. It is one reason why arguments continue to flourish about whether or not *A Midsummer Night's Dream* was originally commissioned to celebrate an aristocratic wedding (Chambers 1: 358). Evidence to support such claims remains inconclusive (if tantalizing), and it seems safer to assume with Louis Montrose that Shakespeare, the public playwright, would have wanted to write plays with broad appeal, plays suitable for private performance at court or an aristocratic household (*Purpose* 160-61). Even so, flattery of royal personages is much less characteristic of plays written for the public theaters where kings and queens never came. Furthermore, it is important to recognize that the play's treatment of *its* fairy queen is far more complex and ambivalent than mere flattery would warrant. Hence scholars have seen real if ambiguous tensions in the play's relations to the monarch, perhaps fueled by what Montrose has called "processes of disenchantment," which are "increasingly evident in Elizabethan cultural productions of the 1580s and 1590s" (*Purpose* 165). It has been important for recent scholarship to explicate the play's varied strategies of allusion and disenchantment, to note the tensions of class, gender, and generation often embedded in the play's metaphorical language or, as with the Amazons and the Indian boy, given importance through reference rather than representation. In such metaphors and allusions we may trace the cultural dialogue in which the play is rooted.

In the commentary and documents of this volume, we have sought to include what seem to us the most important of the many perspectives introduced by such recent historical scholarship, though to do them all justice would require many more pages and many more documents than we have space for. Suffice it to say that we, like others before us, see the play's text saturated by the massive, overarching social and cultural changes occurring in post-Reformation England over the course of the sixteenth century. While it may always be difficult to detail the effect of such changes on the production of specific literary texts, it is almost impossible to overstate their overall transformation of cultural practices. As historian Charles Phythian-Adams has suggested,

> for urban communities in particular, the middle and later years of the sixteenth century represented a more abrupt break with the past than any period since the era of the Black Death or before the age of industrialization. Not only were specific customs and institutions brusquely changed or abolished, but a whole, vigorous,

and variegated popular culture, the matrix of everyday life, was eroded and began to perish.

(57)

In England, the kind of changes that we highlight in this volume were wrought, directly and indirectly, by the Protestant Reformation—what happened during the 1530s when the English abandoned their allegiance to Roman Catholicism and created the national church, today's Church of England. We understand that Reformation not merely as a change in religious practice and doctrine, but rather as a large-scale social, cultural, and intellectual transformation. The revolutionary changes of most interest to us here include (but obviously are not limited to) the following: a transformation of holiday customs, festive practices, and the official calendar; the disappearance of monastic ways of life, especially for women; the centralization of state power around a charismatic ruler and the regularization of the patriarchal nuclear family; and a massive redefinition of supernatural agency and the proper objects of belief.

A history of the English Reformation is of course well beyond our intentions or authority. But our selection of documents is intended to illustrate our firm conviction—and that of other historical scholars of the play—that the Protestant Reformation spreads across the cultural map of early modern England like the letters on a road map, which get harder to see as they increase in size and sprawl across the page. The Reformation's influence on the play is so pervasive and widespread as to be almost invisible. This influence extends, for example, well beyond the obvious effect on the play's representation of marriage and the family (which we document especially in Chapter 3) into such apparently unlikely areas as the play's representation of holiday customs (Chapter 1), its allusive treatment of the Amazons (Chapter 3), and its characterization of the fairies (Chapter 4).

The Reformation's several effects on early modern English culture are of course interrelated. In the later Middle Ages, some 9,300 English men and women (or about 0.26 percent of the population) lived in monasteries or convents, with convents numbering approximately 138 (Crawford, *Women and Religion* 219, n.10). After the dissolution of monastic ways of life, many adults of both sexes, but women especially, found their life choices significantly constrained. Convent life had offered women an honored vocation, a large degree of self-government under the authority of abbesses and prioresses, and independence from the demands of family (Crawford, *Women and Religion* 22). The modern model of an affectionate marriage within a small, nuclear household became the newly normative—and even perhaps the only truly acceptable—basis of mature social identity. This relatively new cultural insistence upon marriage for women suggests why the defeat of the Amazons, that community of self-governing women, should serve as historical precursor for the opening events of the play. The state's dissolution of the conventual way of life may also account for Theseus's disparagement of female celibacy when he informs a defiant Hermia of the harsh Athenian law concerning women's marriages. It is your choice, Theseus informs her without a trace of irony, whether to die by state-sponsored execution (its exact means unspecified), to "live a barren sister all your life" (1.1.72), or to marry the man whom father Egeus wants as son-in-law. Students may gauge the extent of this social transformation by remembering Chaucer's Wife of Bath, who begins her own self-portrait as a much-married woman by defending marriage as a worthy way of life for men and women against the superior perfection of virginity. "Virginitee is greet perfeccion, / And continence eek with devocioun," she admits, but defiantly declares "I wol bistowe the flour of al my age, / In the actes and the fruyt of mariage" (*Wife of Bath's Prologue* 105-06, 113-14). In England two centuries later, she need not have bothered to defend herself or the goodness and necessity of marriage.

Of other major changes brought about in the wake of the Reformation most relevant to *A Midsummer Night's Dream,* we have selected documents that highlight the change in belief practices implied in the play's treatment of the supernatural. As we will spell out in chapter 4, change in the official religion changed the consensus about the nature of supernatural agency. Belief in fairies, like belief in witches, became a matter of real debate instead of a matter of indifference or neutral disagreement. Medieval Catholicism had considered belief in fairies as paganism. Ironically, now that Catholicism was itself the superseded religion in England, Protestant reformers identified it with superstitious beliefs and practices. Placating fairies with gifts of food, as country people were said to do, now smacked of ignorant superstition or worse. But such disagreement about the supernatural is linked—as we shall see—to redefinitions of the natural and a reexamination of the possible. Are marvels the direct work and judgment of God, people increasingly began to wonder, or events susceptible to scientific explanation?

It is this complex of interlinked and overlapping historical issues on which we focus in the following chapters. Chapter 1 has the most general application to English culture, since it concerns holiday celebrations at a moment in the nation's social history when festive practices—May Day observances, civic theatricals, royal entertainments—had begun to divide and differentiate, had begun to signify "popular" or "elite." Chapter 2 takes up the play's representation of male hierarchy and narratives of male development, both the normative development of an upper-class English male and the exceptional but still broadly symbolic development of a legendary hero such as Theseus. The social tensions surrounding the proper formation of the male subject surface in the fairies' custody dispute over the Indian boy. (They would have not quarreled at all, we must remember, had the child been a girl: Oberon's court is a household of male intimates.) Chapter 3 turns to women, first to representations of those who, both alone and in communities, sought to elude or resist marriage, then to representative selections from the literature that

prescribed the duties of daughters and wives and narrated the exemplary lives and deaths of dutiful wives. Chapter 4 is occupied by many elements of the play's dazzling supernaturalism. We understand the play's magic as motivated, at least in part, by a rich post-Reformation debate about the causes of things (especially extraordinary or monstrous things). By highlighting this debate, we seek to offer an alternative to the folkloric interpretations that have sentimentalized the fairies—and often the rest of the play as a result. We define the play's make-believe as an intervention in competing post-Reformation beliefs and practices with the fairies as unknowing players in the religious controversies of late Elizabethan culture. In this context, the following parts of the play come together: Titania's allusions to the wet summers and successive bad harvests of the mid-1590s, the comic treatment of current theological debates about the scope and nature of supernatural agency, Ovidian mythological narratives about wonderful metamorphoses, Bottom's transformation and erotic encounter with Titania, the sin of bestiality, and contemporary theories of monstrous birth.

Romantic comedy's representation of love and marriage cannot escape the determinations of its historical moment, even when the romantic comedy in question is, like *A Midsummer Night's Dream,* explicitly distanced in time and place from the society where it was first performed. Thus when Titania and Oberon meet onstage for the first time and, for their benefit and our own, rehearse the grounds of their profound marital quarrel, we learn that their separation has had disastrous consequences in the natural order:

> No night is now with hymn or carol blessed.
> Therefore the moon, the governess of floods,
> Pale in her anger, washes all the air,
> That rheumatic diseases do abound.
> And thorough this distemperature we see
> The seasons alter. . . .

> (2.1.102-07)

These references to wet weather, bad air, and poor harvests must have reminded Shakespeare's audiences of the succession of stormy springs and cold, wet summers that had caused several years of harvest failure not just in England but also in many parts of northern Europe. These events in nature had affected them all. Perhaps the lines evoked, more generally, the sense of crisis that hung over the last decade of the sixteenth century. For Europeans living in those years, and for the historians who have studied them, the 1590s seem to have been a terrible time. Political disorder, religious warfare, widespread inflation in the price of basic goods, collapse of the agricultural economy in many countries, subsistence and mortality crises, recurrent epidemics of plague—all these factors in combination created a general sense of crisis, even of catastrophe. Predictions of the end of the world were not uncommon (Clark, "Introduction" 4). England did not suffer the depopulation that afflicted other parts of Europe, including northern Ireland; indeed London was then undergoing a population explosion thanks to an influx of newcomers from elsewhere in England and abroad. To many, the urban landscape was violent and crime-infested, inundated with foreigners, threatened by rioting apprentices and other sources of unrest (some included in this category the theaters themselves). England was also spared the internal religious warfare that devastated France, though it too suffered ferocious ideological conflicts between Protestantism and Catholicism of the sort that had spawned warfare on the continent. But overseas warfare—naval expeditions against Spain, military involvement in the Netherlands and France, and recurrent forays against the Irish—took a high toll on English society in the 1590s. It hindered trade, raised taxes, and took a steady stream of able-bodied men out of the labor force only to return some of them, much less able-bodied, as veterans.

A Midsummer Night's Dream, written during difficult years, cannot help being influenced by them, especially since the perception of crisis was a contemporary one. More to the point, Titania's obvious allusions to the recent bad weather seem to invite an audience's critical attention, to offer up the play's action and characters as magical encodings of their own time and space. This impression is reinforced by the play's unusually specific allusions to Queen Elizabeth, mentioned above. But the allusion seems to function here almost as a disclaimer, preventing the scandalous liaison between Titania and Bottom from being understood as a satiric attack on Queen Elizabeth and her manner of bestowing favors and attention upon favorites. The disclaimer cannot work, except tactically, of course. In Elizabethan England, no representation of a fairy queen could ever claim *not* to concern the real queen at some level. The question, as always, is to figure out just what social meanings are encoded in fictive transformations of the real.

Bibliography

Spenser, Edmund. *The Faerie Queene.* London, 1596.

Chambers, E. K. *The Elizabethan Stage.* 4 vols. Oxford: Oxford UP, 1928.

Clark, Peter. Introduction. *The European Crisis of the 1590s: Essays in Comparative History.* Ed. Clark. London: Allen, 1985.

Crawford, Patricia. *Women and Religion in England 1500-1720.* London: Routledge, 1993.

Hendricks, Margo. "'Obscured by Dreams': Race, Empire, and Shakespeare's *A Midsummer Night's Dream.*" *Shakespeare Quarterly* 47 (1996): 37-60.

Leinwand, Theodore. "'I believe we must leave the killing out': Deference and Accommodation in *A Midsummer Night's Dream.*" *Renaissance Papers,* 1986. 11-30.

Montrose, Louis Adrian. *The Purpose of Playing: Shakespeare and the Cultural Politics of the Elizabethan Theatre.* Chicago: U of Chicago P, 1996.

Phythian-Adams, Charles. "Ceremony and the Citizen: The Communal Year at Coventry, 1450-1550." *Crisis and Order in English Towns, 1500-1700: Essays in Urban History.* Ed. Peter Clark and Paul Slack. London: Routledge, 1972. 57-85.

CHARACTER STUDIES

Jan Kott (essay date 1987)

SOURCE: Kott, Jan. "The Bottom Translation." In *The Bottom Translation: Marlowe and Shakespeare and the Carnival Tradition,* translated by Daniela Miedzyrzecka and Lillian Vallee, pp. 29-68. Evanston, Ill.: Northwestern University Press, 1987.

[*In the following essay, Kott examines the significance of Bottom's metamorphosis in* A Midsummer Night's Dream, *particularly focusing on why Shakespeare alluded to both St. Paul and Apuleius in reference to Bottom's transformation.*]

I

"Love looks not with the eyes, but with the mind" (1.1.234).[1] This soliloquy of Helena's is part of a discourse on love and madness. Does desire also look with "the mind" and not with "the eyes"? Titania awakens from her dream, looks at the monster, and desires him. When Lysander and Demetrius awaken, they see only a girl's body and desire it. Is desire "blind" and love "seeing"? Or is love "blind" and desire "seeing"? "And therefore is wing'd Cupid painted blind" (1.1.235). Puck is the culprit in *A Midsummer Night's Dream,* for he awakens desire by dropping a love potion into the eyes of the sleeping lovers. In the poetic rhetoric of *A Midsummer Night's Dream,* "blind Cupid" is the agent of love. Are Puck and Cupid interchangeable?

Helena's soliloquy is recited by a young actress or, as in Elizabethan theater, by a boy acting the woman's part. The soliloquy is the voice of the actor. But it is not, or not only, the voice of the *character.* It is a part of a polyphonic, or many-voiced, discourse on love. In *A Midsummer Night's Dream* this discourse is more than the poetic commentary to the events taking place onstage. And the action onstage is more than illustration of the text. The discourse and the action not only complement each other but also appear to contradict each other. The dramatic tension and the intellectual richness result from this confrontation of discourse and action.

The same similes and emblems recur from the first to the last act of the play. *Emblem* may be the most appropriate term, for Cupid is the most significant image in this discourse. This "child" (1.1.238), "the boy Love" (1.1.241), waggish, foreswearing, and beguiling, repeats the post-classical icon of the blind or blindfolded Cupid.

From the early medieval poem, "I am blind and I make blind" to Erasmus' *Praise of Folly,* the icon is constant: "But why is Cupide alwaies lyke a yonge boie? why? but that he is a trifler, neither doyng, nor thynkyng any wyse acte" (20.20).[2] But this blind or blindfolded Cupid, associated in the Middle Ages with personifications of evil and darkness—Night, Infidelity, and Fortune—became by the Renaissance a sign with two contradictory values set in semiotic opposition. "Blind" Cupid does "see," but only at night, as in one of the most evocative lines in Marlowe's *Hero and Leander,* "dark night is Cupid's day"; or, once again he "sees" but "with an incorporeal eye," as in Pico della Mirandola.[3] This second Cupid, blind but seeing "with the mind," appears soon after the first in Helena's soliloquy:

> Things base and vile, holding no quantity,
> Love can transpose to form and dignity.

> (1.1.232-33)

Who and what is spoken of? Hermia, who is "sweet" and "fair," is hardly "base and vile." Helena does not know yet that Hermia is soon to be her rival. The "real" Helena, a character in the comedy, cannot here be referring to Hermia. The voice of the actor speaking of the madness of Eros forecasts Titania's infatuation with the "monster." But not only Bottom was "translated" that night. "Bless thee, Bottom, bless thee! Thou art translated" (3.1.113). "Translation" was the word used by Ben Jonson for metaphor. But in Shakespeare, "translation" is the sudden discovery of desire. Both couples of young lovers were "translated": "Am I not Hermia? Are you not Lysander?" (3.2.273). Bottom's metamorphosis is only the climax of the events in the forest. This "night-rule" (3.2.5) ends immediately after Bottom's return to human shape. Oberon and Titania "vanish." Theseus and Hippolyta return with the beginning of the new day in place of their night doubles. The lovers wake up from their "dream." And Bottom too wakes up from his: "I have had a dream, past the wit of man to say what dream it was. Man is but an ass if he go about to expound this dream . . . The eye of man hath not heard, the ear of man hath not seen, man's hand is not able to taste, his tongue to conceive, nor his heart to report, what my dream was" (4.1.204-6, 209-12).

The source of these astonishing lines is well known. "It must be accepted," wrote Frank Kermode in his *Early Shakespeare* (1961), "that this is a parody of 1 Corinthians 2:9-10": "Eye hath not seen, nor ear heard, neither have entered into the heart of man the things which God hath prepared for them that love him. But God hath revealed *them* unto us by his Spirit: for the Spirit searcheth all things, yea, the deep things of God."

Kermode quoted the King James version. In Tyndale (1534) and in the Geneva New Testament (1557) the last verse reads, "the Spirite searcheth all thinges, ye the bot-

ome of Goddes secrettes."[4] The "Athenian" weaver probably inherited his name from Paul's letter in old versions of Scripture. The spirit which reaches to "the botome" of all mysteries haunts Bottom. But just "translated" into an ass, Bottom translates Paul in his own way: "I will get Peter Quince to write a ballad of this dream: it shall be called 'Bottom's Dream,' because it hath no bottom" (4.1.212-15).

But Bottom was not the only one in *A Midsummer Night's Dream* to read 1 Corinthians. We find another echo of Paul's letter in Helena's soliloquy:

> Things base and vile, holding no quantity,
> Love can transpose to form and dignity.

Paul had written, "And base things of the world, and things which are despised, hath God chosen, *yea,* and things which are not to bring to naught things that are" (1 Cor. 1:28). In Tyndale and in the Geneva Bible this verse starts, "and vile thinges of the worlde." "Things base," in Helena's lines, appears to be borrowed from the Geneva Bible, and "vile" repeats the wording of the Authorized Version.

For an interpreter a "text" does not exist independently of its readings. Great texts, and perhaps even more so quotations from classical texts, literal or parodistic, form, together with their readings, a literary and cultural tradition. The classical texts are constantly rewritten, they are "the writerly text," to use Barthes's term.[5] Interpretations and commentaries become a part of their life. Classical texts and quotations continuously repeated are active in intellectual *emanation* which gives them new meaning and changes old ones. This emanation is the history of the classical text as well as the history hidden in the literary text. Classical texts converse among themselves. But borrowings and quotations are never neutral. Each quotation enlists its own context to challenge the author's text for better understanding or for mockery. The literary tradition, "the writerly text," works forward and backward, constructing and destroying the classical texts, illuminating or disintegrating them, consecrating or desecrating, or both. The literary history is, in a very literal sense, the eating and digesting of the classical texts.

The verse from Corinthians parodied by Bottom and the biblical "things base and vile" in Helena's lines refer to Bottom's transformation and to Titania's sudden infatuation with the monster—both borrowed from Apuleius' *The Golden Ass.* Shakespeare might have read Apuleius in Latin or in Adlington's translation of 1566.[6] The riddle of *A Midsummer Night's Dream* is not only why Paul or Apuleius was evoked in it but also why *both* were evoked and involved in the dramatic nexus of Bottom's metamorphosis.

Both texts, Corinthians and *The Golden Ass,* were widely known, discussed, and quoted during the Renaissance. From the early sixteenth century until the late seventeenth century, both texts were read in two largely separate intellectual traditions having two discrete circuits, and interpreted in two codes which were complementary but contradictory. The first of these codes, which is simultaneously a tradition, a system of interpretation, and a "language," can be called Neoplatonic or hermetic. The second is the code of the carnival or, in Mikhail Bakhtin's terms, the tradition of *serio ludere.*

> The carnival attitude possesses an indestructible vivacity and the mighty, life-giving power to transform. . . . For the first time in ancient literature the object of a *serious* (though at the same time comical) representation is presented without epical or tragical distance, presented not in the absolute past of myth and legend, but on the contemporary level, in direct and even crudely familiar contact with living contemporaries. In these genres mythical heroes and historical figures out of the past are deliberately and emphatically contemporarized . . .
>
> The serio-comical genres are not based on *legend* and do not elucidate themselves by means of the legend—they are *consciously* based on *experience* and on *free imagination*; their relationship to legend is in most cases deeply critical, and at times bears the cynical nature of the expose. . . . They reject the stylistic unity. . . . For them multiplicity of tone in a story and a mixture of the high and low, the serious and the comic, are typical: they made wide use . . . of parodically reconstructed quotations. In some of these genres the mixture of prose and poetic speech is observed, living dialects and slang are introduced, and various authorial masks appear.[7]

II

Paul's letter to the Corinthians is often invoked in the writings of Neoplatonists. In Mirandola, Ficino, Leone Ebreo, and Bruno, Paul can be found next to the Sibyl of the *Aeneid,* King David, Orpheus, Moses, or Plato. For the hermetics and Florentine philosophers, as for Lévi-Strauss, "myths rethink each other in a certain manner" ("d'une certaine manière, les mythes se pensent entre eux").[8] While icons and signifiers are borrowed from Plato and Plotinus, Heraclitus and Dionysius the Areopagite, the Psalms, Orphic hymns and cabalistic writings, the signified is always one and the same: the One beyond Being, unity in plurality, the God concealed. At times the method of the Neoplatonists resembles strangely the belief of poststructuralism and the new hermeneutics—that the permutation of signs, the inversion of their value and exchanges performed according to the rules of symbolic logic, will, like the philosopher's stone, uncover the deep structure of Being.

The blind Cupid of desire, the emblem of Elizabethan brothels, unveiled divine mysteries to Ficino and Mirandola. The "things base and vile" signify in this new hermetic code the "botome of Goddes secrettes." "Man," wrote Ficino, "ascends to the higher realms without discarding the lower world, and can descend to the lower world without foresaking the higher."[9]

As an epigraph to *The Interpretation of Dreams,* Freud quotes from the *Aeneid*: "*Flectere si nequeo superos,*

Acheronta movebo [If I am unable to bend the gods above, I shall move the Underworld.]" Neoplatonic "topocosmos" reappear in Freud's "superego" and the underworld: the repressed, the unconscious, the id. In *Three Contributions to the Theory of Sex* Freud wrote: "The omnipotence of sex nowhere perhaps shows itself stronger than in this one of her aberrations. The highest and lowest in sexuality are everywhere most intimately connected ('From heaven through the world to hell')."[10]

In the Neoplatonic exchange of signs between heaven, earth, and hell, the celestial Venus is situated above, the Venus of animal sex below the sphere of the intellect. As in a mountain lake whose depths reflect the peaks of nearby mountains, the signs of the "bottom" are the image and the reflection of the "top." *Venus vulgaris,* blind pleasure of sex, animal desire, becomes "a tool of the divine," as Ficino called it, an initiation into mysteries which, as in Paul, "eye hath not seen, nor ear heard." "Love is said by Orpheus," wrote Mirandola, "to be without eyes, because he is above the intellect." Above and at the same time below. For the Neoplatonists the descent to the bottom is also an ascent into heaven. Darkness is only another lighting. Blindness is only another seeing.[11] Quoting Homer, Tiresias, and Paul as examples, Mirandola wrote: "Many who were rapt to the vision of spiritual beauty were by the same cause blinded in their corporeal eyes."[12] To the cave prisoners of Plato's parable, everything seen is but a shadow. Shadows are nothing but misty reflections of true beings and things outside the cave. But the shadow indicates the source of the light. "Shadow," a word frequently used by Shakespeare, has many meanings, including "double" and "actor." Oberon, in *A Midsummer Night's Dream,* is called the "king of shadows," and Theseus says of theater: "The best in this kind are but shadows" (5.1.210). Theater is a shadow, that is, a double. "Revelry" also means "revelation." In the Neoplatonic code the "revels" and plays performed by the actor-shadows are, like dreams, texts with a latent content.

> And it may be said therefore that the mind has two powers. . . . The one is the vision of the sober mind, the other is the mind in a state of love: for when it loses its reason by becoming drunk with nectar, then it enters into a state of love, diffusing itself wholly into delight: and it is better for it thus to rage than to remain aloof from that drunkenness.

This paraphrased translation by Ficino from the *Enneads* of Plotinus could also be read as a Neoplatonic interpretation of Apuleius' *Metamorphoses.* In his famous commentary on the second Renaissance edition of *The Golden Ass* in 1600, Beroaldus quotes amply from Plato, Proclus, and Origen and sees in Apuleius' *Metamorphoses* the covert story and the mystical initiation into the secrets of divine love: "For Plato writes in the *Symposium* that the eyes of the mind begin to see clearly when the eyes of the body begin to fail."[13]

This commentary might surprise a reader not familiar with the Neoplatonic exchange of signs, who reads in a straightforward way the crude story of Lucius transformed into an ass. His mistress, a maid in a witch's house, confused magic ointments and transformed him into a quadruped instead of a bird. Beaten, kicked, and starved by his successive owners, he wanders in his new shape through Thessaly all the way to Corinth. He witnesses kidnappings, murders, and rapes; sits with bandits in their cave; attends the blasphemous rituals of sodomites and eunuch priests, and nearly dies of exhaustion harnessed with slaves in a mill-house.

The *Satyricon* and *The Golden Ass* use the device of fictional autobiography. Each successive episode, like the picaresque novella later, yields a dry picture of human cruelty, lust for power, and untamed sex. Transformed into a thinking animal, Lucius wanders among unthinking men-animals. The most revealing episode is the meeting between Lucius, who performs tricks as a trained donkey in the circus, and the new Pasiphaë, a wealthy Corinthian matron who, like Titania under the influence of the love potion, has a specific urge for animal sex: "Thou art he whom I love, thou art he whom I onely desire."

The infatuation of lunar Titania with a "sweet bully Bottom" ("So is mine eye enthralled to thy shape" [3.1.134]) is written under the spell of Apuleius: "how I should with my huge and great legs embrace so faire a Matron, or how I should touch her fine, dainty and silke skinne with my hard hoofes, or how it was possible to kisse her soft, her pretty and ruddy lips, with my monstrous great mouth and stony teeth, or how she, who was so young and tender, could be able to receive me."[14]

Lucius is fearful that his monstrous endowment might "hurt the woman by any kind of meane," but the Greek Titania hastens to dispel his fears: "I hold thee my cunny, I hold thee my nops, my sparrow, and therewithal she eftsoones embraced my body round about." Even the grotesque humor of this strange mating was repeated in *Midsummer Night's Dream*:

> Come, sit thee down upon this flowery bed,
> While I thy amiable cheeks to coy,
> And stick musk-roses in thy sleek smooth head,
> And kiss thy fair large ears, my gentle joy.

> (4.1.1-4)

But *The Golden Ass* contains yet another story inserted into the realistic train of Lucius' adventures in the ass's shape. The love story of Cupid and Psyche, an *anilibus fabula,* or "pleasant old wives' tale," as Adlington calls it, may be the oldest literary version of the fable of "Beauty and the Beast."[15] The fable is known in folk traditions of many nations and distant cultures; catalogs of folk motifs place it in Scandinavia and Sicily, in Portugal and Russia. It also appears in India. In all versions of the fable, a young maiden who is to marry a prince is forbidden to look at her husband at night. In the daytime, he is a beautiful youth. At night she is happy with him, but never sees him and is anxious to know with whom she is sleeping.

When she lights the lamp in the bedroom, the lover turns out to be an animal; a white wolf, a bear, an ass in one Hindu version, and most often a monstrous snake. When the wife breaks the night-rule, the husband/night animal departs or dies. In *The Golden Ass* this tale is told by "the trifling and drunken woman" to a virgin named Charite, abducted on the eve of her wedding and threatened with being sold to a brothel. This shocking, realistic frame for the mythical tale of Cupid and Psyche is a true introduction for the testing of *caritas* by *cupiditas,* or of the "top" by the "bottom," in *Metamorphoses.*

Venus herself was jealous of the princess Psyche, the most beautiful of all mortals. She sent out her own son, winged Cupid, to humiliate Psyche and with one of his "piercing darts" to make her fall madly in love "with the most miserablest creature living, the most poore, the most crooked and the most vile, that there may be none found in all the world of like wretchedness." Afterward, like Shakespeare's Titania, she would "wake when some vile thing is near" (2.2.33). But Cupid himself fell in love with Psyche and married her under the condition that she would never cast her eyes upon him in bed. Psyche broke her vow and lit a lamp. A drop of hot oil sputtered from the lamp and Cupid, burnt, ran off forever.

The story of Psyche ends with her giving birth to a daughter called Voluptas. The story of Lucius ends with his resumption of human form and his initiation into the mysteries of Isis and, after the return to Rome, into the rites of Osiris. Initiations are costly, but Lucius, a lawyer in the *collegium* established by Sulla, is able to pay the price of secret rites. The story of Psyche, the most beautiful of all mortal maidens, leads from beauty through the tortures of love to eternal pleasure. The story of Lucius, always sexually fascinated by hair before his own transformation into a hairy ass, leads from earthy delights to humiliating baldness: he is ordered twice to shave his head, once as a high priest of Isis and once for the rites of Osiris.

For Bakhtin, the tradition of *serio ludere* starts with Petronius and Apuleius. But which of the two metamorphoses in *The Golden Ass* is serious and mystical, and in which does one hear only the mocking *risus*?

For Beroaldus, *Metamorphoses* is a Platonic message of transcendent love, written in a cryptic language on two levels above and below reason. From Boccaccio's *Genealogia Deorum* (1472) to Calderón's *auto sacramental,* where the story of Psyche and Amor symbolizes the mystical union of the Church and Christ and ends with the glorification of the Eucharist, Apuleius was often read as an orphic, Platonic, or Christian allegory of mystical rapture or divine fury. But for at least three centuries *The Golden Ass* was also read in the code of "serious laughter." In *Decameron,* two novellae were adopted from Apuleius. In *Don Quixote,* the episode of the charge on the jugs of wine was repeated after *Metamorphoses.* Adaptations are innumerable: from Molière's *Psychè,* La Fontaine's *Les*

Amours du Psychè et Cupide, Le Sage's *Gil Blas,* to Anatole France's *La Rôtisserie de la Reine Pedauque.*[16]

In both the intellectual traditions and the codes of interpretation there are exchanges of icons and signs between the "top" and "bottom," the above and below reason. In the "Platonic translation," where the "above" *logos* outside the cave is the sole truth and the "below" is merely a murky shadow, the signs of the top are the ultimate test of the signs of the bottom. *Venus vulgaris* is but a reflection and a presentiment of the Celestial Venus. In *serio ludere* the top is only *mythos;* the bottom is the human condition. The signs and emblems of the bottom are the earthly probation of the signs and emblems of the top. *Venus celestis* is merely a projection, a mythical image of *amore bestiale*—the untamed libido. The true Olympus is the Hades of Lucian's *Dialogues of the Dead* or of Aristophanes' *Frogs,* where the coward and buffoon Dionysus appears in the cloak of Hercules. Having its origins in Saturnalia, *serio ludere* is a festive *parodia sacra.*

In hermetic interpretations, the story of Psyche and Cupid is a mythic version of Lucius' metamorphosis. The transformation into a donkey is a covert story whose mystical sense is concealed. Within the "carnival" as a code, ritual and poetry, Lucius' adventures in an ass's skin form an overt story concealing the hidden mockery in the tale of Amor and Cupid.

Psyche's two sisters, jealous of her happy marriage, insinuate to her that she shared her bed with a snake and monster. The poor woman does not know what she is really feeling since "at least *in one person* she hateth the beast (*bestiam*) and loveth her husband." As in dreams, the latent content of the story of Psyche and Cupid becomes manifest in Lucius' adventures. The signs of the top are an inversion and a displacement of the signs of the bottom. Like the Corinthian matron fascinated by "monstrosity," and like Titania aroused by Bottom's "beastliness," Psyche loved the beast and hated the husband "in one person." The evil sisters, like a Freudian analyst, uncovered her deep secret: "this servile and dangerous pleasure [*clandestinae Veneris faetidi periculesique concubitus*] . . . do more delight thee."

In the Neoplatonic metaphysics as well as in the *serio ludere* of the carnival, the microcosm represents and repeats the macrocosm, and man is the image of the universe. In the vertical imagery man is divided in half: from the waist up he represents the heavens, from the waist down hell. But all hells, from the antique Tartarus through the hells of Dante and Hieronymus Bosch, are the image of Earth.

> Down from the waist they are Centaurs,
> Though woman all above:
> But to the girdle do the Gods inherit,
> Beneath is all the fiend's:
> There's hell, there's darkness.
>
> (*King Lear* 4.6.123-30)

In both systems the signs of the above and the below, the macro and the micro, correspond to each other and are interchangeable. But their values are opposed both in the Neoplatonic code and in the carnival tradition and, to a certain extent, in the poetics of tragedy and comedy. From the Saturnalia through the medieval and Renaissance carnivals and celebrations, the elevated and noble attributes of the human mind are exchanged—as Bakhtin shows convincingly—for the bodily functions (with a particular emphasis on the "lower stratum": defecation, urination, copulation, and childbirth). In carnival wisdom they are the essence of life: a guarantee of its continuity.

Titania, like Psyche, was punished. The punishment is infatuation with the most "base and vile" of human beings. But this vile and base person is not transformed Cupid but the Bacchic donkey. Like the Corinthian matron of Apuleius, Titania sleeps with this carnival ass. In Shakespeare's adaptation of *The Golden Ass,* Psyche and the lascivious Corinthian matron are combined into the one person of Titania. In *serio ludere* piety and reverence do not exist as separate from mockery. Seriousness is mockery and mockery is seriousness.

The exchange of signs in *serio ludere* is the very same translation into the bottom, the low, and the obscene that takes place in folk rituals and carnival processions.[17] The masterpiece of carnivalesque literature is Rabelais' *Gargantua and Pantagruel.* In the sixth chapter of the first book, Gargamelle feels birth pangs:

> A few moments later, she began to groan, lament and cry out. Suddenly crowds of midwives came rushing in from all directions. Feeling and groping her below, they found certain loose shreds of skin, of rather unsavory odor, which they took to be a child. It was, on the contrary, her fundament which had escaped with the mollification of her right intestine (you call it the bumgut) because she had eaten too much tripe.[18]

Gargantua's mother had gorged herself so much the previous evening that the child found its natural exit blocked in this carnival physiology.

> As a result of Gargamelle's discomfort, the cotyledons of the placenta of her matrix were enlarged. The child, leaping through the breach and entering the hollow vein, ascended through her diaphragm to a point above her shoulders. Here the vein divides into two: the child accordingly worked his way in a sinistral direction, to issue, finally, through the left ear.

In medieval moral treatises and sermons, the mystery of the virgin birth was explained again and again as the Holy Ghost entering the Virgin through her ear—invariably, through her left ear. The Holy Ghost descended to the Virgin Mary from the top to the bottom so she could conceive immaculately. A blow from the anus in Rabelais' *parodia sacra* propelled Gargantua from the bottom to the top so the child of carnival could be born in the upside-down world.[19] In this bottom translation, earthly *pneuma* replaced the divine one and the movement along the vertical axis of the body, and of the cosmos as well, was reversed. Rabelais appeals directly to Corinthians. The patron saint of this carnival birth was Paul.

> Now I suspect that you do not thoroughly believe this strange nativity. If you do not, I care but little, though an honest and sensible man believes what he is told and what he finds written. Does not Solomon say in *Proverbs* (14:15): *Innocens credit omni verbo,* the innocent believeth every word, and does not St. Paul (1 Corinthians 13) declare: *Charitas omnia credit,* Charity believeth all?[20]

In carnivalesque literature, the first letter to the Corinthians is quoted as often as in the writings of the Neoplatonists. And the choice of the most favored quotes is nearly the same:

> Where *is* the wise? where *is* the scribe? where *is* the disputer of this world? hath not God made foolish the wisdom of the world?
>
> (1.20)

> And base things of the world, and things which are despised, hath God chosen, *yea,* and things which are not, to bring to naught things that are.
>
> (1.28)

> If any among you seemeth to be wise in this world, let him become a fool, that he may be wise. For the wisdom of this world is foolishness with God.
>
> (3.18-19)

For Florentine Neoplatonists, Paul is the teacher of *supra intellectum* mysteries. But in the carnival rites, the fool is wise and his madness is the wisdom of this world.[21] For Rabelais, and perhaps even more so for Erasmus, the letter to the Corinthians was the praise of folly: "Therefore *Salomon* beyng so great a kynge, was naught ashamed of my name when he saied in his XXX chapitre, '*I am most foole of all men*:' Nor *Paule doctour of the gentiles . . .* when writing to the Corinthians he said: '*I speake it as unvise, hat I more than others, etc.,*' as who saieth it were a great dishonour for him to be ouercome in folie" (109.29 f.). In Erasmus' *Moriae encomium* Folly speaks in the first person and in its own name. In this most Menippean of Renaissance treatises, Folly appeals to Paul's "foolishness of God" on nearly every page. Near the end of *The Praise of Folly,* Erasmus describes heavenly raptures which, rarely occurring to mortals, may give the foretaste or "savour of that hieghest rewarde" and which, as in Paul, "was neuer mans eie sawe, nor eare heard." But Erasmus' Folly, ever cynical and joyful, is more interested in returning to earth and awakening than in mystical raptures.

> Who se euer therefore haue suche grace . . . by theyr life tyme to tast of this saied felicitee, they are subjecte to a certaine passion muche lyke vnto madnesse . . . or beyng in a truance, thei doo speake certaine thynges not hangyng one with an other . . . and sodeinely without any apparent cause why, dooe chaunge the state of theyr countenaunces. For now shall ye see theim of glad chere, now of as sadde againe, now thei wepe, now thei laugh, now thei sighe, for briefe, it is certaine, 192that they are wholly distraught and rapte out of theim selues.
>
> (128.4 ff.)

Bottom speaks much as Folly after awakening from his own dream:

> Man is but an ass, if he go about to expound his dream. Methought I was—there is no man can tell what. Methought I was—and methought I had—but man is but a patched fool if he will offer to say what methought I had.
>
> (4.1.205-9)

We may now once more evoke the striking and ambivalent image of the return to daybreak after the mystical orgasm in *The Praise of Folly.*

> In sort, that whan a little after thei come againe to their former wittes, thei denie plainly thei wote where thei became, or whether thei were than in theyr bodies, or out of theyr bodies, wakyng or slepyng: remembring also as little, either what they heard, saw, saied, or did than, sauyng as it were through a cloude, or by a dreame: but this they know certainely, that whiles their mindes so roued and wandred, thei were most happie and blisfull, so that they lament and wepe at theyr retourne vnto theyr former senses.
>
> (128.16 ff.)

Let us now hear once more Bottom speak to his fellows:

BOTTOM:

> Masters, I am to discourse wonders: but ask me not what; for if I tell you, I am not a true Athenian. I will tell you every thing, right as it fell out.

QUINCE:

> Let us hear, sweet Bottom.

BOTTOM:

> Not a word of me.

The Praise of Folly, dedicated to Thomas More, was published in London in Chaloner's translation in 1549 and reprinted twice (1560, 1577), the last time almost twenty years before *A Midsummer Night's Dream.* It is hard to conceive that Shakespeare had never read one of the most provocative books of the century.[22] Bottom's misquote from Corinthians appears after his sudden awakening after the stay in "heaven." But what kind of heaven, the sexual climax in animal shape or mythical rapture? Apuleius, Paul, and Erasmus meet in Bottom's monologue. Of all encounters in *A Midsummer Night's Dream,* this one is least expected. "I have had a most rare vision. I have had a dream." The same word "vision(s)" was already uttered by Titania in a preceding scene, upon her waking from a "dream": "My Oberon, what visions have I seen! / Methought I was enamour'd of an ass" (4.1.75-76).

III

From Saturnalia to medieval *ludi* the ass is one of the main actors in processions, comic rituals, and holiday revels. In Bakhtin's succinct formula the ass is "the Gospel—symbol of debasement and humility (as well as concomitant regeneration)." On festive days such as the Twelfth Night, Plough Monday, the Feast of Fools, and the Feast of the Ass, merry and often vulgar parodies of liturgy were allowed. On those days devoted to general folly, clerics often participated as masters of ceremony, and an "Asinine Mass" was the main event. An ass was occasionally brought into the church, and a hymn especially composed for the occasion would be sung:

> Orientis partibus
> Adventavit Asinus
> Pulcher et fortissimus
> Sarcinis aptissimus.

The symbolism of the carnival ass and sacred drôlerie survived from the Middle Ages until Elizabethan times.[23] At the beginning of Elizabeth's reign donkeys dressed up as bishops or dogs with Hosts in their teeth would appear in court masques. But more significant than these animal disguises, which were a mockery of Catholic liturgy, was the appearance of the Bacchic donkey onstage. In Nashe's *Summer's Last Will and Testament*, performed in Croyden in 1592 or 1593, a few years before *A Midsummer Night's Dream*, Bacchus rode onto the stage atop an ass adorned with ivy and garlands of grapes.

Among all festival masques of animals the figure of the ass is most polysemic. The icon of an ass, for Bakhtin "the most ancient and lasting symbol of the material bodily lower stratum," is the ritualistic and carnivalesque mediator between heaven and earth, which transforms the "top" into the earthly "bottom." In its symbolic function of translation from the high to the low, the ass appears both in ancient tradition, in Apuleius, and in the Old and New Testaments as Balaam's she-ass, and as the ass on which Jesus rode into Jerusalem for the last time. "Tell ye the daughter of Si-on, Behold thy King cometh unto thee, meek, and sitting upon an ass, and a colt foal of an ass" (Matt. 21:5). Graffiti from the third century on the wall of the Palace of Caesars on the Palatine in Rome represent Jesus on the cross with an ass's head. In the oldest mystic tradition an ass is a musician who has the knowledge of the divine rhythm and revelation. An ass appears in the medieval *Processus prophetarum* and speaks with a human voice to give testimony to the truth in French and English mystery plays.[24] In Agrippa's *De vanitate scientiarum* (1526) we find the extravagant and striking "The Praise of an Ass" (*Encomium asinu*), which is a succinct repetition of and analogue to Erasmus' *Encomium moriae*.

The bodily meets with the spiritual in the *figura* and the masque of the ass. That is why the mating of Bottom and the Queen of the Fairies, which culminates the night and forest revelry, is so ambivalent and rich in meanings. In traditional interpretations of *A Midsummer Night's Dream*, the personae of the comedy belong to three different "worlds": the court of Theseus and Hippolyta; the "Athenian" mechanicals; and the "supernatural" world of Oberon, Titania, and the fairies. But particularly in this traditional interpretation, the night Titania spent with an ass in her "consecrated bower" must appear all the stranger and more unexpected.

Titania is the night double of Hippolyta, her dramatic and theatrical paradigm. Perhaps, since during the Elizabethan period the doubling of roles was very common, these two parts were performed by the same young boy. This Elizabethan convention was taken up by Peter Brook in his famous production. But even if performed by different actors, Hippolyta's metamorphosis into Titania and her return to the previous state, like Theseus' transformation into Oberon, must have seemed much more obvious and natural to Elizabethan patrons than to audiences brought up on conventions of the fake realism of nineteenth-century theater. A play on the marriage of the Duke of Athens with the Queen of the Amazons was most likely performed at an aristocratic wedding where courtly spectators knew the mythological emblems as well as the rules of a masque.

Court masques during the Tudor and Elizabethan period were composed of three sequels: (1) appearance in mythological or shepherds' costumes; (2) dancing, occasionally with recitation or song; and (3) the ending of the masque, during which the masquers invited the courtly audience to participate in a general dance. Professional actors did not take part in masques, which were courtly masquerades and social entertainment. "Going off" or "taking out," as this last dance was called, ended the metamorphosis and was a return of the masquers to their places at court.

The disguises corresponded to social distinctions. The hierarchies were preserved. Dukes and lords would never consent to represent anyone below the mythological standing of Theseus. Theseus himself could only assume the shape of the "King of the Fairies" and Hippolyta that of the "Queen of the Fairies." The annual Records at the Office of the Revels document the figures that appeared in court masques. Among fifteen sets of masking garments in 1555, there were "Venetian senators," "Venuses," "Huntresses," and "Nymphs." During the Jacobean period Nymphs of English rivers were added to the Amazons and Nymphs accompanying Diana, and Oberon with his knights was added to Actaeon and his hunters. In 1611, nearly fifteen years after *A Midsummer Night's Dream*, young Henry, the king's son, appeared in the costume of the "faery Prince" in Jonson's *Oberon*.[25]

The most frequently portrayed and popular figure of both courtly and wedding masque was Cupid. In a painting of the wedding masque of Henry Unton in 1572, the guests seated at a table watch a procession of ten Cupids (five white and five black) acompanied by Mercury, Diana, and her six nymphs.[26] From the early Tudor masque to the

Members of the Festival Company in Act V, scene i of the 1960 Stratford Festival production of A Midsummer Night's Dream.

sophisticated spectacles at the Jacobean court, Cupid appears with golden wings, in the same attire, and with the same accessories: "a small boye to be cladd in a canvas hose and doblett sylverd over with a payre of winges of gold with bow and aroves, his eyes binded."[27] This Cupid—with or without a blindfold—would randomly shoot his arrows at shepherdesses, sometimes missing:

> But I might see young Cupid's fiery shaft
> Quenched in the chaste beams of the watery moon;
> And the imperial votaress passed on.

> (2.1.161-63)

But the Renaissance Cupid, who appears eight times in the poetic discourse of *A Midsummer Night's Dream,* has a different name, a different costume, and a different language as a person onstage. The blindfolded Cupid is "Anglicised" or "translated" into Puck, or Robin Goodfellow. On the oldest woodcut representing the folk Robin Goodfellow, in the 1628 story of his "Mad Pranks and Merry Jests," he holds in his right hand a large phallic candle and in his left hand a large broom. He has goat horns on his head and a goat's cloven feet. He is wearing only a skirt made of animal skins and is accompanied by

black figures of men and women dressed in contemporary garments and dancing in a circle. This "folk" Robin Goodfellow is an Anglicized metamorphosis of a Satyr dancing with Nymphs.

This oldest image of Robin Goodfellow might refresh the imagination of scenographers and directors of *A Midsummer Night's Dream* who still see Puck as a romantic elf. But this engraving is equally important for the interpretation of the play, in which Shakespeare's syncretism mixes mythological icons of court masques with the pranks and rites of carnival. In *A Midsummer Night's Dream* the love potion replaces the mythological arrow. In poetic discourse this love potion still comes from the flower which turns red from Cupid's shaft. Shakespeare might have found the "love juice" in Montemayor's pastoral *Diana,* but he transposed the conventional simile into a sharp and evocative gesture, a metaphor enacted onstage: Puck's squeezing the juice from the pansy onto the eyelids of the sleeping lovers.

"And maidens call it 'love-in-idleness'" (2.1.168). The pansy's other folk names are "Fancy," "Kiss me," "Cull me" or "Cuddle me to you," "Tickle my fancy," "Kiss me ere I arise," "Kiss me at the garden gate," and "Pink of my John."[28] These are "bottom translations" of Cupid's shaft.

But in the discourse of *A Midsummer Night's Dream* there is not one flower, but two: "love-in-idleness" and its antidote. The opposition of "blind Cupid" and of Cupid with an "incorporeal eye" is translated into the opposition of mythic flowers: "Diana's bud o'er Cupid's flower / Hath ever such force and blessed power" (4.1.72-73).

The Neoplatonic unity of Love and Chastity is personified in the transformation of Venus into virginal Diana. Neoplatonists borrowed this exchange of signs from a line in Virgil's *Aeneid,* in which Venus appears to Aeneas, carrying "on her shoulder a bow as a huntress would" (1.327). In the semantics of emblems, the bow, as the weapon both of Cupid-love and of Amazon-virgo, was a mediation between Venus and Diana. The harmony of the bow, as Plato called it, was for Pico "harmony in discord," a unity of opposites.[29] From the union of Cupid and Psyche, brutally interrupted on earth, the daughter Voluptas was born in the heavens; from the adulterous relation of Mars and Venus, the daughter Harmony was born. Harmony, as Neoplatonists repeated after Ovid, Horace, and Plutarch, is *concordia discors* and *discordia concors.*

For Elizabethan poets and for carpenters who designed court masques and entertainments, this exchange of icons and emblems became unexpectedly useful in the cult of the Virgin Queen. The transformation of Venus into Diana allowed them to praise Elizabeth simultaneously under the names of Cynthia/Diana and Venus, the goddess of love. In Paris's judgment, as Giordano Bruno explicated in *Eroici furori,* the apple awarded to the most beautiful goddess was symbolically given to the other two goddesses as well: "for in the simplicity of divine essence . . . all these perfections are equal because they are infinite."[30]

George Peele must have read Bruno. In his *Arraignement of Paris,* the first extant English pastoral play with songs and dances by nymphs and shepherdesses, Paris hands the golden prize to Venus.[31] Offended, Diana appeals to the gods on Olympus; the golden orb is finally delivered to Elizabeth, "queen of Second Troy." The nymph Elise is "Queen Juno's peer" and "Minerva's mate": "As fair and lovely as the Queen of Love / As chaste as Dian in her chaste desires" (5.1.86-87).

In Ovid's *Metamorphoses,* "Titania" is one of Diana's names. The bow is an emblem of the Queen of Amazons. In the first scene of act 1, Hippolyta in her first lines evokes the image of a bow: "And then the moon, like to a silver bow / New bent in Heaven, shall behold the night / Of our solemnities" (1.1.9-11). Liturgical carnival starts with the new moon after the winter solstice. The new moon resembles a strung bow. The moon, the "governess of floods" (2.1.103), is a sign of Titania; her nocturnal sports are "moonlight revels" (2.1.141). In the poetical discourse the bow of the Amazons and the bow of the moon relate Hippolyta and Titania.

A sophisticated game of the court, with allegorical eulogies and allusions, is played through the exchange of classical emblems called "hieroglyphiches" by Ben Jonson. Greek Arcadia was slowly moving from Italy to England. Mythical figures and classical themes in masques, entertainments, and plays easily lent themselves to pastoral settings. But in this new pastoral mode the "Queen of the Fairies" was still an allegory of Elizabeth. For the Entertainment of Elvetham behind the palace at the base of wooded hills, an artificial pond in the shape of a half-moon had been constructed. On an islet in the middle, the fairies dance with their queen, singing a song to the music of a consort:

> *Elisa* is the fairest Queene
> That euer trod vpon this greene . . .
> O blessed bee each day and houre,
> Where sweete *Elisa* builds her bowre.

The queen of the fairies, with a garland as an imperial crown, recites in blank verse:

> I that abide in places under-ground
> Aureola, the Queene of Fairy Land
> . . . salute you with this chaplet,
> Giuen me by Auberon, the fairy King.

The Entertainment at Elvetham took place in the autumn of 1591, only a few years before even the latest possible date of *A Midsummer Night's Dream.* Even if Shakespeare had not attended it, this magnificent event was prepared by poets, artists, and musicians with whom he was acquainted. The quarto with the libretto, the lyrics, and the songs of the four-day spectacle in Elizabeth's honor was published and twice reprinted.[32] Oberon, Titania, and the fairies entered the Shakespearean comedy not from old romances such as *Huon of Bordeaux,* but from the stage, perhaps from Greene's play *James IV* in which Oberon dances with the fairies, and most certainly from that masque.

In masques and court pastorals, among the mythological figures next to Cupid we always find Mercury. In *A Midsummer Night's Dream* the place usually assigned to the messenger of the gods is empty. But Mercury is not merely the messenger, the *psychopompos* who induces and interrupts sleep as Puck and Ariel do.[33] Hermes-Mercury belongs to the family of tricksters. The trickster is the most invariable, universal, and constant mythic character in the folklore of all peoples. As a mediator between gods and men—the bottom and the top—the trickster is a special broker: he both deceives the gods and cheats men. The trickster is the personification of mobility and changeability and transcends all boundaries, overthrowing all hierarchies. He turns everything upside-down. Within this world gone mad a new order emerges from chaos, and life's continuity is renewed.[34]

> Jack shall have Jill,
>   Nought shall go ill;
> The man shall have his mare again, and all shall be well.
>
>   (3.2.461-63)

In the marvelous syncretism of *A Midsummer Night's Dream,* Puck the trickster is a bottom and carnivalesque translation of Cupid and Mercury.[35] The Harlequin, Fool, and Lord of Misrule—called in Scotland the Abbot of Unreason—belong to this theatrical family of tricksters. The Lord of Misrule was the medieval successor of the *Rex* of the Saturnalia. Puck's practical joke ("An ass's noll I fixed on his head" [3.2.17]) has its origin in the oldest tradition of folk festivities. In the Feast of Fools, or *festum asinorum,* the low clerics parodied the Holy Offices while disguising themselves with the masks of animals.[36] Mummery, painting the face red or white or covering it with grotesque or animal masks, is still often seen during Twelfth Night, Ash Wednesday, or Valentine's Day.

But putting on an ass's head was not only a theatrical repetition of mockeries and jokes of the Feast of Fools or the day of Boy-Bishop. Another universal rite is also repeated when a "boore," a thing "base and vile," or a mock-king of the carnival was crowned, and after his short reign, uncrowned, thrashed, mocked, and abused. As the drunken Christopher Sly, a tinker, is led into the palace in *The Taming of the Shrew,* so the bully Bottom is introduced into Titania's court of fairies. A coronet of flowers winds about his hairy temples, and the queen's servants fulfill all his fancies. Among Bottom's colleagues is also another "Athenian" tinker, Tom Snout. Like Christopher Sly and all mock-kings abused and uncrowned, Bottom, a weaver, wakes from his dream having played only the part of an ass at the court entertainment.

No one created Shakespearean scenes as strange and uncanny as those of Fuseli. "Fuseli's Shakespearean characters," wrote Mario Praz in *Il patto col serpente,* "stretch themselves, arch and contort, human catapults about to burst through the walls of the narrow and suffocating world, oppressed by the pall of darkness on which speaks Lady Macbeth . . . It is a demonic world of obsessions, a museum filled with statues of athletes galvanised into action, galloping furies, falling down onto prostrate corpses in yawning sepulchres."[37] But this demonic world of Shakespeare was recreated by Fuseli not only in his drawings and paintings of *Macbeth, Lear,* and *Richard III*: fear and trembling, rebellion and frenzy are also present in Fuseli's scenes from *A Midsummer Night's Dream.*

The famous Fuseli painting *Titania caressing Bottom with an ass's head* was executed three months after the siege of the Bastille. Titania in a frenetic dance assumes the pose of Leonardo's *Leda.* With only a small transparent sash around her left hip and covering her pudenda, she is almost nude, but her hair is carefully coiffed. She sees no one, her eyes are half closed. The fairies, Pease blossom, Cobweb, Moth, and Mustardseed, are not from fairyland, but from a rococo party at Court, or from some bizarre masquerade with dwarfs and midgets. At least two fairies wear long robes of white mousseline with decolleté necklines and the English hats seen in the vignettes of Pamela and Grandisson.

Next to Titania sits the huge Bottom, hunched over. He is pensive and sad. He looks as though, by some strange and unpredictable turn of events, he has found himself at a feast whose sense he does not grasp. In another painting by Fuseli, from 1793-94, Bottom looks even more alienated. Titania, naked from the waist up, embraces him lasciviously, and Pease-blossom, once again with a hat à la mode, scratches his scalp between his "fair, large ears." But Bottom, with the enormous legs of a rustic, does not belong to the orgy of Titania's court. The strangest being in this painting is a small homunculus with the head of an insect and open legs with masculine genitalia. What is the most strange and unexpected in Fuseli's vision is the atmosphere of fear and trembling at the mating of Titania and Bottom as on the last night at Court before the revolution.

This "insolite" syncretism of *A Midsummer Night's Dream,* as seen by Fuseli, was recreated by Rimbaud in one of the most enigmatic of his *Illuminations* under the title *Bottom*:

> Reality being too prickly for my lofty character, I became at my lady's a big blue-gray bird flying up near the moldings of the ceiling and dragging my wings after me in the shadows of the evening.
>
> At the foot of the baldaquino supporting her precious jewels and her physical masterpieces, I was a fat bear with purple gums and thick sorry-looking fur, my eyes of crystal and silver from the consoles.
>
> Evening grew dark like a burning aquarium.
>
> In the morning—a battling June dawn—I ran to the fields, an ass, trumpeting and brandishing my grievance, until the Sabines came from the suburbs to hurl themselves on my chest.[38]

The raped Sabines from the new suburbs throw themselves upon the neck of the lost ass whining and running on the green. All metamorphoses from *The Golden Ass* and *Beauty and the Beast* are evoked in this short poem in prose. It is the most succinct and astonishing "writerly text" of *A Midsummer Night's Dream.* Rimbaud, with rare intuition, discovered both the mystery and the sexuality ("a network with a thousand entrances") of the strange translation of Bottom.

In traditional performances of *A Midsummer Night's Dream,* which present Bottom's night at Titania's court as a romantic ballet, and in the spectacle staged by Peter Brook and many of his followers which emphasizes Titania's sexual fascination with a monstrous phallus (mea culpa!),[39] the carnival ritual of Bottom's adventure is altogether lost. Even Lucius, as a frustrated ass in Apuleius, was amazed at the sexual eagerness of the Corinthian matron who, having "put off all her garments to her naked skinne . . . began to annoint all her body with balme" and caressed him more adeptly than "in the Courtesan schooles." Bottom appreciates being treated as a very important person, but is more interested in the frugal pleasure of eating than in the bodily charms of Titania.

In Bottom's metamorphosis and in his encounters with Titania, not only do high and low, metaphysics and physics, pathos and burlesque, meet, but so do two theatrical traditions: the masque and the court entertainment meet the carnival world turned upside-down.[40] In masques and entertainments, "noble" characters were sometimes accompanied by Barbarians, Wild Men, Fishwives, and Marketwives. At the Entertainment of Elvetham an "ugly" Nereus showed up, frightening the court ladies.[41] But for the first time in both the history of revels and the history of theater, Titania/Diana/the Queen of Fairies sleeps with a donkey in her "flowery bower."[42] This encounter of Titania and Bottom, the ass and the mock-king of the carnival, is the very beginning of modern comedy and one of its glorious opening nights.

IV

A musical interlude accompanies the transition from night to day: "To the winding of horns [within] enter THESEUS, HIPPOLITA, EGEUS, and Train" (stage direction, 4.1.101). In this poetic discourse, the blowing of the hunters' horns, the barking of the hounds, and the echo from the mountains are translated into a musical opposition in the Platonic tradition of "discord" and "concord." In this opposition between day and night, not the night but precisely the musical orchestration of daybreak is called discord by Theseus and by Hippolyta. For Theseus this discord marks "the musical confusion / Of hounds and echo in conjunction" (4.1.109-10). "I never heard," replies Hippolyta, "so musical a discord, such sweet thunder" (4.1.116-17). Only a few lines further, when Lysander and Demetrius kneel at Theseus' feet after the end of "night-rule," the "discord" of the night turns into the new "concord" of the day: "I know you two are rival enemies. / How comes this gentle concord in the world?" (4.1.142).[43]

Both terms of the opposition, "concord" and "discord," are connected by Theseus when Philostrate, his master of the revels, hands him the brief of an interlude to be presented by the "Athenian" mechanicals:

"A tedious brief scene of young Pyramus
And his love Thisbe; very tragical mirth"?
Merry and tragical? Tedious and brief?
That is hot ice and wondrous strange snow!
How shall we find the concord of this discord?

(5.1.56-60)

This new *concordia discors* is a tragicomedy, and good Peter Quince gives a perfect definition of it when he tells the title of the play to his actors: "Marry, our play is 'The most lamentable comedy, and most cruel death of Pyramus and Thisbe'" (1.2.11-12). Although merely an Athenian carpenter, as it turns out, Quince is quite well-read in English repertory, having styled the title of his play after the "new tragical comedy" *Damon and Pithias* by Edwards (1565), or after Preston's *Cambises* (published ca. 1570), a "lamentable comedy mixed full of pleasant mirth."[44] The same traditional titles, judged by printers to be attractive to readers and spectators, appeared on playbills and title pages of quartos: *The comicall History of the Merchant of Venice* or *The most Excellent and lamentable Tragedie of Romeo and Juliet*. The latter title would fit better the story of Pyramus and Thisbe.

We do not know, and probably will not discover, whether *Romeo and Juliet* or *A Midsummer Night's Dream* was written earlier. History repeats itself twice, "the first time as tragedy, the second as farce." Marx was right: world history and the theater teach us that *opera buffa* repeats the protagonists and situations of *opera seria*. The "most cruel death" of Romeo and Juliet is changed into a comedy, but this comedy is "lamentable." The new tragicomedy, "concord of the discord," is a double translation of tragedy into comedy and of comedy into burlesque. The burlesque and the parody are not only in the dialogue and in the songs; the "lamentable comedy" is played at Theseus' wedding by the clowns.

Burlesque is first the acting and stage business. A wall separates the lovers, and they can only whisper and try to kiss through a "hole," a "cranny," "chink." This scene's crudity is both naive and sordid, as in sophomoric jokes and jests where innocent words possess obscene innuendo. Gestures here are more lewd than words.

The Wall was played by Snout. Bottom, who also meddled in directing, recommended: "Let him hold his fingers thus" (3.1.65-66). But what was this gesture supposed to be? Neither the text nor the stage directions ("Wall stretches out his fingers" [stage direction, 5.1.175]) are clear. In the nineteenth-century stage tradition, the Wall stretched out his fingers while the lovers kissed through the "cranny." In Peter Hall's Royal Shakespeare Company film (1969), the Wall holds in his hands a brick which he puts between his legs. Only then does he make a "cranny" with his thumb and index finger. But it could have been yet another gesture. The "hole," as the letter V made by the middle and index finger, would be horizontal and vertical. As Thomas Clayton argues, Snout in the Elizabethan theater of clowns straddled and stretched out his fingers between his legs wide apart. "And this the cranny is, right and sinister" (5.1.162). Snout, although an "Athenian" tinker, had a touch of Latin or Italian and knew what "sinister" meant.[45]

Romeo could not even touch Juliet when she leaned out the window. The Wall scene ("O kiss me through the hole of this vile wall" [198]) is the "bottom translation" of the balcony scene from *Romeo and Juliet*. The sequel of suicides is the same in both plays. But Thisbe "dies" differently. The burlesque Juliet stabs herself perforce with the scabbard of Pyramus' sword.[46] This is all we know for certain about how *A Midsummer Night's Dream* was performed in Shakespeare's lifetime.

The lovers from Athens did not meet a lion during their nightly adventure as Pyramus and Thisbe did in their forest, nor a dangerous lioness as Oliver and Orlando did in the very similar forest of Arden in *As You Like It*. But the menace of death hovers over the couple from the very beginning: "Either to die the death, or to abjure" (1.1.65).

The *furor* of love always calls forth death as its only equal partner. Hermia says to Lysander: "Either death or you I'll find immediately" (2.2.155); Lysander says of Helena: "Whom I do love, and will do till my death" (3.2.167); Helena says of Demetrius: "To die upon the hand I love so well" (2.1.244), and again: "tis partly my own fault. / Which death, or absence soon shall remedy" (3.2.243-44). Even sleep "with leaden legs and batty wings" is "death counterfeiting" (3.2.364).

In this polyphony of sexual frenzy, neither the classical Cupid with his "fiery shaft" nor the Neoplatonic Cupid with his "incorporeal eye" is present any longer. Desire ceases to hide under the symbolic cover. Now is the action of the body which seeks another body. In the language of the earthly gravitation, the eye sees the closeness of the other body, and the hand seeks rape or murder. The other is the flesh. But "I" is also the flesh. "My mistress with a monster is in love" (3.2.6).

"Death" and "dead" are uttered twenty-eight times; "dying" and "die" occur fourteen times. The field of "death" appears in nearly fifty verses of *A Midsummer Night's Dream* and is distributed almost evenly among the events in the forest and the play at Theseus' wedding. The frequency of "kill" and "killing" is thirteen, and "sick" and "sickness" occur six times. In *A Midsummer Night's Dream,* which has often been called a happy comedy of love, "kiss" and "kissing" occur only six times, always within the context of the burlesque; "joy" occurs eight times, "happy" six, and "happiness" none.

The forest happenings during the premarital night are only the first sports in *A Midsummer Night's Dream*; the main merriment is provided by clowns. In the "mirths," in the forest and at court, Bottom is the leading actor. While rehearsing his part in the forest, "sweet Pyramus" was "translated" into an ass. He "dies" onstage as Pyramus, only to be called an ass by Theseus: "With the help of a surgeon, he might yet recover, and prove an ass" (5.1.298-300).

If Bottom's metamorphoses in the forest and at court are read synchronically, as one reads an opera score, the "sweet bully" boy in both of his roles—as an ass and as Pyramus—sleeps with the queen of the fairies, is crowned and uncrowned, dies, and is resurrected onstage. The true director of the night-rule in the woods is Puck, the Lord of Misrule. The interlude of Pyramus and Thisbe was chosen for the wedding ceremonies by Philostrate, the master of revels to Theseus. Within *A Midsummer Night's Dream,* performed as an interlude at an aristocratic wedding, the play within a play is a paradigm of comedy as a whole. The larger play has an enveloping structure: the small "box" repeats the larger one, as a wooden Russian doll contains smaller ones.

The change of partners during a single night and the mating with a "monster" on the eve of a marriage of convenience do not appear to be the most appropriate

themes for wedding entertainment. Neither is the burlesque suicide of the antique models of Romeo and Juliet the most appropriate merriment for "a feast of great solemnity."[47] All dignity and seriousness vanish from the presentation of the "most cruel death of Pyramus and Thisbe." The night adventure of Titania and two young couples is reduced to a "dream." "And think no more of this night's accidents / But as the fierce vexation of a dream" (4.1.67-68).

"The lunatic, the lover and the poet, / Are of imagination all compact" (5.1.7-8). These lines of Theseus, like those of Helena's monologue from the first scene in act 1, are a part of the poetic metadiscourse whose theme is self-referential: the dreams in *A Midsummer Night's Dream* and the whole play. And as in Helena's soliloquy, Neoplatonic oppositions return in it. Ficino, in *In Platonis Phaedrum* and in *De amore,* distinguishes four forms of inspired madness: *furor divinus,* the "fine frenzy" of the poet; "the ravishment of the diviner"; "the prophetic rapture of the mystic"; and the "ecstasy of the lover," *furor amatorius.*[48]

Even more important than the repetition of Neoplatonic categories of "madness" is the inversion by Theseus/Shakespeare of the values and hierarchy in this exchange of topos:

> The poet's eye, in a fine frenzy rolling,
> Doth glance from heaven to earth, from earth to
>   heaven;
> And as imagination bodies forth
> The forms of things unknown, the poet's pen
> Turns them to shapes, and gives to airy nothing
> A local habitation and a name.
>
> (5.1.12-17)

As opposed to the "fine frenzy" of the Platonic poet, Shakespeare's pen gives earthly names to shadows, "airy nothing," and relocates them on earth.[49] The "lunatic" who "sees more devil than vast hell can hold" (5.1.9) replaces Neoplatonic mystics. The frenzied lover "sees Helen's beauty in a brow of Egypt" (5.1.11). All three—"the lunatic, the lover and the poet"—are similar to a Don Quixote who also gave to "phantasies," shadows of wandering knights, the "local habitation and a name"; who saw a beautiful Dulcinea in a coarse country maid; and, like a Shakespearean madman who in a "bush supposed a bear" (5.1.22), would charge windmills with his lance, taking them to be giants, and stormed wineskins, thinking them to be brigands.

> Lovers and madmen have such seething brains,
> Such shaping phantasies, that apprehend
> More than cool reason ever comprehends.
>
> (5.1.4-6)

In this metadiscourse, which is at the same time self-defeating and self-defending, a manifesto of Shakespeare's dramatic art and a defense of his comedy are contained. "More than cool reason ever comprehends" is not the Platonic "shadow" and the metaphysical *supra intellectum* of Pico and Ficino. "More than cool reason ever comprehends" is, as in Paul, the "foolish things of the world" which God designed "to confound the wise." This "foolishness of God," taken from the Corinthians, read and repeated after the carnival tradition, is the defense of the Fool and the praise of Folly.

The lunatics—the Fool, the Lord of Misrule, the Abbot of Unreason—know well that when a true king, as well as the carnival mock-king, is thrown off, he is turned into a thing "base and vile, holding no quantity"; that there are "more devils than vast hell can hold" and that Dianas, Psyches, and Titanias sleep not with winged Cupids but with an ass. "Bless thee, Bottom, bless thee! Thou art translated." You are translated. But into what language? Into a language of the earth. The bottom translation is the wisdom of Folly and delight of the Fool.

V

Bottom, soon after his death onstage, springs up and bids farewell to Wall with an indecent gesture. Thisbe is also resurrected; her body cannot remain onstage. The merry, joyful, and playful Bergomask ends the clowns' spectacle. It is midnight, and all three pairs of lovers are anxious to go to bed. In a ceremonial procession they leave the stage, illuminated by the torchbearers.

The stage is now empty for a moment. If *A Midsummer Night's Dream* was performed in the evening during the wedding ceremony, the stage was by then cast in shadows. Only after a while does Puck, the Master of night-rule, return to the stage.

> Now the hungry lion roars
> And the wolf behowls the moon . . .
> Now is the time of night
> That the graves, all gaping wide,
> Every one lets forth his sprite
> In the church-way paths to glide.

> (5.1.357-58, 365-68)

The somber line of Puck would be more appropriate for the night when Duncan was murdered than as a solemn "epithalamium" for the wedding night of the noble couple. The "screeching loud" (5.1.362) of the owl and "the triple Hecate's team" (5.1.370) are evoked in Puck's lines, as they were on the night of the regicide in *Macbeth*. It is the same night during which Romeo and Juliet, and Pyramus and Thisbe, committed suicide, during which Hermia might have killed Helena and Demetrius might have killed Lysander.[50]

Hecate is *triformis*: Proserpina in Hades, Diana on earth, and Luna in the heavens, Hecate/Luna/Titania is the mistress of this midnight hour when night starts changing into a new day. But it is still the night during which elves dance "following darkness like a dream" (5.1.372). Wedding follows the evocation of the rite of mourning.

Puck is holding a broom in his hand; the broom was a traditional prop of the rural Robin Goodfellow: "I am sent

with broom before / To sweep the dust behind the door" (5.1.375-76). In this sweeping of the floor there is a strange and piercing sadness. Puck sweeps away dust from the stage, as one sweeps a house. Sweeping away recurs in all carnival and spring rituals in England, France, Italy, Germany, and Poland. The symbolism of sweeping is rich and complex. A broom is a polysemic sign. But invariably sweeping away is a symbol of the end and of the beginning of a new cycle. One sweeps rooms away after a death and before a wedding. Goethe beautifully shows this symbolism of sweeping on Saint John's Night:

> Let the children enjoy
> The fires of the night of Saint John,
> Every broom must be worn out,
> And children must be born.

In Eckermann's *Conversations with Goethe,* Goethe quotes his poem and comments: "It is enough for me to look out of the window to see, in the brooms which are used to sweep the streets and in the children running about the streets, the symbols of life ever to be worn out and renewed."[51] Puck's sweeping of the stage with a broom is a sign of death and of a wedding which is a renewal. This is but the first epilogue of *A Midsummer Night's Dream.*

There is yet another. Oberon and Titania, with crowns of waxen tapers on their heads, enter the darkened stage with their train. They sing and dance a pavane. At a court wedding they might have invited the guests to participate in the dance together: "Every fairy take his gait" (5.1.402). Peter Brook, in his famous staging, had the house lights come up while the actors stretched their hands out to the audience and threw them flowers.

Titania and Oberon appear for the second time in the play as the night doubles of their day shapes. If they are the same pair of actors who play Theseus and Hippolyta, Puck's soliloquy would give them enough time to change their costumes. The enveloping structure of the play had led, with astounding dramatic logic, to its final conclusion. Theseus and Titania, Philostrate, Hermia and Helena, Lysander and Demetrius—the spectators onstage of the "most lamentable comedy"—are the doubles of the audience watching *A Midsummer Night's Dream* in the house. The illusion of reality, as in Northrop Frye's succinct and brilliant formulation, becomes the reality of illusion. "Shadows"—doubles—are actors. But if actors-shadows are the doubles of spectators, the spectators are the doubles of actors.

> If we shadows have offended,
> Think but this, and all is mended,
> That you have but slumbr'd here,
> While these visions did appear.

> (5.1.409-12)

Only Puck is left on the stage. This is the third and last epilogue. "Gentles, do not reprehend" (5.1.415). As in *As You Like It* and *The Tempest,* the leading actor asks the public to applaud. But who is Puck in this third and last epilogue?

The spirit Comus (Revelry), to whom men owe their revelling, is stationed at the doors of chamber . . . Yet night is not represented as a person, but rather it is suggested by what is going on; and the splendid entrance indicated that it is a wealthy pair just married who are lying on the couch . . . And what else is there of the revel? Well, what but the revellers? Do you not hear the castanets and the flute's shrill note and the disorderly singing? The torches give a faint light, enough for the revellers to see what is close in front of them but not enough for us to see them. Peals of laughter arise, and women rush along with men, wearing men's sandals and garments girt in a strange fashion; for the revel permits women to masquerade as men, and men to "put on women's garb" and to ape the talk of women. Their crowns are no longer free but, crushed down to the head on account of the wild running of the dancers, they have lost their joyous look.[52]

This quotation is from Philostratus, the Greek Sophist and scholar (ca. 176-245), whose *Imagines* became, during the Renaissance in Latin translation, one of the most popular textbooks and models for ancient icons of gods and mythical events. The most famous and most frequently quoted chapter of *Imagines* was "Comus." Shakespeare could not have found a more appropriate name for Theseus' Master of the Revels. Philostratus became Philostrate at the "Athenian" court, so that in a system of successive exchanges he would be transformed into Puck, Lord of Misrule, and return in the epilogue to his antique prototype, the god of revelry and the festivities, Comus of the *Imagines* written by Philostratus the Sophist.[53]

There will always remain two interpretations of *A Midsummer Night's Dream*: the light and the somber. And even as we choose the light one, let us not forget the dark one. Heraclitus wrote: "If it were not to Dionysus that they performed the procession and sang the hymn to the pudenda, most shameful things would have been done. Hades and Dionysus are the same, to whichever they rave and revel."[54] In the scene described by Philostratus, Comus is holding a torch downward. He is standing with his legs crossed, in a slumbering stance, at the entrance to the wedding chamber. His pose is that of a funerary Eros of Roman sarcophagi.[55] At the end of *A Midsummer Night's Dream*'s first epilogue, Puck could assume the pose of the funerary Eros. Shakespeare is a legatee of all myths.

In both interpretations of *A Midsummer Night's Dream,* the bottom translation is full of different meanings. All of them, even in their contradiction, are important. The intellectual and dramatic richness of this most striking of Shakespeare's comedies consists in its evocation of the tradition of *serio ludere*. Only within "the concord of this discord" does blind Cupid meet the golden ass and the spiritual become transformed into the physical. The *coincidentia oppositorum* for the first time and most beautifully was presented onstage.

Notes

1. All quotations from *A Midsummer Night's Dream* are taken from *The Arden Shakespeare,* ed. Harold F. Brooks (London: Methuen, 1979).

2. *The Praise of Folie,* "A booke made in Latine by that great clerke Erasmus Roterodame. Englisshed by sir Thomas Chaloner knight. Anno 1549." All quotations after Clarence F. Miller ed. (London: Oxford University Press, 1965).

3. Erwin Panofsky, "Blind Cupid," in *Studies in Iconology: Humanistic Themes in the Art of the Renaissance* (1939; rpt. New York: Harper & Row, 1972), pp. 95-128; Edgar Wind, "Orpheus in Praise of Blind Love," in *Pagan Mysteries in the Renaissance* (New York: Norton, 1968), pp. 53-80.

4. Frank Kermode, "The Mature Comedies," *Early Shakespeare* (New York: St. Martin's, 1961), pp. 214-20; Paul A. Olsen, "*A Midsummer Night's Dream* and the Meaning of Court Marriage," *ELH* 24 (1957): 95-119.

5. "The commentary on a single text is not a contingent activity, assigned the reassuring alibi of the 'concrete': the single text is valid for all the texts of literature, not in that it represents them (abstracts and equalizes them), but in that literature itself is never anything but a single text: the one text is not an (inductive) access to a Model, but entrance into a network with a thousand entrances." Roland Barthes, *S/Z,* trans. Richard Miller (New York: Hill & Wang, 1974), p. 12.

6. *The Xi Bookes of The Golden Asse, Conteininge the Metamorphosie of Lucius Apuleius.* "Translated out of Latine into Englishe by William Adlington. Anno 1566." Rpt. 1571, 1582, 1596. All quotations after Ch. Whibley ed. (London, 1893).

7. Mikhail Bakhtin, *Problems of Dostoevsky's Poetics,* trans. R. W. Rotsel (Ann Arbor: Ardis, 1973), pp. 88-89.

8. Claude Lévi-Strauss, *Le Cru et le cuit* (Paris: Plon, 1964), p. 20.

9. Quoted in Panofsky, "Blind Cupid," p. 137.

10. *The Basic Writings of Sigmund Freud* (New York: Random House, 1938), p. 572.

11. "Perhaps good king Oedipus had one eye too many" (Hölderlin, *In Lovely Blueness*).

12. Wind, "Orpheus," p. 58.

13. Ibid., pp. 58-59.

14. Shakespeare's borrowings from *The Golden Ass* in *A Midsummer Night's Dream* (the meeting with the Corinthian lady, and the story of Psyche) were first noted by Sister M. Generosa in "Apuleius and *A Midsummer Night's Dream*: Analogue or Source. Which?" in *Studies in Philology* 42 (1945): 198-204. James A. S. McPeek, "The Psyche Myth and *A Midsummer Night's Dream*," *Shakespeare Quarterly* 23 (1972): 69-79.

15. Emmanuel Cosquin, *Contes populaires de Lorraine* (Paris: V. F. Vieweg, 1886), 1:xxxii and 2:214-30.

16. Elizabeth Hazelton Haight, *Apuleius and His Influence* (New York: Cooper Square, 1963), pp. 90 ff.

17. "The theme of role reversal was commonplace in folk imagery from the end of the Middle Ages through the first half of the nineteenth century: engravings or pamphlets show, for instance, a man straddling an upside-down donkey and being beaten by his wife. In some pictures mice eat cats. A wolf watches over sheep; they devour him. Children spank parents. . . . Hens mount roosters, roosters lay eggs. The king goes on foot." Emmanuel Le Roy Ladurie, *Carnival in Romans,* trans. M. Finey (New York: Braziller, 1979), p. 191. "Hot ice" and "wondrous strange snow" (5.1.59) belong to this carnival language.

18. Passages from *Gargantua and Pantagruel* in Jacques Leclerq's translation (New York: Heritage Press, 1964).

19. From twelfth-century liturgical songs (*Gaude Virgo, mater Christi / Quae per aurem concepisti*) up to Molière's *The School for Wives* ("She came and asked me in a puzzled way . . . if children are begotten through the ear") we have an interrupted tradition, first pious, later parodic, of the virgin conceiving through the ear. See Gaston Hall, "Parody in *L'Ecole des femmes*: Agnès's Question," *MLR* 57 (1962): 63-65. See also Claude Gaignebet, *Le Carnaval* (Paris: Payot, 1974), p. 120.

20. Rabelais possibly feared that the joke went too far, and this entire passage, beginning with "Does not Solomon" disappeared from the second and subsequent editions of *Gargantua*. Rabelais also ironically quotes from Corinthians in chapter 8, at the end of the description of his medallion with a picture of the hermaphrodite.

21. "Rabelais' entire approach, his *serio ludere,* the grotesque mask, is deeply justified by his conviction that true wisdom often disguises itself as foolishness. . . . Because he is the most foolish, Panurge receives the divine revelation: the 'Propos des bien yvres,' apparent gibberish, contains God's truth." Florence M. Weinberg, *The Wine and the Will: Rabelais's Bacchic Christianity* (Detroit: Wayne State University Press, 1972), p. 149.

22. Ronald F. Miller, in "*A Midsummer Night's Dream*: The Fairies, Bottom and the Mystery of Things," *Shakespeare Quarterly,* vol. 26 (1975), pointed out the possibility of a relation between Chaloner's translation and Bottom's monologue. This essay is perhaps the most advanced attempt at an allegorical, almost Neoplatonic interpretation of *A Midsummer Night's Dream*; the "mystery of the fairies" points to "other mysteries in the world offstage" (p. 266).

23. Mikhail Bakhtin, *Rabelais and His World,* trans. Helene Iswolsky (Cambridge, Mass.: MIT, 1968), pp. 78, 199; Enid Welsford, *The Fool* (London: Faber & Faber, 1935), pp. 200 ff.; E. K. Chambers, *The Medieval Stage* (Oxford: Oxford University Press, 1903), 1:13-15.

24. Hardin Craig, *English Religious Drama of the Middle Ages* (Oxford: Clarendon, 1960), p. 68; Anderson, pp. 20-21. See also Grace Frank, *The Medieval French Drama* (Oxford: Oxford University Press, 1954, rpt. 1967), pp. 40-42: "At Rouen the play, preserved in several manuscripts, is frankly entitled *Ordo Processionis Asinorum,* although Balaam is only one of the more than twenty-eight characters involved. . . . The ass itself was not necessarily a comic figure; it served as the mount of the Virgin for the Flight into Egypt and of Christ for the Entry into Jerusalem; moreover it was associated with the ox in *praesepe* observances and at all times has been regarded as a faithful, patient beast of burden. But at the feast of the subdeacons the ass undoubtedly became an object of fun, a fact apparent from later church decrees forbidding its presence there."

"Quite probably the appearance of Balaam and his *obstinata bestia* in the prophet play owes something to the revels of the Feast of Fools: though the *Ordo Prophetarum* is the older ceremony, it seems likely that the use of the ass there was introduced late, perhaps as a kind of counter-attraction to the merrymaking of the subdeacons, 'an attempt to turn the established presence of the ass in the church to purposes of edification, rather than ribaldry' (Chambers, ii. 57). In any case the curious title of the Rouen play must be due to the conspicuous figure of Balaam and his *asina,* a beast that seems to have wandered into the prophet play from the Feast of Fools."

25. E. K. Chambers, *The Elizabethan Stage* (Oxford: Clarendon, 1923), 1:158 ff, 192. According to Chambers, Henry had appeared earlier in Daniel's masque *Twelve Goddesses* (1604), "taken out" and as a child "tost from hand to hand," 1:199.

26. Chambers, *The Elizabethan Stage,* 1:163-64: The reproduction of a painting on frontispiece in vol. 1.

27. Letter of George Ferrars, appointed Lord of Misrule by Edward VI. Quoted: Enid Welsford, *The Court Masque* (New York: Russell & Russell, 1927), p. 146.

28. *A Midsummer Night's Dream,* ed. Henry Cuningham, Arden Shakespeare (London: Methuen, 1905), note to 2.1.168. The poetic name of the love-potion flower was "lunary." In Lyly's *Sapho and Phao*: "an herbe called Lunary, that being bound to the pulses of the sick, causes nothing but dreames of wedding and daunces" (3.3.43); in *Endymion*: "On yonder banke neuer grove any thing but Lunary, and hereafter I neuer haue any bed but that banke" (2.3.9-10). *The Complete Works of John Lyly,* ed. R. Warwick Bend (Oxford: Clarendon, 1902), 3:38, 508.

29. The harmony of the string symbolized for the Neoplatonists the *concordia discors* between the passions

and the intellect: the bow's arrows wound, but the bowstring itself is held immobile by the hand and guided by the controlling eye. Wind, "Orpheus," pp. 78f, 86f.

30. Ibid., p. 77.

31. In *The Arraignement of Paris,* performed at court ca. 1581-84, published in 1584, Venus bribes Paris. In this "Venus show," Helena appears accompanied by four Cupids. The court masque is mixed with pastoral play. Yet perhaps for the first time the "body" of a nymph who fell unhappily in love appears on stage with a "crooked churl"—a folk Fool. But even if Peele's play did not influence Shakespeare, it does nevertheless demonstrate how, at least ten years before A Midsummer Night's Dream, Neoplatonic similes of blind and seeing Cupid became a cliché of euphuistic poetry. ("And Cupid's bow is not alone in his triumph, but his rod . . . His shafts keep heaven and earth in awe, and shape rewards for shame" [3.5.33, 36]; "Alas, that ever Love was blind, to shoot so far amiss!" [3.5.7].) Only Shakespeare was able to put new life into these banalities.

32. The entertainment at Elvetham was prepared by, among others, Lyly, Thomas Morley, the organ player and choirmaster in St. Peters, and the composers John Baldwin and Edward Johnson. Ernest Brennecke, "The Entertainment at Elvetham, 1591," in *Music in English Renaissance Drama* (Lexington: University of Kentucky Press, 1968), pp. 32-172.

33. The *locus classicus* of Hermes, the *psychopompos* who induces and dispels dreams, is in the first lines of the last book of the *Odyssey*: "Meanwhile Cyllenian Hermes was gathering in the souls of the Suitors, armed with the splendid golden wand that he can use at will to cast a spell on our eyes or wake us from the soundest sleep. He roused them up and marshalled them with this, and they obeyed his summons gibbering like bats that squeak and flutter in the depths of some mysterious cave" (*Odyssey,* trans. R. V. Rieu [Baltimore: Penguin, 1946]).

34. "Fundamentally trickster tales represent the way a society defines the boundaries, states its rules and conventions (by showing what happens when the rules are broken), extracts order out of chaos, and reflects on the nature of its own identity, its differentiation from the rest of the universe." Brian V. Street, "The Trickster Theme: Winnebago and Azanda," in *Zandae Themes,* ed. André Singer and Brian V. Street (Oxford: Oxford University Press, 1972), pp. 82-104. "Thus, like Ash-boy and Cinderella, the trickster is a mediator. Since his mediating function occupies a position half-way between two polar terms, he must retain something of that duality—namely an ambiguous and equivocal character." Claude Lévi-Strauss, *Structural Anthropology* (New York: Basic, 1963), p. 226.

35. Puck was originally played by a mature actor, not by a young boy. Only since the Restoration has a bal-

lerina played the part of Puck, as well as Oberon. Peter Brook, in his *Midsummer Night's Dream* (1970), repeated the Elizabethan tradition and had Puck's role performed by a tall and comical actor, John Kane ("thou lob of spirits" [2.1.16]).

36. See Anderson, p. 20.

37. Mario Praz, "Fuseli," in *Il patto col serpente* (Milan: Mondadori, 1972), p. 15. See also T. S. R. Boase, "Illustrations of Shakespeare's Plays in the Seventeenth and Eighteenth Centuries," in *Journal of the Warburg and Courtauld Institutes,* vol. 10 (1947). See also *John Heinrich Fuseli (1741-1825)* (Musée du Petit Palais, 1975.)

38. Rimbaud, *Complete Works,* trans. Wallace Fowlie (Chicago: University of Chicago Press, 1966), p. 227. On the impact of Fuseli on Gautier and on the debt of Rimbaud to Gautier, see Jean Richer, *Etudes et recherches sur Théophile Gautier prosateur* (Paris: Nizet, 1981), pp. 213-23.

39. "In the most solid and dramatic parts of his play [*MND*] Shakespeare is only giving an idealized version of courtly and country revels and of the people that played a part in them." Welsford, *The Court Masque,* p. 332. The most valid interpretation of the festive world in Shakespeare's plays remains still, after over thirty years, C. L. Barber's *Shakespeare's Festive Comedy.*

40. See Jan Kott, "Titania and the Ass's Head," in *Shakespeare Our Contemporary* (New York: Doubleday, 1964), pp. 207-28.

41. On the second day of interrupted spectacles Nereus appeared "so ugly as he ran toward his shelter that he 'affrighted a number of the country people, that they ran from him for feare, and thereby moved great laughter'" (Brennecke, "Entertainment," p. 45). Snout's fears that the ladies will be frightened by a lion are usually considered to be an allusion to the harnessing of a black moor to a chariot instead of a lion during the festivities of the christening of Prince Henry in 1594; perhaps it is also an amusing echo of "ugly" Nereus who frightened the ladies at Elvetham.

42. Even in Ben Jonson, who introduced the "anti-Masque," or false masque (in *The Masque of Blackness,* 1605), figures of the "anti-Masque" never mix with persons of the masque: they "vanish" after the "spectacle of strangenesse," before the allegories of order and cosmic harmony start. As Jonson emphasized:

> For Dauncing is an exercise
> not only shews ye mouers wit,
> but maketh ye beholder wise
> as he hath powre to rise to it.

(*Works* [1941], 7:489)

See John C. Meagher, "The Dance and the Masques of Ben Jonson," *Journal of the Warburg and Courtauld Institutes* 25 (1962): 258-77.

43. For Shakespeare's use of the terms "concord" and "discord" with musical connotations, see: *Richard II,* 5.5.40 ff., *Two Gentlemen of Verona* 1.2.93 ff., *Romeo and Juliet* 3.5.27, *The Rape of Lucrece,* line 1124. See also E. W. Naylor, *Shakespeare and Music* (New York: Da Capo, 1965), p. 24.

44. Grimald's *Christus Redivivus,* performed in Oxford in 1540 (published in 1543), bears the subtitle "Comoedia Tragica." This is probably the earliest mixture in England of "comedy" and "tragedy" in one term. For the history of titles used by Peter Quince, it is interesting to note *The lamentable historye of the Pryunce Oedipus* (1563) and *The lamentable and true tragedie of M. Arden of Feversham in Kent* (1592). *The tragedy of Pyramus and Thisbe,* published by Geoffrey Bullough (*Narrative and Dramatic Sources of Shakespeare* [London, 1966], 3:411-22) as an "Analogue" to *A Midsummer Night's Dream,* bears the subtitle: "Tragoedia miserrima." Chambers suspects that it is a seventeenth-century product, perhaps by Nathaniel Richards. Bullough holds that it dates from the sixteenth century. Richards' authorship appears to me out of the question; the language and Latin marginalia suggest that this "Tragoedia miserrima" is earlier than *A Midsummer Night's Dream.*

45. Thomas Clayton, "'Fie What a Question That If Thou Wert Near a Lewd Interpreter': The Wall Scene in *A Midsummer Night's Dream,*" *Shakespeare Studies* 7 (1974): 101-12; I. W. Robinson, "Palpable Hot Ice: Dramatic Burlesque in *A Midsummer Night's Dream,*" *Studies in Philology* 61 (1964): 192-204.

46. The last words of Juliet ("O happy dagger, / This is thy sheath; there rest, and let me die") are not the most fortunate, and almost ask for burlesquing.

47. Three other interludes for wedding entertainments offered by Philostrate seem even less appropriate for the occasion. The strangest one is the first: "'The battle with the Centaurs, to be sung / By an Athenian eunuch to the harp'" (5.1.44-45). Commentators and notes invariably referred one to Ovid's *Metamorphosis* (12.210 ff.) or else to the "Life of Theseus" in North's *Plutarch.* But the *locus classicus* of this battle with centaurs in the Renaissance tradition was quite different. It is Lucian's *Symposium* or *A Feast of Lapithae,* in which the mythical battle of the Centaurs with the Lapiths is a part of a satirical description of a brawl of philosophers at a contemporary wedding: "The bridegroom . . . was taken off with head in bandages—in the carriage in which he was to have taken his bride home." *The Works of Lucian of Samosata,* trans. H. W. Fowler and F. G. Fowler (Oxford: Oxford University Press, 1905), 4:144. In Apuleius' *The Golden Ass* unfortunate Charite also evokes the wedding interrupted by Centaurs in her story of her abduction by bandits from her would-be wedding: "In this sort was our marriage disturbed, like the marriage of Hypodame."

Rabelais in *Gargantua and Pantagruel* also evokes that unfortunate wedding: "Do you call this a wedding? . . . Yes, by God, I call it the marriage described by Lucian in his *Symposium.* You remember; the philosopher of Samosata tells how the King of the Lapithae celebrates a marriage that ended in war between Lapithae and Centaurs" (4.15). Shakespeare's ironical intention in evoking this proverbially interrupted marriage appears self-evident.

48. Panofsky, "Blind Cupid," p. 140; and Kermode, *Shakespeare, Spenser, Donne* (London: Routledge & Kegan Paul, 1971), p. 209: "To Pico, to Cornelius Agrippa, to Bruno, who distinguished nine kinds of fruitful love-blindness, this exaltation of the madness of love was both Christian and Orphic."

49. Michel Foucault, in *The Order of Things* (1966; New York: Vintage, 1971), discusses in his chapter on *Don Quixote* this new confrontation of poetry and madness, beginning at the age of Baroque: "But it is no longer the old Platonic theme of inspired madness. It is the mark of a new experience of language and things. At the fringes of a knowledge that separates beings, signs, and similitudes, and as though to limit its power, the madman fulfills the function of *homosemanticism*: he groups all signs together and leads them with a resemblance that never ceases to proliferate. The poet fulfills the opposite function: his is the allegorical role; beneath the language of signs and beneath the interplay of their precisely delineated distinctions, he strains his ears to catch that 'other language,' the language, without words or discourse, of resemblance" (pp. 49-50). But the poet in Theseus' lines is compared to the madman, and his function is to destroy the "allegorization." The exchange between the noble functions of mind and the low function of body is a radical criticism of all appearances, and an attempt to show a real similitude of "things" and "attitudes."

50. Cf. the recitation of "fatal birds" by Bosola to the Duchess of Malfi in her cell before her strangling: "Hark, now everything is still, / The schreech owl, and the whistler shrill / Call upon our dame, aloud, / And bid her quickly don her shroud" (*The Duchess of Malfi* 4.2.179 ff.). An epithalamium, which bade such creatures to be silent on the wedding night, is astonishingly similar to the foreboding of the fearful events. In the carnival rites often, especially in the South, the images of death and wedding meet.

51. *Conversations with Goethe,* January 17, 1827. Quoted by Bakhtin, in *Rabelais,* pp. 250-51.

52. Philostratus, *Imagines,* trans. Arthur Fairbanks (London: Heinemann, 1931), pp. 9 ff. Philostratus, a Greek writer (ca. 170-245), author of *The Life of Apollonius of Tyana* and of *Imagines,* was well known during the Renaissance. *Opera quae extant* in Greek with Latin translation had been published in Venice, 1501-4, 1535, 1550, and in Florence in 1517.

The "Stephani Nigri elegatissima" translation had at least three editions (Milan, 1521, 1532; Basel, 1532). *Imagines* was translated into French by de Vigenere: at least one edition (Paris, 1578) dates from before *A Midsummer Night's Dream* (Paris, 1614; L'Angelier rpt., New York: Garland, 1976). *Imagines* was extensively commented upon and quoted by Gyraldus and Cartari, whose *Le imagini dei degli antichi* often reads like a transcript of Philostratus. *Imagines* was highly esteemed by Shakespeare's fellow dramatists. Jonson directly quoted Philostratus six times in his abundant notes to his masques (i.e. in a note to "Cupids" in *The Masque of Beauty,* 1608: "especially *Phil.* in Icon. Amor. whom I haue particularly followed in this description." *Works,* Hereford and Simpson, ed. [Oxford: Oxford University Press, 1941], 7:188). See Allan H. Gilbert, *The Symbolic Persons in the Masques of Ben Jonson* (Durham, N.C.: Duke University Press, 1948), pp. 262-63. Samuel Daniel referred to *Imagines* and followed very precisely its image of Sleep in *The Vision of the Twelve Goddesses* (1604): "And therefore was Sleep / as he is described by Philostratus in *Amphiarai imagine* / apparelled." *A Book of Masques* (Cambridge: Cambridge University Press, 1967), p. 28.

53. For over a hundred years commentaries suggested the source of the name Philostrate is borrowed from Chaucer's *The Knight's Tale.* But Chaucer's lover, who goes to Athens under the name of Philostrate, and Shakespeare's master of the revels have nothing in common. The author of *Imagines* as a possible source for the name of Philostrate is a guess one is tempted to make. Philostratus' "Comus" is generally thought to be the main source for the image of Comus opening Jonson's *Pleasure Reconcild to Vertue* (1618) and for Milton's *Comus* (1634). *A Midsummer Night's Dream* and the two plays have often been compared: Jonson's *Pleasure* with *Comus* (Paul Reyher, *Les Masques anglaises* [Paris, 1909; New York: B. Blom, 1964], pp. 212-13; Welsford, *The Court Masque,* pp. 314-20; the editors of Jonson, *Works,* 2:304-9); *A Midsummer Night's Dream* with *Comus* (Welsford, *The Court Masque,* pp. 330-35; Glynne Wickham, *Shakespeare's Dramatic Heritage* [London: Routledge & Kegan Paul, 1969], pp. 181-84). But the real link between these three plays is the passage on Comus in *Imagines* (1.2). See also Stephen Orgel, *The Jonsonian Masque* (Cambridge, Mass.: Harvard University Press, 1965), pp. 151-69. Orgel compares the passage on Comus from Philostratus with Cartari's *Le imagini* and describes the iconographic tradition stemming from *Imagines.*

54. Fragment B 15. Quoted from Albert Cook, "Heraclitus and the Conditions of Utterance," *Arion,* n.s. 2/4 (1976): 473.

55. Wind, "Orpheus," pp. 104, 158.

Philip C. McGuire (essay date 1989)

SOURCE: McGuire, Philip C. "Egeus and the Implications of Silence." In *Shakespeare and the Sense of Performance,* edited by Marvin Thompson and Ruth Thompson, pp. 103-115. Newark: University of Delaware Press, 1989.

[*In the following essay, McGuire explores the ways in which Egeus's silence in Act IV, scene i has been interpreted by modern directors.*]

One way to glimpse what the future might hold for performance-centered criticism of Shakespeare's plays is to ponder the challenges posed by a silence that occurs in act 4, scene 1 of *A Midsummer Night's Dream,* soon after Duke Theseus and his hunting party find the four young lovers asleep on the forest ground following their baffling experiences of the night before. Lysander, "Half sleep, half waking" (4.1.146),[1] begins to explain that he and Hermia were fleeing "the peril of the Athenian law" (152) that sentences Hermia to death or to a life of perpetual chastity if she persists in refusing to marry the man her father has chosen to be her husband. Egeus, Hermia's father, interrupts, fiercely calling upon Theseus to apply the law most rigorously: "Enough, enough, my lord! you have enough. / I beg the law, the law, upon his head" (153-54).

During act 1, Theseus had warned Hermia that "the law of Athens" was something "Which by no means we may extenuate" (1.1.119-20). Now, however, after hearing Demetrius, Egeus's choice to be Hermia's husband, explain that his love for Hermia has "Melted" (4.1.165) away, Theseus proceeds to set aside the very law upholding an Athenian father's right to "dispose" (1.1.42) of his daughter that he had earlier declared himself powerless to "extenuate." Theseus declares,

> Egeus, I will overbear your will,
> For in the temple, by and by, with us,
> These couples shall eternally be knit. . . .
>
> (4.1.178-80)

What is Egeus's response to Theseus's decision to disregard not only his will but also Athenian law? In both the Quarto of 1600 and the Folio of 1623—the two texts of *A Midsummer Night's Dream* surviving from Shakespeare's time that are considered independently authoritative[2]—Egeus says nothing. The agreement between Quarto and Folio gives us as much certainty as we can get that Egeus's silence is an authentic feature of *A Midsummer Night's Dream,* but probing that silence in an effort to determine its specific meaning(s) and effect(s) brings us face-to-face with bedeviling uncertainties.

Evidence from Shakespeare's era prevents us from assuming that Egeus's silence is in and of itself definitive evidence that he withholds assent to a wedding that Theseus will no longer allow him to prevent. The marriage ritual set down in the 1559 *Book of Common Prayer*—like many of the rituals observed these days—specified functions for the bride's father that he is to carry out in silence. After bringing his daughter to the altar, the father "stands by in mute testimony that there are no impediments to the marriage."[3] A logical response to the question "Who giveth this woman to be married to this man?" is for the bride's father to say "I do," but the response the ritual calls for him to make is nonverbal; he is to relinquish his daughter without speaking. However, since what happens in act 4 is not a marriage ceremony, we cannot take evidence of the kind provided by the 1559 *Book of Common Prayer* as certain proof that Egeus's silence establishes his consent.

Recent productions of *A Midsummer Night's Dream* demonstrate the range of alternative meanings and effects that can emerge from Egeus's silence. In Richard Cottrell's 1980 production for the Bristol Old Vic Company, Egeus said nothing after hearing Theseus "overbear" his will, but before exiting with Theseus, Hippolyta, and their attendants, Egeus embraced Hermia. In an act that suggested the traditional wedding ceremony, Egeus then relinquished his paternal authority by placing his daughter's hand in Lysander's. With that action he gave Hermia to the man whom he had earlier denounced before Theseus for having "filched my daughter's heart, / Turned her obedience (which is due to me) / To stubborn harshness" (1.1.36-38). The Egeus of that production was a father who had come to accept without reservation the combination of ducal authority and erotic attraction that was soon to make his daughter Lysander's wife.

Elijah Moshinsky's 1981 production for the BBC-TV/New York Life series "The Shakespeare Plays" enacted alternatives that are different but equally consistent with the silence that the Quarto and the Folio assign to Egeus. After hearing Theseus's words authorizing her marriage to Lysander, Hermia moved to her father and they embraced. The reconciliation implicit in those gestures took on an added dimension when, before exiting, Egeus kissed his daughter's hand. In the opening scene, Theseus had warned Hermia "To fit your fancies to your father's will" (1.1.118). By kissing Hermia's hand, the Egeus of Moshinsky's production conveyed that he would now "fit" *his* will not only to the duke's authority but also to his daughter's "fancies."

In Celia Brannerman's 1980 production for the New Shakespeare Company at the Open Air Theatre in Regent's Park, London, Egeus, in his silence, submitted obediently but without any enthusiasm to Theseus's dictate. Egeus did not move to embrace Hermia after hearing Theseus declare, "Egeus, I will overbear your will." He did allow Hippolyta to take his hand in a comforting gesture that also implied that he would remain a valued member of Athenian court. Egeus exited with Theseus and Hippolyta, but there was no reconciliation between father and daughter, and Hermia's father did not acknowledge her husband-to-be.

The most acclaimed of recent productions of *A Midsummer Night's Dream*—Peter Brook's for the Royal Shake-speare Company in the early 1970s—enacted possibilities radically different from those already described.[4] When Theseus finished announcing ". . . by and by, with us, / These couples shall eternally be knit," Egeus stepped from where he had been standing between Theseus and Hippolyta and strode toward the exit downstage right. He paused briefly, even expectantly, as he heard Theseus begin to speak again—"And, for the morning now is something overworn" (181). Once it was clear, however, that Theseus was simply announcing the cancellation of the hunting, Egeus continued to make his departure. Before Theseus could call, "Away, with us to Athens" (183), Egeus was gone, leaving through an exit different from the one used moments later, first by Theseus and Hippolyta and then by the four lovers as they returned "to Athens." In the specific context established by that production, Theseus's words "Three and three, / We'll hold a feast in great solemnity" (183-84) registered the fact that "Three and three" did not include Egeus. The exit that Egeus made in Brook's production established that he was withdrawing from Athenian society.

The standard tactic for discriminating among alternatives such as those acted out in the four productions I have cited, for deciding which is "right" and which "wrong," which honors Shakespeare's intentions and which violates them, is to scrutinize the words of the play for evidence of what Shakespeare himself intended. When we look to those words, however, we find that neither the Folio nor the Quarto gives information of the caliber we need. Because each gives Egeus nothing to say, there are no words of his to scrutinize. The stage directions in the Quarto and the Folio are also of limited utility. They give no precise sense of how the silent Egeus makes his exit, and they help to drive home how little the words others speak reveal about Egeus's response to Theseus's decision authorizing Hermia's marriage to Lysander.

The Folio specifically requires that Egeus enter in act 4, scene 1 with Theseus: *"Enter Theseus, Egeus, Hippolita and all his traine."*[5] The stage direction for the exit to be made after Theseus overrules Egeus is less precise: *"Exit Duke and Lords."* There is, perhaps significantly, no specific mention of Egeus. Egeus could be one of those *"Lords"* who exit with Theseus—as happened in Elijah Moshinsky's 1981 production for BBC-TV. In such a case, Egeus remains a member of Athenian society, whether or not he accepts Hermia's marriage to Lysander.

However, nothing in the Folio *requires* that Egeus departs with Theseus. By first specifically including Egeus among those who enter with Theseus and by then not specifically listing him as one of those who leave with Theseus, the Folio allows for the possibility—enacted in Brook's production—that Theseus [*sic*] makes an exit separate from Theseus and those who go with him. Such an exit—which the Folio permits but does not mandate—would establish that Egeus's response to Theseus's exercise of ducal authority is to withdraw from Athens. Earlier Lysander and Hermia had fled from Athens in order to escape the punishments proscribed by "the sharp Athenian law" (1.1.162). The law they fled is the law that Egeus invokes when he calls for "the law, the law" upon Lysander's head, and it is that law that, overbearing Egeus's will, Theseus sets aside. The Athens to which Hermia and Lysander return is an Athens that will officially accept and validate their marriage: "In the temple, by and by, with us," Theseus says, "These couples shall eternally be knit." It is also the Athens from which Egeus could choose to withdraw. If he does, then Egeus in his silence is, like Malvolio and Jacques, a man who excludes himself from a renewed social order in which he is welcome to participate. We might even see in such an Egeus a forerunner of those tragic fathers, Lear and Brabantio, who cannot bring themselves to accept a daughter's will.

The corresponding stage directions in the Quarto are, if anything, open to even more diverse possibilities. The Quarto reads: "*Enter* Theseus *and all his traine*"—a phrasing that does not single out Egeus and Hippolyta as the Folio does. The Quarto provides no stage directions for the exit beyond what is implicit in Theseus's final words in the scene:

> Away, with us, to *Athens*. Three and three,
> Weele holde a feast, in great solemnitie. Come *Hyppolita.*

As stage directions, Theseus's words were inconclusive. "Away, with us, to *Athens*," for example, may be words of reassurance to Egeus—an effort to include him that Egeus may either accept or refuse. The words could also be an order from the Duke to Egeus, a command that he may or may not obey. In the opening scene, after what might be called Hermia's trial, Egeus leaves with Theseus, emphasizing his allegiance by declaring, "With duty and desire we follow you" (1.1.127). His words on that occasion resonate against the silence with which Hippolyta responds to Theseus's words calling for her to depart with him, "Come, my Hippolyta" (1.1.122). Hippolyta again says nothing when in act 4 Theseus says, "Come *Hyppolita*." This time, however, Egeus is silent too. He may wordlessly obey or he may wordlessly disobey the words that Theseus may direct to him: "Away, with us, to *Athens*." However, those words need not be addressed specifically to Egeus. Spoken to Hermia after Egeus has departed in anger, they could be Theseus's effort to ease whatever anguish Hermia feels at the departure of her embittered father: "Away, with US, to *Athens*."[6] Thus, like the Folio, the Quarto allows the possibility that Egeus exits with Theseus and his "*traine*" but does not require it. Also, like the Folio, the Quarto does not require that Egeus exit apart from them either.

If we seek to clarify the meanings and effect of Egeus's silence by looking at the wedding festivities of act 5, we find differences between the Quarto and the Folio that compound our difficulties.[7] The Folio begins act 5 with a direction that specifies the presence of Egeus: "*Enter Theseus, Hippolita, Egeus and his Lords.*" The corresponding stage direction in the Quarto, however, reads "*Enter* Theseus, Hyppolita, *and* Philostrate." There is no specific mention of Egeus as there is in the Folio, and there is no term equivalent to the "*Lords*" of the Folio that can be taken to include Egeus. In the Quarto Philostrate is the only person present to overhear the conversation between Theseus and Hippolyta, while the Folio requires that at least several be present, one of whom must be Egeus. Thus, the Folio, in contrast to the Quarto, establishes a situation in which Egeus stands by without speaking as he and others hear the Duke, who has overruled his will and Athenian law in order to permit Hermia's marriage, explain that he "never may beleeve" the lovers' account of what transpired during their night in the woods. Egeus must come to terms with a marriage that is one of the consequences of "Fairy toyes" in which Theseus himself does not believe.

Egeus's absence from festivities celebrating three weddings, one of which is his daughter's, is certainly compatible with interpreting Egeus's silence after Theseus overrules him as a refusal to accept Hermia's marriage to Lysander. The Quarto, then, justifies a production like Brook's in which Egeus, embittered at having Theseus "overbear" his will, ignores his daughter and withdraws from Athens rather than accept Hermia's marriage to Lysander. A father absent from his daughter's nuptial festivities would be another of those elements in *A Midsummer Night's Dream* that call attention to the darker, destructive possibilities inherent in the dynamics of sexual attraction and the processes of familial and communal renewal that the wedding revels and the play itself celebrate.[8]

Egeus's absence from the wedding festivities poses what I should like to call a dramaturgical problem: what means does Shakespeare provide to give that absence theatrical impact, to make it register on those watching a performance? One way to appreciate the problem is to try to remember whether Egeus was absent from the wedding festivities in the last performance of *A Midsummer Night's Dream* you saw. Shakespeare faced the same problem in act 5 of *The Merchant of Venice,* and there he insured that Shylock's absence would be an element of the audience's experience by having characters refer to Shylock. Lorenzo tells Jessica that the moonlit night they are enjoying together at Belmont reminds him of the night in Venice when she left her father to run away with him:

> In such a night
> Did Jessica steal from the wealthy Jew,
> And with an unthrift love did run from Venice
> As far as Belmont.
>
> (5.1.15-18)[9]

Antonio refers explicitly to his bond with Shylock when he offers to guarantee Basanio's fidelity to Portia by entering into another bond on his behalf:

> I once did lend my body for his wealth,
> Which but for him that had your husband's ring

Had quite miscarried. I dare be bound again,
My soul upon the forfeit, that your lord
Will never more break faith advisedly.

(249-53)

After Portia and Nerissa reveal the parts they played at
Shylock's trial, Nerissa explains to Lorenzo and Jessica
how the sentence imposed on Shylock benefits them:

There do I give to you and Jessica
From the rich Jew, a special deed of gift,
After his death, of all he dies possessed of.

(291-93)

There are no equivalently direct references to the absent
Egeus in act 5 of the Quarto version of *A Midsummer
Night's Dream*. Twice, however, what characters say could
refer to Egeus. Early in act 5, Theseus asks, "Where is our
usual manager / Of mirth?" The possibility that Egeus is
the *usual* manager of mirth cannot be ruled out conclusively, but even if Theseus's question does refer to the
absent Egeus, a reference so oblique is unlikely to register
with much force on a theatre audience. A second possible
reference to the absent father comes after the end of the
play-within-the-play, when Snug, stepping out of his role
as Lion, explains why Wall is not one of those "left to
bury the dead": "No, I assure you," he tells Demetrius and
others in the Athenian audience, "the wall is downe that
parted their fathers." Again, however, if this is a reference
to Egeus, it is indirect and of questionable theatrical
impact.

Words, however, are not the only means at a dramatist's
disposal. Doubling Egeus with another character is a tactic
available to Shakespeare that could use the visual dimension of drama in order to draw attention to Egeus's
absence.[10] Doubling Egeus and Philostrate, for example,
would create a theatrical situation in which seeing Philostrate, whom Theseus calls upon in the Quarto to provide
the wedding entertainment, could also make the audience
conscious that Egeus has absented himself from the nuptial
merriment. Brook's production of *A Midsummer Night's
Dream* doubled Egeus and Peter Quince. The presence
during act 5 of the novice director who struggles to bring
theatrical order out of the impulses and imaginings of the
rude mechanicals was a visual reminder of the absent
father who had tried to make his daughter's fancy and
sexual energies fit his will. I might also point out that the
visual parallels generated by doubling Egeus would
enhance the theatrical effectiveness of what are otherwise
no more than possible, very indirect verbal references to
him in the Quarto.

The Folio—in contrast to the Quarto—not only calls for
Egeus to be present during act 5 but also provides a means
for directing attention to him by giving him words to speak
that the Quarto assigns to Philostrate. Clearly, by mandating the presence of Egeus during the wedding festivities,
the Folio rules out the possibility that Egeus's response
when Theseus overrides his will is to withdraw *perma-*

nently from Athens. Even if the silent Egeus stalks off
alone when he exits in act 4, he must, according to the
Folio, be present in act 5. The presence of Egeus increases
the possibility—more difficult to envision if, as the Quarto
permits, he is absent—that he is fully reconciled to the
marriage of Hermia and Lysander. The Folio has Egeus
provide the list of "sports" from which Theseus selects the
nuptial entertainment. In the Folio, it is Egeus, not Philostrate, who explains how the play of Pyramus and Thisby
can be "merry" and "tragicall" as well as "tedious" and
"briefe." As part of that explanation, Egeus confesses that
watching the play in rehearsal "made mine eyes water: /
But more merrie teares, the passion of loud laughter /
Never shed."

Although the Folio certainly allows for full reconciliation
between father and daughter, it does not mandate it. The
first words that Egeus speaks are in response to the ducal
command "Call *Egeus*." Egeus answers, "Heere mighty
Theseus," and by stressing "mighty," the actor playing
Egeus can make his reply a telling reference to the power
Theseus exercises, power capable of overriding both a
father's will and the law upholding that father's right to
exercise his will. Even Egeus's account of how his eyes
watered is less conclusive than it first appears. The phrase
"more merrie teares" can be spoken so that it implies that
Hermia's father has also shed other, less merry tears. Note,
too, that while "more" can serve as an adverb of comparison, it can equally well function as an adjective meaning
"additional." When it does, the sentence of which it is a
part says that Egeus has not shed any merry tears since the
rehearsal.

For me the most persuasive evidence for the possibility
that Egeus's presence at the wedding festivities can signify
nothing more than dutiful obedience to his duke is the fact
that all the words he speaks are addressed to "mighty Theseus." He never speaks to Hermia or Lysander, and neither
of them ever speaks to him.[11] Thus, Egeus's acts of speaking during act 5 also establish a silence that he maintains
toward his daughter and her new husband and that they
maintain toward him.

An especially important set of differences between Quarto
and Folio turns on how the list of possible entertainments
is presented. In the Folio Theseus asks Egeus what
entertainments are available, while the Quarto has him ask
Philostrate. In the Quarto Philostrate provides a "briefe"
from which Thesus proceeds to read out the titles of the
various sports, interspersing comments on each. The Folio
changes what the Quarto presents as a single speech given
by Theseus into a dialogue involving Lysander and Theseus. Lysander reads out the titles, and Theseus responds
to each. What needs emphasis is that Egeus himself never
carries out Theseus's charge that he "SAY, what abridgement have you for the evening" (my emphasis). That
charge is the first of a series of questions Theseus asks:
"What maske? What musicke? How shall we beguile /
The lazie time, if not with some delight?" The questions can be
asked very rapidly, but if Theseus pauses after each ques-

Act I, scene i of A Midsummer Night's Dream.

tion, waiting for an answer that does not come before asking the next, the lines can emphasize that when Egeus does at last speak, he does not "Say" what the entertainments are. Instead, he says, "There is a breefe how many sports are rife *[sic]*: / Make choice of which your Highnesse will see first."

By having Lysander be the one who then reads out what is in the brief, the Folio establishes a situation in which Hermia's new husband speaks what her father was called upon to say. Although it is clear that Lysander reads from the brief to which Egeus refers, it is not clear how that document gets into Lysander's hands, and it is equally unclear what significance emerges from the fact that Lysander rather than Egeus says what the "sports" are. Does Egeus himself hand the brief to Lysander and by that action both acknowledge and (literally) give his voice to Lysander? Does giving the brief to Lysander indicate that Egeus is declining to read it himself—a reluctance to speak that could echo his silence after Theseus overbears his will? Instead of giving the brief to Lysander, Egeus might place it on a table—"THERE is a briefe . . ." (my emphasis)—and Lysander could then step forward and read it. Another possibility is that Lysander snatches the brief from Egeus before he has a chance to read it, in effect taking Egeus's voice and his place as he has taken his daughter. Perhaps Egeus hands the brief—deferentially?

defiantly?—to Theseus, who then passes it to Lysander. Such a sequence could establish a harmony between father and son-in-law centered on the figure of the duke. Alternatively, however, the same set of actions could convey that Theseus's response to an Egeus unwilling or unable to bring himself to "Say" what entertainment is available is to confer new status upon Lysander by giving him the opportunity to "Say" what Egeus will not.

By requiring the presence in act 5 of an Egeus who speaks, the Folio rules out the possibility that Egeus withdraws permanently from Athens rather than be present for a wedding he does not want, but the Folio leaves us unable to determine whether Egeus is present at his daughter's wedding festivities as a rejoicing father or as a dutiful courtier. Thus, neither the Folio nor the Quarto provides information that allows us to decide how Shakespeare wanted Egeus to respond to Theseus's decision authorizing Hermia's marriage to Lysander and to the marriage itself once it is performed. Even if we could convince ourselves that we had divined Shakespeare's intentions, the differences between the Quarto and the Folio suggest that those intentions did not remain fixed and constant but were fluid and changing. The Folio may be a revision of the Quarto, but if it is, the revising process was not one that worked toward clearer definition and greater specificity of intention. The aim of any revision that may have occurred seems to have been to give Egeus's response to Hermia's wedding—whatever that response is—greater theatrical effectiveness by requiring that, after his silence in act 4, he be present and speak during act 5.[12]

The differences in how the Quarto and the Folio present Egeus in act 5 are radically incompatible. There is no way to halve those differences nor to mediate them away by conflating the two texts. Egeus cannot be absent as well as present. The dialogue between Theseus and Hippolyta cannot be a relatively private conversation that only Philostrate is present to overhear and a public exchange that takes place in the presence of Egeus and the "Lords." Nevertheless, recent editors—among them Madeleine Doran,[13] David Bevington,[14] G. Blakemore Evans,[15] Stanley Wells,[16] and R. A. Foakes[17]—have concurred in providing a stage direction at the beginning of act 5 that follows the Quarto in requiring the presence of Philostrate and follows the Folio in specifying the presence of others identified as lords and attendants. As a result of such conflation, the beginning of act 5 available to the vast majority of scholars, students, and theatre artists is significantly different from the two beginnings with the best claim to being Shakespeare's—the one in the Quarto and the one in the Folio.[18]

We can, of course, deal with the problems posed by Egeus's silence and the differences between the Quarto and the Folio by dismissing them as trivial. Egeus is a minor character, such a line of thinking would run, and his response to the wedding that Theseus declares will take place is a peripheral matter of no major significance. The inadequacy of such reasoning comes into focus if we think of *A Midsummer Night's Dream* in terms of the three phases that the anthropologist Arnold van Gennep has identified as the components of all rites of passage: separation, transition, and reincorporation.[19] Lysander and Hermia enter the woods as part of a conscious decision to separate themselves from Athens, and once in the woods they, as well as Helena and Demetrius, undergo experiences that ultimately permit the four young lovers to pair off as male and female: each "Jill" ends up with a "Jack." Theseus then makes possible the reincorporation of Lysander and Hermia into an Athens they had fled when he overrules Egeus and sanctions their marriage. The postnuptial festivities of act 5, which is set in Athens, make that reincorporation manifest, but the precise nature of that reincorporation varies according to how Egeus responds to his daughter's marriage.

If Egeus's silence and (in the Quarto) his absence from the wedding signifies his permanent withdrawal from Athens, *A Midsummer Night's Dream* is a play in which marriage and the movement toward it occasion an irreparable break between father and daughter. The family composed of father and daughter fragments as the more inclusive social unit of the city accepts and validates the formation of a new family through marriage. Reincorporation coincides with Egeus's withdrawal. Athens loses a citizen in the process of acquiring a new couple with the potential to bring forth offspring who will be part of the next generation of Athenians. Renewal of the city becomes possible through a process of change that exacts a lasting cost.

The reincorporation that occurs in *A Midsummer Night's Dream* is radically different, however, if Egeus and Hermia are reconciled and he wholeheartedly accepts her marriage. In such a case, the family unit into which Hermia was born survives her entry into the marital family that she and Lysander form. The social unit of the family—in both its natal and its marital embodiments—and the social unit of the city emerge from the process of renewal intact and regenerated.

Should Egeus do no more than obediently submit to Theseus's authority, a third variety of reincorporation takes place. The continuing estrangement of father and daughter testifies to the shattering of the natal family, but the city itself remains capable of including both the embittered but dutiful father and the marital family her marriage to Lysander brings into existence. Egeus loses Hermia, and Hermia loses Egeus, but Athens loses no one. The city itself benefits as the result of a process that sees one family break apart as a new family that will help to ensure the city's future comes into being.

We are accustomed to thinking of Shakespeare's plays as works that he himself completed in all important details, and we routinely expect—if we do not demand—that those who study, teach, edit, and (especially) perform his plays will honor Shakespeare's intentions as codified in the words he wrote. Once we accept the importance to Egeus, however, the limits of the concepts of completeness and

intentionality become inescapable. The very words mandating that Egeus respond to Theseus's decision to "overbear" his will and (in the Folio) to the fact of Hermia's marriage do not give us information adequate to determine what Shakespeare wanted those responses to be, yet those responses are essential components of the play's vision. In this instance, the notion of fidelity to Shakespeare's intentions does not suffice, and as we try to come to terms with the consequences of that insufficiency, one of our first priorities must be to rethink, to reenvision the relationship between Shakespeare and those who perform what we reflexively call *his* plays. Perhaps because of Shakespeare's own dramaturgical design, perhaps because of the accidents of textual transmission, the Quarto and the Folio present circumstances requiring that those who perform *A Midsummer Night's Dream* be responsible for determining what Egeus's responses are. The only way to know with anything approaching precision what those responses are is to know how the play has been performed, to take into account what actors actually do or have done. The responses enacted will vary—I would even say must and should vary—from performance to performance, production to production. Each time specific alternatives from among the panoply of available responses are enacted, *A Midsummer Night's Dream* achieves a particular state of completion, an actual coherence of vision, that it does not have in either its Quarto or its Folio manifestation. Those who perform the play endow it with essential, necessary details that Shakespeare's words require but do not themselves furnish. In so doing, theatre artists do more than serve as agents obediently implementing Shakespeare's intentions. They act as virtual cocreators with him, bringing to completion a process that he initiated. As they do, *A Midsummer Night's Dream* becomes their play as well as his and challenges all who study what we (misleadingly) call "Shakespeare's" plays to come to terms with their character as works that come into being through a process that is collaborative, collective, and communal in nature.

Notes

1. The modern edition of *A Midsummer Night's Dream* from which I quote is Madeleine Doran's in William Shakespeare, *The Complete Works,* The Pelican Text revised, gen. ed. Alfred Harbage (New York: Viking Press, 1977).

2. A second quarto of *A Midsummer Night's Dream* was printed in 1619 with the false date of 1600 on the title page. Since it was based on the first, it has no independent authority.

3. Lynda E. Boose, "The Father and the Bride in Shakespeare," *PMLA* 97 (1982): 326. In this impressive essay, Boose observes, "Hence in *A Midsummer Night's Dream,* a play centered on marriage, the intransigent father Egeus, supported by the king-father figure Theseus, poses a threat that must be converted to a blessing to ensure the comic solution" (327). I am less certain than she is that the conversion she says must happen actually takes place.

4. See *Peter Brook's Production of William Shakespeare's "A Midsummer Night's Dream" for the Royal Shakespeare Company: The Complete and Authorized Acting Edition,* ed. Glen Loney (Chicago: Dramatic Publishing Company, 1974), 67b.

5. Quotations from the Folio follow *The Norton Facsimile: The First Folio of Shakespeare,* ed. Charlton Hinman (New York: Norton; London: Paul Hamlyn, 1968). Quotations from the Quarto of 1600 follow *Shakespeare's Plays in Quarto: A Facsimile Edition of Copies Primarily from the Henry E. Huntington Library,* ed. Michael J. B. Allen and Kenneth Muir (Berkeley and Los Angeles: University of California Press, 1981).

6. Rather than italicize words that I emphasize, I have resorted to capitalizing all letters in them. This enables me to preserve the italicization present in the Folio. It should be noted, however, that we cannot be sure that in Shakespeare's time italicization was an indication of emphasis.

7. I am deeply indebted to Barbara Hodgdon. Her essay "Gaining a Father: The Role of Egeus in the Quarto and Folio," *Review of English Studies,* n.s. 37 (1986): 534-42, has enriched my understanding of Egeus's role in act 5 of the Folio.

8. Those elements include Titania's account of how the changeling boy's mother died giving birth to him (2.1.135-37), the deaths of the lovers Pyramus and Thisby in the play-within-the-play, and Oberon's closing incantation against birth defects:

> So shall all the couples three
> Ever true in loving be;
> And the blots of Nature's hand
> Shall not in their issue stand.
> Never mole, harelip, nor scar,
> Nor mark prodigious, such as are
> Despisèd in nativity
> Shall upon their children be.

(5.1.396-403)

9. Quotations follow Brent Stirling's edition of *The Merchant of Venice* in William Shakespeare, *The Complete Works,* Pelican Text revised.

10. For a discussion of doubling in various plays by Shakespeare, including *A Midsummer Night's Dream,* see Stephen Booth's "Speculations on Doubling in Shakespeare's Plays," in *Shakespeare: The Theatrical Dimension,* ed. Philip C. McGuire and David A. Samuelson (New York: AMS Press, 1979), 103-31. An expanded version of that essay was published as appendix 2 in Booth's book, *"King Lear," "Macbeth," Indefinition, and Tragedy* (New Haven: Yale University Press, 1983), 129-55.

11. In fact, Hermia, like Helena, says nothing at all during act 5. In both the Quarto and the Folio we have a situation in which two brides remain silent throughout festivities celebrating their weddings. Their silence is all the more intriguing when set against their insistence on speaking at other moments in the play. In act 1, for example, Hermia first asks Theseus's pardon, then "made bold" by "I know not" "what power," goes on "In such a presence here to plead my thoughts" (1.1.59, 61). The silence of Hermia and Helena accentuates the fact that Hippolyta, who remained silent during Hermia's trial in act 1, is the only bride who speaks during the festivities. For a discussion of Hippolyta's silence in act 1, see chapter 1, "Hippolyta's Silence and the Poet's Pen," in my *Speechless Dialect: Shakespeare's Open Silences* (Berkeley and Los Angeles: University of California Press, 1985), 1-18.

12. In "Gaining a Father," Barbara Hodgdon points out that by requiring Egeus's presence the Folio raises the issue of when and how he makes his exit. She comments on several possibilities, and the point I should like to emphasize is that his final exit, whenever and however it occurs, is made in silence and is therefore open to various, even conflicting alternatives.

13. P. 169: *"Enter Theseus, Hippolyta, and Philostrate [with Lords and Attendants]."*

14. *The Complete Works of Shakespeare,* ed. Hardin Craig and David Bevington, rev. ed. (Glenview, Illinois; Brighton, England: Scott, Foresman and Company, 1973), 201: *"Enter* THESEUS, HIPPOLYTA, *and* PHILOSTRATE, [Lords, *and* Attendants]."

15. *The Riverside Shakespeare* (Boston: Houghton Mifflin, 1974), 241: *"Enter* THESEUS, HIPPOLYTA, *and* PHILOSTRATE, [Lords, *and* Attendants]."

16. New Penguin edition (Harmondsworth, Middlesex: Penguin Books, 1967), 107: *"Enter Theseus, Hippolyta, Philostrate, Lords, and Attendants."*

17. The New Cambridge Shakespeare (Cambridge: Cambridge University Press, 1984), 115: *"Enter* THESEUS, HIPPOLYTA, PHILOSTRATE, *Lords and Attendants."*

18. The New Oxford Shakespeare (William Shakespeare, *The Complete Works,* gen. ed. Stanley Wells and Gary Taylor [Oxford: Clarendon Press, 1986], 371), comes close to following the Folio: *"Enter Theseus, Hippolyta, [Egeus], and attendant lords."*

19. Boose, "Father and the Bride," 325. Another way of establishing the importance of Egeus is to link him with the issue of authority; see Leonard Tennenhouse, "Strategies of State and Political Plays: *A Midsummer Night's Dream, Henry IV, Henry V, Henry VIII,"* in *Political Shakespeare: New essays in cultural materialism* (Ithaca and London: Cornell University Press, 1985), 109-28.

PRODUCTION REVIEWS

John Bemrose (review date 1999)

SOURCE: Bemrose, John. "What Muddled Dreams May Come." *Maclean's* 112, no. 20 (17 May 1999): 61.

[*In the following review, Bemrose assesses the 1999 film version of* A Midsummer Night's Dream, *starring Kevin Kline and Michelle Pfeiffer and directed by Michael Hoffman. Bemrose praises the performances of Kline as Bottom and Pfeiffer as Titania, but finds fault with the rest of the film, which seems to be, in Bemrose's opinion, a battle between a "tedious Hollywood costume drama" and an effort to remain true to Shakespeare's play.*]

After *Shakespeare in Love, Hamlet, Romeo + Juliet* and all the other recent plunderings of Shakespeare, it was only a matter of time until someone got around to making a new version of *A Midsummer Night's Dream.* After all, it is the most perennially popular of Shakespeare's comedies, with a ready-made audience of millions who have studied it in school, or seen it acted in theatres great and small around the world. To watch Bottom, Puck and the quarrelling lovers is for many people like resuming an old friendship. Several cinematic versions have been made of the play: film audiences would seem to be ever-ripe ground for Shakespeare's intoxicating mix of romance and broad humour. And so *A Midsummer Night's Dream* hits the screen once more, ambitiously directed by Michael Hoffman and starring Kevin Kline and Michelle Pfeiffer.

Those two might seem unlikely Shakespeareans, but both have acted the bard before, and they bring an exquisite tenderness to the famous meeting between Titania, Queen of the Fairies, and her ass-eared lover, Bottom. The major problems that afflict this film lie elsewhere. In fact, *A Midsummer Night's Dream* feels like two movies under the guise of one. One is a standard and fairly tedious Hollywood costume drama where the pretty locations, computer-driven special effects and booming operatic score, courtesy of Verdi and Puccini, matter most. The other movie is recognizably Shakespearean, where the momentum of the play's language and story is trusted to do its work. At the best of times, these two strands marry to generate some fine scenes. But too often the movie jolts along with a divided mind, never quite sure whether it wants to be a sugary Hollywood fantasy or guts-and-soul Shakespeare.

The split is clear right from the opening scene, which borrows heavily from Kenneth Branagh's 1993 version of *Much Ado About Nothing.* Both films are set in the dry hills of Tuscany, and both open with an exuberant rush of operatic music. But while Branagh ultimately gives primacy to the text of the play, *Dream's* camera lingers typically over the preparations for the wedding feast of Duke Theseus (David Strathairn). So great is the press of

servants and cooks that Theseus' famous opening speech to his bride, Hippolyta (Sophie Marceau), has to be breathed privately into her ear. There is nothing wrong with this, except that the actors seem unaware that they are speaking poetry: their conversation mumbles along like something overheard on a crowded bus.

The acting improves when the action shifts to the enchanted woods ruled over by the King of the Fairies, Oberon (Rupert Everett), and his mischievous executive assistant, Puck (a balding, behorned Stanley Tucci). Puck, of course, plays havoc with the four young lovers (Calista Flockhart, Anna Friel, Christian Bale, Dominic West) who are there to sort out their amorous complications. In a nice touch, Hoffman has them riding bicycles, and when Puck—who has never seen a bicycle before—steals one to carry out his errands, the film strikes a pleasing irony. After all, the rogue could fly if he wanted to, but instead he pedals around the woods in a transport of childlike joy.

Left to themselves, the actors might have saved this *Dream.* But time and again, it strays off into long uninteresting silences, or invented (but unnecessary) scenes, backed by passages of gorgeous music meant to manipulate our feelings. At such times, the whole enterprise falls flat, and the attempt to revive it with cute special effects (the worst portrays the fairies as a travelling crowd of Tinkerbell-like points of light) only makes matters worse. The best films of Shakespeare's plays know how to surf the powerful, unrelenting wave of his language. This *Midsummer Night's Dream* tries to find its magic elsewhere—and falls under a spell of confusion it cannot break.

Richard Alleva (review date 1999)

SOURCE: Alleva, Richard. Review of *A Midsummer Night's Dream. Commonweal* 126, no. 12 (18 June 1999): 20-1.

[*In the following review, Alleva offers a mixed assessment of Michael Hoffman's 1999 film adaptation of* A Midsummer Night's Dream. *The critic censures some of the actors' performances, most notably Michelle Pfeiffer's "gracelessly spoken performance" as Titania. Alleva further claims that while Kevin Kline reduces Bottom to an emotionally fragile clown, this approach works well in Hoffman's production.*]

Judged by the film he has made from it, two elements of *A Midsummer Night's Dream* seem to have fascinated the director Michael Hoffman nearly to the exclusion of everything else in the play: the supernatural sylvan community ruled by Oberon and Titania, and the character of Bottom the weaver.

Up to the moment when the camera enters the forest, this production is a typical example of the cute modernization of Shakespeare. Instead of ancient Athens, Hoffman sets the story in an imaginary Tuscan town called Monte Athena at the turn of the century. Its ruler, Theseus, is no warrior hero but a harassed bureaucrat, and his bride-to-be, Hippolyta, is a bluestocking chafed by masculine traditions. The men wear boaters and the women corsets; bicycles and phonographs are important props; the music of Bellini, Donizetti, and Verdi fills the soundtrack.

As usual with such modernizations, some things in the play fit the director's scheme and some, egregiously, don't. Among the former: the rebellion of Hermia against a parental authority still powerful and, especially in southern Europe, still backed by the law in 1900. The craftsmen trying to put on a play are archetypal in any setting of any era. Less convincing is the threat of a death sentence for Hermia's defiance, though the alternate punishment of convent confinement is more plausible. Some of Hoffman's inventions fit neither the text nor his updating. Since we already accept the convention that these Italians are speaking Elizabethan English, why does Hoffman have villagers in the background chatter in Italian? When Lysander and Hermia camp down for the night, why does Hermia disrobe in the quickly cooling damp forest? (To add sex to a PG-13 movie, I hear you muttering. But surely a Hollywood producer would never stoop so low!) And, of course, to eliminate even more glaring incongruities, Hoffman has scissored away at the text and so, many verbal enchantments have disappeared. (One mustn't object that Shakespeare must be cut for the screen. Not after Kenneth Branagh's four-hour *Hamlet*.).

But, once the action shifts to the moonlit forest, we begin to discover that Hoffman has something fresh to bring to the play.

Initially startling is how unsupernatural, even flat-footed, the sprites and dryads and fairies seem. When Puck, well played by Stanley Tucci as a lecherous satyr, encounters one of Titania's nymphs, he comes on to her like a spiv trying to pick up a secretary on her lunch hour. A few seconds later, he's urinating against a tree. Oberon and Titania may be less vulgar, yet the fairy Queen, in Michelle Pfeiffer's gracelessly spoken performance, seems middle-class in her shrewishness rather than regally furious, like a Scarsdale matron whose ex-husband has missed his last two alimony payments; while Oberon takes on the manner of an overripe lounge lizard (but, granted this approach, skillfully done by Rupert Everett).

This mundanity is a function not of the director's incompetence but of his strategy. Hoffman sees the fairy world simply as a kingdom in exile, driven into the woods by the triumph of Christianity. These ousted deities, denied the fealty of mortals and confined to a sylvan ghetto, have become clumsy, enervated, aimless, petty, and irritable. (I began to wonder why the wings hadn't dropped off the fairies long ago.) In Shakespeare's text, Titania denies her mate the little page boy because of her regard for her friend, the lad's dead mother. But here, with that motive deemphasized, the real cause of the quarrel seems to be a kind of cabin fever. After sixteen hundred years of exile in

a very small forest, Oberon and Titania just can't stand the sight of each other.

It is a severe reduction of Shakespeare's multilayered emotionality, but Hoffman's cleverness often prevails. For instance, being a community of exiles longing for news of home, the fairy folk have smuggled things out of Monte Athena in order to find out what mortals are up to nowadays. Titania may be able to command lightning and rain but she and her nymphs can't work the phonograph filched from the villa of Theseus. When Bottom finally winds the contraption up and plays "Casta Diva," the nymphs look at him with new respect. He may not be the most glamorous lover Titania's ever had, but he sure is a handy guy to have around. (Shakespeare's term for working man, "mechanical," here takes on new meaning.).

The highest compliment I can pay to the characterization of Nick Bottom as redesigned by Hoffman and actor Kevin Kline is also a backhanded one: Having banished Shakespeare's conception from their production, they have contrived a not unworthy substitute. The fellow you encounter in the play—surely Shakespeare's greatest purely comic character, for Falstaff is tragicomic—is a glorious monster of happy fatuity, deaf to all criticism, laving himself in fantasies of theatrical triumph, capable of receiving the amorous caresses of a goddess as but his due. But Kline's weaver, to the contrary, feels himself precariously situated in society (a local star but also a clown to be mocked), and has an all-too-fragile ego. When a mischief-maker pours wine on the weaver and ruins his best suit, Kline crumbles and goes home to sulk. (Shakespeare's Bottom would have received the drenching as a tribute: "Lo, how the commonality lauds me in manner Bacchic!") This local-yokel hambone and would-be Lothario of Kline's is a relative of the overgrown boys in Fellini's *I Vitelloni,* tugging at the restraints of small-town life and yearning for a future of sensual bliss or artistic renown. (And Roger Rees's Peter Quince—a lovely, subtle piece of work—seems directly inspired by *Vitelloni's* Leopoldo, the aspiring poet.) This new characterization, though a reversal of what's in the play, nevertheless works on screen. When Kline is wooed by Titania, he wonderfully conveys a loser's amazement at suddenly winning. The comedy of Shakespeare's weaver is that he gets exactly what he thinks he deserves. But the pathos of Kline's Nick Bottom is that he achieves what he never imagined would come to him.

Whenever the fairies and Bottom aren't together on screen, the movie trudges. I've seen the lovers' spats and the performance of *Pyramus and Thisbe* work better in college productions than they do here. Above all, what this film lacks is a sense of ritual and mystery. With the special effects now available to any big-budget movie, Hoffman can convey Titania's wrath at her husband with lightning and thunder, but the insipid kiss and quick fade into the distance with which he stages their reconciliation doesn't distill the essence of "Come, my queen, take hands with me, / And rock the ground whereon these sleepers be." Hoffman's cinematic shorthand doesn't rock the ground or us.

Thanks to much of the acting (I also liked David Strathairn's fusspot Theseus and Dominic West's dark, incisive Lysander) and to the director's flashes of invention, this movie is mainly amusing and worth seeing. But check your local video store or library for the BBC's 1982 *Dream*, directed by Moshinsky and featuring the best Nick Bottom (Brian Glover's) I've ever seen. It's easy to be amused by any moderately well-done production of this play. Dare to be awed.

Jim Welsh (review date 1999)

SOURCE: Welsh, Jim. Review of *A Midsummer Night's Dream*. *Literature/Film Quarterly* 27, no. 2 (1999): 159-61.

[*In the following review, Welsh compares Michael Hoffman's 1999 film adaptation of* A Midsummer Night's Dream *to the 1935 Max Reinhardt-William Dieterle film production. The critic contends that the more recent version of the play is generally less compelling, despite the success of Calista Flockhart's Helena.*]

Does Hollywood love Shakespeare, as some have suggested, or does Hollywood simply love *Shakespeare in Love*? John Madden's film was a surprise success, both at the box office and at the Academy Awards. *Shakespeare in Love* was made on a budget of $38 million and took in over $68 million in domestic revenues. Hollywood "loves" Shakespeare because Hollywood loves money, and *Shakespeare in Love* won the Oscar jackpot. Hence the current "Bard Boom" has little to do with the real Shakespeare and a whole lot to do with speculative greed.

In 1998 the much admired *Shakespeare in Love* put an appealing human face on the Droeshout engraving of the balding Bard, indulging in a biographical fantasy that made the Bard a sexy and energetic young lover who knew how to thrill with his quill. Call it the reinvention of Shakespeare, done with nimble dialogue and astonishing theatrical flourishes sufficient to dazzle the Motion Picture Academy. Newsweek credited the film with starting the so-called "Bard Boom," even though the current Shakespeare revival has been going on for at least a decade, starting with Kenneth Branagh's *Henry V* in 1989.

One commentator rightly described *Shakespeare in Love* as a Shakespeare-highlight film, and so it is—a mishmash of the best bits of Romeo and Juliet squeezed into a faux-biographical framework, mostly invented, mostly fanciful. Kit Marlowe shows Will the way to shape his tragedy of star-crossed lovers, for example, according to Marc Norman and Tom Stoppard, who turn the boy Bard into slick Willy, a lovesick puppy pining androgenously for blonde bombshell Viola DeLesseps (Gwyneth Paltrow), a poetry groupie who earns her hour on the stage before being sent to Virginia Beach and an arranged marriage in the *Brave New World*. The script is certainly clever. *Shakespeare in Love* interfaces amusingly with *Romeo and Juliet* and *Twelfth Night* to provide in-your-face entertainment, distorting the facts in a determined effort to popularize the Bard.

Can the recent adaptation of *A Midsummer Night's Dream* compete with this slick confection? That's part of the challenge. Another challenge for Hoffman is to match the enchantment of earlier screen adaptations of the play, especially the Max Reinhardt-William Dieterle production put together by MGM in 1935, embellished with Felix Mendelssohn's incidental music, a Russian ballet troupe, and a cast that included the leading comic character actors of the day. Small wonder, then, that Hoffman's film, though often charming and amusing in its way, comes up short.

Hoffman moves the action forward in time and sets it in late 19th-Century Tuscany, but does the Italianate setting make sense? The MGM version was given a God-knows-where setting that was vaguely and humorously "Athenian," though this Athens seemed to border a mad German Black Forest setting of gnomes, trolls, fairies, and unicorns. Once the boundaries were firmly set, the film carefully made clear visual and musical transitions between the kingdoms of Theseus and Oberon. In this film the forest was a magical place, something other than a bicycle park on a quaint Italian holiday.

In Hoffman's film the roles of both Theseus and Oberon are strangely reduced. Shakespeare's Duke Theseus is a powerful warrior who has defeated the Amazon Queen Hippolyta in battle and is then determined to marry her and make merry. Hoffman's Theseus (David Strathairn) lacks the grandeur and the comic pomposity of Shakespeare's Theseus, and his lines are so abridged in keeping with the new setting that he appears to be merely the maitre d' of a swanky Italian resort, not a ruler truly in charge, but a stiff, wooden mannequin oddly detached from the festivities of his own nuptials. Hippolyta (Sophie Marceau) is likewise translated into a genteel, aristocratic lady, rather too frail to be imagined wearing Amazon battle-garb.

Rupert Everett's Oberon is perhaps nearer the mark, but more naked than lordly, and not nearly so sinister as Victor Jory's Oberon in the MGM version, attended by bat-winged spirits in contrast to the airy spirits of Titania, his Fairy Queen. Michelle Pfeiffer's Titania is overly made-up as she sweeps her monsterous lover—Kevin Kline with funny ears and a hairy face—into the privacy of her bower, where she discovers her ass-eared lover's other endowments (perhaps suggesting Jan Kott's lusty and bestial reading of the play). The long and the short of it is that Kline is obviously up for the role and makes a fine Bottom, but his Bottom is topped by Jimmy Cagney's performance in 1935, and one suspects Kline knows it, since he seems at times to be imitating Cagney. Though Roger Rees is not bad as Peter Quince, the "rude mechanicals" are altogether eclipsed by the comic talents of the 1935 film, with memorable turns by Hugh Herbert and Joe E. Brown, camping it up as Thisby. As Puck, Stanley Tucci looks like Mr. Spock with horns, oversized, rather than sprightly. Tucci gives a thoroughly professional and carefully modulated performance, but this Vulcanized Puck is no Mickey Rooney, whose performance was outrageously overdone and over the top, campy but fun.

Midsummer Night's Dream should be more fun than the current adaptation is. The only advantage it may have over the 1935 version is the casting of the confused and enchanted lovers. Calista Flockhart is outstanding as Helena. Christian Bale and Dominic West manage to personalize the look-alike beaux Demetrius and Lysander, and Anna Friel pouts mightily as the much-abused Hermia. In the final forest frenzy they muck about in a way that amusingly recalls Peter Hall's 1968 Royal Shakespeare adaptation.

But, again, I stress, the "Bard Boom" did not start last year after Hollywood had tired of exploiting Jane Austen, as witnessed by Branagh's realistic *Henry V* and his ambitious (if somewhat bloated and extravagant) *Hamlet,* Oliver Parker's *Othello* (with Branagh as Iago), and Trevor Nunn's miraculous *Twelfth Night,* which set a standard for both *Shakespeare in Love* and *A Midsummer Night's Dream* to live up to. The fallout of *Shakespeare in Love* will involve several more pictures. Opening almost concurrently with *A Midsummer Night's Dream,* was *10 Things I Hate About You,* which attempted to translate *The Taming of the Shrew* into a teenpix set at "Padua High," Shakespeare rendered *Clueless,* in other words.

Forthcoming titles promised by USA Today (29 January 1999) may be of more academic interest. Anthony Hopkins will undertake *Titus Andronicus* (described, not too promisingly, by Julie Taymor as "the *Pulp Fiction* of its day") and Ethan Hawke will presume to play Hamlet (a courageous move, given the definitive treatment of Kenneth Branagh, but this one is said to be "transplanted to Manhattan." One vividly recalls the freaky "transplantation" of Baz Luhrmann's *Romeo + Juliet* and hopes for the best.) Meanwhile, Branagh apparently intends to transform *Love's Labor's Lost* into a 1930's styled musical, with Alicia Silverstone and the music of Irving Berlin. How long will it be before the Shakespeare boom goes bust?

Russell Jackson (review date 2000)

SOURCE: Jackson, Russell. "Shakespeare at Stratford-upon-Avon: Summer and Winter, 1999-2000." *Shakespeare Quarterly* 51, no. 2 (2000): 217-29.

[In the following review, Jackson comments on Michael Boyd's 1999-2000 stage production of A Midsummer Night's Dream. *Boyd discusses the production's emphasis on the sexuality of the forest and its inhabitants and its use of dance and movement as unifying elements within the play.]*

In my previous report on Shakespeare at Stratford-upon-Avon I wondered more in sorrow than in anger what kind of artistic policy the RSC might lay claim to.[1] Whether or not in the course of the "Summer Festival Season" the company found a policy, they certainly acquired a stage, which may amount to the same thing. The 1500-seat proscenium-arch main house, with whose architecture directors and designers have struggled since it opened in 1932, was remodeled under the direction of the company's resident designer, Anthony Rowe. For the summer season the company installed a deep, elliptical platform stage, on which the principal action of each play was performed. The space upstage of the proscenium arch was relegated to providing background images or (for long stretches of some of the season's plays) simply closed off from view. In order to make the actors visible to spectators at the back of the topmost level, the new platform was higher than in previous attempts to bring the stage forward (such as that of the 1976 season). Consequently, the front two rows of stalls on either side of it became "restricted-view" seats, and the performers' horizontal sight line was slightly above the heads of the audience in the middle and rear stall seats.

But two other elements of the past twelve months' work in Stratford were definitely signs of policy: an increased attention to clarity of speech (reinforced by company voice classes) and the designation of the main season, from March to September, as a "summer festival." The voice work—together with the remodeled stage—addressed directly some criticisms made in recent years by giving speech and action priority over scenic display. The renaming amounted to a repackaging of the company's scheduling so that it at least seemed coherent, even as it revived a concept that the RSC left behind some two decades or more ago. Four Shakespeare plays over four months, all given in the largest of the Stratford spaces, were well attended. By the end of the period tickets for most performances (particularly *Timon of Athens*) were hard to come by, but this was still a considerable retrenchment on previous scheduling in terms of the number of productions and performances. The choice of Shakespeare plays (*A Midsummer Night's Dream, Antony and Cleopatra, Othello,* and *Timon of Athens*) was complemented by at least three later plays with a bearing on the dramatist's work: Schiller's *Don Carlos* in the Other Place and Eliot's *The Family Reunion* and a dramatized selection of Ted Hughes's *Tales from Ovid* in the Swan. Schiller's play includes variations on *Hamlet*—a gloomy prince, the expectancy and rose of a not-very-fair state, is kept back from university in an oppressive court and has major problems with parents and paramour. There are also occasional smacks in it of *The Winter's Tale, Othello,* and *King Lear,* echoes of the last allowing John Woodvine as King Philip, both fearsome and pitiable, to suggest what he might do with a Shakespearean role that has yet to come his way. *Tales from Ovid,* adapted by Simon Reade and the director Tim Supple, was an eloquently spoken and choreographed ensemble piece, full of striking and simple story-telling devices for its tales of the gods' interference with humans and the sometimes terrifying consequences. It also included some larky male nudity (Pan and his newly acquired disciple Midas) and powerful erotic images (in the Semele episode, for example). In addition to these productions, the season included a powerful new adaptation of Aphra Behn's *Oroonoko* and a new work, *Warwickshire Testimony,* by April di Angelis at The Other Place. Greg Doran directed a stylish, dark *Volpone* at the Swan, with Malcolm Storry as Volpone and Guy Henry as Mosca.

In the opening scene of *A Midsummer Night's Dream,* directed by Michael Boyd with designs by Tom Piper, Athens was distinctly chilly. The courtiers, in heavy overcoats and fur hats, stood stiffly at attention in front of the curving wall of plain white that bounded the back of the forestage. Snow fell from the dark sky visible above the wall. The bursts of applause with which the courtiers reacted to Theseus's and Hippolyta's speeches were prompted by a bowler-hatted, white-gloved master of ceremonies. This looked like Moscow, *circa* 1956, in a court where the stern Athenian law would be enforced with a kind of frigid absolutism. Hippolyta (Josette Simon) did not appear to be unduly displeased with her lot as the intended bride of Theseus (Nicholas Jones), but the harsh treatment of Egeus's daughter clearly disturbed her. She moved to Hermia's side during Theseus's harangue (he seemed embarrassed to have to deliver it), and as she left the stage, she lingered to look at the prospective victim.

With the move to the forest the curved wall of doorways at the back remained in place, but flowers suddenly sprang up through holes in the stage. One of the Athenian court ladies, wearing an all-enveloping overcoat, fur hat, and gloves, came on and began to pick them. The master of ceremonies, still in bowler hat and coat, accosted her—and they began to tear off each other's outer garments until she was revealed (once her spectacles were removed) as a very flirtatious and *décolleté* First Fairy and he as the barechested Puck. Only the impending arrival of Oberon and Titania (doubled with Theseus and Hippolyta) prevented them from having sex there and then. It was probably this moment of passion suddenly unbridled that provoked a teacher with a party of schoolchildren to make a protest—subsequently nurtured into a flurry of press interest—about the wholesale lubricity of the production. In fact, the director hardly went any further than other recent interpreters of the play, and there was a clear distinction between mortal passions before and after fairy influence. Hermia's insistence that Lysander "lie further off" and his clumsy attempts to lie closer when they decide to go to sleep were not played leeringly, and although Helena went into the woods wearing a short red dress and high heels—perhaps hoping this would get her man for her—it was the wood and its inhabitants that held the key to sexuality. In order to administer the juice of the vision-altering flower, Puck arrived onstage dressed as a gardener, with a wheelbarrow, a watering can, and a substantial plant, its roots clogged with soil. He pulled Lysander's coat up over his face, heaped some dirt on top of his head, "planted" the flower, and watered it in like a good

gardener. The mayhem of the long lovers' scene (3.2) was appropriately acrobatic (Hermia being pitched head over heels offstage at one point) but scarcely erotic. However, goings-on elsewhere in the wood seemed to have some effect on these lovers. When Puck rearranged the recumbent and disheveled mortals after their night of confusion, he entwined them suggestively, having planted the antidote to the magic flower firmly over Lysander's groin. After all, these are the "lovebirds" that, as Theseus observes when he finds them, have begun "to couple now."

Titania's seduction of Bottom (David Ryan) was as physically direct as has become customary, and her bower was a solid and commodious bed that descended from the flies: as the first part of the performance ended, she and Bottom were clearly already getting on well. When the bed was lowered again in 4.1, Titania's arms were hanging over the side as she sprawled in an attitude of satisfied exhaustion. Bottom appeared in a dressing-gown and smoking a post-coital cheroot, with the smug air of one relaxing after a job well done. It was clear that some of the fairy attendants fancied similar treatment from him and had to be kept in check.

The woodland selves of all the Athenians seemed transformed and enhanced by the production's doubling. This was simply effected by change of costume (Oberon had long tails to his coat and a tattoo-like mark on his bald head), a pattern of stylized movement using the whole stage, and the equipping of each fairy with a repeated gesture, half nervous tic, or half "magic" pass of the hands. The "fairy" who had been Egeus, for example, held his right hand in the air above his head and shook it as though inducing some kind of hypnotic trance: touchingly, he seemed to echo (and counterpose) his mortal self by holding this hand in benediction over Hermia. Oberon was as smoothly spoken and assured as Theseus had been, with the added abilities to be invisible, to fly (courtesy of a chair lowered from the flies), and to move through the earth (on a ladder that rose through a trap for him to ascend Titania's bower). Titania was only slightly less inhibited in demeanor than Hippolyta: Josette Simon took the stage in the first scene with an assurance befitting an Amazonian queen, captured or otherwise, while Theseus seemed a little nervous and hesitant once Egeus's demand for judgment against Hermia had placed him on the spot. Puck found aerial travel rather more troublesome: after collecting the magic flower, he arrived bedraggled and still sweating. Bottom, with asinine teeth, luxuriant facial hair, and eminently strokable ears, was an amiable monster for Titania to love. There were moments of darkness in the production (notably when Demetrius threatened Hermia with a knife), and the lovers' dismay and physical distress were not merely a matter of torn clothes and besmirched faces. On balance, though, this was no nightmare.

Dance and movement were a well-conceived unifying element. In their first scene the "hard-handed men of Athens" entered in a line, solemn and sober-suited, then turned to face the audience and performed a stamping line-dance reminiscent of *The Full Monty*. Later, disconsolate at the absence of Bottom, their chief actor, they made a half-hearted attempt at the same routine. In a pleasing *coup*, "Pyramus and Thisbe" was performed in Elizabethan dress, with Peter Quince looking somewhat like Shakespeare. After an appropriately hilarious rendition of the tragedy (Bottom lost his sword blade, Thisbe had to make do with the hilt), the bergamask consisted of a version of the men's steps seen in 1.2, which then became a solemn fandango-like number as Bottom—with some temerity—held out his hand to Hippolyta. When she took it and joined in, the dance turned into the more "primitive" stamping, hip-gyrating dance with which Oberon and Titania had rocked the ground in 4.1: the woodland had invaded the palace. At the end of the play, when the fairy king and queen returned, dance was varied into another ritualistic mode, again evoking fertility rites, as with sweeping gestures they waved fronds of greenery over their heads to scatter "field-dew" across the stage.

Notes

1. See my "Shakespeare at Stratford-upon-Avon, 1996-98: or the Search for a Policy," *Shakespeare Quarterly* 50 (1999): 185-205.

Mark Thornton Burnett (essay date 2000)

SOURCE: Burnett, Mark Thornton. "Impressions of Fantasy: Adrian Noble's *A Midsummer Night's Dream*." In *Shakespeare, Film, Fin de Siècle,* edited by Mark Thornton Burnett and Ramona Wray, pp. 73-101. London: Macmillan, 2000.

[*In the following essay, Burnett discusses Adrian Noble's 1996 film version of* A Midsummer Night's Dream, *noting that while Noble's 1994-95 Royal Shakespeare Company stage production of the play was lauded by critics, the film adaptation received primarily negative reviews. Burnett reevaluates the film, praising it as a reinvention of the comedy "for the millennium."*]

When Adrian Noble's *A Midsummer Night's Dream* was performed by the Royal Shakespeare Company as part of its 1994-5 Stratford-upon-Avon and touring programme, the production attracted widespread acclaim. Eminent critics joined to sing the praises of a 'magnificent', 'notable', 'outstanding', 'stunning' and 'vibrant' reinterpretation of Shakespeare's play.[1] No doubt spurred on by this theatrical success, the RSC, in collaboration with Channel Four, quickly set about transferring the production to celluloid. The film version of *A Midsummer Night's Dream,* again directed by Noble, was commercially released to a limited number of cinemas in 1996 and, in 1997, made its way to a TV showing and the video market. But the passage from stage to screen proved an unhappy experience. As a film, *A Midsummer Night's Dream,* contrary to the expectations aroused by the reception of its previous incarnation, was roundly criticized. Directorial inadequacy had resulted in a

'botched' creation (stated *The Daily Telegraph*), an 'unmitigated disaster' (asserted *The Observer: Review*) and a 'highbrow pantomime' (agreed *The Sunday Times: Culture*).[2] Concluded *The Times*: 'Noble still thinks like a primitive', offers us a reading of the play that is 'charmless under the camera's close scrutiny' and 'puts the Bard's cause back a hundred years'.[3] Such a chorus of condemnation invites a considered response. In this essay, I aim to redress the filmic reputation of Noble's *A Midsummer Night's Dream* by concentrating on its stylistic felicities and postmodern aspirations. Rather than putting the Bard's cause back a hundred years, I will suggest, the film reinvents Shakespeare for the millennium, both recalling high Victorian decadence and looking ahead to the dawning of the new century. Before that argument can be developed, however, we need to return to the play itself.

In the opening scenes of *A Midsummer Night's Dream,* Egeus, outraged at his daughter Hermia's reluctance to accept his choice of marriage partner, accuses her lover, Lysander, of having 'stolen the impression of her fantasy'.[4] This printing metaphor is quickly taken up by Theseus, who reminds Hermia that her 'father should be as a god; / One that composed your beauties—yea, and one / To whom you are but as a form in wax / By him imprinted' (I.i.47-50). Thus does the play evoke women's positions in relation to patriarchal discipline and perceived malleability in the hands of fathers and governors alike. But the metaphors deployed here also suggest the role of the imagination in the artistic process: at one and the same time Hermia is a pawn in a struggle for an appropriate alliance and the raw material out of which will be fashioned a new entity. Indeed, the shaping 'imagination' (V.i.8) can be seen as essential to the action as a whole. It is not accidental that the 'mechanicals' are made up of carpenters and joiners (both types of artist). Nor is it irrelevant that Theseus should, towards the conclusion, play a variation upon his original argument, claiming that 'Lovers and madmen have such seething brains, / Such . . . fantasies, that apprehend / More than cool reason ever comprehends' (V.i.4-6). In many ways, the power struggles of *A Midsummer Night's Dream* are conducted through representations of the myriad 'forms' (V.i.15) that the creative faculty is driven to produce.

In New Historicist criticism, in particular, these struggles have been read in terms of contemporary anxieties that obtained in the Elizabethan state. Louis Montrose, in a 1996 study, approaches *A Midsummer Night's Dream* by mapping the various contexts—the interplay among discourses of gender, social status and theatricality—that were a 'condition of the play's imaginative possibility'.[5] However, it also needs to be recognized that, as much as the play's prevailing concerns are in dialogue with the cultural complexion of the 1590s, they have an equally significant contextual location in later historical periods. Taking the various 'impressions' or 'forms' made by 'fantasy' or the 'imagination', Noble's filmic *A Midsummer Night's Dream* serves them up as a postmodern mixture of childhood reminiscences, self-conscious literary allusions, sexual awakenings and reminders of a turn-of-the-century environment.

Chiefly, it is through the interpolated character of the Boy (Osheen Jones) that the film manages to rewrite the play's imaginative topos. The film opens with the Boy asleep in his bedroom, which is crowded with books, puppets, a rocking-horse and a miniature theatre. It quickly modulates to the scene of the play itself—the Athenian court. By placing the Boy first under and then at the table in this aristocratic world, the film grants him a key responsibility in the ensuing narrative: his is the guiding perspective, to the extent that he is capable, dramaturge-like, of giving birth to fairies from the bubbles created by his own toy pipe. At other points, the Boy assumes a more directive role still, as when he pushes Bottom's motorbike and propels forward a spherical moon, suggesting the centrality of the child's imperatives and projections to the play's unfolding events. Like Puck (Barry Lynch), the Boy has the power to activate and to generate. He 'bodies forth' (V.i.14) in the 'empty space' of his invention both the personalities and the properties that will people his dream.[6]

Crucial to the film are the ways in which the Boy's imaginative energies simultaneously empower and enslave. Even as he authors the 'forms' of his 'fantasies', appropriately envisioning the fairies as much younger versions of himself (their baggy trousers recall infants in diapers), the Boy is represented as the 'changeling' (II.i.120) over whom Titania (Lindsay Duncan) and Oberon (Alex Jennings) fight. During the realization of Titania's speech about the 'votaress' of her 'order' (II.i.123), the camera focuses in on a conventionally 'Indian' (II.ii.124) image of the Boy in a turban—his distraught expression indicates his alarm at becoming the object of the King and Queen's dissension. In addition, when the toy theatre is magically transported to the forest, the Boy must struggle with Oberon for ownership of the puppets' strings. Oberon's seizure of a model figure from the theatre implies that he has no qualms in usurping the Boy's manipulative privileges. Power in Noble's conception of things is a matter of contest, and no one is permitted to exercise a secure and unchanging control. If, in the play, then, tensions cluster about the father's hopes for his daughter, in the film, they are extended to encompass wider generational conflicts and the predicament of a child in a divided familial landscape. In common with other recent 'Shakespearean' films, such as Lloyd Kaufman's *Tromeo and Juliet* (1996) and Jocelyn Moorhouse's *A Thousand Acres* (1998), Noble in *A Midsummer Night's Dream* deploys the Bard to hint at the increasing untenability of the late twentieth-century nuclear family as a practical ideal. For all his imaginative abilities, the Boy is still subject to the crises and estrangements of his adoptive parents.

To shore up the role of the Boy in the imaginative process, the film draws upon a variety of motifs from children's literature. Its opening frame of the Boy asleep is lent additional force by the copy of *A Midsummer Night's Dream*, illustrated by Arthur Rackham, which lies beside him on the bedclothes. When he falls through the night sky and a chimney pot to encounter the 'mechanicals', the descent of Alice down the rabbit hole in Lewis Carroll's *Alice's Adventures in Wonderland* (1865) and the depiction of the tornado in L. Frank Baum's *The Wonderful Wizard of Oz* (1900) are brought to mind. (Crying 'Mummy!' and screaming as he is pitched into darkness, the Boy seems on the point of entering not so much his dream at this point as his nightmare.) Each pivotal moment is accompanied by allusions to narratives that either evoke childhood richly or appeal to a collective children's memory. For instance, the flying umbrellas used by the fairies for their wonder-inducing entrances and exits recall P. L. Travers' *Mary Poppins* (1934); the departure of Bottom (Desmond Barrie) and Titania across the water in an upturned umbrella is reminiscent of Edward Lear's sea-loving and moon-seeking animals, the owl and the pussy-cat; and the scene of Bottom flying across the moon on his motorbike harks back to the escape of 'E. T.' in the film of the same name. The result is less an experience of Shakespeare as it is an intertextual rehearsal of familiar children's stories, past and present. In this way, Noble's *A Midsummer Night's Dream* pushes back the perimeters of what constitutes 'Shakespeare', combining elements from 'high' and 'low' cultural traditions and mixing 'old' and 'new' representational materials.

The film's investment in the trappings of childhood has a three-fold effect. First, the echoes of both literary and filmic forms point to the ways in which the imaginative impetus has assumed a wide range of manifestations across history. On the one hand, *A Midsummer Night's Dream* longs nostalgically for the heyday of children's literature in a late Victorian context; on the other, it revels in the possibilities afforded by a unprecedented wave of children's films, as references to 'E. T.' and *Home Alone* suggest.[7] (In this connection, the print culture outlined at the start is placed in a rivalrous relationship to the power of alternative media and new informational practices.) It is as if Noble seeks a mode of production that addresses the 'special effects' requirements of a younger, cinematically demanding spectator, while also answering to the more intellectual expectations of the twentieth-century Shakespearean filmgoer. The invocation of popular literary predecessors argues for the Bard's perennial appeal; the use of technological wizardry discovers the dramatist being appropriated to satisfy a modern sensibility.

Motifs from children's literature speak to the implied child in the audience in more specific ways, however. At a secondary level, the narratives alluded to in *A Midsummer Night's Dream*, like the film itself, work to equip the Boy (and thus the generation he represents) with important social skills and interpersonal capacities. Like Alice and Dorothy, to whom, in his parentless condition, he is allied, the Boy undergoes a series of extraordinary dislocations, as a result of which he is finally able to confront 'reality' in a more self-aware and constructive fashion than before.[8] This, of course, is the pattern elaborated in children's stories in their more traditional guise. As Paul Schilder states of the *Alice* stories, 'the child uses Carroll's . . . anxiety situations in a way similar to the manner in which the child uses *Mother Goose Rhymes*. They take them as an understood reality which one can hope to handle better after one has played and worked with it.'[9] It is also the pattern characteristic of the fairy-tale, a form with a similar educative aspect. Bruno Bettelheim has said of fairy-tales that they explore the 'need . . . to find meaning in our lives'. By suggesting 'solutions to perturbing problems', he argues, such tales reveal the 'struggle to achieve maturity' and 'caution against the destructive consequences if one fails to develop higher levels of responsible self-hood'.[10] Although *A Midsummer Night's Dream,* in its self-conscious elaboration of a child's experiences, follows neither of these trajectories exactly, the Boy's experiments with his creative abilities, involvement in his adoptive parents' conflicts and property disputes with a father figure reveal more than a passing resemblance to the generic processes whereby other fictional children are enabled to foster their personal development. They show the Boy testing and stretching the boundaries of childhood, striving towards a realizable autonomy.

A key element of the child's development is the confrontation with his or her own sexuality. In this regard, the third effect of Noble's investment in the cultural production of childhood comes into play. Through amalgamating a Shakespearean art form with the stuff of childhood 'fantasies', the director reactivates the sexual dimensions that underlie all mythic archetypes. In his classic *The Uses of Enchantment,* Bruno Bettelheim posits that fairy tales negotiate the uncertain sexual terrain between childhood, adolescence and adulthood, at times concerning themselves with specific crises such as 'Oedipal anguish'.[11] With reference to *Alice in Wonderland,* A. M. E. Goldschmidt makes more detailed claims for the sexual import of children's stories: the lock and the key, and the descent down the well, he contends, belong to 'the common symbolism of . . . coitus'.[12] Nowhere in Noble's *A Midsummer Night's Dream* are obviously Oedipal crises hinted at; however, the film abounds in scenes of sexual revelation and voyeurism, which read in many ways as a working through of Goldschmidt's critical position. Sexuality in *A Midsummer Night's Dream* is initially brought to the Boy's attention via moments of heterosexual tension and displaced masculinity. Thus the Boy undergoes something of a primal scene when, at the start, he is privy to the chief protagonists' 'nuptial' (I.i.1) plans: Hippolyta's reference here to the 'silver bow / New-bent' (I.i.9-10) is, in Lindsay Duncan's delivery, made to bristle with all the erotic energy of unconsummated desire. More obscurely, perhaps, sexuality is paraded before the Boy during the rehearsals of the 'mechanicals', which take place in the war-time austerity of a corrugated hut. As Noble admitted in interview, a *Dad's Army* effect was aimed for in these scenes, and certainly the fire extinguishers, dartboards and old sporting trophies that adorn the hut walls appear as telling indicators of the 1940s.[13] But the temporal markers are also instrumental in constructing the 'mechanicals' as sexual

outcasts, who can have no place in the war effort. The effeminacy of Francis Flute (Mark Letheren), it is implied, identifies him as an unfit soldier, while the braggadocio of Bottom, the film suggests, constitutes the sublimated sexuality of a man debarred from the battlefield. Because the Boy is simultaneously the voyeuristic auditor of the rehearsals, the film allows him to bear witness to a range of expressions of sexuality, from pre-marital badinage to compensatory theatricals. His is the blank page on which *A Midsummer Night's Dream* writes a vicarious experience of sexuality's frustrations and possibilities.

Nor do glimpses into the sexual world of adulthood end with the opening scenes. What might be termed a floating phallus is, via visual details and linguistic emphases, frequently tied to the Boy, suggesting a particularly forceful engagement with the archetypal paradigms that inform mythic narratives. The elongated handle of the sumptuous red parasol in which Titania drapes herself first suggests the male member, and the spectacle is lent an additional phallic flavour by the arch rendering of the accompanying song: 'You spotted snakes with double tongue, / Thorny hedgehogs, be not seen' (II.ii.9-10). That which the film suggests at the level of metaphor it soon takes up in physical action. Once Bottom, as an ass, has been granted a view of Titania's pudenda, he is spurred on to penetrate her violently from the rear. Given the graphic nature of Bottom's transformation, it therefore seems appropriate that the recollection of his 'vision' (IV.i.203) should be imbued with a sexual charge: with its bawdy 'methought I had' refrain, his account is presented as a reverie upon the delights of priapic tumescence. Dovetailing with, and suffused through, these moments are the Boy's responses. In them, an audience is prompted to discover the 'impression' of an awakening consciousness, one poised between the child's sense of sexual wonder and the adult's knowledge of sexual practice. Indeed, at one point the Boy actually assumes the phallic qualities that characterize his adult counterparts. Coming across Hermia (Monica Dolan) as she dreams of the 'crawling serpent [at her] breast' (II.ii.152), the Boy, magician-like, subjects her to levitation, thereby becoming, through a process of association, the phallus that is at the heart of the nightmare. Confirming the connection are the broader visual links forged between the Boy's stripy pyjamas, the strip flooring and the snaky implications of the parasol handle. Part of the business of achieving sexual responsibility, it might be argued, is knowing what to do with the phallus, and this is borne out in *A Midsummer Night's Dream* in which the Boy is chief participant in a number of organ-oriented scenarios. Dominated and dominant in his imagined universe, the Boy is forewarned of both the pleasures and the dangers of his future maturity.

Such is the nature of Noble's direction, moreover, that the Boy's experience is not restricted to examples of heterosexual behaviour alone. The film, in fact, is equally rife with interludes of homoerotic attraction. Perhaps inspired by recent queer appropriations of Shakespeare, Noble chooses to have Demetrius (Kevin Doyle) highlight the phrase, 'cheek by jowl' (III.ii.338), as part of a homerotic alliance with Lysander (Daniel Evans) against Helena (Emily Raymond). Similarly, just before he is turned into an ass, Bottom struggles to rid himself of Puck, who has climbed aboard his back. The implication is that the same-sex combination of fairy and mortal sets the seal on the weaver's subsequent bestial metamorphosis. While the Boy is not directly involved in these scenes, the underlying idea is still that sexuality is an uncertain property, that a child's gendered identity may be 'shape[d]' (V.i.16) by the external factors with which it comes into contact.

Cumulatively, and not surprisingly, the shifting sexual perspectives that characterize Noble's *A Midsummer Night's Dream,* as well as its ironic rewritings, invocations of modes of artistic production, confoundings of the states of 'fantastic' and 'real', conjurations of competing temporal markers and signifiers, and manipulations of forms of history mark the film out as a peculiarly postmodern phenomenon. As the late twentieth century draws to a close, Shakespeare and postmodernity, in fact, have become increasingly familiar bedfellows. In an age of post-capitalist 'mechanical reproduction', discussion invariably attends to the ways in which the dramatist operates less as a point of origin than as a prompt for all manner of cultural associations, a commodity that can be copied and imitated as well as applied and exploited.[14] Richard Burt's *Unspeakable ShaXXXspeares: Queer Theory and American Kiddie Culture* (1998), a study of the semantics of Shakespearean authority in modern American culture, is indicative of this shift in the critical mindset. If hybridity, pastiche, pluralism, cultural ransacking and the recourse to other texts and images are the defining marks of postmodernity, then the *mise-en-scène* of Noble's film makes a timely contribution to the postmodern debate.[15]

Through its self-conscious deployment of a number of representational 'forms', *A Midsummer Night's Dream* makes newly relevant the play's 'antique fables' and 'fairy toys' (V.i.3). In particular, by granting the parentless Boy some of the power of the dramaturge himself, it questions the extent to which Shakespeare still signifies an 'original', the 'parent' (II.i.117) to which the later development of the 'great literary tradition' can be traced. Even the set design functions as an important element in the film's interrogative confrontation with the Bard's mythic status. Numerous mirrors festoon the Athenian and forest interiors. At court, Helena contemplates her reflection in a glass; in the forest, Bottom glimpses pursuing fairies in the mirror of his motorbike. Privileging mirrors in this way serves a meta-cinematic purpose. It urges us to be sensitive to another reflective surface (the lens of the camera) and thus to recognize the constructed nature of the visions the film provides. Mirrors in *A Midsummer Night's Dream,* then, provoke an attempt to distinguish the authentic from the counterfeit, to adjudicate between the various accretions of Shakespearean doubling, reproduction and imitation in postmodern culture. Noble reminds his audience that he deals not so much in Shakespeare as in the meanings that a filmic engagement with the Bard

might stimulate. 'Forgeries' (II.i.81), in short, *A Midsummer Night's Dream* implies, may eventually prove more resilient than the 'originals' to which they are parodically related.

Postmodernity, as critics have recently argued, cannot be linked to the twentieth century in its entirety. For it acquires much of its impact from an association with specifically *fin-de-siècle* anxieties. As Hillel Schwartz observes, 'what the postmodernist narrative celebrates is suspiciously millennial: a world of unending variety . . . a world of transitive and playful identities, a world unencumbered by traditional demarcations of space or normative experiences of time'.[16] Ever alert to the implications of such connections, Noble's *A Midsummer Night's Dream* elaborates its material in not one but several end-of-century modes. In itself, of course, as a play dating from 1594-5, *A Midsummer Night's Dream* is a millennial production, written in a decade of economic crisis. Ian Archer sums up the contemporary climate in the following terms: 'Harvest failures spelt impoverishment for the mass of the people, and crime soared . . . Poor harvests in 1594 and 1595 were followed by two years of dearth in 1596 and 1597.'[17] The play is acutely responsive to this situation, and Titania's extended meditation on 'Contagious fogs' (II.i.90), the bank-breaking 'river' (II.i.91), rotting 'green corn' (II.i.94), 'distemperature' (II.i.106) and altered 'seasons' (II.i.107) can be profitably read as a nervous reaction to a desperate moment in England's economic fortunes. Noble's filmic *A Midsummer Night's Dream,* too, works to acknowledge the speech's point of origin in the fraught years of the 1590s. As Lindsay Duncan as Titania intones the celebrated words, the camera pans out to show mists gathering ominously over the sea and the music swells to climax on a foreboding note. True to the film's postmodern credentials, however, the montage here simultaneously invites spectators of the 1990s to assimilate messages pertinent to their historical location. For a late twentieth-century audience, the visual conjunction between water and fog points to chemically induced 'natural' disasters in the same moment as it precipitates memories of the Holocaust and fears of the imminent apocalypse.

Both the 1590s and the 1990s, however, are arguably overshadowed in the film by references to the nineteenth century's final decade. From the very start of *A Midsummer Night's Dream,* it is the symbolic appurtenances of the 1890s that predominate. The Boy's copy of the play, for instance, emblazoned with the name of Arthur Rackham, evokes that turn-of-the-century artist who enjoyed considerable success with his illustrated edition, published in 1900, of *Fairy Tales of the Brothers Grimm.*[18] The turn of the century is returned to again in the borrowing from L. Frank Baum's *The Wonderful Wizard of Oz,* also published in 1900, and finds cinematic confirmation in the scenes set at the Athenian court. Here, the cast-iron fireplaces, chandeliers, red and green corridors, sash windows, four-panelled doors and tessellated floors function as carefully chosen signifiers of a decadent late Victorian historical juncture: not surprisingly, Theseus comes into this *Homes and Gardens* setting dressed as a Wilde-attired aesthete. Commenting on the 1890s, Robert Newman observes: 'In ways that present striking parallels to the 1590s and the 1990s, the 1890s attempted to constrain threats to the social order in a context marked by shifting articulations of gender, sexuality, class and ethnicity.'[19] Newman does not elaborate, but it may be that he has in mind the traditional construction of the 1890s as a period in which the splendours of imperialism were beginning to be tarnished, in which fears of 'anarchism' circulated, in which established religion was on the decline, in which the so-called 'New Woman' was paving the way for the Suffragettes and in which belief was fading in the power of the middle classes.[20] As a transitional moment in history, then, the 1890s lend themselves well to the premeditated imperatives and overall effect of Noble's *A Midsummer Night's Dream*. Taking off from the 1590s, the film addresses the 1990s via a detour of the 1890s, borrowing from a spectrum of fantastic 'impressions' to reflect upon the future 'forms' that the 'Shakespearean' imagination will surely adopt or may never assume.

Nowhere are the connections between imagination and reproduction, overlapping sexualities and historical time-frames, and autonomy and domination more precisely illustrated than in the film's final moments. Earlier in the film, we have seen both the Boy and Puck as auditors at the rehearsals of the 'mechanicals', suggesting that each is an influence upon the ultimate shape of the play-within-a-play. This idea is elaborated upon in the closing stages of *A Midsummer Night's Dream*, where the imaginative impetus features not so much as an autonomous endeavour as an aspect of collaborative enterprise. Reciprocity is hinted at when Philostrate (Barry Lynch) takes the Boy's hand and leads him into the theatre where the amateur theatricals are about to take place. The theatre itself is an enlarged version of the toy theatre, earlier seen in the forest scenes and the Boy's bedroom. Such a shift in scale implies that the Boy's power will be diminished while that of the 'mechanicals' is about to be increased: no longer is a child able to aspire to absolute control over the imaginative experience. Nor is an audience frustrated in its meta-theatrical suspicions. As the performance begins, the Boy is seen in the wings raising the curtain and generally pulling at the ropes of the stage machinery. Even if he is able to conjure images and sequences from his favourite texts, the film suggests, the Boy requires the assistance of a host of underlings to bring his visions to life. Bruno Bettelheim has argued that fairy stories enable children to achieve 'meaningful and rewarding relations with the world around' them, since they concentrate on integrating isolated 'personalities' with the social and cultural collective.[21] A comparable operation can be detected in Noble's film, for it is only when he participates in a joint venture, rescinding theatrical authority to the 'mechanicals', that the Boy's dream can be fully realized.

Closely allied to his newly collaborative role is the Boy's developing grasp of the potential consequences of adult sexual conduct. The phallus, the film implies, cannot

forever float irresponsibly, but must form part of an integrated whole. When the hymenal wall has been broken and the bloody 'mantle' (V.i.274) connoting deflowerment has been cast upon the stage, therefore, the mood of levity lifts, the Boy and the theatre audience becoming sober, calm and quiet. Along with his aristocratic auditors, the Boy hovers on the cusp of a liminal moment, an incipient awareness of the relationship between sexuality and mortality.

Illuminating still further the Boy's imaginative collaboration and evolving sexual identity is the film's concluding emphasis upon the restorative power of familial relations. Even before the closing celebrations, the Boy has been prepared for the healing of fractured families, having overheard the prediction made by Oberon that the lovers will soon be 'Wedded with Theseus all in jollity' (IV.i.91). At the end, the focus of the film thus moves away from the isolation of the Boy in his private box and toward his incorporation within a series of new family scenarios. Once the 'mechanicals' have concluded their performance, the back of the theatre gives way to reveal a magical, moon-lit stretch of water. The liquid spectacle suggests rebirth, and this is clarified in the accompanying shot of the Boy being embraced by Oberon, Titania, Puck and the fairies. Picking up upon the references to 'nativity' (V.i.403) in Oberon's benediction, the film constructs the assembly as a welcoming family, as a parent, child and sibling group that only now can announce itself with certainty. Given its postmodern credentials, however, *A Midsummer Night's Dream* does not settle upon one family alone. The film's very last image is of the Boy in the lap of another family: returned to the theatre, he is cradled by the whole cast for the curtain call. It is, of course, to the cinema spectators that the cast appeals for applause, a move which neatly identifies us as the key collaborative element in the exercise of imaginative judgement.

With these final moments, the film blurs purposefully once again the dividing-lines between its 'realities' and 'fantasies', court and forest locations, and characters and institutions. It hints, in fact, at the interchangeability of Shakespearean representations, reminding us, at a deeper level of its fabric, of the collaborative transferability of a production that, via a complex of funding agencies, managed to gravitate from a stage performance to a screen presentation. The play, *A Midsummer Night's Dream,* the film wants to suggest, does not only exist on the printed page; rather, it consorts with, and is revitalized by, the new media and technologies that have revolutionized the twentieth century. As the clock chimes twelve in the closing sequence, harking back to the striking of midnight in the Boy's bedroom at the start, it seems as if one era has ended and another is about to commence.

Notes

1. Michael Coveney, 'Filth well worth revelling in', *The Observer,* 7 August 1994; Louise Doughty, 'Dream lovers', *The Mail on Sunday: Review,* 7 August 1994; John Gross, 'Heady stuff, this reality',

The Sunday Telegraph, 21 August 1994; *The Sunday Times,* 7 August 1994.

2. *The Daily Telegraph,* 26 December 1997, p. 31; *The Observer: Review,* 1 December 1996, p. 12; *The Sunday Times: Culture,* 1 December 1996, p. 9.

3. *The Times,* 28 November 1996, p. 39.

4. *A Midsummer Night's Dream,* ed. Stanley Wells (Harmondsworth: Penguin, 1978), I.i.32. All further references appear in the text.

5. Louis Montrose, *The Purpose of Playing: Shakespeare and the Cultural Politics of the Elizabethan Theatre* (Chicago and London: University of Chicago Press, 1996), p. 160.

6. I am recalling here, of course, Peter Brook's famously unadorned production of *A Midsummer Night's Dream* in 1970-1 and the title of his book, *The Empty Space* (Harmondsworth: Penguin, 1980).

7. On the *Home Alone* parallel, see Richard Burt, *Unspeakable ShaXXXspeares: Queer Theory and American Kiddie Culture* (New York: St. Martin's Press, 1998), p. 3. *Peter Pan* (1953), *Pinocchio* (1940) and *Time Bandits* (1981) would be related films which transport a parentless child from 'reality' into an imaginative landscape.

8. For further Alice/Dorothy parallels, see Martin Gardner, 'A child's garden of bewilderment', in Sheila Egoff, G. T. Stubbs and L. F. Ashley (eds), *Only Connect: Readings of Children's Literature* (New York: Oxford University Press, 1969), p. 153.

9. Paul Schilder, 'Psychoanalytic Remarks on *Alice in Wonderland* and Lewis Carroll', in Robert Phillips (ed.), *Aspects of Alice: Lewis Carroll's Dreamchild as seen through the Critics' Looking-Glasses, 1865-1971* (Harmondsworth: Penguin, 1981), p. 343.

10. Bruno Bettelheim, *The Uses of Enchantment: The Meaning and Importance of Fairy Tales* (New York: Vintage, 1977), pp. 3, 5, 183.

11. Bettelheim, *Uses of Enchantment,* p. 115.

12. A. M. E. Goldschmidt, '*Alice in Wonderland* Psychoanalysed', in Phillips (ed.), *Aspects of Alice,* p. 330.

13. Matt Wolf, 'From Stratford', *The Times,* 19 December 1995.

14. I draw here, of course, on Walter Benjamin's essay, 'The Work of Art in the Age of Mechanical Reproduction'. See his *Illuminations,* ed. Hannah Arendt (London: Fontana/Collins, 1982), pp. 219-53.

15. See Zygmunt Bauman, *Intimations of Postmodernity* (London and New York: Routledge, 1992), pp. 187-8; Hans Bertens, *The Idea of the Postmodern: A History* (London and New York: Routledge, 1995), pp. 54, 161; Angela McRobbie, 'Postmodernism and popular culture', in Lisa Appignanesi (ed.), *Postmodernism: ICA Documents 5* (London: ICA, 1986), pp. 54-7.

16. Hillel Schwartz, 'Economies of the Millennium', in Charles B. Strozier and Michael Flynn (eds), *The Year 2000: Essays on the End* (New York and London: New York University Press, 1997), p. 315.

17. Ian Archer, 'The 1590s: Apotheosis or Nemesis of the Elizabethan Régime?', in Asa Briggs and Daniel Snowman (eds), *Fins de Siècle: How Centuries End* (New Haven and London: Yale University Press, 1996), pp. 65, 71.

18. It might be suggested that Rackham is a particularly appropriate artist for the film to invoke. One of his reflections on his art—'[I believe] in the educative power of imaginative . . . pictures . . . for children in their most impressionable years'—is conducted in language redolent of Shakespeare's play. See Margaret Drabble (ed.), *The Oxford Companion to English Literature* (Oxford: Oxford University Press, 1985), pp. 806-7.

19. Robert Newman, 'Introduction', in Robert Newman (ed.), *Centuries' Ends, Narrative Means* (Stanford: Stanford University Press, 1996), p. 7.

20. See Asa Briggs, 'The 1890s: Past, Present and Future in Headlines', in Briggs and Snowman (eds), *Fins de Siècle,* pp. 157-95.

21. Bettelheim, *Uses of Enchantment,* pp. 11, 14.

THEMES

James A. S. McPeek (essay date 1972)

SOURCE: McPeek, James A. S. "The Psyche Myth and *A Midsummer Night's Dream*." *Shakespeare Quarterly* 23, no. 1 (winter 1972): 69-79.

[*In the following essay, McPeek explores Shakespeare's treatment of the Psyche myth in* A Midsummer Night's Dream, *contending that the play provides a mythic translation of the Psyche legend.*]

In the phantasmagoria of *A Midsummer Night's Dream* scholars have discerned and analyzed the elements of several antique fables and fairy toys, but they seem largely to have neglected the curious and extensive relationship of this dreamworld to the story of Psyche and its matrix in Lucius Apuleius' *Golden Ass.* Many will concede that though Shakespeare may have known other stories about ass-headed men,[1] Apuleius' account of his adventures affords the most likely source for Titania's infatuation with a monster, as well as for some other motifs, as Sister M. Generosa has shown.[2] But the relationship of the *Dream* to the story of Psyche appears deeper than that of a series of casual resemblances, such as might be based on vague recollection.

If one looks below the texture of the language, which tends to obscure the outlines of the story, one finds remarkable similarity between many events of the myth and the main adventures of the drama. In effect, it may be urged that the fundamental pattern of the myth and the patterns of the main stories in the play are similar in several interlocking ways, and that if Shakespeare did not consciously recall the Psyche tale as he wrote, he nevertheless had in mind many of its archetypal features, so that the *Dream* in part becomes yet another example of what Northrop Frye designates as displaced myth. The general impression is not that of an ordering of the play to correspond to the structure of the myth, but rather as if the mosaic of the myth had been shattered into its original *tesserae,* which Shakespeare has picked up and arranged to suit his own design. With his usual independence in deriving material from his sources, Shakespeare largely avoids borrowing the phrasing of the story, but his apparent use of a few terms suggests that he may have known the Latin text[3], and the possible use of William Adlington's preface to his translation of the work indicates that he may have also known that version (1566), which was reprinted for the third time in 1596[4]. The parallels are numerous and vary from notable resemblances to vague likenesses; but one does not have to defend the validity of all the parallels to sustain the thesis that Shakespeare probably had read *The Golden Ass* and that he has given the Psyche tale a truly mythic translation in *A Midsummer Night's Dream.*

The reshaping of the Psyche myth in the play is dreamlike and strange in its new arrangements, but yet essentially true to the original story. The tale itself in its telling is associated with dreams. Before the story begins, the captive Charites has been distressed by a shocking dream-vision (Bk.iv, sec.27; 42-43). The "trifling old woman" set to guard her counsels her not to be afraid of strange visions and dreams, and then to revive her spirits tells her the tale of Psyche.

The Psyche image itself, the concept of the devoted woman patient in adversity and unfailingly true to her love, becomes an important construct in *A Midsummer Night's Dream,* involving both mortals and fairies. First let us consider it as embodied in the mortal women of the drama. It will perhaps be granted that in developing his archetypal pattern of the fair Helena and the dark Hermia Shakespeare was not interested in creating character, but rather in giving a composite impression of woman, universal woman in all her variety. The two are contrasted without prejudice (tall and short, fair and dark, phlegmatic and waspish); it is clear that one is not to be preferred to the other. For all their external differences they are "two lovely berries on one stem", and they are manifest Psyches in

their unfailing constancy to their lovers (Demetrius and Lysander change their loves, but Helena and Hermia remain true). If the persistence of Helena in following the estranged Demetrius to the woods may seem at first to associate her more notably with the Psyche pattern, later on the plight of Hermia, bedraggled and torn by briars, hopelessly searching for Lysander, redresses the balance.

At the outset in the myth and in the play, Psyche and Hermia are in somewhat similar circumstances. Hermia is faced with the necessity of complying with her father's wish that she wed Demetrius or die (Theseus offers her a third choice of becoming a devotee of Diana), and she spiritedly accepts the alternatives to marriage. Psyche is seemingly faced with the necessity of marrying a Serpent, a bridal of death, arranged for her by her father (against his wishes), courageously accepts her lot, and becomes, for a period, a votaress of Venus.

Helena and Hermia make use respectively of the monster and serpent images[5], images of central importance to the Psyche tale and to the drama. These images are frequently employed by Shakespeare throughout his plays, sometimes, as with the serpent image, tracing to unambiguous sources, such as the stories of the serpents strangled by Hercules and the Serpent of Eden. The usages in *A Midsummer Night's Dream,* considered singly, may seem adventitious; taken together, in conjunction with other resemblances, they seem somehow to reflect the myth. In soliloquy Helena sees herself as being like a monster: remarking that she must be ugly as a bear, she considers it no wonder that Demetrius flies from her as from a monster (II.ii.94-97). One is reminded that all things fear the power of the fierce serpent who is to be the husband of Psyche—a slight resemblance by itself; but when one recalls the apparent fact that the monster image as applied to Bottom is based on Apuleius, the resemblance seems more plausible. But Helena will not give up her pursuit; in her unswerving devotion, as she remarks earlier, Demetrius is all her world and his face banishes night ("It is not night when I do see your face", II.i.220-226). In comparable mood Psyche courts Cupid: "I little esteeme to see your visage and figure, little doo I regarde the night & darkness thereof, for you are my onely light" (Bk. V.7; 50). Later, Demetrius equates Helena's beauty with that of Venus (III.ii.60-61), and Oberon promises that (like Psyche) Helena shall rival Venus in beauty, that she shall "shine as gloriously / As the Venus of the sky" (III.ii.106-107).

In her turn, Hermia dreams that a serpent is eating her heart away while Lysander sits smiling at the deed (a forecast of his later mocking of her). She wakens to find Lysander gone without a word to her ("gone? No sound, no word?"), and, after almost fainting from fear, she sets out to find him or die (II.ii.145-156). In her search she meets Demetrius and applies the serpent image to him as a possible slayer of Lysander (III.ii.70-73). After she finds Lysander, now devoted to Helena, he mocks her and rejects her as a "Vile thing", like a serpent ("Vile thing, let loose, / Or I will shake thee from me like a serpent", III ii.260-

261). In the myth, it will be recalled, Psyche is convinced by her sisters that her unseen husband is indeed the creature ("the most miserablest creature livinge, the most poore, the most crooked, and the most vile", IV.31; 44ᵛ) that Venus would have her love, the dire Serpent of the Oracle of Apollo, who will devour both her and her child at its birth (V.18; 51). When she discovers his true identity and accidentally awakes him, he flies from her "without utteraunce of any woorde" (V.23; 53). She catches him as he rises into the air but shortly loses her grip and falls. Cupid pauses a moment to rebuke her and mock her for her folly, and then flies away, leaving her grief-stricken and lamenting. After he is out of sight, she first attempts suicide, but presently sets out to seek her alienated husband.

And Shakespeare's fairies, who preside over the fortunes of these mortals both in fickle love and in true love (as is fitting since there is magic in both states), exhibit action, themes, and imagery that are also paralleled in the myth. The fairies themselves have a mythic parallel in the unseen servitors who wait on Psyche and provide her with every need and luxury (V.3; 46ᵛ). That Shakespeare would translate these creatures to fairies follows the practice of English authors from the time of *Sir Orfeo* and Chaucer in reshaping classical myth. It is interesting that at the end of the play Shakespeare visualizes his fairies as attendants of Hecate: "And we fairies that do run / By the triple Hecate's team . . ." (V.i.390-391). Though Shakespeare's fairies are visible to the audience, like the servants of Psyche they are never seen by any of the characters except Bottom, and he finally remembers them only as a dream. In the shaping of the drama, aspects of both Venus and Psyche are fused in the person of Titania (it will be remembered that Psyche is a surrogate of Venus in the myth, IV.28; 43ᵛ), while Cupid plays a triple role in Oberon, Puck, and the Indian boy.

With his power over fickle love as well as true love Oberon is a manifest Cupid figure. His lieutenant Puck, as Sister M. Generosa has pointed out, has the propensities of Cupid added to his folklore characteristics. When Venus calls Cupid to her aid in taking vengeance on Psyche for usurping worship due her, Apuleius describes his nature in terms broadly suggestive of Puck's behavior: "And by and by she called her winged sonne Cupide, rashe inough, and hardie, who by his evil manners, contemninge all publique iustice and lawe, armed with fire & arrowes, runninge up and downe in the nightes from house to house, and corruptinge the lawfull marriages of every person, doth nothinge but that whiche is evill, who although that he weare of his owne proper nature sufficient prone to woorke mischiefe, yet she egged him forwarde with woordes" (IV.30; 44). Puck's delight later on in maneuvering the crossed loves completes his fashioning as a Cupid.

Venus urges Cupid to shoot his arrows at Psyche to make her fall in love with the "most miserablest", the "most vile" of creatures. Then she goes off to the sea where sea gods and goddesses flock to her and follow her:

Sic effata . . . proximas oras reflui litoris petit, plantisque roseis vibrantium fluctuum summo rore calcato, ecce iam profundum⁶ maris sudo resedit vertice, et ipsum quod incipit velle, et statim, quasi pridem praeceperit, non moratur marinum obsequium. Adsunt Nerei filiae chorum canentes . . . et auriga parvulus delphini Palaemon; . . . iam passim maria persultantes Tritonum catervae Talis ad Oceanum pergentem Venerem comitatur exercitus

(IV. 31).

Adlington, as usual, translates very freely, omitting some significant details in the opening sentence:

When she had spoken these woordes, she . . . took her voiage towardes the sea.

When she was come to the sea, she began to call the Goddes & Goddesses, who were obedient to her voyce. For incontinent came yᵉ daughters of Nereus singing with tunes melodiously . . . Palemon, the driver of the Dolphin, the trumpetters of Triton leapinge hither and thither. . . . Such was the cõpany which followed Venus marchinge towardes the Occean sea

(44ᵛ).

Gaselee fills out the missing details in his revision of Adlington:

When she had spoken these words, she . . . took her voyage towards the shore hard by, where the tides flow to and fro: and when she was come there, and had trodden with her rosy feet upon the top of the trembling waters, then the deep sea became exceeding calm upon its whole surface, and at her will, as though she had before given her bidding, straightway appeared her servitors from the deep. . . .

Similarly, when Oberon, like Venus, wishes to take vengeance on Titania for denying him his right to the Indian boy, he calls Puck to his aid. He first reminds Puck of an earlier experience by the sea (II.i.148-160):

> Thou rememb'rest
> Since once I sat upon a promontory
> And heard a mermaid, on a dolphin's back
> Uttering such dulcet and harmonious breath
> That the rude sea grew civil at her song,
> And certain stars shot madly from their spheres
> To hear the sea-maid's music.

Puck.

> I remember.

Ob.

> That very time I saw (but thou couldst not)
> Flying between the cold moon and the earth
> Cupid, all arm'd. A certain aim he took
> At a fair Vestal, throned by the West,
> And loos'd his love-shaft smartly from his bow,
> As it should pierce a hundred thousand hearts.

It seems generally accepted that Shakespeare may have remembered here impressions, however derived, from the entertainments for Elizabeth at Kenilworth (1575)[7] and El-vetham (1591),[8] spectacles that presented singing mer-maids, dolphins, Tritons, fireworks (shooting stars), and spells supposedly calming the seas—pageants similar to the one described by Apuleius. On the other hand, Apuleius clearly provides adequate background for most of the action and imagery of this episode as part of the continuing story. In his account we have Venus' summoning Cupid to aid her in taking vengeance on Psyche, her urging Cupid to aim his arrows at Psyche so that she will love the vilest of creatures, the pageant of Venus by the sea with her calming the waters, her melodious Nereids, and a dolphin ridden by Palemon. Furthermore, Psyche is described (in the following paragraph) as essentially a fair Vestal (a virgin of solitary life and of divine beauty). In aiming at her, as in aiming at Elizabeth, Cupid (in effect) missed his mark. All the images in the *Dream* are accounted for save for the shooting stars. In sum, though Shakespeare may have recalled the descriptions of the water pageants at Ke-nilworth and Elvetham, it seems very likely also that he knew this episode in Apuleius.

The Indian boy seems a marvellous objectification of one side of Oberon-Cupid's nature, in relation to Titania as a Venus figure. The quarrel between Oberon and Titania for possession of the Indian boy clearly represents a conten-tion for mastery, Oberon asserting his male supremacy ("Am I not thy lord?") and Titania insisting, in her turn, on matriarchal rule ("If you will patiently dance in our round", II.i.140).[9] If Oberon were to submit and allow Ti-tania to retain the boy (a young Cupid figure who may be considered symbolic of Cupid himself under Venus' control), he would acknowledge the matriarchal rule, very much as Cupid does, so long as he lies wounded, virtually a prisoner in his mother's palace. But Oberon-Cupid rejects the dominance of Titania-Venus, and taking the Indian boy (the young Cupid should not remain indefinitely under feminine rule, as Juno and Ceres remind Venus in the myth, V.31; 56), he becomes truly Titania's lord, and the contention is over. The Indian boy, son of a votaress of Ti-tania, seems almost a fulfillment in the play of Venus' threat to replace Cupid with the son of one of her retainers (V.29; 55). In her final patient submission to Oberon's will (IV.i.60-66), Titania becomes a Psyche, whose patient submission to the will of Venus attests her worthiness of Cupid's love.

Titania functions also as a Venus figure in representing Nature herself. Even her name, a patronymic of Diana as Shakespeare would have known from Ovid[10], is one of the names used to designate "the natural mother of all things", as Apuleius calls her (XI.4; 117), known variously as Ceres, Venus, Diana, and other goddesses. The creatures of nature are Titania's fairy servitors (II.i.8-15), and sum-mer itself attends on her state (III.i.158). Her division with Oberon has reversed the seasons and created general disorder:

> Hoary-headed frosts
> Fall in the fresh lap of the crimson rose;
> And on old Hiems' thin and icy crown

> An odorous chaplet of sweet summer buds
> Is, as in mockery, set. The spring, the summer,
> The childing autumn, angry winter change
> Their wonted liveries; and the mazed world
> By their increase, now knows not which is which.
> And this same progeny of evils comes
> From our debate, from our dissension;
> We are their parents and original.

(II. i. 107-117)

Even the phrasing in the last lines of this quotation seems to recall the language of Apuleius or that of his translator. Through their quarrel, Titania declares, she and Oberon are the "parents and original" of this "progeny of evils". Early in the myth Venus is inflamed to fury by the worship of Psyche, an anger which has been the cause for the desolation and desecration of her temples (IV.29; 43[v]). This disorder, though not described specifically as affect-ing the seasons, is reflected in all human affairs which "are now become no more gratious, no more pleasant, no more gentle, but incivill, mõstrous & horrible: moreover the marriages are not for any amitie, or for love of procre-atiõ, but ful of envy, discorde, & debate" (V.28; 54[v]). Venus' anger is the greater since she is the mother of all, "the originall parent of all these elementes" (IV.30; 44), as Adlington translates Apuleius' phrasing, "rerum naturae prisca parens, en elementorum origo initialis." Shake-speare's phrase, "parents and original", is somewhat closer to the Latin in pattern. Later, in Book XI, Venus (to use one of her many names) speaks of herself as the "natural mother of all things, mistris and governesse of all the El-emenentes, the initiall progeny of worldes", a fairly literal translation of Apuleius' "rerum naturae parens, elemen-torum omnium domina, saeculorum progenies initialis" (XI.4; 117). Though it cannot be proved that Shakespeare expropriated the word *progeny* from this source for his phrase "progeny of evils", its use in this special context offers an interesting parallel. Possibly Apuleius' phrase, "governesse of all the Elementes", may have begotten Ti-tania's epithet for the moon, "governess of floods", in the same speech.

In the same picture of Venus, Apuleius describes the god-dess as crowned like Flora with garlands interlaced with flowers (Hiems uses such a chaplet in mockery), and apostrophizes her at length as controlling the stars, the seasons, the winds, seeds, and all life. After the "devine image" has departed, all things rejoice (and a reversal of seasons is suggested): "For after the horefrost, ensued the whote and temperat Sunne. . . . The barrein and sterrill were contented at their shadowe, rendering swete and pleasant shrilles: The seas were quiet from wyndes and tempestes: The heaven had chased away the cloudes, and appeared faire and cleare with his propre light" (XI.7; 118). Though Shakespeare doubtless remembered the inclement seasons of 1594-1595[11], these passages may have been stimulating to his imagination also, and it would appear that Apuleius' Venus could well be the parent and original of Shakespeare's concept of a bounteous goddess of nature which underlies his vision of Titania as the Fairy Queen.

Titania is also a Psyche figure in several aspects of the action. In the myth when Psyche is first conveyed to the paradisal garden of Cupid, she is laid on a "bedde of most sweete and fragrant flowers." Though Apuleius does not name the flowers, he at once reiterates and emphasizes the image:

. . . florentis caespitis gremio leniter delapsam reclinat

(IV.35).

Psyche teneris & herbosis locis, in ipso toro roscidi graminis suave recubans, tanta mentis perturbatione sedata, dulce conquievit

(V.1).

. . . she was laide in a bedde of most sweete and fragrant flowers.

Thus fayre Psyches beinge sweetely couched emongst the softe and fragrant flowers, and havinge quallified the troubles and thoughtes of her restles minde, was now well reposed

(46).

After awaking from a refreshing sleep, she espies a pleasant wood of mighty trees, and in it a "Princely edifice" not built by human hands. Entering this heavenly palace, she is waited on by unseen servants and entertained by their song and music; and after going to bed, she becomes the bride of an unseen husband, the supposed Serpent Bridegroom of the oracle, as Venus would have it, the "most vile" creature alive, "tamque infimi ut per totum orbem non inveniat miserae suae comparem" (IV.31).

Titania's experiences are curiously akin. In the Palace woods of Theseus, Titania is lulled to sleep by fairy song on a bank of wild thyme (a resilient herbal couch) and oxlips, muskroses, and other "sweete and fragrant flowres" (as Apuleius has precondensed the exquisite excursus). While Titania sleeps, Oberon squeezes the juice of his flower on her eyelids and conjures her to fall in love with whatever she sees on awakening: "Wake when some vile thing is near" (II.ii.35). She wakens to love, not a serpent bridegroom, but another monster, Bottom the ass-man, a mock figure of the Golden Ass[12].

With this event the action and imagery relating Titania to Psyche take on a mocking tone and are applied by inversion to Bottom. As observed above, unseen servants attend on Psyche, ministering to her every desire, providing her all sorts of delicacies and wines, while invisible musicians sing and play on various instruments, giving her the impression that she is surrounded by a multitude (V.2-3; 46ᵛ-47). The palace is a storehouse of jewels and gold at her disposal. In the play Titania bids her elves and fairies wait on Bottom. They are to bring him jewels from the deep (Venus is attended, we remember, by servitors from the sea), and sing while he sleeps on pressed flowers. Does he wish to hear music? or would he like something to eat? The queries remind one of those addressed by the unseen voices to Psyche. Unlike Lucius, who retains his

human appetites in food, Bottom prefers good dry oats, hay, and pease to the dainties Titania would offer him, such as new nuts from the squirrel's hoard (IV.i.33-38). For the detail of the new nuts, as Sister M. Generosa has shown, Shakespeare probably remembers the episode immediately following the Psyche story (VI.28; 65ᵛ) in which Charites promises Lucius that if he aids her in escaping the robbers, she will splendidly dress his forehead and mane, deck him with gold to shine like the stars, and bring him daily kernels of nuts and other dainties in her silken apron.

Moreover, for the scenes of Titania's dotage on Bottom, as Sister M. Generosa has indicated, Shakespeare may also have remembered the story of the noblewoman of Corinth (X.21-22; 109-110), who anoints Lucius' body and nose with balm, looks at him with burning eyes while uttering passionate endearments, and "eftsones embraced [his] bodie round about." In her dalliance with Bottom Titania "coys" his cheeks, garlands his head with muskroses (Lucius is always seeking for a garland of roses to eat to effect his remetamorphosis into man), and kisses his "fair large ears". As he goes to sleep, Titania declares her doting love for him, while clasping him in her woodbine embraces. The resemblances in manner are patent, the essential difference between the two episodes being that Shakespeare's delicate scene from its first staging up to recent times has apparently conveyed to its audiences and readers no hint of forbidden lust (Jan Kott's view presents a Shakespeare all too modern).

It is noteworthy also that on awakening from his transformation Bottom realizes that he has had a wondrous experience, which he interprets as a "most rare vision", a dream that no man can expound: "The eye of man hath not heard, the ear of man hath not seen, man's hand is not able to taste, his tongue to conceive, nor his heart to report what my dream was" (IV.i.212-214). Bottom the ass-man has seen the Fairy Queen. Lucius is more articulate about his experience, and he too has a most rare vision. In his sleep the "queene of heaven" appears to him in all her glory to answer his prayers for restoration to his human shape, and when he wakes he marvels at the details of his vision (XI.7; 118). Later on, in describing his initiation into the mysteries of the goddess, he will not reveal the details lest his reader's ears and his own tongue incur the "paine of rashe curiositie" (XI.23; 123ᵛ).

The ending of the main action of the drama and the conclusion of the Psyche myth also have an extensive dreamlike correspondence. After bewildered wandering in a drooping fog (created by Puck at Oberon's command) as black as Acheron (a common metonymy for Hades), the lovers are overcome by "death-counterfeiting sleep"; then Puck crushes the herb of true love into Lysander's eye (III.ii.355-369; 370-463), and after the lovers are wakened by Theseus to meet their true loves, they return to Athens to enjoy a bridal blest by supernatural beings. Oberon meanwhile tells Puck that when he saw Titania in her dotage, he taunted her, and she responded with gentle patience to his mocking and yielded him the Indian boy. Then Oberon removes the hateful imperfection from her eyes, awakens her, and after music charming the lovers into yet deeper sleep he announces his intention of blessing the house of Theseus to "all fair posterity". In the ensuing scene, Theseus quickly overrules Egeus' earlier objection to the marriage of Hermia and Lysander and announces the nuptial feast and the imminent marriages, which in due course are blest by the fairies in their concluding song and dance.

All these events have notable parallels in the myth. After returning from Hades, Psyche opens the box given her by Proserpina for Venus, and, according to Adlington, an infernal sleep invades all her members: "and by and by she opened the boxe, where she coulde perceave no beautie nor any thinge els, save onely an infernall and deadly sleepe, whiche immediatly invaded all her members as sone as the boxe was uncovered, in such sort that she fel downe on the gronnde, & lay there as a sleepinge corps" (VI.62). The Latin is yet more pertinent: "nec quicquam ibi rerum nec formositas ulla, sed infernus somnus ac vere Stygius, qui statim coperculo revelatus invadit eam crassaque soporis nebula cunctis eius membris perfunditur et in ipso vestigio ipsaque semita collapsam possidet; et iacebat immobilis et nihil aliud quam dormiens cadaver" (VI.21).

In brief, Psyche was invaded by an infernal and Stygian sleep, a *dense fog of sleep* (*crassa soporis nebula*) which poured over her entire body so that she fell to the ground like a sleeping corpse (that is, in a "death-counterfeiting sleep"). Did Shakespeare remember this metaphor when he had Puck overcast the night with the drooping fog black as Acheron, fog that helps to produce a death-counterfeiting sleep for the lovers? In any event, when Cupid comes upon Psyche in her deathlike trance, he wipes the sleep from her face, wakens her, taunts her gently about her reckless curiosity, and then goes off to arrange all things for them with Jupiter, who overcomes the objections of Venus to the marriage by making Psyche immortal at a celestial banquet attended by the gods and goddesses, the Graces, and the Muses (VI.22-24; 62-63).

Finally, it seems possible that in evaluating the significance of his translation of Apuleius, Adlington may have influenced Shakespeare to some degree in his summing up of the fundamental meaning of *A Midsummer Night's Dream*. In his preface "To the Reader," an apologia for the apparent frivolity of the text of *The Golden Ass*, Adlington expresses fear lest men may scorn his work as an idle fable and himself for his attention to such trifling toys; but he finds his justification in the praiseworthy intent of the author. Through this thing of jest, he says, men may come to know their present estate and be transformed to their better selves. But listen to Adlington:

> . . . fearinge lest the translation of this present booke (which seemeth a meere iest and fable, and a woorke woorthy to be laughed at, by reason of the vanitie of the Author, mighte be contemned & despised of all

men, and so consequently, I to be had in derisiõ to occupy my selfe in such frivolous and trifling toyes: but on the other side, when I had throughly learned the intent of the Author, and the purpose why he invented so sportfull a iest: I was verely perswaded, that my small travell, should not onely be accepted of many, but the matter it selfe allowed, & praised of all. Wherefore I intend (God willinge) as nighe as I can, to utter and open the meaning thereof to the simple and ignorant, whereby they may not take the same, as a thing only to iest and laugh at (for the Fables of Esope & the feiginge of Poetes, weare never writen for that purpose) but by the pleasauntnes therof, be rather induced to the knowledge of their present estate, and thereby trãsforme them selves into the right and perfect shape of men. . . . Verely under the wrappe of this transformation, is taxed the life of mortall men, when as we suffer our mindes so to be drowned in the sensuall lusts of the fleshe . . . we leese wholy the use of reason and vertue (which proprely should be in man) & play the partes of bruite and savage beastes"

(Aii-Aiii).

It would appear that in this passage Adlington offers Shakespeare sentiments and a pattern for some of his reflections on the fundamental meaning of his drama. After their return from the woods, Theseus and Hippolyta reflect on the meaning of the fantastic adventures of the lovers. The rational Theseus is openly scornful of "these antique fables", "these fairy toys." Lovers and madmen, he says, imagine such fantasies, inexplicable by "cool reason". Hippolyta, however, perceiving a deeper meaning to the story, protests this attack on the powers of fantasy and imagination:

> But all the story of the night told over,
> And all their minds transfigured so together,
> More witnesseth than fancy's images
> And grows to something of great constancy;
> But howsoever, strange and admirable.

The experiences of the lovers were not, she says, their idle imaginings, mere fables and fairy toys; the transfiguring of their minds, their spiritual metamorphoses into their right and perfect shapes, if one may adapt Adlington's phrasing, is something that hints of cosmic mystery, truly strange and admirable. In just such a mood, Apuleius tells us, the people and the religious, moved by the miracle of his transformation, wondered at the visions that had taken place in the night, attesting the favor of the goddess: "then the people began to mervell, and the religious honored the Goddesse for so evident a miracle, they wondred at the visions which they sawe in the night, and the facilitie of my reformation, whereby they rendered testimony of so great a benefite which I received of the Goddesse" (XI.13; 120).

In his mythic translation of the various effects of Apuleius' story, Shakespeare seems to have accepted the moral intention of Adlington's preface as a guide, for he has refined the coarseness of the original, leaving little that could offend the most delicate sensibility. Lucius, prior to his final transformation, is lustful both as man and ass. No one can imagine a more unlustful creature than Bottom. And though Titania, an unlustful Venus, brings Bottom to her bower and coys his amiable cheeks, in her way she intends to reform his grosser nature: "And I will purge thy mortal grossness so / That thou shalt like an airy spirit go" (III.i.163-164).

Notes

1. See *A Midsummer Night's Dream by William Shakespeare,* ed. G. L. Kittredge (Boston, 1939), p. xi. My citations of the play are to this text.

2. Sister M. Generosa "Apuleius and *A Midsummer Night's Dream*: Analogue or Source, Which?" *SP,* XLII (1945), 198-204.

3. For the Latin passages in the present study I have used the Latin text prepared by Gaselee, *Apuleius The Golden Ass Being the Metamorphoses of Lucius Apuleius With an English Translation by W. Adlington,* Loeb Cl. Lib. (Cambridge, Mass., 1965). Citations of this text will follow its uses. The research of T. W. Baldwin (as Sister M. Generosa notes) makes it apparent that Shakespeare could have known the Latin text, since, assuming the availability of the work, Vives commends Apuleius to the student for logic and Erasmus recommends imitating him for matter (*William Shakspere's Small Latine & Lesse Greeke,* II (Urbana, 1944), 26, 185, 247). It is interesting to find that Adlington may have borrowed some ideas from Erasmus for the composition of his preface "To the Reader" (cf. Erasmus, *Opera,* I (1703), 358; Baldwin, II, 247).

4. The *STC* lists printings in 1566, 1571, 1582, 1596. My citations of Adlington are to the 1566 text, whose title-page reads: "The xi Bookes of / the Golden Asse, / Conteininge the Metamorphosie / of Lucius Apuleius, enterlaced / with sondrie pleasaunt and delecta- / ble Tales, with an excellent / Narration of the Mari- / age of Cupide and / Psiches, set out / in the iiii. / v. and vi. Bookes. / *Translated out of Latine into Englishe / by William Adlington. / Imprinted at London in Fleetstreate, / at the signe of the Oliphante, / by Henry* VVykes. / Anno. 1566." (*STC* 718, Huntington Lib. 12926, Univ. of Mich. Microfilm 10596.) Citations of this text will follow its uses in this study, preceded by references to the Latin text (see note 3).

5. The numerous monster images in Shakespeare's plays preceding and following *MND* seem unrelated to the Psyche story except for the one notable usage in *Rom.* of the theme of the bridal of death and its mysterious palace: "Shall I believe / That unsubstantial Death is amorous, / And that the lean abhorred monster keeps / Thee here in dark to be his paramour? / For fear of that I still will stay with thee / And never from this palace of dim night / Depart again" (V.iii.102-108). There appears also no discernible relationship between Shakespeare's other numerous uses of the serpent image and that of the Psyche story.

6. Koehler's emendation for the early textual reading, *profundi.* The early texts (those that Shakespeare might have known) at this point read "ecce iam profundi maris sudo resedit vertice", a clause which seems to mean essentially, as Gaselee notes, that Venus took her seat on the sea, a meaning that does not fit the context. Koehler's emendation offers the improved (and expected) sense that with the coming of Venus the waters became entirely calm.

7. In his *Letter* on the entertainment for Elizabeth at Kenilworth Castle in 1575, Laneham describes a pageant in which appeared a "swimming mermayd" (a boat), along with Triton who charged the waters to be still during the Queen's presence; then Arion on a dolphin ship sang a "delectable ditty . . . well apted to a melodious noiz" (John Nichols, *The Progresses and Public Processions of Queen Elizabeth,* London, 1823; repr. New York: Burt Franklin, I (1966), 457-458). Gascoigne (*The Princely Pleasures at the Courte of Kenelwoorth,* Nichols, I, 485-523) visualizes Proteus rather than Triton as the singer on the back of a dolphin (a boat so fashioned). Gascoigne also represents Triton in Neptune's name charging the winds and waters to be calm during the Queen's presence, and both Laneham and Gascoigne remark the exhibition of fireworks over the waters (pp. 435, 494).

8. Edith Rickert argues that Shakespeare was recalling instead the festival of Elvetham ("Political Propaganda and Satire in *A Midsummer Night's Dream*", *MP,* XXI (1923), 53-87, 133-154), which has a speaking Nymph of the sea, Neaera, on a ship (possibly a dolphin ship, though not so described in Nichols, III, 111); Nereus and two "Echoes" sing. Elaborate fireworks burn in the water (p. 118), and the Fairy Queen Aureola says that "amorous starres fall nightly in [her] lap" (p. 119).

9. On the conflict between Eros and Aphrodite, see Erich Neumann, *Amor and Psyche, The Psychic Development of the Feminine* (New York and Evanston, 1956).

10. Ovid uses the name for Diana once (*Met.* III. 173) and twice for Circe (*Met.* XIV. 382, 438). Kittredge (p. xiii) objects that Diana is not a satisfactory prototype for Shakespeare's Titania; but Apuleius makes it clear that *Diana* is only one of the names and aspects of Queen Isis (XI. 5; 117). That Shakespeare was aware of the manifold nature of Diana is evident from his association of his fairies with the "triple Hecate" (V.i.390-391; cited earlier in this study).

11. See Kittredge, p. viii; Furness, *A Midsummer Night's Dream,* Variorum ed., pp. 65-66.

12. Sister M. Generosa studies in detail the differences and similarities of Bottom and Lucius. She suggests that Titania's line, "Tie up my love's tongue, bring him silently" (III. i. 206), is perhaps a reminiscence

of the episode in which Lucius betrays his priestly masters by braying (VIII. 29; 86ᵛ). It is curious also that on his transformation into ass, Bottom fancies himself as a singer and sings a lay about various birds. Before his transformation, Lucius expects to be transformed into an owl.

Clifford Earl Ramsey (essay date 1977)

SOURCE: Ramsey, Clifford Earl. "*A Midsummer Night's Dream.*" In *Homer to Brecht: The European Epic and Dramatic Traditions,* edited by Michael Seidel and Edward Mendelson, pp. 214-37. New Haven, Conn.: Yale University Press, 1977.

[*In the following essay, Ramsey examines the scenic structure in* A Midsummer Night's Dream, *maintaining that it expresses diversity and opposition, and yet it also emphasizes harmony and integration. According to the critic, the scenic structure ultimately underscores the play's dual themes of the power of love and the power of imagination.*]

The history of interpretation, and misinterpretation, of Shakespeare's *A Midsummer Night's Dream* demonstrates more strikingly than that of most works a deep truth of literary history: changes in critical fashion, changes in the theory of literature and in approaches to particular literary works, virtually alter those works themselves. Criticism shapes our fundamental responses to the works of art it contemplates. Whatever *Iliad* we hear, it surely is not the poem Homer sang.

In our time we have come increasingly to accept the idea, notably articulated by T. S. Eliot and Northrop Frye, that the "primary context" of any individual work of literature is other literature, that all literature—not just that we call neoclassical—is inherently and inescapably traditional. We are also beginning to see that criticism itself is an intrinsic part of this "primary context," that the history of literature is deeply interfused with the history of interpretation. Thus the *Aeneid,* as well as growing out of the *Iliad,* also recoils upon it. Virgil is involved in an act of criticism as well as an act of creation. Criticism, hardly less than creation itself, is a consequence of and gives expression to our deepest needs—needs that are often unacknowledged. Euripides could not write plays like Sophocles any more than he could accept Homer's gods. The Middle Ages had to moralize Ovid. Shakespeare's plays will mean what we need them to mean.

The *Midsummer Night's Dream* we see and study today is, in an almost literal sense, not the play Coleridge saw and studied, not the play Johnson saw and studied, perhaps not even the play Shakespeare wrote. My point is not simply that modern criticism of *A Midsummer Night's Dream* differs from that of earlier periods. We expect that. The point I want to stress is that the differences are more striking in

the case of this play and therefore that a consideration of it may have much to tell us about the way we think critically today; certainly as much as the way we think critically today has to tell us about *A Midsummer Night's Dream.*

It might be imprudent to claim that today's audiences enjoy *A Midsummer Night's Dream* more than audiences of previous eras, but it does seem clear that today's scholars and critics—and teachers—pay it far more attention. We do know that a shrewd member of one audience three centuries ago could not enjoy it. On Michaelmas Day in 1662 Samuel Pepys wrote this comment in his diary:

> To the King's Theatre, where we saw "Midsummer Night's Dream," which I had never seen before, nor shall ever again, for it is the most insipid ridiculous play that ever I saw in my life. I saw, I confess, some good dancing and some handsome women, and which was all my pleasure.

To give Pepys and the play their due, we can assume that he is likely to have witnessed a very uninspired and truncated version. But a century and a half later we can catch an unquestionably great Shakespearean critic—Coleridge, discussing the dating and sequence of the plays—observing that *A Midsummer Night's Dream* "hardly appeared to belong to the complete maturity of his genius" because when writing that comedy Shakespeare was "ripening his powers" for such works as *Julius Caesar, Troilus and Cressida, Coriolanus,* and *Cymbeline.* As late as 1951, in a standard *Introduction to Shakespeare,* one could find the then still fairly common opinion that the play was mostly a glittering fabric of "moonlight, with a touch of moonshine." But by 1961, in an essay provocatively entitled "The Mature Comedies," Frank Kermode was "prepared to maintain that *A Midsummer Night's Dream* is Shakespeare's best comedy."

If we take *A Midsummer Night's Dream* more seriously than former eras did, it is partly because the idea of comedy, the genre itself, is now taken more seriously. (The same point might be made about romance and about pastoral, the other genres most prominent in *A Midsummer Night's Dream.*) We have begun to glimpse the profound suggestiveness lurking in Socrates' oracular assertion, made in the presence of the drowsy Aristophanes at the close of Plato's *Symposium,* that the genius of comedy and the genius of tragedy is the same. So in our time we find Northrop Frye perceiving a ritual pattern of death-and-resurrection lying behind both comedy and tragedy, and thence arguing that two things follow from this: "first, that tragedy is really implicit or uncompleted comedy; second, that comedy contains a potential tragedy within itself."

Such arguments are briefs for the parity of comedy and tragedy, not their identity. The genius of comedy and tragedy may be the same, they may be equally serious or equally profound, but their forms, their characteristic structures, will be different. The comic muse and the tragic muse dance to different rhythms. So Frye and modern critics like him stress the shape, the characteristic movement, of each genre: whereas the characteristic movement of tragedy is toward isolation, they theorize, that of comedy is toward integration. C. L. Barber describes "saturnalian" movement in Shakespearean comedy, a movement "through release to clarification." Frye, in "The Argument of Comedy," an account now so famous as to have become a shibboleth, speaks of Shakespeare's "drama of the green world" and defines the archetypal pattern of that drama as one of "withdrawal and return": the characteristic action of a Shakespearean comedy, Frye hypothesizes, "begins in a world represented as a normal world, moves into the green world, goes into a metamorphosis there in which the comic resolution is achieved, and returns to the normal world." Perhaps the common thread in such theories is a willingness to take seriously the wish-fulfillment pattern of all comedy. Comedy may only present the "beautiful lie," but for all our cynicism and secularism there is something in each of us that wants to believe in those happy endings. What the modern theorists of comedy are finally claiming is that the comic muse responds to the renewing cycles of time, and so refreshes time.

What of the structure of this particular comedy? I will suggest that the elements of external form in *A Midsummer Night's Dream* correspond to its internal elements, that the play's structure is precisely commensurate with its argument, that its shape *is* its vision. The play's "scenic" structure articulates its thematic design. (By "scene" I mean a formal unit that is both dramatic and spatial.) What we shall find, if we examine the scenic structure of this play, is that the organization of scenes—the juxtaposition and interplay of scenes, the movement between and through them—is everywhere expressive of diversity and variety and opposition, and yet at the same time paradoxically everywhere expressive also of harmony and concord and integration; that is, everywhere expressive of the play's twin themes, the power of love and the power of the imagination.

In focusing on the scenic structure of *A Midsummer Night's Dream,* I am following out the implications of a suggestion made by Madeleine Doran, who reminds us that the original quarto was not divided into acts and scenes. Taking the quarto as the authoritative text and taking a clear stage to represent a change of scene, Doran concludes that there are only seven scenes in the whole play (no other play by Shakespeare has so few scenes). According to Doran's scheme, the play begins and ends, respectively, with two scenes outside the wood (the same two, but in reverse order). Podlike, these first two and last two scenes enclose the core of the play, the three scenes in the wood. If we place the first and last scenes in the court of Theseus, and the second and sixth somewhere inside Athens where Peter Quince and his crew of patches can rehearse (possibly Quince's house), we could diagram the play's scenic structure like this: T;Q// W, W, W //Q;T. Such a scheme crystallizes the fundamental thrust of the play. Thus anatomized, there can be little doubt that its

central action is the movement into and out of the wood. Such a scheme also crystallizes our awareness that there are three major domains within the play: the play occurs in three places only, occupies only three landscapes. Each of these three landscapes constitutes what might be called a separate "world." Such talk of "worlds" seems more persuasive than usual because it is solidly rooted in the spatial and dramatic facts of the play's setting and organization. In *A Midsummer Night's Dream,* there is the world of the court, presided over by Theseus; there is the world of the hardhanded amateur actors, presided over by Peter Quince (this second world, like the first, is inside Athens); and there is the world of the magical wood, presided over by Oberon (this world is outside Athens and obeys none of its rules). These three places or landscapes, these three separate environments or milieus, constitute three different "worlds" in the sense that each projects different values and styles, each offers a different slice or dimension of experience. These three worlds of the play define three separate aspects of reality; they provide three *perspectives on reality.* Each world of the play gives "a local habitation and a name" to, a different way of looking at, apprehending, or organizing human experience. Furthermore, the way the play holds these worlds up against each other, makes them balance and mirror and qualify each other, how the play moves between and through these worlds, is at the heart of its comic meaning.

For a brief and partial illustration, observe the movement of the young lovers through these "worlds": they flee the court or normal world; they enter the wood or "green" world, for them a scene first of confusion, then of resolution; and they finally return to the court where, having been changed, they can be assimilated. Admittedly, this is a rather facile account of the young lovers' experience in the play; experience never reduces itself to a diagram. I ought to indicate that the lovers, after their assimilation into the court world, are entertained by a parody of their incongruous nighttime experience in the wood (one way to take the mechanicals' presentation of the Pyramus and Thisby story). Too, I ought to acknowledge the possibility that the court has changed more than the lovers (all the members of the court did, after all, finally enter the wood), and the possibility that the court—having relaxed its laws and solemnized three weddings—is now free and flexible enough to make room for the young lovers. But even such a facile account can suggest how, by the end of *A Midsummer Night's Dream,* the young lovers, having shuttled between worlds, have undergone a change of perspective; and, in contemplating them, so have we. Matters are not so crystal clear as our diagram because the play throughout manifests an extraordinary diversity, but the notion of perspective may help guide us through the diversity. Indeed, I would be willing to maintain that almost everything in this play can be understood as either the comically incongruous clash, or the richly inclusive fusion, of perspectives.

Together, the first three scenes of *A Midsummer Night's Dream* initiate its first major movement—the entrance into the wood. Individually, each scene defines one of the play's major worlds, one of its main perspectives on reality. The opening lines of the first scene quickly reveal an imposing world, the court of Athens. The first nineteen lines of the play introduce many of its most important concerns; these lines suggest what Theseus and his queen are like, and they orient us in the kind of world Theseus inhabits and controls, the kind of perspective he embodies. Theseus and Hippolyta open the play by speaking of their imminent nuptials:

THESEUS.

> Now, fair Hippolyta, our nuptial hour
> Draws on apace. Four happy days bring in
> Another moon; but O, methinks, how slow
> This old moon wanes! She lingers my desires,
> Like to a stepdame, or a dowager,
> Long withering out a young man's revenue.

HIPPOLYTA.

> Four days will quickly steep themselves in
>   night,
> Four nights will quickly dream away the time;
> And then the moon, like to a silver bow
> New-bent in heaven, shall behold the night
> Of our solemnities.

Then Theseus instructs his master of revels, Philostrate, to stir the Athenian youth to merriment, to

> Awake the pert and nimble spirit of mirth,
> Turn melancholy forth to funerals;
> The pale companion is not for our pomp.

After Philostrate exits, Theseus again addresses his Amazon bride-to-be:

> Hippolyta, I wooed thee with my sword,
> And won thy love doing thee injuries;
> But I will wed thee in another key,
> With pomp, with triumph, and with reveling.

Here in these opening lines we already have the motifs of the moon, desire and dreams, mirth and solemnity. We have a sense of time as both a fructifying and a withering force, as something linked with the rhythms of nature and with the rhythms of human feeling and ceremony. Striking a dominant tone for the whole work, the first line's "nuptial hour" provides an overarching frame, an enveloping action, for the entire play. Partly a Renaissance prince, partly the great hero of antique fables, very much the Theseus of Plutarch and Chaucer, the lord of Athens seems established in these opening lines as a man of action and of reason, of authority and maturity and eloquence, as a figure of measured and civilized dignity. He seems very much in control of his world. Theseus knows what he feels and says what he means. Perhaps what most makes Theseus and Hippolyta imposing here is the cadence of their speech, their poised and urbane idiom. They seem to represent an achieved mastery of experience realized in great magnificence of style.

Here, and in the last scenes of the play too, Theseus is a figure of self-proclaimed potency. Pulsating just under the elegant surface of these first lines are Theseus's assertive energies: he wooed his Amazon queen with his sword, and he can't wait to get her into bed. Control may be less easy than it first appears. Such energies could have a darker, more threatening aspect. They could issue in injuries. In each of the play's first three scenes, we can observe a tendency for irrepressible desires to break out in quarreling or confusion. As modern critics unfailingly point out, these first scenes are haunted by the threat of contention.

Thus, immediately after the opening nineteen lines, Egeus comes in "full of vexation" (1.1.23) and appeals—against his daughter—to "the sharp Athenian law" (1.1.162), which "by no means" may be extenuated, according to Theseus (1.1.117 ff.). What is the "complaint" of Egeus?—simply that Hermia loves someone other than her father's choice. Theseus, less flexible than we might have hoped, leaves the stage ruling that Hermia must accept her father's choice or suffer the penalty of death or "single life." Within a hundred lines, the court—at first a world ruled by thoughts of an imminent "nuptial hour"—has been revealed as a world inimical to young love, a world with little tolerance for "feigning" love or "feigning" verses (1.1.31). The rest of the play will be required to integrate the young lovers into the court. The rest of this first scene alternates, without resolution, between images of love as special pain ("The course of true love never did run smooth," line 134) and images of love as special vision ("Things base and vile, holding no quantity, / Love can transpose to form and dignity. / Love looks not with the eyes, but with the mind," lines 232-34). Let me pause over one image where, as it were, the "pain" and the "vision" come together. I speak of Lysander's description of his plan to flee Athens with Hermia. The urgings of unfulfilled desire drive them out of Athens, one presumes, but an image of beauty and repose—of glittering moonmade reflections—is used to describe the moment of their fleeing; the young lovers intend to flee the city when Phoebe beholds "her silver visage in the wat'ry glass, / Decking with liquid pearl the bladed grass" (1.1.209-11). In the image, if not yet in the action, frustration resolves itself into a dew.

From Theseus's court—a stately, aristocratic world of elegance and authority (though a world not yet elastic enough to accommodate the young lovers)—we pass to another, and startlingly different, version of the "normal" or "first" world. Athens is also the domain of Peter Quince and his handicraftsmen. The second scene of *A Midsummer Night's Dream* takes us into a more "barren sort" (3.2.13) of world. Quince and his "crew of patches" are "hempen homespuns," "rude mechanicals" (3.1.74 and 3.2.9). Quince the Carpenter (and playwright), Snug the Joiner, Bottom the Weaver, Flute the Bellows-Mender, Snout the Tinker, and Robin Starveling the Tailor are "hard-handed men" that "never labored in their minds" until their interlude for Theseus's nuptial (5.1.72-75). In their world one must "hold" or "cut bowstrings" (1.2.111). Their language (unlike that of Theseus and Hippolyta or that of Oberon and Titania) consistently betrays disjunctions between intention and expression, fact and idiom. Today's critics see the mechanicals as well-intentioned literalists and stress the parodic value of their failure to comprehend the nature of dramatic illusion. The mechanicals repair plays much as they might repair houses. Quince's hope that "here is a play fitted" (1.2.66)—"Here is the scroll of every man's name which is thought fit, through all Athens, to play in our interlude before the Duke and the Duchess, on his wedding day at night" (1.2.4-7)—receives this judgment from Philostrate in the last scene: "in all the play / There is not one word apt, one player fitted." Philostrate does admit, however, that he laughed until he cried (5.1.61-70).

Prosaic as the perspective of the mechanicals is, they project a world of sprawling energies. There is something vital about their good will and their rude wit. Like the young lovers, the mechanicals are headed for the wood too, where they expect to "rehearse most obscenely and courageously" (1.2.108). Yet at this point there is a sense in which the mechanicals, compared with the rather stiff, conventional, and undifferentiated lovers of the first scene, convince us that a "paramour" is, indeed, "a thing of naught" (4.2.14). Of course Bottom has his irrepressible desires too—he wants to play every role in Quince's interlude. No one ever had a stronger histrionic appetite than Nick Bottom. In fact, Bottom's irrepressible desires might have led to contentions like those of the first and third scenes (his desires do lead to a modest degree of confusion, one can safely say), if Quince were not able to "manage" his realm better than Theseus does his. Certainly Bottom well deserves the title "my mimic" that Puck gives him (3.2.19).

In a curious sense, Flute's hilarious pronouncement later that Bottom "hath simply the best wit of any handicraft man in Athens" (4.2.9-10) does not seem entirely unjustified. In his inadvertent way, Bottom often stumbles into some of the play's most trenchant utterances. In the third act, for example, Bottom tells Titania that she can "have little reason" for loving him and then utters lines that some critics find definitive of the play's theme:

> And yet, to say the truth, reason and love keep little company together nowadays; the more the pity, that some honest neighbors will not make them friends. Nay, I can gleek upon occasion.
>
> [3.1.129-33]

In a fine recent essay, J. Dennis Huston has demonstrated that one of Bottom's earliest "gleeks" is one of his most trenchant. When Peter Quince tells Bottom that he is set down for Pyramus, Bottom asks, "What is Pyramus? A lover, or a tyrant?" (1.2.22). Apparently Bottom believes that these two parts, lover and tyrant, subsume all the roles a man could play; curiously enough, as Huston demonstrates, the play's opening scenes suggest that Bottom is virtually correct. Egeus surely acts like a tyrant. The behavior of Oberon and Titania in the next scene to some

degree convicts them of the charge of tyranny. If we extend the idea of tyranny to include the caprice of passion's oppressive hold on us when infatuated, then the young lovers tell us something of tyranny too. Perhaps Bottom's query most revealingly recoils upon Theseus himself. Having entered the stage in the first scene as a lover, Theseus leaves it as a tyrant. But Egeus may not be on the stage at the end of *A Midsummer Night's Dream,* and as one of its final delights the play will appear to banish tyranny.

From the homely and literalistic yet strangely life-filled world of the mechanicals, we pass to yet another extraordinarily different scene, the green world of the wood and the exotic perspective of the fairies. Possibly expecting a world of fertility, we find a world of misrule. Oberon and Titania are contentious indeed. Their irrepressible desires for the "sweet" changeling boy have produced the most violent and pervasive disorder of the play, a "distemperature" throughout the natural world. Titania accuses Oberon of love for Hippolyta. Oberon in turn accuses his queen of love for Theseus. Titania's retort to Oberon's charges describes a world upside down, a scene of "brawls," of the "forgeries of jealousy," of "contagious fogs," of flooding rivers, rotting grain, and diseased flocks:

> The human mortals want their winter here;
> No night is now with hymn or carol blest.
> Therefore the moon, the governess of floods,
> Pale in her anger, washes all the air,
> That rheumatic diseases do abound.
> And thorough this distemperature we see
> The seasons alter. . . .
>   . . . . .
> . . . The spring, the summer,
> The childing autumn, angry winter, change
> Their wonted liveries; and the mazèd world,
> By their increase, now knows not which is which.
> And this same progeny of evils comes
> From our debate, from our dissension;
> We are their parents and original.
>
> [2.1.101-17]

The cause of this "progeny of evils," the "little changeling boy," seems out of all proportion to the consequences.

The speech in which Titania explains her fervent determination to keep the changeling boy (2.1.121-37) is one of the most elusive and suggestive in *A Midsummer Night's Dream.* Titania tells Oberon to set his heart at rest; all fairyland cannot buy the child from her because she felt a deep attachment for his mother. Titania's remembrance of the delicately playful, affectionate relationship she had with the boy's mother seems at first to call up a happier and more perfect world:

> His mother was a vot'ress of my order,
> And, in the spicèd Indian air, by night,
> Full often hath she gossiped by my side,
> And sat with me on Neptune's yellow sands,
> Marking th' embarkèd traders on the flood;
> When we have laughed to see the sails conceive
> And grow big-bellied with the wanton wind;

> Which she, with pretty and swimming gait
> Following—her womb then rich with my young
> 　squire—
> Would imitate, and sail upon the land,
> To fetch me trifles, and return again,
> As from a voyage, rich with merchandise.

What Titania provides in these lines is a paradigm of visionary perception, a model of how the optics seeing generate the objects seen, a glimpse of poetic consciousness actively at work. Too, like Bottom, Titania and her votaress have rich histrionic sensibilities. Like Bottom, the votaress is a "mimic," and with her at least imitation becomes transformation. But unlike Bottom, Titania and her votaress cannot be accused of literalness; they laugh all the while. Their visionary consciousness is suffused with self-consciousness.

Perhaps what is most important in Titania's speech is how she subtly, and yet very explicitly, interweaves love and the imagination. She and her big-bellied votaress playfully imagine the ships' sails to be big-bellied: "we have laughed to see the sails *conceive* / And *grow* big-bellied with the *wanton* wind." The pun here on "conceive" is especially suggestive, and pertinent to the whole play. The lover and the poet both "conceive" a world, bring a world into being; each, being a visionary, returns from the voyage of experience "rich with merchandise." But at this very moment Titania pulls us up short with what may be the most sobering and poignant lines in the play. Almost with casualness she reveals that this haunted grove is no paradise, reminds us that we inhabit a mutable, indeed a mortal, world. Titania tells the rest of her votaress's story:

> But she, being mortal, of that boy did die;
> And for her sake do I rear up her boy,
> And for her sake I will not part with him.

For the Renaissance, death is a corollary of the principle of plenitude. A world of growth is a world of change. A fecund world must be a mutable world. Does *A Midsummer Night's Dream* also hint that the reverse might be true? Is a world without change less fecund? Do Titania and Oberon possibly regret their immutability? Are they, like the Wife of Bath, possibly childless? Does their passionate desire for the *changeling* boy suggest that the creatures of eternity are in love with time?

In any event, Titania's loving remembrance of her votaress enforces an awareness of the human need to mythologize experience. Oberon continues in the same vein. He provides his own mythological remembrance of the powers of love and the imagination. Immediately after Titania leaves, Oberon asks Puck if he remembers the time

> 　　I sat upon a promontory,
> And heard a mermaid, on a dolphin's back,
> Uttering such dulcet and harmonious breath,
> That the rude sea grew civil at her song,
> And certain stars shot madly from their spheres,
> To hear the sea maid's music.

> [2.2.240-45]

Oberon has given us a compelling image of art making rude nature harmonious. At the same time the image suggests that the source of the harmony—the sea maid's music—was also a source of disruption. What Oberon then saw from his promontory (we are told that Puck could not see it) was Cupid's empurpling of the pansy—"maidens call it love-in-idleness"—with "love's wound" (2.1.155-74). What Oberon saw, in effect, was a myth about the power of love (a myth designed to recall the change of the mulberry from white to crimson in Ovid's account, in the fourth book of the *Metamorphoses,* of the tragic love of Pyramus and Thisby). And just as certain stars shot "madly from their spheres" to hear the mermaid's song, the juice of love-in-idleness, laid upon sleeping eyelids, will make "man or woman madly dote / Upon the next live creature that it sees." Oberon orders Puck to fetch him this herb, and at this point in the play the invasions of the wood by the Athenians begin.

The rest of the play's movement through this haunted grove will reveal it as simultaneously a scene of confusion and fertility, a place where folly is manifested and constancy is discovered, a place of midsummer madness and magical metamorphoses, of hateful fantasies and most rare visions; the play's movement, all this is to say, will reveal this "green plot" as the natural home of love and the imagination. In these first three scenes, *A Midsummer Night's Dream* has introduced three distinct realms, each radically different from the others, each thoroughly alive. What is most remarkable of all, by playing these three worlds off against each other, Shakespeare has somehow managed to affirm simultaneously their partialness and their integrity. Somehow the play's embrace of incompleteness assures its coherence. Building better than Peter Quince, Shakespeare "fits" all three worlds together on his stage.

These first three scenes get us into the wood. I would like to focus now on the precise moment when we begin to come back out; and then I would like to discuss the way we come out. The pivotal moment in *A Midsummer Night's Dream,* the moment where the movement back out of the wood begins, is that wonderful moment—almost a visual oxymoron—where Titania and Bottom embrace and fall asleep in each other's arms. Thoroughly enamored, Titania makes rapturous love to her ass:

> Sleep thou, and I will wind thee in my arms.
> Fairies, be gone, and be all ways away.
> So doth the woodbine the sweet honeysuckle
> Gently entwist; the female ivy so
> Enrings the barky fingers of the elm.
> Oh, how I love thee! How I dote on thee!

> [4.1.43-48]

Shakespeare has indeed made his world "fit" together. This "sweet sight," as Oberon calls it (4.1.49), is a moment of extreme incongruity, yet also a moment of great inclusiveness. The most diverse, indeed antithetical, perspectives have been fused in this single moment. The

Bernard Behrens as Snug, Chris Wiggins as Snout, Mervyn Blake as Quince, Robin Gammell as Flute, William Needles as Starveling, and Tony Van Bridge as Bottom in Act IV, scene i of the 1960 Stratford Festival production of A Midsummer Night's Dream.

wood has done its utmost magic. I find it significant that Titania's language at the moment of her embrace of Bottom echoes precisely that of the earlier moment at the close of the third scene when Oberon had described her bower. Puck has returned with the love-in-idleness, and Oberon declares that he knows where to find Titania:

> I know a bank where the wild thyme blows,
> Where oxlips and the nodding violet grows,
> Quite overcanopied with luscious woodbine,
> With sweet muskroses, and with eglantine.
> There sleeps Titania sometime of the night,
> Lulled in these flowers with dances and delight;
> And there the snake throws her enameled skin,
> Weed wide enough to wrap a fairy in.

> [2.1.249-56]

Taken together, these two passages go far toward defining the reconciling and transfiguring power that the wood, at its best, is said to possess. After the pivotal embrace of Titania and Bottom, every Jack can begin to have his Jill (as Puck puts it, 3.2.448 ff.), and "all things shall be peace" (as Oberon puts it, 3.2.370-77). Then, but only then, the play's resolutions begin to occur. After the pivotal embrace, but only after this, a sense of inclusiveness begins to dominate the play. After this, but only after this, Oberon can "begin to pity" Titania's "dotage" (4.1.49 ff.). Now the other members of the court can enter the wood. Now all the sleeping lovers can begin to awaken. Now the play begins to drive toward that great final scene in Theseus's hall where love seems to be the common will.

Fundamentally, we get out of the wood by watching a series of dreaming lovers awaken from their visions. First, right after Titania winds Bottom in her arms, Oberon (he now has the changeling boy) releases the fairy queen from her vision. He and Titania dance, and then the "king of shadows" (3.2.347) declares that he and his queen, now "new in amity," will "tomorrow midnight" solemnly and triumphantly dance in Duke Theseus's house and "bless it to all fair prosperity": "There shall the pairs of faithful lovers be / Wedded, with Theseus, all in jollity" (4.1.90-95). At this exact moment the altogether palpable rulers of Athens enter the wood. Theseus and Hippolyta have been engaged in May Day rites, and they have decided to spend the rest of the morning hunting. Anxious to impress Hippolyta, Theseus orders the attendants to uncouple his hounds in the western valley so that his love can hear their "music":

> We will, fair Queen, up to the mountain's top,
> And mark the musical confusion
> Of hounds and echo in conjunction.

This prompts Hippolyta to remember some rather spectacular hounds and hunts in her own past:

> I was with Hercules and Cadmus once,
> When in a wood of Crete they bayed the bear
> With hounds of Sparta. Never did I hear
> Such gallant chiding; for, besides the groves,
> The skies, the fountains, every region near
> Seemed all one mutual cry. I never heard
> So musical a discord, such sweet thunder.

Not to be outdone, Theseus makes strong claims for the extraordinary muscularity, and musicality, of his hounds:

> My hounds are bred out of the Spartan kind,
> So flewed, so sanded; and their heads are hung
> With ears that sweep away the morning dew;
> Crook-kneed, and dew-lapped like Thessalian bulls;
> Slow in pursuit, but matched in mouth like bells,
> Each under each. A cry more tuneable
> Was never holloed to, nor cheered with horn,
> In Crete, in Sparta, nor in Thessaly.
> Judge when you hear. . . .
>
> [4.1.112-30]

Theseus must want to convince Hippolyta that he is as physically impressive, as potent, as his hounds. I suspect this passage puzzled many earlier critics, but modern critics exult over these lines as a remarkable illustration of the play's habitual concern to make concordant music out of potential clamor. This talk of the hounds' "sweet thunder" also serves an important structural function. Here in the third scene from the end of the play we have the enactment of a perceptual and poetic activity very similar to that which occurred in the third scene from the beginning of the play; much as the fairy king and queen had done earlier (in 2.1.121-74), the human king and queen are mythologizing experience. It is entirely characteristic of *A Midsummer Night's Dream* that in one of the passages where the characters most overtly revel in dynamism, the play itself—as an artifact—calls covert attention to its own symmetries.

Theseus and Hippolyta came to the wood to hunt; expecting one kind of "sport," they find another and better game: they find the four young Athenians. Seeing that the young lovers have now more amicably paired up ("Saint Valentine is past. / Begin these woodbirds but to couple now?"), Theseus wonders, "How comes this gentle concord in the world?" (4.1.142 ff.). None of the four young lovers is able to answer him with confidence. All their replies are full of wonder and amazement. For each of them the

visionary experience of the moonlit night in the haunted grove now seems blurred and indistinguishable.

The reply of the one lover most changed during the midsummer night deserves attention. Demetrius confesses that he followed Hermia and Lysander into the wood "in fury," but he now affirms his love for Helena. Anticipating the exchange between Theseus and Hippolyta at the beginning of the last scene, and echoing Hermia's defiance of her father in the first scene ("I know not by what power I am made bold," 1.1.59), Demetrius assures Theseus that, no matter how indefinable, something real has happened to him:

> . . . I wot not by what power—
> But by some power it is—my love to Hermia,
> Melted as the snow, seems to me now
> As the remembrance of an idle gaud,
> Which in my childhood I did dote upon. . . .

Possibly magical, certainly indefinable, but for Demetrius his change of heart seems as natural as growing up. Now that Demetrius has been in the wood, all his faith, all the virtue of his heart, the entire object and pleasure of his eye is "only Helena"; to her

> Was I betrothed ere I saw Hermia:
> But, like a sickness, did I loathe this food;
> But, as in health, come to my natural taste,
> Now I do wish it, love it, long for it,
> And will for evermore be true to it.
>
> [4.1.163-79]

Does Theseus recognize the power Demetrius speaks of? We can never be certain, but it is at this precise moment that he decides to overbear the will of Egeus; he sets aside the "purposed hunting" and rules that "these couples shall eternally be knit" in the same ceremony with him and Hippolyta (4.1.180-88).

The last "lover" to awaken seems the least touched by his vision. Just when we might have allowed ourselves to believe that the stage had emptied, Bottom—irrepressibly histrionic as always—starts up and cries, "When my cue comes, call me, and I will answer" (4.1.2.3 ff.). At first Bottom does not seem to recall his amorous experience with Titania. Not hearing his next cue, he searches frantically all over the stage for his lost companions. But Bottom has been "translated" (3.1.120), and the "change" (3.1.115) wrought in the haunted grove is too intense for even Bottom to ignore. Glimmerings of remembrance begin to steal over him:

> I have had a most rare vision. I have had a dream, past the wit of man to say what dream it was. Man is but an ass, if he go about to expound this dream. Methought I was—there is no man can tell what. Methought I was—and methought I had—but man is but a patched fool if he will offer to say what methought I had. The eye of man hath not heard, the ear of man hath not seen, man's hand is not able to taste, his tongue to conceive, nor his heart to report what my dream was. . . .

Predictably, Bottom misquotes, but one of his sources here is Saint Paul (1 Corinthians 2:9). Realizing that, we can realize that we have just seen still another of the play's "translations"; we have watched the comically irrepressible slide into the profoundly inexpressible.

Bottom's dream may be too unfathomable to expound, but it seems too rare to waste; so having himself made his dream into "material for a performance," as Alexander Leggatt puts it, Bottom will give it to Peter Quince as material for a work of art:

> I will get Peter Quince to write a ballet of this dream. It shall be called "Bottom's Dream," because it hath no bottom; and I will sing it in the latter end of a play, before the Duke. Peradventure, to make it the more gracious, I shall sing it at her death.

Bottom rebounds quickly. He is "a patched fool," but his vitality is, indeed, bottomless.

After Bottom's momentary uncertainties, we return to the daylight world of Athens. After the brief scene (the sixth in the Doran scheme) of the reunion of Bottom with Quince and the other handicraftsmen, we turn to the poised urbanities of Theseus's famous pronouncement on love and the imagination (5.1.2-22). Bottom and Theseus—so unutterably different, yet so curiously alike. Each has the desire, and the capacity, to play many parts. Each is extraordinarily alive, and yet each achieves a kind of repose—each is, in today's vernacular, "unflappable." For all that he is "but a patched fool," Bottom is in some respects a more beguiling interpreter of visionary experience than the rational and detached and self-possessed Duke. Of course Bottom speaks from firsthand experience, whereas the Duke has only been a spectator; but then the Duke may not need magic spells to realize his desires.

Still, for us the Duke is almost too cool a customer. For all Theseus's eloquence, almost no critic today sees his speech as the play's last word on love and the imagination. His pronouncement, from one perspective, is cool reason's cogent demonstration that, as Rosalind disarmingly puts it in *As You Like It* (3.2.376), "Love is merely a madness." Yet, from another perspective, Theseus's pronouncement recoils upon him (he is himself an "antic fable"), and today's critics relish the way Shakespeare has insidiously used this speech to defend his own imaginative achievement. Perhaps imagination and love are forms of lunacy, but as Orlando had just said to Rosalind before she called love a mere madness, "Neither rhyme nor reason can express how much" he loves. Surely *A Midsummer Night's Dream* has apprehended "more than cool reason ever comprehends." Surely Shakespeare wants us to see the value of Theseus's common sense, but just as surely he wants us to see that, behind common sense and beyond cool reason, his imagination has bodied forth the "forms of things unknown," his "pen" has given palpable shape to such "strange" things and given "airy nothing" a "local habitation and a name."

Theseus does not even get the last word here; Hippolyta does:

> But all the story of the night told over,
> And all their minds transfigured so together,
> More witnesseth than fancy's images,
> And grows to something of great constancy;
> But howsoever, strange and admirable.
>
> [5.1.23-27]

It is Hippolyta's speech, not that of Theseus, that today's critics have grown to love. At the very moment of her final words, as if to prove the queen's point, the newly married young lovers, "full of joy and mirth," stroll onto the stage, and the whole last scene is a compelling emblem, visual as well as verbal, of consummation and communion.

A bit later in the scene Theseus *will* get a last word. Just as Hippolyta has amended his view of love and the imagination, he amends hers of plays and players. Wearying of Quince's "tedious brief" interlude, Hippolyta growls, "This is the silliest stuff that ever I heard" (5.1.211). Theseus's response to her remark, and their subsequent exchange, is often perceived today as one of Shakespeare's most incisive comments on the necessary contribution of the audience to the power of any dramatic illusion:

THESEUS.

> The best in this kind are but shadows; and the worst are no worse, if imagination amend them.

HIPPOLYTA.

> It must be your imagination then, and not theirs.

THESEUS.

> If we imagine no worse of them than they of themselves, they may pass for excellent men.

Now more amenable to the imagination than he appeared to be 180 lines earlier, Theseus seems to be acknowledging that we half create what we perceive. The idea of "amendment" will continue to reverberate throughout this final scene (most emphatically at the close in Puck's epilogue), and it might be said that *A Midsummer Night's Dream* is ultimately about the power of love and the imagination to amend the human condition. We might draw a moral for critics, as well as one for audiences, and speculate that criticism, too, must be a history of continuing amendment.

Have we, I wonder, finally accounted for this play's deep hold on the contemporary imagination? I have been trying to suggest that it is the dynamism and perspectivism of the play that fascinate modern critics. I would like further to suggest that the play's affirmations—self-conscious and guarded and mellow as they may be (Shakespeare never wears his heart on his sleeve)—engage us deeply too. The play may speak of things more "strange than true," as Theseus declares (5.1.2); yet as well as being "strange," such things, as Hippolyta urges, are also "admirable." For the play's many ripe sports have abridged at least one evening, have forestalled and perhaps softened the "iron tongue of midnight" (5.1.39 and 365). Even Theseus, about to get Hippolyta into bed at last, slips and can be heard to exclaim "'tis almost fairy time." Shakespeare does not of course expect us to believe literally that the fairies can keep "the blots of Nature's hand" from the "issue" of the newlyweds (5.1.403 ff.), but he may well expect us to agree that his "palpable-gross play hath well beguiled / The heavy gait of night" (5.1.368-69). Wouldn't Shakespeare ask of us, and have us ask in turn, "How shall we beguile / The lazy time, if not with some delight" (5.1.40-41)? We now regard *A Midsummer Night's Dream* as an authentic masterpiece because in it, better than in most works we know, we are persuaded that (to borrow words from Wallace Stevens) "Life's nonsense pierces us with strange relation."

Bibliographical Note

William Shakespeare was born in Stratford-upon-Avon in 1564; he died in Stratford in 1616. *A Midsummer Night's Dream* was probably performed in 1594-95. It was first published in 1600.

I have used the Signet edition, edited by Wolfgang Clemen (New York: New American Library, 1963), but also recommend the Pelican edition for Madeleine Doran's excellent introduction (Baltimore: Penguin, 1959). I am in debt throughout this essay to the felicitous and comprehensive study by David Young, *Something of Great Constancy: The Art of "A Midsummer Night's Dream"* (New Haven: Yale University Press, 1966). His book continues to be the point of departure for all serious study of this play. Most valuable for me among other studies have been essays by J. Dennis Huston, "Bottom Waking: Shakespeare's 'Most Rare Vision,'" in *Studies in English Literature* 13 (1973): 208-22; Frank Kermode, "The Mature Comedies," in *Early Shakespeare,* Stratford-upon-Avon Studies 3, ed. John Russell Brown and Bernard Harris (London: Edward Arnold, 1961); and Paul A. Olson, "*A Midsummer Night's Dream* and the Meaning of Court Marriage," *ELH* 24 (1957):95-119. I owe the point that Demetrius seems to grow up in act 4 to Alexander Leggatt's useful chapter in *Shakespeare's Comedy of Love* (London: Methuen, 1974). On comic structure I refer to C. L. Barber, *Shakespeare's Festive Comedy* (Princeton: Princeton University Press, 1959); to Northrop Frye, *Anatomy of Criticism* (Princeton: Princeton University Press, 1957); and to Frye, "The Argument of Comedy," *English Institute Essays, 1948* (New York: Columbia University Press, 1949).

For general background material on Shakespeare see E. K. Chambers, *William Shakespeare: A Study of Facts and Problems* (London: Oxford University Press, 1930); S. Schoenbaum, *Shakespeare's Lives* (New York: Oxford University Press, 1970); S. Schoenbaum, *William Shakespeare: A Documentary Life* (New York: Oxford University Press, 1975). For Shakespeare's sources see Geoffrey Bullough, *Narrative and Dramatic Sources of Shakespeare,*

6 vols. (New York: Columbia University Press, 1957-). For Elizabethan stage history see E. K. Chambers, *The Elizabethan Stage,* 4 vols. (New York: Oxford University Press, 1923; rpt., 1945); and Enid Welsford, *The Court Masque* (New York: Macmillan, 1927). For additional material on Shakespeare see the bibliographical note to Mark Rose's essay on *Hamlet* in this volume.

Richard H. Cox (essay date 1982)

SOURCE: Cox, Richard H. "Shakespeare: Poetic Understanding and Comic Action (A Weaver's Dream)." In *The Artist and Political Vision,* edited by Benjamin R. Barber and Michael J. Gargas McGrath, pp. 165-92. New Brunswick, N.J.: Transaction Books, 1982.

[*In the following essay, Cox examines the discordant nature of* A Midsummer Night's Dream, *asserting that in Shakespeare's comic treatment of Theseus, and in the serious undertones of his portrayal of the artisans and especially Bottom, the playwright used comedy to teach his audience serious lessons about civic life.*]

> . . . *what hinders one to be merry and tell the truth? as good-natured teachers at first give cakes to their boys, that they may be willing to learn at first the rudiments.*
>
> *Horace*[1]

> . . . *imitation is a kind of play, and not serious . . .*
>
> *Socrates*[2]

I

Political life generally is understood to be a serious matter. And in particular, founders of cities and regimes generally are understood to be serious men undertaking a supremely serious task: Lycurgus, Theseus, and Romulus, in the ancient world, and Washington, Lenin, and Hitler, in the modern world, are so regarded. How, then, are we to understand Shakespeare's playfulness in treating Theseus, legendary founder of Athens, one of the most extraordinary polities that ever existed, in a "comedy"?

This question is the starting point for my musings on *A Midsummer Night's Dream.* The musings are rooted in wonder and perplexity concerning the purpose of this dazzling display of Shakespeare's poetic art and buttressed by certain views I hold concerning how one should go about the study of a play by Shakespeare. Because those views underlie and inform the substance of the musings, it is necessary to say a few words about them at the outset.

It is easy to call Shakespeare a poet, and everyone does. It is a good deal more difficult, as the heap of critical works attests, to specify what Shakespeare himself conceived the poetic art to be: its nature; its purpose; its relationship to other human activities, including the making arts (e.g., carpentry), the doing arts (e.g., ruling), and not least, philosophy, in its original sense of the desire to become wise about the nature of things. It is instructive, on this point, to compare the problem as it pertains to Shakespeare and to Sir Philip Sidney, his distinguished contemporary.

Shakespeare, for whatever reason, left nothing but his poetic works: a series of intelligible yet partially enigmatic compounds of action and speech, much like Plato's dialogues. Sidney, on the other hand, wrote not just poetic works, such as the *New Arcadia,* but also a prose analysis of the poetic art, *An Apology for Poetry* (1595). Sidney argues that the true poet practices the noblest form of the art of imitation: he seeks, by his deeds and words, to teach men to be virtuous. He does so, first, by delighting men with his imitations of virtuous actions and repelling them with his imitations of vicious actions. Having thus enticed men's souls with his "speaking picture,"[3] he then teaches them to seek virtue and flee vice. He does so at the lowest level by artfully drawing upon the soul's general moral tendency to imitate what is good and shun what is bad; and at the highest level, by stimulating the tendency of the reasoning part of the soul to seek the good, in and for itself. The poet, so understood, is the "right popular philosopher." His mode of teaching is intrinsically superior not only to the historian, who necessarily deals in specific cases, but even to the moral philosopher, who seeks to give compelling precepts. Sidney recognizes that the moral philosopher—such as Aristotle, in his treatment of justice in Book V of the *Nichomachean Ethics*—seeks, and may even discover, conclusive definitions of virtue and of vice. But even though the moral philosopher may thus, in principle, furnish men with "infallible grounds of wisdom," these must "lie dark before the imaginative and judging power if they be not illuminated or figured forth by the speaking picture of poesy."[4]

As for "comedy" in particular, it is, according to Sidney, that kind of poetic imitation that fuses actions and speeches that teach us by both "delighting" us, and by moving us to the "scornful tickling" called laughter. In Sidney's own words: "all the end of the comical part of comedy [is] not upon such scornful matters as stirreth laughter only, but mixed with it, that delightful teaching which is the end of poesy."[5]

The task of musing on *A Midsummer Night's Dream* might be easier if we had a comparable argument by Shakespeare to turn to, but we do not. On the other hand, inasmuch as, as one scholar recently has shown,[6] Shakespeare evidently knew and even at times drew upon Sidney's *Apology,* it seems reasonable to consider the possibility that the two poets' understanding of the nature and purpose of poetry is similar if not identical. And yet, however suggestive such a procedure may be, it clearly is inconclusive, and we are thus compelled to recognize that Shakespeare's poetic works directly confront us, time and again, in all their puzzling and beguiling concreteness. If there is a "delightful teaching" imbedded in them, it seems that we must seek it in the interstices of the action and speech that make up the whole of a given work.

How, then, to proceed? I confess that I am not altogether sure, and that what follows on *A Midsummer Night's Dream* is, essentially, a playfully serious set of conjectures. The procedural premises that underlie its substance are these: First, Shakespeare's poetic works present themselves to us as "deeds"—something *done* by him, that is, but presented to us with no explicit explanation as to what the given work, as deed, seeks to do. Second, we thus seem always to have to work our way from the surface of the work toward an attempt to grasp the meaning of its parts, and then toward an understanding of the whole that makes up the context for the parts. Third, Shakespeare's general "deed" in constructing a given work includes specific "deeds": the title, the setting, the names of the characters, the overall movement of the action, the placement as well as the content of the speeches, the interaction of speeches and actions, and the problems posed "in speech" that may be imitated by the "action."[7]

II

A Midsummer Night's Dream is the only play in which Shakespeare treats one of the founders of antiquity.[8] By that deed he singles out Theseus and Athens above all other ancient founders and cities. Furthermore, within the play, Shakespeare makes Hermia, whose name evokes that of the god Hermes, compare Athens to "paradise" (I, i, 205).[9] Nowhere else in the corpus does Shakespeare make a character compare a city to "paradise."

However one eventually construes Hermia's remark, the singling out of Theseus and of Athens is at once compelling and perplexing. It is compelling because it seems fitting: is not Athens *the* glory of the ancient world, indeed, *the* glory of Western civilization? Is it not *the* city renowned in its own time, and ever since, for its architecture, poetry, political greatness, military valor, and not least, for its being *the* city of antiquity famous for "philosophy"?

It is perplexing, however, because of these features of the play—features that constitute specific "deeds" by Shakespeare:

1. The title itself shrouds Theseus and Athens. Stated somewhat differently, Shakespeare's deed in titling this play, in contrast to *Julius Caesar, Timon of Athens,* and *Coriolanus,* wholly obscures the political setting. Furthermore, the title points away from the political world altogether: it suggests darkness, sleeping, and dreaming, rather than the light, wakefulness, and vivid consciousness ordinarily associated with the works of the mind and the body so gloriously displayed by Athens in her greatness.

2. "Midsummer" is connected with the notion "height of madness," as is the lunar month in which "midsummer day," or the summer solstice, occurs. And the word "wood," in addition to its ordinary meaning, in Shakespeare's time, also had the meaning of "madness."[10] Given the fact that the central, longest, and most complex sequence of actions in the play occurs in the "wood" outside the walls of Athens, it seems that a triple madness is pointed to by the season, the moon, and the physical setting of the central action of the play.

3. The greatest part of the action concerns not Theseus and the display of the ruling art, but the adventures of lovers (whether humans or fairies); and even more puzzling, the antics of "rude mechanicals" (III, ii, 9), who have leapt out of their station to engage in a dramatic form of the poetic art.

4. The title, taken literally and in abstraction from the body of the work, evokes the notion of a particular dream that occurs on the eve of the summer solstice. Yet within the body of the play, not only is there no specific reference to that astronomical event—just as, in *Twelfth Night, or What You Will,* there is no specific reference to the Epiphany—but, in fact, Theseus' speech at the moment of discovering the young lovers in the woods seems to change the seasonal locus to that of May Day (IV, i, 133).

5. The title, taken in relation to the epilogue spoken by Puck, suggests that the entire body of the play may be "thought" of as but a "dream." But given Puck's notorious penchant for mischief at the expense of humans, it surely is a problem whether to take him seriously or no. And even if we do, we are left to wonder how to interpret the play's words and deeds in terms of the involuntary activity of dreaming.

Stated in the language Bottom uses at one point, the question is: how to go about "expounding" the meaning of a poetic drama disguised as a "dream"? Or is it a dream disguised as a poetic drama? And whatever it is, how to expound its meaning? Indeed, should one even make the attempt to do so? Should one be warned of the folly one may thereby fall into, warned, that is, by Nick Bottom's wondering speech that he makes when he awakes from *his* "dream": "Man is but an ass, if he go about [t'] expound this dream"? (IV, i, 206-7). But perhaps this is to take seriously what Shakespeare only means to be laughable. Perhaps a man *is* an ass who would apply to the poet's "dream" what the poet makes a weaver turned tragic actor for a day utter in his perplexity. And yet, could it be that a serious warning against "expounding" is meant to be conveyed by the playfulness of Shakespeare's treatment of Nick Bottom? Or is it, possibly, a playful warning against taking poetry seriously? But if the latter, what, then, should one take seriously? Political life? Philosophy? The revealed truth of the Bible? More questions than answers thus bubble up when one permits oneself the luxury of dwelling on titles and on the risible speech of a lowly weaver.

At the risk, then, of imitating Bottom, when one tries to expound on Shakespeare's "dream" one begins to wonder how to reconcile the discord between the sense of the play as a *single dream* and these two qualities of the action: (a) The play includes waking as well as dreaming activity. (b) The dreaming activity, which takes place only in the woods outside the city walls, is multiple: (1) Hermia's dream which occurs when she and Lysander first fall asleep in the woods (II, ii, 144-156); (2) the four lovers' dream-vision of what happened to them in the woods (IV, i, 187-199); (3) Bottom's dream-vision of what happened to *him* in the woods (IV, i, 200-219). If the title is meant to focus on one of these "dreams," it certainly is not obvious which one. A case might be made that the lovers' dream is most

crucial; and yet, to make that case requires that one consider it on its merits in relation to the dream that precedes and the one that follows.

These features of *A Midsummer Night's Dream* suggest that there is a "discord" among its elements. That discord reverberates in the poet's playing on the antinomies of dreaming/waking, madness/sanity, woods/city, fairies/humans, artisans/nobles, and the like. In attempting to discover whether there is an underlying concord in the discord, and whether such a concord might itself convey the kind of "delightful teaching" so praised by Sidney, I have been struck by the pains Shakespeare took to make the artisans play an *integral* part in the action of the whole. On the supposition that such a deed may be rooted in something more than a mere desire to reduce us to the "scornful tickling" Sidney refers to, I will scrutinize Shakespeare's treatment of the denizens of Athens's stalls.

I will begin again, by looking briefly at two classical treatments of Theseus: Plutarch's in his *Lives of the Noble Grecians and Romans,* and Socrates' in Plato's *Republic.* I will do so to throw into sharper relief the strangeness of Shakespeare's comic treatment, a prime element of which is the prominence and the hilarity of the deeds and speeches of the artisans. I will then analyze certain features of the treatment of the artisans; most importantly, their place in the structure, and the nature of the problems that emerge from what they are made to do and say. Next, I will look closely at the most singular of the artisans, Nick Bottom the weaver. And I will conclude with a few observations on why I think that the treatment of the artisans has an underlying, serious purpose that makes the poetic art, strangely, become the ruling art.

III

Plutarch's Theseus—manifestly known to Shakespeare from his partial drawing on Sir Thomas North's translation of the *Lives*—is a fusion of hero and lawgiver. As hero, Theseus, whose descent from the gods is emphatically conveyed by Plutarch, had many adventures, amorous and military. Among the latter was his audacious slaying of the Minotaur, the monster that annually devoured seven each of the cream of Athenian youths and maidens. As lawgiver, Theseus—in North's words—"dyd gather a people together of all nations." Further, he at length resigned his "regall power" to constitute a "common weale or popular estate." The commonwealth had three "orders": noblemen, husbandmen, and artificers. To the noblemen Theseus assigned the judging of "matters of religion," the bearing of civil office, the determination of the laws, and the telling of "all holy and divine things." And thus the noblemen "dyd passe the other [two orders] in honour: even so the artificers exceeded them in number, and the husbandmen in profit."[11] In sum, although Plutarch's account of Theseus emphasizes his giving a place in the civil order to the common people, its focus is simply on Theseus, and its treatment of the common people is not only minimal but utterly sober, as contrasted to Shakespeare's treatment.

Socrates' Theseus—possibly known to Shakespeare—is also a hero and lawgiver, descended of the gods. However, Socrates, in speaking to young Adeimantus about the poetic education of the young in his "city in speech," blames the poets' accounts that portray Theseus, son of Poseidon, and Perithous, son of Zeus, as "eagerly" undertaking "terrible rapes," or as engaging in other "terrible and impious deeds." Socrates then says to Adeimantus: ". . . we should compel the poets to deny either that such deeds are theirs, or that they are children of gods . . ."[12] Thus Socrates' brief account, though it says nothing directly about Theseus in relation to the common people, draws on the civic sense that Adeimantus has of that aspect of the lawgiving activity of Theseus at Athens, and portrays Theseus even more soberly than does Plutarch.

Shakespeare's comic framework for the portrayal of Theseus thus stands out the more sharply when one considers that classical treatments of the ancient lawgiver place him in a strictly sober, heroic context, and that those classical treatments were the very images that educated persons of Shakespeare's time would have brought to the play.[13] It is true, of course, that Shakespeare seems to retain the sense of the heroic, and even the sense of the kinship to the gods (by Theseus' reference to Hercules as his "kinsman"). (V, i, 43ff). Even so, on balance, there is a great tension with the persistent sobriety of the classical treatments.

The tension between the sobriety of lawgiving and the comedy of mad adventures of lovers, fairies, and artisans in the woods is greatest precisely at the point where Theseus is made by Shakespeare to take his greatest political action: Theseus suddenly overrules the ancient marriage laws of Athens. Let us see how and why that is so.[14]

At the beginning of the action, when the play seems to have all the makings of a tragedy—in the mode of *Romeo and Juliet,* for example—Hermia appeals to Duke[15] Theseus to override the ancient law of Athens which requires her either to marry the man her father chooses (Demetrius) instead of the man she loves (Lysander), or else suffer one of two other fates: to be killed, or to live out her life as a cloistered virgin. But Theseus at once replies that not even he has the power to "extenuate" its application (I, i, 120). What is the status of this law that makes it exempt from the power of a god-related heroic duke? It seems that it must be one of those awe-inspiring *nomoi* which exist from the most remote past of the city: a law derived from the gods, or at least having the aura of such divinity. And yet, in the aftermath of the lovers' and the artisans' often hilarious adventures in the woods, and as a prelude to the hilarity of the performance of the artisans' comic-tragedy in the Duke's palace, Theseus peremptorily overrules that ancient law. But then, taken in abstraction from Shakespeare's deliberate framing of Theseus' singular political action, that action must appear as an act of great impiety. Yet precisely by the way in which Shakespeare does frame it—above all by making the last phase of Bottom's adventures with Titania and his wondering and comical

speech about those adventures constitute the immediate dramatic frame for Theseus' action—the impious act is greatly muted.[16]

That Shakespeare's comic framing of this singularly political episode is intended to have that moral effect is reinforced, I believe, by the framing that he also gives to what is, strictly speaking, Hermia's impious act in fleeing the reach of the city's laws. Following this act Hermia has a remarkable dream—the only dream that occurs in the woods as a *natural* dream, rather than as a retrospective, magic-induced dream-vision of waking events that actually occur there.

Hermia flees to the "wood"—the place of madness, in the punning sense of that word—in the company of Lysander. They manifestly intend to defy the city's law that forbids them to marry in opposition to Egeus' will. The lovers lose their way in the woods and at last fall asleep. When Hermia awakes, she is nearly mad with fear. Her fear, at first, is occasioned by starting into bewildered consciousness from a nightmare: a serpent has entered her breast and is eating her heart away; meanwhile, Lysander sits by and only smiles at that cruel act. But Hermia's fear becomes terror when she suddenly realizes that Lysander, who had been asleep nearby, has vanished. Hermia calls to him in great anguish. He does not respond. Hermia then races madly off to find him, determined to meet death if necessary.

Now as I have just summarized this episode, I have deliberately falsified it. I have, that is, torn it out of its framework in the whole play, and in so doing, I have made it appear much more an episode of fear and near-madness than it is when we react to it in that framework. For then we, the auditors/witnesses, are aware of two crucial circumstances: first, that nearly all of what is happening in the woods is somehow under the control of the fairies, and especially Oberon, who has already indicated his benevolence toward the young lovers. Second, that given the hilarity of the earlier deportment of Peter Quince and company, and given the expectation we have of soon seeing them cavort in these same woods, at the rehearsal of their ludicrous play, we have every reason to suppose that no harm can come to Hermia. But our assurance of that is, ultimately, the effect of the poet's deed—his practicing his poetic art on our souls. In particular, he makes us know what Hermia cannot know; and that knowledge *works* in us by causing the painful passions of fear and pity to be replaced, or overridden, by wonder, amusement, and perhaps even laughter.[17]

To restate the preceding point in relation to the problem of impiety: The natural moral consequence of willfully breaking man-made laws is that the offender deserves to be punished by human punishment. But the natural moral consequence of willfully breaking sacred laws is that the offender deserves to be punished by divine punishment. And we know from ancient tragedies that one form of punishment for breaking sacred laws is madness. Hermia, one may say, is portrayed as coming close to madness as an immediate aftermath of her fleeing the sacred law of marriage of the city, yet as being saved from it, in the action within the play, by the poet's deed in causing Oberon to reunite the lovers, and bless them. As for us, Shakespeare's so framing the episode saves us from the sense of dread that ordinarily derives from contemplating just punishment inflicted on one who has broken a sacred law.

To sum up: Shakespeare's comic framing of both Hermia's dream and of Theseus' bold action in overriding the sacred law of marriage gently assuages the awe that the *nomoi* naturally inspire in us. It seems that the poetic art, as practiced by Shakespeare, seeks to *teach* statesmen by indicating to them the reason and the means to assuage that awe.

IV

Now the most hilarious element in the comic framing of Theseus' action is what happens to Nick Bottom, weaver turned tragedian, metamorphosed into an ass/man, and beloved of Titania. In order to see more exactly how that element is integrated into the action and speech of the entire play, we need to look closely at the precision and care with which Shakespeare treats the "rude mechanicals."

Dramatically speaking, the artisans' drollery first bursts upon us as a charming, comical discord in what seems to be an impending tragedy: Peter Quince calls the artisans to order to rehearse their play immediately following Helena's anguished soliloquy, which concludes with her fateful decision to betray Lysander and Hermia by revealing to Demetrius their plan to flee Athens. Historically speaking, the artisans' appearance is even more of a charming, comical discord: we suddenly hear Anglo-Saxon, presumably Christian, artisans who have somehow miraculously been transposed to the ancient pagan Athens of Theseus. Thus they are given, with one exception, Christian names: Peter, Nick (Nicholas), Francis, Tom (Thomas), and Robin (Robert). And each of their English surnames is either a technical word that refers to the art practiced, or alludes to it: Quince comes from *quoins* or *quines,* wedge-shaped blocks of wood used by carpenters; Bottom comes from the *bottom* or core of the skein on which the weaver winds the yarn; Flute comes from the *flute stop* of an organ, which a bellows mender would repair; Snug refers to the compact joining that a joiner would do; Snout refers to a spout of a kettle, a common object mended by tinkers; Starveling alludes to the proverbial leanness of tailors: according to an old phrase, "Nine tailors make a man."[18]

I will comment later on the significance of this specification of the arts practiced by each artisan. For now, it suffices to remark that it is an integral element of the sudden, comic appearance of the artisans; and that the comic turning curiously and unexpectedly produces a shift in the political focus of the action: Up to this point, the focus is wholly on ruler and nobles; now, of a sudden, it is on men who represent the lowest order in the city, which is to say the people, or *demos.*

The initial, sudden shift in the political focus of the action proves, on reflection, to be linked to a *series* of shifts in the locus of the play's action. The action begins inside the city walls at the palace of Duke Theseus. It then moves to Peter Quince's cottage. The next, and much the longest part of the action, takes place outside the city walls in the "wood" of Athens. It then returns to Peter Quince's cottage. And it concludes in the great hall in the Duke's palace. The placement of the action, abstracted, thus proves to be highly symmetrical: palace, to carpenter's cottage, to woods, to carpenter's cottage, to palace. The mediation, then, between the palace, the place of rule, and the woods, the place of nature where no rule as such is characteristic, proves to be the abode of an artisan—and a carpenter, at that, whose natural material is the wood of trees. His art, as carpenter, is indispensable for transforming the natural material into shelter for men. But as such, it is an art that proves, in cities, to be dependent on other arts—on what has come to be called the "division of labor." Shakespeare has seen fit, on the one hand, to make the artisans of this strange Athens practice six related arts that have to do with the provision of shelter and clothing within the city and, on the other hand, in contrast with Plutarch, to exclude any arts that have to do with agriculture. He also has seen fit, on the one hand, to specify the arts of his handicraftsmen and, on the other hand, to give no indication whatever of whether they are truly skilled at their art. Instead, these artisans take on themselves an art—the dramatic part of the art of imitation—for which they are, as their deeds and words at once make apparent, wholly unfit. One must wonder what will happen to Athens, simply in terms of its ability to survive, if Quince and Bottom are as inept at carpentering and weaving as they are at the imitative art. But of course, such a mundane question hardly arises, at least not now. Instead, we are charmed into a blissful state of hilarity by the antics of the group, especially by Nick Bottom. The acme of mirth produced by Bottom in the woods, and at the palace, is already foreshadowed in this opening scene, and comes to a focus on his being transformed in seeking to play many parts, even as Socrates' "democratic man" *does* play many parts in *The Republic*.[19] Bottom is a thespian to keep an eye on.

In any case, the comic quality of the portrayal of the artisans depends decisively on their being made, temporarily, to forego the practice of the *productive* arts in order to engage, with stunning ineptitude, in one of the *imitative* arts—the dramatic art, the imitative art that has the greatest power to move men's souls, which is why Socrates seeks to purge it in his best city (*kallipolis*). Now the artisans' practice of the dramatic form of imitative art takes place in three phases: (1) the statement of the theme and the assignment of the parts (Quince's cottage: II,i); (2) the aborted rehearsal, during which certain problems concerning the presentation of the play are broached (the wood: III,i); (3) the actual presentation of the play (Theseus' palace: V,i). It thus happens that the central segment of the artisans' practice of the dramatic art coincides (1) with the central scene of the entire play (it is the fifth in a series of nine scenes), and; (2) with the central part of the action that takes place in the woods at night. It also thus happens that in a triple sense Shakespeare has formed his play so that the artisans of the city are at the center of the action; and so that at the center of that center, Bottom is made to enter for a time into the fairy world. The *occasion* for Bottom's temporary entry into that world is, of course, the intended rehearsal of the artisans' play. But the proximate *cause* of his entry proves to be the chance intersection of Puck's and Oberon's scheme with that of the artisans. The *effect* is that Bottom's adventures with Titania replace the rehearsal: a ludicrous, magic-induced transformation of a weaver into a man/beast, beloved of a fairy queen, replaces a ludicrous, self-induced transformation of that same weaver into an imitator of a tragic hero. What Shakespeare's purpose is in bringing about such a replacement—one that imitates and plays on the sense of "transformation"—is itself a good question, and one to which I shall turn a bit later, in looking more directly at Bottom's part in the whole action. For now, I observe only that by that transformation of a transformation, Shakespeare causes Bottom to be the *only* human privileged to enter directly into the fairy world. That is startling, when one ponders its political implication: Bottom is made to do that which not even great Duke Theseus, nor Hippolyta, nor any of the four young noble lovers, is permitted to do.

Let us now take a closer look at the central segment of the artisans' practice of the dramatic art. As I have previously noted, it opens as the artisans treat certain problems concerning how to mount their play. Those problems, one may say, are made by Shakespeare to focus on the artisans' curious—to say the least—understanding of how the dramatic art achieves its effects on the souls of the audience. The treatment falls into two phases. In the first phase, Bottom and Snug raise the question of the presumed fearful, even terrible, effect of two episodes on the ladies in the audience: Pyramus' suicide by stabbing, and the lion's roar. Nick Bottom, peerless at his newly-acquired art, divines the solution to both problems: let a prologue be spoken by Quince, which will remove the fear from the ladies' souls by reassuring them that the actions presented are not "real," that Pyramus is really Bottom the weaver, and Lion really Snug the joiner.

In the second phase, two further problems are raised, one by one, by the poet, Peter Quince: how to bring in the needed moonlight, and how to depict the needed wall. Bottom, as eager to solve every problem as he was to play every part, now proposes, as a solution to the first problem, that the moonlight from the sky be permitted to enter the casement window of the chamber in the palace. It is a solution that depends on Quince's having first ascertained—from God help us, a printed almanac, in Thesean Athens!—that the moon "doth shine that night." (III, i, 50-55). Yet Quince does not at once accept Bottom's suggestion; instead, he suggests an alternative: let the moonlight be personified, even as the lion will be personified. The second problem raised in the second phase, that of how to depict the wall, is resolved quickly by Bottom's suggestion that it, too, be personified.

Taking them in abstraction now, Bottom makes three *kinds* of proposals: the use of a prologue, the use of the moonlight from the sky, and the use of a man to personify the wall. His central proposal is set off against Quince's proposal, but no resolution is reached in this central segment of the artisans' practice of the dramatic art. We are thus left to wonder how it will be resolved, and we do not find that out until the night of the performance. Then at last in his prologue Quince tells us, as well as the three newly-married couples, that wall, moonshine, and lion all are to be personified. It thus happens that Quince's proposed personification triumphs over Bottom's proposed reliance on moonlight at the casement. And it thus also happens—oh blessed triumph of Quince over Bottom!— that we, as well as the lovers, are treated to a rare display of the imitative art. That is to say: If Bottom's solution had prevailed, the light of the moon from the casement would surely have been a tame business. But in the event, the triumph of the poet Quince's solution produces some of the most extended mirth in the play; for the personification of moonlight becomes the occasion, not just for the antics of Robin Starveling, the tailor, but for a comic interaction between him and four members of the audience.

I will turn to that interaction in a moment. But it first must be emphasized that Shakespeare's deed in so ordering the treatment of moonlight in the artisans' play is part of a complex *set* of deeds concerning moonlight. Perhaps the most obvious such deed is his setting the longest sequence of his play in the moonlit woods outside of Athens, and his making fairies, human lovers, and artisans alike, speak of the moonlight there on a number of occasions. A less obvious deed is forty-six uses of words referring to moonlight: moon (31), moonbeams (1), moonlight (6), and moonshine (8). This is the densest concentration of words about moonlight in any single play in Shakespeare's corpus, and by a considerable margin. Another less obvious deed is making the majority of these forty-six uses involve the artisans, and above all their comic-tragedy. I doubt that is merely accidental, in a play in which the centrality of the artisans and their play is thrice pointed to by the structure itself. Let us therefore more deliberately explore the emphasis on the moonlight in the artisans' play.

Bottom's first proposal, to use a prologue, depends on the power of speech to persuade the ladies that their fear is groundless. His last proposal, to personify the wall, depends on the power of action and speech to persuade the entire audience that a man dressed in rough garments and made to tell them that he is a massive human artifact *is* that artifact. But his central proposal, to admit moonlight at the casement, depends on the conjunction of two natural conditions being met—the moon has to be in its bright phase, and the sky has to be free of fog or clouds—with the enactment of *Pyramus and Thisby.* But the alternative solution—that of personifying moonlight—depends only on the power of words and deeds to exert a poetic charm. Shakespeare thus sets up a tension between a "natural" and a "poetic" solution, and causes that tension to come to a sharp focus on the artisans' words and deeds concerning the problem of moonlight.

When one scrutinizes the actual presentation of moonlight in the play within a play, three things stand out. First, Quince's poetic solution to the problem of bringing in moonlight contains an astronomical impossibility: On the one hand, Quince makes Moonshine three times claim to be the *crescent* moon (thus echoing the natural crescent moon that Theseus and Hippolyta awaited for their nuptials); and on the other hand, he makes Pyramus speak as though the moon were *full.* (V, i, 238-239, 272-275). Quince either is ignorant of the natural difference between a crescent and a full moon, or has forgotten what he wrote in his speech for Moonshine when he wrote his speech for Pyramus. In either case, the artisan-poet's ineptitude draws our attention all the more sharply to the problem of moonlight in the play within a play. And, as I shall argue a little later, it eventually directs our attention, by reflection, to the problem of moonlight in *A Midsummer Night's Dream* as a whole.

Second, the densest, most complex jesting by the royal and noble members of the audience occurs precisely in the eleven-speech sequence in which Moonshine makes his first appearance.[20] The jests' surface target is Moonshine's perfect ineptitude in the practice of the dramatic art. The jests' deeper target, however, is the artisan's intrinsic ineptitude as a human being. There is a complex interaction between the two levels of jests. That interaction is a remarkable example of Shakespeare's integration of the poetic with the political, as I shall now argue.

The jests' surface target is, to be more precise now, the perfect if wholly unintended comedy of Moonshine's serious attempt thrice to persuade the audience that he is the man in the moon, that the lantern he holds in his hand is the moon itself, and that the moon is in its crescent phase. In reply to Moonshine's central attempt to persuade, Theseus at once mocks Moonshine. The essence of that mocking is the absurdity of the man holding the thing within which he is supposed to be; stated generally, Theseus mocks the fundamental absurdity of making "the whole" be held by or contained in "the part."

Now the sequence which provokes such mocking is, of course, itself a part of the whole enactment of *Pyramus and Thisby.* And the play within a play is, in turn, a part of *A Midsummer Night's Dream.* The Moonshine "part" surely provokes us, as well as the interior audience, to laughter. But more fundamentally, its playing with the problem of the relation of part to whole incites us to thought—if we will let it—concerning the *meaning* of the

play within a play in relation to the *meaning* of the whole of which it is a part. I suggest that the perfect ineptitude of the play within a play is itself part of the perfection of *A Midsummer Night's Dream,* and that that perfect ineptitude is intended to throw light, by reflection, on the problematic character of the realization of poetic perfection.

Nor is that all. The problem of the realization of poetic perfection is intrinsically connected to that of the realization of political perfection. This is revealed by a further analysis of the deeper target of the royal and noble jesting. We must start, here, with this observation about the political situation that is depicted: It is the artisans of Athens, the lowest "part" of the political order—indeed, the part which is only problematically even *in* the political order as such—who unwittingly incite the royal and noble parts of the city to mockery. At the core of that mockery is a punning playfulness concerning the meaning of the "crescent" moon, whether as the thin bow of the waxing moon (which is the exact astronomical sense), or the thin bow of the waning moon (which is the more ambiguous general sense). Now in either case, of course, the "crescent" moon gives very little light. The punning on "crescent," as signifying "little light," is most pointed and revealing in the two-speech dialogue that takes place between the royal couple, Theseus and Hippolyta.

The dialogue begins with the first of three speeches Hippolyta makes about the moon, and the only speech she makes within the eleven-speech sequence with Moonshine. Hippolyta expresses weariness with "this moon," and a punning desire that it would "change"—i.e., that it would quickly enter its last phase and thus disappear for good. Theseus' reply to this central speech of the five-speech rejoinder to Moonshine's central speech proves to be the densest punning speech in the whole of *A Midsummer Night's Dream.* It is, in fact, a complex series of puns on "light," "discretion," "wane," "courtesy," (one of the meanings of *discretion*), "reason," and "time." I will not try to sort out all aspects of this double punning by the rulers of the city, but simply limit myself to these observations: Shakespeare makes the two most "political" characters of his play engage in a brief exchange that dwells, however playfully, on the intrinsic limitation of the artisan who plays Moonshine—on, that is, his weak "light" of "discretion." Yet Shakespeare also makes Theseus, however playfully, indicate that in all civility, yes, even "in all reason," they must accept the presence of that artisan: his "light," it seems, dim though it is, is required by the city.

Third, the playful interaction between politically lowest and politically highest parts of the city concerning the problem of moonlight reaches its climax in Pyramus-Bottom's death scene. His final speech is: "Tongue, lose thy light! / Moon, take thy flight!" Whereupon Moonshine-Starveling, ever eager to please, and blessed, as Theseus observed, with but a "small light" of "discretion," takes his leave of the action, considering himself dismissed by Pyramus-Bottom's imperative. This causes poor Thisby-

Flute to try to discover her dead lover solely by the dim light of the stars, a fact gleefully commented on in Hippolyta's third and last speech on the moon, and Theseus' rejoinder to it.

This final comic collapse of Quince's poetic solution to the problem of bringing in moonlight depends, of course, on Bottom's strangely deranged speech. And the derangement, in turn, depends on the chance event that is wholly unknown to the royal couple, only confusedly known to Bottom, but clearly known to us: Bottom's temporary sojourn in the land of the fairies. For Bottom's unwitting transposition of "moon" and "tongue" is a sign, in speech, of a confusion in the soul that first afflicted him when he awakened in the woods. He then gave the first and most complex of four speeches which reveal that confusion: "The eye of man hath not heard, the ear of man hath not seen, man's hand is not able to taste, his tongue to conceive, nor his heart to report, what my dream was" (V, i, 211-213). All three of the later speeches take place back in the city; all three occur in or with respect to the play within a play; and all three continue the initial emphasis on a confusion, above all, concerning the sense of sight, the sense that is utterly dependent for its function on the existence of external light (whether the sun, in the natural realm, or a lantern, in the artificial realm). That Bottom's sojourn in the fairies' realm has the unexpected effect, at last, of making the moon disappear should make us reflect on Bottom's derangement and on what the disappearance of the moon may signify or point to. That reflection entails a closer consideration, first, of the light that is associated with the events in the woods; and second, of the traditional symbolic sense of light, in relation to the main actions of the play.

The sense of bright moonlight bathing the woods is conveyed by speeches of several of the characters, and is maintained except for one episode: Oberon makes a black fog temporarily cut off all heavenly light around the human lovers, to prevent Lysander and Demetrius from harming each other. The surface sense of the action in the woods thus is that of bright natural moonlight interrupted, for a short time, by the black, magically-induced fog that surrounds the lovers.

Let us consider, next, the traditional symbolic sense of light. According to a common understanding widespread in Shakespeare's time, an understanding going back to antiquity and exemplified in perhaps its most famous form in the eikon or "image" of the cave in Plato's Republic,[21] the sun is symbolically connected to reason and the moon to unreason, or to reason paled by the operations of mere opinions and the force of the passions.[22]

If we now apply this traditional symbolic sense of the meaning of "moonlight" to the surface impression of moonlight bathing the adventures of the human lovers and of Bottom, it seems to make sense: those moonlit adventures result from the wholly unforeseen, fortunate intersection of the humans with the fairies. But by the same token, the happiness of the human lovers, in particular, proves to depend decisively on fortune, not on knowledge, and hence is precarious, to say the least. And when one realizes that bright moonlight is made to give way, for a time, to utter blackness—when no light whatever from the heavens reaches the human lovers—the sense of that precariousness is reinforced. As moonlight—which at least gives the human eye some possibility of engaging in its natural function—gives way to utter darkness, the loss of function of the sense of sight naturally reaches its peak; and by analogy, the dependence of human happiness on the blindness of fortuna reaches its peak. It is true that in this instance the blackness is benevolent and thus not charged with the deepest sense of an utter dependence. But Shakespeare's playing, in two connected contexts, on the theme of the disappearance of the natural light of the heavens should make us consider further the implications of the disappearance of Moonshine from Pyramus and Thisby. To do this, we need to move from the impression of bright moonlight in the woods outside of Athens to an examination of the details of the treatment of moonlight in the play as a whole.

The play begins with Theseus and Hippolyta eagerly awaiting the appearance of the new moon, for the night when the "silver bow" of that moon appears in the heavens will be the night of their nuptials. Now the night in the woods—when Bottom, as well as the lovers, engage in their adventures by bright moonlight—is the night before the nuptials. But in astronomical terms, with respect to the natural phases of the moon, it is impossible for those adventures to take place by moonlight. The moon is invisible for a few nights between the last thin bow of the old and the first thin bow of the new moon. What is more, on the night when the crescent moon appears, it gives little light, and is visible only for a short time, near sunset.

What, then, does Shakespeare do? In his own way, he does what he makes his poetic counterpart, Peter Quince, seek to do. That is, Shakespeare, with consummate skill in the poetic art, calls on the charms of that art to induce in us a waking-dreaming state, such that we will "see" moonlight where, in nature, there can be none. But he also reminds us, by the artisans' bumbling efforts to bring in moonlight, by the jesting of the nobles and the rulers at those efforts, and above all, by the final foolishness of Bottom's inadvertently making the moon disappear, that there is a tension between the natural and the poetic solutions to the problem of bringing in moonlight, and that his own practice of the poetic art is the ultimate cause of making the poetic solution prevail over the natural one. The political bearing of that complex, playful, and imitative treatment of the relation of the poetic art to nature remains now to be explored, above all in its application to Bottom's adventures in the woods.

V

The delightful effect of A Midsummer Night's Dream surely is in part the product of the extraordinary beauty of the poetry, the hilarity of the artisans' adventures, the mischief of Puck, and so on. But it is also in part the product of the supposition, first of all, that war for now is at an end. Theseus has lately been at war, but that has been successfully concluded: indeed, from that war has come not just victory, but the winning of Hippolyta, and thus the prospect of the gratification of wedded erotic love. Second, the city is at peace within. The artisans, so far from being in a state of unrest or rebellion, are obedient. And so are the nobles: Lysander, far from seeking to challenge the rule of Theseus or the ancient laws, instead chooses to lead his love away from the city. Third, the city is possessed, it seems, of sufficient goods for the support of life and is sufficiently free of the ravages of disease that its denizens can indulge themselves in the revelry of feasting and entertainments. In short, the duke and the nobles, but no less the artisans can afford to enjoy the sweets of life.

It might seem that the portrayal of such a condition is easily managed by a poet: all he need do is imagine it, then figure it forth in deeds and words. But such a way of conceiving of the poetic art seems to presuppose that the poet need not be concerned with the problematic basis of such a condition—with the problem, that is, of the degree to which such a condition of civil peace, plenty, health, and leisure, is necessarily, in the real world, dependent on the arduous and often marginally successful transformation of nature by human arts. Is that Shakespeare's understanding of the poetic art? I seriously doubt it, for reasons that I will now elaborate.

A key aspect of Shakespeare's poetic art is his deed in causing Bottom's entry into the fairy world. That entry is central to the action of the play; it elevates Bottom, a mere "rude mechanical," above nobles and duke; it provides the occasion for those experiences that give rise to the first speech in which he confuses the senses; and it thus also lays the basis for his later confused speech which causes the moon to disappear. It is also a key aspect of Shakespeare's poetic art so to construct the play that we are made to be the only humans privileged (1) to *know* what was done and said in the fairy world, and (2) to *hear* Bottom's first confused speech about what happened to him in that world. Our privileged status brings us, in a curious way, closer to Bottom, yet differentiates us from him. That is, we are made to know a great deal *more* than Bottom about what went on in the fairy world, and to know it in a *way* that he is not privileged to do: we are made to know it in a conscious way, whereas Bottom's residual "knowing" is but a dream that is "past the wit of man to say what dream it was." Above all, as I shall now argue, we are thus privileged to know things that connect the fairy world's effects on nature to the ordinary world of human activity and that reveal a dependence of the latter on the former, a dependence that becomes inextricably interwoven with Bottom's adventures.

The revelry at the palace, which marks the threshold of a new generative activity by the three newly married couples, is framed by the adventures with the fairies in the woods and the unusual entry of the fairies into the palace. The revelry presupposes, as I have noted, peace, leisure, and plenty. But such a condition presupposes, in turn, that the ordinary transformation of nature by the human arts—the arts of the city and the arts of the country—has been successful. Whether it also presupposes that such a transformation of nature depends upon forces beyond human control is a question that does not obtrude itself on the revelers. It is we, the privileged ones, who are made to see that "framing" I have referred to, and perhaps to reflect on its connection to the joyousness of the revelers.

In the first part of the fairies' framing of the reverly, we learn, at once, of the quarrel between Titania and Oberon. We also learn that the quarrel can have a devastating effect on the natural world, and therefore also on the human world, especially on the human world's dependence on the transformation of nature through the human arts. In the longest speech in the entire play, Titania articulates the fateful consequences of their lovers' quarrel. The speech begins and ends with an emphasis on the quarrel itself. In between, it is a catalogue of disasters that characteristically accompany the actual quarreling: raging winds, contagious fogs, rampaging rivers, and a profound confusion of the seasons, which destroys the natural cycle of the seasons, and worse still, thus destroys the generative cycle itself. At the center of this "progeny of evils," the effect on humans is brought into sharp and dismaying focus in one of only two passages in the play that refer to the "ploughman": the "ploughman" loses his "sweat"; the cattle and the sheep die in droves from diseases; and the corn rots before it is ripe. As for humans, they are stricken with "rheumatic diseases," a result of the angry activity of the moon, that same heavenly body about whose light Shakespeare takes such pains in every dimension of his "dream."

Titania's speech, given its setting in the woods outside of Athens and its ominous contents, evokes in us, who are the privileged ones, memories of a terrible and altogether real natural catastrophe that did in fact befall that beautiful city. In the early part of the Peloponnesian Wars, in 430 B.C., when Pericles was still the leading man of the city, a devastating plague struck the Athenians. A most remarkable description of that catastrophe, and especially its political effects on civil life—such as the reduction of men to impiety and lawlessness on a great scale—is given by Thucydides. His account, in turn, forms the basis of the stark and even terrifying description of the plague that occurs at the end of one of the great classical philosophical poems, Lucretius' *Of the Nature of Things.*

Lucretius' poem begins with an invocation of Venus, the goddess of love and generation. That invocation becomes the basis of the hymn to Venus in Book IV of Edmund Spenser's *Faerie Queene,* first published in 1596.[23] Listen, for a moment, to Lucretius as transformed by Spenser, Shakespeare's great contemporary:

> Great Venus, queene of beautie and of grace, . . .
> That with thy smyling looke doest pacifie

The raging seas, and makst the stormes to flie;
Thee, goddesse, thee the winds, the clouds doe feare,
And when thou Spredst thy mantle forth on hie,
The waters play, and pleasant lands appeare,
And heavens laugh, and al the world shews joyous
     cheare.
Then doth the daedale earth throw forth to thee
Out of her fruitful lap abundant flowres . . .[24]

The last book of Lucretius' poem begins and ends with passages on Athens, the only book in the poem to be so constructed. At the beginning, Lucretius praises Athens above all cities that have ever existed:

It was Athens of illustrious name that first in former days spread abroad the corn-bearing crops amongst unhappy mankind; Athens bestowed on them a new life and established laws; Athens first gave the sweet consolations of life, when she brought forth a man endowed with such wisdom, who in past days poured forth all revelations from truth-telling lips.[25]

Reflection on this passage shows that, in order of ascending importance, Athens has established the arts, given laws, and brought forth philosophy. Lucretius has in mind, in particular, the philosophy of Epicurus; but that single example seems to stand for the activity of philosophy as such, as the highest human activity. Athens, then, is *the* city of philosophy. Yet the emergence of philosophy decisively presupposes the arts, above all the art of agriculture, and the political art, needed for the establishment of the city as a city. The activity of the founder, it seems, is central to the human activity of bringing forth not just the city, but what the city makes possible, the life of the mind. Theseus may not himself be philosophic, but his actions underlie the emergence of *philosophia,* or the love of being wise.

At the end of Lucretius' last book, however, we see that not even Athens is exempt from the devastation of natural calamities, which destroy the ordered life of the city. Furthermore, it is irony of the deepest kind that the very artisans whose art first gave rise to the settled life of the city should now be the proximate cause of the city's undoing: the calamity proceeds from the country into the city. Listen again to Lucretius:

And in no small degree this affliction was brought from the country into the city, for the fainting crowd of countrymen brought it, gathering from all quarters with seeds of disease. They filled all places and buildings; so, by the stifling heat, death all the more piled them in heaps, being thus packed.[26]

Lucretius' intention in formulating a stark and startling contrast between the loveliness of Venus and of generation at the beginning and the ugliness of plague and civil destruction at the end has been summarized by Leo Strauss in these words:

The plague is as much the work of nature as the golden deeds of Venus, nay, as the understanding of nature. It is doubtful whether philosophy has any remedy against the helplessness and the debasement which afflicts anyone struck by such events as the plague.[27]

Now as we well know, *A Midsummer Night's Dream* ends happily—not with deaths of lovers, let alone plagues and civil destruction, but with revelry. More exactly, as a final counterpoint to the human revelry, it ends with fairies dancing in an unusual place, in the Duke's palace, and with their pronouncement of a remarkable blessing. I will come to that blessing in a few moments. But first, I must take a further look at Titania's speech in relation to the sequence of actions in the whole play. Titania's speech catalogues natural disasters that accompany the quarrel of Oberon and Titania wherever they happen to be. Fortunately for Athens, the natural catastrophes have not as yet visited that fair city, for only belatedly have Oberon and Titania come to Athens from far-off India, and they separate just before, as Titania puts it, they are inclined to "chide downright." (II,i,145). But if the quarrel is not ended very soon, what can prevent catastrophe of the kind so poignantly described in Lucretius?

And now, at this moment of potential peril for the city, lo and behold, it is Bottom to the rescue. Yes, Bottom, that weaver who has left his loom to become a master of the imitative arts. Bottom, who eagerly seeks to play any part and above all a tyrant, but who settles for the part of a tragic lover. Bottom, who will play the part of the lion so well that he will roar as "gently as any sucking dove," so as not to frighten the ladies; or so well as to cause his ruler, the Duke, to say "Let him roar again; let him roar again!" (I,ii,30-73). In any case, it is Bottom, who happens to be the means of reconciliation between Oberon and Titania, hence also the means of forefending against natural catastrophes that may erupt from their quarrels, hence a kind of savior of Athens.

Not that Bottom has any intention of doing all those things, nor, of course, any real understanding of what has happened to him in the woods: he retains only that rare vision, that dream that it is past the wit of man to expound, and which is a strange blend of being lifted up—that is, being loved by a beautiful queen, with many servants at his command—and being driven down—that is, being possessed of the head of an ass, that most foolish, stubborn, and burden-bearing of beasts, which brays and cavorts, but cannot speak, let alone sing a song. Bottom has the consolation, that is to say, of not having lost his humanity, even if he has been made temporarily to wear the revolting head of an ass; for even in his extermity, he retains the faculty of speech, which depends decisively on the faculty of reason.

This is shown in a comic but instructive way in the first exchange between Titania and Bottom. Titania first becomes aware of Bottom's presence when she hears his braying song about the birds. She then sees him and exclaims that her ear is "enamoured" by his song, her eye "enthralled" by his shape, and her soul seized with love for his "fair virtue's force," or the power of his beauty. Bottom modestly replies that Titania has "little reason" for loving him, then indulges in a "gleek," or jest, the core of which is the problem of whether—and if so how—

"reason" and "love" may be "friends." Whereupon Titania says, "Thou art as wise as thou art beautiful," and Bottom again modestly claims "Not so, neither . . ." (III,i,128-150).

This is the only place in *A Midsummer Night's Dream* where someone is called "wise" as well as "beautiful." But for it to be Bottom is ridiculous: we laugh at Titania's remark, for we know that Bottom is no more wise than he is beautiful. The immediate comic effect of this episode depends, I think, on our eyes and our reason being simultaneously exempt from, yet naturally charmed by, the imagined transformations wrought on Bottom and Titania. But the comic effect's basis comes into view only when the charm gives way to reason's natural function of thinking how the effect is rooted in certain absurdities. That is to say that "love" gives way to "reason," or that reason replaces that which is loved merely because it is charming with that which is loved because it is intelligible. But for this to happen, there has at first to be the charmed awareness of the discrepancy between what *we* see and know and what the deranged senses and perception of Titania cause *her* to see and know.

We are reminded of this episode in the perplexed speech Bottom gives on awakening from his adventures with Titania. Bottom is charmed by what he recalls; and he seeks to reason concerning what it means, as well as whether it can be expounded in speech. It happens, however, that Bottom's articulation of the problem of perceiving and expounding is confused in a way that echoes the confusion of the charmed Titania, in that it reveals a derangement of the function of the senses, above all the senses of sight and hearing. Yet Bottom's speech goes beyond Titania's, for it proves to be a parody of one of the most famous passages in the New Testament, Saint Paul's *First Letter to the Corinthians* (chapter II vs. 9): "But as it is written, The things which eye hath not sene, nether eare hathe heard, nether came into man's heart, *are,* which God hathe prepared for them that loue him."[28] In Bottom's confused state that becomes, as we have seen, "The eye of man hath not heard, the ear of man hath not seen, man's hand is not able to taste, his tongue to conceive, nor his heart to report, what my dream was."

Now it is important to observe, first, that the context within which the original biblical verse is found is one of the New Testament's most important treatments of the tension between revelation and philosophy. To be more precise, Saint Paul's first chapter sets forth a profound tension between Christian revelation and Greek philosophy. Thus Saint Paul says: ". . . the Jewes require a signe, and the Grecians seke after wisdome. But we preache Christ cruci-fied: unto the Jewes, even a stombling blocke, & unto the Grecians, foolishnes" (I: 22-23). Second, the parody spoken by Bottom draws our attention to the confusion of the senses; but in so doing, it also draws attention *away* from that which is omitted by Bottom's speech: Saint Paul's decisive emphasis on "the things" God "has prepared for them that love him." Substituted for those

"things" are the things that happened to Bottom in the woods, things that transcend the sphere of the natural understanding, but in a direction that is, by Saint Paul's lights, all but blasphemous. Third, not only has Shake-speare made Bottom's adventure cause a confusion in his soul concerning the senses, but he also has made the adventure somehow add to the senses dwelt on in the biblical original. That is, in Saint Paul's text the senses of sight and of hearing are set in contrast to the "things of God," which are "revealed" to us by "the Spirit." And later in the second chapter, Saint Paul stresses the conflict between that "revealing" and the operations of the soul of the "natural man" to whom such things are "foolishness." (II: 14). But in Bottom's wondering speech the senses of sight, hearing, taste, and touch are dwelt on, thus adding the two senses most integral to the demands of the body. Finally, added to the senses of that "natural man" so excoriated by Saint Paul is the faculty of "conceiving." One wonders whether that faculty is not the root of the "natural man's" temptation to seek after that "wisdom" which the Grecians seek. I know that one ought not to put too much stock in what a confused weaver says in his perplexity. But it is worth recalling that Bottom's parodic speech in the woods outside of Athens provides an integral part of the comic framing for Theseus' overriding the *nomoi* of the city.

I must hasten, however, from the woods to the last sequence in the palace, the sequence in which the fairies leave their natural place in the woods in order to preside—unseen—over the removal of the human lovers to their respective nuptial beds.

Theseus' last speech urges all the lovers at last to bed, and jestingly adds, "'tis almost fairy time," little suspecting that the fairies are indeed close at hand. His last speech then closes with the promise of a whole fortnight of "revels," and new "jollity," as befits ducal and noble nuptials.

Between Theseus' last speech and Oberon's last speech is a single speech by Puck. The beginning of Puck's speech is starkly in contrast to Theseus' benediction, for it evokes the ordinary harshness of the world of nature. It does this, for example, by speaking of a lion's roar, and a wolf's howl. But it does so even more tellingly with respect to the toil of the human arts in extracting the substance of life from nature, with these laconic words: "the heavy ploughman snores, / All with weary task fordone." (V,i,373-74) This is the second and last time in the play that we are reminded of the ploughman, he who practices the art that underlies all the other arts on which the city depends, the art that stands closest to, and has most constantly to contend with, the world of living nature. The exhaustion of the ploughman is begotten of the practice of his art in extracting from nature what nature, in the absence of human art, provides in only the most minimal and problematically available way. That exhaustion is the condition, one may say, for the prolonged amorous revelry that Theseus has promised. But it is also the condition for the leisure in which the practice of the poetic art and the turning to philosophy may take place. When we place the last reference to the ploughman alongside the first reference, we may recall Titania's evocation of the fearful dislocations in nature that may afflict the city; we are reminded, that is, that the descent from the level of mere hard toil on the meager provisions of nature, as nature, to the level of natural catastrophe has been narrowly averted for this lovely city, whose potential for realizing the highest humans are capable of is yet to unfold.

Lest we forget that the saving of Athens took place in the woods, through the fortunate conjunction of the artisans' practice of the dramatic art with the appearance of the fairies, Shakespeare now makes the fairies leave their natural place, come into the palace, the seat of political rule, and pronounce a remarkable blessing on the married couples as their generative activity is about to commence. It is not just that they all will "Ever true in loving be." More remarkable still, the promise is that all their children will be free of the "blots of nature's hand": no deformities, not even a mole, let alone a "mark prodigious," such as is "despised in nativity." (V,i,401-415). The fairies thus assume, for a moment, the role of Venus, the goddess of love and generation. Their blessing on the couples replaces the somber ending of Lucretius' poem, even as Bottom's adventure replaces the rehearsal of the artisans' comic-tragedy.

VI

If action and speech are the warp and the woof of poetic drama, then it seems Shakespeare is a kind of weaver. I will conclude with a few remarks that indicate the way in which Shakespeare's weaving in *A Midsummer Night's Dream* seems to me to be akin to the royal art of weaving that is so praised in Plato's *Statesman*.[29]

When the artisans first enter into the action, Bottom, weaver turned actor, says to Quince, carpenter turned poet: "First, good Peter Quince, say what the play treats on . . ." Quince says: "Marry, our play is *The Most Lamentable Comedy, and Most Cruel Death of Pyramus and Thisby*." We are at once reduced to mirth, by Quince's seriousness, and even more by the title itself: this craftsman has unwittingly given his play a title that contains an arrant self-contradiction, a discord, a confusion of two distinct modes of dramatic poetry, tragedy and comedy. Later, in act V, Philostrate presents a list of possible entertainments to Theseus, who rejects the first three, then comes at last to Peter Quince's opus, now referred to as "A tedious brief scene of young Pyramus and his love Thisby; very tragical mirth." Whereupon Theseus laughingly exclaims:

> Merry and tragical! tedious and brief!
> That is hot ice and wondrous snow.
> How shall we find the concord of this discord?
>
> (IV,i,59-60).

Stated in terms of the conventional names for two essentially different types of poetic drama, Theseus' question

means: How is it possible to reconcile the fundamental discord between the end of tragedy and the end of comedy? The first seeks to move us to a catharsis of fear and pity, felt for those who are intrinsically noble; the second seeks to move us to a catharsis of contempt for those who are base and/or foolish.

The answer to Theseus' question (and to ours) proves to be the artisans' actual performance of their "lamentable comedy": The artisans, that is, inadvertently transform the tragic into the comic, and thus also unintentionally overturn the traditional order of nobility and seriousness of the two forms of poetic drama. The effect of that overturning is to reduce the ruling and the noble parts of the city to mirth and jesting mockery; they are seized with what Sir Philip Sidney called a "scornful tickling." Yet the tickling itself attenuates the hate-filled contempt that higher natures may feel for lower natures. We are reminded of the fundamental political problem represented by such contempt in various places in Shakespeare's "dream," but nowhere more pointedly than in a single remark entrusted to Oberon. Having at first himself been reduced to mirth by the drollery of Titania's loving the ass-headed Bottom, Oberon at last says to Puck that he has begun to feel "pity" for Titania's mad "dotage," which has reduced her to "seeking sweet favours" for Bottom, this "hateful fool." (IV,i,49).

Shakespeare's poetic art causes that same "hateful fool" to be transformed, if only for a time, from a mere "rude mechanical" into an ardent yet ludicrous "hero" (and, as we alone see, into the savior of Athens). Bottom's nature, so transformed, is then briefly joined by the balm and the catharsis of laughter into a tenuous and fragile harmony with the other natures in the city. The comic as well as the fortuitous and transitory character of such a weaving together may well appear to be an exceedingly problematic solution to the fundamental political problem of joining essentially different natures into a well-ordered whole. But even Socrates, confronted with that problem, was compelled to yearn for a poet who could persuade all three kinds of "natures," and not least those of the *demiourgoi*, whose *technai* provide the basis of civil existence, that their place in the city is itself wholly the product of nature, not of human acts, or of accidents. Indeed, Socrates was compelled to make that "noble lie" be the very cornerstone of his "city in speech," the city that is simply *kata phusin*, or according to nature.

To say, then, that Shakespeare's and Socrates' respective poetic solutions to the problem of weaving essentially different natures together in the city are foolish, not least because they are so little likely to become actual, may only be to say that the modern mind's conviction that the solution to that problem is wholly within the power of human art is itself the most comical thing of all; or rather, it would be comical if modern men, who cling with unabated zeal to that conviction bred of the revolutionary possibilities opened by Shakespeare's countryman, Francis Bacon,[30] did not take themselves and their project with such deadly seriousness. I myself wonder, in fact, whether that deadly seriousness is not itself *the* obstacle, today, to every attempt to articulate the problem in the comprehensive terms in which it appears in Shakespeare's "dream."

In any case, if the foolishness of the comic weaving together of natures in the city is foolishness of the first power, then surely it is foolishness raised to the second power to make the poetic art prevail over the natural solution to the problem of bringing in light, and foolishness raised to the third power to make a weaver who has been translated into an ass/man become the savior of the city by his accidental sojourn with a fairy queen in the woods outside of Athens. Yet who among us is so bold, then, as to tell exactly how that city *did* manage to rise from obscurity and ascend to the pinnacle of the possibilities available to human life? The rarity, and even more, the cause of such a remarkable realization have ever since reduced those who truly reflect on it to wonder and perplexity. Shakespeare's comical treatment of ancient Athens at its founding phase thus seems to me itself to be rooted in those states of the soul; and his artful weaving of action and speech seems to me to be his comically serious way of teaching us something about the possibilities, and yet the harsh and perhaps ultimately unpassable limits and dependencies, of life in the city as such.

Shakespeare knew full well that even Athens was at last subject to the ravages of political and natural destruction. He knew it well enough to write a somber work in which a cynic philosopher, Apemantus, says: "The commonwealth of Athens is become a forest of beasts."[31] That Athens thus proved, like the love of unfortunate lovers, to be a "quick bright thing," come, at last, to "confusion" (I,i,149), redirects our attention to the problem of what is highest and what it is rooted in. Or it does so if we will let Shakespeare's "dream" take us outside the city by reducing us to laughter about the things that are inside it. But whether we can learn again to imbibe the delightful *pharmakon* of such laughter is as uncertain as whether a Bottom will come, again, to be in our midst.

Notes

1. *The Satires,* I.1. 24-27, in *The Works of Horace,* trans. C. Smart (New York: Evert Cuyckinck et al., 1821), pp. 6-7.

2. Plato, *The Republic,* trans. Allan Bloom (New York: Basic Books, 1968), 602b.

3. Sir Philip Sidney, *An Apology for Poetry,* ed. Forrest G. Robinson (Indianapolis: Bobbs-Merrill, 1970), pp. 18 and 28.

4. Ibid., p. 28.

5. Ibid., p. 79. Cf. the following statement in James Amoyt's "To the Readers," at the head of Sir Thomas North's rendering of Plutarch's *Lives of the Noble Grecians and Romans,* a statement Shakespeare very likely had read: "such books as yield pleasure and profit, and do both delight and teach, have all that a man can desire why they should be universally liked and allowed of all sortes of men, according to the common saying of the poet Horace: 'that he which matcheth profit with delight, / Doth winne the price in every poynt aright.'" *Plutarch's Lives of the Noble Grecians and Romans Englished by Sir Thomas North anno 1579,* ed. George Wyndham (London: David Nutt, 1895), vol. 1. p. 8.

6. See Alwin Thaler, *Shakespeare and Sir Philip Sidney* (New York: Russell & Russell, 1967), especially pp. 42-48.

7. Jacob Klein's penetrating analysis of "action" and "speech" in Platonic dialogues, and in particular, his treatment of the mimetic function of action in relation to speech, seem to me to be very pertinent to the study of Shakespeare's plays. See Klein's introductory remarks to his *A Commentary of Plato's* Meno (Chapel Hill: University of North Carolina Press, 1965), pp. 3-31.

8. Theseus appears, of course, in the play *The Two Noble Kinsmen,* but given the disputed authorship of that play, I have excluded it. See Hallet Smith's introduction to the play in *The Riverside Shakespeare,* ed. G. Blakemore Evans (Boston: Houghton Mifflin Co., 1974), pp. 1639-41.

9. All citations to the text of Shakespeare's plays are from *The Riverside Shakespeare.* All statements about uses of words in the plays are based on Marvin Spevack's *The Harvard Concordance to Shakespeare* (Cambridge: Harvard University Press, Belknap Press, 1973). The Spevack *Concordance* is keyed to the Evans text. In the speech in which Hermia refers to Athens as "paradise," she is momentarily disenchanted with Athens because of its marriage law. All that is required for that enchantment to resume is for her to be permitted to marry Lysander.

10. See the various articles for these words in the *Oxford English Dictionary.*

11. See Plutarch's "Life of Theseus," pp. 53-54.

12. Plato, *The Republic,* 391c.

13. It is possible that the classical sense of Theseus underlay Samuel Pepys's reaction, in 1622, to Shakespeare's "dream"; for Pepys called it "the most ridiculous play that ever I saw in my life." See Anne Barton's introduction in *The Riverside Shakespeare,* p. 217.

14. See Howard B. White's analysis of *A Midsummer Night's Dream,* in his *Copp'd Hills Towards Heaven: Shakespeare and the Classical Polity* (The Hague: Martinus Nijoff, 1970), Chap. III. I have been much stimulated and influenced by White's general line of thought, but have sought to look more directly and intensively than he did at the specifically comic aspect of the play, and in particular at the comic aspect as it emerges in the treatment of the artisians.

15. The title "duke" seems to be used in this play—and other plays, such as *Twelfth Night, or What you Will*—in sense 1 in the *OED*; "A leader; a leader of an army, a captain or general; a chief, ruler."

16. Act IV, scene i begins with the last phase of Bottom's involvement with Titania, it moves through the key episode in which the ancient law is overriden, and ends with Bottom's soliloquy.

17. See also what I argue, later on, concerning the intended moral effect of Quince's "prologue" that will overcome the fear of the ladies.

18. See the note to I, ii, p. 225 of *The Riverside Shakespeare*; and cf. the edition of the play edited by Sir Arthur Quiller-Couch and John Dover Wilson (Cambridge: Cambridge University Press, 1969), p. 102.

19. *Republic,* 560c-d

20. MOON
This lanthorn doth the horned moon present—

DEM.

He should have worn the horns on his head.

THE.

He is no crescent, and his horns are invisible within the circumference.

MOON.

This lanthorn doth the horned moon present;

Myself the man i' th' moon do seem to be.

THE.

This is the greatest error of all the rest. The man should be put into the lanthorn. How is it else the man i' th' moon?

DEM.

He dares not come there for the candle; for, you see, it is already in snuff.

HIP.

I am a-weary of this moon. Would he would change!

THE.

It appears, by his small light of discretion, that he is in the wane; but yet in courtesy, in all reason, we must stay the time.

LYS.

Proceed, Moon.

MOON.

All that I have to say is to tell you that the lanthorn is the moon. I the man i' th' moon, this thorn-bush my thorn-bush, and this dog my dog.

DEM.

Why, all these should be in the lanthorn; for all these are in the moon.

21. Plato, *The Republic,* 514a-517b.

22. On the title page of Robert Record's *The Castle of Knowledge* (1556), the sun is made to shine above the "sphere of destinye, whose gouenour is knowledge," while the crescent of a new moon is made to shine above the "wheele of fortune, whose ruler is ignorance." On the left side, Urania, or heavenly wisdom, with open eyes, holds a pair of compasses in her right hand, and the handle of the sphere of destiny in her left. On the right side, the goddess Fortuna, blindfolded, holds a cloth in her left hand, and pulls on the cord of the wheel of fortune with her right. The verses at the center treat the contest between the two, and conclude: "The heavens to fortune are not thralle / These spheres surmount al fortunes chance." See plate 16 in *The Riverside Shakespeare,* p. 1134, for a reproduction of Record's title page.

23. See the account of "Lucretius and the Renaissance" in George D. Hadzsits, *Lucretius and His Influence* (New York: Longmans, Green, and Co., 1935), pp. 248-83.

24. Edmund Spenser, *The Faerie Queene,* in *The Complete Poetical Works of Edmund Spenser* (Boston: Houghton Mifflin Co., 1908), Book IV, Canto X, sections xliv-xlv.

25. Lucretius, *De Rerum Natura,* trans. W. H. D. Rouse (Cambridge: Harvard University Press, 1937), VI, ll. 1-9.

26. Ibid., VI, ll. 1259-1265.

27. Leo Strauss, "Notes on Lucretius," in *Liberalism Ancient and Modern* (New York: Basic Books, 1968), p. 83.

28. It is a problem which translation of the Bible Shakespeare used. On balance, the evidence seems to me to point to the Geneva Bible. I have quoted from the 1560 version, published in a facsimile version by the University of Wisconsin Press, 1969. See p. 20 of the introduction for a brief treatment of Shakespeare's use of the Geneva Bible.

29. See especially the last speech by the Eleatic Stranger, at 311b-c.

30. See Howard B. White, *Peace Among the Willows: The Political Philosophy of Francis Bacon* (The Hague: Martinus Nijhoff, 1968) especially chapter 1, "Political Faith and Utopian Thought."

31. *Timon of Athens,* IV,iii,348.

Virgil Hutton (essay date 1985)

SOURCE: Hutton, Virgil. "*A Midsummer Night's Dream*: Tragedy in Comic Disguise." *Studies in English Literature 1500-1900* 25, no. 2 (spring 1985): 289-305.

[*In the following essay, Hutton explores the religious and philosophical issues which he claims Shakespeare deliberately raised in* A Midsummer Night's Dream.]

Even though the seriousness of *A Midsummer Night's Dream* has long been getting its due, T. Walter Herbert is the only critic to treat at length the metaphysical implications as the dominant concern of the play. A rapid survey of the criticism of the play reveals an early concentration on the theme of love, which, with Barber's rejection of love as the play's major motif, gradually yields to a stress on the theme of art (perhaps climaxing with Young's view of the play as Shakespeare's *Ars Poetica*), which in turn may, under the provocation of Herbert's study, shift to a probing of the play's metaphysical dimensions.[1] Herbert opens an inviting prospect for critics by claiming to make statements not about Shakespeare's intentions but only about a contemporary spectator's reactions to the play. Through linking the theme of art with the metaphysical issues raised by Herbert, I will argue that Shakespeare did deliberately raise the philosophical and religious issues so perceptively pondered by Herbert's spectator.

Herbert's spectator sees two contrasting worlds in the play: the comic animist world of Athens, under the guidance of the fairies, and the tragic nonanimist "Babylonian" world in the play-within-a-play of "Pyramus and Thisby," where there is no guidance of any gods or spirits whatsoever. Because "Pyramus and Thisby" is produced by citizen mechanicals, the spectator, with the aid of Herbert's centuries of hindsight, links their soulless play world with the future soulless world of commerce, industry, and technology that they are to construct in real life. Thus, for him, the play provides not merely a representation of contemporary currents of thought and belief but also a prophetic glimpse and warning of the "brave new world" to come. Though accepting some of the premises of this new naturalistic world himself, and though not being able to reconcile his religiously oriented beliefs in a beneficent animist world with the actualities of life around him, Herbert's spectator in the end rejects the Babylonian vision of the mechanicals' play and rests in the more comfortable world of the fairy King.

If one could choose which world to live in, one might certainly, along with Herbert's spectator, prefer the world of benevolent fairies to the fairyless world of "Pyramus and Thisby." But of course we have no such choice. If our world is a world with fairies or gods, none of our beliefs or actions can make it otherwise, any more than Lysander's or Theseus's lack of belief in the fairies prevents them from existing and operating. And if our world is a world without fairies or gods, no beliefs or actions of ours can make it otherwise, just as the godless world of "Pyramus

and Thisby" would not be changed by any appeals for godly aid Pyramus or Thisby might have made. The only choice we have is one of belief, and through *A Midsummer Night's Dream* Shakespeare does seem to offer us this choice, after hinting at his own belief concerning the reality.

For many critics, the choice offered by the play is either between the rational and the irrational or between reason and the imagination. For those stressing the theme of love, rational love is said to triumph over irrational love as the young lovers, after their night of irrationality, return to the bonds of rational love and marriage exemplified by Theseus and Hippolyta. When linked to the theme of art, however, "cool reason" usually loses out to the presumably warmer imagination.[2]

Though both views suffer from the absence of a clear example of dramatized "reason" in the play, the rational-irrational love dichotomy is particularly vulnerable. First, the designation of Theseus as the standard of rational love is unconvincing because Shakespeare does not develop the quality of Theseus's love sufficiently for us to apply any special label to it. Second, at the beginning of the play the young lovers are endeavoring not to avoid marriage but to avoid marriage to parties not of their choice, which seems quite rational. Third, at the end of the play no difference in the quality of the young peoples' love is portrayed. Those who claim that the juice of "Dian's bud" represents rational love as opposed to the irrational love induced by the flower "love-in-idleness" must, like Frank Kermode, pass over with embarrassing silence the fact that Demetrius's charmed eyes are never washed with the antidote.[3]

The dichotomy of reason and imagination also relies heavily on linking Theseus to reason (often tagged "skeptical reason") in opposition to the fairy realm of imagination. But, as some critics have recently pointed out, Theseus represents reason in general no better than he represents reason in love. Huston, for example, likens Theseus's behavior in the first scene of the play to that of an irrational tyrant,[4] and certainly one might easily view Oberon's behavior toward the lovers as more reasonable than Theseus's blustering threats. Even in the opening exchange of Act V, where Theseus is usually labeled the defender of reason and Hippolyta of the imagination, Hippolyta's openmindedness, as Herbert's spectator observes (pp. 160-61), is more reasonable than Theseus's dogmatic dismissal of the evidence.

Here we pause to note that Theseus's unreasonableness lies particularly in his refusal to grant any more reason to the poet's imaginings than to the lunatic's ravings. Hippolyta grants some credibility to the lovers' stories because she discerns an order or pattern in their account—that is, she finds some "reason" in them—that differentiates them from "fancy's images." Shakespeare's point seems to be that the poet's imaginings, unlike the lunatic's, also contain an order or pattern as a result of being under the guidance of reason, and therefore deserve some consideration as purveyors of truth.

After Hippolyta's superior reasonableness here, however, Theseus, during the mechanicals' play, becomes the more reasonable in his gracious tolerance and willingness to mend the mechanicals' efforts with his imagination. No characters consistently embody reason, just as no scenes illustrate a world of reason as opposed to a world of imagination. And this deficiency is to be expected, since Shakespeare's comedies, as well as his tragedies, are devoted to showing that reason and people, like reason and love, in the words of Bottom, "keep little company together now-a-days" (III.i.129-30). Only the play as a whole remains to exemplify that necessary fusion of reason and imagination in art that Hippolyta's speech and Shakespeare's *ars poetica* call for.

But though the reconciliation of reason and imagination remains an important theme, it is not the major concern of the play. In order to be a complete embodiment of Shakespeare's *ars poetica* as well as his defense of poetry, the play would have to go beyond a presentation of mere method. It would have to contain a discernible pattern or order that would produce a meaning beyond "fancy's images." That such a meaning arises from the worlds perceived by Herbert's spectator appears likely not only because the worlds are concretely dramatized within the play but because other interpretations centering on love or the imagination have not been able satisfactorily to account for the carefully constructed parallels, antitheses, and paradoxes generated by the mechanicals' play.

Through the mechanicals' rehearsal scenes, Shakespeare confronts many of the problems and paradoxes arising from the art of drama; I will concentrate on one problem slighted by critics. Once in the first rehearsal scene and twice in the second the mechanicals worry over how to keep their play from frightening the ladies. In considering this worry, critics have largely concentrated on how Shakespeare satirizes the mechanicals' overly literal-minded solution to the problem;[5] but little attention has been devoted to the problem itself, which, though raised so lightly and comically by the mechanicals, is of fundamental importance to any artist.

Behind the mechanicals' concern for "the ladies," which is comparable in some respects to our modern expressions of concern for "the children," lies the general concern over how much should be shown to anyone. And the problem for artists, as with the mechanicals, becomes particularly pressing when their material is perceived as being frightening or offensive. The mechanicals' worry is twofold: first, they fear the effect on the audience (that they will be too frightened to continue watching the play); and second, they fear the repercussions on themselves (that the ladies will have them hanged).

In relation to the first fear, a consideration of Hamlet's "Mousetrap" may prove instructive. There we see a clear example of the audience (Claudius) being so upset by a performance that he cannot see it through. When we ask why, we find that Hamlet's theory of art is to blame. The mirror image he holds up to Claudius is too exact, too close to Claudius's secret reality for him to bear. The theory suits Hamlet's purposes, but it is not appropriate as a general theory of art; for if it succeeds splendidly in art's one traditional aim of instructing Claudius as to his faults, it fails miserably in art's other aim of providing him with delightful entertainment. The mirror must be sufficiently distorted to keep the audience's shoe from pinching so tightly that they cannot enjoy the performance. And even Hamlet's mirror is sufficiently distorted to allow the more innocent spectators to enjoy the performance by preventing them from realizing its sinister purposes.

Hamlet's "Mousetrap" may also illustrate the mechanicals' fear of repercussions. By making Claudius perceive that his crimes are discovered, Hamlet rouses not only Claudius's conscience, but also his determination to kill the one who has revealed knowledge of his guilt. The real death Hamlet faces and the imagined death the mechanicals predict are extreme but realistic manifestations of the resentment aroused toward anyone who exposes the follies and crimes of another too openly. Through censorship, society both reveals where it is most vulnerably fearful and warns artists to avoid portraying these subjects too openly. But of course artists are most attracted to these forbidden subjects because it is obviously just in these areas that society is most in need of enlightenment and instruction. Thus, as many have pointed out, the artist must distort his mirror to penetrate the censorship shield of society just as Freud's dreamwork distorts the dream content in order to deceive the individual's internal censor.

Since they are to provide entertainment for a marriage celebration, the mechanicals fear that the threat of violence, posed by the lion, as well as the actual violence of the onstage suicides of Pyramus and Thisby will be too much for their audience's sensibilities. Shakespeare must share this concern because, if scholarly conjecture is correct, he too is preparing an entertainment to celebrate a marriage, and he would not wish to bathe both the stage and the audience in a bloody tragedy. Yet the seemingly inept decision of the mechanicals to entertain with a tragedy that they must then sweat to divest of its tragic content is also Shakespeare's. And we must ask what he had in mind.

Simply to entertain is the goal of the mechanicals, and, judging from Theseus's assertion that "This palpable gross play hath well beguil'd / The heavy gait of night" (V.i.356-57), they achieve this aim brilliantly. But if we include instruction as a goal of art, their play utterly fails, for, as many critics have observed, the audience of newlyweds gives no indication of receiving any instruction whatsoever. They fail to perceive the parallels between themselves and the story of Pyramus and Thisby. By a clumsy performance and by striving to palliate everything unpleasing to their audience, the mechanicals have so distorted their artistic mirror that the newlyweds do not recognize their own features in it.

Shakespeare's deliberate rather than unwitting decision to include a tragic story within his comedy surely reflects his desire to instruct as well as to entertain; for if a wedding celebration demands entertainment, the newlyweds also need instruction as preparation for sustaining their new commitments. As Hugh Richmond notes, having our obtuse stage audience witness a play-within-a-play is a device, used earlier in *Love's Labor's Lost,* to incite the theater audience to grasp meanings lost to the stage audience.[6] In *A Midsummer Night's Dream,* the theater audience, including perhaps a pair of newlyweds, should be able to observe the pertinent parallels overlooked by the stage couples and to apply to themselves the clear warning of the tragic consequences that may result from rash actions induced by passionate love. From their superior viewpoint the theater audience can then smile at the stage audience, and Shakespeare's instruction neatly gives rise to comic pleasure.

But since such instruction does not seem frightful enough either to drive away the audience or to attract the wrath of society's censorship—if we are to apply the mechanicals' fears over the effect of their play to *A Midsummer Night's Dream* itself, as I believe we should—we must gaze more deeply into Shakespeare's distorted mirror. Here we must return to the speculations of Herbert's spectator over the "Babylonian," godless world of the mechanicals' play, for these speculations uncover strong reasons for Shakespeare's having fears similar to those of the mechanicals concerning the reaction to his play. After perceiving the parallels between the story of Pyramus and Thisby and the adventures of the young lovers watching the skit, Herbert's spectator, through induction, concludes that the tragic outcome of the mechanicals' play can be explained by the one major lack of parallelism: the absence of any benevolent fairies or gods to protect Pyramus and Thisby from the fatal consequences of their misguided assumptions.[7] But Herbert's spectator makes no attempt to decide where Shakespeare stands in relation to the contrasting worlds in the play. We must still ask what it is that Shakespeare tried so cunningly both to present and to conceal.

Pursuing the reasoning of Herbert's spectator a bit further may help. Though the absence of benevolent gods in the mechanicals' play may account for the tragic deaths of the lovers, we need not conclude that such a world of accident must always produce tragic results, for there may be happy as well as unhappy accidents. The crucial point being made is that tragedy can occur only in a world not under the guidance of benevolent gods. Both the world of Lysander and Hermia and the world of Pyramus and Thisby are full of accidents, but the one pair of lovers is saved from their unlucky accidents by the benevolent fairies, whereas the other pair is not. And neither pair is more deserving of help than the other.

Which of these worlds does the play present as an image of reality? If my reasoning in the preceding paragraph is correct, the answer immediately becomes apparent. Our world of daily tragedies is more faithfully mirrored in the godless world of Pyramus and Thisby than in the fairy world of the Athenian woods. C. L. Barber, for instance,

stresses the play's skeptical attitude toward the existence of the fairies,[8] and certainly the fanciful representation of the fairies is not calculated to instill belief in their literal existence. Indeed, it is the presence of the fairies that creates the dreamlike atmosphere of unreality in the play once we move into the woods, and it is this air of fantasy that makes the contrasting tragedy of Pyramus and Thisby appear all the more shocking and realistic.

Shakespeare also, I believe, uses the play's moon symbolism to reinforce the realism of the Pyramus and Thisby tragedy. The opening speeches of *A Midsummer Night's Dream* reveal a moonless or virtually moonless world as Theseus and Hippolyta await the new moon's appearance in four days. This moonlessness emphasizes the realism of the first scene, where the motifs of love and sex are treated by government and parent with the heavy-handed obtuseness so familiar in our society. When, upon the scene's shifting to the woods, the moon, with comic inconsistency, shines brightly overhead, it becomes apparent that Shakespeare is using the moon to signal, among other things, a fantasy world of wish-fulfilling dreams. In the mechanicals' play the moon also plays a singularly important role, though it has not been overly commented on by critics.

As in the main play, the moon makes its entrance when the scene shifts to the night meeting place of the lovers fleeing their parents' cruelty. Ominous signs, however, accompany this moon. It enters not with fairies but with a lion, and it shines not on palace woods but on a tomb. Furthermore, this moon, instead of being associated with the magical moonlight of Act II, is linked to the waning moon of Act I by two speeches of Theseus:

THESEUS:

> but, O, methinks, how slow
> This old moon wanes!

> (I.i.3-4)

THESEUS:

> It appears, by his small light of discretion, that he is
> in the wane.

> (V.i.242-43)

Still, the moon's dim presence preserves a faint atmosphere of romance as it ironically provides just enough light for Pyramus to spy the bloodstained mantle of Thisby. But even this faint glimmer disappears when Pyramus, in the throes of death, orders the moon to depart: "*Pyramus*: Moon, take thy flight. / Now die, die, die, die, die!" (V.i.293-94). And in case the audience has overlooked the moon's obedient departure, Shakespeare has Hippolyta ask "How chance Moonshine is gone before Thisby comes back and finds her lover?" We must supply the answer to Hippolyta's unanswered query. The moon's exit at the crucial moment of Pyramus's death marks the turn to tragedy just as Mercutio's death performs the same function in *Romeo and Juliet.* Here, of course, the multiple distancing of the action enables the comic tone to continue,

Bruno Gerussi as Oberon, Deborah Cass as Titania, Helen Burns as Hermia, Leo Ciceri as Lysander, Peter Donat as Demetrius, and Kate Reid as Helena in Act IV, scene i of the 1960 Stratford Festival production of A Midsummer Night's Dream.

but the symbolic message is clear. The moonless conclusion of "Pyramus and Thisby" represents the intrusion of dark reality into the midst of comic romance, and Pyramus's "now die, die, die, die, die!" becomes the comic equivalent of Lear's "Never, never, never, never, never."

But Shakespeare is not yet through with this moon. At the close of the mechanicals' play we are again reminded that their moon is no longer creating a world of benevolent magic; Theseus pairs the moon with the lion to perform a ritual symbolizing not the joy of restoration but the finality of death: "Moonshine and Lion are left to bury the dead" (V.i.334). And following this symbolic return from fantasy to reality brought about by the tragedy of Pyramus and Thisby, Shakespeare is ready to present the play's final image of the moon—the cold, naturalistic moon that chilled Herbert's spectator:[9]

PUCK:

> Now the hungry lion roars,
> And the wolf beholds the moon.

(V.i.354-55)

Our shock should double when we recall the play's opening promise of a forthcoming new moon, a symbol of renewal suitable for the traditional comic ending. The reversal is so extreme and unexpected that I don't believe it can be satisfactorily explained as merely a foil to heighten our sense of joy. A consideration of Shakespeare's technical strategy here may help.

By abruptly transferring the lion and moon from the play-within-a-play to the main action, Shakespeare heightens the realism of Puck's images through the seeming change from fiction to "fact," from Snug's and Starveling's make-believe back to reality. The use of Puck and then Oberon as spokesmen here further strengthens our acceptance of the realities they describe; the fairies, in contrast with the mechanicals and even with Theseus, give the effect of a godlike chorus.

Comic distancing, however, continues to create the ambivalent tone of tragicomedy. If the fairies as spokesmen add a godlike credibility to their images of disaster, their godlike status also adds credibility to their more happy promises of protection from these disasters, so that we can cheerfully leave our characters to the comic fate of being happy ever after. But still our emotions at the end must remain mixed. For though we can accept the happy prophecies for the characters within the framework of the play, we cannot convincingly apply those prophecies to ourselves within the framework of reality, just as the newly married spectators could not be certain that none of their children would ever suffer any "blots of Nature's hand" (V.i.392). The images of surrounding threats and potential disasters ultimately derive their powerful authority not from the credibility of the speakers but from the everyday evidence of experience, which, paradoxically, refutes the existence of the godlike spokesmen.

For the theater spectators, then, the final effect should be the mingling of comic delight with tragic instruction. Specifically to the newlyweds Shakespeare's message, which of course applies to all, seems clear: in order to have any chance of preserving your marriage and some degree of happiness you must recognize and be ready to meet and endure all sorts of possible calamities that may occur in a world where one cannot count on the continual guidance and aid of benevolent fairies or gods.

The stage spectators experience the delight but fail, for various reasons, to receive the instruction. Distracted by the bungling performance of the mechanicals and blinded by the desire to reinforce their egos after their own recent follies, the stage lovers do not recognize even the most obvious instructive parallels with themselves. But they cannot be faulted for snobbish obtuseness in missing the even bleaker philosophical implications of the wedding entertainment, since they are not in a position to be able to draw the inferences open to Herbert's spectator and to us concerning the presence and absence of the fairy gods in the two stories. Being unaware of the presence of the fairies, the stage spectators cannot perceive that their good fortune resulted from the aid of the fairies, whereas the bad fortune of Pyramus and Thisby resulted from the absence of any such aid. Why then shouldn't the stage lovers be proud of their own sagacity in comparison both with the hapless Pyramus and Thisby and with the clumsy actors portraying them?

Seeing the young lovers, even at the end of the play, so full of ignorance, can we be at all hopeful that their present happiness will outlast even the short night left after the "iron tongue of midnight" has spoken? We can, because, in lieu of the instruction they missed, they have the fairies to protect them from the disasters so common among less fortunate married couples. The prognostication for the newlyweds in the theater audience may be favorable to the extent that they grasp and assimilate the play's instruction, which has been generally neglected, perhaps, because it seems less appropriate to comedy than to tragedy.

In 1957 Frank Kermode was applauding the new serious-ness with which critics were approaching Shakespeare's comedies in general and *A Midsummer Night's Dream* in particular,[10] and succeeding critics have continued to call attention to the dark, nightmarish, and potentially tragic undercurrents of the play. But to my knowledge, Herbert, through his spectator, was the first to apply the term "cosmic comedy" to the play.[11] The term is apt because it recognizes the play's treatment of themes conventionally reserved for tragedy: the nature of the universe; man's relation to the universe; the existence of the gods; man's relation to the gods if they exist; human suffering; and death. Whether or not one wishes to establish a separate genre for such plays, the label, as a working hypothesis for the "intrinsic genre" of the play, to use the term of E. D. Hirsch, Jr.,[12] allows one to see and to take seriously many things in the play that have been overlooked or dismissed because the play is supposed to be merely a comedy.

Critics have seldom expressed difficulty over labeling *A Midsummer Night's Dream* because they have apparently not been sufficiently aware of the play's tragic content. It is time to observe that the esthetic theory stated and exemplified in *A Midsummer Night's Dream* is also operating in a "dark" comedy or "problem" play such as *Measure for Measure*; only in the latter play there is not so great a disparity between the comic surface and the serious undercurrents—the tragic content is not so cautiously disguised. Herbert's spectator begins to suspect that *A Midsummer Night's Dream* may be a cosmic comedy when he hears Titania "bemoan the misplaced seasons and the excessive rain."[13] By creating his fairies in the image of the Homeric gods, Shakespeare provides a broad clue that his play will be cosmic in scope, just as the mechanicals' "Lamentable Comedy" (I.ii.9) and "tragical mirth" (V.i.57)—labels that also fit *A Midsummer Night's Dream*—point to the intrusion of tragic content. Let us consider how the play's fairy world, which represents, I believe, an approach to an ideal world for Shakespeare, contributes to a mingled effect of comic delight and tragic pathos.

Some have seen the workings of Providence in the fairies,[14] but the fairies contrast rather than compare with the gods of conventional Christianity. Most obviously, the fairies are sexual lovers, who, like any man and wife, are in the midst of a domestic quarrel, unlike Christian deities who are not susceptible to such mortal antics. The fairies' susceptibility to sexual involvement with humans is also, of course, Homeric rather than Christian, though the New Testament stories of the virgin birth retain the motif in spiritualized form. Of even greater importance is a difference seldom if ever commented on: the fairies, unlike Christianity's God, do not hesitate to accept responsibility for some of the evils in the world. After enumerating the recent disturbances in the order of nature, Titania, instead of trying to blame "sinful" man, emphatically places the responsibility on herself and Oberon:

TITANIA:

> And this same progeny of evils comes
> From our debate, from our dissension;
> We are their parents and original.

(II.i.115-17)

"Parents" is a key term here because it links the fairies to Egeus, the parent of Hermia, and to the unseen parents of Pyramus and Thisby. Through implication, Shakespeare places the burden of responsibility for the potential tragedy of Hermia and the real tragedy of Pyramus and Thisby on the parents, those who, like the gods, have the most authority and power. In taking responsibility, the fairies further parallel the Homeric gods, who, as symbols of forces beyond human control, are regularly assigned responsibility for the behavior of nature and of humans.

As for lending aid to humans, the fairies, again unlike Christianity's God, are not deterred from preventing a fall into disaster by the excuse that they would thereby be interfering with human "free will." Shakespeare's fairy world humbly concedes that humans are masters neither of their fate nor of their wills, although the characters retain the illusion that they are acting freely. And this situation, though an anathema to some peoples' notions of human dignity and pride, seems to be presented as preferable to one in which the gods, if they exist, sit idly by, for whatever excuses, while Pyramus and Thisby, like Romeo and Juliet, blunder into death.

The Homeric gods too are not deterred from giving aid to humans by any concerns over free will, but the fairies surpass both Christianity's God and the Homeric gods in one important respect: selfless benevolence. The fairies are willing to go out of their way to help hapless humans without first demanding belief or worship or sacrifices. The lovers in *A Midsummer Night's Dream*, far from calling upon the fairies for help, are wholly unaware of the fairies' existence. And the fairies, instead of showing any eagerness to be recognized and worshiped, provide their aid invisibly throughout, except for their appearance to Bottom, who provides no threat to their secrecy. Such altruism sets an ideal standard for gods, who surely should be kind enough to help suffering mortals without prescribing any preconditions or demanding any succeeding gratuities.

Kind as they are, however, the fairies, because they are not omnipotent, cannot totally alleviate the sufferings of mortals, nor can they be held responsible for all of the world's evils. Their sphere of operation is limited both in space (wherever they happen to be) and in time (largely the night). Similarly, the Homeric gods, besides having to contend with each other's interference, suffer at crucial times the limitations of Fate—as when Zeus cannot save his son Sarpedon from being killed in battle—and therefore cannot bear total responsibility for human suffering. Paradoxically, the omnipotent, omniscient God of conventional Christianity, who is most eligible to bear total responsibility for human suffering, is the God who totally declines to accept such responsibility.

Curiously enough, the fairies' lack of omnipotence enhances rather than diminishes the ideal status of their world. For one thing, their world is not subject to the irreconcilable moral and logical dilemmas that automatically arise whenever omnipotence is assigned to any being. For another, the fairies exercise upon our imagination a gentle charm that could not be attached to an omnipotent figure, who must remain as unlovable as an unclimbable cliff. But most importantly, the fairy world represents an ideal because, as many have noted, it symbolizes, like the Homeric world, a union between man and nature. Since nature may be too restrictively understood, however, we must add that the union is between man and the gods, between man and the universe. In Shakespeare's play, the parallels between the fairies and the mortals, like the anthropomorphism of the Homeric gods, establishes this perception of unity, which is perhaps most unforgettably symbolized in the brief twining of Titania around Bottom. Add omnipotence to any of the characters, however, and the attractive vision of unity is irrevocably contorted into absurdity.

Herbert's spectator speculates on how the coming age of science, business, industry, and technology was creating the godless Babylonian world of the mechanicals' play. But in a more fundamental sense the gods had already been stripped away from man by Christianity, which, as it strove to distinguish itself from paganism and as it became more and more rationalized and intellectualized, disparaged the anthropomorphism of previous religions through stressing the differences rather than the parallels between man and God. The persistent belief in fairies, which Shakespeare lovingly exploits, manifests the effort to bring the gods back to earth in an understandable and meaningful relationship with humans, who cannot psychologically sustain a position of isolation from the rest of the universe. As the increasing remoteness of orthodox gods induces a feeling of being unimportantly lost in an indifferent abyss, people seek, by reverting to earlier beliefs or turning to new ones, to re-establish their place in the universe, to re-establish their union with the universe, to become part of things once more.

Shakespeare's ideal world of Homeric fairies fits almost any meaning of "dream" one might think of. It is certainly, to use Freud's terminology, a wish-fulfillment dream that provides at least temporary psychological solace to our waking frustrations. To serve as meaningful wish fulfillment, however, the play must also contain the nightmare world of Pyramus and Thisby, from which we are psychologically protected by the play's equivalent of Freud's dreamwork—the artistic triple distancing of the play-within-a-play.

The play's ideal world is also a dream in the sense of something that in reality does not exist. At the play's end we are allowed to wake up to the fact that the fairy world was but an artistic dream, and it is only then that the play's suppressed content of extreme tragic pathos has a chance to surface. As in the opening of Chaucer's Wife of Bath's tale and in Wordsworth's sonnet, "The world is too much with us," the displacement of the fairies and of the Homeric gods by later beliefs is not seen as an improvement. Rather, all three works, through a recreation of past worlds, stress how much has been lost. Shakespeare's vision, however, may be the bleakest, since it suggests that even these mourned lost worlds never existed except in the mind of dreaming man. The classical story of Pyramus and Thisby seems deliberately chosen to illustrate that the ancient gods were no more benevolent and protective in reality than the more recent gods who presided over the destiny of Romeo and Juliet. And the supposed newly-married couples in the audience will, like the couple in Arnold's "Dover Beach," have to rely on their own resources of love and mutual support to maintain their happiness in an unpromising world.

The final sense of dream I will treat is the one raised in the epilogue—that a dream is something of such little value and significance that one need not pay it serious attention:

ROBIN:

> If we shadows have offended,
> Think but this, and all is mended—
> That you have but slumb'red here
> While these visions did appear.
> And this weak and idle theme,
> No more yielding but a dream
> Gentles do not reprehend.

The irony behind Shakespeare's belittling of his play has regularly been noted, but its relation to the play's theory of art, which demands the employment of sufficient distancing devices to allow the presentation of unsettling views without destroying the purveyance of pleasure, has been overlooked. Under the conventional concern that the performance has not been sufficiently pleasing lies a more serious concern. For, if my reading of the play has any validity, there would be ample reason to fear that some of the audience might be offended by its instruction, and we can recognize how the word dream, from the title to the end of the play, serves as the last layer of defense to ward off any who might be both perceptive enough to grasp the play's serious implications and orthodox enough to protest against them.

Frequently A Midsummer Night's Dream has been interpreted as a defense of the irrational and of the imagination against the attacks of reason. Marjorie Garber, for instance, concludes: "But if illusion and the imagination are not without their dangers, they are nonetheless, in the terms of this play, preferable to their radical opposite, 'cool reason,' in Theseus's phrase." She sees Bottom's efforts to avoid frightening the ladies as resulting from his being "aware of the dangers of imagination and illusion" and wanting to protect the court audience from them just as dreamwork,

she claims, warns us "against the dangers of the irrational."[15] Certainly both illusion and the irrational may be dangerous if mistaken for reality and reason, but Garber's analysis seems slightly awry. Dreamwork does not warn against the irrational; it protects the mind from too direct a confrontation with unpleasant reality. Similarly, Bottom and the mechanicals strive to protect their audience not from illusion but from too clear a confrontation with the terrifying realities of their story; and their imagination must be exercised to discover means to avoid frightening their audience, just as Shakespeare exercised his imagination to present unpleasant messages without frightening away his audience. Here again, reason and the imagination should be seen not as opposing duellists in a game of one-upmanship but as necessary partners in any artistic enterprise.

Without "cool reason" the efforts of the imagination are apt to be wasted, for the careful calculations of reason are needed not only to produce artistic order and meaning out of chaos, but also to determine how much unpleasantness or strangeness an audience can tolerate. In A Midsummer Night's Dream, Shakespeare demonstrates his understanding of the fragile human psyche by not only using the distancing device of a play-within-a-play but also by having the players of this internal drama use distancing devices. But somewhat like the magician who pretends to reveal his secret while continuing to deceive his audience, Shakespeare has so artfully exposed his secrets under the guise of farcical parody that few have grasped what he was up to. In another way, however, Shakespeare's employment of artistic illusion in A Midsummer Night's Dream is the opposite of the magician's: the magician creates the illusion that bodies are being cut in half and heads are being chopped off while in reality no such things are happening at all; Shakespeare creates the illusion that all is well while in reality heads are rolling all over the place. The magician presents comedy under the guise of tragedy; Shakespeare presents tragedy under the guise of comedy.

Notes

1. Henry B. Charlton, *Shakespearian Comedy* (London: Methuen, 1938). Charlton's chapter on the play represents an influential interpretation focusing on the love theme. C. L. Barber, *Shakespeare's Festive Comedy: A Study of Dramatic Form and its Relation to Social Custom* (Princeton: Princeton Univ. Press, 1959); David P. Young, *Something of Great Constancy: The Art of "A Midsummer Night's Dream"* (New Haven: Yale Univ. Press, 1966); T. Walter Herbert, *Oberon's Mazéd World* (Baton Rouge: Louisiana State Univ. Press, 1977). Quotations from the play are from the text in Irving Ribner and George Lyman Kittredge, eds., *The Complete Works of Shakespeare* (Waltham: Xerox, 1971).

2. George A. Bonnard, "Shakespeare's Purpose in Midsummer-Night's Dream," *Shakespeare Jahrbuch* 92 (1956):268-79; Paul A. Olson, "A Midsummer Night's Dream and the Meaning of Court Marriage,"

ELH 24, 2 (1957):95-119; Marjorie B. Garber, *Dream in Shakespeare: From Metaphor to Metamorphosis* (New Haven: Yale Univ. Press, 1974), ch. 2.

3. Frank Kermode, "The Mature Comedies," in *Early Shakespeare,* ed. John R. Brown and Bernard Harris, Stratford-upon-Avon Studies 3 (New York: St. Martin's Press, 1961), p. 218. An attack on Kermode's interpretation is offered by R. W. Dent's "Imagination in *A Midsummer Night's Dream,*" *SQ* 15, 2 (Spring 1964):115-29.

4. J. Dennis Huston, "Bottom Waking: Shakespeare's 'Most Rare Vision,'" *SEL* 13, 2 (1973):217.

5. Barber, pp. 148-51.

6. Hugh M. Richmond, *Shakespeare's Sexual Comedy: A Mirror for Lovers* (Indianapolis: Bobbs-Merrill, 1971), p. 121.

7. Herbert, pp. 53, 143-44.

8. Barber, pp. 123, 140-43.

9. Herbert, pp. 61-62. Here I follow, with Herbert, the Folio's "beholds."

10. Kermode, pp. 214, 220.

11. Herbert, p. 153.

12. E. D. Hirsch, Jr., *Validity in Interpretation* (New Haven: Yale Univ. Press, 1967), pp. 78-89.

13. Herbert, p. 153.

14. John A. Allen, "Bottom and Titania," *SQ* 18 (1967):111; Stephen Fender, *Shakespeare: A Midsummer Night's Dream* (London: Edward Arnold, 1968), pp. 48-49, 54-55.

15. Garber, pp. 82, 84.

A. D. Nuttall (essay date 2000)

SOURCE: Nuttall, A. D. "*A Midsummer Night's Dream*: Comedy as *Apotrope* of Myth." *Shakespeare Survey* 53 (2000): 49-59.

[*In the following essay, Nuttall contends that in* A Midsummer Night's Dream, *Shakespeare used comedy to suppress, however incompletely, the darker aspects of the myths that influence the play.*]

> Hippolyta, I wooed thee with my sword,
> And won thy love doing thee injuries.
> But I will wed thee in another key—
> With pomp, with triumph, and with revelling.
>
> (1.1.16-19)

Thus Theseus, benignly, to Hippolyta in the opening scene of *A Midsummer Night's Dream*. Everyone watching, in 1595 or 1596, would have known that the speaker was an important personage. He enters, splendidly dressed (we may be certain) and, according to the Folio stage direction, 'with others' (rightly interpreted by Theobald as implying a train of attendants). His speech contrives, within a small compass, to be stately. It at once receives from Egeus, a kind of underlining, a graceful, articulate equivalent of loyal (servile?) applause: 'Happy be Theseus, our renowned Duke.' Now we are clearly aware of the exact social status of Theseus, which is of course very high. The cadence of Egeus' words anticipates that of the courtier Amiens in *As You Like it,* 'Happy is your grace', after Duke Senior's similarly stately (if deeply implausible) speech on the merits of the simple life, although, interestingly, Amiens' 'happy' carries, as Egeus' 'happy' does not, a connotation of stylistic felicity. Theseus, then, is a grand fellow of whom we should all take notice. Do we know anything else? Do we know—to put the question more precisely—who he is?

A little more than eighty years after the London audience listened to the words of Shakespeare's Duke of Athens, another audience in another country could be found listening to the words of one Thésée (or Theseus) in another play. This other play—Racine's *Phèdre*—is, to put it mildly, different from Shakespeare's. It is black tragedy. This Theseus is a harsh figure of sexual violence. Racine builds explicitly on Euripides and Seneca.

The full mythological information is made available. Indeed it impregnates the semantic fabric of the drama. This, we are left in no doubt, is the Herculean hero who with his sword defeated the army of women, the Amazons, and afterwards carried off their queen, Antiope, begetting on her his son, Hippolytus—that Hippolytus who describes his father as the deliverer of Crete, 'fumant du sang du Minotaure' (1.i.82). Behind this line stands a passage in Shakespeare's favourite poet, Ovid, beginning,

> Te, Maxime Theseu,
> Mirata est Marathon, Cretaei sanguine tauri
>
> (*Metamorphoses,* vii.433-4)

> You, greatest Theseus, Marathon adores for the blood shed of the Cretan bull.

Racine, however, has actually darkened the bestial allusion. Where Ovid evokes the slaying of the Marathonian bull, Racine slides to the far more frightening Minotaur, half bull, half man (equally part of the Theseus myth). The Minotaur was the creature who lived in the labyrinth, the monstrous issue of the unnatural coupling of Pasiphae with a bull. We now meet perhaps the most grotesque, the most disturbing, of all the Greek myths. When Pasiphae was overcome with lust for the beautiful bull she was at first at a loss how to contrive physical intercourse with the brute. To solve her problem she had a wooden cow constructed, to attract the bull. He mounted the wooden cow and she, straddling within, received the bull's member. The story is so gross that even Ovid seems to flinch from it, in his uncharacteristically hurried account of Pasiphae 'quae torvum ligno decepit adultera taurum', literally, 'who, unchaste, deceived the savage bull with wood' (*Metamorphoses,* viii.132). Theseus was aided in his defeat of this monster by a daughter of the same Pasiphae, Ariadne, whom he later ditched in Naxos. After the death of the Amazon queen Antiope he married (in the normal version of the myth) Phaedra (Racine's Phèdre), another daughter of Pasiphae. She it is, in Racine, who, infected by her terrible lineage ('la fille de Minos et de Pasiphaé', 1.i.36) is incestuously drawn to her son-in-law, Hippolytus. We are, quite obviously, in another world. On the one hand, in the English comedy, we have moonlight, fairies and happy love. On the other, in the French tragedy, we have sexual horror. Can Shakespeare's Theseus be in any sense the same person as the one we meet in Racine?

When we passed from Racine to Ovid we crossed over from drama to narrative poetry. Yet the answer, from the point of view of a mythographer, is, 'Yes, Shakespeare's Theseus is quite clearly the Theseus of Greek myth; it is the same man.' Racine's tragedy is in immediate accord with ancient story. Shakespeare's comedy, perhaps, is not. The first thing Shakespeare's Theseus tells us, however, is that he wooed Hippolyta 'with my sword' (1.1.16). This is—must be—an allusion to the war with the Amazons. Good scholarly editions of the play accordingly cite at this point Shakespeare's source, which is, once more narrative: North's Plutarch.

> Touching the voyage he made by the sea Major, Philochorus, and some other holde opinion, that he went thither with Hercules against the Amazones: and that to honour his valiantnes, Hercules gave him Antiopa the Amazone. But the more part of the other Historiographers, namely Hellanicus, Pherecydes, and Herodotus, doe write, that Theseus went thither alone, after Hercules voyage, and that he tooke this Amazone prisoner, which is likeliest to be true.[1]

At this point we have in North's margin the shoulder-note, 'Antiopa the Amazone ravished by Theseus'. Then, a little later, after the shoulder-note, 'Theseus fighteth a battell with the Amazones', we are told how

> The graves of the women which dyed in this first encounter, are founde yet in the great streete, which goeth towards the gate Piraica, neere unto the chappell of the litle god Chalcodus. And the Athenians . . . were in this place repulsed by the Amazones, even to the place where the images of Eumenides are, that is to saye, of the furies. But on th'other side also, the Athenians comming towards the quarters of Palladium, Ardettus and Lucium, drove backe their right poynte even to within their campe, and slewe a great number of them. Afterwards, at the ende of foure moneths, peace was taken betwene them by meanes of one of the women called Hypollita. For this Historiographer calleth the Amazone which Theseus maried, Hyppolita, and not Antiopa . . . It is very true, that after the death of Antiopa, Theseus maried Phaedra, having had before of Antiopa a sonne called Hippolytus . . .[2]

Far more lightly than Racine but nevertheless unmistakably Shakespeare is touching on this Greek story. Near the

beginning of Act 2 Oberon and Titania are squabbling, each half-accusing the other of adulterous desires. Oberon says,

> How canst thou thus for shame, Titania,
> Glance at my credit with Hippolyta,
> Knowing I know thy love to Theseus?
> Didst thou not lead him through the glimmering night
> From Perigouna, whom he ravishèd,
> And make him with fair Aegles break his faith,
> With Ariadne and Antiopa?
>
>   (2.1.74-80)

The myth wobbles as myths do. Antiope, queen of the conquered Amazons can, as we saw already in Plutarch, reappear with another name, Hippolyta—a name which seems somehow to have moved, with the necessary change of gender, from Hippolytus, Theseus' son. Shakespeare went for 'Hippolyta' in his main action, yet Antiopa is still there in Oberon's speech. Theseus appears alternately as ravisher and bridegroom. Most wonderfully, when the story is told by the king of the fairies, the myth itself is drawn into the distinctive magic of Shakespeare's comedy: Theseus, we learn, was led through a 'glimmering night' by a fairy to his harsh conquests. Titania, it seems, played Robin Goodfellow to the erotic Hercules of antiquity.

Obviously the scholars are not wrong to cite North's Plutarch. But still, it might be said, the source, though certainly that, a source, remains poetically extraneous. Does the Theseus of myth figure in the *theatrical* experience of *A Midsummer Night's Dream*? I think the answer to this question must be blurred. The mythological Theseus will be there for some, not there for others. Those who see only the benign conquering bridegroom will be happy. Others, however, will not be able to help knowing more (and Shakespeare knows that some will know more). The flowery train of names in Oberon's speech especially will be largely dead matter to the former class. To the latter it will work, as allusive poetry properly works, as a series of casements opening on the wild foam of European story. Shakespeare, I am sure, would not have allowed Theseus his reference to the sword used in winning Hippolyta if he had not wanted such thoughts to arise. He reminds us—very swiftly, I grant—of past violence in the opening sequence of the play; it is a prominent, *mind-setting* speech.

And of course if we admit the ravisher Theseus we at once let in a strand of meaning which is as congenial to feminist criticism as it is uncongenial to old-fashioned bardolatry. It is, I suppose, a good rule in criticism to be especially mistrustful of anything you find with delight and, conversely, to be prepared to concede, as it were, with clenched teeth, the presence of undesired matter. It is for the reader to judge which of these injunctions (if either) is being followed in the rest of this essay.

Surely nothing can be more evident—and more obstinately irremovable—than the contrast to which I carefully alluded at the outset. Racine's *Phèdre* and Shakespeare's comedy, whatever off-stage links may be discovered in the hinterland of sources, present substantially different universes. Mythologically this may be the same Theseus, but poetically this is another person altogether. What happens in Theseus' wholly benevolent speech to Hippolyta is a *successful* banishing of the old dark narrative from the play. With these words the myth is turned on its head; the harsh Theseus drops out of sight and the smiling Duke of Athens springs up in its place. What we see is a verbal equivalent of a visual transformation in a masque. Still more it resembles a transition in music (Theseus himself says 'in another key', 1.1.18). The whole point of *A Midsummer Night's Dream* is its gossamer beauty. The twentieth century is marked by a prejudice in favour of the discordant. Shakespeare is saying, as clearly as it can be said, that this is not what he is after. *Préjudice de siècle* is nowhere so evident as in Jan Kott. His notorious description of Titania as 'longing for animal love'[3] (as if Titania were Pasiphae) is simply ludicrous. Has he not noticed that Titania is deluded? She is attracted by what she sees as a wise and beautiful being. She cannot see the grotesque half-donkey available to the rest of us. A play in which Titania said, 'Give me a beast to make love to me' would be essentially different from Shakespeare's. In his words to Hippolyta Theseus actually changes the story itself; it is now another story, one (why should we be so reluctant to receive it?) of happy love.

All of that sounds like good sense. It is, I think, 90 per cent true. This leaves, the alert will perceive, a troubling 10 per cent which I propose now to consider. I have just said that Shakespeare has changed the myth and moved on to new territory. If he had wished simply to produce a new story why did he allow Theseus to mention his sword at all? Why, after the great switch, did he let the word 'ravished' appear in Oberon's speech? Why did he not present a smiling wooer who could quite easily have been called by some other name than Theseus?

When I was trying to describe the transformation of the myth the phrase 'turns all to favour and to prettiness' came into my mind. These of course are the words of Laertes as he looks at Ophelia. The full speech runs,

> Thought and affliction, passion, hell itself
> She turns to favour and to prettiness.

> (*Hamlet* 4.5.186-7)

Laertes is responding to a speech by Ophelia which is, in fact, faintly evocative of the world of *A Midsummer Night's Dream*: it is all flowers and greenery and ends with a snatch from the song 'Sweet Robin'. There is a robin—Robin Goodfellow—in *A Midsummer Night's Dream*. The effect of this sequence of speeches in *Hamlet* is not to enforce the absolute division of tragedy from comedy, *Phèdre* from the *Dream*, but to mediate between them. Just as triple Hecate, goddess of hell in Ovid and Seneca[4] finds her way into *A Midsummer Night's Dream*, drawing the fairies after her from the rising sun (5.2.14), so hell and passion, the stuff of *Phèdre* are the matter of

Ophelia's feat of transformation. If we had no sense of the material, we would not know that a feat had been performed. Of course in the tragic world of *Hamlet*, confronted as we are by the wreckage of Ophelia's mind, we cannot forget these things. In *A Midsummer Night's Dream* it is all so much lighter, so much swifter, that we can forget. Nevertheless *A Midsummer Night's Dream*, likewise, presents not the accomplished fact of terror disarmed but a feat of disarming. To understand the feat, to feel the proper energy within the lines, we must be aware in some degree, if only for a moment, of background terror.

George Herbert in his 'Jordan' poems did not make an editorial decision in advance to exclude all artful ingenuity from his divine poems; instead he risked his soul and made poetry from the act of exclusion. Shakespeare similarly did not decide in advance not to use the old myth. Instead he chose to exhibit the exclusion, as a process within the drama. Having said this, I will now push the thesis a little further. The suppression of dark forces is not only incomplete at the beginning of the play; there is a sense in which it remains incomplete throughout. The play is haunted to the end by that residual ten per cent.

Listen again to Theseus:

> Hippolyta, I wooed thee with my sword,
> And won thy love doing thee injuries.
> But I will wed thee in another key—
> With pomp, with triumph, and with revelling.

I wish now to draw attention to the fact that a certain disquiet can persist, even in the latter, supposedly joyous half of this 'over-turning' speech. Instead of making Theseus say 'I won you by violence but now I will seek to gain your trust by a loving devotion', Shakespeare makes him say, 'I won you with my sword, but now we will proceed in joyous triumph.' The second half of the antithesis actually fails to achieve a fully antithetical status. 'Triumph' remains, obstinately, an arrogant, masculine word. It carries the idea of military victory into the new world of marriage. The actor who delivers this speech is in no danger of kneeling to his lady, as Lear would have knelt to Cordelia. Rather the very words will cause him almost to strut.

Later in the play, in the famous dialogue about the lunatic, the lover and the poet, Theseus (who certainly won the battle of the citations-index since his are the words endlessly quoted in anthologies) uncomprehendingly occludes the far subtler observations of Hippolyta. It is not too much to say that the entire 'Coherence Theory' of truth is sketched in her phrase 'grows to something of great constancy' (5.1.26). Her IQ is as far above Theseus' as her real status is, quite evidently, below. As Graham Bradshaw saw, there is a delicious *gaucherie* in a lover telling his lady, *de haut en bas*, that all lovers are crazy.[5] It is not *galant*.

Thus the new, smiling Theseus remains oddly stiff. He is indeed no longer the ravisher. Nor does he ever come close to bullying Hippolyta. But he is still harshly masculine. We cannot quite say, with a whole heart, 'Now all is well!' It is as if, after all, Shakespeare wants a half-memory to continue, at the edge of consciousness.

Another work famous for turning enmity into beauty and lightness is Pope's *Rape of the Lock,* written, it is said, to laugh quarrelling parties out of their difference. The very title enacts, within a monosyllable, the healing transformation. The word 'rape', then as now, applied to forced sexual intercourse. But as we reach the words 'of the lock' we begin to guess, with relief, that the word is being used in its milder, Latin sense: 'seizure', 'carrying off'. Nevertheless, having achieved the soothing modification and dispelled all anxieties (we might suppose), Pope keeps the harsher meaning alive, at the back of the reader's mind, through imagery of cracked porcelain, scissors ('the glittering forfex') and the like. The alternatives before us are, first, that *A Midsummer Night's Dream* enacts a complete suppression of sexual violence, replacing it with unbroken felicity and, second, that there is indeed just such a suppression but it is laced with a nervous, intermittent memory of the matter suppressed. It will be obvious by now that I am going for the second alternative.

I want at this point to shift focus from Theseus to the fairies. If Theseus is, by mythological birthright, the figure who could have brought a Greek violence into the play had he not been softened, the very English fairies are surely the obvious agents of that softening, powerfully assist the change of tone, embody the opposite principle, the principle of beauty. Once more, however, the absoluteness of our initial distinction will not survive close inspection. The fairies, no less than Theseus, carry the burden of a dark history. Shakespeare's fairies, indeed, are miniature, pretty creatures, but to say this is very like saying that Shakespeare's Theseus is a benign figure. We can no longer assert with Latham that Shakespeare was the first to present minuscule fairies, since earlier examples have been found, but we can say that he chose the then unusual miniature fairy, in preference to the more usual version. And of course Titania, herself a fairy, is clearly full-size; she can entwine Bottom the Weaver in her arms. Even if Peaseblossom and the rest were played by children, children are not nearly small enough to lie in a cowslip's bell (from *The Tempest,* I know, but really a bit of *A Midsummer Night's Dream* which has somehow strayed into *The Tempest,* at 5.1.89). The truth is that Shakespeare knows that one element in the pleasure taken in all this pretty flimsiness will be relief. The fairies of *A Midsummer Night's Dream,* with their redemptive beauty chasing away all tragic elements may be the same people as the fairies who were once feared. At the end of the play Oberon has to promise that no child born from the marriages forged on that magic night will be deformed:

> Never mole, harelip, nor scar,
> Nor mark prodigious, such as are

> Despisèd in nativity
> Shall upon their children be.

> (5.2.41-4)

The promise is urgently required because the fear of these effects is still there—fairies are notorious for pranks, but the infliction of a hare-lip on a new born child is something worse than a prank.

In a way everything I have been saying is already present in the phrase, 'The Good Folk', a minor anthropological curiosity in its own right. The fairies were called 'The Good Folk' not because they were benevolent but in the hope of making them so—we can almost say, because they were in fact the reverse of benevolent. The phrase does not occur in *A Midsummer Night's Dream* but 'Goodfellow' does, as another name for Puck. There is a seventeenth-century woodcut of Robin Goodfellow which shows him with horns, shaggy thighs, cloven hooves and graphically emphasized animal genitalia.[6] 'Good Folk', then, is a conciliating, propitiatory description, which can be paralleled in other languages. For example the avenging Furies whom we have already met in Plutarch and can find again in Aeschylus were called the 'Eumenides', 'The Kindly Ones'. In Sophocles' *Oedipus at Colonus* the chorus sings . . .

> As we call them the kindly ones, that they may receive
> the supplicant safe, with kindly heart.[7]

Near the end of the seventeenth century Robert Kirk wrote in *The Secret Commonwealth of Elves, Fauns and Fairies,* 'These sith's or Fairies, they call sluagh-maith or the good people (it would seem, to prevent the dint of their ill attempts: for the Irish use to bless all they fear harme of)'.[8]

We are dealing with a kind of euphemism, but not the kind we employ simply to avoid an undesired image (as in 'passed away' for 'died'). Rather, this euphemism is *put to work* (presumably in the hope of inducing the hearer to conform to the flattering description) with the design of *turning away* hostility. It is therefore an apotropaic euphemism, from the Greek . . . 'turning away'. Richard Wilson applies the term 'apotropaic' to this comedy in his brilliant essay, 'The Kindly Ones: The Death of the Author in Shakespearian Athens'.[9] He observes that the play procedes through a series of rejected scripts, 'Seneca's *Hercules,* Euripides' *Bacchae* . . . all are evaded during the action'.[10] Of course I want to say 'not quite rejected, not exactly evaded', but Wilson is basically right. Duke Theseus performs an *apotrope* of his former self at the beginning of the play. Could *A Midsummer Night's Dream* constitute, as a whole, an *apotrope*? Myths are essentially recounted; the story of the things that happened long ago is told, and re-told. But apotrope is not narrative but action upon those very beings whose exploits are set forth in myth. It is the product of efficacious ritual. Remember here how *drama* in Greek once meant 'doing'. When Theseus re-describes himself in that opening *volta,* in a euphemism which we hope will 'take', like an inoculation,

Shakespeare is perhaps banishing, or 'praying-away' from his drama that mythic darkness which Racine will later let back in. But Shakespeare also knows that the joy and relief consequent upon the *apotrope* will lose their keenness if all sense of danger is lost. Hence the keeping-alive of the disquiet after the opening *apotrope*.

How does Bully Bottom figure in this play of nervous delight? The answer (which may strike the reader as vacuously pious) is 'With a deep, very Shakespearian complex coherence'. Once more, the first thing to be said is that Bottom, translated into the form of a beast, is (hilariously) innocent. He lolls, like some degenerate Roman emperor, in the midst of a feast, as a beautiful woman climbs all over him, and his great hairy head is full of thoughts of food, not sex. He is like a small boy. Yeats famously said (in 'Ego Dominus Tuus') that Keats was like a schoolboy 'with face and nose pressed to a sweetshop window', which makes some sense if one thinks of *The Eve of Saint Agnes*. But, in spite of the notorious 'feast in the dorm' passage, we are in fact clearly aware that Porphyro in that poem is interested in sex as well as food. Bottom is interested only in the jellies and ice-creams (or rather, since the donkey is beginning to take over, in hay).

I am now repeating the move I made at the beginning of this essay. I said then that the most obvious thing—and the most obvious thing can be the most important thing—about Shakespeare's Theseus is that he differs from Racine's Thésée, as *A Midsummer Night's Dream* differs from *Phèdre, toto coelo*. But then I admitted a darker penumbra of meaning. So here, having asserted the comic innocence of Bottom, I must acknowledge that the mere sight of a woman entwined with a beast or half-beast of itself suggests monstrosity. Again I have to ask, are the demons completely removed? Is our laughter simple, unmixed, or is it the louder because energized by a surviving anxiety? Again, I go for the second alternative.

While the 'primary move' of Theseus is from hostility to benevolence, the 'primary move' of Bottom, at the level of action, is in the opposite direction, from human being to beast. That is why the Bottom sequence is immediately funny, as Theseus is not. In Bottom's case there is an element of shock to be surmounted and this supplies the incongruity needed. 'Jupiter / Became a bull, and bellowed', says Florizel in *The Winter's Tale*, (4.4.28) (apparently in the hope of cheering up the rustic Perdita with august precedents of sexual condescension). But Bottom, who becomes not a bull but half an ass, is no Jupiter but a hard-handed mechanical. Yet Europa and the bull, Leda and the swan and all the other ancient stories of bestial coupling remain critically relevant. They are part of the material to be comically inverted or apotropaically defused. Again, a quantum of anxiety survives the *apotrope*. As I have said, it is difficult to look at a woman entwined with something which is turning, as we watch, into an animal—Beauty and the Beast—without worrying. The worry, at the back of one's mind, may be partly about physiology. 'Will she be hurt if they have sexual inter-

course? Oh, no danger of that, I see' (laughter here)—but then the thought returns.

This obstinate refusal ever quite to go away is admirably caught by Peter Holland in his essay, 'Theseus' Shadows in *A Midsummer Night's Dream*'.[11] Holland quotes the sinister jingle of Hughes Mearns,

> As I was going up the stair
> I met a man who wasn't there,
> He wasn't there again today.
> *I wish, I wish he'd stay away.*

For Holland, Seneca's Hippolytus is a shadow—an absence-presence—in the play, 'a man on the stair'. Surely sane persons take care not to be seriously distracted by such things? Holland writes, 'Hippolytus cannot be ignored, but does that mean he should be noticed?' It is a good question. That criticism which soldifies the properly fluid, changes glimpses into full percepts, must be falsifying its material. But meanwhile it remains just (as Holland sees) to register shadows as—merely—shadows. Moreover our relation to these shadows may be more dynamically charged than at first appears. The last line of the jingle expresses a wish. Translate that wish into magical action and you have, once more, *apotrope*.

As the Plutarchian Theseus stands behind the Duke of Athens, so the Golden Ass of Lucius Apuleius stands behind Bottom the Weaver. Once more, the scholarly editions rightly cite Adlington's translation of 1566 as a source. Here is Lucius' account of how he, transformed into an ass, became involved with a lustful matron. In this passage all the anxieties I was just alluding to are explicit.

> Then she put off all her Garments to her naked skinne, and taking the Lampe that stood next to her, began to anoint her body with balme, and mine likewise, but especially my nose . . . Then she tooke me by the halter and cast me downe upon the bed, which was nothing strange unto me, considering that she was so beautifull a matron and I so wel boldened out with wine, and perfumed with balme, whereby I was readily prepared for the purpose: But nothing grieved me so much as to think, how I should with my huge and great legs imbrace so fair a Matron, or how I should touch her fine, dainty and silken skinne, with my hard hoofes, or how it was possible to kisse her soft, pretty and ruddy lips, with my monstrous mouth and stony teeth, or how she, who was young and tender, could be able to receive me.[12]

That last word, 'me', is a euphemism, on Adlington's part, a euphemism of the ordinary kind. The Latin at this point (x.22) is 'Tam vastum genitale'. Remember Pasiphae, within the wooden cow, receiving the organ of the bull. Apuleius, certainly, has not forgotten. He writes how the matron 'had her pleasure with me, whereby I thought the mother of Minotarus [*sic*] did not causelesse quench her inordinate desire with a Bull'.[13] Earlier, when the matron is introduced, she is likened to Pasiphae. Here Adlington says, simply 'as Pasiphae had with a Bull', eliding the note of comic incongruity, essential to the Shakespearian version, which is present in the Latin, *instar asinariae Pasiphaae* 'like some *asinine* Pasiphae'.

With Bottom, as with Theseus, if we read backwards into prior myth, we are led into the world of *Phèdre*. Bottom is a happily averted Minotaur, or Bull, Titania Pasiphae. In Peter Holland's essay the Minotaur is the second major 'shadow' of the play, after Hippolytus.[14] It will be said, 'There is nothing in Shakespeare about a huge penis.' True. But this thought must lie behind the physiological anxiety, the physiological comic incongruity. Titania's words,

> While I thy amiable cheeks do coy,
> And stick musk-roses in thy sleek smooth head

> (4.1.2-3)

are funny because, as she speaks, we are looking at a monstrous, hairy head. She herself betrays, a line later, that even to the eye of infatuation Bottom's ears are oddly large. A moment afterwards he says himself, 'I am marvellous hairy about the face' and the scratchy word 'scratch' appears twice in the same speech (4.1.22-5). A sense of physical incompatibility is present in the faint Ovidian surrealism of Titania's image of 'the female ivy' encircling 'the barky fingers of the elm' at 4.1.42-3. Think of Apollo feeling the breast of Daphne as the bark began to form over it, the heart fluttering under the roughened surface, at *Metamorphoses,* i.554. Horror is successfully averted. We laugh and we are happy. But the horror is there, to be averted, and in some degree survive the act of aversion. The director who caused Bottom to cast on the backcloth a shadow (Peter Holland's word!) that looked for a moment more like a minotaur than a donkey would not, I suggest, be exceeding his interpretative brief.

There is a nasty poem by Martial about a promiscuous lady, one Marulla, whose children can be seen by their looks to have many fathers, none of which is the lady's husband. One with frizzy hair looks like the African cook; another, with flat nose and thickened lips is the very image of Pannicus, the wrestler and so on. The poem includes these lines,

> Hunc vero acuto capite, et auribus longis,
> Quae sic moventur ut solent assellorum
> Quis morionis filium neget Cyrrhae?[15]

And this one with his tapering head and long ears which have a way of twitching like those of an ass, who will deny that he is the son of the idiot Cyrrha?

No grand mythology now, but a sneer at the woman who will go with anyone, even a cretin. Bottom may not be an idiot, which seems to be the sense of *morio* here. But another sense of *morio* is 'one kept as a laughing stock, a fool', and this is not a million miles away from Bottom's function in relation to the grand persons of the play. Although Shakespeare gives him the most profound speech in the comedy, 'It shall be called "Bottom's Dream",

because it hath no bottom' (4.1.213-4), his best friend could not call him wise. When the love-crazed Titania applies this word to him at 3.1.140 ('Thou art as wise as thou are beautiful'), it always gets a laugh. I cite Martial's donkey-man not because I am sure—or even think—that Shakespeare read this poem but because it highlights discomforts of a more trivial kind than those broached in the more ancient myths—discomforts arising from perceived social and intellectual disparity. This is also relevant to the comedy of *A Midsummer Night's Dream.* But the myths, with their deeper violence, though they may seem more remote from comedy, really are more deeply pertinent to the major effects of this play.

It is often said that Shakespeare continued to be an adventurous, experimental poet to the very end. *The Tempest,* his last complete play, is a very strange pastoral. A displaced duke and his entourage find themselves in an uncivilized place, where the issues of nature and nurture are debated and all are sorted out, so that they can begin their lives afresh at the end. Thus far I could be describing *As You Like it.* But we are not in Arden or Arcadia. We are on a supposedly Mediterranean island which is removed by more than Atlantic distances from the North African coast, in a place having its own physical laws and lawlessness—almost an alternative, science-fiction world. *The Tempest,* therefore, is transposed pastoral. But long before all this, *A Midsummer Night's Dream* was also, in its own way, a transposed pastoral. The transposition is achieved by darkening, and by placing the trees closer together. In ordinary pastoral there are spaces for the sheep to crop the grass, spaces for reflection, singing-competitions and so on. But the dense, tangled wood—an Athenian labyrinth to answer that of Crete—is frightening. This is the same wood that we find in Milton's *Comus* or in Kenneth Graham's *The Wind in the Willows*—the Wild Wood. Shakespeare has in this early play given us a Nocturnal Pastoral, itself, generically, a strange thing. Even the weather is unpastorally bad. You hear people say 'Oh, we don't have summers now like the summers I remember in my childhood.' *A Midsummer Night's Dream,* if indistinctly remembered, can seem (there are so many flowers in it) to embody this golden world. Yet if we re-enter the play we meet people complaining, exactly as people complain today, about the rotten weather this year.

> Therefore the winds, piping to us in vain,
> As in revenge have sucked up from the sea
> Contagious fogs which, falling in the land,
> Hath every pelting river made so proud
> That they have overborne their continents.
> The ox hath therefore stretched his yoke in vain,
> The ploughman lost his sweat, and the green corn
> Hath rotted ere his youth attained a beard,
> The fold stands empty in the drowned field,
> And crows are fatted with the murrain flock.
> The nine-men's morris is filled up with mud,
> And the quaint mazes in the wanton green
> For lack of tread are indistinguishable

> (2.1.88-100)

Even this speech, which might seem the purest contemporary realism, has its roots in ancient materials. There is a running reference to ancient plague: the plague of Aegina in Ovid (*Metamorphoses,* vii), the plague of Thebes in Seneca's *Oedipus, Medea* and *Hippolytus* (the last of these is of course *Seneca's* 'Phèdre'). But the reader may say, 'Stop! You are reading backwards again'.

In what sense is *A Midsummer Night's Dream* an apotropaic work? Shakespeare has performed an active, suasive euphemism upon ancient myth, and this, I have suggested is in accord with the element of quasi-ritual efficacy still present in comic drama but absent from pure narrative. But presumably in this irreligious, unsuperstitious age we cannot believe that a full *apotrope,* in the old sense, has occurred. We cannot believe that demons have been driven off, because we do not believe in demons. Could the play, nevertheless, have been a full *apotrope* for the original audience, in the 1590s? I am not sure, but I suspect not. The magic of *A Midsummer Night's Dream* is not like the magic of *The Tempest.* Prospero is a serious (highly fashionable) proto-scientific magician, a little like the real Dr Dee, but the magic and fairies of the earlier play are perceptibly becoming picturesque, the stuff of the old tales at which city people now smile. If that is right, this *apotrope* never had the status of an efficacious ritual, actually turning aside malign spirits. Weakening of belief makes inversion of tone easier. It is obviously a simpler matter to vary a mere tale than to alter a known, inherited truth. If people in the seventeenth century had really believed that, once, Apollo pursued Daphne, it would have been harder for Andrew Marvell in 'The Garden' to turn the myth on its head, suggesting that the god, so far from being frustrated when Daphne was turned into a laurel, was actually pursuing her, with dendrophiliac intent, *because* she was turning into a very attractive plant.

It might be thought that Theseus would have been history not myth for Shakespeare because he is in Plutarch. But it is pretty evident that we are not in the historically constrained environment of *Julius Caesar.* Shakespeare knows his audience will have some notion of Theseus as a character but will have few rigid expectations. But all of this, while it facilitates the transformation we see in *A Midsummer Night's Dream,* seems at the same time to deprive it of apotropaic force.

Indeed, we have made it all too easy. While we may not believe in demons, we still believe in what those demons mean. The fears remain. Could Shakespeare have performed a real *apotrope* not at the level of spirits and demons but at the psychological level? Has he turned away fear, not only within his fiction but in the minds and hearts of those who watch?

Within the fiction he has turned aside not only ancient myth but also incipient tragedy. We have the *Hippolytus* of Euripides and Seneca, the *Phèdre* of Racine, but we know, when we see Duke Theseus smiling on Hippolyta, that we are not going to get Shakespeare's—I suspect that it would

have been called—*Hippolytus and Phaedra.* While Shakespeare is carefully *not* writing *Phèdre* the mechanicals are carefully *not* performing *Romeo and Juliet.* 'I believe we must leave the killing out, when all is done,' says Starveling (3.1.12-13) and they all assent. At the same time Shakespeare is concerned not simply that his audience should be happy but that it should experience the more specific pleasure of relief. The myths, though not felt to be literally true, are still full of meaning and that meaning is black. Shakespeare triumphs over horror not only with humour but with a still-ambiguous beauty, a beauty mediated by the pale fire of moonlight, itself somehow half-way between darkness and day. In America at Halloween little children shriek with alarm at the first appearance of witches and goblins and then the shrieks turn to peals of laughter. Most of them (not all) are, I think, psychically strengthened and protected by the process. A successful *apotrope* of fear is performed. We seem now very close indeed to the real *apotrope* of *A Midsummer Night's Dream.*

It is, however, one thing to comfort a person by saying 'It's all right—wake up—the thing you feared was never real at all' and another to say, 'You can deal with your fear if you *pretend* it isn't there—tell a different story to yourself—give the demons smiling faces.' The former kind gives the more complete victory; indeed it is not so much an *apotrope* as a complete exorcism, or abolition. There is no need, in this scheme, to evoke the notion of suasive euphemism, for there is no malign entity to be flatteringly re-described. But the latter scheme—'Give the demons smiling faces'—implicitly allows that the dark forces continue in existence. We turn them aside, keep them off, at least for a while, by pretending in their hearing—as a placating courtesy—that they are benevolent. Which of these is the scheme of *A Midsummer Night's Dream*? Puck's epilogue in which he draws a line under the whole experience by terming it a *mere* dream—'you have *but* slumber'd here' (Epilogue.3)—is the first. The logic is the re-assuring logic of Theseus' 'lunatic/lover' speech, always obscurely annoying to lovers of poetry. But Hippolyta's reply to Theseus, Bottom's 'It hath no bottom' and Demetrius' love for Helena, which, wonderfully, spills over from the enchanted night into the following, civil day, are the other. These powers and their effects are not, after all, so easily erased. Thus a sense of euphemism survives the close of the play. This entails a negotiation— with a long spoon, as it were—between comedy and tragedy, between comedy and myth, a negotiation, that is, between joy and fear, resulting in an *apotrope* of the latter. Just that, *apotrope,* not abolition.

Notes

1. Geoffrey Bullough, *Narrative and Dramatic Sources of Shakespeare,* vol. 1 (London:, 1957), p. 386.

2. Ibid., pp. 387-8.

3. Jan Kott, *Shakespeare Our Contemporary* (2nd edn (London, 1967)), p. 183.

4. Ovid, *Metamorphoses,* vii.194; Seneca, *Hippolytus,* 406-17.

5. *Shakespeare's Scepticism* (Brighton, 1987), p. 44.

6. Reproduced in Marina Warner, *From the Beast to the Blonde* (London, 1994), p. 257.

7. The Greek is tricky. . . . See Sir Richard Jebb's edn (Cambridge, 1885), p. 85.

8. Ed. Stewart Anderson (Cambridge, 1976), p. 49.

9. In *A Midsummer Night's Dream*, 'New Casebooks', ed. Richard Dutton (London, 1996), pp. 198-222, at p. 213. See also D'Orsay W. Pearson, '"Unkinde Theseus': A Study of Renaissance Mythography", *English Literary Renaissance*, 4 (1974), 276-98; M. E. Lamb, '*A Midsummer Night's Dream*: The Myth of Theseus and the Minotaur', *Texas Studies in Literature and Language*, 21 (1979), 478-91; David Ormerod, '*A Midsummer Night's Dream*: The Monster in the Labyrinth', *Shakespeare Studies*, 11 (1978), 39-52; Barbara A. Mowat, '"A Local Habitation and a Name": Shakespeare's text as construct', *Style*, 23 (1989), 335-51.

10. Ibid., p. 205.

11. *Shakespeare Survey 47* (Cambridge, 1994), pp. 139-51.

12. *The Golden Ass of Apuleius*, translated by William Adlington. The Tudor Translations, ed. W. E. Henley, iv (London, 1893), p. 218.

13. Ibid., p. 217.

14. 'Theseus' Shadows in *A Midsummer Night's Dream*', pp. 149 f.

15. Epigrams. vi.39. 'To Cinna'.

FURTHER READING

Criticism

Burns, Edward. "'Two of both kinds makes up four': The Human and the Mortal in *A Midsummer Night's Dream*." In *'Divers toyes mengled': Essays on Medieval and Renaissance Culture*, edited by Michel Bitot in collaboration with Roberta Mullini and Peter Happ, pp. 299-309. Tours: Publication de l'Université François Rabelais, 1996.

Discusses how rhetoric in relation to emotion and theatrical situation distinguishes the mortals and fairies in *A Midsummer Night's Dream*.

Lamb, Mary Ellen. "Taken by the Fairies: Fairy Practices and the Production of Popular Culture in *A Midsummer Night's Dream*." *Shakespeare Quarterly* 51, no. 3 (fall 2000): 277-312.

Argues that there are profound social and political implications inherent in Shakespeare's dramatic representation of the fairies, particularly Puck, in *A Midsummer Night's Dream*.

Lowenthal, David. "The Portrait of Athens in *A Midsummer Night's Dream*." In *Shakespeare's Political Pageant: Essays in Literature and Politics*, edited by Joseph Alulis and Vickie Sullivan, pp. 77-88. Lanham, Md.: Rowman and Littlefield Publishers, 1996.

Demonstrates the ways in which Shakespeare portrayed Athens as the origin of democracy, philosophy, and drama in *A Midsummer Night's Dream*.

Mahood, M. M. "*A Midsummer Night's Dream* as Exorcism." In *Essays on Shakespeare*, edited by T. R. Sharma, pp. 136-49. Meerut, India: Shalabh Book House, 1986.

Examines *A Midsummer Night's Dream* as a wedding play in which the action serves to exorcise the fear and anxiety associated with the act of marriage.

Mikics, David. "Poetry and Politics in *A Midsummer Night's Dream*." *Raritan* 18, no. 2 (fall 1998): 99-119.

Maintains that Shakespeare employed imagination in *A Midsummer Night's Dream* to demonstrate the superiority of the poet dedicated to synthesis and coordination over the willful, dictatorial politician.

Olson, Paul A. "*A Midsummer Night's Dream* and the Meaning of Court Marriage." *ELH* 24, no. 2 (June 1957): 95-119.

Analyzes *A Midsummer Night's Dream* within the context of the Renaissance tradition of the court marriage, noting how the play's structure and masque elements illuminate the traditional conception of marriage.

Taylor, Marion A. "The Allegorical Roles of Alençon and Queen Elizabeth in *A Midsummer Night's Dream*. In *Bottom, Thou Art Translated: Political Allegory in* A Midsummer Night's Dream *and Related Literature*, pp. 131-65. Amsterdam: Rodopi NV, 1973.

Suggests that Shakespeare addressed Elizabethan political issues in *A Midsummer Night's Dream*, employing Bottom and Titania to represent the Duke of Alençon and Queen Elizabeth.

Weller, Barry. "Identity Dis-figured: *A Midsummer Night's Dream*." *The Kenyon Review*, new series, 12, no. 3 (summer 1985): 66-78.

Examines how devices such as metamorphosis, metaphor, and the physical nature of theatrical performance represent issues relating to identity in *A Midsummer Night's Dream*.

Richard II

For further information on the critical and stage history of *Richard II,* see *SC,* Volumes 6, 24, 39, 52, and 58.

INTRODUCTION

Richard II is the first play of Shakespeare's second tetralogy, a series of four plays based on English history. Unlike the other plays in the series, and despite the political and historical nature of the play, *Richard II* contains no battles; rather, it focuses on the more subtle and psychological aspects of political power. In addition to the scrutiny of the play's historical and political issues, other topics of critical examination include the play's structure, as well as the characters of Richard, his rival Bolingbroke, and the often overlooked York. Additionally, *Richard II* has a lengthy stage history, and is still a popular choice for modern productions.

Often viewed as an intense and focused study of Richard's political fall and Bolingbroke's rise to power, *Richard II* is commonly studied in terms of the conflict between these men and the values each represents. Derek Traversi (see Further Reading) sees the play as the downfall of a traditional conception of royalty, represented by Richard, and the uprising of a new political force, represented by Bolingbroke. In Traversi's analysis of the play and its characters, he concludes that Richard betrays his political office, which he has ineffectively filled, and Bolingbroke, not unlike Richard, proves to be divided between political virtue and the quest for power. Like Traversi, C. W. R. D. Moseley (see Further Reading) is interested in Richard's decline. Moseley focuses on Shakespeare's source adaptations as well as his development of the play's characters, demonstrating the ways in which the audience is led toward sympathy for Richard, despite his failures and faults. While critics such as Moseley concentrate on Richard's personal tragedy, John Palmer (1961) complains that too often, the play is seen solely in terms of Richard as a private individual. Palmer maintains that Richard's actions should be viewed within the context of their political and public ramifications as well. Through the course of his examination, Palmer demonstrates how Shakespeare portrayed Richard as an unfit, futile politician who was unable to effectively deal with the group of ambitious politicians surrounding him. Additionally, Palmer assesses the political motivations and performances of Bolingbroke and others, including Gaunt, Mowbray, York, and Aumerle. While York is sometimes dismissed as weak and feeble, some critics have found his role in the play to be significant. Michael F. Kelly (1972) contends that York serves a pivotal role in the thematic and dramatic development of the play. Specifically, Kelly studies York's position as a staunch but intimidated ally of Richard, and York's subsequent transfer of loyalty to Bolingbroke, arguing that York's shift in attitude spurs a similar response within the audience. Like Kelly, James A. Riddell (1979) finds York to be a crucial character in the play in that he serves as a representative of Christian stoicism and magnanimity. In York's dedication to the principles of magnanimity, Riddell asserts, Shakespeare highlights Richard's deficiencies.

For Elizabethan audiences, *Richard II* was rife with political implications, as it dramatized the conflict between the divinely ordained right of monarchs and the question of the legitimacy of the right to usurp. Robert Ornstein (see Further Reading) explores the appeal of the play's treatment of medieval history to Elizabethan audiences, maintaining that Shakespeare's evocation of this medieval past was not done with political intentions, but simply for artistic pleasure. According to Ornstein, Shakespeare portrayed the complexity of this conflict without offering a solution to the problems associated with political loyalty and disloyalty. Taking another approach to the play's treatment of history and politics, Leeds Barroll (1988) studies the relationship between the play and the Earl of Essex rebellion. Barroll documents the commissioning of a performance of the play just prior to the Essex rebellion (1601), and the subsequent punishments suffered by those involved with the production. In conclusion, Barroll claims that *Richard II* was not a potentially dangerous piece of political propaganda; rather, the individuals who commissioned the performance and the players performing it were thought to be dangerous and engaged in possibly treasonous actions. Critics have also focused on the ceremonial, formal language of *Richard II,* and how such language supports the carefully constructed structure of the play. Margaret Shewring (1996) centers her study on the complementary relationship between the play's patterned poetic language and the artfully balanced structure. Shewring explains that in order to achieve this type of focused structure, Shakespeare simplified history as he found it in his sources, omitting much of the factionalism displayed by the nobility.

Like modern critical analyses of *Richard II,* modern productions also often scrutinize the historical elements of the play, as well as the performances of Richard and Bolingbroke. Ace G. Pilkington (1991) assesses the 1979 BBC production of *Richard II,* directed by David Giles and starring Derek Jacobi as Richard. Pilkington notes the ways in which the production may have been improved with greater resources, comments on the production's concern with history, and praises the performance of Jacobi. Michael Feingold (1998) reviews the Theatre for a New

Audience production directed by Ron Daniels, which was paired with a staging of *Richard III*. Feingold finds that the production was less than effective due to this pairing. Feingold also reviews a production of the play staged at the Pearl Theatre, directed by Shepard Sobel, noting that it had a better grasp of the play as poetry than did Daniels's production, although Daniels's staging is described as more vivid. Robert L. King (1995) reviews The National Theatre production, directed by Deborah Warner, which cast a woman as Richard. King praises Fiona Shaw's depiction of Richard and also applauds the production's respectful and illuminating take on Shakespeare's text. Charles Isherwood (2000) reviews Ralph Fiennes's performance as Richard in Jonathan Kent's production of *Richard II* at the Brooklyn Academy of Music. Isherwood finds Fiennes's portrayal of Richard to be somewhat silly and pompous.

CHARACTER STUDIES

John Palmer (essay date 1961)

SOURCE: Palmer, John. "Richard of Bordeaux." In *Political Characters of Shakespeare*, pp. 118-79. London: Macmillan & Co. Ltd., 1961.

[*In the following essay, Palmer challenges critics who view* Richard II *as the tragedy of one man, and explores the fall of Richard as a king and political figure.*]

Shakespeare's *Richard II* is too often read as the tragedy of a private individual. Attention is focused upon Richard's personality and upon elements in his character which would have been just as interesting if he had never been called upon to play the part of a king. We are fascinated by the unfolding of his brilliant, wayward and unstable disposition, his pathetic lapses from bright insolence to grey despair, the facility with which he dramatises his sorrows and takes a wilfully aesthetic pleasure in his own disgrace. The political implications of the play are correspondingly neglected. And this is only natural. In all simplicity—and in essentials no tragedy was ever simpler—*Richard II* is the story of a sensitive, headstrong, clever, foolish man, graceless in prosperity, in calamity gracious. But this simple story has a setting and the setting is high politics. The fact that Richard is a king not only enhances the pathos of his fall, but sets him in a political environment in which the dramatist is not seldom interested for its own sake.

Men living under Elizabeth would think it strange that anyone should need to insist that *Richard II* is a political play. To Shakespeare's audience its political significance was immediate and tremendous. It went to the heart of a burning question. Ministers of State wrote letters about it.

It was years before the censor of books would allow the most famous of its scenes to be printed. It was played on one occasion as a propaganda piece and became the subject of a state trial. Queen Elizabeth, inspecting the Tower records with William Lambarde at Greenwich, was moved to exclaim: 'I am Richard II, know ye not that?' and to add with displeasure that 'this tragedy was played forty times in streets and houses.'

We are shortly to concentrate on the political aspects of the play which are significant for all times and places. First, however, it seems necessary to ask why *Richard II* should have struck Shakespeare's contemporaries so forcibly not merely as a political play, but as by far the most topical political play of the period.

The ordinary Englishman who saw Shakespeare's tragedy in 1595 had lived in peace under a strong Government—and, what is even more important, an incontestably legitimate Government—for over a hundred years. But he still remembered the government of the house of Lancaster, which had been neither strong nor legitimate, and the hideous interim of civil war before Henry of Richmond married Elizabeth of York and provided England with a dynasty acceptable to God and man. In the years following 1595 the whole kingdom was on tenterhooks. Who was to succeed Elizabeth Tudor? The Virgin Queen was as coy of her successor as she had been of the suitors who years before, in despite of the gossips and in the teeth of her physician, might have helped her to solve the problem in the way of nature. Many were called but none was chosen. All that the Englishman held most dear had found a satisfying symbol in the Tudor monarch, ruling by divine right, holding a sacred office, to question whose authority was treason, to trouble whose peace was an impiety. But the Tudor monarch was about to die childless. Was England to fall back into the old disorder, horror, fear and mutiny which had followed the usurpation of Bolingbroke?

Shakespeare chose this moment to write a play in which a legitimate king is deposed and the dreadful consequences of a disputed succession to the crown foretold with eloquence and particularity. This play, moreover, which was topical enough in 1595, when Robert Cecil was invited to witness it at Channon Row, became yet more topical when in 1601 Essex had it ostentatiously performed at the Globe theatre on the eve of his rebellion. This was miching mallecho and meant mischief. There was no treason in the play, as Elizabeth and her Privy Council well knew, but there was undoubted treason in this particular performance. Essex had already cast himself for the part of Bolingbroke and had even gone so far as to accept in 1599 the dedication of a prose history on the reign of Henry IV in which he was addressed in effect as heir apparent to the throne. The prose history was suppressed and the gentleman who procured the performance of Shakespeare's play in 1601 was afterwards hanged. Neither Shakespeare nor his company, however, was molested. Shakespeare was no more responsible for the scandal caused in London by his *Richard II* in 1601 than for the scandal caused in Paris by his *Coriolanus* in 1935. He had written in each case a political play recognisably true of any period for the kind of situation and the type of public persons presented. Elizabeth disliked the play and very properly, according to her lights, regarded its performance before a select body of conspirators as a hanging matter. But for once the right persons were hanged—not the author, nor even the players, but certain members of the audience, who thus paid the penalty, which some might consider excessive, for confusing a work of art with a political manifesto.

Apart from the special circumstances which gave a topical interest to the play in the last years of Elizabeth, Shakespeare's Richard was bound to make a very strong appeal to his contemporaries on more general grounds. Richard of Bordeaux had towards the end of the sixteenth century become a legendary figure. His deposition had acquired a mystical significance. For over two centuries he had stood to poets and historians, both in England and in France, for a supreme example of that tragical fall of princes which appealed so strongly to the imagination and conscience of the post-mediaeval world. To the legitimists he was a martyr and his enforced abdication a sacrilege. To the Lancastrians his removal was a necessary act of providence. To all alike he was a tragic symbol of the instability of human fortune. Those who took the mystical view of his fall did not hesitate to compare his passion with that of Christ. Even those who, in deference to the house of Lancaster, affected to regard his deposition as a salutary act of state, were deeply affected by this saddest of all stories of the deaths of kings and tended to regard its protagonists as blind agents of a divine purpose rather than conscious masters of the event. Bolingbroke and Richard, in the Tudor imagination, played their parts as in a mystery, Richard accepting his humiliation as a cup that might not pass away and Bolingbroke, unconscious instrument in bringing about a second fall of man, achieving his triumph as a thing pre-ordained. This sacramental approach to the tragedy, which Shakespeare inherited and to which he gave exquisite humanity in the person of Richard, was an essential element in its contemporary appeal.[1]

To most of Shakespeare's countrymen this contemporary aspect of the play is still alive. The English, in dealing faithfully with their kings for over a thousand years of history, have contrived to retain a mystical respect for the royal office without in any way forgoing their right of judgment on the royal person. The waters of the rough rude sea of English politics have washed the balm from half a dozen anointed kings without in any way detracting from the consecration of their successors. God save the King—but God help him if his subjects should find him troublesome. When the occasion arises—and it has arisen no less than four times since Richard died at Pomfret—the English people can always be trusted to demonstrate that a sincere reverence for monarchy is compatible with a distinctly uncivil treatment of the monarch. Nothing in fact so signally illustrates the force of English sentiment for royalty than its successful survival of so many royal

persons who have left their country for their country's good. The emotions aroused in an Elizabethan by the enacted deposition of a king have outlived two revolutions and the importation of two foreign princes.

The central situation in Shakespeare's play thus retains much of its original appeal. But even if this were not the case, the political interest of the play and its relevance to the public life of our own or of any time would be scarcely affected. For Shakespeare's handling of the sacramental aspect of royalty is only one component of his tragedy. His main purpose is to exhibit in Richard the qualities which unfitted him to rule, to show his exquisite futility in dealing with public affairs, to present a playboy politician coping ineffectually with men seriously intent on the business of getting what they want, to contrast the man of imagination who lives unto himself with men of the world who adapt themselves to the event. A play with such a theme is necessarily a political play. *Richard II,* for all its lyrical quality, is concerned with public affairs and with the kind of men who in every generation delude themselves into the belief that they are making history. Over against Richard, whose personal disaster touches the heart of the spectator, Shakespeare has set in juxtaposition a group of politicians and an analysis of political events which claim the attention no less forcibly.

With these preliminary observations in mind let us consider for a moment the opening scene of the tragedy.

Henry, surnamed Bolingbroke, Duke of Hereford and son to John of Gaunt, has publicly accused of high treason no less a person than Thomas Mowbray, Duke of Norfolk. Richard summons them to a hearing. The two men decline to be reconciled and the King is reluctantly obliged to make arrangements for a trial by battle. Such is the bare outline of this short scene of some two hundred lines. It serves its dramatic purpose well enough if we see in it no more than a robustious squabble between two angry noblemen who refuse to be pacified by their sovereign. The essential ingredients of this short scene are crystal clear on the surface—a king who is plainly not master in his own house; two haughty subjects who huff it in the royal presence, professing a reverence for Majesty which nevertheless stops short of obedience; a suggestion that this Richard, who is not sufficiently sure of himself to call his troublesome subjects to order, is quick to see through their assurances of respect; a promise of exciting and turbulent events shortly to follow. Here, surely, is matter enough to fill the first two hundred lines of any play.

But there is more to it than that. Look a little more closely at the political environment into which the dramatist, with his customary abrupt felicity, introduces the hero of his tragedy.

Bolingbroke accuses Mowbray of complicity in the murder of the Duke of Gloucester. He knows perfectly well, however, that Richard himself is by many held responsible for Gloucester's death. In accusing Mowbray, Bolingbroke is covertly attacking the King's government. He is playing the party game of His Majesty's Opposition, using the gestures of the period. Mowbray, of course, knows what Bolingbroke is driving at. So does everybody else. But nobody would think of admitting it. The real issues are not even mentioned. Bolingbroke, attacking the King, accuses his opponent of treason to the King, Mowbray, who is of the King's party and who, if he did not murder Gloucester himself, was at least an accessory to the crime by negligence, affects to be defending himself against a merely personal charge. All that full-blooded talk by Bolingbroke about the devotion of a subject's love and by Mowbray about his spotless reputation is no more than the impassioned rhetoric of two rival politicians assuming in public the attitudes required of them by the situation. The other persons present are equally aware of the facts, but they, too, are expected to assume that Bolingbroke and Mowbray really mean what they say. These are two loyal gentlemen and their good faith must in decency be accepted. Each of them is lying and everyone present knows that they are lying, but each, according to the rules of the game, must be believed. The scene thus reveals itself on examination to be a notably accurate presentation of a familiar—and indeed typical—situation in public life, in which the outward professions of the persons concerned bear little or no relation to their real purposes and passions.

Mowbray has the better platform manner. It has a certain dignity:

> A jewel in a ten-times-barr'd-up chest
> Is a bold spirit in a loyal breast.
> Mine honour is my life; both grow in one;
> Take honour from me, and my life is done.

Bolingbroke is less fruitily impassioned, but no less ready to maintain with conviction that his actions are wholly determined by the loftiest motives. He calls on heaven to be the record of his speech. His divine soul is ready to answer in heaven for the truth and justice of his cause.

Shakespeare here presents the normal behaviour of notable persons discussing a political or diplomatic issue in public. The uninstructed onlooker enjoys the quarrel for its own sake. But the spectator who knows that all this high-and-mighty bickering has no more bearing on the facts of the dispute than the mutual recriminations of rival candidates for a parliamentary seat or the notes exchanged between foreign ministers in a time of international crisis, has, in addition to his enjoyment of the superficial cut-and-thrust of the formal encounter, the extra pleasure of understanding what it is all about. He sees through the pretences of the performers to the real subject matter of the performance.

Shakespeare leaves no doubt in the mind of an alert and intelligent spectator as to the facts of the dispute, but he does not rely on the ability of his audience to grasp them at a first performance. He does not, in fact, let us know immediately, if we did not know it before, that Richard was himself implicated in Gloucester's death. He lets *that* cat out of the bag at a later stage. Shakespeare has the fact well in mind, but it was not essential for him to stress it in the opening scene, where our attention is rightly concentrated on the more superficial aspects of the quarrel and on Richard's manifest inability to quash it. The subtler political implications of the incident are unfolded progressively. Shakespeare was too skilful a dramatist to demand the attention of his audience for more than one important thing at a time.

There is another aspect of this first scene which can only be fully appreciated at a later stage. Its main dramatic purpose is to show Richard facing a political situation with which he is unable to cope successfully. Towards the end of the play we are to see Bolingbroke confronted with a situation precisely similar at all points. We shall then see the usurper dealing promptly and effectively with this mediaeval equivalent of a cabinet crisis. He calls his refractory noblemen to order and successfully handles in five minutes an incident such as had cost Richard his throne.

There is yet another level on which this first simple episode of the play may be appreciated. On the political facts, almost every word uttered by Bolingbroke and Mowbray is a wilful misrepresentation. They nevertheless play their parts with complete conviction and everybody present accepts their posturing as the outcome of a genuine passion for truth and justice. This raises a point which crops up repeatedly in Shakespeare's political plays: how far does he deliberately satirise in his politicians the inconsistency of their professions with their performance? Mowbray is presented as a fine figure of a man and we shall shortly be quoting with admiration some of the moving things he has to say as a patriotic English gentleman. Did Shakespeare intend thereby to emphasise only the more effectively that he was a lamentable impostor?

It is on this third level of appreciation that Shakespeare provides us with surprising examples in many plays of his effortless grasp of the realities of political life. Mowbray and Bolingbroke are not presented as consciously fraudulent persons. They play the game according to the rules of their time and class. Mowbray loves his country, is loyal to the King and entirely convinced of his own honesty. Bolingbroke no less sincerely sees himself as a faithful public servant. He is morally sure of himself and prepared to hazard his life in defence of an honourable cause. Both are equally mistaken in themselves; and the facts, as presented by the dramatist, are not in accord with the pretensions of either party. But no satire is intended. The two men are presented without malice. They are political persons and that is how political persons behave.

The spectator's interest in the scene is naturally concentrated on the part played by Richard himself. The King has little to say, but every word is significant. He promises himself a bad quarter of an hour. The appeal is 'boisterous' and the appellants will be difficult to manage:

High-stomach'd are they both, and full of ire,
In rage deaf as the sea, hasty as fire.

He accepts the rules of the game and plays it with dignity. To Mowbray, who asks leave to present his case against a kinsman of the King, Richard gravely rejoins:

Now, by my sceptre's awe I make a vow,
Such neighbour nearness to our sacred blood
Should nothing privilege him, nor partialise
The unstooping firmness of my upright soul:
He is our subject, Mowbray; so art thou:
Free speech and fearless I do thee allow.[2]

After listening patiently to the accuser and the accused, he attempts with an assumption of playful good humour to reconcile the parties:

Forget, forgive; conclude and be agreed;
Our doctors say this is no month to bleed.

He appeals personally to Mowbray:

RICHARD:

Rage must be withstood:
Give me his gage: lions make leopards tame.

MOWBRAY:

Yea, but not change his spots:

Neither will consent to a peace and Richard finally accepts the inevitable. He closes the proceedings with a set speech in which the formal decencies of a false situation are solemnly maintained:

We were not born to sue, but to command:
Which since we cannot do to make you friends,
Be ready, as your lives shall answer it,
At Coventry, upon Saint Lambert's day:
There shall your swords and lances arbitrate
The swelling difference of your settled hate:
Since we cannot atone you, we shall see
Justice design the victor's chivalry.

Shakespeare makes it very plain that Richard is fully alive to all the political implications of the situation. In his first words to the contending parties he drily dismisses their professions of respect:

BOLINGBROKE:

Many years of happy days befal
My gracious sovereign, my most loving liege!

MOWBRAY:

Each day still better other's happiness;
Until the heavens, envying earth's good hap,
Add an immortal title to your crown!

RICHARD:

We thank you both: yet one but flatters us,
As well appeareth by the cause you come;
Namely, to appeal each other of high treason.

The reproof is shrewd and neatly turned. Richard's position requires him to accept the pleadings of the parties. But he is not going to let anyone imagine that he attaches the slightest value to their professions and, in asking Bolingbroke to state his case, he covertly warns his cousin to remember that, in attacking Mowbray, he is sailing dangerously near the wind:

What doth our cousin lay to Mowbray's charge?
It must be great that can inherit us
So much as of a thought of ill in him.

Bolingbroke prefers his charges and concludes with a vigorously complacent picture of himself as appointed by heaven to chastise an injurious villain by whose contriving his uncle Gloucester had sluiced out his innocent soul through streams of blood:

Which blood, like sacrificing Abel's, cries,
Even from the tongueless caverns of the earth,
To me for justice and rough chastisement;
And, by the glorious worth of my descent,
This arm shall do it, or this life be spent.

Richard is thereby provoked to a further disclosure of his private mind. Bolingbroke is professing his loyalty, but he is in fact challenging the King's man. In a bitter, penetrating aside Richard exclaims:

How high a pitch his resolution soars!

He already divines in Bolingbroke an ambition which reaches instinctively beyond its immediate purpose, and, in assuring Mowbray that he may fearlessly answer the charges brought against him, Richard puts the predestined usurper in his place with a crushing exactitude:

Mowbray, impartial are our eyes and ears:
Were he my brother, nay, my kingdom's heir,—
As he is but my father's brother's son—
Now, by my sceptre's awe I make a vow,
Such neighbour nearness to our sacred blood
Should nothing privilege him.

This king is already showing qualities of mind that put him in a different class from the noble persons surrounding him. He is contemptuous of the game which he is required to play, but plays it becomingly and with a sidelong smile. He may blunder fatally in his handling of persons and events, but there is never any doubt of his intelligence. It is equally clear from the outset that he has the courage of his fitful genius. He sees through these proud, turbulent and practical men of affairs, and he is not afraid to let them know it.

Mowbray's answer to the charges brought against him by Bolingbroke clearly illuminates the harsh political background against which the tragedy of Richard is to be unfolded. Mowbray has been accused of peculation and murder. He admits to having pocketed a quarter of the sum which was earmarked to pay the King's soldiers at Calais, but this, he pleads, was only to recoup himself for expenses incurred on a previous account. Let that pass. On the accusation of murder, he seems unnecessarily candid—until we realise that he is merely stating facts that were common knowledge:

> For Gloucester's death,
> I slew him not; but to mine own disgrace
> Neglected my sworn duty in that case.
> For you, my noble lord of Lancaster,
> The honourable father to my foe,
> Once did I lay an ambush for your life,
> A trespass that doth vex my grievèd soul;
> But ere I last receiv'd the sacrament
> I did confess it, and exactly begg'd
> Your grace's pardon, and I hope I had it.

What could be fairer than that? Mowbray's ingenuous apology is a fair measure of the accepted political standards of the time. He was not guilty of Gloucester's murder, he merely did nothing to prevent it. He had tried to murder Gaunt, but he had apologised to the party concerned and hoped that the incident was closed. It is necessary to keep these facts in mind if we are fairly to judge Richard's less amiable reactions to some of the later speeches and to the conduct in general of his noble kinsmen.

The second scene of the play, which is devoted to a conversation between John of Gaunt and the Duchess of Gloucester, has no other purpose than to underline the political implications of the first. The widowed Duchess urges Gaunt to exact retribution for her husband's death. She belongs to that long line of noble dames used by Shakespeare in his political plays to remind the spectator that there are human, and even moral, considerations which should not be altogether ignored in public life. Gaunt has decided to let the matter rest and, in defending his decision, explicitly insists that Richard himself was a party to the crime:

> But since correction lieth in those hands
> Which made the fault that we cannot correct,
> Put we our quarrel to the will of heaven.
> God's is the quarrel; for God's substitute,
> His deputy anointed in His sight,
> Hath caused his death; the which if wrongfully,
> Let heaven revenge; for I may never lift
> An angry arm against His minister.

The Duchess is unconvinced:

> Call it not patience, Gaunt; it is despair:
> In suffering thus thy brother to be slaughter'd,
> Thou showest the naked pathway to thy life,
> Teaching stern murder how to butcher thee:
> That which in mean men we intitle patience
> Is pale cold cowardice in noble breasts.

The political wisdom of the bastard feudalism of fourteenth-century England could not be more lucidly expressed.

The scene between Gaunt and the Duchess, which discloses the political realities of the dispute between Mowbray and Bolingbroke, is followed by the famous scene in which we are invited to enjoy for its own sake the pagentry of the royal lists at Conventry, where these impressive champions, plated in habiliments of war, commit their several causes to heaven and proceed with high solemnity to face the ordeal by battle. It is a gallant show and Shakespeare is too good a dramatist to spoil its effect by insisting unseasonably that it is also, in effect, an amusingly veracious study in the public deportment of men in high places. Richard ceremoniously invites the champions to declare their business. The defendant in armour and the appellant in armour respond according to the protocol. Each professes his truth and nobility of purpose. Each takes a devoted leave of his sovereign. Mowbray still has the better platform manner:

> However God or fortune cast my lot,
> There lives or dies, true to King Richard's throne,
> A loyal, just, and upright gentleman:
> Never did captive with a freer heart
> Cast off his chains of bondage and embrace
> His golden uncontroll'd enfranchisement,
> More than my dancing soul doth celebrate
> This feast of battle with mine adversary.
> Most mighty liege, and my companion peers,
> Take from my mouth the wish of happy years.
> As gentle and as jocund as to jest,
> Go I to fight; truth has a quiet breast.

The more vigilant spectator may detect a subtle difference in Richard's addresses to the two men. Surely there is a touch of irony in his words to Bolingbroke:

> Cousin of Hereford, as thy cause is right,
> So be thy fortune in this royal fight;

and a touch of affectionate approval in his valediction to Mowbray:

> Farewell, my lord; securely I espy
> Virtue with valour couchèd in thine eye.

But these are hints to the wary. The simple onlooker is absorbed by the knightly courtesy of it all and is as eager for the fight as the champions themselves.

Then comes the grand surprise. The charge is sounded. But stay, the King has thrown his warder down! Defendant and appellant are bidden to lay aside their spears and Richard withdraws with his council while the champions disarm. Presently he emerges and announces his decision. The King, to save his peace, banishes them both—Bolingbroke for ten years and Mowbray for life:

> Draw near,
> And list what with our council we have done.
> For that our kingdom's earth should not be soil'd
> With that dear blood which it hath fosterèd;
> And for our eyes do hate the dire aspect
> Of civil wounds plough'd up with neighbours' swords;
> And for we think the eagle-wingèd pride
> Of sky-aspiring and ambitious thoughts,
> With rival-hating envy, set on you

To wake our peace, which in our country's cradle
Draws the sweet infant breath of gentle sleep;
. . . . .
Therefore, we banish you our territories.

It is a veritable sensation in court.

It should be noted that the King's decision is no sudden freak of temperament but a considered act of state. Richard is acting with the approval of his council and Gaunt himself is a consenting party to the arrangement. When the old man laments that he may not live to see his banished heir again, Richard pertinently reminds him:

Thy son is banish'd upon good advice,
Whereto thy tongue a party-verdict gave.

Richard's interruption of the ordeal by battle at the eleventh hour has often been cited as evidence of his impulsive disposition. But the scene has a greater and very different significance if we suppose that Richard had decided beforehand to quash the proceedings. For him the whole elaborate to-do, with its heralds and trumpets, solemn appeals to heaven, ceremonious farewells and heroic attitudes, was matter for a May morning. He knows that these doughty champions are inflating themselves to no purpose. The actor playing Richard should watch them with a twinkle, impishly awaiting the moment when he will knock the bottom out of all these political high jinks. There is a merry side to the puerility of Richard, the boy-king who would never grow up. The whole scene is in the nature of a practical joke.

We should like to have been present at the cabinet meeting which found so discreet a remedy for a situation which was as embarrassing for Gaunt, leader of the King's opposition, as for the King, leader of his own government. If Mowbray had killed Bolingbroke, Gaunt would have lost his son. If Bolingbroke had killed Mowbray, the King would have lost a loyal servant. All the sleeping dogs, which it is the whole art of politics to let lie, would in either case have been set barking to the discomfiture of both parties. Shakespeare must have been sorely tempted to show us the King and his ministers discussing at length the real issues of the dispute. But he chose to concentrate upon his grand surprise of the interrupted combat and to fix the interest of his public on the gorgeous preliminaries of the tournament. He preferred to present Mowbray and Bolingbroke to the simple spectator as *bona fide* champions and to reveal them to the more judicious as figures of fun only at the eleventh hour.

The dramatist, in the final result, has it both ways—the tournament for what it is worth and, for those who look below the surface, the political comedy as well. It is the reward of an artist who sees things as they are that his rounded achievement defies all the categories. It can be enjoyed as a true and faithful presentment of men and things, as an emotional experience and as an act of judgment. The general effect is a combination of all three.

Shakespeare, having sprung his grand surprise on the audience in the lists at Coventry, instinctively refrains from bringing his champions to earth. From silver trumpets to brass tacks would have been too steep a fall. Bolingbroke and Mowbray maintain their heraldic attitudes to the last. Mowbray in particular is permitted to make a dignified and sincerely affecting retirement from public life:

The language I have learn'd these forty years,
My native English, now I must forgo:
And now my tongue's use is to me no more
Than an unstr4ngèd viol or a harp,
Or like a cunning instrument cased up,
Or, being open, put into his hands
That knows no touch to tune the harmony.

I am too old to fawn upon a nurse,
Too far in years to be a pupil now:
What is thy sentence then but speechless death,
Which robs my tongue from breathing native breath?

He is to the last a faithful subject. He had every right to protest that his sentence was unjust. Richard would undoubtedly have preferred to banish Bolingbroke for life and Mowbray for ten years. But he had been obliged to secure Gaunt's consent to the arrangement and Mowbray had to be sacrificed to the opposition. Mowbray understands and accepts the situation. He cannot explicitly defend himself without exposing the King to further embarrassment. He submits loyally to the decision, though he cannot refrain from suggesting that it was unmerited:

A heavy sentence, my most sovereign liege,
And all unlook'd for from your highness' mouth:
A dearer merit, not so deep a maim
As to be cast forth in the common air,
Have I deservèd at your highness' hands.

Bolingbroke presses his case to the end:

Confess thy treasons ere thou fly the realm;
Since thou hast far to go, bear not along
The clogging burthen of a guilty soul.

But Mowbray is not to be pricked, even at this bitter moment, into making things difficult for his master and confines himself to warning Richard against his enemy:

No, Bolingbroke, if ever I were traitor,
My name be blotted from the book of life,
And I from heaven banish'd as from hence!
But what thou art, God, thou, and I do know;
And all too soon, I fear, the king shall rue.

One cannot help reflecting that, if Richard, for his time of need, had retained by his side so devoted a servant as Thomas Mowbray, Bolingbroke would less easily have compassed his designs.[3]

Bolingbroke's manner of accepting the King's award is highly characteristic. He persists, as we have just noted, in re-affirming the justice of his cause and receives his sentence with a forced humility in which there lurks an element of sly defiance:

> Your will be done: this must my comfort be,
> That sun that warms you here shall shine on me;
> And those his golden beams to you here lent
> Shall point on me and gild my banishment.

You will look in vain, however, for any suggestion that Bolingbroke yet aims higher than a subject should. Richard is alive to his ambition; Mowbray warns the King that he is dangerous. But Bolingbroke gives no sign of his purpose—and for an excellent reason. He is that most dangerous of all climbing politicians, the man who will go further than his rivals because he never allows himself to know where he is going. Every step in his progress towards the throne is dictated by circumstances and he never permits himself to have a purpose till it is more than half fulfilled. From first to last his friends and enemies alike are always more clearly aware of his intentions than the man himself.

This is especially true of Richard, who divines in Bolingbroke the secret, unsleeping treachery of one who plays instinctively for his own hand. Richard's distrust is covertly conveyed in the present scene by his suddenly requiring both parties to swear upon his royal sword that they will not conspire against him in exile. The admonition, administered to Mowbray as well as to Bolingbroke, is in fact addressed to Bolingbroke alone:

> You never shall, so help you truth and God!
> Embrace each other's love in banishment;
> Nor never look upon each other's face;
> Nor never write, regreet, nor reconcile
> This louring tempest of your home-bred hate:
> Nor never by advisèd purpose meet
> To plot, contrive, or complot any ill
> 'Gainst us, our state, our subjects, or our land.

Bolingbroke swears the oath and Richard appears to be satisfied. He even indulges his essential good nature by remitting four years of Bolingbroke's sentence out of consideration for the sorrowing Gaunt. Bolingbroke's comment on Richard's mercy is to observe how fine a thing it is to be an absolute monarch:

> How long a time lies in one little word!
> Four lagging winters and four wanton springs
> End in a word: such is the breath of kings.

Bolingbroke maintains his enigmatic silence even after Richard has departed. His friends press round him with expressions of condolence, but he is not to be drawn into speech. Gaunt is moved to protest against his almost inhuman reticence:

> O! to what purpose dost thou hoard thy words,
> That thou return'st no greeting to thy friends?

Bolingbroke's answer is to play for sympathy as an unhappy man condemned to exile. Gaunt is thereby diverted into uttering words of comfort, exquisitely moving but addressed, we feel, to the wrong person:

> All places that the eye of heaven visits
> Are to a wise man ports and happy havens.
> Teach thy necessity to reason thus;
> There is no virtue like necessity.
>
> Suppose the singing birds musicians,
> The grass whereon thou tread'st the presence strew'd,
> The flowers fair ladies, and thy steps no more
> Than a delightful measure or a dance.

It is difficult to imagine Bolingbroke consoling himself with the accents of divine philosophy or to picture him as taking any pleasure in singing-birds. He quits the stage on a political peroration:

> Where'er I wander, boast of this I can,
> Though banish'd, yet a trueborn Englishman.

So for a moment we take leave of Henry, surnamed Bolingbroke, Duke of Hereford and son to John of Gaunt. During his temporary absence from the scene let us look a little more closely into his character and place in the tragedy.

There are two apparently opposite views of Bolingbroke's conduct in this first of the three plays in which he figures. But the opposition is superficial and it disappears as we begin to grasp his fundamental qualities. Coleridge, significantly enough, puts forward now one and now the other, without seeming to be in any way aware of their inconsistency.

Critics who keep exclusively to the first view describe Bolingbroke as a long-headed conspirator, consciously bent on obtaining the crown from the outset, concealing a fixed purpose under a show of false humility, deliberately advancing step by step to the achievement of his purpose. Coleridge, when he writes of the 'preconcertedness of Bolingbroke's scheme' and the 'decorous and courtly checking of his anger in subservience to a predetermined plan' appears to favour this interpretation. Hazlitt, too, comes very near it when he describes Bolingbroke as 'seeing his advantage afar-off, but only seizing on it when he has it within his reach, humble, crafty, bold and aspiring, encroaching by regular but slow degrees.'

Critics who whole-heartedly espouse the second view see in Bolingbroke a man who, in the words of Dr. Dover Wilson, 'appears to be borne upward by a power beyond his volition.' According to this reading of the character there is no premeditation in the conduct of Bolingbroke, no indication of a deep design. He takes in Shakespeare's tragedy the part assigned to him in the chronicles which saw in the deposition of Richard something more than a story of successful ambition at the expense of an unsuccessful king. It is a view of Bolingbroke in relation to Richard which comes from Holinshed himself, who wrote: 'In this dejecting of the one and advancing of the other,

Lorne Kennedy as Aumerle, Eric Donkin as York, Craig Dudley as Bolingbroke, Stephen Russell as King Richard, Ted Follows as Northumberland, and Richard Hardacre as Fitzwater in Act IV, scene i of the 1979 Stratford Festival production of Richard II.

the providence of God is to be respected and his secret will to be wondered at.'

Shakespeare has created in Bolingbroke a character which fits perfectly into this mystical view of the tragedy, but which can at the same time be enjoyed as faithfully portraying a political opportunist in almost any period or environment. Shakespeare's Bolingbroke, in following his fortune, instinctively adapts himself to the moment. His intentions remain obscure, even to himself, till they are in effect fulfilled. He thus conveys the impression that he is just as much the victim of necessity as master of the event, and Coleridge, who diagnoses premediation, can without essentially contradicting himself also describe him as 'scarcely daring to look at his own views or to acknowledge them as designs.'

For confirmation of a reading in which instinctive premediation is reconciled with an equally instinctive yielding to circumstance we have the final word of Bolingbroke himself. It is the word of a dying king. He looks back over the troubled years of his reign and, though pregnantly

conscious of the 'indirect crook'd ways, whereby he had achieved the crown, he nevertheless meditates on the blindness with which he once pursued his infant fortune, and he goes on to state explicitly that he had acted throughout undesignedly, as a man thrust on by force of circumstance:

> Though then, God knows, I had no such intent,
> But that necessity so bowed the state
> That I and greatness were compell'd to kiss.[4]

The noblemen who assisted Bolingbroke to win the crown also take this view. More than once, telling the story in retrospect, they comment on the way in which circumstances conspired to smooth his way to the throne, so that at the last he only needed to accept what destiny had thrust into his hands. Worcester, for example, meeting the King years later at Shrewsbury, describes the whole process as it struck the men who had contributed to the event:

> You swore to us,
> And you did swear that oath at Doncaster,
> That you did nothing purpose 'gainst the state;
> Nor claim no further than your new-fall'n right,

The seat of Gaunt, dukedom of Lancaster:
To this we swore our aid. But in short space
It rain'd down fortune, showering on your head;
And such a flood of greatness fell on you,
What with our help, what with the absent king,
What with the injuries of a wanton time,
The seeming sufferances that you had borne,
And the contrarious winds that held the king
So long in his unlucky Irish wars,
That all in England did repute him dead:
And from this swarm of fair advantages
You took occasion to be quickly woo'd
To grip the general sway into your hand.

This reading of Bolingbroke is consistent with all that we have yet seen of him in the first Act of *Richard II*. It will become even more explicit as we follow him through the play.

It is Shakespeare's way to concentrate on one thing at a time. The stage is now clear for a firm handling of the political issues which lay behind the King's sentence of exile.[5] The hints already conveyed that Richard divines the character and intentions of Bolingbroke more clearly than Bolingbroke himself now blossom into direct and vivid statement. Richard, King by divine right, has noted in his rival the arts whereby a man may aspire to rule by popular favour. He has observed Bolingbroke's courtship of the common people:

How he did seem to dive into their hearts
With humble and familiar courtesy.
What reverence he did throw away on slaves,
Wooing poor craftsmen with the craft of smiles
And patient underbearing of his fortune.

Off goes his bonnet to an oyster-wench;
A brace of draymen bid God speed him well
And had the tribute of his supple knee,
With 'Thanks, my countrymen, my loving friends';
As were our England in reversion his,
And he our subjects' next degree in hope.

Unfortunately Richard's perceptions have little relation to his conduct. Bolingbroke is dangerous, but Richard, in the Elizabethan sense, is secure. He anatomises in Bolingbroke the qualities that crave wary walking, but carelessly embarks upon a career which is to cost him his life and crown. The Irish are in rebellion. He will cross the sea in person to suppress them, leaving his kingdom open to invasion and his subjects to foot the bill:

We will ourself in person to this war:
And, for our coffers with too great a court
And liberal largess are grown somewhat light,
We are enforced to farm our royal realm;
The revenue whereof shall furnish us
For our affairs in hand: if that come short,
Our substitutes at home shall have blank charters;
Whereto, when they shall know what men are rich,
They shall subscribe them for large sums of gold,
And send them after to supply our wants.

This is bad enough, but worse is to follow. News is brought that John of Gaunt is sick. Richard blithely embraces the occasion:

Now put it, God, in the physician's mind
To help him to his grave immediately!
The lining of his coffers shall make coats
To deck our soldiers for these Irish wars.
Come, gentlemen, let's all go visit him:
Pray God we may make haste, and come too late!

Richard's treatment of the dying Gaunt is one of the prime causes of his downfall. It is also the least amiable episode of his career. Shakespeare, writing the famous scene in which Gaunt with his dying breath celebrates the glories of England, tarnished by an unworthy king, seems deliberately bent on setting us against his hero. Why this exaltation of Gaunt at Richard's expense? No character in Shakespeare has a finer end. The prologue is rich in promise:

O, but they say the tongues of dying men
Enforce attention like deep harmony.

The setting sun, and music at the close,
As the last taste of sweets, is sweetest last;

and the promise is nobly fulfilled in lines quoted by generations of Englishmen, that can never be worn threadbare:

This royal throne of kings, this scepter'd isle,
This earth of majesty, this seat of Mars,
This other Eden, demi-paradise,
This fortress built by Nature for herself
Against infection and the hand of war,
This happy breed of men, this little world,
This precious stone set in the silver sea,
Which serves it in the office of a wall,
Or as a moat defensive to a house,
Against the envy of less happier lands,
This blessèd plot, this earth, this realm, this England,
This nurse, this teeming womb of royal kings,

This land of such dear souls, this dear, dear land,
Dear for her reputation through the world,
Is now leased out,—I die pronouncing it,—
Like to a tenement or pelting farm:
England, bound in with the triumphant sea,
Whose rocky shore beats back the envious siege
Of watery Neptune, is now bound in with shame,
With inky blots and rotten parchment bonds:
That England, that was wont to conquer others,
Hath made a shameful conquest of itself.

For this prophet, new-inspired, Richard has neither respect nor mercy. Clearly he is deeply moved by the speech, but that only makes him all the more savage in retort. He rounds on the sick man in a flash of temper:

And thou a lunatic lean-witted fool,
Presuming on an ague's privilege,
Dar'st with thy frozen admonition
Make pale our cheek, chasing the royal blood

With fury from his native residence.
Now, by my seat's right royal majesty,
Wert thou not brother to great Edward's son,
This tongue that runs so roundly in thy head
Should run thy head from thy unreverent shoulders.

It may be urged in extenuation that Richard had small reason to spare the father of Bolingbroke. When York protests:

I do beseech your majesty, impute his words
To wayward sickliness and age in him:
He loves you, on my life, and holds you dear
As Harry, Duke of Hereford, were he here:

Richard retorts with a touch of shrill hysteria:

Right, you say true: as Hereford's love, so his;
As theirs, so mine; and all be as it is.

There is, however, neither haste nor temper to excuse his reception of the news, a minute or so later, that Gaunt is dead. His comment is touched with feeling for the common lot of man:

The ripest fruit first falls, and so doth he;
His time is spent, our pilgrimage must be.
So much for that;

but there is no yielding on the personal issue. Gaunt is dead. *So much for that*—and Richard at once announces that he will seize his uncle's plate, coin and revenues.

Critics who insist that Shakespeare has an ethical purpose in his tragedies tend to regard this scene, in which Richard shows us the worst of his character, as a deliberate preparation for the retribution which is to follow. But the world in which Shakespeare's characters move is not a moral gymnasium. It is a world in which men and women reveal their hearts and minds, engage our sympathy and evoke our perpetual wonder at the intricate working of simple or subtle souls. The dramatist, in this present instance, while he uncompromisingly exposes the flaws in Richard's character which lie at the heart of his tragic failure, is not bringing him to judgment, but presenting him with a compassionate understanding of his frailty. Richard does not forfeit our sympathy. We feel that his rash, fierce blaze of riot cannot last and this mitigates our censure. Nor is his conduct altogether unjustified. Richard saw in this Galahad of the sceptred isle a political enemy masquerading as a patriot, a cantankerous nobleman whose son had already made mischief in the land and was to make more. Richard's behaviour, heartless and unseasonable enough in all conscience, is that of a spoiled child of fortune, as he then was, resenting a rebuke peculiarly exasperating in that it was, in the specific instance, deserved but, from such a man, misplaced.

The question still remains: why does Shakespeare weight the scales so heavily against Richard in this scene? Why give to Gaunt, at the very moment when Richard is to behave so badly, the finest speech in the play? Why did Shakespeare permit himself an outburst of lyrical ecstasy whereby he risked putting his hero irretrievably in the shade and thus killing his play dead in the first Act?

The answer is to be found in the mood and structure of the tragedy. Gaunt, in his dying speech, is but one of many voices to which a single tune is given: the voice of Mowbray, mourning his exile from England; the voice of Gaunt, declaring his love of England; the voice of Richard, saluting with his hand the dear earth of England. To all these voices is given in turn the chorus-theme which serves as background to the political figures of the story. In every one of Shakespeare's political plays we feel the constant presence of a country and a people. In *Richard II* it assumes a lyrical form, flowering through the texture of the verse on all possible occasions. Shakespeare, coming to Gaunt on his deathbed, saw a magnificent opportunity and seized it without misgiving. He was confident, if he gave the matter a conscious thought, that our sympathy with Richard would survive this splendid interlude and he even contrived that it should reveal the character of his hero to better effect than the more cautious approach which common prudence would have dictated to a journeyman playwright.

The political implications of Richard's decision to seize his uncle's property have now to be considered. But here we must pause to make the acquaintance of a new character, the most important person in the play after Richard and Bolingbroke, and one of the most interesting in the whole gallery of Shakespeare's political portraits.

Edmund of Langley, Duke of York, belongs to a type of politician which has made more English history in the bulk than any other. He is a public figure not from choice but by nativity. Shakespeare found him in the chronicles in the shape of a man who loved hunting and good cheer and avoided the council chamber—just the kind of person, in fact, to provide a contrast in temperament with Richard and in ability with Bolingbroke. York has no refinement of understanding and no political ambition. He is a sturdy, honest, well-meaning man, prompt with sensible advice but easily flustered, shrewd enough to see what's coming but not clever or resolute enough to prevent it. He stands for the average gentleman amateur in public life, as true to his friends and as firm in his principles as the times allow. Normally he makes the best of a bad business—which is usually not so bad after all, either for himself or for the nation. Such men are loyal to a government as long as it has legal or traditional status and the means to enforce it. With every appearance of probity and devotion—by no means wholly assumed—they contrive to find themselves in the long run sturdily swimming with the tide. These men of moderate intelligence and average sensibility are normally the backbone of the English political system. Every now and then a member of this class, of more outstanding ability than the rest, will step forward from the ranks when it becomes necessary to direct the allegiance of a party, a government or a people to new fountains of authority. English history has two illustrious examples of the type in James Monk, who served the Commonwealth till it was time to bring King Charles back to Whitehall, and in John Churchill, who served King James till it was time to call King William from The Hague. The politician who saves his country by turning his coat is God's most precious gift to a people which prefers a change of government to a revolution.

Such a person is Shakespeare's Edmund of Langley, Duke of York. He stays with Richard till Richard can no longer usefully be served and he serves Bolingbroke with an equally good conscience as soon as Bolingbroke has successfully assumed the crown. He needs careful watching, for Shakespeare fits him so smoothly into the pattern of the play that his importance is apt to be overlooked. We discover him, upon his first effective appearance, urging Gaunt not to waste breath in admonishing his wilful nephew:

> Direct not him whose way himself will choose.

This very sound advice comes at the conclusion of a speech engagingly appropriate in the mouth of so representative an Englishman. Richard, York contends, is too full of foreign notions. The royal ear is no longer open to wholesome English counsel:

> No; it is stopp'd with other flattering sounds,
> As praises, of whose taste the wise are fond,
> Lascivious metres, to whose venom sound
> The open ear of youth doth always listen,
> Report of fashions in proud Italy,
> Whose manners still our tardy apish nation
> Limps after in base imitation:
> Where doth the world thrust forth a vanity—
> So it be new, there's no respect how vile—
> That is not quickly buzz'd into his ears?
> Then all too late comes counsel to be heard.

But nobody ever listens to York. Gaunt rejects his warning and, when Gaunt is dead and his property attached, Richard pays no attention to his uncle's protests. York wisely insists that, if the King of England, ruling by right of birth and the feudal law, deprives Bolingbroke of his succession to the estates of his father, he will be destroying not only his own title to the crown but everybody's title to anything at all. The barons of England hold their stake in the country by primogeniture:

> Take Hereford's rights away, and take from Time
> His charters and his customary rights,
> Let not to-morrow then ensue to-day;
> Be not thyself; for how art thou a king
> But by fair sequence and succession?
>
> You pluck a thousand dangers on your head,
> You lose a thousand well-disposèd hearts,
> And prick my tender patience to those thoughts
> Which honour and allegiance cannot think.

York speaks like a true conservative in defence of the traditional rights of property. It cuts him to the heart that

his sovereign, apex of the feudal pyramid, should have such small respect for the broad base on which it rests. He might have added that Richard, in seizing the estates of Bolingbroke, was providing his enemy with an excellent pretext for unlawfully returning to England to claim a lawful inheritance.

Richard's answer has the urchin brevity and wilfulness which characterise all his acts of sovereignty:

> Think what you will, we seize into our hands
> His plate, his goods, his money, and his lands.

York departs, shaking his wise old head. If Richard is determined to ruin himself, he can only wash his hands of the business: 'I'll not be by the while.'

York, however, is not permitted to escape into private life. Richard sends off messengers to effect the seizure of Gaunt's property and announces that to-morrow he will sail for Ireland. What follows is almost a stroke of humour in a play that but rarely invites a smile:

> And we create, in absence of ourself,
> Our uncle York lord governor of England;
> For he is just and always loved us well.

York has just scolded Richard roundly, proffered him advice which has been discourteously rejected and retired with ominous allusions to what must come of the 'bad courses' of his nephew. All this has passed clean over Richard's head. York is his uncle and York shall therefore act as his regent. Richard is quick to utter more than his mind on all occasions and, as is common with free speakers, he attaches little or no importance to what anybody else may say. He is in no way disconcerted by his uncle's reproaches and abrupt retirement. *For he is just and always loved us well.*

The argument urged upon Richard by York is picked up immediately by the Lords Willoughby, Ross and Northumberland as soon as Richard leaves the stage. *Our* lives, *our* children and *our* heirs are threatened, exclaims Northumberland. But he knows of eight tall ships, well furnished by the Duke of Brittany, which are waiting to bring over Bolingbroke and his friends. Here, then, is a means of making things secure for themselves and of serving the nation:

> If then we shall shake off our slavish yoke,
> Imp out our drooping country's broken wing,
> Redeem from broking pawn the blemish'd crown,
> Wipe off the dust that hides our sceptre's gilt
> And make high majesty look like itself,
> Away with me in post to Ravenspurgh.

This is the first effective appearance of a character whose fortunes Shakespeare is to follow through three successive plays. Northumberland, the man who helps to put Bolingbroke on the throne and who afterwards does his best to unseat him, is a man in whom disloyalty is almost a matter of principle. He lives in perpetual discontent with himself, his friends and the world at large. He abandons every cause as soon as he has persuaded his colleagues to take it up. He has thoroughly mastered the art of identifying his private interests and temperamental grudges with a zeal for the public welfare and he performs this act of identification so easily that it needs a wary eye to take and keep the measure of his suave iniquity. He is the sort of political leader who starts a rebellion and leaves his partners to face the consequences. He will take to his bed when his son is fighting at Shrewsbury and steal across the border into Scotland when his friends are marching south to meet his enemies. He is Shakespeare's presentation, valid for any generation, of the malcontent without a cause, the rebel without a conviction. To-day he speaks boldly for the Opposition and abstains from voting against the Government.

The report that Bolingbroke has landed at Ravenspurgh comes to London simultaneously with the news that Northumberland and his party have absconded. York, Richard being by this time away in Ireland, receives the news in a fluster. The nobles are fled. The commons are cold. The coffers are empty. Posts must be sent to the King. Arms must be collected and men mustered.

> If I know
> How or which way to order these affairs,
> Thus thrust disorderly into my hands,
> Never believe me. Both are my kinsmen:
> The one is my sovereign, whom both my oath
> And duty bids defend; the other again
> Is my kinsman, whom the king hath wrong'd,
> Whom conscience and my kindred bids to right.
> Well, somewhat we must do.

York is as distracted in conscience as in counsel. His bewilderment is admirably conveyed. The very verse is disjointed and breathless as the old man turns this way and that. Note the touching futility of the abrupt, disconnected order to his servant:

> Go, fellow, get thee home, provide some carts
> And bring away the armour that is there.

It is a masterly little scene and serves, better than pages of explicit commentary on Richard's fecklessness, to expose the levity with which the King has left his kingdom unprovided.

Meanwhile Northumberland is meeting Bolingbroke at Ravenspurgh. Their first colloquy is a model of political deportment as between masters of the game. Evidently Bolingbroke has not been sparing of his charm and Northumberland, as they come upon the scene in the wilds near Berkeley Castle, repays him in kind:

> I am a stranger here in Gloucestershire:
> These high wild hills and rough uneven ways
> Draw out our miles, and make them wearisome;
> And yet your fair discourse hath been as sugar,
> Making the hard way sweet and delectable;

and Bolingbroke returns:

> Of much less value is my company
> Than your good words.

To them enters Harry Percy, who in years to come will aptly remember this first meeting with Bolingbroke. It is for all present an occasion big with consequence and the use to be made of it by Shakespeare in two histories as yet unwritten affords a remarkable instance of the continuity with which he follows his political characters from play to play. Harry Percy, Bolingbroke and Northumberland, firmly rooted already in his imagination, though they may grow and put forth the shoots proper to their growth, can never change their essential quality.

Northumberland introduces his son:

NORTHUMBERLAND:

> Have you forgot the Duke of Hereford, boy?

PERCY:

> No, my good lord; for that is not forgot
> Which ne'er I did remember: to my knowledge
> I never in my life did look on him.

NORTHUMBERLAND:

> Then learn to know him now: this is the duke.

PERCY:

> My gracious lord, I tender you my service,
> Such as it is, being tender, raw and young,
> Which elder days shall ripen and confirm
> To more approvèd service and desert.

BOLINGBROKE:

> I thank thee, gentle Percy; and be sure
> I count myself in nothing else so happy
> As in a soul remembering my good friends;
> And as my fortune ripens with thy love,
> It shall be still thy true love's recompense:
> My heart this covenant makes, my hand thus seals
>   it.

The Lords Ross and Willoughby are then presented. Percy stands apart and, if the actor knows his business, will seem a trifle impatient of these civilities:

BOLINGBROKE:

> Welcome, my lords. I wot your love pursues
> A banish'd traitor; all my treasury
> Is yet but unfelt thanks, which, more enrich'd,
> Shall be your love and labour's recompense.

ROSS:

> Your presence makes us rich, most noble lord.

WILLOUGHBY:

> And far surmounts our labour to attain it.

BOLINGBROKE:

> Evermore thanks, the exchequer of the poor;
> Which, till my infant fortune comes to years,
> Stands for my bounty.

The scene is well enough in itself, however carelessly we read. But observe how already it hints at a significance for all concerned which only a distant sequel will in the fullness of time reveal. Harry Hotspur describes this very incident years later in terms which show that, tender, raw and young as he may have been at the time, he has already taken the measure of Bolingbroke's ingratiating ways. Hotspur has a natural dislike of humbug and a keen flair for its presence. Forestalling four years of troubled history, let him speak for himself:

> Why, what a candy deal of courtesy
> This fawning greyhound then did proffer me!
> Look, 'when his infant fortune came to age',
> And 'gentle Harry Percy', and 'kind cousin';
> O, the devil take such cozeners!

Hotspur *almost* remembers the very words of Bolingbroke—almost, but not quite perfectly, as is only natural.[6]

The short scene which follows the meeting between Bolingbroke and the absconded peers provides us with a further example of Shakespeare's sureness of touch in the handling of a political situation.

York has come to meet the rebel lords as the King's regent. Bolingbroke respects his loyalty. He does not attempt to force the issue, but with consummate skill he so conducts the interview that York first finds himself committed to neutrality and subsequently drawn into an ambiguous acceptance of the usurper. Bolingbroke does not ask for his support, but York, before he knows it, is being gently urged in the direction of acting as intermediary in procuring Richard's voluntary abdication.

When Bolingbroke kneels to his uncle, York bluntly challenges his false obeisance:

YORK:

> Show me thy humble heart, and not thy knee,
> Whose duty is deceivable and false.

BOLINGBROKE:

> My gracious uncle—

YORK:

>   Tut, tut!
> Grace me no grace, nor uncle me no uncle:
> I am no traitor's uncle; and that word 'grace'
> In an ungracious mouth is but profane.
> Why have those banish'd and forbidden legs
> Dar'd once to touch a dust of England's ground?
> Com'st thou because the anointed king is hence?
> Why foolish boy, the king is left behind,
> And in my loyal bosom lies his power.

But Bolingbroke has taken the measure of this honest champion of things as they are—or ought to be. He strikes instantly at the weak joint in his uncle's armour. He was banished as Hereford. He returns to claim his rights as Lancaster:

> Will you permit that I shall stand condemn'd
> A wandering vagabond; my rights and royalties
> Pluck'd from my arms perforce and given away
> To upstart unthrifts? Wherefore was I born?
> If that my cousin king be King of England,
> It must be granted I am Duke of Lancaster.
>   I am a subject,
> And challenge law: attorneys are denied me,
> And therefore personally I lay my claim
> To my inheritance of free descent.

This is too much for a feudal prince who, as Bolingbroke reminds him, has also a son who looks to inherit his father's lands. York will not admit that Bolingbroke is in the right, but cannot deny that he has a grievance. The rebel lords are prompt with assurances that Lancaster has come only to claim his lawful dues and York throws in his hand:

> Well, well, I see the issue of these arms:
> I cannot mend it, I must needs confess,
> Because my power is weak and all ill left;
> But if I could, by Him that gave me life,
> I would attach you all and make you stoop
> Unto the sovereign mercy of the king;
> But since I cannot, be it known to you
> I do remain as neuter.

Bolingbroke at once presses his advantage:

> But we must win your grace to go with us
> To Bristol castle, which they say is held
> By Bushy, Bagot and their complices,
> The caterpillars of the commonwealth,
> Which I have sworn to weed and pluck away.

YORK:

> It may be I'll go with you: but yet I'll pause;
> For I am loath to break our country's laws.

Thus York, the champion of lawful authority, is drawn into the camp of the usurper and becomes his intermediary with Richard. He goes to Bristol; he is present at the condemnation to death of the caterpillars of the commonwealth, thus condoning what is in effect an act of sovereignty on the part of Bolingbroke; and, before Richard has set foot in his kingdom, he is sending letters to Richard's queen on Bolingbroke's behalf.

Shakespeare, having dealt faithfully with the political issues of his play in the foregoing scenes, now fixes our attention on the absorbing spectacle of a gifted, sensitive and undisciplined character exposed to the high tension of a tragic destiny. Politics, for a while, fall into the background. The reactions of Bolingbroke, York and Northumberland are still worth watching; there is always an interest in observing how public persons demean themselves in the presence of emotions which exceed their comprehension or experience. But the mood of the play changes abruptly at this point. Richard enters upon the coast of Wales; drums and a flourish of trumpets die away into silence; history pauses and tragedy takes the stage.[7]

Richard himself establishes the change of key:

> I weep for joy
> To stand upon my kingdom once again.
> Dear earth, I do salute thee with my hand,
> Though rebels wound thee with their horses' hoofs:
> As a long-parted mother with her child
> Plays fondly with her tears and smiles in meeting,
> So, weeping, smiling, greet I thee, my earth,
> And do thee favour with my royal hands.
> Feed not thy sovereign's foe, my gentle earth,
> Nor with thy sweets comfort his ravenous sense;
> But let thy spiders, that suck up thy venom,
> And heavy-gaited toads lie in their way,
> Doing annoyance to the treacherous feet
> Which with usurping steps do trample thee:
> Yield stinging nettles to mine enemies;
> And when they from thy bosom pluck a flower,
> Guard it, I pray thee, with a lurking adder
> Whose double tongue may with a mortal touch
> Throw death upon thy sovereign's enemies.

It should be borne in mind that the speaker of these lyric numbers has just landed on the shores of his kingdom. He is confronted with a political situation which calls for immediate action. But Richard has no mind or will to spare for the business in hand. He has started upon that dramatisation of himself as a tragic figure which will be henceforth the dominant theme of the play. Narcissus is already absorbed in the contemplation of his royal image. From that nothing will turn him aside. Looking round on his followers, he notes their astonishment that he should be thus wasting the precious hours:

> Mock not my senseless conjuration, lords,

he exclaims and starts off again in full career:

> This earth shall have a feeling and these stones
> Prove armèd soldiers, ere her native king
> Shall falter under foul rebellion's arms.

The Bishop of Carlisle respectfully reminds his sovereign that God preferably helps those who help themselves:

> The means that heaven yields must be embraced,
> And not neglected; else, if heaven would,
> And we will not, heaven's offer we refuse,
> The proffer'd means of succour and redress.

Aumerle is more explicit:

> He means, my lord, that we are too remiss;
> Whilst Bolingbroke, through our security,
> Grows strong and great in substance and in friends.

But Richard's mind and fancy are otherwise engaged:

> Not all the water in the rough rude sea
> Can wash the balm from an anointed king;
> The breath of worldly men cannot depose
> The deputy elected by the Lord:
> For every man that Bolingbroke hath press'd
> To lift shrewd steel against our golden crown,
> God for his Richard hath in heavenly pay
> A glorious angel.

This is Shakespeare's first direct tribute to the sacramental tradition which for his contemporaries was part of the legend that had grown round Richard's deposition. Richard, in his reference to a legion of angels on which he can call for his defence, suggests an analogy between the passion which he is called upon to suffer, and from which he makes no real effort to escape, and that of Christ. These references will become more explicit as the tragedy proceeds.

Bad news now comes by every post. Salisbury reports that the Welshmen who were to have supported Richard are dispersed and fled. Scroop enters. His face promises more evil tidings. All is grist to the mill of Richard's self-centred artistry:

> Mine ear is open and my heart prepared:
> The worst is worldly loss thou canst unfold.
> Say, is my kingdom lost? why, 'twas my care;
> And what loss is it to be rid of care?
> Strives Bolingbroke to be as great as we?
> Greater he shall not be; if he serve God,
> We'll serve Him too, and be his fellow so;
> Revolt our subjects? that we cannot mend;
> They break their faith to God as well as us:
> Cry woe, destruction, ruin and decay;
> The worst is death, and death will have his day.

Scroop tells his lamentable tale. Bolingbroke has a mighty following; the whole kingdom is in arms against the crown. Where, then, asks Richard, are the men of my party? Where is Bagot? What is become of Bushy? Where is Green? Have they, too, made peace with Bolingbroke? Mark what follows:

SCROOP:

> Peace have they made with him indeed, my lord.

RICHARD:

> O villains, vipers, damn'd without redemption!
> Dogs, easily won to fawn on any man!
> Snakes, in my heart-blood warm'd, that sting my
>   heart!
> Three Judases, each one thrice worse than Judas!
> Would they make peace? terrible hell make war
> Upon their spotted souls for this offence!

SCROOP:

> Sweet love, I see, changing his property,
> Turns to the sourest and most deadly hate.
> Again uncurse their souls; their peace is made
> With heads, and not with hands: those whom you
>   curse
> Have felt the worst of death's destroying wound
> And lie full low, graved in the hollow ground.

Richard's vehement cursing of his friends upon an ambiguous report of their behaviour has often been quoted by critics as an instance of the unstable impetuosity of his character. It is even more significant as revealing in Richard a self-absorption so complete that he cannot properly attend to what is being said. No one could possibly have mistaken the meaning of Scroop's 'Peace have they made with him, indeed, my lord' unless he were wholly self-engrossed, or could have failed to receive the news of the death of his hapless followers without some word of regret. But Richard hasn't a syllable or a thought to spare for Bushy or for Bagot. The announcement of their summary execution by Bolingbroke is just another fillip to his climbing sorrow:

> Let's talk of graves, of worms and epitaphs;
> Make dust our paper and with rainy eyes
> Write sorrow on the bosom of the earth.

He sees himself walking in a long procession of kings born to illustrate the tragical fall of princes, who are set on high but who in the end must live with bread, feel want, taste grief, need friends and refuse to be mocked with solemn reverence:

> For God's sake, let us sit upon the ground
> And tell sad stories of the death of kings:
> How some have been deposed, some slain in war;
> Some haunted by the ghosts they have deposed,
> Some poison'd by their wives, some sleeping kill'd;
> All murder'd: for within the hollow crown
> That rounds the mortal temples of a king
> Keeps Death his court, and there the antic sits,
> Scoffing his state and grinning at his pomp,
> Allowing him a breath, a little scene,
> To monarchize, be fear'd and kill with looks,
> Infusing him with self and vain conceit,
> As if this flesh which walls about our life
> Were brass impregnable; and humour'd thus
> Comes at the last, and with a little pin
> Bores through his castle wall, and farewell king!

The Bishop of Carlisle again ventures a rebuke:

> My lord, wise men ne'er sit and wail their woes
> But presently prevent the ways to wail.

Richard, for a moment, condescends to business. His uncle York has an army. Where is he to be found? Scroop informs him that York has abandoned the field. Richard's cup is now full. There is nothing left to mar the luxury of his grief:

> Beshrew thee, cousin, which didst lead me forth
> Of that sweet way I was in to despair!
> What say you now? what comfort have we now?
> By heaven, I'll hate him everlastingly
> That bids me be of comfort any more.

Richard discharges his army and takes refuge in Flint Castle. Thither marches Bolingbroke with York and Northumberland in attendance. York is still loyal to Richard in spirit. Bolingbroke has as yet no formal right to his allegiance. Nor has Bolingbroke laid claim to it. He still entertains the wilful stillness of the man who waits upon his fortune. But Northumberland knows what Bolingbroke will do before Bolingbroke has confessed it even to himself. York knows it, too. There is a characteristic passage between them in which Bolingbroke contrives to remain graciously neutral:

NORTHUMBERLAND:

> The news is very fair and good, my lord:
> Richard not far from hence hath hid his head.

YORK:

> It would beseem the Lord Northumberland
> To say 'King Richard': alack the heavy day
> When such a sacred king should hide his head!

NORTHUMBERLAND:

> Your grace mistakes me; only to be brief,
> Left I his title out.

YORK:

>   The time hath been,
> Would you have been so brief with him, he would
> Have been so brief with you, to shorten you,
> For taking so the head, your whole head's length.

BOLINGBROKE:

> Mistake not, uncle, further than you should.

YORK:

> Take not, good cousin, further than you should,
> Lest you mistake the heavens are o'er our heads.

BOLINGBROKE:

> I know it, uncle, and oppose not myself
> Against their will.

Bolingbroke's message to Richard is a masterpiece of political statement. He comes in all submission, but with an army which he ostentatiously parades before the walls. He comes with a humble request, but, if the request be not granted, he will enforce it at the point of the sword. Let Richard rage in fire, Bolingbroke will weep his waters on the earth:

> Henry Bolingbroke
> On both his knees doth kiss King Richard's hand
> And sends allegiance and true faith of heart
> To his most royal person; hither come
> Even at his feet to lay my arms and power,
> Provided that my banishment repeal'd
> And lands restored again be freely granted:
> If not, I'll use the advantage of my power
> And lay the summer's dust with showers of blood
> Rain'd from the wounds of slaughter'd Englishmen:
> The which, how far off from the mind of Bolingbroke
> It is such crimson tempest should bedrench
> The fresh green lap of fair King Richard's land,
> My stooping duty tenderly shall show.

This is the cue for Richard to resume the stature of a king. York, looking up to the battlements, comments on his royal appearance and yearns to think on what must follow:

> Yet looks he like a king: behold, his eye,
> As bright as is the eagle's, lightens forth
> Controlling majesty: alack, alack, for woe,
> That any harm should stain so fair a show!

Northumberland stands forth to deliver Bolingbroke's message. Richard checks him with a superb gesture:

> We are amazed; and thus long have we stood
> To watch the fearful bending of thy knee,
> Because we thought ourself thy lawful king:
> And if we be, how dare thy joints forget
> To pay their awful duty to our presence?
> If we be not, show us the hand of God
> That hath dismiss'd us from our stewardship;
>
> And though you think that all, as you have done,
> Have torn their souls by turning them from us,
> And we are barren and bereft of friends;
> Yet know, my master, God omnipotent
> Is mustering in his clouds on our behalf
> Armies of pestilence; and they shall strike
> Your children yet unborn and unbegot,
> That lift your vassal hands against my head
> And threat the glory of my precious crown.

Northumberland delivers his master's message, concluding with a solemn oath:

> His coming hither hath no further scope
> Than for his lineal royalties and to beg
> Enfranchisement immediate on his knees:
> Which on thy royal party granted once,
> His glittering arms he will commend to rust,
> His barbèd steeds to stables, and his heart
> To faithful service of your majesty.
> This swears he, as he is a prince, is just;
> And, as I am a gentleman, I credit him.

To which Richard very civilly replies:

> Northumberland, say thus the king returns:
> His noble cousin is right welcome hither;
> And all the number of his fair demands
> Shall be accomplish'd without contradiction:
> With all the gracious utterance thou hast
> Speak to his gentle hearing kind commends.

But the strain of royally maintaining a false show of courtesy is too great. He turns to Aumerle. Has he not debased himself in speaking the traitor fair? Should he not rather defy his enemy? Aumerle counsels prudence. Fight the intruder with gentle words till time brings friends and forces with which to meet him on a more equal footing. Richard, no longer a king who weighs advice, but a man whose pride has been wounded to the quick, cries out:

> O God! O God! that e'er this tongue of mine,
> That laid the sentence of dread banishment
> On you proud man, should take it off again

> With words of sooth! O that I were as great
> As is my grief, or lesser than my name!

Northumberland brings back an answer from Bolingbroke, but Richard cannot wait to receive it. He is again the man of sorrows and has thrown his dignity to the winds:

> What must the king do now? must he submit?
> The king shall do it: must he be deposed?
> The king shall be contented: must he lose
> The name of king? o' God's name, let it go:
> I'll give my jewels for a set of beads,
> My gorgeous palace for a hermitage,
> My gay apparel for an almsman's gown,
> My figured goblets for a dish of wood,
> My sceptre for a palmer's walking-staff,
> My subjects for a pair of carvèd saints
> And my large kingdom for a little grave,
> A little little grave, an obscure grave;
> Or I'll be buried in the king's highway,
> Some way of common trade, where subjects' feet
> May hourly trample on their sovereign's head.

He grows more exquisitely fanciful as self-pity entices him from one conceit to another. He scatters himself, as Coleridge expresses it, into a multitude of images and endeavours to shelter himself from that which is around him by a cloud of his own thoughts. He finds Aumerle, his tender-hearted cousin, weeping beside him and brings him into the picture:

> Or shall we play the wanton with our woes,
> And make some pretty match with shedding tears?
> As thus, to drop them still upon one place,
> Till they have fretted us a pair of graves
> Within the earth; and, therein laid,—there lies
> Two kinsmen digg'd their graves with weeping eyes.

One of the most moving touches in Shakespeare's delineation is Richard's bleak perception, now and then, that his fancies are regarded by those about him as foolishly irrelevant. We have heard him exclaim on a former occasion: *Mock not my senseless conjuration, lords!* Now, again, he becomes abruptly aware that he has lost touch with the real world and is playing his part on a stage before spectators who find him fantastic or even ridiculous:

> Well, well, I see
> I talk but idly, and you laugh at me.

These moments, in which Richard sees himself as possibly the only appreciative witness of his tragedy, are the more affecting as they aggravate rather than restrain his excess of feeling. A brief moment of lucidity is in the present instance followed by an outbreak of almost intolerable hysteria:

RICHARD:

> Most mighty prince, my Lord Northumberland,
> What says King Bolingbroke? will his majesty
> Give Richard leave to live till Richard die?
> You make a leg, and Bolingbroke says ay.

NORTHUMBERLAND:

> My lord, in the base court he doth attend
> To speak with you; may it please you to come
>   down.

RICHARD:

> Down, down I come; like glistering Phaëton,
> Wanting the manage of unruly jades.
> In the base court? Base court, where kings grow
>   base,
> To come at traitors' calls and do them grace.
> In the base court? Come down? Down, court!
>   down, king!
> For night-owls shriek where mounting larks should
>   sing.

Northumberland's comment is drily expressive:

> Sorrow and grief of heart
> Makes him speak fondly, like a frantic man.

King Richard, in the base court, brushes aside Bolingbroke's sustained pretences of respect. He sees himself as the royal martyr, victim of circumstance and the strong hand. Bolingbroke kneels to him:

RICHARD:

> Up, cousin, up; your heart is up, I know,
> Thus high at least, although your knee be low.

BOLINGBROKE:

> My gracious lord, I come but for mine own.

RICHARD:

> Your own is yours, and I am yours, and all.

BOLINGBROKE:

> So far be mine, my most redoubted lord,
> As my true service shall deserve your love.

RICHARD:

> Well you deserve: they well deserve to have,
> That know the strong'st and surest way to get.
> Uncle, give me your hand: nay, dry your eyes;
> Tears show their love, but want their remedies.
> Cousin, I am too young to be your father,
> Though you are old enough to be my heir.
> What you will have, I'll give, and willing too;
> For do we must what force will have us do.

We come now to the famous scene of abdication in Westminster Hall. It is remembered necessarily as a supreme exhibition of Richard's quality. But the political background is worth attention if only for its faithful rendering of the reactions of public men to the impact and artistry of human emotion expressed in beauty and without reserve. Shakespeare, though his eyes are fixed on Richard, never loses sight of the dramatic contrast between his practical politicians and the suffering, wayward spirit of the fallen King. The scene opens, as so many scenes at this particular

point in Shakespeare's plays, with an episode apparently novel but in fact recalling and developing the main initial theme of the tragedy. Bolingbroke is dealing masterfully with precisely the same political situation which confronted Richard at the beginning of the play. Bolingbroke in the first Act charged Mowbray with being privy to the death of Gloucester. Bagot, in the fourth Act, confronts Aumerle with precisely the same charge. Bagot, like Mowbray, denies Aumerle's accusation. Challenges are flung down on either side, but Bolingbroke firmly suppresses the unruly peers:

> Lords appellants,
> Your differences shall all rest under gage
> Till we assign you to your days of trial.

He takes complete control of the situation and incidentally—a revealing touch, this—he adopts the royal 'we' in announcing his decision.

Into this scene, clearly designed to show that Bolingbroke has the political tact and resolution in which Richard has proved so grievously deficient, comes York to announce that an abdication has been arranged:

> Great Duke of Lancaster, I come to thee
> From plume-pluck'd Richard; who with willing soul
> Adopts thee heir, and his high sceptre yields
> To the possession of thy royal hand.
> Ascend his throne, descending now from him;
> And long live Henry, of that name the fourth!

Not by a single word or gesture, though he is already behaving like a king, has Bolingbroke laid any explicit claim to the crown. But now his destiny is plain. His chance has come and he seizes it with the readiness of a patient man who, moving deviously to his journey's end, at last sees the road clear before him:

> In God's name, I'll ascend the regal throne.

But stay; there is a hitch in these well-ordered proceedings. The Bishop of Carlisle bars the way of the usurper. Richard, he protests, is still the King. There is none present noble enough to judge his royal master and, even if Richard were a common thief, he should not be condemned unheard:

> What subject can give sentence on his king?
> And who sits here that is not Richard's subject?
> Thieves are not judged but they are by to hear,
> Although apparent guilt be seen in them;
> And shall the figure of God's majesty,
> His captain, steward, deputy-elect,
> Anointed, crownèd, planted many years,
> Be judg'd by subject and inferior breath,
> And be himself not present?

The Bishop goes on to warn the rebel lords of what must follow the elevation of a traitor:

> Disorder, horror, fear and mutiny
> Shall here inhabit, and this land be call'd

The field of Golgotha and dead men's skulls.
O! if you raise this house against this house,
It will the woefullest division prove
That ever fell upon this cursèd earth.

Northumberland takes it upon himself to order the instant arrest of the Bishop, but Bolingbroke intervenes. It must not appear that he is taking the kingdom by force; there must be no doubt that Richard has in fact voluntarily surrendered his rights. He turns to York:

Fetch hither Richard, that in common view
He may surrender; so we shall proceed
Without suspicion.

Thus is Richard called upon to play the famous scene in which he unkings himself and he plays it with a vengeance. These men have summoned him to comply with a formality. He will shame them, if he can; wring their hearts, if it be possible. In any case, he will make it a bad quarter of an hour for everyone concerned:

Alack, why am I sent for to a king,
Before I have shook off the regal thoughts
Wherewith I reign'd? I hardly yet have learn'd
To insinuate, flatter, bow and bend my limbs:
Give sorrow leave awhile to tutor me
To this submission. Yet I well remember
The favours of these men: were they not mine?
Did they not sometime cry, 'All hail!' to me?
So Judas did to Christ.

York explains the purpose for which he has been called:

To do that office of thine own good will
Which tired majesty did make thee offer,
The resignation of thy state and crown
To Henry Bolingbroke.

'Here, cousin, seize the crown', cries Richard and his fancy takes wings. The crown is a deep well; he and Bolingbroke are two buckets—his own deep down and full of tears, Bolingbroke's empty and mounting aloft in the air. Bolingbroke twice interrupts. Somehow Richard must be kept to the point. 'I thought you had been willing to resign,' he protests. Richard flashes back:

My crown, I am; but still my griefs are mine:
You may my glories and my state depose,
But not my griefs; still am I king of those.

He invites Bolingbroke to meet him in another flight of fancy but Bolingbroke is not to be put off. Bluntly he asks:

Are you contented to resign the crown?

Richard is contented, but after his own fashion:

Now mark me, how I will undo myself:
I give this heavy weight from off my head
And this unwieldy sceptre from my hand,
The pride of kingly sway from out my heart;

With mine own tears I wash away my balm,
With mine own hands I give away my crown,
With mine own tongue deny my sacred state,
With mine own breath release all duteous rites:
All pomp and majesty I do forswear.

God save King Henry, unking'd Richard says,
And send him many years of sunshine days!
What more remains?

Bolingbroke has brought Richard to the point and his work is done. What more remains he leaves to the callously officious Northumberland. Richard's abdication must be justified to the people of England. No one knows that better than Bolingbroke. But this supple, audacious and secret man has the politician's art of allowing others to do the ignoble things necessary for his advancement while he himself remains in the background to reap the profit and show to advantage in gestures of mercy, magnanimity and honest care for the public weal.

A document has been prepared setting forth the misdemeanours of the fallen king. Northumberland suggests that Richard should read the charges:

That, by confessing them, the souls of men
May deem that you are worthily depos'd.

Richard replies:

Must I do so? and must I ravel out
My weaved-up follies? Gentle Northumberland,
If thy offences were upon record,
Would it not shame thee in so fair a troop
To read a lecture of them? If thou wouldst,
There shouldst thou find one heinous article,
Containing the deposing of a king,
And cracking the strong warrant of an oath,
Mark'd with a blot, damn'd in the book of heaven.

He looks round upon the assembled lords. They are obviously feeling the strain. They have no liking for scenes and there has never been such a scene as this. They stand about awkwardly, uneasily, a little pitifully. And Richard, for the third time in the play, sees himself as the Christ betrayed:

Though some of you, with Pilate, wash your hands,
Showing an outward pity; yet you Pilates
Have here deliver'd me to my sour cross,
And water cannot wash away your sin.

Northumberland is inexorable and finally drives Richard to a sudden blaze of human temper, in striking contrast with the mood in which he adorns and cherishes his grief:

NORTHUMBERLAND:

My lord, dispatch; read o'er these articles.

RICHARD:

Mine eyes are full of tears, I cannot see:
And yet salt water blinds them not so much
But they can see a sort of traitors here.

NORTHUMBERLAND:

My lord,—

RICHARD:

No lord of thine, thou haught insulting man.

Soon, however, his imagination is at work again and inspires him to one of his most striking images:

O, that I were a mockery king of snow,
Standing before the sun of Bolingbroke,
To melt myself away in water-drops!

Finally comes his last command:

An if my word be sterling yet in England,
Let it command a mirror hither straight,
That it may show me what a face I have,
Since it is bankrupt of his majesty.

For the men about him how unexpectedly frivolous is this request! And yet how appropriate! Narcissus has reached the supreme moment of his tragedy and calls for a looking-glass.

Bolingbroke sends an attendant for the mirror. Northumberland still presses Richard. Let him read the paper while the glass is fetched. This is too much even for Bolingbroke:

BOLINGBROKE:

Urge it no more, my Lord Northumberland.

NORTHUMBERLAND:

The commons will not then be satisfied.

RICHARD:

They shall be satisfied: I'll read enough,
When I do see the very book indeed
Where all my sins are writ, and that's myself.

The attendant returns and Richard is allowed his most memorable gesture:

Was this face the face
That every day under his household roof
Did keep ten thousand men? Was this the face
That, like the sun, did make beholders wink?
Was this the face that faced so many follies,
And was at last out-faced by Bolingbroke?
A brittle glory shineth in this face:
As brittle as the glory is the face;
    (*Dashes the glass against the ground.*)
For there it is, crack'd in a hundred shivers.
Mark, silent king, the moral of this sport,
How soon my sorrow hath destroy'd my face.

Bolingbroke's comment—

The shadow of your sorrow hath destroy'd
The shadow of your face—

is not intended as a sneer, though behind it lurks the contempt of a realist for the imaginative exercises of the artist. He is not insensitive to the scene and, in reaction against the impression it has made upon him, he is prompted to reflect that it has no dynamic relation to the world of action. He suggests that Richard's sorrow is largely of the imagination. The sorrow may be real, but its expression is histrionic—in fact, a shadow. Richard acknowledges the force of this observation but construes it with a difference:

Say that again.
The shadow of my sorrow! Ha! let's see:
'Tis very true, my grief lies all within;
And these external manners of laments
Are merely shadows to the unseen grief
That swells with silence in the tortured soul.

And now suddenly he is tired of the shadow-show and asks leave to go. 'Whither?' asks Bolingbroke, and Richard, with the petulance of a hurt child, replies: 'Whither you will, so I were from your sights.'

So ends a scene in which Shakespeare's gifts as poet and dramatist are for the first time perfectly united. It goes instantly to the heart, but yields its treasures the more abundantly as it is the more closely studied. It is full of wonders. Not the least is the way in which it combines the sacramental, the aesthetic and the purely human elements in the dramatic character of Richard and the situation in which he finds himself. The speech in which Richard divests himself of crown and sceptre is likened by Walter Pater in his 'Appreciations' to an inverted rite, a rite of degradation, a 'long, agonising ceremony' in which the order of coronation is reversed. The sacramental analogy with Christ's passion has already been noted. The rebel peers who deliver up their lord to his sour cross are thrice stigmatised as Judases in the course of the play. It is Shakespeare's supreme achievement to have retained this mystical aspect of the tragedy and yet in no way to have impaired its humanity. The consecrated king, impiously discrowned, shades away into the poet king, in whom suffering induces a lyric ecstasy; who, in his turn, gives place to the mere human victim of misfortune, subject to everyday infirmities of mind and will, with whom we can live in fellowship. This Richard, who undoes himself with hierophantic solemnity, who humbles, or pities, or exalts himself in imagination, is also the man who turns on Northumberland in a flash of temper and reveals himself, all at once, as a very ordinary creature. Nor do we feel any incongruity or rift in the total performance. The three elements are completely fused. The king, the artist and the man are the person we have come to know as Richard. No play of Shakespeare has a more perfect unity of tone, texture and feeling. Yet no play has drawn upon a greater diversity of thematic material. Shakespeare, deriving from tradition, from recorded facts and from his own mind a bewildering complex of emotions and ideas, has produced a play which is all of a piece.

The scene of Richard's deposition fills, as it should, the whole fourth Act of the tragedy. It is the summit of the play and of Shakespeare's dramatic achievement at the time when it was written.[8] From this summit we descend in the fifth Act to the foregone conclusion of Richard's death and premonitory hints of the expiation which will be required of the usurper in future histories. The descent is well-contrived and there is much to be observed on the way down.

First we are taken to a street in London. Richard, being led to the Tower, is intercepted by his queen.

This is the third appearance of the Queen as a speaking character and her first appearance in a scene with her husband. Shakespeare, happily misled by his authorities, has given her a part in the play for which there is no warrant in history. Richard's first queen, Anne, dearly loved and extravagantly mourned, had been dead seven years. His second queen, Isabella, was only nine years old. Shakespeare, in presenting Richard as a king who failed in his public office, felt the need of showing him also in a more intimate relationship. Here, too, was an opportunity of adding a touch, here and there, to that English background against which the whole tragedy is played. The Queen, in her garden at Langley, lies full in the fresh green lap of fair King Richard's land, which, like Prospero's island, is full of noises heard above the brazen clamour of its barons and in the hushed pauses of their plotting. From the scene in which a pride of rebel lords sets forth to meet Bolingbroke we are taken to a scene in which a forsaken wife is grieved and anxious for 'sweet Richard'. From the scene in which Richard comes lamentably down to the court where kings grow base we are taken to where a queen and her ladies devise pastimes. A gardener binds up his dangling apricocks and thinks it a pity that the commonwealth cannot be trimmed and dressed as neatly as his hedges and borders. No one can fail to feel in his heart, though he may not be aware of its peerless cunning, the effect of the speech with which the scene at Langley concludes. The Queen has heard that Richard is deposed. The gardener, who has commented so wisely and gently on the faults which have ruined his master, looks sadly after his mistress:

> Here did she fall a tear; here, in this place,
> I'll set a bank of rue, sour herb of grace:
> Rue, even for ruth, here shortly shall be seen,
> In the remembrance of a weeping queen.

Dynasties change; the masters of England have opened the purple testament of bleeding war, which will not be closed for a hundred years to come; a simple plain man, in compassion for a weeping queen, sets a sweet herb. Only a moment before she has upbraided him as a 'little better thing than earth' for his evil tidings and called down God's curse upon his flowers. He has accepted her rebuke and bears no malice. In this garden at Langley England is wise and kind; there is here a fragrance which will outlive the futilities of history.

Shakespeare thus prepares us for a last meeting between husband and wife and we realise, when the Queen speaks, if we have not already done so, that Richard is a man beloved:

> But soft, but see, or rather do not see,
> My fair rose wither.
>
>   Thou most beauteous inn,
> Why should hard-favour'd grief be lodged in thee,
> When triumph is become an alehouse guest?

Shakespeare here gives us but a glimpse of that lovely quality in Richard which fascinated the chroniclers and survived a hundred years of Lancastrian detraction. Yet he does not falter in his portrayal of Richard's blemishes of mind and will. Now or never Richard should forget himself and speak from the heart. But no; he is still the absorbed spectator of his own tragedy, in which he is now all set to play the penitent:

>   Learn, good soul,
> To think our former state a happy dream;
> From which awak'd, the truth of what we are
> Shows us but this! I am sworn brother, sweet,
> To grim Necessity, and he and I
> Will keep a league till death. Hie thee to France
> And cloister thee in some religious house:
> Our holy lives must win a new world's crown.

The Queen very naturally resents this performance:

> What! is my Richard both in shape and mind
> Transform'd and weaken'd? hath Bolingbroke deposed
> Thine intellect? hath he been in thy heart?
> The lion dying thrusteth forth his paw
> And wounds the earth, if nothing else, with rage
> To be o'erpower'd; and wilt thou, pupil-like,
> Take thy correction mildly, kiss the rod,
> And fawn on rage with base humility,
> Which art a lion and a king of beasts?

But Richard is incorrigible:

> Good sometime queen, prepare thee hence for France:
> Think I am dead and that even here thou tak'st,
> As from my death-bed, thy last living leave.
> In winter's tedious nights sit by the fire
> With good old folks, and let them tell thee tales
> Of woeful ages, long ago betid;
> And ere thou bid good night, to quit their griefs,
> Tell thou the lamentable tale of me,
> And send the hearers weeping to their beds.

At this point Shakespeare brings on to the stage the man of all others most fitted to impersonate the new political order. Northumberland arrives with fresh instructions from Bolingbroke. Richard is to be taken to Pomfret. This is Richard's cue for prophecy. Retribution inevitably attends the success of wicked men. Triumph, the alehouse guest, has no abiding place:

> Northumberland, thou ladder wherewithal
> The mounting Bolingbroke ascends my throne,

The time shall not be many hours of age
More than it is, ere foul sin gathering head
Shall break into corruption: thou shalt think,
Though he divide the realm and give thee half,
It is too little, helping him to all;
And he shall think that thou, which know'st the way
To plant unrightful kings, wilt know again,
Being ne'er so little urged, another way
To pluck him headlong from the usurped throne.
The love of wicked men converts to fear;
That fear to hate, and hate turns one or both
To worthy danger and deservèd death.

Northumberland is not, however, a man to be moved by premonitions. He has come to execute an order. 'My guilt be on my head and there's an end,' he answers curtly, and, when the Queen begs that Richard may go with her to France, he retorts with a shrug for her simplicity: 'That were some love, but little policy.'

We are not to see Richard again till we find him playing his last part in the solitude of his prison at Pomfret. But Shakespeare has much to do in the interval. He has first to show us two celebrated companion portraits, one of Bolingbroke in his triumph and the other of Richard in his fall. It is York who executes the commission. Here is Bolingbroke:

Then, as I said, the duke, great Bolingbroke,
Mounted upon a hot and fiery steed,
Which his aspiring rider seem'd to know,
With slow but stately pace kept on his course,
Whilst all tongues cried 'God save thee, Bolingbroke!'
You would have thought the very windows spake,
So many greedy looks of young and old
Through casements darted their desiring eyes
Upon his visage, and that all the walls
With painted imagery had said at once
'Jesu preserve thee! welcome, Bolingbroke!'
Whilst he, from the one side to the other turning,
Bareheaded, lower than his proud steed's neck,
Bespake them thus: 'I thank you, countrymen':
And thus still doing, thus he pass'd along.

And here is Richard:

As in a theatre, the eyes of men,
After a well-grac'd actor leaves the stage,
Are idly bent on him that enters next,
Thinking his prattle to be tedious;
Even so, or with much more contempt, men's eyes
Did scowl on Richard: no man cried 'God save him!'
No joyful tongue gave him his welcome home;
But dust was thrown upon his sacred head;
Which with such gentle sorrow he shook off,
His face still combating with tears and smiles,
The badges of his grief and patience.

York has accepted the situation and finds God's purpose at work even in the humiliation of his late master:

That had not God, for some strong purpose, steel'd
The hearts of men, they must perforce have melted,
And barbarism itself have pitied him.

But heaven hath a hand in these events,
To whose high will we bound our calm contents.

Nor has he long to wait for an opportunity to demonstrate his loyalty to the new dynasty. For Bolingbroke is already threatened with conspiracy. Richard's friends, headed by the Abbot of Westminster, are plotting a restoration and York's own son, Aumerle, is involved. His father counsels him to accept the accomplished fact:

Well, bear you well in this new spring of time,
Lest you be cropp'd before you come to prime.

But York, even as he delivers this advice, sees dangling from his son's bosom a seal. He demands to see the writing and presently he is spelling out proof that his son, and a dozen other lords, have sworn to kill Bolingbroke at Oxford. He calls for his boots. The King must be warned. It is bad enough that Richard should have been deposed. And now before anyone has had time to settle down under the new dispensation, here is yet another attempt to upset the established order. Is treason to become the fasion in England?

The scenes in which Aumerle's conspiracy is plotted, discovered, reported to Bolingbroke and suppressed are usually omitted on the stage. It is assumed that the interest of the audience is so strongly absorbed by Richard's personal tragedy that the political results of his abdication can be ignored. This was not Shakespeare's intention. It must again be insisted that *Richard II* is a political play, with a political theme which had a poignant interest for an Elizabethan audience. Bolingbroke has deposed a king ruling by right of birth and consecration. The consequences were to be written red in the history of England for the next hundred years and to haunt the memories of Englishmen for as long again. The scenes in which Bolingbroke is confronted with civil war as an immediate result of his usurpation are essential to Shakespeare's design. It is, moreover, dramatically interesting to see how Bolingbroke handles this dangerous conspiracy while we still have vividly in mind the conduct of Richard in a similar situation. Bolingbroke thanks York for his intelligence:

O loyal father of a treacherous son!
Thou sheer, immaculate and silver fountain,
From whence this stream through muddy passages
Hath held his current and defiled himself!

Bolingbroke is fulsome in his acknowledgment of a service rendered and turns the moral situation inside out. York, who deserted Richard, is praised for his loyalty. Aumerle, who has remained true to his allegiance, is abused for treachery. Bolingbroke pardons Aumerle, but suppresses the insurrection with an iron hand.

Shakespeare's presentation of Aumerle's conspiracy has yet another dramatic purpose. It supplies the crowning motive for his instigation of Exton to the murder of Richard. Characteristically it is an ambiguous instigation:

Have I no friend will rid me of this living fear?

He looks round and there is Exton to overhear and execute his thought. He has been moved to the deposition of a king without explicitly avowing his intention. He is moved to the crowning act of murder in the same somnambulist fashion and, when the deed is done, can in a sense, disavow the intention:

> They love not poison that do poison need,
> Nor do I thee: though I did wish him dead,
> I hate the murderer, love him murderèd.

He can even regard the act as though it had been performed not by, but upon, him:

> Lords, I protest, my soul is full of woe,
> That blood should sprinkle me to make me grow.

Richard, soliloquising in his prison at Pomfret, is like an actor reviewing the scenes in which he has played and reflecting on their relation to reality. He is still dramatising his own introverted responses to the tragedy that has befallen him and he discusses how these histrionic intro-versions may be prolonged into the solitude in which he finds himself:

> I have been studying how I may compare
> This prison where I live unto the world.
>
> Thus play I in one person many people
> And none contented: sometimes am I king;
> Then treasons make me wish myself a beggar,
> And so I am: then crushing penury
> Persuades me I was better when a king;
> Then am I king'd again: and by and by
> Think that I am unking'd by Bolingbroke,
> And straight am nothing: but whate'er I be,
> Nor I nor any man that but man is
> With nothing shall be pleased, till he be eased
> With being nothing.

How apt is this annihilating conclusion of a self-centred mind, brooding in a wilful seclusion from its kind! These still-breeding thoughts are doomed to sterility and can bear no fruit! The man who lives in imagination only has no place in the world of experience. Richard is himself aware at last of the cause of his ruin. The friendly music that breaks upon his solitude sets him thinking how differ-ent his story might have been if he had kept his ears open to the harmonies and rhythms of the life about him:

> Music do I hear?
> Ha, ha! keep time: how sour sweet music is,
> When time is broke and no proportion kept!
> So is it in the music of men's lives.
> And here have I the daintiness of ear
> To check time broke in a disorder'd string;
> But for the concord of my state and time
> Had not an ear to hear my true time broke.
> I wasted time, and now doth time waste me;

and he concludes upon a note of genuine human feeling:

> This music mads me; let it sound no more;
>
> Yet blessing on his heart that gives it me!
> For 'tis a sign of love.

It is not without significance that this sign of love has come to Richard from a man whom he did not even remember, a poor groom of the stable who with much ado had obtained leave to visit his royal master. This poor groom had seen Bolingbroke in his coronation, riding on roan Barbary. Richard has here the cue for a last exquisite fancy. But what he has to say is for the first time touched with a wistful charity towards man and beast:

RICHARD:

> Rode he on Barbary? Tell me, gentle friend,
> How went he under him?

GROOM:

> So proudly as if he disdain'd the ground.

RICHARD:

> So proud that Bolingbroke was on his back!
> That jade hath eat bread from my royal hand;
> This hand hath made him proud with clapping him.
> Would he not stumble? would he not fall down,
> Since pride must have a fall, and break the neck
> Of that proud man that did usurp his back?
> Forgiveness, horse! why do I rail on thee,
> Since thou, created to be awed by man,
> Wast born to bear?

For Richard now it is finished. There is a brave blaze of anger at the last. He beats the keeper who comes to him with a poisoned dish. He strikes down two of the men who come to murder him and it is Exton himself who strikes him down. He dies a king, whose sanctity no abdication can compromise before God:

RICHARD:

> That hand shall burn in never-quenching fire That stag-
> gers thus my person. Exton, thy fierce hand Hath with
> the king's blood stain'd the king's own land. Mount,
> mount, my soul! thy seat is up on high, Whilst my
> gross flesh sinks downward, here to die.

The character of Richard has provoked comparisons which, however, only serve to stamp him as unique among the creations of Shakespeare. His futility as a man of action has led many critics to put him in the same gallery with Henry VI, Marcus Brutus and Hamlet. But to none of these three men does he bear any real resemblance except for the fact that they, too, were men unfitted to play the part imposed on them by circumstance.

Henry was a saint and a scholar, required to assert his authority over a full-blooded, termagant queen and as graceless a set of political ruffians as ever reached high of-fice in the land. He loved books, hated war, sought peace and believed in justice. He grieved not for himself, but for a kingdom in disorder and cruelties committed in his name. His weakness, as the world assesses weakness, was that of the altruist. He was a model of non-resistance and a pattern of humility in a society which believed only in power. Hazlitt once observed how Shakespeare, dealing with men who on a superficial view seem much of the same complexion and who appear in almost identical situations, presents characters wholly distinct. It is possible to go further. These characters, who tend to be hung in the same gallery, are often more remarkable for their essential differences than for any real similarity. Even when appearing to make the same speech to the same occasion, they talk a different language in a different mood and with a wholly different meaning. Turn back to the speech in which Richard rejects the splendours of royalty:

> I'll give my jewels for a set of beads.

Consider the catalogue of precious things which Richard is prepared to discard—his gorgeous palace, his gay apparel, his figured goblets. His subjects he will exchange for a pair of carvèd saints. Every epithet expresses the sophistication of an aesthete whose hermitage is presented as pleasantly to the fancy as the palace for which it is bartered. Consider, too, the flagellant self-pity of the epithets that come last of all—the *little, little* grave, an *obscure* grave. The words themselves and the fall of the lines in which they bloom like flowers in an exotic garden betray their derivation. This is not the utterance of an afflicted heart, seeking peace in surrender and simplicity, but of a man who finds consolation in a wilfully induced luxury of grief. We follow the working of an imagination that wantons in the pleasures of the humble.

Read now the similar, but how different, speech of Henry on the battlefield at Towton. Henry sorrows, not for himself, but for the strife and treachery in which he is entangled. He has so little wish to be king—a part in which Richard postured as readily as in any other—that he feels he is doing well for his family in agreeing that his son shall be disinherited. He sincerely envies a man who can live remote from great affairs and, unlike Richard, who, seeing himself in a bedesman's grown, merely changes his apparel, he shares with all his heart the rustic joys and sorrows of a simple hind. His imagination looks abroad into the world for things outside himself, whereas Richard looks always within himself for his own reflection.

The speech in which Henry's mood is crystallised is of a limpid simplicity. There is hardly an epithet. The picture is seen for itself and needs no touch of the self-conscious artist:

> O God! methinks it were a happy life,
> To be no better than a homely swain.
>
> So many hours must I tend my flock,
> So many hours must I take my rest;
> So many hours must I contemplate;
> So many hours must I sport myself;
> So many days my ewes have been with young;

So many weeks ere the poor fools will ean;
So many years ere I shall shear the fleece.

And to conclude, the shepherd's homely curds,
His cold thin drink out of his leather bottle,
His wonted sleep under a fresh tree's shade,
All which secure and sweetly he enjoys,
Is far beyond a prince's delicates,
His viands sparkling in a golden cup,
His body couchèd in a curious bed.[9]

The comparison with Brutus serves only to mark an equally essential contrast. Brutus failed as a politician because he had fixed principles and a rigid mind. Richard failed because he had no principles at all and a mind of quicksilver. Brutus misjudged political events and public persons because he saw them always in the light of his own convictions. Richard could read the hearts and purposes of the men about him, but having no convictions, only imaginative reactions to events and persons, was unable to use his insight effectively. Brutus was shut off from the world by his philosophy, Richard by his absorption in the play of a self-regarding fancy.

The comparison with Hamlet, more often drawn by the critics, is more delicately fallacious. Goethe compared Hamlet, on whom a tragic duty has been imposed, to a beautiful vase in which an acorn has been planted. The acorn in growing shivers its frail container into fragments. Yeats compares Richard to a vessel of porcelain, contrasting him with Henry V, the vessel of clay, which Shakespeare was to fashion later. Here are two poets, writing respectively of the two characters, using quite independently the same image.

Hamlet and Richard are admittedly alike in their nervous sensibility, their preoccupation with things imagined rather than things experienced, their habit of dramatising the issues presented to them, their constant outpouring of heart and mind in words of incomparable felicity, their chameleon changes of mood and temper, their stultification and defeat by grosser spirits. But how superficial are these likenesses compared with the fundamental difference in texture of the two characters! To put them together is to compare a wilful child 'pretending' in a playroom with a grown man searching into the depths of his nature and the ultimate mysteries of human life. Richard is interested only in himself and the figure he cuts in a world of his own contriving. Hamlet's interest is universal. Unlike Richard, who moves always from the general to the particular—the particular being his own destiny and passion—Hamlet moves as inevitably from the particular to the general. The tragedy in which he is immersed is his cue for infinite speculation. His personal wrongs are viewed as an epitome of all the ills that flesh is heir to. His hesitations and misgivings prompt him to analyse the source of all the hesitations and misgivings which distract the human mind. There is no character in all Shakespeare's plays so self-centered as Richard; no character less self-centered than Hamlet, who, in brooding on his own problem, sees it instinctively as the problem of every man;

who, in the bitterness of his own suffering, can lose himself in the woes of Hecuba or follow the dust of Alexander till it be found stopping a hole to keep the wind away. No character in all Shakespeare's plays is less capable than Richard of meeting and speaking with men as they are. Hamlet, on the contrary, meets every man for what he is and is instantly on speaking terms with them all—from Osric, the waterfly, to a ghost from the grave. Richard's imagination, governed by his sensibility, turns perpetually inward as inevitably as Hamlet's imagination, governed by his intellect, turns perpetually outward. To Richard nothing has interest or significance but what concerns himself. To Hamlet nothing has interest or significance till it can be related with the scheme of things entire.

If these characters, superficially alike, prove on closer acquaintance to be essentially different, it is equally true that characters superficially different often prove to be in essentials more truly comparable. No two men could seem more unlike in their disposition and fortune than Richard of Bordeaux and Richard of Gloucester. Yet here, surely, are two portraits which might with advantage be hung side by side. The contrast between them serves only to emphasise their fundamental kinship. Both are men of the artist type, the first working in imagination and the second in action. Both are egocentric, the one concentrating upon a self-created image within the mind which changes its form to reflect sensations and experiences passively received, the other concentrating upon the impact of his mind and will upon the external world of men and events. Each is the child of Narcissus: Richard, the fair rose, who calls for a mirror that he may see the brittle glory of a face that did keep ten thousand men every day under his household roof; Richard Crookback, enamoured of his own deformity, who calls on the fair sun to shine out that he may see his shadow as he passes from one piece of mischief to another.

Thus, the two Richards present in their contraries the same fundamental truth. The man who is self-centred in imagination and the man who is self-centred in action are equally out of touch with reality, and equally doomed to destruction. The first withdraws from reality to live in a false world of his own creation. The other loses the real world in an effort to fashion it according to his own will and pleasure.

Notes

1. The blending of the mystical and the realist approach to the tragedy of Richard is finely described by Dr. Dover Wilson in his introduction to the play in the New Cambridge Edition. This introduction, in its handling of the sources of the play, relating them to the finished tragedy and throwing into relief the contemporary ideas and tendencies from which it emerged, is a masterpiece of Shakespearean criticism.

2. Note the political irony of this rejoinder. Mowbray is *defending* the King. Richard graciously gives him permission to do so and assures him that he will not allow himself to be moved by any partiality for his kinsman, Bolingbroke, who is *attacking* him.

3. Shakespeare undoubtedly had this thought in mind. Years later Mowbray's son, in rebellion against Henry IV, recalls the lists at Coventry and the part played in that scene by his father:

> The king that loved him, as the state stood then,
> Was force perforce compell'd to banish him:
> And then that Henry Bolingbroke and he,
> Being mounted and both rousèd in their seats,
> Their neighing coursers daring of the spur,
> Their armèd staves in charge, their beavers down,
> Their eyes of fire sparkling through sights of steel
> And the loud trumpet blowing them together,
> Then, then, when there was nothing could have stay'd
> My father from the breast of Bolingbroke,
> O, when the king did throw his warder down,
> His own life hung upon the staff he threw;
> Then threw he down himself and all their lives
> That by indictment and by dint of sword
> Have since miscarried under Bolingbroke.

This is only one of many references back to *Richard II* which occur throughout the two succeeding plays. Shakespeare's tetralogy—*Richard II*, the First and Second Parts of *Henry IV* and *Henry V*—is a sequence not only in history but in theme and motive. In all four plays the dramatist looks forward and backward and carries in his mind all that has gone before and all that is to come. Thus we are able to find in the fourth Act of the third play of the series a passage which reveals what was present in his mind, though not explicitly stated, when he was writing the first Act of the first play.

4. See below, p. 210.

5. The editors who divided Shakespeare's plays into Acts should, as Dr. Johnson has pointed out, have concluded Act I with the banishment of Bolingbroke and started Act II with Richard's subsequent comments on the episode. They chose instead to include in Act I the short scene with Aumerle. This scene in time, temper and subject should obviously be Scene I of Act II and not, as printed in all editions, Scene IV of Act I.

6. The scene in which Hotspur recalls his first meeting with Bolingbroke (*I Hen. IV,* Act I, Sc. III) is more extensively quoted in the chapter on Henry of Monmouth. See below, p. 201.

7. Again the division into Acts is injudicious and illogical. The scene in which Bushy and Green are condemned to death, which is Act III, Sc. I, of the play, should quite obviously be Act II, Sc. IV. This scene concludes the political manoeuvres of Bolingbroke and his confederates and leaves all clear for Richard's return, when he will take the centre of the

stage and focus our attention henceforth on the tragedy of his fall from power.

8. The scene has, of course, a long and curious history. It was omitted from early published editions of the play and not printed till 1608, five years after the death of Elizabeth. There is no reason to believe, however, that it was not acted upon the stage in 1595—indeed, it was almost certainly this scene which made the play so dangerously topical and accounted for its performance no less than forty times in the years immediately following its production. Another fact about this scene of interest to the literary historian is that it drew from Dr. Johnson perhaps the most unfortunate of his comments upon Shakespeare. Part of it he declares is 'proper', but part 'might have been forborne without much loss'. He concludes with the observation: 'The author, *I suppose,* intended to write a very moving scene.' The eighteenth century has never so unhappily condescended to the genius of the sixteenth than in Johnson's criticism of this particular play. He seems to have had no idea, first to last, what it was all about. He found Richard 'imperious and oppressive' in prosperity, but in his distress 'wise, patient and pious'—a view of the character which makes complete nonsense of the tragedy from start to finish and which drove Dr. Johnson to his final conclusion: 'nor can it be said much to affect the passions or enlarge the understanding.'

9. Hazlitt, comparing these two speeches, writes: 'This (Henry's speech) is a true and beautiful description of a naturally quiet and contented disposition and not like the former (Richard's speech) the splenetic effusion of disappointed ambition.'

Michael F. Kelly (essay date 1972)

SOURCE: Kelly, Michael F. "The Function of York in *Richard II.*" *Southern Humanities Review* VI, no. 3 (summer 1972): 257-67.

[*In the following essay, Kelly studies the crucial role York plays in the dramatic and thematic developments of* Richard II. *Kelly contends that York's shift in attitude and loyalty, from Richard to Bolingbroke, encourages a parallel response in the audience.*]

The thematic and dramatic development of *Richard II* depends on the pivotal role played by the Duke of York. While he guides audience response, structurally he is also a pivot upon which the transfer of power turns, and thematically he appears for a time to be a spokesman for the play's political lesson. Many scholars who have written on *Richard II* have been able to dispose of him with a sentence or two, usually to the effect that York is a pitiable old man who is simply caught in the middle of a political revolt.[1]

Although the play's structure and theme have been the subject of critical debate, York is consistently ignored.[2] *Richard II* is, as I see the play, structured on three different turning points. As early as the second act Bolingbroke has led a successful invasion of England, and he is a *de facto* king, which he demonstrates in III.i, with an act of semi-regal authority, the execution of Bushy and Green. The "transfer of real power,"[3] in the words of Peter Ure, has occurred. In IV.i, Richard's self-deposition accomplishes the *de jure* transfer of power. The power does not, however, pass directly from Richard to Bolingbroke, but passes from Richard to York to Bolingbroke. Between the *de facto* and *de jure* transfer of power York gradually moves from a position as a staunch though fearful ally of the diminishing Richard to a new role as a loyal supporter of Bolingbroke. And while York moves, he carries the audience with him, *i.e.,* his shift in attitude stimulates a similar response in the audience. He likewise becomes a spokesman for the nation. Thus while the central focus of the play is on Richard's decline, Shakespeare makes the audience aware of the political implications of the action, namely that the doctrine of divine right may be inadequate. As a pivotal character York affects what this play has to say about politics and how we respond to what it has to say.

The significance of York is initially suggested by the gradually developed contrast between him and Gaunt. In the opening of I. ii, when the Duchess of Gloucester is urging Gaunt to seek justice for the death of her husband, Gaunt indicates his unwillingness to cooperate with her:

> God's is the quarrel—for God's substitute,
> His deputy anointed in His sight,
> Hath caused his death; the which if wrongfully,
> Let heaven revenge, for I may never lift
> An angry arm against His minister.[4]
>
> (11. 37-41)

The expression of faith in the divine right is mirrored frequently by Richard and Carlisle, and enacted by Gaunt himself in II. i as he is about to die. This latter scene demonstrates most vividly the difference between Gaunt and York. The following exchange occurs at the opening of II. i:

GAUNT.

> Will the King come, that I may breathe my last
> In wholesome counsel to his unstaid youth?

YORK.

> Vex not yourself, nor strive not with your breath;
> For all in vain comes counsel to his ear,
>
> (11. 1-4)

and he concludes his comments to Gaunt:

> Direct not him whose way himself will choose:
> 'Tis breath thou lack'st and that breath wilt thou lose.
>
> (11. 29-30)

Although York says nothing in these lines to indicate that he will shift allegiance, he reveals himself as a man of more realistic perception than Gaunt, who performs the limited role of spokesman for divine right. York's realistic attitude enables him in the later stages of the play to accept Bolingbroke, though he ultimately accepts him on other grounds. After the encounter between Richard and Gaunt and after Gaunt is removed, Richard announces his intent to confiscate and use the whole estate of Gaunt. At this point York himself delivers his lament:

> How long shall I be patient? ah, how long
> Shall tender duty make me suffer wrong?
> Not Gloucester's death, nor Hereford's banishment,
> Nor Gaunt's rebukes, nor England's private wrongs,
> Nor the prevention of poor Bolingbroke
> About his marriage, nor my own disgrace,
> Have ever made me sour my patient cheek
> Or bend one wrinkle on my sovereign's face.
>
> (11. 163-170)

York is, of course, speaking for himself, but the grievances he cites are generally such that they touch all England. Richard has, in effect, violated the justice for which the King should stand. In this speech, a ritualistic lament with its repetition and parallelism, York achieves symbolic value as a spokesman for a suffering England, and he sustains this value through the rest of the play. This scene is also extremely important in that York here gains audience sympathy and acceptance as a wise and realistic man, in effect a moderator of audience response.

Further on in this same scene York pointedly tells Richard that by seizing Gaunt's estate he has violated the principle of succession, the principle on which his own kingship rests (11. 186-208). (York is later able to ignore this principle in his support of Bolingbroke, whose possession of the crown does not depend upon proper succession but power.) York warns Richard where he stands in the kingdom and in his personal estimation:

> You pluck a thousand dangers on your head,
> You lose a thousand well-disposed hearts,
> And prick my tender patience to those thoughts
> Which honour and allegiance cannot think.
>
> (11. 205-208)

He senses that his allegiance to Richard is weakening and in his comment foreshadows his coming shift. The logic does not affect Richard, but it does convince the audience.

In a later scene the test of York's honor and allegiance is more fully delineated in the conflict between duty which binds him to Richard and conscience which would lead him to support Bolingbroke. Near the end of II. i, after York has warned Richard of impending disaster, the king appoints York Lord Governor of England while he goes to the war in Ireland. This appointment is significant for several reasons. First, York's role as symbol of England is underscored as he becomes an official representative of England. Second, he is acting in an official capacity for

Richard which is later balanced by his acting officially for Bolingbroke. When Richard makes the appointment, he does so because York "is just and always lov'd us well" (1.221). His appointment of the "just" York mirrors one of the larger ironies of Richard's character, his failure to carry thought into action, as he here implicitly recognizes the necessity for justice but in his own behavior acts unjustly. The fact of York's appointment should dispel the view of York as a doddering old man. Donald Reiman, commenting on this question, notes that "Richard, contrary to popular opinion, is not behaving foolishly when he creates York lord governor during the King's absence in Ireland, for he recognizes that York, despite his reservations about Richard's reign, will do all in his power to fulfill his oath to defend the kingdom and York is the only man whom the king can trust, who has any support among the country at large."[5]

York next appears in II.ii, where he is described by Richard's Queen as entering "with signs of war about his aged neck" (1. 73), as he is now aware of what the arrival of Bolingbroke at Ravenspurgh bodes for his country. York comments in woeful tones:

> Here am I left to underprop his land,
> Who weak with age cannot support myself.
> Now comes the sick hour that his surfeit made,
> Now shall he try his friends that flatter'd him.
>
> (11. 82-85)

York's self-deprecating comments ought not be taken as a literally accurate description of himself. Certainly York is old, but he does have a strength of character which he reveals in his confrontation with Bolingbroke, and he has a strength of body which enables him later to make a furious ride to the king to accuse his son of treason. He is able to support himself, though the overwhelming burden of supporting the reign of Richard in its "sick hour" arouses in him a sense of weakness. York further laments his difficulties:

> God for his mercy, what a tide of woes
> Comes rushing on this woeful land at once!
> I know not what to do. . . .
>
> (11. 97-99)

The final statement of this passage is one of the first real statements of the ambiguity of York's situation as well as the hopelessness of it. He enlarges upon this ambiguity a few lines later, echoing his earlier statement on honor and allegiance:

> Both are my kinsmen:
> Th' one is my sovereign, whom both my oath
> And duty bids defend; th' other again
> Is my kinsman, whom the King hath wrong'd,
> Whom conscience and my kindred bids to right.
>
> (11. 111-115)

In this comment York is clearly going beyond the blind and unthinking acceptance of divine right as expressed

William Needles as the Bishop of Carlisle, Steve Ross as Sir John Bagot, Geordie Johnson as Richard II, Jordan Pettle as Sir John Bushy, and Donald Carrier as Sir Henry Greene in Act I, scene iii of the 1999 Stratford Festival production of Richard II.

earlier by Gaunt. Yet he cannot easily resolve this conflict by making an abrupt shift in allegiance. His loyalty is not easily displaced, but all he can do is say, "Well, somewhat we must do" (1. 115), and he orders Bushy, Green, and Bagot to "muster up your men" (1. 117). York's refusal to relinquish his role as Lord Governor and to give up the cause of opposing Bolingbroke underscores his basic loyalty to Richard and emphasizes the significance of his coming shift in allegiance. Even the men who have been the flatterers and false counselors of Richard admire York's constancy and sympathize with his plight as Green comments after York has left the scene:

> Alas, poor Duke! The task he undertakes
> Is numb'ring sands and drinking oceans dry;
> Where one on his side fights, thousands will fly.

> (11. 144-146)

Green's estimate of York's situation is, of course, accurate. The images of "numb'ring sands" and "drinking oceans dry" help to draw audience sympathy to him as an impossible underdog who in spite of overwhelming odds is will-

ing to enter the fray. Of course he never really fights, but he is nonetheless the most sympathetic character on the scene. Richard at this point gets no sympathy, since he has put York in this unenviable position of defending a defenseless country.

York next appears in an encounter with Bolingbroke in II.iii, when he comes to learn Bolingbroke's intent. When York enters, Bolingbroke kneels to him as the Lord Governor, but York, seeing the pretense immediately, upbraids him:

> Show me thy humble heart, and not thy knee,
> Whose duty is deceivable and false.

> (11. 83-84)

When Bolingbroke later asks York what his offence is, York unhesitatingly tells him treason and rebellion. Even after Bolingbroke declares as his sole intent the regaining of his stolen inheritance, York remains adamant, helpless as he is to back up his words with act:

My lords of England, let me tell you this:
I have had feeling of my cousin's wrongs,
And labour'd all I could to do him right.
But in this kind to come, in braving arms,
Be his own carver, and cut out his way,
To find out right with wrong—it may not be.
And you that do abet him in this kind
Cherish rebellion, and are rebels all.

(11. 139-146)

In addressing himself to the "lords of England," he is extending his accusation, and in the formal introduction to his speech he is acting as the Lord Governor. Yet York, as we have already seen, is a realist. He understands the character of Richard and knows he is deaf to any sound advice. He understands the situation confronting him:

Well, well, I see the issue of these arms.
I cannot mend it, I must needs confess,
Because my power is weak and all ill left.
But if I could, by Him that gave me life,
I would attach you all, and make you stoop
Unto the sovereign mercy of the king;
But since I cannot, be it known unto you
I do remain as neuter.

(11. 151-158)

Here, for the first time, York makes a definite shift in his position going from loyalty to Richard to neutrality. He realistically recognizes that he can do nothing against Bolingbroke but nevertheless tells him what he would do if he could. At the close of this scene York agrees to go with Bolingbroke to Bristow Castle, but he is still unwilling to commit himself to Bolingbroke's position:

It may be I will go with you; but yet I'll pause,
For I am loath to break our country's laws.
Nor friends, nor foes, to me welcome you are.
Things past redress are now with me past care.

(11. 167-170)

In his adoption of neutrality York is abdicating his authority as Lord Governor and recognizing that Bolingbroke is the *de facto* king. He is now "loath to break our country's laws," but he sees that they are going to be broken. Through his eyes we see the situation as unfortunate but unavoidable. York's course of action is the only one, or at least we are made to think so.

By the end of Act II, York has gone from simple loyalty to a loyalty in ambiguity, to neutrality. He appears next at Bolingbroke's camp at Bristol in III.i, in which Bolingbroke orders the execution of Bushy and Green. York plays no role and voices no opinions, but by his silent presence he acknowledges Bolingbroke as the *de facto* king. *De jure*, York himself possesses the power which Bolingbroke is exercising, but in his silent acceptance he gives proof of his neutrality and abdication of authority. In III.ii Richard returns to his kingdom only to find himself all but dispossessed. After vacillating between hope and despair, he seems to gain control of himself:

This ague fit of fear is overblown;
An easy task it is to win our own.
Say, Scroope, where lies our uncle with his power?

(11. 190-192)

This optimism is promptly dispelled by Scroope who, after an ominous preface, responds to Richard:

Your uncle York is join'd with Bolingbroke,
And all your Northern castles yielded up,
And all your southern gentlemen in arms
Upon his party.

(11. 200-203)

York's shift in allegiance has finally occurred and the news of it is a crushing blow to Richard's hope, as he is now no longer able to generate within himself even the false hope of success, nor do his followers, Carlisle and Aumerle particularly, make any attempt to rouse him to defend his position. In reaction to Scroope's information he simply says. "Thou has said enough" (1. 203). Richard seems to recognize the significance of York's change of allegiance. When the man of whom he said earlier, "he is just and always lov'd us well" (II.i. 221), has deserted him, he no longer can hope for success. Richard concludes III.ii with a despairing lament:

He does me double wrong
That wounds me with the flatteries of his tongue.
Discharge my followers; let them hence away,
From Richard's night, to Bolingbroke's fair day.

(11. 215-218)

Richard at this point abdicates *de facto* his role as king of England, almost simultaneously with his knowledge of York's shift of loyalty from Richard to Bolingbroke.

In the next scene, III.iii, Richard and Bolingbroke meet before Flint Castle where Richard gives himself over into the power of Bolingbroke. But before Richard enters York makes several relevant comments. Northumberland, in addressing Bolingbroke, says, "Richard not far from hence hath hid his head" (1. 6). York immediately picks up the mode of reference to the King and says:

It would beseem the Lord Northumberland
To say "King Richard." Alack the heavy day
When such a sacred king should hide his head.

(11. 7-9)

Even though York has joined Bolingbroke, he still maintains respect for the King as divinely anointed. His shift has been political and not philosophical, as is later revealed more fully in his comments on the necessity for loyalty to Bolingbroke. The tone of regret in York's statement significantly places him in contrast with others, notably Carlisle, who continue in their rhetorical proclamations of divine right. When Richard does appear later in the scene, York again expresses a similar sentiment:

Yet looks he like a king. Behold, his eye,
As bright as is the eagle's, lightens forth

Controlling majesty. Alack, alack, for woe,
That any harm should stain so fair a show!

(11. 68-71)

Saddened though he is, implicit in his statement, "Yet looks he like a king" and his phrase "so fair a show," is York's recognition that the image of the king is not sufficient to meet the demands of political necessity, or, as Traversi states it, his consciousness "of the gap that already separates appearance from reality."[6] In saying this York is again controlling audience response. Certainly it is regrettable that Richard has lost his power; York even encourages our sympathy. Yet he has made us aware that Bolingbroke's ascendancy is an unavoidable political reality.

York next appears in IV.i, after Bolingbroke has for the moment settled the contention between Bagot and Aumerle. He enters in an official capacity to address Bolingbroke:

Great Duke of Lancaster, I come to thee
From plume-pluck'd Richard, who with willing soul
Adopts thee heir, and his high sceptre yields
To the possession of thy royal hand.
Ascend his throne, descending now from him,
And long live Henry, fourth of that name!

(11. 107-112)

York functioned as Lord Governor of England in the absence of Richard, thus acting for Richard. In the above passage he is functioning as a mediator between Richard and Bolingbroke, thus acting for both men. Later in this same scene, Bolingbroke asks that Richard be brought in and York offers to "be his conduct" (1. 157). In making this suggestion, he is offering himself to the service of Bolingbroke. When Richard and York re-enter, Richard asks why he has been sent for and York again responds, as a spokesman for the new king:

To do that office of thine own good will
Which tired majesty did make thee offer:
The resignation of thy state and crown
To Henry Bolingbroke.

(11. 177-180)

York's shift in allegiance is now complete. And he has brought the audience to the same point, namely a recognition that Bolingbroke's rise and Richard's decline have been the necessary product of the political situation created by Richard himself. In Act II he had solemnly warned Richard of what lay ahead if he pursued his intended course. York's subsequent actions as representative and mediator have kept him before us, and they have grown out of his premise that Richard's behavior has pricked his "tender patience to those thoughts / Which honour and allegiance cannot think" (II.i. 207-208).

In the final act of the play, York enacts his loyalty to the new king. Previously he has given only vocal or official support, but in Act V he tries to have his own son Aumerle executed for his treasonous plot. Even before this, however, York appears with the Duchess of York in his castle describing the triumphant entry of Bolingbroke into London at a "stately pace," "Whilst all tongues cried 'God save thee, Bolingbroke!'" (V.ii. 11). The tone of this description is, of course, an indication of his admiration of the new king, and it also amplifies the relationship between York and the people of England. He has seen Bolingbroke from the same point of view as the common people, and his tongue seems to be one with theirs as they cry "God save thee, Bolingbroke!"

After describing Bolingbroke, York comments on how dust was thrown upon Richard's "sacred head" (1. 30). In a passage highly relevant to the thematic issues of the play, York continues:

Which with such gentle sorrow he shook off,
His face still combating with tears and smiles,
The badges of his grief and patience,
That had not God for some strong purpose steel'd
The hearts of men, they must perforce have melted
And barbarism itself have pitied him.
But heaven hath a hand in these events,
To whose high will we bound our calm contents.
To Bolingbroke are we sworn subjects now,
Whose state and honour I for aye allow.

(11. 31-40)

This speech emphasizes, on one hand, one of the central paradoxes of the play, namely that while Richard is losing his royal and official stature, he simultaneously gains sympathy, ironically through York. While inducing audience sympathy, York is also attempting to hold a providential view of history in which the deposing of a rightful monarch by power politics can be regarded as a working out of a divine plan for England. The sympathy expressed is York's, not the commoners' of England, because "God for some strong purpose steels / The hearts of men." In his further comments York again explicitly states his new allegiance and his motivation. Earlier he seemed to act out of political necessity as a part of the working of God's "high will." In adopting this position York places himself in a dilemma. He desires to have both the old and the new, a king to whom loyalty is divinely required, but also a king who has achieved his crown through political power and military force. Even in his ambiguous position, York acts contrary to the orthodox Tudor doctrine in his support of a king who has gained his throne by deposing a divinely ordained king. Yet it is at this point that York disqualifies himself has a spokesman for the play. He sees Bolingbroke perhaps as the nation saw him, but seemingly not as Shakespeare saw him.

Later in V.ii York questions Aumerle about the letter protruding from his garment. When Aumerle refuses to respond to York's satisfaction, he snatches the letter and, upon reading it, reacts violently with "Treason, foul treason! Villain! Traitor! Slave!" (1. 73). The spontaneity of this reaction to the letter is indicative of his new kind of acceptance of Bolingbroke. Earlier in the play he gives evidence of an emotional attachment and affection for Richard, but until this point he has offered primarily an intellectual acquiescence to Bolingbroke. His response to the letter suggests that now he possesses a similar kind of wholehearted, emotional devotion to his new ruler. His response is not, as Coleridge suggested, one of "abstract loyalty,"[7] however misguided the loyalty may be. In the ensuing action York vows to reveal the treasonous plot to Bolingbroke, but his wife makes an emotional appeal to York as the father of Aumerle. He is deaf to all such appeals and responds:

> Away, fond woman! Were he twenty times my son,
> I would appeach him.

> (11. 101-102)

York's willingness to have his son executed implies, of course, that his confused loyalty is destructive, but the great irony here is that his loyalty is to a man who is king not by virtue of his being divinely anointed but of his possessing political and military power. Yet the basis of York's loyalty is something akin to divine right, the working of God's "high will."

The ensuing scene in which York and his Duchess alternately appeal to the king for justice and mercy is a ritual enactment, superficially of York's new loyalty and, more profoundly, of the confusion of York's position. He demands of his son a complete loyalty to Bolingbroke. Aumerle is, in a sense, doing the same thing Bolingbroke has done, except that Aumerle is attempting to place Richard, the divinely anointed, back on the throne. York is condemning the very action he himself has only shortly before condoned. Thus, York's answer to the question of the right to depose is ambiguous. The answer of the whole play is correspondingly ambiguous since at the play's end Bolingbroke has brought some greatly needed stability and strength to the throne, but the ominous warnings of Carlisle (IV.i. 115-149) and Richard (V.i. 55-60) temper any optimism about a glorious and peaceful reign for Henry IV.

Some significance may also be attached to the fact that, in this same scene, Bolingbroke gives York an official function in the new government. After granting pardon to Aumerle, he orders York:

> Good uncle, help to order several powers,
> To Oxford, or where'er these traitors are.

> (11. 140-141)

Whereas earlier York had acted for Bolingbroke in a ritualistic capacity in speaking for the court at Richard's deposition, he now assumes an active role in the defense of the new king. He thereby balances his earlier role as Lord Governor without means to fulfill his function. Now as a deputy for Bolingbroke he is again in the role of the defender of his country, but, we may assume, with the necessary means.

This analysis of the multiple and interdependent functions of York in *Richard II* provides both some new insights

into the complexities of that play, and also some insights into Shakespeare's dramatic art. Shakespeare's handling of York demonstrates, I believe, his concern with how an audience responds to character and action. In a general sense, York is some indication of Shakespeare's intention while still being an integral part of the action.

Notes

1. Samuel Taylor Coleridge, *Lectures on Shakespeare,* etc. (London: Everyman Library, 1907), pp. 116-117; Peter Ure, intro., *King Richard II* (Cambridge, Mass.: Arden Shakespeare), p. lxxiii; Derek Traversi, *Shakespeare from Richard II to Henry V* (Stanford, 1957), p. 45.

2. Lily B. Campbell in *Shakespeare's Histories* (San Marino, 1947), p. 211, sees the central issue of the play as the deposition of a king and the central scene as the deposition scene, a scene of sacrilege which produced the War of Roses. E. M. W. Tillyard in *Shakespeare's History Plays* (London, 1944), p. 261, views the play primarily as a struggle between Richard and Bolingbroke climaxed in the deposition scene, and he concludes that "in doctrine the play is entirely orthodox." Irving Ribner in *The English History Play in the Age of Shakespeare* (Princeton, 1957), p. 156, observes that "when Shakespeare came to write *Richard II* he could regard the deposition of Richard as an historical *fait accompli* which was sinful and which ultimately resulted in the horror of the War of Roses, . . . but which in its immediate effects was good for England because it replaced a weak and ineffective king with a strong and efficient one." Peter Ure, in his introduction to the new Arden *Richard II,* commenting on the structure of the play, notes that the political climax of the play occurs when the news arrives that Bolingbroke has gained control of the land.

3. Ure, p. lxii.

4. All quotations from the play are from *King Richard II,* ed. Peter Ure (Cambridge, Mass.: Arden Shakespeare, 1956).

5. "Appearance, Reality, and Moral Order in *Richard II,*" *MLQ,* [*Modern Language Quarterly*] XXV (1964), 36.

6. Traversi, p. 35.

7. Coleridge, p. 117.

James A. Riddell (essay date 1979)

SOURCE: Riddell, James A. "The Admirable Character of York." *Texas Studies in Literature and Language* 21, no. 4 (winter 1979): 492-502.

[*In the following essay, Riddell defends the character of York against negative criticism, and asserts that York exemplifies the Christian ideal of magnanimity.*]

Coleridge's high opinion of the character of York in *Richard II* has been shared by few critics in the past century. Although it is unlikely that anyone today would be as shrill (but at the same time obsequious) in disagreeing with Coleridge as Swinburne finally was, the essense of his view persists today. The figure of York, said Swinburne, "is an incomparable, an incredible, an unintelligible and a monstrous nullity. Coleridge's attempt to justify the ways of York to man—to any man of common sense and common sentiment—is as amusing in Coleridge as it would be amazing in any other and therefore lesser commentator."[1] It seems often to be the case that the more a critic admires Richard, the less he admires York. Swinburne thought that Shakespeare's "attention and sympathy" were directed away from other characters because his interest "was wholly concentrated on the single figure of Richard" (*Study*, p. 41). If, like Pater and Yeats,[2] one finds Richard to be a poet (therefore sincere and attractive), one may subsequently find York to be a politician (therefore hollow and repellent). As Mark Van Doren puts it: "[Richard] is a touching person. . . . And the Duke of York, fussing like old Capulet over the grievous state of the realm, . . . is not so much a sorrower as a worrier; he is perhaps a parody, in the decrepit key, of Richard's full-noted grief."[3] In the years since Van Doren's judgment York has even been seen as so feeble and spineless that he must reflect some reservations Shakespeare had about traditional notions of order and ceremony.[4] Or (when York's inner feelings are analyzed rather than Shakespeare's) he has been seen as doggedly pursuing the punishment of his son as a way of expiating his own guilt.[5] More charitably, and most commonly, York has been seen as being merely weak and/or confused.[6]

To be sure, a few modern critics have expressed higher opinions of York's character, notably Peter Ure and Norman Rabkin. Rabkin sees York as being one of "Shakespeare's 'reflector' characters, who . . . epitomizes and directs our shifting sympathies. Like us York begins with a poignant sense of loyalty to the crown; like us he soon finds his sympathy virtually exhausted and declares an end to his former approval."[7] Ure refers us to Coleridge's observations, saying that they "are not likely to be bettered."[8] Perhaps they will not be bettered; however, they are no more than lecture notes and are so brief that they stand merely as assertions, with no evidence to convince anyone not already disposed to agree with them. Coleridge's fragmentary comments are:

> The admirable character of York. Religious loyalty struggling with a deep grief and indignation at the king's vices and follies; and adherence to his word once given in spite of all, even the most natural feelings. . . .

> York's character. The weakness of old age and the overwhelmingness of circumstance struggling with his sense of duty; and the function of both exhibited in boldness of words and feebleness in act.[9]

Coleridge was right, but for reasons that may never have entered his mind.

Before I proceed, however, I should like to mention that critics of York, those who disagree with Coleridge, exist entirely outside the play of *Richard II*: no character in the play has a bad word to say about York, either to his face or behind his back.[10] Indeed, when anyone in the play has occasion to characterize York, it is always in terms of approbation. The Duchess of Gloucester, Woodstock's widow, calls him "good old York."[11] The gardener, whose comments on the state of the realm appear to be so sane, talks of the "good Duke of York" (III.iv.70). Richard, wisely or not, does leave York in charge of his kingdom. Bolingbroke, sincerely or not, is always respectful of his uncle York, as Richard is not of his uncle Gaunt. (As I discuss the character of York in this article, I hope that it will become clear that Richard could have been wise in placing trust in him and Bolingbroke could have been sincere in respecting him.)

Those who contend that York is feeble, or worse—often much worse—usually fault him for his behavior on two occasions: when he takes Bolingbroke into Berkeley Castle after withdrawing himself from conflict between Richard and Bolingbroke, and when he discloses to Henry that his son Aumerle has subscribed to plot against Henry. These are taken to be examples of his feebleness of spirit and feebleness of wit. It is, however, on precisely these two occasions that York demonstrates Christian stoicism and magnanimity (the former being an aspect of the latter), as would have been more immediately apparent to a sixteenth-century audience than to a modern one. Almost every contemporary author who touched upon the conduct of great men emphasized the significance of magnanimity, and it is from the point of view of this virtue, as it was perceived by Shakespeare's contemporaries, that I wish here to consider York's actions.[12] The classical antecedents for the sixteenth-century writers who dealt with magnanimity were preponderantly Roman, rather than Greek, and among the Romans none so important as Cicero, and then Seneca. Two qualities of magnanimity that Cicero stresses are that it is a passive as well as an active virtue and that its chief end is not personal satisfaction but rather the sustaining of the commonweal.[13] As an active virtue magnanimity involves heroic exploits. As a passive virtue it involves an aloofness towards either the praises or the scorn of others, and, furthermore, a stoical capacity to accept one's own strengths or weaknesses, one's fortunes, indifferently. Thus, for instance, one faces death, as any other misfortune, with equanimity. As La Primaudaye says: "When a man is past all hope of saving his life, . . . perfect Magnanimitie alwaies knoweth how to finde out a convenient remedie and wise consolation, not suffering himselfe to be vexed therewith."[14]

If a man is to face the loss of his life without suffering himself to be vexed, he surely must face any lesser calamity with patience and resolve. In the light of this consideration, it is plausible that York's behavior towards Bolingbroke when they meet in front of Berkeley Castle is a manifestation of York's magnanimity. In Thomas Lodge's translation of Seneca there is a passage that bears on this aspect of magnanimity:

These things which we undertake are to bee estimated, and our forces are to be compared with those things which wee will attempt. For there must alwais be a greater force in him that beareth, then in the burthen. These waights must need beare him down, that are greater then he is that carrieth them. Besides there are some affaires that are not so great as they are fruitfull, and breed many other businesse, and these are to be avoyded, from whence a new and divers occasion of trouble ariseth: neither must thou adventure thither, whence thou canst not freely returne againe. Set thy hand to these things, whose end thou mayest either effect or at least-wise hope. These things are to be left that extend themselves farther then the act, and end not there where thou intendest they should.[15]

What York is able to undertake, admonition and rebuke, he proceeds with; what he is unable to undertake, armed resistance, he abandons. Helpless to control events (through no fault of his own but age), he resigns himself to them, and in the conflict between Richard and Bolingbroke declares himself "neuter":[16]

YORK

> Well, well, I see the issue of these arms.
> I cannot mend it, I must needs confess,
> Because my power is weak and all ill left.
> But if I could, by Him that gave me life,
> I would attach you all, and make you stoop
> Unto the sovereign mercy of the king;
> But since I cannot, be it known unto you
> I do remain as neuter. So, fare you well,
> Unless you please to enter in the castle,
> And there repose you for this night.

BOL.

> An offer, uncle, that we will accept.
> But we must win your grace to go with us
> To Bristow castle, which they say is held
> By Bushy, Bagot, and their complices,
> The caterpillars of the commonwealth,
> Which I have sworn to weed and pluck away.

YORK

> It may be I will go with you; but yet I'll pause
> For I am loath to break our country's laws.
> Nor friends, nor foes, to me welcome you are.
> Things past redress are now with me past care.

(II.iii.151-70)

Given the circumstance in which York finds himself, his observation in the last line amounts to an expression of "perfect Magnanimitie." He has assessed his opportunities, has realized that the burden is too great for him possibly to bear, and has acquiesced, without recrimination, without distress.

This is a quality of York which was introduced into this part of the story by Shakespeare. It is well known that he altered the role of York from that which he found in his sources. In Holinshed, the reasons given for York's action (or inaction) when he was to confront Bolingbroke are quite different: "The Duke of Yorke, whome king Richard had left as governour of the realme in his absence, hearing that his nephue the duke of Lancaster was thus arrived, and had gathered an armie, he also assembled a puissant power of men of armes and archers . . . but all was in vaine, for there was not a man that willinglie would thrust out one arrow against the duke of Lancaster, or his partakers, or in anie wise offend him or his freends."[17] The significant effect of Shakespeare's alteration, I suggest, is to place emphasis on York's making a decision rather than having his troops make it for him, and, more important, to place emphasis on the reason York made his decision as he did. What we see in the play but do not see in Holinshed is York's patience, his magnanimity.

If York is perceived as being magnanimous, his actions in "appeaching" his son of treason are not only consistent with his character, but also provide further evidence of its excellence. I do not mean to suggest that the York-Aumerle-Henry episode reflects only York's magnanimity. York, as is the case with other venerable counselors in Shakespeare, is shown to be occasionally foolish, even ridiculous. Like Gonzalo in *The Tempest,* he becomes a victim of his own high-mindedness by persisting too narrowly in it. York neglects to eschew anger in his diligent attempt to provide for the good of the commonweal. His excess, however, should not subvert our understanding of his virtue. I think that we should see York as an example of magnanimous man, but one who is slightly flawed—ironically by a passionate devotion to a virtue the central quality of which is dispassion. Beyond this, however, we see York taking action when there is every reason to believe that the action will be fruitful. Furthermore, the action he takes is at the expense of his personal benefit, for the benefit of the king, the law, the commonweal. In this he is something like the prince whose virtue provides an example in the courtesy book of Bertrand de Loque:

> *Zaleucus* enacted his lawes, that whosoever should bee found to commit adultery, should have both his eies put out: it fell out that his owne sonne was convinced of this crime, wherefore his father would in any wise have the law executed upon him: and sure so it had bin, had not the importunate praiers of his people, entreating him to remit wholly the culpe, moved him some thing in the matter: but see what hee accorded unto the people, because he would not have his lawes violated, and to be made without effect: to satisfy the law, hee put out one of his own eies, and commaunded that his sonne should have one of his eies put forth in the like manner.[18]

Fully as persistent as Zaleucus in upholding the law of the state, York demands the death of Aumerle for treason. Here, again, Shakespeare's use of his sources is instructive. There is nothing in the chronicles to suggest that Aumerle was an only son, and indeed historically he had a younger brother. However, Shakespeare focuses our attention on the absolute nature of York's commitment by making Aumerle an only son and by causing the Duchess to dilate upon the implication of the fact, in particular emphasizing that she and her husband can no longer have children. York is willing, in short, to sacrifice his entire posterity for the sake of the commonweal.

If, indeed, Shakespeare intended his audience to perceive York as being magnanimous, what is the purpose? I think that Rabkin's notion about York being a "reflector" character is close to the mark. However, I would alter his evaluation somewhat, and would suggest that York is a kind of measure against which Richard—or one significant quality of Richard—can be judged. I suggest that Richard's chief failing is his lack of magnanimity as a king. It is now a commonplace that in *Richard II* Henry's decisiveness as king is set off against Richard's indecisiveness. But there is a much more comprehensive statement about Richard's character implicit in the contrast between him and York. York is not a king, and so the contrast is not one to be drawn between men of equal station. Nor is York a gardener, and so the contrast cannot be seen as allegorical, drawn between one at the top and one near the bottom of the order of mankind. We are to be informed by the quality of York's spirit, and that can be seen through his devotion to the principles of magnanimity. The more we are reminded of York's devotion to those principles, the more we are invited to recognize Richard's indifference to them. Jacques Hurault's rather full description of a magnanimous man is virtually a catalogue of qualities Richard should possess but does not:

> Magnanimitie or noblemindedness is the meane betweene bacemindednes and overloftines. . . . The nobleminded man advanceth not himselfe for honor, riches, or prosperity, neither maketh he the greater account of himself for them; if he fall from his degree or loose his goods, he stoopeth not for it; for he is upheld with a certain force and stoutnes of mind. Contrariwise, the baceminded or faint-hearted man, becometh wonderfully vainglorious of every little peece of good fortune or advauncement that befalleth him, and at every little losse that betideth him, he shrinketh and is cast downe like an abject, as if he lost al, because he hath not the force of mind, to beare his fortune either good or bad.[19]

Richard, however, is not borne up by stoutness of mind when he falls from degree. His stooping behavior in the deposition scene, furthermore, is the opposite of York's behavior when he reflects upon the losses Richard has exacted from him, and from his brothers and Bolingbroke as well. York has asked:

> How long shall I be patient? ah, how long
> Shall tender duty make me suffer wrong?
> Not Gloucester's death, nor Herford's banishment,
> Nor Gaunt's rebukes, nor England's private wrongs,
> Nor the prevention of poor Bolingbroke
> About his marriage, nor my own disgrace,
> Have ever made me sour my patient cheek,
> Or bend one wrinkle on my sovereign's face.
>
> (II.i.163-70)

York refuses to make public, or even to take personally, his private losses; tender duty compels that he forbear. Richard, on the other hand, insists upon making personal his public losses, and, worse, upon making a public display of his personal grief. It is an understatement to say that he has not "the force of mind to beare his fortune either good or bad."

Hurault continues with a list of qualities that a magnanimous man should possess:

> The nobleminded man hath six properties: the first is, that he thrusteth not himself into perils rashly and for small trifles, but for great matters, whereof he may have great honor and profit. . . . The second propertie of the nobleminded, is to reward vertuous persons, and such as have imploied themselves in his service. Whereunto a king ought to have a good eie. . . . The third propertie of the nobleminded, is to do but little, and not to hazard hisselfe at all times. For a man cannot do great things easily and often. The fourth property, is to be soothfast, and to hate lying and all the appurtenances thereof, as flatterers, talebearers, and such others, which ought to be odious, most cheefly unto princes, who should be a rule to other men.
>
> (sigs. VI-VIᵛ)

Although there is not at every point a convenient comparison to be made between York and Richard, the pattern is apparent; there are, of course, more examples of Richard's behavior than of York's. In Hurault's summary, the first and third properties are much alike, as are the second and fourth. In both (or all) respects, Richard's faults are clear. He pursues his Irish wars, where the gain to be realized cannot be great but where the hazard to himself is likely to be, and does prove, disastrous. His eye for good service, as shown many times in the play, is altogether false. The seductive flattery of Bushy, Bagot, and Greene is preferred to the sound advice of counselors such as Gaunt or York, as York reminds Gaunt just before Richard pointedly ignores Gaunt's appeal from his deathbed. York poses his argument in explicitly patriotic language; the distinction between indifference to flattery and susceptibility to it is set in terms of sound English values as opposed to frivolous foreign ones. When Gaunt hopes that his "death's sad tale may yet undeaf [Richard's] ear," York replies:

> No, it is stopp'd with other flattering sounds,
> As praises, of whose taste the wise are fond,
> Lascivious metres, to whose venom sound
> The open ear of youth doth always listen,
> Report of fashions in proud Italy,
> Whose manners still our tardy-apish nation
> Limps after in base imitation.
>
> (II.i.16-23)

Later in the scene, when Northumberland, Willoughby, and Ross determine to join forces with Bolingbroke, they do so citing Richard's being "not himself, but basely led / By flatterers" (ll.241-42) as justification. Through the very fact that he is not a "rule to other men," he is perceived as an example of misrule, an invitation to rebellion.

Hurault's final properties are also relevant:

> The fifth property of the nobleminded, is that he is no great craver nor no great borrower; assuring himself that nothing is so deerly bought, as that which is gotten by intreatance. . . . The sixt propertie of the nobleminded, is that he passeth not whether he be praised or dispraised, so long as he himselfe do well.
>
> (sig. VI^v)

Richard is a great craver, as witness, for instance, his seizure of the "royalties and rights" of Bolingbroke, which subsequently will contribute greatly to his own danger, as York accurately predicts:

> If you do wrongfully seize Herford's rights,
> Call in the letters patents that he hath
> By his attorneys-general to sue
> His livery, and deny his off'red homage,
> You pluck a thousand dangers on your head,
> You lose a thousand well-disposed hearts,
> And prick my tender patience to those thoughts
> Which honour and allegiance cannot think.
>
> (II.i.201-08)

The sixth property touches upon all of those in Hurault's catalogue, and is the one most obviously wanting in Richard. Richard's love of praise is, if anything, doubly evident in his inability to distinguish praise from flattery, as we are reminded throughout the play. Richard, in fact, courts attention of any sort, so long as it is personal. When he looks into the mirror in the deposition scene he is searching for praise *or* dispraise, rather than disinterested counsel. And in his final appearance (V.v), the implied dispraise of even an animal causes Richard dismay, and provokes his trivial lament that his royal horse, Barbary, has willingly borne Bolingbroke to be crowned.

I do not mean to suggest that Shakespeare rigorously followed Hurault, or any other guide to the proper behavior of magistrates. Nor do I insist that at all times York is held up as a figure against which Richard can be measured. I do believe, however, that both characters are more accurately perceived if one considers how the principles of magnanimity apply to each. Magnanimity is a state of mind; although its manifestations in a prince are of necessity different from its manifestations in lesser creatures, they are the result of the same impulse. Therefore when we see York's exemplary devotion to the principles of magnanimity, we are reminded of Richard's neglect of those principles—if, as members of a sixteenth-century audience would be, we are aware of what the principles are.

Notes

1. A. C. Swinburne, *Three Plays of Shakespeare* (London: Harper, 1909), p. 71. In this volume, published in the year of his death, Swinburne carried to an extreme the misgivings he felt about the character of York some thirty years previously: "It is for me at least impossible to determine what I doubt if the poet could for himself have clearly defined—the main principle, the motive and the meaning of such characters as York, Norfolk, and Aumerle" (*A Study of Shakespeare* [1880; rpt. London: Heinemann, 1920], p. 39).

2. Walter Pater, *Appreciations: With an Essay on Style* (London: Macmillan, 1889), pp. 196-212 *passim*; W. B. Yeats, *Ideas of Good and Evil* (London: Bullen, 1903), pp. 156-67 *passim*.

3. Mark Van Doren, *Shakespeare* (New York: Holt, 1939), p. 95.

4. S. C. Sen Gutpa, *Shakespeare's Historical Plays* (London: Oxford Univ. Press, 1964), p. 117; Sheldon P. Zitner, "Aumerle's Conspiracy," *SEL* [*Studies in English Literature*], 14 (1974), 254-56.

5. Harold C. Goddard, *The Meaning of Shakespeare* (Chicago: Univ. of Chicago Press, 1951), p. 158; James Winny, *The Player King* (London: Chatto and Windus, 1968), p. 76; Roy Battenhouse, "Tudor Doctrine and the Tragedy of *Richard II*," *Rice University Studies: Renaissance Study in Honor of Carroll Camden,* 60, No. 2 (1974), 46.

6. For instance: Derek Traversi, *Shakespeare: From Richard II to Henry V* (Stanford: Stanford Univ. Press, 1957), p. 28; A. P. Rossiter, *Angel with Horns* (London: Longmans, 1961), p. 27; M. M. Reese, *The Cease of Majesty* (London: Arnold, 1961), p. 250; A. Norman Jeffares, "In One Person Many People: King Richard the Second," *The Morality of Art: Essays Presented to G. Wilson Knight,* ed. D. W. Jefferson (New York: Barnes and Noble, 1969), p. 56; Robert Ornstein, *A Kingdom for a Stage* (Cambridge, Mass.: Harvard Univ. Press, 1972), p. 123.

7. Norman Rabkin, *Shakespeare and the Common Understanding* (New York: Free Press, 1967), p. 87.

8. *King Richard II,* ed. Peter Ure, New Arden Shakespeare (London: Methuen, 1956), p. lxxii, n.2.

9. *Coleridge's Shakespeare Criticism,* ed. T. M. Raysor (London: Constable, 1930), I, 153, 154.

10. It may be argued that York's wife faults him. That argument, however, turns against itself, as the essence of her complaint is that he acts too much upon principle, rather than upon sentiment as she does. Her dispraise, I intend to demonstrate, does more to call attention to a strength of York's character than to a weakness of it.

11. I.ii. 67. All references to *Richard II* are to Ure's edition.

12. The term *magnanimity* can be applied not only to a concept, but also to various manifestations of that

concept, and, depending upon context, could refer to qualities as diverse as physical courage, generosity, or humility. It is the concept with which I am concerned here; although a discussion of it must necessarily be made in terms of its manifestations, no one of those should be construed as its full definition.

13. *De Officiis,* I.65 and I.88. Section numbers are from the Loeb edition (London: Heinemann, 1913). In *Honor and the Epic Hero* (New York: Holt, Rinehart, 1960), Father Maurice B. McNamee points out differences between Aristotelian and Ciceronian concepts of magnanimity (chap. 3). The views of Cicero, and of Romans in general, are those which most affected political and moral treatises of Shakespeare's time.

14. Pierre de la Primaudaye, *The French Academie,* trans. T[homas] B[owes], 4th ed. (1602), sig. T7.

15. *The Workes* (1614), sig. Hhh4.

16. This term, it is well to observe, has a precise political meaning; see *OED* [*Oxford English Dictionary*]: "2. Taking neither one side nor the other; not declaring oneself on, or rendering assistance to either side." It is perverse, I think, to argue as Wilbur Sanders does that the political meaning is subverted by "grammatical senses of the word" (*The Dramatist and the Received Idea* [Cambridge: Cambridge Univ. Press, 1968], p. 184). He finds the sense of neuter gender particularly damaging, "for it is a man who speaks, claiming a kind of 'neutrality' which is proper only to inanimate nature, impossible to man," as though a political act were impossible to man. Zitner's wry comment, "'I do remain as neuter,' says York with formidable insight" (p. 245), makes a point only if one forces onto the term a definition unknown in Shakespeare's time. York's invitation to Bolingbroke, issued to one who is neither friend nor foe, is quite consistent with York's mere acceptance of that which is beyond his control.

17. Geoffrey Bullough, *Narrative and Dramatic Sources of Shakespeare,* III (London: Routledge, 1960), pp. 398-99.

18. Bertrand de Loque, *Discourses of Warre and Single Combat,* trans. J[ohn] Eliot (1591), sig. D4. The chief concern throughout the text was indicated by Eliot, in his dedication to Essex. It was, he hoped, "now as fit to be perused as patronized by some magnanimous Martialist of our own Countrie. It may please you then (Right Ho.) to read these Treatises in a rude stile, and shew them your favourable countinance, that they maie passe to the view of all valiant warriours (in whose number our countrie counteth your Lo. formost for your forwardly indevours and approved magnanimitie)" (sig. A2ᵛ).

19. Jacques Hurault, *Politicke, Moral, and Martial Discourses,* trans. Arthur Golding (1595), Sig. V1.

PRODUCTION REVIEWS

Ace G. Pilkington (essay date 1991)

SOURCE: Pilkington, Ace G. "The BBC *Richard II.*" In *Screening Shakespeare from* Richard II *to* Henry V, pp. 29-63. Newark: University of Delaware Press, 1991.

[*In the following essay, Pilkington offers a detailed assessment of the highlights and deficiencies of the 1979 BBC production of* Richard II, *directed by David Giles and starring Derek Jacobi as Richard.*]

FACTORS SHAPING THE PRODUCTION

John Wilders told me in a June 1987 interview that two of the constraints on the BBC *Richard II* were (as might be expected from the general background of the series) time and money. He used the Mowbray-Bolingbroke confrontation as an example of a scene where "the camera tended simply to shift in a rather automatic way from one to another." And he went on to argue "that if more had been done with having many more cameras and many more camera angles and more interesting lighting and so on, it wouldn't have been quite such a routine, workaday production." He pointed out, however, that "we would not only have needed a bigger budget, a much bigger technical crew, but it would also simply have taken a very great deal more time in rehearsal and the actual recording it."

As John Wilders indicates, the production could have been improved with more time to rehearse and film. The coordination required among director, actors, and camera crew cannot be achieved without careful planning, no matter how capable the artists involved may be; the choreography required on a soundstage must be almost balletic in its precision. Actors must, of course, hit marks to remain within the effective range of the camera. This is complicated when an actor crosses from one part of the set to another; it becomes still more complex when groups are involved. For instance, in a three shot, the actors must carefully restrict their movements and stay close together. They must also keep to the prearranged schedule, delaying or speeding up their dialogue and inserting pauses to allow the camera the time it needs for changes of movement and focus.[1] It is worth remembering in this context that the BBC productions were sometimes taped in blocks of as much as fifteen minutes.

There are, indeed, many signs in *Richard II* of the haste that lack of money creates. The framing is often sloppy, the actors sometimes shuffle to get out of the way of the camera and each other, there is a worrisome sameness to the camera angles, and, especially in the early scenes, actors are often crammed into shots for no reason other than to add more costumes and bodies. Thus, through most of Bolingbroke's early speeches, he is in two and three shots with stony-faced actors who look blankly away from the action and even down at the floor in what seems much closer to actors' boredom than courtiers' embarrassment. Reaction shots in general tend to be slow (and with the notable exception of Jacobi's) not well thought out. There is perfunctory pointing of a camera at an actor as an illustration to go with a particular line instead of using the reaction shot as a means (like lines and often equally important) of advancing plot and characterization.

Here, for example, are some of the problems that occur in the first three scenes:

At 1.1.36, "And mark my greeting well," the back of a head bobs between Bolingbroke and the camera and then moves away again. At 1.2.9, "Finds brotherhood in thee no sharper spur?" there is an unsteady camera movement. At 1.2.58, "Yet one word more," Gaunt is partly out of the frame, the most common type of trouble.[2]

At 1.3.7, "Marshal, demand of yonder champion," Richard's face is too distant to be clearly visible in the shallow focus this production often employs. This too is a frequent difficulty, as the following examples show. At 1.3.78, "God in thy good cause make thee prosperous," Richard is visible in the background during Gaunt's speech, an excellent idea that comes to nothing because the king's features are so blurred as to be indistinguishable. At 1.3.116, "Attending but the signal to begin," Richard signals, but his face is again unclear.

At 1.3.141, "Till twice five summers have enriched our fields," there is a cut to Richard, but in the background Gaunt's shoulder and a fringe of hair rock in and out of the frame, partly, no doubt, as a result of the crowded acting conditions. At 1.3.166, "Within my mouth you have enjailed my tongue," Mowbray is in a two shot with a bored actor who looks down. This is a repeated difficulty; there are many useless faces. Shortly after this, for example, Bolingbroke is in a shot that should belong to him, but two less important actors are seen more prominently than he is. At 1.3.179, "Lay on our royal sword your banished hands," Gaunt is the cause of a similar problem; he is visible, shuffling from one foot to the other in a way unmotivated by anything but finding an unobtrusive place to stand.

At 1.3.268, "Will but remember me what a deal of world," there is a more complicated difficulty than sloppy framing. Bolingbroke turns upscreen to speak to Gaunt, and as a result, we lose most of his expression. This would be an excellent place to employ a reverse angle shot, perhaps giving the film a three-dimensional feeling by shooting the reverse angle over Gaunt's shoulder. The result of that strategy would have been to add visual variety plus give us more of Gaunt's expression than we had of Bolingbroke's and all of Bolingbroke's reaction as well.

The difficulties I have so far listed might most readily be ascribed to a too-short shooting schedule. However, there is an overall problem of attitude as well, which appears most clearly in 2.1. This scene should, in my opinion, have been reshot, but, as I'm about to argue, it should first have been rethought. It follows the most cleverly filmed of the early scenes, the king and his courtiers in the baths, and has in addition Shakespeare's excellent stage (and even better screen) transition from Richard's "Pray God we may make haste and come too late!" to Gaunt's "Will the King come" to start things off. One of Giles's better ideas was the juxtaposition of the informalities at the baths with the informalities we see in the dress and attitudes of the two brothers. It is a vital scene for the plot, containing important confrontations and strong performances, made more prominent still by the decision to use this scene (or at least the first two-thirds of it) as the end of part 1 in the three-part structure, which the BBC imposed on the play. But the filming is marred not only by absence of time but also by the presence of Messina's conception of television Shakespeare as a "front row in the stalls with two fine actors shouting at each other."[3]

For instance, at 2.1.11, "More are men's ends marked than their lives before," York crosses downscreen between Gaunt and the camera on Gaunt's line for no discernible reason, and then Gaunt looks back to where York had been to deliver his next line. Surely something odd must have happened to leave two veteran actors in such straits. At 2.1.72, "What comfort, man? How fares it with aged Gaunt?" there is a desperate camera movement to bring a sliver of Richard to the screen while he speaks his line. At 2.1.113, "Landlord of England art thou now," there is another example of confusion. Gaunt, who has been advancing on Richard during his speech, steps back at this point, which happens also to be the time when the camera switched to Richard for a reaction shot. Since Gaunt and the camera operator had not synchronized their movements and since only one camera appears to have been involved, Gaunt was left very clumsily out of frame before an equally clumsy cut to Richard.

At 2.1.117, "Darest with thy frozen admonition," the camera is shooting over Gaunt's shoulder at Richard, who is upscreen, but instead of a shot that might have given us the two of them reacting to each other, all we get is the back of Gaunt's head. In fact, we do not see Gaunt's face from this point until the last half of 2.1.124. Far too often in this scene we are deprived of Gaunt's face, of Richard's, or of both. At 2.1.141, "I do beseech your Majesty, impute his words," there is a similar problem. York is shouting upscreen at Richard, who is facing the wall.

Much in this scene was not caught by the camera. At 2.1.148, "Nay, nothing, all is said," we fail to get Richard's first reaction to Gaunt's death because Richard is out of focus. At 2.1.151, "Be York the next that must be bankrout so!" we have only the back of York's head. At 2.1.155, "So much for that," Richard moves quickly offscreen and then back; the camera can't keep up. At 2.1.175, "Than was that young and princely gentleman," York moves completely out of frame. At 2.1.181, "Which his triumphant father's hand had won," we have the back of Richard's head, while York is turned upscreen with his hand blocking what little we might otherwise have seen of his profile. At 2.1.184, "O, Richard, York is too far gone with grief," York now turns downscreen and his face falls out of the frame. At 2.1.200, "Now afore God—" York follows Richard behind the other actors and neither is visible.

Many of the problems with what otherwise could have been a very strong scene come directly from giving the audience a seat in the stalls while two actors shout at each other. There is plenty of shouting, and the camera (there often appears to be only one) does seem to have been confined to the front seats of a hypothetical theater: it is capable of moving in for close-ups but not of shooting from the wings, from the back of the stage, or from anywhere overhead. As a result, we are burdened with the difficulties of the stage and television together. We have not the freedom of watching anything the director does not show us, and the sight lines are so clumsy and the camera's freedom of access so limited that much of the scene is not visible to anybody. Undoubtedly many of these problems could have been corrected with longer shooting time and more retakes, but many of the difficulties could also have been eliminated if the initial idea had been to film television rather than to record a stage production from the front rows.

In fairness to David Giles and his company, I should point out that the problems I have so far listed are at their worst in the early scenes of *Richard II*. There is a steady decline in the number of technical mistakes through the four BBC Shakespeares he directed and a corresponding increase in the flexibility of camera placement. In addition, the efficient handling of many specialized group shots in the difficult circumstances of *Richard II* demonstrates his expertise.

Several critics commented on Giles's skill. For Clive James, Giles "showed his firm hand immediately, framing the actors' faces as closely as possible while they got on with . . . speaking the text."[4] Jorgens similarly praises the "scene where Bolingbroke sentences Bushy and Green to death." He points to "the confident use of the camera, which includes and excludes characters with precision," providing "a striking contrast with the randomness of earlier productions."[5] I have indicated that it also provides a contrast (if not a striking one) with some other scenes in this production, but I do not mean to deny Giles's effectiveness. He should certainly be credited with the victories and finesses that emerged from a rough process.

In addition to the neat juxtaposition of informal scenes from Richard in the baths to Gaunt and York alone together, Giles has made other interesting connections. The last part of 2.1, from 224 to the end (the plot of the three conspirators), was cut away and set at the beginning of part 2, in Westminster, the Cloisters.[6] And this whole miniscene was cleverly handled. We begin with Northumberland in close-up, speaking, it would seem, to himself.

Then Ross, on his first line, turns back into the screen to make it a two shot, and finally Willoughby neatly steps in for a three shot. There is movement provided soon after by Northumberland crossing correctly behind prior to the three of them walking off as a group. Once they are all onscreen, their three faces are adroitly crammed together, providing a visual illustration for Ross's "We three are but thyself, and speaking so / Thy words are but as thoughts" (2.1.275-76). This visual concentration also helps to make them seem more positive, more certain of the success of that coming man (in two of the word's senses), Bolingbroke. The elimination of the first ninety-nine lines of 2.2 gives Giles an all-but-perfect jump cut from the absolute plan for action of Northumberland, Ross, and Willoughby to York's plaintive "I know not what to do" (2.2.100).

That Giles is also capable of handling larger groupings is proved with the arrival of Bolingbroke in 2.3. The whole scene is nicely done, with especially crisp camera movement between Bolingbroke and York during their confrontation. At 2.3.122, "If that my cousin king be King in England," we get a three shot with Northumberland cannily watching Bolingbroke's persuasion from the background. When Ross and Willoughby are added, we have a neat five shot with Bolingbroke standing silent in front while other voices speak his arguments for him. It is a visual summary of the progress from the three conspirators' certainty to York's dithering, Bushy, Bagot, and Green's fear, and the arrival of Bolingbroke himself. The film has told us, even without the text, that one of the next moves will be against the favorites.

Michael Manheim points to the symbolic use of long shots and close-ups as the strength in the filming of 3.3: "That both Richard and Northumberland are seen at a distance establishes the highly political, patently insincere nature of their exchange." When "close-ups take over . . . Richard speaks his real feelings to his entourage."[7] A similar juxtaposing of private and public takes place in 4.1 when Bolingbroke, who has been using his private voice, switches at 4.1.199, "Are you contented to resign the crown?" to a public style of declamation, a contrast that the intimacy of television easily heightens. Giles has demonstrated his skill by achieving more than might be expected in such difficult circumstances.

In addition to time and money, there were other factors in the construction of the BBC's *Richard II*. The decisions made by the designers and directors in that first season reflected the concerns of the producer and his corporate sponsors, which were in turn dictated by the audience expectations they perceived and hoped to fulfill. Messina's initial idea for the series had involved an open-air production of *As You Like It,* which meant, according to set designer Tony Abbott, "that the studio productions must be able to go alongside the ultra-realism of the location productions."[8] Here again is the feeling of restriction I noted earlier. Despite William Walton's music for the opening, despite the reassuring presence of John Gielgud, there is a sense of smallness, of sameness, so that there will be fewer visual styles in a whole season of different plays than in Olivier's *Henry V*. The decision, however, was part of the producer's concern for the expectations of his audience. And according to at least one reviewer, Messina may not have been conservative (or consistent) enough. Philip Purser complained that if the BBC had decided to limit itself to "reliable texts in a straightforward studio setting—an acoustic cube as the modern equivalent of Shakespeare's wooden 'O,'" it should not then go "frolicking off on location in Scotland for 'As You Like It.'"[9]

Tony Abbott describes the style that finally emerged in *Richard II* as "stylised realism."[10] That there were distinct limitations both on the realism and the stylization is clear from the handling of the tournament scene (1.3). David Giles says the scene was "an absolute swine." He goes on to explain the impossibility of doing the scene realistically in a television studio but points out that they used real horses to avoid the alternate danger of too much stylization, because "if we had gone too stylised with the list scene we would have had to stylise the play all the way through." Giles is apparently aware that a mixture of styles in the same film (or the same season) was not one of his options.

He is also suspicious of too much stylization because "on television where what you see is a real head against a bit of stylised background you can only stylise if you design it shot by shot." Though later productions in the series, such as *The Winter's Tale* (and his own *Henry V*), tend to contradict Giles's initial assumption, it seems to me that his comments are another example of the pressure of truncated rehearsal and shooting schedules. He continues, "There certainly wasn't time for that here and I'm not sure I'd have wanted to do that anyway."[11] He is slightly defensive and almost apologetic about the only part of the filming that was noticeably unusual.

Perhaps David Giles has good reason to sound apologetic. It was, in fact, this sequence that prompted those remarks by Cedric Messina about "arty-crafty" shooting, which I have already quoted. After discussing what he saw as the healthy habit of shooting for fifteen minutes without a break, Messina mentioned that Richard's soliloquy had been cut into ten different shots; he then went on to defend this seeming deviation from his policy of plain shooting: "We've done nothing sensational in the shooting of it— there's no arty-crafty shooting at all."[12]

Again, such comments indicate Messina's attempts to fulfill the expectations of his mass audience. He says he hoped the productions would "stimulate people who . . . notice *Hamlet* advertised in their neighborhood theatre to say, 'I saw it on the box; I think it's a good play. Let's go in and see it.'"[13] Apparently, as Messina envisions the viewing experience, his audience must be introduced to art gradually, with no visual shocks to warn them that they have switched to something different from their ordinary fare.[14]

David Giles's decision about the costumes for *Richard II*, which brought him into conflict with the overall costume policy and with Robin Fraser-Paye, the costume designer for the production, tends to support my reading of Messina's remarks. Giles said he did not want the costumes to resemble *The Book of Hours* but

> to look as much like clothes as possible.[15] Robin . . . said to me, "But they're extraordinary clothes." I said, "Yes, I know . . . and I do know Richard spent £2000 on one suit . . . but I want them to look real—everyday clothes that the audience can accept."[16]

In this case the goal for the costumes in the histories "to be historically accurate to the period in which the play is set"[17] had to give way to what Giles (and Messina behind him) thought his "unsophisticated" audience could accept as real clothes.[18] Robin Fraser-Paye solved the problem by toning down the color palette and omitting the more extreme fashions.[19]

Many of the decisions that moved the production toward realism and away from "arty-crafty" shooting were also designed (as might be expected) to reduce the director's impact and importance. David Bevington, for example, calls Giles's direction (of *1H4* but the description applies equally well to *R2*) "low-key" and his "interpretation less insistent than that in the [stage] productions of Burrell, Seale, Hall, Hands, Nunn and others."[20] I see this reduction of the director's influence as designed because of Messina's obvious desire to avoid "arty" direction and let "the plays speak for themselves." Of course, plays do not speak, actors do, and this too is clearly one of Messina's designs—to let the actors speak to the audience with as little interference as possible. In the process David Giles has become much less important than some of his stage counterparts, while the actors have emerged as—to some extent—auteurs.

There is nothing particularly unusual about the actor as auteur; both Olivier and Welles might—by stretching a point—be so described. Indeed, Patrick McGilligan argues that a performer who "shifts meanings, influences the narrative and style of a film and altogether signifies something clear-cut to audiences despite the intent of writers and directors" is an auteur.[21]

Obviously, Orson Welles and Laurence Olivier do much more than this, while the actors in the BBC Shakespeares do less. But McGilligan discusses an intermediate situation, where the actor may also be an auteur. In the work of three Warner Brothers directors of the thirties and forties—William Keighley, Roy Del Ruth, and Lloyd Bacon—McGilligan identifies a straightforward, quick style of making movies, which "gave the actors . . . free rein to interpret their roles: indeed, there was little time for anything else."[22] Bacon, for example, shot *Picture Snatcher* in fifteen days,[23] a feat that is perhaps comparable to filming a Shakespeare play in six (allowing for the relative difficulty of the material and for the fact that Bacon had no time for separate rehearsal).

In short, given the preconceptions of the producer (including a bias toward realism that foregrounds the individual performance at the expense of any overall pattern), the extremely brief time allowed for shooting, the tendency to film the plays in large chunks when possible and to do retakes only when absolutely necessary, and keeping in mind that many of the actors had more experience with the material than the director did, it makes sense to look at the BBC *Richard II* (and the other plays of the second tetralogy) as the result of a combined effort. Of course, any film is a combined effort of many artists, but in the circumstances I have just described, the impact of any one of the chief players might be as great or greater than that of the director, and any analysis of the film must be arranged accordingly.

A clear example comes in Michael Manheim's review of *Richard II*. It is one of the most favorable reviews the production received, and it is undoubtedly strongly influenced by Manheim's admiration for the cast in general and Jacobi in particular. He ascribes the film's success to "the superb realization of the characters" and goes on to say, "Derek Jacobi is for me the best Richard witnessed in over thirty years."[24] Cedric Messina had to some extent anticipated this, calling the play "the tragedy of one man."[25]

What emerges from this description of the making of the BBC *Richard II* is the clear subordination of an individual production to an overall "house style." It might well be argued that such subordination is dangerous. As Messina himself had said, "Each play creates its own problems,"[26] and shaping *Richard II* perforce to fit the preconceptions of BBC television realism meant rejecting a number of other forms the production could have taken. It might have been more logical to look first at the text and only then to determine the film to be made from it.

In examining Shakespeare's aims in the play, Stanley Wells says, "Shakespeare made a decision of fundamental importance. He decided to write this play entirely in verse." He goes on to discuss the effects of this degree of "stylisation and artificiality in the language," maintaining that "a number of the characters are so lacking in individuality that they seem mainly or entirely choric in function."[27]

However, since pointing up such a choric function or foregrounding the stylization of the language can be undertaken by actors only when directorial decisions have paved the way, certain elements in *Richard II* were, of necessity, played down or shut out. Messina no doubt viewed this as part of the process of meeting the expectations of his various audiences, "what the layman would expect to see when he hears the name of . . . Richard II." Hence, "in all the histories the aim is to be historically accurate to the period in which the play is set."[28] This principle (violated only when even stronger audience expectations got in the way) emerged in tragedies with historical settings as well, even when the tight budget might not have seemed able to support it. Russell Miller "was told by a disgruntled employee" that during the making of *Romeo and Juliet,* the only researcher was in the British Museum, "wading through

Italian books to try and find out what a town square was like in Italy in the fifteenth century. And she can't even speak Italian."[29]

Costume designer Odette Barrow indicates the kind of detail that was expected in the "semidocumentary style" for *1 Henry IV*:

> I had a problem with Hotspur. Historically, when his mother died he incorporated her arms with his. But Shakespeare manages to have her appear in Part 2 *after* Hotspur's death; so we thought, well, we'll have to give him his arms as they were before she died. So far as history is concerned his arms at the battle of Shrewsbury are therefore inaccurate, but as far as Shakespeare is concerned, they're right.[30]

Clearly, David Giles was not meant to be an auteur, making Shakespeare's material his own after the fashion of Orson Welles. Many of the options that would have made a directorial imprint possible had been eliminated. There was not even the inspiration of continuity, of seeing *Richard II* as the beginning of a four-part sequence. Despite Cedric Messina's description of the histories as a "sort of Curse of the House of Atreus in English,"[31] there was initially no plan to produce the plays in the second tetralogy as a group. It is true that many of the actors do continue throughout the series, and Giles did direct all four; however, at the time he made *Richard II,* he "was not expecting to continue with the three Henrys."[32] Thus, it is not safe to regard decisions in *Richard II* as direct preparations for the later plays. The omission of Henry's reference to Hal, the inclusion of his mention of Glendower, and the change of actors in the part of Hotspur are therefore likely to be influenced by factors other than the connection between *Richard II* and *1 Henry IV.* For example, the choice of Tim Pigott-Smith for Hotspur was probably the result of his success as Angelo in the first season's production of *Measure for Measure.*

The central interpretation that grew from David Giles's *Richard II* was, as I have indicated, as much a matter of what could not be done (or what was not allowed) as of what could. It had to fit (or at least seem to fit) Messina's vision of audience expectations, and it had to take into account the naturalism of the production and the interpretive importance (and even control) of the actors, especially Derek Jacobi. It also had to fit in with the BBC's emphasis on the history of the period in which the play was set. In the circumstances, it is not surprising that the central interpretation which emerged was the result of cooperation between Giles and Jacobi (who had read history at university) and that it used the play's historical background as a starting point. In a way, Giles's creative use of history anticipated Jonathan Miller, who was able to work within the restrictions of BBC house style by focusing on the history of Shakespeare's period. Miller said, "It's the director's job, quite apart from working with actors . . . to act as the chairman of a history faculty and of an art-history faculty."[33]

THE CRITICS, GILES, AND HISTORY

One logical means for charting the central interpretation of the BBC *Richard II* is to look at the critics' reactions. Often, the unfavorable responses are even more revealing than the favorable ones because they show where the critic's expectational text has been revised by Giles and company. Malcolm Page is right when he says, "Commentators gave moderate praise to the television *Richard*, grudgingly observing that it was rather better than others of the first six."[34] But as Manheim's judgment makes clear, Page is describing a consensus or average from which individual conclusions diverged widely.

The most sweeping condemnations were made (as might be anticipated) in those instances when Giles seemed to be deliberately revising the expectational text. Sheldon P. Zitner criticizes the whole of the BBC second tetralogy and *Richard II* in particular for "the effort to 'clarify' the text." However, the example he gives is surprising: "the camera cuts to Bolingbroke in exile, informing us that before he returns to England he knows about the death of his father and about Richard's proposal to confiscate his property. Not so in Shakespeare."[35] And not so in the BBC *Richard II* either. As happens disconcertingly often in Shakespeare film criticism, a check of the production in question fails to verify the description of events. Bolingbroke's first appearance after the death of Gaunt is in 2.3 with the scene's first line, "How far is it, my lord, to Berkeley now?" There simply is not an interpolated French scene, and, in any event, how would such a scene without lines indicate Bolingbroke's royal ambitions? But Zitner's hypersensitivity to the remote (and in this case nonexistent) possibility is revealing.

At least part of Zitner's objection is expressed more directly by Martin Banham: "When a television (or, to be fair, a film) director . . . shapes our image of the action, he is intruding his own interpretation of what is significant." Banham sees in this the danger that the director will "interfere with our imaginative liberties" and may even destroy "the sensitive integral framework of the play itself." He maintains that one result of this interference "has been to give these Shakespearean productions on television a linear feeling."[36]

This comment seems to me to come (on one level at any rate) from an uncritical idealization of the stage and an equally uncritical condemnation of television and film. Surely, as John Barton's 1973-74 production of *Richard II* for the Royal Shakespeare Company makes clear, a stage director may also interfere with the audience's "imaginative liberties."[37] In fact, as David Bevington's analysis indicates, David Giles's "low-key" direction results in an interpretation that is "less insistent" than that of many of his stage counterparts.

Nevertheless, several factors contribute to the feeling that Giles has more control than is actually the case. I have already pointed out that the shooting schedule and the conscious decisions of Messina and of Giles himself effectively reduced the impact of the director on the films of the second tetralogy. But the large number of close-ups, the small number of reverse-angle shots, and the use of "a very long lens on the camera, so what you see in focus is clear but everything else is blurred" for exterior shots,[38] all added up to what Samuel Crowl called a "claustrophobic *Richard II*."[39] While that adjective may be too strong, there is a closeness (and even, perhaps, a visual flatness) about the production that can give the misleading impression of a linear progression imposed on the viewer by the director.

I do not, of course, wish to suggest by this that David Giles did not make directorial decisions, some of which had strong impact. It is likely to be certain key decisions Giles made that are annoying Banham, even though he does not directly say so. Michael Manheim, who approves of those decisions, praises Giles for serving "as teacher as well as director." We are, he says, being taught history we may not have learned "when, following Bolingbroke's accusation that Norfolk has murdered the Duke of Gloucester, Giles has the camera switch not to Norfolk but to Richard, the real culprit in Gloucester's death."[40] Such a camera movement will not work, of course, unless the actor playing Richard is ready for it and shares the director's vision of the historical events that preceded the opening of the play. But Giles and Jacobi did have a shared vision that shaped the film.

It is in all probability this shape that Banham dislikes. He finds the "linear feeling" uncomfortable because the line moves away from his expectational text. One of the strongest objections to the production from another critic hits at this precise issue of the interpretation of the history behind the history play. Pointing to Cedric Messina's conventional description of the history plays and a television talk given by Paul Johnson as a curtain raiser for *Richard II*, Graham Holderness argues that "the second tetralogy emerges from this production as a constituent element in an inclusive and integrated dramatic totality, illustrating the violation of natural social 'order' by the deposition of a legitimate king."[41] Additionally, he maintains that the naturalistic conventions which Messina and Giles favor further endorse this ideology,[42] and he contrasts this with what he sees as the more open and radical version of history and history plays that emerged from Jane Howell's direction of the first tetralogy.[43] I find some of Holderness's assumptions concerning the BBC *Richard II* useful because, though I believe his reading to be incorrect, I think the part of the filmtext that makes him uneasy is the center of the interpretation which Giles and Jacobi created.

Certainly, a naturalistic style of production can be used to endorse Tillyard's thesis, but style does not guarantee the political nature of content. As Henry Fenwick points out, "television casting is able to open up hitherto neglected portions of the play," and one of the examples he gives is "the tiny part of the Duchess of Gloucester played by Mary Morris."[44] The naturalistic television scene (1.2) foregrounds the Duchess of Gloucester's grief, Richard's guilt, and John of Gaunt's expressed belief that God will avenge Richard's crime as emphatically as the same scene was foregrounded in John Barton's stylized and nonnaturalistic stage production.[45] A good Tillyardian or even a director who wanted to simplify characterizations might have been expected to cut the scene.

Despite Cedric Messina's remarks about an English Curse of the House of Atreus, there was no concerted effort to produce a version of the second tetralogy conforming to Tillyard's Elizabethan world picture. In fact, the emphasis on the history of the period resulted in the contradiction of many of Tillyard's points.

Paul Johnson did say (as Holderness indicates), "According to the orthodox Tudor view of history the deposition of the rightful and anointed King, Richard II, was a crime against God, which thereafter had to be expiated by the nation in a series of bloody struggles."[46] But shortly before that he had called Richard "an ideologue, a fanatic, an early supporter of the theory that kings ruled by divine right." He also accused Richard of "illegal exactions and confiscations" and of exploiting parliament "to commit judicial murder against the nobles and despoil their estates."[47] It would seem that the "orthodox Tudor view of history" was not shared by Paul Johnson.

His remarks do, however, fit the interpretation of history that Giles and Jacobi had worked out. To understand how far this is from the "world picture" it is necessary only to contrast it with Tillyard on the same subject: "Shakespeare knows that Richard's crimes never amounted to tyranny and hence that outright rebellion against him was a crime. He leaves uncertain the question of who murdered Woodstock."[48]

The radio curtain raiser to the BBC *Richard II* was given by Ian Richardson, who, with Richard Pasco, alternated the roles of Richard and Henry in John Barton's "radical" stage production. Richardson also failed to adhere to the Tillyardian party line, saying on the subject of Gloucester's death, "Richard had ordered it and so Mowbray from sheer loyalty keeps his mouth shut."[49] He committed further heresies when he suggested that "Richard plucks defeat from the jaws of victory and wilfully destroys himself," and "It's important for Henry Bolingbroke to have had no hand in Richard's overthrow, at least as direct instigator, if he is to maintain the audience's sympathy within Shakespeare's moral framework."[50]

If, in fact, Cedric Messina and the other administrators of the series were bent on "an inclusive and integrated dramatic totality," they seem to have consistently chosen the wrong people for their purposes. David Giles and Derek Jacobi agreed early in rehearsals that Richard was indeed guilty and that his emotion in the first scene is, in Giles's words, "high tension because it is the moment he's been waiting for so long,"[51] with the clear implication that what Richard has been awaiting is revenge. Nor would the two of them have found a defender of Tillyard's orthodoxy in the series literary consultant, John Wilders.

Wilders's wide range of responsibilities included trimming "the texts to fit the two-and-three-quarter hour time slot allotted for productions," plus advising "directors of the series . . . on interpretation of difficult passages, rhythms, cuts, and relevant bibliographical sources" and "holding a 'literary clinic' to help actors make sense of Shakespeare's language."[52] It is probably safe to assume that one reason for John Wilders's appointment to the post of literary consultant was the appearance in 1978 of his book *The Lost Garden,* an elegant study of Shakespeare's English and Roman history plays that strongly attacks Tillyard's thesis.

It is, nevertheless, correct, I think, to see the BBC version of the second tetralogy and especially *Richard II* as productions of the history plays which are very much concerned with history. The background material I have presented up to this point indicates no less. Robert Hapgood said, commenting on *Richard II,* "The best of the Shakespeare Plays histories have been enlightened costume dramas, at ease with their historical ambience yet not at the expense of . . . dramatic strengths."[53]

I also agree with Holderness (with the reservations my discussion so far makes clear) when he says that the emphasis on history is the result of the plays being "produced in 'classic drama' style with predominantly naturalistic devices of acting, *mise-en-scène,* and filming."[54] Extreme stylization of the kind Stanley Wells discusses was ruled out by Messina's house style. At the same time, the emphasis on history and the semidocumentary style that went with it would have pushed many directors (as it later did Jonathan Miller) to consider the historical possibilities inherent in the current play. David Giles and Derek Jacobi created their interpretation within the imposed limits of the BBC Shakespeares, but despite that (and, in fact, partly because of that) they produced a new Richard and an original *Richard II.*

As might be expected in the circumstances, Giles and Jacobi have done their best to maintain the interpenetration that has long existed between Shakespeare's histories and history itself. As Peter Saccio says in *Shakespeare's English Kings,* "far more than any professional historian . . . Shakespeare is responsible for whatever notions most of us possess about the period and its political leaders."[55] Or as J. L. Kirby, himself a professional historian, writes in *Henry IV of England,* "From Shakespeare, of course, we can never escape whether we wish to or not."[56]

More important, though, for this study than the effect of Shakespeare on the writing of history is the impact of history on *Richard II* in its BBC incarnation. David Giles assumed that a modern audience was at a disadvantage because "the first third of the play depends on a circumstance which isn't fully explained in the play and which was close to the Elizabethan audience—the murder of Gloucester. To them it was the beginning of the Wars of the Roses."[57]

While this is hardly a startling position from which to begin,[58] it pushes the performance in definite directions.

For example, in 1963, John Gielgud talked of Richard being "only lightly sketched at first in a few rather enigmatic strokes."[59] This attitude pushed to its extreme (as it was by John Neville, playing the role at the Old Vic in 1955)[60] leads to the idea of two Richards—a pre-Ireland and post-Ireland one—the relevance of character in the latter half of the play having no relevance to the actions in the first half.

David Giles and Derek Jacobi took a precisely opposite view. As Giles says, "Derek and I both agree that the key section for Richard is the opening section of the play—the first three scenes."[61] This at once introduces a series of subtextual messages into the performance, which may be expected to alert even audience members who come to the play unprovided with the historical background. Instead of an impartial king attempting to resolve a dispute between two important nobleman—well or ill, weakly or powerfully, as actor, as poet, or as aesthete, according to the nature of the production—we now have a politician, manipulating royal justice to serve his own partly concealed purposes.

In a careful analysis of these subtextual (and in the case of historical information, extratextual) possibilities, John Russell Brown pointed out in 1966 that in the first scene Richard's protestations "may carry subtextual impressions of irony, apprehension or antagonism. Bolingbroke's accusations may seem aimed at the King rather than Mowbray, and Mowbray's confidence to stem from royal support rather than his own innocence."[62]

Brown's words could easily serve as a description of the relevant portion of the BBC *Richard II*. Only one significant element is missing, and Brown picks that up in his comments on scene 3: "Bolingbroke's submission . . . may seem to veil a rivalry with the King himself."[63]

Such a shift in perspective makes for what amounts to a reinterpretation of the motives for various actions in the play (and behind it) and a reassessment of Richard himself. Thus, as Andrew Gurr, editor of the New Cambridge *Richard II,* notes concerning the duel, "Richard cannot afford to have either man win, and therefore chooses to send both into the silence of exile for his own political safety."[64] Such a view of the character is a long way from the picture of a histrionic Richard who stops the fight to make himself the center of attention and is even further from the vision of a political incompetent who makes dim and whimsical decisions. If this Richard belongs in the company of Hamlet and Coriolanus, where Yeats placed him,[65] it is because he too is involved in a battle of mighty opposites. In that case, even his most seemingly self-indulgent moments may shield something more than emotion. Gurr argues, for example, that "Richard calls for the mirror in order to evade Northumberland's insistence that he read the Articles listing his misdeeds."[66] Gurr is not commenting on the BBC *Richard II,* but his words are an accurate description of what happens in the production, nevertheless. In fact, the Richard who emerges from these critical comments, the BBC film, and recent histories[67] is an altogether more dangerous character than a man who, as Theodore Weiss put it, "is Shakespeare's most thoroughgoing study of the absorption in words."[68]

HISTORY AS SUBTEXT

The version of history Giles and Jacobi used (and which became a kind of parallel text behind the filmtext) differs from that of Tillyard and other familiar sources in the placing of emphases and the conclusions it reaches. Despite the fact that Giles and Jacobi were contradicting the expectational texts of some of their viewers (including not a few critics), the coherent historical text that was available to them provided a workable interpretation for the play and also fitted in neatly with the BBC emphasis on history. This was true in part because the play is much closer to being historically accurate than many literary critics have realized.

Richard's whole career is seen in this view as a struggle to impose his royal (and therefore divine) will on his recalcitrant subjects. There was an escalating series of clashes between Richard and his nobles. The first—in 1386—involved Arundel and Thomas, duke of Gloucester, and left Richard fuming under the rule of an executive commission for one year. He was compelled to accept this by the threat of deposition, and one chronicle says Richard thought of asking the opposing lords to dinner and murdering them but gave up the idea as unworkable.[69]

The second clash came in November of 1387, when Richard challenged the commission with a royal army in Cheshire and the signatures of many of the country's justices on a document that declared the commission imposed on the king to be not only illegal but also treasonous.[70] Gloucester and Arundel joined with Warwick, swiftly bringing their own troops to London and "appealing" five of Richard's closest advisors (who were supposedly behind the king's dangerous policies) of treason. Caught without an army of his own, Richard agreed to put the matter to Parliament and until that time to "take the case into his own hands."[71]

However, as soon as the three "appellant" lords had withdrawn their army, Richard let his favorites escape and summoned the royal army of Cheshire archers.[72] It was at this point, in December 1387,[73] that Henry Bolingbroke and Thomas Mowbray joined the appellants. The king's men were defeated at Radcot Bridge, and again Richard found himself pressured to agree to demands by the threat of deposition.[74]

It took Richard ten years to prepare his revenge, building up his royal power to the point of tyranny. He now had a formidable force of Cheshire archers, and Parliament had, at his request, redefined interference in the royal household as treason.[75] Bruce suggests that Richard "had never fully recovered from the trauma of the Apellants' revolt,"[76] and the meeting of the five appellants for dinner at this time (and Mowbray's report of it to Richard) pushed him into action. In July of 1397, the three original appellants were themselves appealed of treason. Warwick confessed and was banished, Arundel was executed, and Gloucester, imprisoned in Calais, died mysteriously, almost certainly on Richard's orders.[77]

The next step was to compel Parliament to repeal the general pardon granted after the 1388 Parliament and, in effect, to brand "anyone who had interfered with the king's prerogative, or had persuaded him to do anything against his will"[78] as a traitor. Parliament was forced to agree to what Richard wanted by the presence of four thousand archers with bent bows and arrows drawn to their ears.[79] The repeal of the general pardons put most of the people of southeast England in Richard's power,[80] a power he employed in various profitable ways. He sold pardons, neglected to record the sales, and sold pardons to the same men (and whole counties) again; and, finally, he had blank charters[81] drawn, signed, and stored in chests for later use.[82]

With Richard censoring all foreign mail and "sheriffs . . . being made to swear to imprison at once anyone whom they heard speak ill of the king,"[83] Mowbray told Bolingbroke of Richard's intention to punish them for their part in Radcot Bridge.[84] Remembering Mowbray's hand in the destruction of the three elder appellants, Bolingbroke reported his words to John of Gaunt, who, in turn, reported them to the king. Then, it was simple for Richard to force a quarrel and banish both men.[85]

Giles and Jacobi have made their view of Richard's history clear. Speaking of Richard and the five appellant lords, Giles says,

> One he has executed, one is in the tower, Gloucester has just been murdered, and now of the five only Mowbray and Bolingbroke, the two youngest, are left. Derek and I both agreed that the key section for Richard is the opening section of the play—the first three scenes. He said, "Why is he so angry in the first scene?" and I said, "He isn't—it's just high tension because it is the moment he has been waiting for so long."[86]

Giles goes on to give additional insights into his view of Richard and also his directorial decisions: "it's easier on television . . . because by focusing on Richard . . . and by using a major actress like Mary Morris . . . in a part that's usually skimped over on stage, the audience does gather something of what has happened."[87]

As Giles's remarks indicate, the entire production and not just Jacobi's performance was affected by the historical interpretation (or reinterpretation). Part of the originality of accepting this plausible and well-documented version of history as the blueprint for a production of *Richard II* is that it means treating Shakespeare's play as a serious attempt to set out the facts as well as to get at the truth, an attitude that many critics have been unwilling to adopt. The play is, in fact, more accurate than many critics believe it to be,[88] and this accuracy fitted in neatly with the semidocumentary style the BBC *Richard II* employed.

F. W. Brownlow (among others) finds the play unhistorical, objecting to the view of Thomas of Woodstock as a "plain well-meaning soul" and maintaining that John of Gaunt was never noted for public spirit or high principle. He believes "such changes of character are more damaging to the play's historical truth than are details like the alterations of Queen Isabella's and Henry Percy's ages, because they mean that Shakespeare can never treat properly the political realities of the reign."[89] Saccio is similarly unhappy with Gaunt, since Shakespeare has not followed Holinshed, "who with far greater historical accuracy, depicts Gaunt as a contentious and ambitious baron."[90]

Surely in the special circumstances of 2.1.128 Gaunt ought to be allowed to call his murdered brother a "plain well-meaning soul." "Plain" after all, may be used to describe behavior such as Kent's in *King Lear* 2.2, where he is repeatedly called "plain" by Cornwall and by himself. Just such plain speaking seems to have been one of Gloucester's faults. Kirby says he "possessed neither common sense nor the respect for the King's estate which had been shown by his brother, John of Gaunt."[91]

But perhaps in Gaunt's last moments, when he himself has been doing some plain speaking to the king, Gloucester's freedom of speech seems more attractive and his critical viewpoint the correct one. It is often dangerous for any critic to assume he knows history better than Shakespeare shows it.[92] As Marie Louise Bruce says about Gloucester, "From a twentieth century viewpoint a curiously unattractive character, at the time his honesty of purpose was to make him seem to many . . . 'the best of men' and 'the hope and solace of the whole community of the realm.'"[93] In that light, John of Gaunt's words are not only historical but also moderate.

The portrait of Gaunt himself is equally easy to defend. Even Saccio admits that he was "fundamentally loyal to his nephew, and remained Richard's faithful advisor throughout the 1390s."[94] Both Kirby and Bruce see him as a moderate influence, whose absence in Portugal allowed more extreme factions to chart the country's course.[95] The critical confusion about Gaunt comes from paying too much attention to his early career and not enough to his later one. His reputation (if not his nature) seems literally to have suffered a sea change. In the summer of 1381, as Kirby says, "John of Gaunt had become the best hated man in England."[96] But by the time he was preparing to leave for Portugal "with the prospect of seeing the last of him for a while everyone liked the duke of Lancaster."[97] On his return to England, as a result of his vast new wealth and his daughters' powerful marriages on the Iberian peninsula, he assumed precisely the role in English politics that Shakespeare gives him. The former hatred of Gaunt "paled into insignificance." He became "a legendary figure admired by nearly all, and with this new image went a new, more sober approach to politics. In England from now on he was to play the part of the most respected elder statesman."[98]

Even in the minor details, Shakespeare's picture is accurate. The Duchess of Gloucester suspects Gaunt's motives for peacefully accepting her husband's murder, telling him, "That which in mean men we entitle patience / Is pale cold cowardice in noble breasts" (1.2.33-34). In his campaign of terror, Richard put York and Gloucester in fear of their lives, and they were both "to besmirch the memory of their dead brother"[99] as a result of that fear. It seems safe to say of many of Shakespeare's historical figures what Marie Louise Bruce says of his York, that the portrait "of the bumbling, well-intentioned duke unhappily trying to choose between duty and inclination and in the end taking the only course open to him appears to be remarkably accurate."[100] Though there are clearly elements in the play that benefit from the kind of stylization John Barton's production gave it, there are also elements that can be most easily seen when the emphasis is placed on history and naturalism, as it was in the BBC film.

BOLINGBROKE AND YORK

Giles's interpretation of *Richard II* and his emphasis on history has not only produced an effective Richard but also given other characters firmer ground to stand on than they usually have. I have previously mentioned the Duchess of Gloucester, but two other characters were specially important to this production, the Duke of York and, of course, Henry Bolingbroke. In Michael Manheim's words, "Charles Gray brings new dimensions to the character of York, that loved but lightly regarded political weathervane whose rationalizations of his gross betrayal of Richard never make him forfeit the affection his avuncular bumblings draw from us."[101]

Partly, of course, this is because David Giles and Derek Jacobi have given us a different kind of Richard, but partly too it is because York has been allowed his full part, including the semicomic 5.3, which is often cut. We thus have the full range of the character from the man who, despite his fear of the king, is pushed by his brother's death into speaking the truth, to the bemused uncle who first berates and then befriends Bolingbroke, and finally to the bewildered husband, father, and subject whose shifting loyalties have brought him literally to his knees.

Stanley Wells says that in the scenes "concerned with Aumerle's conspiracy and his mother's attempts to save him from its consequences" there is a not altogether successful attempt "to achieve a subtle fusion of seriousness and comedy for which he [Shakespeare] cannot command the necessary technical resources, so that the comedy tends to submerge the seriousness." But as Wells goes on to argue, "there are good reasons for including the scenes, and the awkwardnesses . . . can be mitigated by tactful acting."[102] One of the strengths of the small screen is evident here because the comedy can be underplayed in a fashion that would not work in a large theater and because York can be pointed out and his character deepened in other scenes in ways that would be difficult if not impossible on stage. For instance, at 4.1.238, "Though some of you, with Pi-

late, wash your hands," we have a close-up of York bowed over his clasped hands, which he is clearly washing with his own tears.

The same grief emerges in this very different setting as York sits, wearing an informal robe and telling the Duchess the story of Richard's humiliation while she stitches at her embroidery. At 5.2.30, "But dust was thrown upon his sacred head," York's tears begin, and he unsuccessfully searches both of his sleeves for a handkerchief, which the Duchess then supplies. Aldous Huxley says, "We participate in a tragedy; at a comedy we only look."[103] But there is a sense in which we participate more fully in this tragedy of a fallen king because we see it, in part, from the vantage of a domestic comedy. Very few members of Shakespeare's audiences now or at any time will have been firsthand participants in royal intrigues; almost everyone, however, will have experienced the varieties of family tensions. In the context of this naturalistic production, the scenes fit neatly, and the historical footnote of the handkerchief (invented by Richard himself and typical of the attention to historical detail in this film) adds an extra bit of intimate irony.

We are also given a chance to see Bolingbroke from a new perspective. (In this context, it is unfortunate that his reference to his problems with his own son was cut.)[104] At 5.3.64, "And thy abundant goodness shall excuse," he puts his hand on York's shoulder and shakes him affectionately. It is the kind of gesture not often associated with Henry IV, and certainly not with the stiff, self-contained king whom Finch has created. However, throughout the scene Finch manages an undercurrent of exasperation and humor, and at the end, it seems entirely right for him to add the monosyllable "Ha!" to Shakespeare's text while clutching his head.

The praise for Jacobi's Richard usually includes kind comments for Finch's Bolingbroke as well. According to Jack Jorgens he "brought his tough, terse manner from his performance in Polanski's *Macbeth*."[105] For Clive James, Jon Finch was "the revelation of the evening." He went on to argue that if the actor playing Bolingbroke was to do more than look worthy and staunch, "he must play the role on two levels, speaking what is set down for him and transmitting his ambitions . . . by other means." According to James, Finch found those means: "even when he was standing still you could tell he was heading for the throne of England by the direct route."[106] For Michael Manheim also, Finch was a paradigm of political ambition: "Finch's Bolingbroke is a full embodiment of the new Machiavellian ideal in Shakespeare's time."[107]

Finch was probably chosen for Macbeth because "Polanski was insecure about the idea of working with anyone strongly identified as a Shakespearean actor,"[108] and Finch, in his turn, "was understandably insecure when he came to work alongside Sir John Gielgud and Derek Jacobi."[109] But when Gielgud praised Finch's verse speaking at the read through, Finch says, "I couldn't believe it. It immediately

Richard II in Act V, scene v of Richard II, *engraving.*

made me feel better and I was relaxed during the rest of the rehearsals."[110]

In fact, Finch's limited Shakespearean experience and his lack of drama school training may in some ways have been an advantage for his role in this production. In their *Macbeth* "Polanski and Tynan . . . insisted that the lines be spoken almost as natural speech,"[111] which was a suitable style to bring to the naturalistic BBC *Richard II*. Perhaps an additional advantage for Finch was that he did not bring a firm "expectational text" with him; his Bolingbroke was not already set in a pattern that would have clashed with Jacobi's Richard. As David Gwillim (the BBC's Prince Hal) points out, "Knowing the play . . . cuts both ways: if you have a clear vision of the play that's fine, but on the other hand you can have a *set* vision of the play as opposed to any sense of exploration."[112]

However, despite critical "readings" of Finch's performance that are colored by memories of the dark ambition he showed in Polanski's film, he appears to be a relatively unambitious Bolingbroke. Critical responses to both Finch and Jacobi are here being dictated at least partially by the expectational text: Richard is often weak and so Jacobi's Richard is; Bolingbroke is just as often pointed toward power, and so that must be Finch's direction as well.

There is, though, more to it than that, and while Clive James and Michael Manheim have (I think) got their explanations slightly muddled, I have no serious quarrel with their perceptions. Because of the *strength* of Jacobi's Richard, because Jacobi is playing so thoroughly to the subtext of the conflict between Richard and his cousin, there is a greater than usual political tension between the two of them, which can easily be misread as Bolingbroke's desire for the crown. In fact, Bolingbroke is locked in a political struggle with the king that is far more complicated (and certainly less superficially ambitious) than any Machiavellian desire to charm the people and harm the king on the way to the throne.

The historical reinterpretation of Richard that this production invites also requires a reinvestigation of Bolingbroke, and because of this, Finch's almost unreadable sternness becomes an advantage. Clive James says "there is a good case for asking the actor playing Bolingbroke to content himself with standing around looking worthily staunch."[113] This production makes the case for doing so stronger than usual, and on one level Finch's performance could be described in just those terms. His reactions to his banishment comprise realistic exasperation, not the frustrated ambition he reveals as Macbeth. Even when Richard puts the crown into his hands, he looks as he might have looked if, when they were boys, his cousin king had just given him a favorite toy—there is a mixture of surprise and joy.

On another level, of course, Finch's Bolingbroke is moving purposefully—and even perhaps virtuously—toward the crown. When I say virtuously, I mean to suggest that there are arguments by which he had a right to act as he did. Historically, there was disagreement (and this production certainly emphasizes Shakespeare's references to the subject) as to whether Mortimer or Lancaster was the rightful heir. In the event, the burden of restoring law fell on the adult claimant, Henry Bolingbroke, and much of England saw him as a savior.[114] Whether or not he later felt guilt for taking and keeping the crown (and Shakespeare, history, and the BBC suggest that he did), many Renaissance political theorists would have absolved him of guilt, as Roland Mushat Frye indicates in an extended discussion of the subject. As he says in commenting on John of Gaunt's refusal to act against Richard, literary historians have used "passive resistance as the panacea for too many problems and ills." He points to "the influence of E. M. W. Tillyard and Lily B. Campbell" but concludes that "developments in the history of political thought have made such major advances since the time of Tillyard that reassessments can and must now be made."[115]

Tillyard's thesis requires us not only to ignore theories of politics but also to suppress facts of history. One of the values of this *Richard II* and of Finch's Bolingbroke is the chance to look at both in a new light. Finch may be especially effective here because he did not bring with him into the production a preconceived notion of the nature of Bolingbroke, because he was not during this performance planning to carry the role forward into the two parts of *Henry IV* and was not therefore affected by the pressure of the other role, and because the part he was playing was rather close to the "usual heroic, rather swashbuckling parts he plays in films."[116]

GILES, JACOBI, AND RICHARD II

In a production where the acting consistently received greater praise than anything else, Derek Jacobi has equally consistently been praised as the outstanding performer. Jack Jorgens found him "superb at rendering the arc of Richard's development."[117] And Clive James said, "Derek Jacobi gave intelligent, fastidiously articulated readings from beginning to end."[118]

Clive James goes on to point up one of the sources of the strength of Jacobi's performance: "each turn of thought [was] given its appropriate vocal weight by the actor and its perfectly judged close-up by the director."[119] Such a critical comment offers evidence of the success of the Giles-Jacobi partnership and also indicates the value of their shared interpretation. Jacobi, who had played the part of Richard II on radio but not on stage, was probably chosen for the role by Messina because of the triumph of "his television Claudius and his stage Hamlet."[120] And while, as Clive James says, this Richard "managed to make you not think of Jacobi's Claudius,"[121] Jacobi's Hamlet was waiting in the wings and from time to time doing a bit of prompting. While every actor must draw from his own central image to fill the mirrors of his roles, and Jacobi's Benedick, Prospero, Hamlet, and Richard have their overlapping edges, there seems a special connection between Jacobi's active, political Hamlet and his other king involved in a struggle of mighty opposites.

From Derek Jacobi's point of vantage as actor, the part of Hamlet has one of the same difficulties that he found with Richard: "So much has happened in *Hamlet* before the play starts."[122] About the same problem in *Richard II,* he said, "the first three scenes all contain allusions to the death of Gloucester, which happened before the play started." Jacobi goes on to elucidate the problems: "He [Richard] doesn't say very much . . . but the man's got a lot to hide and a lot to lose and a lot to gain from the situation, and it's completely understated by Shakespeare."[123] Given this vision of two characters who must play to the subtext as a means of explaining what has happened before the start of the action, of two men who are striving against great odds to fulfill themselves as kings and who find themselves in deadly political battle as a result, it is not surprising that Jacobi should use some of the same devices. The comparison not only illuminates Jacobi's acting style, but it also helps to explain the Richard that Jacobi as star and Giles as director created.

Thus, faced in both productions with the problem of successfully communicating a subtext, of suggesting that the character he is playing is at once more complicated and more powerful than he immediately appears to be, Jacobi has employed the device of sarcasm. Indeed, for Jacobi, sarcasm is more than a device, it is a whole armory of weapons—broadsword, rapier, dagger, and even shield. His Hamlet is arguably the most consistently sarcastic version of the Danish prince yet committed to film, and his Richard is also to this manner born. Jacobi's sarcasm as a means of emphasis has two major advantages: it sends a message of hostility that is easily read by the audience, and it announces itself as either the expression of superior power, superior insolence, or the two together.

So, in *Hamlet,* Jacobi's "Not so, my lord. I am too much in the sun" (1.2.67) immediately signals Hamlet's hostility toward the king, even (in my experience) for student audiences who have never seen the play before and who do not understand the pun. With "I shall in all my best obey *you,* madam" (1.2.120), which is delivered with all the nastiness of a knife blow and which Claudius is compelled to meet smiling, the battle is truly joined, and the audience settles down to watch the outcome.

The effect Jacobi achieves in *Richard II* is similar, allowing for the difference in his position. Here his attack is softer, less abrasive because he *is* king and his position adds emphasis, but the harsh message is still there. He does, of course, send other messages too. At 1.1.15, "Then call them to our presence," he sounds more eager than apprehensive because this is a confrontation he has been awaiting. Following Bolingbroke's compliments at 1.1.20-21, Richard turns to Mowbray, expecting more of the same, not even commanding the flattery but only waiting for it. The attitude is very much like the one Ian Richardson cultivated for the part. In his words, the sovereign "never needed to ask for anything. . . . I never looked to see if my commands were executed because I knew they would be."[124] That Jacobi bothers to look is the only sign of his tension.

Giles and Jacobi gradually build up the connections between Richard and Mowbray. At 1.1.79, "Which gently laid my knighthood on my shoulder," there is a cut from Mowbray to Richard. At 1.1.84-86, we get the first full flash of Richard's sarcasm in defense of Mowbray (though it can also be taken as an incitement to Bolingbroke, a stirring of the quarrel and a means of pushing it to extremes). At 1.1.100, "That he did plot the Duke of Gloucester's death," there is (as Michael Manheim has noted) a cut to Richard and only then to Mowbray. At 1.1.109, Jacobi's slightly worried reading of "How high a pitch his resolution soars!" suggests that there is something more than a well-pointed camera that links him to Mowbray. There is still more evidence at 1.1.131, "Since last I went to France to fetch his Queen," where a cut to Richard suggests satisfaction on his part and complicity or at least an understanding with Mowbray. In the same speech there is another cut to Richard and an even stronger signal. At 1.1.134, "Neglected my sworn duty in that case," Richard looks at Mowbray in what must (by now) be taken as a stern warning.

Jacobi has, however, sarcastically signaled that there is another, equally important issue. He puts Bolingbroke in his place at 1.1.116-17, "Were he my brother, nay, my kingdom's heir, / As he is but my father's brother's son." The camera cuts to John of Gaunt as a visual explanation of the relationship, but Richard's sarcasm suggests that something more is happening than meets the camera's eye. That impression is confirmed at 1.1.122, when Richard says, "He is our subject, Mowbray, so art thou," with a special emphasis on "subject" that clearly implies that someone somewhere has doubts about that subjection.

Historically, Shakespeare, the BBC production, and Derek Jacobi are essentially right; the issue was uncertain. As Bruce says, "Since William the Conqueror no one as distantly related to the king as the earl of March had succeeded to the throne and the custom of primogeniture had not always been followed."[125] So there was a reason for Richard to remind his audience of what he considered to be the proper order and succession of things. When Roger Mortimer, earl of March, died in Ireland on 20 July 1398, leaving only a child heir,[126] preparations for the combat between Mowbray and Bolingbroke were going forward; Richard had an even stronger reason on 16 September 1398, the day of the duel,[127] to get his dangerous cousin away from the throne.

With such preparation, the second scene will be watched more closely than it often is, clearly the intention of both Jacobi and Giles. Jacobi continues to build on what are now textual as well as subtextual impressions in the third scene. His hand-holding with the queen may be taken as an indication of the health of their relationship and a refutation in advance of the charge of homosexuality; it may also be seen as his indifference to a ritual he has already decided to abort. At 1.3.119, "Let them lay by their helmets and their spears," his decision seems firm, and there is no indication of sudden impulse or the process of thinking to a decision, two reactions at which Jacobi is particularly adept.

In addition, his antipathy for the House of Lancaster, father and son, has come much closer to the surface. The embrace he has for his cousin at 1.3.54 is extremely sketchy, and at 1.3.224, "Why! uncle, thou hast many years to live," he is as close to being sarcastic as he is far from being sympathetic. Almost he anticipates his wish for Gaunt's death. With Mowbray's half-spoken sense of betrayal by the king he trusted (1.3.155, "All unlooked for from your Highness' mouth") and Richard's cynical determination to be rid of Mowbray and Bolingbroke, we are left with a relatively dark public portrait of the sun king.

The public portrait of the king becomes effectively (and viciously) private in 1.4. The scene begins with Jacobi's laugh climbing above and dominating the laughter of his courtiers. It is the first indication we have had that the king may lose control, but, oddly, this seemingly unplanned mirth soon emerges as one more device in the power struggle. Jacobi has forged a link between Richard's insecurity and his attempts to make himself even more powerful than he already is.

Jacobi employs laughter as a weapon in *Hamlet* as well as *Richard II,* and again its use is broader and more obvious in the prince than the king. In *Hamlet,* for example, at 1.2.94, "'Tis unmanly grief," Hamlet laughs at the king in a thoroughly disrespectful but slightly hysterical and therefore presumably forgivable manner. He tries a similar ploy on the king after the play within the play. At 3.2.275, "Give me some light," the king approaches Hamlet, studies him by the light of a torch, and in response, Hamlet

covers his face with his hands and then laughs foolishly. The silly laughter turns to triumph as the king exits.

The BBC *Richard II* describes the setting for 1.4 (their scene 5) as "Interior. A Room in the King's Palace."[128] It is clearly, however, a representation of Richard's famous bathhouse, with the king and his favorites draped Roman fashion. This at once makes a number of suggestions not necessarily present in Shakespeare's text.

At 1.4.11, Aumerle's report of Bolingbroke's "Farewell," there is a cut to Jacobi for an extended reaction shot. Lying on his back with his head over the edge of a table and the camera shooting down at him as he looks awkwardly up, he appears particularly vulnerable, while his long fit of laughter seems a part of that vulnerability. The laughter is, though, both a sign of his uncertainty and one means to his ends, the ridicule and destruction of Bolingbroke and Richard's other enemies. Again, the insecurity and the attempt to gain greater power are presented as cause and effect.

Richard's resentment (or at least his show of it) continues to build throughout the scene. At 1.4.31, "Off goes his bonnet to an oyster-wench," he uses a parodic gesture and sarcastic emphasis to suggest his disgust. By 1.4.35, "As were our England in reversion his," his emotion has reached to royal rage, a danger to his self-control and his control of others and, more than that, an indication of his true feelings and insecurities. At this point Jacobi's Richard disguises himself in the same mask of laughter that his Hamlet uses. It is a means of undermining the seriousness of his own emotion, of reducing the importance of the situation, and as he had done earlier in the scene, of making the very suggestion of ambition in Bolingbroke seem ridiculous, a laughable stupidity. Coming as it does shortly after this, Richard's decision to go to Ireland himself has an air of relief about it. It follows Green's "Well, he is gone, and with him go these thoughts" (1.4.37) and suggests a brief vacation for Richard from his long revenge.

That there is to be no such vacation, that, in fact, Richard's vengeful, insecure nature and central position will not allow it, becomes clear with the news of Gaunt's illness. Jacobi's taking of the news is one of his neatest bits of characterization. From 1.4.59, "Now put it, God, in the physician's mind," he moves from a quiet acceptance of the news to the thought of Gaunt's death, the satisfaction that death will provide, and the use he can make of it. And he does all of this, arcing from stillness to an almost childish glee, with an eye on his courtiers to make sure they share his antipathies and intentions. The strength of Jacobi's performance as Richard is clearly visible here. In a scene that is not too far removed from the melodrama of Don John in *Much Ado About Nothing* and his "Would the cook were o' my mind!" (1.3.68), Jacobi conjures a Renaissance prince and a charming tyrant.

I emphasize that Jacobi's Richard is a legitimate king who maintains himself by tyrannous means, a dispenser of justice who suborns murder, and a man whose power has become so great that it must decline. The tension in the early scenes between the Richard who accepts absolute obedience as his due and the Richard who carefully maneuvers to conceal his crime has already begun to send these messages. Like those other Shakespearean tyrants Richard III and Macbeth, Richard II falls as a result of harshness, not weakness. In trying to grasp all, he threatens too many people and ends by clutching nothing. As A. R. Humphreys puts it, "at the beginning he is decisive even to ruthlessness, and it is his very energy of action which, when ill-directed, endangers his kingdom."[129]

One of the specially interesting facets of Jacobi's performance is that he manages to demonstrate that the Richard in the second half of the play is the same as the Richard in the first half. This Richard has always oscillated between a vision of himself as a divinely supported, all-powerful king and a picture of himself as a nameless beggar. In trying desperately to rise to the height of one, he has fallen almost to the depth of the other.

By 2.1, the family contentions and Richard's tyrannous intentions are very much out in the open. In this production Gaunt's accusation is coupled with the strong memory of the Duchess of Gloucester's, and their two dying voices convict Richard of a crime that his casual acceptance of Gaunt's mortal illness has helped us to believe he could easily commit. The first of several strong reactions to this situation from Jacobi's Richard comes at 2.1.123, where the last line of that verbal assault on Gaunt, "Should run thy head from thy unreverent shoulders," has a regal ferocity that explains his two uncles' fear of him and lets us know that Gaunt's death is near indeed when he dares to challenge the king as he does. At 2.1.145-46, "Right, you say true, as Hereford's love, so his, / As theirs, so mine; and all be as it is," Richard's voice is under control, but his anger is still stinging him into telling the truth without his usual rhetoric. He has calmed down for 2.1.153-55, and we have another of the excellent Jacobi-Giles reaction shots; there is some shock for him in this death he has wished for, perhaps even a suggestion that his wish is the cause, but again we see him thinking, walling himself off from everything but his royal purposes. The message that emerges is a deadly callousness: "So much for that" (2.1.155). He is not to be deflected by his Uncle York's tears or even by what seems to be semirebellion from this most placid of his relatives. There is nothing undecided about this Richard or about his "Think what you will, we seize into our hands / His plate, his goods, his money, and his lands" (2.1.209-10). It needs only his casual dismissal of the queen to send him off to Ireland as an unsympathetic tyrant.

One of the advantages of this Giles-Jacobi strategy now becomes apparent: the two halves of the play, pre-Ireland and post-Ireland, hold together. The audience has been asked to work out the nature of Richard before his military voyage, and the clues provided by Shakespeare and the production have proved pretty conclusively what he is.

As I have already pointed out, Jacobi's Richard (and Shakespeare's Richard, for that matter) is clearly identified as a tyrant. For the historical Richard, the use of the Cheshire archers or mercenary troops was one such indication. Shakespeare's Richard repeatedly makes decisions that are enforced by his power as kind and not supported by the people or advisers such as York and Gaunt. As a result, Richard's fear of the love the common people have for Bolingbroke, like "Claudius' twice stated recognition of Hamlet's popularity . . . indicates the tyrant's fear of being supplanted."[130] Also like Claudius, Richard surrounds himself with flatterers and wastes the substance of his country, in his own words, on "too great a court / And liberal largess" (1.4.43-44). Gaunt's condemnation of him rises to the height of wishing for his retroactive deposition: "O, had thy grandsire with a prophet's eye / Seen how his son's son should destroy his sons, / From forth thy reach he would have laid thy shame, / Deposing thee before thou wert possessed" (2.1.104-8). In the crime of murder to which Gaunt refers and in the crime of seizing Lancaster's lands just after Gaunt's death, Richard commits the tyrant's unforgivable sin of destroying the order of the commonwealth he is set to rule and preserve.[131]

The rest of the film is (at least from Richard's point of view) a matter of why and wherefores. It is one thing to create and label a tyrant;[132] it is another to explain him, especially if that explanation is, as Richard's must be, something more than the itch of ambition or some other tragic flaw of the flesh.

Richard's return in 3.2 becomes in this production the means to an explanation; the stress of crisis is used to break through to the why of his earlier actions. Part of Richard's complexity (and no doubt one of the sources of the many suggestions that he is an actor-king)[133] comes from the control he exercises over his words and emotions and from the use he makes of them even when they are not in his complete control. Until now Richard has had no reason, either political or personal, to talk about the divine rights of kings. Now his private obsession becomes public; nor can it rightly be called an obsession, an abnormality, except in the intensity of his belief and the insensitivity of his actions. Gaunt and York share his point of view,[134] and even those very practical politicians, Bolingbroke and Northumberland, want Richard's acquiescence and royal sanction for his own deposition. In this production his speeches to the English earth and his dependence on plagues and angels must be seen not as vain posturing but as the misty periphery of his beliefs, a mixture of wishful fantasy and literal expectation. For Jacobi's Richard, like his historical counterpart, the boundaries of the world are immense, stretching from fear of being deposed and becoming nothing to an ecstatic state in which all his royal words could come divinely true. It is the arc of alternation between these two states that Jacobi has managed to travel.

In the context of 3.2, Richard's appeal to God to end Gaunt's life and Jacobi's almost stunned pause when he receives the news suggest Richard may have been willing to believe in the power of his own prayer. His actions through the rest of the production argue a vacillation between faith in his practical political (and, failing that, divine) support and a desperate uncertainty caused by the fear that at long last he will conclusively lose the battle to hold his throne (his identity as person, priest, and king) while holding down his subjects; thus the alternation between hope and despair, frenzied activity and passive suffering in 3.2. A particularly effective collaboration of director and star to demonstrate this occurs at 3.2.63, "How far off lies your power?" when Richard in an anxiety of optimism thrusts his arm out of the frame (at last an effective use of what has happened often accidentally), reaching to Salisbury as to a more than physical savior.

The danger in the man is demonstrated once more at 3.2.129, "O, villains, vipers, damned without redemption!" as Jacobi works himself up to a terribly active anger that ends in the threat of political execution, which he clearly means to carry out. If another revolution of the wheel (always possible while life remains) brings Richard to the top, Bolingbroke will certainly suffer the fate Richard had momentarily intended for Bushy, Bagot, and Green.

At 3.3.132-40, which begins with "O God! O God! that e'er this tongue of mine," the fury of Jacobi's Richard is again obvious and indeed barely contained, but he follows Aumerle's advice that it is wiser to delay to a better time than to force battle now and so die. This is very much the sort of policy Richard has pursued before, and always, in spite of humiliations and threatened depositions, he has been able to emerge more powerful in the end. No doubt he hopes beneath all the words of despair that this new deposition will prove impermanent. One of Jacobi's neatest demonstrations of this part of Richard's nature comes at 5.5.105, "How now! What means Death in this rude assault?" He turns his back to the murderers, reading the line as though he is resigned to die without a struggle. Then suddenly, on the next line, he turns to face the murderers again, beating them and making use of the surprise to seize a weapon.

The historical interpretation begun in the early scenes carries through consistently and successfully in the second half of the play. The tension between Richard and Bolingbroke does not relax, though the roles are reversed. Jacobi's Richard (like his Hamlet) is adept at maintaining political pressure even when he is at a disadvantage.

At 3.3.71, he has already insisted on an obeisance from Northumberland. At 3.3.171-72, with double-edged irony he has called Northumberland "Most mighty prince" and his hated cousin "King Bolingbroke." As he marches energetically down a stone staircase, Richard describes himself (equally energetically) as Phaethon, a sun king "Wanting the manage of unruly jades" (3.3.178). This is not self-pity but a simple act of placing the blame where he feels it belongs; he is a divinity betrayed by baseness, as his reference to Christ and Judas (where, interestingly, Christ's situation is found to be preferable, His troubles

less severe) makes plain in 4.1.170. The same point is made in a different way at 5.1.35-36, "A king of beasts indeed: if aught but beasts, / I had been still a happy king of men." In each of these instances Jacobi's sarcasm is itself a judgment; he is categorizing and chastising what he sees as political injustice. His will is still active, still struggling against circumstance, and though waves of despair wash over him, he is not yet ready to sink.

Thus, in his encounter with Bolingbroke in 3.3, he repeats and expands his earlier accusations against his cousin. "Up, cousin, up, your heart is up, I know, / Thus high at least" (3.3.192-93). In his fuller accusation, which begins at 3.3.198, he reaches with "Cousin, I am too young to be your father, / Though you are old enough to be my heir" (3.3.202-3), an almost exact restatement of his earlier indications of Bolingbroke's royal ambition. Far from giving up, this Richard is naming Bolingbroke's crime as his only immediate means of combating it. Part of the strength of Richard's conviction of his own divine mission is clearly visible once we realize that he cannot totally accept the possibility of being deposed. For Jacobi's Richard, naming the crime—which is also a blasphemy—should almost have the power to stop the criminal, as he has earlier said that his very presence in England will stop "this thief, this traitor, Bolingbroke" (3.2.47).

Perhaps the greatest strength of this production and of Jacobi's acting is the coupling of the sympathy that these scenes usually generate for Richard with a firm conviction in the audience that Bolingbroke is ending a tyranny; the very lines that make us pity Richard's loss of power show us how dangerous he has been and would be again in wielding it. This is especially true in 4.1, where we seem to see Richard breaking down, stripping away the layers of pretence that have surrounded his essential personality, but at the same time we perceive (in this production at any rate) his political maneuverings and his outmaneuvering of both Bolingbroke and Northumberland, who must win by force what Richard has kept them from gaining by any other means.

Jacobi's Richard takes command of the scene immediately on his entrance, and his bitter reading of the biting lines, his taunting emphasis at 4.1.181, "Here, cousin, *seize* the crown," show him to be an exceptionally dangerous adversary still.[135] He does everything that can be done in the circumstances to undermine Bolingbroke. He is compelled to give some small support to the new king, but he retracts everything he says both before and after he says it. Jacobi believes that though Richard is at "rock bottom" in the deposition scene, "he gives a marvellous account of himself." Jacobi sees Richard as an actor thinking, "'If I've got to go, I'm going to go in style,'" an attitude he says he found "fascinating. . . . All the emotions are absolutely real for him—but he can switch it on."[136] This is an explicit statement of what we have earlier seen Jacobi's Richard do, that is, turn a real emotion, fear or doubt, for instance, into a weapon in a political situation.

Indeed, much of Bolingbroke's silence seems enforced by the energy of Richard's speech, and only that withdrawal into stillness keeps the new king from being made to look ridiculous. Northumberland too, who tries to force Richard to read a list of his crimes and, in fact, claps the king on the shoulder just after 4.1.220, like a buff-jerkined officer apprehending a malefactor, is repeatedly baffled. Richard first turns against him the accusation of deposing a true king then delays with "Mine eyes are full of tears, I cannot see" (4.1.243), at which point Northumberland casts his eyes up to heaven in frustration. At last Richard tears the list of crimes from his hands and throws it to the floor. The request for the looking glass is another tactic of delay and another opportunity to display the perfidy of his enemies.

The end result of the historical, naturalistic interpretation that Giles and Jacobi have created has been a more coherent and complex protagonist than is sometimes the case. This Richard is a legitimate king whose insecure position, echoed in his oscillations between confidence and despair, makes him a tyrant. His belief in his divine right to power and his fear lest he lose all are at once terrifying and pathetic. His insecurities—internal and external—force him to reach for absolute power and finally mean his downfall. In the desperate attempt to make himself perfectly secure financially, militarily, and therefore personally, he has threatened and alienated most of his supporters. Bolingbroke does not succeed because of his own superior ability or because of Richard's incompetence but because he offers an alternative to tyranny. The production succeeds because it offers a consistent and believable Richard who is set in an understandable historical context.

Notes

1. Mary Ellen O'Brien, *Film Acting: The Techniques and History of Acting for the Camera* (New York: Arco, 1983), 100.

2. It happens, for instance, at 1.3.183, 207, 216, 242, 249, 254, 295, 303, 305, and 307.

3. Cited Carr, Review of *Measure for Measure,* 5.

4. Clive James, *The Crystal Bucket: Television Criticism from the "Observer," 1976-79* (London: Jonathan Cape, 1981), 158.

5. Jorgens, "BBC-TV Shakespeare," 414.

6. BBC *R2,* 49.

7. Michael Manheim, review of *Richard II,* by William Shakespeare, BBC-TV/Time-Life Inc. Production, PBS Stations, 28 March 1979, "The Shakespeare Plays on TV: Season One," *Shakespeare on Film Newsletter* 4, no. 1. (1979): 5.

8. Fenwick, *R2,* 19.

9. Purser, "Going Round Again," 13.

10. Fenwick, *R2,* 20.

11. Ibid.

12. Cedric Messina, "Interview," 136-37.

13. Ibid., 137.

14. In Messina's defense, I note that even some reviewers were by no means eager for the Bardathon. Philip Purser described the project as "an admirable service to Shakespeare, but not necessarily a service to television" ("In Tight Focus," *Sunday Telegraph,* 17 December 1978, 15). And Russell Miller felt that at least some of the plays could be dispensed with. "Titus Andronicus [*sic*] is widely considered to be unwatchable and Timothy of Athenea [*sic*] is unlikely to attract a mass audience. So why include them?" ("BBC's Schoolgirl Juliet," 32).

15. Evidently one other motive here is to avoid copying the Olivier *Henry V,* which had used *The Book of Hours.*

16. Fenwick, *R2,* 20-21.

17. Ibid., 20.

18. A similar example emerges from the first season's production of *Julius Caesar.* The director, Herbert Wise, was chosen by Messina largely because of his experience with *I Claudius.* "'If anybody knows a toga, he does,' says Messina" (Henry Fenwick, "The Production," in *The BBC TV Shakespeare: "Julius Caesar"* [London: British Broadcasting Corporation, 1979], 20). Wise rejected the idea of dressing the play in Elizabethan costume with the words, "I don't think that's right for the audience we will be getting. . . . For an audience many of whom won't have seen the play before, I believe it would only be confusing" (20).

19. Fenwick, *R2,* 21.

20. David Bevington, *The Oxford Shakespeare: "Henry IV, Part I"* (Oxford: Oxford University Press, 1987), 84-85.

21. Patrick McGilligan, *Cagney: The Actor as Auteur* (New York: Da Capo Press, 1979), 199.

22. Ibid., 202.

23. Ibid.

24. Manheim, "Shakespeare on TV," 5.

25. Fenwick, *R2,* 24.

26. Wilders, "Shakespeare on the Small Screen," 57.

27. Stanley Wells, *Royal Shakespeare: Four Major Productions at Stratford-upon-Avon* (Manchester: Manchester University Press, 1979), 68-69.

28. Fenwick, *R2,* 20.

29. Russell Miller, "BBC's Schoolgirl Juliet," 32.

30. Fenwick, *1H4,* 21.

31. Ibid., 19.

32. Ibid., 20.

33. Jonathan Miller, "Interview; Jonathan Miller on *The Shakespeare Plays*," with Tom Hallinan, *Shakespeare Quarterly* 32 (1981): 137.

34. Malcolm Page, *"Richard II": Text and Performance* (London: Macmillan, 1987), 55. Sean Day-Lewis said, for example, "In my view the first season has contained three duds ('Romeo and Juliet,' 'As You Like It,' and 'Julius Caesar') and three successes ('Richard II,' 'Measure for Measure,' and 'Henry VIII')" ("Years of the Bard," *Daily Telegraph*, 5 March 1979, 11).

35. Sheldon P. Zitner, "Wooden O's in Plastic Boxes: Shakespeare and Television," *University of Toronto Quarterly* 51 (1981): 7.

36. Banham, "BBC Television's Dull Shakespeare," 50.

37. For discussions of this much-praised production, see Peter Thomson, "Shakespeare Straight and Crooked: A Review of the 1973 Season at Stratford," *Shakespeare Survey* 27 (1974): 151-54; Wells, *Royal Shakespeare,* 64-81; Page, *R2,* 57-68; and Richard David, *Shakespeare in the Theatre* (Cambridge: Cambridge University Press, 1978), 164-74.

38. Fenwick, *1H4,* 20.

39. Samuel Crowl, Review of *Henry IV, Part 1,* by William Shakespeare, BBC-TV/Time-Life Inc. Production, PBS Stations, 26 March 1980, "The Shakespeare Plays on TV: Season Two," *Shakespeare on Film Newsletter* 5, no. 1 (1980): 3.

40. Manheim, "Shakespeare on TV," 5.

41. Holderness, "Radical Potentiality," 197.

42. In Holderness's own words, "Messina saw the history plays conventionally as orthodox Tudor historiography, and the director employed dramatic techniques which allow that ideology a free and unhampered passage to the spectator" (Ibid., 197).

43. Ibid.

44. Fenwick, *R2,* 24.

45. In 1973, "Gloucester's widow was played as a ghost, emerging from the downstage grave-trap with a skull in her hand, and speaking with the aid of echo effects" (Thomson, "Shakespeare Straight and Crooked," 152). "This created a melodramatic impression which exemplified the dangers of stylisation, and in 1974 she simply entered from the wings and spoke quietly, though she still carried the skull" (Wells, *Royal Shakespeare,* 69).

46. Paul Johnson, *"Richard II,"* in *Shakespeare in Perspective,* ed. Roger Sales vol. 1, (London: British Broadcasting Corporation, 1982), 35.

47. Ibid., 34.

48. E. M. W. Tillyard, *Shakespeare's History Plays* (London: Chatto and Windus, 1951), 261.

49. Ian Richardson, *"Richard II,"* in *Shakespeare in Perspective,* ed. Roger Sales vol. 1, (London: British Broadcasting Corporation, 1982), 39.

50. Ibid., 41, 43.

51. Fenwick, *R2,* 22.

52. "Wilders Interview at MLA," *Shakespeare on Film Newsletter* 4.1 (1979): 3.

53. Robert Hapgood, "Shakespeare on Film and Television," in *The Cambridge Companion to Shakespeare Studies,* ed. Stanley Wells (Cambridge: Cambridge University Press, 1986), 279.

54. Holderness, "Radical potentiality," 197.

55. Peter Saccio, *Shakespeare's English Kings: History, Chronicle, and Drama* (New York: Oxford University Press, 1987), 4.

56. J. L. Kirby, *Henry IV of England* (London: Constable, 1970), 2.

57. Fenwick, *R2,* 22.

58. Richard David, for example, maintains that the issues in *Richard II* "cannot be appreciated without some identification with the Elizabethans" (*Shakespeare in the Theatre,* 45).

59. John Gielgud, "King Richard the Second," in *Shakespeare "Richard II": A Casebook,* ed. Nicholas Brooke (London: Macmillan, 1978), 77.

60. In John Neville's words, "there are two different characters. . . . We quite blatantly made no attempt to link the two; he came back from Ireland a different man" (cited in Page, *R2,* 20).

61. Fenwick, *R2,* 22.

62. John Russell Brown, "Narrative and Focus: *Richard II,"* in *Shakespeare "Richard II": A Casebook,* ed. Nicholas Brooke (London: Macmillan, 1978), 84.

63. Ibid., 85.

64. Andrew Gurr, ed., *King Richard II* (Cambridge: Cambridge University Press, 1984), 22.

65. W. B. Yeats, "At Stratford-on-Avon (1901)," in *Shakespeare "Richard II": A Casebook,* ed. Nicholas Brooke (London: Macmillan, 1978), 70.

66. Gurr, *King Richard II,* 22.

67. J. L. Kirby's *Henry IV of England* (1970) and Marie Louise Bruce's *The Usurper King: Henry of Bolingbroke, 1366-99* (London: Rubicon Press, 1986) share this vision of Richard. I am not making the claim that Kirby's book influenced the production or that the production influenced Bruce's book. I am using them only as parallel examples of a particular interpretation that can be a means of organizing both historical and theatrical materials.

68. Theodore Weiss, *The Breath of Clowns and Kings: Shakespeare's Early Comedies and Histories* (London: Chatto and Windus, 1971), 260.

69. Bruce, *Usurper King,* 69.

70. Ibid., 71.

71. Ibid., 72.

72. Ibid., 73.

73. Kirby, *Henry IV,* 25.

74. Bruce, *Usurper King,* 75-76, 80.

75. Ibid., 156.

76. Ibid., 160.

77. Kirby, *Henry IV,* 45.

78. Bruce, *Usurper King,* 164.

79. Ibid., 165.

80. Ibid., 172.

81. "So called not because it was empty of words . . . but because it gave Richard carte blanche to do more or less as he wished with the property of the unfortunate person whose name appeared on it" (ibid., 172-73).

82. Ibid., 172-73.

83. Ibid., 173.

84. Kirby, *Henry IV,* 46.

85. Ibid., 47-49. Mowbray's punishment was more severe in fact than Shakespeare shows it to be. Mowbray was allowed to live only in Prussia, Bohemia, Hungary, or among the Saracens (Bruce, *Usurper King,* 188). As Kirby rather caustically remarks, "There would soon be insufficient countries in Europe to house all the exiles whom Richard fondly hoped to keep apart" (*Henry IV,* 49).

86. Fenwick, *R2,* 22.

87. Ibid., 23.

88. Richard Last writes in his review of the BBC *Richard II,* "Apart from historical shortcomings (Shakespeare seems to have stood in the same relationship to the Tudors as Shostakovich to the Soviet tyrants)" ("'Shakespeare' Creates Boxed-In Feeling," 15).

89. F. W. Brownlow, *Two Shakespearean Sequences: "Henry VI" to "Richard II" and "Pericles" to "Timon of Athens"* (London: Macmillan, 1977), 98.

90. Saccio, *Shakespeare's English Kings,* 20.

91. Kirby, *Henry IV,* 24. Bruce says he "outspokenly criticised Richard, whom he despised as an incompetent ruler" (*Usurper King,* 62). But his criticisms could well have been the plain truth. In Kirby's words, "Richard had already shown himself completely lacking in all those qualities of tact and statesmanship that were required of a king" (*Henry IV,* 24).

92. Even that other Gloucester in *Richard III,* which is sometimes supposed to be the least historical of the history plays, has gotten support in Desmond Seward's 1983 biography, *Richard III: England's Black Legend* (London: Country Life Books, 1983). Seward says, "Shakespeare was nearer the truth than some of the King's latter-day defenders" (15).

93. Bruce, *Usurper King,* 62.

94. Saccio, *Shakespeare's English Kings,* 20.

95. Kirby, *Henry IV,* 23, and Bruce, *Usurper King,* 61.

96. Kirby, *Henry IV,* 18.

97. Bruce, *Usurper King,* 59.

98. Ibid., 96.

99. Ibid., 166.

100. Ibid., 211.

101. Manheim, "Shakespeare on TV," 5.

102. Wells, *Royal Shakespeare,* 74.

103. Aldous Huxley, *The Devils of Loudun* (London: Chatto and Windus, 1952), 324.

104. Cutting the reference to Hal is curious in a production of *Richard II* that was to be followed immediately by *1 Henry IV.* Perhaps the cut was designed (like the omission of Exeter's penitence and his praise of Richard at 5.5.113-18, and the list of executed traitors given to Henry IV at 5.6.5-18) to present Bolingbroke in a favorable light.

105. Jorgens, "The BBC-TV Shakespeare Series," 413.

106. James, *Crystal Bucket,* 158-59.

107. Manheim, "Shakespeare on TV," 5.

108. Barbara Leaming, *Polanski: The Filmmaker as Voyeur* (New York: Simon and Schuster, 1981), 121.

109. Fenwick, *1H4,* 24.

110. Ibid.

111. Leaming, *Polanski,* 121.

112. Fenwick, *1H4,* 24.

113. James, *Crystal Bucket,* 158-59.

114. Bruce, *Usurper King,* 204.

115. Roland Mushat Frye, *The Renaissance "Hamlet": Issues and Responses in 1600* (Princeton: Princeton University Press, 1984), 45.

116. Fenwick, *2H4,* 20.

117. Jorgens, "BBC-TV Shakespeare," 413.

118. James, *Crystal Bucket,* 158.

119. Ibid.

120. Fenwick, *R2,* 25. Messina says, "I wanted from the first to get Derek Jacobi," and Jacobi was, in fact, the first actor to be cast (Fenwick, *R2,* 25).

121. James, *Crystal Bucket,* 158.

122. Derek Jacobi, "Hamlet," in *Shakespeare in Perspective,* ed. Roger Sales vol. 1, (London: British Broadcasting Corporation, 1982), 186.

123. Fenwick, *R2,* 22-23.

124. Richardson, *R2,* 40.

125. Bruce, *Usurper King,* 149-50.

126. Kirby, *Henry IV,* 52.

127. Bruce, *Usurper King,* 185.

128. BBC *R2,* 43.

129. A. R. Humphreys, *Shakespeare: "Richard II"* (London: Edward Arnold, 1967), 31.

130. Frye, *Renaissance "Hamlet,"* 38-39.

131. Ibid., 40.

132. As Marie Louise Bruce puts it "to disinherit Henry was even more perilous, because the injustice of it outraged public opinion and made the king seem more than ever a tyrant" (*Usurper King,* 194). This is an unthinkable thought, to which even York has been pushed.

133. The historical Richard was, as perhaps all kings must be, an actor. But there is evidence that hypocritical performance was part of his nature. Marie Louise Bruce refers to "yet another of the king's beloved charades. . . . With artistry he acted the part of the wronged monarch finally driven to magnanimous mercy at the pleas of his stricken subjects" (ibid., 125).

134. Gaunt himself was a "staunch believer in royal absolutism" (ibid., 153).

135. Bolingbroke is, as Shakespeare is about to demonstrate, peculiarly vulnerable to counterrevolutions. As Ruth Bird relates, "while Richard was a captive at Conventry, a deputation arrived from London to beg for the execution of Richard before he is brought any further," because they feared his retaliation if he regained power (*The Turbulent London of Richard II* [London: Longman, Green and Co., 1949], 110).

136. Fenwick, *R2,* 26.

Robert L. King (review date 1995)

SOURCE: King, Robert L. Review of *Richard II. The North American Review* 280 (November-December 1995): 41-2.

[*In the following review, King offers a positive assessment of the National Theatre's staging of* Richard II, *directed by Deborah Warner and starring Fiona Shaw as an impressive Richard.*]

The National Theatre presented *Richard II* in repertory with Skylight in the smallest of its three houses, the Cottesloe. Of all Shakespeare's kings, Richard is the most dependent on speech to assert a self because for much of the play he has no real power. The director, Deborah Warner, who had her King Lear enter in a party hat and wheelchair, cast a woman in the title role, the justly acclaimed Fiona Shaw. Richard seemed ready to take a wild ride. From the seating arrangement to Shaw's forceful resistance to death, however, the production honored and illuminated Shakespeare's text. The audience at floor level was divided into four sections, two on either side of a rectangular space with open areas at either end and small spaces between them. Boarded in the front, they were slightly oversized jury boxes, apt places for evaluating competing speech. I think that the Warner/Shaw Richard sprang, almost literally, from Henry IV's characterization of him in *1 Henry IV*: "The skipping King, he ambled up and down / With shallow jesters and rash bavin wits." In one exit, Shaw did indeed skip like a boy miming a horse ride, and she did an impromptu jig to mock the Irish before her courtiers, "shallow jesters" whose flattering emptiness came through strongly. In the first scenes, Shaw seemed like an adolescent boy, bemused by all the serious talk going on around her. She was a youth reciting a well-worn truth, smug and casual, when she told the banished Mowbray, "It boots thee not to be compassionate." The delivery of many of her early lines was equally self-satisfied, specifically when Richard exercised or delegated power, and this tone sharply and appropriately set up the longer and more desperate speeches as kingly power wanes and is transferred. In a more direct anticipation, Warner had Shaw admire herself in a small mirror in scene one; when this image is later smashed, we appreciate its deeper meaning for Richard. Swathed in bolts of white, her hair close-cropped, Shaw—taller by far than the historical Richard—never exploited her sex. She did kiss Bolingbroke full on the mouth in scene one, held him in a full embrace and kissed him in the deposition scene. They kept the contested crown between them by the pressure of their waists. The suggestion that Richard is physically attracted to Bolingbroke and Shaw's actual clinging to him offered fresh insights about Richard, one part "skipping" and one part "king," enamored of the power he would not use effectively. Surely Shaw conveyed much of the role's poignant ambivalence because she is a woman but mostly because she acts so well. . . .

Michael Feingold (review date 1998)

SOURCE: Feingold, Michael. "Here's Richardness." *The Village Voice* 43, no. 10 (10 March 1998): 141.

[*In the following review, Feingold appraises two productions of* Richard II, *one by the Theatre for a New Audience at New York City's St. Clement's Theater, directed by Ron Daniels, and the other staged by the Pearl Theatre. Feingold observes that while both plays had their strengths as well as effective scenes, each seemed to lose something as it went on. Reviewing Pearl's production, directed by Shepard Sobel, Feingold states that while it was not as vivid as Daniels's production, it had a stronger grasp of the play as poetry.*]

To have one company play *Richard II* and *Richard III* in alternation makes sense. The two unheroic heroes are opposite extremes on the spectrum of kingship: the king who gives up all too easily and the shameless one who stops at nothing. Each has an antagonist, too, with a slight resemblance to the other, which makes double-casting logical: Tough, pragmatic Bolingbroke is a Richard III with moral scruples, while "deep revolving" Buckingham shows twinges of Richard II's faintness of heart. Richard II—often, though not here, played as a crypto-queer—sloughs women off, preferring his "caterpillars"; Richard III, embittered by his ineligibility as a wooer, takes pleasure in abusing them, for which they exact due revenge in curses and confrontations. As those suggest, both plays are feats of rhetoric, studies in the poetics as well as the ethics of kingship. Visions, dreams, and prophecies dog the characters' tracks; in more than one dispute, the moral victor is the one with the quickest verbal comeback. If the action, in its bleakness and violence, suggests a prelude to *King Lear,* the language rings with echoes of the innocently playful *Love's Labour's Lost.*

The other reason *R2* and *R3* should be played in rep is that the undertaking is big, bold, and difficult. New York, the most complacent and money-minded of all the world's great theater cities, doesn't face such a challenge very often. Our serious companies hang on by a shoestring, while what should be our major theaters cozy up to the public with anodyne new plays and sentimental rehashes of Broadways past, leaning on star actors and making no pretense of forming a company—essential for Shakespeare, who created his plays for one.

Theatre for a New Audience has assembled for its two-play rep a core group of strong professionals with a supporting cast mostly of non-Equity newcomers. The inevitable imbalance in the playing makes an apt reflection of Ron Daniels's productions, each of which is full of strong choices and effective scenes but seems to diminish as it goes on; pairing the two has given each a bit less than it deserves.

Neil Patel's set is dominated, for *R2,* by a vast, circular cathedral window—removed, for *R3,* to create a gaping hole, ruins from the Yorkist wars still smoldering in it. So we know this is a land where kingship is sanctified by God, and dethroning a legitimate king will catapult us into moral chaos. The only problem is that Richard II isn't much of a god-king, and Daniels's perspective doesn't give us a clue to his inner failings, which are the source of his toppling. While Richard strives manfully to be just and wise during the Mowbray-Bolingbroke feud, his heart is elsewhere, and any interpretation depends on which elsewhere the director chooses. The true king whom Richard becomes at the end is a soul of a different order.

Not much of this is visible in Daniels's treatment, busy adumbrating an absolute moral order to which none of the characters, not even John of Gaunt, really subscribe. While this relativism might set up Richard's downfall—he's disillusioned when he sees that it's all a pose—Daniels doesn't use it that way. We don't get a Richard bearing the seeds of self-destruction at the start, nor a transcendent Richard at the cursory end. So we aren't prepared when the astonishing thing happens: In the middle, Richard is in love with poetic irony, and in Steven Skybell we have an actor for whom poetic irony is like a second central nervous system. From the despair before his surrender through the desperate farewell to his queen, Skybell is enthralling—burning the way tears can burn, funny as only the blackest despair can be funny.

If Daniels is uncertain about the nature of R2's rise and fall, *R3* leaves him even more constrained: Here is a character who never alters, morally or otherwise. Shaw's image of the play as an ultimate version of Punch and Judy points unerringly to its only source of tension: Richard's relations with the audience. Unlike his coevals, we know what he's up to. If there's no surprise for us in how he's received, no change in tone from the tragedy he inflicts to the comedy he shares with us, the actor has nowhere to go. Christopher McCann, a great hand at chilling mordancy, is no ingratiating comic. A cool, close-to-the-vest Bolingbroke, his moral disquiet bubbling up from below, he makes an oddly monochrome Richard, seemingly entangled in an inner agenda almost as complex as his physical twists and hobbles. He drives forcefully down this one-lane path, barely stopping to deceive the others, let alone amuse us. Skybell, his Buckingham, can hardly get a word of encouragement in before his almost automatic rejection.

Luckily, R3 is woman-hounded, and Daniels supplies three splendid actresses to stop him in his tracks. Laurie Kennedy, Duchess of York in both plays, rings as true in the comedy of Aumerle's pardon in *R2* as she does while cursing her own son in *R3*. Pamela Payton-Wright's slow, grave ferocity is the next best thing to the grandeur Margaret of Anjou requires. *R3*'s Elizabeth has to mix canny strength with suppressed hysteria; my only quibble about Sharon Scruggs, towering in her strength, is that at points she lets the hysteria out.

Helmar Augustus Cooper comes off strongly as both a bluff Northumberland and a ruefully empathetic Brakenbury. In *R2,* Graham Brown is a movingly crestfallen Duke of York; Robert Stattel, as John of Gaunt, handles the famous speech with such elegant theatricality that it nearly renews itself. The rest are negligible, except for Tom Hammond, a touching Bagot and a creepily servile Catesby. Patricia Dunnock's strained Queen Isabel and Lady Anne confirm what *Strictly Dishonorable* revealed: her gift is for light comedy.

Stattel, doubling as the Bishop of Carlisle, does less well with *R2*'s visionary foreshadowing of the civil wars to come. That John Wylie, taking on the same dual role in the Pearl's *R2,* succeeds hauntingly with it shows you what a small-scale troupe can bring Shakespeare that those who think bigger often can't. Directed by Shepard Sobel, the Pearl's version is stiff-jointed, nowhere near as vivid in its physicality as Daniels's. But Murrell Horton's designs—lush gold and ochre costumes against bare black panels—rivet the eye, and the sense of the play as poetry is often a good deal stronger than at St. Clement's. Bradford Cover has seized on just the aspect of Richard that Daniels downplays: his actorish manner. Cover is a showy performer, and R2 loves showing off; for him every event is a new role, exploited by Cover with skill and vocal grace. Though lacking Skybell's fiery anguish, he's actually more moving at the end, as Hope Chernov's delicate, restrained Queen is throughout. (Caveat: In prior seasons, I've translated for the Pearl.)

Here, too, the supporting cast is often less than it should be—Seth Jones, the Bolingbroke, is so good in quiet moments that you wonder why he yells so much—but the presence of a permanent company gives a feeling of everyone working together, on a mission both important and pleasurable, that show-by-show enterprises can never quite evoke. The final argument against Daniels's exciting conception is that it would make most sense for a resident acting troupe.

Such a troupe, of course, requires actors, which was one of the two things wrong with Gregory Wolfe's ingenious, misguided *R3* for the young company called Moonwork Inc. The other was the central premise—that Shakespeare only makes sense if you dress it in glib contemporary analogies, like turning the kings into Mafia dons. Yeah, you can predict the rest: The Lord Mayor's plea was covered on CNN, and Margaret's curse came via Internet. It would all be very convincing, if John Gotti lived at 1600 Pennsylvania Avenue. Or if the cast had had the suppleness of voice and passion that you need for Shakespeare—which it didn't, except for Gregory Sherman's Pacino-ish Richard and Paula Stevens's crisp Elizabeth. Still, a young group's reach should exceed its grasp. Criticism, like *R2*'s gardener, just has to bind up the unruly children sometimes.

Charles Isherwood (review date 2000)

SOURCE: Isherwood, Charles. "Fiennes Plays Politics at BAM." *Variety* 380, no. 5 (18-24 September 2000): 45, 47.

[*In the following review, Isherwood comments on the Brooklyn Academy of Music production of* Richard II, *directed by Jonathan Kent and starring Ralph Fiennes as Richard. Isherwood focuses on Fiennes's performance, finding that while it was "compelling," Fiennes's portrayal of the king was silly and pompous.*]

It's probably just a coincidence, but the Almeida Theater Co.'s current engagement at the Brooklyn Academy of

Music is wittily timed. As the peculiar form of theater known as election-year politics heads into its third act, the company is performing two stern Shakespearean essays on political no-no's. *Coriolanus* offers a lesson in the importance of pandering to public opinion (hardly a necessary admonition these days, admittedly), while *Richard II* warns strongly against the dangers of presuming too much on dynastic privilege—a fault attributed to both of our presidential hopefuls at some time.

But it's hardly their topicality that has made the shows a virtual sellout for the company's monthlong run: It's the presence in the rifle roles of Ralph Fiennes, the movie star who is also an Almeida regular. Fiennes, who won a Tony for the company's *Hamlet* on Broadway, is here delving into more exotic Shakespearean territory, and delivers compelling—if not equally satisfactory—performances in pair of roles that at first blush appear to be entirely antithetical.

Richard is a sort of proto-Hamlet, a man who's inept and heedlessly immoral in action but (eventually) touched with genius as a poet; Coriolanus is brilliant whenever battle is joined, but self-destructive when he lets his words expose his proud soul. The plays themselves, in fact, are as divergent as their central characters. *Richard II* is written entirely in verse, and for a play that depicts a civil war, it's oddly free of alarums and excurions. Its chief interest lies in its lyrical depiction of the spiritual awakening of the title character. By contrast, the later tragedy *Coriolanus* and its hero are notably short on lyricism. It's a play of deeds, not words, of politics more than poetics.

The two make an intriguing pair, and Fiennes and Jonathan Kent, who directs both, allow the audience to take in both the concordances and the discordances between them. On a superficial level, both Richard and Coriolanus are miserable players of politics, Richard because he feels his divine right places him above consideration of the public weal, Coriolanus because he believes his martial prowess and his honor are all-justifying—and can only be tainted by the humbling necessities of political maneuvering. But it's how these two men, similarly ill-suited to their public roles, meet their similarly unhappy fates that distinguishes them. One is undone because he cannot betray his integrity; the other discovers his integrity only when he is undone.

Kent's *Richard II* unfolds in the twilight gloom pierced with sharp shafts of light that seems to be de rigueur for Shakespeare productions these days. Here the dank atmosphere is certainly justified by the play: The England of *Richard II* is a country in deep decline, a place where the golden light of regency has been dimmed by evil influences.

Fiennes, an actor who has specialized in both good and bad guys with an aura of sensitivity, would seem a natural fit for Richard. Perhaps that's why he seems to go out of his way to de-emphasize this trait. From his first entrance, sitting with stiff pomp on a gothic throne, attired in florid silks that set him strikingly apart from the rest of the court, Fiennes' Richard is a distinctly silly king. His petulance comes most strongly to the fore when Richard reacts with childish peevishness to Gaunt's deathbed reprimands: Fiennes adds his own flourishes to Shakespeare's boldly drawn picture of a royal tantrum—he sticks out his tongue at the dying man before gleefully usurping his wealth to fill the royal coffers.

Fiennes' showily comic, nearly hysterical Richard certainly gives the production a vivid focus, particularly amid a supporting cast too prone to loud and generic declaiming. And it's certainly grounded in the text of the first two acts, in which the ineptness and immorality of the king is plainly seen to be draining the lifeblood from the kingdom. But Shakespeare's Richard begins a journey toward illumination well before Fiennes' does; Fiennes' decision to accentuate Richard's antic neuroses intermittently throughout many of the character's great lyrical speeches leaves the play without any consistent emotional depth—any poetry of the soul to match its magnificent words—until virtually its last moments.

Suffering turns a miscreant monarch into a poet who sees deeper into the nihilistic corners of existence than almost any of Shakespeare's characters, and certainly anyone in the play. So it's a pity that Fiennes continues to obscure this spiritual awakening almost indefinitely, negating it with trivializing comic shtick all the way into the play's penultimate act (a sarcastic hand to his ear awaiting a royal greeting that he knows will not come, for instance, in the renunciation scene). "My grief lies all within," says Richard toward the close of this scene, and Fiennes has suggested that it's here that the character's transformation finally takes place; but this is to ignore too much of the reflective poetry that precedes it, and to rob us of a more psychologically nuanced—to say nothing of sympathetic—portrait of a man spiritually ennobled by grief and misfortune.

What is lost becomes instantly clear in Fiennes' last scene, when Richard, robbed of his royal robes, stands chained to the floor of his cell and imprisoned in a shaft of light. Fiennes delivers the deposed king's last great speech with great sensitivity, meticulously navigating his way through its dense philosophy with both a clear-sighted intelligence and a bruised, spiritual majesty. "I wasted time, and now time doth waste me," he says with a piteous humility. The play's emotional impact finally arrives in its full measure, but it's too little, too late.

There is a similar, and more apt, emphasis on comedy in Kent's *Coriolanus*. The play has at times been pegged as a satire, and Fiennes gives full and delicious scope to the warrior Coriolanus' wry, disgusted encounters with the Roman tribunes and the people. Also delightfully dry is Oliver Ford Davies as Menenius. Indeed, Davies plays similar roles in both plays—as the Duke of York in *Richard II,* he displays much of the same fatigued, ironical

pragmatism that he does as the peace-making Menenius in *Coriolanus*. While great leaders rise and fall, and revolutions wax and wane, the subtle, unassuming performances of this capable actor suggest that there will always be men of intelligence, effort and good will who are ground beneath the wheels of the state even as they are instrumental in keeping it on course.

On the whole, the company fares far better in *Coriolanus* than in *Richard II* (with the curious exception of Linus Roache, who makes little of the major role of Bolingbroke in *Richard II* and scarcely more of Aufidius in *Coriolanus*; his classical verse technique seems to consist primarily of twisting the volume knob up and down haphazardly). David Burke's Comidius and the wily tribunes of Alan David and Bernard Gallagher are effective, but the standout supporting performance in *Coriolanus* comes from Barbara Jefford as a fire-breathing Volumnia, a mother who most willingly suckled a bloodthirsty warrior and just as willingly betrays him.

But it's Fiennes' mesmerizing Coriolanus that gives the production both its energy and, more surprisingly, its humanity. Fiennes does not offer us merely a bellowing warrior whose excessive pride is his single and simple tragic flaw. He's suitably bloodthirsty as needed (in Kent's boldly drawn conception, Fiennes looks spookily like Carrie at the prom during the Romans' initial battles with the Volscians), but there is a vivid, quixotic nobility in this warrior's pride, and his disdain for public approbation seems to stem from an authentic sensitivity rather than simple churlishness.

With his eyes afire and, in a particularly effective piece of staging, his back turned to public ceremony, Fiennes' Coriolanus is also loyal to a vision of human possibility that everyone else has long since forsaken in favor of more smudged, dissimulating, dishonest personae. Shakespeare's attitude toward the vacillating populace in this play is more nuanced than in others, but in an age when politicians are too wont to follow rather than lead the public, the proud integrity of Fiennes' Coriolanus asserts itself as admirable—even thrilling—and his treatment at the hands of the Romans' is consequently more pitiable.

We share his benumbed march toward vengeance, and when Volumnia bears down upon him with her plea for mercy to Rome, this most political of Shakespeare plays reaches a devastating emotional climax. The hero's mother's strange love, it's easy to see, resulted in a man whose pride may just hide a bone-deep insecurity—he still needs a mother's approval more than anything else. Fiennes plays the scene with shattering stillness, finally crumpling into Volumnia's breast as he capitulates, making us aware that Coriolanus' assent is both an act of mercy and a plea for mercy: Both know his capitulation will cost him his life. It's a deft, brilliant stroke that crowns a thoroughly captivating performance.

Shakespeare productions ultimately rise or fall on their allegiance to the playwright's greatest gift, the truths he tells of the curious workings of human hearts. It's here, surprisingly, that Fiennes' Richard II falls a little short, while his Coriolanus, the manifestly more inhuman hero, succeeds—much like the warrior who bested a city of Volscians—against all odds.

THEMES

Leonard Barkin (essay date 1978)

SOURCE: Barkin, Leonard. "The Theatrical Consistency of *Richard II.*" *Shakespeare Quarterly* 29, no. 1 (winter 1978): 5-19.

[*In the following essay, Barkin studies the emotional impact of* Richard II, *and claims that the play possesses inherent theatrical and logical unity in terms of the emotional responses displayed by the characters on stage and the emotional interaction between the characters and audience members.*]

For some years, critics analyzing Shakespeare's plays and teachers teaching them have labored under a self-induced pressure to approach the plays as *theatre.* Such an injunction is properly justified by appeals both to the historical circumstances under which the plays were composed and to the theatrical liveliness of the texts themselves. And some of the finest Shakespearean criticism of the post-war period has been inspired by this theatrical awareness.

Though theatrical criticism embraces a great range of approaches, it often involves a tendency to equate theatre with theatrical *effects.* Consequently, we have come to look to this school of criticism for an explanation of the path between the text and the theatrical result, whether in gesture, blocking, visual matters, actors' approaches to individual roles, or directorial conception. But it is important to remember that creative artists in the theatre do not spend all their time producing theatrical effects; in fact, they also expend a great deal of energy looking for theatrical *causes.* If in theatrical criticism we choose effects as our only goal, we omit a crucial phase in theatrical practice: the search for inherent theatrical values or meanings in the text without any prejudice as to their specific realization on stage.

Foremost among these theatrical causes is what we might call "emotional consistency." Dramatic action, besides being the raveling and unraveling of a fictional narrative, consists of a sequence of emotional responses, both among the characters on stage and between stage characters and members of the audience. In Shakespeare's dramas, these responses are ordered by a grand design; I call this design the play's "consistency." As used here, "consistency" has two relevant meanings: texture and logical continuity.

In scrutinizing *Richard II,* I aim to describe its emotional texture and to prove its theatrical continuity. For evidence inside the play, I rely heavily on systems of emotional response, both among the characters and between them and us. Analysis of theatrical causes can point to particularly apposite theatrical effects. Once we understand a play's theatrical causes and effects, we will have gone a long way toward defining a stage meaning for the play—that is, a way of seeing the play's totality that is at once true to the spirit of the work and susceptible to theatrical realization.

The emotional consistency I propose for *Richard II* concerns a history of violent or passionate energies suppressed and then released in both physical violence and comedy. We do not tend to think of *Richard II* as a violent play, of course. Whether in the study or in the theatre, *Richard II* has a justified reputation for being poetic, cerebral, wistfully tragic. But when we concentrate our attention exclusively on the mellifluous language, the history of ideas, the suffering misfitted king, we close our eyes to much of the power, and specifically the stage power, contained in the text.[1] The early parts of the play, both in events and in theatrical style, are characterized by an increasing emphasis on violence and passion desired or imminent but not realized. The personality of Richard and the ritualistic style of the drama act, each in its own way, to inhibit such realization.[2] Once Richard is excluded from control of England (and the play), however, all the passionate energies explode with a force all the greater for their suppression. The result is a transformation of England and—more important for our purpose—a change in the drama's ritualistic style. As *Richard II* concludes, we find ourselves in a dramatic world where violence is real, joined with new forms of complexity and that familiar close relative of violence, comedy.

I

The play opens with two powerful noblemen who want to slaughter each other. We soon learn that the violence they desire is itself due to an act of violence, the murder of the king's uncle. But the original event stands in the past, where throughout the play its actuality—its course, motives, perpetrators—remains hopelessly elusive. Meanwhile, the present desire for violence is suppressed in various ways. At first, the king tries simply to cancel all eruption of violence. Having heard the word "blood" eight times in some hundred lines, he tries to stop the blood before it flows:

> Let's purge this choler without letting blood—
> This we prescribe, though no physician;
> Deep malice makes too deep incision.
> Forget, forgive, conclude and be agreed:
> Our doctors say this is no month to bleed.[3]

>   (I. i. 153-57)

Indeed he is no physician. Ignoring the very proper medical value of bleeding, the king fails in his efforts to convince his patients to abjure violence altogether.

If we try to be alive to theatrical "causes," we can hardly fail to notice that throughout the first half of *Richard II* much of the dramatic power results from the confrontation between passion or violence and some sort of chilling force bent on their suppression. Consider in the opening scene, first, the immense passion of the two combatants, second, what we might call the *genius loci* (that is, the awesome decorum of the throne room, where violent passion does not belong), and, third, a quality peculiar to this particular occupant of the throne room, an infuriating, almost flippant self-possession that suggests he is deaf and blind to the passions around him. Virtually all of Richard's responses to the outbursts of Bolingbroke and Mowbray can be effectively delivered in a cool, almost playful, and altogether inscrutable way, an insouciant style in which the king tries to deny violence but ends by provoking it all the more. To the first ceremonial well-wishing by the two disputants, Richard answers, "We thank you both, yet one but flatters us, / As well appeareth by the cause you come" (I. i. 25-26). Richard toys with the intensity and gravity of their concerns, reducing their great argument until it concentrates upon him and upon the trivial and court-centered issue of flattery. The tone of Richard's other comments (which, by the way, are very few in number) is much the same:

> What doth our cousin lay to Mowbray's charge?
> It must be great that can inherit us
> So much as of a thought of ill in him.

> (I. i. 84-86)

After a particularly complete and violent accusation by Bolingbroke, Richard muses "How high a pitch his resolution soars!" (I. i. 109). The king persists in a kind of aesthetic appreciation of the passions he is observing, as though the disputants were a pair of successful actors.

Richard chills the emotions but does not pacify them. When absolute peace fails, he resorts to a compromise between peace and war, the trial by combat, which amounts to a postponement and a ritualization of the disputants' desires for violence. The scene in the lists at Coventry offers us the perfect theatrical metaphor for the emotional tension we observed in the first scene. What has been a merely conversational conflict now becomes the keystone of the stage business itself. Shakespeare develops the formality of the trial proceedings to their ultimate extension by using repeated expressions, formal constructions, old-fashioned language, and all the trappings of verbal ceremony. Lest we be hypnotized by the printed page, however, we should remember that the theatrical requirements of the scene are likely to rigidify the formality of the ritual even more than the language does. The vertical structure of the set composition, the ubiquitous armor, the trumpets and banners, the presence of a large number of supernumeraries who are dehumanized into absolute military posture: all of these elements offer an unavoidable sense of chilling indifference to the passions that originated the quarrel and the violence that may arise from it. The emotions that surface from under all the armor

and ceremony are still fiery hot, but the king has succeeded in containing them even more effectively than in the first scene. His decision to terminate the trial by combat is no more than a natural outgrowth of the institution itself: he reduces it entirely to its ritual aspects and deprives it of its natural, and bloody, resolution. In one action he attempts to separate the two combatants from each other and, just as important, to separate the whole problem of violence—including Mowbray, Bolingbroke, and the murder of Gloucester—from himself and his court.

II

But the emotional tension between violent desires and chilly suppression is not limited to the principal scenes of Richard's kingly ascendance. Virtually every scene in the first two acts of *Richard II* is characterized by the same sort of affective tension. The conversation between the Duchess of Gloucester and John of Gaunt, which occupies the second scene, is swimming in violence, with many repetitions of words like "blood," "slaughter," "murder," and "butcher." The subject here, of course, is violence in the past, but there is no dearth of onstage passion from the Duchess, who wants to see her husband's death avenged. For this scene, then, she is the Mowbray-Bolingbroke figure:

> O, sit my husband's wrongs on Herford's spear,
> That it may enter butcher Mowbray's breast!
> Or if misfortune miss the first career,
> Be Mowbray's sins so heavy in his bosom
> That they may break his foaming courser's back
> And throw the rider headlong in the lists.

> (I. ii. 47-52)

All this passionate intensity is again contrasted with a figure in possession of more practical power who refuses to respond to the emotions. "Venge my Gloucester's death," says the Duchess; Gaunt responds, "God's is the quarrel." A desire for violence is once more thrown against unshakable inaction, and a firm intention not to act has the practical power to contain the violence.

In his death scene, however, Gaunt shifts from his earlier position and becomes the passionate figure playing to a flippant and unresponsive Richard. The king reverts to his tone at the play's opening, a light-hearted sort of teasing that attempts to treat Gaunt's death as an aesthetic experience. For the first time, Richard's composure is actually breached:

> A lunatic lean-witted fool,
> Presuming on an ague's privilege,
> Darest with thy frozen admonition
> Make pale our cheek, chasing the royal blood
> With fury from his native residence.

> (II. i. 115-19)

The image is a significant one. The suppression of violence is beginning to tell, even on Richard; and the royal blood, which has already been insistently connected both with continuity and with violence among the Plantagenets, is asserting itself, if only negatively, in the king's involuntary responses. But again the suppression of violence wins out. Gaunt's privilege to speak passionately in the king's presence is due only to the imminence of his own death, an event over which the king has no power. Gaunt's death soon silences the outburst.

The second scene of Act II is clearly intended to parallel the second scene of Act I. Again a passionate woman, in this case the Queen, confronts rational and unresponsive comforters who do not comfort her. Bushy does not urge her to appeal to God, as did Gaunt to the Duchess of Gloucester, but rather offers a consolation much like Theseus' speech in Act V of *A Midsummer Night's Dream,* suggesting that her imagination is creating more griefs than she has any real reason to feel. Considering that this consolation comes just when Bolingbroke's first successes against Richard are about to be announced, the viewer will see that the Queen's imagination is far more reliable than Bushy's reality. Realizing that her fears are justified, the Queen turns on her comforters with a violent image of her own:

> So, Greene, thou art the midwife to my woe,
> And Bolingbroke my sorrow's dismal heir;
> Now hath my soul brought forth her prodigy,
> And I, a gasping new-deliver'd mother,
> Have woe to woe, sorrow to sorrow join'd.
>
> (II. ii. 62-66)

This monstrous birth, and the passion of its expression, are contrasted with the chilliness of Bushy's "Despair not, madam" and the passive piety of York's "Comfort's in heaven and we are on the earth, / Where nothing lives but crosses, cares, and grief" (II. ii. 78-79).

In the next scene, it is again York who acts as the chilling force. Of all the characters in the play, he is the one who is most extremely torn between opposing points of view, capable of speaking with the greatest passion about both the wrongs of King Richard and the crime of usurpation. The result of these conflicting passions is an internal suppression of violence. "I do remain as neuter" (II. iii. 158), he says, reminding us that he is himself the product of an immovable object and an irresistible force and that he will try to take his stand against the rising tide of rebel violence. By the end of Act II, just before Bolingbroke's triumphs begin, we have witnessed a considerable increase in the ability of the blocking individual to suppress passion and violence; but we have not left behind the emotional tension between violent desires and an opposition to them that declares itself neuter.[4]

III

The middle of the play becomes a series of provocations to violence; Richard meets them with retreat and self-denial. While Bolingbroke is executing villainous Plantagenet allies, Richard is making his own deposition inevitable by yielding to all demands before his rival can

even make them. All of Richard's great speeches are concerned with escapism, with undoing, with self-annihilation. So this is the one play in the tetralogy that has no battles. In an almost Chekhovian way, any form of decisive narrative action is eschewed. Thus, the main event of the plot, Richard's deposition, is never actually introduced as a possibility. Around the middle of the play it is suddenly taken for granted. Shakespeare has deliberately rejected the powerful theatrical effect of a discovery, a single instant when either Richard or Bolingbroke first confronts the possibility of deposition.[5] When the decisive moment actually arrives, it is almost comically anticlimactic. Almost as if he had just thought of it, Bolingbroke says, "In God's name, I'll ascend the regal throne" (IV. i. 113). Shortly thereafter Richard interrupts the formal abdication ceremony to say, "Give me the crown. Here, cousin, seize the crown" (IV. i. 181).

Through this central phase of the play, significant changes take place in the theatrical mood of the drama. The great scenes for which the play is often remembered—Richard's passionate lyrical performances in III. ii, III. iii, and IV. i—represent the high point in the play's ritualistic style, but they also mark the beginning of its obsolescence. Up through this point Shakespeare has realized a ritualistic form of drama by banishing violence (indeed any form of decisive action) from the narrative. The result has been a remarkably decorous dramatic structure, one that is free of such elements as comic subplots, multiple points of view, and villains we love to hate. But just as Bolingbroke becomes increasingly powerful, and rebellion, with its violent implications, is loose in the land, the mode and style of the play become more diffuse.

IV

As we move toward Acts IV and V, the nature of the theatrical experience changes in three interconnected ways. First, violence ceases to be effectively suppressed. Though it is not until the end of the play that blood is actually shed on the stage, the offstage presence of violence is more imminent; meanwhile, potentially violent human passions become frequent on stage. Second, comedy becomes possible in the world of the play. As actions become more extreme and reality more distanced from ritual, the incongruities turn toward irony and even laughter. Third, the play's concentrated focus upon the king as single individual and as political/cosmic principle is eased, and the view of the world is much broadened. As the range of interest widens in this latter part of the play, there are frequent ironic attempts to deflect our concern about monarchic and historical questions, deflating the seriousness with which such questions can be handled.

The clearest manifestations of these new dramatic qualities are to be found in the multiple challenges in the first scene of Act IV and in the Aumerle rebellion in Act V. For years stage producers have looked at these episodes and despaired. Faced with seemingly manic scenes in the final minutes of such a sublime drama, they have had a number of choices. They could (and often have) cut the scenes, since they seem unnecessary to the plot. They could stage them in a solemn fashion befitting the high tragic tone of Richard's own final scenes, even though such solemnity seems completely out of place and must be justified by appeal to such untheatrical notions as the history of ideas or the quaint oddity of the distant past. Or they could follow their theatrical instinct and present these scenes in a raucous style, running considerable risks with both critics and audiences. It seems to me that there has been no need to fear incongruity. The frenzy, the bathos, the comedy of these episodes represent Shakespeare's most salient demonstration of the fact that passion and violence have been loosed into the world. The more hectic and funny the staging of these scenes, the more powerful the message.[6]

The judgment scene at the opening of Act IV parallels the first scene of the play. In both instances, the ruler is engaged in the solemn business of ascertaining the truth by means of a type of legal proceeding. Richard handles it clumsily, of course, and, what is more serious, cannot deal justly, since (like the judge Oedipus) he is himself the culprit. Bolingbroke has none of these problems, and the later scene begins by glorifying his order and rationality just as these qualities were glorified at the opening of Act III, when Bolingbroke was judging Bushy and Greene. But things get out of hand. Aumerle is accused of complicity and throws his gage down. Bolingbroke tries to prevent Bagot from responding in kind (in one rather helpless line, and he will not speak again for another sixty lines), and all he gets for his trouble is to have Fitzwater throw his gage down. Soon others jump into the fray. Percy throws his gage down. "Another Lord," whom Shakespeare does not even bother to name, throws his gage down. Then a new party, Surrey, is heard from, and new reversals begin:

SURREY.

> My Lord Fitzwater, I do remember well
> The very time Aumerle and you did talk.

FITZ.

> 'Tis very true; you were in presence then,
> And you can witness with me this is true.

SURREY.

> As false, by heaven, as heaven itself is true.

FITZ.

> Surrey, thou liest.

> > (IV. i. 60-65)

Surrey seems to be cooperating and corroborating; Fitzwater is delighted to have an unimpeachable witness; Surrey says exactly the opposite of what the set-up has led us to expect; and Fitzwater ought to be the absolute picture of frustration.

Now I am not saying that this scene is irrepressibly hilarious, but I do think it has strong comic properties. Surely it becomes a parody of the play's opening. The repetition of a single physical action often leads to laughter in the theatre, and the throwing down of gages in this scene has the effect of mocking all the pomposity that we, as members of the audience, have been willing to swallow for three acts. In addition, there is a strongly comic quality to the chain-reaction effect in the scene. We begin with Bolingbroke and Bagot; Bagot involves Aumerle; Aumerle involves Fitzwater; Fitzwater involves Surrey. Aumerle even runs out of gages and has to borrow one. Each time a new combatant becomes involved, the previous ones drop out of the picture and are left, as I see it, standing awkwardly around. The climax comes when the argument reduces itself to a battle between Surrey and Fitzwater, who are, after all, non-entities with only the remotest connection to the original scene in which Gloucester's death was plotted. An uncontrollable domino effect of relatively trivial human passions has deflected the play from its central thematic concerns and the new ruler from the serious business of ordering England. It is significant for both the meaning and the chaotic humor of the scene that Bolingbroke, who sets it in motion, becomes a silent and almost helpless spectator by the time the scene ends.[7]

The episode involving Aumerle and the Duke and Duchess of York occupies a quite remarkable amount of space in the closing scenes of the play.[8] From the moment when York discovers his son's involvement in the conspiracy against King Henry, circumstances produce the release of violent energies. "Treason, foul treason! Villain! Traitor! Slave!" (V. ii. 72), the Duke calls out, and we begin to see the incongruous image of an aged man—indeed, one who has vehemently defined himself as neutral—in a physical frenzy. From here on, the frenzy is accompanied by rough humor. Again, the bathetic comedy derives from deflection. Just as the gage-throwing deflects our attention from the real issue (the murder of Gloucester) to a repeated chivalric act and to individuals who are increasingly remote from the murder of Gloucester, so here, in both the Aumerle scenes, our attention is deflected from the real issue of rebellion and the family bond. The first deflection concerns York's boots:

YORK.

> Bring me my boots: I will unto the king
> *His man enters with his boots.*

DUCH.

> Strike him, Aumerle. Poor boy, thou art amaz'd.
> Hence, villain! never more come in my sight.

YORK.

> Give me my boots, I say.

> > (V. ii. 84-87)

We are invited to forget about Aumerle, about rebellion, and even about York's journey to the king. Instead the focus is on a mute servant, involved in the action in a remote and inconsequential way. The Duchess, taking out her frustration on the servant and the boots, is all the more frustrated because she cannot induce her son to beat up the poor servant. The Duke, oblivious to the meaning of the boots, just continues wanting them.

Then the Duchess, in her eagerness to save Aumerle from his father's wrath, deflects the issue in a new direction:

> But now I know thy mind: thou dost suspect
> That I have been disloyal to thy bed,
> And that he is a bastard, not thy son.
> Sweet York, sweet husband, be not of that mind;
> He is as like thee as a man may be,
> Not like to me, or any of my kin,
> And yet I love him.

(V. ii. 104-10)

Cuckoldry, particularly with the resulting issue of dubious parentage, is a stock comic topic, and in this situation, the advanced age of the participants renders doubly absurd the Duchess' assumptions about passionate jealousy. The speech culminates in a series of comic reversals. Since the Duchess is so passionately defending her son, we assume that she is very close to him in spirit and, presumably, in stage position. But the climax of her argument depends on her proving that the young man's real closeness is to his father (imagine her pushing the inert Aumerle up against his father). Then in a fit of hyperbole, the Duchess asserts that she has no stake in him at all (perhaps pushing the two of them further away from her). Finally she recognizes the absurdity of arguing passionately for her son and denying her maternity, so she reverses again, says "And yet I love him," and, following this little staging of the scene, pulls son, and perhaps father too, back to herself. All the while—judging from York's next comment, "Make way, unruly woman!"—she is blocking the door. The scene culminates in a rush of great energy as all three characters, two of them quite aged, engage in a race to reach the king.

When the York frenzy is transferrd from its own home to the king's palace, its mood becomes even more incongruous. With the entrance of the Yorks, a low-keyed, wistful scene about a wayward son is interrupted by a piece of slapstick about a wayward son. If at first the matter of Aumerle's pardon is treated solemnly, it is soon rendered absurd by the stage business of the kneeling. The kneeling here is precisely equivalent to the gage-throwing in Act IV, scene i: it is a repeated physical action producing a chain reaction.[9] Aumerle's first genuflection is accompanied by a slightly incongruous physical image:

> For ever may my knees grow to the earth,
> My tongue cleave to my roof within my mouth,
> Unless a pardon ere I rise or speak.

(V. iii. 29-31)

The unmistakable hyperbole in this plea is properly deflated when Bolingbroke gives the pardon with greater alacrity than Aumerle expected. As a consequence, this eternal cleaving of knees and tongue to their respective grounds lasts approximately fifteen seconds.

But the main event is yet to come. The Duchess enters and kneels immediately:

BOL.

> Rise up, good aunt.

DUCH.

> Not yet, I thee beseech:
> For ever will I walk upon my knees,
> And never see day that the happy sees
> Till thou give joy—until thou bid me joy,
> By pardoning Rutland my transgressing boy.

AUM.

> Unto my mother's prayers I bend my knee.

YORK.

> Against them both my true joints bended be.

(V. iii. 90-96)

The king is tired of petitioners who get their way by kneeling, but the Duchess is relentles and goes her son's hyperbole one further by vowing to walk on her knees—an action she might even illustrate to prove the seriousness of her intent. With the corroborative kneeling of Aumerle and the counter-kneeling of York, we reach comic chaos. The immense long-windedness of the Duchess—38 lines, all spoken from her knees—reinforces the absurdity, especially since we know the pardon has already been given. Again there is a deflection from the main issues and individuals. At a time when our attention ought to be focused on the idea of rebellion and on the opposition of Bolingbroke and Aumerle, we are concerned instead with kneeling. Aumerle is altogether silent, and the King of England is reduced to saying nothing but "Rise up, good aunt," "Good aunt, stand up," and "Good aunt, stand up." Frenzy has invaded the king's sanctuary, and bathos has invaded the sanctuary of the play.

V

But what has become of Richard in the midst of all this bathos? As the protagonist in a tragedy of personal suffering and insight, he does not belong to the chaotic Lancastrian world. It is therefore interesting to note that Richard is not immune. In the same scene (IV. i) that includes the multiple gage-throwing, Richard himself stage-manages an episode that might profitably be realized in the theatre as cynical, comic, or at least bathetic:

RICH.

> Give me the crown. Here, cousin, seize the crown.
> Here, cousin,
> On this side my hand, and on that side thine.
> Now is this golden crown like a deep well
> That owes two buckets, filling one another,
> The emptier ever dancing in the air,
> The other down, unseen, and full of water.
> That bucket down and full of tears am I,
> Drinking my griefs, whilst you mount up on high.

Bol.

> I thought you had been willing to resign.

Rich.

> My crown I am, but still my griefs are mine.
> You may my glories and my state depose,
> But not my griefs: still am I King of those.

Bol.

> Part of your cares you give me with your crown.

Rich.

> Your cares set up, do not pluck my cares down.
> My care is loss of care, by old care done;
> Your care is gain of care, by new care won.
> The cares I give, I have, though given away,
> They 'tend the crown, yet still with me they stay.

Bol.

> Are you contented to resign the crown?

Rich.

> Ay, no; no, ay; for I must nothing be.
> Therefore no "no", for I resign to thee.

                    (IV. i. 181-202)

Richard has been asked to resign his "state and crown / To Henry Bolingbroke." Though he is generally a master of the abstract statement, he chooses on this occasion to construe "crown" not as metonymy but as the physical object itself. He then subjects Bolingbroke to a tug-of-war which either lasts for the whole twenty lines or else forces his antagonist into the rather sheepish gesture of letting go of the crown during one of his impatient one-line speeches. Meanwhile Richard trivializes his language, eschewing Christ and the heavens and concentrating for the moment on buckets going up and down in a well.[10] Richard even captures the seesaw effect of a tug-of-war in the language he uses. The image of one bucket up and one down is complemented by a rash of contrasts, contradictions, oxymorons, and lines broken in two halves by caesuras. "Ay, no; no, ay" (IV. i. 201) serves as the climax of this style and sentiment. All these linguistic effects seem perfectly suited to the stage business of a wavering tug-of-war.

However we might stage the scene, it is at least clear from Bolingbroke's responses that he thinks Richard is taunting him. Richard is daring his rival to hold on to the crown, and Bolingbroke is forced to recognize and take part in the charade in a vividly physical way. Richard holds on tight, first as an act of physical defiance, to prove that he is still alive and still a man, and second as a means of forcing Bolingbroke to re-enact, in an almost self-parodic fashion, his usurpation. Bolingbroke begins the episode half-heartedly, as if humoring a madman, but continues the tug-of-war because he too comes to recognize its symbolism; he has been trapped into doing battle for his manhood. Just when the new king's actual strength is about to win out, Richard willingly lets go, making it clear that his

imagination has moved to other, more abstract charades. Bolingbroke is left with a victory so childish and (suddenly) unsymbolic that it is worse than a defeat.

These associations of Richard with the physically chaotic in the last acts are, of course, the exception rather than the rule. Shakespeare is not content merely to transform a ritualistic play into a bathetic one; instead, he uses the last two acts to polarize his theatrical styles. As more violence and comedy enter the new world of Bolingbroke's rule, Richard's part in the drama becomes increasingly pure and abstract. By the end of the fourth act, Richard has reduced himself imaginatively to nothing; his poetry has reached a pinnacle of solipsism and abstraction; as a consequence, he has become sequestered from the frenzy of the narrative and from the play's new styles. When we see him in his last scene, soliloquizing in prison about matters of the greatest intellectual abstraction, he forms a very striking theatrical contrast to the kind of drama that is becoming typical of the Lancastrian rule.

Yet abstraction and physicality are yoked together again in Richard's death scene. Consider the stage direction and Richard's gloss upon the stage business:

> *The murderers rush in.*

Rich.

> How now! what means death in this rude assault?
>
>   (V. v. 105)

Shakespeare has made enthusiastic use of the historical tradition, derived from Holinshed and Hall, that Richard slew a number of his would-be murderers. In a decisive break with the philosophizing and elegiac mood of the previous hundred lines, Shakespeare injects physical energy into Richard's last moments. Richard has just cursed Henry and struck his jailor for refusing to act as a food taster, and he is now clearly preparing for a last burst of violent energy. The scene ought to become frenzied, as the original stage directions suggest. *"Here Exton strikes him down,"* we are told, and we observe the play's first onstage act of violence. In the theatre, this act produces at last a real release, in blood, of tensions that the whole play has been building, and it would be a mistake to shrink away from a considerable fight amongst Richard and his three assassins. If I wanted to produce the play in a radically arresting fashion, I would make Exton a half-comic bungler who has found the physical task of murdering Richard no easy matter. He laboriously decides in the previous scene to commit the murder; he accomplishes it in a clumsy way with macabre humor; and he brings his good deed to the new king only to be severely reproved. He is a picture of the little man who tries to play by the rules only to find the rules changed. If the scenes are staged properly, we can come to see their similarity to the kind of frenzied semi-comic dramaturgy in the Aumerle episode.

Once the onstage murder has occurred, violence is truly loosed into the world of the play:

BOL.

> Kind uncle York, the latest news we hear,
> Is that the rebels have consum'd with fire
> Our town of Ciceter in Gloucestershire. . . .
>   (*Enter* Northumberland) . . .

NORTH.

> The next news is, I have to London sent
> The heads of Salisbury, Spencer, Blunt and
>   Kent. . . .
>   (*Enter* Fitzwater.)

FITZ.

> My lord, I have from Oxford sent to London
> The heads of Broccas and Sir Bennet Seely,
> Two of the dangerous consorted traitors
> That sought at Oxford thy dire overthrow. . . .
>   (*Enter* Percy . . .)

PERCY.

> The grand consiprator, Abbot of Westminster, . . .
> Hath yielded up his body to the grave.
>
>   (V. vi. 1-21)

This represents the real *grand guignol* or satyr-play ending of *Richard II*. Violence and theatrical bathos unite. A lengthy series of violent deaths is underlined by a succession of vivid announcements about the victims' heads being shipped to London. Meanwhile, the entrance of breathless messengers reminds us of the earlier sequences involving gage-throwing and kneeling: the repeated mechanism of these sequences suggests that violence and comedy are, in this play at least, potentially close relatives.[11]

VI

I have tried to draw a line of stage affinities, an underplot of theatrical causes, along with some possible theatrical effects, in *Richard II*. The motif of suppressed passion in the early part of the play is balanced and resolved in the later portions of the play by a series of explosive releases, including the judgment scene and the tug-of-war with the crown in IV. i, the Aumerle episode in V. iii, the murder of Richard in V. v, and the bloodbath (V. vi) to which the rebels are treated at the end. What all these explosive releases have in common is a kind of theatrical mood or emotional consistency, and this mood demands realization on stage. But the effect of these episodes goes beyond the realm of mood: they help establish Shakespeare's vision of kingship in the modern world. While the world has become raucous and destructive, the new king has tried to dissociate himself from violence at every turn. He has disdained the multiple gage-throwing by appealing to evidence rather than to mere strife:

> These differences shall all rest under gage
> Till Norfolk be repeal'd—repeal'd he shall be,

> And, though mine enemy, restor'd again
> To all his lands and signories.
>
>   (IV. i. 86-89)

He has dissociated himself from the multiple kneeling by uttering some of the most perceptive dramatic criticism of the play to be found within it:

> Our scene is alt'red from a serious thing,
> And now chang'd to "The Beggar and the King" . . .
>
>   (V. iii. 77-78)

And he has tried in the same scene to avoid Richard's mistakes by going beyond mere banishment of his enemies—that is, Aumerle's fellow-conspirators:

> Destruction straight shall dog them at the heels. . . .
> They shall not live within this world, I swear.
>
>   (V. iii. 137, 140)

Finally, in punishing Exton, he has tried to dissociate himself from the murder of Richard:

> They love not poison that do poison need,
> Nor do I thee. Though I did wish him dead,
> I hate the murtherer, love him murthered.
>
>   (V. vi. 38-40)

There is no doubt that Bolingbroke has been to some extent justified in each of these dissociations. Shakespeare takes great pains to establish the newly violent world, but he also seems intent on reminding us that the new king is a man of order, reason, and sensitivity. But the violence is already beginning to taint the king. He will never find out the truth about the murder of Gloucester because the one man who could tell all has slipped through his fingers and died in Venice. He cannot completely rid his realm of dangerous people; he is trapped, for instance, into pardoning Aumerle. He even ends the play with a series of banishments, since he is unable to execute Carlisle and Exton. In all these respects he resembles his predecessor. Richard could not or would not get at the truth about Gloucester; he was condemned to fostering enemies; and he was foolish enough to banish enemies instead of committing the clean break so eloquently favored by the gardener. Finally, Bolingbroke will be plagued to the end of his days by Richard's death, precisely as Richard was by Gloucester's.

Yet if the figures are similar, they relate very differently to the ground. Henry IV has, by accident or design, created the style of the modern world, though he is personally unsympathetic to that style. The plays named after Bolingbroke will celebrate that combination of comedy and bloodshed. What we need to recognize is that the modern world actually begins earlier than the *Henry IV* plays, with the birth of Henry's kingship in *Richard II*.

Notes

1. The present argument runs against the tide of a good deal of criticism tending to see *Richard II* as

extremely unified. Walter Pater is perhaps the most passionate exponent of this view: "The play of *Richard the Second* does, like a musical composition, possess a certain concentration of all its parts, a simple continuity, an evenness in execution, which are rare in the great dramatist. . . . It belongs to a small group of plays, where, by happy birth and consistent evolution, dramatic form approaches to something like the unity of a lyrical ballad, a lyric, a song, a single strain of music" (*Appreciations* [London: Macmillan, 1901], pp. 202-3). We remake Shakespeare in the image of our own times; and while Pater may have yearned for the lyric unity he saw in *Richard II,* we may be erring in our own desire to find twentieth-century tensions and paradoxes in everything. Writing a half-century later, John Dover Wilson nonetheless agrees with Pater: "the tragedy of King Richard the Second has all the air of being composed in a single mood" (Introduction to *King Richard II* [Cambridge: Cambridge Univ. Press, 1939], p. xiv). But a number of twentieth-century critics do find a multiplicity of materials and styles in the play. M. C. Bradbrook, in *Shakespeare and Elizabethan Poetry* (London: Chatto and Windus, 1951), pp. 135-40, bases her whole discussion of the play on a certain kind of complexity: "It is the multiplicity of points of view which gives its tragic character to this play: even as on the early stage a multiple setting allowed the dramatist to set several scenes on the stage side by side, so this multiple characterization allows the dramatist several centres of sympathy" (p. 136). As my argument will show, I do not find this thesis entirely convincing. Much of the material in the play is powerfully homogeneous; hence, the effectiveness of the heterogeneous elements. A. P. Rossiter (*Angel with Horns,* ed. Graham Storey [London: Longmans, 1961]) goes even further, declaring that "most critics" have felt "some kind of discontinuity, or inconsistency" in the play. For his own opinion he declares, "Whether you approach *Richard II* from the angle of the texture of the verse, the verse-styles, character, plot or themes, you encounter what geologists call 'unconformities'" (p. 23). He sees these largely as between the first two acts and the last three, a point of view I share in some respects.

2. It is interesting to note that those who argue for a homogeneous *Richard II* nearly always see the unified tone as being one of pure ritual, a style in which the play has often been staged. John Dover Wilson, for instance, tells us that "*Richard II* ought to be played throughout as a ritual. As a work of art it stands far closer to the Catholic service of the Mass than to Ibsen's *Brand* or Bernard Shaw's *Saint Joan*" (p. xiii). Not surprisingly, this approach has appealed greatly to theatre people: it seems to offer a direct theatrical key to all the action. Sir John Gielgud begins his fascinating little essay saying that "Richard the Second is a ceremonial play" (*Stage Direc-*

tions [London: Mercury Books, 1963], p. 28). John Russell Brown, in *Shakespeare's Plays in Performance* (Baltimore: Penguin Books, 1969), uses a discussion of the play to illustrate the theatrical value of emblematic ceremony. He feels that the visual power of these ceremonies is so great that it has the natural effect upon an audience of inspiring belief, particularly in the case of the Bolingbroke ceremonies near the close of the play. I believe very firmly in the theatrical power of these rituals, but I think that they exist in a state of dynamic tension with (a) anarchic, non-ritual forces and (b) corrupted values that cheapen the ritual. A. P. Rossiter (p. 38) points out that "only six scenes out of nineteen can be called 'ritualistic' or formalized"; and Paul Jorgensen ("Vertical Patterns in *Richard II,*" *Shakespeare Association Bulletin,* 23 [1948], 134) questions the rituals themselves: "There is something not entirely convincing about the pomp and gorgeous decorativeness of the play. Its most exalted scenes leave one uncertain as to the dignity of the participants, uneasy as to the appropriateness of solemn emotion." Let us then see *Richard II* as a play of attempted ritual.

3. Citations are to Peter Ure, ed., *King Richard II,* the Arden Edition (London: Methuen, 1956).

4. Even the language the characters use testifies to the presence of violence and the effort to suppress it. Theoretically, language offers an alternative to violence: Bolingbroke and Mowbray are invited to talk their differences out, so that they will not come to blows; and in another sense, later in the play, Richard's linguistic artistry demonstrates his distance from the world of violent action. Language indeed seeks to contain violence, then, particularly when Richard uses elaborately formal constructions in order to regulate the passions around him: "Face to face, / And frowning brow to brow, ourselves will hear / The accuser and the accused freely speak. / High-stomach'd are they both and full of ire, / In rage, deaf as the sea, hasty as fire" (I. i. 15-19). The formal language precisely parallels the formal ritual; and like the ritual, it is broken by what it attempts to contain. But language, far from containing violence, may be the means by which violence enters the play (the frequent repetitions of "blood," for instance). Or else words may be violent acts in themselves. Richard responds to Gaunt's tongue-lashing: "Wert thou not brother to great Edward's son, / This tongue that runs so roundly in thy head / Should run thy head from thy unreverent shoulders" (II. i. 121-23); and York attacks Northumberland for failing to use the proper title of respect for the king: "The time hath been, / Would you have been so brief with him, he would / Have been so brief with you to shorten you, / For taking so the head, your whole head's length" (III. iii. 11-14). In both cases, language is aggression, and it is met with an equal, physical counter-aggression.

5. Brents Stirling, in "Bolingbroke's 'Decision,'" *Shakespeare Quarterly,* 2 (1951), 27-34, does a very interesting job of tracing the complex ways in which the notion and then suddenly the reality of deposition enters the world of the play. To his argument it might be added that in the theatre this circuitous path can be very surprising, like the forcible omission of an obligatory scene.

6. My theatrical understanding of the second half of the play is heavily influenced by an interest in the "Northern" tradition of comedy, bloodshed, and in chaos, often associated with the later Middle Ages. The classic treatment of this tradition is, of course, Johan Huizinga, *The Waning of the Middle Ages* (London: Edward Arnold, 1924): "Towards the end of the Middle Ages feudal and hierarchic pride had lost nothing, as yet, of its vigour; the relish for pomp and display is as strong as ever. . . . So violent and motley was life, that it bore the mixed smell of blood and of roses. The men of that time always oscillate between the fear of hell and the most naive joy, between cruelty and tenderness, between harsh asceticism and insane attachment to the delights of this world, between hatred and goodness, always running to extremes" (pp. 18-19). Better than anything, these images describe my sense of the play's multiplicity; and were I actually producing it along these lines, I would make heavy use of the chaotic atmosphere of late medieval Europe, juxtaposing blood and beauty, prophecy and farce. It is interesting that Peter Brook (*The Empty Space* [New York: Avon, 1969], p. 78) speaks in much the same terms about Shakespeare: "It is through the unreconciled opposition of Rough and Holy, through an atonal screech of absolutely unsympathetic keys that we get the disturbing and the unforgettable impressions of his plays. It is because the contradictions are so strong that they burn on us so deeply."

7. Bolingbroke's handling of this quarrel is often taken as a sign of his political effectiveness. John Russell Brown (*Shakespeare's Plays,* p. 142) finds Henry's silence to be one of "his most arresting contributions," but to me it reads otherwise.

8. The Aumerle episode has had a very bad press. It is often cut in production, and those who argue for the ritual homogeneity of the play not infrequently resort to justification by multiple authorship or multiple sources. For some theatrical history, and also a negative opinion on both the Aumerle and the gages scenes, see A. C. Sprague and J. C. Trewin, *Shakespeare's Plays Today* (London: Sidgwick and Jackson, 1970), pp. 41-43. The most enthusiastic treatment, and one that parallels many of my conclusions here, is Sheldon P. Zitner's "Aumerle's Conspiracy," *SEL* [*Studies in English Literature*], 14 (1974), 239-57. I very much agree with the basic premise: "The Aumerle scenes, with the exception of the set pieces that open each, are I think fully intended farce, sometimes roaring, sometimes savage, but farce with such salt and savor as to distress the taste for pageant, pathos, and elevated death the play otherwise appeals to and satisfies" (pp. 243-44). Some of Zitner's most eloquent arguments concern the ways in which the episode acts as a kind of mock-heroic, "a deliberate send-up of the Elizabethan big bow-wow style, the Senecanizing ornamented bombast that was first the liberation and then the plague of English tragedy" (p. 250).

9. In this connection, Zitner makes a valuable point about the historical Richard II's "obsession with genuflection" (p. 250). With or without real history, we ought to note that kneeling is a highly charged symbolic issue in a play about definitions of royalty; and so, while kneeling deflects attention from the main concerns, it also symbolizes them.

10. Wolfgang Clemen, in an extremely persuasive treatment of the play (*The Development of Shakespeare's Imagery* [London: Methuen, 1951], pp. 53-62) takes the tug-of-war quite seriously as an example of Richard's ability to create a kind of acted-out imagery that arises directly from real situations. I agree with the seriousness of the content but wish to emphasize the potential bathos of the dramatic event.

11. Eric Bentley (appropriately enough a Brechtian) is one of the few to spot the essential brutality of this final scene. He sees it as "the spirit of politics and war—dog eat dog" (*In Search of Theater* [New York: Knopf, 1953], p. 127).

Leeds Barroll (essay date 1988)

SOURCE: Barroll, Leeds. "A New History for Shakespeare and His Time." *Shakespeare Quarterly* 39, no. 4 (winter 1988): 441-64.

[*In the following essay, Barroll investigates the relationship between the Earl of Essex rebellion and* Richard II.]

> History must be detached from the image that satisfied it for so long, and through which it found its anthropological justification: that of an age-old collective consciousness that made use of material documents to refresh its memory; history is the work expended on material documentation (books, texts, accounts, registers, acts, buildings, institutions, laws, techniques, objects, customs, etc.) that exists, in every time and place, in every society, either in a spontaneous or in a consciously organized form. The document is not the fortunate tool of a history that is primarily and fundamentally *memory*; history is one way in which a society recognizes and develops a mass of documentation with which it is inextricably linked.
>
> Michel Foucault, *The Archaeology of Knowledge*

Because what we see as "history" is focused, hued, elongated, and foreshortened by our own sense of what we are scanning, we bring back from our viewing something of what we have brought to it.[1] Yet it is just this redundance that holds so much promise as we seek to reassemble our sense of Shakespeare's relationship to his time. Our awareness of the varying histories to be drawn from texts that have survived from the late sixteenth and early seventeenth centuries—an awareness achieved by our entertaining, if only for heuristic purposes, a number of different narratives—cannot but invert assumptions, add possibilities, and raise those doubts through which one sharpens historical understanding.[2]

In our renewed efforts to relate Shakespeare to the period in which he lived, it is important, I think, to avoid some of the confusions plaguing the new historicism. Unless these confusions are addressed, our efforts to study Renaissance drama in any new way may drift from what I take to be the original intent of new historicists: an approach to historicity as it bears on the study of Shakespeare. So I propose here to consider certain difficulties with which we must deal before we can take full advantage of the exciting options that the new historicism has presented to us all. In this essay I am specifically concerned with whether certain approaches that we have come to identify with the new historicism accord with what historians are calling not the "new historicism" but the "new history."[3] Pursuing this question, I will engage some of our new historical positions in argument; this will be done not to disparage the positions themselves but rather to honor the spirit informing them, even though, at times, their letter seems to me to reside in dubious texts.

Specifically, I shall focus on two historical loci, noting here that I define an historical "locus" as that portion of a surviving text from which an interpreter creates "fact" and derives narrative. The "locus," in this sense, becomes epistemologically interesting because it serves as a differentia of various approaches to history: various kinds of historicism, if we will. Any operation with the locus inevitably generates from it an historical "event" already implicit in the terms that formulated the operation. Both the loci to be considered here have been entered by critics prominently associated with the new historicism and have—unfortunately, I think—been offered as exemplary of the importance and pertinence of new historicism itself.

One locus derives from the reign of Queen Elizabeth: the presentation of Shakespeare's *Richard II* at the Globe on the day before the Essex rebellion. According to one narrative built on these events and appropriated by several approaches to the new historicism, the Earl of Essex frightened the authorities about the political possibilities of drama by using *Richard II* in his effort to seize the crown. The second locus has more widely involved the delineation of an atmosphere, resulting in an assumption about the nature of the new royal court established at the accession of James I. This view emphasizes James I's own relationship to the activities of professional actors and dramatists in an effort to structure larger assumptions about the nature of the early Stuart monarchy, assumptions that have inevitably politicized Shakespeare's drama by relating it to the programs of King James himself.[4]

I

Moving first to that locus associating Shakespeare's *Richard II* with the Essex uprising, I note that it has received a particular interpretation in the writing both of Stephen Greenblatt and Jonathan Dollimore as they construct rationales for their approaches to the study of English Renaissance drama. As a result, the sequence has become something of a cliché in current historical discussions of Shakespeare. In Greenblatt's Introduction to the 1982 anthology *The Power of Forms,* he describes the essays contained therein as giving voice "to what we may call the new historicism, set apart from both the dominant historical scholarship of the past and the formalist criticism that partially displaced this scholarship in the decades after World War Two." Greenblatt states that "the earlier historicism tends to be monological," while the new historicism "tends to ask questions about its own methodological assumptions and those of others." In presenting his own historical example, Greenblatt devotes all but the final paragraph of his Introduction to a description of Shakespeare's *Richard II* in its 1601 context. Modern historical scholarship, he observes, does not see Shakespeare's *Richard II* as a threat:

> But in 1601 neither Queen Elizabeth nor the Earl of Essex were so sure: after all, someone on the eve of a rebellion thought the play sufficiently seditious to warrant squandering two pounds on the players, and the Queen understood the performance as a threat. Moreover, even before the Essex rising, the actual [deposition] scene (IV.i.154-318 in the Arden edition) was carefully omitted from the first three quartos of Shakespeare's play and appears for the first time only after Elizabeth's death.[5]

In the 1985 anthology *Political Shakespeare,* edited by Jonathan Dollimore and Alan Sinfield, Dollimore's essay entitled "Introduction: Shakespeare, Cultural Materialism and the New Historicism," employs the locus similarly:

> A famous attempt to use the theatre to subvert authority was of course the staging of a play called *Richard II* (probably Shakespeare's) just before the Essex rising in 1601; Queen Elizabeth afterwards anxiously acknowledged the implied identification between her and Richard II, complaining also that "this tragedy was played 40 times in open streets and houses." As Stephen Greenblatt points out, what was really worrying for the Queen was both the repeatability of the representation—and hence the multiplying numbers of people witnessing it—and the *locations* of these repetitions; "*open* streets and houses."[6]

Quoting Greenblatt, Dollimore reiterates: "Can 'tragedy' be a strictly literary term when the Queen's own life is endangered by the play?" (p. 8).

This continual adduction and uniform interpretation of the Essex locus presents, I think, important reasons why any historical method must first deal with its own theoretical premises—especially given the seeming solidity of the "fact" that serves as the cornerstone of the foregoing remarks. J. G. Droysen long ago suggested that the use of any historical text to establish the immutability of a fact is redundant; thus, this curious privileging of one account of the Essex conspiracy in approaches opting for *new* ways of making history about Shakespeare's milieu produces an ironic effect.[7] For the statements about Shakespeare's *Richard II* uncritically organize and promulgate from one Essex locus nothing more than a time-honored and traditionally tendered narrative about the earl and his connection with Shakespeare's drama, a narrative promoted by a nineteenth-century aristocratic ideology that constantly sought to raise Shakespeare to the status of confidant with the peerage.

To comment on the univocal readings of the Essex locus now characterizing some approaches to the new historicism, I shall offer an alternate account of the Essex affair as it might impinge upon Shakespeare's *Richard II.* For though acknowledging that no single narration (or many single ones) can rise above the theoretical problems inherent in the structuring of narrative itself, I urge that it is methodologically important to break this traditional story of the *Richard II* performance out of its amber, that we must de-ossify a narrative before it is ironically re-ossified through our own efforts to use it as the way to illustrate the analytic promise of the new historicism.

There has been, since the 1930s, little systematic study of the texts detailing the entire episode in which the Earl of Essex attempted to seize control of Queen Elizabeth's person and of her closest advisors, but the pertinent documents have long been calendared. Fifty years ago, in fact, they caused a lively (and now surprisingly ignored) debate regarding the relationship of Shakespeare's *Richard II* to the Essex uprising.[8] And circumstances offer not one "basic history" of the Essex situation but two sets of texts. One set (only a portion of which is currently in use) is that describing *Richard II* in its relationship to the Essex conspirators. But another—very different—set of documents presents information about other Crown activity vis-à-vis Essex, again connected with the story of the unthroning of the historical Richard II, and this set has nothing to do with drama or the playhouse. Both groups of material further illustrate, I think, those methodological complexities in the making of narrative currently being addressed by historical theory.[9]

Let us look at the material. The first set of records alludes to the performance of *Richard II* and pertains to the Essex conspiracy. As I read them, these records tell, very briefly, that on the Thursday or Friday before the Essex uprising of Sunday, February 8, 1601, five or six of the followers of the Earl of Essex visited several members of Shakespeare's company and offered them 40s., more than twice as much as the players would usually earn for a play, if they would consent to perform the out-of-date *Richard II* on Saturday afternoon.[10] The actors agreed. On Saturday, February 7, eleven of the conspirators had a midday meal together in London and crossed the Thames by boat to the Bankside theatre area where they went to the Globe and saw the play *Richard II* (presumably Shakespeare's). On Sunday morning the Essex uprising began. After it had been quelled, the Privy Council began to collect testimony. Eight to ten days later three depositions separately describing the *Richard II* performance had been taken. The first two depositions were by two conspirators, while the third was by one of the Lord Chamberlain's players, Shakespeare's fellow actor, Augustine Phillips. In aggregate, all three depositions make up the record of the events I have just recounted. They constitute the locus.

From this composite narrative (often, in much current commentary on the subject, treated as having derived from one account) critics have been quick to build an interpretation that emphasizes the importance of drama as a "power to subvert." But certain questions put to these same documents may complicate any monological history recently inferred from the *Richard II* performance. For example, how did the Crown dispose of those persons involved with the *Richard II* performance? The answer seems to be that of the eleven conspirators known to have attended the performance or who could be considered connected with it, all were punished for their involvement in the uprising as well as for whatever was offensive about their attending the play. Four of those associated with the performance were executed, but they had been closely involved in the Essex conspiracy as a whole. The large majority were punished by being fined various sums, presumably scaled according to their ability to pay, and then were freed within six months.

One of the executed playgoers was Gilly Meyricke, Essex's steward, who showed in the total of his testimony that he was privy to almost everything Essex had been planning. Another of the four executed conspirators who attended the *Richard II* performance was Christopher Blount, brother to Charles Blount (8th Lord Mountjoy and Penelope Rich's lover) and husband to the Countess of Leicester, the Earl of Essex's and Penelope's mother; in the Essex plot Christopher Blount had accepted a definite assignment in the seizing of the royal palace. Another executed playgoer was Captain Thomas Lea, who actually tried to enter the privy chambers to assassinate the queen. Also executed was Henry Cuffe, to whom Lea reported. But although these four conspirators, Meyricke, Blount, Lea, and Cuffe, were closely involved in the plot, their specific relationship to the performance of *Richard II* seems incidental. Cuffe, for instance, did not go to the play, only to the midday meal beforehand. Lea did not go to the midday meal, only to the play, while Gilly Meyricke arrived at the play late.[11]

Another question that might be asked of the material constituting this locus is: who were involved in the plot but did *not* attend this performance of *Richard II,* and how were these men disposed of? The absences—perhaps caused by great responsibilities in the conspiracy—suggest again the complex limitations of the texts in hand. Absent from the group named by the deponents as involved in *Richard II* were the Earl of Essex and Sir Charles Danvers (both executed); the earl closest to Essex, Southampton (not executed but sentenced to the Tower for life); and two other earls close to Essex and Southampton: the Earl of Rutland and the Earl of Bedford. Both were spared but paid huge fines.[12] Absent from the play, then, were the most prestigious conspirators of the Essex plot.

To ask a different kind of question: assuming a minimal correlation between a person's attendance at the *Richard II* performance and his presumed involvement in the conspiracy, what evidence do we have as to how the Privy Council viewed the subversive performance itself? For example, how did the Privy Council dispose of those who, according to testimony, actually instigated the *Richard II* episode? According to the player Augustine Phillips, the chief instigators and bargainers who actually came to the playhouse to arrange and pay for the performance were three persons not described as having attended: the two younger Percies (brothers of the Earl of Northumberland) and Lord Monteagle (married to the sister of one of the conspirators, Francis Tresham, who would hold Sir Thomas Egerton prisoner at Essex House on the morning of the rebellion). These three nobles—Charles and Jocelyn Percy, third and sixth sons of the Earl of Northumberland, and William Parker, Lord Monteagle—were neither executed nor put in the Tower for life. Despite the fact that they were part of the Essex conspiracy and, in addition, had actually caused *Richard II* to be performed, they were fined only moderate amounts and freed within six months to walk the streets, long before Elizabeth's death.[13] If the performance of *Richard II* was indeed dangerous to the state, those who raised the danger were treated rather lightly.

To put a final question to the locus: The original depositions that long ago alerted scholars to a possible relationship between *Richard II* and the Essex conspiracy do not indicate which of the original deponents were then required to return for a second deposition, a not unusual order when the Council wished to follow up a line of inquiry; which conspirators in this instance did Council members wish to question further? They were Gilly Meyricke and William Constable. But in his later appearance, Meyricke, Essex's steward, was questioned about almost everything concerning the uprising except the *Richard II* performance. William Constable, operating in a much more restricted sphere than Meyricke (Constable had been to the play, spent the night for the first time in his life at Essex's house, and marched with the rebels the next day), was not asked about the play again either. He was queried exclusively about his friends and co-conspirators in York-shire.[14] In other words, once identified as a conspirator via the play incident, Constable was now questioned not about *Richard II* but about his knowledge of northern conspira-tors who would have had nothing to do with a play at the Globe.

The direction of this interrogation suggests to me that, from the Privy Council's point of view, commissioning Shakespeare's *Richard II* just before the Essex uprising

was not a severely punishable offense in itself, and thus the play may not have been regarded as dangerous propaganda. In the papers of the Privy Council of England, furthermore, minutes of the discussion on March 11, 1601, about what to do with the remaining persons imprisoned for the Essex plot are followed by notations in the text matter-of-factly authorizing pay to John Heminge and the rest of Shakespeare's fellows "for their interludes and plaies" shown during the recent Shrovetide following the Essex uprising. Behind this notation lies the fact that the acting company gave the traditional play at court before the queen on Shrove Tuesday night, February 24, the day Elizabeth had again signed Essex's death-warrant and the eve of Essex's execution on Ash Wednesday, February 25.[15]

Another example of the complications that the documents introduce into too straightforward a narrative is Francis Bacon's pamphlet about the conspiracy written in 1601. In the pamphlet he inveighed against Gilly Meyricke and charged that Meyricke personally "procured to be played" the performance of *Richard II*—but not, presumably, as Greenblatt and also Dollimore seem to have implied, for the purpose of "wrest[ing] legitimation from the established ruler" by infecting the populace (Greenblatt, p. 3). Bacon wrote, rather, that Meyricke commanded the performance because "so earnest hee was to satisfie his eyes with the sight of that tragedie which hee thought soone after his lord should bring from the stage to the state."[16] Francis Bacon's words suggest that the performance had a primary psychological function that might be of great interest to a Habermas, but Bacon seems not to have seen it as a dangerous incitement to revolution in the streets.

But what of Queen Elizabeth's own alleged claim that "I am Richard II"? This too plays a major part in the traditional narrative that associates Shakespeare's *Richard II* with the Earl of Essex. The story comes from a manuscript held by the Lambarde family—quite a different source than Privy Council records. It tells, in the third person, of William Lambarde, who on August 4, 1601, six months after Essex's death, was presenting the queen with a list of manuscripts contained in the Tower. Her eye fell upon the "Richard II" subdivision of the listing and she remarked, "I am Richard II. know ye not that?" Lambarde, according to the manuscript, responded, "Such a wicked imagination was determined and attempted by a most unkind Gent. the most adorned creature that ever your majestie made"—meaning, perhaps, that Essex had tried to make a Richard II out of Queen Elizabeth. The manuscript then tells us that the queen answered, "He that will forget God, will also forget his benefactors; this tragedy was played 40[tie] times in open streets and houses."[17] Let us waive here an interesting problem in the hermeneutics of historical narrative to grant the manuscript's accuracy and timeliness—Lambarde himself died on August 19, 1601, fifteen days after the interview. Let us also grant for the moment the possibility that Queen Elizabeth was person-ally disturbed by the Richard II story. Let us even grant the improbable supposition that plays (by the Lord

Chamberlain's Servants?) were acted (free) in the public streets and that in 1601 *Richard II,* though old, was acted forty times. Given all of this, was Shakespeare's play the force behind the queen's sensitivity to the Richard II model?

Such need not have been the case. As early as January 9, 1578, Sir Francis Knollys, and at some time before 1588, Henry Lord Hunsdon (future patron of Shakespeare's company) each wrote remarks protesting that he would not give flattering advice to his sovereign, both expressing this sentiment by saying that they would not play the part of "Richard the Second's men." The Richard II model was an old one.[18]

Surely, however, we cannot dismiss Shakespeare's play from the context of contemporary politics, one might object, for Shakespeare's *Richard II* had in it a deposition scene that was suppressed until 1608. At least so goes the traditional narrative.[19] But considering what we can know only from the texts of Shakespeare's quartos of *Richard II* themselves, the concept of a deposition scene as "suppressed" is a curious and distressing intellectual position for critics who are interested in new approaches to and apprehensions of the history of Shakespeare's time. For the traditional view of a suppressed deposition scene is based on a limited concept of textual transmission in Shakespeare's quartos as well as on formalist assumptions about *Richard II* itself.

To advert to the textual situation briefly: the "deposition scene" is absent from the 1597 and the two 1598 quartos of *Richard II* (all printed well before the Essex uprising),[20] but in the next two quartos (1608 and 1615) as well as in the First Folio (1623), 160 added lines—what we call "the deposition scene"—appear. It has been concluded by many critics that because these additional lines were *absent* from the first three printings of Shakespeare's play, they were, in fact, *excised* from these first three printings. Because, in other words, 160 lines describing Richard's resigning of his crown appear for the first time in the 1608 quarto of *Richard II,* their absence from the former quartos has been thought to mean that the sequence was actually suppressed. The generalization that would follow from such a premise is that all new material in revised editions of Shakespeare's plays would represent the surfacing of previously censored sequences—a proposition that can be neither supported nor refuted.

The difficulty of supporting such a proposition may be why the premise of suppression in the case of *Richard II* has traditionally been buttressed by formalist criticism, an approach succinctly illustrated in the words of E. K. Chambers, who in 1931 observed that "the excision" of the deposition scene from the early quartos of *Richard II* left an "obvious scar." And although David Bergeron questioned both the critical and textual assumptions underlying this traditional approach to the *Richard II* quartos over a decade ago, the myth of a suppressed deposition scene still colors some historical perceptions.[21]

At the same time, we must entertain the possibility (implicit, for example, in the premise of two *King Lear* texts) that Shakespeare revised his plays. Shakespeare may have revised *Richard II*—and not necessarily for purposes of subversion. He may have wished to expand the characterization of Richard himself, the 1608 quarto appearing at a time when Shakespeare had recently written *King Lear* and *Antony and Cleopatra,* plays exploring other tragic figures coping with the dilemma of regal status as an objectification of psychic identity, a problem implicit in the *Richard II* addition.[22]

Whatever may be the case with the "deposition scene" itself, the larger question of *Richard II* and the Essex conspiracy can be viewed from an alternate historical locus—and at this point we move to a second set of available documents. These texts embody a response by the authorities to a different version of the story of Richard II, a prose history published in 1599, two years after Shakespeare's play was first printed in quarto and two years before the Essex rebellion. This history, written by the scholar John Hayward and entitled *The first part of the life and raigne of king Henrie the IIII,* covered only the first year of Henry's reign and described at some length the deposition and the killing of Richard II. (Contrary to another traditional assumption in Shakespeare criticism, the surviving documents indicate that it was the depiction of the *murder* more than of the deposition that always concerned authorities.[23]

The publication of Hayward's book correlated with the activities of the Earl of Essex as follows: Briefly, on January 9, 1599, almost two years before the Essex uprising, John Hayward's *Life of Henry IV* was entered in the Stationers' Register for printing. The book appeared by March 1 with a fulsome Latin preface addressed to the Earl of Essex, a preface that had already "given offense" and been ordered excised after 500-600 copies of the book had been sold. The remainder of the issue, another 500-600 copies, nevertheless sold quickly thereafter.

On March 27, 1599, Essex left London for the Ireland campaign with great éclat. By April 8 Hayward's book was still much in demand, and a second printing, including a new "Epistle Apologetical" by Hayward, was planned. Fifteen hundred copies had been produced by Whitsunday (May 27) when the Wardens of the Stationers' Guild confiscated the run and delivered the books to the Bishop of London (in effect censor-in-chief), who had them burned. Then the printer, John Wolfe, was imprisoned for two weeks.[24]

Over the next several months Essex, in Ireland, began having those difficulties with the Crown that resulted in his unauthorized return to London on September 28, 1599, after an absence from England of only six months: March 27 to September 28.[25] As a result of his unwarranted homecoming, Essex was confined to York House, beginning a long period in more or less stringent custody that would be ended only by his rebellion sixteen months later.

Confined through the fall of 1599, he became quite ill from December through March, and this illness prevented arraignment for his conduct in Ireland until June 5, 1600. On that date Essex was tried at York House and dismissed from all his offices, remaining still in loose confinement.

It was after this first trial that the Crown began to move in on John Hayward and his *Life of Henry IV,* more than a year after the book's publication. On July 11, 1600, about a month after Essex's trial and nine months before the uprising, Hayward confessed to a court made up of such personages as the Earl of Nottingham, Sir Thomas Egerton, Robert Cecil, and Sir John Fortescue—respectively, the Lord Admiral, Lord Privy Seal, the Secretary of State, and the Chancellor of the Exchequer—that he had inserted spurious material into his history of Henry IV. Several days later, on July 13, 1600, the author was imprisoned. In that same July, according to Dudley Carleton, because of Hayward's book the queen also took away from Essex the liberty of leaving London that she had granted him hitherto:

> My Lord of Essex remains prisoner, but at his owne custody. the Queen had given him liberty to go into the cuntrie, but recalled it againe upon the taking of Doctor Hayward who for writing Henry the forth was committed to the tower.[26]

The same day Hayward was committed to the Tower, Hayward's printer, John Wolfe, was examined by Sir Edward Coke, who on July 20, seven days later, also examined the censor who had allowed the book.[27] When the articles to support this earlier charge of treason against Essex were drawn up on July 22, 1600, the articles used Essex's alleged implication in Hayward's *Life of Henry IV* as one among a list of points that might strike us as more important items, such as Essex's suspiciously lax campaigning in Ireland.

Months later—seventeen days before the Essex rebellion—Hayward was still in the Tower. He was again exhaustively examined twice, first by Sir Edward Coke and Sir John Peyton, Lieutenant of the Tower, and then by Coke again, about the historical sources for his *Life of Henry IV.* The Crown's interest in Hayward's book makes the attention they will later bestow upon the *Richard II* performance seem, by comparison, trivial.[28]

After the rebellion itself, Hayward's book seems to have remained in the minds of those who proceeded against Essex. In all the testimony before the Privy Council about the performed play, for example, the play was referred to as "Richard II" only by Augustine Phillips, Shakespeare's fellow-actor, who would naturally have been alive to the difference between Shakespeare's *Richard II* and his *Henry IV* plays. But Gilly Meyricke, arch-conspirator, and Sir Edward Coke, the Crown prosecutor (the only Crown official known to have referred to the performed play by its name), spoke of the play as "Henry the 4th" and "a play of Henry the 4th" (Chambers, *WS,* Vol. 2, 324-26). This,

as we know, was the title of the book by John Hayward about King Richard's deposition and death.

After the accession of James I, Hayward's book was reprinted three times, each time fraudulently dated "1599" by three different publishers.[29] Such was, it seems, the remembered notoriety and ongoing demand for this publication. In crucial contrast, there is, first, no evidence that either Shakespeare or his printer was ever arrested or questioned about the printed version of *Richard II* or the performance of the play; nor was there any great demand for the text of Shakespeare's drama at the time immediately preceding or following the rebellion. Nor did the accession of James I immediately provoke editions of Shakespeare's *Richard II.* As we have seen, a quarto was not published until 1608, and, after that, not another until 1615 before the 1623 First Folio.[30]

Indeed, as I read the records, any political relevance Shakespeare's play possessed could well have derived from its similarity to Hayward's history. For it was this book that seems most publicly to have given the topic of Richard II its application to the Essex uprising.[31]

If the Privy Council showed in its responses more concern for the danger represented by Hayward's book than for that occasioned by Shakespeare's drama, then the link between Shakespeare's *Richard II* and the Essex conspiracy is at best an ambiguous representative example in arguments that wish to stress the connection between drama and the power of the state. If one looks beyond the locus that has been used to demonstrate the subversive value of Shakespeare's play, one finds other loci that add new readings of history. One could argue, in fact, that the Elizabethan authorities perceived in connection with the Essex plot a threat much more serious than acted plays: i.e., the printed book.

Since we are concerned with the question of premises underlying the new historicism, it is important to stress this point. The acting of plays was not a social novelty in 1601. The English monarchs had had companies of actors at least since the year 1450, as we can discern from payments made from the accounts maintained at Selby Abbey[32]; the printing of books, while not new and revolutionary, was still a social proposition difficult for the authorities to deal with (as the Marprelate situation of the 1590s reminds us). As Francis Bacon, one of those who held Hayward's *Life of Henry IV* against Essex, observed in the *Novum Organon,* Aphorism 129:

> We should note the force, effect, and consequences of inventions which are nowhere more conspicuous than in those three which were unknown to the ancients, namely, printing, gunpowder, and the compass. For these three have changed the appearance and state of the whole world.[33]

The public playhouse as invented by James Burbage was perhaps equally new, but not, in any event, capable of replicating its product in the way available to the printing

Wilfrid Dube as Groom, John Wojda as Attendant, Gregory Wanless as Bagot, Frank Maraden as King Richard, Marti Maraden as Isabel, and William Needles as John of Gaunt in Act II, scene i of the 1979 Stratford Festival production of Richard II.

press. Thus the printed book's inherent primacy as "media" for the Richard II analogue is certainly witnessed in the remarks made by the printer of Hayward's *Life of Henry IV*: "No book ever sold better"; "The people having divers times since called to procure the continuation of the history by the same author."[34] On the other hand, if we can believe Augustine Phillips, Shakespeare's company was reluctant to put on his *Richard II* in this same period because it "was so old and so long out of use as that they should have small or no company at it." Offer a printer Shakespeare's *Richard II* or Hayward's *Life of Henry IV* in 1601, and there could be little doubt which manuscript would be more attractive. The *Life of Henry IV* was topical, current, scandalous, and suppressed, and it was written, as John Pocock has reminded me, by Sir John Hayward, Doctor of Law, more socially conspicuous than a common player. Shakespeare's *Richard II* was old—apparently not even worth producing on a Saturday afternoon in 1601.

Finally, the impression made by Hayward's *Life of Henry IV* on the minds of Shakespeare's contemporaries is tell-

ingly indicated, I think, by an unwitting confusion exhibited in the abstracts following the earlier trial of the Earl of Essex in 1600, when he was arraigned for leaving Ireland without permission. Even then Essex was berated for his "underhand permitting of that most treasonous booke . . . *Henry the fourth* to be printed and published, being plainly deciphered not onely by the matter, and by the Epistle itself, for what ende and for whose behoof it was made, but also the Erle himself being so often present at the playing thereof, and with great applause giving countenance and lyking to the same."[35] This fascinating statement can be read many ways, perhaps even suggesting that Shakespeare's play was thought to be a *dramatization* of Hayward's book.

Because the epistemic problems posed by the question of historical "evidence" are so great, any description of Essex's relationship to the Richard II story is open to doubt and to complication; there is no way that we can know the "true" story. But it is at least possible that drama may have been significant to the Essex conspiracy not because of the impression the authorities thought plays might make upon the populace, but because of the impression plays made upon certain figures in the circle about Essex. Indeed, one reads of a supper given at Essex House on February 15, 1598, a year before the earl's Irish troubles began, where Essex and his circle saw "two plays which kept them up till 1 o'clock after midnight," plays that in the usual course of events would have been arranged and paid for by the host, who that evening was Essex's steward, Gilly Meyricke, the future playgoing conspirator and the man whom Bacon accused of instigating the *Richard II* performance. In the fall of 1599, after Essex had returned without permission from Ireland and was awaiting trial in London, we hear of the two earls closest to Essex whiling away this time of inactivity in similar pursuits. "My Lord Southampton and Lord Rutland come not to court . . . they pass away the tyme in London merely in going to plaies every day."[36] While, as we have seen, these two nobles were not (ostensibly, at least) involved in the *Richard II* performance, obviously others in the same circle (Essex's steward and those who paid for *Richard II*) seem to have been fascinated by the power of stage plays— upon themselves, at any rate.

Accordingly, in dealing with the *Richard II* incident, we might set aside a theory that foregrounds drama's power over the populace to focus instead on a theory that views the interesting influence of drama upon certain minds. Perhaps the "fact" that we should extract from the situation is the belief by some conspirators that the fictions they viewed on stage had the same power over others as such fictions had over themselves. In analogue, perhaps, to the methodology adopted by Foucault in his history of madness, one might wish to examine the power of drama as it was *misconstrued* by certain members of the Essex circle. Such a study would also take into account the Earl of Bedford's and the Earl of Essex's commitment to shows of chivalry embodied in the Accession Day tournaments, and it would consider the importance of mimetic and quasi-mimetic forms to an Essex group that included in its number so many patrons of the arts, a group led by an earl who had married Sir Philip Sidney's widow. Members of such a group would not be the first to have believed that literary forms and pageants constitute a political power that can influence events.

One might wonder, then, whether the performance of Shakespeare's *Richard II* just before the Essex rebellion caused the Privy Council much concern about the power of drama itself. That Richard II was a suggestive subject in these years is, I think, beyond debate. To try to present the story in any form, as Matthew Black and Peter Ure remind us in the commentaries they have gathered in their respective New Variorum and New Arden editions, is often to incur suspicion. But if we compare the documents surrounding the publication of Hayward's *Life of Henry IV* with those surrounding the 1601 performance of *Richard II*, we find, I think, that they suggest very different political points. In Hayward's case, a *book* was deemed quite dangerous as a medium; in Shakespeare's case, not the play but the persons involved in the production—both

players and those who commissioned the performance— were deemed dangerous because they were doing something they *thought* to be seditious.

II

In the end, current interpretations of the Essex locus seem to be functions of a more general approach to the social role of drama in Shakespeare's lifetime. For if some critics practicing the new historicism have seen *Richard II* as significant to a single political plot in Elizabeth's reign, others writing of James I have implicated drama in the whole fabric of the new king's theory, policy, and practice. Thus, in this more general claim about the political significance of drama to the time of Shakespeare, documents bearing on the king's own tastes, personality, and writing have constituted a pertinent locus. Organized into one familiar narrative, this locus presents a situation in which Shakespeare's dramas, the plays of others, and court masques became important as part of a political dialogue between James I and certain dramatists, or as propagandistic material in the policy programs of the Crown. And crucial to this argument has been the idea of James's personal preference for plays and masques—i.e., of a monarch who was intellectually inclined to the writing of poems, to the reading of history, and therefore to drama too.[37]

"When King James came to the throne," writes Jonathan Goldberg, "his first act in the literary realm was to take the theatres under his patronage," for "as part of his entertainment, James demanded court performance of plays."[38] Indeed, argues Stephen Orgel, "King James wanted the theatrical companies under royal patronage because he believed in the efficacy of theater as an attribute of royal authority." Players, by this token, were the "outward and visible signs of James's sense of his office."[39]

A central text in Goldberg's reading of King James's theatrical orientation has been the *Basilikon Doron*, the long essay on kingship James wrote and dedicated to his then five-year-old son, Prince Henry. Goldberg has emphasized in particular that section of *Basilikon Doron* in which James likens a king to "one set on a stage whose smallest actions and gestures all the people gazingly do behold." To read James's printed statement as a witness to his personal inclinations is in itself troubling. Yet, even if one assumes that in this passage King James is promulgating his partiality to professional acting rather than his sense of kingly responsibilities and techniques, the *Basilikon Doron* is at best ambiguous in showing James's attitude toward actors and plays. Consider a short passage from the *Basilikon* that has not been cited in recent discussions:

> . . . abuse not youreself in making youre sporters youre counsaillouris; specialie delyte not to keepe ordinairlie in youre cumpanie comœdians, or balladins, for the tirans delyted maist in thaime & delyted to make comœdies & tragedies thaimeselfis, [whereupon] the

ansuere that a philosophe gaue ane of thame [there-anents] is nou cum in a prouerbe, reduc me in lato-mias.[40]

To make his point, James turns to the bad example of Nero, a ruler traditionally associated with drama and performance and, of course, with capricious tyranny.

Such a passage, if passages can indeed reveal a writer's personal opinions, serves to complicate the claim that King James held any special brief for drama. But my use of this counter-example is meant primarily to emphasize methodological dangers in assessing the tastes and inclinations of a person removed from us by centuries. Because the complexities of the intertextual relationships between biography and statement are, as I think Dominick LaCapra might agree, beyond our current achievements, it is best not to look for James's person in his *Basilikon Doron*.[41]

However, the question of King James's attitude towards drama (and thus, ultimately, of his attitude towards the plays of Shakespeare) is worth pursuit, and it is therefore worth our time to dissolve the binding rust of "facts" that have long seized up the potential play of other narratives. One such "fact" is the increase in the sheer number of plays presented during the holidays at court after King James came to the English throne, for this surge has traditionally been cited to suggest King James's interest in drama, and, by implication, in the other arts.[42] Before dealing directly with this matter, I shall begin by suggesting that a more general reference to the systematic records of the Scottish Crown and Privy Council—despite their potential for ambiguity and slanting for social purposes—can produce earlier and as potentially relevant documents about King James and drama. In 1589, for instance, when James planned to marry Anna of Denmark in Scotland, he requested of Queen Elizabeth that the acting group Queen Elizabeth's Servants travel to Scotland to provide entertainment at the Scottish royal wedding.[43] This request could suggest that James was intensely interested in drama; it could just as well suggest that he did not support actors in his own household, or that he thought English actors far superior to Scottish. Since I can find few records of dramatic performances at court in James's early Scottish reign, I favor the "absence of household actors" interpretation. Such records as survive from James's Scottish days suggest no great passion in King James of Scotland for plays.[44]

It is extremely important, therefore, that rather than *assuming* James's great interest in the drama when he ascended the English throne, we seek some indication of this interest. One obvious sign has traditionally been taken to be the patenting of Shakespeare and his fellows as the Servants of the King in May 1603, an event that I have found to be extremely complicated but not necessarily any more indicative of the king's personal interests than was an early grant of the office of the Keeper of the Manor House and Park of Temple-Newsham in the County of York, given by the Crown to Thomas Pott, for life, on

May 14, 1603 (five days prior to this patenting); or the grant on May 17, 1603, to Sir Amias Preston, of the Office of the Keeper of Stores and Ordnance in the Tower of London. In these cases, specific financial opportunities had been awarded, as was not the case with the patenting of the King's Servants. Indeed, although the general scholarly assumption has been that King James was the instigator of a relationship between Shakespeare's fellows and the Crown, my own reconstruction of the patenting of the acting company suggests that the king could have had little to do with it—that the event was more in keeping with the style of the Earl of Pembroke, who, with Southampton, became early on one of James's inner (social) circle. Because the basis for this assertion requires too extended a demonstration to rehearse here, I shall merely suggest at this time that our rush to place King James at the center of the patenting process has perhaps led us to ignore other possible narratives describing the creation of Shakespeare's company as "Servants of the King."[45]

But what of the upswing in performances at court after James's accession? As I noted, this is a fact often adduced in our assumptions regarding James's interest in drama. When we put this fact in context, we recall that James, as king of England, now inherited quite a different tradition of court entertainment than obtained in Scotland. In England, the Declared Accounts of the Treasurer of the Chamber had listed Christmas holiday payments to adult players at the English court since 1567.[46] Thus, when a number of plays were performed at Hampton Court during James's first Christmas season (1603-04), this was no great departure in custom. In the Christmas season just before her death the year previous, for example, Queen Elizabeth saw eight plays by five different companies of players between December 26 and Shrovetide, including one on Shrove Sunday, March 6, less than three weeks before her death. Thus, the Venetian ambassador spoke true when he noted that in James's first Christmas season "All these days have been devoted to fetes, banquets, jousts, as is usual in England from St. Stephens [December 26] to Twelfth Night."[47]

It is also true that the number of these dramatic performances during James's Christmas seasons at court was high. But existing financial records suggest that the number of plays seen by the king as compared with the number seen by other members of the royal family when the king was absent complicate our reading of James's response to theatre. During the first and celebratory Christmas of his reign, for example, James personally attended eleven plays by five companies. (As I noted above, during the last Christmas of her reign, Queen Elizabeth saw a total of eight plays by five adult professional companies.[48]) Seven additional plays of that first season, the number that so importantly swells James's reputation as a patron of the drama, were seen not by King James but by the queen and by Prince Henry.

Moreover, an interesting indication of King James's level of enthusiasm for the plays he did see comes from the courtier, Dudley Carleton—the future Lord Roscommon. Describing that first Jacobean holiday season, he wrote John Chamberlain:

> The first holy days we had every night a public play in the great hall, at which the King was ever present and liked or disliked as he saw cause, but it seems he takes no extraordinary pleasure in them.[49]

If Carleton is to be believed, one might ask why James watched plays at all. An important reason, as I see it, was the role of these plays in court activity. Ambassadors, usually at court during Christmas festivities, were especially numerous during the first season of James's reign. Special envoys were present to offer formal congratulations on behalf of their sovereigns upon James's accession to the throne.[50] The first two nights after Christmas, when plays were traditional at the English court, James honored such ambassadors—from Spain and from Savoy on December 26, and from Florence and Poland on December 27. Their entertainment was presented in the form of dinner and a play, as was often the custom.[51] On other evenings during the holidays, the Crown paid for many more performances, but neither James nor the ambassadors were in attendance for many of them.

For example, James missed two plays during the famous Hampton Court Conference, a series of meetings with the prelates of England on January 12, 16, and 18, 1604, to settle matters of religion. Indeed, his own language about holiday entertainment describes not the plays but a battle with the Puritans at this conference:

> We have kept such a *revel* with the Puritans here these two days as was never heard the like, where I have peppered them as soundly as ye have done the Papists there.[52]

It is interesting that James himself applied the word "revel" (ordinarily used to describe holiday court festivities) to describe instead his sense of pleasure in dealing with advocates of the Puritan religious position. Since the conference was held during the winter holidays, James speaks of this activity as if it were his true "revels," showing in his language an exuberance not to be found in Carleton's description of his responses to plays.

After viewing his sixth and seventh plays in this, his first, royal Christmas season, on January 21 and February 2 (Candlemas) when the ambassador from Florence was entertained, the king left the London area, to which he did not return until February 19, Shrove Sunday, when he presided over the traditional celebration of Shrovetide,[53] a celebration made more important by the fact that Shrove Sunday was this year the young Prince Henry's tenth birthday. In the three days before Lent there was one play by the King's Servants, two plays by two children's companies, one by the Prince's Servants, and bearbaiting. But after these events James did not watch another play from Shrove Tuesday, February 21, 1604, until the celebration of All Saints' Day on November 1, 1604. In fact,

throughout his reign King James seldom, if ever, saw plays between Shrove Tuesday and All Saints' Day, a period of more than seven months. Nor had his predecessor, Queen Elizabeth, who, however, waited past All Saints' Day to Advent before she had plays at the palace.

If, then, there was a surfeit of plays during the first Christmas season of James's reign, the surfeit may have been largely enjoyed by the ten-year-old Prince Henry and by his mother, the queen. For if, by the time Prince Henry's birthday had come around on February 19, Shrove Sunday, his father had hitherto presided over seven plays, Prince Henry, who had presumably seen these eight, had also presided himself over seven more on December 30, January 1, 2, 4, 13, 15, and 22. Both king and prince together must have seen the four additional plays at Shrovetide, for Prince Henry would surely have attended his own birthday celebration. Thus the young Prince Henry himself presumably saw eighteen plays, as compared to King James's eleven.[54]

In short, writers who urge King James and his interests as arguments for a role played by drama in King James's philosophy of kingship have not, I think, shown how such a penchant for drama in James is to be found. Indeed, the documents I have presented can be read to suggest that King James held no great brief for plays. The use of the *Basilikon Doron,* then, and of traditionally construed statistics in support of a fundamentally traditional view of James's tastes as centered on drama narrows the opportunity for new narratives that might refine our conception of the scope and role of plays at the royal court. For, as I have urged, a departure from the traditional (parts of) documents and from traditional narratives might lead to a greater variety of contexts in the same documents and even to new texts suggesting different possible relationships between the Crown and drama at court.

One such set of texts—the final set to be considered in this essay—suggests (as I read them) that, under James, the royal "solace" offered by the players was, in fact, replaced by a new kind of restorative. The writings—letters from the collection at Hatfield House and papers held in Italian archives—appear early in James's reign, during the second series of Christmas holidays (1604—05). "Solace" was the term applied to that recreation considered necessary to a monarch who otherwise might become dull and demoralized and, through his or her own ill health, in turn bring sickness to the body politic of which the monarch was the head. This concept of "solace" was integral to many of the documents of the late sixteenth century that dealt with entertainment at court. For example, the Privy Council notice to the Aldermen and Mayor of London of November 1581 urged the financial relief of players to expedite their readiness for court entertainment "with convenient matters for her highnes[s'] solace this next Christmas, which cannot be without their usuall exercise therein."[55] Indeed, the rubric under which the actors were paid for court performances with Crown money was precisely the necessity of the sovereign's solace.

Moreover, it was a concept that was not necessarily confined to specific performances at the palace. The players had to perform when not at court in order to be well-rehearsed for the Christmas solace; therefore players needed their own playhouses and audiences before whom to "practice." In sum, as has long been understood, the idea of the monarch's "solace" was of some importance to the survival of professional drama in the City, and greatly helped to sustain professional drama up to 1642. The concept was well enough known even to be burlesqued in 1626 in a story of the visit of the queen's ape to Looe in Cornwall.[56]

It is, therefore, highly interesting, when we attempt to gauge King James's own attitude towards the drama and towards "solace," to note what the Venetian ambassador Nicolo Molino wrote in code to the Doge of Venice on January 31, 1605, a month or so after James first saw *Othello* and *Measure for Measure*. James had apparently written a letter to the Privy Council reminding its members that he had been in London for nearly three weeks over Christmas (seeing, among other presentations, the plays I have mentioned). But, Molino's report continues, the king "finds this sedentary life prejudicial to his health":

> . . . for in Scotland he was used to spend much time in the country and in hard exercise, and he finds that repose robs him of his appetite and breeds melancholy and a thousand other ills. He says he is bound to consider his health before all things, and so he must tell them that for the future he means to come to London but seldom, passing most of his time in the country in the chase; and as he thus will be far away from court he cannot attend business, and so he commits all to them, relying fully on their [the Council's] goodness and ability.[57]

Corroboration for Molino's account comes from several sources—principally from King James himself, who wrote the Privy Council as early as January 9, 1605, that during his absences "for necessary recreation" they should assemble to conduct business at the court of the queen. In a letter to Robert Cecil, the king later wrote that he would return to London only "if my continual presence in London be so necessary, as my absence for my health makes the Councillors to be without authority or respect."

All this occasioned much comment at court. For example, John Chamberlain wrote to Ralph Winwood on January 26 that "the hunting life" is "the only means to maintain his [James's] health" which must be "spared too much business." For it is this health which is "the health and welfare of us all." Even the Earl of Worcester spoke of hunting and referred to the king's health "that doth necessarily require these recreations."[58]

What seems to have happened, interestingly enough, is that the instrument of solace moved in January 1605 from the domain of stage plays and courtly entertainments to the domain of hunting. And though this new and explicitly stated pre-eminence of the chase would hardly be a death

threat to the drama, which had now established itself as a viable commercial enterprise, the statement by James about the importance of the outdoor life to his health must inform any historical approach to the early seventeenth century that posits a special relationship between the king and the arts. It is clear that any such relationship, if inferred from a view of James as patron and admirer of plays during the period when Shakespeare wrote his great tragedies, will not be a wholly convincing narrative. As far as we can judge from surviving documents, for James, hunting, not plays, was the approved solace.

Whether this publicly stated attitude was a reliable indication of James's private feelings is beside the point. It is enough that a public rhetoric served as a conceptual basis for his absence from palace life and from the attendant ceremony of which drama, in the season we have glanced at, was a significant part. When James was absent from various performances that the queen and the prince attended during the first Christmas of the reign, James was at his hunting lodge at Royston. So we must consider seriously an alternate concept of King James's early reign, a narrative in which hunting (and prelate-baiting) seem to have been entertainment more important to him than ever were the plays that he saw only in the winter holiday season.

III

In the latter part of this essay, I have brought forward a segment of the *Basilikon Doron,* records of payments to players at court during the reign of Elizabeth and the first year of James, and a group of letters both domestic and foreign for the year 1604 to suggest new narratives describing the relationship of the early Stuart Crown to the drama in the time of Shakespeare. As in the previous case of Shakespeare's *Richard II,* where similarly espoused traditional narratives project drama into political importance, I have been questioning the theoretical foundations of some recent approaches to drama and society in the writing we think of as the new historicism. For even though we must value their rhetoric for its power to remind us that the practice of history is a never-resting effort, many of the narratives presented by new historicists are disturbingly unself-conscious and static, constricted by old narratives that tell a traditional story of the drama in a special relationship to the state or to the person of the monarch. The theoretical implications of this problem are very complex,[59] and the ramifications for Shakespeare studies far-reaching, as scholars continue to accept histories formulated many years ago. Even so perceptive a Marxist critic as Walter Cohen, in his *Drama of a Nation,* depends upon old narratives to support his contention about what he describes as the crisis of the public theatre in England in the early seventeenth century. He writes, for example, that

> Following the suppression of playing near the end of the 1590s, the public theaters of England and Spain reopened under tighter royal control. In England, between 1598 and 1604 the state narrowed the right to

patronize acting companies until, in the latter year, this privilege was restricted to the royal family. The number of professional troupes was correspondingly reduced, although especially outside London the absolutist intention of the policy was partially thwarted.[60]

Here he is "citing" unspecified historical texts that indicate a "suppression of playing" in England near the end of the 1590s, although recent historians of the drama have not noted such a phenomenon. Indeed, Cohen's narrative method seems to marginalize those documents that describe instead the *expansion* of the number of permissible companies in London in 1602 and in 1604—once to accommodate the Earl of Worcester's Servants at the time when their patron had recently been made Master of the Horse and joined the Privy Council, and once to accommodate the Duke of Lennox.[61]

It is not my own intent here to deny drama a crucial social role during the career of William Shakespeare. Rather, I am suggesting that those premises underlying some of our recent approaches to Shakespeare seem finally to evade the concerns raised—to cite only a few examples—by Fernand Braudel as long ago as his 1950 survey of the state of post-Rankean historiography, or more recently by Lawrence Stone, or lately by Hans Kellner in his discussion of poststructuralist approaches to narrativity.[62] For to write literary history in terms of any ideology (in other words, to write literary history at all) without a concurrently examined historical method is to fail to consider such points as are at issue between J. L. Gorman and Paul Veyne (most recently expressed in Gorman's review of Veyne's *Writing History*): the problem of the very nature of the material we are to take—or to define—as "history."[63] Such material, such texts, salvaged through the particular narrative predispositions of those individuals who created them during Shakespeare's era and culled by critics today according to their own story-making propensities, inevitably exist in a worrying instability if taken as the unexamined bases of any historicism. And, in the end, any method that accords epistemologically with such aims of "the new history" as are, for instance, finally imagined by Foucault in that avowed rethinking of his own work, his *Archaeology of Knowledge,* must remind itself that what we choose to see as records—or materials for the construction of new narratives—offer only multiple interpretive possibilities.[64] Otherwise we begin our historical narratives by having privileged supposed events into basic "facts," grammatically (in Wittgenstein's sense) reifying what have been only our own causal constructs. The result is not a freeing but a freezing of our conceptual options.

As to the cases I myself have discussed, while I have tried to complicate what I see as a pre-Marxian dependence on the historical roles of dominant personalities such as the Earl of Essex, Queen Elizabeth, or King James I, and while my proposed narratives have attempted to de-center Crown affairs in Shakespeare's drama, I certainly acknowledge the possible existence of a more general truth. Drama, while not necessarily involved topically in court politics, as Jean Howard has put it to me in correspondence, can be

political in the sense of being implicated in ideology and in the production and reproduction of power relations. But the documents that are now before us do not allow us to infer a narrative in which the monarch as authority-figure views drama as a special and vital medium with potentialities for subversion, or for the enhancement of the royal image, or for intellectual entertainment; for such a narrative, we must find out yet other loci, evolve other narratives than those we have examined, and must eschew argument based on formalist criticism of the plays. For the social relevance of drama may have reached beyond political purviews, and the drama of Shakespeare's time may have been used to serve more complicated ends.

If the Essex story indicates a group of nobles and gentlemen whose own inclinations toward drama predisposed them to exaggerate what plays could do, the impetus to bring about the early promotion of Shakespeare and his fellows to the status of "King's Majesty's Players" is even more suggestive. It may have come not from the king but from the peerage. Whether this impulse was as political as the later involvement of the peerage with drama in the 1620s is something I cannot speak of with certainty, although Jerzy Limon's recent study of *The Game at Chess* is extremely suggestive in this respect.[65] But if, for example, we wish to speak in terms of subversion-and-containment models for Shakespeare's time, we might want to think of an agency somewhat different from that suggested by Stephen Greenblatt. For it may have been James, the new-fashioned monarchist with absolutist notions, who was in England, as he had been in Scotland, the subversive force: threatening the established power and order of a circle of oligarchs in the earldom. We might, in fact, wish to consider whether it was the earls of that period, not the king, who attempted to use drama to contain subversion of their own financial and political positions by the monarch and his favorites. James's theories of monarchy were not, after all, traditional ones.

Finally, we might also consider how these interactions were complicated by the advent of another force, the court of James's spouse, Anna of Denmark. With her accession a number of powerful countesses and their husbands, high-ranking earls, came to reside in or around the court for the first time; many of these nobles, of both sexes, had been strong patrons of the arts. It was, in fact, the countesses with Queen Anna who sponsored and enacted the masques Ben Jonson is so often said to have written for King James. Because traditional study of the reign of James has not been a study of the powerful women who were part of the scene, because our interpretations of these years have been skewed in patriarchally inclined directions, our efforts at a new historicism may have overlooked an obvious source of power and patronage that may even have extended to the drama presented at court.[66]

In other words, there are many open questions waiting for engagement with the opportunities of what I think of as the new history. It would be unfortunate were we to restrict the new historicism to those approaches to Shakespeare built upon the unquestioning acceptance of an extremely narrow set of documents, creating a configuration of "events" ensconced in traditional narratives and premised upon elementary concepts of political process. In our effort to work in terms of a new history, we must take care not to succumb to a postmodern form of historical positivism, no matter what its ever-changing faces and modes of appeal. I can only invoke the spirit of the passage from Foucault with which I introduced this essay. A new history does not ask us to follow one overarching theory of culture; it asks us to deal with the profound problems posed by the notion of the historical "event."

Notes

1. Cf. J. L. Gorman, *The Expression of Historical Knowledge* (Edinburgh: Edinburgh Univ. Press, 1982).

2. I am using "narrative" in the sense that Arthur Danto applies it to Hegel's *Reason in History*: see Arthur C. Danto, *Narration and Knowledge* (New York: Columbia Univ. Press, 1985), p. 357.

3. See the series of essays, including that by Jacques Juilliard, "Political History in the 1980's: Reflections on its Present and Future," in *The New History: The 1980s and Beyond,* eds. Theodore K. Rabb and Robert I. Rotberg (Princeton: Princeton Univ. Press, 1982). But see also Louis O. Mink, "History and Fiction as Modes of Comprehension" (1970), now Chapter 2 of *Historical Understanding,* ed. Brian Fay et al. (Ithaca, N.Y.: Cornell Univ. Press, 1987), and Hayden White, *Tropics of Discourse* (Baltimore: Johns Hopkins Univ. Press, 1978). See also the debate occasioned by J. H. Hexter's 1967 review of Morton White's *The Foundations of Historical Knowledge* and Danto's *Analytical Philosophy of History* in *The New York Review of Books* (Feb. 9, 1967), p. 28, and (Mar. 23, 1967), p. 31.

4. See below, pp. 454-61.

5. *The Power of Forms in the English Renaissance,* ed. Stephen Greenblatt (Norman, Okla.: Pilgrim Books, 1982), p. 4; cf. Stephen Orgel's similar use of *Richard II* in the same volume (p. 45).

6. *Political Shakespeare,* eds. Jonathan Dollimore and Alan Sinfield (Ithaca, N.Y.: Cornell Univ. Press, 1985), p. 8. See also Leonard Tennenhouse, *Power on Display* (London: Methuen, 1986), p. 88.

7. Droysen, *Historik,* ed. Rudolf Hubner (Munich, 1967), pp. 133, 167. Claude Lévi-Strauss expands on the concept in *The Savage Mind* (Chicago: Univ. of Chicago Press, 1966), pp. 257-62, as does Paul Ricoeur in "Objectivity and Subjectivity in History" in *History and Truth* (Evanston, Ill.: Northwestern Univ. Press, 1965), pp. 21-40.

8. See E. M. Albright, "Shakespeare's *Richard II* and the Essex Conspiracy," *PMLA* [*Publications of the Modern Language Association*], 42 (1927), 686-728,

followed by an exchange over several years initiated by Ray Heffner, "Shakespeare, Hayward, and Essex," *PMLA,* 45 (1930), 754-80. Much of the pertinent material in the debate is available in the Appendix to the New Variorum *Richard II* (1955).

9. These complexities have been well described in Jean E. Howard's definition in "The New Historicism in Renaissance Studies," *English Literary Renaissance,* 16 (1986), 13-43. See also the issues adverted to by Hayden White in "The Question of Narrative in Contemporary Historical Theory" (1984), now Chapter 2 of White, *The Content of the Form* (Baltimore: Johns Hopkins Univ. Press, 1987) and "Historical Pluralism," *Critical Inquiry,* 12 (1986), 480-93, as well as Louis Mink's "Narrative Form as a Cognitive Instrument" (1978), now in *Historical Understanding.*

10. I am assuming that their offer of two pounds meant two pounds more than their maximum possible take. The actual sum might be important in establishing the actors' motivation as partisan or mercenary. (From 1592-97 the total take for the Rose playhouse—the only Elizabethan playhouse for which statistics are available—averaged 30s. a day: see E. K. Chambers, *The Elizabethan Stage,* 4 vols. [Oxford: Clarendon Press, 1923], Vol. 1, 368-69, hereafter cited as Chambers, *ES.*) According to the player Augustine Phillips, the conspirators offered the actors "xls. more than their ordinary." Does this mean 40s. + 30s.? If so, then this was an extra day's profit, and financial incentive would appear as strong as any partisanship, assuming the Rose figures are representative of Shakespeare's Globe.

11. For the relevant materials, see E. K. Chambers, *William Shakespeare: A Study of Facts and Problems,* 2 vols. (Oxford: Clarendon Press, 1930), Vol. 2, 323-27, hereafter cited as *WS.*

12. See *Acts of the Privy Council of England,* 45 vols. (London: HMSO, 1890-1960), Vol. 31, 228, 249, 250, 483-89, hereafter cited as Dasent; and *Great Britain: Calendar of State Papers (Domestic): Elizabeth,* 7 vols. (London: HMPRO, 1856-1871), Vol. 5, 553, 573, hereafter cited as *SPD.* For the Crown's sense of the roles assigned to the various conspirators, see Francis Bacon's *Declaration* (London: Robert Barker, 1601), sigs. K3 ff.

13. For Tresham, see *DNB* article on Tresham by A. F. Pollard. Monteagle would later be the first person to alert the Crown to the "Gunpowder Plot" in 1605 when warned in a letter by his still-seditiously-active brother-in-law, Francis Tresham, not to go to Parliament on November 5.

14. For the relevant documents, see *Calendar of the Manuscripts of the Most Honourable the Marquess of Bath,* ed. G. Dyfnallt Owen, 5 vols. (London: HMSO, 1980), Vol. 5, 281-82, hereafter cited as *Bath.* For Monteagle, see *Complete Peerage,* ed. H. A.

Doubleday and Lord Howard DeWalden, 13 vols. (London: St. Catherine Press, 1910-59), Vol. 9, 113-19. See also *Calendar of the Manuscripts of the Most Hon. the Marquis of Salisbury,* 23 vols. (London: HMSO, 1883-1976), Vol. 10, 214; Vol. 11, 127, 214; Vol. 14, 170; hereafter cited as *Salisbury.* For Constable, see *SPD,* Vol. 5, 548, 573, 576. For the list of those executed, see *Salisbury,* Vol. 11, 215; for the list of all those implicated in the plot, see *Bath,* Vol. 5, 281-82, and Dasent, Vol. 31, 159.

15. Dasent, Vol. 31, 216-17. This "coincidence" is widely discussed in the debate about *Richard II* and Essex (see note 8, above).

16. Chambers, *WS,* Vol. 2, 326.

17. John Nichols, *The Progresses and Public Processions of Queen Elizabeth,* 3 vols. (London: John Nichols and Son, 1823; originally pub. 1783), Vol. 3, 552. Most scholars who quote this passage break off at this point, but we should note that the queen was not yet finished with talking about Richard II. Here is what follows "in open streets and houses":

Her Majestie demanded "what was *praestita?*"

W.L. He expounded it to be "monies lent by her Progenitors to her subjects for their good, but with assurance of good bond for repayment."

Her Majestie. "So did my good grandfather King Henry VII. sparing to dissipate his treasure or lands." Then returning to Richard II. she demanded, "Whether I had seen any true picture, or lively representation of his countenance and person?"

W.L. "None but such as be in common hands."

Her Majestie. "The Lord Lumley, a lover of antiquities, discovered it fastened on the backside of a door of a base room; which he presented unto me, praying, with my good leave, that I might put it in order with the Ancestors and Successors; I will command Tho. Kneavet, Keeper of my House and Gallery at Westminster, to shew it unto thee." Then she proceeded to the Rolls . . . (p. 553).

18. Outside of drama, the fall of Richard II appeared in the *Mirror for Magistrates* in the 1559, 1563, 1571, 1578, and 1587 editions, the last ones before 1610. The fall was also chronicled in 325 stanzas of the first three books of Daniel's *Civil Wars,* published twice in 1595 and once in 1599 and 1601-02. Halle's *Union of the Two Noble and Illustrate Families of Lancaster and York* told of Richard II, but there were no editions after 1550. Holinshed's *Chronicles of England, Scotland, and Ireland* also described Richard's fall, but there were no editions after 1587. For remarks about "Richard II's men," see Thomas Wright, *Queen Elizabeth and Her Times, A Series of Original Letters,* 2 vols. (London: Henry Colburn, 1838), Vol. 2, 75; and A. Strickland, *Lives of the Queens of England,* 8 vols. (London: Henry Colburn, 1857-1860), Vol. 4, p. 728.

19. For one re-telling of the narrative about the suppressed scene, see the Greenblatt quotation early in this essay. On the question of why the scene was repressed, and by whose agency, is never made clear. We know that the Master of the Revels had to review scripts for objectionable material before they could be staged (the *Sir Thomas More* fragment is the best illustration of this process), but he did not necessarily peruse printed copies of plays; the censorship of printed books was within the purview of the Bishop of London. Yet despite the problem inherent in this distinction, the traditional view of an excised deposition scene has never specified whether the "deposition scene" was never acted, or whether it was simply never printed.

20. See *Richard the Second 1597: Shakespeare Quarto Facsimiles,* ed. Charlton Hinman (Oxford: Clarendon Press, 1966), sig. H2, for the earlier state of the text.

21. See David Bergeron, "The Deposition Scene in *Richard II,*" *Renaissance Papers 1974* (1975), pp. 31-37. A. W. Pollard and P. A. Daniel have also commented on the non-inflammatory nature of the added lines that present not a deposition but an abdication. For these matters, see *Richard II: The Variorum Edition,* ed. Matthew W. Black (Philadelphia: Lippincott, 1955), pp. 369-77. See also note 22, below. In the long run, the whole excision/addition issue revolves around the meaning of the phrase "woeful pageant" that the friends of Richard say they have beheld. In the early (1597) version, the pageant beheld can only be the show by which Bolingbroke has just ascended the throne so unctuously. But the 1608 addition requires this "pageant" to be the attitudinizings of Richard in the 160 added lines. Proponents of the censorship theory, however, argue formalistically that "pageant" makes sense only if it refers to Richard's 160 added/restored lines. But Shakespearean usage most often has "pageant" implying artifice, as when the Venetian senate speaks of the Ottoman naval feint as "a pageant to keep us in false gaze." Having said this, however, I can only reiterate that the issue reduces itself to competing interpretations of dramatic "intent."

22. Ten copies of the 1608 (Q4) edition survive. All ten copies have the 160-line addition. Of these ten, three have title pages missing, six have the original title page, and one has a new title page. The new title page reads "with new additions of the Parliament Sceane, and the deposing of King Richard as it hath been lately acted etc." Of the next (1615) edition (Q5), all fourteen surviving copies have the new title page. The Shakespearean passage, finally, should be compared to the Marlovian passage dramatizing the (apparently uncensored) abdication of a king in *Edward II* in a play published in 1594 and again in 1598.

23. Gilly Meyricke, testifying as to his activities in going to the play said: "the play was of Kyng Harry the

4th, and of the kyllyng of Kyng Richard the second" (Chambers, *WS,* Vol. 2, 324). Sir Edward Coke, in his prosecuting speech against Gilly Meyricke, used his presence at the Shakespeare play as an item in his guilt and referred to "the story of Henry IV being set forth in a play, and in that play there being set forth the killing of the King upon a stage" (pp. 325-26). Again, Coke in a speech at the trial of Essex: "Note but the precedents of former ages, how long lived Richard the Second after he was surprised in the same manner?" (p. 325). See also Robert Cecil's speech in *SPD,* Vol. 5, 556.

24. For these matters, see *SPD,* Vol. 5, 165, 451.

25. It is during this six-month period that one could assume Shakespeare wrote the chorus to Act V of *Henry V* anticipating a general's triumphant return from Ireland: "The Mayor and all his brethren in best sort, / . . . Go forth and fetch their conqu'ring Caesar in; / As by a lower but loving likelihood, / Were now the general of our gracious Empress, / As in good time he may, from Ireland coming, / Bringing rebellion broached on his sword, / How many would the peaceful city quit / To welcome him."

26. For Essex's activities, see *SPD,* Vol. 5, 447-48, and Dasent, Vol. 30, 351. For Hayward's confession, see *SPD,* Vol. 5, 449. Hayward's imprisonment was reported by Robert Whyte, who wrote to his master, Sir Robert Sidney, Sir Philip Sidney's brother and part of the Essex circle (Essex had unsuccessfully supported him for the Lord Chamberlainship), that "the scholier that wrytt Harry the 4th is commytted to the Towre." For Whyte's letter, see *Report on the Manuscripts of Lord De L'Isle and Dudley Preserved at Penshurst Place,* 6 vols. (London: HMSO, 1914-1966), Vol. 2, 475. Carleton's letter is quoted by Margaret Dowling, "Sir John Hayward's Troubles over his *Life of Henry IV," Library,* 11 (1930), 212-24, esp. p. 212.

27. The censor who allowed the book was, interestingly enough, the Samuel Harsnet who was later so zealous in exposing exorcism in a volume Shakespeare is assumed to have read prior to writing *King Lear.* Harsnet had finished the first of his imposture exposés by May 15, 1599, several weeks before the reissue of Hayward's *Life of Henry IV* was burned by the Bishop of London, and during a time when Harsnet wrote a letter begging the Privy Council's forgiveness for his offence.

28. For these matters, see *SPD,* Vol. 5, 449-51, 455, 539, 553. In addition, there also exist two undated lists of notes, one made by Sir John Popham, Lord Chief Justice, and another by Sir Edward Coke, of detailed questions to be put to John Hayward about the text of his *Life of Henry IV. SPD* conjecturally dates these notes as February, 1600, but they could have been taken at any time before Hayward's hearing. Coke's notes, reproduced by Dowling, observe, for example,

that Hayward "selecteth a storie 200 yere olde, and publisheth it this last yere." For the references to *Richard II* as "Henry the 4th," see Chambers, *WS,* Vol. 2, 324-26.

29. William A. Jackson, "Counterfeit Printing in Jacobean Times," *Library,* 15 (1935), 372-76. Pantzer, in the revised *Short Title Catalogue,* numbers the genuine edition as STC 12995 (entered in the Stationers' Register: 9 January 1599). Four other editions are falsely dated 1599 (STC 12995.5-12997a). Further indications of the seriousness with which Hayward's book was taken are the Crown's direction to preachers about the line to take with their congregations about the Essex uprising. These directions included: "Two years since, a history of Henry IV. was printed and published," etc. (*SPD,* Vol. 5, 567). Not only were the preachers directed to argue against this book, but the book was also used by Cecil as part of his speech against Essex; Cecil alluded to Essex's countenancing of the Hayward book and his thinking of himself as Henry IV (*SPD,* Vol. 5, 583-84).

30. Shakespeare's *Richard II* appeared in print in editions prior to the First Folio that were published 1597, 1598, 1598, 1608*, 1615* (* 160 lines added). It should be noted that if ten years intervened between 1598 and 1608 (the time between Q3 and Q4), and seven years intervened between 1608 and 1615 (the time between Q4 and Q5), *Richard II* was not in great demand.

31. The disparity in the treatment of Shakespeare and Hayward by the authorities has led Annabel Patterson to conclude that drama therefore enjoyed a favored position with the Crown. In *Censorship and Interpretation* (Madison: Univ. of Wisconsin Press, 1984), she observes (p. 47) that while the Bishops' Order of 1599 directed that "'noe English historyes be printed excepte they bee allowed by some of her majesties Privie Counsell,'" drama was not mentioned. But the Bishops' Order of June 1, 1599, 1) forbade the publication of any satires; 2) required permission not by the Bishop of London but by the Privy Council for the publication of any history; and 3) forbade that plays be published "except they be allowed by such as have authority." The 1599 orders, then, prohibited satires, made the "allowing" of histories much more difficult than heretofore, and maintained the power of the Bishop of London over printed plays. Meanwhile, *acted* plays continued to be censored by the Master of the Revels. Thus drama had no privileged position with the Crown as regarding censorship. For the text of the 1599 orders, see *A Transcript of the Registers of the Worshipful Company of Stationers,* ed. Edward Arber, 3 vols. (London, 1876), Vol. 3, 316.

32. Appendix C in Glynne Wickham, *Early English Stages: 1300-1600,* 3 vols. (London: Routledge and Kegan Paul, 1959), Vol. I, 332-39.

33. Quoted by Elizabeth L. Eisenstein, *The Printing Press as an Agent of Change,* 2 vols. (Cambridge: Cambridge Univ. Press, 1979), Vol. 1, 43.

34. *SPD,* Vol. 5, 450-51.

35. Chambers, *WS,* Vol. 2, 323.

36. *L'Isle and Dudley,* Vol. 2, 401.

37. The case was argued over thirty years ago by Glynne Wickham, who wrote that at James's accession "almost at a single stroke, the leading actors of the day were snatched out of the hands of their enemies into the sanctuary of the sovereign's personal protection, or that of his family." See Wickham, Vol. 2, part 1, 90-91. For more recent expressions of this assumption about James and the drama, see David Mathew, *James I* (London: Eyre and Spottiswoode, 1967), p. 234; and Ronald D. S. Jack, "James VI and I as Patron," in *Europäische Hofkultur im 16. und 17. Jahrhundert,* eds. August Buck et al., 3 vols. (Hamburg: Kongress des Wolfenbutterler Arbeitskreises für Renaissanceforschung, 1981), Vol. 2, 179-85. For a recent statement to this effect, see Leonard Tennenhouse, "Strategies of State and political plays" in *Political Shakespeare,* p. 116.

38. *James I and the Politics of Literature* (Baltimore: Johns Hopkins Univ. Press, 1983), pp. 231-39. See also Leonard Tennenhouse, *Power on Display* (New York: Methuen, 1986), pp. 159-60.

39. "Making Greatness Familiar," *Pageantry in the Shakespearean Theater,* ed. David M. Bergeron (Athens: Univ. of Georgia Press, 1985), pp. 22-23.

40. *The Basilikon Doron of King James VI,* ed. James Craigie, 2 vols. (Edinburgh: William Blackwood and Sons, 1944), Vol. 1, 197-98.

41. Dominick LaCapra, "History and Psychoanalysis," *Critical Inquiry,* 13 (1987), pp. 222-51, especially on the problem of transference, p. 229 ff.

42. See Wickham, Vol. 2, part 1, 94.

43. *Calendar of the State Papers Relating to Scotland,* 13 vols. (Edinburgh: HMSO, 1898-1969), Vol. 10, ed. M. S. Giuseppi, 157, 179, hereafter cited as *SPS.* Queen Elizabeth's Servants had been in existence since 1582, but after the death of their star, Richard Tarleton, and the rise of Edward Alleyn's company with Marlowe in their repertoire in 1588, this group became somewhat marginal, and operated primarily in the provinces. They were in Carlisle from September 12 to 22, 1589, and were entertained, along with Queen Elizabeth's cannoniers, by the Earl of Bothwell. The company appeared in Scotland and was shown hospitality by one of James's earls, but the group then returned to England. James had gone to Denmark to claim his bride in October 1589 but could not return to Scotland until the spring of 1590 because of the weather, so the players did not perform. Anna Jean Mill, *Mediaeval Plays in Scotland* (Edinburgh: William Blackwood and Sons, 1927), reproduces payment-entries for entertainment in the "Account of the Lord High Treasurer" of Scotland. Between 1581 and 1603 I find three entries: one for dancing, one for a lion-keeper, and, in February 1602/03, one for scarlet cloth to be given to actors. This last warrants further investigation.

44. Eight years later James would strongly overrule the Kirk's attempt to block a performance by actors in Edinburgh, but, as I shall discuss at greater length elsewhere, James was using the actors as a commodity to emphasize and assert the power of Crown over Kirk. See *SPS,* Vol. 13, 569-71. Arthur Melville Clark, in *Murder Under Trust* (Edinburgh: Scottish Academic Press, 1981), has brought together useful references to the role of drama in Scotland before James's accession to the English throne (see pp. 127-64). Clark's narrative, however, does not end but begins with the assumption of the king's interest in plays, nor does Clark use the modern *Calendar of State Papers . . . Scotland.* Had he done so, he would have found, for example, that the players brought up for James's wedding to Anna of Denmark were never received by him and never performed; see above, note 43.

45. This argument was first presented in a paper read to the Shakespeare section of the Modern Language Association in Los Angeles at the annual meeting, 1983.

46. *Dramatic Records in the Declared Accounts of the Treasurer of the Chamber,* 1558-1642, eds. David Cook and F. P. Wilson, Malone Society Collections, 13 vols. (Oxford: The Malone Society, 1961), Vol. 6, 1-42, hereafter cited as *MSC.*

47. See *Calendar of the State Papers of Venice,* ed. Horatio F. Brown, 38 vols. (London: HMSO, 1864-1947), Vol. 10, 129, hereafter cited as *SPV.*

48. *MSC,* Vol. 6, 35-41.

49. See *Dudley Carleton to John Chamberlain,* ed. Maurice Lee, Jr. (New Brunswick, N.J.: Rutgers Univ. Press, 1972), p. 53.

50. Plague had kept the majority of these special ambassadors from making their ceremonial visits because the new king had moved so often from place to place in England during the previous summer and autumn. Ceremony required formal honors and entertainment to be extended to such visiting dignitaries: as Arabella Stuart, the king's first cousin, remarked in a letter to her uncle, the Earl of Shrewsbury, just before these holidays, "the King will feast all the ambassadors at Christmas." See E. T. Bradley, *Life of the Lady Arabella Stuart,* 2 vols. (London: Richard Bentley & Son, 1889), Vol. 2, 195. Volume 2 is an edition of Arabella's letters.

51. An unretrieved dramatic gem entitled *Murderous Michael* (Machiavel?) was acted by the Servants of

the Earl of Sussex before Queen Elizabeth and the French ambassador as far back as March 3, 1579, when Shakespeare was fifteen, for example. See Chambers, *ES,* Vol. 4, 96. For ambassadorial attendance at plays in the season under discussion, see *SPV,* Vol. 10, 128-29.

52. Letter to Lord Henry Howard (the future Earl of Northhampton) in *Letters of King James VI and I,* ed. G.P.V. Akrigg (Berkeley: Univ. of California Press, 1984), pp. 220-21.

53. See the Earl of Worcester's letter to the Earl of Shrewsbury in John Nichols, *The Progresses of King James I,* 4 vols. (London: J. B. Nichols, 1828), Vol. 1, 317, and see also *Carleton,* pp. 53-55.

54. *MSC,* Vol. 6, 113b-120a.

55. Chambers, *ES,* Vol. 4, 283.

56. For a discussion of this well-known theory, see Chambers, *ES,* Vol. 1, 267, 292. John Taylor, in *Wit and Mirth* (London: 1629), wrote that the ape needed practice throughout England to be "better enabled to doe her majesty service thereafter."

57. *SPV,* Vol. 10, 218-19.

58. See *SPD,* Vol. 8, 186; *Salisbury,* Vol. 16, 399; *Memorials of Affairs of State,* ed. Edmund Sawyer (London: 1725), Vol. 2, 46; Edmund Lodge, *Illustrations of British History* (London: 1838), Vol. 3, 136.

59. A recent and very interesting discussion of these implications from the viewpoint of a member of the Konstanz school is H. R. Jauss's *Towards an Aesthetic of Reception,* trans. Timothy Bahti (Minneapolis: Univ. of Minnesota Press, 1982).

60. Walter Cohen, *Drama of a Nation* (Ithaca, N.Y.: Cornell Univ. Press, 1985), p. 265.

61. See *Henslowe's Diary,* ed. W. W. Greg (London: A. H. Bullen, 1904), Vol. 1, 108-90 for numerous references to normal dramatic activity from 1599 on. For Worcester and Lennox, see Chambers, *ES,* Vol. 2, 220, 241.

62. The studies I allude to are Howard, "The New Historicism in Renaissance Studies"; Louis Montrose, "Renaissance Literary Studies and the Subject of History," *ELR,* 16 (1986), 5-12. See also Edward Pechter, "The New Historicism and Its Discontents: Politicizing Renaissance Drama," *PMLA,* 102 (1978), 292-303. For Braudel and Stone, see Fernand Braudel, *On History,* trans. Sarah Matthews (Chicago: Univ. of Chicago Press, 1980), pp. 6-22, and Lawrence Stone, *The Past and the Present* (Boston: Routledge and Kegan Paul, 1981), Part I, as well as his review of Gertrude Himmelfarb's *The New History and the Old* in *NYRB,* December 17, 1987, pp. 59-62. For Hans Kellner, see *History and Theory, Beiheft* 26: *The Representation of Historical Events* (1987), pp. 1-29. Of special pertinence to Tudor and

early Stuart history is the distinction raised by Marshall Sahlins in his study of Hawaiian culture, *Islands of History* (Chicago: Univ. of Chicago Press, 1983), p. 34, in his reiteration of Emil Durkheim's suggestion that societies may not only have their own different human courses but may also require different particular historicities. See E. Durkheim's review of A. D. Zenopol's book in *L'Année Sociologique,* 9 (1905-06).

63. See Gorman's review-article of Paul Veyne, *Writing History* (trans. Mina Moore-Rinvolucri [Middletown, Conn.: Wesleyan Univ. Press, 1984]) in *History and Theory,* 26 (1987), 99-114. Gorman's own views of the nature of historical accounts are to be found in Chapters 3-6 of Gorman, *The Expression of Historical Knowledge.*

64. Michel Foucault, *The Archaeology of Knowledge,* trans. A. M. Sheridan Smith (London: Tavistock, 1972), esp. pp. 202-4, where Foucault succinctly summarizes his aim of allowing history "to be deployed in an anonymity on which no transcendental constitution would impose the form of the subject."

65. *Dangerous matter: English drama and politics in 1623/24* (Cambridge: Cambridge Univ. Press, 1986).

66. I have argued this point most recently in a paper presented at the conference "The Mental World of the Jacobean Court," The Folger Shakespeare Library, March 18, 1988.

Christopher Pye (essay date 1988)

SOURCE: Pye, Christopher. "The Betrayal of the Gaze: Theatricality and Power in Shakespeare's *Richard II.*" *ELH* 55, no. 3 (autumn 1988): 575-98.

[*In the following essay, Pye analyzes the relationship between political power and theatricality in* Richard II.]

I would like to begin this analysis of the relationship between theatricality and power in Shakespeare's *Richard II* by invoking one of those significant and nameless characters who inhabit the margins of Elizabethan political intrigue. In May 1582, during a renewal of Catholic "enterprises" against the English Queen, the crown uncovered its first threat from abroad in the form of a treasonous plot involving the Duke of Guise and the imprisoned Mary. Something caught the eye of Elizabeth's agent at the border. Arthur Kinney recounts that one of the crown's spies,

> keeping watch along the border of Scotland, stopped a suspicious man who posed as a tooth-drawer, discovered he was a servant of [the Spanish Ambassador] Mendoza's, and learned he was carrying letters for Mary and Guise hidden behind the little looking-glass. This was the first indication the English government had of Guise's enterprise.

J. E. Neale adds a further note. Apparently, the suspect was able to bribe his guards and escape with his baggage, but "as luck had it" managed to leave behind the incriminating glass.[1] There is nothing particularly mysterious about this "suspicious man." Indeed, the treasonous puller-of-teeth who escapes with everything except what he has to hide remains inscrutable precisely because he exposes the evidence of his crime a bit too openly. If his deed is uncovered it is only because the investigator of political crimes knew to look closest to home, in the "little looking-glass" where he recognizes himself.

Richard II bears quite directly on this smaller drama of power. It too is preoccupied with treason, with transgressed boundaries, with mirrors that both conceal and betray too much. The anecdote can also help us recognize, however, the outline of a larger drama in the story of a king's fall. For the cunning political go-between, caught on the border with his letters and his glass, can be seen to emblematize the relationship between power and theatricality in Renaissance England. The image of the letter on the other side of the looking glass is an apt figure for the textual and visual structure of theatrical production itself. Moreover, that obscure and in this case treacherous intersection between gaze and text also represents an ideological structure. The glass of the messenger at the threshold, with its power to captivate and betray every inquisitive gaze, would have been an absorbing object for the Renaissance subject insofar as it marked his own political and fundamentally theatrical condition. Ultimately, that may be the function and allure of *Richard II* as well.

The pleasing symmetry between authority and transgression conveyed by the story of a messenger who betrays himself, but in a form that mirrors and implicates any who would search out the crime, might lead us to suspect that we have uncovered a brief moral allegory, not an historical account at all. The self-betraying betrayer was a real enough phenomenon in the age of Elizabeth, yet he often raises the suspicion that the investigator has entered into the workings of some unfathomable fiction. Quoting Muriel Byrne, Lacey Smith comments that "whatever face it assumed . . . Tudor treason tended to be not only unbelievably maladroit but also 'more wildly fantastic than any fiction.' Embedded in this current of deviant malcontent was a self-destructiveness and hysteria that far exceeded mere artless mismanagement and bordered upon the neurotic. . . . Almost without exception, [traitors] behaved . . . as if they were asking to be destroyed." W. K. Jordan suggests that the traitor Seymour "was more than a little mad," and Neville Williams comments that the fourth Duke of Norfolk "behaved as one possessed."[2] What strikes us as "mad" about these real-life figures is precisely their disquieting willingness to conform to their proper role in an ideological fiction, as though each were intent on proving to the death the myth of the sovereign's indestructability. And yet if Richard, a fictitious sovereign, can be taken as evidence, the king himself can be strangely "possess'd . . . to depose [him]self."[3] If there is complicity between authority and transgression it cuts both ways,

and if there is an ideological production unfolding it takes possession of the king as much as it does of the traitor.

The concerns I touch on here—authority, subversion, theatricality—have been elegantly drawn together in the recent work of Stephen Greenblatt. In the Renaissance, Greenblatt argues, "power . . . not only produces its own subversion but is actively built upon it." In reference to Shakespeare's sovereigns he writes that the "ideal image [of the king] involves as its positive condition the constant production of its own radical subversion and the powerful containment of that subversion . . . order is neither possible nor fully convincing without the presence and perception of betrayal."[4] A power thus engaged in staging and overcoming its own subversion depends upon a mobile, improvisatory, and vicarious structure such as theater to realize itself, Greenblatt suggests.[5] Greenblatt's account of the aims of Renaissance power is both accurate and contradictory. If subversion is the "positive condition" of power—if it enables the possiblity of power—how can power be said to "create" that subversion? The contradiction should not be too quickly resolved, either in the direction of authority or subversiveness, for it suggests the possibility of a theater which exceeds the power that institutes it, one which, like the traitor's equivocal glass, betrays the very authority it reflects and confirms. The apparent indeterminacy of such a structure does not at all place it beyond the politics of representation. Insofar as it catches up the subject in its resolutely specular snares, theater sustains the dread that sustains the monarch.

I

Richard II certainly lends itself to Greenblatt's theory of power, for the central question in the drama is whether sovereignty can prove itself absolute by mastering its own subversion. That formulation is severe, particularly since Richard often seems drawn more to the pathos of his fall than to any affirmation of his glory. Yet Richard's rule does assume its most irrefutable form through negation. "Now mark me how I will undo myself," Richard says, as if announcing a sleight of hand:

> I give this heavy weight from off my head,
> And this unwieldly sceptre from my hand,
> The pride of kingly sway from out my heart;
> With mine own tears I wash away my balm,
> With mine own hands I give away my crown,
> With mine own tongue deny my sacred state,
> With mine own breath release all duteous oaths;
> All pomp and majesty I do forswear;
> My manors, rents, revenues, I forgo;
> My acts, decrees, and statutes I deny.
>
> (4.1.203-13)

As Bolingbroke knows, if power is to be transferred legitimately only the king may unking himself. And that is an impossible act. Pompously forswearing all pomp, decreeing the end of all decrees, the king speaks an oath that can't affirm itself except by refuting itself—that can only be spoken in endless self-mockery. At this thoroughly performative moment, Richard's power cannot be denied.

The cunning performativeness of the king's self-subverting oath suggests the grounds of the ancient claim that the king's words have the power to enact what they signify.[6] The speech also suggests that, for all its elaborate hysteria, Richard's more overtly theatrical deposition of himself— his mirror game—reflects some of the serious requirements of absolutism. In the mirror scene, too, the king seems to defy his onlookers to read the moment of his undoing. "Mark," he says again, after dashing the mirror to the ground, "How soon my sorrow hath destroy'd my face" (4.1.290-91). The scene is, of course, an overt bit of theatrics; Richard shatters only the "shadow of [his] face," as the remote and knowing Bolingbroke calmly remarks (4.1.293). But the king's sport beguiles nonetheless.

> Give me that glass, and therein will I read.
> No deeper wrinkles yet? . . .
>   . . . . .
> . . . O flatt'ring glass,
> Like to my followers in prosperity,
> Thou dost beguile me. Was this face the face
> That every day under his household roof
> Did keep ten thousand men? Was this the face
> That like the sun did make beholders wink?
> Is this the face which fac'd so many follies,
> That was at last out-fac'd by Bolingbroke?
> A brittle glory shineth in this face;
> As brittle as the glory is the face,
>   [*Dashes the glass to the*
> *ground*]
> For there it is, crack'd in an hundred shivers.

(4.1.276-77, 279-89)

Richard's melodramatic finale merely confirms his cool mastery of this mirror game. Absorbed perhaps more than the king himself in the specular play of his rhetoric, we had not caught the moment the "flatt'ring" and concealing glass became the brittle face itself. As a result, shattering the fragile glass merely serves to affirm its deceptive powers. The problem for the onlooker is not that Richard's sport seems real, but that its theatrical illusion seems limitless.[7]

The deception is not easily undone. If shattering the hollow glass merely seems to extend its domain, it is because the mirror never-was separable from the response it elicited. Conflating the king's glorious face and its effacement, sovereignty and its negation, the radically indeterminate glass reflects back from the outset nothing more than the marking of it. And as a fathomless mirror of reading, the regal glass proves the king's powers to be unassailable. Richard had set out to "read . . . the very book indeed / Where all [his] sins are writ" (4.1.274-75). Through his self-reading, Richard does indeed mark his cardinal sin—"undeck[ing] the pompous body of a king"— but only by way of an elusive reenactment that erodes all distinction between the king's reading and the event it laments. Through his limitlessly theatrical sport, Richard shows himself still king of his griefs, and still irrefutable master of his own demise.[8]

While all this makes perfect sense in theory, and follows a certain implacable logic, Richard's theatricalizing neverthe-

less continues to feel diversionary, a desperate antic set against a larger political drama over which he has no command. In fact, the king's claim that he "will read enough" by reading himself, that he is "the very book indeed where all [his] sins are writ," is in itself a disavowal. At all costs, the king would avoid reading his crimes in another text, the paper recounting his transgression against the state that Northumberland has been insistently pressing upon him. Richard's self-deposition satisfied all demands but that one. "What more remains," the king asks. "No more," Northumberland replies, "but that you read / These accusations, and these grievous crimes / Committed by your person and your followers / Against the state and profit of this land" (4.1.222-25). Richard's reluctance seems understandable enough. If through his spectacular self-reading Richard can elude all who "stand and look upon [him]," the formal writ would separate the crime from the punishment and thus expose the king indeed.

Still, in seeking to deny his real condition, the king unmasks the more fundamental truth of his theatrical one. For here too Richard confronts a text of his sins that cannot be marked, but whose performative effects even the sovereign now cannot escape. "Gentle Northumberland," Richard says,

> If thy offences were upon record,
> Would it not shame thee, in so fair a troop,
> To read a lecture of them? If thou wouldst,
> There shouldst thou find one heinous article,
> Containing the deposing of a king,
> And cracking the strong warrant of an oath,
> Mark'd with a blot, damn'd in the book of heaven.
> Nay, all of you, that stand and look upon me
> Whilst that my wretchedness doth bait myself,
> Though some of you, with Pilate, wash your hands,
> Showing an outward pity—yet you Pilates
> Have here deliver'd me to my sour cross,
> And water cannot wash away your sin.

NORTHUMB.:

> My lord, dispatch, read o'er these articles.

RICHARD:

> Mine eyes are full of tears, I cannot see.
> And yet salt water blinds them not so much
> But they can see a sort of traitors here.
> Nay, if I turn mine eyes upon myself,
> I find myself a traitor with the rest.
> For I have given here my soul's consent
> T'undeck the pompous body of a king.

(4.1.229-50)

Richard's teary-eyed blindness feels like an evasion, a means of turning a blind eye to the articles being forced on him and of turning from the inscribed history of his crimes against the state to the present occasion of his self-betrayal. Yet Richard's self-protective tears betray him more than he knows. His assertion that his tearsoaked eyes blind him to the text of his crimes directly follows his pronouncement that "water cannot wash away [the] sin" of those who, "with Pilate, wash [their] hands, / Showing an outward pity." Richard's tears do indeed show him to be "a traitor with the rest," but they expose him in spite of himself; the king betrays himself even as he seeks to know himself for the self-betrayer he is.

The curious redundancy of Richard's response inheres in the nature of the crime itself. Richard's tears may blind him to the text of his sins, but in doing so they mimic the "heinous article / Containing the deposition of a king." For that crime is itself "marked" only with a "blot," only by its effacement. In *Richard II* and Elizabethan culture generally the most unspeakable of crimes is always marked in that unmarked form.[9] "If ever I were traitor," Mowbray exclaims, "My name be blotted from the book of life" (1.3.201-2). When York makes Bolingbroke read the "heinous . . . conspiracy" he cannot describe—"Peruse this writing here, and thou shalt know / The treason that my haste forbids me show"—the new king discovers a crime that can be pardoned but still not shown: "thy abundant goodness shall excuse / This deadly blot in thy digressing son" (5.3.47-48, 63-64). The digressing son's own attempt to answer to the sin committed against Richard is doomed to errancy and self-contradiction by the nature of the transgression he would amend. "Is there no plot / To rid the realm of this pernicious blot?" Aumerle asks, after viewing the "woeful pageant" of the king's deposition (4.1.324-25). To "rid" the realm of this "blot" would be to erase it, and to erase a blot is of course to renew it once again. The unmasterable persistence of treason's blot suggests that the mark of the king's undoing had always underwritten his absolute power; when Richard insists that "water cannot wash away" the sins of his betrayers, and that "salt water" blinds his own eyes, he unwittingly echoes his earlier pronouncement, "Not all the water in the rough rude sea / Can wash the balm off from an anointed king" (3.2.54-55).

Ultimately, Richard cannot be the master of his subversion because the crime is inscribed from the outset in his attempt to know it. Richard's tear-blinded sight is intimately bound up with the divisive and self-eluding gesture through which he would see himself for the traitor he is. Self-reflection once again reenacts the loss it would mark, but now the king's response to the text of his sins opens the more extravagant possibility that his grief, and his crime, are not his own. Yet despite the apparent political risks, *Richard II* gravitates toward the galvanizing pathos of these moments when inscription and speculation intersect. In the next section, I will consider a scene that opens out the drama of the betraying gaze in terms of an optical trope—anamorphosis—that bears on the politics of theater itself.

II

At a point well before the king's deposition, the play offers a bolder, though more marginalized, version of the theatricality of grief, one which more explicitly undermines our certainty about the origins of Richard's fall but which

also suggests that such evocative drift need not be confined to the drama of sovereignty. During the brief interlude between her husband's departure for the Irish wars and Bolingbroke's usurping return from banishment, Queen Isabel feels a strange, premonitory sorrow: "Yet again methinks / Some unborn sorrow ripe in Fortune's womb, / Is coming towards me" (2.2.9-11). In this scene, more dramatically, "blinding tears" disturb the boundary between the cause and the effects of loss; the queen's sorrow begets the event that prompts it as its "dismal heir" and "prodigy." And here, too, grief itself assumes an unlocatable form, a "shadow" at once inward and alien. The account of Isabel's prescient sorrow is more than a passing testament to the power of womanly intuition. Disrupting sequence and reference radically, the scene raises the possibility that the play's entire narrative of usurpation and betrayal reflects a more fundamental drama concerning the origins of the political subject.

According to the queen's companion Bushy, Isabel's sense of foreboding does have a source and reference in her husband's departure. Like Bolingbroke, Bushy would reduce grief's elusive power to a play of shadows, here the magnifying and distorting effects of "false sorrow's" tear-stained eye on this recent parting. His account of sorrow's gaze in fact shows just how potently inexplicable the queen's grief is.[10]

> Each substance of a grief hath twenty shadows,
> Which shows like grief itself, but is not so.
> For sorrow's eye, glazed with blinding tears,
> Divides one thing entire to many objects,
> Like perspectives, which, rightly gaz'd upon,
> Show nothing but confusion; ey'd awry
> Distinguish form. So your sweet Majesty,
> Looking awry upon your lord's departure,
> Find shapes of grief more than himself to wail,
> Which, look'd on as it is, is nought but shadows
> Of what it is not; then, thrice-gracious queen,
> More than your lord's departure weep not—more's
>   not seen,
> Or if it be, 'tis with false sorrow's eye,
> Which, for things true, weeps things imaginary.
>
> (2.2.14-27)

As editors have noted, Bushy's oddly overelaborate conceit seems to modulate confusedly between two distinct optical devices. He alludes initially to the properties of a "multiplying glass cut into a number of facets each giving a separate image" to describe the way "sorrow's eyes, glazed with blinding tears, / Divides one thing entire to many objects."[11] Then, turning from the medium to the object of sight, he transforms the perspective glass to a perspective image—an anamorphic representation that assumes a coherent form only when viewed obliquely. Bushy's final application of the extended conceit conflates the two devices, for now "looking awry" on the king's departure errs both because it finds multiple shadows and because it resolves these fragments into recognizable shapes. The double perspective explains how grief can at once create false shadows and take them for the truth. Yet by suggesting that the view that fragments and the one that perceives coherency are equally forms of deception, Bushy raises the possibility that the queen's sorrow is more radically groundless than he intended; seen rightly, grief may be a shadow not of any prior substance at all but simply "of what it is not."

The difficulties extend to Bushy's own discourse, which has a tendency to turn "awry" of its own accord. Contradictions of number and reference in the passage suggest how easily the multiplying and resolving devices slide into one another: "Each substance of a grief hath twenty shadows, / Which shows like grief itself"; "shapes of grief . . . looked at as it is, is nought but shadows." The slippage between the optical figures also seems to entail a confusion between the viewer and the object viewed. When Bushy says that these "perspectives . . . ey'd awry / *Distinguish* form," the perceived form seems to take on the properties of the discerning eye. At the same time, the viewer becomes as multiple and fragmentary as the scene she views: "Your sweet Majesty / . . . Find shapes of grief."

The slippages in the account arise because the two optical structures Bushy describes are in fact one and the same. Pivoting without comment from one perspective device to the other, Bushy at once describes and mimics the moment sorrow's eye turns awry to view its own self-fragmenting vision rightly and in doing so renews the fragmentation it would discern. Seen as a reflexive and endlessly divisive moment, Bushy's anamorphic figure dissolves the distinction between the object and the source of sight. It also undoes the distinction between being caught up in grief's illusions and seeing them for what they are, between grieving and commenting on grief. Because the eye is fundamentally complicit in the fragmentation it would know—because that fragmentation is the condition of seeing truly—looking directly comes to coincide with looking awry; by virtue of his very desire to objectify sorrow's forms, to see grief's confused shadows "as it is," the disinterested analyst of woe remains all the more caught up in the grieving eye's captivating effects.

"In this matter of the visible, everything is a trap," Jacques Lacan remarks, speaking specifically of an anamorphic image—Holbein's "The Ambassadors."[12] Lacan's analysis of the relationship between desire and sight suggestively relates Bushy's apparently marginal and misguided commentary on the optics of sorrow to an entire set of preoccupations marking the advent of the modern subject. According to Lacan, the unitary and self-sufficient Cartesian subject is founded on a visual illusion—the notion that consciousness is capable of "seeing itself see itself" (80, 83). Such a dream of reflexive completeness is possible, Lacan suggests, only through the active suppression of a function of sight that disrupts the very distinction between seeing and being seen, a function Lacan terms "the gaze." In the most general sense, the gaze attests our constitution as fundamentally social beings. Before we are seers, Lacan

says, "we are beings who are looked at in the spectacle of the world" (75).

Lacan's point, however, is not simply that we first conceive ourselves as objects under the gaze of others, for such a formulation would merely displace the problem of the origin of consciousness to other subjects. In a more radical sense, the gaze is the manifestation within the domain of sight of castration's central role in the organization of human desire, and as such recalls in especially palpable form the division and contingency that defines the subject in its essence. According to Lacan, the sensation of being looked at, of falling under a masterful gaze, arises from an alterity and invertedness informing the scopic drive itself; because a condition of being "given-to-be-seen" necessarily precedes and determines the possibility of seeing, sight will always be haunted by its own uncanny reversal into spectacle. As the sign of this division which inhabits and constitutes sight, the gaze amounts to an insistent reminder of the eye's absorption within a function that exceeds and masters it: "it grasps me, solicits me at every moment" (96).

The anamorphic device represents this captivation in pictorial terms. According to Lacan, the anamorphic form asserts its peculiar fascination for the first time "at the very heart of the period in which the subject emerged and geometral optics was an object of research" (88). It does so precisely because it conveys the true relation between sight and desire in the eliding movement beyond those geometrical and perspectival structures that sought to define the subject in a determinate and controlling position. Lacan describes the way Holbein's *vanitas* painting yields its secret—the perspectively elongated image of a skull floating in the foreground—at the moment when the viewer gives up on the obscure form, moves past the painting, and then catches an oblique glimpse of the skull in passing. The skull represents the subject's nothingness, but it conveys this annhilation specifically in the form of a fatal entrapment within the field of pictorial representation. For it is in the movement of escaping the "fascination of the picture" that the observer finds himself inscribed within it, "literally called into the picture, and represented there as caught" (88, 92). The anamorphic viewer renews his captivation and loss just insofar as he seeks to evade it.

By representing sight as something divided and contingent, the anamorphic image evokes the thoroughgoingness of the subject's immersion within what Lacan terms the symbolic order, that is, within the purely differential economy of language; the anamorphic device suggests that even vision is a function of difference. But the conjunction of sight and signifier can work in more than one way. While anamorphosis unsettlingly demonstrates the eye's implication within language, the specular conceit also makes the irrecoverable moment of the subject's entry into the symbolic order legible by casting it in a recursive form, as an instance of loss endlessly returning upon the

William Hutt as Richard II, Jackie Burroughs as the Queen, Tony Van Bridge as Northumberland, Leon Pownall as Hotspur, and John C. Juliani as a Soldier in Act V, scene i of the 1964 Stratford Festival production of Richard II.

self.[13] The captivating effects of Bushy's reflexive conceit carry over into the obsessive "turns" of the queen's language:

BUSHY:

> 'Tis nothing but conceit, my gracious lady.

QUEEN:

> 'Tis nothing less: conceit is still deriv'd
> From some forefather grief; mine is not so,
> For nothing hath begot my something grief,
> Or something hath the nothing that I grieve—
> 'Tis in reversion that I do possess—
> But what it is that is not yet known what,
> I cannot name; 'tis nameless woe, I wot.

(33-40)

For Isabel, Bushy errs because he fails to recognize just how causeless her grief is. Not merely conceit, it is also "nothing less" than conceit; a signifier without a signified, divided and derivative in its essence, the queen's sorrow is

the shadow not of anything that has gone before but solely of "what it is not." Grief's "substance" lies in that movement of self-difference itself, conceived and sustained here in the form of a chiasmic reversal and return. Isabel too mimes the loss she would signify in the empty recurrence of her words: "Though on thinking on no thought I think"; "For nothing hath begot my something grief, / Or something hath the nothing that I grieve"; "But what it is that is not yet known what." Like sorrow's reverting gaze, the queen's words seem to reverse and undo themselves even as they return, to deny even as they echo and affirm themselves.

"'Tis in reversion that I do possess," Isabel says of her own grief. "As were our England in reversion his" (1.4.35), Richard says of Bolingbroke, recalling the departing betrayer's power to "woo" the populace with "craft of smiles / And patient underbearing of his fortune, / As 'twere to banish their affects with him" (1.4.28-30). The idea of possession in "reversion," evolved out of the groundless specularity of the queen's sorrow, also lies at the heart of the play's central political event: the traitor's usurpation.

By perplexing causation itself, however, the legal term also unsettles the distinction between Isabel's shadowy grief and the event it anticipates.[14] Paradoxically, the queen feels that her "forefatherless" grief will nonetheless revert to her as to an original possessor, that her unborn sorrow is also a returning sorrow:

> Yet again methinks
> Some unborn sorrow ripe in Fortune's womb
> Is coming towards me.

As though viewing its conception through an anamorphically divided gaze, the queen feels her grief at once as something that will emerge in the ripeness of time and as something that comes toward her from an already established futurity. Conflating these forms of temporality, Isabel's uncanny evocation gives the impression that her grief generates itself through the movement of its coming back, as if it had the power to undo the course of time itself.

The strangely "banished" form of the queen's own "affects"—her sense that her sorrow originates neither from within nor from without, but in "reversion"—lends credence to her assertion that she has actually given birth to the outward event she foresees:

> So, Greene, thou art the midwife to my woe,
> And Bolingbroke my sorrow's dismal heir;
> Now hath my soul brought forth her prodigy,
> And I, a gasping new-deliver'd mother,
> Have woe to woe, sorrow to sorrow join'd.

> (2.2.62-66)

Isabel imagines her delivery as the joining of inward and outward sorrow at the moment her intimations are borne out by events. But she also feels that her grief has given rise to the event it anticipates. As her "sorrow's dismal heir," Bolingbroke is at once a separate figure to whom sorrow is transferred and the progeny brought forth by grief itself. A yielding up of what has already taken place, the return of what hasn't occurred before—the "prodigality" clearly lies in the manner of this indeterminate birth, not in the figure it brings forth.

Perceived in terms of the queen's premonitory sorrow, the traitor's crime does not involve turning against an already established origin. More baffling, he mocks and derides origination in the manner of his coming forth. But we need not look obliquely through the queen's sorrow to see that this is true. In the course of events, Bolingbroke's return makes Richard's fall a foregone conclusion. From that moment all is lost. Furthermore, for the king, the traitor's arrival is itself a fait accompli. By the time Richard returns from his exploits abroad, Bolingbroke has already intruded at home. York speaks to the grieving queen: "Your husband, he is gone to save far off / Whilst others come to make him lose at home" (2.2.80-81). Richard's missing the moment of Bolingbroke's return is not the result of contrivance or contingency, but instead reflects the originless nature of a loss that, from the mo-

ment it is realized, has already occurred within. Bolingbroke's return precipitates, or coincides with, a flood of belatedly recognized internal woes. A servant follows on York's heels to announce his son's dereliction—"my lord, your son was gone before I came"—and his wife's death—"my lord, I had forgot to tell your lordship . . . an hour before I came the Duchess died" (2.2.86, 93-96). When Richard does arrive, he first realizes his doom not in Bolingbroke's return but in his own untimeliness. Hearing rumors and reading the prodigal signs that "forerun the death or fall of kings," Richard's troops had abandoned him before he appeared: "One day too late, I fear me, noble lord, / Hath clouded all thy happy days on earth. / O call back yesterday, bid time return, / And thou shalt have twelve thousand fighting men!" (3.2.67-70). Perceived at once too soon and too late, the king's loss is as causeless as the queen's. It is time itself, not any event, that effaces sovereignty: "Time hath set a blot upon my pride."

We should be wary, however, of the momentousness this missed moment retains in the drama of kingship. Isabel's prescient grief suggests that that moment possessed solely in reversion may have more to do with the constitution of the subject than with the claims of any sovereign power. Still, for all its disruptions, that scene too has a resonant pathos about it that ultimately feels more comforting than subversive. What is its function? We have seen the way Bushy's visual conceit figures the subject's inscription within the symbolic register in terms of a structure of entrapment. There are prospects for dread in that specular capture. But possibilities for consolation as well. Where there is self-betrayal, even endless self-betrayal, there is a self to be betrayed.

Indeed, conceived as a function of theater explicitly, all that had been a source of prodigal dread can become proof of an equally strange benignity. Thomas Heywood offers a sure proof that theater can be a force for the good in terms that recall *Richard II*'s preoccupation with invasions and critically missed encounters:

> As strange an accident happened to a company . . . who, playing late in the night at a place called *Perin* in *Cornwall,* certaine *Spaniards* were landed the same night unsuspected, and undiscovered, with intent to take in the towne, spoyle and burne it, when suddenly, even upon their entrance, the players (ignorant as the townes-men of any such attempt) presenting a battle on the stage with their drum and trumpets strooke up a lowd alarme, which the enemy hearing . . . amazedly retired, made some few idle shots in bravado, and so in a hurly-burly fled disorderly to their boats. At the report of this tumult, the townes-men were immediately armed, and pursued them to the sea, praysing God for their happy deliverance from so great a danger, who by providence made these strangers the instruments and secondary means of their escape from such imminent mischife, and the tyranny of so remorcelesse an enemy.[15]

Heywood's inclusion of this fabulous tale of coincidental victory among his three sure examples of theater's powers will seem less whimsical if we see in it another account of that prodigal intersection of inward and outward events that marked Isabel's treacherous "birth." Far from being a "strange . . . accident," the story would represent something of the strange truth of the political subject's own theatrical origins.[16] Just as "strangers" can be made the "instruments" of a miraculous escape, theater, then, seems able to fend off the very usurpations it threatens.

III

The elusiveness of the betrayal and loss in *Richard II* does not make it any less an agonistic drama—a drama of guilt and shame. For despite his critics' and Richard's own claims that he is the cause of his undoing, one comes to feel that the king is being accused of a more far-reaching transgression—the crime of making the cause of his crime unknowable. That decidedly redundant form of shame ultimately depends, I will suggest, on the specular nature of theatrical exorbitancy, and lies at the center of theater's power to "new mold the hearts of the spectators."[17]

Gaunt, Richard's most aggrieved critic, spells out the king's transgression in the most explicit and, for our analysis, familiar terms. Richard has reduced England to a kingdom of writs. "This dear, dear land," Gaunt says,

> Is now leas'd out—I die pronouncing it—
> Like to a tenement or pelting farm.
> England, bound in with the triumphant sea,
> Whose rocky shore beats back the envious siege
> Of wat'ry Neptune, is now bound in with shame,
> With inky blots and rotten parchment bonds;
> That England, that was wont to conquer others,
> Hath made a shameful conquest of itself.
> Ah, would the scandal vanish with my life,
> How happy then were my ensuing death!
>
> (2.1.57-68)

Gaunt will accuse the king of the far more dramatic sin of murdering his brother, Richard's uncle, Gloucester. That crime against kindred is no less a self-destructive act. "Like the pelican," Richard has "tapped out" his own blood (2.1.126). Yet according to Gaunt, Richard's binding England with "inky blots and rotten parchment bonds" is the more scandalous sin. We have seen that a blot can be deadly: Bolingbroke speaks of "this deadly blot in thy digressing son." We have also sensed what might make it worse than death—that it figures an event which can't be marked without mimicry and which therefore can't be situated at all. "I die pronouncing it," Gaunt says.

In fact, the marked and unmarked "inky blots" Gaunt describes give such discursive effects a specific judicial and political context, for they draw together the two contradictory aspects of the legal transgression of which the king is accused. Even as Richard submits his rule to the law he voids the law. To supply the war in Ireland, Richard says, "We are enforced to farm our royal realm," and "If that come short, / Our substitutes at home shall have blank charters, / Whereto, when they shall know

what men are rich, / They shall subscribe them for large sums of gold" (1.4.45-50). According to Holinshed, these "blanks" or open-ended charters caused "great grudge and murmering" because the "king's officers wrote in the same what liked them, as well for charging the parties with paiment of monie, as otherwise."[18] The blankness of the writs gives Richard a certain omnipotence. He can assert his power at a remove through substitutes and surrogates, and he can command futurity, subscribing men for their "large sums of gold" as they acquire them. But Richard also depends on "parchment bonds," the contractual agreements between landlord and tenant, to lease out his own royal realm. The danger arises when we draw together these two forms of entitlement. To supply his wants, the king binds himself to the terms of a law which at the same time he makes perfectly arbitrary and groundless.

The contradiction of a law that is as indeterminate as it is binding can be seen to arise from a single act: the king leases out all that he possesses. In doing so, he inscribes himself within the reign of the law he institutes:

GAUNT:

> Why cousin, wert thou regent of the world,
> It were a shame to let this land by lease;
> But for thy world enjoying but this land,
> Is it not more than shame to shame it so?
> Landlord of England art thou now, not king,
> Thy state of law is bond-slave to the law.
>
> (2.1.109-14)

Critics have argued over whether Gaunt here laments a debasement of the king's divine prerogative or a transgression of the state of law, whether *Richard II* conveys the tragic abridgement of a theory of sovereignty based on divine right or on contract.[19] In fact, Gaunt articulates an infraction that problematizes the origins of power altogether by unsettling the distinction between king and law. If Richard were regent of the world, Gaunt suggests, it would be shame enough to let England by lease. But this is a shame beyond shame because the king possesses nothing beyond the land he contracts out. The scandal is that the king has instituted a legal agreement that somehow exceeds and compasses everything, including the act that institutes it, and thus makes his law subject to itself: "Thy state of law is bond-slave to the law."

The exorbitancy of Richard's act is reflected in the exorbitancy of the response it provokes. Gaunt's question, "Is it not more than shame to shame it so," directly follows his evocation of the prophetic grandsire who would have robbed Richard of his shame before he had committed it:

> O had thy grandsire with a prophet's eye
> Seen how his son's son should destroy his sons,
> From forth thy reach he would have laid thy shame,
> Deposing thee before thou wert possess'd,
> Which art possess'd now to depose thyself.
>
> (104-8)

Moments later, Gaunt himself adopts the voice of the vengeful prophet, condemning Richard to live with the foresight that his shame will exceed him: "Live in thy shame, but die not shame with thee! / These words hereafter thy tormenters be!" (135-36). The consequences Richard must suffer for his shameful act—to know that his shame will pass beyond him—echo the doom of the prophet who, foreseeing Richard's act, would lay his shame from him before it occurs. And both are reflected in the shame beyond shame that marks the deed itself. The loss of origins and agency implicit in the notion of a law that encompasses the gesture which institutes it is borne out by the elusiveness of the response the transgression prompts; Richard's shame is to be dispossessed of his shame, to experience shame as something that exceeds him from the outset. Richard's self-conquering act robs him even of the power to claim his guilt as his own.

In a sense, the king executes the perfect crime—one that elides itself as it is committed. We can easily enough imagine how such a transgression might work to prove the irrefutable nature of the king's power. In fact, Richard's "crime" simply unmasks the origins of his power, for in its ideal form sovereignty is embodied exclusively in the self-contradiction of those who seek to undo it. In a passage that draws together the captivations of the anamorphic gaze and the displacements of affect prompted by Richard's act, the king reminds the doubting Aumerle of his ancient power to betray—to expose and undo—treasons with a glance:

> Discomfortable cousin! know'st thou not
> That when the searching eye of heaven is hid
> Behind the globe, and lights the lower world,
> Then thieves and robbers range the world unseen
> In murthers and in outrage boldly here,
> But when from under this terrestrial ball
> He fires the proud tops of the eastern pines,
> And darts his light through every guilty hole,
> Then murthers, treasons, and detested sins,
> The cloak of night being pluck'd from off their backs,
> Stand bare and naked, trembling at themselves?
> So when this thief, this traitor, Bolingbroke,
> Who all this while hath revell'd in the night,
> Whilst we were wand'ring in the Antipodes,
> Shall see us rising in our throne, the east,
> His treasons will sit blushing in his face,
> Not able to endure the sight of day,
> But self-affrighted tremble at his sin.
>
> (3.2.36-53)

The king's penetrating gaze uncloaks the traitor's secret crimes. Furthermore, simply by exposing his deeds the sovereign debilitates the traitor, who is emboldened to commit his outrages only because they remain concealed from himself. In this sense, illuminating the criminal's sins directly, the king's gaze also lets the traitor betray himself through his own trembling self-fearfulness and shame. In a more baffling way, however, the passage suggests that it is the traitor's shame alone that betrays him. The myth of the king as a seeing sun whose gaze is tangible conveys the sources of the sovereign's power in the active subversion of the relation between sight and visibility, and between seeing and being seen. The reversals of sight are conveyed here in the ambiguities of Richard's reference to the "sight of day"—at once the traitor's sight of the king and the king's sight of the traitor—and, more boldly, in the way the blush that rises in the traitor's face to expose him mimics the king's rising as the glowing sun in the east. Later, on the battlements, Richard appears "as doth the blushing, discontented sun" (3.3.63). Seen in this reverting light, the traitor is self-affrighted indeed. The "sight" which he is "not able to endure" is neither the distinct gaze of the king, nor even his secret crimes, but the spectacle of his own revealed, and revealing, shame. Exposed solely by his shame at being exposed, the traitor is betrayed by the very groundlessness of his response. In that sense, there is no secret sin, only a spectacular self-betrayal; if treasons themselves "sit blushing in his face," and "tremble self-affrighted" as though they had a peculiar life of their own, it is because the traitor enacts his crime fully in the hollow and dispossessed mask of his shame.[20]

The sovereign's magic gaze compels the traitor to see that his crime was never anything more than a desire to betray himself. Of course, Richard articulates a myth of sovereign power. It is mythic not because its effects are fanciful, however, but because their potency can't be claimed by the king. In a moment, with the announcement that his own troops have already abandoned him, the king visibly proves the truth of that dispossession he had merely described:

SALISBURY:

> One day too late, I fear me, noble lord,
> Hath clouded all thy happy days on earth.
> O, call back yesterday, bid time return,
> And thou shalt have ten thousand fighting men!
> To-day, to-day, unhappy day too late,
> O'erthrows thy joys, friends, fortunes, and thy state,
> For all the Welshmen, hearing thou wert dead,
> Are gone to Bolingbroke, dispers'd and fled.

AUMERLE:

> Comfort, my liege, why looks your grace so pale?

RICHARD:

> But now the blood of twenty thousand men
> Did triumph in my face, and they are fled;
> And till so much blood thither come again,
> Have I not reason to look pale and dead?
> All souls that will be safe, fly from my side,
> For time hath set a blot upon my pride.
>
> (3.2.67-81)

Time blots the king quite vividly—right before our eyes. According to Richard, his sudden pallor is fully self-explanatory: but now the blood of twenty thousand men triumphed in his face, and now it is gone. For the sovereign who embodies all power, betrayal can only ever have its own cause. But Richard's sudden change is more redundant still. The king's transformation is unsettling because it seems to fulfill the premonition that prompted his troops' flight, and thus it amounts to being at once effect and cause of his fall. As a response which is simultaneously the event that prompts it, the king's change of face momentously demonstrates the irreducibility of the belatedness that haunts him; rather than signifying the king's death, Richard's loss of affect enacts that event directly in its own self-eluding occurrence. It is time's blot, but also a blotting elision of time itself.

Then again, one might argue that this unlocatable sign is actually no sign at all. We know of the king's pallor only through his on-looker's words, for in the theater no player could act such a transformation. But we should be wary of denying the presence of a blot. If Aumerle sees paleness in the place of blushing health, he merely repeats the undecidable form of reading that provoked foreboding in the first place: "The pale fac'd moon looks bloody on the earth" (2.4.10), said the Welsh captain, recounting those equivocal signs which foretell the death of kings. Like Aumerle, we too may be tempted to see death in the king's living face. Our vague misgivings over Richard's reference to the "blood of twenty thousand men" triumphing in his face are compounded a few scenes later when, rising "as doth the blushing, discontented sun" above the battlements for all to read—"mark Richard how he looks"—the king expresses his indignation at Bolingbroke's trespass: "Ere the crown he looks for live in peace, / Ten thousand bloody crowns of mother's sons / Shall ill become the flower of England's face, / Change the complexion of her maid-pale peace / To scarlet indignation" (3.3.96-99). Richard's words confuse the distinction between betrayer and betrayed: the triumphant blood of twenty thousand men is also the blood of the faithful that bedews England's "maid-pale peace," and it is England's "scarlet indignation" at being betrayed that turns her face to blood. They also confuse the distinction between life and death.

The king's spectacular presence is then a spectacularly equivocal one—it is strictly a matter of interpretation. Indeed, the regal presence remains irredeemably "untimely" because, like the sign of treason, it is a sight that cannot be separated from the response it provokes. Does that reduction of the king's living presence to something ghostly and unlocatable—an interpretive phantasm of sorts—make *Richard II* a subversive play? In fact, sovereignty's ideological hold may be most complete at the moment it becomes nothing more than a stagey ghost. The first example Heywood provides of theater's benign potency, as unlikely as the tale of Spanish usurpers, focuses on theater's capacity to captivate the viewer, not the invader:

> To omit all farre-fetcht instances, we wil prove [theater's powers] by a domesticke, and home-borne truth, which within these few years happened. At *Lin* in *Norfolk,* the then Earle of Sussex players acting the old History of Fryer *Francis,* & presenting a woman, who insatiately doting on a yong gentleman, had (the more securely to enjoy his affection) mischievously and secretly murdered her husband, whose ghost haunted her, and at divers times in her most solitary and private contemplations, in most horrid and fearfull shapes, appeared, and stood before her. As this was acted, a townes-woman (til then of good estimation and report) finding her conscience (at this presentment) extremely troubled, suddenly skritched and cryd out Oh my husband, my husband! I see the ghost of my husband fiercely threatning and menacing me. At which shrill and unexpected out-cry, the people about her, moov'd to strange amazement, inquired the reason of her clamour, when presently un-urged, she told them that seven years ago, she, to be possest of such a Gentleman (meaning him) had poysoned her husband, whose fearful image personated it selfe in the shape of that ghost: whereupon the murdresse was apprehended, before the Iustices further examined, & by her voluntary confession after condemned. That this is true, as well by the report of the Actors as the records of the Towne, there are many eye-witnesses of this accident yet living, vocally to confirm it.[21]

Though we have shifted to the more intimate politics of the home front, this account represents a juridical fantasy not unlike Richard's; self-affrighted, treason will out almost of its own accord. Now, it is the ghost of patriarchy, not its dazzling presence, that compels the betrayer to betray herself. In both cases, however, the potency of the spectacle derives from the instability of the theatrical threshold itself. Like the blotted apparition of the king, the phantom husband marks the exact point where the viewer can no longer draw the line between her truth and the theatrical mirror in which she sees herself exposed. She would be possessed of *such* a gentleman, one like that one on the stage, but she is haunted by *that* very ghost. Indeed, the passage hints that it is the phantom of theater itself that inspires dread and compels truth. The ghost of the husband doesn't appear in the shape of that image, his "fearful image personate[s] itself in the form of that ghost"; if a specter is raised here it is that representation might assume a life of its own.

Like the self-betraying betrayer, the phantom king was a real enough figure. According to the theory of the king's two bodies, the prince is most truly present when he is present in his most irreducibly theatrical form—in effigy at his demise.[22] Indeed, when Richard makes his last appearance "all breathless" in the coffin borne by his murderer, the audience would have known that this thoroughly undecidable king had been exhumed forty years after his death and conveyed through the streets of London "in a roiall seat . . . covered all over with blacke velvet, & adorned with banners and divers armes."[23] The phantasmal king may have a certain advantage over the more spectacularly dispossessing figure of the regal sun, for a ghost prompts conscience and so can transform a purely representational effect into a controlled drama of betrayal and shame.

Ultimately, however, the royal phantom's capacity to elicit unreasonable fear and shame depends on the paradoxical nature of its represented presence. While Richard's ghostly transformation amounts to an interpretive moment— something to be read rather than seen—his change of affect nonetheless remains intensely focalized and theatrical, as if inscription were somehow a *spectacularly* unmarkable occurrence.[24] That ambiguous crossing of sight and sign, inscription and speculation, recalls the betrayer's looking glass. But it also underlies the sovereign's theatrical powers, his or her ability to solicit a peculiarly groundless sense of exposure and shame.

We may be able to recover a glimpse of that elliptically specular kingship by recalling that there were in fact two probable sources for Shakespeare's preoccupation with anamorphosis: Holbein's attentuated death's head, of course, but also a ghostly king. Jurgis Baltrušaitis points out that Shakespeare was probably familiar with the famous anamorphic portrait of King Edward VI that hung in Whitehall, where the playwright's company had performed on occasion. The association between anamorphosis and regal portraiture extended back to the origins of the art; the association between anamorphosis and regal ghosts becomes explicit with the proliferation of anamorphic portraits of Charles I after his execution, some joining king and skull in the form of a perspective riddle.[25] A telling slip in the inventory description of the Whitehall portrait hints at the source of the power of these images. The portrait, which included a sighting hole at its edge through which the viewer could obliquely resolve the apparition, is listed: "Edward ye 6th lookeing through a hoole."[26] The possibilities for dread and solace inherent in that fleeting reversal of the gaze—a reversionary possession of sorts—lies at the heart of sovereignty's seductive ensnarements. The specter of sovereignty is a marvelously efficient ideological construct because, along with the threat of its presence, it carries with it the threat that it might disappear.

Notes

1. Arthur F. Kinney, *Elizabethan Backgrounds: Historical Documents of the Age of Elizabeth I* (Hamden, Conn.: Archon Books, 1975), 138; J. E. Neale, *Queen Elizabeth I* (Garden City, N.J.: Doubleday, 1957), 271.

2. Lacey Baldwin Smith, *Treason in Tudor England: Politics and Paranoia* (Princeton: Princeton Univ. Press, 1986), 3, 31; W. K. Jordan, *Edward VI: The Young King* (Cambridge: Harvard Univ. Press, 1968), 381; Neville Williams, *Thomas Howard Fourth Duke of Norfolk* (London: Barrie and Rockliff, 1964), 256. See Smith, 31.

3. *King Richard II,* ed. Peter Ure, The Arden Shakespeare (Cambridge: Harvard Univ. Press, 1956), 1.1.108. All citations of *King Richard II* are to this edition and will be included parenthetically in the text.

4. Stephen Greenblatt, "Invisible Bullets: Renaissance Authority and Its Subversion," in *Political Shakespeare,* ed. Jonathan Dollimore and Alan Sinfield (Ithaca: Cornell Univ. Press, 1985), 24, 30.

5. On the relationship between power and improvisation, see Stephen Greenblatt, *Renaissance Self-Fashioning* (Chicago: Univ. of Chicago Press, 1980), 222-54.

6. On the self-subversive negativity of the performative utterance, see Shoshana Felman, *The Literary Speech Act: Don Juan with J. L. Austin, or Seduction in Two Languages* (Ithaca: Cornell Univ. Press, 1983), 51, 141-45.

7. For a fine account of the "all-pervasive theatricality" of the sovereign presence, see Jonathan Goldberg, *James I and the Politics of Literature* (Baltimore: The Johns Hopkins Univ. Press, 1983), 148.

8. Extending Ernst Kantorowicz's reading in *The King's Two Bodies* (Princeton: Princeton Univ. Press, 1957), Murray Schwartz argues that Richard's act of violence in the mirror scene entails a fragmentation that leads both to purely theatrical assertions of regal identity and to a first recognition of the individual behind such theatricalizing ("Anger, Wounds, and the Forms of Theater in *King Richard II*: Notes for a Psychoanalytic Interpretation," in *Assays: Critical Approaches to Medieval and Renaissance Texts,* vol. 2, ed. Peggy Knapp [Pittsburgh: Univ. of Pittsburgh Press, 1982], 120).

9. Only the most famous of dozens of blotted betrayers, Essex was purportedly urged not to reenter England "because he was not only held a patron of his country, which by this means he should have destroyed; but also should have laid upon himself an irrevocable blot, having been so deeply bound to Her Majesty" ("A Declaration Touching the Treasons of the Late Earl of Essex," in *The Works of Francis Bacon,* ed. James Spedding, Robert Ellis, and Douglas Heath [London: Longmans, 1862], 9: 315).

10. Ernest B. Gilman sees the ambiguous optics of the scene as a figure for the double vision required by the play as it calls on us to accommodate a providential view of history and a view acknowledging the "controlling majesty" of the crown (*The Curious Perspective: Literary and Pictorial Wit in the Seventeenth Century* [New Haven: Yale Univ. Press, 1978], 94-128). Scott McMillin also takes this scene to be central in the play and associates it with Richard's deposition, discerning in it an acknowledgement of unseen dimensions of inwardness and loss that cannot be conveyed by theater ("*Richard II*: Eyes of Sorrow, Eyes of Desire," *Shakespeare Quarterly* 35 [1984]: 40-43).

11. See Ure's note to 2.2.18.

12. Jacques Lacan, *The Four Fundamental Concepts of Psychoanalysis,* ed. Jacques-Alain Miller (New York: W. W. Norton, 1981), 93; further citations are given parenthetically. Stephen Greenblatt also discusses the Holbein portrait, analyzing its systematically estranging effects especially in relation to More's self-conscious theatricalism (*Renaissance Self-Fashioning,* 17-21). On the Holbein image, and on anamorphosis generally, see Jurgis Baltrušaitis, *Anamorphic Art,* trans. W. J. Strachan (New York: Abrams, 1977) and Gilman (note 10), 38-60. Timothy

Murray offers a provocative account of anamorphosis as a model for the reader's voyeuristic, projective relationship to a literary text ("A Marvelous Guide to Anamorphosis: *Cendrillon ou la Petite Pantoufle de Verre*," *Modern Language Notes* 91 [1976], 1276-95).

13. Joel Fineman argues that in the Renaissance a distinctly visionary language ensured a structure of specular reflection through which representation could be seen to "iconically . . . replicate whatever it presents" and within which subversion and difference could be subsumed specifically as *its* difference, as "the difference *of* likeness" ("The Turn of the Shrew," in *Shakespeare and the Question of Theory,* ed. Geoffrey Hartman and Patricia Parker [New York: Methuen, 1985], 151, 153). I am suggesting that the intersection of specular and linguistic structures works to subvert vision, even while it allows that subversion to be figured recursively as a moment of loss returning upon the subject.

14. "Reversion" is "a legal term for the reverting of property to the original owner at the expiry of a grant or on the death of the lessee" (Ure, note to 1.4.35). On the legal concept, see Paul Clarkson and Clyde Warren, *The Law of Property in Shakespeare and the Elizabethan Drama* (Baltimore: The Johns Hopkins Univ. Press, 1942), 72-75.

15. Thomas Heywood, *An Apology for Actors* (1612), ed. Richard H. Perkinson (New York: Scholars' Facsimiles and Reprints, 1941), G 2.

16. In this realm of originally missed occurrences, the true may not be altogether distinct from the accidental. According to Lacan, because it plays a constitutive role, the "encounter, forever missed"—what he calls the "tuché"—remains unassimilable to consciousness and thus always appears to the subject "as if by chance," imposing on all that follows "an apparently accidental origin" (54-55).

17. Heywood, B 4.

18. Geoffrey Bullough, ed. *Narrative and Dramatic Sources of Shakespeare* (London: Routledge and Kegan Paul; New York: Columbia Univ. Press, 1966), 3:394.

19. Donna B. Hamilton summarizes the debate before arguing for a law-based reading of the passage ("The State of Law in *Richard II,*" *Shakespeare Quarterly* 34 [1983]: 5-6).

20. My claim that the seeing sun conveys power through the subversions of the gaze should be compared with Joel Fineman's argument that the motif represents an ideally self-inclusive structure joining beholder and beheld and allowing language to "embody its ideal" (*Shakespeare's Perjured Eye: The Invention of Poetic Subjectivity in the Sonnets* [Berkeley: Univ. of California Press, 1986], 12, 13).

21. Heywood, G 1-2.

22. Ernst Kantorowicz (note 8), 426. On the revival of the theory during Elizabeth's rule, see Marie Axton, *The Queen's Two Bodies* (London: Royal Historical Society, 1977). My argument coincides with Stephen Orgel's account of the monarch's ambiguous relationship to royal display—his or her dependency on an inherently subversive form ("Spectacles of State," in *Persons in Groups: Social Behavior and Identity Formation in Medieval and Renaissance Europe,* ed. Richard C. Trexler [Binghamton: Medieval Texts and Studies, 1985], 102-20). See also David Kastan's account of the threat posed for sovereignty by theater's "counterfeit" representations ("Proud Majesty Made a Subject: Shakespeare and the Spectacles of Rule," *Shakespeare Quarterly* 37 [1986]: 459-75).

23. Raphael Holinshed, *Chronicles of England, Scotland, and Ireland* (London: Johnson, 1808), 3:62.

24. Julia Kristeva describes such a visual cathexis of "symbolic activity itself" as "the hallucination of nothing" (*Powers of Horror: An Essay in Abjection* [New York: Columbia Univ. Press, 1982], 42).

25. Baltrušaitis (note 12), 16, 19, 28, 107. Anamorphic portraits of the Emperor Charles V had been particularly popular.

26. *Inventories and Valuations of the King's Goods, 1641-1651,* ed. Oliver Millar, *Walpole Society* 43 (1972), 197. See Gilman, 248 note 9.

Margaret Shewring (essay date 1996)

SOURCE: Shewring, Margaret. "A Question of Balance: The Problematic Structure of *Richard II*." In *King Richard II*, pp. 2-20. Manchester: Manchester University Press, 1996.

[*In the following essay, Shewring maintains that the language of* Richard II, *patterned and poetic in its nature, complements the play's purposefully and carefully balanced structure.*]

Of all Shakespeare's history plays, *Richard II* is arguably the most difficult to accommodate on the twentieth-century stage. Once 'the most dangerous, the most politically vibrant play in the canon' (Berry, p. 16), this tightly structured, poetic account of monarchy in the late Middle Ages is deeply rooted in the political and cultural moment of the 1590s. Such Elizabethan topicality, potentially subversive in the late sixteenth and early seventeenth centuries, makes the play difficult to stage today.

THE CHALLENGE OF *RICHARD II*

Shakespeare's history plays all pose challenges on the contemporary stage. By their very nature they are retelling events from the past, interpreted through the eyes of an Elizabethan playwright. Any subsequent restaging of the play is, inevitably, both an engagement with its general issues and an interpretation rooted in the moment in which each production is presented. In addition, *Richard II* assumes specific knowledge on the part of its audience: knowledge of the theological and political significance of a medieval king's 'Divine Right' to rule, and knowledge of some of the ways in which King Richard II violated that right, undermining morality and justice by his involvement in a plot to murder his uncle, Thomas of Woodstock, Duke of Gloucester. Shakespeare, writing *Richard II* in 1595, may well have assumed that his audience would be familiar with the anonymous *Woodstock,* a morality play on the same dangerous subject, staged in London in the early 1590s. *Richard II* also assumes a wider knowledge: an understanding of the ways in which issues raised by the historical events of Richard's reign were current in the political thinking of the 1590s. These issues are, in turn, both specific—the extent to which Elizabeth I may be seen to parallel Richard II (see below . . .), and general—debating the roots of monarchical power and its relationship to both religious and secular authority as well as to inherited right and nobility.

Furthermore, *Richard II* is written entirely in a formal verse that is the play's very essence and strength: a mode unfamiliar to a modern audience. This patterned poetic language complements a deliberately balanced structure in which episodes are juxtaposed, mirrored or contrasted as Richard gradually loses the respect and authority appropriate to kingship while Bolingbroke's influence increases and he ascends the throne as Henry IV. The strong narrative line through the play constantly juxtaposes the fates of the two men, not in the ambitious ascent of a 'Grand Staircase' of power (Kott, p. 9) but in the balanced motion of opposed buckets in a deep well. The King sets up this symbolic action, saying to Bolingbroke:

> Here, cousin, seize the crown,
> On this side my hand and on that side thine.
> Now is this golden crown like a deep well
> That owes two buckets, filling one another,
> The emptier ever dancing in the air,
> The other down, unseen and full of water.
> That bucket, down and full of tears, am I,
> Drinking my griefs whilst you mount up on high.

(IV.i.181-8)

Throughout the play Shakespeare gives Richard a language that allows him consciously to shape his personality to fill the role of a king by Divine Right, deposed by a more pragmatic regime. The play's poetry heightens that presentation of kingship through its ceremonially expressive discourse.

The awareness that kingship is a self-conscious, even theatrical, creation is further reinforced by the fact that everyone around Richard speaks to him, and of him, in iconic terms. So Gaunt acknowledges that Richard is 'God's substitute, / His deputy anointed in His sight' (I.ii.37-8) and Bolingbroke envisages his encounter with Richard on an elemental stage:

> Methinks King Richard and myself should meet
> With no less terror than the elements
> Of fire and water when their thundering shock
> At meeting tears the cloudy cheeks of heaven.
> Be he the fire, I'll be the yielding water.

(III.iii.54-8)

Even the Gardeners (an invention of Shakespeare) have a symbolic rather than an everyday role. They too speak in carefully measured verse, not in the colloquial language of the rustic folk in *2 Henry IV.* Moreover, Shakespeare's script frequently emphasises the way in which characters play out their assigned roles, even to the extent that York's description of the change of monarch draws explicitly on theatrical terminology:

> As in a theatre the eyes of men
> After a well-graced actor leaves the stage
> Are idly bent on him that enters next,
> Thinking his prattle to be tedious . . .

(V.ii.23-6)

So Shakespeare draws attention to the theatrical skills required by a monarch while providing the player of Richard's role with all the clues necessary to represent a king on the public stage, whether playing the ruler by Divine Right, the petulant nephew of Gaunt, or the suffering individual who once played the king.

Playing a role that confers political authority is, at any moment in history, a matter of political consequence. Arguably this was particularly so in the turbulent context of the 1590s. Perhaps the most notable instance of such role-playing in these years was the role created for himself by the Earl of Essex in his rebellion against Elizabeth I (see below, pp. 24-8). Shakespeare's contemporaries would have been alert to the significant parallels and contrasts between their own time and the 1390s. His interest in a narrative drawn from two centuries earlier can, therefore, be seen to be political rather than merely antiquarian.

E. M. W. Tillyard has drawn attention to a range of source materials (including Shakespeare's debt to John Bourchier, Baron Berners' early-sixteenth-century translation of Jean Froissart's *Chronicles of England, France, etc.*) to create what Tillyard calls an 'intuitive rendering' (*Shakespeare's History Plays,* p. 253) of a medieval world order. From the perspective of the 1590s such a world order could be seen as representing a nostalgically conceived alternative to current factional and ideological conflict. The aesthetic and artistic achievements of the past, exemplified by the elegance of the perpendicular architecture of the original Palace of Westminster (built in Richard's reign), held a retrospective fascination for some, at least, of Shakespeare's contemporaries—as did the world of chivalry and romance offered by Chaucer and Gower. In *Richard II* the prettified medieval court, with its ceremonial qualities that constituted the public face of medieval kingship, offers a theatrical language for what must have seemed, however inaccurately, the alternative culture of the 1390s. The play juxtaposes two styles of rule, one backward-looking and one pointing to the future. As Robert Ornstein comments:

> Creating through poetic manner the medieval ambiance and setting of his play, Shakespeare is less concerned to individualize the voices of his characters than to project in their sentences the collective consciousness of an age which treasured formality and order, and which found their analogical and symbolic expression everywhere in the universe. More than a dramatic protagonist, Richard is also the poetic voice of his era and the quintessential expression of its sensibility. When he falls, a way of life and a world seem to fall with him.
>
> (p. 102)

In some respects, this attention to the formal concerns of ceremony led Shakespeare towards a simplification of history as he discarded documentary chronicle in favour of a clearly structured, balanced script for performance.

Shakespeare's History

Shakespeare patently knew the details of Richard's life from his accession to the throne in June 1377 at ten years of age (as the eldest surviving son of the Black Prince) to his death on 14 February 1400. He made use of the second edition of Raphael Holinshed's *Chronicles of England, Scotland and Ireland,* printed in 1587, an account indebted to previous histories, notably Edmund Halle's *The union of the two noble and illustre famelies of Lancastre & Yorke,* itself dependent upon Polydore Vergil's history of the Tudor succession, written in 1534 and published, posthumously, by Grafton in 1548. But Shakespeare was selective in his use of this material, drawing directly on less than one-third of Holinshed's narrative.

One aspect of Shakespeare's selectivity is the clarity of focus he gives to the narrative by concentrating almost exclusively on the fortunes of Richard and Bolingbroke, omitting much of the complex factionalism and manipulation of power among the other nobility. So, for example, the contribution made by Northumberland to Bolingbroke's victory is not emphasised in the play. Indeed, when Richard accuses Northumberland of personal ambition and prophesies his impatience in the future (V.i.55-68) it comes as a surprise to the audience in the context of the play's presentation of his character. This is a clear instance of Shakespeare's omitting and reshaping incidents from his sources. No mention is made of the account in Holinshed of Northumberland's duplicity in tricking Richard into leaving Conway Castle and ambushing him, thus putting Richard completely in Bolingbroke's power. In its place Shakespeare develops further the parallel, opposing motion of the fates of the two men as played out in the 'base court' of Flint Castle, where Bolingbroke has found the King not as a result of ambush but by chance. As Bolingbroke, belatedly, kneels to Richard, the King acknowledges the inevitable:

> Fair cousin, you debase your princely knee
> To make the base earth proud with kissing it.

> Me rather had my heart might feel your love
> Than my unpleased eye see your courtesy.
> Up, cousin, up. Your heart is up, I know,
> Thus high at least, although your knee be low.
>
> (III. iii.189-94)

All that remains of the Northumberland portrayed in the sources is his support for Bolingbroke's cause—both personal and military—and his grating insistence, in the deposition scene, that Richard read out the Articles setting down his 'grievous crimes' (IV.i.222).

In a similar way, Shakespeare is selective in his inclusion of roles for Richard's friends and advisers. Throughout his reign the historical Richard was shielded from the people by his Councils. The modern historian Anthony Steel outlines the way in which a group of 'professionals' led Richard's household (see *Richard II,* pp. 220-5). This group, headed by Sir Thomas Percy and including William Scrope, Sir John Bushy, Sir William Bagot and Sir Henry Green, were all active members of their own local communities and were, to a large extent, instrumental in shaping the way in which Richard and Richard's authority were perceived in the country as a whole. In contrast, Shakespeare does not allow his audience to be distanced from Richard by such 'professionals'. Rather, he includes these men only as planets to Richard's sun. Shakespeare's quixotic Richard is personally responsible for his public image and, hence, for the country's judgement on his fitness to rule.

No sub-plot is allowed to distract from the main narrative, a narrative that Shakespeare has chosen to restrict to the last three years of Richard's reign. Steel, summarising the relevant historical evidence, concludes that psychologically 'Richard was clearly not normal in his last three years' (p. 111). Lacking modern historical sources, Shakespeare intuitively documents the emotional strain behind the King's public persona. So Richard, King by Divine Right, gradually loses his right to that God-given authority until he comes to realise, poignantly, in his uncrowning,

> I have no name, no title,
> No, not that name was given me at the font,
> But 'tis usurped . . .
>
> (IV.i.254-6)

The trappings of the public role discarded, the closing scenes present the deposed King isolated in his sorrow and trying to come to terms with his own identity: a private man alone with his private grief.

This juxtaposition of public role and private individual ensures that the play's focus is on the tension between the ideal of monarchy and the idiosyncratic personality of the monarch. Shakespeare makes that tension explicit in an encounter of his own invention, on the occasion of Gaunt's death at Ely House. Shakespeare's Gaunt tries out on York some of the arguments he wants to put to Richard in order to force the young king to understand the consequences of his erratic behaviour and self-conceit. The result is the famous 'sceptred isle' speech (II.i.31-68) which has since been frequently quoted out of context, even to the point where 'in the patriotic 1940s . . . [it] was a standard elocution exercise' (Elsom, p. 79). In the 1590s Gaunt's words would surely have been heard with a greater sense of political urgency. A most telling indication of the dramatist's control of his audience's attention here, and in Gaunt's subsequent encounter with Richard, is that Shakespeare has Gaunt's death take place off stage. The audience's attention is thus focused on the dying Gaunt's last heroic effort to 'undeaf' (II.i.16) the King's ear with 'wholesome counsel' (II.i.2) and on the content of that advice with all its implications for 'time-honoured' right and compromised allegiance that preoccupy both York and Gaunt at their last meeting. Human sympathy is not then elicited by the presentation on stage of the moment of Gaunt's death. Rather, the audience's instinctive support for the absent Gaunt ensures that Richard's wilful disregard for his death is shockingly brutal:

> The ripest fruit first falls, and so doth he.
> His time is spent, our pilgrimage must be.
> So much for that.
>
>   (II.i.153-5)

In a similar reshaping of his sources, Shakespeare develops the role of York as the ageing Gaunt's trusted confidant, as he tries to restrain Richard from seizing on Gaunt's 'plate, his goods, his money and his lands' (II.i.210) and thus disinheriting Bolingbroke, Gaunt's exiled heir. Shakespeare's York serves as a barometer of opinion as his personal loyalty, as well as his whole concept of the appropriate authority of God's deputy on earth, is stretched to the limit by Richard's callous actions. Moreover, Shakespeare extends York's role as a loyal and reasonable subject by implicating the whole York family in the issues raised by the deposition of a rightful king, augmenting the historical source material to include scenes showing the Duke's discovery of his son's treachery to the new king. An important function of these scenes is to 'demonstrate the effects of revolution' (Brown, p. 127) as Richard's fate reverberates through his country, affecting the lives of individual subjects and setting son against father, father against son.

THE PLAY'S FEMALE ROLES

Shakespeare includes scenes which demonstrate the implications of decisions of state as they affect the lives of a small group of noble women—scenes which are (as far as we know) entirely Shakespeare's invention. No direct source has been identified for Gaunt's meeting with the Duchess of Gloucester (I.ii), nor for the Duchess of York's intervention in the fate of Aumerle. Above all Shakespeare has, it seems, conflated Richard's two queens—Anne of Bohemia and Isabella of France—into the person of Isabella in the play. Another printed source, the first edition of Samuel Daniel's epic poem *The First Fowre Bookes of the Civile Wars Between the Two Houses of Lancaster and*

Yorke (1595 version), may have suggested the basis for such a 'composite' persona for the queen. But Shakespeare develops the idea more fully, presumably with performance in mind. Following Richard's formal, public abdication of authority the Queen's grief does much to readjust the audience's balance of sympathy in favour of the deposed King. Historically, Isabella was just twelve years old when Richard was deposed. The depth of emotion expressed in Richard's brief encounter with his wife while on his way to prison does not seem to be appropriate to a child bride. Rather, it seems to derive much from the close relationship of the historical Richard with his first wife, Anne, who was a few months his elder. The encounter in the play reinforces sympathy for Richard's isolation and vulnerability, rather than deflecting that sympathy on to the Queen as might well have been the case had the abandoned Isabella been presented as no more than a child left to fend for herself in her enforced return to France. (The emotional maturity suggested by the writing here may also have been a conscious attempt on Shakespeare's part to add weight to lines to be spoken by a boy player— suggesting adult womanhood rather than emphasising the performer's youth.) In general, Shakespeare's inclusion of parts for strong female characters in *Richard II* (however brief their roles), along with the Groom's visit to the prison cell, ensures a depth of emotion beyond the immediate issues of political expediency.

Equally notable in the context of Shakespeare's selective focus is the absence of a wider range of female characters. Northumberland never mentions Henry Percy's mother, nor does she appear. Nor is there any reference to Bolingbroke's wife (mother of Prince Hal), although Shakespeare's York does refer to some interference by Richard in a planned match between Bolingbroke and a cousin of the King of France (II.i.167-8). Presumably the inclusion of such roles would have dissipated Shakespeare's chosen focus, distracting attention from Richard and his eclipse by Bolingbroke. Above all, Shakespeare's treatment of the historic narrative ensures single-minded concentration on Bolingbroke's rise as the inevitable consequence of Richard's fall. The strength of Shakespeare's script, however, does not lie in its structural clarity alone but in its sense of history's significance in the context of England—'the king's own land' (V.v.110).

THIS ENGLAND

Shakespeare's evocation of the country as a whole can provide one of the greatest challenges in subsequent stagings of *Richard II*. Shakespeare takes care to establish a sense of space, with constant allusion to locations encompassing all of England, from the border counties in the north to the south-west and south-east, as well as Wales and Ireland. Yet the very references that contributed so much to a sense of involvement in 'England' and English values for a Elizabethan audience can sometimes prove more difficult to convey today. This change in performance resonance between Elizabethan times and the twentieth century may serve to confuse rather than to clarify. For example, Richard returning from Ireland sees Barklough-ley Castle—not Berkeley but Harlech. The resonances even of familiar names have also been muffled. So the fact that many of the noblemen's (and clergy's) names imply their home seats—Carlisle, Northumberland, Wiltshire, Worcester, York and Lancaster, Salisbury and Norfolk—all too easily escapes a modern audience. Today, titles evoke social status rather than close identification with specific regions and landed estates, and a person's identity is less likely to be defined by strongly regional roots than by a general sense of being English. We regard the whole of the country as conveniently accessible from its capital. There is little sense of open, rough countryside or of journey-times of several days to travel across the land.

It is in this context that one needs to view a play that, deriving resonance from the allusiveness possible on the essentially bare Elizabethan stage, moves from palace to palace the length and breadth of the country. Scenes are set in such noble homes as Langley, Ely and Pleshey and in the castles of Bristow, Harlech and Flint as well as in the Tower. The seat of government shifts from its traditional location in Westminster Hall to Coventry and Oxford. Travel is undertaken from 'Ravenspurgh to Cotshall' (II.iii.9), London to Pontefract. Indeed, the play frequently refers to journeys—from escorting Hereford to the next 'highway' to his travel to Brittany. York's servant travels to Langley via Pleshey and then to Harlech. The Queen goes to Langley Place (and eventually returns to France). Norfolk (Mowbray) undertakes a series of holy crusades before retiring to Venice, where he dies. Early on, references to travel are merely reported; as the play progresses and the political momentum gathers, we see people in transit—Green, Bushy, Bagot, York and, of course, Harry Percy and his father, Northumberland. In the context of movement and confusion it is not surprising that some information comes too late. The Welshmen have waited ten days and the news they have received is at best muddled, at worst contradictory (II.iv). Bolingbroke himself stumbles upon the King by accident when he seeks shelter at Flint Castle (III.iii). The complex geographical sense conveyed in the play is more than an accumulation of historical detail for its own sake. It serves a structural purpose in embodying the confusion surrounding the final months of Richard's rule as the old order breaks down, in the troubled transition of power leading to the accession of Henry IV.

The names that pose such a challenge to modern interpretation reverberated with significance in the 1590s, carrying associations of space, distance, allegiance, faction, even treason. A good example of the range of implications evoked by the discourse of names is the rapid accumulation of significant historical incidents that are distilled from Holinshed and crowded into a single episode preceding the formal uncrowning ritual that is the play's linguistic, emblematic and political fulcrum. Within these first 150 lines of Act IV Bagot and Fitzwater challenge Aumerle (implicating him in plotting Gloucester's death in Calais), Surrey implicates Fitzwater in the conspiracy,

Bolingbroke repeals the banished Mowbray, Duke of Norfolk, only to learn from the Bishop of Carlisle that Norfolk has died in Venice, York arrives with news of Richard's abdication and Carlisle challenges the validity of such an abdication, thus opposing Bolingbroke's move to ascend the throne. Much of this material is often cut in modern productions in acknowledgement of the need to make concessions to a more limited understanding of the play's historical, geographical and political location.

What audiences past and present need to share, in some measure, is a sense of what it means to be in England. So, in the 'sceptred isle' speech, Tony Church, playing Gaunt in John Barton's production for the Royal Shakespeare Company in 1973/74, found his truth in the speech by emphasising the words 'this England'—not with the hollow poetry of rhetorical celebration often infused into the familiar 'set' speech, but with the emphatic repetition of serious identification with one's own land, belonging to the earth, even in death. Unable to draw on the full strength of implication in Elizabethan performance convention, John Barton's production found a way to substitute an immediacy of reference which urged the audience's involvement with a country whose infinite possibilities are being pawned before their eyes for short-term political expediency.

PAGEANTRY AND POWER ON THE ELIZABETHAN STAGE

Shakespeare was writing for performance in a context in which he was familiar both with the individual members of the Chamberlain's Men—including his fellow sharers—and with the opportunities inherent in the playing conventions of his day. These conventions made possible visual reinforcement of the play's verbal and structural parallels. Shakespeare was in a position, that is to say, to exploit the resources and performance languages of the Elizabethan stage to the full.

For many critics of *Richard II*, an awareness of the ways in which the patterned poetry of the play's language parallels the structural symmetry of the narrative stops short of an understanding of the script's full theatrical potential. For example John Palmer, in common with most critics, emphasises the political incompetence of Richard in the first scene, in contrast with Bolingbroke's skill in controlling a comparable situation later in the play, in which Bolingbroke 'successfully handles in five minutes an incident such as had cost Richard his throne' (p. 124). But Palmer stops short of developing his case into an analysis of the challenges such parallelism offers in performance. 'The *main* dramatic purpose' (*ibid.,* my italics) of the play's opening scene, for the audience in the playhouse, is unlikely to be dependent upon an incident much later in the play. On the bare stage of the Elizabethan popular theatre the opening scene allowed the visual establishment of all the spectacle and pageantry of a strongly hierarchical court, a pageantry shortly to be reinforced by the tournament (I.iii). Of course Shakespeare intended the scene to be memorable—even to reverberate in the audience's memories as Bolingbroke copes with a parallel crisis later in the play. But above all the opening of the play establishes Richard in his public, ceremonial role as king—using all the performance languages available to the Chamberlain's Men performing in an open-air playhouse to a popular audience.

The tournament scene in the Lists at Coventry is the first of a series of key scenes in which the visual and linguistic possibilities of ceremony and authority are exploited to the full in confrontations between Richard and Bolingbroke. These scenes demonstrate significant shifts in the balance of power from the occasion of the Lists to the negotiation at Flint Castle, the capitulation of Richard in the deposition scene and his death in prison with its consequences for Bolingbroke (now Henry IV) in the closing moments of the play. Each scene poses a considerable challenge on the modern stage, as each is conceived primarily in terms of the full potential of Elizabethan theatre conventions.

THE TOURNAMENT: ABSOLUTE POWER

Shakespeare's script repeatedly indicates the need for ceremonial entries, often involving processions. The tournament affords an excellent example of the formality befitting a state occasion where language complements and is complemented by visual display. Each contender presents himself, answering the Marshal's call and formally stating his cause. Each receives his lance from the Marshal and each reiterates his challenge through a Herald. It is in the context of this public language of ceremony that Tillyard's assertion that some of the play's verse is 'indifferent stuff' (p. 168) needs to be understood. Frequently quoted out of context as an assessment of the overall quality of the play's verse, this is rather an acknowledgement of Shakespeare's understanding of the place of repetitive and patterned public language. Such speeches as the challenges formally announced in the Lists are not great poetry; they are an integral component of an occasion in which ceremonial discourse replaces action (the tournament is not fought). Moreover, the verse here does not stand alone; it would have been reinforced by costume appropriate to state pageantry. On the Elizabethan stage 'costumes were the most substantial of the portable properties' used for performance (Gurr, p. 43) and, although we have little detailed knowledge of specific costumes, it seems likely that the Chamberlain's Men would have used rich, colourful robes for the courtiers. These would in all probability have been supplemented by appropriate heraldic devices on banners, standards and flags. Many among the Elizabethan audience would have been aware of the details of heraldry and the hierarchical implications conveyed in the fabric and detail of individual costumes—implications reinforced by Queen Elizabeth I's 1597 Edict 'Enforcing Statues and Proclamations of Apparel' which set out in precise terms what people were permitted to wear, according to their social status and degree. The players, presenting some of the highest nobility in the land, including the monarch, had licence to wear costumes above their own social rank and appropriate to the social positions of the characters they represented. These costumes would have been appropriate to the wealth, order and magnificence of the court, comparable to the clothes worn by courtiers themselves in the streets of London on royal Entries, at aristocratic funerals or for the annual Accession Day Tilts. The stage would have been filled with colour: a splendid show reinforcing Richard's pre-eminence. The supreme demonstration of Richard's control of the public discourse of the tournament is his ability to disrupt the whole formal occasion, causing confusion by the single gesture of throwing his warder down.

FLINT CASTLE: WANING POWER

An equally strong visual statement is made by the pivotal scene in which Richard, standing 'on the walls' of Flint Castle, negotiates with Bolingbroke who waits for him in the 'base Court' (III.iii). The physical structure of the Elizabethan playhouse complements the emblematic significance of this scene as Richard appears 'above' (on the gallery over the rear of the stage), expecting Bolingbroke and Northumberland, on the main stage, to respect his authority and to kneel to him. The blocking (i.e. the positioning and movement of the players on the stage) mirrors not just the formal hierarchy but the relative position of the two main protagonists in relation to the populace. Richard's position is elevated, as he stands at a point traditionally associated with power and divine authority—but distant from the majority of the people. Bolingbroke has already taken over the main stage with its greater proximity to the people (the groundlings). As Richard descends, 'like glistering Phaëton' (III.iii.178), attended by Aumerle, it is he who comes into Bolingbroke's space, where Bolingbroke already has control. The scene exploits, too, the tension between public statement and private emotion. Richard's formal exchange with Bolingbroke, with all its political ramifications, is set alongside the private comments of each to trusted companions. Thus the stage picture becomes an eloquent emblem of the play's central concern—the division between the office of king and the fitness of a particular individual for that office. (Shakespeare's control of the timing of the action in this scene is so masterly that the moment of Richard's descent, covered by no more than two lines of script (III.iii.184-5), has been taken by the committee of academics and architects attempting to reconstruct Shakespeare's Globe in Southwark as a measure of the distance behind the stage between the gallery and the entrance on to the rear of the stage.) In removing the player of Richard, however briefly, from the audience's view while the player of Bolingbroke commands the forestage, Shakespeare allows the audience a prophetic glimpse of what is to come as King Richard retreats into private space, leaving Bolingbroke in control of the public arena.

THE DEPOSITION SCENE: POWER IN ECLIPSE

It is in the deposition scene that all the resources of the play's performance languages come together, posing a challenge to actors and directors alike as Shakespeare presents a ceremonial reversal of ceremony. Drawing on established reversals of ritual used to take away honours conferred by the Church as well as by military and secular authorities, Shakespeare makes the formal declaration in the play's deposition scene a reversal of investiture and coronation. (See Ranald, pp. 170-96). In a play so preoccupied with ceremony, 'the ritual stripping away of Richard's symbolic attributes is infinitely more than mere formality' (*ibid.*, p. 195). Underlining the implications of the deposition by allowing Carlisle to speak passionately about the nature of royal power, Shakespeare goes beyond the chronicle accounts and transmutes the action of Richard's resignation 'into a quasi-religious returning to God of his kingly office' (*ibid.*, p. 191). He even allows Richard to draw parallels between himself and Christ:

> I well remember
> The favours of these men. Were they not mine?
> Did they not sometime cry 'All hail' to me?
> So Judas did to Christ, but he in twelve
> Found truth in all but one, I in twelve thousand none.
>
> (IV.i.167-71)

Shakespeare's sense of stage rhythms and space ensures that the very structure of the scene as a whole underlines the political consequences of the process of deposing a king whilst reasserting the authority of the monarchy. Andrew Gurr's note on the opening moments of IV.i makes this clear. He discusses the processional entry, the need for the royal regalia to be carried in to this judicial meeting of Parliament, and the requirement for 'the presence of the throne, since Parliament was formally *rex in parliamento*, the king, lords and commons together' (p. 137). . . . M. M. Mahood underestimates the significance of this scene which, she argues,

> for all its brilliance, adds very little to the total effect of the play. If *Richard II* was ever acted in the mutilated text represented by the first and second Quartos—and the long and rather irrelevant 'gage' scene which precedes the deposition reads like the padding to an abbreviated text—the loss, though serious, cannot have been structural, for the deposition only repeats the contrast, made in the scene at Flint Castle, between the reality of Richard's inward grief and its sham appearance in a profusion of words.
>
> (p. 87)

This argument depends more on literary interpretation than on a visualisation of the text in performance. It needs to be set against the sense of pageantry and spectacle integral to the structure of the script.

The scene begins with Bolingbroke hearing challengers speak against Aumerle. Far from being 'irrelevant', this episode parallels the opening of the whole play when Richard hears Bolingbroke challenge Mowbray. The narrative parallel invites a visual parallel on stage, suggesting that Bolingbroke should be sitting on the throne at the start of Act IV as Richard is at the opening of the play. 'On the evidence of [line] 113, however, he [Bolingbroke]

must stand uncomfortably in front of the empty seat while acting as judge' (Gurr, p. 137). Thus the *visual* structure implicit in the play is used, in advance of the un-crowning, to separate out the office of kingship from the person of the king. The empty 'state' sharply focuses the potential national crisis.

Alongside the public spectacle and pageantry Shakespeare allows Richard an element of poetic self-indulgence and self-awareness as he confronts the problem of his own identity. The 'mirror scene' within the deposition sequence is Shakespeare's invention, alluding perhaps to the familiar *Mirror for Magistrates* tradition. It offers far more than a contrast between Richard's deep-seated personal grief and 'its sham appearance in a profusion of words' (Mahood). The moment is focused by Shakespeare with the choice of one single domestic, personal property in a context which is dominated by the public trappings emblematic of kingship. Yet even in this personal reflection of self there is also a reflection of the public persona, for the mirror with its framed image of the king's face may suggest, also, the framed portrait or miniature painted by the enhancing hand of a creator of public identity. Bolingbroke's enigmatic yet intensely personal reaction to his cousin's plight emphasises the fragmentation of Richard's self as clearly as Richard's gesture in shattering the mirror:

> The shadow of your sorrow hath destroyed
> The shadow of your face.
>
> (IV.i.291-2)

The role has destroyed its own theatrical presentation, or mask, as the trappings necessary to the identification between the player and the role are systematically removed and the symbols of royal authority change hands.

THE PRISON SCENE: POWER OVER THE SELF

Richard's grief and isolation towards the close of the play find full expression in the performance languages of the Elizabethan popular stage. The trappings of ceremony—the rich costumes, the royal regalia, the deferential language and the presence of friends and favourites—are stripped away. The evocation of the country at large, extending to the invasion of Ireland, is replaced by the confinement of the prison. We are hardly aware of the move from London to Pontefract. With Richard we visualise the bars of the cell. And with Richard we experience his extreme desperation when even that tiny refuge is threatened and invaded. In these closing scenes two facets of the play that have been kept at arm's length—love and violence—are now present. The Queen, previously seen with Richard only on crowded public occasions, turns an empty street into the personal space in which to share her husband's pain. Public 'policy' (V.i.84) has deprived them of their private marriage as well as their royal place, and Richard's memory of the 'pomp' (V.i.78) and pageantry of the wedding now increases the sadness of their separation. The visit of his Groom serves to underline Richard's isolation. The affectionate memory of a retainer can only emphasise Bolingbroke's power to take away all that had supported Richard's authority—even 'roan Barbary' (V.v.78). Similarly the gift of music, as 'a sign of love', is soured by Richard's pain (see V.v.41-67). Yet in his vulnerable isolation Richard finds a personal strength that is both spiritual and physical. The only on-stage violence in the whole play is saved for Richard's attack on his murderers. He kills at least two of them before Exton strikes him down. In that moment Shakespeare ensures that the full consequence of the action is seen for what it is—regicide:

> Exton, thy fierce hand
> Hath with the king's blood stained the king's own
> land.

> (V.v.109-10)

THE KING IS DEAD. LONG LIVE THE KING!

With regicide go rebellion and conspiracy. Shakespeare ensures that Richard's personal tragedy does not, on its own, constitute the play's closing image. The last scene underlines the national significance of the act of deposition as Bolingbroke struggles to control the public presentation of the change of power: a struggle in which he is forced to engage from the moment he ascends the throne. Once again, use of stage space (including the number of players on stage) reinforces the wording of the text. In this final scene Bolingbroke is not seen alone, ruling confidently and securely as King Henry IV; he is embroiled in the consequences of the authority that he has usurped. In a scene reminiscent in structure of that following the return of Richard from Ireland (III.i) York, then Northumberland, then Fitzwater, then Percy and Carlisle and finally Exton, come into the King's presence to bring news. Whereas the news brought to Richard was negative and increasingly dispiriting, each bulletin for the new King confirms Henry's power while also underlining the fact that this power depends upon the use of physical force. Understanding that the force is all too likely to lead to violence on a country wide scale, Henry tries to intervene, at least on a personal level. His punishment for the Bishop of Carlisle is not to be death. Rather, Carlisle is distanced from the sphere of national influence. The presence of Carlisle on stage to hear his sentence is important in terms of the play's structure. It must surely recall for the audience his earlier objections to the reported abdication of Richard and his prophecy that, if Bolingbroke is allowed to ascend the throne of state,

> The blood of English shall manure the ground
> And future ages groan for this foul act.

> (IV.i.137-8)

The final stage picture depends, as in so many key scenes in the play, on the presence of both Richard and Bolingbroke on stage. Richard is brought, once again, into Bolingbroke's presence. The Chamberlain's Men presumably carried the player of the murdered Richard onto the stage on a bier (as would be usual for Elizabethan corpses). If so, at least a proportion of the audience would have seen the faces of both players. Richard's bier alone would have been enough to invoke the memory of regicide and its ability to influence the minds of the living. Even as King Henry gives order for King Richard's state funeral, the threat to national peace is clear:

> Lords, I protest my soul is full of woe
> That blood should sprinkle me to make me grow.
> Come mourn with me for what I do lament,
> And put on sullen black incontinent.
> I'll make a voyage to the Holy Land
> To wash this blood off from my guilty hand.
> March sadly after. Grace my mournings here
> In weeping after this untimely bier.

> (V.vi.45-52)

To an extent the patterned structure of *Richard II*, even in its evident disequilibrium, has provided the audience with some sense of historical order. The new reign, we now learn, may be disturbed in a more comprehensive and turbulent fashion. This is indeed the case in the structural language of the *Henry IV* plays.

FURTHER READING

Criticism

Axline, Kim. "'Sad Stories of the Death of Kings': The Revelation of Humanity in *Richard II*." *On-Stage Studies* 22 (1999): 108-21.

> Examines the way in which Shakespeare, in *Richard II*, used historical fact and political rhetoric as a means of revealing serious human concerns and issues.

Barbour, David. "The Bard Off Broadway." *TCI* 32, no. 5 (May 1998): 26-8.

> Assesses some of the technical aspects of the Theatre for a New Audience's performance of *Richard II* and *Richard III*, finding that the set design allowed for each play to have its own strong identity, and that both the set design and lighting accorded with the production's vision of the play.

Berninghausen, Thomas F. "Banishing Cain: The Garden Metaphor in *Richard II* and the Genesis Myth of the Origin of History." *Essays in Literature* XIV, no. 1 (spring 1987): 3-14.

> Maintains that the play's garden scene (III.iv) is properly understood within the context of a grander Biblical scheme in which it is suggested that England be viewed as a parallel with the Garden of Eden.

Calderwood, James L. "*Richard II* to *Henry IV*: Variations on the Fall." In *Metadrama in Shakespeare's Henriad*: Richard II *to* Henry, pp. 10-29. Berkeley: University of California Press, 1979.

Explores Shakespeare's depiction in *Richard II* of the fall not only of King Richard, but of "kingly speech."

Carr, Virginia M. "The Power of Grief in *Richard II*." *Etudes Anglaises* XXXI, no. 2 (April-June 1978): 145-51.
> Argues that while sorrow is endured without consolation in the play, it serves to teach the characters, giving them both knowledge and dignity.

French, A. L. "*Richard II* and the Woodstock Murder." *Shakespeare Quarterly* 22, no. 4 (autumn 1971): 337-44.
> Claims that while other critics have dismissed the significance of the murder of Thomas of Woodstock, Duke of Gloucester in *Richard II,* the event, while not portrayed, is of vital importance to the understanding of the play.

Jacobs, Henry E. "Prophecy and Ideology in Shakespeare's *Richard II*." *South Atlantic Review* 51, no. 1 (January 1986): 3-17.
> Demonstrates that a shift occurs within *Richard II* from the medieval view of an essentially ordered cosmos held by Richard and his loyalists, to a conception of power as essentially lawless. Jacobs contends that this shift is emphasized through changes in the characters' language, actions, and attitudes.

Moseley, C. W. R. D. "Passing Brave to be a King: Richard II." In *Shakespeare's History Plays*. Richard II *to* Henry V: *The Making of a King,* pp. 112-28. London: Penguin Books, 1988.
> Details Richard's decline throughout the course of *Richard II,* demonstrating the ways in which Shakespeare utilized his source material and crafted his characters in order to develop sympathy for Richard despite the kings shortcomings and transgressions.

Ornstein, Robert. "A Kingdom for a Stage." In Richard II: *Critical Essays,* edited by Jeanne T. Newlin, pp. 45-72. New York: Garland Publishing, Inc., 1984.

> Argues that Shakespeare's recollection of medieval history in Richard II is done for the purposes of artistic pleasure rather than out of a political longing for medieval times.

Rackin, Phyllis. "The Role of the Audience in Shakespeare's *Richard II*." *Shakespeare Quarterly* 36, no. 3 (autumn 1985): 262-81.
> Traces the development of the role of the audience throughout the play, and examines the method by which Shakespeare controlled the process of the audience's interaction with the production.

Rutter, Carol Chillington. "Fiona Shaw's Richard II: The Girls as Player-King as Comic." *Shakespeare Quarterly* 48, no. 3 (1997): 314-24.
> Provides a critique of Shaw's portrayal of Richard II in Deborah Warner's production of *Richard II* in June, 1995, for the National Theatre, contending that Shaw's innovative performance offered new insights on the "player king."

Traversi, Derek. "*Richard II*." In *Twentieth Century Interpretations of* Richard II: *A Collection of Critical Essays,* edited by Paul M. Cubeta, pp. 41-57. Englewood Cliffs, N.J.: Prentice-Hall, Inc., 1971.
> Examines *Richard II* as the conflict between a traditional conception of royalty, represented by Richard, and the uprising of a new political force, represented by Bolingbroke.

Zitner, Sheldon P. "Aumerle's Conspiracy." *Studies in English Literature 1500-1900* XIV, no. 2 (1974): 239-57.
> Studies the significance of the two Aumerle scenes in Act V, which are frequently omitted from performances of *Richard II*. Zitner identifies the farcical elements of the scenes, noting the ways in which the scenes both diminish and enrich the play.

The Two Noble Kinsmen

For further information on the critical history of *The Two Noble Kinsmen,* see *SC,* Volumes 9, 41, 50, and 58.

INTRODUCTION

One of Shakespeare's least known plays, *The Two Noble Kinsmen* is believed to have been written by both Shakespeare and John Fletcher. Although most scholars accept the idea of joint authorship, some critics claim that Shakespeare had no part in the writing of the play. Not only is the question of the nature of Fletcher and Shakespeare's collaboration a topic of critical debate, but the concept of collaboration itself has been examined as a theme of the play. Other areas of critical investigation include the theme of friendship and the play's genre. In his introduction to *The Two Noble Kinsmen,* G. R. Proudfoot (1970) discusses the ways in which the play diverges from the formula of tragicomedy, noting that unlike other contemporary tragicomedies, *The Two Noble Kinsmen* sustains its somber quality through the play's ending. After reviewing the play's relation to Chaucer's *The Knight's Tale,* and surveying its themes, Proudfoot concludes that the play is notable not for its characters, but for its masterful control of tragicomic effects. In reviews of modern productions of *The Two Noble Kinsmen,* the portrayal of the relationship between the two kinsmen, Palamon and Arcite, is frequently of major interest.

The issue of collaboration, in terms of the authorial relationship between Shakespeare and Fletcher, and as a theme in the play, has been explored by critics such as Charles H. Frey (1989) and Donald K. Hedrick (1989). Frey argues that the play exhibits a strategy designed to deflect the audience's attention away from the nature of the authors' collaboration (with each other and/or with their source material) in order to direct attention to the more important collaboration between the producers of the play and the audience. Hedrick takes a different approach to the issue of collaboration, claiming that *The Two Noble Kinsmen's* thematic exploration of the nature of artistic rivalry suggests that Shakespeare did not collaborate in the writing of the play. Hedrick goes on to explain that Fletcher's coauthor "is wholly unskilled in the degree and kind of indirect, inferential, second-order speech acts characteristic of Shakespeare." Additionally, Hedrick employs the feminist theory of homosociability as a tool for dissecting the play's depiction of collaboration as a subtext, maintaining that such an approach further underscores the improbability of Shakespeare's joint authorship. Just as Hedrick's analysis includes a discussion of the homosocial relationships in *The Two Noble Kinsmen,* Alan Stewart (1999) similarly investigates the nature of the idealized male friendship between Palamon and Arcite. Stewart examines the failure of their friendship, and suggests that the relationship is doomed because of the conflict between humanist and chivalric notions of male friendship, and the realities of male relations and kinship bonds in Jacobean England.

The nature of the relationship between Palamon and Arcite is just as fascinating to modern producers of the play as it is to Shakespearean scholars. One production of *The Two Noble Kinsmen,* directed by Tim Carroll and performed at the Globe Theater, has been assessed by Matt Wolf (2000) and Lois Potter (2001). Potter praises the performances of Jasper Britton as Palamon and Will Keen as Arcite, observing their ability to establish a good relationship with the audience and applauding their treatment of the relationship's mixture of tragic and comic elements. Potter additionally states that Kate Fleetwood's performance as the Jailer's Daughter underscored the serious issue of the character's madness, and comments that as a whole the production was satisfying. In Wolf's favorable appraisal of the production, he offers high praise for Britton's Palamon and describes the production as "enchanting."

OVERVIEWS AND GENERAL STUDIES

G. R. Proudfoot (essay date 1970)

SOURCE: Proudfoot, G. R. Introduction to *The Two Noble Kinsmen,* by John Fletcher and William Shakespeare, edited by G. R. Proudfoot, pp. xxi-xxiv. London: Edward Arnold, 1970.

[*In the following excerpt, Proudfoot reviews the themes and characters found in* The Two Noble Kinsmen, *observing that the play's impressiveness stems not from its characters, but from its adroit handling of tragicomic effects.*]

The Two Noble Kinsmen belongs to the vogue of tragicomedy that began about 1609 with the revival of the old play of *Mucedorus* and with the writing of *Cymbeline* and *Philaster.* It differs from these plays in sustaining to the end a somber note which they dispel in the resolution of their plots. *The Knight's Tale* prescribed the death of Arcite, but the death sentence imposed on the losers in the tournament is not in Chaucer and the emphasis on mortality which pervades Act I is present only at the end of the tale.

Where Chaucer is concerned with the subtle workings of Fortune, the play lays its emphasis on the destructive power of love. "Is this winning?" cries Emilia, as she is awarded to Arcite and Palamon is led to execution. Palamon too, when he is reprieved and Arcite is dead, is conscious mainly of regret:

> O cousin,
> That we should things desire, which do cost us
> The loss of our desire! That nought could buy
> Dear love, but loss of dear love!
>
> (V.iv.109-112)

The theme of the bitterness of love is not illustrated only by the cousins' destructive rivalry. Palamon's prayer to Venus in V.i invokes her power in grotesque images which stress the need to placate a deity so inimical to rationality and human dignity. As C. Leech has pointed out, the same destructive power of Venus is exemplified in pathetic and comic terms in the "pretty" distemper of the Jailer's daughter.[1]

To offset the picture of irrational and destructive passion, Act I introduces, in the marriage of Theseus and Hippolyta, a love that asserts the natural order instead of disrupting it. Theseus has "shrunk" the Queen of the Amazons into "the bound she was o'erflowing" and Hippolyta, whose subjection to Theseus is voluntary, is ready to postpone her "joy" in order that Theseus may aid the three Queens before concluding the wedding ceremony. Sexual love is here shown under the control of reason, but another love is also exemplified which is not destructive because it is asexual. I.iii is largely devoted to the description of such love, between Theseus and Pirithous, and between Emilia and "the maid Flavina," who died in childhood innocence. The contrast between childish innocence and sexual experience recalls passages in Shakespeare's late plays; in *The Winter's Tale,* where Polixenes evokes his early friendship with Leontes, before sexual maturity taught them "the doctrine of ill-doing"; or in *Cymbeline,* where the jealous passion of Posthumus contrasts with the innocent fraternal love of Guiderius and Arviragus for Imogen in her disguise as Fidele.

P. Edwards gives a convincing account of the design of the play: "We are given, clearly enough, a life in two stages: youth, in which the passion of spontaneous friendship is dominant, and the riper age in which there is a dominant sexual passion, leading to marriage where it can. The movement from one stage to the next, the unavoidable process of growth, is a movement away from innocence, away from joy."[2] Edwards attributes this central idea to Shakespeare, but concedes that Fletcher's treatment of it in the middle acts is superficial and regrets that "Shakespeare did not write the whole of the play." In Acts I and V the main conflicts are thematic. They involve Mars,

patron of the soldiers—Theseus, Pirithous, Palamon and Arcite—and upholder of military honor, and Venus, whose power over the senses and passions is inimical both to honor and to the chaste bonds of friendship. The climax of the thematic conflict is reached in V.i with the prayers of Arcite, Palamon, and Emilia to their divine patrons.

The strangest effect of collaborative authorship is that the central action involving Palamon and Arcite does not seem to bear any essential relation to this broader thematic conflict. Palamon is, indeed, presented as a lover and Arcite as a soldier (at III.vi.282-285) but the distinction is merely nominal. The reason for this is that one principle governing the writing of the later acts is that of suspense. The characterization of the kinsmen as "twins of honor" is designed to establish the conflict between them as one of personal merit and to keep its outcome uncertain for as long as possible. This end could be achieved only by minimizing differences between them and by leaving in the background their respective association with Venus and Mars. Even that small degree of moral superiority enjoyed by Palamon in Chaucer is suppressed as the cousins are not bound by an oath "Neither of us in love to hyndre oother,"[3] although the result is to reduce Palamon's outraged "I saw her first" to the level of the ridiculous. The uncertainty of the outcome is urged by Emilia's doubts in IV.ii and V.iii and by the description of the knights in IV.ii: Palamon's first knight is duly described as a lover, Arcite's as a soldier, but the third knight is described as a composite of lover and soldier and is assigned to neither party. Palamon is to be the winner, and in retrospect we can see this as the proper outcome, if only because the Jailer's daughter has weighted the scales in his favor; but the process of maintaining suspense led Fletcher to alienate sympathy from him in Act III, where his uncontrolled fury at Arcite's "falsehood" contrasts unpleasantly with Arcite's self-possession.

Chaucer's Emilie is vowed to virginity: so is Emilia in Act I and Act V, scene i, of the play. Elsewhere she is shown to be susceptible to the charms of both lovers. She is faced with two choices, between marriage and virginity and between Palamon and Arcite: both choices are made for her by the gods, but only after her perplexity has been presented at length. In the end, like Silvia in *The Two Gentlemen of Verona,* she is reduced to the status of a possession and is restored to Palamon by Arcite as "your stol'n jewel."

The impressiveness of *The Two Noble Kinsmen* lies not in its characters, who are not compelling either as psychological studies or as emblematic figures, but in its mastery of the tragicomic effects, pathos and suspense, and especially in its success, against the odds, in persuading us that its story, which teeters constantly on the verge of absurdity, is a fit vehicle for a poetic exploration of the inscrutability of the gods and of the dangerous power of love. The success is precarious and the tone of heroic hyperbole which makes it possible is sustained only at the cost of emotional involvement and of that range of ironic awareness which usually characterizes Shakespeare's earlier handling of similar themes.

The Two Noble Kinsmen is not best approached as a sequel to *The Winter's Tale* and *The Tempest: Cymbeline* and *Philaster* bear closer affinities to it both in theme and in tone. Its use of elaborate stage spectacle is one of its closest points of contact with Shakespeare's late plays. The Shakespeare scenes, as T. Spencer remarked, "are static and, though with splendor, stiff," expressing themselves in gesture and tableau rather than in action.[4] Their visual impact is often one of incongruous juxtaposition: the wedding procession is stopped by the mourning Queens in I.i; the bridegroom is summoned from the scaffold in V.iv. Such images must have had a peculiar power in the London of 1613, which had within the previous year seen the wedding festivities of its princess postponed for the funeral of the Prince of Wales.

Notes

1. C. Leech, ed., *The Two Noble Kinsmen* (New York, 1966), xxxii-xxxiii.

2. P. Edwards, "On the Design of *The Two Noble Kinsmen*," *A Review of English Literature,* V (1964), 103-104.

3. F. N. Robinson, ed., *The Works of Geoffrey Chaucer* (London, 1957), *The Knight's Tale,* l. 1135.

4. T. Spencer, "*The Two Noble Kinsmen,*" *Modern Philology,* XXXVI (1939), 257.

PRODUCTION REVIEWS

Matt Wolf (review date 2000)

SOURCE: Wolf, Matt. "The Actor's the Thing at Shakespeare's Globe." *Variety* 380, no. 3 (4-10 September 2000): 32-4.

[*In the following excerpted review, Wolf assesses Tim Carroll's production of* The Two Noble Kinsmen *at the Globe Theater, offering his praise of Jasper Britton's performance as Palamon and finding the production as a whole "enchanting."*]

Among the various criticisms made of Shakespeare's Globe over the four seasons that the rebuilt playhouse has been attracting summertime hordes, one lament has more or less stuck: the theater's inability to attract name performers to a venue seemingly bigger than any individual who might appear there. (Vanessa Redgrave's presence this summer as Prospero was very much the starry exception, not the rule.) Still, as the Royal Shakespeare Co. learned ages ago, if you're not going to entice the heavy

hitters, why not do the next best thing and create them? With that in mind, one will remember the Globe's Y2K repertoire as the season that cemented artistic director Mark Rylance's very real stature even as it heralded the thirty something Jasper Britton as a star.

Son of Tony Britton, the long-established English thesp, Britton fils is hardly unknown. Last season, he was a more-than-reliable participant in Trevor Nunn's inaugural National Theater ensemble, playing (among other roles) Shakespeare's sore-ridden Thersites and, later, a duck-hungry cat—the latter as part of the menagerie in the Olivier Award-winning musical, "Honk!" And in the Globe's season-opening *Tempest,* Britton cut the best Caliban I have yet seen—a mud-caked, half-naked creature as prone to poetry as he was to a guttural growl.

Virtually all the Globe company—Redgrave excepted (her next venture, the Trevor Nunn-National Theater *The Cherry Orchard* opens in three weeks)—have been cast across two productions, so it's with great warmth that one welcomes Britton back in *The Two Noble Kinsmen,* along with Tim Carroll's entire production. The likable curiosity that is the Shakespeare-John Fletcher text is not easily separated from Britton and Co.'s playing of it. "My argument is love," soliloquizes Britton's imprisoned Palamon, nephew to Theban king Creon and friend-turned-rival to his newly banished cousin, Arcite (Will Keen). And with Britton in the driver's seat (as he speaks it, a potentially banal utterance like "oh, good morrow" sounds inimitably droll), the play brooks little debate: love's ardor—and its attendant risks—have rarely been so enchanting.

Those perils, as it happens, are sizable, including a joust to the death, not to mention an admirer in demented pursuit—Kate Fleetwood's vibrantly acted Jailer's Daughter, a sort of hyper-bawdy Ophelia—who responds (typical Shakespeare flourish, this) to the subterfuge of disguise. And yet, one is always aware of an unabashed romanticism underscoring even the doomiest moments in a rewrite of Chaucer's *The Knight's Tale* that a rain-soaked evening—of which this London summer has had no shortage—can't keep from seeming choice.

Lois Potter (review date 2001)

SOURCE: Potter, Lois. "This Distracted Globe: Summer 2000." *Shakespeare Quarterly* 52, no. 1 (spring 2001): 124-32.

[*In the following excerpted review of* The Two Noble Kinsmen, *directed by Tim Carroll for the Globe Theater, Potter comments on the director's excising of the text, noting that Carroll valued simplicity over spectacle.*]

The Globe season of 2000 paired two famous Shakespeare plays about madness, metatheatricality, and exotic travel (*Hamlet* and *The Tempest*) with two rarities: a Fletcher-Shakespeare collaboration (*The Two Noble Kinsmen*), whose most popular character has always been an Ophelia-like madwoman; and *The Antipodes,* a Brome comedy of the next generation about the cure of a hero who has gone mad from reading travel literature. Whether these interconnections were intended or merely the product of casting needs and directorial schedules, the result was a season of unusual coherence, though, at the same time, each play could be enjoyed on its own terms. Even if metatheatricality had not been a theme of the plays, it would have been a theme of the season, since the Globe rarely fails to make one conscious of its ongoing experimentation with the relationship between actors and audience.

The Two Noble Kinsmen, directed by Tim Carroll, was the second production by the Red Company—without Vanessa Redgrave but with Yolanda Vasquez, who joined the company to play Hippolyta. Carroll trimmed the play not only of lines (particularly Shakespearean ones) but also of scenes (much of 1.1 and the whole of 1.2, which seems to have been a late decision) and of characters. The disappearance of the three knights who are supposed to support Palamon and Arcite in their combat meant that the heroes addressed to us, not to their followers, the speeches in the temple and (in Palamon's case) on the scaffold—a breaking of the dramatic illusion which the Chaucerian part of the play does not normally allow. At first viewing, I wondered how well the audience could understand what was going on, but I was in the yard on the second occasion and felt a remarkable degree of warmth toward the production. People were of course understanding what was there, not wondering about what wasn't. Though Carroll cut what he found boring, he did not remove what was merely difficult. Thus, Palamon retained his lines about the eighty-year-old man and his young bride, and Pirithous had most of his great final speech about the horse that goes mad. Moreover, the lines that did remain were given their full value, with, for example, beautiful orchestration of voices at antiphonal moments, as in 3.6 when Hippolyta, Emilia, and Pirithous were asking mercy for Palamon and Arcite.

While most productions of this play go on the assumption that it was meant to be spectacular, Carroll opted for extreme simplicity. The "signs" given by the gods in the temple scene (5.1), for instance, were simple and unspectacular (a brief flare-up of flame for Arcite, smoke for Palamon, and, for Emilia, a rose whose petals crumble in her hand). The one scenic device was a structure suggesting a crude siege tower or catapult, topped with the giant skull of a horse and a tail. At times, it recalled the Greek theater's *ekkyklema,* a rolling platform apparently used to reveal characters who were unable to enter under their own power: the half-dead kinsmen were first seen lying at its base in 1.4. But it could also be representational: the prison of the kinsmen or a maypole in the morris-dance scene, with red streamers emerging from its mouth. As something primitive and incomprehensible, like Peter Shaffer's Equus, it represented the three gods who are addressed in the temple scene. In the final scene it became both Palamon's scaffold and, by a turn as sudden as that

of the story, the place where Arcite lay dying. It towered over Pirithous as he gave his famous speech, powerfully delivered by Jonathan Oliver, whose slow and precise treatment of the climax left no doubt about exactly what had happened and how horrendous it was.

Because Carroll chose to cut 1.2, Jasper Britton and Will Keen, as Palamon and Arcite, first appeared in the prison scene, which was well balanced between idealism and egotism: Palamon's reaction to Arcite's declaration of love for Emilia—"I saw her first"—was so perfectly timed that it got not only laughter but applause for the neatness with which it followed the vows of eternal friendship the two men had just been exchanging. Both characters easily established a good relationship with their audience—though I saw a few ominous signs that Britton might be planning to introduce more of the show-stealing behavior that had worked for his Caliban: there was a little too much giggling in 3.3 where the two men drink to "the wenches we have known" and the laughter at "How do I look?" in 3.6 where they arm each other for a fight that they don't really want nearly overpowering the pathos of the situation. But the remarkable mixture of comic and tragic in their relationship and its consequences was probably better judged than I have ever seen it before.

It helped that other characters treated them with sympathy. Martin Turner was an unusually likeable and attractive Theseus, fully conscious of the cost of war (here made visible by the body bags for the three kings). When in 1.4 he announced his intention of posting back to Athens, the tone in which he named the city evoked not only Hippolyta's presence there but the extent to which Athens represented something valuable, the complete opposite of bloodstained, warlike Thebes. He was himself aware, rather than a butt, of the irony in his situation, as he was forced to modify his principles in the light of one complicated dilemma after another: "And, by my honour—*once again*—it stands." Carroll brought out his three-way relationship with Hippolyta and Pirithous (he danced with both of them in the forest), and Emilia's simple, lyrical speech about her eleven-year-old love for another girl, beautifully spoken by Geraldine Alexander, suggested that bisexuality was a natural state in the world of Athens. Emilia's reluctance to marry either kinsman was fully understandable in the context of her Amazonian background, which was more emphasized than usual. She kicked off her shoes with relief at the beginning of the garden scene (2.2) and put them on with reluctance in 4.2 when told to go meet her suitors.

The director intelligently gave Palamon a brief snatch of song at his first appearance to explain why the Jailer's Daughter later refers to his singing, and the young woman (who is never named) echoed it later, when she had gone mad for love of him. In this notoriously show-stealing role, which includes three consecutive soliloquies, Kate Fleetwood played to the whole house effectively but was admirably disciplined in avoiding the temptation to exploit her relationship with the audience. The fact that her madness made her so miserable gave her as much in common with Hamlet as with Ophelia and kept the part from becoming an occasion for cheap laughs about sex-starved women. Paul Chahidi, playing the wooer who impersonates Palamon out of a desperate desire to cure the Daughter's madness, said in a post-performance talk that the actors themselves had had no idea how the audience would take the play and were surprised at how many laughs they got. The basic question about all Fletcherian drama—"Just how funny is it supposed to be?"—is still being answered in different ways by different directors. This production was probably the most completely satisfactory that I have seen, though admittedly some of its success was the result of knowing what to cut. Despite its simplicity, it achieved some fine effects, as when the fragile beauty of the solo voice in the opening wedding song was followed by a chorus, placed all round the second gallery, scattering paper petals over the wedding party as it entered through the yard. This procession was appropriately mirrored in Arcite's funeral procession at the end, which took all the characters out of the yard; the Jailer's Daughter and her Wooer brought up the rear, garlanded for their wedding but sufficiently serious and perturbed to leave open the question of her recovery.

THEMES

Charles H. Frey (essay date 1989)

SOURCE: Frey, Charles H. "Collaborating with Shakespeare: After the Final Play." In *Shakespeare, Fletcher and The Two Noble Kinsmen*, edited by Charles H. Frey, pp. 31-44. Columbia: University of Missouri Press, 1989.

[*In the following essay, Frey examines the issue of collaboration in* The Two Noble Kinsmen, *arguing that the play exhibits a strategy designed to deflect the audience's attention away from the nature of the authors' collaboration (with each other and/or with their source material) in order to direct attention to the more important collaboration between the producers of the play and the audience.*]

Collaborate has two main meanings for us: (1) to work with another on a project to be jointly accredited; and (2) to cooperate with the enemy. If Shakespeare collaborated in the writing of *The Two Noble Kinsmen* (as the title page of the Quarto tells us he did), then to what degree should the project be "jointly accredited"? "Hardly at all" has been the main modern response to this question, for most of the scholarly energy, if not total human energy, devoted to this play has been concerned with separating out the respective contributions of the collaborators. This very effort *not* to "jointly accredit" suggests that the coauthors are in some crucial way dissimilar. The presumed col-

laborator of Shakespeare's is often described as a wretched contriver of vastly inferior verse and drama. As a typical commentator in the nineteenth century put it: "In *The Two Noble Kinsmen*, the degradation of Shakspere's work by the unclean underplot of Fletcher is painful, and almost intolerable."[1] Such description renders Fletcher tantamount to Shakespeare's enemy. Shakespeare, at least, is often treated as if he risked severely tainting his own labor by joining it to another's.

It is amusing that the precise seams between Shakespeare's work and that of his presumed collaborator are often unrecognizable in the sense that, after more than a century of effort, scholars still cannot agree as to which author or authors wrote which parts of *The Two Noble Kinsmen*. Some say Shakespeare wrote all of it; some say he wrote none of it; many divide the play between Shakespeare and Fletcher, but few agree as to the precise division. And whether the two presumed authors would have kept their fingers or suggestions out of each other's scenes may be doubted. Still, the conviction that any collaboration by Shakespeare must in part bear the opprobrious taint of collaborating with the enemy, or at least with an undesirable, remains widespread.

But if we think of Shakespeare as collaborating only to his and our detriment, because we think that whoever he collaborated with necessarily compromised the purity of his unique genius, then do we also assume by probable implication that other persons in Shakespeare's working environment—actors in his company who limited his conception and, possibly, persuaded revision of parts; audiences whose comprehension and taste limited Shakespeare's otherwise infinite range; colleagues or source authors or court authorities whose ideas were cruder than the Bard's yet still influenced him—do we assume that such persons were also alien to or restrictive upon Shakespeare's otherwise unhampered expression of genius? Was Shakespeare, a free spirit capable of moving beyond the collaborations of tradition and ideology, forced nonetheless or even quite willing perhaps to collaborate with the enemy of limitation by coauthority? Or might such colabor, on the contrary, often have rendered "Shakespeare's" contribution less page-bound, more active, accessible, and public? less high-and-mighty in diction and skepticism, more body-voiced, and more emotionally real and grounded than possible from a silent authorial text? Any playwright of other than closet drama *chooses* to be a collaborator (even a closet dramatist collaborates with the audience he imagines), and if Shakespeare chose to collaborate not only with scribes, copyists, actors, other shareowners, varied audience cliques, and so on, but also with a specific or several specific coauthors, who are we to single out the coauthor or authors for special opprobrium and for separatist treatment? Do we know no other ways to give power, coherence, allegiance, credit to a work product than to trace it to an individuating source?

In the case of other kinds of work products, surely, we do jointly credit our labor. Indeed, probably most human labor is jointly credited in significant ways. We look at a road, a car, a building, at most of the things we use, and we jointly credit their makers. We look at each other or at ourselves and jointly credit pairs of parents for our being. Only in certain, specialized classes of labor can we retain any, if often a false, sense of authorship. The word *collaborate* derives from the Latin verb *laborare,* to labor, and this word seems to connect not only with ancient imagery of grasping but also with a whole host of loosely related terms derived from an "l-e-b" stem, terms that suggest a rhythm of grasping and letting go, terms like *lap, lip, labial, lapse, lobe, slump, slab, slip,* and *sleep. Labor* in many associations seems to connect to actions influenced by gravity or other forces beyond personal control or will—as in the labor of love and labor of birth where the sense of individually willed effort fuses with the mandates of extrapersonal forces. Birth labor is straining work and at the same time a gift of nature whereby one mother is made two (or more) persons and two parents are made three (or more) persons. Still, despite the colabors of love and birth and their joint accreditings, we beholders of birth take up attribution study the moment the child issues. We say the new child, or work of art, has one parent's eyes, or another's nose, or voice. By analogy, then, a collaborative literary work may be considered, in our culture, connected in each part to a single authorial parent.

The Prologue to *The Two Noble Kinsmen* works with several images of colabor, including that of the play itself as child of various breeders. Before such an image is reached, however, the play is compared not to the child but to, of all things, the maidenhead of the child's mother:

> New plays and maidenheads are near akin—
> Much follow'd both, for both much money gi'n,
> If they stand sound and well. . . .
>
> (Pro. 1-3)

The potential mother's maidenhead—both her virginity and, more literally, her hymen—is valuable if it stands sound and well, if under the stress of "first night's stir" (Pro. 6) it really stands up to the push of breeding and thus constitutes proof of virginity, because then any child that results from the "stir" should have a known paternity. That is, new plays are like hymens in a patriarchy: men may be assumed to value them when they give proof of authorship. The very first lines of the play, then, raise a question of collaboration: how can one know whether the issue held forth by paired collaborators really is the product of each? This question could, of course, apply to declared coauthors of a play, such as Shakespeare and Fletcher, but here it applies in the first instance to a different pair of collaborators: the "new play" itself as wife and the audience as husband who seeks proof of authenticity in the play.

Now, "much money" is given, I assume, not to the play itself or, in terms of the metaphor, to the virginal wife, but rather to the one(s) who present and guarantee the play or maid to the husband. And that underlying or covert as-

sumption naturally directs attention, in the patriarchal economy of the metaphor, to the status of the "breeder" (Pro. 10) of the play/maid. Would the breeder(s) be likely to have produced honest, modest, chaste offspring? What is the status of the breeder?

As if this last question had been raised explicitly, the Prologue immediately identifies not the playwright(s) but an ancestor, Chaucer, as the pure and noble "breeder" (Pro. 10) of the play that now is both "like her" (the virgin) and also "our play." As the new play evolves, in the Prologue from "maidenhead" to "her" to "our play" with Chaucer as its breeder, the implicit image widens from the audience as husband giving "much money" for the new, virginal play toward Chaucer as breeding "it" (Pro. 10) and then to Chaucer as giving not the play but rather the "story" that itself lives, like a chaste wife, "constant to eternity" (Pro. 14). Just where the playwright(s) may fit into this procreative tangle remains mysterious, however, for, insofar as the playwright(s) may be identified with the father who takes "much money" for being able to provide a virgin daughter, the playwright(s) may seem quite the patriarchs, but, insofar as the playwright(s) may be identified with the play itself, "our play," or with the "story" as "constant to all eternity," then to that extent the playwright(s) would seem feminized to the special maternal source and sole knower(s) of legitimacy. As the Prologue proceeds, this feminized role for the playwright(s) seems to be the one that is developed:

> If we let fall the nobleness of this,
> And the first sound this child hear be a hiss,
> How it will shake the bones of that good man. . . .
>
> (Pro. 15-17)

Now the play is a "child" whom the "writer" (Pro. 19) or writers must protect from bastardizing hisses by refusing to "let fall" the nobleness of "this" (breeder? story? child? retelling?). It sounds as if the writer(s) may control the nobleness of the play in some way analogous to the way in which the maid controls the "honor" of the first night.

An alternative reading of the Prologue could place the writer(s) of this new play as male(s) sub-breeding the play from the "constant" female story sired by Chaucer. This seems the direction taken by the continuing Prologue:

> For, to say truth, it were an endless thing
> And too ambitious, to aspire to him,
> Weak as we are, and almost breathless swim
> In this deep water.
>
> (Pro. 22-25)

This sounds like male emulation of a progenitor. The focus has shifted from inquiring whether the new play, as maiden, catches up the nobility and purity of her ancestor, Chaucer, to inquiring whether "we"—writer(s) and, perhaps, actors—may gain some strength to compete with Chaucer.

Such strength is to be gained here not from coauthorial collaboration but rather from collaboration with the audience. Whereas at first the audience was invited to judge the quality of the play by the purity and nobility of its authorship, now the audience is invited to participate in providing "breath" or inspiration:

> Do but you hold out
> Your helping hands, and we shall tack about
> And something do to save us. . . .

(Pro. 25-27)

One could summarize the argument of the Prologue thus: "You in the audience would like to know for certain the paternity of a new play such as ours, wouldn't you? Well, it does have a particularly famous and noble ancestor, and it would be a shame if his nobility were somehow compromised in our retelling. But, really, we can't emulate him exactly, so you'd better decide you will help by applauding and appreciating what you get here. Let Chaucer sleep, and you be content."

I am arguing, obviously, that the Prologue to *The Two Noble Kinsmen* anticipates, indirectly, the major critical debate on the play, namely, the debate over the nobility of its authorship. While later generations of readers have pondered the relative merits of two possible coauthors, the Prologue sets up a rivalry between two generational levels of authorship—Jacobean and medieval—and then submerges that rivalry through an extended plea for a supervening collaboration, that between the immediate producers of the play and the watching throng. This argument, that the basic strategy of the Prologue is to deflect attention and inquiry from one pair of collaborators to other pairs (and specifically from authorial collaboration to responsive collaboration), informs the more extended argument of my essay: that a dominant internal strategy of the play is to deflect our attention from the "right" collaborative couple to a "wrong" one and that a potentially useful external strategy for our treating the play is to deflect attention from the "right" collaborative couple, the presumed coauthors and their relative merits, to the "wrong" collaborative pair, modern productions of the play (including texts, performances, teachings, and criticism) and their varied audiences.

The play opens with the wedding celebration of Theseus and Hippolyta, whom Theseus has conquered and who now collaborates with her former enemy. The first character we actually see is Hymen, god of marriage but also god of the "maidenhead" proposed first for examination by the Prologue. At issue, then, is issue: whether the "firstborn child" (1.1.7) and "Nature's children sweet" (1.1.13) will bless the royal couple and be free from "the sland'rous cuckoo" (1.1.19).

Somewhat as inquiry into the relations of the new play and its "husband" shifted to inquiry into the status of a third party, the bride's breeder, so now attention on ritually banishing any taint from the royal coupling shifts to Theseus's "gentility" (1.1.25), to Hippolyta's "mother's sake" and Hippolyta's wish that her "womb may thrive

with fair ones" (1.1.27), and on to a third focus (or couple), Emilia and "the love of him whom Jove hath mark'd / The honor of your bed, and for the sake / Of clear virginity" (1.1.29-31). In equational terms, the Prologue's "husband" is to Theseus as the new play is to Hippolyta, and as attention is deflected in the Prologue from the maidlike new play to its noble breeder and then onward from purity of authorial collaboration to collaboration of a third party (the audience), so here in the opening scene attention is deflected from Hippolyta to her "mother's sake" and then onward from the royal progenitive pair to a distinctly "third" relation, the bride's *sister* and her as yet unknown husband, a relation that turns out to be the true focus of interest.

As, in the Prologue, the test of "goodness" for the play/ maid turned from her physical virginity to the nobility of her paternal breeding, so in the opening scene attention turns from the panoply of physically present signs—Hymen, the wheaten garlands, white robes, and so on (all suggesting virginity)—to the wider context of noble breeding. Purely physical virginity may help the husband to feel assured of his paternity, but beyond that assurance lies the desire to be assured of gentle or noble offspring. In the Prologue, that desire evolved into a registry of the play/ maid's male ancestral line; in the opening scene, that desire evolves, via the Theban Queens, somewhat more comprehensively into mention both of Theseus's "gentility" (1.1.25) and of Hippolyta's "mother's sake" (1.1.26). According to the Queens, if Theseus would demonstrate the nobility of his breeding ("gentility" as "extraction" as in Orlando's usage in the opening scene of *As You Like It*), then he must heed the Queens' demands for help. If Hippolyta would give sign to the world that her mother bore noble offspring and if Hippolyta would hope herself to do so, then she must heed the Queens' demands. Gentility and nobility are not just secrets in the blood, for they are made manifest only through behavior, action. As Duke Vincentio says in *Measure for Measure*: "if our virtues / Did not go forth of us, 'twere all alike / As if we had them not" (1.1.33-35). There must be some outward and visible sign of the inward condition, a sign signaling beyond physical beauty toward a volitional virtue.

To recapitulate my argument thus far: (1) attention to *The Two Noble Kinsmen* has centered on the issue of collaboration and, more specifically, the question of to what extent Shakespeare's authorship may be in evidence; (2) the play's Prologue almost anticipates that question when the Prologue interrogates the ancestry, authorship, and breeding of the piece in terms showing how naturally we tend to test aesthetic or artistic merit by our conception not merely of immediate purity or virginity of the piece itself but also of its patriarchal blood-lines (if Chaucer made it, it must be good); (3) intermediary breeders between the noble grandauthor (Chaucer) and the present incarnation or child can prevent the nobleness from "falling," prevent it not by themselves aspiring to claim authorial or genetic nobility but rather by soliciting the enthusiasm of the contemporary audience and letting the child play to that;

(4) the play's opening scene sets up a similar dynamic in that the initial focus on Hippolyta's maidenhead or hymen as guarantor of noble progeny widens into a focus on her and her husband's nobility of ancestry and then into a focus on the deeds that must be done to give outward signs of the inward nobility.

One of the things this argument may have obscured is the imprecision of analogies between artistic collaborations and procreative couplings. Theseus and Hippolyta are man and woman, capable of engendering offspring (though Hippolyta as an Amazon would catch up attributes of the male gender). By verbal sleight of hand, the Prologue inserts differential sexuality into the authorship of the play: first the new play is likened to a maid whose husband seems to be the audience following and giving money; then the new play turns into the offspring of Chaucer. The missing term becomes the play's mother. Implicitly, the playwright(s) would occupy that position if the metaphor of human sexual procreation were to remain in mind. Sexual difference thins out, however, from the Prologue as he proceeds to convert the playwright(s) to the masculinized force that could blast Chaucer's bays (Pro. 20) and to the male writer(s) who could "aspire to him" (Pro. 23). The audience, moreover, asked to help the play-producing swimmers or sailors (again plainly men), would also seem to be imagined as men in a male environment. Compare the Epilogue's final words: "Gentlemen, good night" (Epi. 18).

The shocking, even brutal, invocation of the hymenal site as source and test of siring standards becomes subordinated first to a consideration of patriarchal bloodlines or gentility and then to an almost parthenogenetic vision of men—Chaucer and the writer(s)—seeking to create what is worthy through their own actions and presenting it to other men. This movement away from what might be called heterosexual anxiety toward what might be termed homosocial hoping is a movement of the main action of the play where the initial view of Hymen and the bride and groom seems to slip out of focus as attention turns to Emilia and Flavina and then to Palamon and Arcite and the bonds of their brotherhood.

The essential collaboration for the extension of the human race is between men and women, as is evident in the opening images of both Prologue and play. The image of the two different sexes collaborating equally in essential creation may underlie much of our cultural imagery of colabor—as when the Prologue first posits a two-gendered origin for the play or when critics such as Dowden distinctly feminize the "beauty" of "the young Fletcher in conjunction with whom Shakspere worked upon *The Two Noble Kinsmen*."[2] Thus searching for the Shakespearean portion of the play is also searching for the man's (or "real man's") part.

Apart from making babies, however, much of the most revered colabor in Shakespeare's society (if not also our own) took place among same-sex groups, and the colabor or action that was deemed ennobling as the proof of high blood was, in that patriarchal context, the colabor of men in the church, in legal institutions, or in battle. Thus, to prove his "gentility," Theseus (who has already "shrunk" the Amazon Hippolyta back into the woman's bound she was overflowing [1.1.83]) will take his army of men to attack Thebes. Emilia, furthermore, declares that she will never "take a husband" (1.1.205) unless Theseus takes the petitioned action, as if the war against Thebes were an act emblematic (or even productive) of man's progenitive honor, an act allowing Emilia to choose a worthy mate. Palamon and Arcite, similarly, mull over causative connections between male actions—infamous or heroic—and their impact on male blood. The Theban tyrant Creon is one, says Palamon, who subsumes the heroism of others into his own bodily substance, "who only attributes / The faculties of other instruments / To his own nerves and act" (1.2.67-69). Arcite would have the pair leave the court:

> for our milk
> Will relish of the pasture, and we must
> Be vile, or disobedient—not his kinsmen
> In blood unless in quality.
>
> (1.2.76-79)

Here is made explicit not only the notion that male heroic action directly influences nobility of blood but also the notion that male blood catches up the essential defining power for the quality of offspring. Palamon and Arcite are like two mother cows concerned for their calves and fearful that their environment will taint their "milk," which controls the worth of their physical and spiritual inheritance and bequest.

Both the Prologue and the developing play (as well as traditional criticism of the play) are founded on the grossly patriarchal paradox that the qualities of biological (and artistic) offspring are to be judged, ultimately, not on their own merits or on the apparent merit (virginal status) of any mother but only on the noble breeding of the male ancestors of both mother and father. Such breeding is proved, however, not simply through blood relationships but rather through heroic (martial) male action that ennobles the hero's "milk," that purges and purifies the hero's "blood" (1.2.72, 109). The quest for being, for knowing who the ancestors are, turns to a quest for doing, for knowing what the ancestors (male) have done to qualify themselves as noble, so that the outcome of all heterosexual collaboration can be judged, finally, only on the basis of prior homosocial collaboration in heroic (all-male) action.

It is true that *The Two Noble Kinsmen* presents in its first scene a brief and tantalizing glimpse of noble worth and purity of breeding established not through all-male action but through heroic struggle directly with the female (the Amazon), but this possibility is elided, as it were, through the recycling of Theseus, to prove his "gentility," into battle with a male antagonist. Still, does not the glimpse toward the society of the "most dreaded Amazonian" (1.1.77) constitute a quicksilver admission or presupposition for the play that women may relish their own society, just as men may relish theirs, and that the business of breeding could be reframed as a subordinate kind of collaboration in life? Hippolyta comes to Theseus not alone but paired with a sister—as if Amazonian society were not quite atomized—and not just with a sister, but with a sister who (unlike the standard marriage-eager sister of much comedy) prefers members of her own sex, declaring "the true love 'tween maid and maid may be / More than in sex dividual" (1.3.81-82).

Further subverting the centrality of cross-gendered collaboration is the friendship or doubling between Theseus and Pirithous. If this were a standard romance, the bride's sister, Emilia, would fall in love with and marry the groom's best friend, Pirithous. But here the main collaborative energy of each is distinctly same-gendered. The "knot of love" between Theseus and Pirithous "may be outworn, never undone" (1.3.41). "Love"—among these Greeks, if not elsewhere—centers itself ambiguously among cross-gendered and same-gendered pairs. The hymenal imperative, the command to breed bravely, seems to motivate the main physical action, but the emotional and spiritual centers of love seem to slip between same-gendered pairs.

How to reconcile the patriarchal dictate for a colabor of man and woman toward noble offspring with the supervening demands of same-sex friendships becomes a central problem of the play as it fusses over the meaning of the love between its titular heroes. Though they are true cousins, the sons of sisters, Palamon and Arcite are first presented as "dearer in love than blood" (1.2.1). The twinning of their souls makes them almost one and leads to strange locutions of oneness. Arcite says to Palamon in prison: "The sweet embraces of *a* loving wife . . . shall never clasp *our* necks" (2.2.30-32); "Were we at liberty, / A wife might part us lawfully" (2.2.88-89): "We are one another's wif*e*, ever begetting / New births of love" (2.2.80-81).

After Palamon spies Emilia and falls for her, Arcite exclaims: "am not I / Part of your blood, part of your soul? You have told me / That I was Palamon, and you were Arcite." Palamon answers, "Yes." And Arcite continues:

> Am not I liable to those affections,
> Those joys, griefs, angers, fears, my friend shall
>   suffer?

PAL.

> Ye may be.

ARC.

>   Why then would ye deal so cunningly,
> So strangely, so unlike a noble kinsman,
> To love alone?

>   (2.2.186-91)

Arcite's question, out of context, sounds funny, perhaps, but the play seems seriously to be asking: If two males think of themselves almost as identical twins and also as soul mates, then will they not share an identity of desire? Just before seeing Emilia, Palamon says to Arcite: "Is there record of any two that lov'd / Better than we do, Arcite?" Arcite replies:

>   Sure there cannot.

PAL.

> I do not think it possible our friendship
> Should ever leave us.

ARC.

>   Till our deaths it cannot,
>   *Enter* Emilia *and her* Woman [*below*].
> And after death our spirits shall be led
> To those that love eternally. Speak on, sir.

[EMIL.]

> This garden has a world of pleasures in't.
> What flow'r is this?

WOMAN.

>   'Tis call'd narcissus, madam.

EMIL.

> That was a fair boy certain, but a fool
> To love himself.

>   (2.2.112-21)

The inward-looking love of Palamon and Arcite for each other may be a kind of narcissus-like self-love. Just as Palamon raises the issue of whether anything could part their friendship, Emilia enters the garden of time and its worldly pleasures. Arcite continues to affirm a spiritual love between himself and Palamon that will join them in an eternal company. But Palamon has launched his desire now into the garden. When Arcite follows him there, "falling" also in love with Emilia, Arcite quite seriously seems to imagine an equality of love capable of being shared by the two kinsmen, at least for a moment. Since Palamon is made to assume an exclusivity in love the question is soon dropped whether three persons could ever share in an identity, a singleness, of love.

Arcite for an instant hints, however, at a way that both he and Palamon could share a love for Emilia. He says to Palamon: "I will not [love her] as you do—to worship her / As she is heavenly and a blessed goddess; / I love her as a woman, to enjoy her. / So both may love" (2.2.162-65). But Palamon does not really love so spiritually. He insists that he has taken "possession" of all Emilia's beauties. And of course the kinsmen imagine heterosexual love in the context of wives and issue. When Arcite pictures neither of the two kinsmen having a wife, he laments, and perhaps laments primarily, that then, as he says, shall "no issue know us" (2.2.32). Still, Palamon and Arcite could conceivably collaborate in a love for Emilia, in a ménage à trois that produced issue. She herself makes no persistent distinction between them and cannot choose one over the other "but must cry for both" (4.2.54). What makes such a solution repellent, finally, is the anticollaborative convention of paternity that is assumed on all sides. When Arcite in prison laments the prospect of having no wife and no issue, he describes such issue as "figures of ourselves" (2.2.33), sons who could remember what their fathers were (2.2.36). As images of particular selves, garnered in necessity from only one man's sperm, children cannot have collaborative biological fathers. Yet any number of collaborative parenting arrangements could be imagined. Arcite's concern for identifiable paternity is at base an economic convention of ownership; he wants to be able to say (even though he never can be sure) what issue he can assume belong to him as extensions of his physical being. Thus, when the Prologue of *The Two Noble Kinsmen* speaks of the play as a child with Chaucer as breeder and the author(s) implicated in the breeding process, it invokes and we pursue our deep assumptions about impossibilities of collaborative fatherhood in one sense and improprieties of it in another. That a play is not literally a child, that any spermatic analogies between artworks and children are extremely questionable, and that possible collaboration on a play may indeed challenge our assumptions about the nature of fatherhood, breeding, and authorship seem to be issues that the Prologue taken together with the action of the play invites us to consider.

It so happens that another triangle of lovers in the play comments on the colabors of Palamon and Arcite over Emilia as well as on the possible colabors of producers of this play. The Jailer's Daughter loves Palamon, and she in turn is loved by the character known only as her Wooer. Palamon does not, so far as we know, return her love. The heavy middle of the play is dominated by the very physical passion of the Jailer's Daughter, who longs to lose her maidenhead only by Palamon: "Let him do / What he will with me, so he use me kindly, / For use me so he shall, or I'll proclaim him, / And to his face, no man" (2.6.28-31). In her madness, her talk becomes increasingly bawdy: "I must lose my maidenhead by cocklight" (4.1.112); "I'll warrant ye he had not so few last night / As twenty to dispatch. He'll tickle't up / In two hours, if his hand be in" (4.1.137-39); "now direct your course to th' wood, where Palamon / Lies longing for me. For the tackling / Let me alone" (4.1.144-46). Insofar as the Jailer's Daughter fails to retain, in the terms of the Prologue, much maidenly modesty, she seems to become sexually initiated in the course of the play. When her Wooer substitutes himself for Palamon, and when the couple exits with the mad Daughter plainly intended to go to bed with the Wooer (on Doctor's orders), then we are presented with a strangely collaborative love triangle. The Wooer collaborates, acceptably to the Daughter, with her image of Palamon (as the Wooer's friends all collaborate in her projection). Whose child might she consider any issue to be? Palamon's? Her love gives and hence finds nobility where it wills? Nothing is good or bad but that her think-

ing, to adapt Hamlet's phrase, makes it strangely so? This is a version of marriage plus sex à trois.

Consider now a different analogy among the triangles. As the Jailer's Daughter yearns for Palamon, so Palamon yearns for Emilia. And as the Wooer steps in for Palamon, so might Arcite step in for Emilia. The notion of Arcite as Palamon's "wife" might seem farfetched were it not for Arcite's explicit mention in prison of them being one another's wife. Arcite, furthermore, though he prays to Mars and wins the fight with Palamon, is consistently imaged as feminine in his beauty. Emilia says of him: "His mother was a wondrous handsome woman, / His face, methinks, goes that way" (2.5.20-21). He has a "sweet face" (4.2.7); his brow is "arch'd like the great-eyed Juno's" (4.2.20); he is "gently visag'd" (5.2.41). Arcite, in praying to Mars, speaks, moreover, of winning a garland described as the "queen of flowers" (5.1.45). And Emilia specifically compares Arcite to Ganymede (4.2.15), Jove's page, who "set Jove afire" (4.2.16). Palamon, furthermore, brings to the final combat a group of helpers who are distinctly feminine in appearance. One has thick-curled yellow hair and the face of a "warlike maid" (4.2.106), pure red and white and with no beard. Another is white-haired with arms that gently swell "like women new conceiv'd, / Which speaks him prone to labor" (4.2.128-29). Is it not thus suggested that Palamon's friends resemble male brides? If he could not accept Arcite as collaborator in his love for Emilia, might he accept Arcite as himself an equivalent love? When Arcite dies, Palamon says to Emilia: "To buy you I have lost what's dearest to me" (5.3.112); Emilia thinks of herself as having cut from Palamon "A life more worthy . . . than all women" (5.3.143). And Palamon at the end laments that "we should things desire which do cost us / The loss of our desire!" (5.4.110-11).

A further analogy applies that lament to the probable collaboration of Shakespeare and Fletcher. We might think of ourselves as readers or viewers of the play in a position analogous both to that of the Jailer's Daughter longing for Palamon and to that of Palamon longing for Emilia. If we so strongly and singly desire only Shakespeare in the play and will accept no collaborators, then we may find ourselves desiring what costs us the loss of our desire. Our desire need not be primarily to identify our author and his intents. In some important way, all our origins are collaborative. Recognizing that fact, we are freed to make what we can and will out of our own state and being. As interpreters, if we search for intention or original meaning, we may resemble children questioning their paternity. If we concern ourselves less with an authority embedded in history or in tradition and more with what we now make of the little we can know of that authority and tradition, then we may accept, like the Jailer's Daughter, an object of our desires who may be counterfeit but who also responds to those desires with genuine reward.

One result of such thoughts is, I believe, a felt imperative to make real for oneself the play's emphasis on the emptiness of possessive desire. Desire to know authority, to have authority, to obtain power, is seen as laughably inane in *The Two Noble Kinsmen*. Theseus speaks of the gods "who from the mounted heavens / View us their mortal herd" (1.4.4) as if we were simply ridden and driven by overmastering and uncontrollable forces, and this despite the counterdrive of characters in the play to "master" their own affections and make them bend (1.1.229). The Jailer's Daughter decries "What pushes are we wenches driven to / When fifteen once has found us!" (2.4.6-7). Theseus speaks of Palamon and Arcite having "the agony of love about 'em" (3.6.219). And, in one of the greatest speeches in the play, the address of Palamon to Venus, Palamon refers to the lead-heavy yoke of love that stings like nettles (5.1.97) and to the way Love makes its chase this world "and we in herds thy game" (5.1.132). Though in this aspect the play seems bleak and sad, a moral it teaches is, I think, to question and resist, when possible and appropriate, the neediness of desire, the wanting to own, the promotion of self-interest over collaboration, and the desire for authority, all of which puts us in power struggles, rivalries, and other appetitive uses of our energy. At the end of the play, Theseus advises: "Let us be thankful / For that which is" (5.4.134-35). Such ungreedy emotional expenditure has not been prominent in the play save perhaps in Theseus's charity to the three Queens and in the mad largess of the Jailer's Daughter toward the captive Palamon. Still, the play seems to laud loving as giving, and I would use that notion to commend a similar relationship between us and Shakespeare.

Just as the Prologue turned from an inquiry into the noble breeding of the play toward a plea for collaborative help from the audience to authenticate the play's "content," so current readers and watchers of the play might usefully turn from inquiring mainly into the play's authorship toward collaborative creation of its contemporary significance. Instead of seeking, worshiping, or emulating Shakespeare's authority, why should we not instead give of ourselves to his plays in the spirit of accepting collaboration? When we read or watch silently, for example, do we behave primarily as consumers, taking it all in, voyeuristically, as if we were not really part of it, but only observing and soaking up the authority of the master author or of professional performers? I would encourage a wholly different stance toward the reading and seeing of Shakespeare, a stance of much more active colabor with Will.

One example of such collaboration would be voiced reading, particularly the sort of voiced reading that relishes the capacity of interjections, oaths, expletives, nonsense words, soundplay, meter, freely chosen tonalities, and all the paralinguistic features of Shakespearean speech to force our own collaborative creation of significance.[3] Another example of such collaboration would be to read aloud while standing or walking. Or if one ventured to try out or figure forth certain gestures, postures, or actions in the text, one could immeasurably increase one's sense of life there. In the words of the Prologue: "Do but you hold out / Your helping hands" and greater "content" shall follow.

In the field of English studies, we have barely begun to emulate the great collaborative shift from authorial inquiry to our own psychosomatic, helping-hands response so plainly mandated by the Prologue and perhaps also indicated as a megatrend by the many contemporary de-centerings of traditional sources of authority ("man," Western canonical tradition, God, nature, patriarchalism, and so on). Ironically, as readers we are much less inhibited from holding out our hands in the creation of significance than we are as spectators. Yet I would argue that, against the recognition of what might be created through genuine, living collaboration between spectators and actors, modern Shakespeare audiences tend to be much too observant of conventions relevant only to viewing TV, film, and representational theater where the audience pretends it isn't there. Elizabethan audiences wrote down lines in their table books, made faces and joked at the actors, cried out, wept loudly, laughed uproariously. Nuts were cracked, hands were clapped, apples were thrown, hisses were common, and, at the play's end, audiences would sometimes sing and dance.

Such carryings on might be thought terribly intrusive upon the actors' concentration and any sense of rapt communication with the throng. And there were, certainly, moments of utter silence and stillness. The Elizabethan actors did take a lot of abuse, but also they received from the audience an incredible tide of real, full, warm attention and energy. Each side, performers and spectators, opened itself to the other and collaborated in a vital way. It is hard for us to picture the difference between modern playing conditions and Shakespearean ones. As Bernard Beckerman has written:

> Today as much as possible the actor will try to maintain the illusion that he is facing a fellow actor and not facing the audience. The flat picture frame of our theater encourages this illusion. In the Elizabethan theater the actor had to turn out, that is, orient himself to the circumference of auditors, if he were to be seen at all. This condition reinforced the conventional or ceremonial manner in acting.

> By turning out, the actor emphasized the stage as a setting behind him rather than an environment around him. This was in accord with the demands of the plays. . . .

> On stage, he shared his experience directly with the audience. He was part of an elaborate pageant taking place in a far-off land against an opulent backdrop. Yet on an emotional level he communicated intimately and directly with the audience. In more or less unrestrained utterance he portrayed extremes of passion.[4]

Each side, in other words, presented itself to the other, through voice contact, movement, and interchange of energies. Today, if a modern Shakespeare audience would seek more than a tepid experience of mild, quiet Bardolatrous reverence, such an audience could hardly do better than to agree to seek maximum openness and mutual commitment to vulnerability with the acting troupe as expressed through direct eye contact, appropriate sound interchanges, and relaxed, small-scale gestural mimicries or incorporations of the actions performed. If we would explore the potential emotion in Shakespeare's plays, we must reappropriate their life and their significance in dynamic debate with cultural authorities of presumed authorship, scholarship, or stage professionalism. Shakespeare can live fully only in our eyes, our voices, our bodies and in the feelings stored and working there. Shakespeare inheres in the full, participatory collaboration between the page, the stage, and our capacities to give, to go forth from ourselves in forms of charity and good humor that are not only learned or socially constructed but also unlearned or deconstructed. Let Shakespeare collaborate and merge with his colaborers. Let us collaborate and colabor with Shakespeare. After the final play, what else is left?

Notes

1. Edward Dowden, *Shakspere: A Critical Study of His Mind and Art* (New York: Harper, 1881), 360.

2. Ibid., 379.

3. See Terence Hawkes, *That Shakespeherian Rag: Essays on a Critical Process* (London and New York: Methuen, 1986), 73-91.

4. *Shakespeare at the Globe: 1599-1608* (London: Macmillan, 1966), 129, 156.

Donald K. Hedrick (essay date 1989)

SOURCE: Hedrick, Donald K. "'Be Rough With Me': The Collaborative Arenas of *The Two Noble Kinsmen.*" In *Shakespeare, Fletcher and* The Two Noble Kinsmen, edited by Charles H. Frey, pp. 45-77. Columbia: University of Missouri Press, 1989.

[*In the following essay, Hedrick contends that* The Two Noble Kinsmen's *thematic exploration of the nature of artistic rivalry suggests that Shakespeare did not collaborate in the writing of the play. Hedrick focuses on the play's treatment of the subject of collaboration, and on the relationship between cooperation and competition explored in the play.*]

To the extent that necessity is socially dreamed, the dream becomes necessary.

—Guy Debord, *Society of the Spectacle*

I. COLLABORATION VERSUS AUTHORSHIP

In describing *The Two Noble Kinsmen,* one might well follow Pierre Macherey's prescription that a literary work be treated as "the product of a specific labor," thereby avoiding an account of artistic creativity that in humanist fashion "omits any account of production."[1] I want to provide such a description, however hindered by the formidable obstacle that the historically specific circumstances of the labor producing this work—usually assumed to be a collaboration of Shakespeare and Fletcher—are wholly lost, as are

for the most part the circumstances of collaboration between any Elizabethan playwrights. As indexes to such practices, we have but a few, scattered facts together with the plays themselves. *The Two Noble Kinsmen* may be our best theoretical index.

The account I want to provide is neither an attribution study nor a thorough "reading," but rather a selective analysis based on my interest in the audience strategies or rhetoric of Renaissance spectacle. By the "spectacular" I refer to the economy of visual practices constituted by the agency of all participants (including managers, actors, patrons, texts, artists, audiences, judges, administrators), practices whose end is in decision and judgment. These decisions take different forms, such as taste in artistic spectacle, "calls" in athletic spectacle, and consent in political and legal spectacle. The prizes respectively conferred on the spectators—genius, fanhood, and citizenship—may be as substantive as any of those for the performers.

I propose that this play represents the general practices and perhaps the immediate circumstances of its production. It may even be that it is designed for its historical audience, or at least part of the audience, to recognize these circumstances through the play "translucently,"[2] although such a possibility could hardly be confirmed from the chiefly "internal" evidence and interpretation I give. Along the way I will make several claims useful to a "reading" and to attribution study. Specifically, I claim that the play thematically explores the nature of artistic rivalry, in such a way as to suggest strongly that one of its collaborators was not, as is customarily thought, Shakespeare.[3] The former analysis is not dependent on this incidental claim, whose value depends on an unincluded analysis on new stylistic grounds—rejecting Shakespeare on the basis of speech act theory, by demonstrating that Fletcher's unidentified coauthor is wholly unskilled in the degree and kind of indirect, inferential, second-order speech acts characteristic of Shakespeare. These sorts of acts constitute the informal logic of natural conversation, where speakers reconstruct, reinterpret, and draw inferences from each other's words; where speech acts appear as other forms (assertions as questions, requests as assertions, and so on); and where conversational "maxims," such as the principle requiring one to be relevant to the topic at hand, are often violated for effect and meaning. (See Appendix for examples and discussion.)

Conversation is, not coincidentally, the consummate form of a collaborative practice that includes a competition or rivalry. As such, it too participates thematically in a play about a rivalry between friends. In addition to its reliance on speech act theory—introduced as a language model that vastly improves upon the models grounding earlier style study—the present analysis uses the feminist theory of "homosociability" in order to read systematically the play's representation of collaboration as a professionalist subtext, a reading that adds further weight to the case against Shakespeare as coauthor. Finally, another detachable section—a speculative "Coda"—advances the case by a circumstantial scenario based on the theme.

As a detective enterprise in collaborative work, attribution study typically locates discoverable stylistic differences resulting from two writers combining efforts to produce a spectacle. For *The Two Noble Kinsmen,* aside from the disputes about the names of the writers, there has been some consensus along these lines: (1) the play is written in two distinct styles, (2) one of the styles is more Shakespearean than the other, and (3) there is some rough parity in their quality.[4] I propose to recuperate the collective force of these views by seeing them not as the discoveries of scholars but rather as the special features of the spectating experience for the historical audience, including the writers themselves. The motivating question is this: What if such features of writing were meant to be seen? What if dual authorship does not merely *produce* the show, but *constitutes* the show? The scholarship on this question has provided important insights while evading their force— that the play presents its differences as spectacle. I propose that *The Two Noble Kinsmen* is less significant as a collaboration on spectacle than it is as a spectacle of collaboration.

Collaboration itself, I want to show, appears as a subject for scrutiny in the play. This obsessive topic corresponds, moreover, to the play's valorization of a certain nobility, whose representation is the chief addition to Chaucer and which is always accompanied by a radical anxiety concerning any collaborative production of meaning and value. That is, when *The Two Noble Kinsmen,* unlike *The Knight's Tale,* strives to idealize friendship and nobility, it reflects an anxiety about the way they are produced— specifically, in an artistic, competitive, and "homosocial" labor. This specific mode of labor is at the same time the mode of production of the two noble collaborators of *The Two Noble Kinsmen.* The play is their title match.

The rivalry of Palamon and Arcite for the hand of Emilia is, of course, the central action, shared by both Chaucer's tale and *The Two Noble Kinsmen.* The major thematic shift is signaled by the term *noble* in the play's title, since the rivals' nobility and magnanimity are continually studied, as if transposing the story's arms contest into a Renaissance magnanimity contest. Noble gestures, which are selfless and unnecessary, punctuate the entire story—from Theseus's willingness to interrupt his wedding at the pleas of the three widowed Queens for noble burials of their husbands, to Palamon and Arcite's decision to fight for their own kinsman Creon despite his moral inferiority, to the fraternity-style, charitable collection of the knights contributing to the madwoman's dowry. The most spectacularly magnanimous gesture is undoubtedly the scene of the two kinsmen arming each other for their combat, a scene vastly enlarged from the wordless event merely mentioned by Chaucer. Here again we see the play's added fascination with the dramatic ironies of honor between antagonists. What the play chiefly adds, then, is an exaggeration of the paradoxicality of the rivalry, fluctuating as

it does between reluctance, assertiveness, nostalgic goodwill, and hostility.

With this addition, the play raises the question of differences in nobility between the two without ever fully clarifying, fixing, or dramatizing those differences. (Hence the interpretive debate about their distinguishability.) For Chaucer the differences were more thematic, functioning more as instantiations of courtly love questions such as "Who loves truly? the one who loves his object as a human or the one who loves his object as a goddess?"; or, "Who is worse? the imprisoned one who sees his beloved, or the free one banished from his beloved?" For *The Two Noble Kinsmen,* we seem to be invited only to search for differences in noble style, as Emilia searches for them, as if constructing an indecisive though discriminating audience. Stressing the paradoxical rivalry, the play reduces the consequentiality of any differences. It does this not only by the trick ending in which the military victor dies while the loser wins the girl, as in Chaucer, but especially by its changes. Emilia's indecision, for instance, is as anguished as her preference is fickle. In the play's added subplot, moreover, the Jailer's Daughter does see difference between Palamon and Arcite, but the difference is inconsequential since in her madness she accepts the unnamed Wooer as the surrogate Palamon and is thus fooled into sleeping with him. In both plots there is an ultimate failure—through indecision or through madness—to establish differences. A female failure resolves male rivalry.

In its deliberate exaggeration of the themes of noble indifference, selection by destiny, and courtesy between rivals, the play approaches self-parody, an internal pressure best defined and completed by the play's reception in Jonson's contemporaneous *Bartholomew Fair.* Jonson's allusion signals the main direction of the change from Chaucer, in the rivalry between Winwife and Quarlous for the hand of Grace Wellborn. Interrupting their sword fight, Grace coolly describes both her Emilia-like indecision and its solution: she will also let fate decide, but in a literary way, having each of them write down ("conceive") a word, one of which the next random passerby is to mark. Quarlous picks his word "out of the *Arcadia,* then: 'Argulus,'" and Winwife "out of the play: 'Palamon'" (translating their competition into a competition between literary works). Their absurd hostility-cum-courtesy is a condensation of *The Two Noble Kinsmen.* The situation in which one helps the other produce one's own defeat—a chief paradox of *The Two Noble Kinsmen*—is the ground of Jonson's amusement at Grace's cheery mediation: "Because I will bind both your endeavors to work together, friendly and jointly, each to the other's fortune, and have myself fitted with some means to make him that is forsaken a part of amends."[5] This world is so noble that no one ever loses in it.

The reluctance of the rivalry, and the simultaneous heightening and dissolution of difference, corresponds to the play's elevation of nobility defined as a kind of collaboration among the noble.[6] To understand this "collaboration," however, it is useful to interrogate the term, its uses and associations. Current interest in the subject spans the arts and may be part of a general cultural project of overcoming a textual ideology linked to Romantic and modern notions of individual authorship and genius. Allied to such interests are recent, poststructuralist interrogations of authorship itself, including the "death" of the "author" and his replacement by textuality, or by an "author-effect" in which his identity is institutionally and ideologically constituted, his roles or practices dispersed.[7] Coincidentally, such theoretical claims correspond to recent shifts in Shakespeare studies, where author-centered meaning is reduced by comparison with the meanings produced by the institution itself. Shakespeare's art accordingly can be seen as more of a workshop product of the theatrical company and, bringing in the other side of the stage, as the collaborative product of interchange with the audience, a view growing out of Collingwood's aesthetics.[8] But all such shifts, I believe, demonstrate a premature mystification of collaboration, particularly insofar as, by stressing cooperation, they filter out an oppositional character to the term, one that is revived in the European association of *collaboration* with subversion or treason. In a word, we will soon require more of Jonson's critique of mystified collaboration, expressed in his parody of *The Two Noble Kinsmen.*

How broadly may the term be applied to Elizabethan drama? G. E. Bentley, on the subject of collaboration, concludes, "Every performance in the commercial theatres from 1590 to 1642 was itself essentially a collaboration; it was the joint accomplishment of dramatists, actors, musicians, costumers, prompters (who made alterations in the original manuscripts) and—at least in the later theatres—of managers."[9] Although this is a persuasive view, we need not stop at a consideration of practices exclusively "internal" to the theater companies. We might also include involvement by the nobility and royalty—positive as in commissioned performances and texts, negative as in censorship. This mixture of encouragement and control, cooperation and competition, had an unofficial form as well, if we can believe Dekker's mention of tavern "revels masters" whose criticism influenced playwriting and revision.[10] Indeed, the Elizabethan theater seems to have been as oppositional as it was cooperative. There was cutthroat competitiveness among rival companies at the very beginning of the institution, not to speak of the rivalries among actors, between men's and boys' companies, and between public and private theaters. Plays combated plays, in arenas where bears combated dogs, and fencers combated each other. We have not yet thoroughly explored the implications of a situation in which dramatic texts were themselves arenas for actors, in a setting where wagers were sometimes placed on competing actors, who may have supplemented their salaries by bets that they would outdo others in some role.[11]

The term *collaboration,* with its current positive associations, was not the term applied to the joint authorship of plays, nor did we have the term until two centuries later. Henslowe, recording payments to collaborators, doesn't call them that but simply registers their names with their full or installment payments during or after the composition.[12] Yet we have a recoverable technical term for "coworker" from Jonson himself. The term is *co-adjutor,* significantly used by him in the prologue to *Volpone,* where he demotes this and corollary terms in a boast that he wrote the play all by himself in only five weeks:

> From his owne hand, without a co-adiutor,
> Nouice, iourney-man, or tutor.[13]

As an index to the times, Jonson may be less representative because of his role as a self-classicizing playwright writing on the side of individual genius in a bookish theater.[14] But his remarks nevertheless carry general significance, even though it may be vain, as Bentley asserts, to speculate about procedures of collaboration from this list. The list presupposes, we might say, a range of possibilities rather than a standard method; more importantly, it signals a power differential and a potential rivalry between coworkers, proceeding from the more equitable to the more power-differentiated relationships. Bentley, in his discussion of what is known about Elizabethan collaboration, argues there must have been a standard procedure and that collaboration itself was the standard mode of authorship, on the grounds that as many as half of the plays were coauthored. But Bentley's claims evade the force of the brute evidence he furnishes—that if half of the plays were coauthored, half were not. What we can infer is not the existence of some procedural norm, but the existence of a system in which modes of production are themselves in competition for privilege. Authorship competing with collaboration was the Elizabethan theatrical situation thematized, as we shall see, in *The Two Noble Kinsmen.*

II. CONVERSATION AND CONTEST, OR HOW MEN DO THINGS WITH WORDS

Among all the productive modes of collective effort, perhaps the most common is the practice of conversation, that is, the joint production of utterances among at least two participants. One of the singular accomplishments of Shakespeare that has received little sustained attention among scholars is his ability to represent natural conversation naturally. Throughout the canon he is increasingly attentive to the informal logic, and indeed the collaborative nature, of ordinary talk, including its capacity for the anticollaborative or competitive construction of meaning (best exemplified by Hamlet, or by fools).[15] It is this informal logic with its attendant violations of conversational maxims, as indicated earlier, that led me to conclude that the non-Fletcherian portions of the play were quite un-Shakespearean—that speakers in these portions simply did not do to each others' words as much as Shakespeare can have his speakers do. (See my Appendix for more on this stylistic criterion to add to those such as vocabulary, image clusters, and metrics.)

Martin Turner as Theseus, Yolanda Velasquez as Hippolyta, Geraldine Alexander as Emilia, and Jonathan Oliver as Pirithous in the 2000 production of
The Two Noble Kinsmen *at Shakespeare's Globe.*

For the present purposes, it is sufficient to observe the general phenomenon that conversation is a mode of the production of meaning in which team cooperation and individual competitiveness are in a positive tension. This aspect of conversation enables it to participate significantly in the matrix of competitive-cooperative forces in the play. But the notion of conversation as a form of contest requires translation into a narrower context here: namely, in *The Two Noble Kinsmen* conversation is to be understood as masculine conversation in specifically masculine contexts. The reason for this will become clearer when the concept of conversation is linked to a thematic reading of the play in terms of "homosociability."

Competing readings of *The Two Noble Kinsmen* yield the customary themes of humanist literary studies. One such reading—that the play exemplifies the (late Shakespearean) theme of the passage from innocence to a joyless experience—is especially relevant to the present concerns.[16] The timeless theme of passage, however, here acquires a gendered form. A feminist version of this narrative paradigm is provided in Eve Kosofsky Sedgwick's concept of "male homosocial desire," by which she means all forms of male bonding, located within a standard cultural narrative of a

"male path through heterosexuality to homosocial satisfaction," a path that while compulsory in most cultures is nevertheless a "slippery and threatened one."[17] Mapping this cultural narrative onto the action of the play brings into relief the way in which the contest over Emilia later becomes a contest among all chivalric values. Since those are presumably male values, this path corresponds to Sedgwick's theory of "homosocial desire." Finally, I want to translate this "desire" into the terms of a specifically artistic desire.

More evident in *The Two Noble Kinsmen* than the theme of lost innocence is the play's pervasive representation of the male world of contests. Their frequency has been noticed by Paul Bertram, who thereby deduces thematic unity and the play's single authorship by Shakespeare.[18] (The argument is flawed in its assumption that a main theme could not be jointly achieved.) He notes, for example, that the wedding festivities and the war against Creon are "sports craving seriousness and skill." There are also the "games of honor" that Palamon and Arcite say they will miss, Arcite's wrestling at the May "pastimes," and Theseus's hunting expedition in the third act. Even the morris entertainment becomes a contest for exhibiting skill and prowess, with the schoolmaster Gerrold (who has difficulty when forced to collaborate with rustics) in something like Theseus's role in the final tournament. Other games and sports include the Wooer's fishing after being deserted by the Daughter, the couples' chase game of "barley-break" (known also as "last couple in hell"), and the Wooer's invitation to supper and cards. While noting the relation of such contests to the interest in heroic values, Bertram is finally content to generalize about the enduring significance of play in all human cultures.

What is lost by this generalization is the problematization of gender-specific play throughout *The Two Noble Kinsmen*, where the paradoxes of a self-defeating victory are foregrounded, simultaneously defining and threatening the male world of collaboration and contest.[19] Early in the play we observe this fascination with paradox, in Palamon's comments on the military veterans now begging in the streets of Thebes: "scars and bare weeds / The gain o' th' martialist, who did propound / To his bold ends honor and golden ingots, / Which though he won, he had not; and now flurted / By peace, for whom he fought" (1.2.15-19). And Emilia, lamenting the loss that wins her a husband, concludes the spectacle: "Is this winning?" (5.3.138). Palamon universalizes, "O cousin, / That we should things desire which do cost us / The loss of our desire!" (5.4.109-11). And Arcite makes the paradox an economic one: "Emily, / To buy you, I have lost what's dearest to me, / Save what is bought; and yet I purchase cheaply, / As I do rate your value" (5.3.111-14). Such paradoxes require, I believe, a more gender-specific consideration.

Working from an unswerving humanist essentialism,[20] Bertram simplifies the play's treatment of noble values. But he does so in an instructive way when observing the theme of "admiration-turning-to-emulation." We identify the theme in 1.3 when Emilia tells how she and her childhood friend imitated one another in everything. Its fullest treatment, however, is the dialogue between Palamon and Arcite in which, as they arm each other, they recall earlier encounters:

PAL.

Methinks this armor's very like that, Arcite,
Thou wor'st that day the three kings fell, but lighter.

ARC.

That was a very good one, and that day,
I well remember, you outdid me, cousin;
I never saw such valor. When you charg'd
Upon the left wing of the enemy,
I spurr'd hard to come up, and under me
I had a right good horse.

PAL.

You had indeed,
A bright bay, I remember.

ARC.

Yes. But all
Was vainly labor'd in me; you outwent me,
Nor could my wishes reach you. Yet a little
I did by imitation.

PAL.

More by virtue.
You are modest, cousin.

ARC.

When I saw you charge first,
Methought I heard a dreadful clap of thunder
Break from the troop.

(3.6.70-84)

To concentrate on a theme of emulation of the dialogue, however, is to risk losing sight of the deliberate way that the escalating compliments begin to perform the very rivalry bringing Palamon and Arcite to combat in the first place. As Arcite describes how Palamon "outwent" him in the arena of battle, both begin to transform their conversation into another arena, each outdoing the other by competitive memory and by the one-downsmanship of humility. What follows after the passage Bertram cites is therefore crucial, for Palamon appropriates Arcite's metaphor of thunder in order to say that Arcite was actually first in the charge, just as lightning comes before thunder:

PAL.

But still before that flew
The lightning of your valor. Stay a little;
Is not this piece too strait?

ARC.

No, no, 'tis well.

PAL.

I would have nothing hurt thee but my sword,
A bruise would be dishonor

ARC.

Now I am perfect.

PAL.

Stand off then.

(3.6.84-89)

In complimenting each other they disarm each other while arming each other, acting out an emulation bound up in principle with a rivalry both constructive and destructive. A speech about competition, in the homosocial recursive economy of language, itself becomes a competition. Not accidentally, the scene also figures as an aesthetics of military equipment, a discriminating evaluation of war materials by joint recollections of former armor and former horses. The conversation builds to its natural conclusion in action—a military fashion show of sorts, with Palamon admiring how well his assistance has adorned Arcite.

In recapturing the past, this dialogue echoes other reminiscences in the play, notably in 3.3 when Palamon, having just been released by the doting Jailer's Daughter, is eating the food Arcite brings to strengthen him for their fight. Jarring to critics because of its snickering, locker-room tone, the scene portrays Palamon and Arcite gossiping about former girlfriends, about getting wenches pregnant, and about "hunting" in the woods. Here they employ what socio-linguists term the "topping constraint" in competitive story chaining.[21] They license this competitive discourse with an initial agreement to police their conversation by having "no more of these vain parleys" over Emilia. And they agree to have "no mention of this woman" and to "argue that hereafter" (3.3.5ff.). But they cannot keep cooperation and competition apart. Their nostalgia immediately sours when the topic of Emilia comes up "naturally"—that is, as a result of the logic of competitive conversation. Once again they are at each other's throats with insults and threats as memories of conquest intrude on present cooperation.

An even more important instance of the collaboration/competition matrix is found in the scene in which the rivalry begins:

Pal.

    I saw her first.

                                    . . . . .

Arc.

    I saw her too.

                                            (2.2.160-61)

The issue of who went into battle first will repeat this issue of who saw Emilia first. In the logic of the spectacle, a competition is countered by an emulation, itself another competition. Chaucer's debate about which lover loves truly is emended into a seeing contest or spectacular competition. Thus, women produce not only *sight* but also *sighting,* or competitive male work. They are the agency through which the claims of *seeing first* and *seeing too* are pitted against one another, juxtaposing competition and collaboration.

Aggressive vision is also assigned to the Jailer's Daughter, who is quick to distinguish between the two prisoners in another spectacular moment: "No, sir, no, that's Palamon. Arcite is the lower of the twain; you may perceive a part of him. . . . It is a holiday to look on them. Lord, the diff'rence of men!" (2.1.49-54). Her unfeminine, unhesitant vision is reprimanded by her father, who tells her not to point at them because they would not do so to her. In contrast to Emilia, she is not reluctant to distinguish noble men in competitive and hierarchical terms. But that reluctance is, in Emilia, a positive force, a noble indecision. Indeed, the Jailer's Daughter's failure to be thus reluctant seems allied to her very madness. True nobility makes men difficult to distinguish. Emilia's indecisiveness honors the homosocial community of noble men; the other woman's decisiveness disrupts it. The latter imagines distinctions between Palamon and Arcite that aren't there, while failing to see those that are there between Palamon and the Wooer.

Because of its anxiety about collaborative speech and vision, the play intermittently must present a frictionless conversation, different from its idealization of a "rough" one. This style is by and large a female one, signaled at the outset by the resolutely cooperative entreaties of the three Queens. We also find it in the prison scene when, before the men see Emilia, they are collaborating together on a meditation, a resignation to a fate that will keep them not only from corruption but also from either "business" or a "wife [who] might part us lawfully," followed by a list of natural evils such as sickness (2.2.88ff.). Arcite compares women to "liberty and common conversation, / The poison of pure spirits" (2.2.74-75), insofar as both seek to mislead youth. Accordingly, he goes on to imagine the opposite of "common conversation," that is, a high-minded conversation of further collaborative meditations. This future talk is thought of as the product of an all-male generation:

Arc.

                            What worthy blessing
    Can be, but our imaginations
    May make it ours? And here being thus together,
    We are an endless mine to one another;
    We are one another's wife, ever begetting
    New births of love; we are father, friends, acquain-
        tance;
    We are, in one another, families;
    I am your heir and you are mine; this place
    Is our inheritance . . .

                                            (2.2.76-84)

Despite the imagery of this, we need not look for a homo-erotic or homosexual subtext, if we acknowledge the governing structure of "male homosocial desire." Arcite is daydreaming an idealized arena of labor that dissolves all other social structures but that lacks usual competitive forces. The vision is one of artistic collaboration between comparably talented coadjutors, a vision that is itself collaboratively produced as the two men work together on an acceptable metaphor for their present enclosure. (Arcite begins, "Let's think this prison holy sanctuary" [2.2.71].) But the entire play will move toward its proper enclosure— the field—as the true metaphor for male homosocial satisfaction and its "new births of love." The momentary vision of sanctuary, like other nostalgias for a pure cooperation, will not survive conversation.

In its representation of arenas for speech, vision, and love, *The Two Noble Kinsmen* inevitably focuses on *titles,* a theme that has been well demonstrated by Bertram. In its primary sense *title* signifies a victory, as in Palamon's prayer to Mars that he "be styl'd the lord o' th' day" (5.1.60). The adjunct sense of ownership is also included, as Palamon uses the term when he accuses Arcite of being as "false as thy title to" Emilia (2.2.172), and as Arcite uses the term, responding that his is "as just a title to her beauty" (2.2.180, ownership of spectacle). In a later scene he reasserts the claim of "good title" (3.1.112). One of the Knights will describe the shifts of "Fortune, whose title is as momentary / As to us death is certain" (5.4.17-18). Theseus will tell one of the Queens that to be mastered by the senses is to "lose our human title" (1.1.233) and will later tell Emilia that she must attend the final spectacle since she is "the price and garland / To crown the question's title" (5.3.16-17). Allowing Theseus's metaphor of herself as the "treasure" that "gives the service pay," she will nevertheless deny that she must be present at the homosocial arena: "Sir, pardon me, / The title of a kingdom may be tried / Out of itself" (5.3.32-34). Emilia is reluctant to be a spectator, fearing that she will influence the outcome of the contest if she herself becomes a spectacle for the two rivals as they fight. Hippolyta alludes to other "title" matches, lamenting that she would rather see a fight for a different prize: "They would show / Bravely about the titles of two kingdoms" (4.2.144-45). The metaphor of contested kingdoms echoes Arcite's description of the horses Emilia gave him as fitting to be "by a pair of kings back'd, in a field / That their crowns' titles tried" (3.1.21-22).

The title-seeking of the two "bold titlers" (5.3.83) is represented also at the important level of conversation and language, where we again find the struggle between collaboration and competition. Rivalry mixed with respect motivates, moreover, the exchanges of the two men when they select titles of address for one another. "Noble kinsmen," "sir," "cousin," and proper names alternate in their polite address in the arming scene, where the shifts between formal and informal address again signal their bond and their distance. Palamon even adopts an old, punning form of address to embody the dilemma: "Cozener Arcite" (3.1.44). Turning address itself into yet another contest, their final farewell before the tournament again turns magnanimously competitive:

Pal.

> You speak well.
> Before I turn, let me embrace thee, cousin.
> This I shall never do again.

Arc.

> One farewell.

Pal.

> Why, let it be so; farewell, coz.

Arc.

> Farewell, sir.
>
> (5.1.30-33)

But to win a title is, in the arena of the play, for the other to lose a title, a "paradox" emblematized in the tournament's un-Chaucerian rule that the loser shall die. Fame and the memory of name are contrasted to the forgetting of a name, as Arcite describes:

Arc.

> I am in labor
> To push your name, your ancient love, our kindred,
> Out of my memory, and i' th' self-same place
> To seat something I would confound.
>
> (5.1.25-28)

When they speak of who loses, the talk again acquires its competitive edge, where to praise the other requires one to debase oneself. Thus, in the arming scene Palamon first wishes an honorable place for whichever man is defeated, offering forgiveness in advance if he himself is killed:

Pal.

> If there be
> A place prepar'd for those that sleep in honor,
> I wish his weary soul that falls may win it.
>
> (3.6.98-100)

After a handshake, however, the conversational rivalry continues, as Arcite competes by announcing an even more spectacular resignation to fate: if he loses, he will accept from his opponent what would be a patently unjust title:

Arc.

> If I fall, curse me, and say I was a coward,
> For none but such dare die in these just trials.
> Once more farewell, my cousin.

Pal.

> Farewell, Arcite.
>
> (3.6.104-7)

The absurdity of such exchanges, with Palamon not reacting to this outrageous request, can be accounted for as a desperate artistic attempt, bordering on self-parody, to imagine a transcendent *Sprezzatura.*

Just as title and form of address are used as weapons in the collaborative-competitive arena, so are the speech acts of praise and blame. When Palamon and Arcite first meet after prison, the rapid shifts between flattery and insult may seem an impoverished psychological verisimilitude, but the intention seems to be to represent the paradox of productive rivalry. When Arcite generously offers to bring files to remove Palamon's shackles, to feed, clothe, and even perfume him until he's ready to fight to the death for Emilia, Palamon momentarily demands that the rivalry be conducted with *fitting* conversation, that is, with a hostility to match the forthcoming combat:

Pal.

> Most certain
> You love me not; be rough with me, and pour
> This oil out of your language. By this air,
> I could for each word give a cuff, my stomach
> Not reconcil'd by reason.
>
> (3.1.101-5)

Proceeding with invincible politeness, Arcite begs pardon that his language is not rough, using polite language to apologize for polite language. He explains that he does not even chide his own horse to spur him. Palamon has located language itself in the system of a homosocial labor aesthetic, as a rough "spur" to inspire an escalating greatness in both opponents. To request to be used roughly is the paradigmatic magnanimous gesture of this competitive-cooperative arena. The entire play dreams of a contradictory speech act—"[Please] be rough with me"—as the figure of ideal social relations, the social dream noted in the present essay's epigraph. This is what men do with words.

We see the female antithesis of this complex mode of speech when the deluded Jailer's Daughter goes off to sleep with the man she thinks is Palamon, requesting to him, "But you shall not hurt me," and replying to his assurance, "If you do, love, I'll cry" (5.2.111-12). The pacific mode of action and discourse, linked to women and to madness, is specifically devalued by its juxtaposition with the male dream.

Collaborative-turned-competitive discourse also dominates the prison scene, where the dialogue upon the sighting of Emilia shifts from iteration to one-upmanship:

ARC.

> She is wondrous fair.

PAL.

> She is all the beauty extant.

> (2.2.147)

As they have produced collaborative warfare, meditations, and viewings, so Palamon and Arcite here create collaborative judgment and value. Here, as elsewhere in the play, it is difficult to distinguish between the cousins, and their competitive descriptions increase the stakes in the rivalry at the same time they constitute the value of its object:

PAL.

> What think you of this beauty?

ARC.

> 'Tis a rare one.

PAL.

> Is't but a rare one?

ARC.

> Yes, a matchless beauty.

PAL.

> Might not a man well lose himself and love her?

ARC.

> I cannot tell what you have done; I have,
> Beshrew mine eyes for't! Now I feel my shackles.

PAL.

> You love her then?

ARC.

> Who would not?

> (2.2.153-58)

The tone of this scene is hard to grasp, probably because it is a version of the artificial conversation game known as the "vapors," or sustained contradiction or nonacceptance of whatever your partner says—the game that Jonson spoofs in the same play wherein he spoofs *The Two Noble Kinsmen*. At once imitative and adversarial, such collaborative labor proceeds almost tentatively, as if the production of value is too important to be assigned to a single member of the team. It may be that the love judgments of the men are undermined in the scene, as if neither would be in love if the other were not, but it seems rather that we are invited merely to admire their high masculine spirits. Indeed, this collaborative work seems more a sign of nobility than a deviation from it. Dependence on the other's judgment does not by itself seem to be the object of an implied critique, at least not in the parallel circumstance of Emilia's indecisiveness about the two men. Her indecision is another collaboration. Choice is not simply choice for her but choice in an arena, even when she is alone, soliloquizing over their two pictures in yet another spectacular contest. While she debates their looks—now preferring Arcite's sweeter face, now Palamon's more sober face—at one point she indicates that her choice is not merely influenced, but actually constituted, by the audience observing the choice. Significantly, the choice is gender specific, so that for the male audience she says she loves Arcite, the worshiper of Mars, and for the female audience she says she loves Palamon, the worshiper of Venus:

> For if my brother but even now had ask'd me
> Whether I lov'd, I had run mad for Arcite;
> Now if my sister—more for Palamon.
> Stand both together: now, come ask me, brother—
> Alas, I know not! Ask me now, sweet sister—
> I may go look! What a mere child is fancy,
> That having two fair gauds of equal sweetness,
> Cannot distinguish, but must cry for both!

> (4.2.47-54)

Emilia in her anxiety of choice focuses on the aspect of the arena that makes choice impossible—its bifurcated audience. To seek common values in such a situation is ultimately delusory. The spectacle is constituted by the spectator; the answer to a question depends on who is asking. Along with her own reluctance to be a spectator at the tournament, for fear of becoming a distraction, Emilia's representation of the power of the audience reflects the authors' similar ambivalence toward their audience—an ambivalence, it might be added, far more Jonsonian than Shakespearean, tending more toward hostility than toward generosity. In the audience's power, we learn from the Prologue and Epilogue, rests the play's victory, or its defeat.

III. Nurturing Competition: Beyond the Spectacular Arena

Having located a gender-specific thematization for *The Two Noble Kinsmen,* we might expect some direct correspondence of cooperation with the female, competition with the male. But this equation breaks down in the play's more complicated versions of spectating. Ultimately, the play presents not a gendered division of labor and identity but rather a purified labor and identity that, by balancing cooperation and competition, usurp the realm of the female, who accordingly disappears as the requisite audience constituting the male homosocial arena. The purified or idealized arena is always endangered by a non-idealized, specifically bifurcated audience for whom every performance will always carry a specifically bifurcated significance. Men and women, seeing two different shows in the same arena, place bets on different contestants. In such a spectacle, winning is always losing. The male appropriation of the two oppositional terms—emulation and competition, or oily and rough language—forms the spectacular dream of a nurturing competition, hence raiding the customary, envied social slot of the female. No wonder that Emilia is an anxious, unwilling audience. Reduced, or elevated, to being the contested "kingdom," she is included as a spectator only to be excluded as a judge or collaborator, not only "guiltless of election" but also denied the construction of value. Emilia leaves the arena to the men, letting "the event," which Arcite calls "that never-erring arbitrator" (1.2.114) and which is doubtless a male version of Fortune, decide.

The Two Noble Kinsmen is largely about differentiating and electing men by their qualities. This activity is carried out aside from the main plot in a rather odd extension of Chaucer's descriptions of the assistant knights at the final tournament. In this undramatic section of the play we hear lengthy descriptions of the men's features and clothing, from which we are apparently, as implied spectators, to judge manliness. Many of the details are drawn from Chaucer, but the features are distributed among three instead of two men, as if specific actors may have been intended. The descriptions involve such an exerted delicacy of distinction that judgment itself becomes a noble performance, a skill best exemplified in the ability to read paradox: "when he smiles / He shows a lover, when he frowns, a soldier" (4.2.135-36). The slightest shades of color are deployed in the judgment, demonstrating noble discrimination: "He's white-hair'd, / Not wanton white, but such a manly color / Next to an aborn" (4.2.123-25). The arena is significantly a male aesthetic one, a decadent patriarchal aesthetics.[22] We have observed that the indecision of Emilia acknowledges the community and variety of male virtues while at the same time stereotyping her feminine inconstancy. Still worse is the Jailer's Daughter, who, unintentionally inconstant, chooses too soon and gullibly accepts cheap substitutes. Failing at noble judgment, these women are inferior audiences.

The men, of course, differentiate themselves through combat, which is itself a mode of spectacle. When Theseus interrupts Palamon and Arcite's duel in the forest, he merely defers it; by ordering a tournament, he shifts the mode from private duel to public spectacle. (For the audience, however, it is the second combat that, because offstage, is "private.") The stakes are the same but mediated differently: the loser expects to lose life and title, but only in the private spectacle will he die by the other's hand, the destructiveness unmediated. In spectacular terms the viewing of a contest is itself a contest of viewing, reminding us of the rivals' obsession about who saw the beloved one first. Public spectacle is an arena of audience bifurcation constructed by the male value of priority, where rival viewing replaces rival combat. The issue for the two kinsmen is chiefly whether Palamon's seeing Emilia first counts as a victory, an idea rejected by Arcite with this military analogy:

Arc.

> Because another
> First sees the enemy, shall I stand still,
> And let mine honor down, and never charge?
>
> (2.2.193-95)

What is not at stake is whether the event counts as a contest. That is, no one asks if love is really like a contest or not. Maintaining the question within the terms of a contest, Arcite only muddles the issue by substituting military conventions, but he does so by devaluing spectating and by locating a mimetic component within a competition. In its spectacular economy, the enemy is exchanged for the loved one.

Fight in *The Two Noble Kinsmen* is invariably allied to sight, a conjunction we see in a repetition of phrases by different speakers anticipating the final tournament: the Messenger warns the Doctor that he may "lose the noblest sight / That ev'r was seen" (5.2.99-100), to which the Doctor promises, "I will not lose the fight" (5.2.103; some later editions emend this to "sight"). The following scene begins with Pirithous asking Emilia, "Will you lose this sight?" (5.3.1). Emilia's indecision figures as a self-contesting vision:

> . . . I
> Am guiltless of election. Of mine eyes
> Were I to lose one, they are equal precious,
> I could doom neither. . . .
>
> (5.1.153-56)

The idea of an internal visual contest rehearses the values of the homosocial arena, and accordingly the figure of her fear is reversed by Palamon when he expresses his absolute willingness to destroy the enemy, even if it were a part of himself: "weren't one eye / Against another, arm oppress'd by arm, / I would destroy th' offender, coz, I would, / Though parcel of myself" (5.1.21-24). The dream of the arena is thus repeated in and on the male body. The cultural narrative of an achieved homosocial satisfaction is accompanied by anxiety about the proliferation of arenas, which create competitive viewing, even within one subject.

The anxiety is relieved by a desire to reduce the internal violence of competitive viewing by reducing the event either to a private spectacle or to a public spectacle viewed by a unified, noble audience capable of drawing distinctions but for whom choice remains a rough, noble performance. The dream of homosocial performance requires a homogeneous audience. Appropriately, the Epilogue to the whole play is addressed only to the "gentlemen."

A version of the nostalgia for a single audience is found in the prison scene when Palamon, lamenting that they can't see Thebes, speaks of spectacle lost: never again to see "the hardy youths strive for the games of honor, / Hung with the painted favors of their ladies, / Like tall ships under sail" (2.2.10-12). Palamon collaboratively reminisces about a race, another of the play's numerous contests, in which he and Arcite outran their competitors as well as the audience of ladies:

> . . . then start amongst 'em
> And as an east wind leave 'em all behind us,
> Like lazy clouds, whilst Palamon and Arcite,
> Even in the wagging of a wanton leg,
> Outstripp'd the people's praises, won the garlands,
> Fre they have time to wish 'em ours.
>
> (2.2.12-17)

This vision reconciles collaboration and competition by turning a public race into a private one, unifying the spectators by erasing them. To erase the spectators is to erase the fact of Palamon and Arcite's own competition. Since we never hear which of the two won, their rivalry has been substituted by the rivalry with others. Rough with each other, they spur each other's victory beyond the others, and beyond the competitive judgments of the bifurcated spectators. Like Emilia, the audience is denied the power of observing winning. Especially noteworthy is the play's inclusion of a scene in which the dominant male homosocial vision is explicitly contrasted with the extramural, female alternative. I refer to Hippolyta and Emilia's commentary praising the friendship between Theseus and Pirithous, which, with differences, reminds the women of the childhood friendship between Emilia and a certain Flavina. Hippolyta pictures the men's friendship as a world of sport and labor, describing their having "cabin'd / In many as dangerous as poor a corner," "skiff'd / torrents," and fought together (1.3.35-40). She pictures their ideal male friendship as a self-supporting but self-contesting bondedness: "Their knot of love / Tied, weav'd, entangled," and not to be unwoven (1.3.41-42). Anticipating the imagery of the arming scene, Emilia compares the men's friendship to women's own: "Theirs has more ground, is more maturely season'd, / More buckled with strong judgment, and their needs / The one of th' other may be said to water / Their intertangled roots of love" (1.3.56-59).

In her extended description of her own friendship, Emilia emphasizes a different sort of collaboration, if it can be called collaboration. She pictures this female friendship as a mirror rather than a knot, emulation rather than self-contestation. In their innocent admiration, the two girls would imitate each other in specular spectatorship:

Emil.

> What she lik'd
> Was then of me approv'd, what not, condemn'd,
> No more arraignment. . . .
>
> (1.3.64-66)

Her idealized memory constitutes a homosocial aesthetics when she describes a flower she would put between her breasts, with Flavina longing to do just the same: she would "commit it / To the like innocent cradle, where phoenix-like / They died in perfume" (1.3.69-71). Cradled, these flowers are both children and works of art. Emilia and her friend would copy each other's fashions ("On my head no toy / But was her pattern"). And they would copy each other's music, both copied or "stolen" tunes ("Had mine ear / Stol'n some new air") as well as original ones ("or at adventure humm'd [one] / From musical coinage, why, it was a note / Whereon her spirits would sojourn (rather dwell on) / And sing it in her slumbers" [1.3.71-78]). The images of friendship are consistently those of artists working together.

Friendship, a given in Chaucer, is the subject under investigation by *The Two Noble Kinsmen* through juxtapositions with artistic labor, originality, and collaboration. Both female-female and male-male friendships are thus explicitly idealized and at the same time subjected to an implicit comparison or competition. The play adds a new love-debate to Chaucer by asking: "Which friendship is best?" Emilia, introducing this rivalry between friendships, suggests the priority of the female, claiming, "the true love 'tween maid and maid may be / More than in sex [dividual]" (1.3.81-82). Broadly speaking, a self-contesting but collaborative mode is pitted against a narrowly imitative one lacking priority or leader. The former will turn out to be the preferred mode, as we might expect when we hear Palamon declare that he will never imitate bad manners because he never stoops to any imitation whatsoever: "Either I am / The forehorse in the team, or I am none / That draw i' th' sequent trace" (1.2.58-60). Scorning the textual realm of the sequent trace, his speech diminishes in advance the mimetic values of female friendship, while the female mode of reproductive "sequent traces" is nevertheless given its due, however anxiously.

Fear of the imitativeness idealized in the Flavina-Emilia relationship takes a different form in another of the play's literalized artistic collaborations—the dance. When the Jailer's Daughter declares "I'll lead" (3.5.90) and presumably dances the Third Countryman (who replies "Do, do") offstage after her last line, her madness is gender defined, or gender violating. Her aggressive desire not to be a "sequent trace," allied to the hopeless madness of electing Palamon as her lover, signals an invasion of the homosocial arena that at the same time validates the male traits she appropriates. She is accordingly represented as a kind of mad artist, whose audience admires her mad pageants and especially her originality—as the Doctor exclaims, "How her brain coins!" (4.3.40). Her artistic assistant is the fantasy horse that she says can dance, read, and write (5.2.47ff.). This gift, which she believes Palamon has given her for releasing him from prison, is nicely contrasted to the pair of horses given by Emilia to Palamon and intended for use in military collaboration. But the Jailer's Daughter suffers spectacular indignities, ranging from sleeping with the mere image of Palamon to being herself an image appropriated for the performance of the rustics, who decide that she is just the right thing for a winning show:

3. COUN.

> If we can get her dance, we are made again.
> I warrant her, she'll do the rarest gambols.

1. COUN.

> A mad woman? We are made, boys!

>   (3.5.74-76)

Where the sequent trace or copy is not idealized as in the Flavina passage, it is denigrated and again linked to a version of artistic production. When the Doctor advises that the nameless Wooer pretend to be Palamon by adopting his title ("Take upon you, young sir her friend, the name of Palamon") and by singing the songs Palamon sings (4.3.75ff.), the imposture taints the very ideal of copy. That this imposture is connected to the realm of art, and even to inferior art, is more noticeable in a later scene when, at the Wooer's protest that he has no voice to sing like Palamon, the Doctor advises him to sing anyway: "That's all one, if ye make a noise" (5.2.16). In another example, Emilia, walking outside the prison just before the rivalry is initiated, speaks with her waiting woman about the flower Narcissus and its story of self-mimetic exclusion: "a fair boy certain, but a fool / To love himself. Were there not maids enough?" (2.2.120-21). Emilia asks the woman if she can "work such flowers in silk" for a "gown full of 'em" and admires their color (2.2.127). But to "take out" or copy in this way is, of course, a devalued female and schoolboy labor. It will figure as such in the brute sexual jesting of the countrymen, who prescribe a male folk remedy to cure another problem woman, a jealous wife, by handing her one's erect penis:

3. COUN.

>   Ay, do but put
> A fescue in her fist, and you shall see her
> Take a new lesson out, and be a good wench.

>   (2.3.33-35)

In this joke, female art is performed by means of male technology; that is, the woman is temporarily both armed and disarmed by the masculine instrument of copy.

Despite such superficially evenhanded evaluations of both male and female forms of homosocial friendship, *The Two Noble Kinsmen* works to "ground" or privilege male friendship and the collaborative arena in which spectating is purified of a female emulation, or emulation is purified of a female spectating. The purification takes the final form of nurturing competition. We are tempted to conclude from such a play that women are the objects of this male rivalry. And our conclusion would be supported by a literalized reading of Theseus, for example when he urges Emilia's attendance at the tournament, saying, "You are . . . the price and garland / To crown the question's title" (5.3.16-17). In spectacular rather than metaphorical terms, however, we see them not as valued objects but as empty circles enclosing value, like the numerous garlands, arenas, and other round enclosures of the play. By spectacular inversion, women stand for the dream of a purified male arena.

I have tried thus far to show the ways that collaboration and competition "intertangle": in speaking, in spectating, in being either performer or audience, in love and friendship. But in these examples of the paradoxes of a noble male rivalry, we have repeatedly encountered specifically artistic constructions of that rivalry. In other words, the category of artistic labor has swallowed up or included all other categories of practice, revealing the entire play as a study of the satisfactions achieved from a male labor that is specifically artistic. Moreover, the labors of *The Two Noble Kinsmen* are quite pointedly theatrical, spectating events so that the play is self-referential and, more significantly, self-endorsing. The conditions of dual authorship, then, are represented within the play as a residue of anxiety and perhaps as the intentional effect of spectacular translucency. If the effect is intentional, then some specific audience—the theater audience, the company, the managers, or the writers themselves—is intended to wonder at the writers' high, competitive collaboration. (The sustained effect of this attempt to enforce wonder may even account for the responses of some modern readers who find the play insufferable.)

The arming scene in act 3, continually circled about and reviewed by the present study for various purposes, turns out to be even more crucial for the professionalist subtext of the play since it exhibits not only the paradoxes of a nurturing rivalry but also a specifically male technology in a backstage performance of a *tekhne* or skill. The scene's clever premise is the alternation of polite discourse with the stage business of arming each other to kill—and what is more ironic, to kill one another. The dialogue is obsessed with the aesthetics of weapons and armor. The muted (or inept) comic effect is one of cumulative, involuted ironies, resulting from the participants' exaggerated, well-meaning, and temporary deference. We have already observed moments of an emulation that arouses spectacular virtue and competitions of humility. Palamon, in order to outdo Arcite's generous wish for an honorable "place" for the loser, whoever it should be, offers to accept the title of *coward* should be himself lose in order to show that these are "just trials" (3.6.105). His humility legitimates, just as brash-ness does, the entire male arena. We might once again formulate the speech act here as a *request to be rough,* an act reconciling collaboration and competition in speech and action. The conversation of the scene is punctuated with physical gestures that contain and license, like the conversation itself, whatever is rough:

ARC.

               Do I pinch you?

PAL.

               No.
     . . . . .

ARC.

               I'll buckle't close.

PAL.

  By any means.
     . . . . .

PAL.

               Good cousin, thrust the buckle
Through far enough.

ARC.

               I warrant you.
     . . . . .

PAL.

  Thank you, Arcite.
  How do I look? Am I fall'n much away?

ARC.

  Faith, very little. Love has us'd you kindly.

PAL.

  I'll warrant thee, I'll strike home.

ARC.

               Do, and spare not.
  I'll give you cause, sweet cousin. . . .

PAL.

  Is not this piece too strait?

ARC.

          No, no, 'tis well.

               (3.6.55-86)

I will not examine the dialogue's sexual innuendo, assum-ing that is what is operating in these double entendres, although I would argue that the probable tone of this pas-sage is intended to produce a homosocial locker-room snickering for the male audience rather than a homosexual reference to the characters. For the present purposes, one sees that their conversation embodies both the visions as well as the tensions of the collaborative arena in which the two contests of private victory and collaborative victory are entangled. The involutions brought about by this ideal-ized magnanimity are evident enough here and once again bound up with art.

When Arcite begins by offering, "I'll arm you first" (3.6.53), we observe how important priority is to these collaborative competitors as artist-soldiers. We are perhaps expected to notice that the more one helps one's opponent to arm, the greater the risk to the self, and the more noble one's victory will be in the end. Politeness is radically consequential: the better, more confident fighter facilitates, through his nobility, his own defeat. What is more, in this rough use, the fight stands for the friendship, as Arcite implies when he responds to Palamon's wish that he could thank him for his services with embraces rather than blows: "I shall think either, / Well done, a noble recompense" (3.6.23-24). Blows and embraces are interchangeable, both capable of being artistically "well done."

Watching these artist-figures, as it were, behind the scene, we conclude that more important than the choice of women (ultimately decided merely by fate, not by skill) is the choice of arms. The latter is performed in delicate negotia-tion:

PAL.

  I am well and lusty: choose your arms.

ARC.

               Choose you, sir.

PAL.

  Wilt thou exceed in all, or dost thou do it
To make me spare thee?

ARC.

               If you think so, cousin,
  You are deceived, for as I am a soldier,
  I will not spare you.

PAL.

               That's well said.

ARC.

               You'll find it.

               (3.6.45-49)

To choose first in this game (like being the starting player in collaborative art) is to confess a desire for better arms, thereby conceding one's inferiority. But cooperation and competition threaten to cancel each other out in a comedy of painful deferentiality where competitive magnanimity trips over itself. A new convention deconstructs gender division by dictating that the more deferential contestant is the more masculine contestant. On the other hand, an act of deference—letting the other choose first—could just as well be read as a strategy for victory, which implies that the other must repay, or outdo, the gesture by letting up in combat. All this male comedy depends on an awareness of the self-interfering character of a collaborative, competitive magnanimity. It addresses a male audience, assumed to be both amused and obsessed by such rituals of deference.

At the end of the cited passage the temporary dispute is resolved by a return to the first rule—contractual roughness—followed immediately by Palamon's aesthetic judgment of Arcite's conversational move. Deference, the spectacular acknowledgment of another's authority, again contains within it a potential alternative reading: to acknowledge the authority is to authorize it, and by authorizing one becomes its author. In this arena politeness threatens to subvert, and speech turns on noble gesture to disarm it. With Emilia, Palamon, and Arcite we might ask, "Is this winning?" as they tangle themselves within the involutions of a mimetic and competitive magnanimity. To "defy in fair terms" (3.6.25) is the oxymoron upon which both the play and its discourse are constructed.

IV. MEN'S TOURNAMENT OF ART

To view the men's final tournament is not only to be a part of it, as Emilia fears, but also to constitute it as a tournament, which, Theseus tells her rather unconvincingly, could not exist as a private contest: "You must be there; / This trial is as 'twere i' th' night, and you / The only star to shine" (5.3.18-20). In her absence the event is perhaps only semipublic. In any case, if viewed, this "deed of honor" becomes a work of art:

THE.

> She shall see deeds of honor in their kind,
> Which sometime show well, pencil'd.

> (5.3.12-13)

Whether this means (1) "a mere sketch will represent them," or (2) "as long as they are depicted in word or image," his comment valorizes the event as public spectacle of men's art.

The desire to reconcile rough behavior with cooperative behavior ultimately determines Theseus's novel ground rules for the tournament—a game that requires critical explanation beyond what it has so far received.[23] For the contest he orders that a "pyramid" or obelisk be constructed and that each man, with the assistance of his three knights, attempt to force his opponent to touch the pillar first. While Chaucer stages a bloodless, ordinary tournament between Palamon and Arcite and their one hundred knights, *The Two Noble Kinsmen* creates a peculiar contest with significant structural relations to the many other contests of the play. Among the "games of honor" about which the two men are most nostalgic are racing and combat. Theseus interrupts their actual combat, changes the game, and adds an audience. The form of the new game is significant: the fight around an object mirrors the rivalry over the love-object. Beyond that, the new game is a synthesis of

relations: the contest whose object is a common goal (love) and the contest whose object is the elimination of the other (war) are combined in the form of the pillar spectacle, which is an inverted race—by forcing the other man toward a single object that he resists, one *escapes* rather than *seeks* the "goal." Fighting not to touch the column is a physical embodiment of the deferential or self-defeating rivalry characterizing the male arena and its goal of homosocial satisfaction. The game reflects and reverses the play's obsessions. On the one hand, to spur the other on with rough talk and opposition, thus reconciling competition and collaboration, is to reverse the game of the obelisk, in which one resists with all one's strength moving in the direction that one's opponent is pushing. On the other hand, the game is a remarkable embodiment of the idealized rivalry: it replaces swordsmanship's more single-directed thrusting with the tactical give-and-take of something more like wrestling. In such a contest momentary cooperation or passivity, like a polite gesture, can be a feint in order to use, as in the martial arts, an opponent's full momentum against him. Passivity is not the opposite of power, but just one more of the tools in its box. On the other hand, full cooperation, or cooperation at just the wrong moment, is fatal. Thus, this tournament figures both the idealized form and the attendant anxiety of a collaborative-competitive enterprise. The project of *The Two Noble Kinsmen* is twofold: the construction of a dream arena for homosocial labor, and the design of just the right dream game to play in it.

A metaphor for artistic collaboration, the pillar contest contrasts with the singing contest that Theseus uses for the play's ultimate figure of the rivalry between Palamon and Arcite. Summarizing the fight as a nurturing competition, Theseus narrates an aspiring, self-undoing contest that proceeds toward undifferentiation and absence of priority, a knot of love rendering useless the judgment of spectators, like the race that left all the spectators behind:

> I have heard
> Two emulous Philomels beat the ear o' th' night
> With their contentious throats, now one the higher,
> Anon the other, then again the first,
> And by and by out-breasted, that the sense
> Could not be judge between 'em. So it far'd
> Good space between these kinsmen, till heavens did
> Make hardly one the winner.

> (5.3.123-30)

The play returns to the circumstances of its production through the striking analogy of a singing contest. A bold tale in which the heavens intervene to make losing into winning, in which the power of spectating to decide a contest is neutralized, and in which an audience is too noble to assign either man victory, is a tale serving as the ideal vehicle for an artistic project in which group and individual success are both interdependent and at odds. The final tournament is, ultimately, an inverse spectacle of fame, since the obelisk, the icon of eternal fame, is to be avoided rather than sought. More precisely, the pillar of fame is what one spurs the other to touch by working in selfless collaboration. By the special rules of the contest, however, to touch the male monument is to lose girl, friend, and life, in a repetition of the play's paradoxes of losing by winning, and vice versa. By a complicated representation of nobility and noble contests, *The Two Noble Kinsmen* rereads Chaucer as a stalemate dream permitting continued life within the contradictions that produce value and meaning in an arena of artistic, competitive, and male homosocial labor. Circumstances, not people, conspire to reconcile collaboration and competition perfectly.

But the idealizations of male production, and the consequent reduction and exclusion of female spectatorship, do not tell the full story. *The Two Noble Kinsmen* outdoes its own representations by an even more extravagant mystification of its own artistic labor. In the last degree of mystification of this labor, art takes on the character of the radical other, the mimetic female kingdom in which differentiation and competition with the other dissolve. The highest representation of a mystified homosocial labor, what such representation dreams to become a metaphor of, is paradoxically female labor, whose product is a child who is also a work of art but not a victory. The hyperidealized work, then, inevitably draws a physically sensuous imagery from lovemaking, like the flower imagery of Emilia and Flavina. We have already noted how Palamon and Arcite's collaborative meditation is regarded as their child: "We are one another's wife, ever begetting / New births of love" (2.2.80-81). In another instance, when we hear a description of physical male beauty such as the messenger gives of the freckle-faced knight attending Palamon, and when that description strives for its most mystified status, the imagery again turns toward pregnancy:

> . . . his arms are brawny,
> Lin'd with strong sinews; to the shoulder-piece
> Gently they swell, like women new-conceiv'd,
> Which speaks him prone to labor, never fainting
> Under the weight of arms. . . .

(4.2.126-30)

The Two Noble Kinsmen desires to be another "new birth of love" of a collaborative homosocial labor. Accordingly, it produces at the end a boy, who appears to be a child actor (comparing himself to a "schoolboy" in his dumbfounded fear) to deliver the Epilogue, which is conventionally apologetic and which teasingly calls for a judgment of the entire spectacle. The homosocial arena surrounds both story and play as the boy addresses his "good night" only to men—unlike typically Shakespearean epilogues addressing both sexes.

The Prologue (whether or not it is a later addition) also introduces the ideal of a homosocial birth by comparing the staying power of the play to the staying power of a wife's modesty after the marriage day ("New plays and maidenheads are near akin" [Pro. 1]), before turning to an announcement of the play's source and competitive patriarch, Chaucer ("a poet never went / More famous yet

'twixt Po and silver Trent" [Pro. 11-12]), who is significantly termed the play's "noble breeder and a pure" (Pro. 10). The Prologue reinforces the desired, collaborative nobility of the writers by expressing the fear that if they fail ("if we let fall the nobleness of this") Chaucer himself will lose fame: "O, fan / From me the witless chaff of such a writer / That blasts my bays and my fam'd works makes highter / Than Robin Hood!" (Pro. 18-21). Originality and unoriginality are reconciled, as are the productive modes of competition and collaboration. In the spirit of the play, the Prologue thus constructs a selflessness by which one noble assists and advances the other. The fear of an aspiring artistic epigone is also uttered: "it were an endless thing / And too ambitious, to aspire to him, / Weak as we are, and almost breathless swim / In this deep water" (Pro. 22-25). Repeating the motif of athletic effort, while transferring it to the realm of writing, the Prologue goes on to ask for its own assistants ("your helping hands" [26]), to rescue it from drowning.

Representing itself as a collaborative birth of homosocial satisfaction, of "noble breeders" who bond together even across time to do noble things with each other's words in conversation, *The Two Noble Kinsmen* thus translucently represents the circumstances, and reveals the anxieties, of an idealized collaboration and, by extension, of the specific collaboration of its two authors. My interpretation, in sum, suggests a collaborative contest between rivals and friends of more comparable professional stature—not between the retiring master impresario and the young playwright who was replacing him. This particular professionalist subtext would be odd for a retiring, but not for an aspiring, playwright.

In any case, whoever dreamed it, the play is a compulsory dream for a masculinist theater, a masque of labor for reconciling collaboration and authorship. The inescapable deconstructive conclusion is that its oppositions interanimate one another—that collaboration is the ground of individual authorship, as individual authorship is the ground of collaboration. Let us escape from such a conclusion. We do so by recognizing that the special tension is only significant insofar as the binaries are not logical but historical. That is, this writing occurs at a time when half the plays were produced in one mode, half in the other, and when their interdependency was institutional and gender-specific rather than always rhetorical. Grounded in these facts, even a fanciful conjecture is more historical than an endless play of figures.

In this spirit I offer such a conjecture, having concluded that *The Two Noble Kinsmen* is a title match and spectacle of professional collaboration with some rules, some spectators, some judge, and some prize.

V. CODA

A play that presents art as the children of men's labor imagines a system devoid of paternity or legitimacy questions; yet, ironically, its own paternity has been most seriously in doubt. The play touches on paternity suits of its own—from the Prologue, in which the writer or writers defer to Chaucer, mentioning him only as its "noble breeder," to Palamon's odd prayer before battle to Venus, whose power enabled a gouty, deformed, eighty-year-old man to have a child by his child-bride—or so it is said:

> This anatomy
> Had by his young fair fere a boy, and I
> Believ'd it was his, for she swore it was,
> And who would not believe her?
>
> (5.1.115-18)

The madness of the Jailer's Daughter raises other paternity questions. She praises Palamon because all the maids of the town are supposedly in love with him, and she muses that he has made "at least two hundred" of them pregnant (4.1.129). If she swears they are his, who would not believe her? When we last see her, she goes off to sleep with the nameless Wooer, about whom she says, "We shall have many children" (5.2.94). Those children may get different answers from mother and father when they inquire as to their paternity. Who you are depends on who is asking.

The title page of the first and only published quarto of *The Two Noble Kinsmen* indicates Shakespeare as its breeder, along with Fletcher. But the publisher twelve years later sold his copyright without Shakespeare's name. Title pages were often inaccurate, and dispute still exists about the play's style or styles.[24] The inaccuracy of title pages at the time reinforces the present claim that the era was as divided as its plays were between the values of single authorship and those of collaboration. Writers of Shakespeare's time, like poststructuralists, were groping toward concepts of authorship. Title pages are sites of conflict over sovereignty and must have been subject to whatever forces of circumstance and competition existed in each case. Jonson shows us the territorial thinking when, in order to keep his single-title authorship of *Sejanus,* he painstakingly rewrote all his collaborator's passages, in what he implies is a generous prevention of a "usurpation," as he calls it. The title page is thus yet another arena where we often find the residues of some power relation: there, a coauthor might somehow lose his title; or writers who contributed different amounts (if the records of differing payments are indicative), not to mention different qualities, might win equivalent titles as authors.[25]

Let the reluctant rivalry of *The Two Noble Kinsmen* represent its writers' competitive and collaborative feelings, an anxious and intertangled knot of ambition to promote the self, the other, and the play. Stage a tournament for writing, and let the splendid choice of arena for the tournament be Chaucer's tale of deep play between friends where everything is at stake. Expand the old tale with considerations of a collaborative artistic nobility and, risking your own defeat, spur on your co-adjutor. Dwell on these paradoxes for your spectators, who may have bet on writers as they bet on actors, and win points by show-

ing magnanimity as you show off your style. The audience will know the circumstances of the collaboration: the private spectacle and contest behind the public one. The collaborators should both be of a comparable age— Fletcher and the other one—but more important than age is that they should both be arriving at a propitious moment to whet professional desire. (The King's Men in 1613 had arrived at a professional watershed. They were about to lose, or had just lost, their chief playwright, a sovereign of sorts and very successful. Fletcher's old collaborator Beaumont was no longer collaborating for he had married and left the arena. Fletcher himself may have just married. That year their theater was to burn down, and they would by the summer of 1614 have a new arena.)

Let there be some ground rules for the exercise of power. If there were usual procedures of collaboration (Bentley conjectures, without real evidence, that there were) let them be followed, but there will still be decisions to make, such as the choice of which acts each will write (usually thought to be a common means of division). Let the decision be made like a choice of arms, magnanimously, so that to choose first hints of one's weakness or lack of self-confidence. It is no special honor to go first. Let the weaker man have the positional or material advantage, at least the first and last acts, usually attributed for the most part to Fletcher's collaborator. Let your own writing spur on the other's. Let winning be everything, and nothing. Yet you must win; by making moves that the other won't match, by appropriating his moves, and even by writing him into an occasional corner. Let Shakespeareans attempt to explain inconsistent elements either as failures of design or as harmonious parts of an unobvious, organic unity—as if collaborative work is somehow on principle pacific and never dialogic; as if the paradigm for writing is editing; as if there were no place for, or no consequences of, professional envy, the emotion producing the chance conclusion of the play when a little "envious flint," envious of the horse dancing "to th' music / His own hooves made (for, as they say, from iron / Came music's origin)" (5.4.59-61), terrifies Arcite's horse, which throws the winner to his death. Let Fletcher win.

What prize? The 1634 title page of the play is a page of titles. "Written by the memorable Worthies of their time; Mr. *John Fletcher,* and Mr. *William Shakespeare Gent.*" One of its titles is *Gentleman,* applying, if it does, to Fletcher as well as Shakespeare, whose earlier personal ambition was a coat of arms. The other title is appropriate for military champions; the "Nine Worthies" were also contemporarily known as "The Nine Nobles." In a contest for fame, through a play that represents its own contest for fame around a "pyramid," one of the collaborators will lose title, fame, and, in the arena of the book, his name. His work is subsumed under the title of an artistic sovereign or master. In Italian Renaissance workshop paintings, novice work was treated this way; in fact, the signature of the master from some workshops actually confirms that the painting was not his but the work of assistants. In other cases, a master might sign, with his own signature, a student's work that particularly impressed him. What seems to us dishonest or cavalier merely operated in an unfamiliar system of honorable collaboration. We understand only with difficulty an era of artistic production in which the status of authorship was not as fixed as it now is, or was in contention, as is suggested by the circumstances of Elizabethan collaboration.

At about this time Fletcher becomes the new main playwright of the King's Men, replacing Shakespeare. He may have collaborated in the same year as *The Two Noble Kinsmen* on a play with Nathan Field and Philip Massinger.[26] Field, an actor-playwright, may have received Shakespeare's shares to the company, as Fletcher received his position. Massinger, by some scholars assigned the non-Fletcherian parts of the play, was buried, in a gesture of spectacular friendship, in a single grave with Fletcher.[27] The year 1613 was something of a watershed in the circumstances of Fletcher's dramatic career. After his collaborations of this and the preceding years, his usual practice changed to single authorship. Let Shakespeare, as artistic sovereign, be the judge of this masque of labor, this title match and tour de force of collaboration about collaboration. (But if Shakespeare was coauthor after all, let Fletcher be termed "coadjutor" in the term's other, power-differentiated sense, signifying the assistant to an aging and feeble bishop, an "assistance" in preparation for taking over the position.) Let Shakespeare judge between suitors, as Elizabeth did for Sidney's *Lady of May,* in which the judging sovereign is written into the spectacle, though the actual judgment left to her. Let the weaker collaborator honor the judge by displaying a familiar dense style and echoing some familiar moments of the master. Let the translucent play imply how hard it will be for a noble judge to decide between such emulous Philomels. If he has to decide between the styles of the future, let Shakespeare elect what some see as a cheap theatricality, over what some see as "the voice and music of the master."[28] If someone magnanimously swears the child is his, who would not believe him?

After all of this dreaming, let Shakespeare, for a moment reversing the direction of the cultural narrative in which he and his coworkers were all spectacularly inscribed, leave the powerful arena of artistic satisfaction and return home to three women.

APPENDIX: SHAKESPEAREAN CONVERSATION AND *THE TWO NOBLE KINSMEN*

The following is a brief discussion of a stylistic criterion that best distinguishes, I believe, the dialogue of the non-Fletcherian parts of *The Two Noble Kinsmen* from Shakespeare, thus arguing against Shakespeare's coauthorship. The criterion is the representation of natural conversation, a stylistic determinant not captured by any traditional stylistic tests of authorship, yet one crucial to the study of Shakespeare's language. A full discussion of Shakespeare's habit and skill at this can be found in my "Merry and Weary Conversation: Textual Uncertainty in *As You Like*

It, II.iv.," *ELH* 46 (1979): 21-34. I must forego the possibility of proof here for several reasons: one can notice the differences in ability to represent conversation only in large stretches of text; procedures for identifying chains of speech acts would require an enormous interpretive apparatus; and in this case I am suggesting what is *not* there, an evidentiary situation entirely different from demonstrating what is there.

I can, however, give the reader a few guides to perform his or her own examination of the difference. First, one can recognize that one of the major skills Shakespeare developed was to represent the dialogic nature of conversation, including intentional or unintentional violations of straightforward communication such as topic changing, giving more or less information than is requested, breaking the established tone, answering questions with questions, and so on. In addition to showing how we do things to others' words in our speech, he becomes much more subtle at what are known as "indirect speech acts," in which an utterance takes a different form than its actual pragmatic force or point. In a direct speech act, for example, a question-form is used to ask a question ("What day is it today?"). In an indirect speech act, a question-form might be used for an entirely different point—to thank, to command, to request, and so on ("Can you pass the salt?" is a request that only looks like a question). To see Shakespeare's remarkable development at portraying the messy—though perhaps logical even in its messiness—sequence of real speech, one might compare the flat dialogue of the proposition scene of King Edward and Lady Grey in *3 Henry VI* (3.2) with the subtleties of the proposition scene of Angelo and Isabella in *Measure for Measure* (3.1). Since both scenes portray conversation at cross-purposes, the latter stands out in relief.

The non-Fletcherian parts of *The Two Noble Kinsmen,* while rich in a Shakespeare-style poetic diction and complex syntax, are almost entirely devoid of the misconstructions, inference-drawings, and indirect modes of conversation that occur in what is summed up in the idea of "uptake." Typically, the dialogue there is more limited to direct speech acts, in patterns of question/answer, assertion/agreement or disagreement, and topic/comment, requiring less sense of the context in order to convey complete meaning. Even the occasional interruption of dialogue is achieved mechanically, chiefly to convey information:

PAL.

> . . . that which rips my bosom
> Almost to th' heart's—

ARC.

>   Our uncle Creon.

PAL.

>   He,
> A most unbounded tyrant, whose successes
> Makes heaven unfear'd . . .

>   (1.2.61-64).

A few brief instances from later Shakespeare plays may attune one to the skills Shakespeare had by that time developed, unevident in *The Two Noble Kinsmen*. (Fletcher, though otherwise stylistically quite distinct from Shakespeare, is actually much closer to Shakespeare in this.)

1. SURRY.

May it please your Grace—

KING.

No, sir, it does not please me.
I had thought I had had men of some understanding

. . .

(*Henry VIII*, 5.2.169-70)

The interruption is fully charged, as a deliberate refusal to accept a stock politeness, by taking the word *please* literally. The linguistic moment is fully dramatic, when an attempt to seize the floor and change the direction of conversation is abruptly warded off by the king, who willfully reads the conventional indirect speech act (a request to be heard) as if it were the direct one of its verbal form (a request to please).

2. ANNE.

Pray do not deliver
What here y'have heard to her.

OLD L.

What do you think me? *Exeunt*

(*Henry VIII*, 2.3.106-7)

Shakespeare can even end a scene with a question, unlike a beginner at representing dialogue. But it is an indirect speech act—not really a question, but a promise not to tell. It carries with it a clear-cut tone, full implications of the spirit of the woman, and an index to their relationship. For a lesser writer the form of her response might simply be an agreement, however emphatically expressed, that she would not tell.

3. Subtle construction of oblique reference in conversation is represented in *Pericles* when Boult, who has just gotten customers for the virginal Marina's services, makes a very indirect request that he might try her out first, a request only developed as such in their shared, oblique language moves:

BOULT.

But, mistress, if I have bargain'd for the joint—

BAWD.

Thou mayst cut a morsel off the spit.

BOULT.

I may so.

BAWD.

Who should deny it?

(4.2.129-33)

By force of the delicacy of the context and evasion of responsibility, the process of request and permission doesn't even take on the speech act forms of request or permission. The bawd's final permission is masked as a question.

4. As the plot develops in *The Tempest* to kill Alonso, questions and answers are again obliquely used:

ANTONIO.

What a sleep were this
For your advancement! Do you understand me?

SEBASTIAN.

Methinks I do.

(2.1.267-69)

The question here, superficially about understanding words, is actually a plea for consent to an assassination not spoken about as such. Sebastian's tentative reply is a partial denial, at that moment, of consent. We understand not that he is unclear about the point of Antonio's speech, but that he is hesitant to accept its clear proposal.

Readers are invited to compare these examples and others they can readily find, where there is such a striking residue of meaning outside the linguistic forms themselves, to the conversational sequences of the supposedly Shakespearean scenes in *The Two Noble Kinsmen*.

Notes

1. Pierre Macherey, *A Theory of Literary Production* (London, Henley, and Boston: Routledge, 1978), 51, 58.

2. Donald K. Hedrick, "The Masquing Principle in Marston's *The Malcontent*," *English Literary Renaissance* 8 (1978): 24-42.

3. The version of this paper presented at the seminar on *The Two Noble Kinsmen* in 1985 is largely unchanged with respect to its subsidiary claims against Shakespeare's coauthorship on stylistic and thematic grounds. I want to thank Charles Frey for his critique of the reading, but especially for challenging me at that time to provide an alternative candidate. Although I believed that the kind of study I had done relieved me of the obligation to seek a different author, I began to study evidence about one of the candidates mentioned in the "Coda," Nathan Field. I learned that he had never been considered, that other collaborations of his had been only recently identified, and, most striking, that the nineteenth-century stylistic foundation of the case for Shakespeare—a supposedly thorough comparison of the text's style

with all other authors of the period—while still treated as authoritative and relied on by serious scholars and editors of the play, had never actually been carried out.

I have left the fanciful "Coda" virtually unrevised, to reflect my original thinking. If Field was Fletcher's coauthor, its conjectures nevertheless remain surprisingly apt, except that Field would have been younger than his collaborator, hence more aspiring and less a professional equal. The "Coda" remains fanciful, of course, in its fiction of a kind of playwriting contest with Shakespeare as judge, but I think there may be a larger, nonliteral truth to it. We have more work to do in understanding the institutional base of the drama of the time.

Nathan Field, ambitious artistic upstart in Jacobean theater, a self-confessed aspirant to write tragicomedy like that of his friend Fletcher, and the only major actor-playwright immediately following Shakespeare, was working with Fletcher, as we now know, at the time of *Kinsmen*. He had already tried his hand at adapting Chaucer for the stage, unlike Shakespeare, and had done so working with Fletcher. His poetic style was the only remaining one like Shakespeare's, whose influence is readily argued from plot borrowings, neologizings, and from Field's having memorized Shakespeare in order to act in his plays. Recognized stylistic features of Field, such as "clotted" rhetoric and uncertain tone, have been consistently remarked in the non-Fletcherian parts of *Kinsmen*. The lengthy actor-oriented stage directions we find in *Kinsmen* are a signature, as are other themes, motifs, bawdy style, sexual themes, and Jonsonian misogyny. Major metrical and vocabulary tests (including double endings, *o'th'*, *'em, hath* and *doth*, and unique inventions) support the claim. Field's theatrical connections to Henslowe and others, his move to Shakespeare's company (where he may have received Shakespeare's shares), and his early disappearance support his candidacy as Fletcher's collaborator on this play. His cheeky personal spirit of outrageously noble gestures, his self-fashioning as Bussy D'Ambois (the character he starred as), all imbue *The Two Noble Kinsmen*. The thematic concerns I first recognized in the play turned out to be his "identity themes." In his self-fashioning to fill the gap left by Shakespeare, Field, I believe, deserves study as the first Shakespearoid writer.

The evidence I summarize here was presented in a paper given at the Shakespeare Association Meeting in Montreal, 1986: "The Politics of Attribution: Authorial Image and the Competitive Field of *The Two Noble Kinsmen*."

4. For the development of the consensus, see David V. Erdman and Ephim G. Fogel, eds., *Evidence for Authorship: Essays on Problems of Attribution, with an Annotated Bibliography of Selected Readings* (Ithaca: Cornell University Press, 1966), 486-94.

5. Ben Jonson, *Bartholomew Fair*, in *Drama of the English Renaissance: The Stuart Period*, ed. Russell A. Fraser and Norman Rabkin (New York: Macmillan, 1976), 4.3.71-74.

6. In the visual arts of the Renaissance and modern eras, see for example *Collaboration in Italian Renaissance Art*, ed. Wendy Stedman Sheard and John T. Paoletti (New Haven: Yale University Press, 1978), and Cynthia Jaffee McCabe, *Artistic Collaboration in the Twentieth Century* (Washington, D.C.: Smithsonian, 1984).

7. See Roland Barthes, "The Death of the Author," in *Image-Music-Text* (New York: Farrar, 1977), and Michel Foucault, "What Is an Author?" in *Textual Strategies: Perspectives in Post-Structuralist Criticism*, ed. Josue V. Harari (Ithaca: Cornell University Press, 1979).

8. R. G. Collingwood, "The Artist and the Community," in *The Principles of Art* (1938; rpt. New York: Oxford University Press, 1972).

9. G. E. Bentley, *The Profession of Dramatist in Shakespeare's Time: 1590-1642* (Princeton: Princeton University Press, 1971), 198-99.

10. Thomas Dekker, *The Gull's Hornbook*, in A. M. Nagler, *A Source Book in Theatrical History* (New York: Dover, 1952), 135.

11. B. L. Joseph, *Elizabethan Acting*, 2d ed. (London: Oxford University Press, 1964), 94.

12. Bentley, *Profession of Dramatist*, 199ff.

13. *The Works of Ben Jonson*, ed. C. H. Herford and Percy Simpson (Oxford: Clarendon, 1937), vol. 5, Pro. 15-18.

14. Timothy Murray, "From Foul Sheets to Legitimate Model: Antitheater, Text, Ben Jonson," *New Literary History* 14 (1983): 641-64.

15. For Shakespearean conversational analysis, see my "Merry and Weary Conversation: Textual Uncertainty in *As You Like It*, II.iv." *Early Literary History* 46 (1979): 21-34; or Keir Elam, *Shakespeare's Universe of Discourse: Language-Games in the Comedies* (Cambridge: Cambridge University Press, 1984).

16. Philip Edwards, "On the Design of *The Two Noble Kinsmen*," *A Review of English Literature* 5 (1964): 89-105.

17. Eve Kosofsky Sedgwick, "Sexualism and the Citizen of the World: Wycherly, Sterne, and Male Homosocial Desire," *Critical Inquiry* 11 (1984): 228-29. See also Sedgwick, *Between Men: English Literature and Male Homosocial Desire* (New York: Columbia University Press, 1985).

18. Paul Bertram, *Shakespeare and "The Two Noble Kinsmen"* (New Brunswick: Rutgers University Press, 1965).

19. For a gender-specific reading of the play's world, see Charles Frey, "'O sacred, shadowy, cold, and constant queen': Shakespeare's Imperiled and Chastening Daughters of Romance," in *The Woman's Part: Feminist Criticism of Shakespeare,* ed. Carolyn Ruth Swift Lenz, Gayle Greene, and Carol Thomas Neely (Urbana: University of Illinois Press, 1980), 305-12.

20. I follow the critique of this intellectual tradition offered by Jonathan Dollimore in *Radical Tragedy: Religion, Ideology and Power in the Drama of Shakespeare and His Contemporaries* (Brighton, U.K.: Harvester, 1984), 156ff.

21. Livia Polanyi, "The Nature of Meaning of Stories in Conversation," *Studies in Twentieth Century Literature* 6 (Fall 1981-Spring 1982): 59.

22. For an account of the Renaissance view of performance judgment as just another kind of performance, see Frank Whigham, "Interpretation at Court: Courtesy and the Performer-Audience Dialectic," *New Literary History* 14 (1983): 623-39. For insight into the relation of masculinist aesthetics and warfare I am indebted to poet Jonathan Holden's studies of contemporary sensibilities, especially the essay on the ways American boys satisfy the "aesthetic impulse" with warplanes: "Boyhood Aesthetics," *Iowa Review* 12 (1981): 135-46.

23. The strongest and most illuminating discussion of the form of the contest is by Paula S. Berggren, "'For what we lack, / We laugh': Incompletion and *The Two Noble Kinsmen,*" *Modern Language Studies* 14 (1984): 3-17. Berggren recognizes the physical character of the game as "strength working against itself" (7) and as a reversal of phallic assertion in having a goal one loses by touching. Her investigation of possible sources of the game identifies it as historically unique to the play.

24. For a summary of the developing issues and positions, see Proudfoot, "Introduction" to *The Two Noble Kinsmen,* xiii-xix; the annotated bibliography in Erdman and Fogel, *Evidence for Authorship,* 486-94; G. Harold Metz, *Four Plays Ascribed to Shakespeare: An Annotated Bibliography* (New York: Garland, 1982), 135-81; and Hallett Smith, "Introduction" to *The Two Noble Kinsmen,* in *The Riverside Shakespeare,* ed. G. Blakemore Evans (Boston: Houghton Mifflin, 1974). For additional historical materials, see E. K. Chambers, *The Elizabethan Stage* (Oxford: Clarendon, 1923), 3:226-27; E. H. C. Oliphant, *The Plays of Beaumont and Fletcher* (New Haven: Yale University Press, 1927), 325-48; S. Schoenbaum, *Annals of English Drama 975-1700* (London: Methuen, 1964).

25. Bentley, *Profession of Dramatist,* 206, 201.

26. *Henslowe Papers, Being Documents Supplementary to Henslowe's Diary,* ed. Walter W. Greg (London: A. H. Bullen, 1907; rpt. New York: AMS Press, 1975), article 68, pp. 65-66.

27. T. W. Baldwin, *The Organization and Personnel of the Shakespearean Company* (Princeton: Princeton University Press, 1927), 51.

28. Alfred Hart, "Shakespeare and the Vocabulary of *The Two Noble Kinsmen,*" *Review of English Studies* 10 (1934): 274.

Lois Potter (essay date 1992)

SOURCE: Potter, Lois. "Topicality or Politics?: *The Two Noble Kinsmen,* 1613-34." In *The Politics of Tragicomedy: Shakespeare and After,* edited by Gordon McMullan and Jonathan Hope, pp. 77-91. London: Routledge, 1992.

[*In the following essay, Potter explores the topical allusions in* The Two Noble Kinsmen.]

The Two Noble Kinsmen is a play with an almost embarrassingly long literary past, balanced by a theatrical afterlife which is short even by comparison with Shakespeare's other Fletcherian collaboration, *Henry VIII.* We think of it as a dramatization of Chaucer's *Knight's Tale,* and the prologue invites us to admire it for his sake, but in fact everyone who tells the tale attributes it to someone else. It can be traced, in some form or other, as far back as the earliest Greek legends of Thebes. Antiquity seems to be one of its claims to attention in the first edition of 1634. Not only does the prologue refer to 'Chaucer, of all admired', it also calls Shakespeare and Fletcher (the latter less than ten years dead) 'the Memorable Worthies of their Time'. Despite this pedigree, the play effectively disappears from theatrical history after its revival, heavily adapted by Davenant, in the early years of the Restoration. Subsequent revivals, where they occur, get so little critical attention as to make its stage history almost completely obscure. One reason, I think, is its doubly double focus of attention: two heroes, two authors. Its title, by contrast with that of *Henry VIII,* indicates that there will be no part to serve as a vehicle for a star actor; its dual authorship means that readers can adopt a more critical view than they would allow themselves with a play attributed to Shakespeare alone.

The politics of both theatre and criticism are thus bound up with the history of *The Two Noble Kinsmen.* I shall return to them at the end of this essay, but first it seems important to consider whether the play can be described as inherently political. Normally a story about the love of two men for one woman, when it has no larger dynastic implications, is seen as comic. This play is tragicomic, not in the sense of Shakespeare's late romances, but because its ending is tragic for one hero, comic for the other. Indeed, to call the ending comic at all is possible only if one accepts that marriage is always by definition a happy ending. Arcite's death comes just in time to save Palamon from death, because Theseus has insisted that the conflict shall be all or nothing: the loser and all his friends are to die on the block. In Chaucer's version of the story, Mars and Venus are overridden by the more powerful and sinister figure of Saturn, who provides the solution to the plot by sending the monster which frightens Arcite's horse so that he is killed in the moment of his triumph. But the playwrights omit Saturn and apparently go back to Boccaccio's *Teseida,* where Mars is responsible for Arcite's victory and Venus for Palamon's final triumph. Thus, the gods are left equally balanced, both having fulfilled the letter though not the spirit of their promises. Theseus has to acknowledge that 'the gods have been most equal', but he also recognizes that their decisions do not bear examination:

> Let us be thankful
> For that which is, and with you leave dispute
> That are above our question.

(V.vi.134-6)

This main plot is set against another story, which seems to be original. The Jailer's Daughter helps Palamon to escape from prison because she is in love with him, goes mad in the woods out of frustration, and is finally 'cured', if that is the word, by a doctor who makes her think that her long-suffering suitor, a man of her own class, is Palamon. Her story is kept so completely separate from the rest of the play that Richard Proudfoot has suggested it may be a later addition.[1]

A story which on one level is trivial, yet which is taken immensely seriously by all its characters and expressed in language of tremendous—almost portentous—solemnity, naturally makes one wonder whether it 'means' more than it says. The search for a political meaning is often a last resort when a work seems not to make aesthetic sense. Often, however, finding topical meanings in a Renaissance play is taken to be the same thing as establishing a political meaning. This is obviously too simple: recognizing the resemblance of a fiction to reality is not in itself going to affect one's attitude to that reality. Since we have reasonably good evidence about the dates of some early performances of *The Two Noble Kinsmen* up to its first publication in 1634, I propose to look at some of the ways in which it might have seemed topical at these various dates, and then to consider whether they can be made to add up to a genuinely political statement.

The time-lag between the play's first performance (*c.* 1613) and its publication means that its political meaning was initially controlled by the company which produced it. The approximate period of the play's premiere can be deduced to have been some time after 20 February 1613, that being the date of Beaumont's *Masque of the Inner Temple* from which it apparently borrows its morris dance interlude, and some time before the first performance of *Bartholomew Fair* (October 1614), in which Jonson seems to comment rather sarcastically on the story. A well-known and widely accepted view of the play's first occasion is that, as Richard Proudfoot, Muriel Bradbrook, and Glynne Wickham have suggested, it was a response to the death of Prince Henry in November 1612 and the marriage of his sister Elizabeth to Frederick the Elector Palatine in February 1613.[2] On Wickham's theory, the play would have been taken as an allegory of Elizabeth's reluctance to leave her brother even for the man she loves, and the resolution of her problem by death. Elizabeth is Emilia, Henry is Arcite, and the Palsgrave is Palamon; young Prince Charles has no part in the story according to Wickham, but it would be possible to argue that, whereas the Palsgrave replaces Henry as the object of Elizabeth's love, Prince Charles replaces him in his political role. On this account, then, the play would have had a basically consoling purpose.

Proudfoot and others suggest that *The Two Noble Kinsmen* may have been put together hastily, after the Globe fire of June 1613, either for the Blackfriars season that autumn or for the opening of the new Globe in 1614. Perhaps some of the discontinuities in the play are the result of revisions necessitated by the company's reduced circumstances. The scene in which the combatants are described by Pirithous and an anonymous messenger is one which Gary Taylor thinks shows evidence of revision.[3] It might have replaced a more elaborate pageant-like entry, like those of the knights in *Pericles,* whose shields are described by Thaisa. The final trial by combat is also replaced by description: we experience it, with Emilia, only through offstage shouts. It is true, of course, that other Jacobean plays, like *Bussy d'Ambois, Cymbeline,* and *The Winter's Tale,* show a tendency to classicizing and refinement in the replacement of action by messenger scenes; it can also be argued that Emilia's presence alone onstage heightens her role and emphasizes the suspense of the scene. But why bother to reduce Chaucer's enormous tournament to a fight between the two heroes with three friends each, if not to enable it to be performed? *The White Devil* had already displayed fighting at the barriers, and *The Devil's Law-Case* would later include an elaborate trial by combat for several duellists. It is at least arguable that the play, originally envisaged as a spectacular feast for the eyes, was revised, whether before its first performance or in later revivals, into a more small-scale, psychological drama.

Several features of *The Two Noble Kinsmen* might have offered its first audiences visual reminders of the elaborate celebrations for the royal wedding. The most obvious would have been the morris dance, probably using the same costumes and characters as Beaumont's highly successful masque. *The Lord's Masque,* which Campion wrote for the same occasion, includes a woodland setting with a thicket out of which a wild man comes (like Palamon in Act III of *The Two Noble Kinsmen*) and, more interestingly, a final scene in which statues of the bridegroom and bride are seen on either side of a silver obelisk. The obelisk stands for fame, Campion's notes explain, and in Ripa's *Iconologia* an obelisk or pyramid (the two terms were interchangeable) symbolizes 'the glory of princes'.[4] As Theseus describes his projected tournament (III.vi.292-4), its central feature is to be a 'pyramid', but he also refers to it as a 'pillar' and it would make a lot more sense to pin one's opponent against an obelisk than to try and flatten him against a pyramid. It is possible, then, that there may have been some intention of reusing the obelisk from the masque in this final scene.

The fact that 'funerals' and 'nuptials' could be made to rhyme led a number of writers to greet the wedding of Elizabeth and Frederick with reminders of the sorrow that they had just passed through and of the importance of submitting to the will of fate.[5] Thomas Heywood's *A Marriage Triumphe Solemnized in an Epithalamium* (1613) not only links the funeral with the marriage but also recalls that the princess herself has replaced, in her name, the much-lamented Queen Elizabeth.[6] Rather interestingly, he also introduces widowed queens into his poem, complimenting the Palsgrave for defending them against 'the triple-headed *Gerion*'. This idea is borrowed from Spenser, who had already depicted Belgia as a widow in Book V of *The Faerie Queene*. The widowed queen is of course a common symbol for a country without a ruler.

We know of a couple of possible revivals between that first performance and the play's first printing in 1634. There is some evidence—a fragment of a note—that it may have been given a court performance in 1619 or 1620. If this did happen, the three widowed queens might have turned out to be its most important feature. In 1619, Frederick's acceptance of the crown of Bohemia had precipitated the Thirty Years War. His wife pleaded with her father and brother for help, and on 27 May 1620 a letter to the same effect arrived from the Protestant princes of Germany. Prince Charles took part in a special tilt on 20 June 1620, partly to display his skill and partly to lead the recruiting campaign which started almost immediately after the receipt of the message from Germany. To recall the circumstances of Elizabeth's wedding at this time would have been to invoke the warlike sentiments for which Prince Henry had been so much admired and the popular support for the war. By comparison both with Chaucer and with Lydgate's *Siege of Thebes*, which is a sort of *Knight's Tale, Part One*, the authors of *The Two Noble Kinsmen* seem positively in favour of the purifying effect of Mars, who, as Arcite puts it, rids the world of the pleurisy of people. Other topical possibilities may also be noted. The death of Queen Anne in 1619 would provide another example of royal grief to be transcended. The depiction of ideal friendship in Theseus and Pirithous would have been particularly appropriate to the role which Buckingham had assumed by 1619 in his relations with both James I and the Prince of Wales. Whereas Palamon and Arcite fight for a ruler they despise and a country they see as corrupt, Theseus and Pirithous are associated throughout, despite all the legends to the contrary, with pure friendship and just causes. Moreover, Theseus, in his ability to maintain a perfect balance between married love and ideal friendship, might be taken as James's ideal self-image.

The stage directions of the printed text include the names of two actors who are known to have 'overlapped' in the King's Men only in 1625-6, so there seems some evidence that the play had a revival at that time.[7] The play would have been equally topical at this revival. The pattern of death and replacement in the royal family had worked itself out yet again in a particularly spectacular way. James I died in March 1625; Charles was married to Henrietta Maria by proxy on 1 May. Moreover, his marriage was another example of a second choice: as everyone knew, England's negotiations with the French princess had started only after the breakdown of those with the Spanish infanta began to seem inevitable. Henrietta Maria arrived in England on 13 June, when the plague had already taken hold to such an extent that Charles's first Parliament had to move from Westminster to Oxford and was finally adjourned early because fewer and fewer members dared to attend it. The second Parliament closely followed his coronation in early February 1626. The chief business which Charles urged it to perform on both occasions was the voting of subsidies for the Protestant cause in Europe. The defeat of the Bohemian army at the Battle of White Mountain in November 1620 had made Frederick and Elizabeth exiles and their cause was thus even more urgent than in 1619/20.

By the time the play was printed in 1634, some twenty years after its first performance, Elizabeth of Bohemia was not only symbolically but literally a widowed queen, living at The Hague. Following the assassination of the Duke of Buckingham in 1628, Charles and Henrietta Maria had reconciled their differences and begun to lead an exemplary married life. Its most immediate results were the births of the future Charles II in 1630, of Mary (the future Princess of Orange) in 1631, and of the future James II in 1633. Thus the royal family of 1634 precisely duplicated the royal family of 1612, with an elder son, a daughter, and a second son. This is not the kind of fact likely to be overlooked by court poets, always desperate for new things to say on the subject of each royal birth. For instance, William Cartwright's poem on the birth of the Duke of York recalls that his title was also the one by which the present king was known until his brother's death made him Prince of Wales, and hopes, with what seems crashing tactlessness, that there will be 'no imitation of the father here'. Interchangeability had already been the theme of a number of the poems written on Henry's death. Campion's words for Coperario's *Songs of Mourning* (1613) urged Charles to:

> Follow, O follow yet thy brother's fame;
> But not his fate. Let's only change the name,
>   And find his worth presented
>   In thee, by him prevented.

The Caroline court, however isolated it may seem from some kinds of reality, was sharply aware of the pattern of death and renewal and could see the threat of the son to the father as already present even on the apparently joyous occasion of childbirth. Henry King begins his poem on the birth of the Prince of Wales by explaining that he has been late in writing it because he felt almost disloyal in rejoicing at an event which, by implication, foretold the death of the king:

each following Birth
Doth sett the Parent so much neerer Earth:
And by this Grammer, wee our Heires may call
The smiling Preface to our Funerall.[8]

Yet he goes on to reproach himself for his reluctance to accept this lesson, which is also a lesson for the king himself:

if Fathers should remaine
For ever here, Children were borne in vaine;
And wee in vaine were Christians, should wee
In this world dreame of Perpetuitye.

Decay is Nature's Kalendar, nor can
It hurt the King to think He is a Man:
Nor grieve, but Comfort Him to heare us say
That His owne Children must His Scepter sway.

(II.49-56)

As W. P. Williams has argued, Fletcherian tragicomedy is 'a form which expresses the unity and simplicity of hereditary succession: a happy outcome which cannot occur without the death of a predecessor'.[9] *The Two Noble Kinsmen* is unusual among tragicomedies in that it does not deal with the question of hereditary succession. It is indeed possible that the marriage of Emilia will turn out to have consequences for the succession in Athens, especially if the audience is meant to be aware of what will eventually happen to the son of Theseus and Hippolyta. This possibility is not developed in the play, probably because its medieval sources dominate its classical ones. But the fact that the story deals with replacement on the horizontal rather than the vertical plane would have made it, if anything, still more relevant at the time of its publication in 1634. Its appearance followed closely on two important court performances. One was a revival of Fletcher's *The Faithful Shepherdess,* which has as its title character a woman whose chastity and fidelity to the memory of her dead lover give her a special charismatic power in a world of confused sensuality. The other was a new work, which offers a different view of fidelity: Walter Montagu's famous *Shepheard's Paradise.* Since this play was written for, and specifically identified with, the queen and her ladies, it seems worth looking more closely at what it shows of the Caroline court's self-image in the early 1630s.

Though Montagu's play was privately performed in January 1633, it was not published until 1659. At that time, its publisher, Thomas Dring, prefaced it with an epistle virtually guaranteed to discourage anyone from reading it; the play, he explains, is addressed

to the inspir'd and more refin'd part of men! Such as are capable to be ravish'd when they find a fancy bright and high, as the *Phoebus* that gave it: Such as have experienced those extasies and Raptures, which are the very Genius of Poetry; Poetry its selfe being nothing else but a brave and measur'd Enthusiasm; such as know, what it is to have the Soul upon the wing (suspending its commerce with clay) reaching a room

almost as lofty as the proper Scene of Spirits, till warm'd with divine flames, it melts it selfe into numbers as charming as the Harmony of those Spheres it left beneath it: Such as are thus qualified, may here read upon the square; Others will find themselves unconcern'd.[10]

Not surprisingly, readers then and since have decided that they were not refined enough to cope with *The Shepheard's Paradise.* Yet, contrary to what one might expect from Dring's rhetoric, the play is surprisingly balanced in its attitude to the super-refined love it depicts. The character who most completely embodies its principles is the court poet, Martirio. But his verses are greeted with amusement by everyone, including the brilliant Bellesa herself—the part played by the queen and therefore, presumably, the one uncriticizable character. After Martirio has read verses defining the nature of his love for a mistress he refuses to name, she declares that 'they that could understand these verses might know your Mistress, the impossibilities to me seem equall' (IV.95). What the poet's lines most suggest, in fact, is an uninspired equivalent of Marvell's 'Definition of Love', since its point is that the impossibility and the loftiness of the love go together. The play's hero, having heard the poem, cross-examines Martirio about his love: didn't it, he asks, start in the senses and then become platonic only when the lover found that it could *not* be satisfied? Perhaps, he suggests, 'It was necessity, not choice that drew it up so high.' Martirio replies with dignity that 'my love had ne're so low a thought, as hope' (IV.96). Bellesa later tells him that he exists at 'such a transcendent height above all sense' that nothing should surprise him (IV.106). This attitude to 'transcendent' love is not unlike that of some of Chaucer's sophisticated characters, such as Theseus in *The Knight's Tale.* Near the end of the play, an elderly courtier arrives in search of an unusually large number of misplaced princes and princesses. Asked whether he has ever been in love, he replies devastatingly, 'Nevere Sir, I have not known so light a griefe in all my life' (V.141).

Part of Montagu's plot must have struck its courtly audience as remarkably familiar. The hero has obtained his father's permission to travel, with a close friend who is equally dear to both of them, in an effort to forget an unsuccessful love. Under assumed names, they come to a place called the Shepheard's Paradise, which was created specifically as a refuge for unhappy lovers. It is not a totally platonic society; each year, on the day when the new queen is chosen, lovers can ask to be released from their vows and marry. There is a clear sense that both kinds of life are valid. Once he has met Bellesa, who has just been chosen queen of the shepherds because of her exceptional beauty, the prince falls in love with her. She is equally taken with him, though she conceals the fact that she is the woman he was originally supposed to marry and that she had left court in disguise when she learned of his love for someone else, both in order not to create a political scandal and because she didn't fancy being second best. She and the prince discuss his problems as if he were a third party, reaching the conclusion that he is entitled to love a second time, and that the second love may well be more mature than the first. Clearly, the Caroline court was entertaining itself with its own story. As the witty Bellesa, Henrietta Maria is shown to have complete control over the play's interpretation. But Montagu's transformation of the unromantic facts about the royal marriage into a pastoral romance is the more effective precisely because it retains the capacity to laugh at the excesses of love.

The leading actor of the King's Men, Joseph Taylor, was also the director of *The Shepheard's Paradise,* and conducted rehearsals at court from 15 September 1632 until it was finally performed, on 9 January 1633. His fellow-actors must therefore have known a good deal about this play, even if they never saw either of its two private performances. As a reward for Taylor's help, they were given the splendid costumes worn by the aristocratic actors, which they used in their revival of Fletcher's *The Faithful Shepherdess,* played at court on Twelfth Night 1634. The fact that Montagu's play was not published at this time may have been due to its status as a private affair or to the controversy over Prynne's *Histrio-Mastix* in which it became embroiled. However, a new quarto of *The Faithful Shepherdess* appeared in 1634, with a reference to the court performance on its title-page and a new prologue and verses written specially for it.

The publication of the quarto of *The Two Noble Kinsmen* in 1634 can be seen in the context of these events and of other publications of those years: its printer, Thomas Cotes, was also the printer of the second Shakespeare Folio in 1632 and of *Pericles* in 1635. The title-page of the quarto does not mention a court performance, but it explicitly calls the play a tragicomedy, associating it with a type of drama that Fletcher claimed was too refined for its first audiences, and it names Shakespeare and Fletcher ('the two memorable worthies of their age') in terms which appeal to contemporary nostalgia. Even the Chaucerian source would have had both a nostalgic and an elitist appeal. This was a period when he was thought of above all as the poet of courtly love, as is evident, for example, in the references to him in Jonson's *New Inn* (1629).[11] Moreover, the difficulty of his 'antique' language added to his prestige: in 1635, Francis Kynaston published a Latin translation of the first two books of *Troilus and Criseyde.* Both Chaucer and the play based on his story were thus being appropriated by a courtly society sophisticated enough to recognize and enjoy the fact that its values might appear absurd to the uninitiated.

The evidence I have been amassing about the play's several occasions shows, I think, that a plot involving the conjunction of death and marriage in a royal household would rarely have been anything but topical in the early seventeenth century—or, probably, at any other time, except the reign of Elizabeth I, the last of the Tudors. In so far as both Chaucer and the Jacobean dramatists demonstrate the need to accept the fact that human life consists of the processes of death and renewal, they are

Hugh Quarshie as Arcite and Gerard Murphy as Palamon in the 1986 production of The Two Noble Kinsmen *at the Swan Theatre.*

simply stating, in elegantly tragic language, something with which no one could disagree. The theme can be applied specifically either to the situation of the royal family or to that of the actors themselves, who had lost the Globe in 1613, Burbage in 1619, and Fletcher in 1625. It would probably have had a resonance for most members of the audience. The very abundance of these possible allusions might perhaps reinforce a conservative attitude. '*Plus ça change. . . .*' The play's most famous couplet—

This world's a city full of straying streets,
And death's the market-place where each one meets.

(I.iv.15-16)

—expresses its dominant paradox: characters are constantly being urged to choose one road or another (friendship or love, Palamon or Arcite, Venus or Mars, getting married or fighting a war), but all choices are tragic.

The emphasis on the all-or-nothing nature of the decisions which are forced on the characters is something which Chaucer added to Boccaccio, but Boccaccio retains, as Chaucer does not, the sense of the dark Theban legend in the background of the chivalric romance. The harshness of the play may be due to a similar awareness on the part of at least one of the authors. Hippolyta, commenting on the fighters who are coming to the ceremonial fight, says that

> They would show
> Bravely about the titles of two kingdoms.
>
> (IV.ii.145-6)

Symbolically, women and cities are interchangeable, and in the Theban legend it is over Thebes itself that the brothers Eteocles and Polynices destroy each other. Boccaccio's *Teseida* makes the point that Palamon and Arcite are the last of the Theban line, and traces their conflict to the initial curse of the dragon's seed as well as comparing it to the hatred between Polynices and Eteocles (V.lvii-lix). Chaucer seems to think of Thebes as surviving the war and remaining a possible home for the two men—Theseus comments on the absurdity of Palamon and Arcite remaining in Athens when they could be living there in comfort, and Palamon's marriage to Emilia appears to be part of a treaty between the two countries. Boccaccio, however, had made it clear that the city is utterly destroyed by Theseus, and in the play Arcite knows that it is 'but a heap of ruins' (II.iii.20). If neither of the authors knew Boccaccio, one or both might have read Lydgate's *Siege of Thebes,* which was printed in Speght's edition of Chaucer (1598 and 1602).[12] They would also have known the source which he follows, Statius's *Thebaid,* probably the bloodiest of classical epics.

The analogy between fighting for love and fighting for power seems, at least at first sight, to point towards the political absolutism from which both David Norbrook and Erica Sheen are anxious to dissociate Shakespeare. In particular, the equality between the two heroes, which makes it so impossible to choose between them, is depicted as ultimately a source of destruction, not co-operation. Similarly, in *Antony and Cleopatra,* many characters appear convinced that the greatest danger to the peace of the world is not Antony's love for Cleopatra but the absolute equality that exists between him and Octavius, forcing their two stars to 'divide / Our equalness to this' (by 'this', the speaker, Octavius, means Antony's death (V.i. 477-8)). Coriolanus speaks of the confusion which results 'when two authorities are up, / Neither supreme' (III.i.112-13). The danger of absolute equality is not a purely Jacobean theme, however; it can be traced back through other Shakespearian works, at least as far as the 'two households, both alike in dignity' of *Romeo and Juliet,* which, at the end, are raising golden statues, of equal value, to the young people who have been destroyed by the feud. Perhaps the most interesting example of dangerous equality comes in *King John,* where the equation of the besieged city and the woman is particularly clear. The citizens of Angiers react to the armies of England and France much as Emilia does to Palamon and Arcite:

> Heralds, from off our towers we might behold
> From first to last the onset and retire
> Of both your armies, whose equality
> By our best eyes cannot be censured.
> Blood hath bought blood and blows have answered
>   blows,
> Strength matched with strength and power confronted
>   power.

> Both are alike, and both alike we like.
> One must prove greatest. While they weigh so even,
> We hold our town for neither, yet for both.
>
> (II.i.325-33)

In this case, however, the armies react by rejecting the option of total destruction (either of themselves or of the city) in favour of compromise and a dynastic marriage, and the Dauphin and Blanche suddenly discover a whole vocabulary of courtly love with which to deal with the situation. As in *Antony and Cleopatra* later, this turns out only to postpone the conflict. *King John,* however, ends with the war finely balanced, with defeats on both sides. Only the principle of hereditary succession offers hope of a new beginning in this play. By contrast, *The Two Noble Kinsmen,* which cannot invoke this principle, seems to demonstrate the danger of multiplicity. 'Doubtless / There is a best,' says Emilia (I.iii.47-8), referring to the apparent equality in Theseus's division of his love between Pirithous and Hippolyta. Her words recall the reaction of the Citizen of Angiers to the contending claims of the French and English armies: 'One must prove greatest.' That emotional claims should be as absolutist and irreconcilable as those of warring states explains the more 'tragic' sense of the play in those parts generally agreed to be Shakespeare's—that is, the first and last acts.[13] Absolutism is tragic and Shakespearian; compromise is comic and Fletcherian: this largely summarizes the critical response to the play.

But this is to discuss the Chaucerian plot in isolation. In practice, our sense of the play's politics must depend on how we see the relation of the story of Palamon and Arcite to the story of the Jailer's Daughter. Barry Kyle's RSC production (1986) saw a pattern which made a point about the 'politics of gender': his final tableau juxtaposed Emilia and the Jailer's Daughter, each dressed as a bride, each being tricked or forced into a marriage she did not really want. Alternatively, the two plots can be contrasted in terms not of gender but of class, as exemplified in the Daughter's traditional plebeian obsession with sex and the more refined love of the three aristocratic characters. The distinction is blurred at one point, when Fletcher makes the two men exchange rakish reminiscences of 'the wenches / We have known in our days' (III.iii.28-9), but it holds substantially true. At the one point where Palamon shows any awareness of the Daughter's existence, just before his expected execution, he and his friends offer the Jailer money towards her marriage. Before doing so one of the knights asks the inevitable question: 'Is it a maid?' Palamon says that he thinks so, but in fact he is probably wrong by this time, since her doctor has just given the almost unheard-of prescription of sex before marriage, telling the wooer moreover that as she's probably not 'honest' anyway it doesn't matter what he does to her. The Daughter's final scene can perhaps be described as an example of the 'politics of genre'. When she takes the suitor for Palamon, she asks him whether the doctor is his cousin Arcite, and the doctor, falling in with the role-playing, replies:

Yes, sweetheart,
And I am glad my cousin Palamon
Has made so fair a choice.

(V.iv.91)

This is, surely, the play's alternative ending—what *could* have happened if women were allowed to court men, if the two kinsmen had not been so noble, if the play had been a comedy.

The contrast between the two plots is thus a parallel to the contrasting attitudes frequently set up in Chaucer himself, for instance in *The Parliament of Fowles,* where the noble birds are prepared to die for love whereas the plebeian ones argue, 'But [unless] she wol love hym, lat hym love another!' (line 567). But is one plot being used to ridicule the other? Are the two noble kinsmen fools to commit themselves to an uncompromisingly destructive code of conduct, or is the girl a fool to let herself be tricked into a happy ending which depends on deception and compromise? Critics of the play used to be disgusted by the Daughter's behaviour and, still more, by her cure, but in modern productions it is easily the most touching and successful part of the play. It is possible, I think, that it may even have had this effect in its own time. The play's epilogue, in which the speaker compares himself to a schoolboy who is 'cruel fearful' about its reception, must have been intended for a boy actor, and the obvious choice would be the one playing the Daughter. That the dramatists gave her three soliloquies in a row suggests an astonishing reliance on the abilities of this particular boy. If he scored as great a personal success as Imogen Stubbs did in the 1986 RSC revival, the balance between the two plots, and their apparently opposing attitudes to love, might have remained unresolved. Whether audiences found the Daughter's final situation tragic or comic would depend on whether they wanted to make her story, as Barry Kyle's production did, part of the tragedy of the play. The fact that Davenant's Restoration adaptation arranged a happy ending for the character who corresponds to her (though only after raising her social status) also suggests another way of making the two stories harmonize generically instead of contradicting each other. Another point about performance, of course, is that the differences between the two actors of Palamon and Arcite will inevitably work against any idea of the interchangeability of the two men. The play may be intended to invite the audience to debate which is the more attractive, just as Chaucer's characters occasionally ask the readers of the *Canterbury Tales* to answer what are really unanswerable questions, such as the one the Knight asks at the end of the first book of his *Tale*: Which is better, to be in prison and see Emily, or to be free and banished from her sight? The impossibility of choice is balanced by the inevitability of the need to choose.

Our sense of uneasiness at the end of the play is not only the result of these various kinds of uncertainty. Political meaning is, as I have tried to show, a matter of context, and the context of *The Two Noble Kinsmen,* for us, is the politics of literary criticism. Our awareness that the play is the work of at least two authors makes nonsense of any attempts to ignore the question of intention. Is the extraordinary balance of forces in the play deliberate, or was there a struggle between the two authors on the level of language, genre, and political meaning, corresponding to the struggle between the two heroes and the gods whom they represent? The fact that we cannot possibly answer this question does not prevent us from asking it. It is uncertainty on this point that makes critic after critic discuss *The Tempest* as 'Shakespeare's last play', in spite of the existence of the two later collaborative works. This is the result of our own politics, which demand commitment and distrust pluralism. To suspend judgement is felt to be irresponsible: we *must* interpret, and this means discriminating between Shakespeare and Fletcher; it means finding a meaning in the play or, if there are more possible meanings than one, giving priority to the one belonging to the dramatist who long since won the trial by combat. Like Theseus, we want a straightforward decision about property: Who has a 'right' to Emilia, who is (as the prologue puts it) the 'breeder' of the play? Like Emilia, we are sure that 'Doubtless / There is a best', even if they are 'both too excellent', and we must destroy one in order to reward the other. Maybe, in view of the recent controversies about Shakespearian authorship, we are afraid of repeating the mistake of the Jailer's Daughter, letting ourselves be led off by a false Palamon. But when we set Shakespeare and Fletcher against each other, as if the result of their combat could at last give us an answer to this curious play, we are colluding with precisely the same destructive absolutism whose consequences *The Two Noble Kinsmen* has so vividly depicted.

Notes

Shakespeare's plays are quoted from *The Complete Works,* ed. Stanley Wells and Gary Taylor (Oxford: Oxford University Press, 1986).

1. Richard Proudfoot, 'Shakespeare and the new dramatists of the King's Men, 1606-1913', in J. R. Brown and B. Harris (eds), *Later Shakespeare,* Stratford upon Avon Studies (London: Arnold, 1966), 250-1.

2. John Fletcher and William Shakespeare, *The Two Noble Kinsmen,* ed. Richard Proudfoot, Regents Renaissance Drama Series (London: Arnold, 1970); M. C. Bradbrook, 'Shakespeare as collaborator', in *The Living Monument: Shakespeare and the Theatre of his Time* (Cambridge: Cambridge University Press, 1976); Glynne Wickham, '"The Two Noble Kinsmen" or "A Midsummer Night's Dream, Part II"?', in G. R. Hibbard (ed.), *Elizabethan Theatre* (London: Macmillan, 1980) vol. VII, 167-96.

3. See Stanley Wells and Gary Taylor, with John Jowett and William Montgomery (eds), *William Shakespeare: A Textual Companion* (Oxford: Oxford University Press, 1987), 633.

4. Walter R. Davis (ed.), *The Works of Thomas Campion* (New York: Norton, 1967), 259 and n.

5. See, for example, Augustine Taylor, *Epithalamium upon the All-Desired Nuptials, etc.* (London, 1613), a collection of poems by divers hands on the wedding of Princess Elizabeth and the Palsgrave.

6. Thomas Heywood, *A Marriage Triumphe. Solemnized in an Epithalamium* (London, 1613).

7. See Proudfoot's edition of *The Two Noble Kinsmen,* xii.

8. Henry King, 'By Occasion of the young Prince his happy Birth. May 29. 1630', ll.23-6, *The Poems of Henry King,* ed. Margaret Crum (Oxford: Clarendon Press, 1965), 73-5.

9. William Proctor Williams, 'Not hornpipes and funerals: Fletcherian tragicomedy', in Nancy Klein Maguire (ed.), *Renaissance Tragicomedy: Explorations in Genre and Politics* (New York: AMS Press, 1987), 143.

10. Walter Montagu, *The Shepheard's Paradise. A Comedy. Privately Acted before the late King Charles by the Queen's Majesty and Ladies of Honour* (London, 1659; misprinted as 1629).

11. Caroline F. E. Spurgeon, *Five Hundred Years of Chaucer Criticism and Allusion 1357-1900,* 2 vols (Cambridge: Cambridge University Press, 1925).

12. Geoffrey Chaucer, *The Workes of our antient and learned English Poet, Geffrey Chaucer, newly Printed. In this Impression you shall find these Additions: 1. His Portraiture and Progenie shewed. 2. His Life collected. 3. Arguments to every Booke gathered. 4. Old and obscure Words explained. 5. Authors by him cited, declared. 6. Difficulties opened. 7. Two Bookes of his neure before printed* (London, 1598).

13. See, for example, Ann Thompson, *Shakespeare's Chaucer: A Study in Literary Origins* (Liverpool: Liverpool University Press, 1978), 172.

Alan Stewart (essay date 1999)

SOURCE: Stewart, Alan. "'Near Akin': The Trials of Friendship in *The Two Noble Kinsmen.*" In *Shakespeare's Late Plays: New Readings,* edited by Jennifer Richards and James Knowles, pp. 57-71. Edinburgh: Edinburgh University Press, 1999.

[*In the following essay, Stewart investigates the nature of the failure of Palamon and Arcite's idealized male friendship depicted in* The Two Noble Kinsmen, *suggesting that the relationship was doomed because of the conflict between humanist and chivalric notions of male friendship, and the realities of male relations and kinship bonds in Jacobean England.*]

Critics have never been happy with *The Two Noble Kinsmen.*[1] It has traditionally been regarded as an unsatisfac-tory play, compromised, in Ann Thompson's words, by 'many tensions and inconsistencies';[2] to at least one critic, it remains 'that most distressing of plays'.[3] Despite its use of an archetypal story of two male friends brought into conflict over a woman, already tried and tested by Boccaccio (in the *Teseida*) and Chaucer (*Knight's Tale*), its telling here has seemed less than successful. Theodore Spencer went so far as to complain that the story of Palamon and Arcite 'is intrinsically feeble, superficial, and undramatic'.[4] The characters themselves have been 'dismissed as virtually interchangeable emblems of Platonic love and chivalric courtesy—Tweedledum and Tweedledee as Kenneth Muir once called them'.[5] Some have attributed this to the inherent contradictions of the play's genre, tragicomedy.[6] Some have attributed it to its collaborative authorship by Fletcher and Shakespeare, as if each playwright wrote in solitary ignorance of his partner's work, and the play necessarily betrayed that process.[7] This approach makes possible, for example, the argument that Shakespeare composed the first exchange between Palamon and Arcite, but that Fletcher was responsible for their apparently contradictory quarrel in the prison scene.[8]

I prefer to follow the approach of Richard Hillman, who has argued that 'it is . . . possible, especially in a post-modern critical climate, to take the play's internal jars, whatever their origin . . . as integral to the text we have, not as blocking the text that might have been'.[9] I shall argue that, rather than being a failed attempt at a play about idealised male friendship, *The Two Noble Kinsmen* is rather a play about a failed attempt at idealised male friendship. In turn, I shall suggest, this failure derives from the juxtaposition of both classical-humanist and chivalric modes of male friendship with the realities of social relations, and a particular form of kinship, in Jacobean England.

The Two Noble Kinsmen contains a proliferation of variations on that classical and then humanist theme of *amicitia,* the idealised male friendship celebrated in such key Renaissance pedagogical texts as Cicero's *De amicitia* and *De officiis* and Seneca's *De beneficiis.*[10] First, Theseus and Pirithous present an established example of *amicitia,* a legendary male couple revered alongside Orestes and Pylades, Damon and Pythias, and Scipio and Laelius. Pirithous operates to Theseus as *alter ipse,* another himself, to the extent that he stands in as Theseus at his friend's wedding to Hippolyta, because Theseus is honour-bound to avenge the deaths of the husbands of the three queens. In Emilia's words 'The one of th'other may be said to water / Their intertangled roots of love' (I, iii, 58-9).

Second, we encounter the female friendship of Emilia and Flavina. Emilia tells of her love for the innocent 'play-fellow' (I, iii, 50) of her childhood who died young:

What she liked
Was then of me approved; what not, condemned—
No more arraignment. The flower that I would pluck
And put between my breasts (then but beginning
To swell about the blossom), oh, she would long

Till she had such another, and commit it
To the like innocent cradle, where phoenix-like
They died in perfume.

(I, iii, 64-71)

This intense female friendship, located in early pubescence and now irretrievably lost, occupies the same elegiac space as those in earlier Shakespeare plays: Rosalind and Celia in *As You Like It*, and Helena and Hermia in *A Midsummer Night's Dream*, for example.[11]

But the central friendship is that of Palamon and Arcite. As they are imprisoned together, Arcite gives one of the most passionate friendship speeches in English literature:

And here being thus together,
We are an endless mine to one another;
We are one another's wife, ever begetting
New births of love; we are father, friends, acquain-
    tance,
We are, in one another, families;
I am your heir and you are mine. This place
Is our inheritance; no hard oppressor
Dare take this from us; here, with a little patience,
We shall live long and loving.

(II, ii, 78-86)

Palamon answers, 'Is there record of any two that loved / Better than we do, Arcite?', to which Arcite affirms, 'Sure there cannot.' 'I do not think it possible', continues Palamon, 'our friendship / Should ever leave us'. 'Till our deaths it cannot', declares Arcite, 'And after death our spirits shall be led / To those that love eternally' (II, ii, 112-17). The tale of Palamon and Arcite as told in this play thus echoes that quintessential humanist fiction of the two male friends, temporarily rent asunder by the intrusion of a woman, who then go on to make up, usually with one of them marrying the woman, and the other marrying his friend's sister. Perhaps the most famous example is the story of Titus and Gisippus, told by Boccaccio in his *Decameron,* and then Englished by Thomas Elyot, and placed centrally in his influential *Boke Named the Gouernour.*[12] The moral of such tales is that, despite the claims of family and marriage, male friendship will emerge as the supreme affective force in the lives of the two men.

This superabundance of friendships should, I suggest, raise our suspicions from the start, as couple after couple are introduced displaying apparently textbook adherence to the model. As Theodore Spencer wrote incisively in 1939, '[o]ne of Shakespeare's favourite dramatic devices in his mature work is to establish a set of values and then to show how it is violated by the individual action which follows'.[13] Here, these three instances are introduced precisely to point up the relative failings of two of them. In the case of Emilia and Flavina, the elegiac tone points to the futility of a female version of *amicitia*, always already lost. But more importantly, in Palamon and Arcite something is terribly wrong. From the declaration just quoted, the eternal friendship of Palamon and Arcite lasts exactly two more lines, by which time Palamon has caught

sight of Emilia, and Arcite has to urge him (unsuccessfully) to 'forward' with his speech. Their subsequent quarrel over Emilia, leading to an illegal duel, and ultimately to the strange death of Arcite—rather than to the usual double marriage—indicates clearly that all is not well in this telling of their friendship.

The reason for this, I shall suggest, is that in Palamon and Arcite we see a literary, humanist template sitting uncomfortably on a particular Jacobean social reality. The story of Palamon and Arcite is subtly nuanced in each of its retellings. As Eugene Waith notes, in Boccaccio's *Teseida*, it is 'basically a tale of lovers'; in Chaucer's *Knight's Tale*, the relationship is a 'chivalric bond of blood-brotherhood'.[14] In Shakespeare and Fletcher's version, I suggest, Palamon and Arcite are, first and foremost, as the title makes quite clear, *kinsmen,* and as they constantly reiterate, *cousins.* In this chapter, I shall argue that we can make far more sense of *The Two Noble Kinsmen* if we stop thinking of it as a play about friendship, and approach it instead as a play about the problems of kinship, and specifically the problems of cognatic cousinage.[15]

The Two Noble Kinsmen operates, as much of Jacobean England operated, within a culture where women (and figuratively, their virginity) were passed between families in marriage for financial gain; in the upper middling classes and above, these transactions were often complex and lengthy affairs, as befitted such important exchanges of lands, goods and cash. From the first words of the prologue, *The Two Noble Kinsmen* situates itself centrally within such a culture:

New plays and maidenhead are near akin:
Much followed both, for both much money gi'en,
If they stand sound and well. And a good play,
Whose modest scenes blush on his marriage day
And shake to lose his honour, is like her
That after holy tie [the wedding] and first night's stir
Yet still is Modesty and still retains
More of the maid, to sight, than husband's pains.

(Prologue, ll. 1-8)

The action of the play is inserted into an interrupted marriage (once again, as in *A Midsummer Night's Dream,* Theseus and Hippolyta have to wait!); the action is concluded when Emilia is exchanged between her new brother-in-law Theseus and the surviving kinsman, Palamon. (Although Arcite appears to give Emilia to Palamon with his dying breath—'Take her. I die' (V, iv, 95)—in fact it is Theseus who endorses the match). Even the Jailor's Daughter becomes marriageable because Palamon, in gratitude for her actions in springing him from gaol, gives 'a sum of money to her marriage: / A large one—a gift, of course, not directly to the woman, but to her father, in order that he might marry her to the advantage of both father and daughter (IV, i, 21-4). When Palamon and Arcite are imprisoned, they first bewail the fact that they must remain bachelors; as Arcite puts it:

here age must find us
And, which is heaviest, Palamon, unmarried.
The sweet embraces of a loving wife,
Loaden with kisses, armed with thousand Cupids,
Shall never clasp our necks; no issue know us;
No figures of ourselves shall we e'er see,
To glad our age, and like young eagles teach 'em
Boldly to gaze against bright arms and say,
'Remember what your fathers were, and conquer!'

(II, ii, 25-36)

Much critical work has been done to illuminate this com-modification of women in marriage, most notably Gayle Rubin's reworking of the anthropological work of Claude Lévi-Strauss to uncover the 'traffic in women', and Eve Sedgwick's combining of this with René Girard's triangu-lar formulation to reread male rivalry over women as the prime feature of male homosociality.[16] In her study of quattrocento and cinquecento Florence, Christiane Klapisch-Zuber has shown how these abstract structures operated in practice. 'In Florence', she writes, 'men *were* and *made* the "houses". The word *casa* designates . . . the material house, the lodging of a domestic unit . . . But it also stands for an entire agnatic kinship group. 'These houses, and kinship in general, were 'determined by men, and the male branching of genealogies drawn up by contemporaries shows how little importance was given, after one or two generations, to kinship through women'. She illustrates graphically how, as they married, women moved between houses—both lineage groups and the physical buildings—demonstrating both the stability of the house, and the radical discontinuity of the lives of the women exchanged between them:

> In these *case,* in the sense of both physical and the symbolic house, women were passing guests. To contemporary eyes, their movements in relation to the *case* determined their social personality more truly than the lineage group from which they came. It was by means of their physical 'entrances' and 'exits' into and out of the 'house' that their families of origin or of al-liance evaluated the contribution of women to the great-ness of the *casa*.[17]

Although the importance of kinship in the English mid-dling classes is thought to have been diminishing during this period, in the upper classes it still held sway. As Keith Wrightson writes, '[i]t is undoubtedly true . . . that both the titular aristocracy and the upper gentry were deeply preoccupied with ancestry and lineage and that they tended to recognise a wide range of kinsmen',[18] indeed Anthony Fletcher has asserted that in Sussex county society 'kin-ship was the dominant principle'.[19] Mervyn James writes that the deepest obligation in any man's life was:

> to the lineage, the family and kinship group. For this, being inherited with the 'blood', did not depend on promise or oath. It could neither be contracted into, nor could the bond be broken. For a man's very being as honourable had been transmitted to him with the blood of his ancestors, themselves honourable men. Honour therefore was not merely an individual possession, but

that of the collectivity, the lineage. Faithfulness to the kinship group arose out of this intimate involvement of personal and collective honour, which meant that both increased or diminished together. Consequently, in criti-cal honour situations where an extremity of conflict arose, or in which dissident positions were taken up involving revolt, treason and rebellion, the ties of blood were liable to assert themselves with a particular power.[20]

Viewed in this English social context, rather than in its humanist literary context, the play reads rather differently. The first words uttered by Arcite put in place a competi-tion between affective and familial links: 'Dear Palamon, dearer in love than blood / And our prime cousin' (I, ii, 1-2). The 'love' that Arcite feels for Palamon is greater than the claim of 'blood', the fact that they are first cousins. Yet they refer to themselves constantly in kinship terms (at least thirty-eight times in the course of the play): 'cousin', 'coz', 'noble cousin' (II, ii, 1), 'gentle cousin' (II, ii, 70 and III, vi, 112), 'fair cousin' (III, vi, 18), 'sweet cousin' (III, vi, 69), 'Clear-spirited cousin' (I, ii, 74), 'My coz, my coz' (III, i, 58), 'kinsman' (III, vi, 21), 'noble kinsman' (II, ii, 193 and III, vi, 17).[21] Even when the two are estranged during their competition for Emilia, they are 'Traitor kinsman' (III, i, 30) and 'base cousin' (III, iii, 44) and Palamon can punningly answer Arcite's 'Dear cousin Palamon' with 'Cozener Arcite' (III, i, 43-4), reminding us that the root of 'cozening' is the cozener's claim to be his victim's long-lost cousin.[22]

'Cousin', like 'kinsman', is a deliberately vague term in early modern English, one that can refer to any loose fam-ily connection: Anthony Fletcher writes that in Sussex, 'stress on cousinage in correspondence and account keep-ing became a mere mark of courtesy. The tight circles of intimate friendship, which were more significant for the dynamics of country affairs, ran within the wider circles of blood'.[23] But these men are not merely 'kinsmen': they share a very particular relationship—to Theseus, they are 'royal german foes' (V, i, 9), implying a close cousin relationship, and in the Herald's words, 'They are sisters' children, nephews to the King' (I, iv, 16). This echoes the Chaucerian source, where they are described as being 'of the blood riall / Of Thebes, and of sistren two yborne' (II. 1018-19).[24] This point is reiterated strikingly as Palamon and Arcite go through the ritual motions before their at-tempted duel: Palamon asserts:

> Thou art mine aunt's son
> And that blood we desire to shed is mutual,
> In me thine and in thee mine.

(III, vi, 94-6)

In other words, their blood relationship derives from the female line—in Roman or Scottish law terms, their kin-ship is *cognatic,* rather than *agnatic* (through the male line). Palamon and Arcite are an example, therefore, of what we might call 'cognatic cousinage'.

There is no doubting of course that the kin relationship of cousins german, or first cousins, is extremely close, so close that if one were male and one female, then their right to marry each other would be disputed. However, seen in terms of a culture that exchanges women between patriarchal houses, cousins german whose kinship is cognatic occupy a strangely distant relationship: they are necessarily born into different houses, because their mothers married into different houses. This means, then, that the connection between the two cousins is not necessarily mutually beneficial—what benefits one need not benefit the other.

The peculiarity of this particular kinship relationship—its intense affective claims belied by its signal lack of practical utility—can be glimpsed in the tortuous interactions of two contemporary cousins german: Sir Robert Cecil and Francis Bacon. Cecil was the son of William Cecil, Lord Burghley, by his second wife Mildred Cooke; Bacon was the son of Sir Nicholas Bacon, Lord Keeper, by his second wife Anne Cooke. Mildred and Anne were sisters, two of the renowned and learned daughters of Sir Anthony Cooke, and thus Robert and Francis were first cousins, an instance of cognatic cousinage. But this apparently close family connection was put under great strain after the premature death of Francis's father in February 1579. Left without adequate provision by his father, and unable to call on his estranged elder half-brothers after a dispute about the will, Francis naturally turned to his uncle, Lord Burghley. Throughout his correspondence of the 1580s and early 1590s there are unveiled hints that Burghley might want to become a surrogate parent to his poor nephew. Instead, however, Francis was to be consistently disappointed by his uncle, who put his energies behind his own son, and other protégés. Francis in turn was forced to look for support beyond his immediate family, and turned in 1588 to Elizabeth's new young favourite, Robert Devereux, the second earl of Essex.[25]

Essex backed Francis in his bid to become Attorney-General in 1593 and 1594. It soon became clear, however, that Burghley and Cecil were backing another candidate, Edward Coke. This situation produced some highly charged encounters between Bacon's supporters (including Essex and Bacon's mother) and Coke's supporters (Burghley and Cecil). Such an encounter is recorded for us by one of Essex's intelligencers, Anthony Standen, to whom Essex related the anecdote.[26] At the end of January 1593, in the privacy of a shared coach, Sir Robert asked Essex who his candidate was for the vacant post of Attorney-General. Essex affected astonishment, declaring that he 'wondered Sir Robert should ask him that question, seeing it could not be unknown unto him that resolutely against all whosoever for Francis Bacon he stood'.

Sir Robert affected amazement. 'Good Lord', he replied, 'I wonder your Lordship should go about to spend your strength in so unlikely or impossible a matter.' It was out of the question, he continued, that Francis Bacon should be raised to a position of such eminence, since he was simply too young and inexperienced (Francis was thirty-three at the time). Essex readily admitted that he could not

think of a precedent for so youthful a candidate for the post of attorney. But he pointed out that youth and inexperience did not seem to be hindering the bid by Sir Robert himself ('[a] younger than Francis, of lesser learning and of no greater experience') to become principal secretary of state, the most influential of all government posts. Cecil retaliated immediately:

> I know your lordship means myself. Although my years and experience are small, yet weighing the school I studied in and the great wisdom and learning of my schoolmaster, and the pains and observations I daily passed, yet I deem my qualifications to be sufficient. The added entitlement of my father's long service will make good the rest.

Unconvinced, Essex passionately reaffirmed his support for Bacon. 'And for your own part Sir Robert', he concluded, 'I think strange both of my Lord Treasurer and you that can have the mind to seek the preferment of a stranger before so near a kinsman as a first cousin.'

This exchange demonstrates vividly both the symbolic and the practical implications of various relationships between kinsmen. It testifies to the real practical value of the closest kin relationships: Cecil's career is quite explicitly acknowledged as his birthright, because of his father's success. Cognatic cousinage, however, is more complex. On the one hand, we see here the social expectations of the relationship, and of its powerful affective pull ('strange [that] you . . . can have the mind to seek the preferment of a stranger before so near a kinsman as a first cousin'). On the other, we witness the ineffectiveness of this claim in practical terms: Burghley and Cecil are never swayed to support Bacon (Bacon was not to reach public office for another twelve years, and his career only took off following Cecil's death in 1612). Although the situation was thought unfair by many, Bacon had no legal or moral claim on his cognatic relatives.

The Two Noble Kinsmen is not about either of the cousins' attempting to use the other in any practical sense. As Jeffrey Masten has pointed out, their similarity, a standard trope of *amicitia* literature, is indeed deployed to suggest that they will inevitably enter into competition:

ARCITE

> . . . am not I
> Part of your blood, part of your soul? You have told me
> That I was Palamon, and you were Arcite.

PALAMON

> Yes.

ARCITE

> Am not I liable to those affections,
> Those joys, griefs, angers, fears, my friend shall suffer?
>
> (II, ii, 187-91)[27]

However, the futility of their kinship is signalled throughout the play by a skilfully maintained figurative representation. As the chapters in this collection by Helen Hackett and Gordon McMullan amply illustrate, the late plays return insistently to figures of maternity and manliness. These two sisters' sons, who, as we have already seen, describe themselves as their aunts' sons, are constantly referred to in terms of their mothers. When asked what she thinks of Arcite, Emilia answers that 'Believe, / His mother was a wondrous handsome woman; / His face, methinks, goes that way' (II, v, 19-21) (although Hippolyta then contends that 'his body / And fiery mind illustrate a brave father' (II, v, 212)). Later Emilia describes Palamon as being 'swart and meagre, of an eye as heavy / As if he had lost his mother' (IV, ii, 27-8). Together, she insists, 'Two greater and two better never yet / Made mothers joy' (IV, ii, 63-4).

When Palamon berates the kind of men who boast of their sexual conquests, those 'large confessors', he 'hotly ask[s] them / If they had mothers—I had one, a woman, / And women 'twere they wronged' (V, i, 105-7). To Palamon the image of womanhood is his mother.

Firmly established as mothers' boys, the masculinity of both Palamon and Arcite is steadily chipped away throughout the play by a number of analogies, several with Ovidian overtones: as Jonathan Bate argues, '[c]ollaboration with Ovid is one of the marks of Fletcher and Shakespeare's collaboration with each other'.[28] When they are in prison, delineating their *amicitia, Arcite* exclaims that 'We are one another's wife, ever begetting / New births of love' (II, ii, 80-1). Two classical archetypes of passive male sexuality, Narcissus and Ganymede, are reiterated. Immediately after Arcite and Palamon assert their status as wives to each other, Emilia picks some narcissus from the garden, asserting that 'That was a fair boy certain, but a fool / To love himself. Were there not maids enough?' (II, ii, 120-2), referring of course to the myth of Narcissus dying while longing for his own reflection, having rejected the women who loved him. The connection is made explicit when Emilia later compares pictures of her two suitors—Palamon may be to Arcite 'mere dull shadow; / . . . swart and meagre, of an eye as heavy':

> As if he had lost his mother; a still temper;
> No stirring in him, no alacrity;
> Of all this sprightly sharpness, not a smile.
> Yet these that we count errors may become him:
> Narcissus was a sad boy, but a heavenly.
>
> (IV, ii, 26-32)

As the work of James Saslow, Leonard Barkan and Bruce R. Smith has shown, Ganymede had become by the Renaissance a standard figure for sodomitical, and specifically passive sodomitical, identification.[29] In the same speech, Emilia compares Arcite to Ganymede, one of the 'prettie boyes / That were the darlinges of the gods'. In Golding's words:

> The king of Gods [Jupiter] did burne ere while in loue
>   of *Ganymed*

> The *Phrygian,* and the thing was found which *Iupiter* that sted,
> Had rather be then that he was. Yet could he not beteeme
> The shape of any other bird than Eagle for to seeme:
> And so he soring in the ayre with borrowed wings trust vp
> The *Troiane* boy, who stil in heauen euen yet doth beare his cup,
> And brings him *Nectar,* though against Dame *Iunos* wil it bee.[30]

Emilia declares:

> What an eye,
> Of what a fiery spark and quick sweetness,
> Has this young prince! Here Love himself sits smiling;
> Just such another wanton Ganymede
> Set Jove afire with, and enforced the god
> Snatch up the goodly boy, and set him by him,
> A shining constellation. What a brow,
> Of what a spacious majesty, he carries,
> Arched like the great-eyed Juno's, but far sweeter,
> Smoother than Pelops' shoulder!
>
> (IV, ii, 12-21)

We move from the beautiful shepherd boy Ganymede snatched up to become Jove's cupbearer in the heavens, to Jove's own wife Juno, to the ivory shoulder that replaced the shoulder of Pelops served up by his father Tantalus (and as ever, we are not sure here whether the smooth shoulder is the succulent one eaten, or the ivory replacement).[31] Palamon and Arcite are led through a serious of analogies that cast them as women, or as passive male bodies eaten by men or made love to by men, or as men in love with their own reflection. These images multiply through the play, and no amount of recognition for Arcite's potential prowess as a wrestler is going to shake them off.

What effect might this have on a reading of *The Two Noble Kinsmen*? I return to the speech I quoted earlier, where Palamon and Arcite pledge eternal friendship. It is indeed a remarkable and passionate speech, but we need to see it in context. It comes during the couple's imprisonment: at the beginning of the scene (II, ii), Palamon bewails their situation ('Oh, cousin Arcite, / Where is Thebes now? Where is our noble country? / Where are our friends and kindred?' (II, ii, 6-8)) and Arcite agrees that their 'hopes are prisoners with us' (II, ii, 26), lamenting the fact that they will never marry, nor have children, nor hunt again. It is only then that Arcite exclaims:

> Yet, cousin,
> Even from the bottom of these miseries,
> From all that Fortune can inflict upon us,
> I see two comforts rising, two mere blessings,
> If the gods please: to hold here a brave patience
> And the enjoying of our griefs together.
> While Palamon is with me, let me perish
> If I think this our prison!
>
> (II, ii, 55-62)

Palamon replies:

> Certainly,
> 'Tis a main goodness, cousin, that our fortunes
> Were twined together; 'tis most true, two souls
> Put in two noble bodies, let 'em suffer
> The gall of hazard, so they grow together,
> Will never sink; they must not, say they could.
> A willing man dies sleeping and all's done.

(II, ii, 62-8)

It is then that they go on to 'make this prison holy sanctuary / To keep us from corruption of worse men' (II, ii, 71-2), and go into their passionate speech of friendship. As this preamble shows, however, the speech is a set piece, arrived at only after despair has cast them down, and as a pragmatic response to their dire situation. Friendship in the classic Ciceronian mould is only an option once imprisonment takes away their social agency. It does not stand up to comparison with the successful friendship of Theseus and Pirithous, or with the elegaic friendship of Emilia and Flavina, which have been carefully set up before precisely to demonstrate the failings of Palamon and Arcite's friendship; the first oblique comment on their declaration of friendship is Emilia's discussion of Narcissus. And even within the speech just quoted we can sense something awry: these two friends are 'two souls / Put in two noble bodies' (II, ii, 64-5), when the classic formulation of friendship is a single soul in two bodies. The hyperbole of being each other's wife, family, heir is merely a response to the deprivation of social agency; the minute that a way back into the real world is spied (in the form of Emilia, marriage to whom will ensure not only freedom but social success in Athens) the eternal friendship is shelved.

While the influence of Ciceronian *amicitia* is evident throughout, the play's immediate source requires that the authors also deal with the male friendship associated with chivalric codes. Here again, all is not as it might be. Chaucer's *Knight's Tale* has an ending which can still been seen as happy within the expectations of its genre: one knight wins his lady in honourable chivalric contest, but dies in an accident; after a suitable period, the lady is granted to the honourable loser. Much has been written about the chivalric elements of *The Two Noble Kinsmen*: it has been seen as linked to a neo-chivalric movement associated with Prince Henry;[32] it has even been read as a *roman à clef* of international politics, with Arcite as Henry, who has to die before his sister Elizabeth (Emilia) can marry her betrothed Frederick (Palamon).[33] In *The Two Noble Kinsmen*, the elements are similar to Chaucer's, but their treatment is noticeably different, and the end result unsettling: as Philip Finkelpearl has written, '[a]lthough the knightly code may originally have been designed to curb uncivilized instincts, here it sanctions and dignifies the urge of revenge, murder, and suicide'.[34]

Richard Hillman sees the fundamental contradictions as suggestive of an unbridgeable gap between medieval and Jacobean notions of chivalry: '[p]recisely by endlessly trying and failing to measure up to the inherited images of romance perfection, these pale Jacobean imitations deconstruct the very business of image-making. They are trapped by their own attempted appropriation of a medieval past'.[35] The kinsmen's 'failure to measure up' is, moreover, treated harshly, even callously. The chivalric contest now carries a death penalty for the loser, and there is virtually no time lost between the winner's death and the loser's marriage. The death of one knight, an incidental detail in Chaucer (since it does not matter who marries the lady), here becomes essential to the happy ending. Significantly, a successful conclusion can only come at what Palamon calls the 'miserable end of our alliance' (V, iv, 86), the accident in which Arcite is fatally injured. Even here, the nature of his death—Arcite is left hanging upside down from his mount, after the horse rears away from a spark from the cobbles ('Arcite's legs, being higher than his head, / Seemed with strange art to hang' (V, iv, 78-9))—suggests something less than chivalric. As Richard Abrams notes,' [b]y the play's end, disabused of *The Knight's Tale's* heroic mystique, we recognise the strangeness of a world where a question of love-rights is automatically referred to a determination of which kinsman is the stronger fighter'.[36]

Arcite must die for Palamon to win: as Palamon laments, 'That we should things desire, which do cost us / The loss of our desire! That nought could buy / Dear love, but loss of dear love' (V, iv, 110-12). *The Two Noble Kinsmen* demonstrates, and demands, highly developed understanding of concepts of friendship and kinship, developed enough to accommodate both parody and sincerity about such concepts. The friendship of Palamon and Arcite is no more than a game to while away long hours of incarceration; their constantly reiterated claims to kinship dissolve in the face of a prize (Emilia) that might benefit them as individuals and their immediate family groups; the play's happy ending necessitates the dissolution of their 'alliance'. Fletcher and Shakespeare indulge their audience in the comfortable humanist myth of *amicitia,* and the reliable codes of chivalric courtship, only to force that audience to accept the fact that ultimately these are no more than myths and codes, and that they cannot thrive together. We are faced with the sobering fact that artistic closure is not always compatible with social reality: to secure our desired happy ending, there may be fatalities.

Notes

1. For the limited critical bibliography to 1990 see Proudfoot, '*Henry VIII*', pp. 391-2. The only monograph devoted to the play is Bertram, *Shakespeare and 'The Two Noble Kinsmen'*.

2. Thompson, *Shakespeare's Chaucer*, p. 166.

3. Donaldson, *The Swan at the Well*, p. 50.

4. Spencer, '*The Two Noble Kinsmen*', p. 256.

5. Wickham, '*The Two Noble Kinsmen*', p. 168.

6. See *The Two Noble Kinsmen*, ed. Potter, 'Introduction', pp. 2-6.

7. Spencer, '*The Two Noble Kinsmen*', p. 255. See also *The Two Noble Kinsmen*, ed. Potter, pp. 24-34. The

'collaboration' argument is also used to explain away the problematic Jailer's Daughter subplot, but my focus here is on the Palamon and Arcite story.

8. Waith, 'Shakespeare and Fletcher', pp. 239-42; Hillman, 'Shakespeare's romantic innocents', p. 73.

9. Hillman, 'Shakespeare's romantic innocents', pp. 70, 71.

10. The classic survey of male friendship in Renaissance English literature remains Mills, *One Soul in Bodies Twain.*

11. For a discussion of this genre see Miller, *Stages of Desire,* Ch. 5.

12. See Elyot, *Boke Named the Gouernour* (1531); for the importance of this story, see Hutson, *The Usurer's Daughter,* Ch. 2.

13. Spencer, '*The Two Noble Kinsmen*', p. 270.

14. Waith, 'Shakespeare and Fletcher', p. 236.

15. The importance of kinship rather than friendship in *The Two Noble Kinsmen* is stressed in Mills, *One Soul in Bodies Twain,* pp. 322-3, but he does not address the particular nature of this kinship.

16. Rubin, 'The traffic in women'; Sedgwick, *Between Men.*

17. Klapisch-Zuber, *Women, Family, and Ritual,* pp. 117-18.

18. Wrightson, *English Society,* pp. 44-51, p. 47.

19. Fletcher, *A County Community,* p. 48.

20. James, *Society, Politics and Culture,* p. 325.

21. For other use of 'cousin' and 'coz' see II, ii, 4; II, ii, 63; II, ii, 96; II, ii, 107; II, ii 126; II, ii, 131; III, i, 43; III, i, 69; III, iii, 1; III, iii, 20; III, iii, 23; III, vi, 1; III, vi, 44; III, vi, 47; III, vi, 53; III, vi, 61; III, vi, 73; III, vi, 82; III, vi, 117; III, vi, 262; III, vi, 299;V, i, 23;V, i, 31;V, iv, 93;V, iv, 109.

22. Similarly, 'cousinage' can refer to the writ whereby a legal claim for land is made by one claiming to be a cousin to the deceased.

23. Fletcher, *A County Community,* p. 48.

24. References are to *The Riverside Chaucer.*

25. See Jardine and Stewart, *Hostage to Fortune.*

26. See Anthony Standen to Anthony Bacon, 3 February 1593/4, Lambeth Palace Library MS 650, fols 80-2 (art. 50). This incident is discussed at greater length in Jardine and Stewart, *Hostage to Fortune,* pp. 11-17.

27. Masten, *Textual Intercourse,* p. 49.

28. Bate, *Shakespeare and Ovid,* p. 265.

29. See Saslow, *Ganymede in the Renaissance*; Barkan, *Transuming Passions*; Smith, *Homosexual Desire,* Ch. 3.

30. Golding, *The XV Bookes* (1603), sig. Q8ᵛ (Book X, 11.155-61).

31. For Pelops, see Golding, *The XV Bookes,* sig. K8ᵛ (Book VI, ll. 515-25).

32. See for example Hillman, 'Shakespeare's romantic innocents', p. 79; Finkelpearl, 'Two distincts, division none', pp. 184-99.

33. Wickham, '*The Two Noble Kinsmen'*, passim.

34. Finkelpearl, 'Two distincts, division none', p. 191.

35. Hillman, 'Shakespeare's romantic innocents', p. 71.

36. Abrams, 'Gender confusion', p. 75.

Bibliography

PRIMARY

Chaucer, Geoffrey. *The Riverside Chaucer,* edited by F. N. Robinson. Oxford: Oxford University Press, 1987, 3rd edition.

Elyot, Thomas. *Boke Named the Gouernour.* London: 1531.

Golding, Arthur, translator. *The XV Bookes of P. Ouidius Naso, Entituled Metamorphosis.* London, 1603.

Shakespeare, William. *The Two Noble Kinsmen,* edited by L. D. Potter. London: Routledge, 1997.

SECONDARY

Abrams, Richard. "Gender confusion and sexual politics in *The Two Noble Kinsmen.*" In *Drama, Sex, and Politics, Themes in Drama 7,* edited by James Redmond, pp. 69-76. Cambridge: Cambridge University Press, 1985.

Barkan, Leonard. *Transuming Passions: Ganymede and the Erotics of Humanism.* Stanford Calif.: Stanford University Press, 1991.

Bate, Jonathan. *Shakespeare and Ovid.* Oxford: Clarendon Press, 1993.

Donaldson, E. Talbot. *The Swan at the Well: Shakespeare Reading Chaucer.* New Haven: Yale University Press, 1985.

Finkelpearl, Philip J. "Two distincts, division none: Shakespeare and Fletcher's *The Two Noble Kinsmen* of 1613." In *Elizabethan Theater: Essays in Honor of S. Schoenbaum,* edited by R. B. Parker and S. P. Zitner, pp. 184-99. Newark: University of Delaware Press, 1996.

Fletcher, Anthony. *A County Community in Peace and War: Sussex 1600-1660.* London: Longman, 1975.

Hillman, Richard. "Shakespeare's romantic innocents and the misappropriation of the romance past: the case of *The Two Noble Kinsmen.*" *Shakespeare Survey* 43, (1991): 69-80.

Hutson, Lorna. *The Usurer's Daughter: Male Friendship and Fictions of Women in Sixteenth-Century England.* London: Routledge, 1994.

James, Mervyn. *Society, Politics and Culture: Studies in Early Modern England.* Cambridge: Cambridge University Press, 1986.

Jardine, Lisa, and Alan Stewart. *Hostage to Fortune: The Troubled Life of Francis Bacon, 1561-1626.* London: Gollancz, 1998.

Klapisch-Zuber, Christiane. *Women, Family, and Ritual in Renaissance Italy,* translated by Lydia Cochrane. Chicago: University of Chicago Press, 1985.

Masten, Jeffrey. *Textual Intercourse: Collaboration, Authorship, and Sexualities in Renaissance Drama.* Cambridge: Cambridge University Press, 1997.

Miller, Carl. *Stages of Desire: Gay Theatre's Hidden History.* London: Cassell, 1996.

Mills, Lauren J. *One Soul in Bodies Twain: Friendship in Tudor Literature and Tudor Drama.* Bloomington, Ind.: Principia Press, 1937.

Proudfoot, G. R. "*Henry VIII (All is True), The Two Noble Kinsmen,* and the apocryphal plays." In *Shakespeare: A Bibliographical Guide,* edited by Stanley Wells, pp. 381-403. Oxford: Oxford University Press, 1990.

Rubin, Gayle. "The traffic in women: notes on a 'political economy' of sex." In *Towards an Anthropology of Women,* edited by Rayna Reiter. New York: Monthly Review Press, 1975.

Saslow, James M. *Ganymede in the Renaissance: Homosexuality in Art and Society.* New Haven: Yale University Press, 1986.

Sedgwick, Eve Kosofsky. *Between Men: English Literature and Male Homosocial Desire.* New York: Columbia University Press, 1985.

Smith, Bruce R. *Homosexual Desire in Shakespeare's England: A Cultural Poetics.* Chicago: University of Chicago Press, 1991.

Spencer, Theodore. "*The Two Noble Kinsmen.*" *Modern Philology* 36 (1938-9): 255-76.

Thompson, Ann. *Shakespeare's Chaucer: A Study of Literary Origins.* Liverpool: Liverpool University Press, 1978.

Waith, Eugene M. "Shakespeare and Fletcher on love and friendship." *Shakespeare Studies* 18, (1986): 235-50.

Wickham, Glynne. "*The Two Noble Kinsmen* or *A Midsummer Night's Dream, Part II?*" In *The Elizabethan Theatre VII: Papers given at the Seventh International Conference on Elizabethan Theatre held at the University of Waterloo, Ontario, in July 1977,* edited by G. R. Hibbard, 167-96. London: Macmillan, 1980.

Wrightson, Keith. *English Society 1580-1680.* London: Hutchison, 1982.

FURTHER READING

Criticism

Bachinger, Katrina. "Maidenheads and Mayhem: A Morris-Dance Reading of William Shakespeare's and John Fletcher's *The Two Noble Kinsmen.*" *Salzburger Studien zur Anglistik und Amerikanistik* 16 (1990): 23-38.

> Suggests a reading of *The Two Noble Kinsmen* that explains both its contemporary and modern appeal, and centers on the Morris dance, with its masque and antimasque elements, as a significant element in the play.

Cutts, John P. "Shakespeare's Song and Masque Hand in *The Two Noble Kinsmen.*" In *English Miscellany: A Symposium of History, Literature and the Arts,* edited by Mario Praz, pp. 55-85. Rome: Edizioni di Storia e Letteratura, 1967.

> Assesses the play in terms of its relationship to the other plays performed by the Kings Men under James I's reign, and examines the use of the elements of masque, music, and song in these plays.

Green, Susan. "'A mad woman? We are made, boys!': The Jailer's Daughter in *The Two Noble Kinsmen.*" In *Shakespeare, Fletcher and* The Two Noble Kinsmen, edited by Charles H. Frey, pp. 121-32. Columbia: University of Missouri Press, 1989.

> Examines the role of the Jailer's Daughter in *The Two Noble Kinsmen,* and discusses the way in which assessment of her role in the play speaks to the authorship controversy.

Steyn, Mark. Review of *The Two Noble Kinsmen. The New Criterion* 19, no. 2 (October 2000): 45-9.

> Reviews the production of the play directed by Tim Carroll at the Globe Theater in London, commenting that only Jasper Britton (as Palamon) and Will Keen (as Arcite) appeared comfortable with the play's language.

Underwood, Richard Allan. The Two Noble Kinsmen *and Its Beginnings.* Salzburg, Austria: Salzburg University, 1993, 208 p.

> Book-length analysis of the collaboration between John Fletcher and William Shakespeare on the *The Two Noble Kinsmen.*

Waith, Eugene M. Introduction to *The Two Noble Kinsmen,* by William Shakespeare and John Fletcher, edited by Eugene M. Waith, 233 p. Oxford: Clarendon Press, 1989.

> Offers a detailed overview of *The Two Noble Kinsmen,* including discussion of trends in the critical interpretation of the play, and the way the collaboration between the two authors is manifested in the text.

Shakespearean Criticism
Cumulative Character Index

The Cumulative Character Index identifies the principal characters of discussion in the criticism of each play and non-dramatic poem. The characters are arranged alphabetically. Page references indicate the beginning page number of each essay containing substantial commentary on that character.

Character Index

Jaques
As You Like It
love-theme, relation to **5:** 103; **23:** 7, 37, 118, 128
as malcontent **5:** 59, 70, 84
melancholy **5:** 20, 28, 32, 36, 39, 43, 50, 59, 63, 68, 77, 82, 86, 135; **23:** 20, 26, 103, 104, 107, 109; **34:** 85; **46:** 88, 94; **57:** 31
pastoral convention, relation to **5:** 61, 63, 65, 79, 93, 98, 114, 118
Seven Ages of Man speech (Act II, scene vii) **5:** 28, 52, 156; **23:** 48, 103, 105, 126, 138, 152; **46:** 88, 156, 164, 169
Shakespeare, relation to **5:** 35, 50, 154; **48:** 42
as superficial critic **5:** 28, 30, 43, 54, 55, 63, 65, 68, 75, 77, 82, 86, 88, 98, 138; **34:** 85

the jennet
Venus and Adonis See **the courser and the jennet**

Jessica
The Merchant of Venice **4:** 196, 200, 228, 293, 342; **48:** 54, 77; **53:** 159, 211; **66:** 171

Joan of Arc
Henry VI, Parts 1, 2, and 3 **16:** 131; **32:** 212; **60:** 33

John (Don John)
Much Ado about Nothing **8:** 9, 12, 16, 17, 19, 28, 29, 36, 39, 41, 47, 48, 55, 58, 63, 82, 104, 108, 111, 121; **67:** 169

John (Friar John)
Romeo and Juliet
detention of **5:** 448, 467, 470

John (King John)
King John **41:** 205, 260
death **9:** 212, 215, 216, 240; **56:** 345
decline **9:** 224, 235, 240, 263, 275; **68:** 19, 38, 73
Hubert, scene with (Act III, scene iii) **9:** 210, 212, 216, 218, 219, 280
moral insensibility **13:** 147, 163; **68:** 2, 38
negative qualities **9:** 209, 212, 218, 219, 229, 234, 235, 244, 245, 246, 250, 254, 275, 280, 297; **56:** 325; **68:** 62, 64
positive qualities **9:** 209, 224, 235, 240, 244, 245, 263

John of Lancaster, Prince
Henry IV **49:** 123
and betrayal **49:** 123

Julia
The Two Gentlemen of Verona **6:** 450, 453, 458, 476, 494, 499, 516, 519, 549, 564; **40:** 312, 327, 374; **54:** 325, 332

Juliet
Romeo and Juliet See **Romeo and Juliet**

Launcelot Gobbo
The Merchant of Venice See **Gobbo**

Kate
The Taming of the Shrew
characterization **32:** 1; **43:** 61; **64:** 244, 296, 343, 352
final speech (Act V, scene ii) **9:** 318, 319, 329, 330, 338, 340, 341, 345, 347, 353, 355, 360, 365, 381, 386, 401, 404, 413, 426, 430; **19:** 3; **22:** 48; **54:** 65; **55:** 299, 331; **64:** 296
love for Petruchio **9:** 338, 340, 353, 430; **12:** 435; **55:** 294
portrayals of **31:** 282
shrewishness **9:** 322, 323, 325, 332, 344, 345, 360, 365, 370, 375, 386, 393, 398, 404, 413; **64:** 283
transformation **9:** 323, 341, 355, 370, 386, 393, 401, 404, 407, 419, 424, 426, 430; **16:** 13; **19:** 34; **22:** 48; **31:** 288, 295, 339, 351; **55:** 294, 315; **64:** 233, 244, 273, 283, 320

Katherine
Henry V **5:** 186, 188, 189, 190, 192, 260, 269, 299, 302; **13:** 183; **19:** 217; **30:** 278; **44:** 44; **67:** 23
Henry VIII
characterization **2:** 18, 19, 23, 24, 38; **24:** 129; **37:** 109; **41:** 180; **61:** 119, 136
Hermione, compared with **2:** 24, 51, 58, 76
politeness strategies **22:** 182; **56:** 262
religious discourse **22:** 182
as tragic figure **2:** 16, 18

Kent
King Lear **25:** 202; **28:** 223; **32:** 212; **47:** 9

King
All's Well That Ends Well **38:** 150; **55:** 148

King Richard II
Richard II See **Richard**

King Richard III, formerly Richard, Duke of Gloucester
Richard III See **Richard**

Lady Faulconbridge
King John **68:** 50

Lady Macbeth
Macbeth See **Macbeth (Lady Macbeth)**

Laertes
Hamlet **21:** 347, 386; **28:** 290; **35:** 182; **59:** 26

Launce and Speed
The Two Gentlemen of Verona
comic function of **6:** 438, 439, 442, 456, 458, 460, 462, 472, 476, 478, 484, 502, 504, 507, 509, 516, 519, 549; **40:** 312, 320

Lavatch
All's Well That Ends Well **26:** 64; **46:** 33, 52, 68; **55:** 143

Lavinia
Titus Andronicus **27:** 266; **28:** 249; **32:** 212; **43:** 1, 170, 239, 247, 255, 262; **62:** 225, 233, 242; **68:** 268

Lawrence (Friar Lawrence)
Romeo and Juliet
contribution to catastrophe **5:** 437, 444, 470; **33:** 300; **51:** 253; **60:** 96
philosophy of moderation **5:** 427, 431, 437, 438, 443, 444, 445, 458, 467, 479, 505, 538
as Shakespeare's spokesman **5:** 427, 431, 437, 458, 467

Lear
King Lear **61:** 176
curse on Goneril **11:** 5, 7, 12, 114, 116
death of **60:** 2; **66:** 260
love-test and division of kingdom **2:** 100, 106, 111, 124, 131, 137, 147, 149, 151, 168, 186, 208, 216, 281; **16:** 351; **25:** 202; **31:** 84, 92, 107, 117, 149, 155; **46:** 231, 242; **61:** 194
madness **2:** 94, 95, 98, 99, 100, 101, 102, 103, 111, 116, 120, 124, 125, 149, 156, 191, 208, 216, 281; **46:** 264
as scapegoat **2:** 241, 253
self-knowledge **2:** 103, 151, 188, 191, 213, 218, 222, 241, 249, 262; **25:** 218; **37:** 213; **46:** 191, 205, 225, 254, 264; **54:** 103; **60:** 65, 75; **61:** 215, 220, 250
spiritual regeneration **54:** 103; **60:** 65, 75

Leontes
The Winter's Tale
characterization **19:** 431; **43:** 39; **45:** 366; **68:** 309, 324
jealousy **7:** 377, 379, 382, 383, 384, 387, 389, 394, 395, 402, 407, 412, 414, 425, 429, 432, 436, 464, 480, 483, 497; **15:** 514, 518, 532; **22:** 324; **25:** 339; **36:** 334, 344, 349; **44:** 66; **45:** 295, 297, 344, 358; **47:** 25; **57:** 294; **68:** 309, 324
Othello, compared with **7:** 383, 390, 412; **15:** 514; **36:** 334; **44:** 66; **47:** 25
repentance **7:** 381, 389, 394, 396, 402, 414, 497; **36:** 318, 362; **44:** 66; **57:** 294

Lord Chief Justice
Henry IV
as keeper of law and justice **49:** 133

Lorenzo
The Merchant of Venice **66:** 171

the lovers
A Midsummer's Night Dream **58:** 151, 169

Lucentio
The Taming of the Shrew **9:** 325, 342, 362, 375, 393

Lucio
Measure for Measure **13:** 104; **49:** 379; **65:** 19

Lucrece
The Rape of Lucrece
chastity **33:** 131, 138; **43:** 92
as example of Renaissance virtù **22:** 289; **43:** 148
heroic **10:** 84, 93, 109, 121, 128; **59:** 175, 193
patriarchal woman, model of **10:** 109, 131; **33:** 169, 200
Philomela **59:** 193
self-perception **48:** 291
self-responsibility **10:** 89, 96, 98, 106, 125; **33:** 195; **43:** 85, 92, 158; **59:** 206

Richard (King Richard III, formerly Richard, Duke of Gloucester)

Henry VI, Parts 1, 2, and 3

characterization **3:** 35, 48, 57, 64, 77, 143, 151; **22:** 193; **39:** 160, 177

as revenger **22:** 193

soliloquy (3 Henry VI, Act III, scene ii) **3:** 17, 48

Richard III

ambition **8:** 148, 154, 165, 168, 170, 177, 182, 213, 218, 228, 232, 239, 252, 258, 267; **39:** 308, 341, 360, 370, 383; **52:** 201, 223

attractive qualities **8:** 145, 148, 152, 154, 159, 161, 162, 165, 168, 170, 181, 182, 184, 185, 197, 201, 206, 213, 228, 243, 252, 258; **16:** 150; **39:** 370, 383; **52:** 272, 280; **62:** 104

credibility, question of **8:** 145, 147, 154, 159, 165, 193; **13:** 142

death **8:** 145, 148, 154, 159, 165, 168, 170, 177, 182, 197, 210, 223, 228, 232, 243, 248, 252, 258, 267

deformity as symbol **8:** 146, 147, 148, 152, 154, 159, 161, 165, 170, 177, 184, 185, 193, 218, 248, 252, 267; **19:** 164; **62:** 110

inversion of moral order **8:** 159, 168, 177, 182, 184, 185, 197, 201, 213, 218, 223, 232, 239, 243, 248, 252, 258, 262, 267; **39:** 360; **52:** 205, 214

as Machiavellian villain **8:** 165, 182, 190, 201, 218, 232, 239, 243, 248; **39:** 308, 326, 360, 387; **52:** 201, 205, 257, 280, 285; **62:** 2, 60, 78, 110

as monster or symbol of diabolic **8:** 145, 147, 159, 162, 168, 170, 177, 182, 193, 197, 201, 228, 239, 248, 258; **13:** 142; **37:** 144; **39:** 326, 349; **52:** 227, 272; **66:** 286

other literary villains, compared with **8:** 148, 161, 162, 165, 181, 182, 206, 213, 239, 267

role-playing, hypocrisy, and dissimulation **8:** 145, 148, 154, 159, 162, 165, 168, 170, 182, 190, 206, 213, 218, 228, 239, 243, 252, 258, 267; **25:** 141, 164, 245; **39:** 335, 341, 387; **52:** 257, 267; **62:** 78

as scourge or instrument of God **8:** 163, 177, 193, 201, 218, 228, 248, 267; **39:** 308; **62:** 60

as seducer **52:** 223, 227; **62:** 91, 104

self-esteem **52:** 196; **62:** 78

as Vice figure **8:** 190, 201, 213, 228, 243, 248, 252; **16:** 150; **39:** 383, 387; **52:** 223, 267; **62:** 78

Richard Plantagenet, Duke of York

Henry VI, Parts 1, 2, and 3 See **York**

Richmond

Richard III **8:** 154, 158, 163, 168, 177, 182, 193, 210, 218, 223, 228, 243, 248, 252; **13:** 142; **25:** 141; **39:** 349; **52:** 214, 257, 285; **66:** 286

the Rival Poet

Sonnets **10:** 169, 233, 334, 337, 385; **48:** 352

Roman citizenry

Julius Caesar

portrayal of **7:** 169, 179, 210, 221, 245, 279, 282, 310, 320, 333; **17:** 271, 279, 288, 291, 292, 298, 323, 334, 351, 367, 374, 375, 378; **22:** 280; **30:** 285, 297, 316, 321, 374, 379; **37:** 229

Romeo and Juliet

Romeo and Juliet

characterization **65:** 159

death-wish **5:** 431, 489, 505, 528, 530, 538, 542, 550, 566, 571, 575; **32:** 212

first meeting (Act I scene v) **51:** 212

immortality **5:** 536

Juliet's epithalamium speech (Act III, scene ii) **5:** 431, 477, 492

Juliet's innocence **5:** 421, 423, 450, 454; **33:** 257; **65:** 201

maturation **5:** 437, 454, 467, 493, 498, 509, 520, 565; **33:** 249, 257; **65:** 159

rebellion **25:** 257

reckless passion **5:** 419, 427, 431, 438, 443, 444, 448, 467, 479, 485, 505, 533, 538, 542; **33:** 241

Romeo's dream (Act V, scene i) **5:** 513, 536, 556; **45:** 40; **51:** 203

Rosaline, Romeo's relationship with **5:** 419, 423, 425, 427, 438, 498, 542, 575

Rosalind

As You Like It **46:** 94, 122

Beatrice, compared with **5:** 26, 36, 50, 75

charm **5:** 55, 75; **23:** 17, 18, 20, 41, 89, 111

disguise, role of **5:** 75, 107, 118, 122, 128, 130, 133, 138, 141, 146, 148, 164, 168; **13:** 502; **23:** 35, 42, 106, 119, 123, 146; **34:** 130; **46:** 127, 134, 142; **57:** 23, 40

femininity **5:** 26, 36, 52, 75; **23:** 24, 29, 46, 54, 103, 108, 121, 146

as Ganymede **60:** 115

love-theme, relation to **5:** 79, 88, 103, 116, 122, 138, 141; **23:** 114, 115; **34:** 85, 177

rustic characters

As You Like It **5:** 24, 60, 72, 84; **23:** 127; **34:** 78, 161

A Midsummer Night's Dream **3:** 376, 397, 432; **12:** 291, 293; **45:** 147, 160

Scroop

Henry V See **traitors**

Sebastian

The Tempest See **Antonio and Sebastian**

Shylock

The Merchant of Venice

alienation **4:** 279, 312; **40:** 175; **48:** 77; **49:** 23, 37; **66:** 91

ambiguity **4:** 247, 254, 315, 319, 331; **12:** 31, 35, 36, 50, 51, 52, 56, 81, 124; **40:** 175; **53:** 111; **66:** 87, 110, 117

ghettoization of **53:** 127; **66:** 78

forced conversion **4:** 209, 252, 268, 282, 289, 321; **66:** 110, 144, 180, 292; **68:** 275

Jewishness **4:** 193, 194, 195, 200, 201, 213, 214, 279; **22:** 69; **25:** 257; **40:** 142, 175, 181; **48:** 65, 77; **66:** 87, 110, 117, 126, 292

master-slave relationship **53:** 136

motives in making the bond **4:** 252, 263, 266, 268; **22:** 69; **25:** 22; **66:** 59, 110

as outsider **53:** 127, 224; **66:** 87, 144, 158, 165

as Puritan **40:** 127, 166

as scapegoat figure **4:** 254, 300; **40:** 166; **49:** 27

as traditional comic villain **4:** 230, 243, 261, 263, 315; **12:** 40, 62, 124; **40:** 175; **66:** 87, 117

as tragic figure **12:** 6, 9, 10, 16, 21, 23, 25, 40, 44, 66, 67, 81, 97; **40:** 175; **66:** 87, 117, 124, 126, 153, 180, 292

Sicinius

Coriolanus See **the tribunes**

Silvia

The Two Gentlemen of Verona **6:** 450, 453, 458, 476, 494, 499, 516, 519, 549, 564; **40:** 312, 327, 374; **54:** 325, 332

Silvius

As You Like It See **pastoral characters**

Sly

The Taming of the Shrew **9:** 320, 322, 350, 370, 381, 390, 398, 430; **12:** 316, 335, 416, 427, 441; **16:** 13; **19:** 34, 122; **22:** 48; **37:** 31; **50:** 74; **64:** 244, 343, 352

soldiers

Henry V **5:** 203, 239, 267, 276, 281, 287, 293, 318; **28:** 146; **30:** 169

Speed

The Two Gentlemen of Verona See **Launce and Speed**

Stephano and Trinculo

The Tempest

comic subplot of **8:** 292, 297, 299, 304, 309, 324, 328, 353, 370; **25:** 382; **29:** 377; **46:** 14, 33

Stephen Gardiner

Henry VIII See **Gardiner**

Talbot

Henry VI, Parts 1, 2, and 3 **39:** 160, 213, 222; **56:** 85, 145; **60:** 33

Tamora

Titus Andronicus **4:** 632, 662, 672, 675; **27:** 266; **43:** 170; **62:** 233; **68:** 268

Tarquin

The Rape of Lucrece **10:** 80, 93, 98, 116, 125; **22:** 294; **25:** 305; **32:** 321; **33:** 190; **43:** 102; **59:** 180

Petrarchan lover **48:** 291

platonic tyrant **48:** 291

Satan role **48:** 291

Thaisa

Pericles **66:** 201

Thersites

Troilus and Cressida **13:** 53; **25:** 56; **27:** 381; **59:** 265

Theseus

A Midsummer Night's Dream

characterization **3:** 363; **58:** 151, 220

Hippolyta, relationship with **3:** 381, 412, 421, 423, 450, 468, 520; **29:** 175, 216, 243, 256; **45:** 84

as ideal **3:** 379, 391

Shakespearean Criticism
Cumulative Topic Index

The Cumulative Topic Index indentifies the principal topics of discussion in the criticism of each play and non-dramatic poem. The topics are arranged alphabetically. Page references indicate the beginning page number of each essay containing substantial commentary on that topic. A parenthetical reference after a topic indicates that the topic is extensively discussed in that volume.

Topic Index

Topic Index

Topic Index

Topic Index

Topic Index

Shakespearean Criticism
Cumulative Topic Index, by Play

The Cumulative Topic Index, by Play identifies the principal topics of discussion in the criticism of each play and non-dramatic poem. The topics are arranged alphabetically by play. Page references indicate the beginning page number of each essay containing substantial commentary on that topic. A parenthetical reference after a play indicates which volumes discuss the play extensively.

All's Well That Ends Well (Volumes 7, 26, 38, 55)

appearance versus reality **7**: 37, 76, 93; **26**: 117
audience perspective **7**: 81, 104, 109, 116, 121
bed-trick **7**: 8, 26, 27, 29, 32, 41, 86, 93, 98, 113, 116, 126; **13**: 84; **26**: 117; **28**: 38; **38**: 65, 118; **49**: 46; **54**: 52; **55**: 109, 131, 176
Bertram
  characterization **7**: 15, 27, 29, 32, 39, 41, 43, 98, 113; **26**: 48; **26**: 117; **55**: 90
  conduct **7**: 9, 10, 12, 16, 19, 21, 51, 62, 104; **50**: 59; **55**: 143, 154
  desire **22**: 78
  transformation or redemption **7**: 10, 19, 21, 26, 29, 32, 54, 62, 81, 90, 93, 98, 109, 113, 116, 126; **13**: 84
comic elements **26**: 97, 114; **48**: 65; **55**: 148, 154, 164
conclusion **38**: 123, 132, 142; **54**: 52; **55**: 148, 154, 170
dark elements **7**: 27, 37, 39, 43, 54, 109, 113, 116; **26**: 85; **48**: 65; **50**: 59; **54**: 30; **55**: 164, 170
Decameron (Boccaccio), compared with **7**: 29, 43
desire **38**: 99, 109, 118; **55**: 122
displacement **22**: 78
education **7**: 62, 86, 90, 93, 98, 104, 116, 126
elder characters **7**: 9, 37, 39, 43, 45, 54, 62, 104
gender issues **7**: 9, 10, 67, 126; **13**: 77, 84; **19**: 113; **26**: 128; **38**: 89, 99, 118; **44**: 35; **55**: 101, 109, 122, 164
genre **48**: 65
Helena
  as agent of reconciliation, renewal, or grace **7**: 67, 76, 81, 90, 93, 98, 109, 116; **55**: 176; **66**: 335
  as dualistic or enigmatic character **7**: 15, 27, 29, 39, 54, 58, 62, 67, 76, 81, 98, 113, 126; **13**: 66; **22**: 78; **26**: 117; **54**: 30; **55**: 90, 170, 176
  as "female achiever" **19**: 113; **38**: 89; **55**: 90, 101, 109, 122, 164
  desire **38**: 96; **44**: 35; **55**: 109, 170

pursuit of Bertram **7**: 9, 12, 15, 16, 19, 21, 26, 27, 29, 32, 43, 54, 76, 116; **13**: 77; **22**: 78; **49**: 46; **55**: 90
virginity **38**: 65; **55**: 131, 176
virtue and nobility **7**: 9, 10, 12, 16, 19, 21, 27, 32, 41, 51, 58, 67, 76, 86, 126; **13**: 77; **50**: 59; **55**: 122
implausibility of plot, characters, or events **7**: 8, 45
irony, paradox, and ambiguity **7**: 27, 32, 58, 62, 67, 81, 86, 109, 116
King **38**: 150; **55**: 148
language and imagery **7**: 12, 29, 45, 104, 109, 121; **38**: 132; **48**: 65
Lavatch **26**: 64; **46**: 33, 52, 68; **55**: 143
love **7**: 12, 15, 16, 51, 58, 67, 90, 93, 116; **38**: 80; **51**: 33, 44
merit versus rank **7**: 9, 10, 19, 37, 51, 76; **38**: 155; **50**: 59
"mingled yarn" **7**: 62, 93, 109, 126; **38**: 65
morality plays, influence of **7**: 29, 41, 51, 98, 113; **13**: 66
mythic or mythological elements **60**: 169
naturalism **60**: 169
opening scene **54**: 30
Parolles
  characterization **7**: 8, 9, 43, 76, 81, 98, 109, 113, 116, 126; **22**: 78; **26**: 48, 73, 97; **26**: 117; **46**: 68; **55**: 90, 154
  exposure **7**: 9, 27, 81, 98, 109, 113, 116, 121, 126
  Falstaff, compared with **7**: 8, 9, 16
reconciliation **7**: 90, 93, 98; **51**: 33
religious, mythic, or spiritual content **7**: 15, 45, 54, 67, 76, 98, 109, 116; **66**: 335
romance or folktale elements **7**: 32, 41, 43, 45, 54, 76, 104, 116, 121; **26**: 117
sexuality **7**: 67, 86, 90, 93, 98, 126; **13**: 84; **19**: 113; **22**: 78; **28**: 38; **44**: 35; **49**: 46; **51**: 44; **55**: 109, 131, 143, 176
social and political context **13**: 66; **22**: 78; **38**: 99, 109, 150, 155; **49**: 46
staging issues **19**: 113; **26**: 15, 19, 48, 52, 64, 73, 85, 92, 93, 94, 95, 97, 114, 117, 128; **54**: 30
structure **7**: 21, 29, 32, 45, 51, 76, 81, 93, 98, 116; **22**: 78; **26**: 128; **38**: 72, 123, 142; **66**: 335
youth versus age **7**: 9, 45, 58, 62, 76, 81, 86, 93, 98, 104, 116, 126; **26**: 117; **38**: 109

Antony and Cleopatra (Volumes 6, 17, 27, 47, 58)

allegorical elements **52**: 5
All for Love (John Dryden), compared with **6**: 20, 21; **17**: 12, 94, 101
ambiguity **6**: 53, 111, 161, 163, 180, 189, 208, 211, 228; **13**: 368
androgyny **13**: 530
Antony
  characterization **6**: 22, 23, 24, 31, 38, 41, 172, 181, 211; **16**: 342; **19**: 270; **22**: 217; **27**: 117; **47**: 77, 124, 142; **58**: 2, 41, 118, 134
  Cleopatra, relationship with **6**: 25, 27, 37, 39, 48, 52, 53, 62, 67, 71, 76, 85, 100, 125, 131, 133, 136, 142, 151, 161, 163, 165, 180, 192; **27**: 82; **47**: 107, 124, 165, 174
  death scene **25**: 245; **47**: 142; **58**: 41; **60**: 46
  dotage **6**: 22, 23, 38, 41, 48, 52, 62, 107, 136, 146, 175; **17**: 28
  nobility **6**: 22, 24, 33, 48, 94, 103, 136, 142, 159, 172, 202; **25**: 245
  political conduct **6**: 33, 38, 53, 107, 111, 146, 181
  public versus private personae **6**: 165; **47**: 107; **58**: 41; **65**: 270
  self-knowledge **6**: 120, 131, 175, 181, 192; **47**: 77
  as superhuman figure **6**: 37, 51, 71, 92, 94, 178, 192; **27**: 110; **47**: 71
  as tragic hero **6**: 38, 39, 52, 53, 60, 104, 120, 151, 155, 165, 178, 192, 202, 211; **22**: 217; **27**: 90
audience response **48**: 206; **58**: 88
Caesar **65**: 270
Cleopatra
  Antony, relationship with **6**: 25, 27, 37, 39, 48, 52, 53, 62, 67, 71, 76, 85, 100, 125, 131, 133, 136, 142, 151, 161, 163, 165, 180, 192; **25**: 257; **27**: 82; **47**: 107, 124, 165, 174
  characterization **47**: 77, 96, 113, 124; **58**: 24, 33, 59, 118, 134
  contradictory or inconsistent nature **6**: 23, 24, 27, 67, 76, 100, 104, 115, 136, 151, 159, 202; **17**: 94, 113; **27**: 135
  costume **17**: 94
  creativity **6**: 197; **47**: 96, 113

Topic Index, by Play

Topic Index, by Play

Topic Index, by Play

ISBN 0-7876-5999-1

90000

9 780787 659998